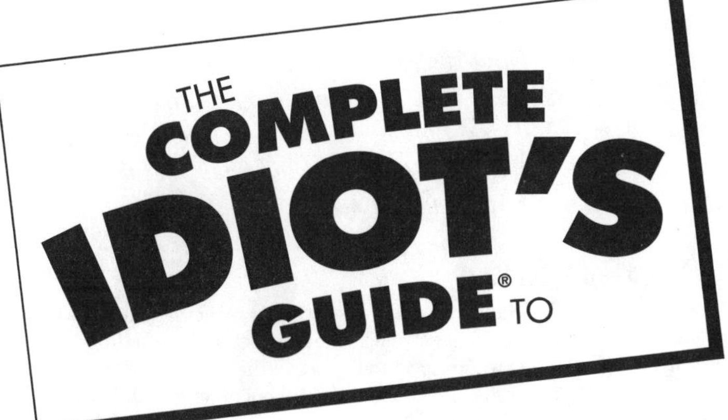

Conversational Japanese

by Naoya Fujita, Ph.D.

A Pearson Education Comp

This book is dedicated to:
My wife Naoko and son Hayato (Ken) for their love and support,
My parents, Akio and Shigeyo Fujita for helping me become who I am,
The Tabuse and Kito families for their encouragement, and finally but not least important,
All my students, who have taught me how to teach Japanese!

International Standard Book Number: 0-02-864179-5
Library of Congress Catalog Card Number: 2002106351

04 03 02 8 7 6 5 4 3 2 1

Interpretation of the printing code: The rightmost number of the first series of numbers is the year of the book's printing; the rightmost number of the second series of numbers is the number of the book's printing. For example, a printing code of 02-1 shows that the first printing occurred in 2002.

Printed in the United States of America

For marketing and publicity, please call: 317-581-3722

The publisher offers discounts on this book when ordered in quantity for bulk purchases and special sales.

For sales within the United States, please contact: Corporate and Government Sales, 1-800-382-3419 or corpsales@pearsontechgroup.com

Outside the United States, please contact: International Sales, 317-581-3793 or international@pearsontechgroup.com

Publisher: *Marie Butler-Knight*
Product Manager: *Phil Kitchel*
Managing Editor: *Jennifer Chisholm*
Senior Acquisitions Editor: *Renee Wilmeth*
Development Editors: *Alex Kent, Michael Thomas*
Senior Production Editor: *Christy Wagner*
Copy Editor: *Rhonda Tinch-Mize*
Illustrator: *Chris Eliopoulos*
Cover/Book Designer: *Trina Wurst*
Indexer: *Brad Herriman*
Layout/Proofreading: *Angela Calvert, John Etchison*

Contents at a Glance

Appendixes

Contents

Appendixes

Foreword

The Complete Idiot's Guide to Conversational Japanese is a highly practical yet academically disciplined guide to the study of the Japanese language and culture. It will satisfy readers who demand language skills they can use now and who also wish to build a solid foundation should they pursue advanced instruction later.

Some of the chapters introduce an extremely useful repertoire of practical phrases in Japanese together with culturally correct, highly valuable pieces of advice. The hypothetical situations covered range from ordering at a restaurant and visiting a Japanese family to making complaints at a hotel and placing an emergency telephone call. Readers can verbally practice conversation with the accompanying CD.

The book also contains several chapters that introduce highly articulate and precise, yet magically simplified, rules of grammar. For instance, the author offers a simple rule on word order—place every verb at the end of a sentence and let other phrases appear freely. Although this approach may sound simplistic, it is a quite reasonable and appropriate suggestion that can be warranted by modern linguists.

Naoya Fujita is a new breed of expert on the Japanese language. He has solid background not only in Japanese pedagogy and Japanese linguistics, but also in the general theory of linguistics. Having learned and taught in both Japan and the United States, he also knows the mentality of the people from both countries inside out.

Finally, this book can also be recommended to serious students of Japanese (even at the college level) as a highly sophisticated reference to be used outside the classroom. It could prove to be the best secret weapon in your college courses that you've ever had. (But be careful. Your knowledge of Japanese could surpass that of your teacher's, which can be dangerous!) This book deserves to be called *The Complete Guide to Japanese for Smart Learners.*

Yoshihisa Kitagawa, Associate Professor of Linguistics, Indiana University

Introduction

Welcome to *The Complete Idiot's Guide to Conversational Japanese!* This book is neither an ordinary language textbook nor merely a phrasebook for travelers. It is a unique tool to get the most out of learning Japanese on your own in a fun way.

How is this book different from other books? Language textbooks are often designed for a classroom, and a teacher guides you through lessons over a long period of time. Because of this, such books tend to contain too much information for a self-study learner to absorb. On the other hand, phrasebooks for travelers are often designed to give you a minimally sufficient set of expressions. They tend to have too little information for a serious self-study learner who is eager to understand not only phrases and expressions, but also the *structure* of the language. Life is not easy. It's too much of one thing, and not enough of the other! This book was written to give you the most valuable information, as well as some insights into the structure of the language—and maybe make your life a little bit easier, too!

The Complete Idiot's Guide to Conversational Japanese has three notable characteristics. First, the tone of the book is not overly academic, so it's easy to read through each chapter. There are many helpful tips and a lot of cultural information throughout the book so that you won't end up just memorizing dry sentence patterns.

Second, this book is not a plain list of unconnected phrases. Learning a language is like solving a jigsaw puzzle with lots of pieces. Once you find the core piece, completing the rest of the puzzle becomes easier! In language learning, the "core piece" is grammar. I introduce all the essential grammatical concepts first, with easy-to-understand explanations. This will enable you to understand sentence patterns that are newly introduced in subsequent chapters. I strongly encourage you to thoroughly read those chapters and come back to them if you need to. Don't miss the core piece of this puzzle!

Third, this book is designed to serve as a powerful survival tool. Ordinary phrasebooks can give you commonly used expressions that might suffice in many situations. However, life sometimes does not go as smoothly as you wish. If you merely memorize phrases without understanding the structure of the language, how can you survive in an unexpected situation? As a language teacher, I want you to learn the language as a survival tool. I want you to be able to handle any situation that you might come across. This is possible if, and only if, you have a grasp on the structure of the language, namely the grammar. Once you are comfortable with basic grammatical concepts, you can apply that knowledge to any situation using the necessary vocabulary. Between the main text and the English-Japanese and Japanese-English dictionaries, you will have the essential vocabulary you need.

I kept these three points in mind while preparing this book. Go through each chapter and learn patterns and expressions. Make sure that you speak aloud when memorizing them. That's the only way to achieve proficiency. In addition, do all the exercises to check your understanding of newly introduced items.

Japanese Sounds and Characters

Japanese is not a language relative to English or any of the Western languages. This means that Japanese has a distinct sound system. Chapter 3 is devoted to the sound patterns of Japanese and the pronunciation of each sound. Don't overlook this chapter. With full understanding of all the sounds through repeated practice, you will be able to understand Japanese speakers, and they will understand your Japanese as well.

The Japanese writing system is also uniquely different from English or any Western language. Having taught Japanese for over 15 years, I am fully aware that learning the Japanese writing system takes time. The main objective of this book is to help you learn conversational Japanese. Because I want you to focus on speaking and listening, all the vocabulary and examples are presented in *romanized* characters. However, in Appendix A, I provide a concise section on the writing system. This section explains what the writing system looks like and provides a list of basic Japanese alphabets.

If you're interested in learning the Japanese writing system along with conversation, I suggest that you start with an elementary writing textbook for nonnative speakers. But even if you want to learn the writing system, you should begin to learn the sound system and basic conversation first. This way, you can identify each character more easily. Remember, the other way (writing first, speaking second) simply does not work.

In the English-Japanese and Japanese-English dictionaries, each entry accompanies words written in *kana* (native Japanese alphabets) and *kanji* (imported Chinese characters). You can use the dictionaries to become familiar with the writing system. In addition, when you need to show a certain word to a Japanese speaker, you can show the Japanese characters in these dictionaries.

The Audio CD

This book comes with a supplementary CD. Look for the icon in each chapter and listen to the corresponding segment on the CD. Make sure that you listen to the same segment and say it repeatedly until you internalize it. This way, you will significantly improve both your listening and speaking skills. After you study each chapter thoroughly using the CD, try listening to the CD alone and see how much you can pick up.

How This Book Is Organized

This book is divided into six parts, each of which focuses on a particular theme.

Part 1, "Before You Get Started: The Basics," provides essential background information about the language. You will learn about Japanese people and their mentality, land, and language in detail. By knowing these facts, you can eliminate common myths and get yourself ready to learn the language. In Chapter 3, you will also be introduced to the Japanese sound system, both its pronunciation and intonation. Don't overlook this chapter! Make sure that you go over each sound with the accompanying CD.

Part 2, "The Survival Skills: Grammar," is the backbone of this book. These chapters provide the fundamental concepts of the grammar. You can skip other chapters as you wish, but I suggest that you don't skip these chapters because the mastery of subsequent chapters depends on how much you understand the material here!

Part 3, "Getting to Know People," enables you to greet people, exchange self-introductions, talk about yourself, and ask people questions. Most of the expressions covered in these chapters are "fixed" or "ritualized" expressions. Learning these essential phrases will enable you to engage in conversation smoothly and comfortably to get to know people.

Part 4, "The Essentials for Traveling," provides valuable tips for traveling and introduces a number of expressions useful at an airport, hotel, and bank, as well as for traveling around Japan. Specifically, you learn how to go through Immigration and Customs at the airport, give directions to a cab driver, make a hotel reservation, exchange currency, and so on.

Part 5, "Japanese for Fun," enables you to have fun in Japan when shopping, dining, and spending leisure time. In particular, you learn how to buy things, order food at a restaurant, make a plan for various cultural events, and so on. For those who would like to do a home stay in Japan, Chapter 20 will prepare you to live in a Japanese house by taking you on a virtual house tour.

Part 6, "Troubleshooting," focuses on possible inconveniences you might encounter in Japan and gives you solutions or tips for handling such situations. In particular, you learn how to deal with medical and other emergencies, how to make a phone call, how to make a complaint at places such as a hotel or restaurant, and so on.

If you read this book from beginning to end, doing the exercises and memorizing vocabulary, you will be able to travel in Japan and do most activities on your own with confidence. So believe in yourself! I know you can do it.

Sidebars

In addition to grammatical explanations, exercises, and newly introduced phrases and vocabulary, there are four types of useful information provided in sidebar format throughout the book. Look for the following:

Green Tea Break

These sidebars are for fun! Here, you'll find interesting cultural remarks or notes on useful customs. These sidebars will help you become accustomed to Japanese society.

Shortcuts to Success

Useful learning tips are provided in these sidebars. These tips will enable you to learn aspects of the language quickly and effectively.

Huh?

These sidebars provide definitions or explanations of unfamiliar or foreign words or concepts.

Lifesavers

These sidebars provide cultural or learning tips that help you avoid making unnecessary mistakes.

Acknowledgments

During the production of this book, I have benefited greatly from a number of people, especially Melissa Bernhardt, Natsuko Alipio, Joyce Gabriel, Amanda Mobbs, Mason Jones, Gardner Robinson, Ron Wise, Daniel Bial, Rhonda Tinch-Mize, and Renee Wilmeth. My special thanks go to Development Editors Mike Thomas and Alex Kent and Senior Production Editor Christy Wagner for their wonderful work and professionalism. Alex Kent also produced the CD, working with voice actors Yuko Takahashi and Hiroyuki Nakai, and recording engineer Wes Talbot of Music Media (Northampton, MA). My thanks also go to Hiroyuki Nakai for the technical editing of the Japanese portions of the manuscript. Finally, I would like to extend my special thanks to Rebecca Forrey-Roofener, my assistant, who did an excellent job going through the entire manuscript and giving me thoughtful comments and input. Thank you all!

Special Thanks to the Technical Reviewer

The Complete Idiot's Guide to Conversational Japanese was reviewed by experts who double-checked the accuracy of what you'll learn here, to help us ensure that this book gives you everything you need to know about learning conversational Japanese. Special thanks are extended to The Language Lab.

Trademarks

All terms mentioned in this book that are known to be or are suspected of being trademarks or service marks have been appropriately capitalized. Alpha Books and Pearson Education, Inc., cannot attest to the accuracy of this information. Use of a term in this book should not be regarded as affecting the validity of any trademark or service mark.

Part 1

Before You Get Started: The Basics

We'll start out with some background on the Japanese language, as well as the society and people. You don't have to worry about memorizing anything yet! Just read the chapters and familiarize yourself with Japan and Japanese because the knowledge will enable you to learn the language comfortably in the subsequent chapters.

In Chapter 3, I'll introduce the "sounds" of Japanese and show you how the sound inventory is organized. Spend some time learning Japanese sounds, and you will be able to listen to and understand people, as well as have them understand what you say. If you can't pronounce basic sounds correctly, you can't communicate with Japanese speakers, no matter how many words and phrases you memorize! So spend time on this chapter and become comfortable with the pronunciation. Also, don't forget to listen to the CD!

Chapter 1

Can I *Really* Learn Japanese on My Own?

In This Chapter

- The Five Golden Rules for the successful mastery of Japanese
- Five guidelines for using this book
- The top 10 reasons to learn Japanese

I am a Japanese teacher. I have seen thousands of students learn Japanese. But I am also a student—of English. I started learning English as an adult. Based on my experience as a language teacher and student, I believe that a "good" learner intuitively knows the Five Golden Rules for the successful mastery of Japanese.

The Five Golden Rules

Rule 1: Be confident! Believe in yourself. Believe that you will master the language in the near future.

Rule 2: Be brave! Don't be afraid of making mistakes.

Rule 3: Be persistent! Stick to one book or methodology from beginning to end. Make a habit of studying the material every day.

Green Tea Break

Your Japanese will significantly improve if you have a Japanese friend who can point out your mistakes. However, culturally speaking, many Japanese people find it extremely rude to correct someone. The ideal solution is to find a Japanese conversation partner whose English is not very good so that you can correct each other's mistakes without hesitation or intimidation.

If you don't speak, of course, you won't make mistakes. But if you do speak, you might make mistakes and learn from them. After I realized this simple yet important fact, I no longer feared making mistakes. I knew I would not make the same mistakes again or that I would at least be aware of those possible pitfalls. So here is my motto:

Better to be embarrassed now than sorry later!

When I speak English, I still make mistakes and occasionally experience embarrassing moments. People might laugh at me, but I always tell them, "Hey, I'm not a native speaker of English anyway. Given that, don't you think my English is pretty good?"

Rule 3: Be Persistent!

There is no mystery to mastering a foreign language. You have to make a habit of practicing it every day, just like brushing your teeth before going to bed. It can be any kind of practice—memorizing new vocabulary, reading a short passage, or watching a video. Only 30 minutes of exposure to the language every day leads to 183 hours of learning per year. That's 30 hours more than the total hours a college student is exposed in a language class! Needless to say, the more you are exposed to Japanese, the faster you can speak it. But the key issue here is consistency.

Consistency is important not only because of continual exposure to the language, but also because it encourages reinforcement of previously acquired skills. In this sense, learning a language is like learning to type. The more you practice typing, the faster and more accurately you will type.

Also, the balance between *input* and *output* is important. Input is what you learn (knowledge) and output is what you produce based on your knowledge. Without output, your skills will easily become rusty. Make it a habit to use the language whenever you get the chance!

Huh?

A **synonym** is a word that means the same or nearly the same as another word. A fluent speaker is often very good at using synonyms.

Rule 4: Be Creative!

How many English words do you know? You probably can't count all of them, but most likely you don't know them all. Yet, you have no problem communicating with people in English. For instance, even if you don't know the word "sermonize," you can convey the same meaning by substituting the *synonym* "preach" for it.

If you see a different icon, right-click your site in VS and choose Use IIS Express. If you don't see the icon in the tray, click the arrow near the other icons in the Windows tray and click the Customize option. Then set IIS Express System Tray to Show Icon and Notifications. The icon belongs to the built-in web server called IIS Express. This web server has been started by VS automatically to serve the request for your page. You learn more about how the web server processes your page later in this chapter.

That's it. You just created your very first ASP.NET website with Visual Studio.

How It Works

Although the website you created in this Try It Out is quite simple, the process that eventually results in the page `Default.aspx` being displayed in your browser isn't so simple. All by itself, an ASP.NET page (also referred to as an ASPX page because of its extension, or a *Web Form*) can't do much. It needs to be processed and served by a *web server* before your browser can display it. That's why VS automatically started up IIS Express to handle the request for the page. Next, it started up your default web browser and directed it to the address of the web server (`http://localhost:49474/Default.aspx` in the Try It Out example), although the actual port number in the address may change every time you start the web server because it is randomly chosen by VS.

It's important to realize that the ASPX file you modified in VS is not the same as the one that eventually gets displayed by the browser.

When you create a page in VS, you add markup to it. The markup in an ASPX page is a combination of HTML, code for ASP.NET Server Controls (which you learn more about in this chapter and in Chapter 4), code written in Visual Basic.NET or C#, and more.

When you request an ASPX page in your browser, the web server processes the page, executes any server-side code it finds in the file, and effectively transforms the ASP.NET markup into plain HTML that it then sends to the browser, where it is displayed. In the preceding Try It Out, the resulting HTML causes the browser to display the current date and time. *HTML*, or *HyperText Markup Language*, is the language that browsers use to display a web page. You learn how HTML looks and how to use it later in this chapter.

To see how the final HTML differs from the original ASPX page, open the source for the page in your browser. In most browsers, you can bring up the source window by right-clicking the page in the browser and choosing View Source or View Page Source. This brings up your default text editor, showing the HTML for the page.

If you already closed your browser after the preceding Try It Out, press Ctrl+F5 in VS to open the page and choose View Source.

Scroll down in the source file until you see the line with the Welcome text. Notice how instead of the code between the tags, you now see the actual date and time:

```
<h2>Hello World</h2>
<p>Welcome to Beginning ASP.NET 4.5 on 8/31/2012 2:13:15 AM</p>
```

When the web server processed the page, it looked up the current date and time from the server and inserted it in the HTML that got sent to the browser. Depending on the language settings of your Windows installation, you may see the date and time formatted differently to accommodate the Windows Regional Settings.

In the following section, you see how ASP.NET works in much more detail.

AN INTRODUCTION TO ASP.NET 4.5

When you type a URL like `www.wrox.com` in your web browser and press Enter, the browser sends a request to the web server at that address. This is done through *HTTP*, the *HyperText Transfer Protocol*. HTTP is the protocol by which web browsers and web servers communicate. When you request the URL, you send a request to the server. When the server is active and the request is valid, the server accepts the request, processes it, and then sends the response back to the client browser. The relationship between the request and response is shown in Figure 1-8.

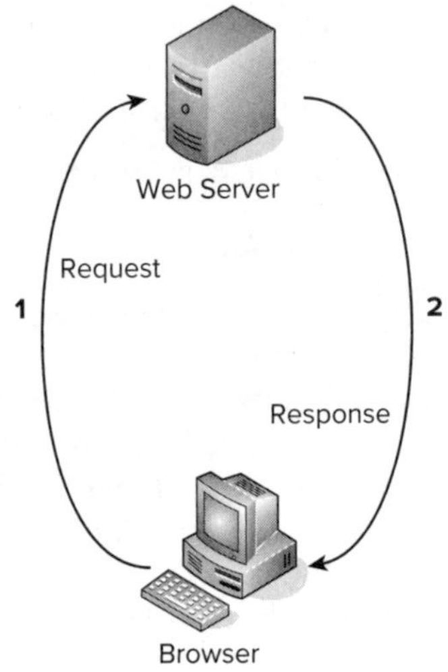

FIGURE 1-8

Because you are using IIS Express, the server and the client are really the same machine. However, in a real-world scenario, you'll host your website on an external web server where it can be accessed by many different clients.

For simple, static files, like HTML files or images, the web server simply reads the file from its local hard drive and sends it to the browser. However, for dynamic files, such as ASPX pages, this is obviously not good enough. If the web server were to send the ASPX file directly to the browser as a text file, you wouldn't have seen the current date and time in the browser, but instead you would have seen the actual code (`<%: DateTime.Now.ToString() %>`). So, instead of sending the file directly, the web server hands over the request to another piece of software that is able to process the page. This is done with a concept called *Application Mapping* or *Handler Mapping*, where an extension of a file (`.aspx` in this example) is mapped to an application that is capable of handling it. In the case of an `.aspx` page, the request is eventually handled and processed by the ASP.NET run time, part of the Microsoft .NET Framework designed specifically to handle web requests.

During the processing of the page, three main areas can influence the way the page eventually ends up in the browser:

- **Static text.** Any static text, like HTML, CSS, or JavaScript code you place in a page, is sent to the browser directly. You learn more about HTML, CSS, and JavaScript (a programming language used at the client) in this and subsequent chapters, including Chapter 3, which gives you a detailed look at CSS.
- **ASP.NET Server Controls.** These controls are placed in your ASPX page and when they are processed, they emit HTML that is inserted in the page. You learn more about server controls after the discussion of HTML in this chapter, and Chapter 4 is devoted entirely to ASP.NET Server Controls.
- **Programming code.** You can embed code, like Visual Basic .NET or C#, directly in a page, as you saw in the previous Try It Out. In addition, you can place code in a separate code file. The official term for this code file is *Code Beside*. However, most developers refer to this as the *Code Behind* file, which is the term I'll stick to in this book. This code can be executed by the run time automatically, or based on a user's action. Either way, execution of the code can greatly influence the way the page is displayed, by accessing databases, performing

calculations, hiding or showing specific controls, and much more. You learn more about this Code Behind file in the next chapter, and programming your ASP.NET web pages is discussed in great detail in Chapter 5.

Once the page is done processing, and all the HTML for the page has been collected, the HTML is sent back to the browser. The browser then reads it, parses it, and, finally, displays the page for you to look at.

Because HTML is so critical for displaying web pages, the next section gives you an overview of HTML.

Understanding HTML

HTML is the de facto language for creating web pages and is understood by every web browser that exists today. Since the beginning of the '90s it has been the driving force of the World Wide Web, the part of the Internet that deals with web pages. HTML documents are simple text files that contain markup, text, and additional data that influences that text. The most recent version of HTML is HTML5. Although the specification of HTML5 is still under development, a lot of modern browsers support important parts of this specification, and this support increases with each new release of those browsers. Despite the fact that not all browsers support HTML5 fully, it is really the future of HTML-based applications, and therefore I use it in this book and for the Planet Wrox demo website. Don't worry about the limited browser support too much. All major browsers support all of the HTML5 features you use in this book, or support can easily be simulated by a script library called Modernizr, which you see later in the book.

HTML Elements and Tags

HTML uses text surrounded by angle brackets to indicate how your content should be *rendered* (or displayed) in the browser. The text with angle brackets is referred to as a *tag*; a pair of tags holding some text or other content is referred to as an *element*. Take another look at the HTML you saw in the previous Try It Out where you opened the source window for the page in the browser:

```
<h2>Hello World</h2>
<p>Welcome to Beginning ASP.NET 4.5 on 8/31/2012 2:13:15 AM</p>
```

The first line of this example contains an `<h2>` element with an opening tag (`<h2>`) and a closing tag (`</h2>`). This element is used to signify a heading at the second level (if you scroll up a bit in the final source in the browser, you also see an `<h1>` element). Notice how the element is closed with a similar tag, but with an additional forward slash (/) in it: `</h2>`. Any text between these opening and closing tags is considered part of the element, and is thus rendered as a heading. In most browsers, this means the text is rendered in a larger font. Similar to the `<h2>` tag are tags for creating headings up to level six, such as `<h1>`, `<h3>`, and so on.

Below the heading element, you see a `<p>` element, which is used to denote a paragraph. All text within the pair of `<p>` tags is considered part of the paragraph. By default, a browser renders a paragraph with some additional margin spacing at the bottom, although you can override that behavior.

Many tags are available in HTML, too many to cover them all here. The following table lists some of the most important tags and describes how they can be used. For a complete list of all HTML elements, take a look at the website of the organization that maintains the HTML standard: `www.w3.org/TR/html5/index.html`.

TAG	DESCRIPTION	EXAMPLE

`<html>`	Used to denote the start and end of the entire page.	`<html>`
		`...All other content goes here`
		`</html>`

`<head>`	Used to denote a special section of the page that contains data about the page, including its title and references to external resources. The contents of this element are not directly output on screen but influence the looks and behavior of the page, as you'll see later. This element is placed inside the `<html>` element.	`<head>`
		`...Content goes here`
		`</head>`

`<title>`	Used to define the title of the page. This title will appear in the browser's title bar. This element is placed inside the `<head>` element.	`<title>`
		`...Welcome to Planet Wrox 4.5`
		`</title>`

`<body>`	Used to denote the start and end of the body of the page. Its content is what you see in the browser. This element is placed inside the `<html>` element.	`<body>`
		`...Page body goes here`
		`</body>`

`<header>`	Used to denote the header of a page. This element and all remaining elements in this table are placed inside the `<body>` element.	`<header>`
		`...<img src="Logo.png" … />`
		`</header>`

`<section>`	Used to denote various sections in your page. You can have multiple sections per page.	`<section>`
		`...Content goes here`
		`</section>`

`<aside>`	Used to denote content that is not part of the core page, but presented as an aside.	`<aside>`
		`...<img src="Banner.png" … />`
		`</aside>`

TAG	DESCRIPTION	EXAMPLE
<article>	Used to denote the main piece of content in a page.	<article> ...Main page content goes here </article>
<footer>	Denotes the footer section of a page.	<footer> ...Content for footer goes here </footer>
<a>	Used to link one web page to another or to create links within a page.	<a href="http://www.wrox.com"> Visit the Wrox site </a>
<img>	Used to embed images in a page.	<img src="Logo.gif" />
<strong> <em>	Used to format text in a bold or italic font.	This is <strong>bold text</ strong> while <em>this text is in italic</em>
<form> <input> <textarea> <select>	Used for input forms that enable users to submit information to the server.	<input type="text" value="Some Text" />
<table> <tr> <th> <td>	These tags are used to create a layout with a table. The <table> tag defines the entire table, the <th> is used to denote header cells, and the <tr> and <td> tags are used to define rows and cells, respectively.	<table> <tr> <td>This is a Cell in Column 1</td> <td>This is a Cell in Column 2</td> </tr> </table>
<ul> <ol> <li>	These three tags are used to create numbered or bulleted lists. The <ul> and the <ol> tags define the looks of the list (either unordered, with a simple bullet, or ordered, with a number), and the <li> tag is used to represent items in the list.	<ul> <li>First item with a bullet</li> <li>Second item with a bullet</li> </ul> <ol> <li>First item with a number</li> <li>Second item with a number</li> </ol>
<span>	This tag is used to wrap and influence other parts of the document. It appears as inline, so it adds no additional line break on the screen.	<p>This is some normal text while <span style="color: red;">this text appears in red </span></p>

(continued)

(continued)

TAG	DESCRIPTION	EXAMPLE

`<div>`	Just like the `<span>` tag, the `<div>` tag is used as a container for other elements. However, the `<div>` acts as a block element, which causes an explicit line break before and after the `<div>` element by default.	`<div> This is some text on 1 line</div>`
		`<div>`
		`This text is put directly under the previous text on a new line.`
		`</div>`

`<audio>`
`<video>`
`<source>`
	Used to embed audio and video files in your web page. The `<source>` element is used to define multiple types of audio and video resources.	`<video src="Somevideo.mpg" />`

HTML Attributes

In addition to the HTML elements, the examples in the preceding table also showed you HTML attributes. *Attributes* contain additional information that changes the way a specific element behaves. For example, with the `<img>` tag that is used to display an image, the `src` attribute defines the source of that image. Similarly, the `<span>` tag contains a `style` attribute that changes the color of the text to red. The value of the `style` attribute (`color: red;`) is part of a cascading style sheet (CSS), which is discussed in much more detail in Chapter 3. Just as with the HTML elements, there is a long list of available attributes and the elements to which they apply on the W3C website: `www.w3.org/TR/html5/index.html#attributes-1`.

You don't need to memorize all these elements and attributes. Most of the time, they are generated for you automatically by VS. In other cases, where you need to enter them by hand, VS offers you IntelliSense to help you find the right tag or attribute. IntelliSense is discussed in the next chapter.

HTML Comments

In order to comment something out in HTML, you wrap it in comment tags, like this:

```
<!-- This is a comment -->
```

Code you comment out is not processed by the browser (and thus isn't visible), but it's still sent to the browser (and thus is viewable by the end user). Because it is still sent to the browser, it adds to the page size, so you should use comments sparingly. In later chapters you see how to comment out code at the server so it's not sent to the client.

The Rules of HTML5

The rules of HTML5 are pretty simple, and most of the time VS helps you get it right or shows you a list of errors and suggestions for how to fix them. HTML5 is actually more relaxed than the previous version of HTML (called XHTML, which in turn was a reformulation of HTML 4.01 with XML rules) when it comes to enforcing rules.

Close Your Elements

Most elements in HTML must be closed. So when you start with a `<div>` tag, you must use `</div>` somewhere later in your page. Some exceptions exist (such as the `<p>` element if it's directly followed by some other elements), but I prefer to consistently close my tags. This is also the case for elements that don't have their own closing tags, like `<img>` or `<br>` (to enter a line break). In HTML5, these tags can be written as *self-closing tags*, where the closing slash is embedded directly in the tag itself as in `<img src="Logo.gif" />` or `<br />`.

Usage of Attributes

Whenever you write an attribute in a tag, you can write the value wrapped in double quotes, single quotes, or no quotes at all. For example, when writing out the `<img>` tag and its `src` attribute, you can write it like this:

```
<img src="Logo.gif" />
```

You could also use single quotes to enclose the attribute value, like this:

```
<img src='Logo.gif' />
```

Both options work, as long as you use the same type of quote on both ends of the value. For values that don't contain a space, you can also leave out the quotes:

```
<input value=yes>
```

It's also sometimes necessary to nest single and double quotes. For example, when some special ASP .NET syntax requires the use of double quotes, you should use single quotes to wrap the attribute's value:

```
<asp:Label ID="TitleLabel" runat="server" Text='<%# Eval("Title") %>' />
```

You see this syntax used a lot more in later chapters in this book.

For consistency, this book uses double quotes where possible in all HTML that ends up in the client, as this is generally the accepted standard.

Nest Your Elements Correctly

When you write nested elements, make sure that you first close the inner element you opened last, and then close the outer element. Consider this correct example that formats a piece of text with both bold and italic fonts:

```
<strong><em>This is some formatted text</em></strong>
```

Notice how the `<em>` tag is closed before the `<strong>` tag. Swapping the order of the closing tags leads to invalid HTML:

```
<strong><em>This is some formatted text</strong></em>
```

Add a DOCTYPE Declaration to Your Page

A `DOCTYPE` gives the browser information about the kind of HTML it can expect. By default, VS adds a `DOCTYPE` for HTML5 to your page:

```
<!DOCTYPE html>
```

The DOCTYPE greatly influences the way browsers like Internet Explorer render the page, so if you're seeing odd behavior on your page, check that your page has the correct DOCTYPE.

You can view the complete HTML5 syntax rules at the W3C site at www.w3.org/TR/html-markup/syntax.html.

Besides HTML, an ASP.NET web page can contain other markup as well. Most pages will have one or more ASP.NET Server Controls to give them some additional functionality. The next section briefly looks at these ASP.NET Server Controls, but you get an in-depth look at them in Chapter 4.

A First Look at ASP.NET Markup

To some extent, the markup for ASP.NET Server Controls is similar to that of HTML. It also has the notion of tags, elements, and attributes, using the same angle brackets and closing tags as HTML does. One big difference is that the ASP.NET tags start with an asp: prefix. For example, a button in ASP.NET looks like this:

```
<asp:Button ID="Button1" runat="server" Text="Click Me" />
```

Note how the tag is self-closed with the trailing slash (/) character, eliminating the need to type a separate closing tag. If you wanted to, you could use a separate closing tag, though.

When a server control is processed, it returns HTML. So, the code for the same button ends up like this when rendered in the browser:

```
<input type="submit" name="Button1" value="Click Me" id="Button1" />
```

The process of converting the server control to its HTML representation is similar to the code you saw earlier that displayed the current date. The server control is processed at the server by the ASP .NET handler. This processing results in HTML, which is sent to the browser, where it's displayed. You see more of this in Chapter 4.

Now that you understand the basics of an ASP.NET page and the HTML that it generates, it's time to look at VS again. Knowing how to use the application and its many tools and windows is an important step in building fun, good-looking, functional websites.

A TOUR OF THE IDE

Visual Studio is by far the most extensive and feature-rich *integrated development environment (IDE)* for building ASP.NET web pages. The abbreviation IDE refers to the way all the separate tools you need to build complex web applications are integrated in a single environment. Instead of writing code in a text editor, compiling code at the command line, writing HTML and CSS in a separate application, and managing your database in yet another, VS enables you to perform all of these tasks, and more, from the same environment. Besides the efficiency this brings because you don't have to constantly switch tools, this also makes it much easier to learn new areas of VS, because many of the built-in tools work in the same way.

The Main Development Area

To get familiar with the many tools that are packed in VS's interface, take a look at Figure 1-9. It shows the same screen you got after you created your first website in VS, but now it highlights some of the most important screen elements. If you are already familiar with a previous version of Visual Studio, you could skip this section and pick up again at the next Try It Out exercise later in this chapter.

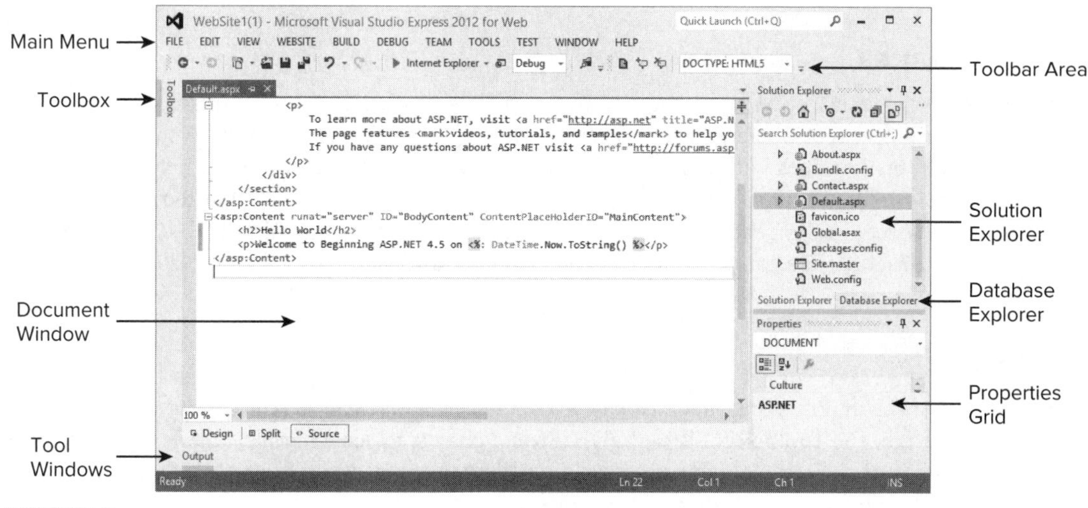

FIGURE 1-9

If you had a previous version of Visual Studio installed, your screen may look different, because Visual Studio 2012 is able to import settings from older versions.

Choosing Your Development Profile

Because VSEW targets people new to ASP.NET development as well as seasoned web developers, you can choose among different developer profiles: Basic Settings, Code Only, and Expert Settings. In Basic Settings mode, many menu items you don't frequently use have been hidden or are placed in their own submenu. The Code Only profile is great for pure coding sessions where you're not interested in many of the design features of VSEW, such as Design View or the Toolbox. Expert Settings mode gives you access to the full functionality of VSEW. You can switch between settings using the Tools ➪ Settings menu. This book assumes you are using Expert Settings mode right from the beginning. You may not need all the features you see right from the start, but you sure will use most of them by the end of the book. Because the menu items change location depending on the profile you choose, I decided to use Expert Settings mode right away, to make it easier to refer to a specific menu item or feature. You don't have this option in the commercial versions of Visual Studio — Expert Settings is on by default.

The Main Menu

At the top of the application, right below the Windows title bar, you see the main menu. This menu bar contains familiar items you find in many other Windows applications, like the File, Edit, and Help menus as well as menus that are specific to VS, such as the Website and Debug menus. The menu changes dynamically depending on the task you're working on, so you'll see menu items appear and disappear as you work your way through the application. You can use the Help ➪ Set Help Preference menu to configure online and offline help. Offline help needs to be installed first, and online help requires a connection to the Internet.

The Toolbar Area

Right below the menu, you see the toolbar area, which is capable of showing different toolbars that give you quick access to the most common functions in VS. In Figure 1-9, only two of the toolbars are enabled, but VS comes with many other toolbars that you can use in specific task-oriented scenarios. Some toolbars appear automatically when you're working on a task that requires a particular toolbar's presence, but you can also enable and disable toolbars to your liking. To enable or disable a toolbar, right-click an existing toolbar or the menu bar and choose the toolbar from the menu that appears.

The Toolbox

On the left of the main screen, tucked away at the border of VS, you see the tab for the Toolbox. If you click the tab, the Toolbox folds out, giving you a chance to see what it contains. If you click the little pin icon in the upper-right corner of the Toolbox (or any of the other panels that have this pin icon), it gets pinned to the IDE so it remains open.

Just as with the menu bar and the toolbars, the Toolbox automatically updates itself to show content that is relevant to the task you're working on. When you're editing a standard ASPX page, the Toolbox shows the many controls you have available for your page. You can simply drag an item from the Toolbox and drop it on a location of your page where you want it to appear. These controls are discussed in great detail in Chapter 4. Note that each Toolbox category also contains a Pointer icon. This isn't a control itself, though. In other designers for Visual Studio (such as Win Forms) this icon is used to get out of control drawing mode, but it has little use in ASP.NET. The Toolbox contains multiple categories, with tools that you can expand and collapse as you see fit to make it easier to find the right tool. You can also reorder the items in the list, add and remove items from the Toolbox, and even add your own tools to it. Customizing the IDE is discussed later in this chapter.

If the Toolbox is not visible on-screen, press Ctrl+Alt+X to open it or choose View ➪ Toolbox, provided you have chosen the Expert Settings option in the Tools ➪ Settings menu.

The Solution Explorer

At the right of the screen, you see the Solution Explorer. The Solution Explorer is an important window because it gives you an overview of the files that comprise your website. Instead of placing all your files in one big folder, the Solution Explorer enables you to store files in separate folders, creating a logical and organized site structure. You can use the Solution Explorer to add new files to your site, move existing files around using drag and drop or cut and paste, rename files and delete them from the project, and more. Much of the functionality of the Solution Explorer is hidden behind its right-click menu, which changes depending on the item you right-click.

At the top of the Solution Explorer, you see a small toolbar that gives you quick access to some functionality related to your website, including refreshing the Solution Explorer window, an option to nest related files, and two buttons that enable you to copy and configure your website. Most of this functionality is discussed later in the book.

You can access the Solution Explorer by choosing View ➪ Solution Explorer from the main menu or by pressing Ctrl+Alt+L.

The Database Explorer

This window, hidden behind the Solution Explorer in Figure 1-9, enables you to work with your databases. If you have a commercial version of Visual Studio, such as Visual Studio 2012 Professional, this window is called the Server Explorer and may be located at the left of your screen.

You can access the Database Explorer by choosing View ➪ Database Explorer or by pressing Ctrl+Alt+S. The Database Explorer is discussed in more detail in the chapters about databases, starting with Chapter 12.

The Properties Grid

With the Properties Grid, you can view and edit the properties of many items in Visual Studio, including files in the Solution Explorer, controls on a web page, properties of the page itself, and much more. The window constantly updates itself to reflect the selected item. You can quickly open the Properties Grid by pressing F4. You can use this same shortcut to force the Properties Grid to show the details of a selected item.

The Document Window

The Document Window is the main area in the middle of the application. This is where most of the action takes place. You can use the Document Window to work with many different document formats, including ASPX and HTML files, CSS and JavaScript files, code files for VB and C#, XML and text files, and even images. In addition, you can use the same window to manage databases, create copies of your site, view the pages in your site in the built-in mini-browser, and much more.

The Document Window is a tabbed window by default, which means it can host multiple documents, each one distinguished by a tab with the filename at the top of the window. The right-click menu of each tab contains some useful shortcuts for working with the file, including saving and closing it and opening the file's parent folder in Windows Explorer.

To switch between documents, you can press Ctrl+Tab, click the tab for the document you want to see, or click the down arrow in the upper-right corner of the Document Window, next to the Solution Explorer, shown in Figure 1-9. Clicking the down arrow reveals a list of open documents so you can easily select one.

Another way to switch documents is to press Ctrl+Tab and then hold down the Ctrl key. On the window that pops ups, you can select a document you want to work with in the right-hand column. You can then use the cursor keys to move up and down in the list with open documents. This makes it super easy to select the correct file.

On the same dialog box, you see a list with all active tool windows. Clicking one of the windows in the list shows it on-screen, moving it in front of other windows if necessary.

To get a quick preview of a document without opening it for editing, click the file you want to see in the Solution Explorer once. You can see that a file is in preview mode by its tab, which is docked to the right of the row with tabs as opposed to the left for open files.

At the bottom of the Document Window in Figure 1-9, you see three buttons called Design, Split, and Source. These buttons appear automatically when you're working with a file that contains markup, such as ASPX and HTML pages. They enable you to open the Design View of a page (giving you an idea of how the page will look in the browser), its Markup View (the HTML and other markup), or both at the same time. How this works is explained in more detail in Chapter 2, but for now, it's important to realize you can switch among Markup, Split, and Design View by clicking one of the three buttons. The Markup View is also often called the Source View or Code View window. However, to avoid confusion with the code editor that is used to edit Code Behind files, this book uses the term Markup View exclusively.

The Start Page

Whenever you start up VS, the Start Page is loaded in the Document Window. With the Start Page, you can quickly create new and open existing websites and other projects. The Start Page also provides a number of links to related news and information about web development. To reopen the Start Page, choose View ➪ Start Page.

To get a feel for how you can use all these windows, the following Try It Out shows you how to build a simple web page that contains a few ASP.NET Server Controls.

TRY IT OUT Creating Your First ASP.NET Web Page

This Try It Out exercise guides you through creating a new website with a single page that contains a number of ASP.NET Server Controls. You see how to use windows like the Document Window and the Solution Explorer, and how to use the Toolbox and the Properties Grid to add ASP.NET Server Controls to the page and change their looks.

1. Start VSEW or Visual Studio 2012.
2. If you're using the Express edition, choose Tools ➪ Settings and choose Expert Settings to turn on the developer profile that gives you access to the full feature set of VSEW.
3. On the File menu choose New Web Site. Depending on configuration, you may have to choose File ➪ New ➪ Web Site instead. This triggers the New Web Site dialog box.
4. In this dialog box, make sure that ASP.NET Empty Web Site is selected and not the ASP.NET Web Forms Site item that you used in a previous exercise. Ensure that File System is chosen in the Web Location drop-down list. Click OK to create the new site.
5. Next, right-click the new website in the Solution Explorer. Make sure you click the website (labeled WebSite2) and not the parent Solution element. It's the highlighted element in Figure 1-5. From the context menu that appears, choose Add ➪ Add New Item.

6. In the new window that appears, click Web Form and type **ControlsDemo** as the name. The ASPX extension is added for you automatically when you click the Add button. You can leave the other settings in the dialog box at their default settings. The page should open in Markup View, showing you the default HTML, like the `<html>`, `<head>`, `<title>`, and `<body>` elements that VS adds there for you automatically when you create a new page.
7. Switch the page to Design View by clicking the Design button at the bottom of the Document Window.
8. If the Toolbox isn't open yet, press Ctrl+Alt+X to open it or click the Toolbox tab to show it and then click the pin icon in the top-right corner to make the Toolbox visible at all times. Drag a `TextBox` and a `Button` from the Standard category of the Toolbox into the dashed area in the Design View of the page. You should end up with a Design View that looks similar to Figure 1-10.

FIGURE 1-10

9. Right-click the button in Design View and choose Properties. In the Properties Grid, locate the `Text` property under the Appearance category (shown in Figure 1-11) and change it from Button to Submit Information. As soon as you press Tab or click somewhere outside the Properties Grid, the Design View of the page is updated and shows the new text on the button.

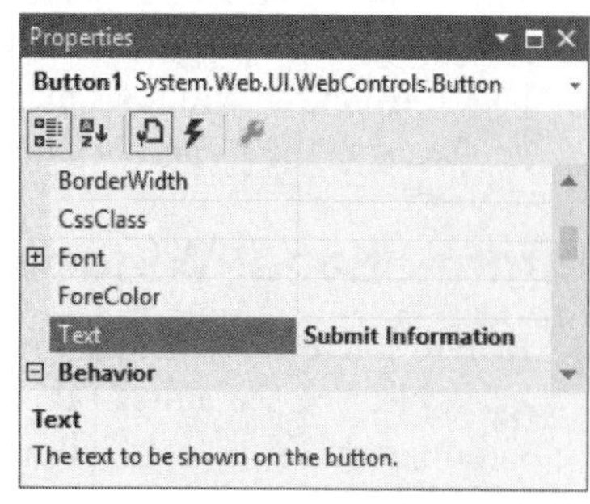

FIGURE 1-11

10. Press Ctrl+F5 to open the page in your default browser. Note that it's not necessary to explicitly save the changes to your page (although it's a good idea to do this often anyway using the shortcut Ctrl+S). As soon as you press Ctrl+F5 to run the page, VS saves all changes to open documents automatically.
11. Type some text in the text box and click the button. Note that after the page has reloaded, the text is still displayed in the text box. Other than that, not much has happened because you didn't write any code for the button yet.

How It Works

When you dragged the `Button` and the `TextBox` from the Toolbox on the page in Design View, VS added the corresponding code for you in Markup View automatically. Similarly, when you changed the `Text` property of the button in the Properties Grid, VS automatically updated the markup for the control in Markup View. Instead of using the Properties Grid, you could also have typed the text directly between the quotation marks of the `Text` property in Markup View.

After changing the `Text` property, your page should contain this code in Markup View:

```
<asp:TextBox ID="TextBox1" runat="server"></asp:TextBox>
<asp:Button ID="Button1" runat="server" Text="Submit Information" />
```

When you press Ctrl+F5 to view the page in the browser, the web server receives the request, the page is processed by the ASP.NET run time, and the resulting HTML for the page is sent to the browser.

After you type in some text and click the button, the same process is more or less repeated: The web server receives the request, the page is processed, and the result gets sent back to the browser. When you click the button, you cause a *postback* to occur, where any information contained in the page — such as the text you typed in the text box — is sent back to the server. ASP.NET reacts to the postback by rendering the page again. However, this time it prepopulates controls, like the `TextBox`, with the values that were sent to the page.

Take a look at the resulting HTML for the page after the postback, using the browser's View Source command (rerun the page from VS by pressing Ctrl+F5 if you already closed it). You should see code similar to this:

```
<input name="TextBox1" type="text" value="Hello World" id="TextBox1" />
<input type="submit" name="Button1" value="Submit Information" id="Button1" />
```

Just as with the earlier example, you can see that the resulting HTML is substantially different from the original ASPX markup.

Postbacks are an important concept in ASP.NET, and you see more about them in other chapters, including Chapter 4.

VSEW hosts many more windows and tool panels than those you have seen so far. The next section briefly touches upon some of the windows you'll most frequently use when building ASP.NET web pages. All of the windows mentioned are accessible from the main View menu in VS or VSEW if you're using the Expert Settings mode.

Informational Windows

In addition to the windows that are visible by default when you start VS, many more windows are available. You see most of them in action in the remainder of this book, but some are worth highlighting now. You access all windows that are discussed next from the main View menu.

The Error List

The Error List gives you a list of the things that are currently somehow broken in your site, including incorrect markup in your ASPX or HTML files and programming errors in VB or C# files. This window can even show you errors in XML and CSS files. The Error List shows its messages in three categories — Errors, Warnings, and Messages — that signify the severity of the problem. Figure 1-12 shows the Error List for a page that has some problems with its CSS and XHTML.

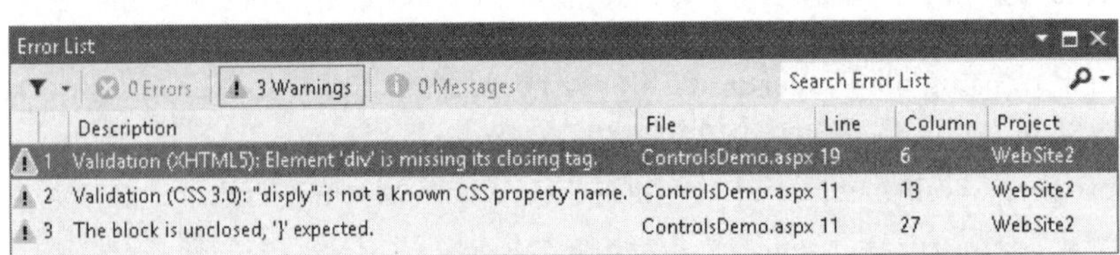

FIGURE 1-12

The Output Window

When you try to build your site using the Build menu, the Output window tells you whether or not the build succeeded. If the build failed, for example because you have a programming error, it tells you why the build failed. In the commercial versions of Visual Studio, the Output window is used for other information as well, including the status of external plug-in programs. Building — or compiling — websites is discussed later in this book, including in Chapter 19, which deals with deployment of your website.

The Find Results Window

The Find and Replace features of VS are invaluable tools when it comes to managing the content of your site. You will often need to replace some text in the current document or even in the entire site. Find in Files (Ctrl+Shift+F) and Replace in Files (Ctrl+Shift+H) both output their results in the Find Results window, as shown in Figure 1-13.

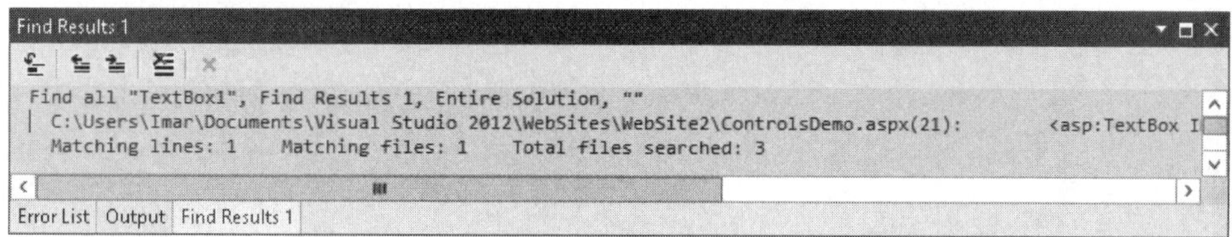

FIGURE 1-13

Because having several informational windows open at the same time may take up precious screen space, it's often a good idea to dock them. This way, only one of them is visible at a time, while you still have quick access to the others. You learn how to customize the IDE, including the docking of windows, next.

CUSTOMIZING THE IDE

Although the standard setup of Visual Studio and its tool windows is pretty useful, there's a fair chance you want to customize the IDE to your liking. You may want to move some of the windows to a location where they are easier to reach, or you may want to open additional windows you frequently use. Visual Studio is fully customizable and enables you to tweak every little detail of the IDE. In the next section, you learn how to perform the most common customization tasks.

Rearranging Windows

To give each window the location it deserves, you can drag and drop them in the main IDE. Simply grab a window's title bar or its bottom tab and drag it in the direction of the new location. Once you start dragging, you see that Visual Studio gives you visual cues as to where the window will end up (see Figure 1-14).

If you drag the window over one of the four square indicators at the sides of the middle indicator, the window will be docked *next to* the existing window. Once you drop it, the window pops to its new location. If you drop the window on the square in the middle of the large indicator, the window docks *with* that window, sharing the same screen space. Each window has its own tab, as you can see with the windows at the bottom of Figure 1-14.

In addition to docking windows with others in the IDE, you can also have floating windows. To change a docked window into a floating one, drag it away from its current location and drop it somewhere in the IDE without hitting one of the visual cues on the screen. You can also choose Window ➪ Float from the main menu or right-click the window's title bar and choose Float.

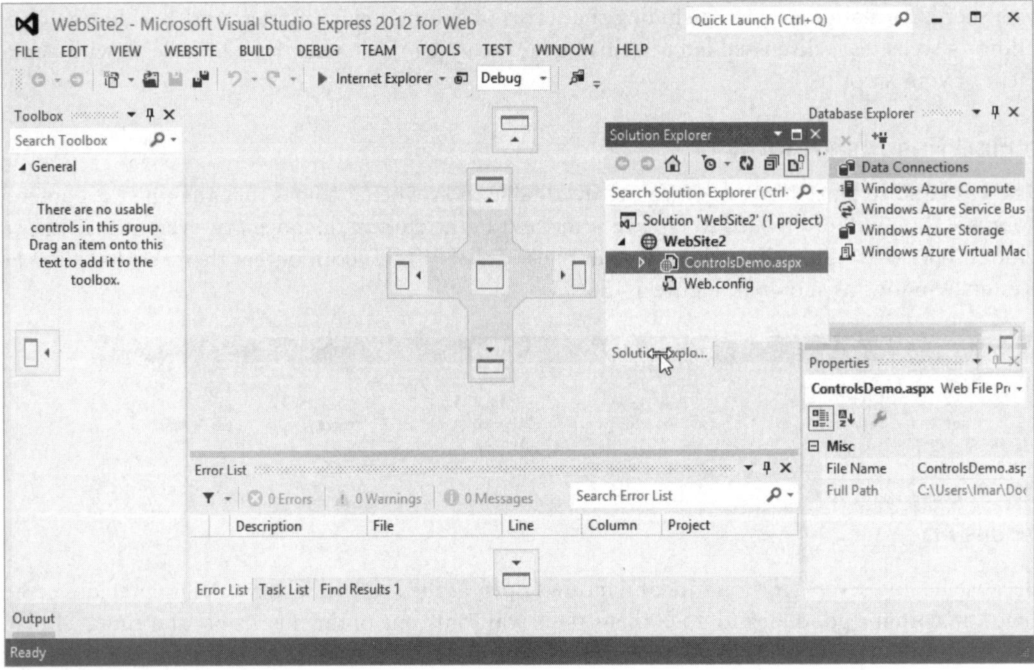

FIGURE 1-14

To restore a floating panel to its previous docked location, right-click its title bar and choose Dock or choose Window ➪ Dock from the main menu. Make sure you don't choose Dock as Tabbed Document for the tool windows, like the Toolbox or the Solution Explorer, or they'll end up in the main Document Window. This makes it difficult to use these tool windows together with an open file because the two windows will share the same space.

Modifying the Toolbox

You can modify the Toolbox as well. By default, the items are sorted alphabetically, but you can reorder them using drag and drop. To do this, open the Toolbox (press Ctrl+Alt+X) and drag an item (such as the `TextBox` under the Standard category) to a different location. You can also delete items from the Toolbox by right-clicking them and choosing Delete from the context menu. Don't worry about items getting lost forever; you can reset the Toolbox again by choosing Reset Toolbox from the same menu.

You can also add your own items to the Toolbox. The most common use for this is code snippets. Simply highlight some text or code in the Document Window and drag it to the Toolbox. You can then right-click the item and choose Rename Item to give it a more meaningful name that you can easily recognize.

To avoid cluttering up the Toolbox with your own code snippets, consider creating a separate category for them. You can do this by choosing Add Tab from the Toolbox's right-click menu. Enter a name and press Enter, and your Toolbox tab is ready for use.

In the next Try It Out exercise, you get the chance to play around with the Visual Studio IDE so you can customize it to your liking.

TRY IT OUT Customizing the IDE

In this exercise you practice opening and rearranging the windows in the VS IDE. Don't be afraid to mess things up. A little later in this chapter, instructions are given on how to reset the IDE to the way it was when you opened it the first time.

1. If you closed your website since the previous Try It Out, open it again, or create a new one using the File menu.
2. From the View menu, choose Error List to open the Error List window. If you don't see the Error List item directly, choose Tools ➪ Settings ➪ Expert Settings first. Notice how the Error List gets docked below the Document Window by default.
3. From the same View menu, choose Task List. By default, it is docked in the same space as the Error List, with the tabs for both windows next to each other.
4. Click the tab of the Task List and, while holding down your mouse button, drag the Task List away from its location in the direction of the Document Window. Once you release the window, it appears as a floating window in the IDE. To restore the window, drag it back on the center square of the Error List. To change the order in which tabs appear in a tab group, drag a tab over the other tabs and release it at the desired location.
5. If you want, you can repeat the previous steps for other windows that are visible in the IDE by default or for the ones you find under the View menu. Spend some time familiarizing yourself with all the different windows and how you can arrange them on-screen. Because you'll be working a lot with these windows in the remainder of this book, it's good to be familiar with their locations.
6. Next, open the `ControlsDemo.aspx` page (or add a new ASPX first if you created a new website) from the Solution Explorer by double-clicking it. When the page opens, the Toolbox becomes visible automatically. If it doesn't, press Ctrl+Alt+X to open it.
7. Right-click the Toolbox and choose Add Tab. Type **`HTML Fragments`** as its new name and press Enter. This adds a new category to the Toolbox that behaves just like all the others.
8. With the Document Window showing your ASPX page in Markup View, type **`<h1>`** directly after the opening `<div>` tag. Note that Visual Studio automatically inserts the closing `</h1>` for you. You should end up with code in Markup View looking like this:

```
<form id="form1" runat="server">
  <div>
    <h1></h1>
  </div>
```

9. Highlight the opening and closing `<h1>` tags, and then drag the selection from the Markup View window onto the new Toolbox tab you created in step 7. The selection shows up as Text: `<h1></h1>`.
10. Right-click the Toolbox item you just created, choose Rename Item, and type **`Heading 1`** as the name.
11. Put your cursor in the Document Window again and press Ctrl+K directly followed by Ctrl+D to format the document in the Document Window. Alternatively, choose Edit ➪ Format Document

from the main menu. This formats the document according to the rules you have set in the Text Editor Options dialog box. Formatting is also available for a number of other document types, including C# and VB.NET code, and CSS and XML files.

From now on, whenever you need a heading in your document in Markup View, simply place the cursor in the Document Window where you want the heading to appear and double-click the appropriate heading in the Toolbox.

> **NOTE** *This exercise serves as an example of adding code to the Toolbox. For an* `<h1>` *element, you might prefer to type the code directly in the code editor. Alternatively, you could use a code snippet. Enter* `h1` *in the editor and then press Tab. Visual Studio expands the code for the heading to* `<h1></h1>` *and positions your cursor between the two tags so you can start typing the heading right away.*

How It Works

Most of the steps in this Try It Out are self-explanatory. You started off by opening a few windows that you frequently need when building websites. You then used the drag-and-drop features of the IDE to rearrange the window layout according to your personal preferences.

You then added an HTML fragment to a custom tab in the Toolbox. When you drag any markup to the Toolbox, Visual Studio creates a Toolbox item for it that contains the selected markup. Whenever you need a copy of that markup in your page, simply double-click the item or drag it from the Toolbox into Markup View. This is a great time saver for HTML fragments that you frequently use. You typically use this technique for larger blocks of code; for elements like the `<h1>`, Visual Studio has a better tool called Code Snippets, which you meet later in this book.

At the end you used Visual Studio's document formatting option to change the layout of the code in the document. This helps to keep the code organized and easier to read. You can fully change how the code is formatted by using the Options dialog box accessible through Tools ➪ Options. Then expand the path Text Editor ➪ HTML ➪ Formatting, and click Tag Specific Options.

Besides the window layout and the Toolbox, Visual Studio enables you to customize a lot more in the IDE. The following section explains how to customize three other important IDE features: the Document Window, toolbars, and keyboard shortcuts.

Customizing the Document Window

Visual Studio gives you great flexibility with regard to how text is displayed in the Document Window. You can change things like font size, font color, and even the background color of the text. You can access the Font and Colors settings by choosing Tools ➪ Options, and then choosing Environment ➪ Fonts and Colors.

One thing I like to customize in the Document Window is the tab size, which controls the number of spaces that are inserted when indenting code. To change the tab size, choose Tools ➪ Options, and then under Text Editor choose All Languages ➪ Tabs. I usually set the Tab and Indent Size to 2 spaces, leaving the other settings in the Tab panel untouched. Another thing I like to customize is the number of line breaks before and after HTML elements. The Options window gives you full control over this: Select Text Editor ➪ HTML ➪ Formatting and then click Tag Specific Options. In the list on the left you can select a tag and then with the settings on the right you can control how the tag is formatted. The Preview box makes it easy to see how the various settings change the formatting.

With the exception of the Tab Size being set to 2 and the number of line breaks around a few HTML elements, all screen shots in this book show the default setup of VSEW.

Customizing Toolbars

You can customize toolbars in three ways: you can show or hide the built-in toolbars, you can add and remove buttons on existing toolbars, and you can create your own toolbars with buttons you often use.

Enabling and Disabling Toolbars

You disable and enable existing toolbars by right-clicking any existing toolbar or the menu bar and then selecting the appropriate item from the list. Once the toolbar is displayed, you can use its drag grip at its left to drag it to a new location within the Toolbar area.

Editing Existing Toolbars

If you feel that an existing toolbar is missing an important button or that it contains buttons you rarely use, you can customize the buttons on the toolbar. To do this, right-click any toolbar or the menu bar, choose Customize, switch to the Commands tab, and select the toolbar you want to modify from the Toolbar drop-down. With the command buttons at the right, you can add new and remove existing commands, or change their order.

Creating Your Own Toolbars

Creating your own toolbar is useful if you want to group some functions that you frequently use. To create a new toolbar, open the Customize window as explained in the preceding section. Click the New button and type a name for the toolbar. Then switch to the Commands tab and modify your toolbar as you would do with existing toolbars.

Customizing Keyboard Shortcuts

Another setting many developers like to change is keyboard shortcuts. Keyboard shortcuts are a great way to save time because they enable you to perform a task with a simple keyboard command instead of reaching for the mouse and selecting the appropriate item from the menu. To change the keyboard shortcuts, choose Tools ➪ Options, expand Environment, and click Keyboard. Locate the command for which you want to change the shortcut in the list of commands. Because this list contains many items, you can filter the list by typing a few letters from the command. For example, typing `print` in the Show Commands Containing field gives you a list of all print-related commands.

Next, in the Press Shortcut Keys field, type a new shortcut and click Assign. Visual Studio enables you to enter a double shortcut key for a single command. For example, you can bind the command Close All Documents to the command Ctrl+K, Ctrl+O. To perform this command, you need to press both key combinations in rapid succession. Although a double shortcut key may seem like overkill, it greatly increases the number of available shortcut keys.

Resetting Your Changes

Don't worry if you feel that you have messed up Visual Studio by trying out the numerous customization options. You have many ways to restore Visual Studio to its previous state.

Resetting the Window Layout

The command Reset Window Layout, accessible from the Window menu, resets all windows to the position they were in when you first started Visual Studio. This command is useful if you misplaced too many windows and ended up with a cluttered IDE.

Resetting the Toolbox

If you removed an item from the Toolbox by mistake or even deleted an entire tab, you can reset the Toolbox to its original state by right-clicking the Toolbox and choosing Reset Toolbox. You need to think twice before you use this command because it also deletes all your custom code snippets.

Resetting All Settings

If you followed along with the previous Try It Out exercises, and then started experimenting with the customization possibilities, your IDE is now probably in one of two states: It either looks exactly the way you want it, or it looks like a complete mess. In the latter case, it's good to know that it is easy to clean up the chaos.

To completely revert all Visual Studio settings to the way they were right after installation, choose Tools ➪ Settings ➪ Import and Export Settings or Tools ➪ Import and Export Settings, depending on the version of VS you're using. Then choose the Reset All Settings option and click Next. If you want, you can create a backup of the existing settings; otherwise, choose No, Just Reset Settings. You get another screen that enables you to choose among a number of settings collections. Choose Expert Settings or Web Development because these options give you access to all the features you need to follow along with this book. Finally, click Finish. This action causes all settings to be reset to their defaults, including the window layout, Toolbox and Toolbox customizations, shortcut keys, and everything you may have changed in the Visual Studio Options dialog box. So, use this command only when you're really sure you want a fresh, new setup of Visual Studio.

With some basic knowledge about ASP.NET pages and Visual Studio, it's time for some real action. In the next chapter, you see how to create ASP.NET websites and web pages in much more detail. You learn how to organize your site in a logical and structured way, how to add the many different types of files to your site and how to use them, and how to connect the pages in your site.

However, before you proceed to the next chapter, there is one more important topic you need to look at: the sample application that comes with this book.

THE SAMPLE APPLICATION

Building websites is what this book is all about, so it makes a whole lot of sense that this book comes with a complete and functional sample site that is used to showcase many of the capabilities of ASP.NET.

The sample site you build in this book is called Planet Wrox, a site that serves as an online community for people interested in music. The site offers the following features to its visitors:

- Reviews about CDs and concerts that have been posted on the site by the administrator.
- The Gig Pics section, an online photo album where users can share pictures taken at concerts.
- The ability to switch between the different graphical themes that the site offers, giving you a chance to change the look and feel of the site without altering the content.
- The ability to store musical preferences that influence the information users see on the site.
- Access to bonus features for registered users.

The site enables the administrator (that is, you, the owner of the site) to do the following:

- Add and maintain the reviews.
- Manage the different musical genres in the system.
- Manage photo albums created by visitors to the site.

Figure 1-15 shows the Planet Wrox homepage.

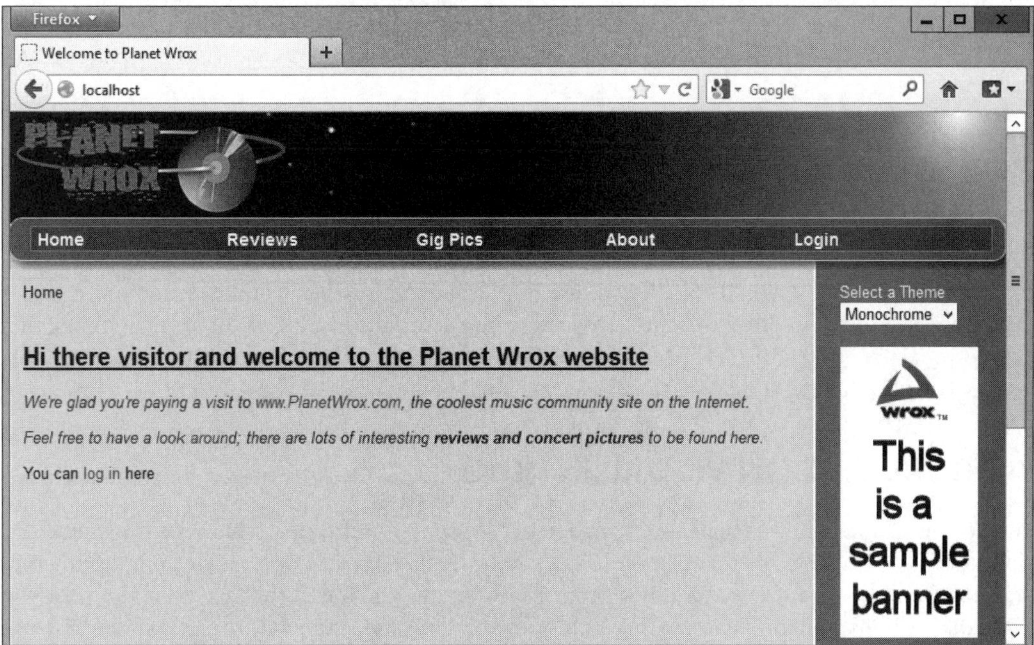

FIGURE 1-15

Figure 1-16 shows another page from Planet Wrox, but with a different theme applied. This page enables users to enter their personal information and specify preferences with regard to their favorite musical genres.

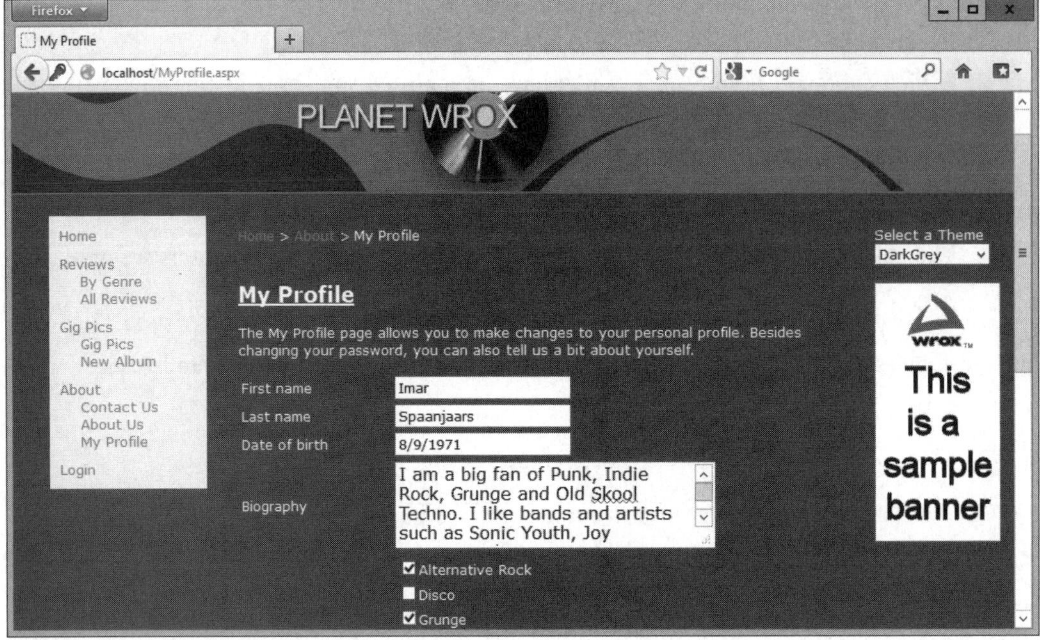

FIGURE 1-16

You can find an online running example of the site at `www.PlanetWrox.com`. There you can play around with the site from an end user's perspective.

You can also download the source for the sample application and all other examples from this book from the Wrox website at `www.wrox.com/remtitle.cgi?isbn=1118311809`.

By the end of this book, you'll be able to build all of the functionality from the sample site (and hopefully even more) in other websites. Don't worry if it sounds like an awful lot of complex things. I guide you, step by step, from the beginning of the application all the way to the last feature. As long as you keep having fun doing this, I'm sure you'll make it all the way.

PRACTICAL TIPS ON VISUAL STUDIO

Most of the chapters in this book end with a short section of useful tips. These are tips that either didn't fit in anywhere in the text or encourage you to further explore or test out things. Sometimes they may seem irrelevant or hard to understand at first, but you'll find that as you make your way through this book and look back at tips from previous chapters, things start to make sense. Don't worry if you don't understand certain things completely the first time you see them. Give the idea some thought and revisit the topic a few days later. Hopefully, by letting the ideas sink in a little, things start to make more sense automatically. This applies not only to the Practical Tips section, but to the entire book.

- Before you move on to the next chapter, play around with Visual Studio some more. Add a couple of pages to your site, drag and drop some controls from the Toolbox onto your pages, and view them in your browser. That way, you'll have a better understanding of the tools and the many controls available when you start the next chapter.
- Familiarize yourself with the many options to tweak the Visual Studio IDE. When building websites, you spend most of your time in this IDE, so it makes sense to tweak it as much as possible to your liking. Don't be afraid to mess it up; you can always revert to previous settings.
- Take some time to browse through the settings you find in the Options dialog box of Visual Studio (accessible through the Tools ➪ Options menu). Many of the settings are self-explanatory and can really help in further tweaking the IDE.

SUMMARY

This chapter covered a lot of important ground to get you started with ASP.NET 4.5 and Visual Studio. It started off with a brief history of the Microsoft .NET Framework in general and ASP .NET in particular.

You then learned how to acquire and install Visual Studio, which is the most extensive and versatile tool available for creating ASP.NET 4.5 web pages. To enable you to work with it effectively, this chapter showed you how to use and customize the main features of the IDE. In subsequent chapters, you use and extend this knowledge to work with the many tools found in VS.

It's important to understand how a page in Visual Studio makes it to your web browser. Some knowledge of the web server that serves the request and how the page is processed to deliver the final HTML in the browser is critical to understanding ASP.NET. This chapter gave you a short introduction to the way a web page is requested and served to the browser.

In the next chapter, you get a much more detailed explanation of creating websites.

EXERCISES

1. Explain the differences between the markup of a page in Visual Studio and the final HTML page in the browser.
2. Imagine you have a number of HTML fragments that you expect to use a lot throughout the site. What's the best way to make these fragments available in Visual Studio?
3. Name three ways you can reset some or all of the IDE customization settings.
4. If you want to change the property of a control on your page, for example the text of a button, which two options do you have available to make the change?

You can find answers to these exercises in Appendix A.

▶ WHAT YOU LEARNED IN THIS CHAPTER

Attribute	Extra information in a tag to define or change its behavior
Element	A pair of tags holding some text or other content
HTML	HyperText Markup Language: the language that browsers use to display a web page
HTTP	HyperText Transfer Protocol: the protocol by which web browsers and web servers communicate
IDE	Integrated development environment: an integrated collection of applications and tools to develop applications
JavaScript	A programming language used to interact with a web page in the client's browser
Tag	Text surrounded by angle brackets to create HTML elements
Visual Studio 2012	The development environment to build .NET applications
Visual Studio Express 2012 for Web	The free version of Visual Studio that enables you to build ASP.NET web applications

2

Building an ASP.NET Website

WHAT YOU WILL LEARN IN THIS CHAPTER:

- The different project types you can choose from as a starting point for your ASP.NET websites
- The different project templates that are available to jump-start your site development
- The numerous file types available in ASP.NET and what they are used for
- Ways to create structured websites that are easy to manage, now and in the future
- How to use the designer tools to create formatted web pages

WROX.COM CODE DOWNLOADS FOR THIS CHAPTER

You can find the wrox.com code downloads for this chapter on the Download Code tab at `www.wrox.com/remtitle.cgi?isbn=1118311809`. The code is in the Chapter 2 download.

To create good-looking, functional, and successful websites, you have to understand a number of important technologies and languages, including HyperText Markup Language (HTML), ASP.NET, cascading style sheets (CSS), a server-side programming language such as C# or VB, and a client-side language such as JavaScript. This and upcoming chapters provide a solid foundation in these technologies, so you should be comfortable with the most important concepts once you've finished this book.

Besides these technologies, you also have to understand the Visual Studio IDE that was introduced in the previous chapter. You need to know how to create sites, add pages, and manage all the toolbars and windows that Visual Studio (VS) offers you. In addition, you need to know how to build and design web pages in VS with HTML and server controls.

This chapter shows you, in detail, how to create and manage your websites. It also shows you how to create your ASP.NET web pages and add markup to them, enabling you to create useful web pages that can present information to users and react to their response.

Although you already created your first ASP.NET website in the previous chapter, this chapter starts off with another in-depth look at creating a new website. Because you have many choices to make when you start a new site, it's important to understand all the different options and pick the right one for your scenario.

CREATING WEBSITES WITH VISUAL STUDIO 2012

The preceding chapter gave you a quick overview of creating a website in VS. You simply chose New Web Site from the File menu, selected a language, selected the standard ASP.NET Web Forms Site template, and clicked OK. However, there's more to the New Web Site dialog box than you saw in the previous chapter. You may have noticed that you can choose among a number of different templates that enable you to create different kinds of sites. But before looking at the different templates on which you can base your new website, you need to know a little more about the different *project types* that are available in VS.

Different Project Types

In Visual Studio 2012 you can choose between two types of projects for creating ASP.NET Web Forms websites: *Web Application Projects* and *Web Site Projects*.

Web Application Projects

Web Application Projects make it easier for developers who work in teams or who need more control over the contents of the site and their compilation and deployment processes to build websites with VS. The whole website is managed as a project, with a single project file that keeps track of all the content of the website.

In VS, you create a new Web Application Project through the File ➪ New Project dialog box. In that dialog box, click your preferred programming language (either Visual Basic or Visual C#) and click the Web category, where you'll find a number of ASP.NET web application templates. One of the available project templates is the ASP.NET MVC 4 Web Application, which creates an application based on the *Model View Controller* pattern, another popular style of web application development. MVC is not used or discussed in this book, but if you want to learn more, check out `www.asp.net/mvc`.

Web Site Projects

Web Site Projects represent a project in VS for a website. You create a new Web Site Project by choosing File ➪ New Web Site or File ➪ New ➪ Web Site from Visual Studio's main menu.

A Web Site Project site is simply a Windows folder with a bunch of files and subfolders in it. There is no collective file (known as the *project file* with a `.vbproj` or `.csproj` extension) that keeps track of all the individual files in the website. You just point VS to a folder, and it instantly opens it as a website. This makes it very easy to create copies of the site, move them, and share them with others, because no dependencies exist with files on your local system. Because of the lack of a central project file, Web Site Projects are usually simply referred to as websites, which is the term I use in the remainder of this book.

Choosing between Web Site Projects and Web Application Projects

Because you have two options to choose from, you may be wondering which project type you should pick. In general, the Web Site Project is a bit easier to work with. Because it's just a folder, it's easier to copy the files to a different location, such as another development workstation or a production server. Also, changes to the code files are picked up by the web server and applied automatically without a formal deployment process. The Web Application Project, on the other hand, works better if you work with a team of developers on the same site, because it dictates a more formal development and deployment process and has better support for working with Source Control versioning systems, such as Microsoft's Team Foundation Server.

This book uses the Web Site Project model because it's easier to work with if you're new to ASP .NET. However, you'll find that sites built using the Web Application Project model have a lot in common with Web Site Projects, which means you can use the knowledge you gain from this book to build sites with the Web Application Project model as well. You must use the Web Site Project model if you want to follow along with this book. When not referring to a specific project type, I'll use the terms website and web application interchangeably throughout this book when referring to websites in general.

Now that you know about the different project models, the next thing to consider is the different *website templates* and their options.

Choosing the Right Website Template

The New Web Site dialog box in VS contains different website templates, each one serving a distinct purpose.

Figure 2-1 shows the New Web Site dialog box in VS. You can open this dialog box by choosing File ➪ New Web Site or File ➪ New ➪ Web Site, depending on your version of VS. If your dialog box doesn't look like Figure 2-1, make sure you chose File ➪ New Web Site and not File ➪ New Project.

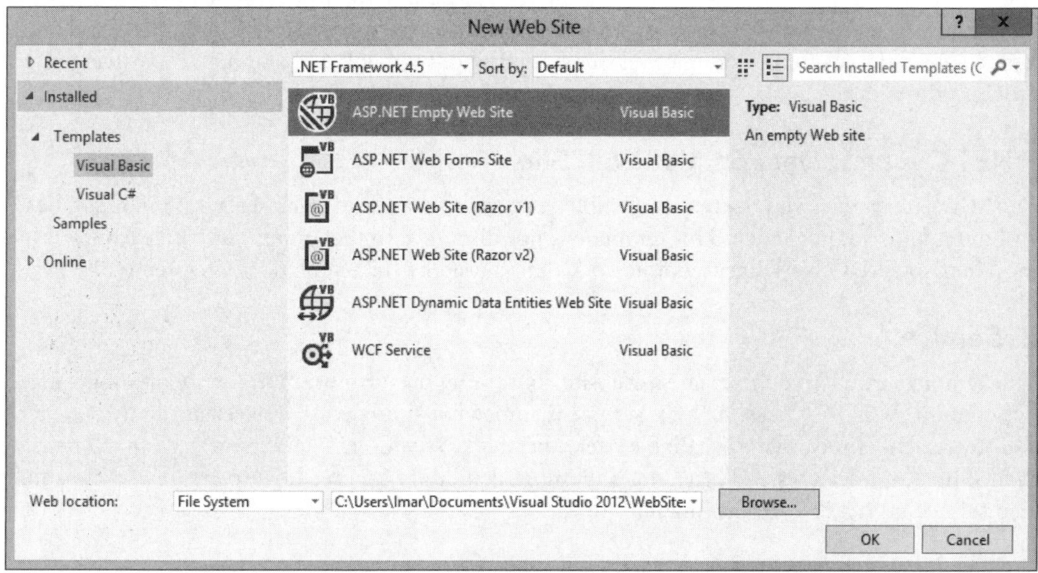

FIGURE 2-1

In the left-hand section you can choose between Visual Basic and Visual C# as the programming language for your site. The section in the middle shows the ASP.NET website templates that are installed by default. Each of them is discussed in the next section. When you have created your own templates (which you learn how to do in Chapter 6), or have templates installed from other parties, they show up in this area as well.

The ASP.NET Empty Web Site template is used throughout this book for the Planet Wrox website. The others are described briefly in the following sections so you know how they can be used. The exact list of installed templates on your system depends on the version of Visual Studio and the installed components. Don't worry if you have other templates as long as you have the ASP.NET Web Forms Site and the ASP.NET Empty Web Site items.

ASP.NET Web Forms Site

This template enables you to set up a basic ASP.NET website. It contains a number of files and folders to jump-start the development of your site. The different file types are all discussed later in this chapter. The special `App_Data` folder and the functionality of the pages in the `Account` folder are discussed later in this book.

This template is a good starting point once you start developing real-world ASP.NET websites.

ASP.NET Web Site (Razor v1 / Razor v2)

You use these templates to create sites using Microsoft's Web Pages framework. You can learn more about Web Pages in my book *Beginning ASP.NET Web Pages with WebMatrix* (Wrox, 2011, ISBN: 978-1-118-05048-4).

ASP.NET Empty Web Site

The ASP.NET Empty Web Site template gives you nothing but a single configuration file (`Web.config`). The ASP.NET Empty Web Site template is useful if you have a bunch of existing files you want to use to create a new website or when you want to create your site from scratch. You use this template as the basis for the sample website you build in the book and add files and folders as you progress through the book.

ASP.NET Dynamic Data Entities Web Site

This template enables you to create a flexible yet powerful website to manage data in a database without a lot of manual code. This template is not discussed in this book, but you learn more about the Microsoft ADO.NET Entity Framework that is used by the template in Chapter 14.

WCF Service

This template enables you to create a website containing one or more Windows Communication Foundation (WCF) Services. A WCF Service is somewhat similar to a web service in that it enables you to create methods that are callable over a network. However, WCF Services go much further than simple web services and offer you a lot more flexibility. You see how to create and consume a web service from a browser in Chapter 10.

Although it seems you have to make a clear choice up front for the right website template, this isn't really the case. Because an ASP.NET website in VS is essentially just a reference to a folder, it's easy to add types from one template to another. For example, it's perfectly acceptable (and very common) to add a web service file to a standard ASP.NET Web Forms Site or an ASP.NET Empty Web Site, as you see in Chapter 10.

Creating and Opening a New Website

You have a number of different ways to create new and open existing websites. The choices you have here are largely influenced by the way you access the website (either on your local machine with Visual Studio on it or on a remote machine), and whether you want to use *IIS Express* (the built-in web server that ships with VS) or the full version of IIS—the web server that comes with Windows.

All the examples in this book assume that you open sites from your local hard drive and that you use IIS Express, a trimmed down version of IIS, because it's very convenient to develop sites with it. However, Chapter 19 shows you how to use and configure the full version of *Internet Information Services*, or *IIS* for short. This advanced web server comes with most editions of Windows and is mostly used for production hosting of your websites on the server editions of Windows, because it's capable of serving web pages in high-traffic scenarios.

Creating New Websites

The next Try It Out section guides you through creating the Planet Wrox website, which is the project you work on in this book. All exercises in the remainder of the book assume you have this website open in VS, except where stated otherwise. The exercise instructs you to store your website in a folder called `C:\BegASPNET\Site`. Take note of this folder name, because it's used throughout this book. If you decide to use a different folder, be sure to use your own location whenever you see this folder name in the book. Also make sure you don't use special characters like the hash (`#`) or insert a space in the folder name because you'll run into trouble when developing your site. Finally, make sure you don't create this folder under your Windows `Documents` folder (typically at `C:\Users\`*`UserName`*`\Documents`), because you'll run into problems later when accounts other than your own need access to your site.

TRY IT OUT Creating a New ASP.NET 4.5 Website

1. Start by creating a folder called **`BegASPNET`** in the root of your C drive using Windows Explorer or My Computer. Inside the folder, create another folder called **`Site`**. You should end up with a folder called `C:\BegASPNET\Site`. If you followed the instructions from the "Introduction" section of this book and unpacked the source for this book, you already have the `BegASPNET` folder, which in turn contains the `Source` and `Resources` folders. You still need to create the `Site` folder, though. If you want to follow along with VB.NET and C# at the same time, you can create two folders, `BegASPNETVB` and `BegASPNETCS`, and use two instances of Visual Studio.
2. Start Visual Studio and choose File ➪ New Web Site or File ➪ New ➪ Web Site, depending on your version of VS.

> ***COMMON MISTAKES*** *Don't mistakenly create a new Web Application Project using File ➪ New Project, because this project template is not compatible with the exercises in this book.*

3. In the target framework drop-down list at the top of the screen, select .NET Framework 4.5.
4. In the Installed Templates area on the left, choose between Visual Basic and Visual C#. All the examples in this book are shown in both programming languages, so you can choose the one you like best.
5. In the area in the middle select ASP.NET Empty Web Site.
6. In the Web Location drop-down list, make sure that File System is selected. The other two options (HTTP and FTP) enable you to open a site running on IIS (either on your local machine or on a remote server using the so-called Microsoft FrontPage Server Extensions) and open a site from an FTP server, respectively.
7. Click the Browse button next to the location text box, browse to `C:\BegASPNET\Site` (the folder you created in the first step of this exercise), and click Open.

   Your final screen should look like the one in Figure 2-2, except that you may have chosen Visual C# instead of Visual Basic.

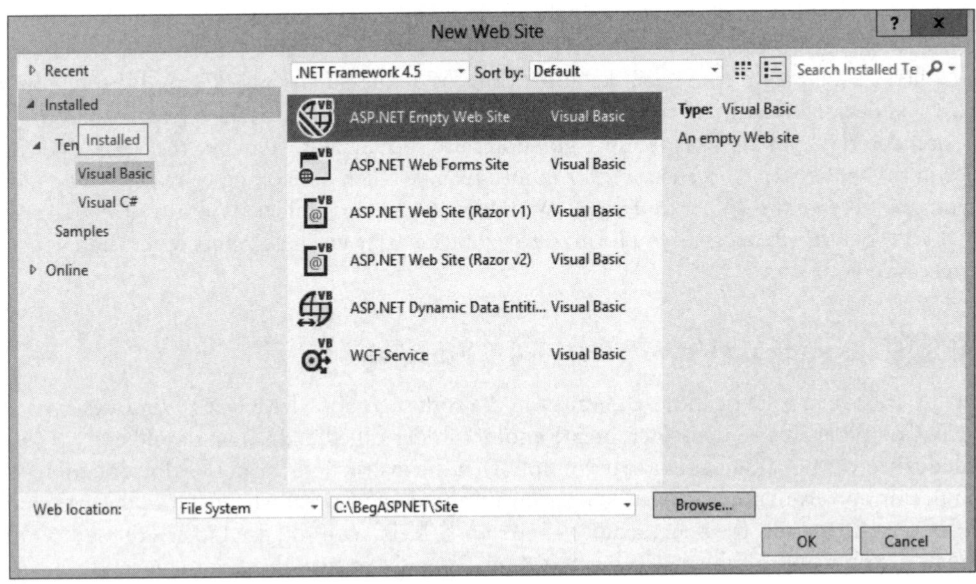

FIGURE 2-2

8. Click OK and VS creates the new site for you.

How It Works

As soon as you click OK, VS creates a new, empty website for you. This new website contains nothing but a configuration file (called `Web.config`). In the Solution Explorer, your website now looks like Figure 2-3. If you don't see the top-level Solution node, choose Tools ➪ Options in VS, and in the Projects and Solutions category select Always Show Solution.

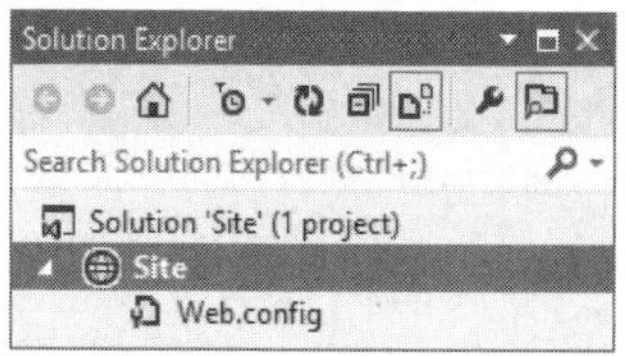

FIGURE 2-3

Because a website based on the Empty Web Site template is just a simple Windows folder that VS looks at, the actual folder on disk contains the same file. No additional files are used to create the site, as shown in Figure 2-4, which shows File Explorer displaying the files in the folder `C:\BegASPNET\Site`.

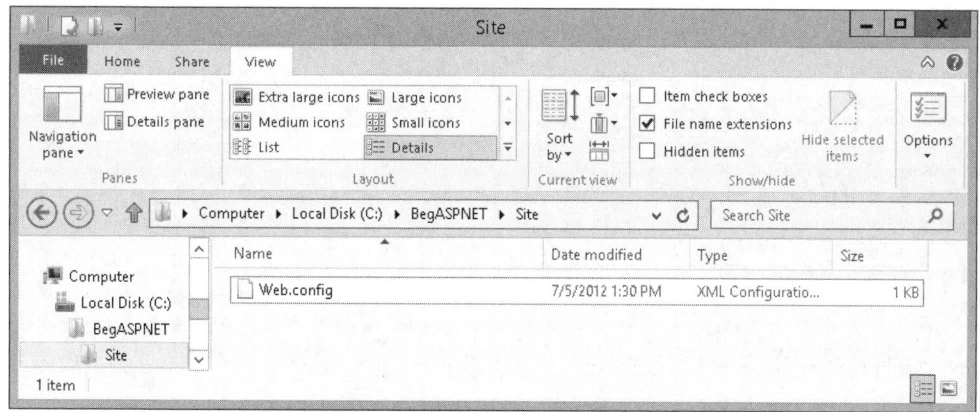

FIGURE 2-4

If you don't see the `.config` extension of the web file, don't worry. You see how to view file extensions in a later exercise.

As you progress through this book, you'll add new files and folders to the site. These additional files and folders show up in the Solution Explorer and will appear in the Windows folder at `C:\BegASPNET\Site` as well.

Opening websites based on the Web Site Project template is very similar to creating new ones. In the next section, you get a quick overview of opening existing sites in VS.

Opening Existing Websites

Just as with creating new sites, opening an existing site in VS gives you a few options with regard to the source location of the website. You can choose to open a site from the local filesystem, from a local IIS web server, from a remote server using FTP, from a remote site using the Microsoft FrontPage Server Extensions, or from a central Source Control system such as Microsoft's Team Foundation Server. Figure 2-5 shows the Open Web Site dialog box in VS.

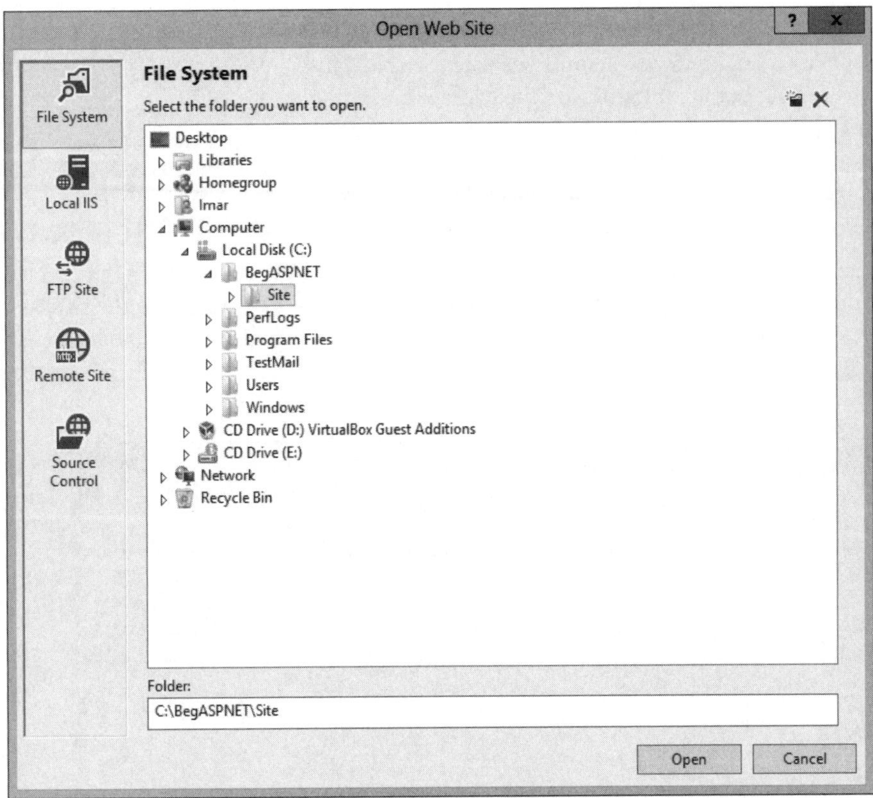

FIGURE 2-5

To get to this dialog box, choose File ⇨ Open Web Site in VS (don't accidentally choose File ⇨ Open Project because that menu item is used to open Web Application Projects instead). All the examples in the book assume that you always open the Planet Wrox website from the local filesystem, using the File System button, which is the first button in the left column of the window. Then in the right pane, locate your website (`C:\BegASPNET\Site` in this example) and click the Open button.

The site you created in the previous Try It Out is a very bare-bones site. To make it more useful, you need to add files to it. The many file types you have at your disposal and the way they are added to the site are the next topics of discussion.

WORKING WITH FILES IN YOUR WEBSITE

An ASP.NET 4.5 Web Forms Site consists of at least a single Web Form (a file with an `.aspx` extension), but usually it consists of a larger number of files. Many different file types are available in VS, each offering a distinct functionality. In the next section, you see the most important file types that are used in VS. In addition, you learn a few different ways to add these files to your site.

The Many File Types of an ASP.NET 4.5 Website

To give you an idea of how many different files you can use in ASP.NET, Figure 2-6 shows the dialog box that enables you to add new files to the site (accessible by right-clicking your website in the Solution Explorer and choosing Add ➪ Add New Item or by choosing Website ➪ Add New Item from the main menu).

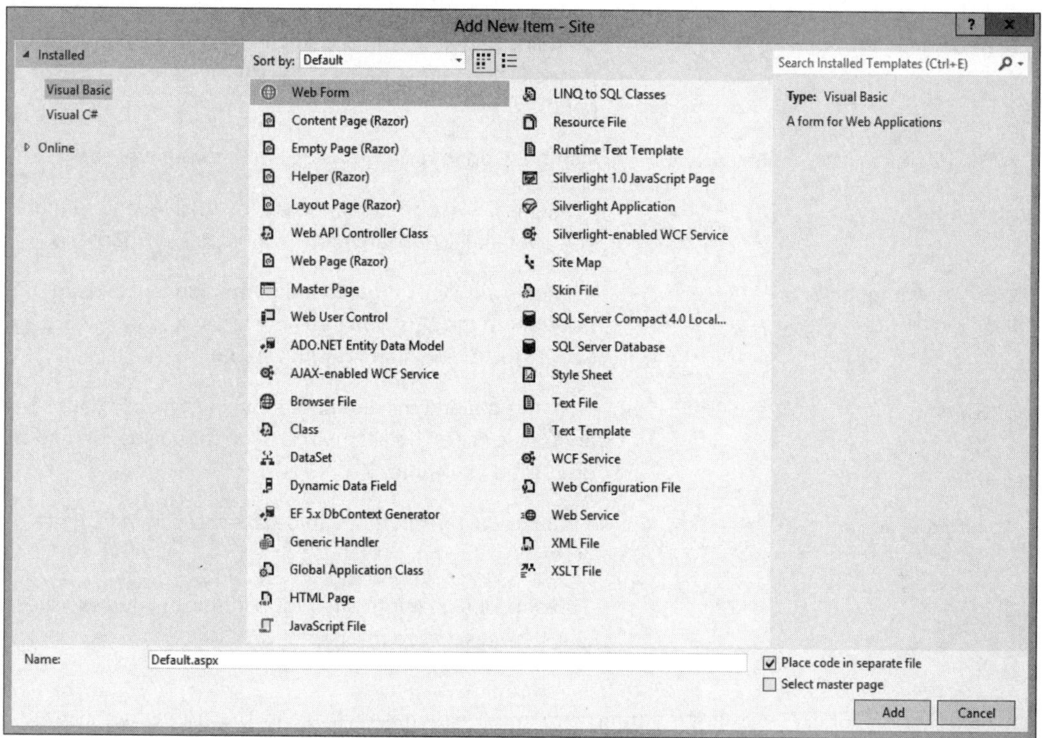

FIGURE 2-6

To make it easier to find the type of file you're looking for, you can use the search box at the top-right corner of the dialog box. Simply enter a few letters of the type you're looking for and hit Enter. VS filters the list of files to those matching your search phrase.

The files you can add to a site can be grouped in a few different categories. The most important files—the ones you use throughout the examples in this book—are discussed next.

Web Files

Web files are specific to web applications and can either be requested by a browser directly, or are used to build up part of the web page that is requested in the browser. The following table lists the various web files you typically use in an ASP.NET Web Forms website and their extensions, and describes how each file is used.

FILE TYPE	EXTENSION	DESCRIPTION
Web Form	`.aspx`	The workhorse of any ASP.NET website; represents the pages that your users view in their browsers.
Master Page	`.master`	Enables you to define the global structure and the look and feel of a website. You see how it can be used in Chapter 6.
Web User Control	`.ascx`	Contains page fragments that can be reused in multiple pages in your site. Chapter 8 is entirely devoted to user controls.
HTML Page	`.htm` / `.html`	Can be used to display static HTML in your website.
Style Sheet	`.css`	Contains CSS code that enables you to style and format your website. You learn more about CSS in Chapter 3.
Web Configuration File	`.config`	Contains global configuration information that is used throughout the site. You see how to use the `Web.config` later in this book, starting with Chapter 4.
Site Map	`.sitemap`	Contains a hierarchical representation of files in your site in an XML format. The site map is used for navigation and is discussed in Chapter 7.
JavaScript File	`.js`	Contains JavaScript that can be executed in the client's browser.
Skin File	`.skin`	Contains design information for controls in your website. Skins are discussed in Chapter 6.

The next Try It Out exercise shows you how to add a new master page to the site, which is used throughout the book.

TRY IT OUT Adding Files to Your Site

1. If it is not still open, open the Planet Wrox website you created earlier by choosing File ➪ Open Web Site. Make sure that you open the site from the filesystem, locate the folder that contains your site (`C:\BegASPNET\Site`), and click the Open button.
2. In the Solution Explorer, right-click your site and choose Add ➪ New Folder.

> ***COMMON MISTAKES*** *Make sure you click the actual site and not the* `Web.config` *file or the Solution node at the top (see Figure 2-3) or you won't get the correct menu item.*

3. Type **`MasterPages`** as the name of the folder and press Enter. Then right-click this new folder and choose Add ➪ Add New Item. Alternatively, you can choose File ➪ New File or Website ➪ Add New Item from Visual Studio's main menu, or you can click the new folder in the Solution Explorer once to put the focus on it and then press Ctrl+Shift+A.
4. In the dialog box that appears, click Master Page and type **`Frontend`** as the name. VS automatically adds the `.master` extension for you when you add the file. Verify that under Installed Templates you have selected the language you want to use for this site and that Place Code in Separate File in the bottom-right corner is checked. Finally, click the Add button. The master page is added to the site, and is opened automatically for you in the Document Window.

How It Works

This simple exercise showed you how to add a new item to your website. Although at this stage the site isn't very exciting yet, the file you added forms the basis for the rest of the book. The next sections briefly look at the remainder of the file types.

Code Files

Adding code files to the site is identical to how you add web files. The following table describes the various types of code files.

FILE TYPE	EXTENSION	DESCRIPTION
WCF Service	`.svc`	Can be called by other systems, including browsers, and can contain code that can be executed on your server. WCF services are covered in Chapter 10.
Class	`.cs` / `.vb`	Can contain code to program your website. Note that Code Behind files (discussed later) also have this extension because they are essentially class files. C# uses files with the `.cs` extension and Visual Basic uses `.vb` files.
Global Application Class	`.asax`	Can contain code that is fired in response to interesting things that happen in your site, such as the start of the application or when an error occurs somewhere in the site. You see how to use this file in Chapters 11 and 18.

Besides the Code Files category, there is one more group of files worth looking into: Data Files.

Data Files

Data files are used to store data that can be used in your site and in other applications. The group consists of the XML files, database files, and files related to working with data.

FILE TYPE	EXTENSION	DESCRIPTION
XML File	`.xml`	Used to store data in XML format. In addition to plain XML files, ASP.NET supports a few more XML-based files, two of which you briefly saw before: `Web.config` and the site map.
SQL Server Database	`.mdf`	Files with an `.mdf` extension are databases that are used by Microsoft SQL Server. Databases are discussed in Chapter 12 and later.
ADO.NET Entity Data Model	`.edmx`	Used to access databases declaratively, without the need to write a lot of repetitive code. Technically, this is not a data file, because it does not contain the actual data. However, because it is tied to the database so closely, it makes sense to group it under this header. You learn more about the ADO.NET Entity Framework in Chapter 14.

As you saw in the previous Try It Out, adding a new file of any of these types is really easy. It's just as easy to add existing files to the site.

Adding Existing Files

Not every file you create in your website has to be brand new. In some cases it makes sense to reuse files from other projects. For example, you may want to reuse a logo or a CSS file across multiple sites. You can easily add existing files by right-clicking the website in the Solution Explorer and choosing Add ➪ Add Existing Item. In the dialog box that appears, you can browse for the files, and optionally select multiple files by holding down the Ctrl key. Finally, when you click Add, the files are added to the website. You can also use copy and paste to copy files from a folder on your local disk to a website in VS. Simply highlight the files in Windows Explorer, press Ctrl+C to copy the files, switch to VS, click the website in the Solution Explorer (or on a subfolder of your site), and press Ctrl+V. The files are then copied into your website's folder.

However, there is an even easier way to add files to the site, which can be a great time saver when you need to add multiple existing files and folders to your site: drag and drop. The following Try It Out shows you how this works.

TRY IT OUT Adding Existing Files to Your Site

1. In Windows, minimize all open applications, right-click your desktop, and choose New ➪ Text Document. If you don't see this option, simply create a new text document using Notepad and save it on your desktop.

2. Rename the file **Styles.css**. Make sure the `.txt` extension is replaced by `.css`. If you don't see the initial `.txt` extension and the icon of the file doesn't change from a text file to a CSS file (by default this is the same icon as a text file with a gear symbol on top of it, but you may have software installed that changed the icon for CSS files), Windows is configured to hide extensions for known file types. If that's the case, open up Windows Explorer in Windows 7, click the Organize button, and then choose Folder and Search Options. Switch to the View tab and deselect the option labeled Hide Extensions for Known File Types. For Windows 8 you find the option called File Name Extensions on the View tab of the Ribbon bar of the File Explorer, shown in Figure 2-4. You now may need to change the name of the file from `Styles.css.txt` to **Styles.css**.

   When you change the file extension from `.txt` to `.css`, Windows may give you a warning that the file becomes unusable if you proceed. You can safely answer Yes to this question to continue.

3. Rearrange VS so you can see part of the desktop with the CSS file as well. You can use the Restore Down button next to the Close button on the Windows title bar of VS to get it out of full screen mode.

4. Click the CSS file on the desktop and, while holding down the mouse button, drag the file into the Solution Explorer. Make sure you drag the file into the Solution Explorer and not into other parts of VS, or the file won't be added. For example, when you drag it into the Document Window, VS simply opens the file for you, but doesn't add it to the site.

5. When you release the mouse while over the website node or an existing file in the Solution Explorer, the CSS file is added to your site.

> ***NOTE*** *If you are using Windows 7 and run VS as an administrator, this might not work because Windows doesn't allow the Windows Explorer and VS to communicate. In that case, add existing files using the Add Existing Item menu discussed earlier or use copy and paste.*

How It Works

Although this seems to be a simple exercise that uses basic Windows skills, it serves to show that VS creates *a copy* of the file when it adds it to the site. So, the original `Styles.css` file on the desktop is not affected when you make changes to the copy in VS. This way, it's easy to drag and drop files from existing websites into your new one without affecting the originals. The same applies to files you add using the Add Existing Item dialog box in VS.

If you have added files to your website's folder outside of VS, they may not show up right away. You can get a fresh copy of the file list by clicking the Refresh button on the Solution Explorer's toolbar.

Organizing Your Site

Because of the many files that make up your site, it's often a good idea to group them by function in separate folders. For example, all style sheet files could go in a folder called `Styles`, `.js` files could go in `Scripts`, user controls could go in a `Controls` folder, and master pages could be stored in a folder called `MasterPages`. This is a matter of personal preference, but structured and well-organized sites are easier to manage and understand. The next Try It Out explains how you can move files around into new folders to organize your site.

TRY IT OUT Organizing Your Website

1. Right-click the Planet Wrox site in the Solution Explorer and choose Add ⇨ New Folder.
2. Type **`Styles`** as the new folder name and press Enter.
3. Create another folder, called **`Controls`**. These two folders are used in the remainder of this book.
4. Drag the `Styles.css` file that you added earlier and drop it into the `Styles` folder.

   If everything went well, your Solution Explorer should look like Figure 2-7.

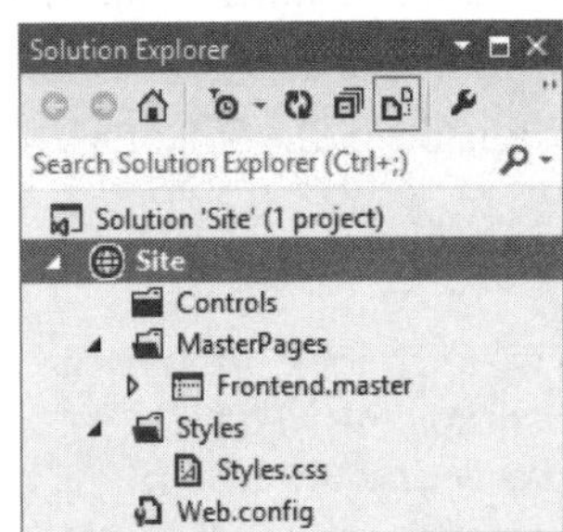

FIGURE 2-7

If your Solution Explorer looks different from the one shown in Figure 2-7, follow this Try It Out again until your site looks exactly the same, with the same folder structure and files in it. Future Try It Out exercises in this book assume you have the correct folders and files in your website.

How It Works

Structure and organization are important to keep your sites manageable. Although you may be tempted to add all of your files to the root of your project, it's better not to do this. With a very small site, you may not notice any difference, but as soon as your site begins to grow, you'll find it becomes a lot harder to manage when it lacks structure. Placing related files in separate folders is the first step to an organized site. Storing files of the same type in a single folder is only one way to optimize your site. In later chapters, you see that separate folders are also used to group files with similar functionality. For example, all files that are accessible only by an administrator of the site are grouped in a folder called `Management`.

The drag-and-drop features of VS make it easy to reorganize your site. Simply pick up one file or multiple files and drop them in their new location. If you continue to apply these kinds of organization practices while expanding your site, you'll find that tomorrow or six months from now, you won't have any problems locating the right file when you need it.

Special File Types

Some of the files listed in the previous section require that you put them in a special folder instead of the proposed optional organizational folder structure. The IDE warns you when you try to add a file outside of its special folder, and offers to create the folder and put the file there. For example, when you try to add a class file (with a `.vb` or `.cs` extension), you get the warning shown in Figure 2-8.

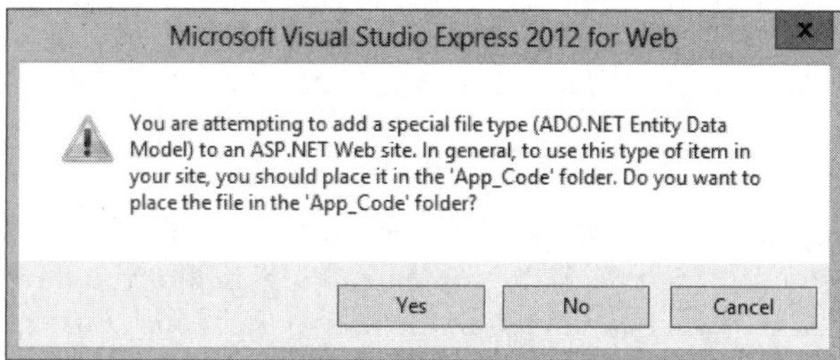

FIGURE 2-8

When you get this dialog box, always click Yes. Otherwise, your file won't function correctly. You get similar dialog boxes for other file types, including skin and database files.

Now that you have a good understanding of the different types of files that make up your website, it's time to look at one of them in much more detail: `.aspx` files, also known as Web Forms.

WORKING WITH WEB FORMS

Web Forms, represented by `.aspx` files, are the core of any ASP.NET 4.5 Web Forms website. They are the actual pages that users see in their browsers when they visit your site.

As you saw in the previous chapter, Web Forms can contain a mix of HTML, ASP.NET Server Controls, client-side JavaScript, CSS, and programming logic. To make it easier to see how all this code ends up in the browser, VS offers a number of different views on your pages.

The Different Views on Web Forms

VS enables you to look at your Web Form from a few different angles. When you have a file with markup—like a Web Form or master page—open in the Document Window, you see three buttons at the bottom-left corner of the window. With these buttons, visible in Figure 2-9, you can switch between the different views. This figure shows a master page, which you'll learn more about in Chapter 6.

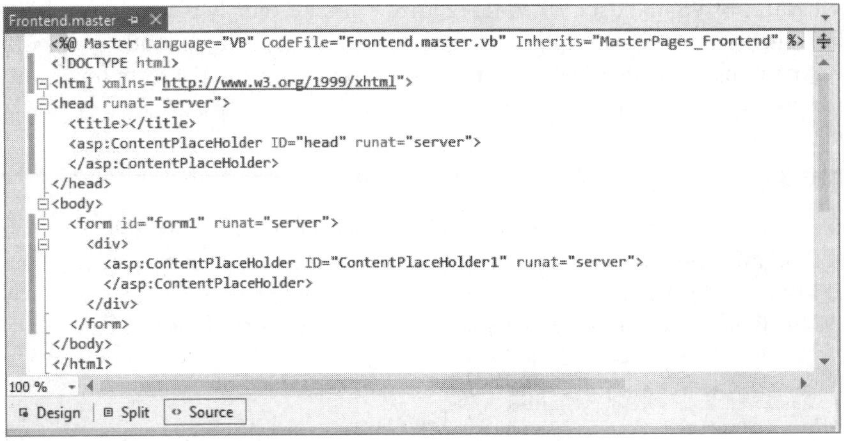

```
Frontend.master
<%@ Master Language="VB" CodeFile="Frontend.master.vb" Inherits="MasterPages_Frontend" %>
<!DOCTYPE html>
<html xmlns="http://www.w3.org/1999/xhtml">
<head runat="server">
  <title></title>
  <asp:ContentPlaceHolder ID="head" runat="server">
  </asp:ContentPlaceHolder>
</head>
<body>
  <form id="form1" runat="server">
    <div>
      <asp:ContentPlaceHolder ID="ContentPlaceHolder1" runat="server">
      </asp:ContentPlaceHolder>
    </div>
  </form>
</body>
</html>
100 %
Design | Split | Source
```

FIGURE 2-9

Source View is the default view when you open a page. It shows you the raw HTML and other markup for the page, and is very useful if you want to tweak the contents of a page and you have a good idea of what you want to change and where. As I explained in the previous chapter, I use the term Markup View rather than Source View to refer to the markup of ASPX and HTML pages.

The Design button enables you to switch the Document Window into Design View, which gives you an idea of how the page will end up. When in Design View, you can use the Visual Aids and Formatting Marks submenus from the main View menu to control visual markers like line breaks, borders, and spaces. Both submenus offer a menu item called Show that enables you to turn all the visual aids on or off at once. Turning both off is useful if you want to have an idea of how the page ends up in the browser. You should, however, use Design View only to get *an idea* of how the page will end up. Although VS has a great rendering engine that renders the page in Design View pretty well, you should always check your pages in different browsers as well, because what you see in VS is the markup for the page before it gets processed. Server controls on the page may emit HTML that changes the look of the page in the browser. Therefore, it's recommended to view the page in the browser as often as possible so you can check if it's going to look the way you want it. It's also recommended to test your site in as many different browsers as you can get your hands on, because there may be small differences between them in the way they render a web page. The Planet Wrox website has been developed and tested against recent versions of Microsoft Internet Explorer, Firefox, Google Chrome, Safari, and Opera. You'll see screenshots of these browsers at various places in the book.

The Split button enables you to look at Design View and Markup View at the same time, as you can see in Figure 2-10.

Split View is great if you want to see the code that VS generates when you add controls to the Design View of your page. The other way around is very useful too: When you make changes to the markup of the page in Markup View, you can see how it ends up in Design View. Sometimes Design View becomes out of sync with Markup View. If that's the case, a message appears at the top of Design View. Simply clicking the message or saving the entire page is enough to update the Design window.

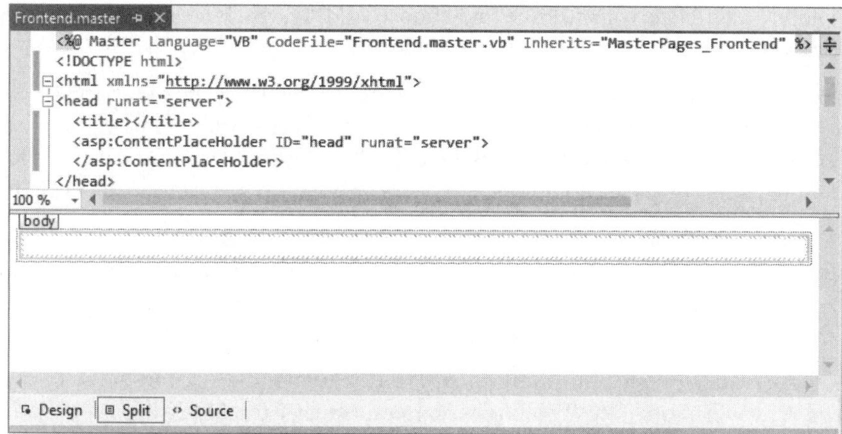

FIGURE 2-10

You can cycle through the three different modes using the Ctrl+Page Up and Ctrl+Page Down keys.

If you want your pages to open in a different view than Markup View, choose Tools ⇨ Options. Then expand HTML Designer, and in the General category, set your preferred view. Alternatively, enter **HTML Designer General** in the Quick Launch text box (which you can access by pressing Ctrl+Q) at the top-right of VS and then click the item in the list that appears.

In addition to the HTML and other markup you see in the Markup View window, a Web Form can also contain code in either C# or Visual Basic .NET. Where this code is placed depends on the type of Web Form you create. The next section explains the two options you have in more detail.

Choosing between Code Behind and Pages with Inline Code

Web Forms come in two flavors: either as an `.aspx` file with a *Code Behind* file (a file named after the Web Form with an additional `.vb` or `.cs` extension) or as `.aspx` files that have their code embedded, often referred to as Web Forms with *inline code*. Although you won't see much code until Chapter 5, it's important to understand the difference between these types of Web Forms. At first, Web Forms with inline code seem a little easier to understand. Because the code needed to program your website is part of the very same Web Form, you can clearly see how the code relates to the file. However, as your page gets larger and you add more functionality to it, it's often easier if you have the code in a separate file. That way, it's completely separate from the markup, enabling you to focus on the task at hand.

In the next exercise, you add two files that demonstrate the difference between Code Behind and inline code.

TRY IT OUT Adding Web Forms with Code to Your Site

The files you add in this exercise aren't needed for the final application. To avoid cluttering up the project, you should put them in a separate `Demos` folder.

1. In the Solution Explorer, right-click your website and choose Add ➪ New Folder. Name the folder **Demos** and press Enter.
2. Right-click the `Demos` folder and choose Add ➪ Add New Item. In the dialog box that appears, choose your preferred programming language on the left, click the Web Form template, and name the file **CodeBehind.aspx**. Make sure that the check box for Place Code in Separate File is selected. Finally, click the Add button. The page should open in Markup View so you can see the HTML for the page.
3. At the bottom of the Document Window, click the Design button to switch the page from Markup View into Design View. The page you see has a white background with a small, dashed rectangle at the top of it. The dashed rectangle represents the `<div>` element you saw in Markup View.
4. From the Toolbox, drag a `Label` control from the Standard category and drop it in the dashed area of the page. Remember, you can open the Toolbox with the shortcut Ctrl+Alt+X if it isn't open yet. In Design View, your screen should now look like Figure 2-11.

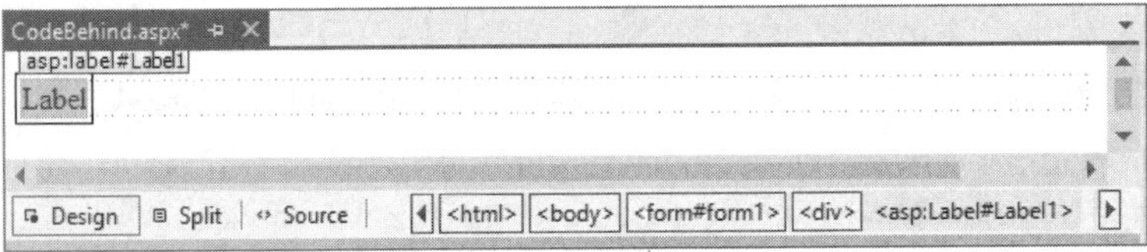

FIGURE 2-11

5. Double-click somewhere in the white area *below* the dashed line of the `<div>` element. VS switches from Design View into the Code Behind of the file and adds code that fires when the page loads in the browser:

VB.NET

```
Protected Sub Page_Load(sender As Object, e As EventArgs) Handles Me.Load

End Sub
```

C#

```
protected void Page_Load(object sender, EventArgs e)
{

}
```

Although this odd syntax may look a little scary at this point, don't worry about it too much now. In most cases, VS adds it for you automatically, as you just saw. In later chapters, you see exactly how this code works, but for now it's important to realize that the code you're going to place between the lines that start with `Protected Sub` and `End Sub` in Visual Basic and between the curly braces in C# will be run when the page is requested in the browser.

All code examples you see from now on include a Visual Basic (VB.NET) and a C# version, so always pick the one that matches your programming language.

6. Place your cursor in the open line in the code that VS created and add the bolded line of code that assigns today's date and time to the label, which will eventually show up in the browser:

VB.NET

```
Protected Sub Page_Load(sender As Object, e As EventArgs) Handles Me.Load
  Label1.Text = "Hello World; the time is now " & DateTime.Now.ToString()
End Sub
```

C#

```
protected void Page_Load(object sender, EventArgs e)
{
  Label1.Text = "Hello World; the time is now " + DateTime.Now.ToString();
}
```

Note that as soon as you type the `L` for `Label1`, you get a list with options to choose from. This is part of Visual Studio's *IntelliSense*, a great tool that helps you rapidly write code. Instead of typing the whole word `Label1`, you simply type the letter `L` or the letters `La` and then you pick the appropriate item from the list, visible in Figure 2-12.

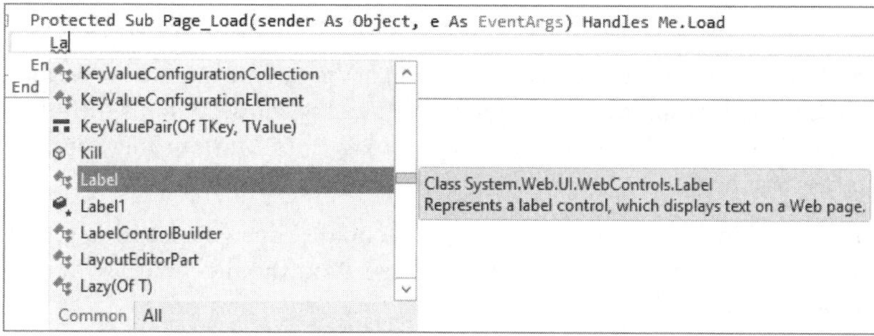

FIGURE 2-12

To complete the selected word, you can press Enter or Tab or even the period. In the latter case, you immediately get another list that enables you to pick the word `Text` simply by typing the first few letters, completing the word by pressing the Tab or Enter key. This feature is a real productivity tool because you can write code with a minimum of keystrokes. IntelliSense is available in many other file types as well, including ASPX, HTML, CSS, JavaScript, and XML. In many cases, the list with options pops up automatically if you begin typing. If it doesn't, press Ctrl+Spacebar to invoke it. If the list covers some of your code in the code window, press and hold the Ctrl key to make the window transparent.

7. Right-click the `CodeBehind.aspx` page in the Solution Explorer and choose View in Browser (Internet Explorer). Depending on the default browser you've configured for your computer, the browser name in the parentheses may be different. I'll simply refer to this menu item as View in Browser from now on.

8. Click Yes if you get a dialog box that asks if you want to save the changes, and then the page will appear in the browser, similar to the browser window you see in Figure 2-13.

FIGURE 2-13

If you don't see the message with the date and time appear or you get an error on the page in the browser, make sure you saved the changes to all open pages. To save all pages at once, press Ctrl+Shift+S or click the Save All button on the toolbar (the one with the multiple floppy disk symbols). Additionally, make sure you typed the code for the right language. When you created this new page, you chose a programming language that applies to the entire page. You can't mix languages on a single page, so if you started with a Visual C# page, make sure you entered the C# code snippet in step 6.

9. Setting up a page with inline code is very similar. Start by adding a new Web Form to the `Demos` folder. Call it **`CodeInline.aspx`** and make sure you uncheck the Place Code in Separate File option.

10. Just as you did in steps 3, 4, and 5, switch the page into Design View, drag a label inside the `<div>` element, and double-click the page somewhere outside the `<div>` that now contains the label. Instead of opening a Code Behind file, VS now switches your page into Markup View and adds the `Page_Load` code directly in the page.

11. On the empty line in the code block that VS inserted, type the bolded line you see in step 6 of this exercise. Make sure you use the correct programming language. You should end up with the following code at the top of your `.aspx` file:

VB.NET

```
<script runat="server">
  Protected Sub Page_Load(sender As Object, e As EventArgs)
    Label1.Text = "Hello World; the time is now " & DateTime.Now.ToString()
  End Sub
</script>
```

C#

```
<script runat="server">
  protected void Page_Load(object sender, EventArgs e)
  {
    Label1.Text = "Hello World; the time is now " + DateTime.Now.ToString();
  }
</script>
```

12. Right-click the page in the Solution Explorer and choose View in Browser. Alternatively, press Ctrl+F5 to open the page in your browser. You should see a page similar to the one you got in step 7.

How It Works

At run time, pages with inline code behave the same as pages that use Code Behind. In both cases, the ASP.NET run time sees the `Page_Load` code and executes any code it finds in it. In the Try It Out, this meant setting the `Text` of `Label1` to a welcome message and today's date and time. The biggest difference between the two options is where the code is stored. With pages with inline code, all code and markup is stored in the same file on disk. When using Code Behind, the VB or C# code you write is stored in a separate file named after the Web Form.

Because pages with Code Behind are easier to manage, I'll use them exclusively for the Planet Wrox website.

In this example, the C# code looks very similar to the VB.NET code. The code that sets the `Label`'s text is almost identical in the two languages. One difference is that VB.NET uses an ampersand (`&`) to glue two pieces of text together, but C# uses the plus (`+`) character. You can also use the plus character in VB.NET to concatenate strings together, but with a few caveats, as you'll learn in Chapter 5. The other difference is that in C# code lines must be terminated with a semicolon (`;`) to indicate the end of a unit of code, but Visual Basic uses the line break. If you want to split a long line of code over multiple lines in Visual Basic, you can use the underscore (_) character. In earlier versions, VB.NET required the underscore in a lot of different places. However, in recent versions of Visual Basic, the designers of the language have greatly reduced the number of places where you must use an underscore.

One place where you do need the underscore if you want to split code over multiple lines is right before the `Handles` keyword that you saw earlier:

```
Protected Sub Page_Load(sender As Object, e As EventArgs) _
       Handles Me.Load
  Label1.Text = "Hello World; the time is now " & DateTime.Now.ToString()
End Sub
```

Note that in your pages you don't have to use the underscore to break a long line. However, I'll add it to some of the examples in this book because the book's pages are not wide enough to show the entire code statement on a single line. You'll see more of these underscores in other Visual Basic examples in the remainder of this book. If you decide to manually type the underscore to make your own code more readable, don't forget to type a space before the underscore or your code won't work.

In C#, you don't need this character because the language itself allows you to break long lines simply by pressing Enter. This is because C# uses a semicolon to denote the end of a line instead of a line break in the source.

You opened the page in your browser using the right-click View in Browser option or by pressing Ctrl+F5. With the View in Browser option, you always open the page you right-click. With the Ctrl+F5 shortcut, you open the page that is currently the active document in the Document Window, the page that is currently selected in the Solution Explorer, or the file that has been set as the Start Page for the website. Additionally, all open files are saved automatically, and the site is checked for errors before the requested page is opened in the browser.

You can assign a page as the Start Page by right-clicking it in the Solution Explorer and choosing Set As Start Page. If you want to control this behavior at a later stage, right-click the website in the Solution Explorer and choose Property Pages. In the Start Options category, you can indicate that you want the currently active page to open, or you can assign a specific page, as shown in Figure 2-14.

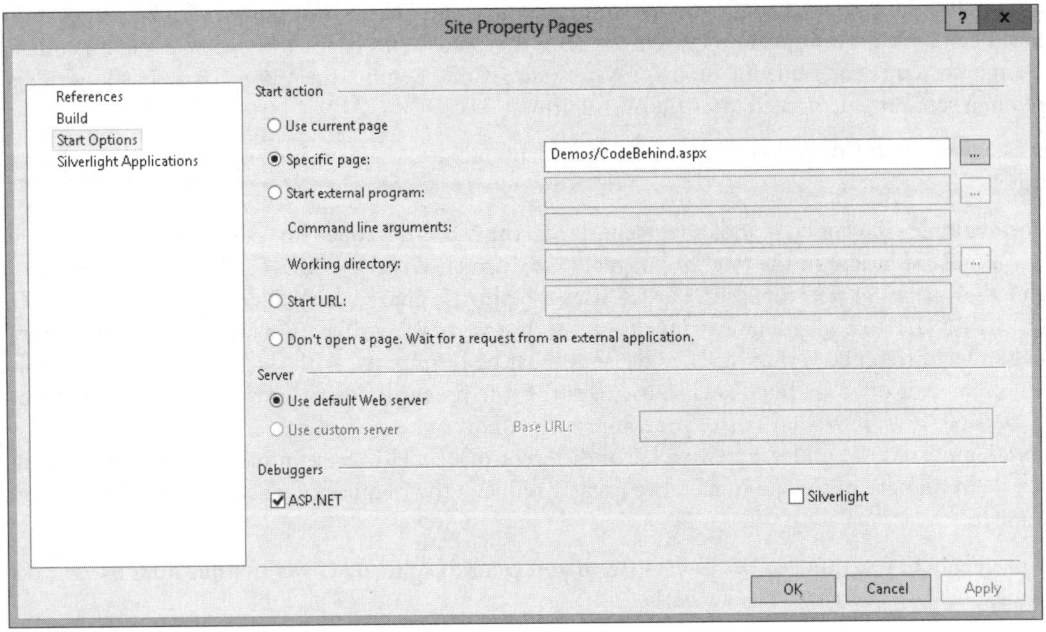

FIGURE 2-14

In the previous exercise, you learned how to add a page that contains a simple `Label` control. Additionally, you saw how to write some code that updates the label with today's date and time. You can ignore this code for now; it only served to demonstrate the differences between Code Behind and inline code. In Chapter 5, you learn more about programming in Visual Basic and C#.

To make compelling pages, you obviously need a lot more content than just a simple `Label` control that shows today's date and time. The next section shows you how to add content and HTML to your pages and how to style and format it.

Adding Markup to Your Page

You have a number of ways to add HTML and other markup to your pages. First of all, you can simply type it in the Markup View window. However, this isn't always the best option, because it forces you to type a lot of code by hand. To make it easier to insert new HTML in the page and to apply formatting to it, the Design View window offers a number of helpful tools. These tools include the Formatting toolbar and the menu items Format and Table. For these tools to be active, you need to have the document in Design View. If you're working in Split View mode, you have to make sure that the Design View part has the focus, or you'll find that most of the tools are not available.

Inserting and Formatting Text

You can type text in both Design View and in Markup View. Simply place the cursor at the desired location and start typing. When you switch to Design View, the Formatting toolbar becomes available, with the options shown in Figure 2-15.

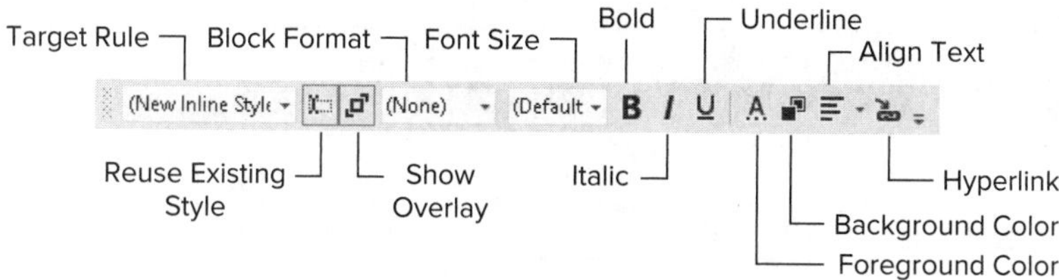

FIGURE 2-15

Many of the buttons on the toolbar function exactly the same as in other editing environments. For example, the B button formats your text with a bold font. Similarly, the I and the U buttons italicize and underline your text, respectively. The drop-down list labeled Block Format enables you to insert HTML elements like `<p>` for paragraphs, `<h1>` through `<h6>` for headings, and `<ul>`, `<ol>`, and `<li>` for lists. You can choose an item from the drop-down list directly to have it inserted in your page, or you can select some text first and choose the appropriate block element from the list to wrap the selected text inside the tags.

In the next Try It Out, you see how to work with these tools to create the homepage of the Planet Wrox website.

TRY IT OUT Adding Formatted Text

In this Try It Out, you create a Web Form called `Default.aspx` and add some basic content to it.

1. Add a new Web Form with the Add New Item dialog box to the root of the site and call it `Default.aspx`. Make sure you check off the Place Code in Separate File option and click Add. Switch to Design View using the Design button at the bottom of the Document Window.

2. Click inside the dashed rectangle until you see the glyph showing that the `<div>` element is currently active. At the same time, the tag navigator at the bottom of the code window should highlight the last block with the text `<div>` on it, as shown in Figure 2-16.

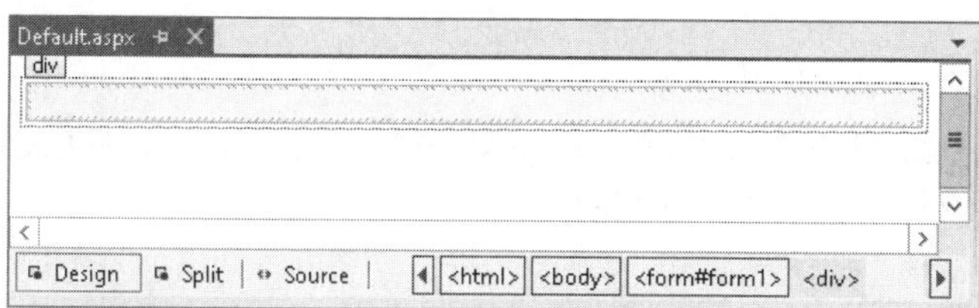

FIGURE 2-16

3. Type **`Hi there visitor and welcome to Planet Wrox`** and highlight the text using the mouse. From the Block Format drop-down list (visible in Figure 2-15) choose Heading 1 <h1>. Note that a small glyph with the text `h1` appears right above the text, to indicate that VS created a heading for you automatically. Figure 2-17 shows the Design View with the `<h1>` element.

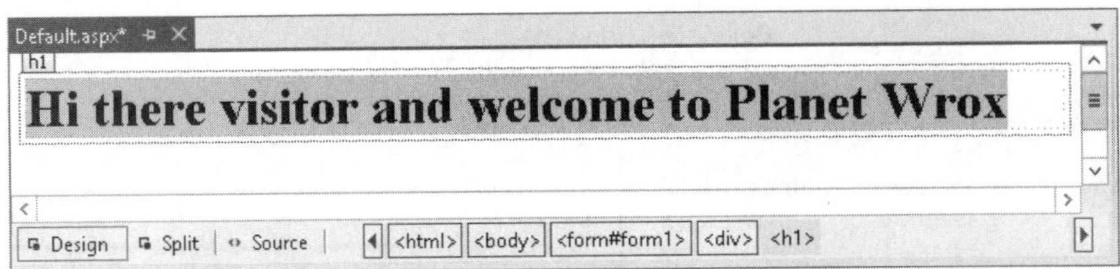

FIGURE 2-17

4. Position your cursor at the end of the heading after the word `Wrox` and press Enter. A new paragraph (indicated by a small glyph with the letter `p` on it) is inserted for you so you can directly start typing.

5. Type the text shown in Figure 2-18 (or make up your own) to welcome the visitor to Planet Wrox. Notice how the text `www.PlanetWrox.com` turns blue as soon as you type the comma to indicate VS has recognized it as a web address and has turned it into a link. You can press Enter to start a new paragraph. Select the text "paying a visit," click the Foreground Color button on the Formatting toolbar, and select a different color in the dialog box that appears. Then select some other text, such as "reviews and concert pictures," and click the Bold button. When you're done, your Design View should show something similar to Figure 2-18.

FIGURE 2-18

The code for the homepage should now look more or less similar to the following (the code has been reformatted a bit to fit the space in the book):

```
<div>
  <h1>Hi there visitor and welcome to Planet Wrox</h1>
  <p>
    We&#39;re glad you&#39;re
          <span class="auto-style1">paying a visit</span> to
          <a href="http://www.PlanetWrox.com">www.PlanetWrox.com</a>,
          the coolest music community site on the Internet.
  </p>
  <p>
    Feel free to have a look around; there are lots of interesting
        <strong>reviews and concert pictures</strong> to be found here.
  </p>
</div>
```

At the top of the file you should also see a `<style>` element, which is discussed next.

6. Open the page in your browser by pressing Ctrl+F5, or by right-clicking the page in the Solution Explorer and choosing View in Browser.

How It Works

When you use the various Formatting toolbar buttons, like Foreground Color, VS inserts the appropriate HTML and CSS code for you. For example, when you click the B button, VS inserts a pair of `<strong>` tags around the selected text. When you click the I button, VS adds a pair of `<em>` tags to italicize the text. In this exercise, VS also inserted a `class` attribute (shown in the previous code example) that points to a class called `auto-style1` when you changed the text color. The code for this style has been added to the top of your file and looks similar to this:

```
<style type="text/css">
  .auto-style1
  {
    color: #FF0000;
  }
</style>
```

Your code may look slightly different if you chose a different color. The code you see here is explained in the next chapter. For now, just remember that this code sets the color of the text it is applied to as red. If the opening curly bracket is on the same line as the class, choose Tools ➪ Options ➪ Text Editor ➪ CSS ➪ Formatting and set the Formatting Style to Expanded. This is just a matter of preference and doesn't change the effect of the code.

Note that VS replaced the apostrophe character (') in "we're" in the welcome message with its HTML-compatible variant: `'`. Using this kind of code enables you to insert characters in your page that a browser may have trouble displaying, or that have special meaning within HTML itself, like the ampersand character (`&`), which is written as `&`. When you type text in Design View, VS automatically inserts the coded equivalents of relevant characters for you; however, if you type in Markup View directly, you'll have to do this yourself.

Don't worry if your code looks different from what is shown here. Many settings in VS influence the code that is generated for you.

So far, the exercises have been concerned with adding and styling text in your page. However, VS enables you to insert other HTML elements as well, like tables and bullets. The next section shows you how this works.

Adding Tables and Other Markup

HTML tables are great if you need to present structured or repeating data, like a list of products in a shopping cart, photos in a photo album, or input controls in a form. There is a lot of debate on the Internet about whether you should use tables to lay out your page as well. For example, if your page contains a header with a logo, a main content area, and a footer at the bottom, you could use a table with three rows to accomplish this. In general, it's considered bad practice to use tables for this purpose because they add a lot of extraneous markup to the page and are often difficult to maintain. Besides, quite often the same result can be accomplished using CSS, which you learn about in the next chapter. Despite the disadvantages that tables may bring, they are still an invaluable asset in your HTML toolbox when it comes to displaying tabular or otherwise structured information.

TRY IT OUT Using the Format and Table Menus

In this exercise, you learn how to add tables to your page using the Table menu and how to add rows and columns. Additionally, you learn how to add other structured elements, such as bulleted lists.

1. In the `Demos` folder, create a new Web Form called **`TableDemo.aspx`**. Make sure it uses Code Behind by checking the Place Code in Separate File option.
2. Switch the page to Design View, click inside the dashed rectangle that represents the standard `<div>` tag in the page, and choose Table ➪ Insert Table. The Insert Table dialog box appears, as shown in Figure 2-19.

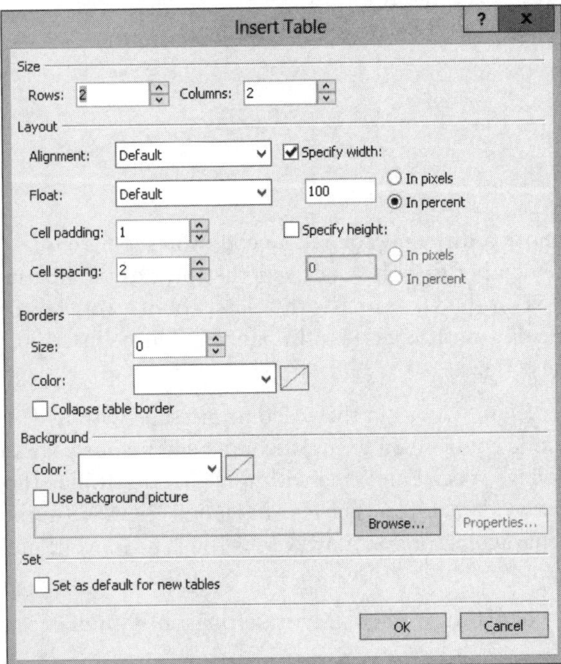

FIGURE 2-19

3. Set Rows to 3 and leave Columns set to 2. Leave all other settings at their defaults and click OK. The table gets inserted in the page.
4. If you see only a single table cell, and not the entire table with three rows and two columns, you need to enable Visual Aid for tables. To do this, choose View ➪ Visual Aids ➪ Visible Borders from the main menu to turn the borders on. Your Design View should now look like Figure 2-20.

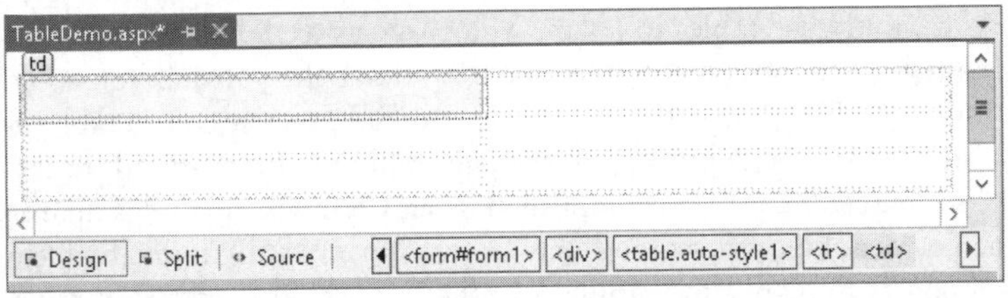

FIGURE 2-20

5. Drag the right border of the very first cell in the table to the left. You'll see a visual indicator showing the width of the cell. Keep dragging it to the left until it has a width of 200 pixels, as in Figure 2-21.

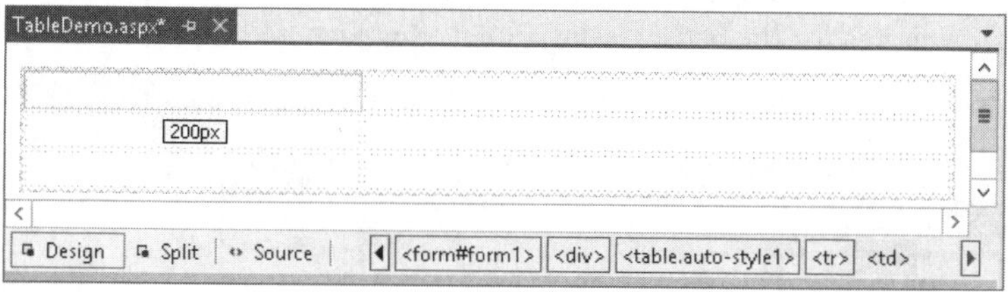

FIGURE 2-21

6. To add more rows or columns to the table, you can right-click an existing cell. From the pop-up menu that appears, choose Insert to add additional rows or columns at different locations. Similarly, you can use the Delete, Modify, and Select options to delete rows or columns, merge cells, and make selections. For this exercise, you don't need to add additional rows or columns, although it's okay if you have already done so.
7. Place your cursor in the first cell of the first row and type the words `Bulleted List`.
8. Place your cursor in the second cell using the mouse. Alternatively, you can press Tab to move the cursor to the next cell. From the Format menu, choose Bullets and Numbering.
9. Switch to the Plain Bullets tab, click the picture with the round, solid bullets (see Figure 2-22), and click OK.

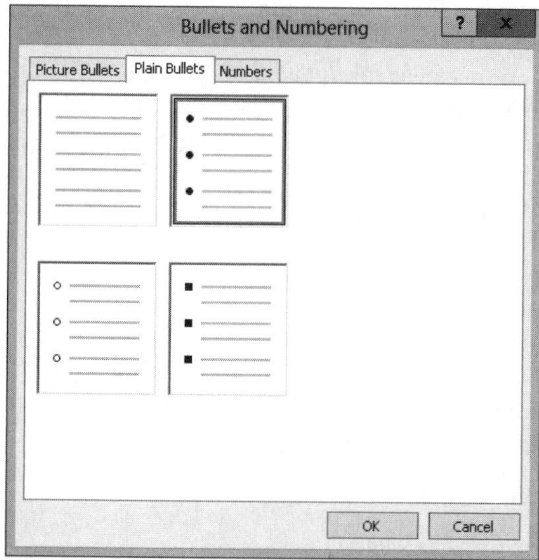

FIGURE 2-22

10. Type some text, like your favorite musical genre (Punk, Rock, Techno, and so on), and press Enter. VS inserts a new bullet for you automatically, so you can continue to add new items to the list. Add two more genres, so you end up with three bullets.

11. Repeat steps 7 through 10, but now create a numbered list. First, type **`Numbered List`** in the first cell of the second row, then position your cursor in the second cell of the same row, and choose Format ➪ Bullets and Numbering. Switch to the Numbers tab (visible in Figure 2-22 behind the Plain Bullets tab) and click the second picture in the first row, which shows a standard numbered list, and click OK. Type a few items for the list, pressing Enter after each item.
12. Open the page in the browser by pressing Ctrl+F5. You should see a screen similar to Figure 2-23.

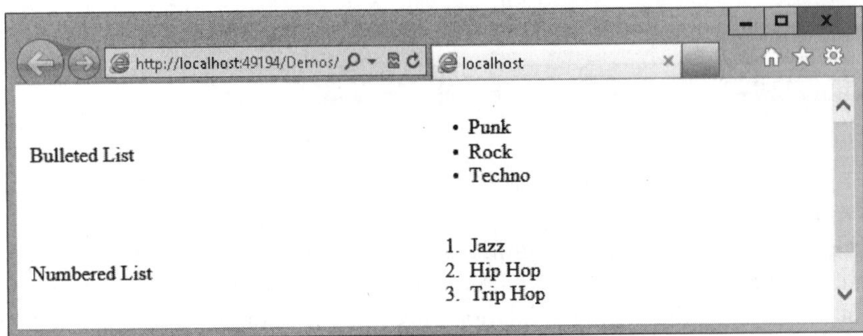

FIGURE 2-23

How It Works

When you visually insert page elements like tables or lists through the available menus, VS inserts the required markup for you in Markup View. When you insert a table, VS adds a `<table>` element and a number of `<tr>` and `<td>` elements to define rows and cells, respectively. It also applies a `class` attribute pointing to a CSS style that defines the table's width. It created another style for the `<td>` elements when you dragged the column width to be 200 pixels. Similarly, when you insert a list, VS inserts an `<ol>` element for *numbered* or *ordered lists* and a `<ul>` element for *bulleted* or *unordered lists*. Within these elements, `<li>` elements are used to define each item in the list.

Besides the HTML tags you have seen thus far, there is another important tag you need to look at: the `<a>` tag, which is used to create links between pages.

Connecting Pages

An important part of any website is the links that connect the pages in your site. Links enable your visitors to go from one page to another, in the same site or to a completely different site on the Internet. You have a few ways to create links between pages, including:

- The HTML `<a>` element, explained in this chapter.
- Using the `<asp:HyperLink>` control, discussed in Chapter 7.
- Programmatically through code. This is discussed later in the book.

The following exercise shows you how easy it is to link from one page to another.

TRY IT OUT Linking Pages

In this Try It Out, you modify the `TableDemo.aspx` page you created earlier by adding text that links to another page. Once you run the page in the browser and click that link, the new page replaces the old one.

1. Open the `TableDemo.aspx` page from the `Demos` folder.
2. If necessary, switch to Design View.
3. In the first cell of the third row, type the text **`Link`**.
4. In the second cell of the same row, type the text **`Go to the homepage of Planet Wrox`** and highlight it with your mouse.
5. On the Formatting toolbar, click the Convert to HyperLink button. It's located near the end of the toolbar and has a link icon and a small arrow on it.
6. In the dialog box that appears, click the Browse button, browse to the `Default.aspx` page in the root of your site, and click OK. Next, click OK again to close the Hyperlink dialog box. The Design View of your page should look similar to the one displayed in Figure 2-24.

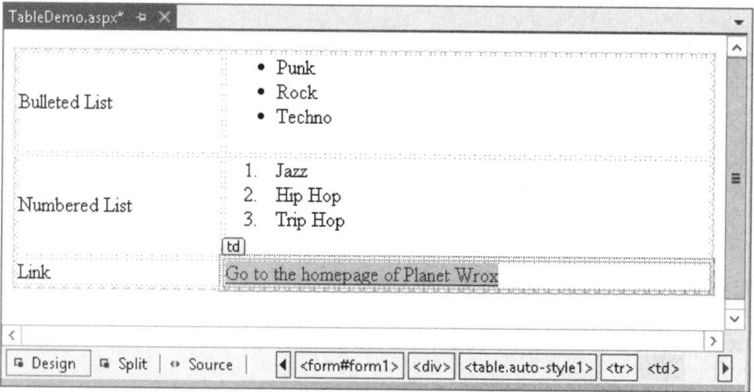

FIGURE 2-24

7. Switch to Markup View and notice how the HTML for the link has been inserted:

```
<a href="../Default.aspx">Go to the homepage of Planet Wrox</a>
```

Note that the `href` attribute points to the page you want to link to.

8. If you want to change the page being linked to from Markup View, click somewhere between the opening and closing quotes of the `href` attribute and press Ctrl+Spacebar. A dialog box pops up that enables you to select another page within your site. Alternatively, you can click the Pick URL option and browse for the new page somewhere in your site.
9. Right-click the `TableDemo.aspx` page in the Solution Explorer and choose View in Browser. When the page has finished loading, click the Go to the homepage of Planet Wrox link. The request is sent to the web server and, as a response, you now get the homepage of the website.

How It Works

Links between pages are likely one of the most important elements in a web page, because they enable you to create a connection between a page in your site and another page, whether that page lives in your own site or on a completely different server somewhere on the Internet. For simple links that should appear somewhere in your page, the HTML `<a>` tag with an `href` attribute set is the easiest to set up. When the user clicks such a link, the browser requests the new page from the server and displays it. The double dots (`..`) in the `href`'s value are a way to refer to the parent directory. The full `href` attribute means "go up one level in the folder hierarchy and then select the file `Default.aspx`." You see a lot more about links and how they work in Chapter 7.

You're not limited to linking to pages in your own site. If you want to link to external pages instead, simply replace the `href` attribute value with the full address of the page, as shown in the following example:

```
<a href="http://www.wrox.com">Go to the Wrox homepage</a>
```

For external links, it's important to include the `http://` prefix; otherwise, the browser goes out looking for a file or folder called `www.wrox.com` on your own website.

You'll use the things you learned in this chapter about page creation and formatting in the next chapter, which deals with designing your web pages using CSS.

Besides the visual tools, like the Formatting toolbar and the Table menu, Visual Studio has another great way to quickly insert code in your pages: code snippets. Code snippets enable you to insert large chunks of code with just a few keystrokes. You see code snippets at work in the next chapter.

PRACTICAL TIPS ON WORKING WITH WEB FORMS

Here are some tips for working with Web Forms:

- Favor Web Forms with Code Behind over those with inline code. Although at first you may not notice a big difference in working with them, as your site and pages start to grow, you'll find that it's easier to work with a page where the code is separated from the markup.
- Spend some time familiarizing yourself with the different menu items of the Format and Table menus. Most of them generate HTML elements that are inserted into your page. Take a look at the HTML elements and attributes that have been generated for you, and try to change them directly in the code, and through the menus and toolbars. This way, you get a good feel for the various tags available and how they behave.
- Experiment with links to connect pages in your site. Notice how VS creates different links depending on the location of the page you are linking to. Chapter 7 deals with linking and the various ways to address pages in your site in much more detail.

SUMMARY

This chapter introduced you to some important topics that help you build maintainable and structured ASP.NET websites. Understanding the differences between the various project types and templates enables you to kick-start a web project with just the files you need.

The same applies to the different file types you can add to your site. Because each file type serves a specific purpose, it's important to realize what that purpose is and how you can use the file.

One common activity that you'll perform when building ASP.NET web pages is adding markup to the page. As you saw in this and the previous chapter, markup comes in a few flavors, including plain HTML and ASP.NET Server Controls. Knowing how to add this markup to your page using the numerous menu options and toolbars that VS offers is critical in building good-looking web pages.

Now that you have a solid understanding of creating and modifying Web Forms, it's time to look at how you can turn those dull black-and-white pages with a few controls into attractive web pages. The next chapter shows you how to work with the many CSS tools found in VS to create the desired effect.

EXERCISES

1. Name three important files in the Web Files category that you can add to your site. Describe the purpose of each file.
2. What do you need to do to make a piece of text both bold and italicized in your web page? What will the resulting HTML look like?
3. Name three different ways to add existing files to an ASP.NET website in VS.
4. What are the different views that VS offers you for your ASPX pages? Does VS offer other views as well?

You can find answers to these exercises in Appendix A.

▶ WHAT YOU LEARNED IN THIS CHAPTER

Code Behind	A page model where server-side code is stored in a separate code file
Design View	Gives you a graphical representation of your page
File Types	ASP.NET supports many different file types, including Web Forms (`.aspx`), master pages (`.master`), CSS files (`.css`), JavaScript (`.js`), and SQL Server databases (`.mdf`)
Inline Code	A page model where server-side code is stored in the same file as the markup
Markup View	Enables you to look at the markup of your page
Project Templates	Jump-start your web development by setting up a site targeting a specific scenario
Project Types	Visual Studio offers two project types: Web Application Projects and Web Site Projects
Split View	Enables you to look at Markup View and Design View at the same time
Web Form	Presents the user interface of your website at the client

3

Designing Your Web Pages

WHAT YOU WILL LEARN IN THIS CHAPTER:

- What CSS is and why you need it
- How CSS looks and how to write it
- The different ways to add CSS code to your ASP.NET pages and to external files
- The numerous tools that VS offers you to quickly write CSS

WROX.COM CODE DOWNLOADS FOR THIS CHAPTER

You can find the `wrox.com` code downloads for this chapter on the Download Code tab at `www.wrox.com/remtitle.cgi?isbn=1118311809`. The code is in the Chapter 3 download.

The pages you created in the previous two chapters look pretty plain and dull. That's because they lack styling information and therefore default to the standard layout that the browser applies. To spruce up your pages, you need a way to change their presentation in the browser. The most common way to do this is by using the *cascading style sheets* (*CSS*) language. CSS is the de facto language for formatting and designing information on the web, including ASP.NET web pages. With CSS you can quickly change the appearance of your web pages, giving them that great look that your design or corporate identity dictates.

Solid support for working with CSS was initially added in Visual Web Developer (VWD) 2008, one of the predecessors of VS Express 2012 for Web. This support has been further enhanced in the previous version of Visual Studio, VWD 2010. The new VS 2012 builds on top of this CSS support and improves it in a number of ways, making the CSS editor a first-class citizen in VS, with editor features similar to other languages such as C# and VB. The CSS tools enable you to create your CSS code visually, making it much easier to style your pages without the need to know or remember every little detail of CSS.

To understand the relevance of and need for CSS in your ASP.NET websites, you need to understand the shortcomings of HTML first. The next section looks at the problems that plain HTML presents, and how CSS is able to overcome these issues.

WHY DO YOU NEED CSS?

In the early days of the Internet, web pages consisted mostly of text and images. The text was formatted using plain HTML, using tags like `<b>` to make the text bold, and the `<font>` tag to influence the font family, size, and color. Web developers soon realized that they needed more power to format their pages, so CSS was created to address some of HTML's styling shortcomings.

Problems of HTML Formatting

One of the problems with using HTML for formatting is that it offers only a limited set of options to style your pages. You can use elements like `<i>`, `<b>`, and `<font>` to change the appearance of text and use attributes like `bgcolor` to change the background color of HTML elements. You also have a number of other attributes at your disposal for changing the way links appear in your page.

Obviously, this feature set isn't rich enough to create the attractive web pages that your users expect and demand.

Another problem of HTML with a lot more impact on how you build your web pages is the way the styling information is applied to the page. By design, HTML forces you to embed your formatting in your HTML document, making it harder to reuse or change the design later. Consider the following example:

```
<p><font face="Arial" color="red" size="+1">
  This is red text in an Arial type face and slightly larger than the default text.
</font></p>
```

The problem with this code snippet is that the actual *data* (the text in the `<p>` element) is mixed with the *presentation* (the formatting of the text with the `<font>` tag in this example). Ideally, the two should be separated, so each of them is easier to change without affecting the other.

Imagine you used the `<p>` and `<font>` elements to mark up the first paragraph of every page in your site. What happens when you decide to change the color of the font from red to dark blue? Or what if your corporate identity dictates a Verdana font instead of Arial? You would need to visit each and every page in your site, making the required changes.

Besides maintainability, another problem with HTML formatting is the fact that you can't easily change the formatting at run time in the user's browser. With the HTML from the previous code snippet, there is no way to let your visitor change things like the font size or color, a common request to help people who are visually impaired. If you want to offer your visitors an alternative version of the page with a larger font size or a different color, you'd need to create a copy of the original page and make the necessary changes.

The final problem with HTML formatting is that the additional markup in your page adds considerably to the size of the page. This makes it slower to download and display because the information needs to be downloaded with each page in your website. It also makes it harder to maintain your pages because you'd need to scroll through large HTML files to find the content you need.

To summarize, formatting with HTML suffers from the following problems:

- Its feature set severely limits the formatting possibilities that your pages require.
- Data and presentation are mixed within the same file.
- HTML doesn't enable you to easily switch formatting at run time in the browser.
- The required formatting tags and attributes make your pages larger and thus slower to load, display, and maintain.

Fortunately, CSS enables you to overcome all of these problems.

How CSS Fixes Formatting Problems

CSS is designed to format your web pages in almost every possible way. It offers a rich set of options to change every little aspect of your web page, including fonts (size, color, family, and so on), colors and background colors, borders around HTML elements, positioning of elements in your page, and much more. CSS is widely understood by all major browsers today, so it's *the* language for visual presentation of web pages and very popular among web developers.

CSS overcomes the problem of mixed data and presentation by enabling you to define all formatting information in external files. Your ASPX or HTML pages can then reference these files and the browser will apply the correct styles for you. With this separation, the HTML document contains *what* you want to display, and the CSS file defines *how* you want to display it, enabling you to change or replace one of the two documents, leaving the other unmodified. In addition, you can place CSS directly in an HTML or ASPX page, which gives you a chance to add small snippets of CSS exactly where you need them. You should be cautious when placing CSS directly in an HTML or ASPX page, because you can then no longer control style information from a single, central location.

Because you can place all CSS code in a separate file, it's easy to offer the user a choice between different styles—for example, one with a larger font size. You can create a copy of the external style sheet, make the necessary changes, and then offer this alternative style sheet to the user. You see how this works in Chapter 6 when ASP.NET Themes are discussed.

Another benefit of a separate style sheet file is the decrease in bandwidth that is required for your site. Style sheets don't change with each request, so a browser saves a local copy of the style sheet the first time it downloads it. From then on, it uses this *cached* copy instead of requesting it from the server over and over again. Sometimes this caching can work against you when the browser doesn't download the latest CSS files with your changes. If you find that the browser is not picking up the changes you made to a CSS file, use Ctrl+F5 or Ctl+R in the browser (not in VS) to get a fresh copy from the server.

Now that you have seen why CSS is so important, it's time to find out how it looks and how to use it.

AN INTRODUCTION TO CSS

In terms of syntax, CSS is an easy language to learn. Its "grammar" consists of only a few concepts. That makes it relatively easy to get started with. What makes CSS a bit more difficult is the way all major browsers render a page. Although virtually every modern desktop browser understands CSS, they all have their quirks when it comes to displaying a page according to the CSS standard. This standard, maintained by the same organization that maintains the HTML standard, the *World Wide Web Consortium*, or *W3C* for short, comes in three different versions: 1.0, 2.1, and 3.0. From these three versions, 2.1 is the most applicable today. It contains everything that version 1.0 contains but also adds a lot of possibilities on top of that. It's also the version that VS uses and generates by default. Version 3.0 is currently under development and it's expected to take some time before the major browsers have solid support for it.

Before you look at the actual syntax of CSS, it's a good idea to see an example first. In the following exercise, you write a simple ASPX page that contains some CSS to format the contents of the page. This helps in understanding the CSS language, which is discussed in full detail in the section that follows.

TRY IT OUT Writing Your First CSS

In this Try It Out you write some CSS that changes the appearance of a header and two paragraphs. You'll hand code the page for now; the second half of this chapter shows you how to use the CSS tools available in VS.

1. In the `Demos` folder of the Planet Wrox project, create a new Web Form called `CssDemo.aspx`. For this exercise, it doesn't matter if you choose inline code or Code Behind.

2. Make sure the page is in Markup View and then locate the closing `</title>` tag in the source. Position your cursor at the end of the line and press Enter to create an empty line between the `<title>` and `<head>` tags. On this new line type the word **`style`** and then press Tab. VS completes the `<style>` element for you. Press Enter twice to create some room between the tags and then complete the block as follows:

```
  <title></title>
  <style type="text/css">

  </style>
</head>
```

> ***NOTE** This code completion feature uses code snippets that enable you to associate a piece of code (like the `<style>` element) with an identifier (like `style` in this example). Code snippets are very useful for inserting pieces of code quickly by typing only the short identifier. Many more code snippets are available, and where appropriate I'll point them out throughout this book.*

Instead of using the style code snippet, you can also type the full code yourself. Note that as soon as you type the opening angle bracket (<), a list pops up that enables you to select the `<style>` tag. The same applies to the `type` attribute; simply type the letters **`ty`** and the `type` attribute is preselected in the list. All you need to do to complete the word is press the Tab or Enter key. And, once more, the same help is available for the attribute value `text/css`. Simply select it in the list and press Tab or Enter, and the value is inserted for you automatically, nicely surrounded by the double quotes.

3. Next, between the opening and closing `<style>` tags, type the following bolded CSS code:

```
<style type="text/css">
  h1
  {
    font-size: 20px;
    color: Green;
  }

  p
  {
    color: Blue;
    font-style: italic;
  }

  .RightAligned
  {
    text-align: right;
  }
</style>
```

Take great care when typing this code, because CSS is rather picky about syntax. The first item in the list is an `h1` tag to style a heading at the first level, so it gets a size of 20 pixels and is displayed in a green font. Notice the colon between `font-size` and `20px` and that the line is closed with a semicolon.

The second item in the list simply contains the letter `p` and defines the look and feel for all `<p>` elements in the page.

The last item is prefixed with a period (.) followed by the text `RightAligned`. This item is used to right-align some text in the page. Because CSS is case sensitive, it's important to type this exactly as shown here, with a capital R and A, or the CSS code won't line up with the HTML shown in the next step.

Note that as soon as you type the hash symbol (#) after the `color` property, a color picker pops up to help you to select a color as shown in Figure 3-1. For now, just close the color picker by pressing Esc and manually complete the code. You see more of this color picker later in this chapter.

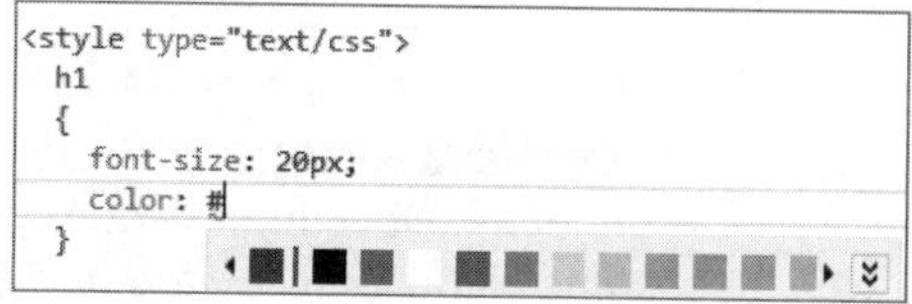

FIGURE 3-1

4. Scroll down in the page a bit until you see the opening `<div>` tag. Right after this tag, type the following bolded code:

```
<div>
  <h1>Welcome to this CSS Demo page</h1>
  <p>CSS makes it super easy to style your pages.</p>
  <p class="RightAligned">
    With very little code, you can quickly change the looks of a page.
  </p>
</div>
```

Instead of typing in this code directly, you can also use the Formatting toolbar while in Design View to create elements like `<h1>` and `<p>`. For now, you need to switch to Markup View to add `class="RightAligned"`, but in later exercises in this chapter you see how you can have the IDE write this code for you.

5. If you switch to Design View (or Split View), you'll see that the designer shows your text with the formatting defined in the `<style>` element of the page. Figure 3-2 shows the page in Split View so you can see the code and the design at the same time.

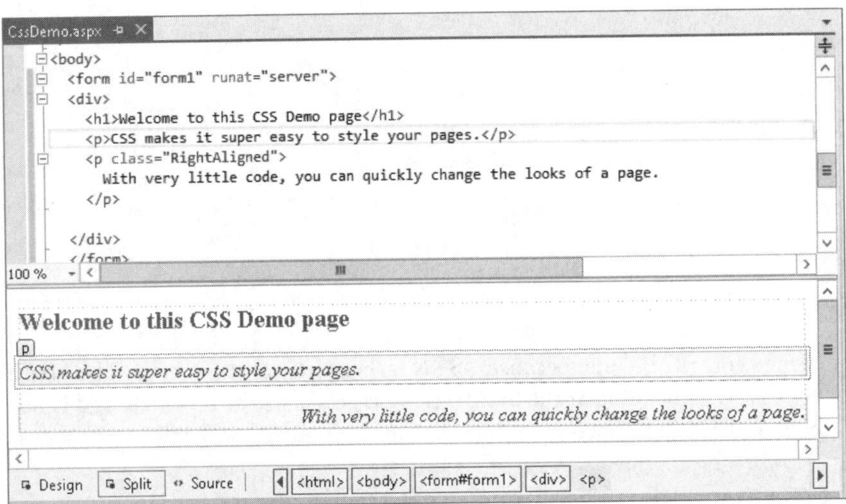

FIGURE 3-2

Although this black-and-white book makes it difficult to see different font colors, in Figure 3-2 you can see clearly that the `<h1>` has a larger font size. The figure also shows that all paragraphs are now displayed with an italic font. Finally, you can see that the last paragraph is aligned to the right of the window, because the `class` attribute on the tag is set to `RightAligned`.

> **COMMON MISTAKES** *If you don't see the last paragraph glued to the right border of the Document Window make sure you typed* `RightAligned` *exactly the same in the* `<style>` *tag and in the* `class` *attribute. Because CSS is case sensitive, there's a big difference between* `RightAligned` *and* `rightaligned`.

6. Press Ctrl+F5 to view `CssDemo.aspx` in your browser. The page you see in the browser is identical to the preview you got in the Design View of VS.

How It Works

Although the code you typed in this exercise is relatively simple, there's a lot going on under the hood of the browser (and the Design View of VS) to make this possible. You started by adding some styles to the `<head>` section of the page:

```
<style type="text/css">
  h1
```

```
    {
      font-size: 20px;
      color: Green;
    }

  ...
</style>
```

The <style> tag is used to wrap a style sheet that is embedded in the page with its type attribute set to text/css. This text/css value is currently the only applicable type for a <style> block and tells the browser to interpret the code that follows as CSS.

The code block from h1 until the closing curly brace (}) between the <style> tags is called a *rule set* or simply a *rule*. The rule in this code snippet defines the appearance for all <h1> elements in your page. The h1 at the top of the code block is called a *selector* and is used to indicate to what element the formatting should be applied. In this case, the selector maps directly to an HTML element, but many other selectors are available, as you see in the next section. Figure 3-3 shows how the elements are related to each other.

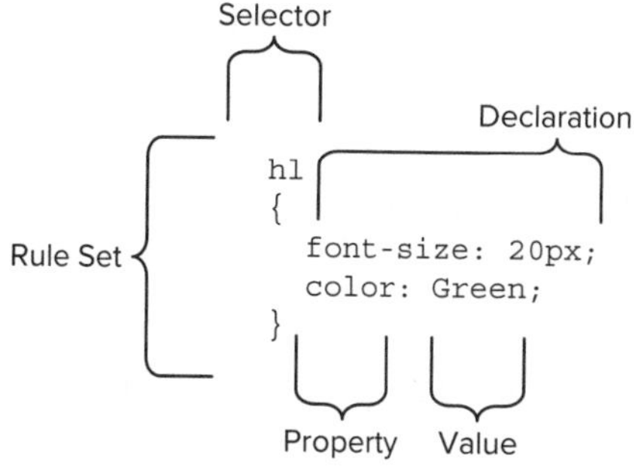

FIGURE 3-3

Between the curly braces you see the style information that should be applied to the heading. Each line between the curly braces is called a *declaration*. A declaration consists of a *property*, followed by a colon, and then followed by a *value*. The semicolon (;) at the end of a declaration separates it from the next declaration and is required on all declarations except for the last one in the rule set. However, for consistency, it's a good idea to add it to all declarations, which is what I'll do in the remainder of this book.

When the browser loads this page, it also reads in the styles you defined between the <style> tags. Then, whenever it comes across an HTML element that matches the selector, it applies the CSS rules to that element. So, for the <h1> and <p> elements, their respective rules are applied. This causes the heading to turn green with a large font, while the paragraphs turn blue with an italic font.

But why does the last paragraph turn blue *and* get right-aligned? In CSS, you can have rules coming from different sources. The last <p> element gets its style information from the standard p selector in the style definition. So, the p rule gives the paragraph a blue and italic font. However, it also has a *class* defined. This class, called RightAligned, links to a Class selector .RightAligned (note the leading period) in the style sheet and causes the text to be aligned to the right of the window. You see more of Class and other selectors in the next section. In the end, the last <p> element gets its rules from two selectors at the same time. You can make up and assign your own class names (as shown with the RightAligned class), giving you the flexibility to design your pages and elements exactly how you want them.

The next section digs a lot deeper in the syntax of CSS, giving you a much more detailed view on selectors, properties, and values.

CSS — The Language

As you saw in the previous Try It Out exercise, a cascading style sheet is actually a collection of rules. A rule is a combination of a selector and one or more declarations, which in turn can be broken down to a property and a value. You're probably getting a little dizzy from all the new terms that were introduced in the past few paragraphs, so in the next section, you see most of them again, with a detailed explanation and code examples that show you what they are used for and how they work.

The Style Sheet

The style sheet contains all the relevant style information that should be applied to page elements. In its simplest form, a style sheet looks like this:

```
h1
{
  color: Green;
}
```

A style sheet can also contain more than one rule, as you saw in the previous exercise. At the same time, each rule can contain multiple declarations, enabling you to group them under a single selector:

```
h1
{
  font-size: 20px;
  color: Green;
}
```

The code you just saw is functionally identical to this:

```
h1
{
  font-size: 20px;
}
h1
{
  color: Green;
}
```

The condensed form, where the two declarations are grouped under the same selector, is much easier to read, understand, and maintain, so it's advisable to use this syntax as much as possible.

To be able to style an element on a page, a browser has to know three things:

- What element of the page must be styled?
- What part of that element must be styled?
- How do you want that part of the selected element to look?

The answers to these questions are given by selectors, properties, and values.

Selectors

As its name implies, a selector is used to select or point to one or more specific elements within your page. A number of different selectors are available, giving you fine control over what elements you want to style. The selector answers the first question: What element of the page must be styled? The next section shows you the four most important types of selectors.

The Universal Selector

The Universal selector, indicated by an asterisk (*), applies to all elements in your page. You can use the Universal selector to set global settings like a font family. The following rule set changes the font for all elements in your page to Arial:

```
*
{
  font-family: Arial;
}
```

The Type Selector

The Type selector enables you to point to an HTML element of a specific type. With a Type selector, all HTML elements of that type will be styled accordingly.

```
h1
{
  color: Green;
}
```

This Type selector now applies to all `<h1>` elements in your code and gives them a green color. Type selectors are not case sensitive, so you can use both `h1` and `H1` to refer to the same heading. I prefer to use all lowercase for my Type selectors though, so that's what you'll see in this book.

The ID Selector

The ID selector is always prefixed by a hash symbol (#) and enables you to refer to a single element in the page. Within an HTML or ASPX page, you can give an element a unique ID using the `id` attribute. With the ID selector, you can change the behavior for that single element, like this:

```
#IntroText
{
  font-style: italic;
}
```

Because you can reuse this ID across multiple pages in your site (it only has to be unique within a single page), you can use this rule to quickly change the appearance of an element that you use once per page, but more than once in your site, for example, with the following HTML code:

```
<p id="IntroText">I am italic because I have the right ID.</p>
<p id="BodyText">I am NOT italic because I have a different ID.</p>
```

In this example, the `#IntroText` selector changes the font of the first paragraph — which has the matching `id` attribute — but leaves the other paragraph unmodified. ID selectors are case sensitive, so make sure that the `id` attribute and the selector always use the same casing.

Notice that the selector uses a hash symbol (#) in its name, but you don't use this symbol in the `id` attribute.

The Class Selector

The Class selector enables you to style multiple HTML elements through the `class` attribute. This is handy when you want to give the same type of formatting to a number of unrelated HTML elements. The following rule changes the text to red and bold for all HTML elements that have their `class` attributes set to `Highlight`:

```
.Highlight
{
  color: Red;
  font-weight: bold;
}
```

The following code snippet uses the `Highlight` class to make the contents of a `<span>` element and a link (`<a>`) appear with a bold typeface:

```
This is normal text but <span class="Highlight">this is Red and Bold.</span>
This is also normal text but
   <a href="CssDemo.aspx" class="Highlight">this link is Red and Bold as well.</a>
```

Notice that the selector uses a period in its name, but you don't use this period when referring to the selector in the `class` attribute. The `class` attribute is very useful because it enables you to reuse a piece of CSS for many different purposes, regardless of the HTML element that uses the class. Class selectors are case-sensitive so make sure you type them correctly (or let IntelliSense help you pick the classes from the list when possible).

CSS supports more types of selectors, giving you even more control over the elements you want to target, but the four different types you just saw are the most widely used.

Grouping and Combining Selectors

CSS also enables you to *group* multiple selectors by separating them with a comma. This is handy if you want to apply the same styles to different elements. The following rule turns all headings in the page to red:

```
h1, h2, h3, h4, h5, h6
{
  color: Red;
}
```

Moreover, with CSS you can also *combine* selectors, enabling you to hierarchically point to a specific element in a page. You can do this by separating the selectors with a space. The following example targets all `<p>` elements that fall within a `<section>` element with an `id` of `MainContent`, leaving all other paragraphs unmodified. Also note there's no space between `section` and `#MainContent`. This results in that part of the selector targeting a `<section>` element with an `id` of `MainContent`.

```
section#MainContent p
{
  font-size: 18px;
}
```

Note that combining is very different from grouping. Grouping is just a shortcut to avoid typing the same declarations over and over again, whereas combining enables you to target specific elements in your document.

With combining, you're not limited to ID and Type selectors; you can also use it with the other selectors, as is demonstrated with the following example:

```
section#MainContent p.Attention
{
  font-weight: bold;
}
```

This rule changes all paragraphs with the class `Attention` within the `<section>` element with its `id` set to `MainContent` and leaves all others untouched. The following HTML snippet uses this rule to show the effect:

```
<section id="MainContent">
  <p class="Attention">My class is Attention, so my text is bold.</p>
  <p>My text is not bold, as it lacks the Attention class.</p>
</section>
<p class="Attention">I am NOT bold because I don't fall within MainContent.</p>
```

The second question that needs to be answered to apply a certain style in your page is about what part of the element must be styled. You do this with properties.

Properties

Properties are the part of the element that you want to change with your style sheet. The CSS specification defines a long list of properties (VS's IntelliSense list shows more than 100 items), although you won't use all of them in most websites. The following table lists some of the most common CSS properties and describes where they are used.

PROPERTY	DESCRIPTION	EXAMPLE
`background-color` `background-image`	Specifies the background color or image of an element.	`background-color: White;` `background-image: url(Image.jpg);`
`border`	Specifies the border of an element.	`border: 3px solid Black;`
`color`	Changes the font color.	`color: Green;`
`display`	Changes the way elements are displayed, enabling you to hide or show them.	`display: none;` This causes the element to be hidden, and not take up any screen space.
`float`	Enables you to "float" an element in the page using a left or right float. Other content is then placed on the opposite side.	`float: left;` This setting causes other content following a float to be placed at the top-right corner of the element. You see how this works later in the chapter.

continues

(continued)

PROPERTY	DESCRIPTION	EXAMPLE

`font-family`
`font-size`
`font-style`
`font-weight`
	Changes the appearance of fonts used on your page.	`font-family: Arial;`
		`font-size: 18px;`
		`font-style: italic;`
		`font-weight: bold;`

`height` `width`	Sets the height or width of elements in your page.	`height: 100px;` `width: 200px;`
`margin` `padding`	Sets the amount of free space inside (padding) and outside (margin) of an element.	`padding: 0;` `margin: 20px;`
`visibility`	Controls whether an element is visible in the page. Invisible elements still take up screen space; you just don't see them.	`visibility: hidden;` This causes the element to be invisible. However, it still takes up its original space in the page. It's as if the element is still there, but completely transparent.

Fortunately, VS helps you to find the right property with its many CSS tools, so you don't have to remember them all.

> ***NOTE*** *Many more selectors and properties are available in CSS than I have described here. For more detail on CSS, consult VS's IntelliSense lists or take a look at* `www.w3schools.com/cssref/`.

For a property to be useful, you need to give it a value, which answers the third question: How do you want the part of the selected element to look?

Values

Just as with properties, values come in many flavors. The values you have available depend on the property. For example, the `color` attribute takes values that represent a color. This can be a named color (such as `White`), a hexadecimal number representing a red, green, and blue (RGB) component (such as `#FF0000`), or you can set it using the CSS `rgb` notation. The following examples are all functionally equivalent and set the color of the `h1` element to red:

```
h1
{
  color: Red;
}

h1
{
```

```
  color: #FF0000;
}

h1
{
  color: rgb(100%, 0%, 0%);
}
```

You can also specify the transparency of a color using the `rgba` notation where the fourth parameter is a decimal number between `0` (fully transparent) and `1` (no transparency) like this:

```
color: rgba(255, 0, 0, 0.50);
```

Using named colors can increase the readability of your CSS code, but because you're limited to a relatively short list of named colors, you often need the hexadecimal notation to get the exact color you want. Later in this chapter you see how to use the built-in color picker to create the exact color you need.

Many other values are possible as well, including size units (`px`, `em`, and so on), font families, images (which take the form of `url(SomeImage.jpg)`), or so-called enumerations like the `border-style`, which enables you to set a border style such as `solid`, `dashed`, `double`.

Using Shorthand

Many of the CSS properties enable you to write a shorthand version as well as a more expanded version. Take, for example, the `border` property. In its shortest form, you can set the `border` property like this:

```
border: 1px solid Black;
```

This `border` property applies a border to all four sides of an HTML element. The border size is `1px`, the style is `solid` (some of the other options include `dashed`, `dotted`, and `double`), and the border color is set to `Black`.

This is an easy way to quickly set all four borders of the HTML to the same values. However, if you want more control over the individual borders and their properties, you can use the expanded version:

```
border-top-width: 1px;
border-top-style: solid;
border-top-color: Black;
border-right-width: 1px;
border-right-style: solid;
border-right-color: Black;
border-bottom-width: 1px;
border-bottom-style: solid;
border-bottom-color: Black;
border-left-width: 1px;
border-left-style: solid;
border-left-color: Black;
```

This long version causes the exact same style to be applied: a solid black border on all four sides with a thickness of 1 pixel. In most cases, you should favor shorthand notation over its expanded counterpart, because it's much easier to read and maintain. However, if you need absolute control over the border — for example, if you want a 2-pixel dashed border on the left and top sides, and a green, solid border on the right and bottom sides of the HTML element — it's good to know that you can set each `border` property of all four directions individually. You can also mix these options. The following example sets the border on all four sides to a 1-pixel solid black line, and then overrides just the color of the left border:

```
border: 1px solid Black;
border-left-color: Blue;
```

Other CSS properties that support shorthand include `font`, `background`, `list-style`, `margin`, and `padding`. If you're unsure whether a property supports shorthand, consult the IntelliSense pop-up list that appears by pressing Ctrl+Space when you're entering a property in a CSS file or a `<style>` block.

Although at times it seems you need to write CSS by trial and error, and just hope for the right result, there's actually a quite accurate model behind CSS that determines how items should be laid out on the page. This model is called the *CSS Box Model*.

The CSS Box Model

The CSS Box Model describes the way three important CSS properties are applied to HTML elements: padding, border, and margin. Figure 3-4 shows a graphical representation of the box model.

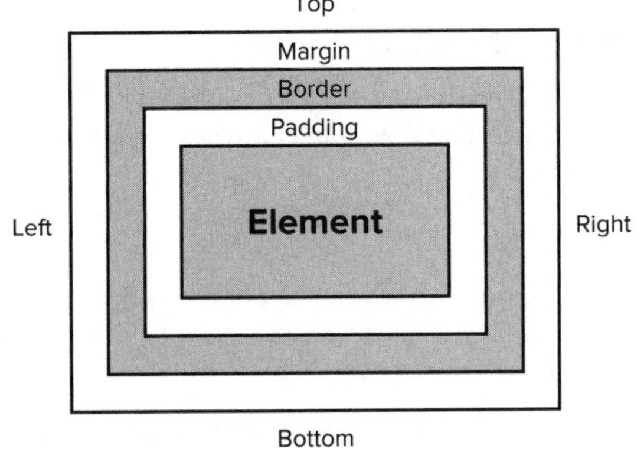

FIGURE 3-4

In the middle there is an HTML element like a `<p>` or a `<div>` with a certain height and width. Just around it there is *padding*; the whitespace that surrounds the element within its border. Immediately after the padding you can see the *border* and finally on the outside there is the *margin*, which defines the room between an element (including its padding and border) and its surrounding elements. The three outer properties of an element — padding, border, and margin — add up to the space that an element takes up in the page. To see how this works, consider the following CSS and HTML:

```
.MyDiv
{
  width: 200px;
  padding: 10px;
  border: 2px solid Black;
}
...
<div class="MyDiv">Element</div>
```

This renders a rectangle in the browser with the `<div>` element surrounded by a black border of two pixels, as shown in Figure 3-5.

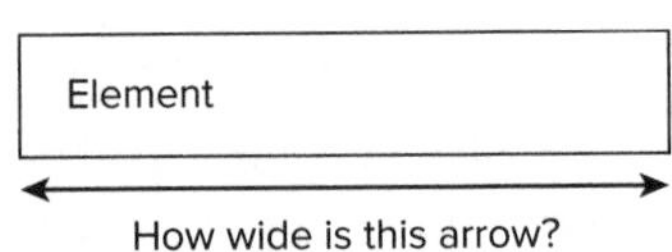

FIGURE 3-5

Before you read on, try answering the question: How wide is the arrow below the <div> element?

If you guessed 224 pixels, you are correct. The width of the arrow is the sum of three values: the width of the actual element (200 pixels), plus the width of the padding surrounding it on both sides (two times 10 pixels), plus the width of the borders on both sides (two times 2 pixels), resulting in a total width of 224 pixels. So, if you wanted the entire box to be 200 pixels wide instead, you'd need to set the `width` property of the `MyDiv` selector to `176px`. Outside the border of the element, `margin` could further influence the gap between this element and its surrounding elements.

The example shows the effect on the width only, but the same principles apply to the height of elements. Keep this box model in mind when laying out your pages. When things end up wider or taller than you anticipated, check the `width`, `height`, `padding`, `border`, and `margin` properties in the CSS style sheet.

In the next exercise, you modify the site's homepage that you created in the previous chapter. You add the basic layout for the site, which is then styled using a style sheet. In Chapter 6 you use this page again when you upgrade it to a master page.

TRY IT OUT Styling the Planet Wrox Homepage

In this exercise you modify two files. First, you add the basic layout elements to the `Default.aspx` page to create room for a header, a menu, the main content area, a sidebar, and a footer. Then you modify the `Styles.css` file from the `Styles` folder to change the size and location of these elements. Finally, you attach the style sheet to the page, so the style information is applied when the page is viewed in the designer or in a browser.

1. Open the `Default.aspx` file from the root of your website and, if necessary, switch to Markup View.

2. Modify the code within the `<form>` element so it ends up like this:

```
<form id="form1" runat="server">
  <div id="PageWrapper">
    <header>Header Goes Here</header>
    <nav>Menu Goes Here</nav>
    <section id="MainContent">
      <h1>Hi there visitor and welcome to Planet Wrox</h1>
      ...
    </section>
    <aside id="Sidebar">Sidebar Goes Here</aside>
    <footer>Footer Goes Here</footer>
  </div>
</form>
```

   Make sure that the welcome message you added in the previous chapter ends up between the opening and closing tag of the `MainContent` `<section>` element. If you were already familiar with versions of HTML before HTML5, you may a bit surprised by the new elements such as `header`, `section`, and `footer`. These elements were introduced in HTML5 to give a better semantic structure to your documents. Refer to Chapter 1 for a quick introduction to HTML5.

3. Open the `Styles.css` file from the `Styles` folder. If you added some code to this file earlier, remove that code first.

4. At the top of the CSS file, type the following code that uses an ID selector to select the `header` element:

```
header
{

}
```

5. Position your mouse between the curly braces, right-click, and choose Build Style from the context menu. The Modify Style dialog box shown in Figure 3-6 appears.

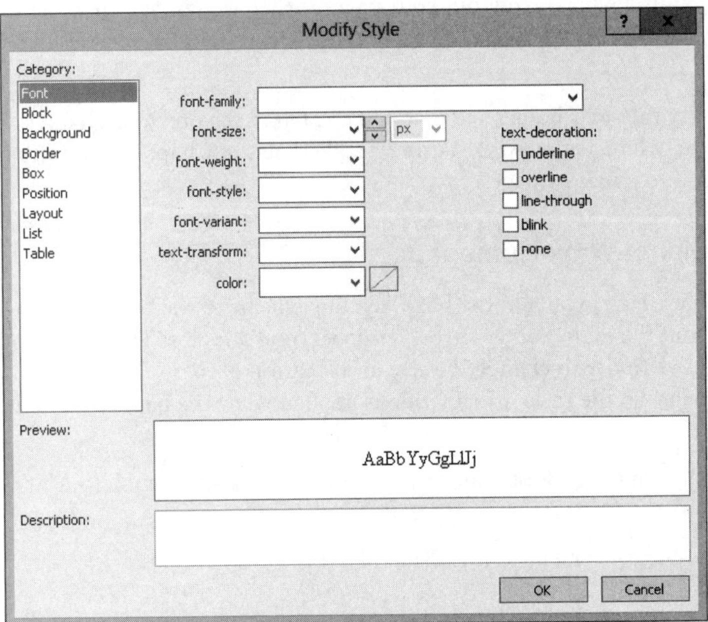

FIGURE 3-6

6. In the Category list on the left, click Background and then open the drop-down list for the background color. From the color picker that appears, click the Silver color, as shown in Figure 3-7.

   Alternatively, you can type the hexadecimal color code for Silver (`#C0C0C0`) in the background-color text box directly.

7. Switch to the Position category by clicking it in the list on the left. The panel that appears enables you to set position-related information, including the height and width. Under width, enter **`844`** and make sure that px is selected in the drop-down list at the right. For the height, enter **`86`**. Click OK to dismiss the dialog box and to insert the declarations into your code, which now looks like this:

```
header
{
  background-color: #C0C0C0;
  width: 844px;
  height: 86px;
}
```

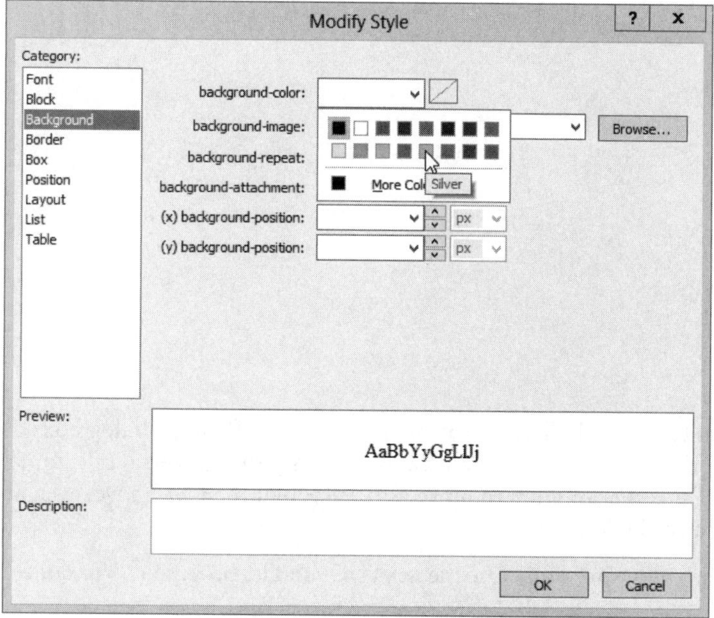

FIGURE 3-7

8. Repeat steps 4 through 7, this time creating the following rules. If you prefer, you could also type in this code directly in the code editor.

```
*
{
  font-family: Arial;
}

h1
{
  font-size: 20px;
}

#PageWrapper
{
  width: 844px;
  margin: auto;
}

nav
{
  width: 844px;
}

section#MainContent
{
  width: 664px;
  float: left;
```

```
}

aside
{
  background-color: Gray;
  width: 180px;
  float: left;
}

footer
{
  background-color: #C0C0C0;
  width: 844px;
  clear: both;
}
```

The `float` and `clear` properties are in the Layout category of the Modify Style dialog box, whereas the `text-decoration` property is in the Font category. Since the Universal selector (`*`) applies to all elements in your site, it's common to move it to the top of the CSS above, even above the header selector, which you could do now.

9. When you're done creating the rules, save and close the `Styles.css` file, because you're done with it for now.

10. Open the `Default.aspx` file again and switch to Design View. From the Solution Explorer, drag the `Styles.css` file from the `Styles` folder onto the page. You should immediately see the Design View change to reflect the code you wrote in the style sheet. When you drop the style sheet on the page, VS inserts code in the `<head>` section of the page in Markup View that attaches the style sheet to the document:

```
<head runat="server">
  <title></title>
  <style type="text/css">
    .auto-style1
    {
      color: #FF0000;
    }
  </style>
  <link href="Styles/Styles.css" rel="stylesheet" type="text/css" />
</head>
```

You can also drag an existing style sheet from the Solution Explorer directly in the `<head>` section of a page in Markup View. When you do that, VS adds the same `<link>` element although the order of the attributes could be slightly different.

11. Since the site uses HTML5, you need a browser that supports this latest HTML version for the page to render correctly. For older browsers, such as Internet Explorer 8 and below, you can use a nifty JavaScript library called *Modernizr*. One of the many features of this library is dynamically adding support for new HTML elements such as `nav`, `section` and `aside` through JavaScript.

Adding Modernizr to your site is very easy using the Package Manager Console that ships with Visual Studio. To add the library, follow these steps:

1. Choose Tools ➪ Library Package Manager ➪ Package Manager Console.
2. Type the following command and press Enter:

```
Install-Package Modernizr
```

3. After a short delay, your site is expanded with a file called `packages.config` that keeps track of the installed packages and a `Scripts` folder that now contains the file `modernizr-2.6.2.js`. Note: your version number could be different if a newer version of Modernizr has been released by the time you read this book. To add this library to your page, open `Default.aspx` in Markup View and drag the file from the Solution Explorer to the `head` section of the code, directly after the link to the style sheet. You should end up with this code:

```
  <link href="Styles/Styles.css" rel="stylesheet" type="text/css" />
  <script type="text/javascript" src="Scripts/modernizr-2.6.2.js"></script>
</head>
```

You should add the Modernizr library to your site even if you have a modern web browser. Since you can't control the browsers visiting your site, you want to make sure everybody sees your site as intended. Adding Modernizr fixes the HTML5 compatibility issues for older browsers while hardly causing any overhead. You can learn more about Modernizr on its website at `http://modernizr.com/`. You'll see a lot more about the Package Manager Console in Chapter 11.

12. Finally, save the changes to all open documents (press Ctrl+Shift+S) and then request `Default.aspx` in your browser. Your screen should look similar to Figure 3-8, which shows the page in Mozilla Firefox.

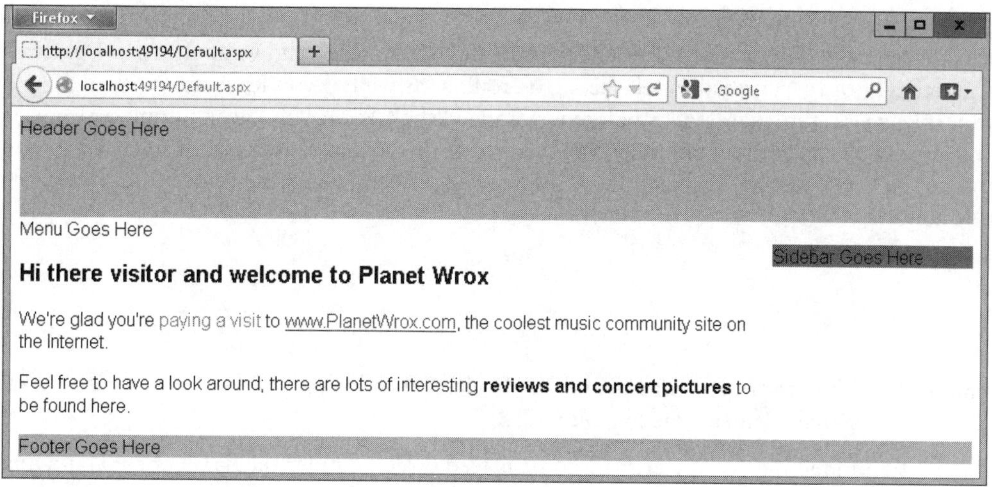

FIGURE 3-8

How It Works

The Style Builder makes it easy to select CSS properties and change their values. You don't need to memorize every little detail about CSS, but instead you can create your CSS code visually. Once you get a better understanding of CSS and its many properties and values, you may find yourself entering CSS in the CSS file directly, because that's often quicker to do.

Note that the `header`, `PageWrapper`, `nav`, and `footer` elements have an exact width of 844 pixels. This way, the site fits nicely on screens with a size of 1024 x 768 pixels, a common screen size for many of today's computers, without being squeezed between the Windows borders. Systems with bigger screens simply center the site in the available space. This centering is done by the `PageWrapper` element, which has its `margin` set to `auto`. This means that the available space on the left and right sides (but not at the top and bottom) is equally divided, effectively centering the `PageWrapper` element in the middle of the browser window.

Note also that the `MainContent section` and the `aside` are positioned next to each other. You do this with the CSS `float` property:

```
section#MainContent
{
  width: 664px;
  float: left;
}

aside
{
  background-color: Gray;
  width: 180px;
  float: left;
}
```

This tells the `MainContent` to "float" on the left side of content that follows it, effectively placing the `aside` to the right of it. You need to tell the `aside` to float as well; if you leave it out, it will be placed at the left of the page, right where it was before you applied the CSS. If you have multiple `aside` elements in your site (which is a common practice), you can target this `aside` that acts as a sidebar by adding an `id` attribute (such as `Sidebar`) just as I did with the `MainContent section` element and then update the CSS as follows:

```
aside#Sidebar
{
  ...
}
```

The combined width of the `MainContent` and `aside` elements adds up to 844 pixels, which is exactly the width of their parent element: the `PageWrapper`.

To end the float and tell the `footer` element to be placed directly under the `MainContent` and `aside` elements, the `clear` property is used to clear any float (left or right) that may be in effect:

```
footer
{
  background-color: #C0C0C0;
  width: 844px;
  clear: both;
}
```

The gray backgrounds are just temporarily added to the code, so it's easier to see what <div> ends up where. In future exercises, you modify the CSS file again to fit the scheme of the Planet Wrox website.

To tell the browser what styles to apply, you link the style sheet in the head of the page:

```
<link href="Styles/Styles.css" rel="stylesheet" type="text/css" />
```

This tells the browser to look in the `Styles` folder for a file called `Styles.css` and apply all rules in that file to the current document. Once the browser has downloaded the CSS file, it applies all the styles it finds in there to your HTML elements, resulting in the layout shown in Figure 3-8.

In this exercise, you saw how to link an external style sheet to a page using the <link> tag. However, you have more ways to include style sheets in your web pages.

Adding CSS to Your Pages

The first way to add CSS style sheets to your web pages is through the <link> element that points to an *external* CSS file, as you saw in the previous exercise. Take a look at the following <link> to see what options you have when embedding a style sheet in your page:

```
<link href="StyleSheet.css" rel="Stylesheet" type="text/css" media="screen" />
```

The `href` property points to a file within your site, just as you saw in the previous chapter when you created links between two pages. The `rel` and `type` attributes tell the browser that the linked file is in fact a cascading style sheet. The `media` attribute is quite interesting: it enables you to target different devices, including the screen, printer, handheld devices, and even Braille and aural support tools for visually impaired visitors. The default for the `media` attribute is `screen`, so it's OK to omit the attribute if you're targeting standard desktop browsers.

You briefly saw the second way to include style sheets at the beginning of this chapter: using *embedded* <style> elements. The <style> element should be placed at the top of your ASPX or HTML page, between the <head> tags. Within the <style> tags, you can write the exact same CSS you saw earlier. For example, to change the appearance of an <h1> element in the current page only, you can add the following code to the <head> of your page:

```
<head runat="server">
  <title></title>
  <style type="text/css">
    h1
    {
      color: Blue;
    }
  </style>
</head>
```

The third way to apply CSS to your HTML elements is to use *inline styles* with the `style` attribute that you saw in the previous chapter. Because the `style` attribute is already applied to a specific HTML element, you don't need a selector and you can write the declaration in the attribute directly:

```
<span style="color: White; background-color: Black;">
    This is white text on a black background.
</span>
```

Choosing among External, Embedded, and Inline Style Sheets

Because you have so many options to add style sheets to your site, what's the best method to use? In general, you should give preference to external style sheets over embedded styles, which in turn are preferred over inline styles. External style sheets enable you to change the appearance of the entire site through a single file. Make one change to your external style sheet file, and all pages that use this style sheet pick up the change automatically.

However, it's perfectly acceptable to use embedded and inline styles as well in certain circumstances. If you want to change the look of a single page, without affecting other pages in your site, an embedded style sheet is your best choice. The same applies to inline styles: if you only want to change the behavior of a single element in a single page, and you're pretty sure you're not going to need the same declaration for other HTML elements, you could use an inline style.

An important thing to consider is the way that the various types of style sheets override each other. If you have multiple identical selectors with different property values, the one defined last takes precedence. For example, consider a rule defined in an external style sheet called `Styles.css` that sets the color of all `<h1>` tags to green:

```
h1
{
  color: Green;
}
```

Now imagine you're attaching this style sheet in a page that also has an embedded rule for the same `h1` but that sets a different color:

```
<link href="Styles/Styles.css" rel="stylesheet" type="text/css" />
<style type="text/css">
  h1
  {
    color: Blue;
  }
</style>
```

With this code, the color of the actual `<h1>` tag in the page will be blue. This is because the embedded style sheet that sets the color to blue is defined later in the page, and thus overrides the setting in the external file. If you turn the styles around like this,

```
<style type="text/css">
  h1
  {
    color: Blue;
  }
</style>
<link href="Styles/Styles.css" rel="stylesheet" type="text/css" />
```

the heading will be green, because the setting in the external style sheet now overrules that of the embedded style.

The same principle applies to inline styles. Because they're defined directly on the HTML elements, their settings take precedence over embedded and external style sheets.

It's also good to know that CSS generally overrules attributes on HTML elements. For example, if you have a CSS rule that sets the width and height of an image, the `height` and `width` attributes on the `img` element are ignored. For example the image in this code snippet ends up as a 100-pixel square:

```
img
{
  height: 100px;
  width: 100px;
}
...
<img src="SomeImage.jpg" width="200px" height"200px" />
```

> ***NOTE*** *There's a lot more to CSS than what is shown here. To learn more about CSS, pick up a copy of* Beginning CSS: Cascading Style Sheets for Web Design, 3rd Edition *Wrox, 2011 by Richard York and Ian Pouncey (ISBN: 978-0-470-89152-0).*

In general, it's recommended that you attach external files at the top of the `<head>` section, followed by embedded style sheets. That way, the external file defines the global look of elements, and you can use embedded styles to overrule the external settings on a page-by-page basis.

VS makes it easy to move embedded style sheets to an external CSS file, something you learn how to do in the next section, which discusses the remainder of the CSS tools in VS.

WORKING WITH CSS IN VISUAL STUDIO

The previous version of VS already had a number of great tools on board to make working with CSS as easy as possible, including:

- The *CSS Properties Grid*, which enables you to change property values.
- The *Manage Styles window*, which enables you to organize styles in your site, changing them from embedded to external style sheets and vice versa; reorder them; link existing style sheets to a document; and create new inline, embedded, or external style sheets.
- The *Apply Styles window*, which you can use to choose from all available styles in your site and quickly apply them to elements in your page.
- The *Style Builder*, which you can use to visually create declarations, as you saw earlier.

In VS 2012, the CSS tools have been greatly enhanced and now support the following options as well:

- *Hierarchical indenting*, which makes your CSS code easier to understand.
- Smarter *IntelliSense* features, which makes it easy to enter CSS code manually.
- A number of helpful editor features such as the ability to easily comment and uncomment code, wrap code in collapsible regions, a color picker, and code snippets.

The next sections give you a detailed look at these tools.

Using the CSS Editor

The CSS text editor in VS hosts a number of powerful features, demonstrated in the next Try It Out exercise.

TRY IT OUT Trying Out the CSS Editor

In this exercise you modify the `Styles.css` file you created earlier by adding a few new styles. Along the way you're introduced to a number of the CSS editor features listed earlier.

1. Open the `Styles.css` file from the `Styles` folder and locate the `section#MainContent` selector. Right below its closing curly brace, add the following CSS selector that targets links (a elements) in the `MainContent` section:

```
section#MainContent a
{

}
```

2. Between the opening and closing curly brace type **`color`**, followed by a colon (**`:`**) and then by a hash symbol (#). As soon as you type the hash symbol, VS presents you with a color picker. If you click the down arrow at the right of the color picker, it expands and shows more options, visible in Figure 3-9.

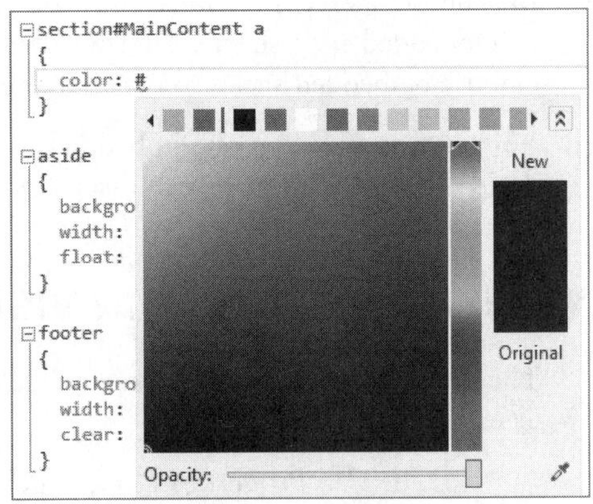

FIGURE 3-9

This color picker has a few interesting features. Firstly, the top row of colored squares contains a list of colors that are defined in your style sheet. This is a great way to quickly pick a color you've already been using for another selector. The list of recognized colors is then followed by a vertical bar, which in turn is followed by some default colors that VS adds for you. In Figure 3-9 you can see two recognized colors: a light and a dark shade of gray. The other colors are all defaults. Secondly, you can mix your own color by dragging the mouse over the large square in the middle as well as over the colored vertical bar on the right. Finally, using the tiny color picker icon at the bottom right of the screen, you can quickly select a color from any other Windows application or your desktop. This is a great way to retrieve the color from an image you may have opened in some graphics program, for example.

If you want to type in your own color information, simply ignore the color picker (or close it by pressing the Esc key).

For this exercise, click a green square, which inserts the hexadecimal value (such as `#4cff00`) for the color for you. Complete the line of code by entering a semicolon and then press Enter.

3. On this new line type the letter **`t`**. This brings up the IntelliSense list and shows you all properties that start with the letter t as shown in Figure 3-10.

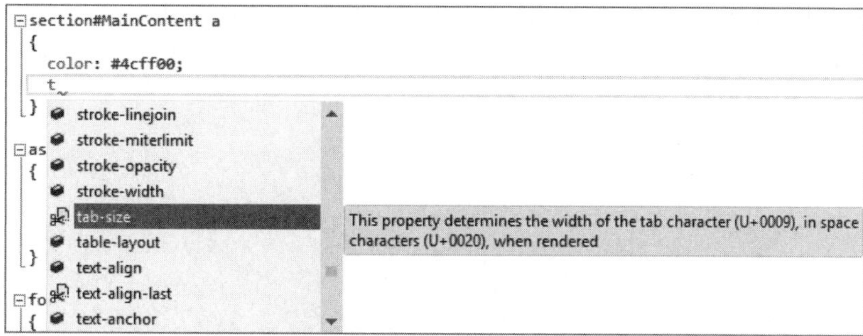

FIGURE 3-10

Next, type the letter `d`. The list is filtered further as you can see in Figure 3-11.

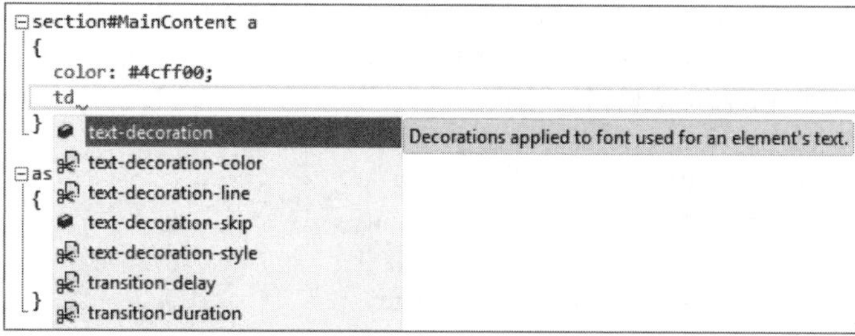

FIGURE 3-11

Notice how this filtering is done in a pretty smart way. The filter does not only limit the list to properties that start with or contain the letters td (which in this case don't exist), but it also supports what is called a *title case search* where it lists items that have each word in the property begin with the letters you're searching for. In this case, `td` matches items such as `text-decoration` as well as `transition-delay`. If you type `tdc` instead, the list would only show `text-decoration-color`. The same applies to all other CSS properties. For example, `bc` would give you `background-color`, `bbw` gives you `border-bottom-width`, and so on. This makes it extremely easy to write CSS code with only a few keystrokes.

Note how some items in the list have an icon with a pair of scissors instead of the standard property icon. The scissors icon indicates a code snippet that you can expand by pressing tab twice. Doing so inserts browser-specific CSS into the file that is used for CSS properties that are not yet widely implemented by all browsers.

Continue this exercise by selecting `text-decoration` from the list. You can double-click the value, press Enter, or press Tab, and VS completes the property for you. Next, type a colon and then **`underline`** as the value for the `text-decoration` property. Close the line with a semicolon. Your final code should now look like this:

```
section#MainContent a
{
  color: #4cff00;
  text-decoration: underline;
}
```

4. Add two more style rules below the one you just created with the following code:

```
section#MainContent a:visited
{
  color: #FF0000;
  text-decoration: underline;
}

section#MainContent a:hover
{
  color: #FFA500;
  text-decoration: underline;
}
```

5. Next, choose Edit ➪ Format Document from the main menu. Alternatively, press Ctrl+K followed by Ctrl+D. This shortcut and menu command are available for other types of files as well, such as HTML, ASPX, Visual Basic, and C# files. When executed, they format the document according to the settings for that particular file type. In the case of CSS, it formats your code by placing the opening curly brace at a consistent location, and indenting and formatting the individual rules. It also performs what's called a *hierarchical indent*. To best understand how this works, take a look at Figure 3-12, which depicts the `section#MainContent` rule set as well as the new selectors for the a elements you added earlier after you've formatted the document.

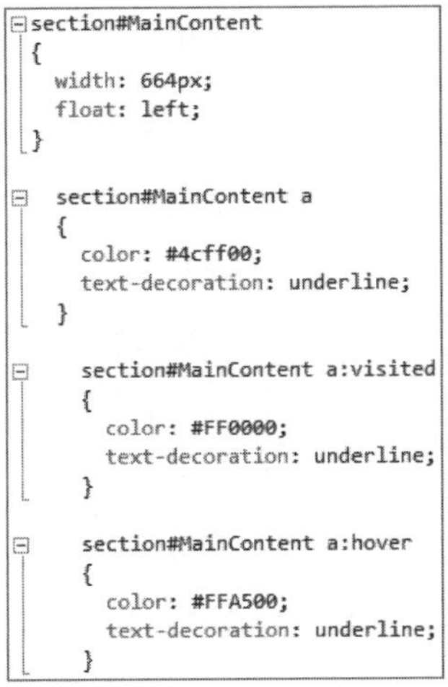

```
section#MainContent
{
  width: 664px;
  float: left;
}

  section#MainContent a
  {
    color: #4cff00;
    text-decoration: underline;
  }

    section#MainContent a:visited
    {
      color: #FF0000;
      text-decoration: underline;
    }

    section#MainContent a:hover
    {
      color: #FFA500;
      text-decoration: underline;
    }
```

FIGURE 3-12

Notice how the `section#MainContent a` rule set has been indented below the `section#MainContent` rule set. This helps to understand the relationship between the two selectors used by the rule set (`section#MainContent a` only targets a elements within a parent `section` element with an `id` of `MainContent`). Likewise, the `section#MainContent a:visited` and `section#MainContent a:hover` rule sets are indented below the a element because they can be considered "children" of the a element. If you don't like this behavior, you can turn it off using Tools ➪ Options ➪ Text Editor ➪ CSS ➪ Formatting. Alternatively, press Ctrl+Q to put focus on the Quick Launch box, type **CSS Formatting** and press Enter. This opens the same Options dialog box. While you're there, spend some time browsing around the items under the Text Editor node to get an idea of how you can change the formatting of the many languages that VS supports.

6. The final two editor features worth showing here are regions and comments. If your CSS code becomes unwieldy, it may help to wrap some parts of the code that belong together in a region. A region in VS can then be collapsed to hide the code, and expanded again when you need to change it. To create a region, you wrap the code in a `region` / `endregion` pair using CSS comment syntax. For example:

```
/*#region Name Of Region */
 … Your CSS code here
/*#endregion*/
```

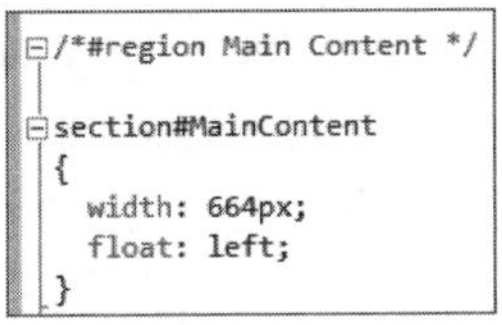

```
/*#region Main Content */

section#MainContent
{
  width: 664px;
  float: left;
}
```

FIGURE 3-13

For this exercise, add the opening region statement with a name of Main Content (`/*#region Main Content */`) right above the `section#MainContent` rule set, and the closing statement

(/*#endregion*/) below the section#MainContent a:hover rule set. Once the region is created, in Figure 3-13 you now see a minus (-) icon in the gutter next to the text editor.

You can now collapse the region by clicking the minus icon. VS hides the code block and shows the name of the region instead, as shown in Figure 3-14.

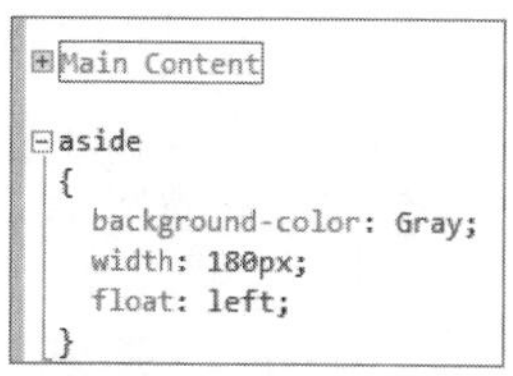

FIGURE 3-14

This makes it really easy to get some code out of the way when working with large code files. Note: regions are also supported by other file types such as C# and VB files although each language uses a slightly different syntax.

The region feature in VS makes use of standard CSS comments syntax. This means that the browser ignores the region code as well as its name.

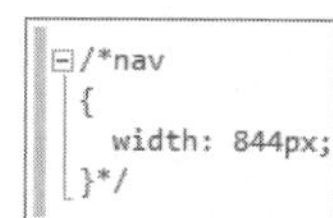

FIGURE 3-15

To comment out other code (so it's not interpreted by the browser), select some text and then press Ctrl+K followed by Ctrl+C (for Comment). The code is then commented out using /* and */, as shown in Figure 3-15.

To uncomment the code again, press Ctrl+K followed by Ctrl+U (for Uncomment). Both commands are also available in the Edit ➪ Advanced menu and on the Styles toolbar. You can also start a comment manually by typing /*. VS then inserts the closing */ for you automatically.

7. Save the changes to the CSS file. You can leave the region code in, but make sure you uncomment any code you may have commented out in the preceding step.

8. Switch to the Default.aspx page and, if necessary, switch to Design View. Select the text "look around" in the paragraph. If you typed something else in an earlier Try It Out, select that text instead. At this stage, all that's important is that you have some text to turn into a link.

9. On the Formatting toolbar, click the Convert to Hyperlink button (with the link symbol and arrow on it), click the Browse button in the dialog box that appears, and select Default.aspx in the root of the site. This way, the link points to the same page it's defined in, which is fine for this exercise. Click OK twice to dismiss the dialog boxes.

10. Save the changes to all open documents (choose File ➪ Save All from the main menu or press Ctrl+Shift+S) and then request Default.aspx in your browser by pressing Ctrl+F5. You should see the page appear with the "look around" link underlined, as shown in Figure 3-16, which shows the page in Google Chrome.

11. Hover your mouse over the "look around" link; note that it turns to orange.

12. Notice how the link to www.PlanetWrox.com is green (provided you haven't visited this site before), whereas the link to Default.aspx is red (because you're currently viewing Default.aspx, the browser marks this page as "visited".) If you visit the Planet Wrox website and then come back to your Default.aspx page again, the link to the Planet Wrox site will have turned red as well. Hovering over it still turns it to orange. If you want to test the page in another browser, right-click Default.aspx in the Solution Explorer and choose Browse With from the context menu. If your alternate browser is listed there already, select it from the list and then click Browse. Optionally, you can make this browser your default by clicking the Set as Default button.

If your browser is not listed, click the Add button and then the ellipsis next to the Program Name box to search for your favorite browser. When the browser is displayed in the list, click it to select it and then click Browse to open the page in that browser. The page should now appear in your alternate browser.

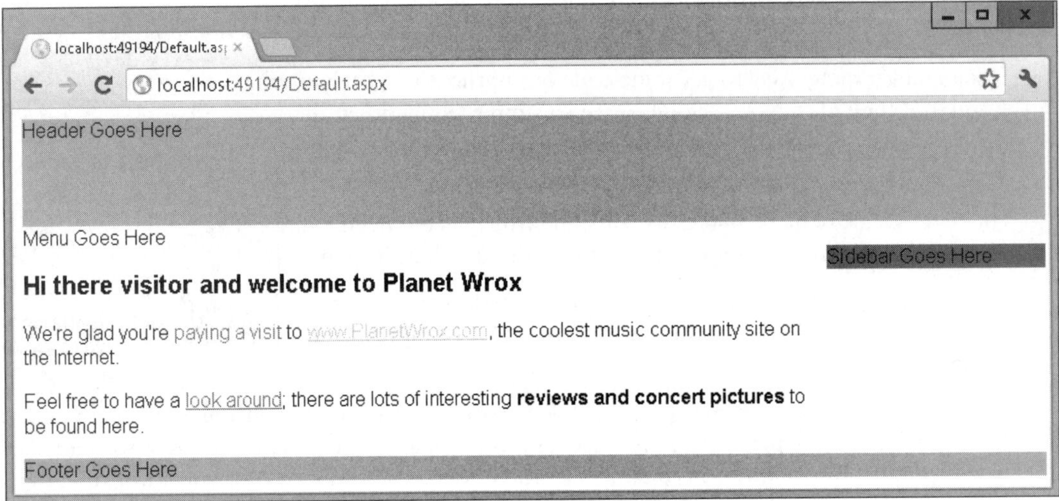

FIGURE 3-16

How It Works

This exercise started off by showing you some of the features of the CSS editor in VS. The IntelliSense list filtering and title case search are great time savers when writing CSS code. You'll need some time to get used to them, but once you have the hang of it you don't want to work without them.

The `:hover` and `:visited` parts on the `a` selector you added are probably new to you. These selectors are called *pseudo class selectors*. The `a:visited` selector is applied only to links that the user has already visited in the browser. The `a:hover` selector is applied only to the `<a>` tag when the user hovers the mouse over the link.

When you open the page in the browser, the updated style sheet is downloaded and the browser then applies the `a:visited` rule set to all links in the `MainContent section` you visited before. When you hover your mouse over a link, the rule set `section#MainContent a:hover` is applied, causing the link to turn orange.

Viewing your pages in different browsers is a good thing to do. Although modern browsers tend to render a page more and more similarly, subtle differences exist that you need to be aware of and handle in your HTML and CSS code. Installing a few different browsers on your system (Internet Explorer, Firefox, Safari, Opera, and Chrome, for example), assigning them to the Browse With dialog box as shown in this Try It Out, and testing your pages in these browsers as often as you can will help to ensure your pages look exactly right in the majority of the browsers.

Useful as external style sheets may be, sometimes you really want to use embedded or inline styles instead. Creating and managing those styles, explained in the next section, is just as easy.

Creating Embedded and Inline Style Sheets

When you're working with a page in Design View, you often need to make minor tweaks to part of the page, like styling a piece of text, aligning an image, or applying a border to an element. At this stage, you need to make a decision about whether to create an inline, embedded, or external style sheet. As you saw earlier, you should opt for external or embedded style sheets if you envision you're going to reuse a style later. VS doesn't care much, though. It enables you to create styles at all three levels. Even better, it enables you to easily upgrade an embedded style to an external one, or copy inline style information to a different location, giving you great flexibility and the option to change your mind later.

In the next exercise, you see how to create inline and embedded style sheets. You see later how to move those styles to an external style sheet, enabling other pages to reuse the same styles.

TRY IT OUT Creating Embedded and Inline Styles in a Page

In this Try It Out, you add a style rule to the `<h1>` element of the page, to remove the default margin that a browser draws around the heading. In addition, you style the first paragraph using a `class` attribute, giving it a different look to make it stand out from the other paragraphs on the page.

1. Go back to VS and make sure that the `Default.aspx` page is open in Design View.
2. Click once on the `<h1>` element in the Document Window to select it and then choose Format ➪ New Style. The New Style dialog box appears (visible in Figure 3-17), which is pretty similar to the Modify Style dialog box you saw earlier.

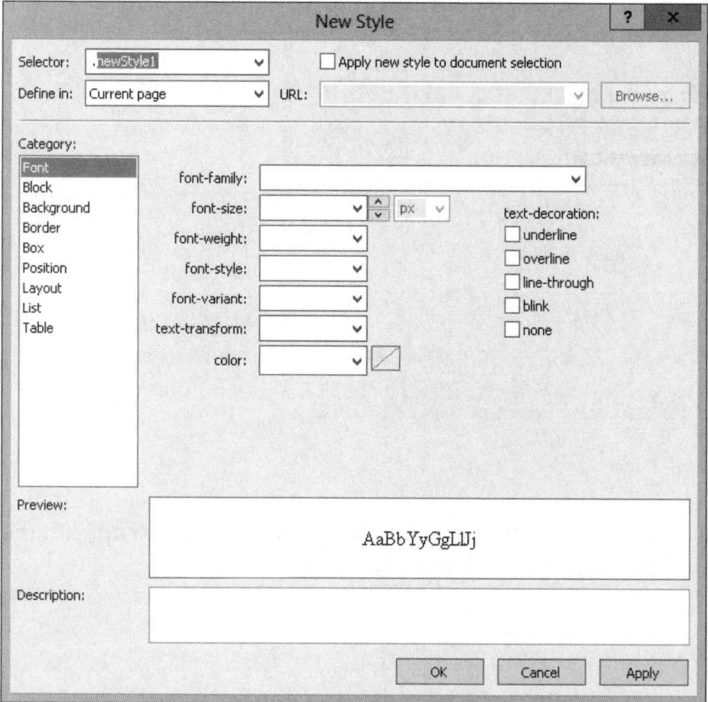

FIGURE 3-17

3. At the top of the screen, open the Selector drop-down list and choose (inline style). It's the first item in the list. This ensures that the new style is applied as an inline style to the `<h1>` element.

4. Switch to the Box category, shown in Figure 3-18.

   This dialog box has a handy diagram that serves as a refresher on the CSS Box Model, showing you where the properties `padding`, `border`, and `margin` end up.

   By default, browsers draw some white space above or below an `<h1>` element, but the actual amount differs between browsers. To give each browser the same consistent settings, you can reset the padding to 0 and then apply a little bit of margin at the bottom of the heading, which creates some distance to the elements following it. To do this, set padding to **0** in the top box and clear the value from the drop-down list next to the text box. By leaving the Same for All option selected, VS creates a shorthand declaration for you. Then uncheck Same for All for the margin section, enter **0** for the top, right, and left boxes, and clear the value from the drop-down next to each value. Next, enter **10** for the bottom text box and make sure px is selected in the drop-down list. Your screen should now look like Figure 3-18.

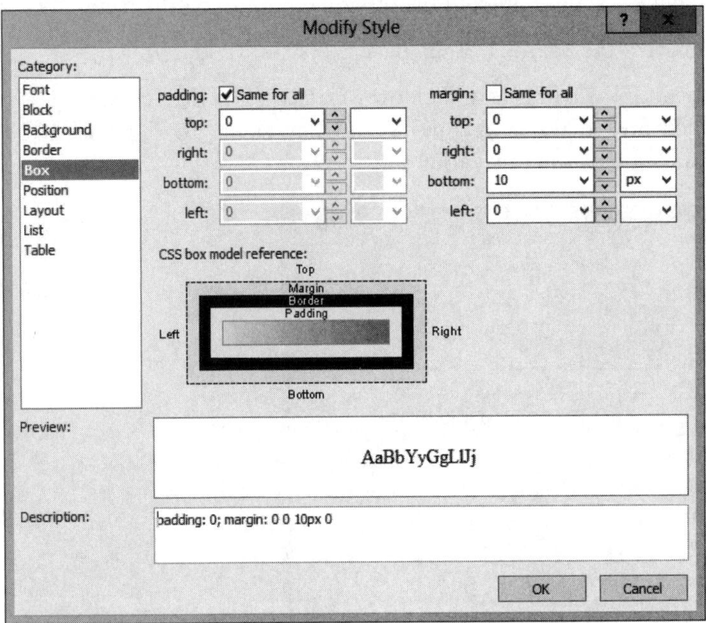

FIGURE 3-18

Click OK to close the dialog box and apply the changes to the heading. You end up with the following `<h1>` element with an inline style in Markup View:

```
<h1 style="padding: 0; margin: 0 0 10px 0">
  Hi there visitor and welcome to Planet Wrox
</h1>
```

5. Next, in Design View, select the first paragraph by clicking it. A small glyph appears to indicate you selected a `<p>` element, as visible in Figure 3-19. The Tag Selector at the bottom of the Document Window should highlight the `<p>` element.

FIGURE 3-19

6. With the paragraph still selected, choose Format ➪ New Style from the main menu. This time, instead of creating an inline style, type the text **`.Introduction`** in the Selector box that is visible in Figure 3-20. Don't forget the dot (`.`) in front of the selector's name.
7. At the top of the screen, select the check box for Apply New Style to Document Selection. With this setting on, the new class you're about to create is applied to the `<p>` element that you have selected.
8. From the font-style drop-down list, choose italic. Your New Style dialog box should now look like Figure 3-20.

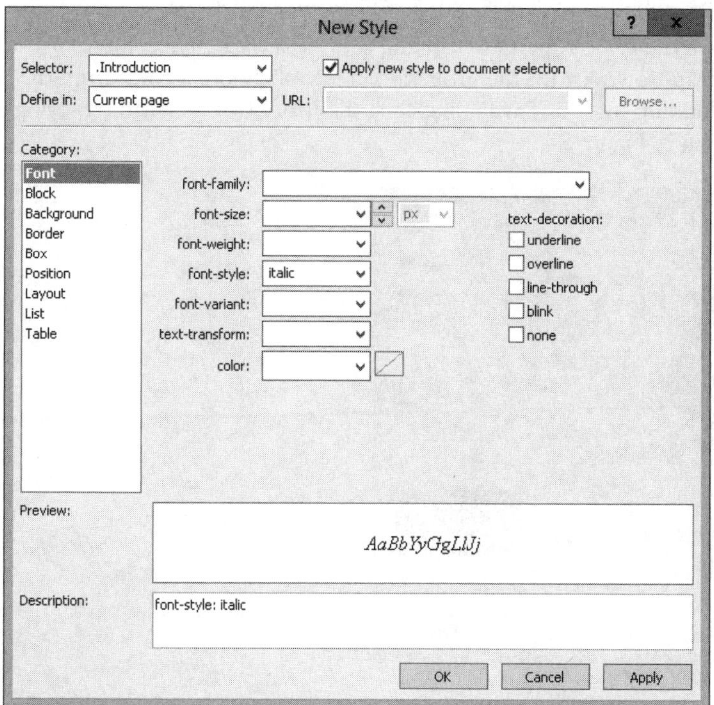

FIGURE 3-20

9. Finally, click OK. Note that the entire paragraph is now displayed with an italic font.
10. With the `<p>` element still selected, open the CSS Properties Grid (see Figure 3-21) by choosing View ➪ CSS Properties. This grid gives you an overview of all the CSS properties and shows which ones are currently active for your page.

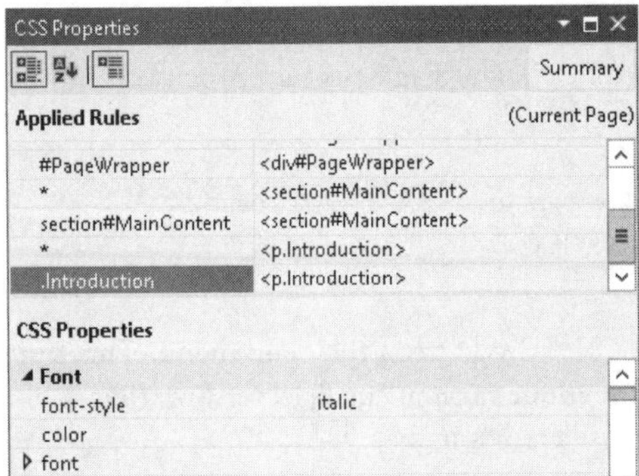

FIGURE 3-21

This grid shows a list of applied rules in the top part of the window in the order in which they are applied. The bottom part of the window is used to show the CSS properties for those rules. In Figure 3-21 you see the rules that are applicable to the `.Introduction` selector.

11. Locate the `color` property in the CSS Properties Grid and set it to a dark blue color, like `#003399`. To achieve this, open the drop-down list for the property value and choose a color from the color picker. If the color you're looking for is not available, click the More Colors button to bring up the extended color picker, shown in Figure 3-22.

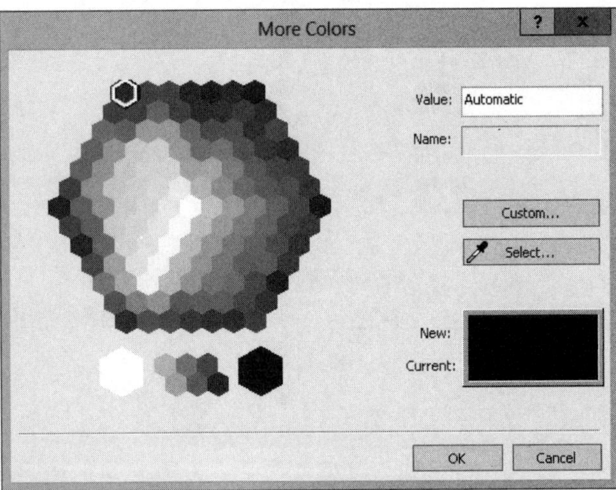

FIGURE 3-22

Instead of using the color picker, you can also type a value in the Properties Grid directly. This is how many of the properties work in the CSS Properties Grid: they let you enter values directly or enable you to change the value visually using a drop-down list or a button with ellipses at the end of the property's value box. Figure 3-23 shows the different options you have for the `font-style` property in a convenient drop-down list.

Take special note of the three buttons at the top of the window, because they house some useful functionality. The first two buttons enable you to switch between categorized mode and alphabetical mode, making it easier to find the right property. The third button enables you to display the applied properties at the top of the list or at their default location in the list.

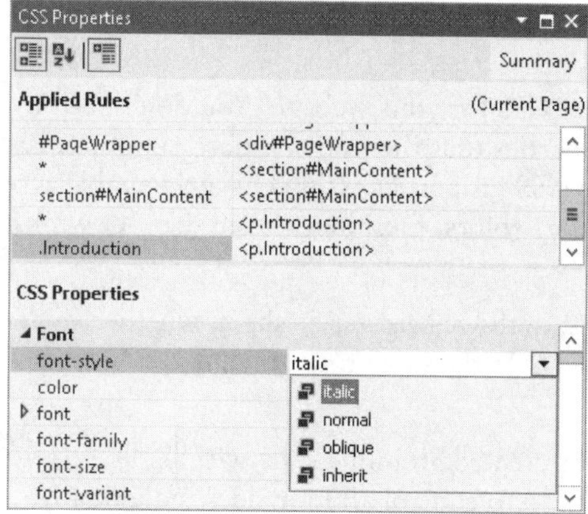

FIGURE 3-23

12. Finally, save all changes and open `Default.aspx` in your browser (see Figure 3-24). You'll see that the first paragraph is now displayed with a blue and italic font except for the link in the text, which is green or red depending on whether you visited that site before. Additionally, if you followed all the instructions from the previous chapter, the text "paying a visit" is red, set by the embedded CSS class.

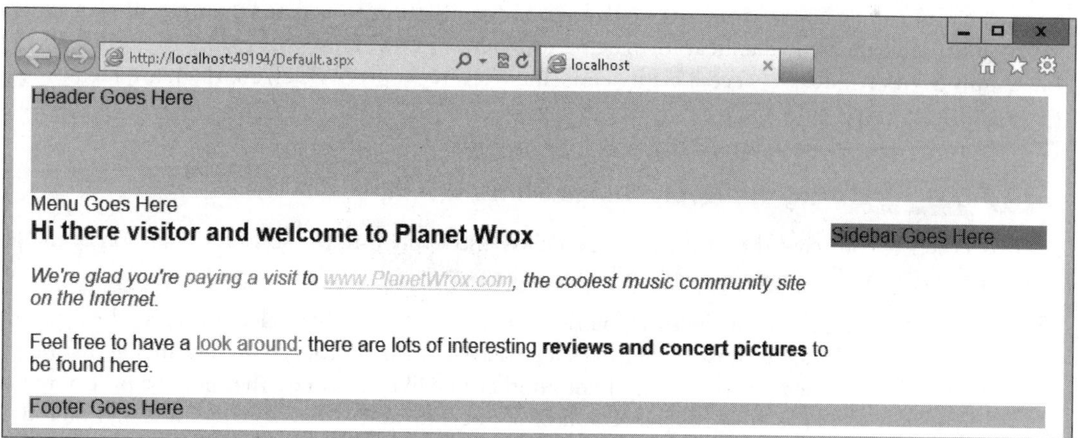

FIGURE 3-24

13. Switch back to VS and look at your page in Markup View. In the `<head>` section of the page, you should see the following embedded style sheet:

```
.Introduction
{
  font-style: italic;
  color: #003399;
```

```
    }
  </style>
  <link href="Styles/Styles.css" rel="stylesheet" type="text/css" />
```

How It Works

The numerous tools that VS offers make it easy to write CSS for your website. You don't need to hand code anything, or remember all the different properties that the CSS standard supports. Instead, you can simply choose them from different lists on the CSS Properties Grid. This grid enables you to enter values manually but also offers handy tools to select colors, files, items from drop-down lists and more.

All changes you make in the Properties Grid are applied to the relevant style sheet, whether you're working with an inline, embedded, or external style sheet. At the same time, the Design View is updated to reflect the new CSS options you have set.

When you look at the `<h1>` element, you can see that VS created an inline style with `padding` set to `0` to affect all four sides at once, and `margin` set to `0 0 10px 0` to control all four sides individually.

Once you have created a bunch of useful and reusable styles, you need a way to apply your existing styles to other pages or HTML elements. You see how this works next.

Applying Styles

If you have some experience with Microsoft Word, you may be familiar with the Styles dialog box, which lists all available styles and enables you to apply them to selected portions of text. This way, you can quickly apply identical formatting to blocks of text. This works similarly in VS. With the Apply Styles window — accessible by choosing View ➪ Apply Styles from the main menu — you can easily apply style rules to elements in the page.

TRY IT OUT Using the Apply Styles Window

In this exercise, you reuse the `.Introduction` class and apply it to the second paragraph of the page as well. That way, both paragraphs end up looking the same.

1. Still in `Default.aspx`, make sure you're in Design View and then select the second paragraph of the page by clicking it. Ensure that the Tag Selector at the bottom of the Document Window shows that the `<p>` element is selected, and not another one like `<strong>` that may be part of the `<p>` element. If you have only one paragraph of text, create a new one first (by pressing Enter after the first paragraph in Design View), enter some text, and then select that paragraph.
2. Open the Apply Styles window by choosing View ➪ Apply Styles. Make sure the window is not accidentally docked in the main Document Window, but either floats or is placed at the side of the Document Window. This window shows all the selectors it finds in the current page and any attached style sheet. If you don't see all the styles shown in Figure 3-25, click the Options button and choose Show All Styles.

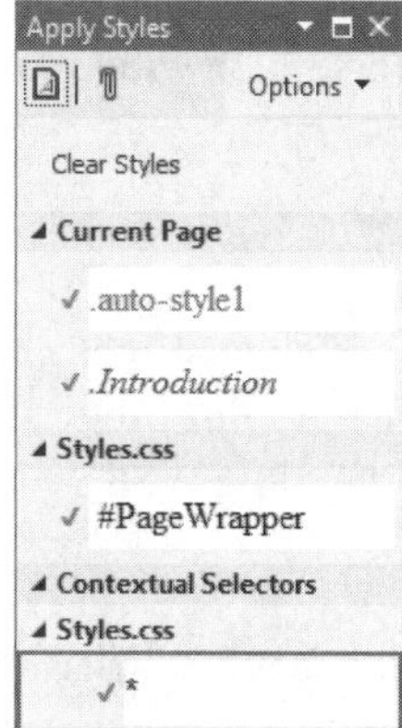

FIGURE 3-25

3. Click the `Introduction` class in the CSS Styles list. VS adds a `class` attribute to the `<p>` tag:

```
<p class="Introduction">
  Feel free to have a <a href="Default.aspx">look around</a>; there are lots of
  interesting <strong>reviews and concert pictures</strong> to be found here.
</p>
```

   If you want to apply multiple classes, hold down the Ctrl key while clicking one of the other classes in the list. This applies a list of classes separated by a space to the element's `class` attribute. You can follow the same steps to apply the selected style in Markup View as well.

4. Using the Clear Styles button, you can quickly remove existing classes and inline styles from a tag. Consider the HTML fragment you saw in the previous chapter when you used the Formatting toolbar to format text in the page. If you used the Foreground Color button, you ended up with code similar to this:

```
We&#39;re glad you&#39;re <span class="auto-style1">paying a visit</span>
```

   To remove the `class` attribute, select the `<span>` tag in the Tag Selector, or simply click the `<span>` tag in Markup View and then click Clear Styles in the Apply Styles window, which you can see below the toolbar in Figure 3-25. You'll end up with this HTML:

```
We&#39;re glad you&#39;re paying a visit
```

   Because an empty `<span>` around the text has no use, VS removes it for you as well. In addition, VS also removes the `auto-style1` rule because it's no longer used by any code on the page.

   Removing style attributes from HTML elements works the same way.

How It Works

Once again, VS is able to keep all relevant windows in sync: the Design View, Markup View, and the various CSS design tools. When you apply a class from the Apply Styles window, VS adds the requested class to the selected HTML element in Markup View. It then also updates the Design View window. Similarly, when you remove a selector or a declaration from an embedded style in Design View, both the Design View and the CSS tools windows are updated.

The final CSS functionality you need to look at in this chapter is located on the Manage Styles and Apply Styles windows. Besides helping you attach CSS files to your documents, these windows enable you to manage your styles easily.

Managing Styles

Because it's so easy to add new inline and embedded styles, your pages may quickly become a mess with styles all over the place. To achieve reusability, you should move as much of your inline and embedded styles as possible to an external style sheet. This is exactly what the Apply Styles and Manage Styles windows enable you to do.

TRY IT OUT Managing Styles with the Manage Styles and Apply Styles Windows

Earlier in this chapter, you modified the `<h1>` element and applied padding and margin to the heading. However, `Default.aspx` is not the only page that could benefit from this style for a heading, so it makes sense to move it to the `Styles.css` file. Similarly, the `Introduction` class seems reusable enough to include it in the `Styles.css` file so other pages can access it. This Try It Out shows you how to move styles around in your site.

1. Make sure that `Default.aspx` is still open and switch to Markup View if necessary.
2. Locate the `<h1>` element and click it once. VS highlights the tag in the Tag Selector at the bottom of the Document Window to indicate it's the active tag.
3. Open the Apply Styles window by choosing View ➪ Apply Styles from the main menu. Alternatively, if you have the window docked with other windows, simply click its tab to make it active. Again, make sure the window is not accidentally docked in the main Document Window, but either floats or is placed at the side of the Document Window. At the bottom of the Apply Styles window, you'll see an inline style appear (see Figure 3-26).

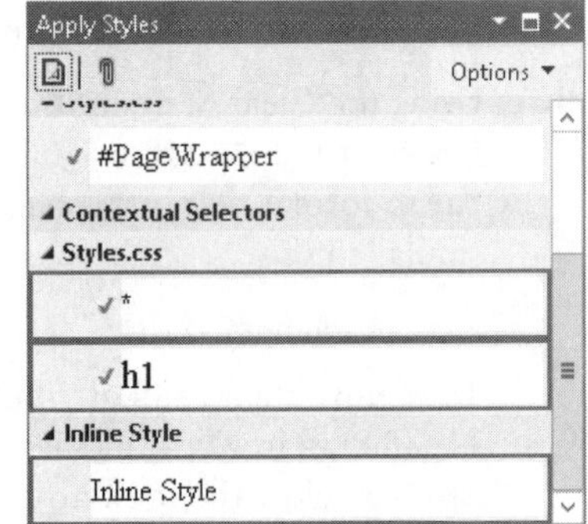

FIGURE 3-26

4. Right-click Inline Style and choose New Style Copy. The New Style dialog box appears, enabling you to create a new style based on the current selection. At the top of the window, choose `h1` from the Selector drop-down list, and from the Define In drop-down list choose Existing style sheet. From the URL drop-down list, choose Styles/Styles.css. If that item isn't available, click the Browse button to locate and select it. Your dialog box should end up like Figure 3-27.
5. Click OK to close the dialog box. VS creates a copy of the `h1` style and places it in the `Styles.css` file. VS creates a new selector for `h1` in the `Styles.css` file instead of adding the padding and margin info to the existing rule set. If you want, you could combine the two selectors into one manually.
6. In the Apply Styles window, right-click Inline Style again, and this time choose Remove Inline Style from the context menu. This removes the style attribute from the `h1` element.

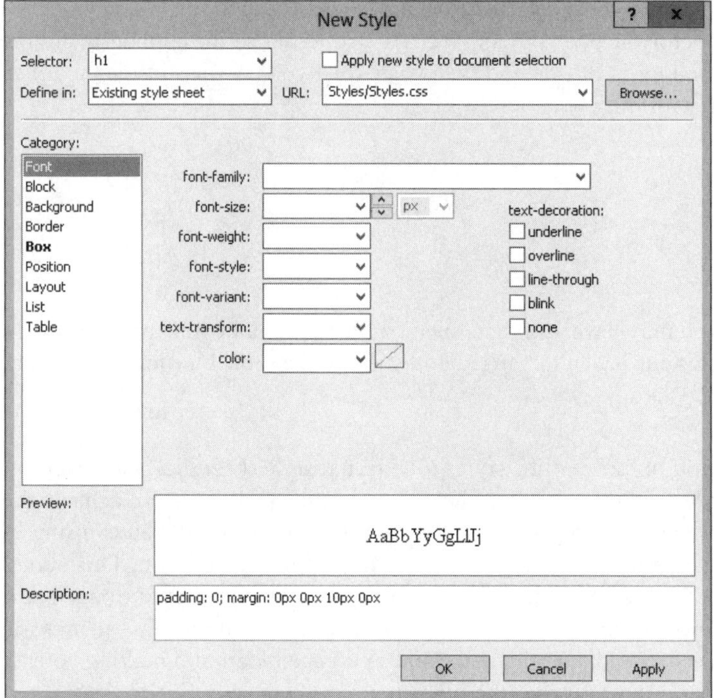

FIGURE 3-27

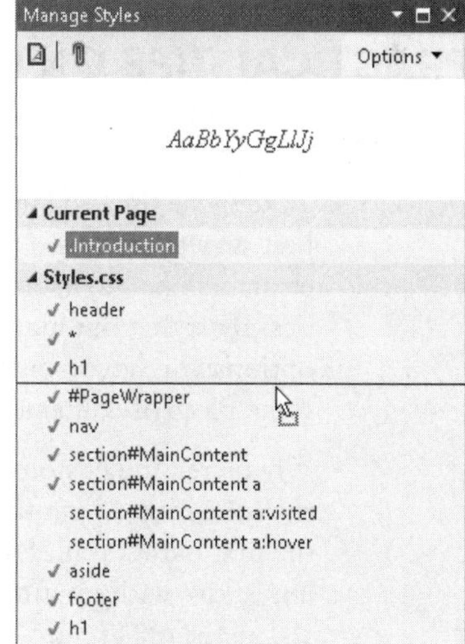

FIGURE 3-28

7. From the main menu, choose View ➪ Manage Styles. Again, make sure the window is placed beside the Document Window and not docked *in* the Document Window. Under the Current Page item, locate the `.Introduction` selector.

8. Click the `.Introduction` selector once, and then drag it into the area for `Styles.css`, for example dropping it after the `h1` selector. Note that VS draws lines between the selectors as you hover over them to indicate the point where the selector will end up. Figure 3-28 shows how the `.Introduction` selector is dragged from the current page into `Styles.css`, between the `h1` and `#PageWrapper` selectors.

9. Once you drop the selector in the `Styles.css` section of the Manage Styles window, the associated style is removed from your current page, and then inserted in `Styles.css`. Because that CSS file is included in your current page using the `<link />` element, you won't see a difference in Design View. You can now remove the empty `<style>` element from `Default.aspx`, because it's not needed anymore.

10. If you haven't already merged the two `h1` selectors, open `Styles.css` and scroll down to the end of the file. Copy the two lines for the `padding` and `margin` properties to the clipboard and then delete the entire selector. Scroll up in the file and then paste the two CSS rules inside the other `h1` selector. You should end up with this code:

```
h1
{
  font-size: 20px;
  padding: 0;
  margin: 0 0 10px 0;
}
```

11. Save any pending changes you may have and then open `Default.aspx` in your browser by pressing Ctrl+F5. Note that the paragraphs haven't changed and still use the same blue and italic font.

How It Works

Unfortunately, VS doesn't allow you to move inline styles to external style sheet files. However, by creating a copy of the existing style, and then deleting the original inline style, you can achieve the same effect. Moving embedded or external style sheets between files is a lot easier. You can simply drag a style from one file to another, and VS will automatically move the code for you. This makes it extremely easy to organize your CSS. Instead of leaving all your embedded CSS in your page because you're afraid to touch it, you can now simply drag and drop it into an external file. This makes it a lot easier to reuse those styles in other pages, decreasing page size and page bloat, and making your site a lot easier to manage. Obviously, it's important that the file you are moving your CSS to is attached to the pages you're working with.

PRACTICAL TIPS ON WORKING WITH CSS

Follow these tips to make the most of CSS:

- Take some time to familiarize yourself with the many properties that CSS supports. The best way to do this is to create a brand-new page in your `Demos` folder, create a few HTML elements like `<div>` and `<p>` tags, and then simply experiment with all the different properties. By trying out many of the properties on the CSS Properties Grid, you get a feel for what options you have available. This makes it easier later if you want to apply a certain effect to some piece of content.
- When creating custom CSS classes, try to come up with names that describe the behavior of the rule, rather than the look and feel. For example, a class called `.Introduction` to style the first paragraph of a page is a good description. It enables you to change the underlying values without affecting the actual meaning of the name. But classes with names like `.BlueAndItalic` are guaranteed to give you problems later. What if you decide to change the blue to black later? You either end up with a very odd class name not describing its own

behavior, or you'll need to rename the class and then update the entire site, changing references to the old class to `.BlackAndItalic`.

- Try to create smaller and reusable rule sets that you can combine if required, rather than creating large, monolithic rules that can only be used on a single UI element. For example, instead of creating a style like this:

```
.ImportantHeading
{
  color: Red;
  font-size: 20px;
  font-weight: bold;
}
```

You're better off creating a few lightweight rules that are easier to reuse:

```
h1
{
  font-size: 20px;
}

.Attention
{
  color: Red;
  font-weight: bold;
}
```

When you apply the `.Attention` class to a heading like this: `<h1 class="Attention">`, you get the exact same behavior you got when you gave it the `ImportantHeading` class. However, with the separate `Attention` class, you have created a reusable rule that you can apply to other elements that need the user's attention, like `<p>` or `<span>` elements.

SUMMARY

This chapter gave you a good look at CSS, the most important language for styling your ASPX and HTML web pages.

CSS enables you to overcome the limitations of HTML with respect to styling your web pages because it is designed to minimize page bloat, give you greater control over the look of your page, and generally help you create websites that load quicker and that are easier to maintain.

Once you have a good understanding of the CSS terminology, you'll find it's easy to work with the many CSS tools that VS has on board. Tools like the Manage Styles and Apply Styles windows, the Style Builder, and the smart IntelliSense in the code editor make writing and managing CSS very easy.

You can apply CSS not only to HTML as you've seen in this chapter, but also to ASP.NET Server Controls. The CSS you apply to those controls eventually ends up in the browser as plain HTML where the same principles apply as those you've seen in this chapter. The next chapter gives you a detailed look at the many available ASP.NET Server Controls.

EXERCISES

1. What is the main benefit of using an external style over embedded style sheets?

2. Write a CSS rule that changes the appearance of all headings at level one (`h1`) in your page to the following:

    - The heading uses an Arial font face.
    - The heading should be blue.
    - The heading must have a font size of 18 pixels.
    - The heading has a blue, thin border at the top and left sides.

    For the last requirement, check out VS's IntelliSense list in a CSS file to discover another shorthand version for the `border` property.

3. Which of the two following rules is easier to reuse across pages in your website? Can you explain why?

```
#MainContent
{
  border: 1px solid Blue;
}

.BoxWithBorders
{
  border: 1px solid Blue;
}
```

4. VS enables you to attach an external style sheet to a page in a number of different ways. Can you name two different options to do this?

You can find answers to these exercises in Appendix A.

▶ WHAT YOU LEARNED IN THIS CHAPTER

CSS	Cascading style sheets, the language used to lay out web pages in the browser
CSS Box Model	The model on which the dimensions of elements are calculated with regard to height, width, padding, border, and margin
Declaration	A combination of a property and a value that determines the styling for the element to which the declaration applies
Embedded style sheets	CSS code that is defined in a page in a `<style />` element. Usually referred to as embedded styles.
External style sheets	CSS code that is defined in a separate file and then included in a page using the `<link />` element
Inline style sheets	CSS code that is defined directly on an element using the `style` attribute. Usually referred to as inline styles.
Rule set	A combination of a selector and one or more declarations wrapped in a pair of curly braces
Selector	A CSS construct to point to one or more elements in the page. Different selectors exist, including the Universal selector, the ID and Class selectors, and the Type selector.

Working with ASP.NET Server Controls

WHAT YOU WILL LEARN IN THIS CHAPTER:

- What ASP.NET Server Controls are
- The different kinds of server controls you have at your disposal
- The common behavior shared among most of the server controls
- How the ASP.NET run time processes the server controls on your page
- How server controls are able to maintain their state across postbacks

WROX.COM CODE DOWNLOADS FOR THIS CHAPTER

You can find the `wrox.com` code downloads for this chapter on the Download Code tab at `www.wrox.com/remtitle.cgi?isbn=1118311809`. The code is in the Chapter 4 download.

ASP.NET Server Controls are the workhorses of ASP.NET. Almost all the Web Forms pages you build in Visual Studio (VS) will contain one or more server controls. These controls come in all sorts and sizes, ranging from simple controls like a `Button` and a `Label` to complex controls like the `TreeView` and the `ListView` that are capable of displaying data from a data source (like a database or an XML file). You see these controls in Chapters 7, 13, and 14.

The architecture of ASP.NET Server Controls is deeply integrated into ASP.NET, giving the controls a feature set that is quite unique in today's technologies for building websites. This chapter shows you what server controls are, how they work, and which ones are available out of the box when you install VS.

The chapter starts off with a general discussion of server controls. You see how to define them in your code by adding them to Design or Markup View.

The section that follows gives you a thorough look at the many controls that are available in the VS Toolbox.

INTRODUCTION TO SERVER CONTROLS

It's important to understand how server controls operate and how they are completely different from the way you define controls in other languages like classic ASP or PHP (another popular programming language for creating dynamic websites).

For example, to influence the text in a text box in these languages, you would use plain HTML and mix it with server-side code. This works similarly to the example in Chapter 2 where the current date and time are displayed on the page. To create a text box with a message and the current time in it in classic ASP, you can use the following code:

```
<input type="text" value="Hello World, the time is <%=Time()%>" />
```

As you can see, this code contains plain HTML, mixed with a server-side block, delimited by `<%` and `%>` that outputs the current time using the equals (=) symbol. This type of coding has a major disadvantage: the HTML and server-side code is mixed, making it difficult to write and maintain your pages. Although this is a trivial example in which it's still easy to understand the code, this type of programming can quickly result in very messy and complex pages.

Server controls work differently. In ASP.NET, the controls "live" on the server inside an ASPX page. When the page is requested in the browser, the server-side controls are processed by the ASP.NET run time—the engine that is responsible for processing requests for ASPX pages. The controls then emit client-side HTML code that is appended to the final page output. It's this HTML code that eventually ends up in the browser, where it's used to build up the page.

So, instead of defining HTML controls in your pages directly, you define an ASP.NET Server Control with the following syntax, where the italicized parts differ for each control:

```
<asp:TypeOfControl ID="ControlName" runat="server" />
```

For the controls that ship with ASP.NET 4.5 you always use the `asp:` prefix followed by the name of the control. For example, to create a `TextBox` that can hold the same welcome message and current time, you can use the following syntax:

```
<asp:TextBox ID="Message" runat="server" />
```

Note that the control has two attributes: `ID` and `runat`. The `ID` attribute is used to uniquely identify a control on the page, so you can program against it. It's important that each control on the page has a unique ID; otherwise the ASP.NET run time won't understand what control you're referring to. If you accidentally type a duplicate control ID, VS signals the problem in the error list. The mandatory `runat` attribute is used to indicate that this is a control that lives on the server. Without this attribute, the controls won't be processed and will end up directly in the HTML source. If you ever feel you're missing a control in the final output in the browser, ensure that the control has this required attribute. Note that for non-server elements, like plain HTML elements, the runat attribute is optional. With this attribute, non-server controls can be reached by your programming code. You learn more about this later in the book.

You can easily add the runat attribute to an existing element using a code snippet by typing runat and pressing the Tab key.

The preceding example of the TextBox uses a self-closing tag where the closing slash (/) is embedded in the opening tag. This is quite common for controls that don't need to contain child content such as text or other controls. However, the long version, using a separate closing tag, is acceptable as well:

```
<asp:TextBox ID="Message" runat="server"></asp:TextBox>
```

You can control the default behavior of closing tags per element using Tools ➪ Options ➪ Text Editor ➪ HTML ➪ Formatting ➪ Tag Specific Options.

You can program against this text box from code that is either placed inline with the page or in a separate Code Behind file, as you saw in Chapter 2. To set the welcome message and the time, you can use the following code:

VB.NET

```
Message.Text = "Hello World, the time is " & DateTime.Now.TimeOfDay.ToString()
```

C#

```
Message.Text = "Hello World, the time is " + DateTime.Now.TimeOfDay.ToString();
```

The definition of the control in the markup section of the page is now separated from the actual code that defines the text displayed in the text box, making it easier to define and program the text box (or any other control) because it enables you to focus on one task at a time. You can either declare the control and its visual appearance in the markup section of the page, or program its behavior from a code block.

In general, controls defined in Markup View are not case-sensitive, although some of the values you can set are case-sensitive. I prefer to use the capitalization as suggested by IntelliSense. Note that when using C#, properties you use in the Code Behind are case-sensitive.

You see how server controls send their underlying HTML to the client in the next exercise.

TRY IT OUT Working with Server Controls

In this exercise, you add a TextBox, a Label, and a Button control to a page. When you request the page in the browser, these server controls are transformed into HTML, that is then sent to the client. By looking at the final HTML for the page in the browser, you'll see how the HTML is completely different from the initial ASP.NET markup.

1. Open the Planet Wrox project in Visual Studio.
2. In the Demos folder in the Solution Explorer, create a new Web Form called ControlsDemo.aspx. Choose your programming language and make sure the Web Form uses Code Behind.

3. Switch to Design View. From the Standard category of the Toolbox, drag a `TextBox`, a `Button`, and a `Label` control onto the design surface within the dashed lines of the `<div>` tag that was added for you when you created the page.

   Type the text **`Your name`** in front of the `TextBox` and add a line break between the `Button` and the `Label` by positioning your cursor between the two controls in Design View and then pressing Enter. If you're having trouble positioning the cursor between the controls, place it *after* the `Label` control and then press the left arrow key twice. The first time you press it, the `Label` is selected; the second time, the cursor is placed between the two controls, enabling you to press Enter. Your Design View should now look like Figure 4-1.

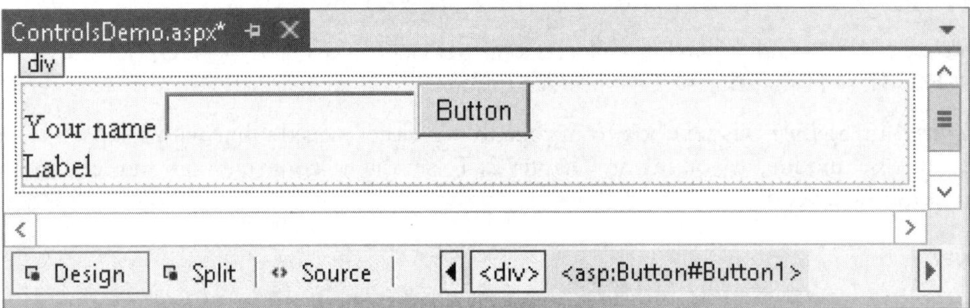

FIGURE 4-1

   Right-click the `Button` control and choose Properties to open up the Properties Grid for the control. Pressing F4 after selecting the `Button` does the same thing. The window that appears, shown in Figure 4-2, enables you to change the properties for the control, which in turn influences the way the control looks and behaves at run time.

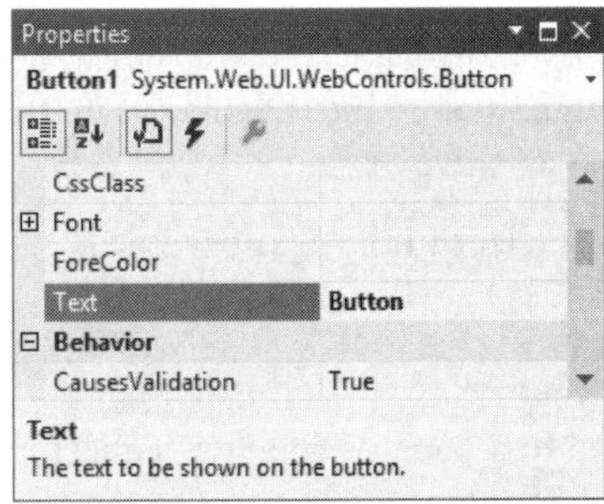

FIGURE 4-2

5. Set the control's `Text` property to **`Submit Information`** and set its `ID` (which you'll find all the way down at the bottom of the list wrapped in parentheses) to **`SubmitButton`**.
6. Change the `ID` of the `TextBox` to `YourName` using the Properties Grid.

7. Clear the `Text` property of the `Label` using the Properties Grid. You can right-click the property's label in the grid and choose Reset, or you can remove the text manually. Set its `ID` to `Result`.

8. Still in Design View, double-click the `Button` control to have VS add some code to the Code Behind of the page that will be fired when the button is clicked in the browser. You see later how to accomplish the same thing from Markup View. Add the bolded line of code to the code block that VS inserted for you:

   VB.NET

   ```
   Protected Sub SubmitButton_Click(sender As Object,
             e As EventArgs) Handles SubmitButton.Click
     Result.Text = "Your name is " & YourName.Text
   End Sub
   ```

   C#

   ```
   protected void SubmitButton_Click(object sender, EventArgs e)
   {
     Result.Text = "Your name is " + YourName.Text;
   }
   ```

   Note that the VB.NET example doesn't need an underscore here to split the code over two lines. In older versions of VB.NET, the underscore was required to split this code over two lines.

9. Save the changes to the page and then open it in the browser by pressing Ctrl+F5. Don't click the button yet, but open up the source of the page by right-clicking the page in the browser and choosing View Source or View Page Source. You should see the following HTML code (I changed the formatting slightly so the HTML fits on the page):

   ```
   <div>
     Your name <input name="YourName" type="text" id="YourName" />
     <input type="submit" name="SubmitButton" value="Submit Information"
                          id="SubmitButton" />
     <br />
     <span id="Result"></span>
   </div>
   ```

10. Switch back to your browser, fill in your name in the text box, and click the button. When the page is done reloading, open up the source for the page in the browser again using the browser's right-click menu. The code should now look like this:

    ```
    <div>
      Your name <input name="YourName" type="text" value="Imar" id="YourName" />
      <input type="submit" name="SubmitButton" value="Submit Information"
                           id="SubmitButton" />
      <br />
      <span id="Result">Your name is Imar</span>
    </div>
    ```

    Note that the two bold lines have changed, and now show the name you entered in the text box. You can ignore the other HTML in the page for now.

How It Works

As its name implies, an ASP.NET Server Control lives on the server in your ASPX page where it can be processed by the ASP.NET run time. When you request a page in the browser, the run time creates an in-memory representation of the ASPX file with the controls you created. When the run time is about to send the HTML to the browser, it asks each of the controls in the page for their HTML, which is then injected in the final response. For example, when the `Label` control is asked for its HTML the first time it loads, it returns the following:

```
<span id="Result"></span>
```

Although you defined the `Label` control with the `<asp:Label>` syntax, it ends up as a simple `<span>` element in the browser. Because the `Text` property of the `Label` control is empty, you don't see any text between the two `<span>` tags. The same applies to other controls; an `<asp:TextBox>` ends up as `<input type="text">`, whereas the `<asp:Button>` ends up as `<input type="submit">`.

When you click the button, the control causes a *postback*, which sends the information for the controls in the page to the server, where the page is loaded again. Additionally, the code that you wrote to handle the button's `Click` event is executed. This code takes the name you entered in the text box and then assigns it to the `Label` control as shown in this C# example:

```
Result.Text = "Your name is " + YourName.Text;
```

Don't worry about the syntax for the code that handles the button's `Click` event for now. In Chapter 5, you see how this works, and why you need this code.

At this stage, the `Label` control contains the text you entered in the text box, so when it is asked for its HTML, it now returns this:

```
<span id="Result">Your name is Imar</span>
```

You get a more in-depth look at postbacks later in this chapter when the ASP.NET state engine is discussed.

A CLOSER LOOK AT ASP.NET SERVER CONTROLS

Because you'll be working with server controls most of the time when building your ASP.NET Web Forms pages, you need to know in detail how they work and how to use them. In the next section, you see how to add the controls to your pages and change the way they behave in the browser. In the section that follows, you get an overview of the behavior that all server controls have in common. Once you understand this shared behavior, it's easy to apply this knowledge to other, new controls as well, enabling you to get up to speed with them very quickly.

Defining Controls in Your Pages

As demonstrated in the previous Try It Out, you can simply drag controls from the Toolbox onto the design surface of the page. This makes it very easy to add a bunch of controls to a page to get you started. However, because of the way the design surface works, it's sometimes difficult to add them exactly where you want them. For example, it can be difficult to drag a control between the opening and closing tags of an HTML element. Fortunately, you can just as easily drag a control from the Toolbox in Markup View. Additionally, you can also type the control's markup directly in Markup View, letting IntelliSense and code snippets help you with the different tags and attributes. You'll also find that the Properties Grid works in Markup View. Simply click the relevant markup, and the Properties Grid is updated to reflect the tag you clicked. This makes it easy to change the properties of the control, while you can still see exactly what markup gets generated for you. If you've worked with older versions of VS, you'll appreciate one great new feature in VS 2012: you can now bind handlers (such as the `Click` event used in the preceding exercise) directly in Markup View without switching to Design View. You'll also be able to access the Smart Tasks panel for the controls from code. You see more of these features later in this chapter.

If you look at the Properties Grid for some of the controls in a page, you'll notice that many of them have similar properties. In the next section, you see exactly what these properties are and what they are used for.

Common Properties for All Controls

Most of the server controls you find in the VS Toolbox share some common behavior. Part of this behavior includes the so-called *properties* that define the data a control can contain and expose. You learn more about properties and other behavior types in the next chapter. Each server control has an ID to uniquely identify it in the page, a `runat` attribute that is always set to `server` to indicate the control should be processed on the server, and a `ClientID` that contains the client-side ID attribute that is assigned to the element in the final HTML. In versions of ASP.NET up to 3.5 this `ClientID` was always generated for you automatically. However, in ASP.NET 4 a new `ClientIDMode` property was introduced that gives you more control over the ID of an element at the client. You see how this works in later chapters. The `runat` attribute is technically not a property of a server control, but is necessary to indicate that the markup for the control should be processed as a server control and not end up as plaintext or HTML in the browser.

Besides these properties, many of the server controls share more properties because they share the same `Control` base class. The next chapter digs deeper into base classes and inheritance. The following table lists the most common shared properties and describes what they are used for.

PROPERTY	DESCRIPTION
`AccessKey`	Enables you to set a key with which a control can be accessed at the client by pressing the associated letter.
`BackColor` `ForeColor`	Enables you to change the color of the background (`BackColor`) and text (`ForeColor`) of the control.

`BorderColor`
`BorderStyle`
`BorderWidth`
	Changes the border of the control in the browser. The similarities with the CSS border properties you saw in the previous chapter are no coincidence. Each of these three ASP.NET properties maps directly to its CSS counterpart.

continues

(continued)

PROPERTY	DESCRIPTION
`CssClass`	Enables you to define the HTML `class` attribute for the control in the browser. This class name could then point to a CSS class you defined in the page or an external CSS file.
`Enabled`	Determines whether the user can interact with the control in the browser. For example, with a disabled text box (`Enabled="False"`) you cannot change its text.
`Font`	Enables you to define different font-related settings, such as size, family and whether or not the font should be bold.
`Height` `Width`	Determines the height and width of the control in the browser.
`TabIndex`	Sets the client-side HTML `tabindex` attribute that determines the order in which users can move through the controls in the page by pressing the Tab key.
`ToolTip`	Enables you to set a tooltip for the control in the browser. This tooltip, rendered as a `title` attribute in the HTML, is shown when the user hovers the mouse over the element.
`Visible`	Determines whether or not the control is sent to the browser. You should really see this as a server-side visibility setting because an invisible control is never sent to the browser at all. This means it's quite different from the CSS `display` and `visibility` properties you saw in the previous chapter that hide the element at the client.

To see how all these attributes end up in the browser, consider the following markup for a `TextBox` server control:

```
<asp:TextBox AccessKey="a" BackColor="Black" ForeColor="White" Font-Size="30px"
  BorderColor="Yellow" BorderStyle="Dashed" BorderWidth="4" CssClass="TextBox"
  Enabled="True" Height="40" Width="200" TabIndex="1" ToolTip="Hover text here"
  Visible="True" ID="TextBox1" runat="server" Text="Hello World">
</asp:TextBox>
```

When you request the page with this control in the browser, you end up with the following HTML:

```
<input name="TextBox1" type="text" value="Hello World" id="TextBox1" accesskey="a"
  tabindex="1" title="Hover text here" class="TextBox" style="color:White;
  background-color:Black;border-color:Yellow;border-width:4px;
  border-style:Dashed;font-size:30px;height:40px;width:200px;"
/>
```

This results in the text box shown in Figure 4-3.

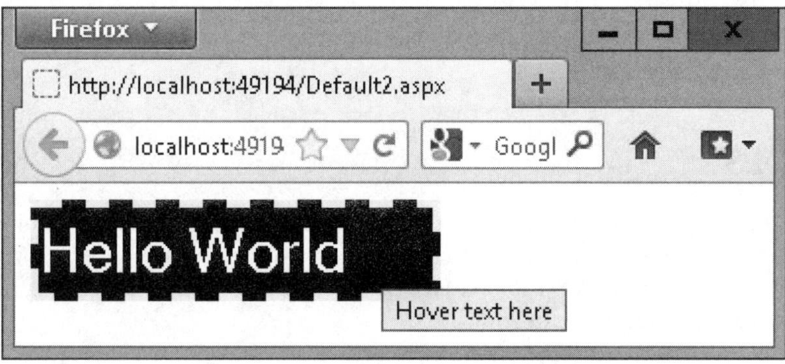

FIGURE 4-3

Note that most of the server-side control properties have been converted into CSS inline styles with the `style` attribute.

When building websites, it's quite uncommon to define a `TextBox` in this manner. As you learned in the previous chapter, you should avoid inline styles as much as possible, and opt for external cascading style sheets instead. You can accomplish the exact same behavior with this server-side control:

```
<asp:TextBox ID="TextBox1" AccessKey="a" CssClass="TextBox" TabIndex="1"
  ToolTip="Hover text here" runat="server" Text="Hello World">
</asp:TextBox>
```

And the following CSS class:

```
.TextBox
{
  background-color: Black;
  color: White;
  font-size: 30px;
  border-color: Yellow;
  border-style: Dashed;
  border-width: 4px;
  height: 40px;
  width: 200px;
}
```

Obviously, the second example is much easier to read, reuse, and maintain. If you want another text box with the exact same look, you simply assign `TextBox` to the `CssClass` of that control. Also, notice I left out the `Enabled` and `Visible` properties. Both default to `True`, so there's no need to explicitly state that in the control declaration.

Although it's recommended to use CSS classes instead of these inline styles, it's good to know about the server-side control properties in case you need fine control over them. If you change the control's properties programmatically (as you learn how to do later), they still end up as inline styles, and thus possibly override settings in embedded or external style sheets.

Now that you have seen the generic behavior that all server controls share, it's time to look at the large number of controls that ship with ASP.NET 4.5.

TYPES OF CONTROLS

Out of the box, ASP.NET 4.5 comes with a large number of server controls, supporting most of your web development needs. To make it easy for you to find the right controls, they have been placed in separate control categories in the VS Toolbox (accessible by pressing Ctrl+Alt+X). Figure 4-4 shows the Toolbox with all the available categories.

Note that depending on your version of Visual Studio, you may have other categories as well.

A handy new feature in VS 2012 is the ability to search in the Toolbox. Just type in a few letters of the control you're looking for in the Search text box at the top of the control, and VS filters the list with controls matching your criteria.

In the following sections, you see the controls in each category and the tasks for which they are designed.

With the discussion of the various controls, you see a mention of the properties of a control. For example, a `TextBox` has a `Text` property (among many others), and a `ListBox` has a `SelectedItem` property. Some properties can only be set programmatically and not with the Properties Grid. Reading and changing control properties programmatically is discussed in detail in the next chapter.

Standard Controls

The Standard category contains many of the basic controls that almost any web page needs. You've already seen some of them, like the `TextBox`, `Button`, and `Label` controls earlier in this chapter. Figure 4-5 shows all the controls in the Standard category.

Many of the controls probably speak for themselves, so instead of giving you a detailed description of them all, the following sections briefly highlight a few important ones.

Simple Controls

The Toolbox contains a number of simple and straightforward controls, including `TextBox`, `Button`, `Label`, `HyperLink`, `RadioButton`, and `CheckBox`. Their icons in the Toolbox give you a good clue as to how they end up in the browser. In the remainder of this book, you see these controls used many times. In ASP.NET 4.5 the `TextMode` property of the `TextBox` control has been expanded to support new HTML5 types such as `DateTime`, `Email`, and `Number`. You see more about this later in the book.

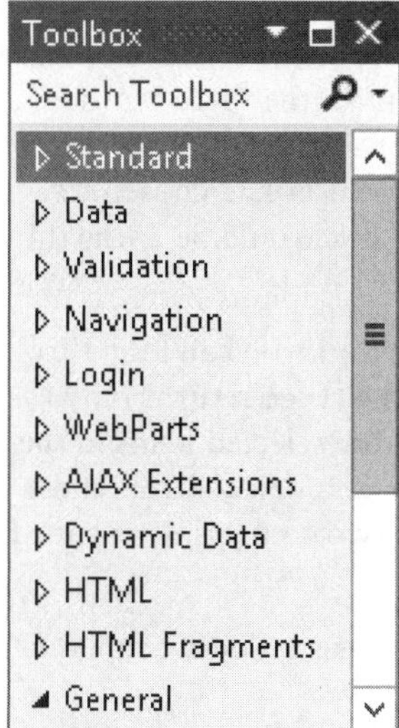

FIGURE 4-4

FIGURE 4-5

List Controls

The standard category also contains a number of controls that present themselves as lists in the browser. These controls include `ListBox`, `DropDownList`, `CheckBoxList`, `RadioButtonList`, and `BulletedList`. To add items to the list, you define `<asp:ListItem>` elements between the opening and closing tags of the control, as shown in the following example:

```
<asp:DropDownList ID="FavoriteLanguage" runat="server">
  <asp:ListItem Value="C#">C#</asp:ListItem>
  <asp:ListItem Value="Visual Basic">Visual Basic</asp:ListItem>
  <asp:ListItem Value="CSS">CSS</asp:ListItem>
</asp:DropDownList>
```

The `DropDownList` enables a user to select only one item at a time. To see the currently active and selected item of a list control programmatically, you can look at its `SelectedValue`, `SelectedItem`, or `SelectedIndex` properties. `SelectedValue` returns a string that contains the value for the selected item, like `C#` or `Visual Basic` in the preceding example. `SelectedIndex` returns the zero-based index of the item in the list. With the preceding example, if the user had chosen C#, `SelectedIndex` would be 0. Similarly, if the user had chosen CSS, the index would be 2 (the third item in the list).

For controls that allow multiple selections (like `CheckBoxList` and `ListBox`), you can loop through the `Items` collection and see what items are selected. In this case, `SelectedItem` returns *only the first* selected item in the list; not all of them. You learn how to access all the selected items in the next exercise. Note that in the browser, both the `DropDownList` and the `ListBox` control render as a `<select>` element. Attributes such as `size` and `multiple` set by these two controls determine the appearance and behavior of the HTML element in the browser.

The `BulletedList` control doesn't allow a user to make selections, and as such doesn't support these properties.

To see how to add list items to your list control, and how to read the selected values, the following exercise guides you through creating a simple Web Form with two list controls that ask users for their favorite programming language.

TRY IT OUT Working with List Controls

In this exercise you add two list controls to a page. Additionally, you add a button that, when clicked, displays the selected items as text in a `Label` control.

1. In the `Demos` folder, create a new Web Form called **`ListControls.aspx`**. Make sure you create a Code Behind file by checking the Place Code in Separate File option.
2. Switch to Design View and drag a `DropDownList` from the Toolbox onto the design surface of the page within the dashed border of the `<div>` element that is already present in your page.
3. Notice that as soon as you drop the `DropDownList` control on the page, a pop-up menu appears that is labeled DropDownList Tasks, as shown in Figure 4-6.

   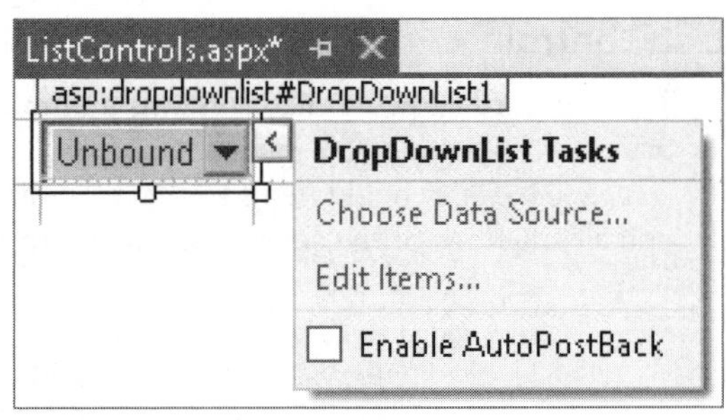

   FIGURE 4-6

   This pop-up menu is called the *Smart Tasks* panel. When it appears, it gives you access to the most common tasks of the control it belongs to. In the case of the `DropDownList`, you get three options. The first option enables you to bind the control to a data source, which is demonstrated in Chapter 13. The second item enables you to manually add items to the list, and the last option sets the `AutoPostBack` property of the control. With this option checked, the control submits the page in which it is contained back to the server as soon as the user chooses a new item from the list. Note that the browser must have JavaScript enabled for this to work.

The Smart Tasks panel appears only for the more complex controls that have a lot of features. You won't see it for simple controls like `Button` or `Label`. To reopen the Smart Tasks panel, right-click the control in the designer and choose Show Smart Tag. Alternatively, click the small arrow at the top-right corner of the control, visible in Figure 4-6, or press Shift+Alt+F10 when the control is selected. You can also open the Smart Tasks panel from markup view. Simply click anywhere on the opening or closing tag of a control or other piece of markup and press Ctrl+Dot (Ctrl+.). Alternatively, hover over the tiny blue rectangle at the start of the opening tag and then click the grey arrow that appears.

On the Smart Tasks panel of the `DropDownList`, click the Edit Items link to bring up the ListItem Collection Editor, shown in Figure 4-7.

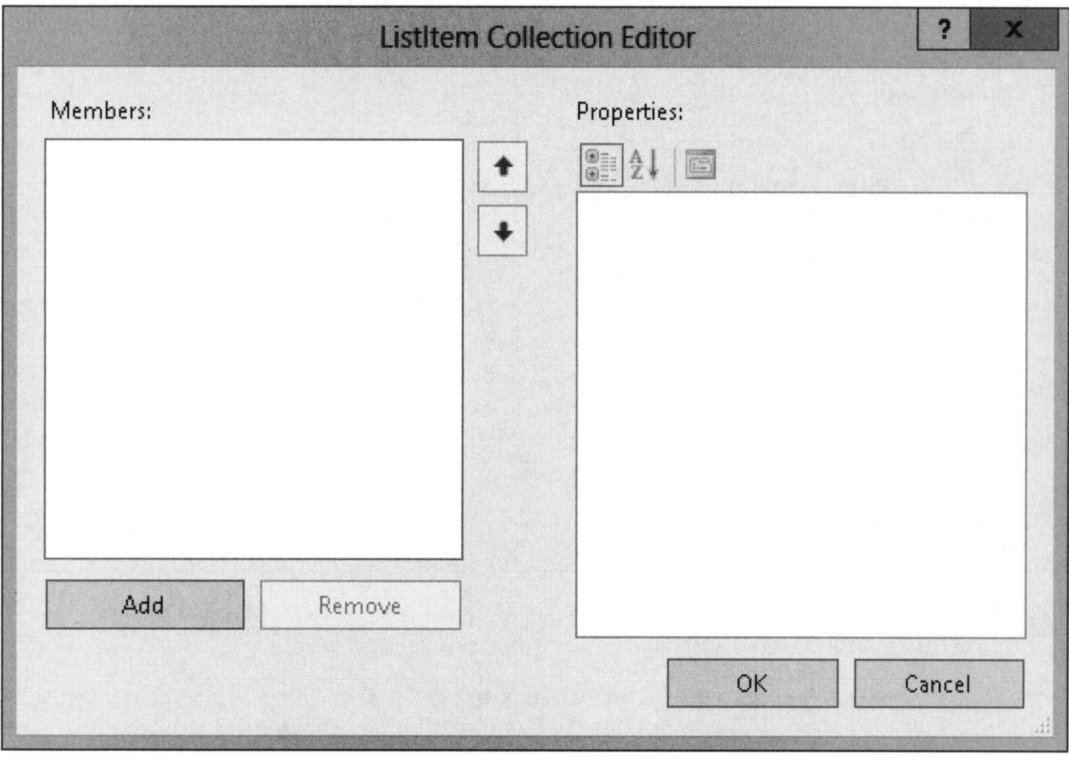

FIGURE 4-7

This dialog box enables you to add new items to the list control. The items you add through this window are added as `<asp:ListItem>` elements between the tags for the control.

4. Click the Add button on the left side of the screen to insert a new list item. Then in the Properties Grid on the right, enter **C#** for the `Text` property and press Tab. As soon as you tab away from the `Text` property, the value is copied to the `Value` property as well. This is convenient if you want both the `Text` and the `Value` property to be the same. However, it's perfectly OK (and quite common) to assign a different value to the `Value` property.

5. Repeat step 4 twice, this time creating list items for **Visual Basic** and **CSS**. You can use the up and down arrow buttons in the middle of the dialog box to change the order of the items in the list. Finally, click OK to insert the items in the page. You should end up with the following code in Markup View:

```
<asp:DropDownList ID="DropDownList1" runat="server">
  <asp:ListItem>C#</asp:ListItem>
  <asp:ListItem>Visual Basic</asp:ListItem>
  <asp:ListItem>CSS</asp:ListItem>
</asp:DropDownList>
```

6. In Markup View drag a `CheckBoxList` control from the Toolbox directly into the code window, right after the `DropDownList`.

7. Copy the three `<asp:ListItem>` elements from the `DropDownList` you created in steps 4 and 5 and paste them between the opening and closing tags of the `CheckBoxList`. You should end up with this code:

```
  <asp:ListItem>CSS</asp:ListItem>
</asp:DropDownList>
<asp:CheckBoxList ID="CheckBoxList1" runat="server">
  <asp:ListItem>C#</asp:ListItem>
  <asp:ListItem>Visual Basic</asp:ListItem>
  <asp:ListItem>CSS</asp:ListItem>
</asp:CheckBoxList>
```

8. Switch to Design View and drag a `Button` from the Toolbox in Design View to the right of the `CheckBoxList` control. The `Button` will be placed below the `CheckBoxList`. Next, drag a `Label` control and drop it to the right of the `Button`. Create some room between the `Button` and the `Label` by positioning your cursor between the controls and then pressing Enter twice. Double-click the `Button` to open the Code Behind of the page.

9. In the code block that VS added for you, add the following bolded code, which will be executed when the user clicks the button:

VB.NET

```
Protected Sub Button1_Click(sender As Object, e As EventArgs) _
          Handles Button1.Click
  Label1.Text = "In the DDL you selected " &
                      DropDownList1.SelectedValue & "<br />"

  For Each item As ListItem In CheckBoxList1.Items
    If item.Selected = True Then
      Label1.Text &= "In the CBL you selected " & item.Value & "<br />"
    End If
  Next
End Sub
```

C#

```
protected void Button1_Click(object sender, EventArgs e)
{
  Label1.Text = "In the DDL you selected " +
```

```
            DropDownList1.SelectedValue + "<br />";

    foreach (ListItem item in CheckBoxList1.Items)
    {
      if (item.Selected == true)
      {
        Label1.Text += "In the CBL you selected " + item.Value + "<br />";
      }
    }
}
```

Notice how in the VB.NET code the underscore is needed to split the code over two lines. VB.NET requires the underscore if you want to move the `Handles` keyword to its own line.

10. Save the changes to the page and then request it in the browser. Choose an item from the `DropDownList`, check one or more items in the `CheckBoxList`, and click the button. You should see something similar to Figure 4-8, which shows the page in Firefox.

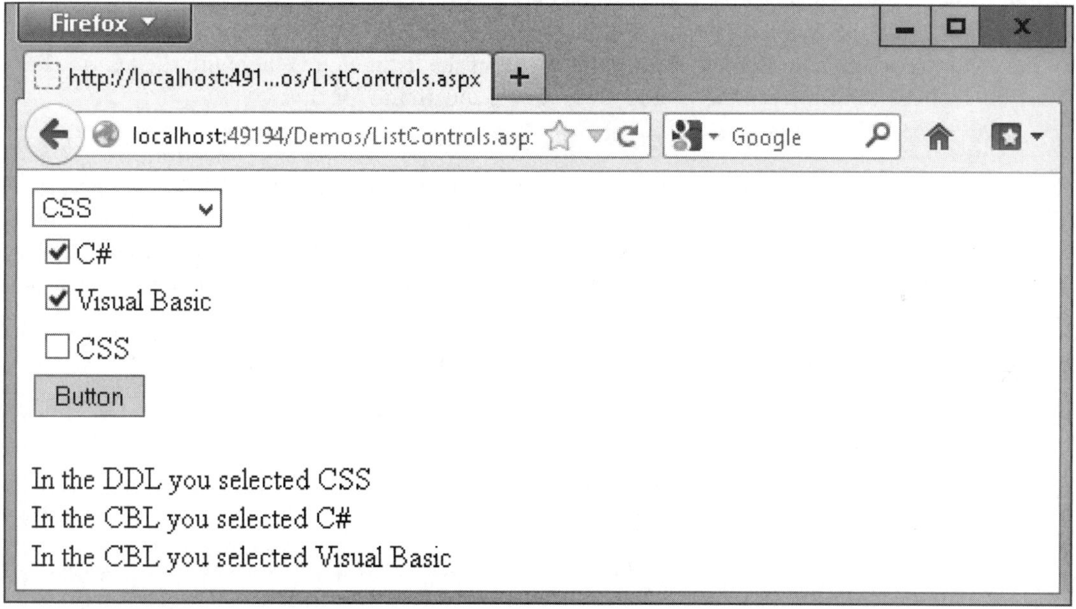

FIGURE 4-8

How It Works

The various list controls all use `<asp:ListItem>` elements. That makes it easy to reuse them by copying them from one control to another. Because the `DropDownList` supports only one selected item at a time, it's pretty easy to get its selected value. All it takes is a single line of code (shown in C#):

```
Label1.Text = "In the DDL you selected " + DropDownList1.SelectedValue + "<br />";
```

The CheckBoxList control enables a user to select multiple items at once. Therefore, you need a bit more code to *loop over the collection of items*, checking the Selected property of each item (again shown in C#):

```
foreach (ListItem item in CheckBoxList1.Items)
{
  if (item.Selected == true)
  {
    Label1.Text += "In the CBL you selected " + item.Value + "<br />";
  }
}
```

The CheckBoxList and the other list controls have an Items collection that contains all the items you defined in the code. So, given the code from this Try It Out, CheckBoxList1 contains three items, for C#, Visual Basic, and CSS, respectively. Each ListItem in turn contains a Selected property that determines whether or not the user has checked the item in the list.

Using a foreach loop (For Each in VB.NET), you can iterate over the collection of ListItem elements, testing the Selected property one by one. If the item was selected in the list, its Selected property is true (True in VB) and its Value is appended to the text of the Label. Notice the use of += (&= in VB.NET) in the last code example to assign the Value of the list item together with the text to the Label control's Text property. The += and &= syntax is shorthand for this:

```
Label1.Text = Label1.Text + "In the CBL you selected" + item.Value + "<br />";
```

This code takes the current text from the Label control, appends the literal text "In the CBL you selected" to it, then appends the value of the item using item.Value and finally appends the literal text "<br />". It then reassigns the entire string back to the Text property of the label. Using the += syntax is often a bit easier to write and understand, but the longer version is common as well.

Both VB.NET and C# have support for a for each loop, although both languages use a slightly different syntax. In the next chapter, you learn a lot more about looping and other language constructs.

Also of note is the way the ListItems are set up. In the first example, before the Try It Out, you saw ListItem elements with both a value and text:

```
<asp:ListItem Value="C#">C#</asp:ListItem>
<asp:ListItem Value="Visual Basic">Visual Basic</asp:ListItem>
<asp:ListItem Value="CSS">CSS</asp:ListItem>
```

When you add items to the list yourself with the ListItem Collection Editor, you don't get the Value attributes:

```
<asp:ListItem>C#</asp:ListItem>
<asp:ListItem>Visual Basic</asp:ListItem>
<asp:ListItem>CSS</asp:ListItem>
```

You didn't get the Value attribute because you didn't supply an explicit value for the item in the ListItem Collection Editor. If you omit the Value, the text between the opening and closing tags of the ListItem is used implicitly as the value, which is fine in many cases. However, it's also quite common to have a different Value and Text property in the list. For example, when you have a list with countries, you could use the full name of the country as the Text (like The Netherlands) and use the official country code (nl) as the Value for the drop-down list. You see the list controls at work in other chapters in this book.

Container Controls

Quite often it's desirable to group related content and controls. You can do this by putting the controls (and other markup) in one of the container controls, like the `Panel`, the `PlaceHolder`, the `MultiView`, or the `Wizard`. For example, you can use the `PlaceHolder` or the `Panel` control to hide or show a number of controls at once. Instead of hiding each control separately, you simply hide the entire container that contains all the individual controls and markup. Both of these controls have their own advantages and disadvantages. The good thing about the `PlaceHolder` control is that it emits no HTML of its own into the page, so you can use it as a container without any side effects in the final page. However, it lacks design-time support, making it hard to manage the controls inside the `PlaceHolder` at design time in VS. In contrast, the `Panel` enables you to easily access all controls and other content it contains but renders itself as a `<div>` element. In many cases this isn't a problem, and can even be useful as you can target that `div` using CSS at the client, so usually you're best off with the `Panel` control because of its design-time support.

The `MultiView` (which can contain one or more `<asp:View>` elements) and the `Wizard` are similar in that they enable you to split up a long page into multiple areas, making it easy to fill in a long form, for example. The `Wizard` has built-in support for moving from page to page using Previous, Next, and Finish buttons, whereas the `MultiView` must be controlled programmatically.

A Closer Look at the Panel Control

In the following exercise, you use a `Panel` control to create a container for other controls and markup. You only add some text for now, but in a subsequent Try It Out exercise you add ASP.NET controls to the panel.

TRY IT OUT Using the Panel Control

In this exercise you see how to use the `Panel` control as a container for some simple text. In addition, you use a `CheckBox` to control the visibility of the `Panel` at the server.

1. Start by creating a new Web Form with Code Behind called **`Containers.aspx`** in the `Demos` folder.
2. Switch the page into Design View and drag a `CheckBox` and a `Panel` control from the Toolbox on the design surface into the dashed `<div>` element.
3. Give the `CheckBox` control a meaningful description by setting its `Text` property to `Show Panel` and set its `AutoPostBack` property to `True` using the Properties Grid. Rather than choosing True from the drop-down list for the property, you can also double-click the `AutoPostBack` property or its value to toggle between `False` and `True`.
4. Set the `Visible` property of the `Panel` control to `False` using the Properties Grid. This hides the `Panel` control when the page first loads.
5. Inside the `Panel` control, type some text (for example, **`I am visible now`**). Note that the panel behaves like the rest of VS's design surface. You can simply add text to it, select and format it, and add new controls to it by dragging them from the Toolbox. The code for the panel should end up like this in Markup View:

```
<asp:Panel ID="Panel1" runat="server" Visible="False">
  I am visible now
</asp:Panel>
```

6. If necessary, switch to Markup View and locate the code for the `CheckBox`. Position your cursor right before the closing forward slash (/) and type **On**, followed by Ctrl+Space. This brings up IntelliSense, as shown in Figure 4-9.

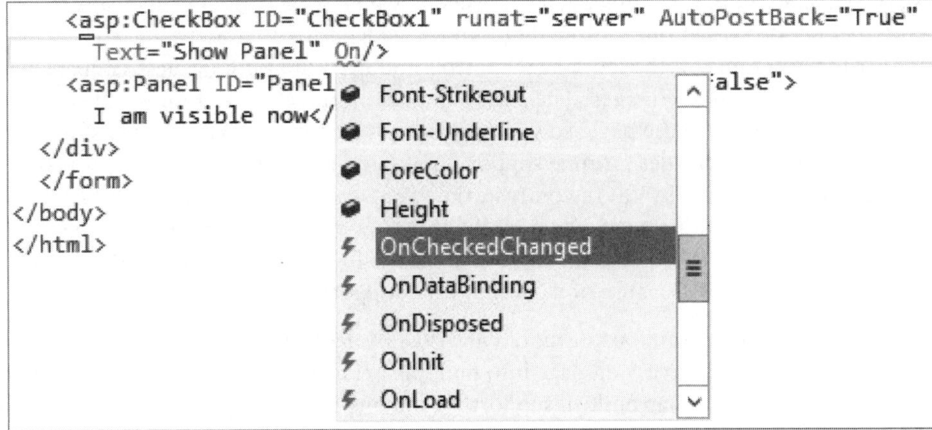

FIGURE 4-9

Select `OnCheckChanged` by pressing Tab or Enter. Next, type an equals sign (=), which brings up IntelliSense again as shown in Figure 4-10. Note that if you're using C#, you may also see a `Page_Load` item in the list of event handlers.

```
<asp:CheckBox ID="CheckBox1" runat="server" AutoPostBack="True"
  Text="Show Panel" OnCheckedChanged=""/>
<asp:Panel ID="Panel1" runat="server"   <Create New Event>
  I am visible now</asp:Panel>
```

FIGURE 4-10

Select the <Create New Event> item and press Tab. VS completes the code as follows:

```
OnCheckedChanged="CheckBox1_CheckedChanged"
```

Although this auto-completion is nice, VS has done something else that's much more useful: when you pressed Tab, it also added the handler code for you in the Code Behind. To see that code, press F7 to switch to Code View.

> ***NOTE*** *I have wanted this feature since the very first version of Visual Studio for .NET, and I am really glad it has been added. With this new feature, the need to switch to Design View and set up the handler by double-clicking a control (as you did in an earlier exercise) or using the Events tab of the Properties Grid (as you see later) has been greatly reduced. This is great for people who prefer hand-coding over the Design View and is especially useful in more complex pages where Design View isn't that useful anyway.*

Note that there is a subtle difference between adding the handler using Markup View and Design View if you're using VB.NET. If you use Markup View, the handler is added to the markup (`OnCheckedChanged="CheckBox1_CheckedChanged"`) and code is added to the Code Behind. When you use Design View, the code in Markup View is not affected, and the code in the Code Behind is annotated with the `Handles` keyword to indicate which event (for instance, the click on a button, the check changed event of a check box, and so on) the code responds to. At run time, however, there is no difference.

7. Next, add the following bolded line within the handler code that VS added for you:

VB.NET

```
Protected Sub CheckBox1_CheckedChanged(sender As Object, e As EventArgs)
  Panel1.Visible = CheckBox1.Checked
End Sub
```

C#

```
protected void CheckBox1_CheckedChanged(object sender, EventArgs e)
{
  Panel1.Visible = CheckBox1.Checked;
}
```

8. Save all your changes and then request the page in the browser by pressing Ctrl+F5.

9. When the page first loads, all you see is the check box and the text beside it. When you look at the HTML for the page in the browser (right-click the page and choose View Source or View Page Source depending on your browser), you'll only see the check box; there's no code for the `Panel` control at this stage sent to the browser. When you click the check box to place a checkmark in it, the page reloads and now shows the text you entered in step 5.

> ***WARNING*** *If nothing happens, go back to the source of the page in VS and ensure that* `AutoPostBack` *is set to* `True` *on the* `CheckBox` *control.*

If you look at the HTML in the browser, you'll see that the text you typed in step 5 is wrapped in a `<div>` element with an `id` of `Panel1`:

```
<div id="Panel1">
  I am visible now
</div>
```

How It Works

In step 4 of this exercise you set the `Visible` property of the `Panel` control to `False`. This means that when the page loads, the control is not visible on the server and thus its HTML never makes it to the browser. When you then check the check box, a postback occurs, which sends the information contained in the form to the server. At the server, some code is run that is fired whenever the check box changes its state from checked to unchecked or vice versa. Inside that code block, the following code is executed (shown in C#):

```
Panel1.Visible = CheckBox1.Checked;
```

This means that the `Panel` is only visible when the check box is checked. When it isn't, the `Panel` is hidden automatically.

As you can see, it's easy to add text and other markup to the `Panel` control in VS. Right now, you only added some plaintext, but in the next section you see how to add a `Wizard` control and how to use it.

Magic with the Wizard Control

The `Wizard` control is a great tool for breaking apart large Web Forms and presenting them as bite-sized chunks of information to the user. Instead of confusing your user with one page with many controls and text on it, you can break the page apart and present each section on a separate wizard page. The `Wizard` control then handles all navigation issues by creating Next, Previous, and Finish buttons automatically. In the following exercise you use a wizard to ask a user for her name and favorite programming language. Although the example itself is pretty trivial, and you could have placed both questions on the same page without confusing the user, the example shows how the wizard works and why it's useful. You can easily apply the same techniques to your own, possibly larger, Web Forms.

TRY IT OUT Using the Wizard to Create Easy-to-Use Forms

In this Try It Out, you place a `Wizard` inside the panel you created in the previous exercise that enables a user to fill in a form that is spread over a couple of pages. The wizard will have two steps where a user can enter details, and a results page that shows the data the user has provided.

1. Make sure you still have `Containers.aspx` page open in Design View. Remove the text "I am visible now" that you entered in the previous Try It Out, and then drag a `Wizard` control from the Toolbox inside the `Panel`. Drag its right edge further to the right, increasing the total width of the control to `500px`. Your page now looks similar to Figure 4-11.

2. Open the `Wizard`'s Smart Tasks panel (click the arrow in its upper right-hand corner) and choose Add/Remove WizardSteps. In the dialog box that follows, click the Add button to insert a third wizard step, shown in Figure 4-12.

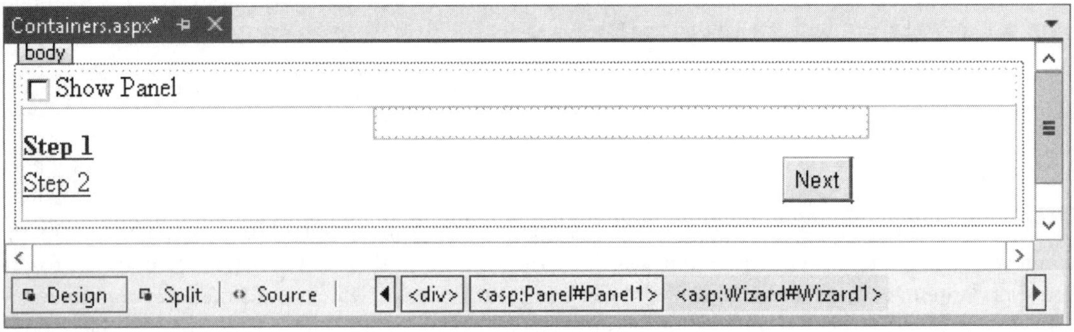

FIGURE 4-11

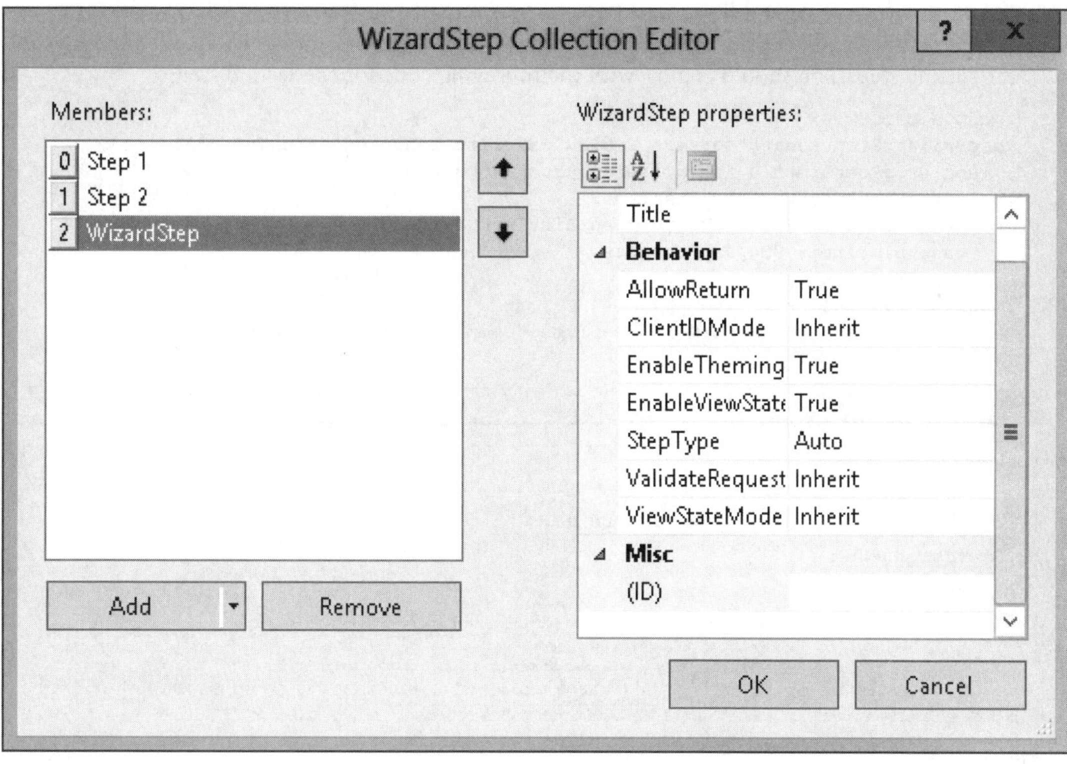

FIGURE 4-12

3. Click the first `WizardStep` labeled Step 1 in the Members list on the left and change its `Title` from Step 1 to **`About You`**. Set the `Title` of the other two steps to **`Favorite Language`** and **`Ready`**, respectively.

4. Change the `StepType` of the second step (now labeled Favorite Language) to **`Finish`**, and of the last step to **`Complete`**. You can leave the `StepType` of the first step set to `Auto`. Click OK to close the WizardStep Collection Editor.

5. In Design View, click About You in the list at the left to make it the active step and drag a `Label` and a `TextBox` to the right side of the `Wizard`. You need to drag them inside the gray rectangle that's in the upper-right corner of the `Wizard`, or the controls won't end up inside the `Wizard`. Set the `Text` property of the `Label` to **`Type your name`** and change the `ID` of the `TextBox` to **`YourName`**. When you're done, your `Wizard` looks like Figure 4-13.

6. Click the Favorite Language item in the list on the left to make it the active step. Add a `DropDownList` to the rectangle with the gray border on the right part of the wizard step. Rename the `DropDownList` by setting its ID to **`FavoriteLanguage`**. Open the Smart Tasks panel of the `DropDownList` control and choose Edit Items. Add the same three items you added in an earlier

Try It Out: for C#, Visual Basic, and CSS, respectively. If you want, you can copy the three items from the page `ListControls.aspx` and paste them between the `<asp:DropDownList>` tags inside the second step. You should end up with the following code for the second step:

```
</asp:WizardStep>
<asp:WizardStep runat="server" Title="Favorite Language" StepType="Finish">
  <asp:DropDownList ID="FavoriteLanguage" runat="server">
    <asp:ListItem>C#</asp:ListItem>
    <asp:ListItem>Visual Basic</asp:ListItem>
    <asp:ListItem>CSS</asp:ListItem>
  </asp:DropDownList>
</asp:WizardStep>
<asp:WizardStep runat="server" StepType="Complete" Title="Ready">
```

FIGURE 4-13

7. For the final step, switch to Markup View. If you try to switch to the last step in Design View, you may notice that the `Wizard` disappears. If that happens, switch to Markup View and set `ActiveStepIndex` to `0` again on the opening tag of the `Wizard` control.

   Inside the last `WizardStep` labeled Ready, drag a label control from the Toolbox and rename it by setting its `ID` to **`Result`**. Alternatively, inside the code for the last step, type the word **`label`** and then press Tab to execute a code snippet for inserting a `Label`. Then add the `ID` attribute manually.

8. Double-click the `Wizard` in Design View and add the following bolded code, which will be executed when the user clicks the Finish button on the last step of the wizard. If you're having problems getting VS to create the correct code for you, as you see it in the next snippet, select the `Wizard`, press F4 to open up the control's Properties Grid, and then click the button with the lightning bolt on it (the fourth button from the left on the toolbar of the Properties Grid), as shown in Figure 4-14.

   This part of the Properties Grid is often referred to as the *Events tab* of the Properties Grid. Locate and double-click

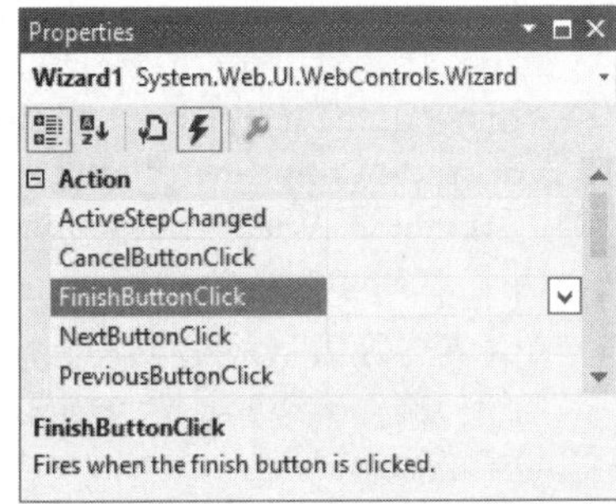

FIGURE 4-14

FinishButtonClick in the Action category. With both methods, you should end up with some code for Wizard1_FinishButtonClick that you need to extend with the following code:

VB.NET

```
Protected Sub Wizard1_FinishButtonClick(sender As Object,
          e As WizardNavigationEventArgs) Handles Wizard1.FinishButtonClick
  Result.Text = "Your name is " & YourName.Text
  Result.Text &= "<br />Your favorite language is " &
                     FavoriteLanguage.SelectedValue
End Sub
```

C#

```
protected void Wizard1_FinishButtonClick(object sender,
             WizardNavigationEventArgs e)
{
  Result.Text = "Your name is " + YourName.Text;
  Result.Text += "<br />Your favorite language is " +
             FavoriteLanguage.SelectedValue;
}
```

9. Switch back to Design View and open the Properties Grid for the Wizard and make sure its ActiveStepIndex is set to 0. The designer remembers the last step you designed and stores the value in the ActiveStepIndex of the Wizard in Markup View. To make sure the Wizard starts on the first page, you should always set the ActiveStepIndex back to 0 (or click the first step in the Wizard control in Design View) before you save your changes and run the page.

10. Save all changes, close all open browser windows, and press Ctrl+F5 to open the page in the browser. Select the check box to make the Panel visible and enter your name on the first wizard page. Click Next and choose your favorite programming language. Notice how there's now a Previous button available that enables you to go back to the first step of the wizard if you want to change your name. Instead of clicking the Next and Previous buttons, you can also click the links on the left of the wizard in the browser. When you click the Finish button, you'll see the results of the information you entered in the wizard (see Figure 4-15).

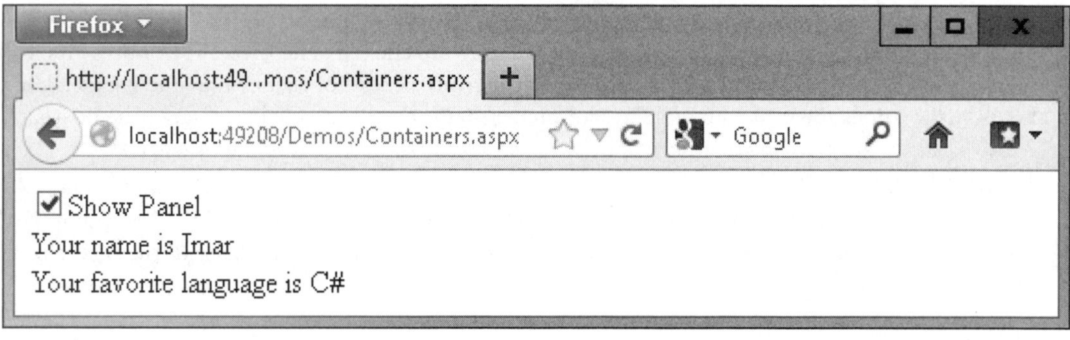

FIGURE 4-15

How It Works

The `Wizard` control takes care of most of the hard work for you. It handles the navigation, determines when to show the correct buttons (Next, Previous, and Finish), and ensures that in the resulting page the values for the controls you added in the wizard steps are still available so you can show them with the label. It does this with a concept called *View State*, something you learn more about toward the end of this chapter.

All you have to do is define the steps and set their `StepType`. You set the `StepType` of the first step to `Auto`. With this setting, the `Wizard` figures out what buttons to show. Because it's the first step in the wizard and there's no previous step to go to, it leaves out the Previous button (this is the equivalent of setting the `StepType` to `Start` manually.) You set the `StepType` of the second step to `Finish`, which tells the `Wizard` to draw a Previous button and a Finish button. When you click the Finish button, the `Wizard` arrives at the last step with its `StepType` set to `Complete`. On this step, the navigation buttons are hidden, and all you see is the label with the result, which was assigned with the code in the Code Behind of the page. In Chapter 5, you learn more about the code in the Code Behind that makes this possible.

In addition to the controls you have seen in the previous sections, a few other controls are worth examining. Not all of them are discussed here in detail because they aren't used any further in this book. A good source of information about these controls is the Microsoft Developer Network (MSDN) site at `http://msdn.microsoft.com`. To find information about controls on this site, use your favorite search engine and then search for *ControlName* Control MSDN. For example, to find more information on the `Wizard` control you'd search for **`Wizard Control MSDN`**. Typically, the MSDN site is at the top of the search results.

Other Standard Controls

This section briefly discusses the remainder of the controls in the Standard category of the Toolbox. You see many of them used in the sample application in the rest of the book.

LinkButton and ImageButton

The `LinkButton` and the `ImageButton` controls operate similarly to an ordinary `Button` control. Both of them cause a postback to the server when they are clicked. The `LinkButton` presents itself as a simple `<a>` element, but posts back (using JavaScript) instead of requesting a new page. The `ImageButton` does the same, but displays an image that the user can click to trigger the postback.

Image and ImageMap

These controls are pretty similar in that they display an image in the browser. The `ImageMap` enables you to define *hotspots* on the image that, when clicked, either cause a postback to the server or navigate to a different page.

Calendar

The `Calendar` control presents a rich interface that enables a user to select a date. You see more of it toward the end of this chapter when the ASP.NET state engine is discussed.

FileUpload

The `FileUpload` control enables a user to upload files that can be stored on the server. You see more of this control in Chapter 14.

Literal, Localize, and Substitute

All three controls look a little like the `Label` control because they can all display static text or HTML. The biggest advantage of the `Literal` is that it renders no additional tag itself; it displays only what you assign to its `Text` property, and is thus very useful to display HTML or JavaScript that you build up in the Code Behind or that you retrieve from a database.

The `Localize` control is used in multilingual websites and is able to retrieve its contents from translated resource files. The `Substitute` control is used in advanced caching scenarios and enables you to update only parts of a page that is otherwise cached completely. Both of these controls fall outside the scope of this book, but for a good discussion of them you may want to get a copy of Wrox's *Professional ASP.NET 4.5 in C# and VB* (ISBN: 978-1-118-31182-0).

AdRotator

The `AdRotator` control enables you to display random advertisements on your website. The ads come from an XML file that you create on your server. Because it lacks advanced features like click tracking and logging that are required in most but the simplest scenarios, this control isn't used much in today's websites.

HiddenField

The `HiddenField` control enables you to store data in the page that is submitted with each request. This is useful if you want the page to remember specific data without the user seeing it on the page. Because the field does show up in the HTML source of the page, and is thus accessible to the end user, you should never store any sensitive data in it.

XML

The `XML` control enables you to transform data from an XML format to another format (like XHTML) for display on a page. Check out *Professional ASP.NET 4.5* for a detailed description.

Table

The `<asp:Table>` control is in many respects identical to its HTML `<table>` counterpart. However, because the control lives at the server, you can program against it, creating new columns and rows dynamically and adding dynamic data to it.

This concludes the discussion of the controls in the Standard category of the Toolbox. In most web pages, you'll be working with at least a few of these controls. The remainder of this section discusses the other categories of the Toolbox. Because most of them are used in some form in the remainder of this book, this chapter just briefly describes their purpose so you get a rough idea what they are used for. You'll find cross-references to the other chapters where you can find out more information about them.

HTML Controls

The HTML category of the Toolbox contains a number of HTML controls that look similar to the ones found in the Standard category. For example, you find the `Input (Button)` that looks like the `<asp:Button>`. Similarly, there is a `Select` control that has the `<asp:DropDownList>` and `<asp:ListBox>` as its counterparts.

In contrast to the ASP.NET Server Controls, the HTML controls are client-side controls and end up directly in the final HTML in the browser. You can expose them to server-side code by adding a `runat="server"` attribute to them. This enables you to program against them from the Code Behind of a Web Form, to influence things like their visibility.

The HTML controls have a lot less functionality than the ones in the Standard category. For example, the `Select` control lacks design-time support for adding new items to the list with the ListItem Collection Editor. This forces you to write the items by hand in the Markup View of VS.

Because the controls in the Standard and HTML category look quite like each other, the next section discusses their differences and gives you some idea of when to favor one category over the other.

How to Choose between Standard and HTML Controls

There seems to be some overlap between the controls in the Standard and HTML categories of the Toolbox. So which ones should you choose and when? Generally, the true server controls in the Standard category offer you a lot more functionality, both in terms of design-time support in VS and what they can do at run time. But this functionality comes at a price. Because of their increased complexity, the server controls take a little more time to process. However, on most websites you probably won't notice the difference. Only when you have a high-traffic website with lots of controls on the page do the HTML controls give you a slightly better performance and consume less memory on the server when compared to the server controls.

In most scenarios, favor the server controls over their HTML counterparts. Because server controls offer more functionality, they give you more flexibility in your pages, enabling you to create a richer user experience. Also, the better design-time support makes it worth choosing these controls.

Choose the HTML controls if you're really sure that you don't need the functionality that the server controls offer you.

The remainder of this section quickly guides you through the other categories in the Toolbox.

Data Controls

Data controls were introduced in ASP.NET 2.0, and offer an easy way to access various data sources like databases, XML files, and objects. Instead of writing lots of code to access the data source as you had to do in earlier versions of ASP.NET, you simply point your data control to an appropriate data source, and the ASP.NET run time takes care of most of the difficult issues for you. You see a lot more about these controls in Chapter 13 and onward.

Validation Controls

Validation controls enable you to rapidly create Web Forms with validation rules that prohibit users from entering invalid data. For example, you can force users to enter values for required fields and check whether the entered data matches a specific format like a valid date or a number between 1 and 10. They even allow you to write custom code to create validation routines that are not covered by the standard controls. The beauty of the validation controls is that they can execute both on the client and the server, enabling you to create responsive and secure web applications. Chapter 9 digs much deeper into these controls.

Navigation Controls

The controls you find under the Navigation category of the Toolbox are used to let users find their way through your site. The `TreeView` control presents a hierarchical display of data and can be used to show the structure of your site, giving easy access to all the pages in the site. The `Menu` control does a similar thing and provides options for horizontal and vertical fold-out menus.

The `SiteMapPath` control creates a "breadcrumb trail" in your web pages that enables your users to easily find their way up in the hierarchy of pages in your site.

You see all of these controls in action in Chapter 7, which deals with navigation in websites exclusively.

Login Controls

Just like the data and navigation controls, the login controls were introduced in ASP.NET 2.0 and are still strongly present in ASP.NET 4.5. With very little effort, login controls enable you to create secure websites where users need to sign up and log in before they can access specific parts of the website (or even the entire website). In addition, they provide the tools for users to change their password, or request a new password if they forget the old one, and enable you to display different data depending on the logged-in status and role of the user. Chapter 16 provides more details about the security features and login controls of ASP.NET.

Ajax Extensions

The Ajax Extensions enable you to create flicker-free web applications that are able to retrieve data from the server from client-side JavaScript without a full postback. You can find the full details on them in Chapter 10.

WebParts

ASP.NET WebParts are a set of controls that enables an end user of a web page to change the appearance and behavior of a website. These controls are outside the scope of this book.

Dynamic Data

The controls in this category are used in Dynamic Data websites. Dynamic Data sites enable you to quickly build a user interface to manage data in a database. These controls are not discussed further in this book. To learn more about them, check out Sams' *ASP.NET Dynamic Data Unleashed*, Oleg Sych and Randy Patterson, 2012 (ISBN: 978-0-672-33565-5).

THE ASP.NET STATE ENGINE

In the previous chapter, you created a page with a `TextBox` and a `Button` control. In the Try It Out, you ran this page in the browser, typed some text, and clicked the button. The button caused a postback to the server, and when the page reloaded, the text was still present in the text box. You pretty much did the same thing with the `Wizard` control in this chapter, where the values from the text box and the drop-down list were maintained as well. If you're familiar with other web technologies like ASP or PHP, this probably surprised you. In those languages, you often need to write lots of code to make this happen. So why and how does this work automatically in ASP.NET?

The text in the text box is maintained by the ASP.NET state engine, a feature that is deeply integrated into the ASP.NET run time. It enables controls to maintain their state across postbacks, so their values and settings remain available after every postback of the page.

What Is State and Why Is It Important?

To understand state, it's important to realize that, by design, HTTP—the protocol used to request and serve pages in a web browser—is *stateless*. What this means is that the web server does not keep track of requests that have been made from a specific browser. As far as the web server is concerned, each request you make to the server by browsing to a page and clicking links to other pages stands on its own. The web server has no recollection of pages you requested previously.

This poses some interesting problems. Consider, for example, a simple login page that enables you to log in to a website, like your favorite web mail program. You can see a sample of the login box in Figure 4-16.

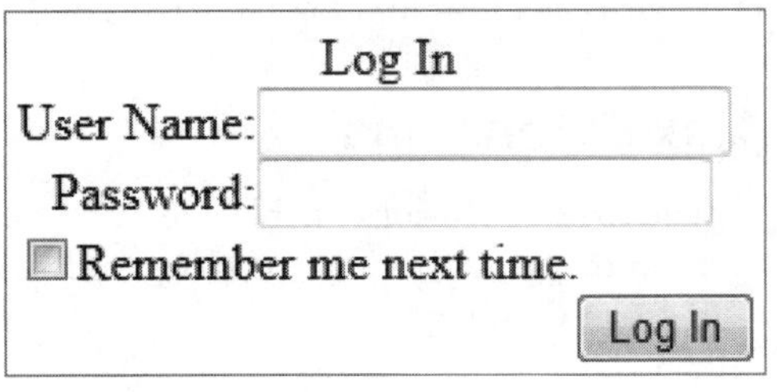

FIGURE 4-16

Now imagine that you try to log in with a correct username but with an incorrect password. The page will then inform you that your login attempt failed. Ideally, you would also want your username to be filled in for you automatically, and you'd want the Remember Me Next Time check box to retain its selection as well. That way, it's easy for the user to enter the correct password and click the Log In button again. This is just a trivial example, but it's easy to come up with many more scenarios where it's useful if controls are able to maintain their own state.

However, by default, a web page or a control cannot do this on its own. Because each request is a standalone request, the server won't fill in the text boxes again after a postback, but will simply serve the page the same way it did when it first loaded it. In other web technologies, like classic ASP or PHP, you could work around this by manually writing code that prepopulates controls after a postback. Fortunately, ASP.NET makes this much easier for you by integrating this functionality in the ASP.NET feature set.

How the State Engine Works

The state engine in ASP.NET is capable of storing state for many controls. It can store state not only for user input controls like a `TextBox` and a `CheckBox`, but for other controls like a `Label` and even a `Calendar`. This is best demonstrated by a demo. The following exercise shows you how to create a page with controls that are capable of maintaining their state. The sections that follow then explain how ASP.NET is able to do this.

TRY IT OUT Examining the ASP.NET State Engine

In this exercise you add `Label`, `Button`, `TextBox`, and `Calendar` controls to the page. These controls are used to demonstrate some of the inner workings of ASP.NET, including postbacks and the way ASP.NET maintains state.

1. Under the `Demos` folder, create a new page called **`State.aspx`**. Make sure it uses Code Behind, and don't forget to choose your preferred programming language.
2. Switch the page to Design View, click inside the dashed `<div>` to put the focus on it, and then choose Table ➪ Insert Table from the main menu. Set Rows to 3 and Columns to 2 and click OK to insert a table with three rows and two columns.
3. In the first cell of the first row, drag a `Label` control from the Toolbox. In the first cell of the second row, drag a `Calendar` control.
4. Note that as soon as you drop the `Calendar` control in the cell, its Smart Tasks panel pops up as shown in Figure 4-17.

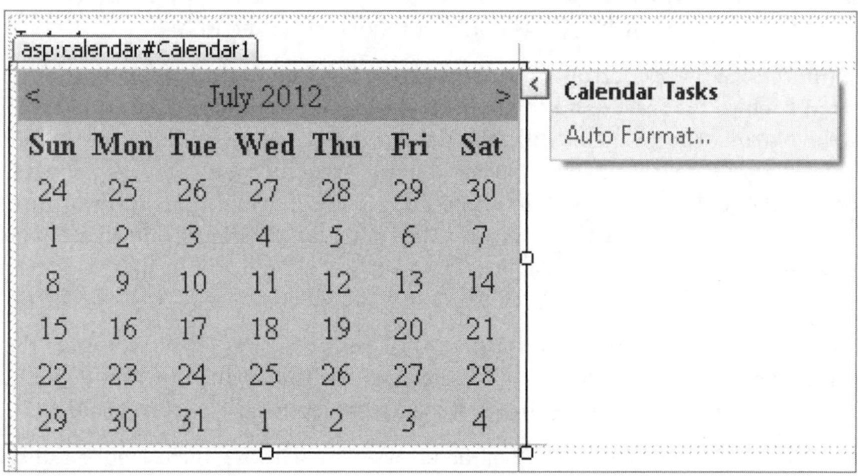

FIGURE 4-17

In the case of the `Calendar` control, you only get one option on this panel, Auto Format, which enables you to change the appearance of the calendar. Click the link, choose from one of the predefined color schemes, like Simple, and click OK.

5. In the first cell of the last row, drag a `TextBox` control.
6. Next, drag `Button` controls into the right column of the first two rows of the table.
7. Click the `Button` in the first row and press F4 to open the Properties Grid. Set the `Button`'s `Text` property to **`Set Date`** and its `ID` to **`SetDate`**. You'll find the `ID` property all the way at the end of the list with properties, or at the beginning if you have the list with properties sorted alphabetically.
8. Repeat the previous step for the other button but call it **`PlainPostback`** and set its `Text` property to **`Plain Postback`**. When you're done, the page should look like Figure 4-18 in Design View.
9. Double-click the Set Date button in Design View and add the following bolded code on the empty line between the code lines that VS inserted for you:

VB.NET

```
Protected Sub SetDate_Click(sender As Object, e As EventArgs) Handles SetDate.Click
  Label1.Text = DateTime.Now.ToString()
End Sub
```

C#

```
protected void SetDate_Click(object sender, EventArgs e)
{
  Label1.Text = DateTime.Now.ToString();
}
```

There's no need to write code for the Plain Postback button.

10. Open the page in the browser by pressing Ctrl+F5. Select a date on the calendar by clicking one of the days. Notice that as soon as you click the date, the page reloads, caused by a postback. You learn more about this in the How It Works section that follows this exercise.
11. Enter some text in the `TextBox` control and then click the Set Date button a few times. Again, the page is posted back to the server and the `Label` is updated with today's date and time each time you click the button. The `TextBox` still shows the text you entered. Wait a few seconds, and then click the Plain Postback button. Once again, a postback occurs, and the page reloads. Now take a look at the text for the `Label`. It still contains the date and time that was displayed when you last clicked the Set Date button. Click the Plain Postback button a few more times and notice that the `Label` doesn't change. The `TextBox` should still display the text you entered.
12. Go back to VS and open the Properties Grid for the `Label` control in Design View. Locate the `EnableViewState` property and set it to `False` by selecting that value from the drop-down list or by double-clicking the property name or its value. Repeat this step for the `TextBox` control.
13. Repeat steps 10 and 11 by reopening the page in the browser and clicking the calendar and the buttons. This time, when you click the Plain Postback button, you'll see that the `Label` control defaults to its initial text: `Label`. The `TextBox`, however, still displays the text you entered.

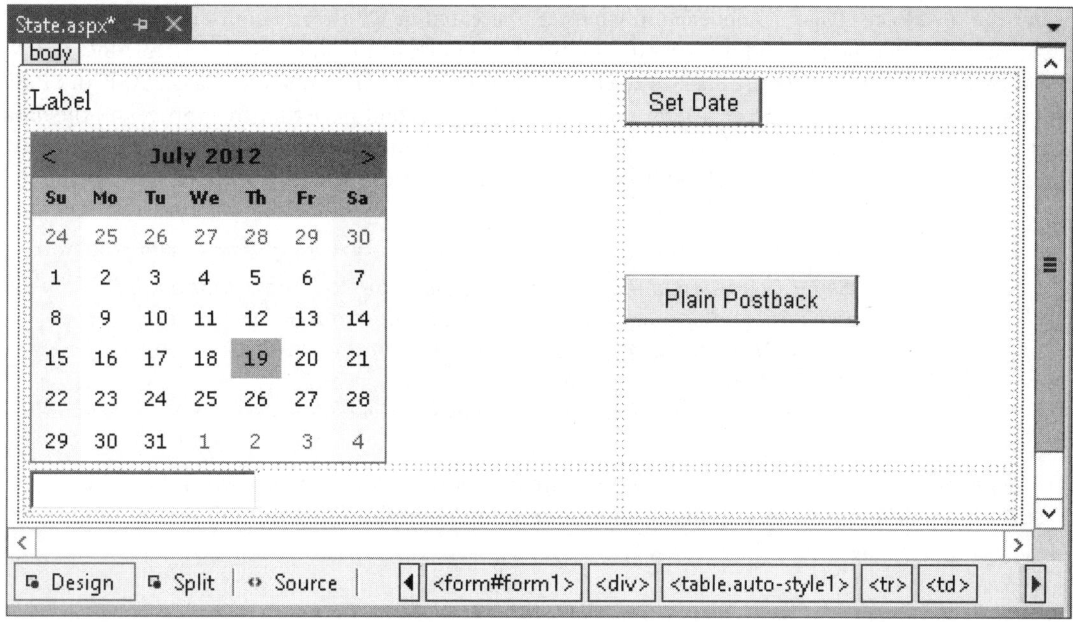

FIGURE 4-18

How It Works

To understand how this all works, you need to look at a few important elements. First, open up the page in the browser again and view its HTML source. You can do this by right-clicking the page in the browser and choosing the View Source or View Page Source menu item. Near the top of the window, you see the following `<form>` element:

```
<form method="post" action="State.aspx" id="form1">
...
</form>
```

The HTML `<form>` element is used to enable a user to submit information from the browser to the server. A user can enter information using controls like text boxes, drop-down lists, check boxes, and so on. A form can be submitted in two ways: with `POST` (as shown in the previous `<form>` element) or with `GET`. In the former case, all data from the form is added to the body of the request and then sent to the server. In the case of the `GET` method, all the data is appended to the actual address of the request. The intricacies of the differences are not that important right now; what's important to understand is what the `<form>` element is used for: it encapsulates form controls whose values are submitted back to the server en masse.

When a control like a `Button` is clicked, it causes a postback to the server. During this postback, all the relevant information in the form is submitted back to the server where it can be used to rebuild the page.

By default, all your ASP.NET Web Forms always use the `POST` method to send data to the server. Also, by default, an entire ASP.NET page always contains exactly one form. Because this is so common, a new page (or Master Page as you learn in Chapter 6) created in VS already contains the `<form>` element, so you don't have to add it yourself. Finally, it's important to understand that an ASP.NET Web Form by default always submits back to itself. In other web environments, like classic ASP and PHP, it's not uncommon to set the `action` attribute of the page to a second page that then processes the data the user has submitted. However, with an ASP.NET page, you'll find that even if you set the `action` attribute in the code explicitly, the ASP.NET run time will revert it to the name of the current page.

> ***NOTE*** *ASP.NET supports a feature called* Cross Page Postbacks *that enables you to submit from one page to another. To learn more about this concept, search the MSDN site for* **Cross Page Postbacks** *or get yourself a copy of* Professional ASP.NET 4.5 *from Wrox.*

The next thing to look at is ASP.NET's View State functionality implemented with the hidden `__VIEWSTATE` field that you see in the HTML source bolded in the following snippet:

```
<form method="post" action="State.aspx" id="form1">
...
  <input type="hidden" name="__VIEWSTATE" id="__VIEWSTATE"
         value="IXcrUZ51B9YmtdoSL9csn2+VrYx5oW32kAw0oRXGsf3F0/W016/upieH7Nht1f
         hyr99U0IRRKmjvYk4FdH5E9ZRucaja0xPkwCyRoNBI3KkidqR5eAVX86D
         qOfE1584eSB0ff3IF4o3Y+ZqD7qZp3A==" />
</div>
```

Although at first the text appears to contain nothing more than random characters, it actually contains useful information. To protect the information stored in this field, ASP.NET has converted the page state in the preceding string. If you were able to look inside the value of the fields, you'd find a value for the `Label1` control with the current date and time.

When your ASP.NET page loads, the ASP.NET run time fills this hidden field with information about the page. For example, it added the value for the `Text` property of the `Label1` control when you caused a postback by clicking the Set Date button. Similarly, it contains the selected date for the `Calendar` control. When the page is then submitted back by a postback, the value in this hidden `__VIEWSTATE` field is sent with the request. Then, when ASP.NET creates the new page on the server, the information from the `__VIEWSTATE` field is read and applied to the controls in the page. This way, a control like the `Label` is able to maintain its text even after the page has been posted back to the server.

The `TextBox` doesn't need View State, though. It's able to maintain its value because the browser submits it to the server with each postback.

To reiterate, here's a rundown of the process that took place in the preceding Try It Out.

1. You requested the page in the browser by opening it from within VS.
2. The browser got the page from the server by making a request for it.
3. The ASP.NET run time read the page from disk, processed it, and sent the resulting HTML to the browser. At this stage, all the controls were set to their default values that were defined in the markup of the page. For example, the `Text` of the `Label` control is set to `Label`.

4. After the page got displayed in the browser, you clicked the Set Date button. This caused a postback to the server.

5. At the server, the page was reconstructed again, similar to the first time it loaded, described in step 3. At this stage, all the controls contain their default values. So, again, the `Label1` control had its `Text` property set to `Label`. Shortly after the defaults have been set, the run time overrides these defaults for controls it finds in View State. However, because this was the first postback and the `Label` control's `Text` property hadn't changed yet, its value was not present in View State. So the `Text` property just contained the default word `Label`.

6. While still processing the same request, the ASP.NET run time fired the code in `SetDate_Click`. As you have seen, this code changed the `Text` property of the `Label` control to the current date and time. The ASP.NET run time sees this change and stores this new value in View State as well, so it stays available for subsequent postbacks.

7. Next, you entered some text and clicked the Plain Postback button. Just as with the other button, this caused a postback to occur. The page was constructed again, and all defaults are set. Again, this means that the `Text` property of the `Label1` control simply contains the word `Label`. However, shortly after that, during the same processing cycle, the ASP.NET run time processes the View State, restoring control values it finds in the hidden `__VIEWSTATE` field. In this example, it found the `Text` property with the current date and time, and assigned it again to the `Label` control. Because the Plain Postback button doesn't change the `Text` of the `Label` anymore, the `Text` property doesn't change: it contains the date and time from the previous postback. The `Text` property of the `TextBox` control is set using the value submitted to the server; that is, this control does not use View State to maintain its value. At the end, the entire page is sent to the browser, where the label correctly displays its previous value.

8. Finally, you turned off the View State for the `Label` and `TextBox` controls by setting `EnableViewState` to `False`. With this setting turned off, the ASP.NET run time doesn't track the `Label` control anymore. So when you click the Plain Postback button, the ASP.NET run time doesn't find any information for the label in View State, which eventually results in the label displaying its own default text: the word `Label`.

Not All Controls Rely on View State

You have to understand that not all controls rely on View State all the time. A number of controls are able to maintain some of their own state, as you saw with the `TextBox` control in the preceding exercise. These controls include, among others, the `TextBox`, `CheckBox`, `RadioButton`, and `DropDownList` controls. They are able to maintain their values because they are rendered as standard HTML form controls in the browser. For example, a `TextBox` server control ends up like this in the browser:

```
<input name="TextBox1" type="text" value="Initial Text" id="TextBox1" />
```

When a page with such a `TextBox` in it is posted back, the browser also sends the value of the control back to the server. The ASP.NET run time can then simply look at that value to prepopulate the text box again, instead of getting the value from View State. Obviously, this is more efficient than storing the value in View State too. If that were the case, the value would get sent to the server twice: once in the text box and once in View State. Especially with large values, this could quickly increase the page's size, and thus its load time. For some features—such as tracking changes made at the client—these controls still need to store their values in View State as well, and do so on a need-to-have basis.

In addition to View State, controls support the concept of *Control State*. Controls use that mechanism to keep track of data they absolutely need to operate correctly. You cannot disable Control State but since only limited amounts of data are stored in Control State, this is not a problem.

A Note about View State and Performance

Because the View State engine adds a considerable amount of information to the page, it's often a good idea to turn it off when you don't need it. This way, you can minimize the size of the hidden `__VIEWSTATE` field, which means the page becomes smaller and thus loads faster in the browser. Note that when you turn of View State you still see the hidden `__VIEWSTATE` field because Control State uses the same field to store its data. Turning off View State is easy, and you can do it at three different places:

- **At the website level**—You can do this in the `Web.config` file in the root of the site by modifying the `<pages>` element under `<system.web>`, setting the `enableViewState` attribute to `false`:

```
<pages enableViewState="false">
  ...
</pages>
```

- **At the page level**—At the top of each page you find the *page directive*, a series of instructions that tell the ASP.NET run time how the page should behave. In the page directive you can set `EnableViewState` to `False`:

```
<%@ Page Language="VB" AutoEventWireup="False" CodeFile="State.aspx.vb"
   Inherits="Demos_State" EnableViewState="False" %>
```

  This option is useful for pages where you're sure you don't need View State at all.

- **At the control level**—Each ASP.NET Server Control enables you to set `EnableViewState` individually, giving you the option to turn it off for some controls, while leaving it on for others.

Once you've turned off View State at a higher level (`Web.config` or page level), setting `EnableViewState` to `True` again at a lower level (the page or a specific control) has no effect. However, using the `ViewStateMode` property you can still accomplish this as follows:

- Do not turn off View State in the `Web.config` file.
- At the page level, set `EnableViewState` to `True` and `ViewStateMode` to `Disabled` like this:

```
<%@ Page Language="C#" ... EnableViewState="True" ViewStateMode="Disabled" %>
```

  This turns off View State for all controls in the page except for those that explicitly enable it again by setting the `ViewStateMode` to `Enabled`.

- For the controls you want to give View State support, set the `ViewStateMode` to `Enabled`, like this:

```
<asp:Label ID="Label1" runat="server" Text="Label" ViewStateMode="Enabled" />
```

If you want to see this at work in your demo page, modify the page directive of `State.aspx` as in the previous example by setting `EnableViewState` to `True` and `ViewStateMode` to `Disabled`. Then create a second `Label` in the page and set `ViewStateMode` for the first to `Enabled`:

```
<asp:Label ID="Label1" runat="server" Text="Label" ViewStateMode="Enabled" />
<asp:Label ID="Label2" runat="server" Text="Label" />
```

In the Code Behind of the page, assign today's date and time to the second label as well:

VB.NET

```
Label1.Text = DateTime.Now.ToString()
Label2.Text = DateTime.Now.ToString()
```

C#

```
Label1.Text = DateTime.Now.ToString();
Label2.Text = DateTime.Now.ToString();
```

Finally, run steps 10 and 11 of the last Try It Out exercise. You'll notice the first `Label` maintains its text, whereas the second defaults back to the text *Label.*

PRACTICAL TIPS ON WORKING WITH CONTROLS

The following list presents some practical tips on working with controls:

- Spend some time trying out the different controls in the Standard category. Although many of them are used and discussed throughout the book, it's good to know how you should use them and how they operate. By experimenting with them now in a few sample pages, you have a head start when the controls reappear in later chapters.
- Consider turning off View State for controls that don't need it. In many cases, you hardly notice the difference, but especially with the data-driven controls discussed in Chapter 13 and onward, disabling View State can seriously decrease the size of your web page, resulting in shorter load times and improved user experience.
- Before you design a complex Web Form with multiple controls to accept user input, step back from your computer and take a piece of paper and a pen to draw out the required functionality. By thinking about the (technical) design of your application before you start coding, it's much easier to create a consistent and well-thought-out user interface. Making considerable changes later in the page if you've taken a wrong route will always take more time than doing it (almost) right the first time.
- Experiment with the View State mechanism to get a better understanding of how it works. Create a couple of pages similar to the one you created in the last exercise. Then turn off View State at the page or control level and see how the page behaves. Take note of the controls, such as `TextBox`, that are capable of maintaining their value even with View State off.

SUMMARY

This chapter gave you a good look at the large set of ASP.NET Server Controls. Because these controls are so important and used throughout every ASP.NET application, it's really critical that you understand what controls you have available in the Toolbox, what they are used for, how they work, and how they maintain their own state.

One of the biggest inventions in ASP.NET is the state engine that enables controls to maintain their state across postbacks. The state engine is a real time-saver and frees you from writing loads of tedious and boring code in every single web page to replicate this behavior. However, you should turn View State off when possible to improve performance.

This chapter also introduced you to some trivial server-side code in Visual Basic and in C#. The next chapter gives you a much better understanding of programming ASP.NET pages. You see how a programming language looks, what elements it contains, and how to write code yourself to use in your ASP.NET pages. And best of all, the examples are presented in Visual Basic and C#, so you're not stuck with a language you may not like.

EXERCISES

1. Name the mechanism that enables server controls to maintain their state.
2. How is the ASP.NET run time able to keep track of control state between postbacks?
3. Name a difference between an `<asp:DropDownList>` and an `<asp:ListBox>`.
4. What property do you need to cause a postback to the server when you change the checked state of a `CheckBox` in the browser?
5. Many server controls have a common set of properties that affects their looks at run time. Name three properties that change styling elements such as color, borders, and size.
6. Instead of setting individual control properties like `BackColor` and `ForeColor`, it's better to set a single CSS-related property. What's the name of this property and what benefit does it give you?

You can find answers to these exercises in Appendix A.

▶ WHAT YOU LEARNED IN THIS CHAPTER

`__VIEWSTATE`	The hidden form field that is used to transfer the state from the server to the client and back.
Container controls	Server controls that serve as a container by wrapping other content and controls.
Events tab	The part of the Properties Grid that lets you set up handlers for control events such as `Click` for a `Button`.
List controls	Server controls that present a list of items to the user. Controls include the `DropDownList`, `CheckBoxList`, and more.
`POST` and `GET` methods	Different methods to submit data from the client to the server. With `POST` the data is added to the body of the request, whereas with `GET` the data is appended to the address of the requested page.
Postback	The process of sending form data from a client browser back to the server.
Server Controls	The work horses of ASP.NET, used to build up the user interface of a web page in the browser.
Smart Tasks panel	The action panel that appears for some controls to help you accomplish common tasks.
View State	The mechanism that enables the ASP.NET controls to store state at the client.

5

Programming Your ASP.NET Web Pages

WHAT YOU WILL LEARN IN THIS CHAPTER:

- How to work with data types, variables, objects, and collections in a programming environment
- Different ways to make decisions in your code
- The options available for creating blocks of functionality that can easily be reused
- Different ways to write well-organized and documented code
- What object orientation is, and how you can use it in your applications

WROX.COM CODE DOWNLOADS FOR THIS CHAPTER

You can find the `wrox.com` code downloads for this chapter on the Download Code tab at `www.wrox.com/remtitle.cgi?isbn=1118311809`. The code is in the Chapter 5 download.

In the previous four chapters, you created a number of Web Forms that contained mostly ASP .NET Server Controls and plain HTML. Only a few of the examples contained actual programming code, written in either C# or Visual Basic (VB.NET), and most of that code was pretty straightforward. However, not all of your pages will always be so simple, and the ability to read, understand, and write code is a critical asset in your web development toolkit.

This chapter teaches you the basics and beyond of programming for web applications. Just as with all the other samples in the book, this entire chapter covers both VB.NET and

C#. For every concept or piece of theory introduced in this chapter, you see an example in both VB.NET and C# at the same time. Which language you prefer is entirely your decision.

> **NOTE** *To get the most out of this chapter, it's recommended that you actually try out the code. You can test most of the examples with a simple ASPX page. Drag a `Label` and a `Button` on your page and double-click the `Button` in Design View. Then type the sample code on the open line of the code block that VS added for you and press Ctrl+F5. After the page has finished loading, click the button and the code will be executed. Some of the examples call fictitious code and won't run correctly. They only serve to illustrate the topic being discussed.*

INTRODUCTION TO PROGRAMMING

To get started with programming, it's critical to understand a common set of terms shared by programmers in all types of languages and applications. The remainder of this chapter introduces you to a relatively large number of terms and concepts. Most of the terminology comes with code examples so you can see how they are used in real code.

It's also important to realize this is not a complete introduction to programming. Not every detail of a programming language is covered. Instead, this chapter focuses on the key concepts that you need to understand to successfully build day-to-day websites. Once you get the hang of that you'll find it's easier to deepen your knowledge about programming by learning the more exotic features of your favorite programming language.

> **NOTE** *If you're interested in learning a lot more about programming in VB.NET or C#, find Beginning Visual Basic 2012 (ISBN: 978-1-1183-1181-3) or Beginning Microsoft Visual C# 2012 (ISBN: 978-1-1183-1441-8), both published by Wrox.*

You add the code you write in this and coming chapters either to the Code Behind of a web page, or in a separate *class file* placed in the special `App_Code` folder. When the ASP.NET run time processes the request for a page containing code, it *compiles* any code it finds in the page, Code Behind, or class files first. When code is compiled, it is being transformed from a human-readable programming language (like C# or VB.NET) into *Microsoft Intermediate Language* (*MSIL*), the language that the .NET Framework run time can understand and execute. The result of the compilation process of an ASP.NET website is one or more assemblies — files with a DLL extension — in a temporary folder on your system. This compilation process takes place only the first time the page is requested after it has been created or changed. Subsequent requests to the same page result in the same DLL being reused for the request. Fortunately, in ASP.NET websites, compilation takes place behind the scenes, so you usually don't have to worry about it.

To get started with programming, the first concepts that you need to look at are data types and variables, because they are the building blocks of any programming language.

> ***NOTE*** *The .NET Framework used by ASP.NET is huge and contains thousands of types with hundreds of thousands of members. Clearly, you cannot memorize all the types in the framework, so you need to make good use of resources like IntelliSense and the online help. Navigating the MSDN site* `(http://msdn.microsoft.com/en-us/library/)` *can sometimes be a daunting task. However, I often find that searching for something like* `typeName type .NET MSDN` *brings up exactly what I need. So, if I wanted to learn more about the* `string` *class, I'd type* `string class .NET MSDN` *in my favorite search engine. Nine out of ten times the first result is a link to the relevant page on the MSDN website, where I can learn more about the class — where it's defined and located and how to use it.*

DATA TYPES AND VARIABLES

At first when you think about data that is used in some programming environment, you may not realize that each piece of data has a *data type*. You may think that a computer would store the text Hello World in exactly the same way as today's date or the number 26; as a series of characters, for example. However, to be able to effectively work with data, many programming languages have different data types, and each data type is constrained to a specific type of information. Out of the box, the .NET Framework comes with a long list of data types that enable you to work with numbers (such as `Int32`, `Int16`, and `Double`), text strings (`Char` and `String`), dates (`DateTime`), true/false constructs (the `Boolean`), and more. A list of the most common types is supplied later in this section.

For each major type of data there is a special data type. To work with that data, you can store it in a *variable* that you need to *declare* first using the required data type. In VB.NET you use `Dim myVariable As DataType`, whereas in C# you use `DataType myVariable` to declare a variable. A valid variable name typically consists of letters, numbers, and underscores, and cannot start with a number. These rules apply to other identifiers as well, such as classes and methods, which you see later. The following example shows you how to declare two variables: an `Integer` (`int` in C#) to hold a number and a `String` (`string` in C#) to hold a piece of text:

VB.NET

```
' Declare a variable of type Integer to hold medium sized whole numbers.
Dim distanceInMiles As Integer

' Declare a variable to hold some text like a first name.
Dim firstName As String
```

C#

```
// Declare a variable of type int to hold medium sized whole numbers.
int distanceInMiles;

// Declare a variable to hold some text like a first name.
string firstName;
```

These two code examples also contain comments, prefixed with a tick (`'`) in VB.NET or two forward slashes (`//`) in C#. You learn more about commenting your code later in this chapter.

After you have declared a variable, you can assign it a value. You can assign types like numbers and booleans directly to a variable. To assign a string to a variable you need to enclose it in double quotes:

VB.NET

```
Dim distanceInMiles As Integer
distanceInMiles = 437

Dim firstName As String
firstName = "Imar"
```

C#

```
int distanceInMiles;
distanceInMiles = 437;

string firstName;
firstName = "Imar";
```

In addition to separate declarations and assignments, you can also declare a variable and assign it a value in one fell swoop:

VB.NET

```
Dim distanceInMiles As Integer = 437
Dim firstName As String = "Imar"
```

C#

```
int distanceInMiles = 437;
string firstName = "Imar";
```

Although a variable name can be nearly anything you like, it's advised that you give each variable a meaningful name that describes its purpose. For example, a string to hold a first name could be called `firstName` and a variable that holds someone's age could simply be called `age`. In .NET it's common to write local variables in what's called *camel case*, which means each word starts with a capital letter except for the first. To help you find the type of the variable later in the code, VS shows a useful tooltip when you hover over a variable in the code editor, making it super easy to find a variable's type. Figure 5-1 shows that the `distanceInMiles` variable in the C# example is of type `int`.

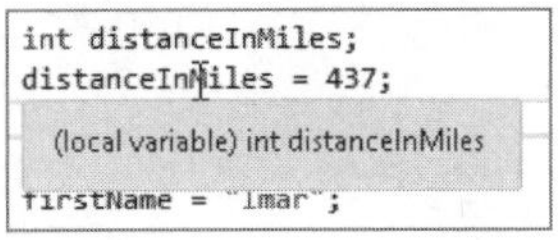

FIGURE 5-1

You're advised not to prefix your variables with letters to indicate the type. For example, write `firstName` and not `sFirstName` for a `String` holding someone's name. This type of notation, called *Hungarian Notation*, is considered outdated. IDEs like Visual Studio, with their smart IntelliSense and other programming tools, don't really require this anymore. Without Hungarian Notation, your code becomes easier to read (`age` is more readable than `iAge`) and easier to maintain because you can change a variable's type without renaming it everywhere it's used.

Microsoft .NET supports a large number of different programming languages, including VB.NET, C#, and others. All these languages are able to communicate with each other. For example, you can write some code in C#, use Visual Studio Express 2012 for Windows Desktop to compile it to a `.dll` file (a file with reusable code that can be consumed by other .NET applications), and then use it in a web application that uses VB.NET as the primary language. Because of this interoperability, it's necessary to agree on some system that enables all .NET programming languages to understand each other. This system is called the *Common Type System* (*CTS*). It's the CTS that defines the data types that are accessible to all CTS-compliant languages. Each language is then free to define a set of *primitive types*, which are essentially shortcuts or aliases for the more complex type descriptions in the .NET Framework. So, even if the CTS defines a type called `System.Int32`, a language like C# is free to alias this type as `int` and VB is free to alias this type as `Integer` to make it easier for a developer to work with it.

The following table lists the most common CTS types in the .NET Framework and their C# and VB.NET aliases. The table also lists the ranges of the variables and what they are used for.

.NET	C#	VB.NET	DESCRIPTION
System.Byte	byte	Byte	Used to store small, positive whole numbers from 0 to 255. Defaults to 0 when no value is assigned explicitly.
System.Int16	short	Short	Capable of storing whole numbers between –32,768 and 32,767. Defaults to 0.
System.Int32	int	Integer	Capable of storing whole numbers between –2,147,483,648 and 2,147,483,647. Defaults to 0.
System.Int64	long	Long	Holds whole large numbers between –9,223,372,036,854,775,808 and 9,223,372,036,854,775,807. Defaults to 0.
System.Single	float	Single	Stores large numbers with decimals between –3.4028235E+38 and 3.4028235E+38. Defaults to 0.0.
System.Double	double	Double	Can hold large fractional numbers. It's not as accurate as the Decimal when it comes to the fractional numbers but when extreme accuracy is not a requirement, you should prefer the Double over the Decimal, because the Double is a little faster. Defaults to 0.0.
System.Decimal	decimal	Decimal	Stores extremely large fractional numbers with a high accuracy. Defaults to 0. This data type is often used to store monetary values.

continues

(continued)

.NET	C#	VB.NET	DESCRIPTION
System.Boolean	bool	Boolean	Used to hold a simple boolean value: True or False in VB, and true or false in C#. Defaults to False.
System.DateTime	n/a	Date	VB.NET has an alias for the System.DateTime data type to store date and time values. C# doesn't define an alias for this type. Defaults to 1/1/0001: 12:00 am.
System.Char	char	Char	Holds a single character. Defaults to Nothing (null in C#).
System.String	string	String	Can hold text with a length of up to 2 billion characters. Defaults to Nothing (null in C#).
System.SByte	sbyte	SByte	Used to store small numbers from –128 to 127. Defaults to 0.
System.UInt16	ushort	UShort	Similar to a System.Int16, but this data type can only store unsigned whole numbers, between 0 and 65,535. Defaults to 0. The other data types prefixed with a U are all unsigned as well.
System.UInt32	uint	UInteger	Capable of storing whole numbers between 0 and 4,294,967,295. Defaults to 0.
System.UInt64	ulong	ULong	Capable of storing whole numbers between 0 and 18,446,744,073,709,551,615. Defaults to 0.
System.Object	object	Object	The parent of all data types in .NET, including the CTS types and types you define yourself. Each data type is also an object, as you learn later in the book. Defaults to Nothing (null in C#).

The standard .NET types are all prefixed with `System` followed by a period. This `System` part is the *namespace* for this data type. You learn what namespaces are and what they are used for later in this chapter.

Sometimes you need to convert data from one type to another. For example, you may have an `Int32` that you need to treat as a `Double`. You can do this in a number of different ways.

Converting and Casting Data Types

The most common way to convert a type is converting it into a `String`. Web applications use string types in many places. For example, the `Text` returned from a `TextBox` is a `String`, and so is the

`SelectedValue` of a `DropDownList`. To get a string representation of an `Object`, you can call its `ToString()` method. Every object in the .NET world supports this method, although the exact behavior may differ from object to object. For now, it's important to understand that `ToString` is a *method* — or an *operation* — on an object, like a `String` or a `Double` and even the parent `Object` itself. You learn more about methods and objects later in this chapter when object-oriented programming is discussed.

Using `ToString()` is easy, as the following example that outputs today's date and time on a `Label` control demonstrates:

VB.NET

```
Label1.Text = System.DateTime.Now.ToString()
```

C#

```
Label1.Text = System.DateTime.Now.ToString();
```

Another way to convert data types is by using the `Convert` *class*.

> ***NOTE*** *Classes are an important concept in .NET, so they are discussed in their own section later in this chapter. For now it's important to understand that a class is like a blueprint for objects that are used in .NET. You can create your own classes, but you will also use many of the standard classes that are part of the .NET Framework.*

The `Convert` class contains functionality to convert a number of data types into another type. The following is a simple example of converting a `String` containing a value that looks like a boolean into a true `Boolean` type:

VB.NET

```
Dim myBoolean1 As Boolean = Convert.ToBoolean("True")  ' Results in True
Dim myBoolean2 As Boolean = Convert.ToBoolean("False") ' Results in False
```

C#

```
bool myBoolean1 = Convert.ToBoolean("True");            // Results in true
bool myBoolean2 = Convert.ToBoolean("False");           // Results in false
```

Besides the `ToBoolean` method, `Convert` offers you a host of other conversion methods, including `ToInt32` (for integer types), `ToDateTime` (for dates), and `ToString`.

Another way to convert one type into another is by using *casting*. With casting you actually force one type into another, which is different from converting, in which the underlying value of a data type is transformed into a new value.

Casting only works for compatible types. You can't, for example, cast a `DateTime` into an `Integer`. You can, however, cast similar types, like a `Double` to an `Integer` or a `String` to an `Object`. The reverse of the latter example isn't always true. Earlier I said that every data type in the .NET Framework is based on the `Object` data type, meaning that, for example, a `String` is an `Object`.

However, not every `Object` is also a `String`. When you try to cast one type into another and get a compilation or runtime error, keep this in mind. Later chapters in this book show you more examples of how to cast compatible types into each other.

To cast one type into another using VB.NET, you have a few options. First, you can use `CType` and `DirectCast`. `CType` is a bit more flexible in that it allows you to cast between two objects that look similar. `DirectCast`, on the other hand, only allows you to cast between compatible types but performs slightly faster. The following VB.NET example shows how this works:

```
Dim o1 As Object = 1
Dim i1 As Integer = DirectCast(o1, Integer)     ' Works, because o1 is an Integer
Dim i2 As Integer = CType(o1, Integer)          ' Works, because o1 is an Integer

Dim o2 As Double = 1
Dim i3 As Integer = DirectCast(o2, Integer)     ' Does not compile, because o2 is
                                                '  not an Integer
Dim i4 As Integer = CType(o2, Integer)          ' Works, because o2 looks like an
                                                '  Integer
```

In the first part of the example, an object called `o1` is declared and assigned the `Integer` value of `1`. Although `o1` exposes itself to the outside world as an `Object`, its underlying value is still an `Integer`. When `DirectCast` is called, the cast succeeds because `o1` is, under the hood, an `Integer`.

In the second example, `o2` is declared as a `Double`, a numeric type that looks somewhat like an `Integer`, but isn't really one. Therefore, the call to `DirectCast` fails because a `Double` cannot be cast to an `Integer`. `CType`, on the other hand, works fine, because the underlying value of the variable `o2` *looks* like an `Integer` and can therefore be cast to one. It's important to realize that if the `Double` type has a decimal part, that part gets lost when casting it to an `Integer`.

The third option to cast in VB.NET is using the keyword `TryCast`, which is somewhat similar to the other two options. When an object cannot be cast correctly, `TryCast` returns `Nothing`, whereas `DirectCast` and `CType` result in a crash of the code.

In C# you have two options to cast objects. The most common way is to put the data type in parentheses in front of the expression you want to cast. This works similar to `CType` in VB.

```
object o1 = 1;
int i1 = (int)o1;                    // Works

double o2 = 1;
int i2 = (int)o2;                    // Works
```

Alternatively, you can use the `as` keyword, which works similarly to `TryCast` in VB.NET in that the code doesn't crash if the cast doesn't succeed. The following sample code shows that you cannot cast an `Integer` to an `ArrayList` (which you meet later in this chapter). Instead of crashing, the variable `myList` simply contains `null` to indicate that the cast operation didn't succeed.

```
object o1 = 1;
ArrayList myList = o1 as ArrayList;  // Doesn't cast, but doesn't crash either.
```

You see more about casting and converting in the remaining chapters in this book.

Using Arrays and Collections

So far the data types you have seen are relatively straightforward and singular objects. For example, you store a value of `True` or `False` in a `Boolean` type, and you store a number like `123` in an `Integer`. But what if you have the need to store lots of integers? You may have the need to do so if you want to store the points of a complex shape like a polygon. Or you may have the need to store all the roles that your application supports in a single variable so you can show them on a web page in the Management section, for example. Here's where arrays and collections come to the rescue.

Defining and Working with Arrays

You can see an array as a big bag or list of the same type of things. You define the data type of the things in the array when you declare it. Each item in the array is identified by a sequential number (its so-called *index*) starting at 0, making arrays *zero-based*. When declaring and accessing an array in VB.NET you use parentheses, whereas in C# you use square brackets. After you have defined the array and populated its elements, you can access the elements by their zero-based element index (0, 1, 2, and so on).

The following code snippet defines an array called `roles` that can hold up to two roles at the same time:

VB.NET

```
Dim roles(1) As String
```

C#

```
string[] roles = new string[2];
```

See the difference between the VB.NET and C# examples? That's not a typo. In VB.NET you define an array's size by specifying the *upper bound*. The upper bound is the last element in the array that you can access. Because arrays are zero-based (that is, you address the first item in the array with an index of 0), it means that if you need room for two items, the upper bound is `1`, giving you the items `0` and `1`.

In C#, on the other hand, you don't define the upper bound but instead you define the *size*. So in C#, you simply specify `2` to get an array with two elements.

Additionally, C# requires you to use the keyword `new`, which instantiates a new array for you. VB.NET does that for you automatically and raises an error if you add the `New` keyword as in the C# example. You see the `new` (`New` in VB.NET) keyword again later in this chapter.

To enter the role names into the array you use the following syntax:

VB.NET

```
roles(0) = "Administrators"
roles(1) = "ContentManagers"
```

C#

```
roles[0] = "Administrators";
roles[1] = "ContentManagers";
```

Just as with the array's declaration, you use parentheses in VB.NET and square brackets in C# to address the elements in the array. Note that `(0)` and `[0]` refer to the first element in the array and `(0)` and `[1]` refer to the second.

By design, arrays have a fixed size. So, given the previous example that defines an array with room for two elements, the following code will throw an error:

VB.NET

```
roles(2) = "Members"      ' Throws an error
```

C#

```
roles[2] = "Members";     // Throws an error
```

This code tries to squeeze a third role into an array that has room for only two. Obviously, that doesn't fit and you'll get an error stating that the "Index was outside the bounds of the array." But what if you need to create more room in the array at a later stage in your code at run time? In VB.NET this is pretty easy. You can use the `ReDim` statement:

```
ReDim Preserve roles(2)
roles(2) = "Members"                    ' Works fine now
```

This line of code re-dimensions the array to its new size: an upper bound of two, thus creating room for a third element. The `Preserve` keyword is necessary to leave the current items in the array intact. Without it, the resized array will be empty.

C# has no direct keyword to re-dimension an array. However, you can leverage the `Array` class of the .NET Framework to resize the array as follows:

```
Array.Resize(ref roles, 3);       // Resize the array so it can
                                  // hold three elements

roles[2] = "Members";             // Works fine now
```

Don't worry about this odd-looking syntax right now; you probably won't need it very often, because the .NET Framework offers alternatives to fixed-size arrays. Since `Array.Resize` is available to VB.NET as well, you have two options to choose from if you're using that language.

When you start working with arrays, you find that they are quick to use at run time, but lack some useful functionality. For example, it's not so easy to add new elements or to remove existing items from the array. Fortunately, the .NET Framework offers a range of useful collections that do give you the feature set you need.

Defining and Working with Collections

Collections are similar to arrays in that they enable you to store more than one object in a single variable. The same bag analogy works for collections: You can simply drop a number of items in a bag, and it will hold them for you. What's different with collections is how they enable you to work with the data in the bag. Instead of simply accessing each item by its index, most collections expose an `Add` method that enables you to add an item to the collection. Similarly, they have `Remove` and

`Clear` methods to remove one or all items from the collection. Just like arrays, they enable you to *iterate*, or loop, over them to access the items in the collection.

When collections were first introduced in the .NET Framework 1.0, the `ArrayList` and `Hashtable` became popular very quickly because they were so easy to use. The `ArrayList` enables you to add arbitrary objects that are then stored in the order in which you add them, whereas the `Hashtable` enables you to store objects referenced by a custom key. The main benefit of these collections over their array cousins is that they can grow on demand. Unlike the previous example, where you needed to resize the array to create room for the third role, the `ArrayList` grows dynamically when required. The following example shows you how this works:

VB.NET

```
Dim roles As New ArrayList()          ' Create a new ArrayList. You don't need
                                      ' to set its size explicitly

roles.Add("Administrators")           ' Add the first role
roles.Add("ContentManagers")          ' Add the second role
roles.Add("Members")                  ' Keep adding roles and the ArrayList
                                      ' grows as necessary
```

C#

```
ArrayList roles = new ArrayList(); // Create a new ArrayList. You don't need
                                   //  to set its size explicitly

roles.Add("Administrators");       // Add the first role
roles.Add("ContentManagers");      // Add the second role
roles.Add("Members");              // Keep adding roles and the ArrayList
                                   // grows as necessary
```

Because this code now calls a method (`Add`) rather than assigning an item to a predefined index in an array, you need parentheses (`()`) in both VB.NET and C#. The usage of methods is discussed later in this chapter.

Although collections solve some of the problems that arrays have, they introduce a few problems of their own. The biggest drawback of the `ArrayList` is that it isn't *strongly typed*. What this means is that you can add *any object* to the list using the `Add` method. This means that the `ArrayList` could hold objects that are of different types at the same time. This may not seem to be a big deal at first, but as soon as you start working with an `ArrayList` that contains multiple types of objects, you'll quickly see why this is problematic. Take the roles example again. With the array and the `ArrayList` versions, the code simply added a few strings containing role names. You can then use these three strings to, say, build up a drop-down list in a Web Form to enable a user to pick a role. So far, so good. But what if one of the items in the list is not a string? What if another developer accidentally wrote some code that adds a `DropDownList` control to the `ArrayList`? Because the `ArrayList` accepts all objects, it won't complain. However, your code will crash if it expects a `String`, but gets a `DropDownList` control instead.

With .NET 2.0, Microsoft introduced a concept called *generics*. Generics are still strongly present in version 4.5 of .NET, helping you overcome the problems that weakly typed collections like the `ArrayList` introduced.

An Introduction to Generics

Since their introduction with .NET 2.0, generics pop up in many different locations in the .NET Framework. Although they are used often in situations where collections are used, the use of generics is not limited to collections; you can also use them for singular types of objects.

Generics are to code what Microsoft Word templates are to word processing. They enable you to write a code *template* that can be used in different scenarios with different types. With generics, you can define a generic code template that doesn't explicitly specify a type. Only when that code is used do you define the type. The main benefit of this is that you can reuse the same template over and over again for multiple data types, without retyping and maintaining multiple versions of the code. In addition to using generics in your own code definitions, you find a host of generics-enabled objects and collections in the .NET Framework, ready to be used by your code.

To understand how you can take advantage of generics, take a look at the following example. It's essentially the same code you saw earlier where the `ArrayList` was used, but this time the type of the list is constrained so it accepts only strings:

VB.NET

```
Dim roles As New List(Of String)

roles.Add("Administrators")
roles.Add("ContentManagers")
roles.Add("Members")
```

C#

```
List<string> roles = new List<string>();

roles.Add("Administrators");
roles.Add("ContentManagers");
roles.Add("Members");
```

Not much code has changed to make the roles list *type safe*. However, with the definition of `List (Of String)` in VB.NET and `List<string>` in C# the new list is now set up to allow only strings to be added through its `Add` method. This compiles fine:

```
roles.Add("Administrators");
```

The following will not compile because `33` is not a String:

```
roles.Add(33);
```

Similar to a generics list of strings, you can also create lists to hold other types. For example:

VB.NET

```
Dim intList As New List(Of Integer)          ' Can hold Integers only
Dim boolList As New List(Of Boolean)         ' Can hold Booleans only
Dim buttonList As New List (Of Button)       ' Can hold Button controls only
```

C#

```
List<int> intList = new List<int>();               // Can hold ints only
List<bool> boolList = new List<bool>();            // Can hold bools only
List<Button> buttonList = new List<Button>();      // Can hold Button controls only
```

> ***NOTE*** *Because there's a lot more to generics than what is shown here, they deserve an entire book of their own. Wrox has released such a book:* Professional .NET 2.0 Generics *by Tod Golding (ISBN: 978-0-7645-5988-4). Although it was originally written for .NET 2.0, you'll find that all the concepts and examples introduced in that book still apply.*

Though the `Add` method is useful to add items to a collection, it can sometimes be a bit tedious if you need to add multiple items to a collection at once. To make this easier, .NET supports *collection initializers*. With a collection initializer, you declare the collection and add some items in one step. You do this by adding the items in a pair of curly braces (prefixed with the keyword `From` in VB.NET) as shown in the following example:

VB.NET

```
Dim myList As New List(Of Integer) From {1, 2, 3, 4, 5}
```

C#

```
List<int> myList = new List<int>() { 1, 2, 3, 4, 5 };
```

Right after this line, the list is populated with the five integers.

Collection initializers are not limited to the `List` class or integers. You can use them with other collection types and data types as well.

The generics examples you have seen barely scratch the surface of what is possible with generics. However, when building ASP.NET websites, you often don't need all the advanced stuff that generics offer you. The `List` collection is so useful it had to be discussed here. Without a doubt, you'll use that collection in your own code one way or another.

STATEMENTS

To make a program or a website do something useful, you need to provide it with code statements that it can execute. Statements cover a wide range of actions, such as show this button, send this e-mail, execute this and that code when a user clicks that button, and so on. However, simply executing these actions is not enough. You often need to execute some code only when a certain *condition* is true. For example, if a visitor to an e-commerce website is buying more than $100 worth of merchandise at one time, she might get a discount of 10 percent. Otherwise, she'll pay the full price. Conditions or decisions are therefore very important statements in a programming language. Another important set of statements is the *loops*. Loops enable you to repeat a certain piece of code a number of times. For example, you can have a loop that goes from 1 to 10, performing some action on each iteration. Or you can loop through the products in a shopping cart, summing up their total price, for example.

The final important set of statements is the *operators*. Operators enable you to do something with your values; or, to be more exact, they enable you to *operate* on them. For example, you use operators to add or subtract values, concatenate (combine) them, or compare them to each other.

The following three sections dig deeper into operators, decision making, and loops.

Operators

The most important operators can be grouped logically into five different types; these types are covered in this section. Of these five types, the assignment operators are probably the easiest to understand and use.

Assignment Operators

The assignment operators are used to assign a value to a variable. This value can come from many sources: a constant value, like the number 6, the value of another variable, or the result of an expression or a function, which are discussed later. In its simplest form, an assignment looks like this, where the number `40` is assigned to the `age` variable:

VB.NET

```
Dim age As Integer = 40
```

C#

```
int age = 40;
```

What if the person this `age` variable is referring to just had his birthday? You'd need to add `1` to the `age` value. That's where arithmetic operators come into play.

Arithmetic Operators

Arithmetic operators enable you to perform most of the familiar calculations on variables and values, like adding, subtracting, and dividing. The following table lists the common arithmetic operators for both VB.NET and C#.

VB.NET	C#	USAGE
+	+	Adds two values to each other
–	–	Subtracts one value from another
*	*	Multiplies two values
/	/	Divides two values
\	n/a	Divides two values but always returns a rounded integer
^	n/a	Raises one value to the power of another
Mod	%	Divides two whole numbers and returns the remainder

The first four operators probably look familiar, and their usage is pretty straightforward. The following code snippet shows the basic operations you can perform with these operators:

VB.NET

```
Dim firstNumber As Integer = 100
Dim secondNumber As Single = 23.5
Dim result As Double = 0
```

```
result = firstNumber + secondNumber      ' Results in 123.5
result = firstNumber - secondNumber      ' Results in 76.5
result = firstNumber * secondNumber      ' Results in 2350
result = firstNumber / secondNumber      ' Results in 4.25531914893617
```

C#

```
int firstNumber = 100;
float secondNumber = 23.5F;
double result = 0;

result = firstNumber + secondNumber;     // Results in 123.5
result = firstNumber - secondNumber;     // Results in 76.5
result = firstNumber * secondNumber;     // Results in 2350
result = firstNumber / secondNumber;     // Results in 4.25531914893617
```

Note that in the C# example you need to add the letter `F` to the value of `23.5`. This tells the compiler you really want it to be a `float` rather than a `double`.

VB.NET also supports the \ operator, which basically performs the division and then drops the remainder from the value, effectively rounding the return value down to the nearest integer.

VB.NET

```
result = firstNumber \ secondNumber      ' Results in 4
```

C# doesn't have a special operator for this. However, when you try to divide two integers, the result is always an integer as well. This means that 7 (stored as an `int`) divided by 2 (stored as an `int`) will be 3. It's important to realize that this rounding occurs, or you may end up with unexpected results.

The final two operators need a bit more explanation. First, the ^ operator — for raising one number to the power of another — is available only in the VB.NET language:

VB.NET

```
Dim result As Double

result = 2 ^ 3                   ' Results in 8 (2 * 2 * 2)
result = 3 ^ 2                   ' Results in 9 (3 * 3)
```

C# doesn't support this operator, but you can easily replicate its behavior using `Math.Pow`, which is made available by the .NET Framework. The following code snippet is functionally equivalent to the preceding one:

C#

```
result = Math.Pow(2, 3);       // Results in 8 (2 * 2 * 2)
result = Math.Pow(3, 2);       // Results in 9 (3 * 3)
```

Of course `Math.Pow` is available to VB.NET as well, so if you're using that language, you have two options to choose from.

The final operator is called the *modulus* operator. It returns the remainder of the division of two numbers, like this:

VB.NET

```
Dim firstNumber As Integer = 17
Dim secondNumber As Integer = 3
```

```
Dim result As Integer = firstNumber Mod secondNumber       ' Results in 2
```

C#

```
int firstNumber = 17;
int secondNumber = 3;
int result = firstNumber % secondNumber;        // Results in 2
```

Simply put, the modulus operator tries to subtract the second number from the first as many times as possible and then returns the remainder. In the preceding example this will succeed five times, subtracting a total of 15, leaving a remainder of 2, which is then returned and stored in the result. The modulus operator is often used to determine if a number is odd or even.

When working with operators, it's important to keep their precedence in mind. To see why this is important, consider the following calculation:

```
2 + 10 * 4
```

What is the outcome of this? You may think the answer is `48` if you first add `2` and `10` together, and then multiply the result by `4`. However, the right answer is `42`; first the multiplication operator is applied on `10` and `4`, resulting in `40`. Then `2` is added, which leads to `42` as the final result. The following table shows the operator precedence for both VB.NET and C#.

VB.NET		C#	
^	Exponentiation	*, /, %	Multiplication, division, and modulus
*, /	Multiplication and division	+, –	Addition and subtraction
\	Integer division		
Mod	Modulus arithmetic		
+, –	Addition and subtraction and string concatenation using the plus (+) symbol		
&	String concatenation		

To force a different operator order, you can use parentheses around expressions. The contents of the expressions are evaluated first, resulting in a different order. For example:

```
(2 + 10) * 4
```

This does result in `48` now, because the addition operator is applied before the multiplication operator.

Both languages also enable you to combine the arithmetic and assignment operators, enabling you to take the value of a variable, perform some arithmetic operation on it, and assign the result back to the variable. The following examples show how this works:

VB.NET

```
Dim someNumber1 As Integer = 3
Dim someNumber2 As Integer = 3
Dim someNumber3 As Integer = 3
```

```
Dim someNumber4 As Integer = 3
someNumber1 += 3          ' Results in someNumber1 having the value 6
someNumber2 -= 3          ' Results in someNumber2 having the value 0
someNumber3 *= 3          ' Results in someNumber3 having the value 9
someNumber4 /= 3          ' Results in someNumber4 having the value 1
```

C#

```
int someNumber1 = 3;
int someNumber2 = 3;
int someNumber3 = 3;
int someNumber4 = 3;
someNumber1 += 3;          // Results in someNumber1 having the value 6
someNumber2 -= 3;          // Results in someNumber2 having the value 0
someNumber3 *= 3;          // Results in someNumber3 having the value 9
someNumber4 /= 3;          // Results in someNumber4 having the value 1
```

C# also enables you to increase a variable's value by `1` using the `++` operator, like this:

C#

```
int someNumber = 3;
someNumber++;          // Results in someNumber having the value 4
```

This construct is used often in loops, as you'll see later in the chapter.

Both languages also use arithmetic assignment operators to concatenate string values, as you'll see shortly.

Another common set of operators is the comparison operators, which enable you to compare values.

Comparison Operators

Just as with the arithmetic operators, VB.NET and C# each have their own set of comparison operators to compare one value to another. A comparison operator always compares two values or *expressions* and then returns a boolean value as the result. The following table lists the most common comparison operators.

VB.NET	C#	Usage
=	==	Checks if two values are equal to each other
<>	!=	Checks if two values are not equal
<	<	Checks if the first value is less than the second
>	>	Checks if the first value is greater than the second
<=	<=	Checks if the first value is less than or equal to the second
>=	>=	Checks if the first value is greater than or equal to the second
Is	is	In VB.NET: Compares two objects. In C#: Checks if a variable is of a certain type

The first thing you'll notice is that C# uses a double equals symbol (==) for the standard comparison operator. This clearly makes it different from the assignment operator. It's a common mistake in C# to use only a single equals symbol if you intend to compare two values. Consider the following example:

```
if (result = 4)
{
  // Do something here with result
}
```

The intention here is to see if `result` equals `4`. However, because the assignment operator is used instead of a proper comparison operator, you'll get the compile error that is displayed in Figure 5-2.

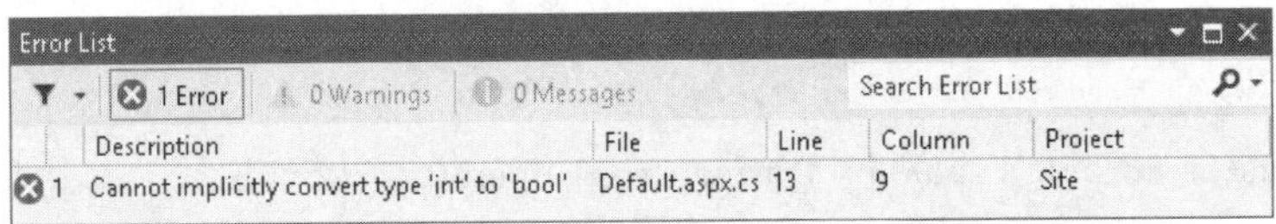

FIGURE 5-2

At first the error message may look a little strange. But if you look at the code a little closer, it starts to make more sense. First, `result` gets assigned a value of `4`. This value is then used for the `if` statement. However, the `if` statement needs a boolean value to determine whether it should run the code inside the `if` block. Because you can't convert an integer value to a boolean like this, you get a compile error. The fix is easy, though; just use the proper comparison operator instead:

```
if (result == 4)
{
  // Do something here with result
}
```

Similar to the simple comparison operator, you can use the other operators to compare values:

VB.NET

```
4 > 5          ' 4 is not greater than 5; evaluates to False
4 <> 5         ' 4 is not equal to 5; evaluates to True
5 >= 4         ' 5 is greater than or equal to 4; evaluates to True
```

C#

```
4 > 5          // 4 is not greater than 5; evaluates to false
4 != 5         // 4 is not equal to 5; evaluates to true
5 >= 4         // 5 is greater than or equal to 4; evaluates to true
```

The `Is` keyword in VB.NET and `is` in C# do something completely different. In VB.NET, `Is` compares two instances of objects, something you learn more about in the second half of this chapter. In C#, you use `is` to find out if a certain variable is compatible with a certain type. You can accomplish that in VB.NET using the `TypeOf` operator. The following two examples are functionally equivalent:

VB.NET

```
Dim myTextBox As TextBox = New TextBox()

If TypeOf myTextBox Is TextBox Then
```

```
  ' Run some code when myTextBox is a TextBox
End If
```

C#

```
TextBox myTextBox = new TextBox();

if (myTextBox is TextBox)
{
  // Run some code when myTextBox is a TextBox
}
```

One of the arithmetic operators enables you to add two values to each other. That is, you use the plus (+) symbol to add two values together. But what if you want to combine two values, rather than add them up? That's where the concatenation operators are used.

Concatenation Operators

To concatenate two strings, you use the + in C# and the & character in VB.NET. Additionally, you can use += and &= to combine the concatenation and assignment operators. Consider this example:

VB.NET

```
Dim firstString As String = "Hello "
Dim secondString As String = "World"
Dim result As String

' The following three blocks are all functionally equivalent
' and result in the value "Hello World"

result = firstString & secondString

result = firstString
result = result & secondString

result = firstString
result &= secondString
```

C#

```
string firstString = "Hello ";
string secondString = "World";
string result;

// The following three blocks are all functionally equivalent
// and result in the value "Hello World"

result = firstString + secondString;

result = firstString;
result = result + secondString;

result = firstString;
result += secondString;
```

In addition to the `&` and `&=` concatenation operators in VB.NET, you could use `+` and `+=` as well. However, depending on the data types of the expressions you're trying to concatenate, you may not get the result you'd expect. Take a look at this code snippet:

```
Dim firstNumber As String = "4"
Dim secondNumber As Integer = 5
Dim result As String = firstNumber + secondNumber
```

Because `firstNumber` is a `String`, you may expect the final result to be `45`, a concatenation of `4` and `5`. However, by default, the VB.NET compiler will silently convert the string `"4"` into the number `4`, after which addition and not concatenation takes place, giving `result` a value of `"9"`, the string representation of the addition.

To avoid this ambiguity, always use the `&` and `&=` operators to concatenate values. Additionally, you can tell VB.NET to stop converting these values for you automatically by adding the following line to the top of your code files:

```
Option Strict On
```

This forces the compiler to generate errors when an implicit conversion is about to occur, as in the previous example.

The final group of operators worth looking into is the logical operators, which are discussed in the next section.

Logical Operators

The logical operators are used to combine the results of multiple individual expressions, and to make sure that multiple conditions are true or false, for example. The following table lists the most common logical operators.

VB.NET	C#	Usage
And	&	Returns True when both expressions result in a True value.
Or	|	Returns True if at least one expression results in a True value.
Not	!	Reverses the outcome of an expression.
AndAlso	&&	Enables you to short-circuit your logical And condition checks.
OrElse	||	Enables you to short-circuit your logical Or condition checks.

The `And`, `Or`, and `Not` operators (`&`, `|`, and `!` in C#) are pretty straightforward in their usage, as demonstrated in the following code snippets:

VB.NET

```
Dim num1 As Integer = 3
Dim num2 As Integer = 7
```

```
If num1 = 3 And num2 = 7 Then       ' Evaluates to True because both
                                    ' expressions are True

If num1 = 2 And num2 = 7 Then       ' Evaluates to False because num1 is not 2

If num1 = 3 Or num2 = 11 Then       ' Evaluates to True because num1 is 3

If Not num1 = 5 Then                ' Evaluates to True because num1 is not 5
```

C#

```
int num1 = 3;
int num2 = 7;

if (num1 == 3 & num2 == 7)          // Evaluates to true because both
                                    // expressions are true

if (num1 == 2 & num2 == 7)          // Evaluates to false because num1 is not 2

if (num1 == 3 | num2 == 11)         // Evaluates to true because num1 is 3

if (!(num1 == 5))                   // Evaluates to true because num1 is not 5
```

The `AndAlso` and `OrElse` operators in VB.NET and the `&&` and `||` operators in C# work very similar to their `And` and `Or` counterparts (`&` and `|`) in C#. The difference is that with these operators the second expression is never evaluated when the first one already determines the outcome of the entire expression. So with a simple `And` operator:

```
If num1 = 2 And num2 = 7 Then
```

both expressions are checked. This means that both `num1` and `num2` are asked for their values to see if they equal `2` and `7`, respectively. However, because `num1` does not equal `2`, there really isn't a point in asking `num2` for its value anymore because the result of that expression will never change the final outcome of the combined expressions. This is where the `AndAlso` (`&&` in C#) operator enables you to short-circuit your logic:

VB.NET

```
If num1 = 2 AndAlso num2 = 7 Then
```

C#

```
if (num1 == 2 && num2 == 7)
```

With this code, the expression `num2 = 7` (`num2 == 7` in C#) is never evaluated because `num1` already didn't meet the required criteria.

This may not seem like a big deal with these simple expressions, but it can be a real performance booster if one of the expressions is actually a slow and long-running operation. Consider this fictitious code:

VB.NET

```
If userName = "Administrator" And GetNumberOfRecordsFromDatabase() > 0 Then
```

C#

```
if (userName == "Administrator" & GetNumberOfRecordsFromDatabase() > 0)
```

The code for this `If` block executes only when the current user is called Administrator and the fictitious call to the database returns at least one record. Now, imagine that `GetNumberOfRecordsFromDatabase()` is a long-running operation. It would be a waste of time to execute it if the current user weren't Administrator. `AndAlso` (`&&` in C#) can fix this problem:

VB.NET

```
If userName = "Administrator" AndAlso GetNumberOfRecordsFromDatabase() > 0 Then
```

C#

```
if (userName == "Administrator" && GetNumberOfRecordsFromDatabase() > 0)
```

Now, `GetNumberOfRecordsFromDatabase()` will only be executed when the current user is Administrator. The code will be ignored for all other users, resulting in increased performance for them.

Most of the previous examples used an `If` statement to demonstrate the logical operators. The `If` statement itself is a very important language construct as well. The `If` statement and other ways to make decisions in your code are discussed next.

Making Decisions

Making decisions in an application is one of the most common things you do as a developer. For example, you need to hide a button on a Web Form when a user is not an administrator. Or you need to display the even rows in a table with a light gray background and the odd rows with a white background. You can make all these decisions with a few different logic constructs, explained in the following sections.

If, If Else, and ElseIf Constructs

The `If` statement (`if` in C#) is the simplest of all decision-making statements. The `If` statement contains two relevant parts: the condition being tested and the code that is executed when the condition evaluates to `True (true` in C#.) For example, to make a button visible only to administrators you can use code like this:

VB.NET

```
If User.IsInRole("Administrators") = True Then
  DeleteButton.Visible = True
End If
```

C#

```
if (User.IsInRole("Administrators") == true)
{
  DeleteButton.Visible = true;
}
```

Note that VB.NET uses the `If` and `End If` keywords, whereas C# uses `if` together with a pair of curly braces to indicate the code block that is being executed. Also, with C#, the parentheses around the condition being tested are required, whereas VB.NET requires you to use the keyword `Then` after the condition.

This code explicitly checks for the value `True` / `true`. However, this is not required and it's quite common to leave it out. The following example is equivalent:

```
If User.IsInRole("Administrators") Then
  DeleteButton.Visible = True
End If
```

C#

```
if (User.IsInRole("Administrators"))
{
  DeleteButton.Visible = true;
}
```

I'll use this succinct version in the remainder of the examples in this chapter. Often you want to perform a different action if the condition is not `True`. Using the negation operator `Not` or `!` you could simply write another statement:

VB.NET

```
If User.IsInRole("Administrators") Then
  DeleteButton.Visible = True
End If
If Not User.IsInRole("Administrators") Then
  DeleteButton.Visible = False
End If
```

C#

```
if (User.IsInRole("Administrators"))
{
  DeleteButton.Visible = true;
}
if (!User.IsInRole("Administrators"))
{
  DeleteButton.Visible = false;
}
```

Clearly, this leads to messy code, because you need to repeat each expression evaluation twice: once for the `True` case and once for the `False` case. Fortunately, there is an easier solution: the `Else` block (`else` in C#):

VB.NET

```
If User.IsInRole("Administrators") Then
  DeleteButton.Visible = True
Else
  DeleteButton.Visible = False
End If
```

C#

```
if (User.IsInRole("Administrators"))
{
  DeleteButton.Visible = true;
}
else
```

```
{
  DeleteButton.Visible = false;
}
```

For simple conditions this works fine. But consider a scenario in which you have more than two options. In those scenarios you can use `ElseIf` in VB.NET or the `else if` ladder in C#.

Imagine that your site uses three different roles: administrators, content managers, and standard members. Administrators can create and delete content; content managers can only create new content, whereas members can't do either of the two. To show or hide the relevant buttons, you can use the following code:

VB.NET

```
If User.IsInRole("Administrators") Then
  CreateNewArticleButton.Visible = True
  DeleteArticleButton.Visible = True
ElseIf User.IsInRole("ContentManagers") Then
  CreateNewArticleButton.Visible = True
  DeleteArticleButton.Visible = False
ElseIf User.IsInRole("Members") Then
  CreateNewArticleButton.Visible = False
  DeleteArticleButton.Visible = False
End If
```

C#

```
if (User.IsInRole("Administrators"))
{
  CreateNewArticleButton.Visible = true;
  DeleteArticleButton.Visible = true;
}
else if (User.IsInRole("ContentManagers"))
{
  CreateNewArticleButton.Visible = true;
  DeleteArticleButton.Visible = false;
}
else if (User.IsInRole("Members"))
{
  CreateNewArticleButton.Visible = false;
  DeleteArticleButton.Visible = false;
}
```

Although this makes your code a bit more readable, you can still end up with difficult code when you have many expressions to test. If that's the case, you can use the `Select Case` (VB.NET) or `switch` (C#) statement.

Select Case/switch Constructs

Imagine you're building a website for a concert hall that has shows on Saturday. During the week, visitors can buy tickets online for Saturday's gig. To encourage visitors to buy tickets as early as possible, you decide to give them an early-bird discount. The earlier in the week they buy their tickets, the cheaper they are. Your code to calculate the discount percentage can look like this, using a `Select Case/switch` statement:

VB.NET

```
Dim today As DateTime = DateTime.Now
Dim discountPercentage As Double = 0

Select Case today.DayOfWeek
  Case DayOfWeek.Monday
    discountPercentage = 40
  Case DayOfWeek.Tuesday
    discountPercentage = 30
  Case DayOfWeek.Wednesday
    discountPercentage = 20
  Case DayOfWeek.Thursday
    discountPercentage = 10
  Case Else
    discountPercentage = 0
End Select
```

C#

```
DateTime today = DateTime.Now;
double discountPercentage = 0;

switch (today.DayOfWeek)
{
  case DayOfWeek.Monday:
    discountPercentage = 40;
    break;
  case DayOfWeek.Tuesday:
    discountPercentage = 30;
    break;
  case DayOfWeek.Wednesday:
    discountPercentage = 20;
    break;
  case DayOfWeek.Thursday:
    discountPercentage = 10;
    break;
  default:
    discountPercentage = 0;
    break;
}
```

For each day where the discount is applicable (Monday through Thursday) there is a `Case` block. The differences between VB.NET and C# syntax are quite small: C# uses a lowercase c for `case` and requires a colon after each case label. Additionally, you need to exit each block with a `break` statement. At run time, the condition (`today.DayOfWeek`) is evaluated and the correct block is executed. It's important to understand that only the relevant block is executed, and nothing else. When no valid block is found (the code is executed on a day between Friday and Sunday), the code in the `Case Else` or `default` block fires. You're not required to write a `Case Else` or `default` block, although it's recommended to do so because it makes your code more explicit and easier to read. The preceding examples could have left it out, because `discountPercentage` already gets a default value of `0` at the top of the code block.

To get a feel for the statements you have seen so far, the following Try It Out exercise shows you how to use them in a small demo application.

TRY IT OUT Creating a Simple Web-Based Calculator

In this exercise you create a simple calculator that is able to add, subtract, multiply, and divide values. You see how to use some of the logical and assignment operators and learn to use the `If` and `Select Case/switch` constructs.

1. Start by creating a new Web Form called `CalculatorDemo.aspx` in the `Demos` folder. Make sure you don't name the page Calculator or you'll run into trouble later in this chapter when you create a class by that name. Once again, make sure you're using the Code Behind model and select the correct programming language.
2. Switch the page to Design View, and click in the dashed rectangle to put the focus on it. Choose Table ➪ Insert Table from the main menu and add a table with three rows and three columns.
3. Merge all three cells of the first row by selecting them with the mouse (either by dragging the mouse or by clicking each cell while holding down the Ctrl key), right-clicking the selection, and choosing Modify ➪ Merge Cells from the menu that appears.
4. Add the following controls to the page, set their ID and other properties as in the following table, and arrange the controls as shown in Figure 5-3.

CONTROL TYPE	CONTROL ID	PROPERTY SETTINGS
Label	ResultLabel	Clear its `Text` property. To do this, right-click the property name in the Properties Grid and choose Reset.
TextBox	ValueBox1	
DropDownList	OperatorList	Add four list items for the following arithmetic operators using the `DropDownList`'s Smart Tasks panel. + - * /
TextBox	ValueBox2	
Button	CalculateButton	Set the `Text` property of the button to **Calculate**.

When you're done, your page should look like Figure 5-3 in Design View.

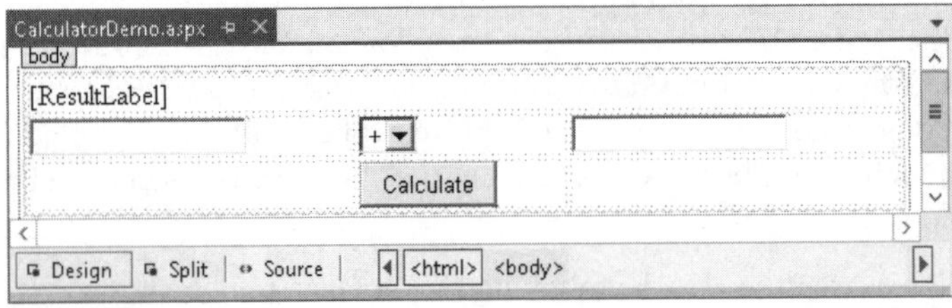

FIGURE 5-3

5. Double-click the Calculate button and add the following bolded code in the code placeholder that VS added for you:

VB.NET

```
Protected Sub CalculateButton_Click(sender As Object,
         e As EventArgs) Handles CalculateButton.Click
  If ValueBox1.Text.Length > 0 AndAlso ValueBox2.Text.Length > 0 Then

    Dim result As Double = 0
    Dim value1 As Double = Convert.ToDouble(ValueBox1.Text)
    Dim value2 As Double = Convert.ToDouble(ValueBox2.Text)

    Select Case OperatorList.SelectedValue
      Case "+"
        result = value1 + value2
      Case "-"
        result = value1 - value2
      Case "*"
        result = value1 * value2
      Case "/"
        result = value1 / value2
    End Select
    ResultLabel.Text = result.ToString()
  Else
    ResultLabel.Text = String.Empty
  End If
End Sub
```

C#

```
protected void CalculateButton_Click(object sender, EventArgs e)
{
  if (ValueBox1.Text.Length > 0 && ValueBox2.Text.Length > 0)
  {
    double result = 0;
    double value1 = Convert.ToDouble(ValueBox1.Text);
    double value2 = Convert.ToDouble(ValueBox2.Text);

    switch (OperatorList.SelectedValue)
    {
      case "+":
        result = value1 + value2;
        break;
      case "-":
        result = value1 - value2;
        break;
      case "*":
        result = value1 * value2;
        break;
      case "/":
        result = value1 / value2;
        break;
    }
    ResultLabel.Text = result.ToString();
  }
```

```
    else
    {
      ResultLabel.Text = string.Empty;
    }
  }
```

6. Save all changes and press Ctrl+F5 to open the page in the browser. If you get an error instead of seeing the page, make sure you typed the code exactly as shown here, and that you named all controls according to the table you saw earlier.

7. Enter a number in the first and second text boxes, choose an operator from the drop-down list, and click the Calculate button. The code in the Code Behind fires and then — based on the item you selected in the drop-down list — the correct calculation is performed and the label is updated with the result.

8. Go ahead and try some other numbers and operators; you'll see that the calculator carries out the right operation every time you click the Calculate button.

How It Works

When you enter two values and click the Calculate button, the following code in the Code Behind fires:

VB.NET

```
If ValueBox1.Text.Length > 0 AndAlso ValueBox2.Text.Length > 0 Then
```

C#

```
if (ValueBox1.Text.Length > 0 && ValueBox2.Text.Length > 0)
```

This code is necessary to ensure that both text boxes contain a value. The code uses a simple `If` statement to ensure that both fields have a value. It also uses `AndAlso` or `&&` to avoid checking the `Text` property of the second `TextBox` when the first is empty. In Chapter 9 you see a much cleaner way to perform this validation. In that chapter you'll also see how to make sure users enter valid numbers, as currently the code crashes when you enter anything that cannot be converted to a `Double`.

The code then declares a `Double` to hold the result of the calculation and then gets the values from the two text box controls, converts the values to a `Double` using the `ToDouble` method of the `Convert` class, and then sets up a `Select Case` (`switch` in C#) block to handle the type of operator you have chosen in the drop-down list:

VB.NET

```
Select Case OperatorList.SelectedValue
  Case "+"
    result = value1 + value2
```

C#

```
switch (OperatorList.SelectedValue)
{
  case "+":
    result = value1 + value2;
    break;
```

For each item in the drop-down list, there is a `Case` statement. When you have chosen the + operator from the list, the code in the first case block fires, and `result` is assigned the sum of the numbers you entered in the two text boxes. Likewise, when you choose the subtraction operator, for example, the two values are subtracted from each other.

At the end, the result is converted to a `String` and then displayed on the label called `ResultLabel`.

The `Select Case/switch` statements close off the discussion about making decisions in your code. There's one more group of statements left: loops that enable you to loop over code or over objects in a collection.

Loops

Loops are extremely useful in many applications, because they enable you to execute code repetitively, without the need to write that code more than once. For example, if you have a website that needs to send a newsletter by e-mail to its 20,000 subscribers, you write the code to send the newsletter once, and then use a loop that sends the newsletter to each subscriber the code finds in a database.

Loops come as a few different types, each with their own usage and advantages.

The For Loop

The `For` loop simply repeats its code a predefined number of times. You define the exact number of iterations when you set up the loop. The `For` loop takes the following format:

VB.NET

```
For counter [ As datatype ] = start To end [ Step stepSize ]
  ' Code that must be executed for each iteration
Next [ counter ]
```

C#

```
for (startCondition; endCondition; step definition)
{
  // Code that must be executed for each iteration
}
```

This looks a little odd, but a concrete example makes this a lot easier to understand:

VB.NET

```
For loopCount As Integer = 1 To 10
  Label1.Text &= loopCount.ToString() & "<br />"
Next
```

C#

```
for (int loopCount = 1; loopCount <= 10; loopCount++)
{
  Label1.Text += loopCount.ToString() + "<br />";
}
```

Although the syntax used in both languages is quite different, both code examples perform the same action: They write out numbers from 1 to 10 on a `Label` control. That is, the loop is started by the assignment of `1` to the variable `loopCount`. Next, the value is converted to a `String` and assigned to the `Label` control. Then `loopCount` is increased by 1, and the loop continues. This goes on until `loopCount` is `10`, and then the loop ends. In this example, hard-coded numbers are used. However, you can replace the start and end conditions with dynamic values from variables or other objects. For example, if you're working with the roles array you saw earlier, you can write out each role in the array like this:

VB.NET

```
For loopCount As Integer = 0 To roles.Length - 1
  Label1.Text &= roles(loopCount) & "<br />"
Next
```

C#

```
for (int loopCount = 0; loopCount < roles.Length; loopCount++)
{
  Label1.Text += roles[loopCount] + "<br />";
}
```

Because arrays are zero-based, you need to address the first item with `roles(0)` in VB.NET and `roles[0]` in C#. This also means that the loop needs to start at `0`. The `Length` property of an array returns the total number of items that the array contains. So when three roles are in the array, `Length` returns 3. Therefore, in VB.NET the code subtracts one from the `Length` and uses that value as the end condition of the loop, causing the loop to run from 0 to 2, accessing all three elements.

The C# example doesn't subtract 1 from the `Length`, though. Instead it uses the expression:

```
loopCount < roles.Length;
```

So, as long as `loopCount` is less than the length of the array, the loop continues. Again, this causes the loop to access all three items, from 0 to 2.

The previous examples loop by adding `1` to the `loopCount` variable on each iteration. To use a greater step increase, you use the keyword `Step` in VB.NET, whereas C# enables you to define the step size directly in the step definition:

VB.NET

```
For loopCount As Integer = 0 To 10 Step 2
  Label1.Text &= loopCount.ToString() & "<br />"
Next
```

C#

```
for (int loopCount = 0; loopCount <= 10; loopCount = loopCount + 2)
{
  Label1.Text += loopCount.ToString() + "<br />";
}
```

This loop assigns the even numbers between 0 and 10 to the `Label` control.

If you are looping over an array or a collection of data, there's another loop at your disposal that's a bit easier to read and work with: the `For Each` or `foreach` loop.

The For Each/foreach Loop

The `For Each` loop in VB.NET and the `foreach` loop in C# simply iterate over all the items in a collection. Taking the roles array as an example, you can execute the following code to print each role name on the `Label` control:

VB.NET

```
For Each role As String In roles
  Label1.Text &= role & "<br />"
Next
```

C#

```
foreach (string role in roles)
{
  Label1.Text += role + "<br />";
}
```

Because the `roles` variable is an array of strings, you need to set up the loop with a `String` as well, as is done with the `role` variable. You would change this variable's type if the collection contained items of a different type.

In addition to the `For` and the `For Each` loops, there is one more loop that you need to look at: the `While` loop.

The While Loop

As its name implies, the `While` loop is able to loop while a certain condition is true. Unlike the other two loops, which usually end by themselves, the `While` loop could loop forever if you're not careful. It could also not execute at all if its condition is never met. The following example shows how to use the `While` loop:

VB.NET

```
Dim success As Boolean = False
While Not success
  success = SendEmailMessage()
End While
```

C#

```
bool success = false;
while (!success)
{
  success = SendEmailMessage();
}
```

This code tries to send an e-mail message using the fictitious `SendEmailMessage` method and will do so until it succeeds — that is, as long as the variable `success` has the value `False` (`false` in C#). Note that `Not` and `!` are used to reverse the value of `success`. The `SendEmailMessage` method is supposed to return `True` when it succeeds and `False` when it doesn't. If everything works out as planned, the code enters the loop and calls `SendEmailMessage`. If it returns `True`, the loop condition is no longer met, and the loop ends. However, when `SendEmailMessage` returns `False`, for example because the mail server is down, the loop continues and `SendEmailMessage` is called again.

To avoid endless loops with the `While` loop, it's often a good idea to add a condition that terminates the loop after a certain number of tries. For example, the following code helps to avoid an infinite loop if the mail server is down:

VB.NET

```
Dim success As Boolean = False
Dim loopCount As Integer = 0
While Not success AndAlso loopCount < 3
  success = SendEmailMessage()
  loopCount = loopCount + 1
End While
```

C#

```
bool success = false;
int loopCount = 0;
while (!success && loopCount < 3)
{
  success = SendEmailMessage();
  loopCount = loopCount + 1;
}
```

With this code, the variable `loopCount` is responsible for exiting the loop after three attempts to call `SendEmailMessage`. Instead of using `loopCount = loopCount + 1`, you can also use the combined concatenation and assignment operators, like this:

VB.NET

```
loopCount += 1
```

C#

```
loopCount += 1;

// Alternatively C# enables you to do this:
loopCount++;
```

All examples have the same result: the `loopCount` value is increased by one, after which the new total is assigned to `loopCount` again.

Besides the `While` loop, you have a few other alternatives, such as the `Do While` loop (`do while` in C#), which ensures that the code to be executed is always executed at least once, and the `Do Until` loop (not available in C#), which goes on *until* a certain condition is true, as opposed to looping *while* a certain condition is true, as is the case with the `While` loop.

Exiting Loops Prematurely

It's common to have the need to exit a loop before it has completely finished. You can do this with `Exit For` in VB.NET and `break` in C#, like this:

VB.NET

```
For loopCount As Integer = 1 To 10
  If loopCount = 5 Then
```

```
      Exit For
    End If
    Label1.Text &= loopCount.ToString() & "<br />"
  Next
```

C#

```
for (int loopCount = 1; loopCount <= 10; loopCount++)
{
  if (loopCount == 5)
  {
    break;
  }
  Label1.Text += loopCount.ToString() + "<br />";
}
```

With this code, the label will only show the numbers 1 to 4, as the loop is exited as soon as `loopCount` has reached the value of 5. Note: This example doesn't have a lot of real-world usage as you would rewrite the code to loop four times only, but it shows the concept quite nicely.

You can use `Continue For` in VB and `continue` in C# to stop processing the current iteration and move on with the next, if available.

So far, the code you've seen has been comprised of short and simple examples that can be placed directly in the Code Behind of a web page; for example, in `Page_Load` or in a `Button`'s `Click` handler that you have seen before. However, in real-world websites, you probably want to structure and organize your code a lot more. In the next section, you see different ways to accomplish this.

ORGANIZING CODE

When you start adding more than just a few pages to your website, you're almost certain to end up with some code that you can reuse in multiple pages. For example, you may have some code that reads settings from the `Web.config` file that you need in multiple files. Or you want to send an e-mail with user details from different pages. So you need to find a way to centralize your code. To accomplish this in an ASP.NET website, you can use functions and subroutines, which are discussed next. To make these functions and subroutines available to all the pages in your site, you need to create them in a special location, which is discussed afterward.

Methods: Functions and Subroutines

Functions and *subroutines* (*subs*) are very similar; both enable you to create a reusable block of code that you can call from other locations in your application. The difference between a function and a subroutine is that a function can return data, whereas a sub can't. Together, functions and subroutines are referred to as *methods*. You'll see that term again in the final part of this chapter that deals with object orientation.

To make functions and subs more useful, they can be *parameterized*. That is, you can pass in additional information that can be used inside the function or subs. Functions and subs generally take the following format:

VB.NET

```
' Define a function
Public Function FunctionName ([parameterList]) As DataType

End Function

' Define a subroutine
Public Sub SubName ([parameterList])

End Sub
```

C#

```
// Define a function
public DataType FunctionName([parameterList])
{

}

// Define a subroutine
public void SubName([parameterList])
{

}
```

The complete first line, starting with `Public`, is referred to as the *method signature* because it defines the look of the function, including its name and its parameters. The `Public` keyword (`public` in C#) is called an *access modifier* and defines to what extent other web pages or code files can see this method. This is discussed in detail later in the chapter. For now, you should realize that `Public` has the greatest visibility, so the method is visible to any calling code.

The name of the function is followed by parentheses, which in turn can contain an optional parameter list. The italic parts in these code examples will be replaced with real values in your code. The parts between the square brackets (`[]`) are optional. To make it a little more concrete, here are some examples of functions and subs:

VB.NET

```
Public Function Add(a As Integer, b As Integer) As Integer
  Return a + b
End Function

Public Sub SendEmailMessage(emailAddress As String)
  ' Code to send an e-mail goes here
End Sub
```

C#

```
public int Add(int a, int b)
{
  return a + b;
}

public void SendEmailMessage(string emailAddress)
{
```

```
    // Code to send an e-mail goes here
}
```

In these code examples it's clear that functions return a value, and subs don't. The `Add` method uses the `Return` keyword (`return` in all lowercase in C#) to return the sum of `a` and `b`. The `Sub` in VB.NET and the `void` method in C# don't require the `Return` keyword, although you can use it to exit the method prematurely.

Finally, both the function and subroutine have a *parameter list* that enables you to define the name and data type of variables that are passed to the method. Inside the method you can access these variables as you would access normal variables. In the case of the `Add` method, you have two parameters: one for the left side of the addition and one for the right side. The `SendEmailMessage` method has only a single parameter: a `String` holding the user's e-mail address.

In earlier versions of VB.NET you would see the keyword `ByVal` in front of each parameter in the parameter list. This is the default type for all parameters, so VS no longer adds it for you. The opposite of `ByVal` is `ByRef`. These keywords determine the way a value is sent to the function or subroutine. When you specify `ByVal`, a *copy* of the variable is made. Any changes made to that copy inside the method are lost as soon as the method finishes. In contrast, when you specify `ByRef`, a *reference* to the variable is sent to the method. Any changes made to the incoming variable reflect on the original variable as well. The following short example demonstrates how this works:

```
Public Sub ByValDemo(someValue As Integer)  ' No ByVal needed as it's the default
  someValue = someValue + 20
End Sub

Public Sub ByRefDemo(ByRef someValue As Integer)
  someValue = someValue + 20
End Sub

Dim x As Integer = 0
ByValDemo(x)

Label1.Text = x.ToString()         ' Prints out 0; A copy of x is sent to ByValDemo,
                                   ' leaving the original value of x unmodified.

Dim y As Integer = 0
ByRefDemo(y)

Label1.Text = y.ToString()         ' Prints out 20; A reference to y is sent
                                   ' to ByRefDemo so when that method modified
                                   ' someValue, it also changed the variable y.
```

C# has a similar construct using the `ref` keyword. The biggest difference from VB.NET is that you need to specify the `ref` keyword in the call to the method as well:

```
public void ByRefDemo(ref int someValue)
{
  someValue = someValue + 20;
}

int y = 0;
ByRefDemo(ref y);                  // Just as in the VB example, y contains 20
                                   // after the call to ByRefDemo
```

Be careful when using reference parameters like this; before you know it the method may change important variables in the calling code. This can lead to bugs that are hard to track down.

To make your sitewide methods accessible to pages in your website, you should place them in a centralized location. The `App_Code` folder of your website is a perfect location for your code.

The App_Code Folder

The `App_Code` folder is a special ASP.NET folder. It's designed specifically to hold code files, like classes that you'll use throughout the site. Code that applies only to one page (like the handler of a `Button` control's `Click` event) should remain in the page's Code Behind, as you have seen so far.

> ***NOTE*** *The `App_Code` folder is specific to Web Site Projects, the project type used for the Planet Wrox sample website. Web Application Projects, on the other hand, don't use or support an `App_Code` folder. However, that project type enables you to create code files in pretty much any other location. When you build sites using the Web Application Project model, you're advised to create a central code folder (called `Code` or `CodeFiles`, for example) to store all your code files. To follow along with the samples in this and later chapters, it's important that you're using a Web Site Project as explained in Chapter 2.*

To add the `App_Code` folder to your site, right-click the site's name in the Solution Explorer and choose Add ➪ Add ASP.NET Folder ➪ App_Code. The folder is added to the site and gets a special icon, shown in Figure 5-4.

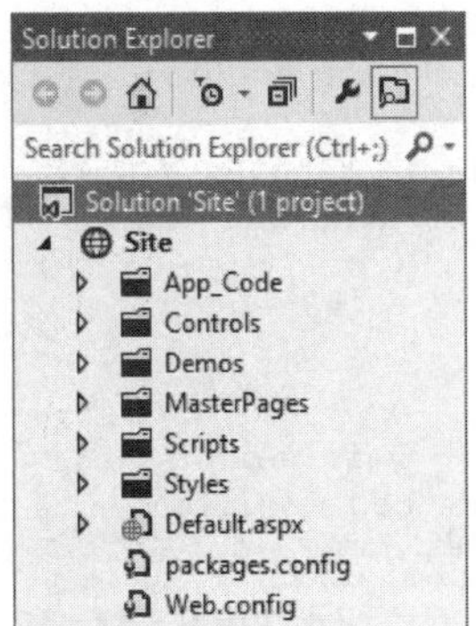

FIGURE 5-4

With the `App_Code` folder in place, you can start adding class files to it. Class files have an extension that matches the programming language you have chosen for the site: `.cs` for C# files and `.vb` for files containing VB.NET code. Inside these class files you can create classes that in turn contain methods (functions and subroutines) that can carry out common tasks. Classes are discussed in more detail in the final section of this chapter; for now, focus on the methods in the code file and how they are called, rather than on why you need to add the code to a class first.

The next exercise shows you how to use the `App_Code` folder to optimize the calculator you created in an earlier Try It Out.

TRY IT OUT Optimizing the Calculator

In this exercise, you create a class called `Calculator` that exposes four methods: `Add`, `Subtract`, `Multiply`, and `Divide`. When the class is set up and is capable of performing the necessary computing actions, you modify the `CalculatorDemo.aspx` file so it uses your new `Calculator` class. Although this is a trivial example when it comes to the amount of code you need to write and the added flexibility you gain by moving your code from the ASPX page to the `App_Code` folder so it can be reused by other applications, it's comprehensive enough to show you the concept, yet short enough to enable you to understand the code. For now, just focus on how the calculator works and how to call its methods. In the section on object orientation later in this chapter, you see exactly what a class is.

1. If you haven't already done so, start by adding an `App_Code` folder to your site by right-clicking the site and choosing Add ➪ Add ASP.NET Folder ➪ App_Code.
2. Right-click this newly created folder and choose Add ➪ Add New Item.
3. In the dialog box that follows, select the appropriate programming language, and click Class.
4. Type **`Calculator`** as the name of the file and click Add. This creates a class file that in turn contains a class called `Calculator`. Note that it's common practice to name classes using what's called *Pascal casing*, where each word starts with a capital letter.
5. Right after the line of code that defines the `Calculator` class, add the following four methods, replacing any code that was already present in the class:

VB.NET

```
Public Class Calculator

  Public Function Add(a As Double, b As Double) As Double
    Return a + b
  End Function

  Public Function Subtract(a As Double, b As Double) As Double
    Return a - b
  End Function

  Public Function Multiply(a As Double, b As Double) As Double
    Return a * b
  End Function

  Public Function Divide(a As Double, b As Double) As Double
    Return a / b
  End Function

End Class
```

C#

```
public class Calculator
{
  public double Add(double a, double b)
  {
    return a + b;
  }

  public double Subtract(double a, double b)
```

```
    {
      return a - b;
    }

    public double Multiply(double a, double b)
    {
      return a * b;
    }

    public double Divide(double a, double b)
    {
      return a / b;
    }
  }
```

6. Next, modify the Code Behind of the `CalculatorDemo.aspx` page so it uses the class you just created. You need to make two changes: First you need to add a line of code that creates an instance of the `Calculator` class, and then you need to modify each `Case` block to use the relevant calculation methods in the calculator:

VB.NET

```
Dim myCalculator As New Calculator()
Select Case OperatorList.SelectedValue
  Case "+"
    result = myCalculator.Add(value1, value2)
  Case "-"
    result = myCalculator.Subtract(value1, value2)
  Case "*"
    result = myCalculator.Multiply(value1, value2)
  Case "/"
    result = myCalculator.Divide(value1, value2)
End Select
```

C#

```
Calculator myCalculator = new Calculator();
switch (OperatorList.SelectedValue)
{
  case "+":
    result = myCalculator.Add(value1, value2);
    break;
  case "-":
    result = myCalculator.Subtract(value1, value2);
    break;
  case "*":
    result = myCalculator.Multiply(value1, value2);
    break;
  case "/":
    result = myCalculator.Divide(value1, value2);
    break;
}
```

7. Save all your changes and open the page in the browser. The calculator still works as before; only this time the calculations are not carried out in the page's Code Behind file, but by the `Calculator` class in the `App_Code` folder instead.

How It Works

The file you created in the App_Code folder contains a class called Calculator. You learn more about classes in the final section of this chapter, but for now it's important to know that a class is like a definition for an object that can expose methods you can call at run time. In this case, the definition for the Calculator class contains four methods to perform arithmetic operations. These methods accept parameters for the left-hand and right-hand sides of the calculations. Each method simply carries out the requested calculation (Add, Subtract, and so on) and returns the result to the calling code.

The code in the Code Behind of the CalculatorDemo.aspx page first creates an *instance* of the Calculator class. That is, it creates an object in the computer's memory based on the class definition. To do this, it uses the New (new in C#) keyword to create an instance of Calculator, which is then stored in the variable myCalculator. You learn more about the New keyword later in this chapter when objects are discussed. Note that the data type of this variable is Calculator, the name of the class.

VB.NET

```
Dim myCalculator As New Calculator()
```

C#

```
Calculator myCalculator = new Calculator();
```

Once the Calculator instance is created, you can call its methods. Just as you saw earlier with other methods, the methods of the Calculator class accept parameters that are passed in by the calling code:

VB.NET

```
Case "+"
  result = myCalculator.Add(value1, value2)
```

C#

```
case "+":
  result = myCalculator.Add(value1, value2);
  break;
```

The Add method then adds the two values and returns the result as a Double, which is stored in the variable result. Just as in the first version of the calculator, at the end the result is displayed on the page with a Label control.

Functions and subroutines are a great way to organize your web application. They enable you to create reusable blocks of code that you can easily call from other locations. Because code you need more than once is defined only once, it's much easier to maintain or extend the code. If you find a bug in a function, simply fix it in its definition in the App_Code folder, and all pages using that function automatically benefit from the change. In addition to the increased maintainability, functions and subs also make your code easier to read: Instead of wading through long lists of code in a page, you just call a single function and work with the return value (if any). This makes the code easier on your brain, minimizing the chance of bugs in your application.

Functions and subs are not the only way to organize code in your .NET projects. Another common way to organize things is to use namespaces.

Organizing Code with Namespaces

Namespaces seem to cause a lot of confusion with new developers. They think they're scary, they think way too many of them exist, or they don't see the need to use them. None of this is true, and with a short explanation of them, you'll understand and maybe even like namespaces.

Namespaces are intended to solve two major problems: to organize the enormous amount of functionality in the .NET Framework and in your own code, and to avoid *name collisions*, where two different types share the same name. One common misconception about namespaces is that there is a direct relation with .NET assemblies (files with a `.dll` extension that are loaded and used by the .NET Framework), but that's not the case. Although you typically find namespaces like `System.Web.UI` in a DLL called `System.Web.dll`, it's possible (and common) to have multiple namespaces defined in a single DLL or to have a namespace be spread out over multiple assemblies. Keep that in mind when adding references to assemblies, as explained later.

To see what a namespace looks like, open one of the Code Behind files of the ASPX pages you've created so far. You'll see something similar to this:

VB.NET

```
Partial Class Demos_CalculatorDemo
    Inherits System.Web.UI.Page
```

C#

```
public partial class Demos_CalculatorDemo : System.Web.UI.Page
{
```

Note that the definition of the class name is followed by the `Inherits` keyword in VB and a colon in C#, which in turn are followed by `System.Web.UI.Page`. You see later what this `Inherits` keyword is used for. In this code, `Page` is the name of a class (a data type), which is defined in the `System.Web.UI` namespace. By placing the `Page` class in the `System.Web.UI` namespace, developers (and compilers) can see this class is about a web page. By contrast, imagine the following (fictitious) class name:

```
Microsoft.Word.Document.Page
```

This code also refers to a `Page` class. However, because it's placed in the `Microsoft.Word.Document` namespace, it's easy to see that it's referring to a page of a Word document, not a web page. This way there is no ambiguity between a web page and a Word document page. This in turn helps the compiler understand which class you are referring to.

Another benefit of namespaces is that they help you find the right data type. Instead of displaying thousands and thousands of items in the IntelliSense list, you get a few top-level namespaces. When you choose an item from that list and press the dot key (.), you get another relatively short list with types and other namespaces that live inside the chosen namespace.

Namespaces are nothing more than simple containers that you can refer to by name using the dot notation. They are used to prefix each data type that is available in your application. For example, the `Double` data type lives in the `System` namespace, thus its fully qualified name is `System.Double`. Likewise, the `Button` control you've added to your web pages lives in the `System.Web.UI.WebControls` namespace, thus its full name is `System.Web.UI.WebControls.Button`.

It's also easy to create your own namespaces. As long as they don't collide with an existing name, you can pretty much make up your own namespaces as you see fit. For example, you could wrap the `Calculator` class in the following namespace (in `Calculator.vb` or `Calculator.cs` in `App_Code`):

VB.NET

```
Namespace Wrox.Samples

  Public Class Calculator
    ...
  End Class

End Namespace
```

C#

```
namespace Wrox.Samples
{
  public class Calculator
  {
    ...
  }
}
```

With the calculator wrapped in this namespace, you could create a new instance of it like this:

VB.NET

```
Dim myCalculator As New Wrox.Samples.Calculator()
```

C#

```
Wrox.Samples.Calculator myCalculator = new Wrox.Samples.Calculator();
```

Although you get some help from IntelliSense to find the `Calculator` class, typing these long names becomes boring after a while. Fortunately, there's a fix for that as well.

After you have created your own namespaces, or if you want to use existing ones, you need to make them available in your code. You do this with the keyword `Imports` (in VB.NET) or `using` (in C#). For example, to make your `Calculator` class available in the Calculator demo page without specifying its full name, you can add the following namespace to your code:

VB.NET

```
Imports Wrox.Samples

Partial Class Demos_CalculatorDemo
  Inherits System.Web.UI.Page
```

C#

```
using Wrox.Samples;

public partial class Demos_CalculatorDemo : System.Web.UI.Page
{
```

With this `Imports/using` statement in place, you can now simply use `Calculator` again instead of `Wrox.Samples.Calculator`.

If you are using C#, you'll see a number of `using` statements by default in the Code Behind of an ASPX page for namespaces like `System` and `System.Web.UI.WebControls`. If you're using VB.NET, you won't see these references. Instead, with a VB.NET website, the default namespaces are included in the machine's global `Web.config` file under the `<namespaces>` element.

Quite often, you know the name of the class, but you don't know the namespace it lives in. VS makes it very easy to find the namespace and add the required `Imports` or `using` statement for you. Simply type the name of the class you want to use and then place the cursor in the class name and press Ctrl+. (Ctrl+Dot). You see a menu appear that lets you select the right namespace, as shown in Figure 5-5.

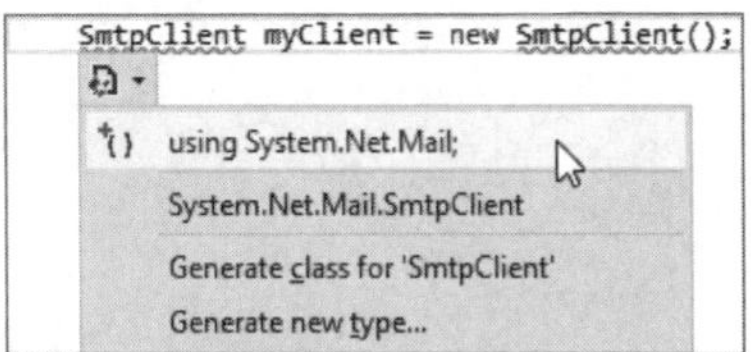

FIGURE 5-5

If the dialog box doesn't offer to add an `Imports` or `using` statement, the assembly that contains the class you're looking for may not be referenced by the project. If that's the case, right-click the website in the Solution Explorer and choose Add Reference. In the dialog box that follows you can choose from the many built-in .NET assemblies on the .NET tab or browse to a third-party assembly using the Browse button. Once the reference is added you should be able to add an `Imports` or `using` statement for the class you're looking for by pressing Ctrl+. again on the class name.

Once you start writing lots of code, you may quickly forget where you declared what, or what a variable or method is used for. It's therefore wholeheartedly recommended to put comments in your code.

Writing Comments

No matter how clean a coder you are, it's likely that someday you will run into code that makes you raise your eyebrows and think, "What on earth is this code supposed to do?" Over the years, the way you program will change; you'll learn new stuff, optimize your coding standards, and find ways to code more efficiently. To make it easier for you to recognize and understand your code now and two years from now, it's a good idea to comment your code. You have two main ways to add comments in your code files: inline and as XML comments.

Commenting Code Inline

Inline comments are written directly in between your code statements. You can use them to comment on existing variables, difficult loops, and so on. In VB.NET, you can comment out only one line at a time using the tick (`'`) character, which you place in front of the text that you want to use as a comment. To comment a single line in C#, you use two slashes (`//`). Additionally, you can use `/*` and `*/` to comment out an entire block of code in C#. The following examples show some different uses of comments:

VB.NET

```
' Usage: explains the purpose of variables, statements and so on.
' Used to store the number of miles the user has traveled last year.
Dim distanceInMiles As Integer

' Usage: comment out code that's not used (anymore).
' In this example, SomeUnfinishedMethod is commented out
' to prevent it from being executed.
' SomeUnfinishedMethod()

' Usage: End of line comments.
If User.IsInRole("Administrators") Then  ' Only allow admins in this area
End If
```

C#

```
// Usage: explains the purpose of variables, statements and so on.
// Used to store the number of miles the user has traveled last year.
int distanceInMiles;

// Usage: comment out code that's not used (anymore).
// In this example, SomeUnfinishedMethod is commented out
// to prevent it from being executed.
// SomeUnfinishedMethod();

// Usage: End of line comments.
if (User.IsInRole("Administrators")) // Only allow admins in this area
{ }

/*
 * This is a block of comments that is often used to add additional
 * information to your code, for example to explain a difficult loop. You can
 * also use this to (temporarily) comment a whole block of code.
*/
```

To comment out the code, simply type the code character (`'` or `//`) at the location where you want the comment to start. To comment out a block of code, select it in the text editor and press Ctrl+K followed by Ctrl+C. Similarly, press Ctrl+K followed by Ctrl+U to uncomment a selected block of code.

Alternatively, you can choose Edit ➪ Advanced ➪ Comment Selection or Uncomment Selection from the main menu.

Inline comments are usually good for documenting small details of your code. However, it's also a good idea to provide a high-level overview of what your code does. For example, for a method called `SendEmailMessage` it would be good to have a short description that explains what the method does and what the parameters are used for. This is exactly what XML comments are used for.

Writing XML Comments

XML comments are comments that you add as XML elements (using angle brackets: < >) in your code to describe its purpose, parameters, return value, and more. The VS IDE helps you by writing these comments. All you need to do is position your cursor on the line just before a class or method and type `'''` (three tick characters) for VB or `///` (three forward slashes) for C#. As soon as you do that, the IDE inserts XML tags for the summary and, optionally, the parameters and return type of a method. Once again, consider a `SendEmailMessage` method. It could have two parameters of type `String`: one for the e-mail address to send the message to, and one for the mail body. With the XML comments applied, the method could look like this:

VB.NET

```
''' <summary>
''' Sends out an e-mail to the address specified by emailAddress.
''' </summary>
''' <param name="emailAddress">The e-mail address of the recipient.</param>
''' <param name="mailBody">The body of the mail message.</param>
''' <returns>This method returns True when the message was sent successfully;
''' and False otherwise.</returns>
''' <remarks>Attention: this method assumes a valid mail server is
''' available.</remarks>
Public Function SendEmailMessage(emailAddress As String,
              mailBody As String) As Boolean
  ' Implementation goes here
End Function
```

C#

```
/// <summary>
/// Sends out an e-mail to the address specified by emailAddress.
/// </summary>
/// <param name="emailAddress">The e-mail address of the recipient.</param>
/// <param name="mailBody">The body of the mail message.</param>
/// <returns>This method returns true when the message was sent successfully;
/// and false otherwise.</returns>
/// <remarks>Attention: this method assumes a valid mail server is
/// available.</remarks>
public bool SendEmailMessage(string emailAddress, string mailBody)
{
  // Implementation goes here
}
```

The cool thing about this type of commenting is that the comments you type here show up in IntelliSense in the code editor when you try to call the method (see Figure 5-6).

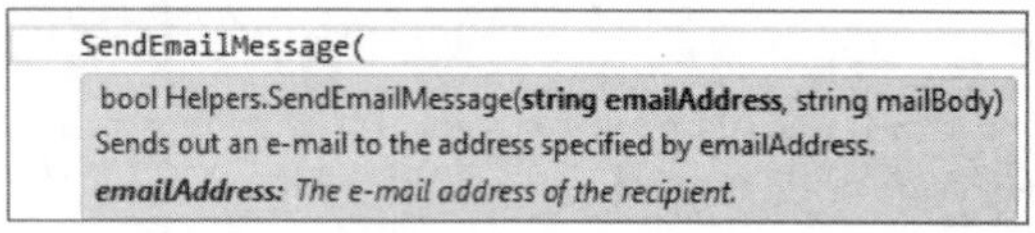

SendEmailMessage(
bool Helpers.SendEmailMessage(**string emailAddress**, string mailBody)
Sends out an e-mail to the address specified by emailAddress.
emailAddress: *The e-mail address of the recipient.*

FIGURE 5-6

This makes it much easier for you and other developers to understand the purpose of the method and its parameters.

In addition to aiding development in the code editor, you can also use the XML comments to create good-looking, MSDN-like documentation. A number of third-party tools are available that help you with this, including Microsoft's own Sandcastle (`http://msdn.microsoft.com/en-us/vstudio/bb608422.aspx`) and Document! X from Innovasys (`www.innovasys.com/`).

OBJECT ORIENTATION BASICS

A chapter about writing code in ASP.NET wouldn't be complete without a section on *object orientation* (OO). Object orientation, or object-oriented programming, is a highly popular style of programming where the software is modeled as a set of objects interacting with each other. Object orientation is at the heart of the .NET Framework. Literally everything inside the framework is an object, from simple things like integers to complex things like a `DropDownList` control, a connection to the database, or a data-driven control.

Because object orientation is such an important aspect of .NET, it's important to be familiar with the general concepts of object-oriented programming. At the same time, you don't have to be an expert on OO to be able to build websites with ASP.NET. This section gives you a 10,000-foot overview of the most important terms and concepts. This helps you get started with object orientation, so you can start building useful applications in the next chapter instead of keeping your nose in the books for the next three weeks.

Important OO Terminology

In object orientation, everything revolves around the concept of objects. In OO everything *is*, in fact, an object. But what exactly is an object? And what do classes have to do with them?

Objects

Objects are the basic building blocks of object-oriented programming languages. Just like in the real world, an object in OO-land is a thing, but stored in the computer's memory. It can be an integer holding someone's age or an open database connection to a SQL Server located on the other side of the world, but it can also be something more conceptual, like a web page. In your applications, you create a new object with the `New` (`new` in C#) keyword, as you saw with the calculator example. This process of creating new objects is called *instantiating* and the objects you create are called instances. You can instantiate complex or custom types like `Calculator`, as well as simple types like `Integers` and `Strings`:

VB.NET

```
Dim myCalculator As Calculator = New Calculator()

Dim age As Integer = New Integer()
```

C#

```
Calculator myCalculator = new Calculator();

int age = new int();
```

Because it's so common to create variables of simple types like `Integer` (`int` in C#) and `String` (`string` in C#), the compiler allows you to leave out the `new` keyword and the assignment. Therefore, the following code is functionally equivalent to the preceding `age` declaration:

VB.NET

```
Dim age As Integer
```

C#

```
int age;
```

All data types listed at the beginning of this chapter except `System.Object` can be created without the `New` keyword.

Once you have created an instance of an object, such as the `myCalculator` object, it's ready to be used. For example, you can access its methods and properties to do something useful with the object. But before you look at methods and properties, you need to understand classes.

Classes

Classes are the blueprints of objects. Just as you can use a single blueprint to build a bunch of similar houses, you can use a single class to create multiple instances of that class. So the class acts as the definition of the objects that you use in your application. At its most basic form, a class looks like this:

VB.NET

```
Public Class ClassName

End Class
```

C#

```
public class ClassName
{
}
```

Because this code simply defines an empty class, it cannot do anything useful. To give the class some behavior, you can give it *fields*, *properties*, *methods*, and *constructors*. In addition, you can let the class inherit from an existing class to give it a head start in terms of functionality and behavior. You'll come to understand these terms in the next couple of sections.

Fields

Fields are simple variables declared at the class level that can contain data. They are often used as backing variables for properties (as you'll see in the next section), but that doesn't have to be the case. Here's a quick example of a field in a `Person` class:

VB.NET

```
Public Class Person
  Private _firstName As String
End Class
```

C#

```
public class Person
{
  private string _firstName;
}
```

Fields are often marked as `Private` (`private` in C#), which makes them visible only in the class that defines them. If you have the need to expose fields to other classes as well, you should use properties, which are discussed next. Later in the chapter you learn more about the `Private` keyword and other access modifiers.

Properties

Properties of an object are the characteristics the object has. Consider a `Person` object. What kind of properties does a `Person` have? It's easy to come up with many different characteristics, but the most common are:

- First name
- Last name
- Date of birth

You define a property in a class with the `Property` keyword (in VB.NET) or with a property header similar to a method in C#. In both languages, you use a `Get` block (`get` in C#) and a `Set` block (`set` in C#) to define the so-called getters and setters of the property. The getter is accessed when an object is asked for the value of a specific property, and the setter is used to assign a value to the property. Properties only provide access to underlying data stored in the object; they don't contain the actual data. To store the data, you need what is called a *backing variable*. This is often a simple field defined in the class that is able to store the value for the external property. In the following example, the variable `_firstName` is the backing variable for the `FirstName` property:

VB.NET

```
Public Class Person
  Private _firstName As String
  Public Property FirstName() As String
    Get
      Return _firstName
    End Get
    Set(value As String)
      _firstName = value
    End Set
  End Property
End Class
```

C#

```
public class Person
{
  private string _firstName;
  public string FirstName
  {
    get { return _firstName; }
    set { _firstName = value; }
  }
}
```

It is common to prefix the private backing variables with an underscore, followed by the first word in all lowercase, optionally followed by more words that start with a capital again. So the `FirstName` property has a backing variable called `_firstName`, `LastName` has one called `_lastName`, and so on. This way, all variables that apply to the entire class are nicely packed together in the IntelliSense list. Simply type an underscore in your code and you'll get the full list of private variables. Note that the underscore is typically not used when defining variables inside a function or a subroutine.

Just like the Public keyword you saw earlier, Private is also an access modifier. You learn more about access modifiers later in this chapter.

The main reason for a property in a class is to *encapsulate* data. The idea is that a property enables you to control the data that is being assigned to it. This way, you can perform validation or manipulation of the data before it's stored in the underlying backing variable. Imagine that one of the business rules of your application states that all first names must be written with the first letter as a capital. In non–object-oriented languages, the developer setting the name would have to keep this rule in mind every time a variable was filled with a first name. In an OO approach, you can make the FirstName property responsible for this rule so others don't have to worry about it anymore. You can do this type of data manipulation in the setter of the property:

VB.NET

```
Set(value As String)
  If Not String.IsNullOrEmpty(value) Then
    _firstName = value.Substring(0, 1).ToUpper() & value.Substring(1)
  Else
    _firstName = String.Empty
  End If
End Set
```

C#

```
set
{
  if (!string.IsNullOrEmpty(value))
  {
    _firstName = value.Substring(0, 1).ToUpper() + value.Substring(1);
  }
  else
  {
    _firstName = string.Empty;
  }
}
```

This code demonstrates that in both VB.NET and C#, the value parameter is accessible, just as a parameter is accessible to a method. The value parameter contains the value that is being assigned to the property. In VB.NET, the value parameter is defined explicitly in the property's setter. In C# it's not specified explicitly, but you can access it nonetheless.

The code first checks if the value that is being passed is not Nothing (null in C#) and that it doesn't contain an empty string, using the handy String.IsNullOrEmpty method.

The code in the If block then takes the first letter of value, using the Substring method of the String class, to which it passes the values 0 and 1. The 0 indicates the start of the substring and the 1 indicates the length of the string that must be returned. String indexing is zero-based as well, so a start of 0 and a length of 1 effectively returns the first character of the value parameter. This character is then changed to uppercase using ToUpper(). Finally, the code takes the remainder of the value parameter using Substring again and assigns the combined name back to the backing variable. In this call to Substring, only the start index is passed, which returns the string from that position to the end.

You can now use code that sets the name with arbitrary casing. But when you try to access the name again, the first name will always begin with a proper first character:

VB.NET

```
Dim myPerson As Person = New Person() ' Create a new instance of Person
myPerson.FirstName = "imar"           ' Accessing setter to change the value

Label1.Text = myPerson.FirstName      ' Accessing getter that now returns Imar
```

C#

```
Person myPerson = new Person();       // Create a new instance of Person
myPerson.FirstName = "imar";          // Accessing setter to change the value

Label1.Text = myPerson.FirstName;     // Accessing getter that now returns Imar
```

For simple properties that don't need any data manipulation or validation, you can use so-called *automatic properties*. With these properties, you can use a much more condensed syntax without the need for a private backing variable. When the code is compiled, the compiler creates a hidden backing variable for you, and you'll need to refer to the public property. Here's the `DateOfBirth` property of the `Person` class, written as an automatic property:

VB.NET

```
Public Property DateOfBirth As DateTime
```

C#

```
public DateTime DateOfBirth { get; set; }
```

The Visual Basic implementation of automatic properties has one advantage over the C# version: You can declare the property and give it a value in one shot. The following snippet defines a `CreateDate` property and assigns it with the current date and time:

VB.NET

```
Public Property CreateDate As DateTime = DateTime.Now
```

To assign a default value to an automatic property in C#, you need to set its value using constructors, which are discussed later.

If you later decide you need to write code in the getter or the setter of the property, it's easy to extend the relevant code blocks without breaking your existing applications. Until that time, you have nice, clean property definitions that don't clutter up your class.

Creating Read-Only and Write-Only Properties

At times, read-only or write-only properties make a lot of sense. For example, the ID of an object could be read-only if it is assigned by the database automatically. When the object is constructed from the database, the ID is assigned to the private backing variable. The public `Id` property is then made read-only to stop calling code from accidentally changing it. Likewise, you can have a write-only property for security reasons. For example, you could have a `Password` property on a `Person` object that you can only assign to if you know it, but no longer read it afterward. Internally, code within the class can still access the backing variables to work with the password value. Another good candidate for a read-only property is one that returns a combination of data. Consider a `FullName` property of a `Person` class that returns a combination of the `FirstName` and `LastName` properties. You use the setter of each individual property to assign data, but you can have a read-only property that returns the concatenated values.

Read-only or write-only properties in C# are simple: Just leave out the setter (for a read-only property) or the getter (for a write-only property). VB.NET is a bit more verbose and wants you to specify the keyword ReadOnly or WriteOnly explicitly. The following code snippet shows a read-only FullName property in both VB.NET and C#:

VB.NET

```
Public ReadOnly Property FullName() As String
  Get
    Return _firstName & " " & _lastName
  End Get
End Property
```

C#

```
public string FullName
{
  get { return _firstName + " " + _lastName; }
}
```

When you try to assign a value to a read-only property, you'll get a compilation error in VS.

Similar to properties, objects can also have methods.

Methods

If properties are the things that a class has (its characteristics), then methods are the things a class can do or the operations it can perform. A Car class, for example, has properties such as Brand, Model, and Color. Its methods could be Drive(), Brake(), and OpenDoors(). Methods give objects the behavior that enables them to do something.

You have already seen methods at work earlier, when this chapter discussed some ways to write organized code using subs and functions. You simply add methods to a class by writing a function or a sub between the start and end elements of the class. For example, imagine the Person class has a Save method that enables the object to persist itself in the database. The method's signature could look like this:

VB.NET

```
Public Class Person
  Public Sub Save()
    ' Implementation goes here
  End Sub
End Class
```

C#

```
public class Person
{
  public void Save()
  {
    // Implementation goes here
  }
}
```

If you want to call the Save method to have the Person object save itself to the database, you create an instance of it, set the relevant properties such as FirstName, and then call Save:

VB.NET

```
Dim myPerson As Person = New Person()
myPerson.FirstName = "Jim"
myPerson.Save()
```

C#

```
Person myPerson = new Person();
myPerson.FirstName = "Jim";
myPerson.Save();
```

The `Save` method would then know how to save the `Person` in the database.

Methods can also have parameters, as you saw earlier in the section on XML comments. The `SendEmailMessage` method accepts two parameters — one for the e-mail address and one for the message body — whose values are then accessible from within the method.

Note that a new instance of the `Person` class is created with the `New` (`new` in C#) keyword followed by the class name. When this code fires, it calls the object's *constructor*, which is used to create instances of objects.

Constructors

Constructors are special methods in a class that help you create an instance of your object. They run as soon as you try to create an instance of a class, so they are a great place to initialize your objects to some default state. Earlier you learned that you create a new instance of an object using the `New` (`new` in C#) keyword:

VB.NET

```
Dim myCalculator As Calculator = New Calculator()
```

C#

```
Calculator myCalculator = new Calculator();
```

The `New` keyword is followed by the object's constructor: the name of the class. By default, when you create a new class file in VS, you get a default constructor for C# but not for VB.NET. That's not really a problem, though, because the compiler generates a default constructor for you if no other constructor exists. A default constructor has no arguments and takes the name of the class in C# and the reserved keyword `New` in VB.NET:

VB.NET

```
Public Class Person
  Public Sub New()

  End Sub
End Class
```

C#

```
public class Person
{
  public Person()
  {

  }
}
```

Although this default constructor is nice for creating standard instances of your classes, sometimes it is really useful to be able to send some information into the class up front, so it's readily available as soon as it is constructed. For example, with the Person class, it could be useful to pass in the first and last names and the date of birth to the constructor so that data is available immediately afterward. To enable this scenario, you can create a specialized constructor. To have the constructor accept the names and the date of birth, you need the following code:

VB.NET

```
Public Sub New(firstName As String, lastName As String, dateOfBirth As DateTime)
  _firstName = firstName
  _lastName = lastName
  _dateOfBirth = dateOfBirth
End Sub
```

C#

```
public Person(string firstName, string lastName, DateTime dateOfBirth)
{
  _firstName = firstName;
  _lastName = lastName;
  _dateOfBirth = dateOfBirth;
}
```

With this code, you can create a new Person object:

VB.NET

```
Dim myPerson As Person = New Person("Imar", "Spaanjaars", New DateTime(1971, 8, 9))
```

C#

```
Person myPerson = new Person("Imar", "Spaanjaars", new DateTime(1971, 8, 9));
```

The constructor accepts the values passed to it and assigns them to the private backing variables, so right after this line of code, the myPerson object is fully initialized.

You can have multiple constructors for the same class, as long as each one has a different method signature.

Visual Basic supports a slightly different syntax to declare and initialize an object in one fell swoop using the Dim *myVariable* As New *ClassName* syntax. The following code is equivalent to the previous instantiation of a Person instance:

```
Dim myPerson As New Person("Imar", "Spaanjaars", New DateTime(1971, 8, 9))
```

In addition to constructors, .NET offers another quick way to create an object and initialize a few properties: *object initializers*. With an object initializer, you provide the initial values for some of the properties at the same time you declare an instance of your objects. The following code creates a Person object and assigns it a value for the FirstName and LastName properties:

VB.NET

```
Dim myPerson As New Person() With {.FirstName = "Imar", .LastName = "Spaanjaars"}
```

C#

```
Person myPerson = new Person() { FirstName = "Imar", LastName = "Spaanjaars" };
```

In VB.NET, you need the `With` keyword in front of the properties list. In addition, you need to prefix each property name with a dot (`.`). Other than that, the syntax is the same for both languages. Object initializers are great if you need to set a bunch of properties on an object quickly without being forced to write specialized versions of the constructors.

Although it's useful to have this `Person` class in your application, at times you may need specialized versions of a `Person`. For example, your application may require classes like `Employee` and `Student`. What should you do in this case? Create two copies of the `Person` class and name them `Employee` and `Student`, respectively?

Although this approach certainly works, it has a few large drawbacks. The biggest problem is the duplication of code. If you decide to add a `SocialSecurityNumber` property, you now need to add it in multiple locations: in the general `Person` class and in the `Employee` and `Student` classes. *Object inheritance*, a major pillar of object orientation, is designed to solve problems of this kind.

Inheritance

Earlier you learned that `System.Object` is the parent of all other data types in .NET, including all the built-in types and types that you define yourself, meaning that each type in .NET (except `Object` itself) inherits from `Object`. One of the benefits of inheritance is that you can define a behavior at a high level (for example in the `Object` class) that is available to *inheriting* classes automatically without the need to duplicate that code. In the .NET Framework, the `Object` class defines a few members that all other objects inherit, including the `ToString()` method.

To let one class inherit another, you need to use the `Inherits` keyword in VB.NET and the colon (`:`) in C#, as shown in the following example that defines a `Student` class that inherits `Person`:

VB.NET

```
Public Class Student
    Inherits Person
```

C#

```
public class Student : Person
{
}
```

To see how inheritance works, think again about the `Person` class shown in earlier examples. That class had a few properties, such as `FirstName` and `LastName`, and a `Save` method. But if it is inheriting from `Object`, does it also have a `ToString()` method? You bet it does. Figure 5-7 shows the relationship between the `Object` class and the `Person` class that inherits from `Object`.

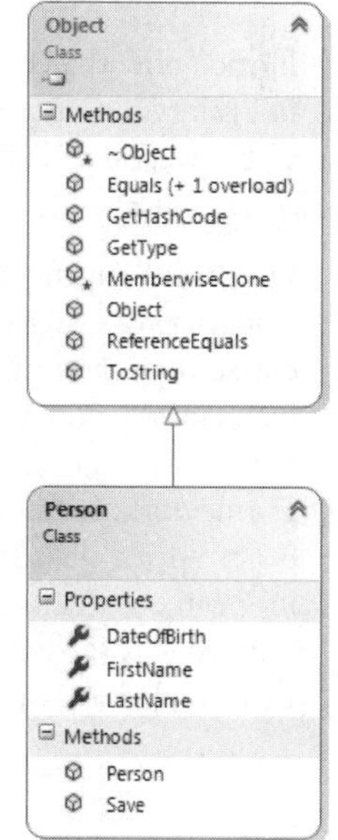

FIGURE 5-7

Figure 5-7 shows that `Person` inherits from `Object` (indicated by the arrow pointing in the direction of the class that is being inherited from), which in turn means that a `Person` instance can do whatever an `Object` can do. So, for example, you can call `ToString()` on your `Person` object:

```
Label1.Text = myPerson.ToString()                ' Writes out Person
```

The default behavior of the `ToString()` method defined in `Object` is to say its own class name. In the preceding example, it means that the `Person` class inherits this behavior and thus says `Person` as its name. Usually, this default behavior is not enough, and it would be much more useful if the `Person` could return the full name of the person it is representing, for example. You can easily do this by *overriding* the `ToString()` method. Overriding a method or property redefines the behavior the class inherits from its parent class. To override a method you use the keyword `Overrides` in VB.NET and `override` in C#. The following snippet redefines the behavior of `ToString` in the `Person` class:

VB.NET

```
Public Overrides Function ToString() As String
  Return FullName & ", born at " & _dateOfBirth.ToShortDateString()
End Function
```

C#

```
public override string ToString()
{
  return FullName + ", born at " + _dateOfBirth.ToShortDateString();
}
```

With this definition of `ToString` in the `Person` class, it no longer returns the word Person, but now returns the full name of the person it is representing:

```
Label1.Text = myPerson.ToString() ' Imar Spaanjaars, born at 8/9/1971
```

Notice how the code uses the read-only `FullName` property to avoid coding the logic of concatenating the two names again. You can't just override any method member you want to. For a method to be overridable, the parent class needs to mark the member with the keyword `virtual` (in C#) or `Overridable` (in VB.NET).

Object inheritance in .NET enables you to create a hierarchy of objects that enhance, or add functionality to, other objects. This enables you to start out with a generic base class (`Object`). Other classes can then inherit from this class, adding specialized behavior. If you need even more specialized classes, you can inherit again from the class that inherits from `Object`, thus creating a hierarchy of classes that keep getting more specialized. This principle works for many classes in the .NET Framework, including the `Page` class. You may not realize it, but every ASPX page you create in VS is actually a class that inherits from the class `System.Web.UI.Page`. This `Page` class in turn inherits from `TemplateControl`, which inherits from `Control`, which inherits from `Object`. The entire hierarchy is shown in Figure 5-8. At the bottom you see the class `MyWebPage`, which could be a Code Behind class of a page such as `MyWebPage.aspx`.

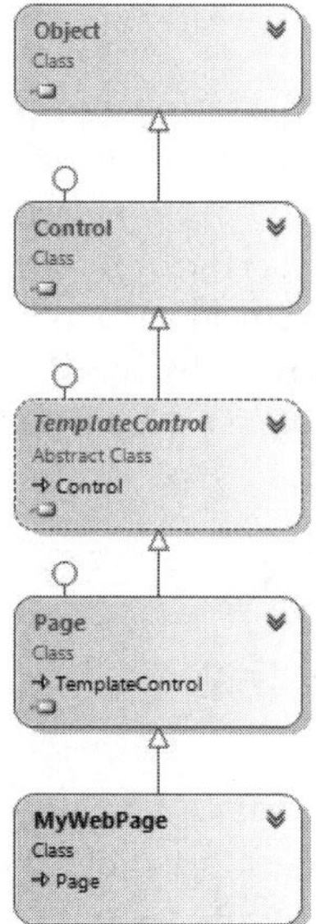

FIGURE 5-8

In Figure 5-8 you can see that `TemplateControl` is an *abstract class* — a class that cannot be instantiated; that is, you cannot use `New` (`new` in C#) to create a new instance of it. It serves solely as a common base class for others (like `Page`) that can inherit from it. The exact classes between `Page` and `Object` are not really relevant at this stage, but what's important is that your page inherits all the behavior that the `Page` class has. The fact that all your ASPX pages inherit from `Page` is more useful than you may think at first. Because it inherits from `Page`, you get loads of properties and methods defined in this class for free. For example, the `Page` class exposes a `Title` property that, when set, ends up as a `<title>` element in the page. Your page can simply set this property, and the parent `Page` class handles the rest for you:

VB.NET

```
Title = "Beginning ASP.NET 4.5 in C# and VB from Wrox"
```

C#

```
Title = "Beginning ASP.NET 4.5 in C# and VB from Wrox";
```

You use inheritance in the next chapter when you create a `BasePage` class that serves as the parent class for most of the pages you create in the Planet Wrox website.

In earlier examples, including the override for the `ToString()` method, you have seen the keyword `Public`. Additionally, when creating backing variables, you saw the keyword `Private`. These keywords are called *access modifiers* and determine the visibility of your code.

Access Modifiers

Earlier in this chapter I mentioned that a core concept of OO is encapsulation. By creating members such as functions and properties, you make an object responsible for the implementation. Other objects interacting with this object consider those methods and properties as black boxes. That is, they pass some data in and optionally expect some result back. How the method performs its work is of no interest to them; it should just work as advertised. To enable an object to shield some of its inner operations, you need a way to control access to types and members. You do this by specifying an access modifier in front of the class, property, or method name. The following table lists the available access modifiers for C# and VB.NET and explains their purpose.

C#	VB.NET	Description
public	Public	The class or member can be accessed from everywhere, including code outside the current application.
protected	Protected	Code with a protected access modifier is available only within the type that defines it or within types that inherit from it. For example, a protected member defined in the `Page` class is accessible to your ASPX page because it inherits from `Page`.
internal	Friend	Limits the accessibility of your code to other code within the same *assembly*. An assembly is a set of one or more compiled code files (either an `.exe` or a `.dll` file) containing reusable .NET code.
private	Private	A class or member that is accessible only within the type that defines it. For example, with the `Person` class, the `_firstName` variable is accessible only from within the `Person` class. Other code, like an ASPX page, cannot access this field directly, and needs to access the public `FirstName` property to get or set the first name of a person.

Of these four access modifiers, only `protected` and `internal` (`Protected` and `Friend` in VB) can be combined. The other two must be used separately. By combining `protected` and `internal`, you can create members that are accessible by the current class and any class that inherits from it in the current assembly only.

Using access modifiers, you can now create properties that are read-only for external code but that can still be set from within the class by marking the getter as private.

As with some of the other OO concepts, you won't be spending half your day specifying access modifiers in your code. However, it's good to know that they exist and what they do. That way, you may have a clue as to why sometimes your classes don't show up in the IntelliSense list. There's a fair chance you forgot to specify the `public` access modifier (`Public` in VB.NET) on the class in that case. The default is `internal` (`Friend` in VB.NET), which makes the class visible to other classes in the same assembly but hides it from code outside the assembly. Adding the keyword `public` or `Public` in front of the class definition should fix the problem.

Events

The final important topic that needs to be discussed in this chapter is events. ASP.NET is an *event-driven* environment, which means that code can execute based on certain events that occur in your application. Events are *raised* by certain objects in the application and then *handled* by others. Many objects in the .NET Framework are capable of raising an event, and you can even add your own events to classes that you write.

To be able to handle an event raised by an object, you need to write an *event handler*, which is basically a normal method with a special signature. You can wire up this event handler to the event using event wiring syntax, although VS takes care of writing that code most of the time for you. When an object, such as a control in a web page, raises an event, it may have the need to pass additional information to the event handler, to inform it about relevant data that caused or influenced the event. You can send out this information using an *event arguments class*, which is the class `System.EventArgs` or any class that inherits it.

To see how all these terms fit together, consider what happens when you click a button in a web page. When you click it, the client-side button in the browser causes a postback. At the server, the `Button` control sees it was clicked in the browser and then raises its `Click` event. It's as if the button says: "Oh, look, everyone. I just got clicked. In case anyone is interested, here are some details." Usually, the code that is interested in the button's `Click` event is your own page, which needs to have an event handler to handle the click. You can create an event handler for the `Button` by double-clicking it in the designer, or you can wire it up using Markup View as you saw in Chapter 4. Alternatively, you can double-click the relevant event on the Events tab of the Properties Grid. You open this tab by clicking the button with the lightning bolt on the toolbar of the Properties Grid (see Figure 5-9.)

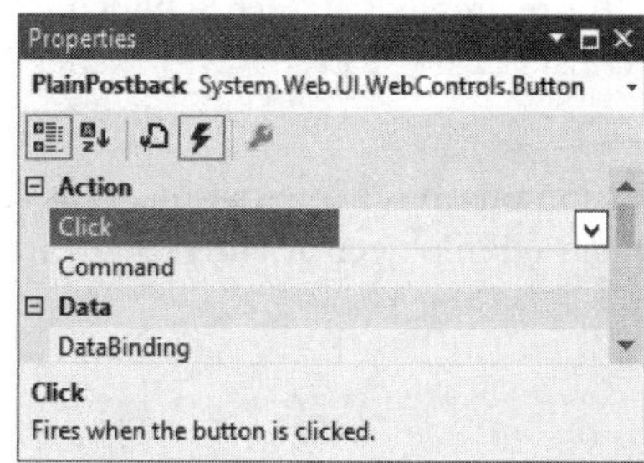

FIGURE 5-9

If you double-click the control in Design View or the event name in the Properties Grid, VS writes the code for the event handler for you. The following snippet shows the handler for a `Button` control's `Click` event in VB.NET and C#:

VB.NET

```
Protected Sub Button1_Click(sender As Object, e As EventArgs) _
        Handles Button1.Click
End Sub
```

C#

```
protected void Button1_Click(object sender, EventArgs e)
{
}
```

In the VB.NET example, you see a standard method with some arguments, followed by `Handles Button1.Click`. This is the event wiring code that hooks up the `Button` control's `Click` event to the `Button1_Click` method. Now, whenever the button is clicked, the code inside `Button1_Click` is executed.

The C# version doesn't have this `Handles` keyword. Instead, with C# you'll find that VS has added the following bold code to the `Button` control in the markup of the page:

```
<asp:Button ID="Button1" runat="server" Text="Button" OnClick="Button1_Click" />
```

With this piece of markup, the compiler generates the necessary code to link up the `Button1_Click` method to the `Click` event of the button. At run time you'll see the exact same behavior: When you click the button, the code in `Button1_Click` is executed. Note that if you wire up an event in Markup View in VB.NET, you get the same behavior as in C#; in that case the `Handles` keyword is omitted from the Code Behind because there's already an `On` handler in Markup View.

You can also see that this `Button1_Click` event handler has two parameters: an `Object` called `sender` and an `EventArgs` class called `e`. This is a standard .NET naming scheme and is followed by all objects that generate events. The `sender` parameter contains a reference to the object that triggered the event, `Button1` in this example. This enables you to find out who triggered an event in case you wired up multiple events to the same event handler.

The second parameter is an instance of the `EventArgs` class and supplies additional arguments to the event. With a button's click, there is no additional relevant data to submit, so the plain and empty `EventArgs` class is used. However, in later chapters (for example, Chapter 9, which deals with data-driven Web Forms), you see some examples of classes that fire events with richer information.

With the concepts of events, you have come to the end of the section on object orientation. This section should have familiarized you with the most important terms used in object-oriented programming. You see practical examples of these concepts in the remainder of this book.

PRACTICAL TIPS ON PROGRAMMING

The following list presents some practical tips on programming:

- Always give your variables meaningful names. For simple loop counters you can use `i`, although `loopCount` probably describes the purpose of the variable much better. Don't prefix variables with the word `var`. All variables are variables, so adding `var` only adds noise to your code. Consider useful names such as `_firstName` and `_categoryId` as opposed to `strFName`, `varFirstName`, or `catI` for private fields, and names like `FirstName` and `Person` for public properties and classes, respectively.

- Experiment and experiment. Even more so than with working with controls and ASPX pages, the best way to learn how to program is by actually doing it. Just type in some code and hit Ctrl+F5 to see how the code behaves. The compiler will bark at you when something is wrong, providing you with useful hints on how to fix it. Don't be afraid to mess anything up; just keep trying variations until the code does what you want it to do. If you can't make your code work, check out Chapter 18, which deals with debugging. You'll find useful tips to locate and fix many of the errors that may occur in your code.
- When writing functions or subroutines, try to minimize the number of lines of code. Usually, methods with more than 40 or 50 lines of code are a sign of bad design. When you see such code, consider the option to move certain parts to their own routine. This makes your code much easier to understand, leading to better code with fewer bugs. Even if a method is used only once, keeping a chunk of code in a separate method can significantly increase the readability and organization of your code.
- When writing comments in your code, try to describe the general purpose of the code instead of explaining obvious statements. For example, this comment (seen many times in real code) is completely useless and only adds noise:

```
Dim loopCount As Integer = 0      ' Declare loopCount and initialize it to zero
```

  Anyone with just a little bit of coding experience can see what this code does.

SUMMARY

Although programming can get really complex, the bare basics that you need to understand are relatively easy to grasp. The fun thing about programming is that you don't have to be an expert to make useful programs. You can start with a simple Hello World example and work from there, each time expanding your view on code a little.

This chapter covered two main topics. First, you got an introduction to programming in .NET using either C# or VB.NET. You saw what data types and variables are and learned about operators, decision making, and loops. You also saw how to write organized code using functions, subs, and namespaces and how to add comments to your code.

The final section of this chapter dealt with object orientation. Though object orientation in itself is a very large subject, the basics are easy to pick up. In this chapter you learned about the basic elements of OO programming: classes, methods, properties, and constructors. You also learned a bit about inheritance, the driving force behind object-oriented design.

In the next chapter, which deals with creating consistent-looking web pages, you see inheritance again when you create a `BasePage` class that serves as the parent for most of the Code Behind classes in the Planet Wrox project.

EXERCISES

1. Considering the fact that the oldest person in the world lived to be 122, what's the best numeric data type to store a person's age? Bonus points if you come up with an even better alternative to store someone's age.

2. What does the following code do?

VB.NET

```
DeleteButton.Visible = Not DeleteButton.Visible
```

C#

```
DeleteButton.Visible = !DeleteButton.Visible;
```

3. Given the following class `Person`, what would the code look like for a new class `Student` that contains a string property called `StudentId`? Make use of inheritance to create this new class.

VB.NET

```
Public Class Person
  Public Property Name As String
End Class
```

C#

```
public class Person
{
  public string Name { get; set; }
}
```

You can find answers to these exercises in Appendix A.

▶ WHAT YOU LEARNED IN THIS CHAPTER

Class	A blueprint for objects in a programming language
Collection	A special data type that is capable of holding multiple objects at the same time
Encapsulation	Hiding the inner workings and data of a class from the outside world in order to better manage and protect that data
Instantiating	The process of creating a new object in memory based on a type's definition
Method	An operation on an object, like `Brake()` for a `Car` class
Namespace	A way to structure classes and other types in a hierarchical manner
Object Orientation	A popular style of programming where the software is modeled as a set of objects interacting with each other
Overriding	Redefining the behavior in a child class of a member defined in a parent class
Property	A characteristic of an object, like the first name of a person

Creating Consistent Looking Websites

WHAT YOU WILL LEARN IN THIS CHAPTER:

- How to use master and content pages that enable you to define the global look and feel of a web page
- How to work with a centralized base page that enables you to define common behavior for all pages in your site
- How to create themes to define the look and feel of your site with an option for the user to choose a theme at run time
- How to create skins to make site-wide changes to control layout
- What the ASP.NET page life cycle is and why it's important

WROX.COM CODE DOWNLOADS FOR THIS CHAPTER

You can find the wrox.com code downloads for this chapter on the Download Code tab at `www.wrox.com/remtitle.cgi?isbn=1118311809`. The code is in the Chapter 6 download.

When you're building a website you should strive to make the layout and behavior as consistent as possible. Consistency gives your site a professional appearance and it helps your visitors to find their way around the site. Fortunately, ASP.NET 4.5 and Visual Studio 2012 offer a number of great features and tools to implement a consistent design, helping you to create great-looking pages in no time.

In previous chapters you learned how to work with VS, HTML5, CSS, and server controls to create your web pages visually. Chapter 5 introduced you to programming in ASP.NET. This chapter is the first that combines these concepts, by showing you—among many other things—how to use programming code to change the appearance of the site.

The first section shows you how to create a master page that defines the general look and feel of a page. The ASPX pages in your site can then use this master page without the need to repeat the general layout. The remaining sections of this chapter build on top of this master page.

CONSISTENT PAGE LAYOUT WITH MASTER PAGES

With most websites, only part of the page changes when you go from one page to another. The parts that don't change usually include common regions like the header, a menu, and the footer. To create web pages with a consistent layout, you need a way to define these relatively static regions in a single template file. Versions of ASP.NET prior to 2.0 did not have a template solution, so you were forced to duplicate your page layout on every single page in the website, or resort to weird programming tricks. Fortunately, this is no longer the case due to *master pages*. The biggest benefit of master pages is that they enable you to define the look and feel of all the pages in your site in a single location. This means that if you want to change the layout of your site—for instance, if you want to move the menu from the left to the right—you need to modify only the master page, and the pages based on this master pick up the changes automatically.

When master pages were introduced in ASP.NET 2.0, they were quickly embraced by the developer community as *the* template solution for ASP.NET pages because they are very easy to use. Even better, VS has great design-time support, because it enables you to create and view your pages at design time during development, rather than only in the browser at run time.

To some extent, a master page looks like a normal ASPX page. It contains static HTML such as the `<html>`, `<head>`, and `<body>` elements, and it can also contain other HTML and ASP.NET Server Controls. Inside the master page, you set up the markup that you want to repeat on every page, like the general structure of the page and the menu.

However, a master page is not a true ASPX page and cannot be requested in the browser directly; it only serves as the template on which real web pages—called *content pages*—are based.

Instead of the `@ Page` directive that you saw in Chapter 4, a master page uses an `@ Master` directive that identifies the file as a master page:

VB.NET

```
<%@ Master Language="VB" %>
```

C#

```
<%@ Master Language="C#" %>
```

Just like a normal ASPX page, a master page can have a Code Behind file, identified by its `CodeFile` and `Inherits` attributes:

VB.NET

```
<%@ Master Language="VB" CodeFile="Frontend.master.vb"
          Inherits="MasterPages_Frontend" %>
```

C#

```
<%@ Master Language="C#" AutoEventWireup="true" CodeFile="Frontend.master.cs"
          Inherits="MasterPages_Frontend" %>
```

To create regions that content pages can fill in, you define `ContentPlaceHolder` controls in your page like this:

```
<asp:ContentPlaceHolder ID="ContentPlaceHolder1" runat="server">
</asp:ContentPlaceHolder>
```

You can create as many placeholders as you like, although you usually need only a few to create a flexible page layout.

The content pages, which are essentially normal ASPX files, without the code that they're going to take from the master page, are connected to a master page using the `MasterPageFile` attribute of the `Page` directive:

VB.NET

```
<%@ Page Title="" Language="VB" MasterPageFile="~/MasterPages/Frontend.master"
        AutoEventWireup="false" CodeFile="Default.aspx.vb" Inherits="_Default">
```

C#

```
<%@ Page Title="" Language="C#" MasterPageFile="~/MasterPages/Frontend.master"
        AutoEventWireup="true" CodeFile="Default.aspx.cs" Inherits="_Default">
```

The page-specific content is then put inside a `Content` control that points to the relevant `ContentPlaceHolder`:

```
<asp:Content ID="Content1" ContentPlaceHolderID="ContentPlaceHolder1"
          runat="Server">
</asp:Content>
```

Note that the `ContentPlaceHolderID` attribute of the `Content` control points to the `ContentPlaceHolder` that is defined in the master page. Right now it points to the default name of `ContentPlaceHolder1`, but in a later exercise you see how to change this.

At run time, when the page is requested, the markup from the master page and the content page are merged, processed, and sent to the browser. Figure 6-1 shows a diagram of the master page with just one `ContentPlaceHolder` and the content page that results in the final page that is sent to the browser.

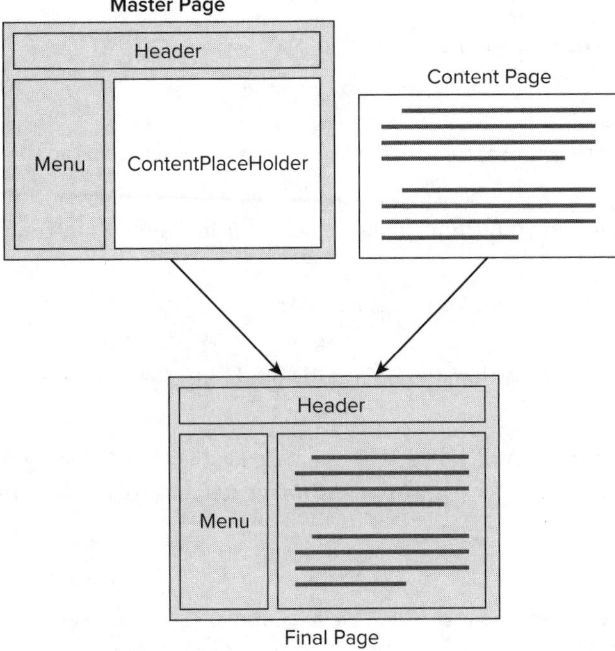

FIGURE 6-1

To see this process in action, the following sections guide you through creating master and content pages.

Creating Master Pages

You can add master pages to the site using the Add New Item dialog box. You can place them in any custom folder in the site, including the root folder, but from an organizational point of view, it's often easier to store them in a separate folder. Just like normal ASPX pages, they support the inline code model as well as the Code Behind model. The master pages used in the Planet Wrox project use the Code Behind model exclusively. In the following exercise, you learn how to create a simple master page and add some HTML to it to define the general structure of the pages in your website.

TRY IT OUT Creating a Master Page

1. Open the Planet Wrox project in Visual Studio if it is not open already.
2. In Chapter 2 you created a folder called `MasterPages` to hold your master pages and then added a single master page to that folder. If you didn't carry out that exercise, add the master page now. To do this, create the `MasterPages` folder in the root of the site, right-click the new folder, choose Add ⇨ Add New Item, and select the Master Page item. Make sure that the master page uses Code Behind and that it is using your preferred programming language. Name the master page **`Frontend.master`**. Finally, click Add.

3. Add the following highlighted code between the <form> tags of the master page, replacing the <div> tags and the ContentPlaceHolder that VS added for you when you created the master page. Note that this is almost the same code you added to Default.aspx in Chapter 3, except for the <asp:ContentPlaceHolder> element and the <a> element within the Header <div>. The <a> element takes the user back to the homepage, and will be styled later.

```
<form id="form1" runat="server">
  <div id="PageWrapper">
    <header><a href="/">Header Goes Here</a></header>
    <nav>Menu Goes Here</nav>
    <section id="MainContent">
      <asp:ContentPlaceHolder ID="cpMainContent" runat="server">
      </asp:ContentPlaceHolder>
    </section>
    <aside id="Sidebar">Sidebar Goes Here</aside>
    <footer>Footer Goes Here</footer>
  </div>
</form>
```

Make sure that you have the ContentPlaceHolder within the MainContent <section> tags. You can drag one from the Toolbox onto the page or enter the code directly, using IntelliSense's helpful hints. In both cases you should give the control an ID of cpMainContent.

4. Next, switch the master page into Design View and then drag Styles.css from the Styles folder in the Solution Explorer onto the master page. As soon as you drop the file, VS updates the Design View and shows the layout for the site that you created in Chapter 3. If the design doesn't change, switch to Markup View and ensure there's a <link> tag in the head of the page pointing to your CSS file:

```
  <asp:ContentPlaceHolder ID="head" runat="server">
  </asp:ContentPlaceHolder>
  <link href="../Styles/Styles.css" rel="stylesheet" type="text/css" />
</head>
```

The page should now look like Figure 6-2 in Design View.

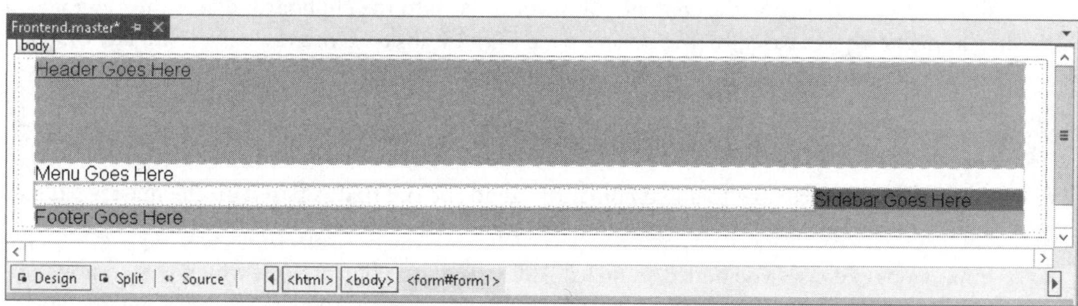

FIGURE 6-2

Note the area with the purple border around it between the menu and the footer region in your Design View. This is the ContentPlaceHolder control that is used by the content pages. You see how to use it in the next exercise.

5. Drag the file modernizr-2.6.2.js from the Scripts folder into the <head> section of the Master Page below the CSS file. Then manually replace the two leading periods with a slash, like this:

```
<script src="/Scripts/modernizr-2.6.2.js"></script>
```

6. You can save and close the master page because you're done with it for now.

How It Works

Within VS, master pages behave like normal pages. You can add HTML and server controls to them, and you can manage the page both in Markup and Design View. The big difference is, of course, that a master page isn't a true page itself; it only serves as a template for other pages in your site.

In the next section you see how to use this master page as the template for a content page.

Creating Content Pages

A master page is useless without a content page that uses it. Generally, you'll have only a few master pages, whereas you can have many content pages in your site. To base a content page on a master page, check the Select Master Page option at the bottom right of the Add New Item dialog box when you add a new Web Form to your site. Alternatively, you can set the MasterPageFile attribute on the page directly in the Markup View of the page. You saw this @ Page directive earlier in this chapter when master and content pages were introduced.

Content pages can only directly contain Content controls that each map to a ContentPlaceHolder control in the master page. These content controls in turn can contain standard markup like HTML and server control declarations. Because the entire markup in a content page needs to be wrapped by <asp:Content> tags, it's not easy to turn an existing ASPX page into a content page. Usually the easiest thing to do is copy the content you want to keep to the clipboard, delete the old page, and then add a new page based on the master page to the website. Once the page is added, you can paste the markup within the <asp:Content> tags. You see how this works in the following exercise.

TRY IT OUT Adding a Content Page

In this Try It Out you see how to add a content page to the site that is based on the master page you created earlier. Once the page is added, you add content to the <asp:Content> regions.

1. In previous exercises you added standard ASPX pages to your project, which should now be "upgraded" to make use of the new master page. If you want to keep the welcome text you added to Default.aspx earlier, copy all the HTML between the MainContent <section> tags to the clipboard (that is, the <h1> and the two <p> elements that you created earlier) and then delete the Default.aspx page from the Solution Explorer. Next, right-click the website in the Solution Explorer and choose Add ➪ Add New Item. Select the correct programming language, click Web

Form, name the page **`Default.aspx`**, and then, at the bottom of the dialog box, select the check boxes for Place Code in Separate File and Select Master Page, as shown in Figure 6-3.

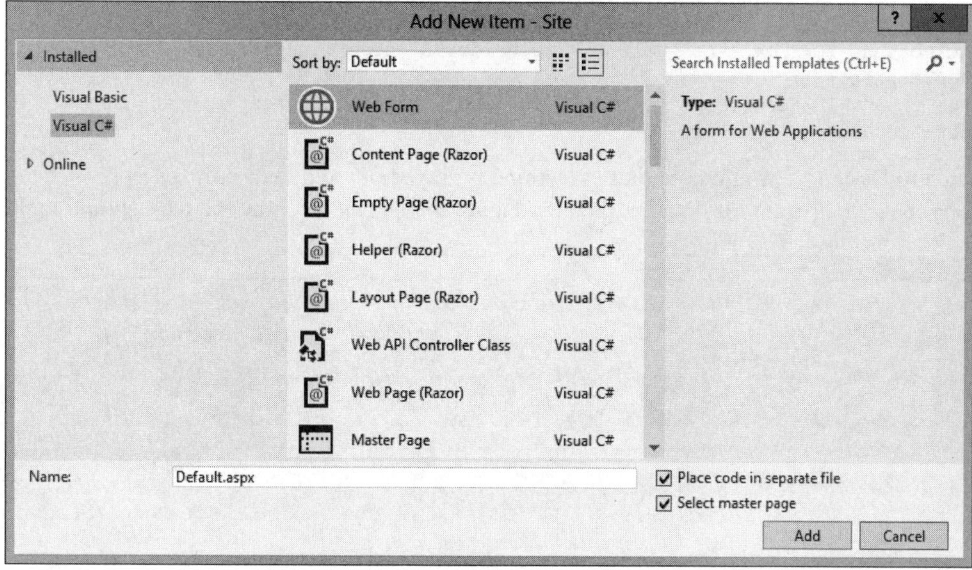

FIGURE 6-3

Finally, click the Add button.

2. In the Select a Master Page dialog box (see Figure 6-4), click the `MasterPages` folder in the left-hand pane, and then in the area at the right, click `Frontend.master`.

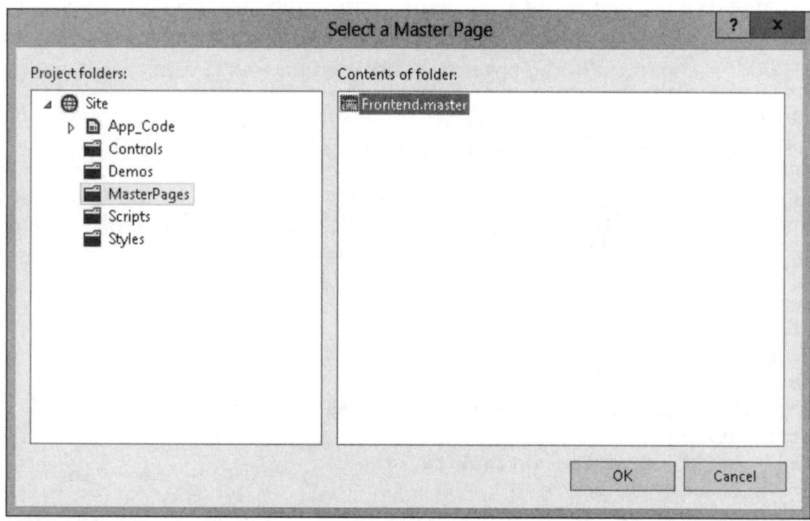

FIGURE 6-4

Click OK to add the page to your website.

Instead of getting a full page with HTML as you got with standard ASPX pages, you now only get two <asp:Content> placeholders as shown in this VB.NET example:

```
<%@ Page Title="" Language="VB" MasterPageFile="~/MasterPages/Frontend.master"
     AutoEventWireup="false" CodeFile="Default.aspx.vb" Inherits="_Default" %>
<asp:Content ID="Content1" ContentPlaceHolderID="head" runat="Server">
</asp:Content>
<asp:Content ID="Content2" ContentPlaceHolderID="cpMainContent" runat="Server">
</asp:Content>
```

3. Switch to Design View and note that everything is grayed out and read-only, except for the <asp:Content> region for cpMainContent. Figure 6-5 shows you how the page should look.

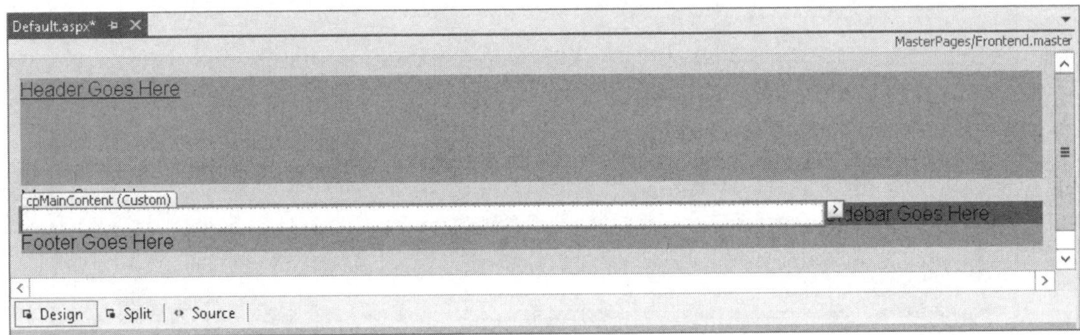

FIGURE 6-5

Also note that VS conveniently lists the master page that this page is based on in the top-right corner of Design View, visible in Figure 6-5. Clicking the name opens the master page in the editor.

4. If you still have the old markup from the Default.aspx on the clipboard, click once inside the cpMainContent placeholder and press Ctrl+V. (Note: you can do this both in Design View and in Markup View). This adds the markup to the page, right between the <asp:Content> tags.

5. Save your changes by pressing Ctrl+S and press Ctrl+F5 to open the page in your browser. The browser should display the page very closely to what you saw in Design View (see Figure 6-5).

6. Now take a look at the HTML for the page in the browser. You can do this by right-clicking the page and choosing View Source or View Page Source. Note that the source of the final page in the browser is a combination of the source of the master page and the content page:

```
<div id="PageWrapper">
  <header><a href="/">Header Goes Here</a></header>
  <nav>Menu Goes Here</nav>
  <section id="MainContent">
    <h1>Hi there visitor and welcome to Planet Wrox</h1>
    <p class="Introduction">
    We&#39;re glad you&#39;re paying a visit to <a
    href="http://www.PlanetWrox.com">
         www.PlanetWrox.com</a>, the coolest music community site on the Internet.
    </p>
    ...
```

The first four lines come from the master page and the bolded lines of HTML code come from the content page.

7. Switch back to VS and create a new page called `Login.aspx` in the root of the site based on the master page. Notice how VS remembered your last settings with regard to the master page and Code Behind (make sure both are checked in case you unchecked them earlier). Switch to Markup View and create an `<h1>` element inside the `cpMainContent` placeholder with the text **`Log in to Planet Wrox`**. There's no need to add any other controls to this page just yet, but it serves as the basis for the login functionality you create in Chapter 16. Without any content in the `MainContent` element, the `Sidebar` will be moved to the left of the page.

8. Go back to `Default.aspx` and switch to Design View. Beneath the welcome text with the header and two `<p>` elements, create a new paragraph (press Enter in Design View) and type some text (for example, **`You can log in here`**). Notice how this new paragraph has a `class` attribute called `Introduction` because VS applies the previous class to new paragraphs automatically. Remove this class using the Clear Styles option of the Apply Styles window, or manually remove it from the code in Markup View.

9. Highlight the words "log in" in Design View and choose Format ⇨ Convert to Hyperlink from the main menu. In the dialog box that follows, click the Browse button and select the `Login.aspx` page that you just created. Click OK twice.

10. Save all changes and press Ctrl+F5 again to view `Default.aspx` in the browser. Then click the link you created in the preceding step. You should now be taken to `Login.aspx`. Note that the general layout, like the header and the sidebar, is maintained. The only thing that changes when you go from page to page is the content in the main content area.

How It Works

When a page based on a master page is requested in the browser, the server reads in both the content page and the master page, merges the two, processes them, and then sends the final result to the browser. In step 6 of this exercise you saw that the HTML in the browser for the requested page contained the markup from both files.

Master pages will save you a lot of work when it comes to updating or radically changing the looks of your site. Because the entire design and layout of your site is defined in the master page, you only need to touch that single file when you want to make any changes. All content pages will pick up the changes automatically.

A Closer Look at Master Pages

So far you've seen a master page with a content placeholder for the main content. But if you look at the master page in Markup View, you'll find another content placeholder in the head section of the page:

```
<head runat="server">
  <title></title>
  <asp:ContentPlaceHolder id="head" runat="server">
  </asp:ContentPlaceHolder>
  ...
</head>
```

This placeholder is added for you automatically to each new master page you create. You can use it in content pages to add page-specific content that belongs between the `<head>` tags of a page, such as CSS (both embedded and external style sheets) and JavaScript. You learn more about JavaScript in Chapters 10 and 11. You need to add content to this placeholder in Markup View, because it's not visible in Design View.

The `ContentPlaceHolder` called `cpMainContent` in the master page currently does not contain any markup itself. However, it doesn't have to be like this. You can easily add your own content there that will serve as the default in your content pages as long as it's not overridden by the content page. For example, you can have the following `ContentPlaceHolder` in a master page:

```
<asp:ContentPlaceHolder ID="cpMainContent" runat="server">
  This is default text that shows up in content pages that don't
  explicitly override it.
</asp:ContentPlaceHolder>
```

When you base a new page on this master page, you won't see this default at first in Markup View. However, you can open the `Content` control's Smart Tasks panel, shown in Figure 6-6, and choose Default to Master's Content.

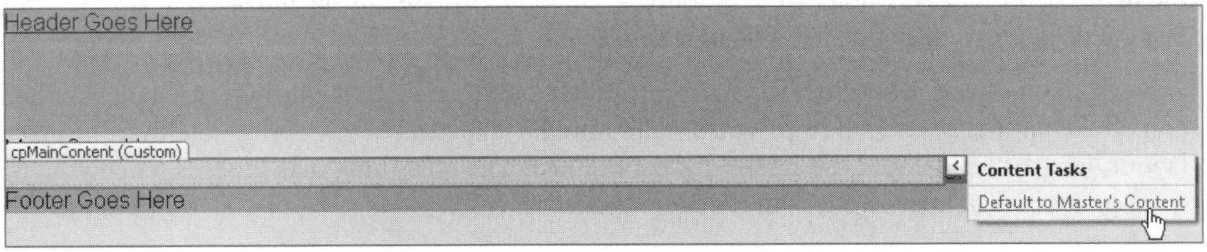

FIGURE 6-6

When you click Yes when asked if you want to default to the master page content, VS removes the entire `Content` control from the Markup View of the page. However, when you request the page in the browser you will still see the default content from the master page. In Design View, the content is still visible, now presented as a read-only area on the design surface. A master page with default content can be useful if you add a new `ContentPlaceHolder` to the master page at a later stage. Existing pages can simply display the default content, without the need for you to touch all these pages. New pages can define their own content. If you don't have default content in the `ContentPlaceHolder` control in the master page and the content page doesn't have a `Content` control for the `ContentPlaceHolder`, no output is sent to the browser.

Once you have defaulted to the master page's content, you can create custom content again by opening the Smart Tasks panel and choosing Create Custom Content. This copies the default contents into a new `Content` control that you can then modify.

Nesting Master Pages

It is also possible to nest master pages. A nested master page is a master that is based on another master page. Content pages can then be based on the nested master page. This is useful if you have a website that targets different areas that still need to share a common look and feel. For example, you can have a corporate website that is separated by departments. The outer master page defines the global look and feel of the site, including corporate logo and other branding elements. You can then have different nested master pages for different departments. For example, the sales department's section could be based on a different master than the marketing department's, enabling each to add their own identity to their section of the site. VS 2012 has excellent Design View support for nested master pages, giving you a good look at how the final page will end up.

Creating a nested master page is easy: check the Select Master Page check box when you add a master page just as you do when you add a normal content page to the site. Then add markup and `ContentPlaceHolder` controls to the `Content` controls at locations that you want to override in the content pages. Finally, you choose your nested master page as the master for new content pages you create. Inside the content page, you only see the `ContentPlaceHolder` controls from the nested master page, not from its parent.

Master Page Caveats

Although master pages are great and can save you a lot of work, you need to be aware of some caveats.

For starters, the ASP.NET run time changes the *client ID* of your controls in the page. This is the `id` attribute that is used in client script to access controls from JavaScript in the browser and with CSS ID selectors. With normal ASPX pages, the server-side ID of a control is usually inserted one-on-one in the final HTML. For example, a `Button` control with a server-side ID of `Button1` in a normal ASPX page defined with this code,

```
<asp:Button ID="Button1" runat="server" Text="Click Me" />
```

ends up with a client-side ID like this in the final HTML:

```
<input type="submit" name="Button1" value="Click Me" id="Button1" />
```

However, the same button inside an `<asp:Content>` control ends up like this:

```
<input type="submit" name="ctl00$cpMainContent$Button1"
     value="Click Me" id="cpMainContent_Button1" />
```

The `name` attribute has been prefixed with the auto-generated ID of the master page (`ctl00`) and both the `name` and the `id` attributes contain the ID of the `ContentPlaceHolder` control (`cpMainContent`).

This means that any client-side code that previously referred to `Button1` should now refer to `cpMainContent_Button1`.

Note that this is not just a master page problem. You'll also run into this behavior in other situations; for example, when working with user controls (discussed in Chapter 8) and data-bound controls (discussed in Chapter 13 and onward).

The second caveat is related to the first. Because the `name` and `id` of the HTML elements are changed, they add considerably to the size of the page. This may not be problematic for a single control, but once you have pages with lots of controls, this could impact the performance of your site. The problem gets worse with nested master pages, where both content controls are appended to the ID. The same button inside a nested master page can end up like this:

```
<input type="submit" name="ctl00$ctl00$cpMainContent$ContentPlaceHolder1$Button1"
      value="Click Me" id="cpMainContent_ContentPlaceHolder1_Button1" />
```

To mitigate the problem, you should keep the IDs of your `ContentPlaceHolder` and `Content` controls as short as possible. To improve readability, this book uses longer names, like `cpMainContent`. However, in your own sites, you could reduce this to `MC` or `cpMC` to save some bandwidth on every request.

> ***NOTE*** *ASP.NET 4 introduced a new feature called* `ClientIDMode` *that helps minimize the problems typically associated with changing client-side IDs. You learn more about this feature in Chapter 8.*

Master pages enable you to define the general look and feel of your site in a single location, thus improving the consistency and maintainability of your site. However, there is another way to improve consistency: centralize the behavior of the pages in your website. You can do this with a so-called base page, which is discussed next.

USING A CENTRALIZED BASE PAGE

In Chapter 5 you learned that, by default, all ASPX pages derive from a class called `System.Web.UI.Page`. This means all of your pages have at least the behavior defined in this class.

However, in some circumstances this behavior is not enough and you need to add your own stuff to the mix. For example, you may have the need to add some behavior that applies to all the pages in your site. Instead of adding this behavior to each and every individual page, you can create a common *base page*. All the pages in your site can then inherit from this intermediate page instead of from the standard `Page` class. The left half of Figure 6-7 shows how an ASPX page called `MyWebPage` inherits from the `Page` class directly. The right half shows a situation where the ASPX page inherits from a class called `BasePage`, which in turn inherits from `Page`.

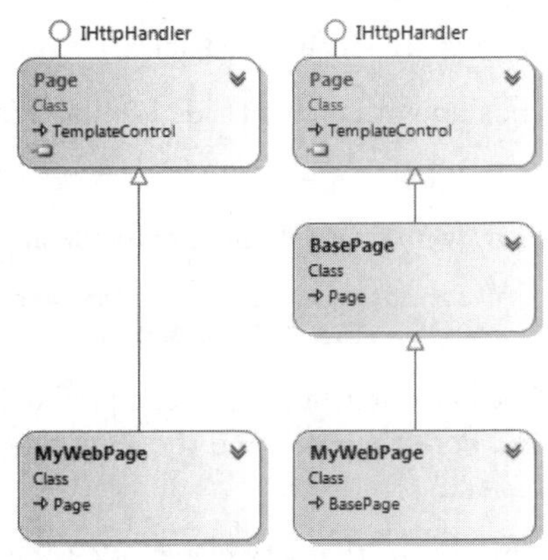

FIGURE 6-7

To have your pages inherit from this base page, you need to do two things:

- Create a class that inherits from `System.Web.UI.Page` in the `App_Code` folder of your website.
- Make the web pages in your site inherit from this base page instead of the standard `Page` class.

In an upcoming exercise you create a new base page class inside the `App_Code` folder. For now, the sole purpose of this class is to check the `Title` of the page at run time to stop pages with an empty title or a meaningless title like "Untitled Page" making it to the browser. Giving your pages a unique and helpful title helps the major search engines to index them, so it's recommended to always include a title in your web pages. Checking the title programmatically is relatively easy to do, which enables you to focus on the concept of inheritance rather than on the actual code. In the section that discusses themes later in this chapter, you modify the base page once more, this time to retrieve the user's preference for a theme.

> ***NOTE*** *Older versions of VS used "Untitled Page" as the default title for new Web Forms. However, starting with the Service Pack 1 release of Visual Studio 2008, the default title is an empty string. I decided to leave the check for "Untitled Page" in the base page so you can see how you can check for unwanted titles.*

Before you can implement the base class, you need to know more about the *ASP.NET page life cycle*, an important concept that describes the process a web page goes through when requested by a browser.

An Introduction to the ASP.NET Page Life Cycle

When you think about how a page is served by a web server to the browser and think of this process as the *life cycle of a page*, you can probably come up with a few important moments in the page's life. For example, the initial request by the browser is the starting point for the page's "life." Similarly, when the page has sent its entire HTML to the browser, its life may seem to end. However, more interesting events are going on in the page's life cycle. The following table describes eight broad phases the page goes through. Within each phase, at least one event is raised that enables a page developer to hook into the page's life cycle and perform actions at the right moment. You see an example of this in the next exercise.

PHASE	DESCRIPTION
Page request	A request to an ASPX page starts the life cycle of that page. When the web server is able and allowed to return a cached copy of the page, the entire life cycle is not executed. In all other situations, the page enters the start phase.
Start	In this phase, the page gets access to properties like `Request` and `Response` that are used to interact with the page's environment. In addition, during this phase the `PreInit` event is raised to signal that the page is about to go into the initialization phase. You use this event later to set the theme of a page.
Page initialization	During this phase, the controls you have set up in your page or added programmatically become available. Additionally, the `Page` class fires three events: `Init`, `InitComplete`, and `PreLoad`.

continues

(continued)

PHASE	DESCRIPTION
Load	During this phase, the control properties are loaded from View State and Control State during a postback. For example, when you change the selected item in a `DropDownList` and then cause a postback, this is the moment where the correct item gets preselected in the drop-down list again, which you can then work with in your server-side code. Also, during this phase the page raises the `Load` event.
Validation	In the validation phase, the Validation controls used to validate user input are processed. You learn about validators in Chapter 9.
Postback event handling	During this phase, the controls in your page may raise their own events. For example, the `DropDownList` may raise a `SelectedIndexChanged` event when the user has chosen a different option in the list. Similarly, a `TextBox` may raise the `TextChanged` event when the user has changed the text before she posted back to the server. When all event processing is done, the page raises the `LoadComplete` event. Also during this phase the `PreRender` event is raised to signal that the page is about to render to the browser. Shortly after that, `SaveStateComplete` is raised to indicate that the page is done storing all the relevant data for the controls in View State.
Rendering	Rendering is the phase where the controls (and the page itself) output their HTML to the browser.
Unload	The unload phase is really a clean-up phase. This is the moment where the page and controls can release resources they were holding on to. During this phase, the `Unload` event is raised so you can handle any cleanup you may need to do.

One thing that's important to realize is that all these events fire *at the server*, not at the client. So, even if you change, say, the text of a text box at the client, the `TextChanged` event of the `TextBox` control will fire at the server after you have posted back the page.

Now you may wonder why you need to know all of this. The biggest reason to have some understanding of the page life cycle is that certain actions can be performed only at specific stages in the page life cycle. For example, dynamically changing the theme has to take place in `PreInit`, as you'll see later. To really understand the ASP.NET page life cycle, you need to know a little more about controls, state, events, and so on. Therefore, you'll revisit the page life cycle again in Chapter 15 where you get a good look at all the different events that fire, and in what order.

In the next exercise, you use the `PreRender` event of the `Page` class to check the title. Because a developer could set the page's title programmatically during many events, checking for a correct title should be done as late as possible in the page's life cycle, which is why `PreRender` is the best event for this.

Implementing the Base Page

Implementing a base page is pretty easy: all you need to do is add a class file to your `App_Code` folder, add some code to it, and you're done. What's often a bit more difficult is to make sure each page in your site inherits from this new base page instead of from the standard `System.Web.UI.Page` class. Unfortunately, there is no way to configure the application to do this for you automatically when using Code Behind, so you need to modify each page manually. Visual Studio makes it a little easier for you by enabling you to export a page template that already contains this code. In the next exercise you add a base page to the site and in a later exercise you see how to export a web form to a template so you can add files that use the base page in no time.

TRY IT OUT Creating a Base Page

1. Right-click the `App_Code` folder in the Solution Explorer and choose Add ➪ Add New Item. Select Class in the Templates list and name the file **`BasePage`**. You could choose another name if you like but `BasePage` clearly describes the purpose of the class, making it easier to understand what it does.
2. Clear the contents of the file, and then add the following code:

VB.NET

```
Public Class BasePage
  Inherits System.Web.UI.Page

  Private Sub Page_PreRender(sender As Object, e As EventArgs) Handles Me.PreRender
    If String.IsNullOrEmpty(Me.Title) OrElse Me.Title.Equals("Untitled Page",
                 StringComparison.CurrentCultureIgnoreCase) Then
      Throw New Exception(
          "Page title cannot be ""Untitled Page"" or an empty string.")
    End If
  End Sub

End Class
```

C#

```
using System;

public class BasePage : System.Web.UI.Page
{
  private void Page_PreRender(object sender, EventArgs e)
  {
    if (string.IsNullOrEmpty(this.Title) || this.Title.Equals("Untitled Page",
                 StringComparison.CurrentCultureIgnoreCase))
    {
      throw new Exception(
            "Page title cannot be \"Untitled Page\" or an empty string.");
    }
```

```
    }

    public BasePage()
    {
      this.PreRender += Page_PreRender;
    }
  }
```

3. Save the file and close it, and then open the `Login.aspx` page that you created earlier. Open its Code Behind file and change the `Inherits` code (the colon [:] in C#) so the login page inherits from the `BasePage` class you created earlier:

VB.NET

```
Partial Class Login
    Inherits BasePage
  ...
End Class
```

C#

```
public partial class Login : BasePage
{
  ...
}
```

4. Save the page and then request it in the browser by pressing Ctrl+F5. If you haven't changed the title of the page earlier, you should be greeted by the error shown in Figure 6-8 in your browser.

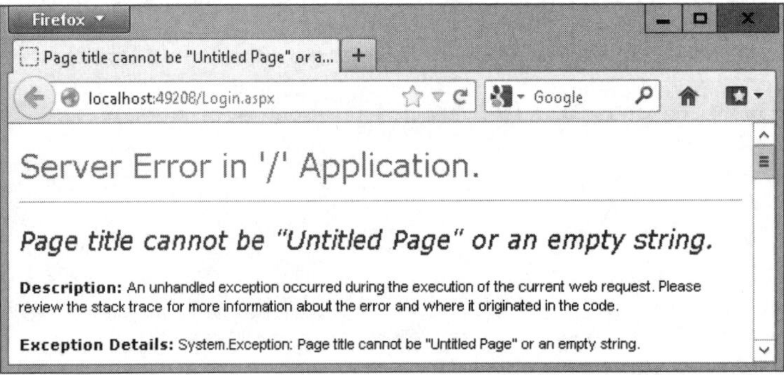

FIGURE 6-8

Instead of this error, you may see an error that displays the source for the `BasePage` class where the title is checked.

5. Go back to VS and open the login page in Markup View. Locate the `Title` attribute in the `@ Page` directive (or add one if it isn't there) and set its value to **`Log in to Planet Wrox`**. The following snippet shows the VB.NET version of the `@ Page` directive but the C# version is almost identical:

```
<%@ Page Title="Log in to Planet Wrox" Language="VB"
    MasterPageFile="~/MasterPages/Frontend.master" AutoEventWireup="false"
    CodeFile="Login.aspx.vb" Inherits="Login" %>
```

6. Repeat steps 3 and 5 for all the pages in your site. To make this a bit quicker, you can use Find and Replace to quickly replace all the occurrences of `System.Web.UI.Page` with `BasePage`. Make sure you don't accidentally replace it in the `BasePage` file in the `App_Code` folder itself. To prevent this from happening, make sure you search only in Code Behind files, like this:
   - Open the Replace in Files dialog box (press Ctrl+Shift+H or select Edit ⇨ Find and Replace ⇨ Replace in Files).
   - In the Find What box, enter **`System.Web.UI.Page`**. In the Replace With text box, enter **`BasePage`**.
   - Expand the Find Options section and in the Look at These File Types text box, enter **`*.aspx.vb`** or **`*.aspx.cs`** depending on the language you use. This leaves the BasePage file, which has a single extension of `.vb` or `.cs`, alone.
   - Click Replace All and then click Yes to confirm the Replace operation.
7. Save the changes you made to any open page and then browse to `Login.aspx` again. If everything worked out as planned, the error should be gone and you now see the login page.

   Remember, though, that all other pages in your site now throw an error when you try to access them. The fix is easy; just give them all a valid `Title`. For pages without a `Title` attribute in their page directive, you need to do this manually. For other pages, with an empty `Title=""` attribute, you can quickly do this by searching the site for `Title=""` and replacing it with something like `Title="Planet Wrox"`. (Don't forget to reset Look at These File Types back to *.*). For pages other than the demo pages you've created so far, you're better off giving each page a unique title, clearly describing the content it contains.

How It Works

By default, all pages in your website inherit from the `Page` class defined in the `System.Web.UI` namespace. This gives them the behavior required to make them act as web pages that can be requested by the browser and processed by the server. Because the inheritance model in .NET enables you to create a chain of classes that inherit from each other, you can easily insert your own base page class between a web page and the standard `Page` class. You do this by changing the `Inherits` statement (in VB) and the colon (in C#) to your new `BasePage`:

VB.NET

```
Partial Class Login
   Inherits BasePage
```

C#

```
public partial class Login : BasePage
```

Inside this new `BasePage` class you add an event handler that is called when the class fires its `PreRender` event. As you learned earlier, this event is raised quite late in the page's life cycle, when the entire page has been set up and is ready to be rendered to the client:

VB.NET

```
Private Sub Page_PreRender(sender As Object, e As EventArgs) Handles Me.PreRender
  ' Implementation here
```

```
End Sub
```

C#

```
private void Page_PreRender(object sender, EventArgs e)
{
  // Implementation here
}
```

Note that Visual Basic uses the `Handles` keyword to tell the compiler that the `Page_PreRender` method will be used to handle the event. In C#, you need to hook up this handler manually. A good place to do this is in the class's constructor:

```
public BasePage()
{
  this.PreRender += Page_PreRender;
}
```

This highlighted line of code serves the same purpose as the `Handles` keyword in VB.NET: it tells the compiler what method to run when the page raises its `PreRender` event.

Inside the event handler, the code checks the current page title. If the page title is still an empty string (the default for any new page you add to your web project) or Untitled Page it *throws an exception.*

VB.NET

```
If String.IsNullOrEmpty(Me.Title) OrElse Me.Title.Equals("Untitled Page",
                    StringComparison.CurrentCultureIgnoreCase) Then
  Throw New Exception(
      "Page title cannot be ""Untitled Page"" or an empty string.")
End If
```

C#

```
if (string.IsNullOrEmpty(this.Title) || this.Title.Equals("Untitled Page",
                  StringComparison.CurrentCultureIgnoreCase))
{
  throw new Exception(
      "Page title cannot be \"Untitled Page\" or an empty string.");
}
```

This code uses the handy `IsNullOrEmpty` method of the `String` class to check if a value is `null` (`Nothing` in VB) or an empty string. It also uses the `Equals` method to check if the page title is equal to Untitled Page. It uses `StringComparison.CurrentCultureIgnoreCase` to do a case-insensitive comparison, so untitled page or Untitled Page would both match.

Notice how the keywords `Me` (in VB.NET) and `this` (in C#) are used. These keywords are context-sensitive and always refer to the instance of the class where they are used. In this example, `Me` and `this` refer to the current instance of the `BasePage` class. This `BasePage` instance has a `Title` property (which it inherits from `Page`) that can be checked for unwanted values. If it still contains the default title (an empty string) or the text "Untitled Page," the code raises (or throws) an exception. This immediately stops execution of the page so you as a page developer can fix the problem by providing a valid title before the page ends up in public. In Chapter 18 you learn more about exceptions and how to prevent and handle them.

To display a double quote (") in the error message, both languages use a different format. In Visual Basic, you need to double the quotes. In C#, you need to prefix the double quote with a backslash (\) to *escape* the double quote. In both cases, a double quote character ends up in the error message.

Because every new page you add to the site should now inherit from this new base page, you should create a page template that already has the correct code in its Code Behind and markup, making it easy to add the correct page to the site right from the start. This is discussed next.

Creating Reusable Page Templates

Visual Studio comes with a great tool to export templates for a number of different file types including ASPX pages, class files, and even CSS files. By creating a custom template, you define the code or markup that you need in every file once and then create new files based on this template, giving you a jump start with the file and minimizing the code you need to type. The next exercise shows you how to create your own templates.

TRY IT OUT Creating a Reusable Page Template

In this exercise you see how to create a template file for all new ASPX pages you add to your site. To avoid conflicts with existing pages in your current site, you create a new temporary page and use that for the template. Afterward, you can delete the temporary file.

1. Add a new Web Form to the root of the site and call it **`Temporary.aspx`**. Make sure it uses Code Behind, uses your programming language, and is based on the master page in the `MasterPages` folder.

2. Open the Code Behind of this new page (by pressing F7) and change the `Inherits` line (the colon in C#) so the page inherits from `BasePage` instead of from `System.Web.UI.Page`. Also rename the class from `Temporary` to **`$relurlnamespace$_$safeitemname$`**:

   VB.NET

   ```
   Partial Class $relurlnamespace$_$safeitemname$
       Inherits BasePage
     ...
   End Class
   ```

   C#

   ```
   public partial class $relurlnamespace$_$safeitemname$ : BasePage
   {
     ...
   }
   ```

   Make sure you don't remove any of the existing code, like the `using` statements or the `Page_Load` method in the C# version.

   Don't worry about any compile errors you may get about unexpected characters like `$`. Once you start adding pages based on this template, `$relurlnamespace$_$safeitemname$` will be replaced by the name of the page you're adding.

3. Switch to Markup View, and change the `Inherits` attribute from `Temporary` to **`$relurlnamespace$_$safeitemname$`** as shown in this C# example:

```
<%@ Page Title="" Language="C#" MasterPageFile="~/MasterPages/Frontend.master"
     AutoEventWireup="true" CodeFile="Temporary.aspx.cs"
     Inherits="$relurlnamespace$_$safeitemname$" %>
```

You must leave the `CodeFile` attribute alone; VS will change it to the right Code Behind file automatically whenever you add a new page to the site.

4. Optionally, add other code you want to add to your pages by default, like a comment block with a copyright notice.

5. Save all changes and then choose File ➪ Export Template. In the dialog box that follows, select Item Template and choose your programming language from the drop-down list at the bottom of the screen, shown in Figure 6-9.

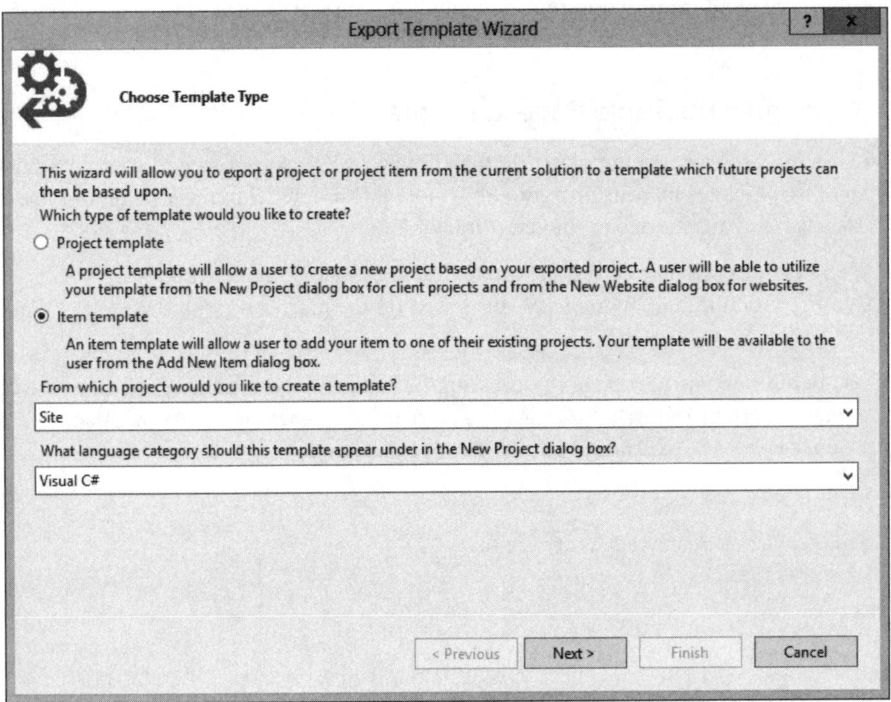

FIGURE 6-9

6. Click Next and place a check mark in front of `Temporary.aspx`, which you find near the bottom of the list. Click Next again to go to the Select Item References dialog box.

7. There is no need to set anything in the Select Item References dialog box now. If you had a web page referencing specific assemblies (`.dll` files) you could pick them here, so VS adds the references for you automatically next time you add a file based on this template. Click Next again to go to the Select Template Options screen. Type **`MyBasePage`** as the new template name, and optionally

type a short note describing the purpose of the template. Make sure the Automatically Import the Template into Visual Studio option is checked. Figure 6-10 shows the final dialog box.

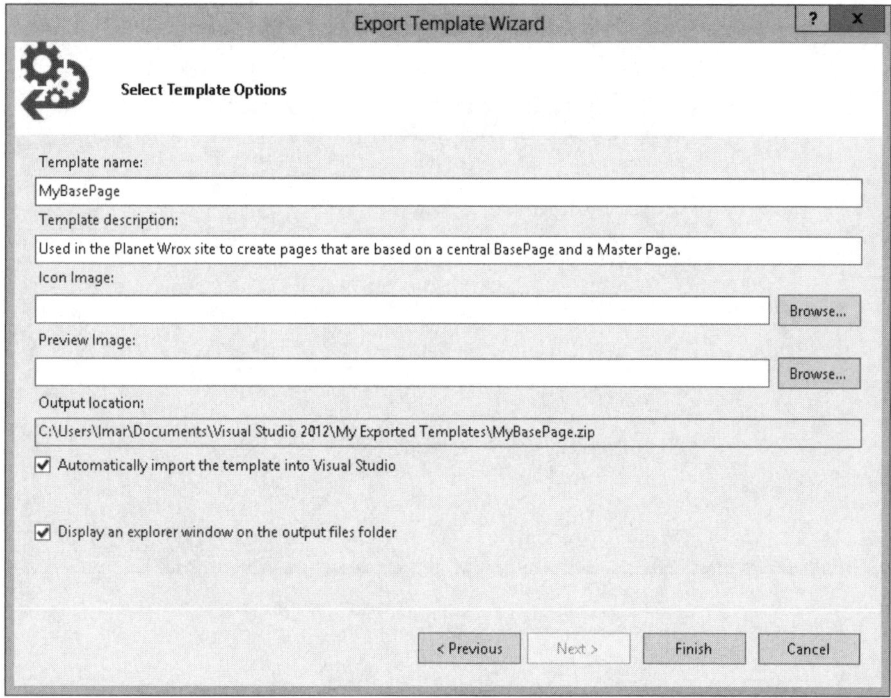

FIGURE 6-10

8. Click Finish to create the template. VS opens a File Explorer (Windows Explorer in Windows 7) showing a copy of the new template as a zip file. You can close that window, because you don't need it.

   If you want to carry out this exercise for both VB.NET and C#, be sure to rename the resulting zip file first before you make an export for the second language; otherwise the zip file gets overwritten. To rename the file, open File Explorer, go to your Documents folder and then browse to `Visual Studio 2012\Templates\ItemTemplates`. You'll find a file called `MyBasePage.zip`, which you can rename to something like `MyBasePageCS.zip`. Note that the file's location is different from the one you see in Figure 6-10; the output location contains just a copy of the exported template that you can use as a backup.

9. Back in VS, delete the temporary file `Temporary.aspx` you created. Then right-click the website in the Solution Explorer and choose Add ➪ Add New Item. Note that your custom template now shows up in the list of templates, shown in Figure 6-11. If you click it, VS shows you the description you gave it earlier. Note: you may have to restart VS and reopen your website for the template to appear.

10. Type a new name for the page, such as **`TestPage.aspx`**, and click Add to add it to your site. Look at the markup and the Code Behind of the file and verify that `$relurlnamespace$_$safeitemn`

ame$ has been renamed to _TestPage to reflect the new name of the page. If everything looks OK, you can delete TestPage.aspx because it's not used in the Planet Wrox website.

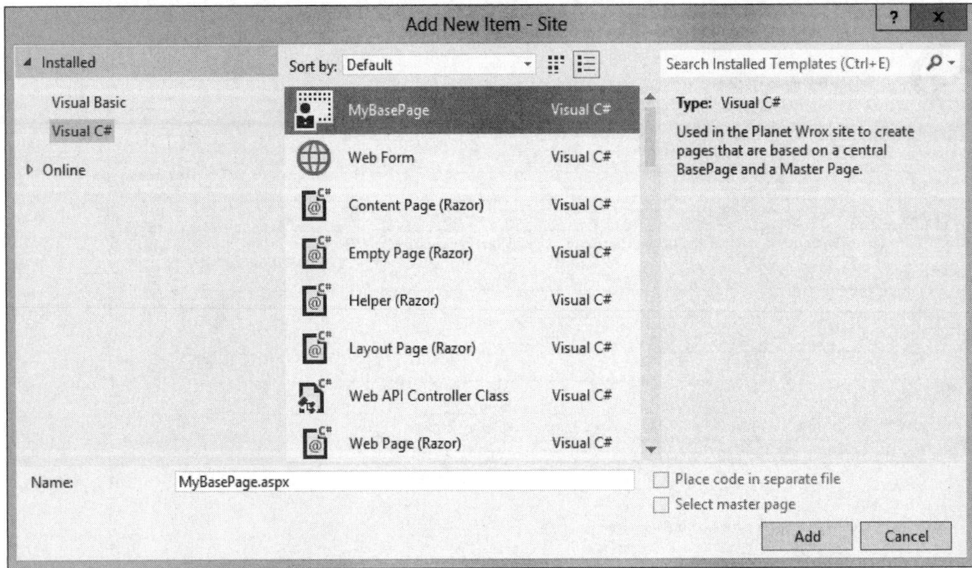

FIGURE 6-11

How It Works

When you export the template, Visual Studio creates a zip file with the necessary files—an ASPX file and a Code Behind file in this exercise. This zip file is then stored in the ItemTemplates subfolder of the Visual Studio 2012 folder under your Documents folder. Some of the files in the zip file contain the placeholders $relurlnamespace$ and $safeitemname$. When you add a new file to the site that is based on your template using the Add New Item dialog box, VS replaces $relurlnamespace$ with the name of the folder (nothing, in the case of a file added to the root of the site) and $safeitemname$ with the actual name of the page. In this exercise, you typed TestPage.aspx as the new name for the page, so you ended up with a class in the Code Behind called _TestPage, which in turn inherits from the global BasePage. The underscore (_) is hard-coded between the two placeholders and is really only needed when adding a Web Form based on this template to a subfolder. However, it's a valid start of a class identifier so you can safely leave it in for pages at the root of your website. If you add a file to a subfolder, such as the Demos folder, the class name is prefixed with the name of the folder so you end up with a class called Demos_TestPage. In addition to $relurlnamespace$ and $safeitemname$, you can use a few other placeholders. Search the MSDN site at http://msdn.microsoft.com for the term $safeitemname$ to find the other template parameters.

If you need to make a change to the exported template, either redo the entire export process, or manually edit the files in the zip file.

With this exported template you now have a very quick way to add pages to your site that inherit from the `BasePage` class. You don't need to manually change the Code Behind of the class file or the markup of the page anymore.

In addition to master pages and the central `BasePage` class, you have more options to create consistent-looking websites. One of them is themes.

THEMES

So far you've seen how to create a master page to define the global look and feel of the pages in your site. You also saw how to centralize the behavior of your pages by using a central base page. However, you have more ways to influence the look and feel of your site: themes and skins. Skins are dealt with later in the chapter because they are an optional part of themes, which need to be discussed first.

A *theme* is a collection of files that defines the look of a page. A theme typically includes skin files, CSS files, and images. You define themes in the special `App_Themes` folder in the root of your website. Within this folder you create one or more subfolders that define the actual themes. Inside each subfolder, you can have a number of files that make up the theme. Figure 6-12 shows the Solution Explorer for a website that defines two themes: Monochrome and DarkGrey.

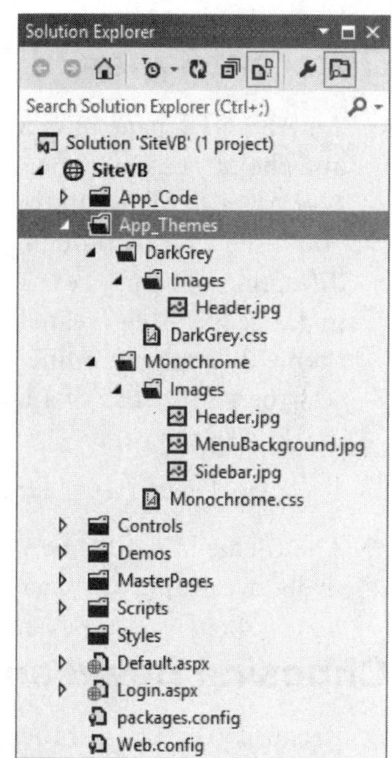

FIGURE 6-12

A link to each CSS file in the theme folder is added to your page's `<head>` section automatically whenever the theme is active. You see how this works later. The images in the theme folder can be referenced from the CSS files. You can use them to change common elements of the website, such as background images, or images used in bulleted lists or navigation lists.

To create a theme, you need to do the following:

- Create the special `App_Themes` folder if it isn't already present in your site.
- For each theme you want to create, create a subfolder with the theme's name, like Monochrome or DarkGrey in Figure 6-12.
- Optionally, create one or more CSS files that will be part of the theme. Although naming the CSS files after the theme helps in identifying the right files, this is not a requirement. Any CSS file you add to the theme's folder is added to the page at run time automatically.
- Optionally, add one or more images to the theme folder. The CSS files should refer to these images with a relative path as explained later.

- Optionally, add one or more skin files to the theme folder. Skins enable you to define individual properties (such as `ForeColor` and `CssClass`) for a specific control that are then applied at run time.

After you have followed these steps, you can configure your site or an individual web page to make use of this theme. To be able to set up the correct theme, you should be aware that two types of themes exist.

Different Types of Themes

An ASP.NET page has two different properties that enable you to set a theme: the `Theme` property and the `StyleSheetTheme` property. Both of these properties use the themes that you define in the `App_Themes` folder. Both of these properties take their default value from the `Web.config` file as you'll see later. Although at first they seem very similar, it's their runtime behavior that makes the difference. The `StyleSheetTheme` is applied very early in the page's life cycle, shortly after the page instance has been created. This means that an individual page can override the settings from the theme by applying inline attributes on the controls. So, for example, a theme with a skin file that sets the `BackColor` of a button to blue can be overridden by the following control declaration in the markup of the page:

```
<asp:Button ID="Button1" runat="server" Text="Button" BackColor="Red" />
```

The theme in the `Theme` property, on the other hand, is applied late in the page's life cycle, effectively overriding any customization you may have for individual controls.

Choosing Between Theme and StyleSheetTheme

Because properties of the `StyleSheetTheme` can be overridden by the page, and the `Theme` in turn can override these properties again, both serve a distinct purpose. You should set the `StyleSheetTheme` if you want to supply default settings for your controls. That is, the `StyleSheetTheme` can supply defaults for your controls, which can then be overridden at the page level. You should use the `Theme` property instead if you want to enforce the look and feel of your controls. Because the settings from the `Theme` cannot be overridden anymore and effectively overwrite any customizations, you can be assured that your controls look the way you defined them in the theme. There is one exception: by setting `EnableTheming` on the control to `False` you can disable theming for that control. You see this property and its effect toward the end of the chapter. The Planet Wrox sample site in this book uses the `Theme` property.

Applying Themes

To apply a theme to your website, you have three different options: at the page level in the `Page` directive, at the site level by modifying the `Web.config` file, and programmatically.

- **Setting the theme at the page level.** Setting the `Theme` or `StyleSheetTheme` property at the page level is easy, just set the relevant attribute in the `Page` directive of the page:

  ```
  <%@ Page Language="VB" AutoEventWireup="false" CodeFile="Default.aspx.vb"
          Inherits="_Default" Theme="DarkGrey" %>
  ```

Replace `Theme` with `StyleSheetTheme` to apply a theme whose settings can be overridden by the individual controls. Figure 6-13 shows that as soon as you type `Theme=`, VS pops up with a list with all the themes it finds in the `App_Themes` folder.

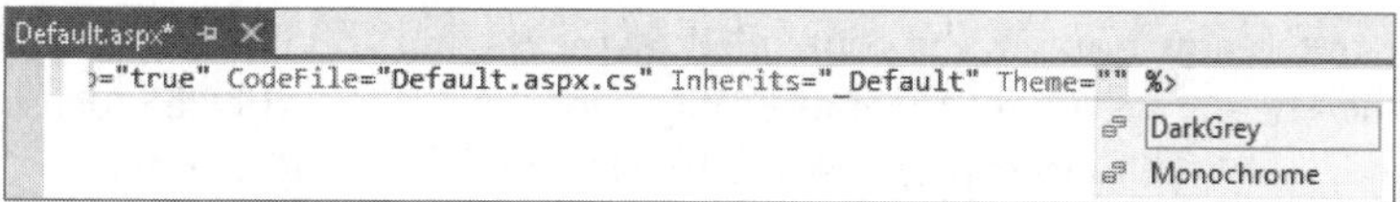

FIGURE 6-13

- **Setting the theme at the site level.** To enforce a theme throughout the entire website, you can set the theme in the `Web.config` file by adding a `theme` or `styleSheetTheme` attribute to the `<pages>` element inside the `<system.web>` element:

```
<pages theme="DarkGrey" styleSheetTheme="DarkGrey">
   ...
</pages>
```

Make sure you type these attributes exactly as shown here because the XML in the `Web.config` file is case sensitive. The attributes you set here are then applied to the `Theme` and `StyleSheetTheme` properties of the `Page` class, as you see later.

- **Setting themes programmatically.** The third and final way to set a theme is programmatically through code. You see how this works in a later exercise.

The next Try It Out exercise shows you how themes work. You create a theme, add the necessary CSS, and then configure the application to use the new theme.

TRY IT OUT Creating a New Theme for Your Website

In this exercise you create two themes: Monochrome and DarkGrey. For each theme, you add the CSS layout, which is applied to the site automatically. You configure the application to use one of the themes and then switch to the other to see the differences.

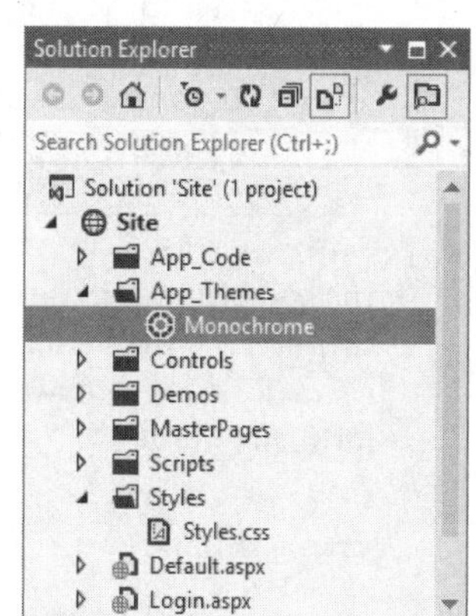

FIGURE 6-14

1. Add the special `App_Themes` folder to your website. To do this, right-click the website in the Solution Explorer and choose Add ➪ Add ASP.NET Folder ➪ Theme. This not only creates the `App_Themes` folder, but immediately creates a subfolder for the theme called `Theme1` by default. Type **`Monochrome`** as the new name instead. Your Solution Explorer should now look like Figure 6-14.
2. From the `Styles` folder, move the `Styles.css` file into this new `Monochrome` folder. You can either drag it directly into the new folder or use Ctrl+X to cut the file, click the `Monochrome` folder, and press Ctrl+V to paste it again. You can leave the empty `Styles` folder because it's used again later.

3. To make it clear later where your CSS is coming from, rename the file from `Styles.css` to **`Monochrome.css`**. You can rename it by selecting it and pressing F2 or by right-clicking it and choosing Rename.

4. Because the main layout is now going to be controlled by the theme, you no longer need the `<link>` element in the `<head>` section of the master page pointing to the old CSS file, so you can remove it. To this end, open the master page, switch to Markup View, and remove the following highlighted line from the code:

```
<head runat="server">
  <title></title>
  <asp:ContentPlaceHolder ID="head" runat="server">
  </asp:ContentPlaceHolder>
  <link href="../Styles/Styles.css" rel="stylesheet" type="text/css" />
```

5. The next step is to apply the theme to the entire website. Open the `Web.config` file from the root of the site and directly inside the `<system.web>` element, create a `<pages>` element with a `theme` attribute pointing to the Monochrome theme. There's no support for themes in IntelliSense in the `Web.config` file so you need to type the name yourself.

```
<system.web>
  <pages theme="Monochrome" />
  ...
```

6. To test the theme, save all your changes and then request the `Default.aspx` page in your browser. The design of the site should be identical to how it was.

> ***COMMON MISTAKES*** *If you get an error about an invalid page title, go back to Visual Studio and change the* `Title` *attribute of the* `@ Page` *directive of* `Default.aspx` *to "Welcome to Planet Wrox." If your design doesn't look as it should, press Ctrl+F5 or Ctrl+R in the browser. This forces a hard refresh, which means you get the latest version of the files from the server instead of a cached local copy of the page.*

Instead of linking to the CSS file from the master page, the CSS is now included in the page source through the theme set in the `Web.config` file. To see how this works, open the HTML source of the page in the browser. At the top you should see the following code (I altered the layout for better readability):

```
<!DOCTYPE html>
<html xmlns="http://www.w3.org/1999/xhtml">
<head>
  <title>Welcome to Planet Wrox</title>
  <script src="/Scripts/modernizr-2.6.2.js"></script>
  <link href="App_Themes/Monochrome/Monochrome.css"
```

```
            type="text/css" rel="stylesheet" />
</head>
<body>
```

Note that a link to the style sheet from the `Monochrome` theme folder is injected in the `<head>` of the page. The ASP.NET run time does this for every CSS file it finds in the currently active theme folder (in alphabetical order), so be sure to keep your theme folder clean to avoid unnecessary files from being included and downloaded by the browser. Also note that the `<link>` is added just right before the closing `</head>` tag. This ensures that the theme file is included after all other files you may have added yourself (through the master page, for example). This is in contrast to how the `styleSheetTheme` attribute works. Because this type of theme allows its settings to be overridden, it's imported at the top of the file, giving room for other CSS files that follow it to change the look and feel of the page.

7. Return to Visual Studio and open the master page file in Design View. Notice how all the design is gone and VS now shows the basic layout of the page again. Unfortunately, VS does not display the theme you've set using the `theme` attribute. However, you can overcome this limitation by setting the `styleSheetTheme` instead. To do this, open the `Web.config` file again, locate the `<pages>` element you created earlier, and add the following attribute:

```
<pages theme="Monochrome" styleSheetTheme="Monochrome" ... />
```

8. Save the changes to `Web.config`, close and reopen the master page, and switch to Design View. You'll see that VS now applies the correct styling information to your pages.

9. To add another theme to the site, create a new folder under `App_Themes` and call it **`DarkGrey`**. Next, open the folder where you extracted the downloaded code that comes with this book. If you followed the instructions in the introduction of this book, this folder is located at `C:\BegASPNET\Resources`. If you don't have these files yet, they are available at `www.wrox.com/remtitle.cgi?isbn=1118311809`. Open the `Chapter 06` folder and then the `DarkGrey` folder. Position the File Explorer and VS side by side and then drag the file `DarkGrey.css` from File Explorer into the `DarkGrey` theme folder in VS. If dragging doesn't work for you, you can use Ctrl+C in File Explorer to copy the file, and then use Ctrl+V in VS to paste the file in the right folder. Your Solution Explorer should now resemble Figure 6-15.

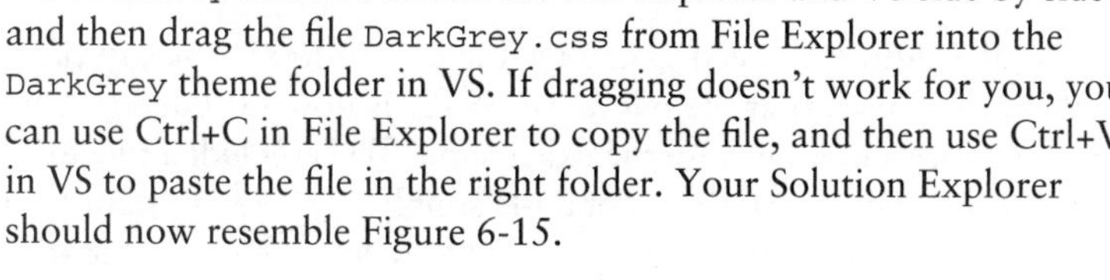

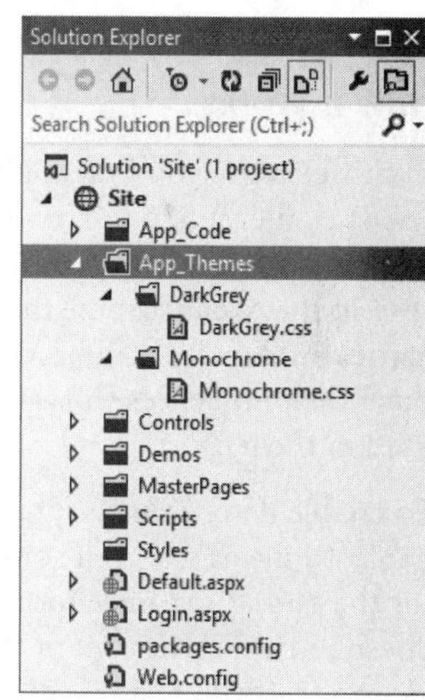

FIGURE 6-15

You add the images that the CSS file refers to in a later exercise.

10. Open the `Web.config` file once more and change both occurrences of `Monochrome` to **`DarkGrey`** in the `<pages>` element. Save the changes again and press Ctrl+F5. Instead of the blue Monochrome theme, you'll now see the site with the DarkGrey theme applied as is visible in Figure 6-16. If you don't see the menu placeholder, the main content, and the sidebar all next to each other, make sure your browser window is wide enough to display all content.

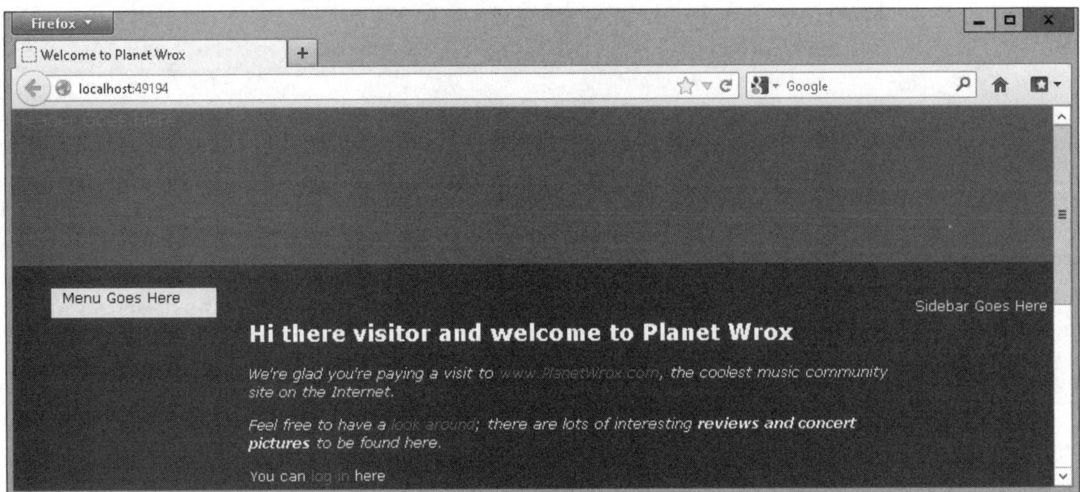

FIGURE 6-16

If you don't see the new theme appear, close all open browsers, ensure you changed `Web.config` correctly, and open `Default.aspx` again. If you still don't see the theme, press Ctrl+F5 or Ctrl+R in your browser to force it to get a fresh copy from the server.

How It Works

In this exercise you first applied the Monochrome theme by changing the `<pages>` element in the `Web.config` file. When the run time sees that a theme is active, it scans the associated theme folder for `.css` files and includes a link to all those files in the page's `<head>` section in alphabetical order. In the case of the Monochrome theme it finds the file `Monochrome.css` and adds it to the `<head>` section automatically. An identical process took place when you changed the theme to DarkGrey. The linked style sheet then influences the way the page is displayed in the browser by changing the layout and colors used in the page.

To enable design-time support in Visual Studio, you need to change the `styleSheetTheme` in the `Web.config` file as well. The only downside of this is that the relevant CSS file is now included *twice*: once for the `Theme` and once for the `StyleSheetTheme`. Because the exact same file is included twice, it doesn't affect the layout of the site. All the selectors in the second file simply overrule those in the first. However, if you feel this duplication is a waste of CPU cycles, you should delete the `styleSheetTheme` attribute from the `Web.config` file when you go live with the application.

The layout of the page is changed radically because of the CSS in the `DarkGrey.css` file. If you want to know what CSS the file contains and what elements of the page it changes, open it up in VS. It has lots of comments describing each selector in detail.

ASP.NET themes are not limited to just CSS files. As you learn next, themes can also contain images and skin files.

Extending Themes

In addition to CSS files and skins (discussed toward the end of this chapter), a theme can also contain images. The most common use of theme images is referring to them from your CSS. To put this to good use it's important to understand how CSS refers to images.

By design, an image referred to by a CSS selector will be searched for relative to the location of the CSS file, unless you give it a path that starts with a forward slash (/) to indicate the root of the site. Consider, for example, the `App_Themes` folder depicted in Figure 6-17.

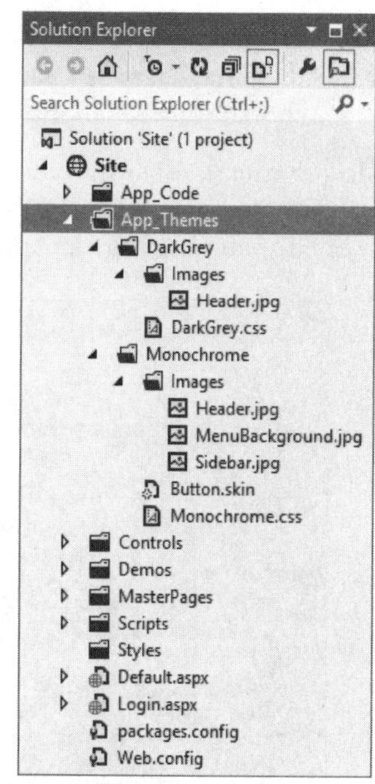

FIGURE 6-17

To refer to the `MenuBackground.jpg` file in the `Images` folder of the Monochrome theme, you can add the following CSS to `Monochrome.css`:

```
nav
{
  background-image: url(Images/MenuBackground.jpg);
}
```

If you wanted to refer to an image in the `Images` folder in the root of the site, you would use this CSS:

```
background-image: url(/Images/MenuBackground.jpg);
```

Note the leading forward slash in front of the image path to indicate the root of the site. This latter syntax is useful if you want to share images between different themes. Simply put them in a folder outside a specific theme, like an `Images` folder at the root, and then use this root-based syntax to refer to them. The next chapter digs a lot deeper into the different forms a URL can take to refer to a resource like an image.

TRY IT OUT Adding Images to Your Theme

In this Try It Out you add the images and CSS files to the site to complete both themes. You overwrite the file `Monochrome.css` in the Monochrome theme, so if you made any customizations you would like to keep, create a backup of it first.

1. Open File Explorer and navigate to the files you extracted from the zip file for this chapter (at `C:\BegASPNET\Resources`). Open the `Chapter 06` folder and then the `Monochrome` folder. Select the `Images` folder and the `Monochrome.css` file.
2. Drag (or copy and paste) the selected folder and files from File Explorer into the `Monochrome` theme folder in VS. Click Yes when you're asked to overwrite `Monochrome.css`.

3. Repeat steps 1 and 2, but this time drag (or copy and paste) only the `Images` folder from the File Explorer's `DarkGrey` folder into the `DarkGrey` theme folder in VS. Your Solution Explorer now looks like Figure 6-17.
4. Open up the master page from the `MasterPages` folder, and remove the text `Header Goes Here` from the `<header>` element. Make sure you don't accidentally remove the `<a>` element, which should now be empty.
5. Request `Default.aspx` in your browser by right-clicking it and choosing View in Browser. You should now see the web page with images from the DarkGrey theme, shown in Figure 6-18, that displays the page in Apple's Safari.

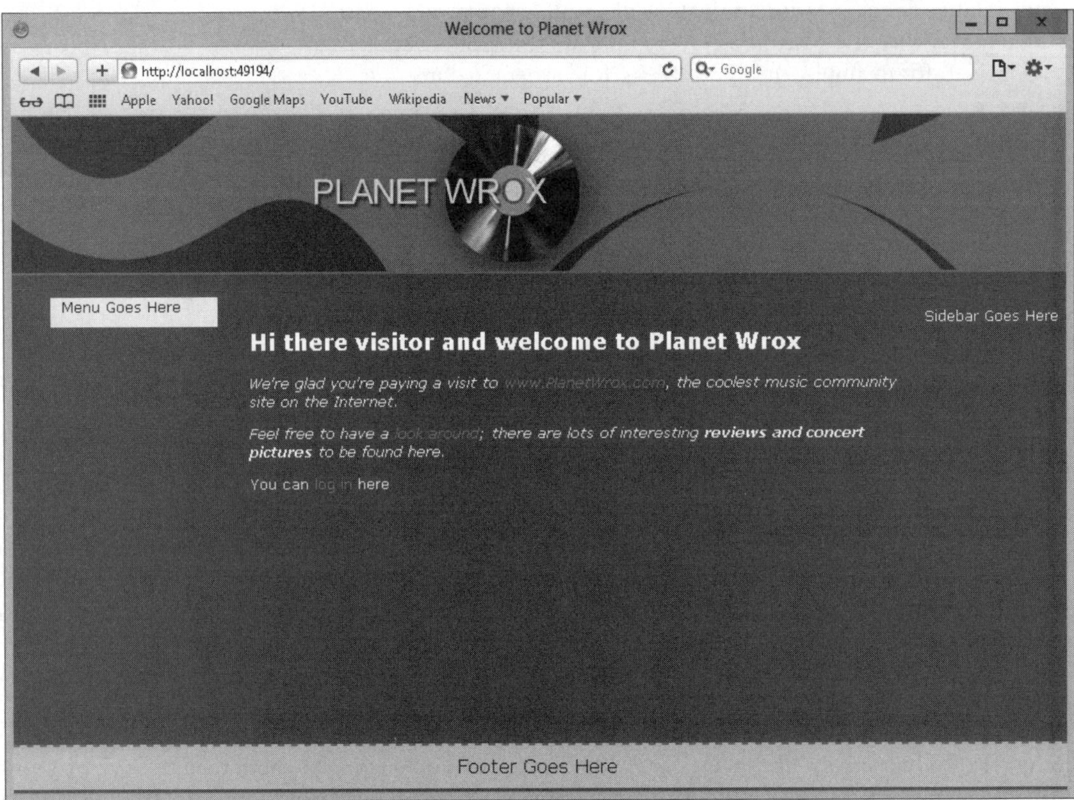

FIGURE 6-18

6. Go back to VS, open the `Web.config` file, and switch the two theme attributes of the `<pages>` element from `DarkGrey` to `Monochrome` again. Open `Default.aspx` in your browser and you'll see the page with the new theme and images as shown in Figure 6-19 that displays the page in Google Chrome. If you still see the old page, press Ctrl+F5 to cause a hard refresh.

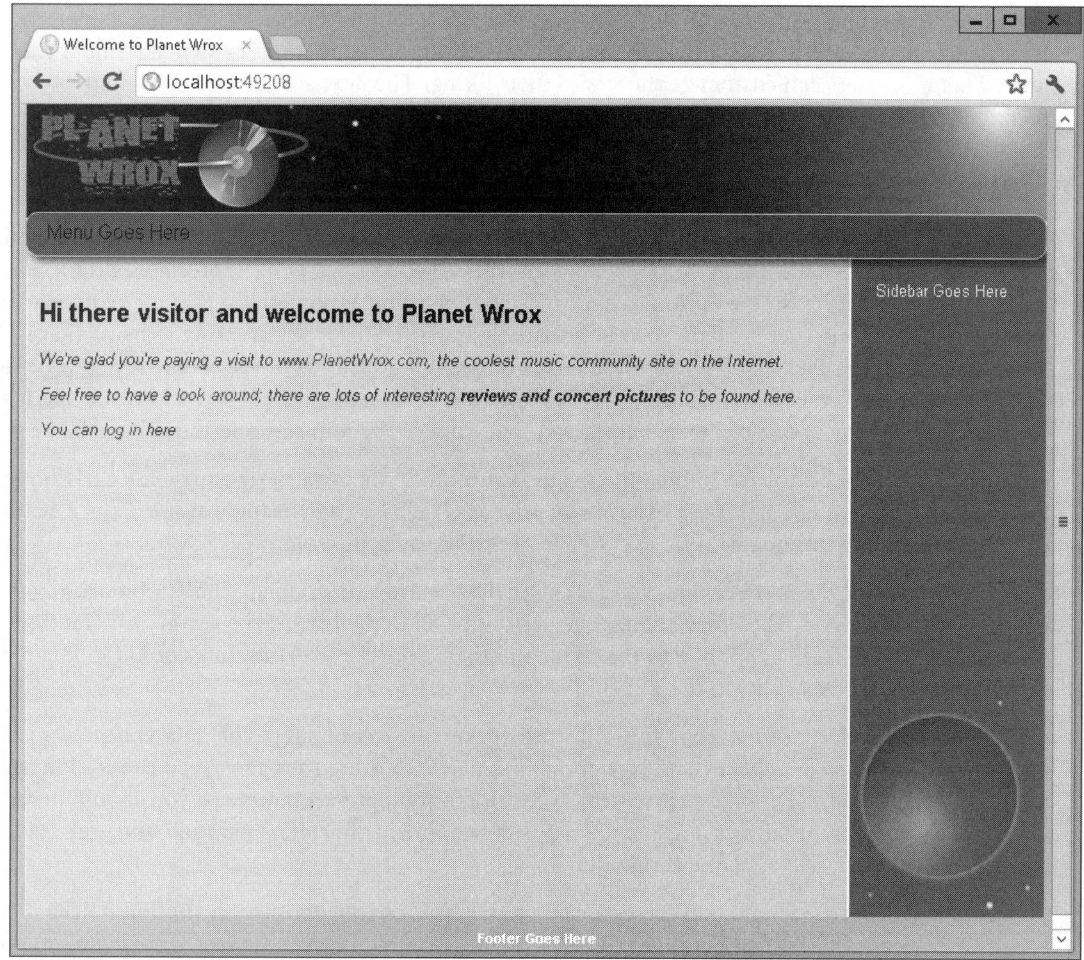

FIGURE 6-19

How It Works

From a theme point of view, nothing has changed in this exercise. Just as you saw before, the theme's style sheet is added to the head of the page. However, this time the style sheet points to images located in the theme folder. The browser reads the CSS file, follows the link to the images, downloads them, and then displays them at the right location as dictated by the various CSS selectors in the code file.

The CSS files you added for both themes contain a lot of comments, so if you want to know what the CSS does, check out the files in the two theme folders.

Useful as themes may be to enable you, the page developer, to quickly change the appearance and even the layout of the site, they become even more useful if you let your users switch them at run time. This way, users can customize the site to their liking. The next section shows you how to accomplish this.

Dynamically Switching Themes

Switching themes at run time has a few benefits. For example, you can please your users by enabling them to choose a theme with the colors and layout they like. Not everyone appreciates a dark background with white text, so the option to change that at run time is something that many people like. However, you can also deploy themes to help visually impaired users. By creating a theme that has a high-contrast color scheme and a large font size, you make it much easier for people to see your site. The themes in the Planet Wrox website only change screen elements like colors and layout, but it's easy to create a copy of one of those themes and then change the font size and the color scheme.

Because of the way themes are applied to a page at run time, you need to set the theme early on in the page's life cycle, in the `PreInit` event to be precise. The base page of the website is once again the ideal location to do this, because every page in the site inherits from this class.

To enable users to change the theme, you can offer them a drop-down menu that automatically posts back to the server when they change the active option in the list. At the server, you get the chosen theme from the list, apply it to the page, and then store the selection in a *cookie* so it can be retrieved on subsequent visits to the website.

Cookies are little pieces of text that you can store on the user's computer. The data you store in a cookie is sent only to the server that set it in the first place, so other sites can't read the cookie from yours. However, because cookies are stored on the user's computer as plaintext, you should never use them to store any sensitive data, such as a password. Storing harmless data like the preferred theme is an excellent use of cookies, though.

To create a cookie so it's stored on the user's computer, you use the `Cookies` collection on the `Response` object. This way, the cookie is sent to the browser along with the response. Here's a quick example:

VB.NET

```
Dim myCookie As HttpCookie = New HttpCookie("CookieName")
myCookie.Expires = DateTime.Now.AddMonths(3)
myCookie.Value = "Cookie value"
Response.Cookies.Add(myCookie)
```

C#

```
HttpCookie myCookie = new HttpCookie("CookieName");
myCookie.Expires = DateTime.Now.AddMonths(3);
myCookie.Value = "Cookie value";
Response.Cookies.Add(myCookie);
```

This code sends the cookie to the browser where it will be stored until it expires, which in this example is three months from the day the cookie is set. For each request to a page, the browser sends this cookie back to the server where you can read it again using the `Cookies` collection of the `Request` object, like this:

VB.NET

```
Dim myCookie As HttpCookie = Request.Cookies.Get("CookieName")
If myCookie IsNot Nothing Then
  Label1.Text = myCookie.Value ' Would display "Cookie value"
End If
```

C#

```
HttpCookie myCookie = Request.Cookies.Get("CookieName");
if (myCookie != null)
{
  Label1.Text = myCookie.Value; // Would display "Cookie value"
}
```

In the following two exercises you see how to implement the functionality to switch themes dynamically. The first exercise guides you through modifying the master page to enable the user to select a theme. This exercise only retrieves the name of the theme the user selects and stores it in a cookie. The second exercise then shows you how to apply that theme at run time to every page that inherits from `BasePage`.

> ***NOTE*** *There has been a lot of debate about cookies and whether or not they can harm your privacy. Generally, cookies are safe, because they only store data that the server that sets it already has. They can't be used to steal sensitive data from your computer if you haven't given this data to the server yourself. In most scenarios, cookies improve the user's browsing experience by remembering little pieces of data instead of asking you every single time you visit a page. Unfortunately, some large corporations like advertising agencies use a unique cookie to track your trails on the web, giving them some global idea of the sites you visit. To ensure that visitors to your site understand what information you have and keep about them, it's usually a good idea to add a privacy statement to your site describing the intent and usage of cookies and any personal data you may keep. Be aware that in Europe you must comply with the "cookie law" that doesn't allow you to create cookies without the user's consent.*

TRY IT OUT Letting the User Select a Theme

In this exercise you add a `DropDownList` control to the master page. This control contains the available themes so a user can choose one. The user's choice is stored in a cookie so it's available again later. The final step is to preselect the correct theme in the drop-down list when the user revisits the page.

1. Open the master page in Markup View and locate the `<aside>` element. Remove the static text `Sidebar Goes Here` and replace it with a `DropDownList` control by dragging it from the Toolbox between the two `<div>` tags. Change the `ID` of the control from `DropDownList1` to `ThemeList`. Type some text (for example, Select a Theme) followed by a line break (`<br />`) in front of the drop-down list to clarify the purpose of the list.
2. Open the control's Smart Tasks panel (in Design View or Markup View), and select Enable AutoPostBack.

3. On the same Smart Tasks panel, click the Edit Items link and insert two items: one with the text Monochrome and one with the text DarkGrey.

4. Double-click the drop-down list in Design View to set up an event handler for the `SelectedIndexChanged` event. Instead of double-clicking, you can also select the `DropDownList`, press F4 to open its Properties Grid, click the button with the lightning bolt to switch to the Events tab, and double-click `SelectedIndexChanged`. Figure 6-20 shows the Properties Grid in Events mode.

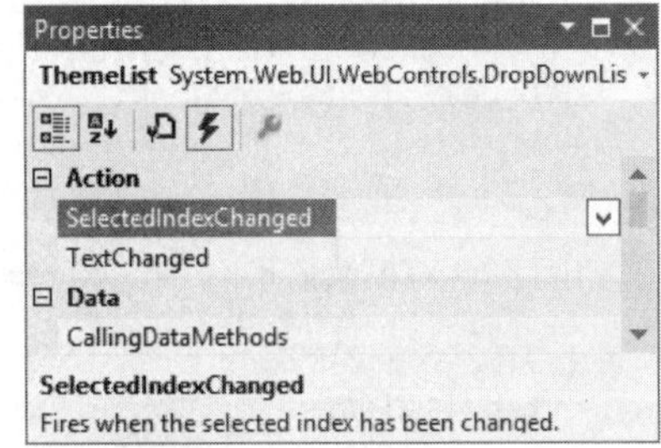

FIGURE 6-20

As you saw earlier, you could also add this event handler in Markup View on the control declaration directly.

Any code you write in the `SelectedIndexChanged` handler fires at the server when the user makes a new selection in the drop-down list at the client. Within the handler block, add the following bolded code that retrieves the selected theme from the list and stores it in a cookie:

VB.NET

```
Protected Sub ThemeList_SelectedIndexChanged(sender As Object,
        e As EventArgs) Handles ThemeList.SelectedIndexChanged
  Dim preferredTheme As HttpCookie = New HttpCookie("PreferredTheme")
  preferredTheme.Expires = DateTime.Now.AddMonths(3)
  preferredTheme.Value = ThemeList.SelectedValue
  Response.Cookies.Add(preferredTheme)
  Response.Redirect(Request.Url.ToString())
End Sub
```

C#

```
protected void ThemeList_SelectedIndexChanged(object sender, EventArgs e)
{
  HttpCookie preferredTheme = new HttpCookie("PreferredTheme");
  preferredTheme.Expires = DateTime.Now.AddMonths(3);
  preferredTheme.Value = ThemeList.SelectedValue;
  Response.Cookies.Add(preferredTheme);
  Response.Redirect(Request.Url.ToString());
}
```

5. Still in the Code Behind of the master page, you need to add some code that preselects the correct item in the list again when the page loads. The best place to do this is in the `Page` class's `Load` event. If you're using C#, the `Page_Load` handler should already be there. When you're using Visual Basic you can add one in two different ways: either double-click the page anywhere in Design View (this works in C# as well), or select (Page Events) from the left drop-down list just above the Document Window in the Code Behind (shown in Figure 6-21), and then choose Load from the second drop-down. This is a nice way to add handlers for other controls as well, like `Button` and `DropDownList` controls.

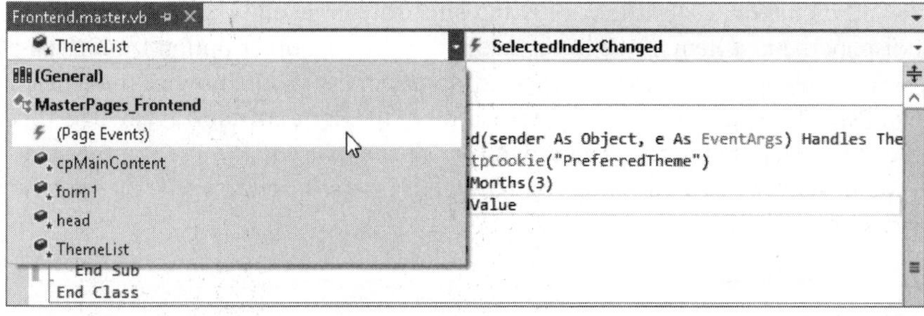

FIGURE 6-21

Within the handler block that VS added for you, add the following code:

VB.NET

```
Protected Sub Page_Load(sender As Object, e As EventArgs) Handles Me.Load
  If Not Page.IsPostBack Then
    Dim selectedTheme As String = Page.Theme
    Dim preferredTheme As HttpCookie = Request.Cookies.Get("PreferredTheme")
    If preferredTheme IsNot Nothing Then
      selectedTheme = preferredTheme.Value
    End If
    If Not String.IsNullOrEmpty(selectedTheme) Then
      Dim item As ListItem = ThemeList.Items.FindByValue(selectedTheme)
      If item IsNot Nothing Then
        item.Selected = True
      End If
      End If
  End If
End Sub
```

C#

```
protected void Page_Load(object sender, EventArgs e)
{
  if (!Page.IsPostBack)
  {
    string selectedTheme = Page.Theme;
    HttpCookie preferredTheme = Request.Cookies.Get("PreferredTheme");
    if (preferredTheme != null)
    {
      selectedTheme = preferredTheme.Value;
    }
    if (!string.IsNullOrEmpty(selectedTheme))
    {
      ListItem item = ThemeList.Items.FindByValue(selectedTheme);
      if (item != null)
      {
        item.Selected = true;
      }
    }
  }
}
```

6. Save all changes and then request `Default.aspx` in your browser again. The drop-down list in the sidebar should display the first item in the list as selected. Select the other option from the list and the page will reload. The item you chose last in the drop-down list should now be preselected in the drop-down list. Close your browser and then browse to `Default.aspx` again. The theme you chose should still be selected in the drop-down list. Notice that you keep seeing the same theme because you haven't written any code yet that applies the selected theme. You see how to do that in a later exercise.

> ***COMMON MISTAKES*** *If you get an error, make sure you have no typos in the code. If nothing seems to happen (for example, the page doesn't post back), check if you set the* `AutoPostBack` *attribute on the* `DropDownList` *control to* `True`*. Also, check the spelling of the name of the cookie (*`PreferredTheme`*) in both code blocks. Finally, if the correct item is not preselected after a postback or after you close and reopen your browser, check you browser's or computer's security settings. You may have configured your browser to delete cookies when you close the browser, or you may have security software running on your machine that blocks cookies altogether. If you can't make it work in one browser, try it in another to rule out problems with the code.*

How It Works

You made three important changes to the master page. First, you added the drop-down list and set `AutoPostBack` to `True`. This causes the page to submit itself back to the server as soon as you choose a new item in the list. When that happens, the code in the `SelectedIndexChanged` handler fires. This code creates a cookie that can be stored on the user's computer. To make the cookie last between browser sessions, you need to set the `Expires` property. In the code example, the cookie is set to expire three months from now, which means the browser will discard it automatically after that period. Every time the user chooses a new theme, this date is extended, setting it for another three months:

VB.NET

```
Dim preferredTheme As HttpCookie = New HttpCookie("PreferredTheme")
preferredTheme.Expires = DateTime.Now.AddMonths(3)
```

C#

```
HttpCookie preferredTheme = new HttpCookie("PreferredTheme");
preferredTheme.Expires = DateTime.Now.AddMonths(3);
```

After the cookie has been created, you can set its `Value` property. In the example, the `SelectedValue` of the `DropDownList` (containing the name of the theme) is stored in the cookie. The cookie is then added to the `Cookies` collection using `Response.Cookies.Add`:

VB.NET

```
preferredTheme.Value = ThemeList.SelectedValue
Response.Cookies.Add(preferredTheme)
```

C#

```
preferredTheme.Value = ThemeList.SelectedValue;
Response.Cookies.Add(preferredTheme);
```

Note that the cookie is added to the `Cookies` collection of the `Response` object that is associated with the response to the user. Later you see how to read this cookie again from the `Cookies` collection of the `Request` object that is associated with the request the user is making for a page.

The final step is to redirect the user to the same page:

VB.NET

```
Response.Redirect(Request.Url.ToString())
```

C#

```
Response.Redirect(Request.Url.ToString());
```

This is necessary because otherwise the new theme won't be applied immediately. Because the theme needs to be set early in the page's life cycle, it can no longer be set for the current request. By redirecting the user to the same page, a new request is made that can successfully apply the selected theme. The next exercise shows you the code to set the selected theme programmatically.

The final change in the master page you made was a modification to the `Page_Load` handler. Inside this method, a `String` variable is declared that holds the currently active theme by looking at `Page.Theme`. This serves as the default theme and will be the one that is preselected in the drop-down list if the user doesn't have a cookie holding her preferred theme. The code then sees if there is a cookie called `PreferredTheme`. If it exists, its value is used to give the string `selectedTheme` a new value. In the end, this `String` variable is then used to find the item in the drop-down list and preselect it.

This way, the drop-down list always displays the currently configured site theme or the item the user has chosen manually, even if she comes back to the site next week. Note the use of the `FindByValue` method on the `Items` collection of the `DropDownList` control. This method returns the item if it is found or `Nothing` (`null` in C#) when the item isn't there. This ensures that if the cookie contains a theme that is no longer available, the code doesn't try to preselect an item in the list that doesn't exist.

With the ability to let a user select a theme in place, the next step is to apply the chosen theme.

As you learned previously, the theme needs to be set in the `PreInit` event, which takes place early in the page's life cycle. Inside this event, you can see if the cookie with the selected theme exists. If it does, you can use its value to set the right theme.

TRY IT OUT Applying the User-Selected Theme

In this exercise, you modify the base page and add some code for the `PreInit` event to set the user's theme.

1. Open the base page file from the `App_Code` folder and add the following code that sets the selected theme during the `PreInit` event. You can add this code before or after the method that checks the page title.

VB.NET

```
Private Sub Page_PreInit(sender As Object, e As EventArgs) Handles Me.PreInit
  Dim preferredTheme As HttpCookie = Request.Cookies.Get("PreferredTheme")
  If preferredTheme IsNot Nothing Then
    Dim folder As String = Server.MapPath("~/App_Themes/" & preferredTheme.Value)
    If System.IO.Directory.Exists(folder) Then
      Page.Theme = preferredTheme.Value
    End If
  End If
End Sub
```

C#

```
private void Page_PreInit(object sender, EventArgs e)
{
  HttpCookie preferredTheme = Request.Cookies.Get("PreferredTheme");
  if (preferredTheme != null)
  {
    string folder = Server.MapPath("~/App_Themes/" + preferredTheme.Value);
    if (System.IO.Directory.Exists(folder))
    {
      Page.Theme = preferredTheme.Value;
    }
  }
}
```

For the C# example, you need to include a `using` statement at the top of the file to bring the `Request` class into scope, like this:

```
using System.Web;
```

2. If you're working with C#, you also need to set up an event handler in the class's constructor for the `PreInit` event, just as you did with the `PreRender` event handler in an earlier exercise. This tells the ASP.NET run time which method will handle the `PreInit` event:

```
public BasePage()
{
  this.PreRender += Page_PreRender;
  this.PreInit += Page_PreInit;
}
```

3. Save changes to all open documents and then request `Default.aspx` in the browser. The page should load with the theme you chose last in the drop-down list in the previous exercise.

4. Choose a new item from the list. The page should reload and should now show the other theme.

   If you find that the page in the browser is showing a combination of the two themes, go back to VS, open `Web.config`, and remove the `styleSheetTheme` attribute from the `<pages>` element, leaving the `theme` attribute in place because it serves as the default for new visitors. If you don't see the theme applied, make sure your page is inheriting the `BasePage` class in the Code Behind.

How It Works

With the hard work of getting the user's favorite theme and storing it in a cookie already done, applying the theme is now very easy. The code in the `PreInit` event handler first verifies whether there is a cookie called `PreferredTheme`. It does this by comparing the return value of the `Get` method to `Nothing` (`null` in C#).

VB.NET

```
Dim preferredTheme As HttpCookie = Request.Cookies.Get("PreferredTheme")
If preferredTheme IsNot Nothing Then
```

C#

```
HttpCookie preferredTheme = Request.Cookies.Get("PreferredTheme");
if (preferredTheme != null)
```

This code uses `Request.Cookies` to read from the cookies that the user's browser sent together with the request. If the cookie exists, its `Value` property is used to set the correct theme:

VB.NET

```
Page.Theme = preferredTheme.Value
```

C#

```
Page.Theme = preferredTheme.Value;
```

Because the theme is set early in the page's life cycle, this setting is applied throughout the page, effectively giving the page the look and feel defined in it. To ensure that the code doesn't try to apply a theme that (no longer) exists, it uses `Directory.Exists` that returns `true` or `false` depending on the presence of the folder on disk. To get at the full path of the theme folder on disk, it uses `Server.MapPath` to translate a virtual path into its physical counterpart. You learn more about virtual paths in the next chapter, while `Server.MapPath` is discussed further in Chapter 9.

With the capability to set the theme programmatically, you're offering your users a quick and easy way to change the page to their liking. The theme affects colors and layout throughout each page in the entire website. Combined with master pages, this gives you a flexible way to influence the look and feel of an entire page. It could also be useful if you were able to change certain controls on a page. For example, you may have the need to give each button in your site the exact same look. This is where the ASP.NET skins come into play.

SKINS

Skins are simple text files that contain markup that enables you to define the look and feel of one or more server controls from a central location. Placed in a theme's folder, they are an integral part of the ASP.NET themes feature. A skin file (with a `.skin` extension) contains the server-side presentational elements of a control. These settings are then applied to all the controls to which the skin applies. To see how this works, consider the following example that defines the skin—or appearance—of a `Button` control:

```
<asp:Button BackColor="#cccccc" ForeColor="#308462" runat="server" />
```

With this skin definition, the buttons in your site will get a `BackColor` of `#cccccc` and a `ForeColor` of `#308462`. All you need to do is create a skin file under your theme's folder, add this markup to it, and that's it. From then on, all the buttons will be changed automatically. Just as with setting the properties on the controls directly as you saw earlier, these properties, like `BackColor` and `ForeColor`, are transformed into client-side HTML and CSS.

Note that this skin markup is similar to the markup of a button. A few differences exist, though. First of all, the control in the skin file cannot have an `ID` attribute. The `ID` is used to uniquely identify a control in a page, and because the skin is applied to all controls, there's no point in giving it an `ID`. Another difference is the number of attributes you can set in the markup. Not all properties of a control are skinnable. For example, you can't set the `Enabled` property of the `Button` through a skin. Microsoft's MSDN documentation lists for each property whether or not they can be skinned. Another way to find out if you can skin a certain property is by simply trying it: just set the property in the skin and if you're not allowed to set it, you'll get an error at run time.

Generally speaking, properties that influence the appearance (`BackColor`, `ForeColor`, `BorderColor`, and so on) can be skinned and properties that influence behavior (`Enabled`, `EnableViewState`, and more) cannot be set.

When you create a new skin file using the Add New Item dialog box, you get a bunch of text wrapped in a server-side comment block. You can safely remove these comments because they only give you a short example of how skins work. You can define multiple controls in a single skin file. However, from a maintainability point of view, it's often easier to name each skin file after the control it represents. For example, you would have a file called `Button.skin` for buttons, `Label.skin` for labels, and so on.

Instead of applying formatting elements directly to the control's properties in the skin and thus to the final markup in the page, it's often better to use the `CssClass` property to point to a CSS class in one of your CSS files. That way, it's even easier to make sitewide changes and you avoid bloating the final HTML. Given the previous example, a file with the following skin definition and a class in the theme's CSS file would give the same effect:

```
<asp:Button CssClass="MyButton" runat="server" />

.MyButton
{
  color: #308462;
  background-color: #cccccc;
}
```

Creating a Skin File

Skin files must be created in the theme's folder directly. You can't store them in a subfolder like you do with the theme's images. In the following exercise you see how to create a simple skin file to change the look and feel of all button controls in the website. Later chapters in this book build on this knowledge by defining more complex skins for other controls like the `GridView`.

When you start typing in a skin file, you'll notice that the familiar IntelliSense doesn't kick in. This makes it slightly difficult to define your controls and their attributes. However, there is a simple workaround:

1. Open Visual Studio's Options dialog box by choosing Tools ➪ Options.
2. Expand the Text Editor category and click File Extension.

3. In the Extension box, type **skin** and then from the Editor drop-down list, choose User Control Editor.

4. Click the Add button and then click the OK button to dismiss the Options dialog box.

From now on, you'll get IntelliSense in skin files (you may need to reopen existing skin files first if you already created one). With this setting on, you may get a warning in the Error List about build providers when you have a skin file open. You can safely ignore this warning, because skins work fine at run time even with these settings in VS.

TRY IT OUT Creating a Skin for the Button Control

To effectively use skins, you should strive to use `CssClass` attributes as much as possible instead of applying inline attributes that all end up in the final HTML of the page, increasing its size and load time. However, to show you how it works in case you do have a special need to add inline attributes, this exercise shows you how to apply both.

1. In the `Monochrome` theme folder, add a new skin file and call it **Button.skin**. You add the file by right-clicking the `Monochrome` folder and choosing Add ➪ Skin File. In the dialog box that follows, type **Button** as the filename and click OK.

2. Delete the entire contents from the file and type the following code:

```
<asp:Button CssClass="MyButton" BackColor="#509EE7" runat="server" />
```

   Note that this markup uses a combination of inline attributes for styling (the `BackColor`) and the `CssClass` to point to a selector in your CSS file. Also note that this control does not have an `ID` attribute. As explained earlier, you can ignore the warning about missing build providers because your skin files will work fine at run time. As soon as you close the skin file, the warning goes away.

3. Open the `Monochrome.css` file from the theme folder and add this CSS selector at the end of the file:

```
.MyButton
{
  color: White;
}
```

4. Create a new Web Form in the `Demos` folder and call it `SkinsDemo.aspx`. Make sure you base it on the exported MyBasePage template you created earlier. Give the page a `Title` of `Skins Demo` and then add a `Button` by dragging it from the Toolbox into the `cpMainContent` area of the page. You end up with this code:

```
<asp:Content ID="Content2" ContentPlaceHolderID="cpMainContent" runat="Server">
  <asp:Button ID="Button1" runat="server" Text="Button" />
</asp:Content>
```

5. Save all changes and then request `SkinsDemo.aspx` in the browser. If necessary, switch to the Monochrome theme. The button you added in step 4 should now have a blue background with white text on it. If the changed colors don't show up, make sure you selected the right theme in the drop-down list and that you added the `MyButton` CSS class to the CSS file of the Monochrome

theme. If you still don't see the changes, press Ctrl+F5 or Ctrl+R to force a fresh copy of the CSS file from the server.

How It Works

To see how it works, you should take a look at the HTML for the page in the browser. The `Button` control has been transformed in the following HTML:

```
<input type="submit" name="ctl00$cpMainContent$Button1" value="Button"
  id="cpMainContent_Button1" class="MyButton" style="background-color:#509EE7;" />
```

Both the `CssClass` and the `BackColor` attributes in the skin have been added to the HTML. The former ended up as a `class` attribute on the button, and the latter has been transformed into a `style` attribute. The `MyButton` class in the CSS file gives the button its white text and the inline style determines the background color of the button. If you choose the DarkGrey theme in the drop-down list and then look at the HTML again, you'll notice it has no `class` and `style` attributes, giving the button its default look.

As you can see, skins are extremely easy to use and enable you to radically change the look of specific controls in your site. But what if you don't want all your buttons to change to blue and white at the same time? What if you need one special button that has a red background? You can do this with *named skins.*

Named Skins

Named skins are identical to normal skins with one exception: they have a `SkinID` set that enables you to refer to that skin by name. Controls in your ASPX pages can then use that `SkinID` to apply that specific skin to the control. The next exercise shows you how this works.

TRY IT OUT Creating a Named Skin for the Button Control

The easiest way to create a named skin is by copying the code for an existing one and then adding a `SkinID` attribute. Be aware that if you copy and paste a skin definition, VS automatically adds an `ID` attribute (that is, if you connected skin files to the User Control Editor as described earlier). This `ID` is not allowed, so you need to remove it.

1. Open `Button.skin`, copy all the code, and paste it below the existing markup.
2. If VS added an `ID` attribute, remove it, together with its value (that is, remove `ID="Button1"`).
3. Remove the `CssClass` attribute and its value, change the `BackColor` of the button to `Red`, and set the `ForeColor` to `Black`.
4. Add a `SkinID` attribute of `RedButton`. You should end up with this code:

   ```
   <asp:Button CssClass="MyButton" BackColor="#509EE7" runat="server" />
   <asp:Button BackColor="Red" ForeColor="Black" SkinID="RedButton" runat="server" />
   ```

5. Save and close the skin file.

6. Open `SkinsDemo.aspx` and add a second button. Set the `SkinID` of this button to `RedButton`. Notice how IntelliSense helps you pick the right `SkinID`. The code for the two buttons should now look like this:

```
<asp:Button ID="Button1" runat="server" Text="Button" />
<asp:Button ID="Button2" runat="server" Text="Button" SkinID="RedButton" />
```

7. Open `SkinsDemo.aspx` in the browser. You should now see two buttons; the blue one you added earlier and the new black on red one. If you don't see the different colors, ensure you have selected the Monochrome theme in the browser.

How It Works

Named skins work almost exactly the same as normal skins. However, with a named skin a control can point to a specific skin in one of the skin files. In the `SkinsDemo.aspx` page, the first button gets its settings from the default, unnamed skin, and the other now gets its settings from the skin with its `SkinID` set to `RedButton`. If you assign a nonexistent `SkinID` to a control, ASP.NET will simply ignore it and not raise an error.

With named skins, you have a very flexible solution at your disposal. With the normal skins, you can quickly change the appearance of all controls in your site. You can then use a named skin to override this behavior for a few controls that you want to look different.

Disable Theming for Specific Controls

If for some reason you don't want to apply a skin to a specific control, you can disable the skin by setting the `EnableTheming` property of the control, like this:

```
<asp:Button ID="Button1" runat="server" EnableTheming="False" Text="Button" />
```

With `EnableTheming` set to `False`, the skin is not applied to the control. CSS settings from the theme's CSS file are still applied, though.

PRACTICAL TIPS ON CREATING CONSISTENT PAGES

The following list provides some practical tips on creating consistent pages:

- When you create a new website, always start by adding a master page that you base all other pages on. Even if you think you have a site with only a few pages, a master page will help you ensure a consistent look across the entire site. Adding a master page at a later stage to the site means making a lot of manual changes to existing pages.
- As soon as you find yourself adding styling information to complex controls like the `TreeView` and `Menu` (discussed in the next chapter) or data-aware controls like the `GridView` (discussed in Chapter 13), consider creating a skin for them. The fact that you can control the layout of all similar controls from a single location makes it a lot easier to update your site. If you want to override the layout for a few controls, you can always use named skins with a `SkinID` or disable the skin entirely by setting `EnableTheming` to `False`.

- When creating skins or setting style properties directly on a control, consider using the `CssClass` property instead, and then moving all styling-related properties to the CSS for the site or theme. This decreases the page's size and makes it easier to make changes to the layout afterward.
- The Export Template feature of Visual Studio is a great time saver. You can use it not only to create a template for an ASPX page and its Code Behind, but also for other files like classes and CSS files, and even a complete website. This enables you to jump-start the creation of new files, saving you from typing the same stuff over and over again.

SUMMARY

The consistent look and feel of all pages in your site is important to give your site a professional and attractive look. This in turn helps your visitors in finding the right information in your site, increasing the chances that they might visit your site again. ASP.NET 4.5 offers a number of great tools to aid you in creating a consistent looking website.

ASP.NET master pages and content pages help you create a layout that is repeated in every page that is based on that master.

Whereas master pages define a centralized look and feel, you use a base page to centralize behavior such as checking the page for invalid titles.

Themes are used to change the look and feel of the pages in your site and the controls they contain. Because themes can contain CSS files, images, and skins, you can change colors, fonts, positioning, and images simply by applying a theme. By making good use of techniques like named skins and the `EnableTheming` attribute, you can create a design that applies to your entire site, while you maintain the flexibility to overrule the design on a control-by-control basis.

The Planet Wrox website is now starting to grow. This means it becomes more difficult for you and your visitors to find the right pages. The next chapter shows you a number of different ways for your users to navigate your site so they won't have any problems finding the page they are looking for.

EXERCISES

1. What's the difference between a `ContentPlaceHolder` and a `Content` control? In what type of page do you use which one?

2. How do you hook up a `Content` control in a content page to the `ContentPlaceHolder` in the master page?

3. Imagine you have created a skin that gets applied to all buttons in your site with the following skin definition:

```
<asp:Button runat="server" CssClass="MyButton" />
```

The imaginary CSS class `MyButton` sets the background color of the button to black and the foreground color to white. To draw attention to a specific button in a page, you decide to give it a red background instead. Which options do you have to control the look of this single button?

4. Explain the differences between setting the `Theme` property and the `StyleSheetTheme` property for a page.

5. Name three different ways to set the `Theme` property for a page and explain the differences between the options.

6. What's the main reason for implementing a base page in your website?

You can find answers to these exercises in Appendix A.

▶ WHAT YOU LEARNED IN THIS CHAPTER

Base page	A class inheriting from the ASP.NET `Page` class that serves as the parent class for your ASPX pages
Content page	An ASPX Web Form that uses a master page to build up its global appearance and layout
Cookies	Little pieces of text that you can store on the user's computer and access again from the server
Master page	A central page that defines the look and feel of content pages that use the master page
Named skin	An ASP.NET skin with an explicit `SkinID` set, enabling you to refer to this skin by its ID
Page life cycle	The series of events that an ASPX page goes through when requested by a browser
Skin	A collection of presentational settings to influence the appearance of controls in the browser
Theme	A collection of CSS styles, skins, and images to change the appearance of pages in your site

7

Navigation

WHAT YOU WILL LEARN IN THIS CHAPTER:

- How to move around in your site using server controls and plain HTML
- How to address pages and other resources like images
- How to use the ASP.NET `Menu`, `TreeView`, and `SiteMapPath` navigation controls
- How to send users from one page to another programmatically

WROX.COM CODE DOWNLOADS FOR THIS CHAPTER

You can find the wrox.com code downloads for this chapter on the Download Code tab at `www.wrox.com/remtitle.cgi?isbn=1118311809`. The code is in the Chapter 7 download.

When your site contains more than a handful of pages, it's important to have a solid and clear navigation structure that enables users to find their way around your site. If you implement a good navigation system, all the disconnected web pages in your project form a complete and coherent website.

When you think about important parts of a navigation system, the first thing that you may come up with is a menu. Menus come in all sorts and sizes, ranging from simple and static HTML links to complex, fold-out menus driven by CSS or JavaScript. But there's more to navigation than menus alone. ASP.NET comes with a number of useful navigation controls that enable you to set up a navigation system in no time. These controls include the `Menu`, `TreeView`, and `SiteMapPath`, which you learn about in this chapter.

Besides visual controls like `Menu`, navigation is also about *structure*. A well-organized site is easy for your users to navigate. The `Web.sitemap` file that is used by the navigation controls helps you define the logical structure of your site.

Another important part of navigation takes place at the server. Sending a user from one page to another in Code Behind based on some condition is a very common scenario. For example, imagine an administrator entering a new CD or concert review in the Management section of the website. When the review is completed, you may want to show the administrator the full details by redirecting her to a new page.

In this chapter, you learn how to use the different navigation options at your disposal. Before you look at the built-in navigation controls, however, you need to understand the different options you have to address the resources in your site, such as ASPX pages and images.

DIFFERENT WAYS TO MOVE AROUND YOUR SITE

The most common way to let a user move from one page to another is by using the `<a>` element. This element has an `href` attribute that enables you to define the address of a page or other resource you want to link to. Between the tags you can place the content you want to link, such as text, an image, or other HTML. The following snippet shows a simple example of the `<a>` element:

```
<a href="Login.aspx">You can log in here</a>
```

With this code in a web page, after users click the text "You can log in here," they are taken to the `Login.aspx` page, which should be in the same folder as the page that contains the link.

The `<a>` element has a server-side counterpart called the `HyperLink`. It eventually ends up as an `<a>` element in the page. The `NavigateUrl` property of this control maps directly to the `href` attribute of the `<a>` element. For example, a server-side `HyperLink` in a content page such as this:

```
<asp:HyperLink runat="server" id="LoginLink" NavigateUrl="Login.aspx">
       You can log in here</asp:HyperLink>
```

produces the following HTML in the browser:

```
<a id="LoginLink" href="Login.aspx">You can log in here</a>
```

Other than the ID that is assigned by the ASP.NET run time, this code is identical to the earlier example. In both cases, the `href` attribute points to the `Login.aspx` page using a relative URL. The next topic describes the differences between relative and absolute URLs.

Understanding Absolute and Relative URLs

Key to working with links in your site is a good understanding of the different forms a *uniform resource locator* (*URL*) to a resource inside or outside your website can take. A URL is used to uniquely identify a resource in your or another website. These URLs are used in different places, including the `href` attribute of a hyperlink or a `<link>` element to point to a CSS file, the `src` attribute pointing to an image or a JavaScript source file, and the `url()` value of a CSS property. A URL can be expressed as a *relative URL* or an *absolute URL*. Both have advantages and disadvantages that you should be aware of.

Relative URLs

In the previous examples you saw a relative URL that points to another resource relative to the location where the URL is used. This means that the page containing the `<a>` element and the `Login.aspx` page should both be placed in the same folder in your site. To refer to resources in other folders you can use the following URLs. All the examples are based on a site structure shown in Figure 7-1.

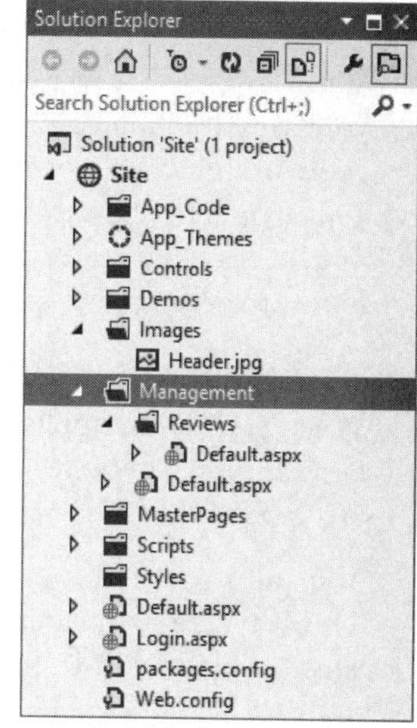

FIGURE 7-1

To link from `Login.aspx` in the root to `Default.aspx` in the `Management` folder, you can use this URL:

```
<a href="Management/Default.aspx">Management</a>
```

To refer to the image `Header.jpg` from `Default.aspx` in the `Management` folder, you can use this URL:

```
<img src="../Images/Header.jpg" />
```

The two leading periods "navigate" one folder up to the root, and then the path goes back in the `Images` folder to point to `Header.jpg`.

For a deeper folder hierarchy, you can use multiple double periods, one for each folder you want to go upward in the site hierarchy, like the following `<img>` element. You can use it to refer to the same image from pages in the `Reviews` folder, which is located under the `Management` folder:

```
<img src="../../Images/Header.jpg" />
```

One benefit of relative URLs is that you can move a set of files to another directory at the same level without breaking their internal links. However, at the same time, they make it more difficult to move files to a different level in the site hierarchy. For example, if you moved the `Login.aspx` page to a separate folder like `Members`, the link to the `Management` folder would break. The new `Members` folder doesn't have `Management` as its subfolder, so `Management/Default.aspx` is no longer a valid link.

To overcome this problem, you can use root-based relative URLs.

Root-Based Relative URLs

Root-based relative URLs always start with a leading forward slash to indicate the root of the site. If you take the link to the `Management` folder again, its root-based version looks like this:

```
<a href="/Management/Default.aspx">Management</a>
```

Note the leading forward slash in front of the `Management` folder to indicate the root of the website. This link is unambiguous. It always points to the `Default.aspx` file in the `Management` folder in the root. With this link, moving the `Login.aspx` page to a subfolder doesn't break it; it still points to the exact same file.

Relative URLs in Server-Side Controls

With ASP.NET Server Controls, you have another option at your disposal to refer to resources in your website: You can use the tilde (~) character to point to the current root of the site. This is especially useful when you run your website as a separate *application folder* under the main website. This would be the case if your main site ran under `www.PlanetWrox.com/Site` rather than under `www.PlanetWrox.com`, for example. To see what that means, consider this image that uses the tilde in its `ImageUrl`:

```
<asp:Image ID="Image1" runat="server" ImageUrl="~/Images/Header.jpg" />
```

When you use an application folder such as `Site`, the image is searched for at `/Site/Images/Header.jpg`. If you reconfigure the site to run without an application folder, the image is looked for at `/Images/Header.jpg` without requiring you to change any code.

You can also use the ~ syntax on regular HTML elements, provided you add the `runat` attribute. This way, the path is processed at the server and then returned to the client. The following example shows a plain HTML link that links to a page in the `Management` folder:

```
<a href="~/Management/Default.aspx" runat="server">Management</a>
```

Previous versions of Visual Studio set up the built-in web server as an application folder, making the use of the tilde a much needed option. However, the new IIS Express that now ships with VS 2012 does not use an application folder by default. So, when you start up the web server by requesting a page, its address will be something like `http://localhost:59898/` and not `http://localhost:59898/Site/`. If you still see the `Site` part in the URL, you may be running the older built-in web server instead. If that's the case, you can switch to using IIS Express by right-clicking the site in the Solution Explorer and then choosing Use IIS Express. The remainder of this book assumes you're using IIS Express and do not have an application folder in the URL for your site.

Absolute URLs

In contrast to relative URLs that refer to a resource from a document or site root perspective, you can also use absolute URLs that refer to a resource by its full path. So instead of directly referring to an image and optionally specifying a folder, you include the full name of the domain and protocol information (the `http://` prefix). Here's an example that refers to the Wrox logo at the Wrox Programmer to Programmer site (`http://p2p.wrox.com`), where you go for questions about this and other Wrox books or for general questions regarding programming:

```
<img src="http://p2p.wrox.com/images/header/wrox_logo.gif" />
```

Absolute URLs are required if you want to refer to a resource outside your own website. With such a URL, the `http://` prefix is important. If you leave it out, the browser will look for a folder called `p2p.wrox.com` inside your *own* website.

Absolute URLs are unambiguous. They always refer to a fixed location, which helps you to make sure you're always referring to the exact same resource, no matter where the source document is located. This may make you think that they are ideal to use everywhere—including references to resources within your own site—but that's not the case. The extra protocol and domain information adds to the size of the page in the browser, making it unnecessarily slower to download. But more important, it creates difficulties if you're changing your domain name, or if you want to reuse some functionality in a different website. For example, if you previously had your site running on `www.mydomain.com` but you're moving it to `www.someotherdomain.com`, you will need to update all the absolute URLs in the entire website.

You will also have trouble with absolute URLs during development. Quite often, you test your website on a URL such as `http://localhost`. If you were to point all your images to that URL, they would all break as soon as you put your site on a production domain like `www.PlanetWrox.com`.

In short, use absolute URLs with caution. You always need them when referring to resources outside your website, but you should give preference to relative URLs within your own projects wherever possible.

Understanding Default Documents

In the context of URLs you should also know about *default documents*. When you browse to a site like `www.domainname.com` you magically see a page appear. How does this work? Each web server has so-called default documents, a list of document names that can be served to a browser when no explicit document name is supplied. So, when you browse to `www.domainname.com`, the web server scans the directory requested (the root folder in this example) and processes the first file from its default documents list it finds on disk. In most ASP.NET scenarios, the web server is set up to use `Default.aspx` as the default document. So, when you browse to `www.domainname.com` on an ASP.NET web server, you are actually served the page `www.domainname.com/Default.aspx`.

In the links you create, you should generally leave out `Default.aspx` when it isn't needed. It decreases the page size, but more important, it makes it easier for your users to type the address.

Now that you have seen how you can use URLs to point to documents and other files, it's time to look at some higher-level controls that make use of these URLs: the ASP.NET navigation controls.

USING THE NAVIGATION CONTROLS

ASP.NET 4.5 offers three useful navigation tools: `SiteMapPath`, `TreeView`, and `Menu`. Figure 7-2 shows basic examples of the three navigation controls, without any styling applied.

The `SiteMapPath` on the left shows the user the path to the current page. This helps if users want to go up one or more levels in the site hierarchy. It also helps them to understand where they are. The `TreeView` can display the structure of your site and enables you to expand and collapse the different nodes; in Figure 7-2 the entire tree is expanded. The `Menu` control on the right initially only displays the Home menu item. However, as soon as you move the mouse over the menu item, a submenu appears. In Figure 7-2 one of these child elements is the Reviews item, which in turn has child elements itself.

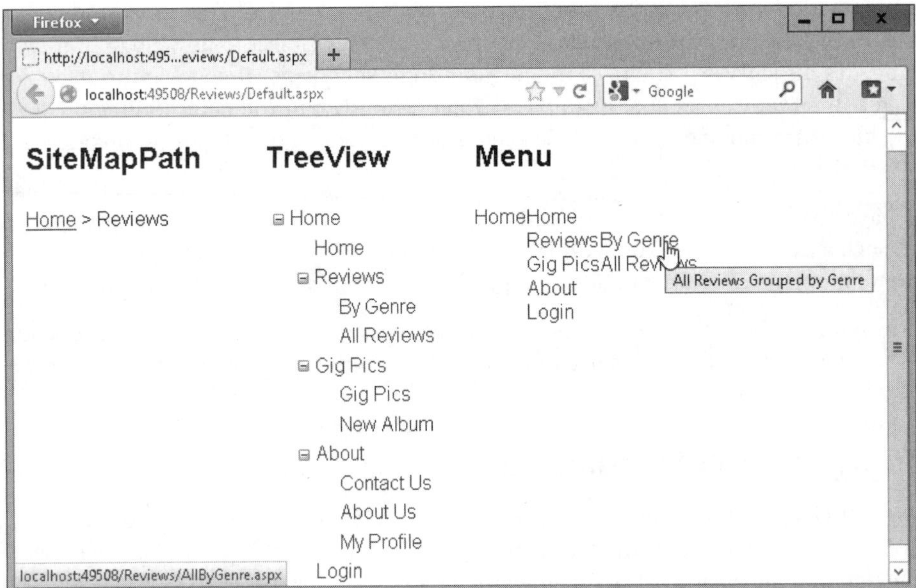

FIGURE 7-2

Although quite different in behavior and appearance, these three navigation controls have part of their design in common.

Architecture of the Navigation Controls

To make it easy to show relevant pages in your site using a `Menu`, a `TreeView`, or a `SiteMapPath`, ASP.NET uses an XML-based file that describes the *logical structure* of your website. By default, this file is called `Web.sitemap`. This file is then used by the navigation controls in your site to present relevant links in an organized way. Simply by hooking up one of the navigation controls to the `Web.sitemap` file, you can create complex user interface elements like fold-out menus or a tree view.

Examining the Web.sitemap File

By default, you should call the site map file `Web.sitemap`. This enables the controls to find the right file automatically. For more advanced scenarios you can have multiple site map files with different names, with a configuration setting in the `Web.config` file that exposes these additional files to the system. In most cases, a single site map file is sufficient. A basic version of the site map file can look like this:

```
<?xml version="1.0" encoding="utf-8" ?>
<siteMap xmlns="http://schemas.microsoft.com/AspNet/SiteMap-File-1.0">
  <siteMapNode url="~/" title="Home" description="Go to the homepage">
    <siteMapNode url="~/Reviews" title="Reviews"
            description="Reviews published on this site" />
    <siteMapNode url="~/About" title="About"
            description="About this site" />
  </siteMapNode>
</siteMap>
```

The site map file contains `siteMapNode` elements that together form the logical structure of your site. In this example, there is a single root node called Home, which in turn contains two child elements, Reviews and About.

Key Elements of the Web.sitemap File

Each `siteMapNode` can have many child nodes (but there can only be one `siteMapNode` directly under the `siteMap` element), enabling you to create a site structure that can be both wide and deep. The `siteMapNode` elements in this example have three of their attributes set: `url`, `title`, and `description`. The `url` attribute should point to a valid page in your website. You can use the ~ syntax you saw in the previous section to refer to application-root–based URLs. The ASP.NET run time doesn't allow you to specify the same URL more than once, but you can work around that by making the URL unique by adding a query string. For example, `~/Login.aspx` and `~/Login.aspx?type=Admin` will be seen as two different pages. You see more of the query string later in this chapter.

The `title` attribute is used in the navigation controls to display the name of the page. You see more about this later when you work with the `Menu`, `TreeView`, and `SiteMapPath` controls. The `description` attribute is used as a tooltip for the navigation elements. Figure 7-2 shows a tooltip for the By Genre item.

The navigation controls work together with the ASP.NET security mechanism. That is, you can automatically hide elements from controls like the `Menu` that users don't have access to. Security is described in more detail in Chapter 16.

The `SiteMapPath` control that displays a breadcrumb (discussed later in this chapter) is able to find the `Web.sitemap` file itself. For the other two navigation controls, you need to specify a `SiteMapDataSource` control (which you can find under the Data category of the Toolbox) explicitly as an intermediate layer to the `Web.sitemap` file.

To create a `Web.sitemap` file, you need to add one to your site and then manually add the necessary `siteMapNode` elements to it. There is no automated way in Visual Studio to create a site map file based on the current site's structure, although third-party solutions exist that help you with this.

TRY IT OUT Creating a Web.sitemap File

In this exercise you add a new `Web.sitemap` file to the site and add a bunch of `siteMapNode` elements to it. This site map serves as the basis for the navigation controls in the site.

1. Right-click the website in the Solution Explorer, choose Add ➢ Add New Item, and click Site Map. Leave the default name set to `Web.sitemap` and click Add. You end up with one root element containing two child nodes in the `Web.sitemap` file.
2. Modify the `Web.sitemap` so it contains this code:

```
<?xml version="1.0" encoding="utf-8" ?>
<siteMap xmlns="http://schemas.microsoft.com/AspNet/SiteMap-File-1.0">
  <siteMapNode url="~/" title="Home" description="Home">
    <siteMapNode url="~/Default.aspx" title="Home"
           description="Go to the homepage" />
    <siteMapNode url="~/Reviews/Default.aspx" title="Reviews"
             description="Reviews published on this site">
      <siteMapNode url="~/Reviews/AllByGenre.aspx" title="By Genre"
```

```
                 description="All Reviews Grouped by Genre" />
      <siteMapNode url="~/Reviews/All.aspx" title="All Reviews"
                 description="All Reviews" />
    </siteMapNode>
    <siteMapNode url="~/About/Default.aspx" title="About"
             description="About this Site">
      <siteMapNode url="~/About/Contact.aspx" title="Contact Us"
                 description="Contact Us" />
      <siteMapNode url="~/About/AboutUs.aspx" title="About Us"
                 description="About Us" />
    </siteMapNode>
    <siteMapNode url="~/Login.aspx" title="Login"
             description="Log in to this web site" />
  </siteMapNode>
</siteMap>
```

Remember, you don't have to type all this code yourself. You can find a copy of the file in this chapter's code file that you can download from the Wrox website.

3. Save the file; you're done with it for now.

> **COMMON MISTAKES** *Make sure you type the code exactly as shown here. Notice that some items, such as the first Home element, contain other child elements and have their closing tag further down in the code. In contrast, items such as By Genre are using self-closing tags and do not have any child elements.*

How It Works

Although you didn't add any spectacular code in the `Web.sitemap` file, a few things are worth discussing. First of all, note that the site map only contains a single root node called Home. This is enforced by the `Web.sitemap` file, which doesn't allow more than one root element. The downside of this is that this single root element will also be the root item of your `Menu` and `TreeView` controls. In Figure 7-2 you can see how all submenus of the `TreeView` fall under the `Home` node. In most websites, however, it's much more common to have the `Home` item at the same level as the others. Therefore, in this exercise you added an additional `Home` node directly under the parent node to align it with the Reviews, About, and Login items. In a later exercise you see how to hide the root element from the controls, enabling you to only show the "first children" of the root node and their children. To overcome the problem that URLs in the `siteMapNode` elements need to be unique, you set one to `~/` and the other to `~/Default.aspx`. Because of the way web servers handle default documents, this eventually points to the same file.

A `Web.sitemap` file all by itself isn't very useful. You need to add navigation controls to your site to make use of the site map. In the next section you see how to use the `Menu` control. Later sections dig into the `TreeView` and `SiteMapPath` controls.

Using the Menu Control

The Menu control is very easy to use and tweak. To create a basic menu, all you need to do is add one to your page, hook it up to a SiteMapDataSource control, and you're done. But at the same time, the control is quite flexible and has around 80 public properties (including the ones shared by all controls) that enable you to tweak every visual aspect of the control. The following table lists the most common properties used with the menu. Refer to the MSDN online help for a complete description of this control.

PROPERTY	DESCRIPTION
CssClass	Enables you to set a CSS class attribute that applies to the entire control.
StaticEnableDefaultPopOutImage	A boolean that determines whether images are used to indicate submenus on the top-level menu items.
DynamicEnableDefaultPopOutImage	A boolean that determines whether images are used to indicate submenus on submenu items.
DisappearAfter	Determines the time in milliseconds that menu items will remain visible after you move your mouse away from them.
MaximumDynamicDisplayLevels	Determines the number of levels of submenu items that the control can display. Useful with very large site maps to limit the number of items being sent to the browser.
DataSourceID	The ID of a SiteMapDataSource control that supplies the data for the menu from the Web.sitemap file.
Orientation	Determines whether to use a horizontal menu with drop-out submenus, or a vertical menu with fold-out submenus.
RenderingMode	Introduced in ASP.NET 4, this property determines whether the control presents itself using tables and inline styles or unordered lists and CSS styles.
IncludeStyleBlock	Introduced in ASP.NET 4, this property gives you full control (and responsibility) in styling the control. When set to False, ASP.NET does not add the embedded style sheet block used to lay out the Menu control, making you responsible for writing the CSS.

The Menu control also has a few properties that start with Static or Dynamic, two of which were shown in the preceding table. The Static properties are used to control the main menu items that appear when the page loads. Because they don't change or get hidden when you hover over them, they are considered static. The submenus are dynamic, because they appear only when you activate the relevant main menu items.

In addition to these properties, the `Menu` control also has a number of style properties that enable you to change the look and feel of the different parts of the menu.

Using the Rendering Mode

Earlier versions of the `Menu` control were criticized because of the HTML they generated. In ASP .NET 2.0 and 3.5, the `Menu` control generated bloated HTML using tables and inline styles. Besides increasing the size of the page unnecessarily, this also meant that the `Menu` was much harder to style using your own CSS. Fortunately, this was fixed in ASP.NET 4 with the introduction of the `RenderingMode` property on the control. By default in new ASP.NET 4 and 4.5 sites, this property ensures the control renders itself as an unordered list using `<ul>` and `<li>` elements. You can override this behavior by setting the `RenderingMode` property to `Table` instead.

You see the `Menu` control and the HTML it generates in the next exercise.

Creating a Basic Version of the Menu Control

To see how the `Menu` control operates, you're best off creating a very basic version first. Once you understand how it works and how it operates under the hood, you can style the menu to your liking so it blends in with the design of the rest of your site.

TRY IT OUT Adding a Menu to the Site

In this exercise, you see how to add a `Menu` control to the master page that uses the `Web.sitemap` file to build up the menu. The `Menu` is added to the `<nav>` element in the master page and presents the menu items horizontally. Because of this orientation, this `Menu` is suitable only for the Monochrome theme. Later you add a `TreeView` to represent the pages in the site, and write some code that shows the `Menu` for the Monochrome theme and the `TreeView` for the DarkGrey theme.

1. Open the master page in Markup View and locate the `<nav>` element. Remove the placeholder text `Menu Goes Here.`

2. From the Navigation category of the Toolbox, drag a `Menu` and drop it between the `<nav>` tags. Set the `CssClass` of the `Menu` control to `MainMenu`:

```
<nav>
  <asp:Menu ID="Menu1" runat="server" CssClass="MainMenu"></asp:Menu>
</nav>
```

3. Switch to Design View. You may notice that the Design View doesn't look like the final page anymore. That's because you may have removed the `styleSheetTheme` attribute from the `<pages>` element in `Web.config`. You can leave it like this for now. With much of the styling already done, this isn't so important. You can still see how the content inside the `cpMainContent` placeholder is

going to end up in the browser. If your Design View does look much closer to the final page, open the `Web.config` file and remove the `styleSheetTheme` attribute from the `<pages>` element.

4. Click the `Menu` control's gray arrow to open its Smart Tasks panel.
5. From the Choose Data Source drop-down list select <New data source>. In the dialog box that appears, click the Site Map icon. Figure 7-3 shows the Data Source Configuration Wizard.

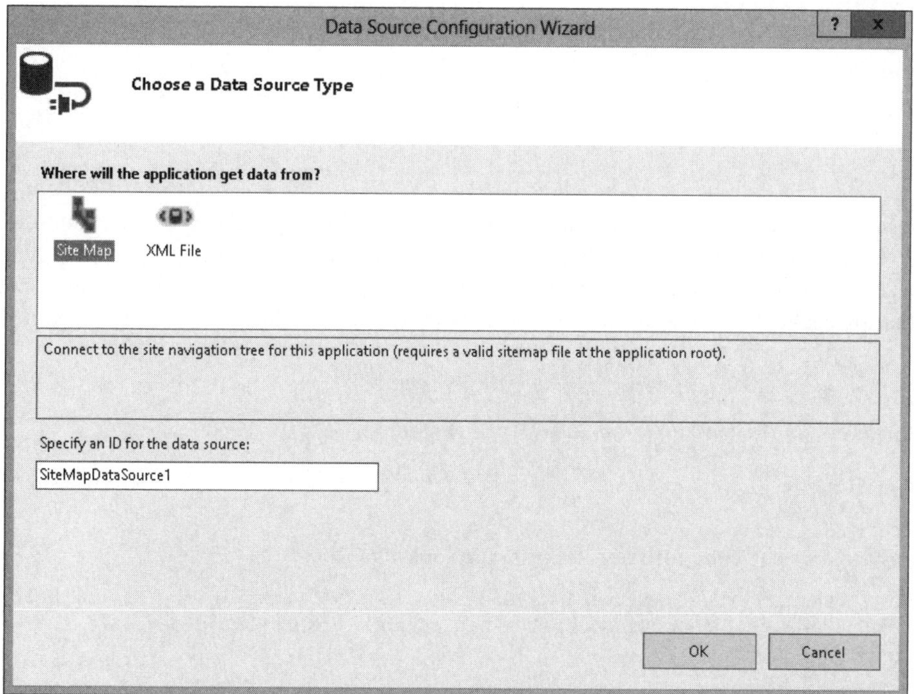

FIGURE 7-3

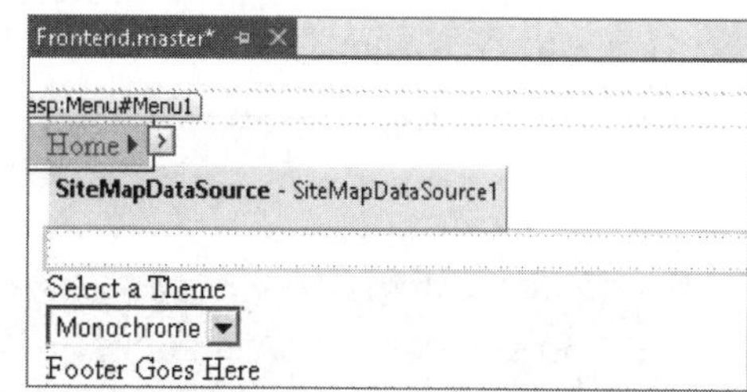

FIGURE 7-4

6. Click OK to close the dialog box.
7. When you return to the page, the `Menu` control now shows the top-level element, Home (see Figure 7-4).
8. Click the `SiteMapDataSource` control once and then press F4 to open or activate the Properties Grid. Change the `ShowStartingNode` property from `True` to `False`. Note that as soon as you do this, the `Menu` control in the designer is updated and shows all direct child menus under the root element: Home, Reviews, About, and Login. Figure 7-5 shows how your `Menu` control should look now.

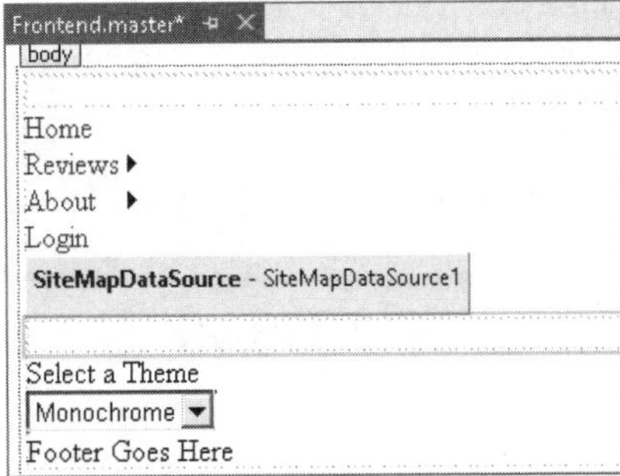

FIGURE 7-5

9. Click the `Menu` control once to select it and then make the following changes to the properties of the control using the Properties Grid. Because the `Menu` control has so many properties, you may find it easier to find them if you sort the list of properties alphabetically in the Properties Grid. You can do that by clicking the second button on the toolbar with an A, a Z, and an arrow on it.

PROPERTY	VALUE
`StaticEnableDefaultPopOutImage`	`False`
`Orientation`	`Horizontal`

When you're ready, the code for your `Menu` should look like this:

```
<asp:Menu ID="Menu1" runat="server" CssClass="MainMenu" Orientation="Horizontal"
      DataSourceID="SiteMapDataSource1" StaticEnableDefaultPopOutImage="False">
</asp:Menu>
```

10. Save the changes to the master page and then request `Default.aspx` in your browser. If necessary, use the Theme drop-down list to make Monochrome the active theme. You should now see the menu in the horizontal menu area. Hover your mouse over the items, and you'll see sub items appear as in Figure 7-6, which shows the page in Google's Chrome browser.

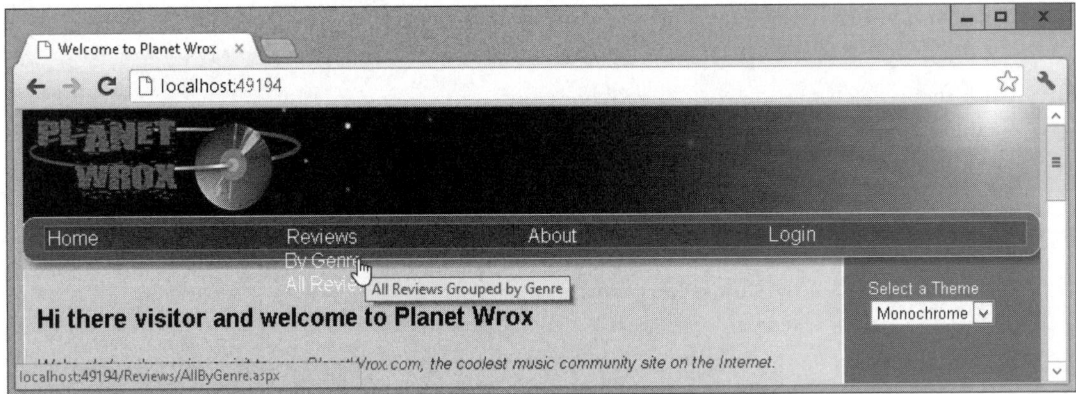

FIGURE 7-6

Note that the text on the sub items is hard to read. That's because the CSS from the Monochrome theme has changed the text of all anchors in the menu area to white and no explicit background color has been set. After you've seen how the `Menu` control works, you get a chance to fix its styling.

Don't worry if the menu doesn't look good in the DarkGrey theme. You see how to implement a different navigation control for that theme later in this chapter.

How It Works

When a page with the menu is sent to the browser, the `Menu` control asks the `SiteMapDataSource`, defined in the same master page, for data. This data source control in turn reads the `Web.sitemap` file and then hands over the data to the `Menu` control. Based on the hierarchical XML, the `Menu` is able to generate the necessary HTML and JavaScript. It generates a `<ul>` element for the top menu items with nested subelements, each containing one or more menu items. The `Menu` control initially hides the submenus. When you hover your mouse over one of the main menu items, the submenu becomes visible. This is done by some JavaScript.

If you search the source of the page for the JavaScript code that hides or shows the menu, you won't find it. So where is the JavaScript that is used to show and hide the relevant menu items? The answer is in the cryptic `<script>` tag in the page that looks similar to this:

```
<script src="/WebResource.axd?d=vxurWY7jjhneEhwNQbmdBEdPSXwLRytjgBhME9lyLool
     &amp;t=633925206143355520" type="text/javascript">
```

This `<script>` tag references a special ASP.NET *handler* called `WebResource.axd`. The seemingly random characters in the query string (the part of the URL after the question mark) tell the ASP.NET run time to fetch a JavaScript file that contains the functionality for the menu. The file doesn't exist on your disk, but is returned by the `WebResource.axd` handler on the fly based on the query string. If you're brave, you can look at the file by requesting it in your browser by copying the value of the `src` attribute and pasting it right after the port number of your website in the browser (for example, `http://localhost:50404`). You can safely ignore the file, because you don't need to make any changes to it for the menu to function correctly. The `WebResource.axd` syntax is also used by other controls, like the `TreeView` that uses it to retrieve the images used in the `TreeView`.

In addition to the JavaScript, you also find a CSS `<style>` block at the top of your page, which sets the default layout for your menu items. Among other things, it removes the default bullet that `<ul>` elements display and removes underlining from the `<a>` elements in the menus.

To better integrate the `Menu` control with the existing design of the Monochrome theme, you can style it using CSS.

Styling the Menu Control

The `Menu` control exposes a number of complex style properties that enable you to change the look of items such as the main and submenu items. You can also define how these items look when they are active (selected) or when you hover your mouse over them. Each of these style properties has a number of subproperties for visual aspects, such as font, color, and spacing. Figure 7-7 shows the

Properties Grid for the `StaticMenuItemStyle` property, which defines the look of the main menu items that are visible when the page first loads.

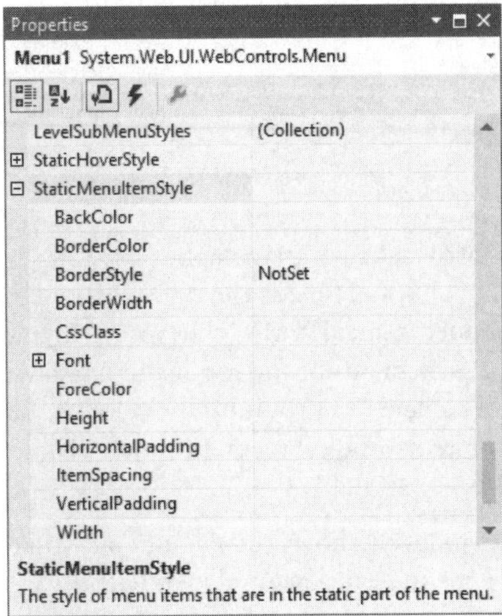

FIGURE 7-7

Most of the properties, like `BackColor`, `ForeColor`, and `Font`, are added to the `<style>` block at the top of the page that contains the `Menu` control. This makes it difficult to reuse the design in other pages or with other themes, so it's much better to use CSS instead. You see how this works next.

TRY IT OUT Styling the Menu Control

In this exercise you add some CSS rules to the `Monochrome.css` file to influence the way the `Menu` control is styled. By default, the `Menu` control adds CSS classes to the menu items, such as `level1` and `level2`, which makes it easy to apply styling at various levels in the menu.

1. Open `Monochrome.css` from the `Monochrome` theme folder and add the following CSS rules. You can leave out the comments placed between `/*` and `*/`, because they only serve to describe the purpose of the selectors. If you don't feel like typing all this CSS, remember you can also get a copy of this file from the code download that comes with this book and copy it from that file into yours. You can find the `Monochrome.css` file in the `Monochrome` theme folder for this chapter. Remember, CSS is case sensitive, so type the selectors exactly as shown here:

```
ul.level1
{
  /* Defines the appearance of main menu items. */
  font-size: 14px;
  font-weight: bold;
  height: 19px;
  line-height: 19px;
}
```

```
ul.level1 .selected
{
  /* Defines the appearance of active menu items. */
  background-color: #509EE7;
}

a.level1
{
  /* Adds some white space to the left of the main menu item text.
     !important is used to overrule the in-line CSS that the menu generates */
  padding-left: 5px !important;
}

a.level2
{
  /* Defines the appearance of the sub menu items. */
  background-color: #555555;
  padding-left: 8px;
}

a.level1:hover, a.level2:hover
{
  /* Defines the hover style for the main and sub items. */
  background-color: #509EE7;
}
```

2. Save and close the file.
3. Next, create the following folders and Web Forms that you'll use in this and later chapters. Use the MyBasePage template to create the new files. Also, in Markup View, give each page a meaningful title to avoid errors later.

FOLDER	FILENAME	TITLE
/About	Default.aspx	About this Site
/About	Contact.aspx	Contact Us
/About	AboutUs.aspx	About Us
/Reviews	Default.aspx	My Favorite Reviews
/Reviews	All.aspx	All Reviews
/Reviews	AllByGenre.aspx	Reviews Grouped by Genre

4. Save all changes and open the `Default.aspx` page from the root in your browser. Your site menu now looks a lot better and more in line with the rest of the Monochrome theme. When you hover the mouse over a main menu, the submenus appear, showing the text on a light gray background. When you hover over a submenu, its background color changes again. Figure 7-8 shows the expanded Reviews menu with the `hover` style applied to the By Genre menu item in Opera.

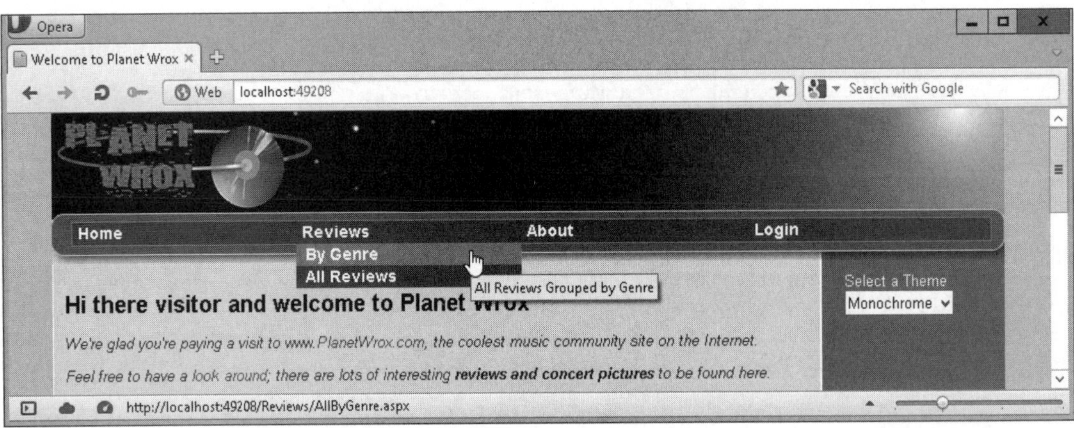

FIGURE 7-8

> ***COMMON MISTAKES*** *If you get an error when you navigate to one of the new pages you created, make sure you gave all of them a valid title. Because they all inherit from the base page, the title is checked when the page loads. If the menu hasn't been updated, press Ctrl+F5 to get a fresh copy of the style sheet from the server.*

How It Works

The `Menu` control renders itself as a series of `<ul>` and `<li>` elements. The menu items themselves are simple `<a>` elements with a `class` attribute to indicate at what level they are. If you look in the HTML for the page in the browser you see something like this:

```
<ul class="level1">
  <li><a title="Go to the homepage" class="level1"
       href="/Default.aspx">Home</a></li>
  <li><a title="Reviews published on this site"
        class="level1" href="/Reviews/Default.aspx">Reviews</a>
    <ul class="level2">
      <li><a title="All Reviews Grouped by Genre"
         class="level2" href="/Reviews/AllByGenre.aspx">By Genre</a></li>
      <li><a title="All Reviews"
         class="level2" href="/Reviews/All.aspx">All Reviews</a>
      </li>
    </ul>
  </li>
  ... <!-- Other menu items go here -->
</ul>
```

Because this code is pure HTML with a few `class` attributes applied, it's easy to style this information using the CSS techniques you learned in earlier chapters. The code you added in step 1 uses a number of selectors to style individual elements of the menu. For example, the main menu items are styled as follows:

```
ul.level1
{
  font-size: 14px;
  font-weight: bold;
  height: 19px;
  line-height: 19px;
}
```

This code is applied to all `<ul>` elements with a CSS `class` of `level1`, which means it's applied to all main menu items such as Home, Reviews, and About. Take a look at the first `<a>` element in the HTML of the menu, which represents the selected Home item. Notice how it has a second `class` called `selected` applied:

```
<a title="Go to the homepage" class="level1 selected"
      href="/Site/Default.aspx">Home</a>
```

Selected items are then given a different color using this CSS selector:

```
ul.level1 .selected
{
  background-color: #BCD1FE;
}
```

The same principle is used for the other selectors, including the pseudo `:hover` selector that applies to `<a>` elements when you hover your mouse over them:

```
a.level1:hover, a.level2:hover
{
  background-color: #BCD1FE;
}
```

To override some of the CSS that the `Menu` control adds to the top of the page, the CSS rule for the static menu items looks like this:

```
a.level1
{
  padding-left: 5px !important;
}
```

The inclusion of `!important` marks this property as more important than the inline style targeting the same menu item. Without `!important`, your menu item has only a tiny bit of padding on the left.

The `Menu` control in horizontal mode is ideal for the Monochrome theme, because it features a horizontal navigation bar. For the DarkGrey theme you can use the same `Menu` and set its `Orientation` to `Vertical`. This creates a vertical menu with the main items stacked on top of each other, whereas the submenus will fold out to the right of the main menus. But instead of the `Menu` control, you can also use a `TreeView` control to display a hierarchical overview of the site map. This control is discussed next.

Using the TreeView Control

A `TreeView` is capable of displaying a hierarchical list of items, similar to how the tree in Windows Explorer looks. Items can be expanded and collapsed with the small plus and minus icons in front of items that contain child elements. This makes the `TreeView` an ideal tool to display the site map of the website as a means to navigate the site. The data used by the `TreeView` control is not limited to the `Web.sitemap` file, however. You can also bind it to regular XML files and even create a `TreeView` or its items (called nodes) programmatically.

The following table lists the most common properties of the `TreeView`. Again, the MSDN online help is a good place to get a detailed overview of all the available properties and their descriptions.

PROPERTY	DESCRIPTION
`CssClass`	Enables you to set a CSS `class` attribute that applies to the entire control.
`CollapseImageUrl`	The image that collapses a part of the tree when clicked. The default is an icon with a minus symbol on it.
`ExpandImageUrl`	The image that expands a part of the tree when clicked. The default is an icon with a plus symbol on it.
`CollapseImageToolTip`	The tooltip that is shown when a user hovers over a collapsible menu item.
`ExpandImageToolTip`	The tooltip that is shown when a user hovers over an expandable menu item.
`ShowExpandCollapse`	Determines whether the items in the `TreeView` can be collapsed and expanded by clicking an image in front of them.
`ShowLines`	Determines whether lines are used to connect the individual items in the tree.
`ExpandDepth`	Determines the level at which items in the tree are expanded when the page first loads. The default setting is `FullyExpand`, which means all items in the tree are visible. Other allowed settings are numeric values to indicate the level to which to expand.

The `TreeView` control has a number of style properties that enable you to change the look and feel of the different parts of the tree. To tell the `TreeView` which items to show, you bind it to a `SiteMapDataSource` control, which is demonstrated next.

TRY IT OUT Building a Navigation System with the TreeView Control

In this exercise, you add a `TreeView` control to the `<nav>` element, right below the `Menu` you created earlier, and then bind the `TreeView` to the same data source as the `Menu`. Next, you write some code that shows either the `Menu` or the `TreeView`, depending on the active theme.

1. Open the master page in Markup View and just below the `Menu` control, add a `TreeView` control by dragging it from the Toolbox.

2. Within the opening and closing tags of the control, add the following `<LevelStyles>` element:

```
<LevelStyles>
  <asp:TreeNodeStyle CssClass="FirstLevelMenuItems" />
</LevelStyles>
```

   The `FirstLevelMenuItems` class selector is defined in the file `DarkGrey.css` that you added in the preceding chapter and is used to create some room above each tree item at the first level.

3. Switch to Design View, click the `TreeView` once, and click the small arrow to open the Smart Tasks panel. From the Choose Data Source drop-down, select `SiteMapDataSource1`, the data source control you created for the `Menu` control (see Figure 7-9).

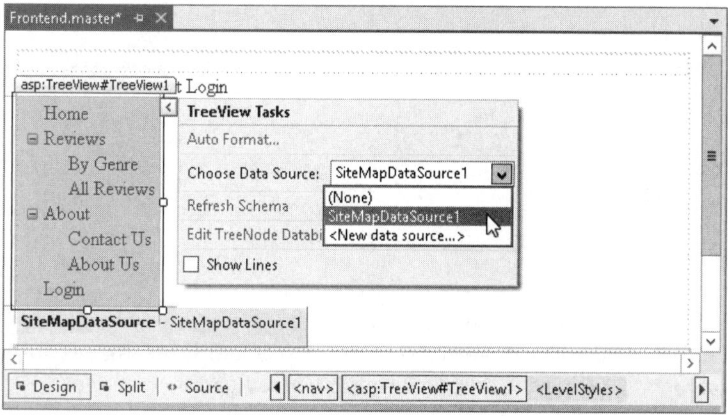

FIGURE 7-9

   As soon as you select the data source, the `TreeView` is updated in Design View; it now shows the correct menu items from the site map file.

4. Open the Properties Grid for the `TreeView` control and set the `ShowExpandCollapse` property to `False`.

5. Click somewhere in the document to put the focus on it, and then press F7 to open the Code Behind of the master page file and locate the `Page_Load` event that you used earlier to preselect the theme in the Theme list. Right below that code, and before the end of the method, add the following bold code that shows or hides the `TreeView` and `Menu` controls based on the currently active theme:

VB.NET

```
        item.Selected = True
      End If
    End If
  End If
  Select Case Page.Theme.ToLower()
    Case "darkgrey"
      Menu1.Visible = False
      TreeView1.Visible = True
    Case Else
      Menu1.Visible = True
      TreeView1.Visible = False
  End Select
End Sub
```

C#

```
        item.Selected = true;
      }
    }
  }
  switch (Page.Theme.ToLower())
  {
    case "darkgrey":
      Menu1.Visible = false;
      TreeView1.Visible = true;
      break;
    default:
      Menu1.Visible = true;
      TreeView1.Visible = false;
      break;
  }
}
```

6. Save all changes and open `Default.aspx` in the browser. Depending on your currently active theme, you should see either the `Menu` or the `TreeView` control. Select a different theme from the list and the page will reload, now showing the other control as the navigation system of the website (see Figure 7-10).

> ***COMMON MISTAKES*** *If you get an error from the code in the* `BasePage` *class that checks the title, make sure you set a valid theme in the* `<pages>` *element in the* `Web.config` *file. If the theme seems to switch when you move from one page to another, make sure your pages inherit* `BasePage`*, which should be the case if you based the new pages on your custom template.*

FIGURE 7-10

How It Works

Just like the `Menu` control, the `TreeView` control can get its data from a `SiteMapDataSource` control, which in turn gets its information from the `Web.sitemap` file. By default, the `TreeView` shows plus and minus signs to indicate that items can be collapsed and expanded. For a site menu this may not make much sense, so by setting `ShowExpandCollapse` to `False`, you effectively hide the images. The `TreeView` enables you to set a number of style properties, including the `NodeStyle`, `RootNodeStyle`, and `LevelStyles` that influence the appearance of individual items in the tree. In this exercise, you used `LevelStyles` to apply a class called `FirstLevelMenuItems` that adds some room above each item at the top level, such as Home and Reviews.

The code in the Code Behind of the master page looks at the current theme by investigating the `Theme` property of the `Page`. When `DarkGrey` is the current theme, the code hides the `Menu` and then displays the `TreeView`. In the `Case Else` / `default` block the reverse is true. This means that for the Monochrome theme and all future themes you may add, the `TreeView` is hidden and the `Menu` is used instead as the navigation system.

The `TreeView` still suffers from the same problems as the `Menu` control in previous versions of ASP.NET in that it generates a lot of bloated HTML. Unfortunately, this control has no `RenderingMode` property, so if you're using the `TreeView` you're stuck with the table-based HTML.

With two of the three navigation controls discussed, the final control you need to look at is the `SiteMapPath` control.

Using the SiteMapPath Control

The `SiteMapPath` control shows you where you are in the site's structure. It presents itself as a series of links, often referred to as a *breadcrumb*. It's a pretty simple yet powerful control with more than 50 public properties you can set through the Properties Grid to influence the way it looks. Just like the `Menu` and `TreeView`, it has a number of style properties you use to change the look of elements like the current node, a normal node, and the path separator.

The following table lists a few of the most common properties of the `SiteMapPath` control.

PROPERTY	DESCRIPTION
`PathDirection`	Supports two values: `RootToCurrent` and `CurrentToRoot`. The first setting shows the root element on the left, intermediate levels in the middle, and the current page at the right of the path. The `CurrentToRoot` setting is the exact opposite, where the current page is shown at the left of the breadcrumb path.
`PathSeparator`	Defines the symbol or text to show between the different elements of the path. The default is the "greater than" symbol (>), but you can change it to something like the pipe character (|).
`RenderCurrentNodeAsLink`	Determines whether the last element of the path (the current page) is rendered as a text link or as plaintext. The default is `False`, which is usually fine because you are already on the page that element is representing, so there's no real need for a link.
`ShowToolTips`	Determines whether the control displays tooltips (retrieved from the description attribute of the `siteMapNode` elements in the `Web.sitemap` file) when the user hovers over the elements in the path. The default is `True`, which means the tooltips are shown by default.

Depending on your personal preferences, you usually don't need to define any of the styles of the `SiteMapPath` control. In the final page in the browser, the `SiteMapPath` consists of mainly anchor tags (`<a>`) and plaintext. If you have set up a specific selector for anchors in your CSS file, the `SiteMapPath` automatically shows itself in line with the other links in the page.

TRY IT OUT Creating a Breadcrumb with the SiteMapPath Control

A good location for the `SiteMapPath` is in the global master page of the site. That way it becomes visible in all your pages automatically.

1. Open the master page in Markup View and locate the `MainContent` `<section>` element. Right after its opening tag, and before the `<asp:ContentPlaceHolder>` tag, press Enter to create some room and drag a `SiteMapPath` from the Toolbox. Right after the `SiteMapPath` add two line breaks (`<br />`). You should end up with code like this:

```
<section id="MainContent">
  <asp:SiteMapPath ID="SiteMapPath1" runat="server"></asp:SiteMapPath><br /><br />
  <asp:ContentPlaceHolder ID="cpMainContent" runat="server">
```

2. Save the changes and then request `Default.aspx` in the browser. Note that the page now shows the path from the root of the site (identified by the Home text) to the current page. Click a few of the items in the `Menu` or `TreeView` control to navigate around the site and you'll see the breadcrumb change for each page. Figure 7-11 shows the breadcrumb for the All Reviews page in Firefox. The All Reviews page is a subelement of Reviews, which in turn falls under the Home root element.

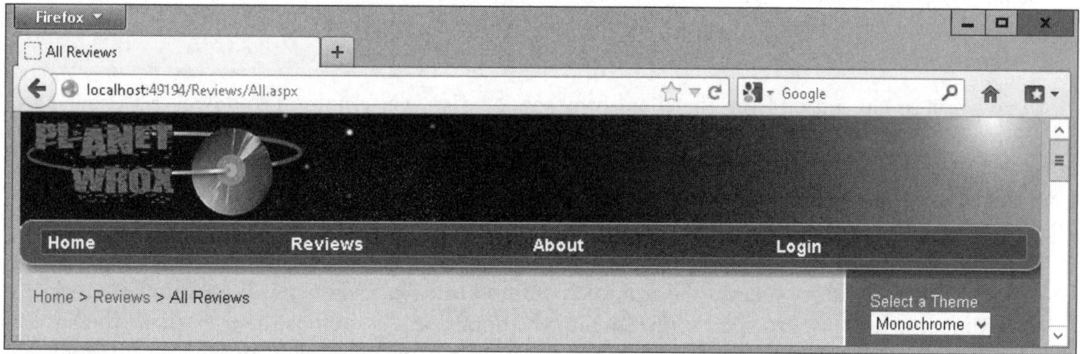

FIGURE 7-11

When you navigate to one of the subpages, you can click the elements of the path to go up one or more levels. Clicking Reviews in the page shown in Figure 7-11 takes you back to the main Reviews page, and clicking Home takes you back to the root of the site.

3. Using the Theme selector, switch to the other theme. Note that the `SiteMapPath` looks pretty much the same, except for the color of the links, which are defined in the CSS file of each theme.

How It Works

The `SiteMapPath` renders as a series of `<span>` elements that contain either a link or plaintext. Here's a part of the HTML code for the `SiteMapPath` from Figure 7-11:

```
<span><a title="Home" href="/">Home</a></span>
<span> &gt; </span>
<span><a title="Reviews published on this site"
          href="/Reviews/Default.aspx">Reviews</a></span>
<span> &gt; </span>
<span>All Reviews</span>
```

The first two menu items (Home and Reviews) are represented by a link (`<a>`) to enable you to navigate to the pages defined in their `href` properties. The final menu item—All Reviews—is just plaintext.

In between the elements you see a `<span>` with the character you set in the `PathSeparator` property. Because this separator character (>) has a special meaning in HTML, its value is encoded to `>` (greater than) to ensure it ends up as a plaintext character in the browser.

If you look at the HTML for the page in your browser, you also see an `<a>` element that enables you to skip links. The `<a>` contains a small image with its `left` property set to a large negative value, so it is outside of the visible browser window and you don't see it. This is useful for vision-impaired users with screen readers because it enables them to skip the navigation and go directly to the content of the page. The `TreeView` and `Menu` controls use an identical approach to prevent a screen reader from reading the entire site structure out loud every time the page loads.

The three navigation controls give you a great feature set for a navigation system in your website from the client side. Both the `Menu` and the `TreeView` controls enable you to quickly display the entire structure of the site so users can easily find their way. `SiteMapPath` helps users understand where they are in the site and gives them an easy way to navigate to pages higher up in the site hierarchy.

In addition to navigating from the client browser, it's also very common to navigate a user to a different page from the server side using code. How this works is discussed in the next section.

PROGRAMMATIC REDIRECTION

Programmatic redirection is very useful and common in ASP.NET pages. For example, imagine a page that enables a user to enter a review into the database. As soon as the user clicks the Save button, the review is saved and the user is taken to another page where she can see the entire review.

ASP.NET supports three major ways to redirect users to a new page programmatically. The first two, `Response.Redirect` and `Response.RedirectPermanent` (which was introduced in ASP.NET 4), send an instruction to the browser to fetch a new page. The third option, `Server.Transfer`, executes at the server. Because there's quite a difference in client- and server-side redirection, the following sections describe them in more detail.

Programmatically Redirecting the Client to a Different Page

Within each ASPX page you have access to a property called `Response`, which you saw earlier when saving the cookie for the selected theme. The `Response` object gives you access to useful properties and methods that are all related to the response from the server to the user's browser. Two of these methods are the `Redirect` and `RedirectPermanent` methods. These methods send an instruction to the browser to request a new page. This is useful if you want to redirect your user to another page in your site or to a completely different website.

The difference between `Redirect` and `RedirectPermanent` mainly has to do with search engine optimization. Using `Redirect` tells the client that the page has moved *temporarily*. You often use this to redirect a user to a new page based on some action. For example, after filling in a contact form, you may want to send the user to `ThankYou.aspx` that displays a message.

`RedirectPermanent` tells the client the page has moved *permanently*. This is useful if you want to tell a search engine to stop looking at an old page, and index the new one instead. For example, imagine your site has a page called `Index.aspx` that you no longer use. Search engines may keep requesting this page. If you add the following code to the Code Behind of `Index.aspx`, clients (including search engines) are sent to `Default.aspx`. Moreover, search engines keep note of the permanency of the redirect and will stop requesting `Index.aspx` and focus on `Default.aspx` instead.

VB.NET

```
Protected Sub Page_Load(sender As Object, e As EventArgs) Handles Me.Load
  Response.RedirectPermanent("Default.aspx")
End Sub
```

C#

```
protected void Page_Load(object sender, EventArgs e)
{
  Response.RedirectPermanent("Default.aspx");
}
```

The two methods each have a second version (called an *overload*) that accepts an additional boolean parameter called `endResponse`, which enables you to execute any remaining code after the redirect action when you pass `False` (`false` in C#) for that parameter. This is usually not necessary, so you're better off calling the first version, which ends the response by default.

Quite often, when you want to send the user to a different page, you want to send some additional information. You can do that by passing it in the *query string*, the part of the address that comes after the page name, separated by a question mark. Consider the following URL:

`http://localhost:49246/Demos/Target.aspx?`**`CategoryId=10&From=Home`**

The entire bold part (after the question mark) is considered the query string. It consists of name-value pairs, each separated from another by an ampersand (`&`). In this case, you have two pairs: `CategoryId` with a value of `10` and `From` with a value of the word `Home`. The page, `Target.aspx` in this example, is able to read these values using `Request.QueryString`. You see how to use the query string in the next exercise.

TRY IT OUT Redirecting the User to Another Page

To give you a closer look at how it works, this exercise shows you how to create a page that redirects from one page to another using `Response.Redirect`. The example uses a temporary redirect (the initial page remains accessible after the redirect), so the code uses `Response.Redirect` instead of `Response.RedirectPermanent`.

1. In the `Demos` folder, create two new Web Forms based on your custom MyBasePage template. Call them `Source.aspx` and `Target.aspx`. Set their `Title` to `Source` and `Target`, respectively.
2. Open `Source.aspx` in Design View and double-click somewhere in the gray, read-only area of the page outside the `ContentPlaceHolder` to set up a `Page_Load` handler. Inside this handler, write the following code that redirects the user to the `Target.aspx` page. To show you how to pass additional data through the query string and how to read that information in the target page, the code passes a query string field called `Test` with `SomeValue` as the value:

VB.NET

```
Protected Sub Page_Load(sender As Object, e As EventArgs) Handles Me.Load
  Response.Redirect("Target.aspx?Test=SomeValue")
End Sub
```

C#

```
protected void Page_Load(object sender, EventArgs e)
{
  Response.Redirect("Target.aspx?Test=SomeValue");
}
```

3. Open `Target.aspx`, switch to Design View, and add a `Label` control to the `cpMainContent` `Content` control. Leave its `ID` set to `Label1`. Set up a `Page_Load` handler similar to the one you created in the previous step by double-clicking the gray, read-only area of the page, and then add the following code:

VB.NET

```
Protected Sub Page_Load(sender As Object, e As EventArgs) Handles Me.Load
  Label1.Text = Request.QueryString.ToString()
End Sub
```

C#

```
protected void Page_Load(object sender, EventArgs e)
{
  Label1.Text = Request.QueryString.ToString();
}
```

4. Save all your changes, go back to `Source.aspx`, and press Ctrl+F5 to open it in the browser. Instead of seeing `Source.aspx`, you now see the page depicted in Figure 7-12.

FIGURE 7-12

Note that the address bar now reads `Target.aspx?Test=SomeValue`, the page you redirected to in the `Page_Load` event handler of the source page. The `Label` in the target page shows the query string that is passed to this page. Notice that `QueryString.ToString()` contains only `Test=SomeValue`. The address and the question mark are not a part of the query string for the page.

How It Works

When you use `Response.Redirect`, ASP.NET sends an instruction to the browser to tell it to fetch a new page. In technical terms, it sends a "302" HTTP status code to indicate the page has moved temporarily. With this instruction it also sends the new URL, so the browser understands what page to fetch next. In this exercise, the new page was `Target.aspx?Test=SomeValue`, which contains both the page name and a query string. The `Target.aspx` page is then requested by the browser, the `Page_Load` event fires, and the query string is displayed on the label in the page. Because of this client redirect, the new page name and query string are fully exposed to the client. If you use `Response.RedirectPermanent`, ASP.NET sends out a "301 Moved Permanently" instruction. For some browsers, this means that if the original page has previously been cached by the browser, you're taken automatically to the new page if you request the original page. Once the browser cache is cleared, a request is made again for the original page. Other browsers may continue to request the original page. Search engines interpret the 301 redirect as "don't bother fetching this page again" and the page will no longer be indexed.

Redirects follow the same naming scheme for URLs as those used in server controls, so you can redirect to a page like `~/Default.aspx` to redirect the user to the file `Default.aspx` in the website's root.

In contrast to `Response.Redirect` and `Response.RedirectPermanent`, there is also `Server.Transfer`, which redirects to another page at the server.

Server-Side Redirects

Server-side redirects are great if you want to send out a different page without modifying the client's address bar. This enables you to hide details of page names and query strings, which may lead to cleaner URLs from a user's point of view. This is often used in so-called URL-rewrite scenarios that are used to create pretty URLs. For example, a user may request a page like this:

```
http://www.domain.com/Cars/Volvo/850/T5/
```

Under the hood the server might transfer to:

```
http://www.domain.com/Cars/ShowCar.aspx?Make=643&Model=984&Type=7345
```

Clearly, the first URL is a lot easier to understand and type in a browser. It also enables a user to guess other URLs that match the same pattern. For example, there's a fair chance you can request a page like this:

```
http://www.domain.com/Cars/Volvo/V70/R/
```

and end up with the right page showing you the Volvo V70 R.

In addition to being easier to understand, server-side transfers may also speed up your site a little. Instead of sending a response to the browser to tell it to fetch a new page, which results in a new request for a page, you can transfer the user directly to a new page, saving you some network overhead.

Server-side transfers are carried out with the `Server` object. Just as the `Request` and `Response` objects you saw earlier give you information about the request and the response, so does the `Server` object provide you with information about the server the page is running on. You can use it to get information about the server name, its IP address, and so on. One of its methods is `Transfer`, which performs a server-side transfer.

You can use `Server.Transfer` only to redirect to other pages within your site. You cannot use it to send the user to pages on different domains. If you try to do so, the ASP.NET run time throws an error.

To see the difference between `Response.Redirect` and `Server.Transfer`, the following exercise shows you how to change the page `Source.aspx` to perform a `Server.Transfer` operation.

TRY IT OUT Server-Side Redirecting

It's easy to change the redirect code so it transfers the user to another page. All you need to do is replace `Response.Redirect` with `Server.Transfer` as demonstrated in this exercise.

1. Open the Code Behind of `Source.aspx` and replace the line with `Response.Redirect` with the following line:

VB.NET

```
Protected Sub Page_Load(sender As Object, e As EventArgs) Handles Me.Load
  Server.Transfer("Target.aspx?Test=SomeValue")
End Sub
```

C#

```
protected void Page_Load(object sender, EventArgs e)
{
  Server.Transfer("Target.aspx?Test=SomeValue");
}
```

2. Save the changes and then press Ctrl+F5 to open `Source.aspx` in the browser (see Figure 7-13).

FIGURE 7-13

The `Label` control displays the query string values that were sent from `Source.aspx` to `Target.aspx`, demonstrating the fact that you are really viewing the output of the `Target.aspx` page. However, the browser's address bar is left unmodified and still shows `Source.aspx`, hiding the new page name and query string values from the user.

How It Works

Instead of instructing the browser to fetch a new page, `Server.Transfer` takes place completely at the server. The output of the old page is discarded and a new page life cycle is started for the page that is being transferred to. This page then generates its content and sends it back to the browser, while leaving the browser's address bar unmodified.

If you look at the emitted HTML in the browser, you see that the form action is set to the new page so any postback that occurs is executed against that page, which in turn changes the address in the address bar:

```
<form method="post" action="Target.aspx?Test=SomeValue" id="form1">
...
</form>
```

> ***NOTE*** *ASP.NET supports a concept called routing that enables you to freely define your own URL structure and link that to pages in your site. For example, you could use routing to implement the car examples shown in this chapter without the downside of the changed* `action` *attribute. Check out this article to learn more about routing:* `http://tinyurl.com/RoutingWebForms`.

With programmatic ways to send a user to another page, you have come to the end of this chapter on navigation. With the concepts shown in this chapter, you have all the knowledge you need to create a highly effective navigation system in your site, from both the client's browser and your own server-side code.

PRACTICAL TIPS ON NAVIGATION

The following list presents some practical tips on navigation:

- When you start building a website that you think will grow in the future, create a logical structure right away. Don't place all files in the root of your website, but group logically related files in the same folder. Such logical grouping makes it easier for you to manage the site and for your users to find the pages they want. Although it's easy to move a page in a `Menu` or `TreeView` using the `Web.sitemap` file, it's more difficult if you are also using programmatic redirects or transfers, because you also need to update the server-side code to reflect the new site structure. To create a solid page structure, you can draw it out on paper before you start with the site, or use site map diagramming tools like Microsoft Visio.
- Try to limit the number of main and sub items that you display in your `Menu` or `TreeView` controls. Users tend to get lost or confused when they are presented with long lists of options to choose from.
- When creating folders to store your pages in, give them short and logical names. It's much more intuitive to navigate to a page using `www.PlanetWrox.com/Reviews` than it is to navigate to a folder with a long name including abbreviations and numbers.

SUMMARY

This chapter familiarized you with navigation in an ASP.NET website. Users don't just type in the address of a web page directly, so it's important to offer them a clear and straightforward navigation system.

A critical foundation for a good navigation system is a good understanding of how URLs work. URLs come in two types: relative URLs and absolute URLs. Relative URLs are used to point to resources within your own site. Absolute URLs enable you to point to resources by their complete location, including protocol and domain information. Absolute URLs are mostly useful if you want to point to resources outside your own website.

ASP.NET offers three navigation controls used in the user interface of a website. These controls enable your users to visit the different pages in your site. The `Menu` control displays either as a vertical or a horizontal menu, with submenus folding or dropping out. The `TreeView` control can show the complete structure of the site in a hierarchical way. The `SiteMapPath` control displays a breadcrumb trail to give users a visual cue as to where they are in the site.

In addition to the built-in navigation controls, you can also send the user to a different page programmatically. ASP.NET supports two major ways to do this: client side using `Response.Redirect` and `Response.RedirectPermanent` and server side using `Server.Transfer`. The redirect methods instruct the browser to fetch a new page from the server, whereas the transfer method is executed at the server.

In the next chapter you learn more about ASP.NET user controls, which enable you to reuse specific code and user interface elements in different pages in your website.

EXERCISES

1. The `TreeView` control exposes a number of style properties that enable you to change items in the tree. Which property do you need to change if you want to influence the background color of each item in the tree? What's the best way to change the background color?

2. What options do you have to redirect a user to another page programmatically? What's the difference between them?

3. You can use the `TreeView` controls in two different ways: either as a list with items and sub items that can be collapsed and expanded by clicking them, or as a static list showing all the items, with no way to collapse or expand. What property do you need to set on the control to prevent users from expanding or collapsing items in the tree?

You can find answers to these exercises in Appendix A.

▶ WHAT YOU LEARNED IN THIS CHAPTER

`Menu` **control**	A navigation control that is able to display data, including data coming from the `Web.sitemap` file, in a horizontal or vertical manner using drop-down or fold-out submenus.
Permanent redirect	A mechanism to inform a client, such as a search engine, that a page has moved permanently, telling the client to stop requesting the old resource.
Server-side transfer	A redirect to another page that takes place at the server without informing the client browser.
`SiteMapDataSource` **control**	The bridge between the `Web.sitemap` file and the navigation controls, such as `TreeView` and `Menu`.
`SiteMapPath` **control**	A navigation control that displays a breadcrumb from the root of the site to the current page, enabling users to move back up in the hierarchy of a site.
Temporary redirect	A mechanism to redirect a client to a new, temporary location.
`TreeView` **control**	A navigation control that is able to display data, including data coming from the `Web.sitemap` file, in a hierarchical way.
`Web.sitemap`	The XML-based file that contains the logical structure of your site. This file drives the other navigation controls.

8

User Controls

WHAT YOU WILL LEARN IN THIS CHAPTER:

- What user controls are, how they look, and why they are useful
- How to create user controls
- How to consume (or use) user controls in your pages
- How you can improve the usefulness of user controls by adding coding logic to them

WROX.COM CODE DOWNLOADS FOR THIS CHAPTER

You can find the wrox.com code downloads for this chapter on the Download Code tab at `www.wrox.com/remtitle.cgi?isbn=1118311809`. The code is in the Chapter 8 download.

In addition to the master pages, themes, and skins discussed in Chapter 6, ASP.NET 4.5 has another feature that enables you to create reusable and thus consistent blocks of information: *user controls.*

User controls enable you to group logically related content and controls together so they can be treated as a single unit in content pages, master pages, and inside other user controls. A user control is actually a sort of mini-ASPX page in that it has a markup section and, optionally, a Code Behind file in which you can write code for the control. Working with a user control is very similar to working with normal ASPX pages, with a few minor differences.

In versions of ASP.NET before 2.0, user controls were often used to create blocks of reusable functionality that had to appear on every page in the site. For example, to create a menu, you would create a user control and then add that control to each and every page in the site. Because of the ASP.NET support for master pages, you don't need user controls for these scenarios anymore. This makes it easier to make changes to your site's structure. Despite the advantages that master pages bring, there is still room for user controls in your ASP.NET websites. For example, you can build a user control that displays a banner that is shown on some, but not all pages as you'll see in this chapter.

By the end of this chapter, you'll have a firm understanding of what user controls are and how they work, enabling you to create functional, reusable blocks of content.

INTRODUCTION TO USER CONTROLS

User controls are great for encapsulating markup, controls, and code that you need repeatedly throughout your site. To some extent, they look a bit like server controls in that they can contain programming logic and presentation that you can reuse in your pages. However, rather than dragging existing ones from the VS Toolbox, you need to create your own user controls and then add them to your ASPX pages, as you learn how to do later in this chapter.

Though master pages enable you to create content that is displayed in all pages in your site, it's common to have content that should appear only on some, but not all, pages. For example, you may want to display a banner on a few popular pages, but not on the homepage or other common pages. Without user controls, you would add the code for the banner (an image, a link, and so on) to each page that needs it. When you want to update the banner (if you want to use a new image or link), you need to make changes to all pages that use it. If you move the banner to a user control and use that control in your content pages instead, all you need to change is the user control and the pages that use it pick up the change automatically. This gives you a flexible way to create reusable content.

User controls have the following similarities with normal ASPX pages:

- They have a markup section where you can add standard markup, server controls, and plain HTML.
- They can be created and designed with Visual Studio in Markup, Design, and Split View.
- They can contain programming logic, either inline or with a Code Behind file.
- They give you access to page-based information like `Request.QueryString`.
- They raise some (but not all) of the events that the `Page` class raises, including `Init`, `Load`, and `PreRender`.

You should also be aware of a few differences. User controls have an `.ascx` extension instead of the regular `.aspx` extension. In addition, user controls cannot be requested in the browser directly. Therefore, you can't link to them. The only way to use a user control in your site is by adding it to a content or master page or another user control (which eventually should be added to a page).

In the remainder of this chapter, you see how to create a user control that is capable of displaying banners. The user control can present itself as a horizontal or vertical banner to accommodate for differently sized regions in your pages. In the next section, you see how to create a user control. The sections that follow show you how to use that control in an ASPX page.

Creating User Controls

You add user controls to the site like any other content type: through the Add New Item dialog box. Similar to pages, you get the option to choose the programming language and whether you want to place the code in a separate Code Behind file. Figure 8-1 shows the Add New Item dialog box for a user control.

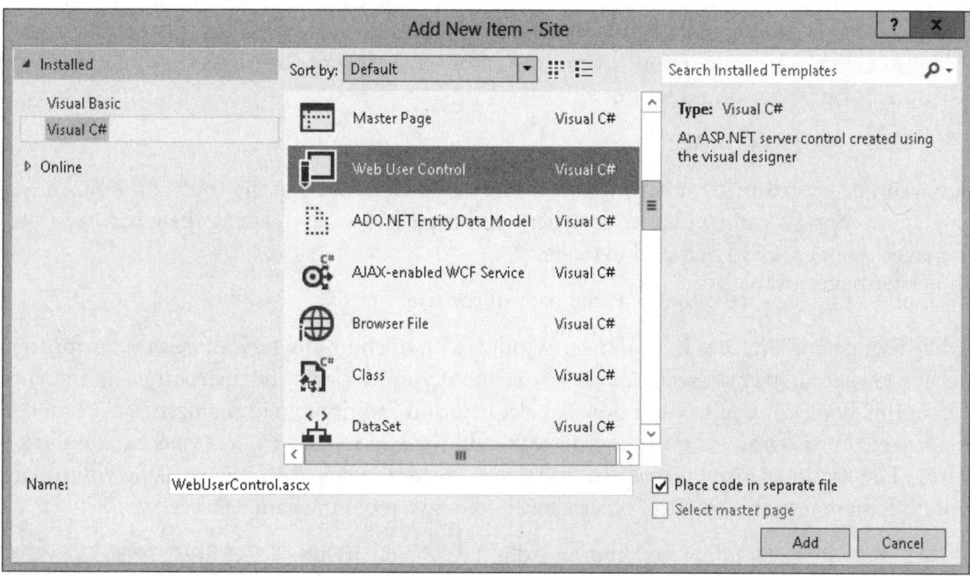

FIGURE 8-1

Once you add a user control to the site, it is opened in the Document Window automatically. The first thing you may notice is that a user control doesn't have an `@ Page` directive, but rather an `@ Control` directive, as shown in this example that uses Code Behind:

```
<%@ Control Language="C#" AutoEventWireup="true" CodeFile="WebUserControl.ascx.cs"
    Inherits="WebUserControl" %>
```

This marks the file as a user control, so the ASP.NET run time knows how to deal with it. Other than that, the directive is similar to a standard ASPX page that doesn't use a master page.

With the user control open in the VS Document Window, you can use all the tools you have used in the previous seven chapters to create pages. You can use the Toolbox to drag controls in Markup and Design View, the CSS windows to change the look and feel and content of the user control, and the Properties Grid to change the properties of controls in your user controls. You can also write code that reacts to the events that the control raises.

To try this out yourself, the next exercise shows you how to create your first user control. In a later exercise, you see how to use the control in ASPX pages in your site.

TRY IT OUT Creating a User Control

In this exercise, you create a basic user control that displays a single vertical banner using an `Image` control. In later exercises, you see how to use this control in your pages and how to add another (horizontal) image.

For this exercise, you need two images that represent banners—one in portrait mode with dimensions of roughly 120 x 240 pixels, and one in landscape mode with a size of around 486 x 60 pixels. The `Resources` folder for this chapter's code download that comes with this book has these two images, but you could also create your own. Don't worry about the exact size of the images; as long as they are close to these dimensions, you should be fine.

1. Open the Planet Wrox site in VS.
2. If you haven't done so already, create a new folder called `Controls` in the root of the site. Although user controls can be placed anywhere in the site hierarchy, placing them in a separate folder makes them easier to find and manage.
3. Create another folder called `Images` at the root of the site.
4. Using File Explorer (Windows Explorer on Windows 7), open up the `Resources` folder for this chapter (at `C:\BegASPNET\Resources\Chapter 08` if you followed the instructions in the introduction of this book). If you haven't done so already, you can download the necessary resources from `www.wrox.com`. Drag (or copy and paste) the files `Banner120x240.gif` and `Banner486x60.gif` from File Explorer into the `Images` folder you created in step 3. If you're using your own images, drag them into the `Images` folder as well and give them the same names.
5. Right-click the `Controls` folder and choose Add ➪ Add New Item. In the dialog box that follows, choose your programming language, click Web User Control, and make sure that Place Code in Separate File is checked, as shown in Figure 8-1. Name the file **`Banner`** and then click Add to add the control to the site. Notice how VS adds the extension of `.ascx` for you automatically if you don't type it in. VS does this for all file types you add through the Add New Item dialog box so you don't need to type the extension yourself. Your Solution Explorer should now look like Figure 8-2.

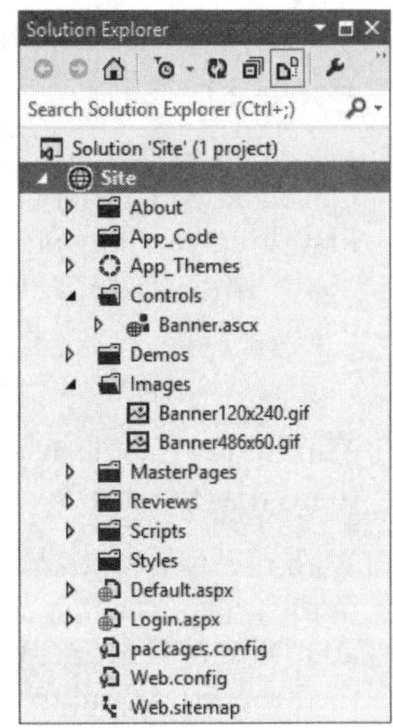

FIGURE 8-2

6. Switch the user control to Design View and drag a `Panel` from the Standard category of the Toolbox onto the design surface. Using the Properties Grid, change the `ID` of the `Panel` to `VerticalPanel`.
7. From the Toolbox, drag an `Image` control into the `Panel`. Select the `Image` and then open the Properties Grid. Locate the `ImageUrl` property and click its ellipsis button, shown in Figure 8-3.

   Browse to the `Images` folder, select the `Banner120x240.gif` image, and click OK to add it to the user control. Your Design View now looks like Figure 8-4.
8. Using the same Properties Grid, locate the `AlternateText` property and type **`This is a sample banner.`** Most browsers display the alternate text (rendered as a client-side `alt` attribute) only

when the image cannot be displayed correctly. Some older browsers show the alternate text as the tooltip for the image when you hover your mouse over it.

9. Switch to Markup View and if your `Panel` control has `Height` and `Width` attributes that were added by default when you dragged it on the page, remove both of them.

10. Wrap the `Image` in a standard `<a>` element and set its `href` attribute to `http://p2p.wrox.com`. If you want, you can use the a code snippet to insert the bare link for you. To do this, type the letter **a** and then press Tab. VS inserts a link for you and enables you to type in the `href` value directly. When you then press Tab again, the content of the link is selected, which you can delete by pressing Del (the `Image` control will be the contents of the link). Finally, cut the closing `</a>` tag and move it to after the image.

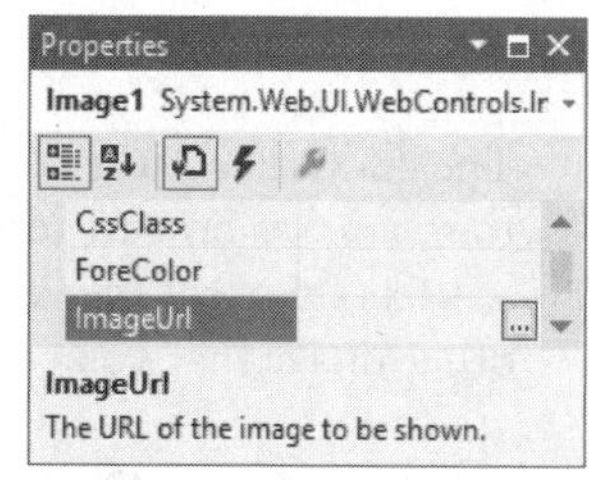

FIGURE 8-3

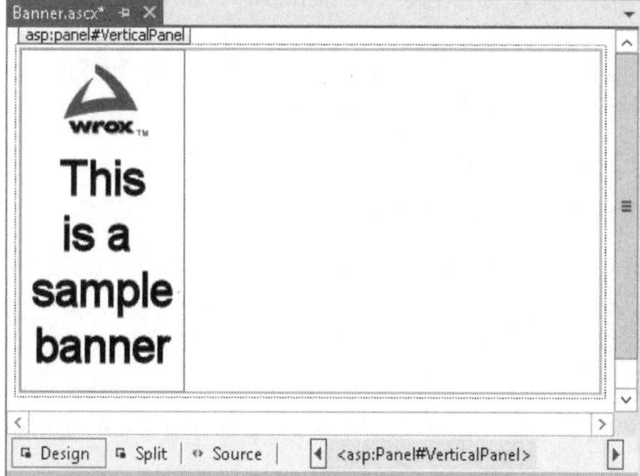

FIGURE 8-4

11. Set the `target` of the anchor tag (`<a>`) to `_blank` to force the browser to open up the page in a new window when the image is clicked. When you're done, the code for the entire user control should look like the following code, except for the `Language` attribute that you may have set to `VB` and the `AutoEventWireup` that is `False` by default in VB.NET:

```
<%@ Control Language="C#" AutoEventWireup="true" CodeFile="Banner.ascx.cs"
      Inherits="Controls_Banner" %>
<asp:Panel ID="VerticalPanel" runat="server">
  <a href="http://p2p.wrox.com" target="_blank">
    <asp:Image ID="Image1" runat="server" AlternateText="This is a sample banner"
            ImageUrl="~/Images/Banner120x240.gif" />
  </a>
</asp:Panel>
```

12. Save the changes by pressing Ctrl+S and then close the user control file by pressing Ctrl+F4.

How It Works

The design experience of user controls in the Visual Studio IDE is identical to that of pages. You can use drag and drop; the Toolbox; the Markup, Split, Design Views; and so on. This makes it easy to work with user controls because you can use all the familiar tools you also use for page development.

The control you just created displays a single image wrapped in an anchor element. In the next section, you see how to add the user control to the master page so it will be displayed in the `Sidebar` `<aside>` element of every page in the site. Later sections in this chapter show you how to add the other image that you can use to display a horizontal banner in individual content pages.

Adding User Controls to a Content Page or Master Page

To use a user control in a content or master page or in another user control, you need to perform two steps. First, you need to *register* the control by adding an `@ Register` directive to the page or control where you want the user control to appear. The second step involves adding the tags for the user control to the page and optionally setting some attributes on it.

A typical `@ Register` directive for a user control looks like this:

```
<%@ Register Src="ControlName.ascx" TagName="ControlName" TagPrefix="uc1" %>
```

The directive contains three important attributes, described in the following table.

Attribute	Description
`Src`	Points to the user control you want to use. To make it easier to move pages at a later stage, you can also use the tilde (~) syntax to point to the control from the application root.
`TagName`	The name for the tag that is used in the control declaration in the page. You're free to make up this name, but usually it is the same as the name of the control.
`TagPrefix`	Holds the prefix of the `TagName` that is used in the control declaration. Just as ASP.NET uses the `asp` prefix to refer to its controls, you need to provide a prefix for your own user controls. By default, this prefix is `uc` followed by a sequential number, but you can also change it to your own liking—for example, to your own company name or a custom abbreviation.

Considering the user control you created in the preceding exercise, your `@ Register` directive could look like this:

```
<%@ Register Src="~/Controls/Banner.ascx" TagName="Banner" TagPrefix="uc1" %>
```

When the control is registered, you can add it to the page using the `TagPrefix:TagName` construct, similar to the way you add standard server controls to a page. Given the `@ Register` directive for the banner control, you need the following markup to add the control to your page:

```
<uc1:Banner ID="Banner1" runat="server" />
```

This is the minimum code needed for a user control in a page. Note that the control is defined by a combination of the `TagPrefix` and the `TagName`. The other two attributes—`ID` and `runat`—are standard attributes that most controls in an ASP.NET page have.

Fortunately, in most cases, you don't have to type all this code yourself. When you drag a user control from the Solution Explorer into a page in Design View, VS adds the required code for you automatically. The following exercise demonstrates how this works.

TRY IT OUT Adding the User Control to Your Page

In this exercise, you add the user control `Banner.ascx` to the master page, so it displays a banner on each page in the site in the sidebar area.

1. Open up `Frontend.master` from the `MasterPages` folder and switch it into Design View.
2. Locate the drop-down list that enables you to select a theme, position your cursor right after the drop-down list, and press Enter three times to create some room.
3. From the Solution Explorer, drag the `Banner.ascx` file from the `Controls` folder into the empty spot you just created. Design View is updated and now looks like Figure 8-5.

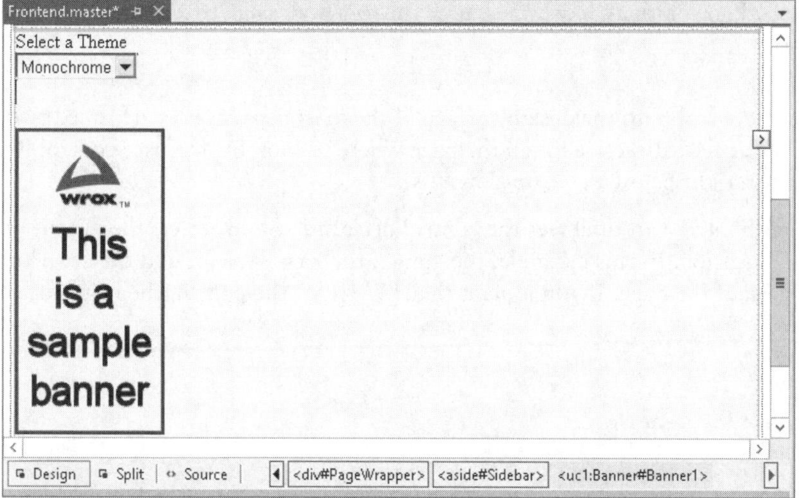

FIGURE 8-5

> ***COMMON MISTAKES*** *If your Design View doesn't look like this, but looks much closer to how the file ends up in the browser, you may still have the* `styleSheetTheme` *set in the* `Web.config` *file. Also, you may have more or fewer options selected in the View ➪ Visual Aids or View ➪ Formatting Marks menu, which may affect your display.*

4. Switch to Markup View and locate the `@ Register` directive at the top of the file. If the `Src` attribute starts with two dots, change them to a tilde (~):

```
<%@ Register Src="~/Controls/Banner.ascx" TagName="Banner" TagPrefix="uc1" %>
```

5. Save the changes to the master page and close it.

6. Open the `Monochrome.css` file from its theme folder and add the following CSS code:

```
img
{
  border: 0;
}
```

7. Copy this rule set to the other theme (add it to `DarkGrey.css`).

8. Save all your changes, right-click `Default.aspx` in the root of your site in the Solution Explorer, and choose View in Browser.

9. The banner is now displayed below the drop-down list. Switch to the other theme and you'll see the same banner appear. When you click the banner, a new window is opened that takes you to the site you linked to in the previous exercise. If you don't see the banner appear at all, check to see if you're running ad-blocking software on Windows or in your browser. For example, Firefox has an add-on called Adblock Plus that may block the banner in your web page based on its dimensions.

How It Works

When you dragged the user control onto the design surface of the master page, VS performed two tasks: first it added the `@ Register` directive to tell the page where to look for the user control. It then added the control declaration right below the drop-down list.

When the page loads, the ASP.NET run time sees the control declaration and injects the output of the control at the specified location. In this example, the `Panel`, the `<a>` element, and the `Image` are inserted in the sidebar region of the page. If you look at the HTML for the page in the browser, you see the following code:

```
</select>
<br /><br />
<div id="Banner1_VerticalPanel">
  <a href="http://p2p.wrox.com" target="_blank">
    <img id="Banner1_Image1" src="Images/Banner120x240.gif"
           alt="This is a sample banner" />
  </a>
</div>
```

The `Panel` control has been transformed into an HTML `<div>` element and the `Image` control into an `<img>` element. Because the anchor element (`<a>`) was defined with plain HTML in the user control, it ends up exactly as you wrote it. The `AlternateText` property has been changed to an `alt` attribute.

Notice how the `id` of the panel has been changed from `VerticalPanel` to the client ID `Banner1_VerticalPanel`. This is necessary to give the `<div>` tag a unique client-side `id` attribute that is used in client-side scripting. The same has happened to the `id` of the `<img>` element. You see more about this in a later section of this chapter.

Normally, when you put an `<img>` element inside an `<a>` element to link it, the browser draws a border around the image. The border is usually blue for unvisited links and purple for links you have visited before, though you could have some CSS code targeting a elements that overrides these default colors. To remove that border completely, you need to add the following CSS:

```
img
{
  border: none;
}
```

When you add a user control to a page, VS usually refers to the control using a relative path. In this exercise, this path first contained two dots (`..`) to indicate the parent folder, followed by the `Controls` folder, and finally by the name of the control:

```
<%@ Register Src="../Controls/Banner.ascx" TagName="Banner" TagPrefix="uc1" %>
```

By changing the two dots to the tilde symbol, it becomes easier to move your pages around in your site because the `Src` attribute now always points to the `Controls` folder at the application's root, no matter where the page that consumes the control is located. If your `Src` attribute already contained the tilde, you don't have to change anything.

Though the tilde syntax makes your pages with user controls a little easier to manage, there is an even easier way to register your user controls sitewide.

Sitewide Registration of User Controls

If you have a control that you expect to use quite often on separate content pages in your site, like the banner in the previous examples, you can register the control globally in the `Web.config` file. This way it becomes available throughout the entire site, without the need to register it on every page. The following exercise shows how to do this.

TRY IT OUT Registering User Controls in the Web.config File

In this exercise, you register the `Banner.ascx` user control in the `Web.config` file. You can then remove the `@ Register` directive from the master page because it isn't needed anymore. After you have changed the `Web.config` file, adding the same user control to other pages will no longer add the `@ Register` directive to the page.

1. Open the `Web.config` file from the root of the site. If you're familiar with versions of ASP.NET prior to .NET 4, you may find the `Web.config` worryingly empty. But don't worry; the functionality it included has not been removed from .NET. The configuration information placed in the website's `Web.config` file has now been moved to the central `Web.config` and `Machine.config` files that apply to the entire machine instead. This gives you a much cleaner configuration file, making it easy to focus on your own stuff that you put in there.

2. Locate the `<pages/>` element that you used in Chapter 6 to apply the theme, and within its tags add the following bolded code that contains a `<controls>` element with a child `<add/>` element.

Note: you may need to change the self-closing tag of the <pages> element to a full closing tag.

```
<pages theme="Monochrome">
  <controls>
    <add tagPrefix="Wrox" tagName="Banner" src="~/Controls/Banner.ascx" />
  </controls>
</pages>
```

3. Save the changes and close the file.
4. Open the master page again in Markup View and locate the `Banner` control in the sidebar area. Change `uc1` to `Wrox`:

```
<Wrox:Banner ID="Banner1" runat="server" />
```

If the declaration for your user control has its own closing tag, VS updates the closing tag for you automatically:

```
<Wrox:Banner ID="Banner1" runat="server"></Wrox:Banner>
```

5. Scroll all the way up in the master page file and remove the entire line with the `@ Register` directive.
6. Save and close the master page.
7. Open `Default.aspx` again in your browser. Note that the banner is still present in the sidebar area.

> ***COMMON MISTAKES*** *If you get an error, verify that you added the correct code at the right location to the* `Web.config` *file. Also, make sure that you changed* `uc1` *to* `Wrox` *in the control declaration and that you deleted the* `@ Register` *directive from the master page.*

How It Works

Without the `@ Register` directive in the master page, the ASP.NET run time scans the `Web.config` file for controls that have been registered there. It then finds the registration of the `Wrox:Banner` control so it is able to successfully find the file using the `src` attribute and add its contents to the page hierarchy.

With the control registration added to the `Web.config` file, it's much easier to move or rename the control. Instead of finding and replacing the `@ Register` directive in all pages that use it, the only thing you need to change is the registration in the `Web.config` file. When you make a change there, all pages using the control will automatically find the new location or name of the user control.

Useful as user controls are, they have a few caveats that you need to be aware of.

User Control Caveats

Earlier you saw that the `ID` of the `Panel` control you added to the page was modified by the ASP.NET run time. Instead of getting a `<div>` element with its `id` set to `VerticalPanel`, you got the following `id`:

```
<div id="Banner1_VerticalPanel">
  ...
</div>
```

In many cases, this isn't problematic because you often don't need the client `id`. However, if you need to access this control from client-side JavaScript or CSS, it's important to understand why this `id` is modified.

Understanding and Managing Client IDs

By design, all elements in an HTML page need to be unique. Giving them an `id` attribute is not required, but if you do so, you have to make sure they are unique. To avoid conflicts in the final HTML code of the page, ASP.NET ensures that each server-side element gets a unique client `id` by prefixing them with the name of their *naming container*. Within a naming container all elements should have unique IDs. VS warns you when you try to add a control that doesn't have a unique server ID. For example, you get an error when you try to add a second panel with an ID of `VerticalPanel` to the user control. But what if you place two `Banner` controls in the same page, or one in the master page and another in a content page? Potentially, you could end up with two client `<div>` elements with an ID of `VerticalPanel`. To avoid this problem, ASP.NET prefixes each element with the ID of its nearest naming container. For the `Panel` inside the user control it means it's prefixed with `Banner1`, the server-side ID of the user control in the master page.

You can use the `ClientID` of a control to get its full client-side `id`. The following snippet shows how to display the `ClientID` of the `Panel` control on a fictitious `Label` control within the `Banner.ascx` user control:

VB.NET

```
Label1.Text = VerticalPanel.ClientID
```

C#

```
Label1.Text = VerticalPanel.ClientID;
```

With this code, the `Label` control's `Text` property will contain `Banner1_VerticalPanel`, the client-side `id` of the `Panel`. You see a more practical example of using `ClientID` in the next chapter.

With an explicit ID, it's easier to predict the final `id` of a client-side HTML element, which in turn makes it easier to reference those elements in JavaScript or CSS.

> ***NOTE*** *Because the ASP.NET run time can change the client* `id` *attributes of your HTML elements, you may have trouble using CSS ID selectors to refer to elements. The easiest way to fix this is to use Class selectors instead of ID selectors. Alternatively, you can use the control's* `ClientID` *when using embedded style sheets.*

ASP.NET 4 introduced a new option to influence the client ID: the `ClientIDMode`.

Introducing ClientIDMode

Starting with ASP.NET 4, each web control now has a `ClientIDMode` property that enables you to determine the way the client ID is made up. You can set the `ClientIDMode` to any of these four values:

VALUE	DESCRIPTION
`AutoID`	Generates the ID as it did in previous versions of ASP.NET.
`Inherit`	With this setting the control inherits its `ClientIDMode` value from its parent control.
`Predictable`	This value is mostly used for data-bound controls (discussed in Chapter 13 and later) and enables you to create predictable client IDs for repeating elements. The client ID of a control is generated by concatenating the client ID of the parent control and the server ID of the control itself. The ID can optionally be extended with a unique value for each element using the `ClientIDRowSuffix` property.
`Static`	With this value the client ID will be exactly the same as the server ID that you set. This enables you to set the client ID explicitly, giving you greater control. However, it doesn't prevent you from assigning the same value twice, which may result in duplicate IDs in the client's HTML. Use with care!

The default value of `ClientIDMode` for the `Page` class is `Predictable` and the default value for a control is `Inherit`. This in turn means that the default ID generation mode for controls is effectively `Predictable` as they inherit that setting from `Page`. If you use Visual Studio to convert a Web project to ASP.NET 4.5 from an earlier version, Visual Studio automatically sets the site default to `AutoID` in the `<pages>` element in the `Web.config` file to maintain backwards compatibility like this:

```
<pages controlRenderingCompatibilityVersion="3.5" clientIDMode="AutoID"/>
```

Currently, the Planet Wrox website doesn't benefit a whole lot from changing the client IDs for any of the existing controls, so there's no need to change any of them right now. However, in later chapters, you use the `ClientIDMode` property again to create cleaner client IDs.

Although the current banner user control makes it easy to display a banner at various locations in your site, it isn't very smart yet. All it can do is display a linked image and that's it. To improve its usability, you can add behavior to the control so it can behave differently on different pages in your site.

ADDING LOGIC TO YOUR USER CONTROLS

Although using controls for repeating content is already quite useful, they become even more useful when you add custom logic to them. By adding public properties or methods to a user control, you can influence its behavior at run time. When you add a property to a user control, it becomes available automatically in IntelliSense and in the Properties Grid for the control in the page you're working with, making it easy to change the behavior from another file like a page.

To add properties or methods to a user control, you add them to the Code Behind of the control. The properties you add can take various forms. In its simplest form, a property looks exactly like the properties you saw in Chapter 5. For more advanced scenarios you need to add *View State properties* which are able to maintain their state across postbacks. In the next two exercises you see how to create both types of properties.

Creating Your Own Data Types for Properties

To make the banner control more useful, you can add a second image to it that displays a horizontal banner. You could also add a property to the control that determines whether to display the vertical or horizontal image. You could do this by creating a numeric property of type `System.Byte`. Then `0` would be vertical and `1` would be horizontal, for example. However, this makes it hard to remember what each number represents. You can make it a bit easier by creating a `String` property that accepts the values `Horizontal` and `Vertical`. However, strings cannot be checked at compile time, so you may end up with a spelling mistake, resulting in an error or in the incorrect banner being displayed. The .NET Framework supplies a nice way to solve this by enabling you to create your own data type in the form of an *enumeration*. With an enumeration, or *enum* for short, you assign numbers to human-friendly text strings. Developers then use this readable text, while under the hood the numeric value is used. The following snippet shows a basic example of an enum (notice how the VB example doesn't use commas, whereas they are required in C#):

VB.NET

```
Public Enum Direction
  Horizontal
  Vertical
End Enum
```

C#

```
public enum Direction
{
  Horizontal,
  Vertical
}
```

With these enums, the compiler assigns numeric values to the `Horizontal` and `Vertical` members automatically, starting with `0` and counting upward. You can also define numeric values explicitly if you want:

VB.NET

```
Public Enum Direction
  Horizontal = 0
  Vertical = 1
End Enum
```

C#

```
public enum Direction
{
  Horizontal = 0,
  Vertical = 1
}
```

The cool thing about enums is that you will get IntelliSense in code files, in the Properties Grid, and even in the code editor for your user controls. Figure 8-6 shows how IntelliSense kicks in for a VB.NET code file.

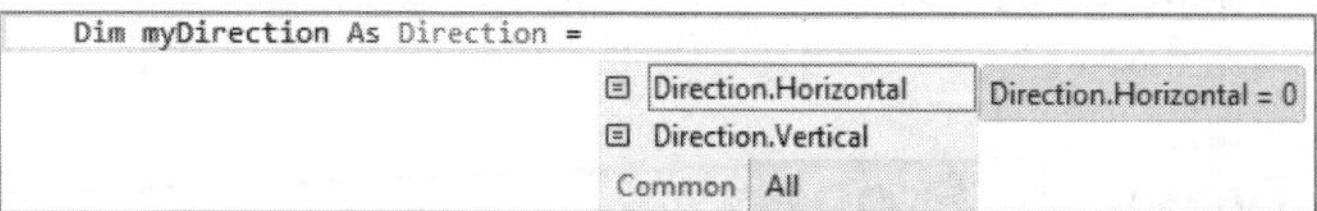

FIGURE 8-6

In Figure 8-7 you see the same list with values from the enum in the Properties Grid.

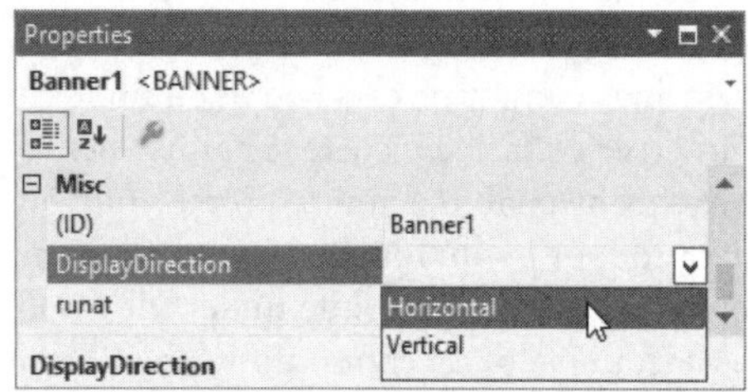

FIGURE 8-7

And in Figure 8-8 you see the same list appear for a property of a user control in Markup View.

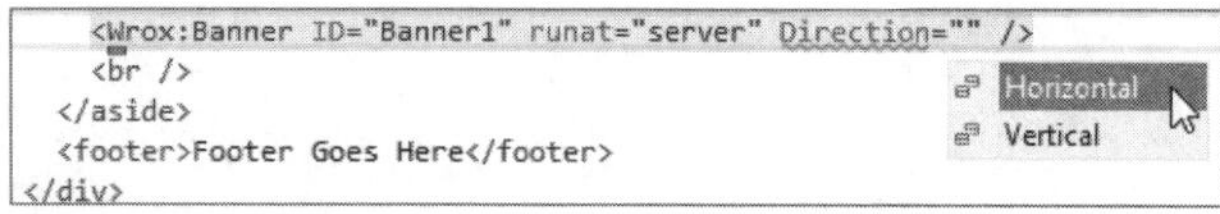

FIGURE 8-8

Just as with other code files like classes, you should put your enums in a file under the `App_Code` folder. If you have more than one of them, you can store them all in the same file or create a separate file for each enum.

Enums are great for simple and short lists. They help you find the right item quickly without memorizing "magic numbers" like 0 or 1, but enable you to use human-readable text strings instead.

In the next exercise, you see how to create an enum and use it in your `Banner` user control.

TRY IT OUT Creating Smarter User Controls

In this exercise, you add a second banner to the user control. This banner displays as a horizontal image inside its own panel. To avoid the two banners showing up at the same time, you add a property that determines which banner to display. Pages that use the control can then define the correct banner.

1. Start by creating an enumeration that contains two members for the different directions: vertical and horizontal. To do this, right-click the `App_Code` folder and choose Add ➪ Add New Item. Choose your programming language and add a class file called **`Direction`**.

2. Once the file opens, clear its contents and add the following code to it:

   VB.NET

```
Public Enum Direction
  Horizontal
  Vertical
End Enum
```

   C#

```
public enum Direction
{
  Horizontal,
  Vertical
}
```

3. Save and close the file.

4. Open the Code Behind for the user control `Banner.ascx` and add the following property. To help you create properties, VS comes with a handy code snippet. To activate the snippet in C#, type **`prop`** and then press Tab twice. VS adds the code structure for an automatic property for you. For VB.NET, you can type **`Property`** and then press Tab. However, this creates a full property rather than an automatic property (which is what is used in this exercise), so you're better off typing in the code manually in this case. Once the code is inserted, you can press Tab again to move from field to field, each time typing the right data type or property name. Complete the code so it looks like this:

   VB.NET

```
Public Property DisplayDirection As Direction
```

   C#

```
public Direction DisplayDirection { get; set; }
```

> ***COMMON MISTAKES*** *Make sure you add the property outside the* `Page_Load` *method (when you're working with C#) but before the closing* `End Class` *(in VB.NET) or the closing curly brace for the class (in C#).*

   Note that the name of the property is `DisplayDirection` and its data type is `Direction`, the enum you defined earlier.

5. Open the Markup View of `Banner.ascx`, copy the entire `<asp:Panel>`, and paste it right below the existing `Panel`. Name the control **`HorizontalPanel`** and set the `ImageUrl` of the image to **`~/Images/Banner486x60.gif`**. If you want to browse for the image instead of typing its path directly, position your cursor in Markup View after the opening quote of the `ImageUrl` attribute's value and press Ctrl+Space. Choosing Pick URL in the menu that appears enables you to browse for a file. Your code should now look like this:

```
<asp:Panel ID="HorizontalPanel" runat="server">
  <a href="http://p2p.wrox.com" target="_blank">
    <asp:Image ID="Image2" runat="server" AlternateText="This is a sample banner"
```

```
            ImageUrl="~/Images/Banner486x60.gif" />
    </a>
  </asp:Panel>
```

6. Switch back to the Code Behind of the control and add the following bolded code to the `Page_Load` handler. In C#, the handler should already be there. In Visual Basic, you can choose (Page Events) from the left drop-down list at the top of the Document Window and Load from the right drop-down list to set up the handler, or you can double-click the user control in Design View.

VB.NET

```
Protected Sub Page_Load(sender As Object, e As EventArgs) Handles Me.Load
  Select Case DisplayDirection
    Case Direction.Horizontal
      HorizontalPanel.Visible = True
      VerticalPanel.Visible = False
    Case Direction.Vertical
      VerticalPanel.Visible = True
      HorizontalPanel.Visible = False
  End Select
End Sub
```

C#

```
protected void Page_Load(object sender, EventArgs e)
{
  switch (DisplayDirection)
  {
    case Direction.Horizontal:
      HorizontalPanel.Visible = true;
      VerticalPanel.Visible = false;
      break;
    case Direction.Vertical:
      VerticalPanel.Visible = true;
      HorizontalPanel.Visible = false;
      break;
  }
}
```

7. Save and close the two files that make up the user control because you're done with them for now.

8. Open up the master page file once more in Markup View and locate the user control declaration. Right after the `runat="server"` attribute, add the following `DisplayDirection` attribute that sets the correct image type:

```
<Wrox:Banner ID="Banner1" runat="server" DisplayDirection="Horizontal" />
```

IntelliSense will help you pick the right `DisplayDirection` from the list. If you don't get IntelliSense, wait a few seconds until VS has caught up with all the changes. Alternatively, save and close all open files (or restart VS), open the master page, and try again.

9. Save all changes and request `Default.aspx` in the browser. Note that the right sidebar area now contains the horizontal image, breaking the layout a little because the image is too wide for the sidebar. If you don't see the banner appear at all, check your system for ad-blocking software that may stop the banner image from appearing.

10. Switch back to the master page and change the `DisplayDirection` from `Horizontal` to `Vertical`. Save your changes and refresh the page in the browser. The sidebar should now display the vertical banner, as shown in Figure 8-9.

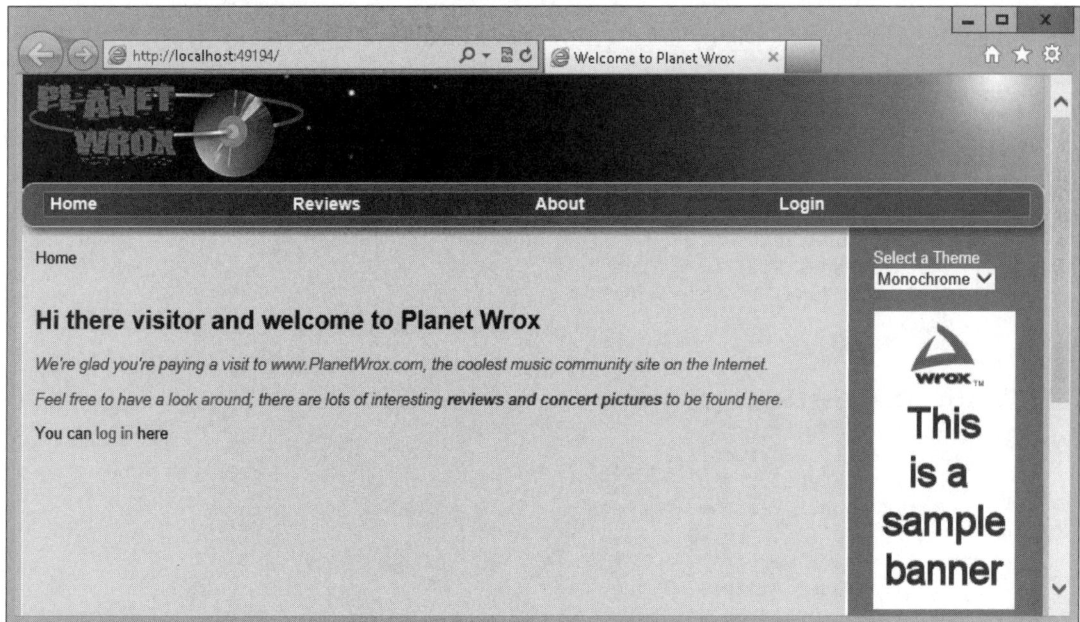

FIGURE 8-9

11. Open the `AboutUs.aspx` page from the `About` folder in Markup View. If you don't have that file, create it first. In the `cpMainContent ContentPlaceHolder`, add some text describing you or your organization and the reason you created the site. Switch to Design View and drop the `Banner.ascx` control from the Solution Explorer onto the design surface, right below the text you just added. VS detects the user control in the master page called `Banner1` and assigns the `ID` of `Banner2` to the user control you just dropped. Notice how you see four banners in Design View; two come from the `Banner` control in the master page and the other two come from the `Banner` control in the About Us page itself. At run time, two of them will be hidden.

12. Select the user control you just added in Design View, open its Properties Grid, and set the `DisplayDirection` to `Horizontal`.

13. Save all your changes and then press Ctrl+F5 to open the About Us page in your browser. In addition to the banner in the right sidebar, you should now also see the horizontal banner appear in the content area.

How It Works

The property called `DisplayDirection` gives your user control some extra behavior. Pages using the control should now set the `DisplayDirection` like this:

```
<Wrox:Banner ID="Banner1" runat="server" DisplayDirection="Horizontal" />
```

When the control instance is created by the ASP.NET run time, the value you set in the control declaration is assigned to the property `DisplayDirection`. If you don't assign a value, the default will be `Horizontal` for the current definition of the `Direction` enum as that's the first item in the list and has an implicit value of zero.

When the page loads, this code in the user control is executed:

VB.NET

```
Select Case DisplayDirection
  Case Direction.Horizontal
    HorizontalPanel.Visible = True
    VerticalPanel.Visible = False
  Case Direction.Vertical
    VerticalPanel.Visible = True
    HorizontalPanel.Visible = False
End Select
```

C#

```
switch (DisplayDirection)
{
  case Direction.Horizontal:
    HorizontalPanel.Visible = true;
    VerticalPanel.Visible = false;
    break;
  case Direction.Vertical:
    VerticalPanel.Visible = true;
    HorizontalPanel.Visible = false;
    break;
}
```

This code uses a `Select Case`/`switch` block to determine which image to show. When the `DisplayDirection` equals `Horizontal`, the `Visible` property of `HorizontalPanel` is set to `True` and the other control is hidden. The same principle is applied to the `Vertical` setting.

Implementing View State Properties

In addition to the `DisplayDirection`, another useful property for the user control would be the URL that the banner links to. In the next section, you see how to implement this and learn how to create a View State property called `NavigateUrl` that is able to survive postbacks.

TRY IT OUT Implementing the NavigateUrl Property

To be able to set the URL that a user is taken to programmatically, you need to be able to access the anchor tag that is defined in the control's markup. To do this, you need to give it an `id` and a `runat="server"` attribute. To be able to programmatically set the new `NavigateUrl` property that you'll add to the `Banner` control and to ensure that this property survives postbacks, you need to implement a View State property. To show you why you need a View State property, the first three steps of this exercise have you modify the About Us page so it sets the `DisplayDirection` of the `Banner` control programmatically. You'll then cause a postback so you can see that the value for the direction gets lost because it doesn't maintain its state in View State. The second part of the exercise then shows you how to implement the `NavigateUrl` property that is able to maintain its state.

1. Open the Code Behind of `AboutUs.aspx` and add the following bolded code to the `Page_Load` event handler. If the handler isn't there yet, switch to Design View and double-click somewhere on the gray area of the page.

   VB.NET

   ```
   Protected Sub Page_Load(sender As Object, e As EventArgs) Handles Me.Load
     If Not Page.IsPostBack Then
       Banner2.DisplayDirection = Direction.Vertical
     End If
   End Sub
   ```

   C#

   ```
   protected void Page_Load(object sender, EventArgs e)
   {
     if (!Page.IsPostBack)
     {
       Banner2.DisplayDirection = Direction.Vertical;
     }
   }
   ```

   Verify that the `Banner` user control has an `ID` of `Banner2` in the Markup View of the page, or update your code accordingly.

2. Switch to Design View and add a `Button` control by dragging it from the Standard category of the Toolbox on top of the `Banner.ascx` control that is placed inside the page (not the one that's defined in the master page). There's no need to write any code for the `Button` control's `Click` event.

3. Save the page and open it in your browser. Because of the code in `Page_Load`, the first time the page loads, the banner at the bottom of the screen displays the vertical banner. Now click the button so the page will reload. This time, the page displays the horizontal image. Because the `DisplayDirection` of the `Banner` control is set in `Page_Load` only when `Page.IsPostBack` is `False`, that setting is lost when you post back, causing the banner to revert to its default setting of `Horizontal`.

4. To avoid this problem with the `NavigateUrl`, you need to implement it as a View State property where the `ViewState` collection is used as the *backing store* to store the underlying value. That way, the value is sent to the browser and back to the server with every request. To implement the property, add the following code to the Code Behind of the `Banner.ascx` user control, right below the `DisplayDirection` property you created earlier.

   Remember, you don't have to type all this code manually because the download that comes with this book contains all the code shown.

   VB.NET

   ```
   Public Property NavigateUrl() As String
     Get
       Dim _navigateUrl As Object = ViewState("NavigateUrl")
   ```

```
    If _navigateUrl IsNot Nothing Then
      Return CType(_navigateUrl, String)
    Else
      Return "http://p2p.wrox.com"   ' Return a default value
    End If
  End Get
  Set(Value As String)
    ViewState("NavigateUrl") = Value
  End Set
End Property
```

C#

```
public string NavigateUrl
{
  get
  {
    object _navigateUrl = ViewState["NavigateUrl"];
    if (_navigateUrl != null)
    {
      return (string)_navigateUrl;
    }
    else
    {
      return "http://p2p.wrox.com";  // Return a default value
    }
  }
  set
  {
    ViewState["NavigateUrl"] = value;
  }
}
```

5. Switch to Markup View of the user control and add `runat="server"` attributes to both links. Give the link in the vertical panel an `id` of `VerticalLink` and the other an `id` of `HorizontalLink`. They should end up looking like this:

```
<a href="http://p2p.wrox.com" target="_blank" runat="server" id="VerticalLink">
...
<a href="http://p2p.wrox.com" target="_blank" runat="server" id="HorizontalLink">
```

6. Switch back to the Code Behind of the user control (press F7) and modify the `Page_Load` handler of the user control so it also sets the `HRef` property of the anchor element:

VB.NET

```
Case Direction.Horizontal
  HorizontalPanel.Visible = True
  VerticalPanel.Visible = False
  HorizontalLink.HRef = NavigateUrl
Case Direction.Vertical
  VerticalPanel.Visible = True
  HorizontalPanel.Visible = False
  VerticalLink.HRef = NavigateUrl
```

C#

```
case Direction.Horizontal:
  HorizontalPanel.Visible = true;
  VerticalPanel.Visible = false;
  HorizontalLink.HRef = NavigateUrl;
  break;
case Direction.Vertical:
  VerticalPanel.Visible = true;
  HorizontalPanel.Visible = false;
  VerticalLink.HRef = NavigateUrl;
  break;
```

7. Save the changes and go back to the Code Behind of `AboutUs.aspx`. Modify the code so it sets the `NavigateUrl` property of the `Banner` control to a different URL. You should overwrite the code that sets the `DisplayDirection`.

VB.NET

```
Protected Sub Page_Load(sender As Object, e As EventArgs) Handles Me.Load
  If Not Page.IsPostBack Then
    Banner2.NavigateUrl = "http://imar.spaanjaars.com"
  End If
End Sub
```

C#

```
protected void Page_Load(object sender, EventArgs e)
{
  if (!Page.IsPostBack)
  {
    Banner2.NavigateUrl = "http://imar.spaanjaars.com";
  }
}
```

8. Save all your changes and then request the `AboutUs.aspx` page in your browser by pressing Ctrl+F5.

> ***COMMON MISTAKES*** *Make sure you get a fresh browser window, so close any windows you may have open first.*

Click the horizontal banner at the left side of the page. A new window pops up, showing the URL you set in the previous step.

9. Close this new window and click the button you added to `AboutUs.aspx` earlier to cause the page to post back to the server. Once the page is reloaded, click the banner image again. You are taken to the same site as in step 8. This illustrates the point that the `NavigateUrl` property is now able to maintain its value across postbacks, unlike the `DisplayDirection` property you added to the user control earlier.

How It Works

In the first three steps, you witnessed the behavior of non–View State properties. You started off by writing some code in the `Page_Load` event handler that sets the `DisplayDirection` programmatically:

VB.NET

```
If Not Page.IsPostBack Then
  Banner2.DisplayDirection = Direction.Vertical
End If
```

C#

```
if (!Page.IsPostBack)
{
  Banner2.DisplayDirection = Direction.Vertical;
}
```

Because of the check for `Page.IsPostBack`, this code only fires when the page loads the first time. It doesn't fire when the page is reloaded due to a postback. When it fires, it sets the `DisplayDirection` property of the `Banner` control so the banner displays the correct image. However, as soon as the page is posted back, this value is lost and the control reverts to its default direction of `Horizontal`. One way to overcome this problem is to make sure the code fires both the first time and on subsequent postbacks. Removing the check for `Page.IsPostBack` is enough to accomplish this. However, this is not always a desired solution. Imagine you're getting the correct display direction from a database. Because fetching data from a database is a costly operation, you want to minimize the number of times you hit the database. In such scenarios, developers are likely to fetch the data only when the page loads the first time and expect it to stay around on subsequent postbacks. That is exactly what the `NavigateUrl` property does. You set its value once and it stays available, even if you post the page back to the server. This is accomplished with a View State property.

To see how this works, take a look at the setter of that property first:

VB.NET

```
Public Property NavigateUrl() As String
  ...
  Set(Value As String)
    ViewState("NavigateUrl") = Value
  End Set
End Property
```

C#

```
public string NavigateUrl
{
  ...
  set
  {
    ViewState["NavigateUrl"] = value;
  }
}
```

When you assign a value to the `NavigateUrl` property, its value is stored in the `ViewState` collection. You can see the `ViewState` collection as a bag that enables you to store data that you can retrieve again after a postback. You identify values in View State using a unique key. In the example the key equals the name of the property so it's easy to see they belong together. Once you assign a value to a View State property, it's stored in the page in the hidden `__VIEWSTATE` field that you learned about in Chapter 4. This means it gets sent to the browser when the page loads and it is sent back to the server when the page is posted back again.

When the postback occurs, the code in `Page_Load` in the user control fires again. Just as with the initial request, the code accesses the `NavigateUrl` property in the `Select Case`/`switch` block:

VB.NET

```
Case Direction.Horizontal
  ...
  HorizontalLink.HRef = NavigateUrl
  ...
```

C#

```
case Direction.Horizontal:
  ...
  HorizontalLink.HRef = NavigateUrl;
  ...
```

The value for `NavigateUrl` is returned by the getter of the property:

VB.NET

```
Public Property NavigateUrl() As String
  Get
    Dim _navigateUrl As Object = ViewState("NavigateUrl")
    If _navigateUrl IsNot Nothing Then
      Return CType(_navigateUrl, String)
    Else
      Return "http://p2p.wrox.com"  ' Return a default value
    End If
  End Get
  ...
End Property
```

C#

```
public string NavigateUrl
{
  get
  {
    object _navigateUrl = ViewState["NavigateUrl"];
    if (_navigateUrl != null)
    {
      return (string)_navigateUrl;
    }
    else
    {
      return "http://p2p.wrox.com";  // Return a default value
    }
  }
  ...
}
```

This code first tries to get the value from View State using `ViewState("NavigateUrl")` in VB.NET or `ViewState["NavigateUrl"]` in C#, which uses square brackets to access items in a collection. If the value that is returned is `Nothing` or `null`, the getter returns the default value for the property: `http://p2p.wrox.com`.

However, if the value is not `Nothing`, it is cast to a string using `CType` in VB.NET and `(string)` in C# and eventually returned to the calling code. At the end, the `NavigateUrl` returned from the View State property is assigned to the `HRef` property of the anchor tag again, which is then used as the URL users are taken to when they click the image.

View State Considerations

Although View State is designed to overcome the problems of maintaining state as outlined in the previous exercise, you should carefully consider whether or not you use it. The values you store in View State are sent to the browser and back to the server on *every* request. When you store many or large values in View State, this increases the size of the page and thus negatively impacts performance. Never store large objects like database records in View State; it's often quicker to get the data fresh from the database on each request than passing it along in the hidden View State field if the amount of data that needs to be stored is large. Also, because the View State is stored within the page and is thus transferred over the wire, you shouldn't use it to store sensitive values such as passwords.

PRACTICAL TIPS ON USER CONTROLS

The following list provides some practical tips on working with user controls:

- Don't overuse user controls. User controls are great for encapsulating repeating content, but they also make it a little harder to manage your site because code and logic is contained in multiple files. If you're not sure if some content will be reused in another part of the site, start by embedding it directly in the page. You can always move it to a separate user control later if the need arises.
- Keep user controls focused on a single task. Don't create a user control that is able to display five different types of unrelated content with a property that determines what to display. This makes the control difficult to maintain and use. Instead, create five lightweight controls and use them appropriately.
- When you create user controls that contain styled markup, don't hardcode style information like the `CssClass` for the server controls contained in the user control. Instead, consider creating separate `CssClass` properties on the user control, which are then used to set the `CssClass` of your server controls. This improves the reusability of your user control, making it easier to incorporate the control in different designs.

SUMMARY

User controls can greatly improve the maintainability of your site. Instead of repeating the same markup and code on many different pages in your site, you encapsulate the code in a single control, which you can then use in different areas of your site.

To improve the usefulness of your controls, you can add behavior to them. It's common to create controls with properties you can set in consuming pages, enabling you to change the behavior of the control at run time. Although View State properties can solve some of the state issues you may come across, you should carefully consider whether you really need them. Because these properties add to the size of the page, they can have a negative impact on your site's performance.

You can further improve the `Banner` control by keeping track of the number of times each image has been clicked. The Planet Wrox site doesn't implement this, but with the knowledge you gain in the chapters about database interaction, this is easy to implement yourself.

In the next chapter you create another user control that serves as a contact form. By building the form as a user control, it's easy to ask your users for feedback from different locations in the site.

EXERCISES

1. In this chapter you saw how to create a standard property and a View State property. What is the main difference between the two? And what are the disadvantages of each of them?

2. Currently, the `DisplayDirection` property of the `Banner` control doesn't maintain its state across postbacks. Change the code for the property so it is able to maintain its state using the `ViewState` collection, similar to how `NavigateUrl` maintains its value.

3. What are the two main benefits of using a custom enumeration like `Direction` over built-in types like `System.Byte` or `String`?

You can find answers to these exercises in Appendix A.

▶ WHAT YOU LEARNED IN THIS CHAPTER

`@ Control` **directive**	A set of instructions that marks a file as a User Control and define its behavior.
`@ Register` **directive**	Used to register user controls and point to their source inside pages, master pages, and other user controls.
`AlternateText`	The property that enables you to set the `alt` attribute on images that is shown when the image cannot be displayed.
`Machine.config`	The central .NET configuration file that applies to your entire system and provides defaults for your website's settings.
User Control	A block of content (stored in a file with an `.ascx` extension and an optional Code Behind file) that can be reused in pages, master pages, and other user controls in your site.
View State Properties	Properties at the page, master page, or user control level that store their values in View State so they can survive postbacks.
`ViewState` **collection**	The `ViewState` collection is the property on the `Page`, `UserControl`, and `MasterPage` classes that enables you to store and retrieve values using View State.

Validating User Input

WHAT YOU WILL LEARN IN THIS CHAPTER:

- What user input is and why it's important to validate it
- What ASP.NET 4.5 has to offer to aid you in validating user input
- How to work with the built-in validation controls and how to create solutions that are not supported out of the box
- How to send e-mail using ASP.NET
- How to read text files

WROX.COM CODE DOWNLOADS FOR THIS CHAPTER

You can find the wrox.com code downloads for this chapter on the Download Code tab at `www.wrox.com/remtitle.cgi?isbn=1118311809`. The code is in the Chapter 9 download.

So far you have been creating a fairly static website where you control the layout and content by adding fixed pages to the site and its navigation menus. But you can make your site a lot more attractive by incorporating dynamic data. This data usually flows in two directions: it either comes from the server and is sent to the end user's browser, or the data is entered by the user and sent to the server to be processed or stored.

Data coming from the server can be retrieved from many different data sources, including files and databases, and is often presented with the ASP.NET data controls. You see how to access databases in Chapter 12 and onward.

The other flow of data comes from the user and is sent to the server. The scope of this information is quite broad, ranging from simple page requests and "Contact Us" forms to complex shopping cart scenarios and wizard-like user interfaces, but the underlying principle of this data flow is basically the same in all scenarios—users enter data in a Web Form and then submit it to the server.

To prevent your system from receiving invalid data, it's important to validate this data before you allow your system to work with it. Fortunately, ASP.NET 4.5 comes with a bag of tools to make data validation a simple task.

The first part of this chapter gives you a good look at the validation controls that ASP.NET supports. You see what controls are available, how to use and customize them, and in what scenarios they are applicable.

The second half of this chapter shows you how to work with data in other ways. You see how to receive the information a user submits to your site and then send it by e-mail and how to customize the mail body using text-based templates.

By the end of the chapter, you will have a good understanding of the flow of information to an ASP .NET website and the various techniques you have at your disposal to validate this data.

GATHERING DATA FROM THE USER

Literally every website on the Internet has to deal with input from the user. Generally, this input can be sent to the web server with a number of different techniques, of which `GET` and `POST` are the most common. In Chapter 4, you briefly saw the difference between these two methods and saw that `GET` data is appended to the actual address of the page being requested, whereas with the `POST` method, the data is sent in the body of the request for the page.

With the `GET` method, you can retrieve the submitted data using the `QueryString` property of the `Request` object, as discussed in Chapter 7. Imagine you are requesting the following page:

```
http://www.PlanetWrox.com/Reviews/ViewDetails.aspx?ReviewId=34&CategoryId=3
```

With this example, the query string is `ReviewId=34&CategoryId=3`. The question mark is used to separate the query string from the rest of the address, and the query string itself consists of name/value pairs separated by an ampersand (`&`). The names and values in turn are separated by the equals symbol (`=`). To access individual items in the query string, you can use the `Get` method of the `QueryString` collection:

VB.NET

```
' Assigns the value 34 to the reviewId variable
Dim reviewId As Integer = Convert.ToInt32(Request.QueryString.Get("ReviewId"))
' Assigns the value 3 to the categoryId variable
Dim categoryId As Integer = Convert.ToInt32(Request.QueryString.Get("CategoryId"))
```

C#

```
// Assigns the value 34 to the reviewId variable
int reviewId = Convert.ToInt32(Request.QueryString.Get("ReviewId"));
// Assigns the value 3 to the categoryId variable
int categoryId = Convert.ToInt32(Request.QueryString.Get("CategoryId"));
```

The `POST` method, on the other hand, gets its data from a form with controls that have been submitted to the server. Imagine you have a form with two controls: a `TextBox` called `Age` to hold the user's age and a `Button` to submit that age to the server. In the `Button` control's `Click` event, you could write the following code to convert the user's input to an integer:

VB.NET

```
Dim age As Integer = Convert.ToInt32(Age.Text)  ' age now holds the user's age
```

C#

```
int age = Convert.ToInt32(Age.Text);           // age now holds the user's age
```

Note that in this case, there is no need to access a collection like `Form` as you saw with the `QueryString` collection earlier. ASP.NET shields you from the complexity of manually retrieving data from the submitted form, and instead populates the various controls in your page with the data from the form.

All is well as long as users enter values that look like an age in the text box. But what happens when a user submits invalid data, either deliberately or by accident? What if a user sends the text *I am 41* instead of just the number 41? When that happens, the code will crash. The `ToInt32` method of the `Convert` class *throws an exception* (an error) when you pass it something that cannot be represented as a number. As soon as the exception is thrown, page execution stops completely. Chapter 18 digs deeper into exception handling.

To avoid these problems, you need to validate all the data that is being sent to the server. When it doesn't look valid, you need to reject it and make sure your application deals with it gracefully.

Validating User Input in Web Forms

People concerned with validating user input often use the mantra: *Never trust user input.* Although this may seem like paranoia at first, it is really important in any open system. Even if you think you know who your users are, and even if you trust them completely, they are often not the only users that can access your system. As soon as your site is out on the Internet, it's a potential target for malicious users and hackers who will try to find a way into your system. In addition to these evil visitors, even your trustworthy users may send incorrect data to your server by accident.

To help you overcome this problem as much as possible, ASP.NET ships with a range of *validation controls* that help you validate data before it is used in your application. In the following sections, you see how to use the standard validation controls to ensure the user submits valid data into the system.

The ASP.NET Validation Controls

ASP.NET 4.5 comes with six useful controls to perform validation in your website. Five of them are used to perform the actual validation, whereas the final control—`ValidationSummary`—is used to provide feedback to the user about any errors made in the page. Figure 9-1 shows the available controls in the Validation category of the Toolbox.

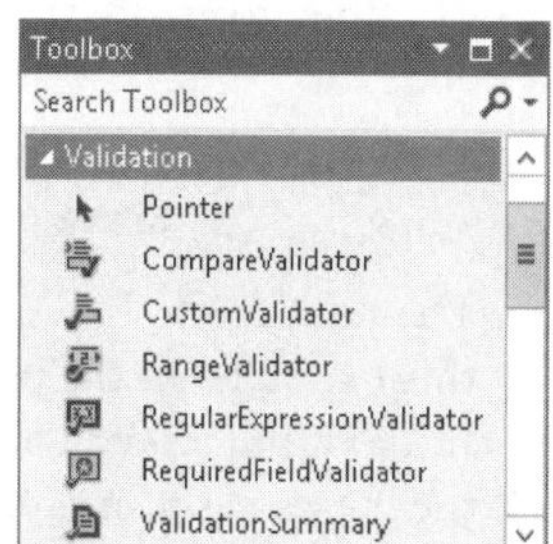

FIGURE 9-1

The validation controls are extremely helpful in validating the data that a user enters in the system. They can easily be hooked to other controls like the `TextBox` or a `DropDownList`; however, they also support custom validation scenarios. Figure 9-2 demonstrates two of the validation controls—`RequiredFieldValidator` and `RangeValidator`—at work to prevent a user from submitting the form without entering required and valid data.

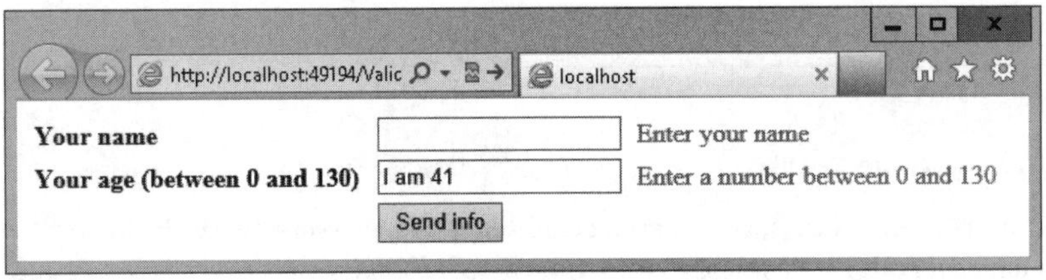

FIGURE 9-2

The great thing about the validation controls is that they can check the input at the client and at the server. When you add a validation control to a web page, the control renders JavaScript that validates the associated control at the client. This client-side validation works on most modern web browsers with JavaScript enabled, including Internet Explorer, Firefox, Chrome, Opera, and Safari. At the same time, the validation is also carried out at the server automatically. This makes it easy to provide your user with immediate feedback about the data using client-side scripts, while your web pages are safe from bogus data at the server.

A Warning on Client-Side Validation

Although client-side validation may seem enough to prevent users from sending invalid data to your system, you should never rely on it as the only solution to validation. It's easy to disable JavaScript in the browser, rendering the client-side validation routines useless. In addition, a malicious user can easily bypass the entire page in the browser and send information directly to the server, which will happily accept and process it if you don't take countermeasures.

In general, you should see client-side validation as a courtesy to your users. It gives them immediate feedback so they know they forgot to enter a required field, or entered incorrect data without a full postback to the server. Server-side validation, on the other hand, is the only real means of validation. It's effectively the only way to prevent invalid data from entering your system.

The following section discusses how you can employ the validation controls to protect your data.

Using the Validation Controls

To declare a validation control in your ASPX page, you use the familiar declarative syntax. For example, to create the `RequiredFieldValidator` control used in Figure 9-2, you need the following code:

```
<asp:RequiredFieldValidator ID="ReqVal1" runat="server" ControlToValidate="YourName"
        ErrorMessage="Enter your name" />
```

The `ControlToValidate` property links this validation control to another control (`YourName` in this example) in the page. When asked to perform its validation, the validation control looks at the value of the linked control and when that value doesn't meet the validation rules you set, it displays the message set in the `ErrorMessage` property by default although you can override this behavior as you'll see later.

To give you an idea of how the validation controls work, the following exercise guides you through the process of using the `RequiredFieldValidator` in a contact form that is placed in a user control. The exercise is followed by an in-depth discussion of the various validation controls.

> ***NOTE*** *Visual Studio comes with a number of useful code snippets that enable you to quickly insert controls like the validation controls in Markup View. In the following exercise, you see how to add the necessary controls using the Toolbox, Design View, and drag and drop, but it's useful to know how to quickly add controls in Markup View as well. For example, to insert a* `TextBox` *in Markup View, type* **`tb`** *or* **`textbox`** *and then press Tab. VS completes the full control code for you. To insert a* `RequiredFieldValidator`*, type the letters* **`req`***, press Ctrl+Spacebar to have VS complete the word* `requiredfieldvalidator` *for you, and then press Tab again to insert the entire tag.*
>
> *If you do this directly below a* `TextBox` *control with its ID set, VS even sets the correct* `ControlToValidate` *attribute for you. This latter trick wouldn't work if you tried it in the next exercise because the various controls are not directly next to each other, but are placed in separate table cells. VS still inserts the code for the* `RequiredFieldValidator` *for you, but you need to set the* `ControlToValidate` *property to the ID of the associated* `TextBox` *manually.*

TRY IT OUT Using the RequiredFieldValidator

In this exercise, you create a user control called `ContactForm.ascx`. You can place it in a web page so visitors to your site can leave some feedback. In later exercises, you extend the control by sending the response by e-mail to your e-mail account.

1. Open the Planet Wrox project and add a new user control in the `Controls` folder. Call the control **`ContactForm.ascx`**. Make sure that it uses your programming language and a Code Behind file.
2. Switch to Design View and insert a table by choosing Table ➪ Insert Table. Create a table with eight rows and three columns.
3. Merge the three cells of the first row. To do this, select all three cells, right-click the selection, and choose Modify ➪ Merge Cells.
4. In the merged cell, type some text that tells your users they can use the contact form to get in touch with you. You could use an `h1` element as a heading above the page to draw the user's attention.
5. In the first cell of the second row, type the word **`Name`**. Into the second cell of the same row, drag a `TextBox` and set its `ID` to `Name`. Into the last cell of the same row, drag a `RequiredFieldValidator` from the Validation category of the Toolbox. Finally, into the second cell of the last row, drag a `Button`. Rename the button to **`SendButton`** by setting its `ID` and set its `Text` property to `Send`. When you're done, your Design View looks like Figure 9-3.

ContactForm.ascx*
Get in touch with us
Use the form below to get in touch with us. Enter your name, e-mail address, and your home or business phone number to get in touch with us.
Name
RequiredFieldValidator
Send
Design
Split
Source
<tr>
<td>
<asp:Button#SendButton>

FIGURE 9-3

6. Click the `RequiredFieldValidator` once in Design View and then open up its Properties Grid by pressing F4. Set the following properties on the control:

PROPERTY	VALUE
`CssClass`	ErrorMessage
`ErrorMessage`	Enter your name
`Text`	*
`ControlToValidate`	Name

Note: you can type in the value for `ControlToValidate` directly or you can pick it from the list by clicking the down arrow.

7. Save the changes to the user control and then close it because you're done with it for now.

8. Add the following CSS declaration to the CSS files for both themes (`Monochrome.css` and `DarkGrey.css`):

```
.ErrorMessage
{
  color: Red;
}
```

Save and close both files.

9. Open `Contact.aspx` from the `About` folder in Markup View and from the Solution Explorer, drag the user control `ContactForm.ascx` between the tags of the `cpMainContent` control. You should end up with this control declaration:

```
<asp:Content ID="Content2" ContentPlaceHolderID="cpMainContent" runat="Server">
  <Wrox:ContactForm ID="ContactForm" runat="server" />
</asp:Content>
```

Visual Studio remembers the last custom prefix you used and reuses that when dragging the user control onto the page. Depending on how you previously configured the `Banner` user control in `Web.config`, your `Wrox:` prefix may be different. That doesn't matter for this exercise. Also note, when you drag the control in Design View, its ID is `ContactForm1`. For this exercise, the actual ID doesn't matter, but beware of the difference when working with the control ID later in this chapter.

10. Open `Web.config` and add or modify the following code under the `<appSettings>` element (which is a direct child of the main `<configuration>` node):

```
<configuration>
  <appSettings>
    <add key="ValidationSettings:UnobtrusiveValidationMode" value="None" />
  </appSettings>
  ...
</configuration>
```

Unobtrusive validation requires jQuery, which is discussed in Chapter 11. Until then, you need to disable it or your pages with validation controls will throw errors.

11. Save your changes and open `Contact.aspx` in your browser. If you get an error, make sure you renamed the `TextBox` to `Name` and that you set the `ControlToValidate` property on the `RequiredFieldValidator` to `Name`.
12. Leave the Name text box empty and click the Send button. Note that the page is not submitted to the server. Instead, you should see a red asterisk appear at the very right of the row for the name field to indicate an error. If the asterisk is not red, press Ctrl+F5 or Ctrl+R to get a fresh copy of the theme's CSS file from the server and click the Send button again.
13. Enter your name and click Send again. The page now successfully posts back to the server.

How It Works

With the `RequiredFieldValidator` attached to the `TextBox` through the `ControlToValidate` property, client-side JavaScript is sent to the browser that validates the control at the client.

The `RequiredFieldValidator` control is able to validate another control like a `TextBox`. It does this by comparing the value of the other control with its own `InitialValue` property and making sure that the other control's value is different. By default, this property is an empty string, which means that anything except an empty string is considered a valid value. Whenever you try to submit the form to the server by clicking the Send button, the validation control checks the control it is attached to. When the text box is still empty, the asterisk from its `Text` property is shown (formatted with the `ErrorMessage` CSS class), and the form is not submitted. You see how to use and display the `ErrorMessage` property later in this chapter. When the user enters something in the `Name` text box, validation succeeds and the page submits to the server successfully.

Using the HTML5 Data Types

HTML5 has introduced a number of new types for the `type` attribute on the `input` element. These new types enable you to determine how a browser should interpret the field so it can render a correct user interface for it. ASP.NET 4.5 supports these new attributes using the `TextMode` property of a `TextBox` control. In addition to the `SingleLine`, `MultiLine`, and `Password` types that have been supported since ASP.NET 1, you can now use the following values as well:

VALUE	DESCRIPTION
Color	Enables the user to choose a color, usually from a color picker.
Date / DateTime / DateTimeLocal / Month / Week / Time	Enables various ways for the user to enter a date or time. Depending on the type, the browser renders a calendar or other specialized control to enter a value.
Email	Enables the user to enter an e-mail address.
Url	Enables the user to enter a web address.
Number	Enables the user to enter a number.
Range	Enables the user to enter a number with a specified range. The browser typically draws a slider control to enter the value.
Search	Enables the user to enter a search term. This typically renders a standard text box but with an option in the right corner to clear the text.

These server-side values for the `TextMode` property are converted into client-side HTML attributes with the same name, but written in lowercase. To see how that looks, consider this `TextBox`:

```
<asp:TextBox runat="server" ID="Email" TextMode="Email" />
```

When rendered in the browser, this control generates the following HTML:

```
<input name="Email" type="email" id="Email" />
```

Based on various values for the `type` attribute, browsers can help the user enter the correct data by drawing a different user interface for the control and by validating the data that is entered. Also, devices with a “soft keyboard”—a keyboard that is displayed on-screen—are able to adapt the keyboard to match the data type for the input control. For example, Apple’s iPad shows a numeric keyboard if you put the focus on a text box with its `type` set to `number`.

Although these new attribute values are a great addition to HTML, you need to be aware of a few caveats. First of all, with HTML5 being so new, not all browsers support these new features. Figure 9-4 shows each of these attributes in the five most popular browsers today. On the first row, you see Internet Explorer 10, Firefox 14, and Chrome 21; and on the second row, you see Safari 5 and Opera 12.

As you can see, some browsers support more of the attributes than others. At the time of writing, Opera and Safari have the best support. Note that not all browsers implement these new types exactly the same. For example, in Firefox you’ll get an error and you won’t be able to submit the page if you enter a value that doesn’t look like an e-mail address in an `input` box with its `type` attribute set to `email`.

Another thing you need to realize is that you should see these new attributes as helpful hints to the user only; you should never solely rely on them for validation purposes. It would be easy for a malicious user to bypass the validation carried out by the browser. In addition, because browser support is still so limited, the validation won't be carried out for all fields in all browsers.

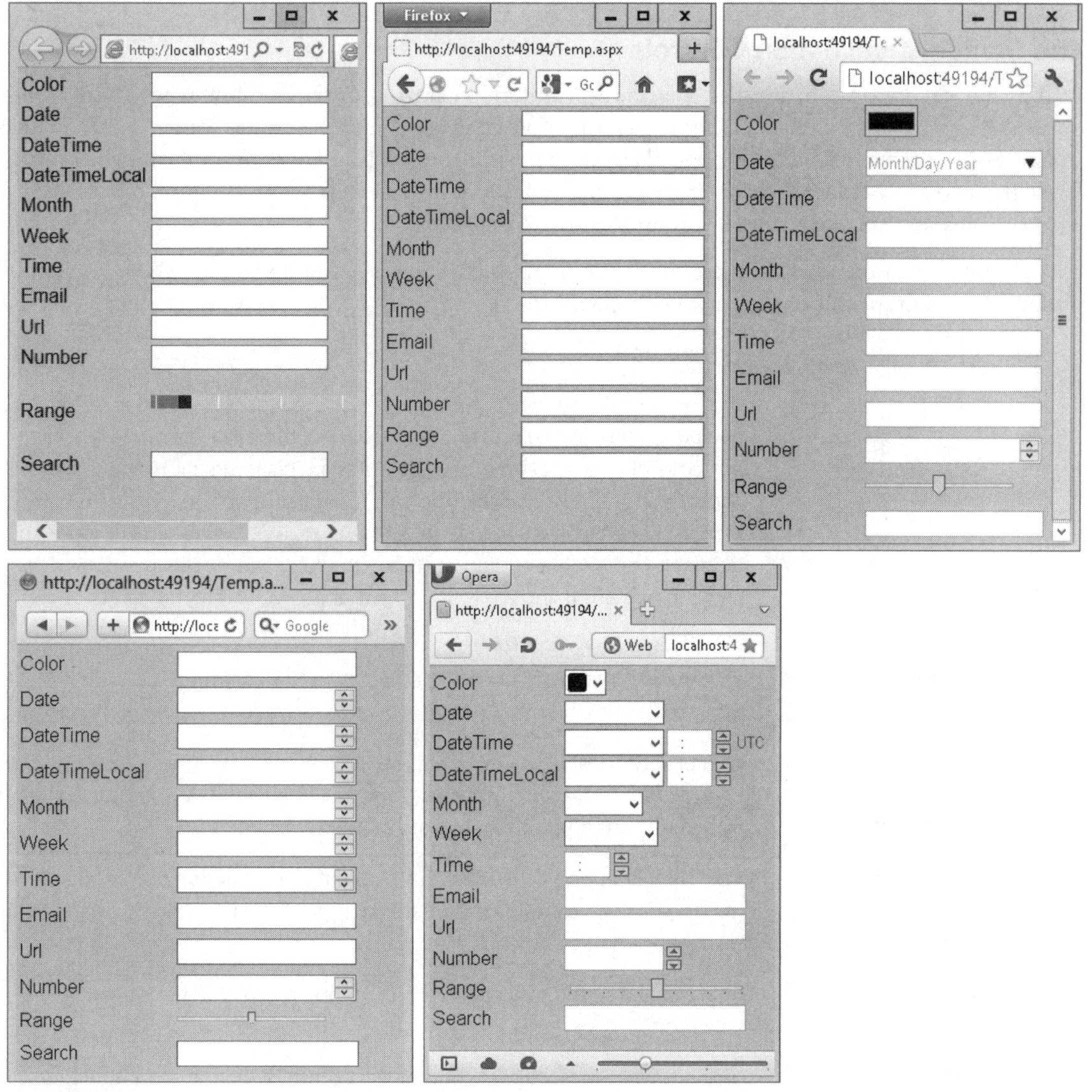

FIGURE 9-4

Given the limited implementation of these new attributes in major browsers, you may wonder if it's worth using them in the first place. My recommendation would be to use them, even though support is somewhat limited. First of all, new versions of browsers are released on a regular basis, bringing better HTML5 support. In addition, other devices such as phones and tablets come to the market with browsers that do have support for these attributes. Finally, using these attributes is pretty much risk-free. The default `type` for an `input` element is `text`, so when a browser encounters a value it doesn't understand, it treats the element as a simple text box.

Because you can't rely on these HTML5 attributes to validate your data, it's important that you use the ASP.NET validation controls. The next section discusses the remaining validation controls that are available in ASP.NET.

The Standard Validation Controls

The five validation controls (the ones in the Validation category of the Toolbox whose names end in `Validator`) ultimately all inherit from the same base class, and thus share some common behavior. Four of the five validation controls operate in the same way, and contain built-in behavior that enables you to validate associated controls. The last control, the `CustomValidator`, enables you to write custom validation rules not supported out of the box.

The following table lists a number of common properties that are shared by the validation controls and that you typically use when working with them.

PROPERTY	DESCRIPTION
`Display`	This property determines whether or not the hidden error message takes up space. With the `Display` set to `Static`, the error message takes up screen real estate, even when it is hidden. This is similar to the CSS setting `visibility: hidden` you saw in earlier chapters. The `Dynamic` setting hides the error message using `display: none` until it needs to be displayed. With a setting of `None`, the control is not visible at all. This is useful if you are using a `ValidationSummary`, which you see later in this chapter.
`CssClass`	This property enables you to set the CSS `class` attribute that is applied to the error message text.
`ErrorMessage`	This property holds the error message used in the `ValidationSummary` control. When the `Text` property is empty, the `ErrorMessage` value is also used as the text that appears on the page.
`Text`	The `Text` property is used as the text that the validation control displays on the page. This could be an asterisk (*) to indicate an error, or text like "Enter your name."
`ControlToValidate`	This property contains the server ID of the control that needs to be validated.
`EnableClientScript`	This property determines whether the control provides validation at the client. The default is `True`.
`SetFocusOnError`	This property determines whether client-side script gives the focus to the first control that generated an error. This setting is `False` by default.

PROPERTY	DESCRIPTION
ValidationGroup	Validation controls can be grouped together, enabling you to perform validation against a selection of controls. All controls with the same ValidationGroup are checked at the same time, which means that controls that are not part of that group are not checked. Consider, for example, a login page with a Login button and fields for a username and password. The same page may also contain a search box that enables you to search the site. With the ValidationGroup, you can have the Login button validate the username and password boxes, whereas the Search button triggers validation for just the search box.
IsValid	You don't typically set this property at design time, but at run time, it provides information about whether the validation test has passed. The Page class also has an IsValid property that returns the combined result of all controls in the page or validation group, as you'll see later.

The Difference between the Text and ErrorMessage Properties

At first glance, these two properties seem to serve the same purpose. Both of them can be used to provide feedback to the user in the form of an error message. But when used in combination with a ValidationSummary control, there's a subtle difference between the two. When you set both the properties at the same time, the validation control displays the Text property, whereas the ValidationSummary uses the ErrorMessage. Figure 9-5 shows a sample login page with two RequiredFieldValidator controls. Both validation controls have their Text property set to an asterisk (*) to give the user a visual cue that there is a problem. The ValidationSummary below the control then displays the full ErrorMessage properties.

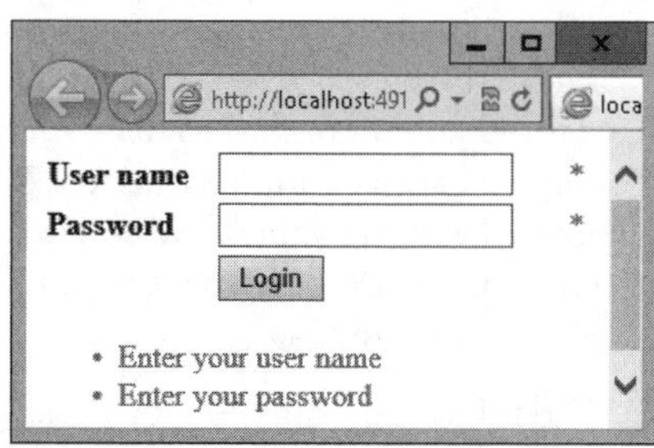

FIGURE 9-5

You've already seen the RequiredFieldValidator at work, so the next sections give you a good look at the three remaining standard validation controls. A later section then shows you how to use the CustomValidator and the ValidationSummary controls.

RangeValidator

The RangeValidator control enables you to check whether a value falls within a certain range. The control is able to check data types like strings, numbers, dates, and currencies. For example, you can use it to make sure a number is between 1 and 10, a character between A and F, or a selected date falls between today and the next two weeks. The following table lists its most important properties.

PROPERTY	DESCRIPTION
`MinimumValue`	This property determines the lowest acceptable value. For example, when checking an integer number between 1 and 10, you set this property to 1.
`MaximumValue`	This property determines the highest acceptable value. For example, when checking an integer number between 1 and 10, you set this property to 10.
`Type`	This property determines the data type that the validation control checks. This value can be set to `String`, `Integer`, `Double`, `Date`, or `Currency` to check the respective data types.

The following example shows a `RangeValidator` that ensures that the value entered in the `Rate` text box is a whole number that lies between 1 and 10:

```
<asp:RangeValidator ID="RangeValidator1" runat="server"
    ControlToValidate="Rate" ErrorMessage="Enter a number between 1 and 10"
    MaximumValue="10" MinimumValue="1" Type="Integer" />
```

RegularExpressionValidator

The `RegularExpressionValidator` control enables you to check a value against a *regular expression* that you set in the `ValidationExpression` property of the control. Regular expressions offer a compact syntax that enables you to search for patterns in text strings. Regular expressions are a complex subject, but fortunately, Visual Studio comes with a few built-in expressions that make it easy to validate values like e-mail addresses and ZIP codes. If you want to learn more about regular expressions, pick up a copy of Wrox's *Beginning Regular Expressions* by Andrew Watt (ISBN: 978-0-7645-7489-4).

The following example shows a `RegularExpressionValidator` control that ensures that a user enters a value that looks like an e-mail address:

```
<asp:RegularExpressionValidator ID="RegularExpressionValidator1" runat="server"
     ControlToValidate="Email" ErrorMessage="Enter a valid e-mail address"
     ValidationExpression="\w+([-+.']\w+)*@\w+([-.]\w+)*\.\w+([-.]\w+)*" />
```

CompareValidator

The `CompareValidator` can be used to compare the value of one control to another value. This is often used in sign-up forms where users have to enter a password twice to make sure they type the same password both times. Instead of comparing to another control, you can also compare against a constant value.

The following table lists the additional properties for the `CompareValidator` control.

PROPERTY	DESCRIPTION
ControlToCompare	This property contains the ID of the control that the validator compares against. When this property is set, ValueToCompare has no effect.
Operator	This property determines the type of compare operation. For example, when Operator is set to Equal, both controls must contain the same value for the validator to be considered valid. Similarly, you have options like NotEqual, GreaterThan, and GreaterThanEqual to perform different validation operations.
Type	This property determines the data type that the validation control checks. This value can be set to String, Integer, Double, Date, or Currency to check the respective data types.
ValueToCompare	This property enables you to define a constant value to compare against. This is often used in agreements where you have to enter a word like Yes to indicate that you agree to some condition. Simply set the ValueToCompare to the word Yes and the ControlToValidate to the control you want to validate and you're done. When this property is set, make sure that the ControlToCompare property is empty because that will otherwise take precedence.

This example shows a CompareValidator that ensures that two TextBox controls contain the same password:

```
<asp:CompareValidator ID="CompareValidator1" runat="server"
    ControlToCompare="ConfirmPassword" ControlToValidate="Password"
    ErrorMessage="Your passwords don't match" />
```

In the following exercise, you see most of these controls at work, except for the RangeValidator. However, its usage is similar to the other validation controls, so it's just as easy to add it to your web page or user control when you need it.

TRY IT OUT Extending the Contact Form

In the previous Try It Out, you started with the basics for the contact form by creating a user control holding a table and a few controls to let users enter their name. In this exercise, you extend the form and add fields for an e-mail address, a home phone number, a business phone number, and a comment. You use the validation controls to ensure that the e-mail address is in a valid format, and that at least one of the two phone numbers is filled in. To make sure users enter a correct e-mail address, they are asked to enter it twice. If you don't like this behavior, you can simply delete the row with the text box for the second e-mail address and ignore the `CompareValidator`.

1. Open `ContactForm.ascx` from the `Controls` folder again and switch to Design View.
2. In the second column, drag five additional `TextBox` controls in the empty table cells between the text box for the name and the Send button. From top to bottom, name the new controls by setting their ID as follows:
   - `EmailAddress`
   - `ConfirmEmailAddress`
   - `PhoneHome`
   - `PhoneBusiness`
   - `Comments`
3. Set the `TextMode` property of the `Comments` control to `MultiLine`, and then make the control a little wider and taller in the designer so it's easier for a user to add a comment.
4. Set the `TextMode` property of the two e-mail fields to `Email`. On browsers that support this, this will validate the value as an e-mail address and may trigger the correct "soft keyboard" to be displayed.
5. In the first cell of the rows to which you added the `TextBox` controls, add text describing the purpose of the `TextBox`. Figure 9-6 shows an example.
6. In the last cell of the row for the first e-mail address, drag a `RequiredFieldValidator` and a `RegularExpressionValidator`. In the last cell of the row for the second e-mail address, drag a `RequiredFieldValidator` and a `CompareValidator`. Finally, in the last cell for the comments row, drag a `RequiredFieldValidator`. When you're done, your form looks like Figure 9-6.

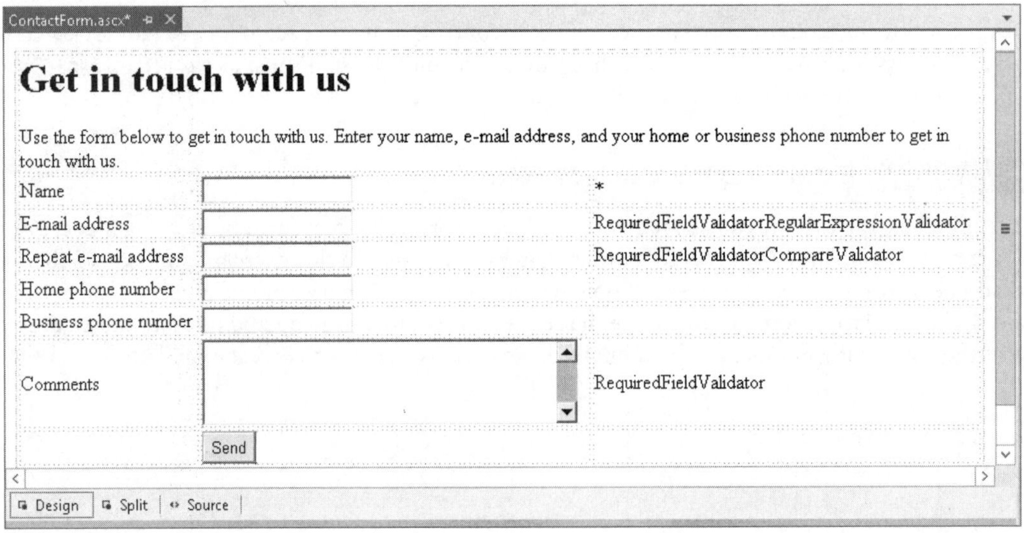

FIGURE 9-6

7. For each of the five validation controls you added, open the Properties Grid and set the `Text` property to an asterisk (`*`), the `Display` property to `Dynamic`, and the `CssClass` to `ErrorMessage`. To do this for all controls at once, select the first validator control, then press the Ctrl key and click the others. When you make changes to the Properties Grid while you've selected multiple controls, the changes are applied to all of them.

8. Next, set the remaining properties for the controls as shown in the following table.

Control	Properties You Need to Set	Values You Need to Set
`RequiredFieldValidator` (for the first e-mail address)	`ErrorMessage:`	Enter an e-mail address
	`ControlToValidate:`	`EmailAddress`
`RegularExpressionValidator`	`ErrorMessage:`	Enter a valid e-mail address
	`ControlToValidate:`	`EmailAddress`
`RequiredFieldValidator` (for the second e-mail address)	`ErrorMessage:`	Confirm the e-mail address
	`ControlToValidate:`	`ConfirmEmailAddress`
`CompareValidator`	`ErrorMessage:`	The e-mail addresses don't match
	`ControlToCompare:`	`EmailAddress`
	`ControlToValidate:`	`ConfirmEmailAddress`
`RequiredFieldValidator` (for the Comments field)	`ErrorMessage:`	Enter a comment
	`ControlToValidate:`	`Comments`

9. Still in Design View, click the `RegularExpressionValidator` once, open its Properties Grid, and locate the `ValidationExpression` property. When you click the property in the grid, the grid shows a button with an ellipsis. When you click that button, you get a dialog box that enables you to select a regular expression, shown in Figure 9-7.

10. Scroll down in the list and then click Internet e-mail address from the list and note that VS inserts a long

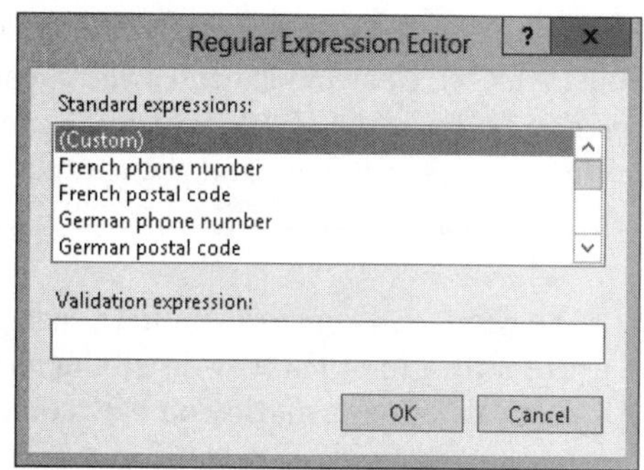

FIGURE 9-7

regular expression in the Validation Expression box. Click OK to add the property to the control and dismiss the dialog box.

11. Save all the changes and then request the `Contact.aspx` page from the `About` folder in your browser. If you get errors, make sure you set all the `ControlToValidate` properties on the relevant controls as shown earlier. Play around with the various validation controls by leaving out required data or by entering bogus data. At this stage, you will only see the red asterisks appear to give an indication of the problem. After you have seen how these validators work, you learn how to use the `ValidationSummary` to provide more detailed information to the user.

    Depending on your browser, you may see other notifications about invalid fields such as colored borders or tooltips explaining the problem. Only when you have entered all required fields and typed the same e-mail address in both text boxes will the page submit to the server.

How It Works

Just like the `RequiredFieldValidator` control, the other validation controls emit JavaScript to the client, which is triggered when you click the Send button or when the value of one of the client controls is changed. The `CompareValidator` works by looking at the value of two different controls. Only when both contain the same data will it return true. It's important to realize that the `CompareValidator` control does not trigger its validation code when the text boxes are empty. Therefore, it's important to hook up a `RequiredFieldValidator` control as well. This control first makes sure the user entered at least some data and then the `CompareValidator` control ensures that the text is the same in both text boxes.

The `RegularExpressionValidator` control works by checking the pattern of the data that it is validating. If you look at the `ValidationExpression` property of the control, you see a long, cryptic string. This pattern ensures that the e-mail address contains some text, optionally followed by some separation character like a dash (-) or period, followed by more text. It also ensures that there's an @ symbol in the address, followed by a domain name, a period, and then at least one more character to represent the top-level domain like `.com`, `.nl`, or `.co.uk`. With this expression, `you@example.com` is considered a valid e-mail address. So is `a@a.a`, whereas `you@you` isn't.

Note that the `RegularExpressionValidator` control only roughly checks the syntax of the e-mail address. It's still perfectly possible to enter a nonexistent e-mail address that just looks valid or even an invalid e-mail address such as `a@a.a`. However, in many cases, this validator is good enough to filter out common typos that users make when entering e-mail addresses.

If you look at the source for the page you see a lot of JavaScript code at the end of the file. With this code, ASP.NET has implemented the client-side validation since the first version of ASP.NET. However, starting with ASP.NET 4.5, you now have another alternative that uses jQuery under the hood. You learn more about jQuery and the alternative validation mechanism in Chapter 11.

The validation controls you have seen so far are very easy to use. You add them to a page, set a few properties, and then they do all the hard work for you. However, they do not support every possible validation scenario you may come up with. For example, what if you wanted to ensure that a user entered at least one of the two phone numbers? And what if you wanted to present your users with a full list of all the errors they made in the form? This is where the `CustomValidator` and the `ValidationSummary` controls come in.

The CustomValidator and ValidationSummary Controls

The `CustomValidator` control enables you to write custom validation functions for both the client (in JavaScript) and the server (using VB.NET or C#). This gives you great flexibility with regard to the data you want to validate and the rules you want to apply.

The `ValidationSummary` control provides the user with a list of errors that it retrieves from the individual validation control's `ErrorMessage` properties. It can display these errors in three different ways: using a list embedded in the page, using a JavaScript alert box, or using both at the same time. You control this setting with the `ShowMessageBox` and `ShowSummary` properties. Additionally, the `DisplayMode` property enables you to change the way the list of errors is presented. The default setting is `BulletList` where each error is an item in a bulleted list, but other options are `List` (without bullets) and `SingleParagraph`.

You learn how to write client- and server-side validation methods and how to use the `ValidationSummary` control in the following exercise.

TRY IT OUT Writing Client- and Server-Side Validation Methods

In this exercise, you see how to use the `CustomValidator` in your page to ensure that at least one of the two phone numbers is entered. The validation is carried out at the client and at the server. Additionally, you see how to use the `ValidationSummary` control to provide feedback to your users about the errors they made in the form.

> ***NOTE*** *This is the first chapter where you'll actually write some JavaScript on your own. Don't worry about it too much because you won't have to write a whole lot of it. The examples should be pretty easy to follow, even if you don't have any prior experience with JavaScript. If you want to learn more about JavaScript, consider getting a copy of* Professional JavaScript for Web Developers, 3rd Edition *by Nicholas C. Zakas (Wrox, ISBN: 978-1-1180-2669-4).*

1. Go back to the `ContactForm.ascx` user control in VS and switch it to Design View. Right-click the row with the `Button` control in it (right-click a cell, not the button) and choose Insert ➪ Row Below from the context menu to insert a new table row. Alternatively, you can click in a cell of the row to select it and then press Ctrl+Alt+down arrow to have the row inserted for you as well.
2. Select the three cells of the row you just inserted, right-click them, and choose Modify ➪ Merge Cells to create a single cell that spans all three columns.
3. From the Validation category of the Toolbox, drag a `ValidationSummary` control into this newly created cell and set its `CssClass` property to `ErrorMessage`.
4. In the empty cell after the text box for the Home phone number, drag a `CustomValidator` control and set the following properties:

PROPERTY	VALUE
CssClass	ErrorMessage
Display	Dynamic
ErrorMessage	Enter your home or business phone number
Text	*
ClientValidationFunction	validatePhoneNumbers

5. Double-click the `CustomValidator` control in Design View to have VS write an event handler for the `ServerValidate` event. Add the following code to the handler:

VB.NET

```
Protected Sub CustomValidator1_ServerValidate(source As Object,
         args As ServerValidateEventArgs) Handles CustomValidator1.ServerValidate
  If Not String.IsNullOrEmpty(PhoneHome.Text) OrElse
              Not String.IsNullOrEmpty(PhoneBusiness.Text) Then
    args.IsValid = True
  Else
    args.IsValid = False
  End If
End Sub
```

C#

```
protected void CustomValidator1_ServerValidate(object source,
                ServerValidateEventArgs args)
{
  if (!string.IsNullOrEmpty(PhoneHome.Text) ||
               !string.IsNullOrEmpty(PhoneBusiness.Text))
  {
    args.IsValid = true;
  }
  else
  {
    args.IsValid = false;
  }
}
```

6. Switch to Markup View of the user control and add the following block of JavaScript code right before the table with the controls:

```
<script type="text/javascript">
  function validatePhoneNumbers(source, args)
  {
    var phoneHome = document.getElementById('<%= PhoneHome.ClientID %>');
    var phoneBusiness = document.getElementById('<%= PhoneBusiness.ClientID %>');
    if (phoneHome.value != '' || phoneBusiness.value != '')
    {
      args.IsValid = true;
    }
    else
```

```
    {
      args.IsValid = false;
    }
  }
</script>
<table class="auto-style1">
```

In JavaScript, it's common to write method names using *camel casing*, where the first word of the method name is written in lowercase, followed by words with the first letter in uppercase.

If you find that VS is adding your opening curly braces ({) at the end of a line, rather than on their own line, choose Tools ⇨ Options from the main menu. Then expand the path Text Editor ⇨ JavaScript ⇨ Formatting and check off both items in the New Lines category. This is purely a formatting preference; the JavaScript runs fine with or without the curly brace on its own line. Note that JavaScript is case sensitive, so make sure you type the code exactly as shown here.

7. Save all the changes by pressing Ctrl+Shift+S, request the `Contact.aspx` page in your browser, and click the Send button. Also note that the `ValidationSummary` control shows a list of all the problems with the data entered in the form. The client-side JavaScript function `validatePhoneNumbers` now ensures that you enter at least one phone number before you can submit the page back to the server. Figure 9-8 shows how the page appears in Google Chrome.

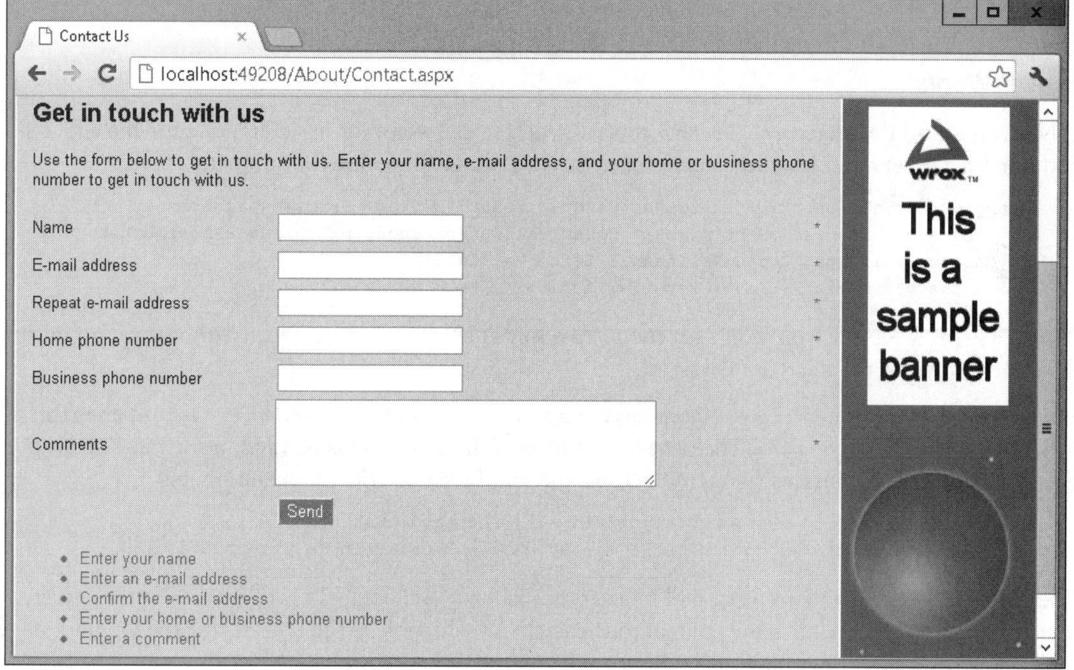

FIGURE 9-8

8. Go back to VS and click the `ValidationSummary` control in Design View. On the Properties Grid, change `ShowMessageBox` to `True` and `ShowSummary` to `False`. (Quick tip: you can easily choose

the next item in a drop-down list on the Properties Grid by double-clicking the value. For booleans, this means that if you double-click False, it turns to True and vice versa). Also, set its `HeaderText` property to **Please correct the following errors:**.

9. Open the page in the browser again and click the Send button once more. Note that instead of the inline list with errors, you now get a client-side alert, shown in Figure 9-9. The list of errors is preceded with the `HeaderText` of the `ValidationSummary`.

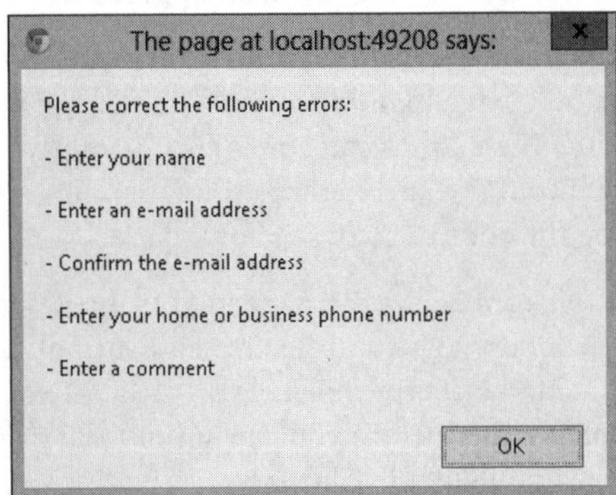

FIGURE 9-9

How It Works

When you added the `CustomValidator` control, you set up two event handlers, one for the client-side and one for the server-side validation check, both in bold in the following snippet:

```
<asp:CustomValidator ID="CustomValidator1" runat="server" ErrorMessage="Enter your
    home or business phone number" ClientValidationFunction="validatePhoneNumbers"
  OnServerValidate="CustomValidator1_ServerValidate"
  Display="Dynamic">*</asp:CustomValidator>
```

If you're using VB.NET, you won't see the `OnServerValidate` attribute because that is set up in the Code Behind using the `Handles` keyword.

The JavaScript function `validatePhoneNumbers` that you set in the `ClientValidationFunction` is triggered at the client when you click the Send button. This function is defined in the markup section of the user control and contains two references to the text boxes for the phone numbers:

```
var phoneHome = document.getElementById('<%= PhoneHome.ClientID %>');
var phoneBusiness = document.getElementById('<%= PhoneBusiness.ClientID %>');
```

The calls to the `ClientID` are wrapped in a server-side `<%= %>` block. This code runs at the server, and then returns the `ClientID` of the control to the client. If you look at the HTML for the Contact page in the browser, you find the following code:

```
function validatePhoneNumbers(source, args)
{
  var phoneHome = document.getElementById('cpMainContent_ContactForm_PhoneHome');
  var phoneBusiness =
        document.getElementById('cpMainContent_ContactForm_PhoneBusiness');
  if (phoneHome.value != '' || phoneBusiness.value != '')
```

Here you can see how the server-side `ClientID` properties of the controls have been transformed into their client `id` counterparts. This is a much better solution than hard-coding the `id` attributes of the text boxes in the final HTML, because they can be changed easily by the ASP.NET run time. You saw how and why this happened in the preceding chapter.

To make the final JavaScript in the browser slightly shorter and easier to read, you can use the `ClientIDMode` property you saw in the preceding chapter to "fix" the IDs of the phone number controls. Because it's unlikely you will have two `ContactForm` user controls in a single page, you can safely assume that you won't end up with two client controls with the same name if you fix the client control IDs. To do this, you need to set the `ClientIDMode` for these two controls to `Static`, like this:

```
<asp:TextBox ID="PhoneHome" runat="server" ClientIDMode="Static" />
...
<asp:TextBox ID="PhoneBusiness" runat="server" ClientIDMode="Static" />
```

Because the control IDs are now fixed, they end up as-is in the final HTML:

```
var phoneHome = document.getElementById('PhoneHome');
var phoneBusiness = document.getElementById('PhoneBusiness');
```

Eventually, the client IDs are passed to the JavaScript function `getElementById` on the `document` object to get a reference to their respective text boxes in JavaScript. In Chapter 11, which deals with jQuery, I discuss an easier alternative to using `getElementById`. The code then examines the `value` properties of these two `TextBox` controls. If one of them is not an empty string, the validation succeeds. But how does the `validatePhoneNumbers` method report back to the validation mechanism whether the validation succeeded or not? When the ASP.NET validation mechanism calls the `validatePhoneNumbers` method, it passes two arguments: `source`, which is a reference to the actual `CustomValidator` in the HTML, and `args`. The `args` object exposes an `IsValid` property that enables you to determine whether or not the validation succeeded:

```
if (phoneHome.value != '' || phoneBusiness.value != '')
{
  args.IsValid = true;
}
else
{
  args.IsValid = false;
}
```

With this code, if both text boxes are empty, `IsValid` is set to `false`, so validation won't succeed, stopping the form from being submitted. If at least one of the text boxes contains a value, `IsValid` is set to `true`. In this example, the `source` argument is not used, but you could use it to highlight or otherwise change the validation control based on whether or not it's valid.

At the server, the `CustomValidator` control calls the server-side validation method, which performs the same check:

VB.NET

```
If Not String.IsNullOrEmpty(PhoneHome.Text) OrElse
             Not String.IsNullOrEmpty(PhoneBusiness.Text) Then
  args.IsValid = True
Else
```

```
  args.IsValid = False
End If
```

C#

```
if (!string.IsNullOrEmpty(PhoneHome.Text) ||
                !string.IsNullOrEmpty(PhoneBusiness.Text)
{
  args.IsValid = true;
}
else
{
  args.IsValid = false;
}
```

By checking the data at the client and at the server, you ensure your system accepts only valid data. Even when the browser doesn't support JavaScript (possibly because the user turned it off deliberately), your data is still checked at the server. However, it's important to realize that you still need to check whether the page is valid before you work with the data submitted to it. You do this by checking the `IsValid` property of the page:

VB.NET

```
If Page.IsValid Then
  ' OK to proceed
End if
```

C#

```
if (Page.IsValid)
{
  // OK to proceed
}
```

The `IsValid` property returns `True` when all the controls in the page or in the active `ValidationGroup` are valid. By checking the `IsValid` property on the server before you work with the data, you can be sure that the data is valid according to your validation controls, even if the user turned off JavaScript in the browser, and sent the form to the server without any client-side checks. You see the `IsValid` property used again later in this chapter, when sending e-mail is discussed.

In addition to the validation controls you have seen so far, ASP.NET comes with another validation mechanism, which is discussed next.

Understanding Request Validation

By design, an ASP.NET page throws an exception whenever one of the controls on a page contains content that looks like HTML tags. For example, you see the error shown in Figure 9-10 when you enter `<h1>Hello World</h1>` or `<script type="text/javascript">alert('Hello World');</script>` as the contents for the comments text box in the contact form.

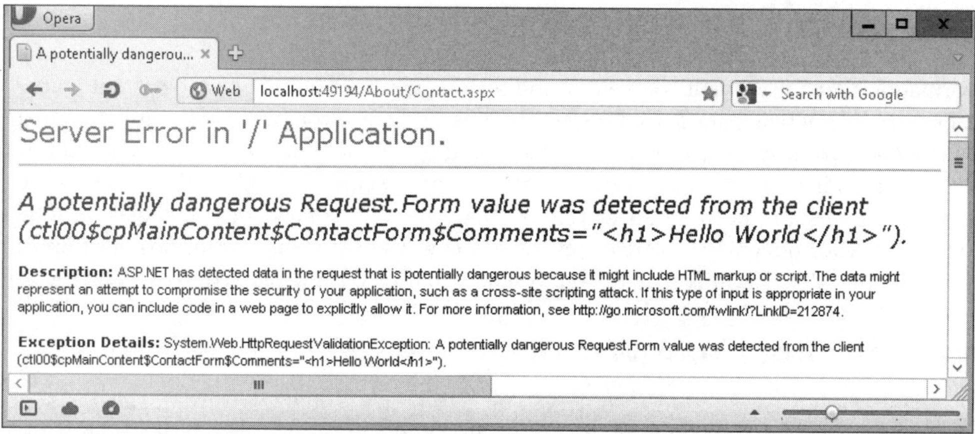

FIGURE 9-10

The ASP.NET run time does this to prevent users from entering HTML or JavaScript that can potentially mess with the design or workings of your website or that could lead to security risks. If you're sure you want to allow your users to enter HTML, you have a few options available. First, you can disable request validation by setting the `ValidateRequest` attribute in the `@ Page` directive to `False`:

```
<%@ Page .... Inherits="Contact" Title="Contact Us" ValidateRequest="False" %>
```

With this setting set to `False`, users can enter HTML without causing an error. In previous versions of ASP.NET, this was the only way to enable a user to send HTML to your page. The downside of this solution is that it's all or nothing. By turning off request validation at the page level, all controls in the page will now accept HTML. This unnecessarily opens up your page for potential abuse. As a good security mechanism, you should allow HTML only for specific fields that you determine explicitly.

Fortunately, ASP.NET 4.5 now makes this very easy; the `Control` class (from which classes such as `TextBox` inherit) has been extended with a `ValidateRequestMode` property that controls the check for invalid data. When set to `Enabled`, the control does not accept HTML; when set to `Disabled` the control does accept HTML, similar to how `ValidateRequest` enabled this for all controls in the page. The final value for `ValidateRequestMode` is `Inherit`, which gives it the value set by the parent of the control such as a `PlaceHolder`. This is convenient because you can wrap multiple controls that should accept HTML in a `PlaceHolder` and then configure the `ValidateRequestMode` on the container instead of on each individual control.

Before you set this property on a control, make sure you really want to allow users to submit HTML in your controls. This opens up your site for Cross Site Scripting attacks when you're not careful. Depending on the situation, you may need to sanitize the data by removing dangerous pieces of code such as `<script>` elements. When displaying the data on a page, you could use a `Literal` control, with its `Mode` set to `Encode` in order for the HTML to be encoded and rendered harmless. With this property set, the text is displayed verbatim, without being interpreted as HTML or JavaScript.

PROCESSING DATA AT THE SERVER

The information that a user inputs on your Web Forms is typically not the only data that makes your website an interactive, data-driven system. In most websites, you have information coming from other data sources as well, such as databases, text, XML files, and web services. In addition, there is also data going out of your system. You may want to send an e-mail to the owner of the website whenever someone posted information through the contact page, or you may want to notify people whenever you add a new feature or review to the website. For these scenarios, it's important to understand how ASP.NET 4.5 enables you to send e-mail. This is discussed in the next section.

Sending E-mail from Your Website

Writing code that sends e-mail from an ASP.NET page is pretty straightforward. Inside the `System.Net.Mail` namespace you find a number of classes that make it easy to create and send e-mail messages. These classes enable you to create new messages; add addressees in the To, Cc, and Bcc fields; add attachments; and, of course, send the messages.

The following table describes four classes that you typically work with when sending e-mail from a .NET application.

CLASS	DESCRIPTION
`MailMessage`	This class represents the message you're going to send. It has properties such as `Subject` and `Body` to set the message contents; `To`, `CC`, and `Bcc` properties to set the addressees; and an `Attachments` collection to attach files to the message.
`MailAddress`	This class represents a sender or receiver address used in the e-mail. It has a few constructor overloads that enable you to set the e-mail address and display name.
`Attachment`	This class represents a file you can attach to a `MailMessage`. When you construct an `Attachment` instance, you can pass in the name of the file you want to send. You then add the attachment to the `MailMessage` using the `Add` method of its `Attachments` collection.
`SmtpClient`	This class is used to send the actual message. By default, an instance of this class checks the `Web.config` file for settings such as the SMTP server (which stands for Simple Mail Transfer Protocol) to send the mail to and an optional username and password that is used for sending e-mail.

Configuring Your Website for Sending E-mail

Although the code to send e-mail is pretty easy, configuring your application and network can often be a bit trickier. The machine you are using to send e-mail must be able to access an SMTP server, either available locally on your network or over the Internet. In most cases, you should use the SMTP server that you also use in your e-mail client (for example, Microsoft Outlook). If you're hosting your site with an external hosting party, you need to use the SMTP server it provides. Contact your network administrator or your ISP if you are unsure about your SMTP server.

When you have the address of the SMTP server, you can configure it globally in the `Web.config` file in the `<system.net>` element. When you are using the SMTP server from your ISP, the configuration setting looks like this:

```
    <system.net>
      <mailSettings>
        <smtp deliveryMethod="Network" from="Your Name &lt;you@example.com &gt;">
          <network host="smtp.example.com" />
        </smtp>
      </mailSettings>
    </system.net>
    ...
  </configuration>
```

You must add the `<system.net>` element as a direct child of the `Web.config` file's root element `<configuration>`. Within `<system.net>` you add a `<mailSettings>` element, which in turn contains an `<smtp>` element. Finally, the `<network>` element has a `host` attribute that points to your SMTP server.

The `<smtp>` element accepts an optional `from` attribute that enables you to set the name and e-mail address of the sender in the format `Name <E-mail Address>`. Because the angle brackets (`< >`) in XML have special meaning, you need to escape them with `<` and `>`. When you send e-mail programmatically, you can override this From address as you see in the next Try It Out exercise.

If your ISP requires you to authenticate before you can send the e-mail or wants you to use a different port number, you can add this information to the `<network />` element:

```
<smtp deliveryMethod="Network" from="Your Name &lt;you@example.com &gt;">
  <network host="smtp.example.com" userName="UserName" password="Password"
          port="587" />
</smtp>
```

The port number varies from server to server. In some cases, you can leave out the `port` attribute and the `SmtpClient` will use the default port number (which is 25). Other port numbers that are frequently used include 465 and 587.

Some mail servers—like the one supplied by Gmail—require you to use *Secure Sockets Layer (SSL)*, a technique that encrypts the data going to the mail server to improve security. In ASP.NET prior to version 4, you had to enable SSL programmatically in your own code. Fortunately, with the inclusion of the `enableSsl` attribute on the `<network />` element, this is no longer the case. To use a Gmail server or any other mail server that requires SSL, you use a `<network />` element that looks like this:

```
<network enableSsl="true" host="smtp.gmail.com" password="Password"
              userName="YourAccountName@gmail.com" port="587" />
```

Don't forget to enter your password and username—which in the case of Gmail is your full Gmail e-mail address. Depending on your settings, you may need to generate an application-specific password, which you can do here: `http://bit.ly/N9Wv35`.

For `Outlook.com` (the former Hotmail), you can use the following settings:

```
<network host="smtp.live.com" password="Password"
    userName="you@yourdomain.com" enableSsl="true" port="587" />
```

And for Yahoo, you can use the following settings:

```
<network host="smtp.mail.yahoo.com" password="Password"
      userName="YourAccountName@yahoo.com"  />
```

During development, there's a much easier way to handle mail sent by your application: drop it in a folder on your local hard drive directly. To do this, create a folder like `C:\TempMail`. You need to create the folder yourself because it won't be created automatically. Then configure the `<smtp />` element as follows:

```
<smtp deliveryMethod="SpecifiedPickupDirectory"
            from="Planet Wrox &lt;planetwrox@example.com&gt;">
  <specifiedPickupDirectory pickupDirectoryLocation="C:\TempMail" />
</smtp>
```

With these settings in `Web.config`, your messages are not sent over the network, but are dropped as physical files (with an `.eml` extension) in the folder you configured in the `pickupDirectoryLocation` attribute. You can read these files with mail clients like Outlook or Windows Live Mail (which you can download from the Internet). I prefer this setting during development over the networked version because mail arrives instantly, and doesn't clutter up my mail account or Inbox. Another alternative is to use a fake development SMTP server such as smtp4dev. You can find out more about this program on their website at `http://smtp4dev.codeplex.com`.

Refer to the online MSDN documentation at `http://tinyurl.com/bu79nkm` for more information about the different settings that the `<mailSettings>` element takes.

Creating E-mail Messages

To create and send an e-mail message, you need to carry out four steps. First, you need to create an instance of the `MailMessage` class. You then configure the message by adding a body and a subject. The next step is to provide information about the sender and receivers of the message, and finally, you need to create an instance of the `SmtpClient` class to send the message. The following exercise shows you how to code these four steps.

TRY IT OUT Sending E-mail Messages

In this exercise, you create a simple page in the `Demos` folder. The code in this page creates an e-mail message that is sent when the page loads. In a later exercise, you modify the contact form so it can send the user's response by e-mail.

1. Under the `Demos` folder, create a new file called `Email.aspx`. Make sure it's based on your own base page template so that it has the right master page and inherits from `BasePage` automatically. Change the page's `Title` to **`E-mail Demo`**.
2. Switch to the Code Behind by pressing F7 and at the top of the file, before the class definition, add the following statement to make the classes in the `System.Net.Mail` namespace available to your code:

VB.NET

```
Imports System.Net.Mail
```

C#

```
using System.Net.Mail;
```

3. Add the following code to a `Page_Load` handler. If you're using VB.NET, you need to set up the handler first using the two drop-down lists at the top of the Document Window (or by double-clicking the page in Design View):

VB.NET

```
Protected Sub Page_Load(sender As Object, e As EventArgs) Handles Me.Load
  Dim myMessage As MailMessage = New MailMessage()
  myMessage.Subject = "Test Message"
  myMessage.Body = "Hello world, from Planet Wrox"
  myMessage.From = New MailAddress("you@example.com", "Sender Name")
  myMessage.To.Add(New MailAddress("you@example.com", "Receiver Name"))

  Dim mySmtpClient As SmtpClient = New SmtpClient()
  mySmtpClient.Send(myMessage)
End Sub
```

C#

```
protected void Page_Load(object sender, EventArgs e)
{
  MailMessage myMessage = new MailMessage();
  myMessage.Subject = "Test Message";
  myMessage.Body = "Hello world, from Planet Wrox";
  myMessage.From = new MailAddress("you@example.com", "Sender Name");
  myMessage.To.Add(new MailAddress("you@example.com", "Receiver Name"));

  SmtpClient mySmtpClient = new SmtpClient();
  mySmtpClient.Send(myMessage);
}
```

Change the e-mail addresses and names in the two lines that set the `From` and `To` addresses to your own. If you have only one e-mail address, you can use the same address for the sender and the receiver.

4. Open `Web.config` and right before the closing `</configuration>` tag, add the following settings:

```
  <system.net>
    <mailSettings>
      <smtp deliveryMethod="Network" from="Your Name &lt;you@example.com&gt;">
        <network host="smtp.example.com" />
      </smtp>
    </mailSettings>
  </system.net>
</configuration>
```

Don't forget to change `smtp.example.com` to the name of your SMTP server. Also, be sure to enter your name and e-mail address in the `from` attribute. If necessary, add the `userName`, `password`, `enableSsl`, and `port` attributes to the `<network>` element as shown earlier.

If you're using Gmail, Outlook.com, or Yahoo, use the settings shown at the start of this section. Otherwise, check with your host for specific requirements concerning the port number when SSL is used; typical port numbers include 465 and 587. The source that comes with this book uses `SpecifiedPickupDirectory` as the delivery method, which means you need to create a folder called `C:\TempMail` in order to send e-mail if you want to run that code.

5. Save all changes, switch back to `Email.aspx`, and request it in your browser. After a while, you should receive an e-mail message at the address you specified in step 3 of this exercise or in your local pickup folder.

> ***COMMON MISTAKES*** *If you get an error, you can check a couple of things. First, make sure you entered the right SMTP server in* `Web.config`*. You may need to talk to your Internet provider or network administrator to get the right address and, optionally, a username and password. Also make sure that the mail server you are using actually allows you to send messages. If you get an error such as "The SMTP server requires a secure connection or the client was not authenticated," your provider may require you to log in or to use SSL to secure the connection. If that's the case, check the username, password, and port number in* `Web.config` *or try setting the* `enableSsl` *attribute of the* `<network />` *element as shown earlier. Different mail servers use different port numbers, so try out the listed port numbers or ask your host which port you should use.*

In some obscure cases, you may receive an error when the name of your development machine contains an underscore. In that case, you either need to rename the machine or use a different SMTP server.

Another reason for problems could be a mismatch between your account name and the address you specify in the `From` property in the code. Some mail servers require these values to be identical.

Finally, if you get the error "The specified string is not in the form required for an e-mail address," check if you entered a valid e-mail address in the `from` attribute in the `Web.config` file. You get this error if you leave out the `@` symbol or make some other syntax error.

If you can't make sending mails from your local machine work, you can always use the `SpecifiedPickupDirectory` delivery option to store the files on your local machine. This way, you need to configure the mail server only when you deploy your website, and it gives you a quick, convenient solution during development.

How It Works

You added the following `Imports` or `using` statement to the Code Behind file:

VB.NET

```
Imports System.Net.Mail
```

C#

```
using System.Net.Mail;
```

This statement is used to make the classes in this namespace available in your code without prefixing them with their full namespace. This enables you, for example, to create a MailMessage instance like this:

VB.NET

```
Dim myMessage As MailMessage = New MailMessage()
```

C#

```
MailMessage myMessage = new MailMessage();
```

Without the Imports or using statement, you would need this longer code instead:

VB.NET

```
Dim myMessage As System.Net.Mail.MailMessage = New System.Net.Mail.MailMessage()
```

C#

```
System.Net.Mail.MailMessage myMessage = new System.Net.Mail.MailMessage();
```

The code in Page_Load creates a new MailMessage object and sets its Subject and Body properties. The code then assigns addresses for the sender and recipient of the e-mail message:

VB.NET

```
myMessage.From = New MailAddress("you@example.com", "Sender Name")
myMessage.To.Add(New MailAddress("you@example.com", "Receiver Name"))
```

C#

```
myMessage.From = new MailAddress("you@example.com", "Sender Name");
myMessage.To.Add(new MailAddress("you@example.com", "Receiver Name"));
```

The From property of the MailMessage is of type MailAddress, so you can assign a new MailAddress directly. The constructor of the MailAddress class accepts the e-mail address and friendly name as strings, so you can create and assign the From address with a single line of code.

The To property of the MailMessage class is a collection, so you cannot assign a MailAddress instance directly. Instead, you need to use the Add method to assign an address. This also enables you to add multiple recipients by calling To.Add multiple times, each time passing in a different MailAddress instance. You use the CC and Bcc properties in a similar way to assign e-mail addresses to the carbon copy and blind carbon copy fields of an e-mail message.

The final two lines of the code send out the actual message:

VB.NET

```
Dim mySmtpClient As SmtpClient = New SmtpClient()
mySmtpClient.Send(myMessage)
```

C#

```
SmtpClient mySmtpClient = new SmtpClient();
mySmtpClient.Send(myMessage);
```

When the Send method is called, the SmtpClient scans the Web.config file for a configured SMTP server or local drop folder. It then contacts that server and delivers the message or saves it locally.

In the preceding Try It Out exercise, the body text for the e-mail message is hard-coded. This isn't always the best solution because it means you need to scan and change your code whenever you want to change the text. It's often better to use a text-based template instead. You see how to do this in the next section.

Reading from Text Files

The .NET Framework comes with a few handy classes and methods that make working with files very easy. For example, the `File` class located in the `System.IO` namespace enables you to read from and write to files, create and delete files, and move files around on disk. This class contains only static methods, which means you don't have to create an instance of the class first. Instead, you call methods directly on the `File` class. For example, to read the complete contents of a text file, you can use the following code:

VB.NET

```
Dim myContents As String = System.IO.File.ReadAllText("C:\MyFile.txt")
```

C#

```
string myContents = System.IO.File.ReadAllText(@"C:\MyFile.txt");
```

In this example, the filename in C# is prefixed with an `@` symbol, to avoid the need to prefix each backslash (\) with an additional backslash. In C#, the backslash has a special meaning (it's used to "escape" other characters that have a special meaning), so to use it in a string, you normally need to prefix it with another backslash. Using the `@` symbol tells the compiler that it should treat each backslash it finds as literal, ignoring the special meaning of the character. It also preserves any line breaks inside the string.

The following table lists the most common methods of the `File` class that enable you to work with files.

METHOD	VALUE
`AppendAllText`	Appends a specified string to a text file. If the file does not exist, it's created first.
`Copy`	Copies a file from one location to another.
`Delete`	Deletes the specified file from disk.
`Exists`	Checks if the specified file exists on disk.
`Move`	Moves the specified file to a different location.
`ReadAllText`	Reads the contents of a text file.
`WriteAllText`	Writes the contents of a string to a new file and overwrites the target file if it already exists.

You can use these methods for all kinds of purposes. For example, when a user has uploaded a file, you can use the `Move` method to move it to a different folder. Additionally, when you want to get rid of uploaded files that you don't need anymore, you use the `Delete` method.

The `ReadAllText` method is useful to read the complete contents of a text file. For example, when sending text by e-mail, you could store the body text of the e-mail in a text file. When you're about to send the e-mail, you call `ReadAllText` and assign the contents that this method returns to the body of the e-mail. You see how this works in the following Try It Out.

TRY IT OUT Sending Mail from the ContactForm User Control

This exercise shows you how to use e-mail to send the user data from the contact form to your own Inbox. As the body of the e-mail message, the code reads in a text file that contains placeholders. These placeholders are filled with the actual user data from the form.

1. Start by adding a new text file to the `App_Data` folder in your website. If you don't have the `App_Data` folder yet, right-click the website and choose Add ➪ Add ASP.NET Folder ➪ App_Data. Create the text file by right-clicking the `App_Data` folder and choosing Add ➪ Add New Item. Then select Text File, name the file **`ContactForm.txt`**, and click Add.
2. Enter the following text in the text file, including the placeholders wrapped in a pair of double hash symbols:

```
Hi there,

A user has left the following feedback at the site:

Name:                ##Name##
E-mail address:      ##Email##
Home phone:          ##HomePhone##
Business phone:      ##BusinessPhone##
Comments:            ##Comments##
```

   Save and close the file.

3. Open the Code Behind of the `ContactForm.ascx` user control and import the following namespaces (no need to type the comments) at the top of the file:

   VB.NET

```
Imports System.IO         ' Provides access to the File class for reading the file
Imports System.Net.Mail   ' Provides access to the various mail related classes

Partial Class Controls_ContactForm
  Inherits System.Web.UI.UserControl
```

   C#

```
using System.IO;          // Provides access to the File class for reading the file
using System.Net.Mail;    // Provides access to the various mail related classes

public partial class Controls_ContactForm : System.Web.UI.UserControl
```

4. Switch to Markup View and add `runat="server"` and `id="FormTable"` attributes to the table with the server controls. This way you can hide the entire table programmatically when the form has been submitted. To do this, locate the opening `<table>` tag and modify it like this:

```
<table class="auto-style1" runat="server" id="FormTable">
```

5. Scroll down to the end of the file and right after the closing `</table>` tag, add a label called `Message`. Set its `Text` property to **`Message Sent`**. Hide the label by setting the `Visible` property to `false`:

```
</table>
<asp:Label ID="Message" runat="server" Text="Message Sent" Visible="false" />
```

6. Switch the control into Design View and set `ShowSummary` of the `ValidationSummary` back to `true` and `ShowMessageBox` to `false`. Because these are the default values, VS removes the attributes from the markup completely. Next, double-click the Send button. Inside the event handler that VS adds for you, add the following code:

VB.NET

```
Protected Sub SendButton_Click(sender As Object, e As EventArgs) _
            Handles SendButton.Click
  If Page.IsValid Then
    Dim fileName As String = Server.MapPath("~/App_Data/ContactForm.txt")
    Dim mailBody As String = File.ReadAllText(fileName)

    mailBody = mailBody.Replace("##Name##", Name.Text)
    mailBody = mailBody.Replace("##Email##", EmailAddress.Text)
    mailBody = mailBody.Replace("##HomePhone##", PhoneHome.Text)
    mailBody = mailBody.Replace("##BusinessPhone##", PhoneBusiness.Text)
    mailBody = mailBody.Replace("##Comments##", Comments.Text)

    Dim myMessage As MailMessage = New MailMessage()
    myMessage.Subject = "Response from web site"
    myMessage.Body = mailBody

    myMessage.From = New MailAddress("you@example.com", "Sender Name")
    myMessage.To.Add(New MailAddress("you@example.com", "Receiver Name"))
    myMessage.ReplyToList.Add(New MailAddress(EmailAddress.Text))

    Dim mySmtpClient As SmtpClient = New SmtpClient()
    mySmtpClient.Send(myMessage)

    Message.Visible = True
    FormTable.Visible = False
  End If
End Sub
```

C#

```
protected void SendButton_Click(object sender, EventArgs e)
{
  if (Page.IsValid)
  {
    string fileName = Server.MapPath("~/App_Data/ContactForm.txt");
    string mailBody = File.ReadAllText(fileName);

    mailBody = mailBody.Replace("##Name##", Name.Text);
    mailBody = mailBody.Replace("##Email##", EmailAddress.Text);
    mailBody = mailBody.Replace("##HomePhone##", PhoneHome.Text);
    mailBody = mailBody.Replace("##BusinessPhone##", PhoneBusiness.Text);
    mailBody = mailBody.Replace("##Comments##", Comments.Text);
```

```
        MailMessage myMessage = new MailMessage();
        myMessage.Subject = "Response from web site";
        myMessage.Body = mailBody;

        myMessage.From = new MailAddress("you@example.com", "Sender Name");
        myMessage.To.Add(new MailAddress("you@example.com", "Receiver Name"));
        myMessage.ReplyToList.Add(new MailAddress(EmailAddress.Text));

        SmtpClient mySmtpClient = new SmtpClient();
        mySmtpClient.Send(myMessage);

        Message.Visible = true;
        FormTable.Visible = false;
      }
    }
```

Again, make sure you replace the e-mail addresses for the `From` and `To` properties of the `MailMessage` with your own. Also, the replace method is case sensitive so make sure you type the placeholders exactly as how you wrote them in the text file.

7. Save all your changes and once again request the `Contact.aspx` page in the browser. Enter your details and click the Send button. You'll see the text Message Sent appear.

8. Check the e-mail account you sent the e-mail to (or look in the folder `C:\TempMail` if you're dropping your mail on disk) and you should see an e-mail message similar to Figure 9-11.

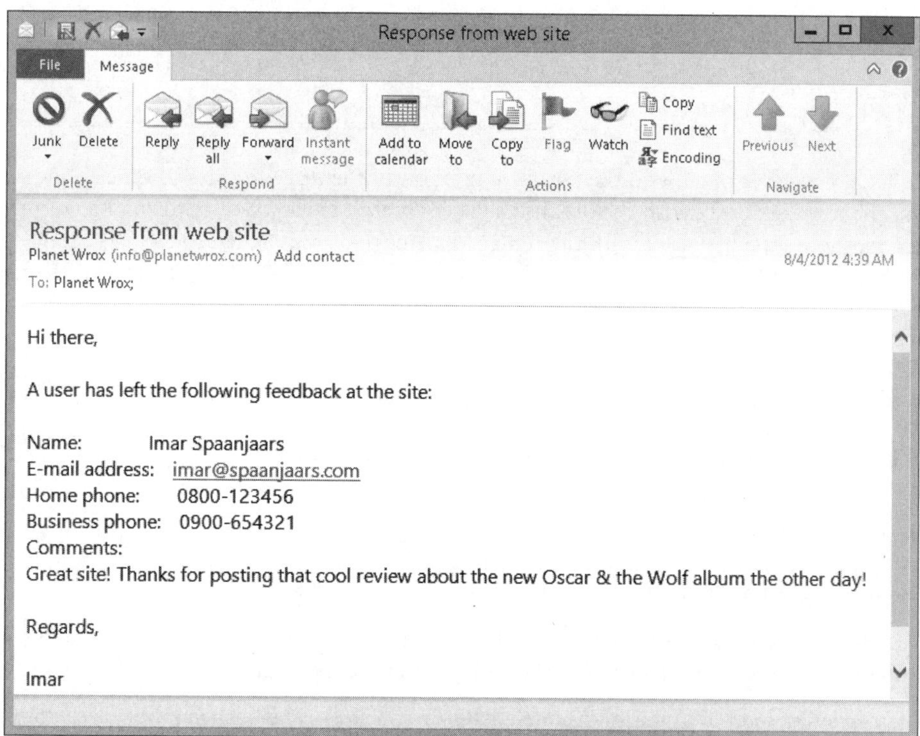

FIGURE 9-11

How It Works

The mail-sending part of this exercise is pretty similar to the demo page you created earlier. What's different, however, is where the body text for the mail message comes from. Instead of hard-coding the body in the Code Behind of the `ContactForm` control, you moved the text to a separate file. This file in turn contains a few placeholders that are replaced at run time with the user's details. To read in the entire file at once, you use the following code:

VB.NET

```
Dim fileName As String = Server.MapPath("~/App_Data/ContactForm.txt")
Dim mailBody As String = File.ReadAllText(fileName)
```

C#

```
string fileName = Server.MapPath("~/App_Data/ContactForm.txt");
string mailBody = File.ReadAllText(fileName);
```

The first line uses `Server.MapPath` to translate a *virtual path* into its *physical* counterpart. By using the virtual path, it's easier to move your site to a different location because it doesn't depend on any hard-coded paths. `Server.MapPath("~/App_Data/ContactForm.txt")` returns a physical path such as `C:\BegASPNET\Site\App_Data\ContactForm.txt`. This path is then fed to the `ReadAllText` method of the `File` class, which opens the file and returns its contents, which are then assigned to the `mailBody` variable.

> **NOTE** *Reading this file every time you need it isn't very efficient. In Chapter 15, you see how to cache the contents of this file so you don't have to read it on every request.*

The code then uses a number of calls to the `Replace` method of the `String` class to replace the static placeholders in the message body with the details the user entered in the contact form. The return value of the `Replace` method—the new text with the replaced strings—is reassigned to the `mailBody` variable. After the final call to `Replace`, the `mailBody` no longer contains the placeholders, but the user's details instead:

VB.NET

```
mailBody = mailBody.Replace("##Name##", Name.Text)
...
mailBody = mailBody.Replace("##Comments##", Comments.Text)
```

C#

```
mailBody = mailBody.Replace("##Name##", Name.Text);
...
mailBody = mailBody.Replace("##Comments##", Comments.Text);
```

The `Replace` method is case sensitive, so if you find that some placeholders are not replaced correctly, make sure you used the same capitalization in the code and in the message body.

The placeholders are wrapped in a pair of double hash symbols (##). The hash symbols are arbitrarily chosen, but help to identify the placeholders, minimizing the risk that you accidentally replace some text that is supposed to be in the actual message.

Once the message body is set up, it's assigned to the `Body` property of the `MailMessage` object, which is then sent using the `SmtpClient`, identical to what you saw in an earlier exercise.

You may have noticed the call to the `ReplyToList` collection of the `MailMessage` instance. This code adds the e-mail address that the user entered in the `EmailAddress` text box to the reply-to list of the mail message. This means that when you receive the message and want to reply to it, the reply gets sent to the user's address instead of to the `From` address you assigned to the message. This is especially useful in contact forms where users enter an e-mail address so you can directly reply to them. You may be tempted to assign the address the user entered to the `From` property directly, but you're advised not to do this. Some mail servers require this address to be your own and thus sending the mail may fail. Also, your message may be rejected when users enter an invalid address. By setting the `From` address to one of your own and adding the user's address to the `ReplyToList`, you create a reliable, yet convenient solution.

When you filled in your details in the contact form and clicked the Send button, you may have noticed some page flicker as the page submits to the server and is then reloaded with the success message. This page flicker can easily be minimized or completely removed using Ajax technologies, which are discussed in the next chapter.

PRACTICAL TIPS ON VALIDATING DATA

The following list provides practical tips on validating data:

- Always validate all user input. Whenever you have a public website on the Internet, you lose the ability to control its users. To stop malicious users from entering bogus data in your system, always validate your users' input using the ASP.NET validation controls.
- Always provide useful error messages in your validation controls. Either assign the error message to the `ErrorMessage` property and leave the `Text` empty, or use a `ValidationSummary` control to show a list of error messages.
- Consider using the `CssClass` attribute of the validation controls to move the style definitions for the error messages to a separate CSS file instead of setting them directly on the validation controls.
- Whenever you are writing code that sends an e-mail message, consider moving the body of the e-mail to a separate text file stored in the `App_Data` folder because it makes your application much easier to maintain.
- When storing data in text or XML files, always store them in the `App_Data` folder that is designed specifically for this purpose. This way, all your data files are nicely packed together. More importantly, by default the web server blocks access to the files in this folder so a visitor to your site cannot request them directly.
- When sending e-mails as a test, always send them to an existing and valid address. Even though an address like `asdf@test.com` may appear to be invalid, there's a fair chance the account exists and is monitored, leading to the possible loss of sensitive data like passwords you may be sending through e-mail.

- Consider using `SpecifiedPickupDirectory` as the `deliveryMethod` for SMTP mail during development. It avoids the need to send messages over the network, resulting in a faster response and a cleaner Inbox.

SUMMARY

User input is an important aspect of most interactive websites. The input comes from different sources in your website: the contact form you created in this chapter, the query string, and other sources. To stop users from entering invalid or even dangerous content into your system, it's important to validate all input before you work with it.

The biggest benefit of the validation controls that ship with ASP.NET 4.5 is that they work at the client and at the server, enabling you to create responsive forms where users get immediate feedback about any errors they make, without the need for a full postback. At the same time, the data is validated at the server, ensuring that data coming from clients that don't use JavaScript is valid as well.

To store the information that users submit to your site, you have a couple of options. The data can be stored in a database or a text file or sent by e-mail. The latter option is particularly useful for contact forms, so you get an immediate alert when someone leaves a comment at your website. Sending e-mail is a breeze with the classes in the `System.Net.Mail` namespace. These classes enable you to create an e-mail message, add subject, body, sender, and recipient information, and then send the message using the `SmtpClient` class.

EXERCISES

1. To make the `ContactForm.ascx` user control even more reusable, you can create a string property on it such as `PageDescription` that enables you to set the name of the page that uses the control. You can then add this string to the declaration of the control in the containing page. Finally, you can add the description to the subject of the message that you send. This way, you can see from which page the contact form was called. What code do you need to write to make this happen?

2. Why is it so important that you check the value of the `IsValid` property of the `Page` when processing data? What can happen if you forget to make this check?

3. What's the difference in behavior between the `To` and the `From` property of the `MailMessage` class?

4. When you use a `CustomValidator`, you can write validation code at the client and at the server. How do you tell the ASP.NET run time what client-side validation method to call during the validation process?

5. How do you tell the validation mechanism that validation succeeded or failed in your `CustomValidator` routines?

You can find answers to these exercises in Appendix A.

▶ WHAT YOU LEARNED IN THIS CHAPTER

Client-side validation	Validation that takes place in the client's browser. Mainly serves as a courtesy to users and offers quick feedback.
`File` **class**	Contains methods that enable you to work with files, including reading and writing text files.
Regular expressions	A compact and flexible, albeit quite complex, syntax for finding strings of text in other strings.
`Replace` **method**	A method on the `String` class to replace one value in a string with another.
Server-side validation	Validation that takes place at the server. You always need server-side validation to protect your data because client-side validation can be bypassed.
SMTP Server	A server responsible for accepting and delivering e-mail.
SSL	A technique to encrypt (and thus protect) data flowing between two machines.
`System.Net.Mail` **namespace**	The namespace for e-mail classes such as `MailMessage`, `MailAddress`, and `SmtpClient`.
Validation controls	A set of ASP.NET Server Controls that enable you to validate user input at the client and at the server.

10

ASP.NET AJAX

WHAT YOU WILL LEARN IN THIS CHAPTER:

- Using the `UpdatePanel` control to avoid page flicker
- Understanding the `ScriptManager` control that enables the Ajax functionality
- Using the `UpdateProgress` control to notify users about progress of an Ajax operation
- Creating WCF services and page methods that are accessible by your client-side script

WROX.COM CODE DOWNLOADS FOR THIS CHAPTER

You can find the wrox.com code downloads for this chapter on the Download Code tab at `www.wrox.com/remtitle.cgi?isbn=1118311809`. The code is in the Chapter 10 download.

Over the past few years, Ajax has popularized itself immensely in the web development community. Although the technology that drives Ajax has been around for quite some time, it wasn't until the beginning of 2005 that it got an official name. Ajax, which stands for *Asynchronous JavaScript And XML*, enables your client-side web pages to exchange data with the server through *asynchronous calls*, which means they don't block the user interface while running. Probably the most popular feature driven by Ajax is the flicker-free page that enables you to perform a postback to the server without refreshing the entire page. Note that the term Ajax doesn't really cover the underlying technology anymore. Asynchronous JavaScript is still used to make the calls, but in many situations XML as the data format has been replaced with JSON, as you see later in this chapter.

To enhance your website with Ajax features you can choose among different Ajax frameworks. In earlier versions of Visual Studio and ASP.NET, Microsoft shipped both a server-side framework as well as a client-side script library for Ajax interactions. This client-side script library—while still present in ASP.NET 4.5—is no longer the recommended solution. Instead, you're encouraged to use jQuery, which is discussed in detail in the next chapter.

The server-side part of Microsoft ASP.NET AJAX gives you a lot more than flicker-free postbacks. In addition to the controls that make flicker-free pages possible, Microsoft ASP.NET AJAX gives you a few more server controls to create rich, interactive, and responsive user interfaces.

THE CORRECT SPELLING OF AJAX

You'll come across two different spellings of Ajax: using Pascal casing, or in all caps. I'll use the term Ajax when referring to the general concept, and I'll use ASP .NET AJAX when specifically referring to Microsoft's Ajax framework.

By the end of the chapter, you should have a good understanding of the various server controls that the ASP.NET AJAX Framework has to offer. You will also have a basic understanding of creating WCF Services and page methods using ASP.NET and how you can call them from client-side JavaScript code.

INTRODUCING AJAX

In the first chapter of this book you learned how browsers interact with the server. The browser makes a request for a page using `GET` or `POST`, as you've seen in Chapter 4 and Chapter 9. The server processes that page and sends back the resulting HTML. The browser then parses that HTML and renders the page to the user, optionally downloading any external resources like images, script files, and cascading style sheets (CSS). When a user interacts with the page (for example, by clicking a button to submit a filled-in contact form) the page is posted back to the server, after which the entire page is loaded in the browser again. The left-hand side of Figure 10-1 shows a visual representation of this process.

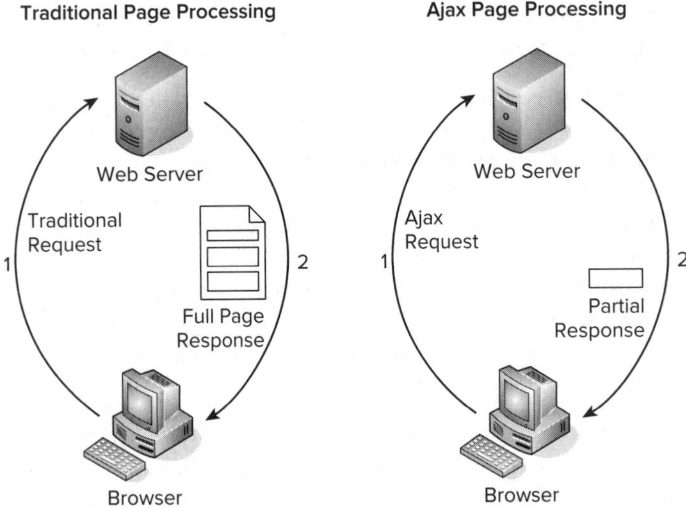

FIGURE 10-1

Even though this model has been used for years to serve web pages, it has a few big drawbacks. First, because the entire page is loaded after a postback, the HTML sent to the browser is much larger than it needs to be. Think back to the contact form you created in the previous chapter. Right after the user has submitted the contact form, the server shows a `Label` control with the text Message Sent. It does that by fully loading a new page that hides the form controls and shows the message. Even though the rest of the page hasn't changed (the menu, the sidebar, the footer, and so on), they are still sent from the server to the client. Ideally, you would only want to send back the HTML that has changed. In the case of the contact form, that could be as little as the text Message Sent. The right-hand side of Figure 10-1 shows how this works. Rather than sending the entire page as a response, the server sends a partial response (containing little more than the text Message Sent), which is then used by the browser to update just the part of the page that has changed, leaving the rest of the page as it was.

The second drawback of a full page reload has to do with the way the browser renders the page. Because the entire page is replaced, the browser has to dismiss the old one and then draw the new one. This causes the page to "flicker," which results in an unattractive user experience. You can deploy Ajax techniques to overcome these two problems, as you see in the remainder of this chapter.

The concepts behind Ajax have been around for many years. Browsers since Internet Explorer 5 have shipped with the `XMLHttpRequest` object that enabled you to make calls to the server from JavaScript to send and receive data. However, people also used other techniques to emulate the behavior of what is now called Ajax, including Macromedia Flash, `iframe` elements, or hidden frames.

However, when the term Ajax was introduced, things really took off. In an attempt to stay ahead of the curve, Microsoft started building ASP.NET AJAX, the Ajax framework that is now fully integrated in ASP.NET and Visual Studio 2012. This framework offers a number of benefits that you as a web developer can take advantage of to create responsive applications.

In particular, ASP.NET AJAX enables you to:

- Create flicker-free pages that enable you to refresh portions of the page without a full reload and without affecting other parts of the page
- Provide feedback to your users during these page refreshes
- Update sections of a page and call server-side code on a scheduled basis using a timer
- Access server-side WCF services and page methods and work with the data they return

The nice thing about ASP.NET AJAX is that it is very easy to get started with. Creating a flicker-free page is a matter of dragging and dropping a few controls from the Toolbox onto your page. When you understand the basics of the Ajax framework, you can extend your knowledge by looking at more advanced topics such as calling WCF services.

USING ASP.NET AJAX IN YOUR PROJECTS

ASP.NET AJAX is fully integrated in ASP.NET and VS, which means you can start using it right away. Each new ASP.NET 4.5 web project you create in VS is already Ajax-enabled. In addition, the Toolbox contains an AJAX Extensions category with a number of Ajax-related controls that you can use in your pages. Visual Studio also has great support for ASP.NET AJAX, giving you IntelliSense for the controls at the server as well as for the client-side JavaScript you'll write to interact with the client page and code running on the server.

Creating Flicker-Free Pages

To avoid full postbacks in your ASPX pages and update only part of the page, you can use the `UpdatePanel` server control. For this control to operate correctly, you also need a `ScriptManager` control. If you're going to use Ajax functionality in many of your ASPX pages, you can place the `ScriptManager` in the master page, so it's available in all pages that are based on this master. You can have only one `ScriptManager` per page, so if you add one to a master page, you can't add another one to a content page. To access a `ScriptManager` control that is defined in a master page from a content page, you can use the `ScriptManagerProxy` control as explained later. You'll find these and other Ajax-related server controls in the AJAX Extensions category of the Toolbox, shown in Figure 10-2.

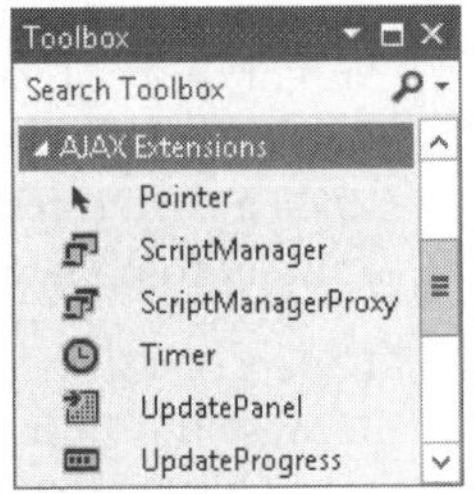

FIGURE 10-2

The following two sections introduce you to the `UpdatePanel` and `ScriptManager` controls. After the introduction you see how to make use of these controls in the pages in your Planet Wrox website. Later sections introduce you to the `UpdateProgress`, `Timer`, and `ScriptManagerProxy` controls.

The UpdatePanel Control

The `UpdatePanel` control is a key component in creating flicker-free pages. In its most basic application, you simply wrap the control around content you want to update, add a `ScriptManager` to the page, and you're done. Whenever one of the controls within the `UpdatePanel` causes a postback to the server, only the content within that `UpdatePanel` is refreshed.

To see what problems the `UpdatePanel` control solves and how it behaves in a client page, the following Try It Out shows a simple example that uses the panel to avoid page flicker during postbacks.

TRY IT OUT Adding an UpdatePanel to a Page

In this exercise, you add a `Label` and a `Button` control to a page. When you click the button in the browser, the `Text` property of the `Label` is updated with the current date and time at the server. To avoid the page flicker typically associated with postbacks, you then wrap the controls in an `UpdatePanel` to see how that control affects the behavior.

1. Open the Planet Wrox website in Visual Studio.
2. In the `Demos` folder, create a new Web Form called `UpdatePanel.aspx` using your custom template. Give the page a `Title` of **`UpdatePanel Demo`**.
3. Switch the new page into Design View and drag a `Label` control and a `Button` control from the Toolbox into the `cpMainContent` placeholder. If the `ContentPlaceHolder` suddenly gets as small as the `Label`, simply drop the `Button` *on top* of the `Label`. The `Button` is then placed before the `Label` but if you now drag the `Label` on top of the `Button` again, the two change places.

4. Use the Properties Grid to clear the `Text` property of the `Label` control. To do this, right-click the `Text` property label in the Properties Grid and choose Reset.

5. Double-click the gray and read-only area of the page in Design View to set up a handler for its `Load` event and add the following code to the handler that VS added for you:

VB.NET

```
Protected Sub Page_Load(sender As Object, e As EventArgs) Handles Me.Load
  Label1.Text = System.DateTime.Now.ToString()
End Sub
```

C#

```
protected void Page_Load(object sender, EventArgs e)
{
  Label1.Text = System.DateTime.Now.ToString();
}
```

6. Save all your changes and press Ctrl+F5 to open the page in your browser. The `Label` displays the current date and time. Click the `Button` control a few times. Note that each time you click the button, the page flickers and is then redrawn, displaying the updated date and time. Now take a look at the HTML that is used by the browser (right-click the page in the browser and choose View Source or View Page Source). Notice how the page contains a `<span>` element with the date and time that was sent from the server.

7. Close your browser, go back into VS, and switch the `UpdatePanel.aspx` page to Markup View. Make some room right before the `Label` control, and then type **`updatepanel`** and press Tab. VS inserts the code for an `UpdatePanel` and a `<ContentTemplate>` for you.

8. Next, cut both the closing `</ContentTemplate>` and the closing `</UpdatePanel>` tags and paste them below the button you created in step 3. You should end up with this markup:

```
<asp:UpdatePanel runat="server">
  <ContentTemplate>
    <asp:Label ID="Label1" runat="server"></asp:Label>
    <asp:Button ID="Button1" runat="server" Text="Button" />
  </ContentTemplate>
</asp:UpdatePanel>
```

9. Right before the opening tag of the `UpdatePanel`, drag a `ScriptManager` from the AJAX Extensions category of the Toolbox. Alternatively, type **`sm`** followed by the Tab key to insert the `ScriptManager` using a code snippet. Your code should look similar to this (although your `ScriptManager` may lack the `ID` attribute and may use a self-closing element when you use a code snippet):

```
<asp:Content ID="Content2" ContentPlaceHolderID="cpMainContent" runat="Server">
  <asp:ScriptManager ID="ScriptManager1" runat="server"></asp:ScriptManager>
  <asp:UpdatePanel ID="UpdatePanel1" runat="server">
```

10. Save your changes and request the page in the browser again. Click the button a few times to update the label with the current date and time. Note that there is no page flicker now, and only the label is updated on the page. If you look at the source in the browser again, you see the `<span>` element that contains the date and time of the very first request. The updates to the label that were

added by clicking the button are not a part of the HTML source because they have been added dynamically by the ASP.NET AJAX Framework to the browser's internal HTML.

How It Works

By wrapping the content in an `UpdatePanel` you define a region in your page that you want to refresh without affecting the entire page. In the example, the `Button` control inside the `UpdatePanel` caused a postback and thus a refresh of just the region in which the control is defined. Rather than replacing the entire page, only the part of the page that is wrapped in the `UpdatePanel` is refreshed, causing a flicker-free reload of the page.

If you analyze the data that gets sent from the server to the browser (using a network analysis tool like Fiddler, which you can download from `www.fiddler2.com/fiddler2/`), you would see that only a limited amount of data gets sent to the client. Rather than the full page (weighing around 12KB), only the following data is sent:

```
1|#||4|232|updatePanel|cpMainContent_ctl00|
<span id="cpMainContent_Label1">4/9/2012 11:56:09 AM</span>
<input type="submit" name="ctl00$cpMainContent$Button1" value="Button"
id="cpMainContent_Button1" class="MyButton" style="background-color:#7A70A4;" />
|0|hiddenField|__EVENTTARGET||0|hiddenField|__EVENTARGUMENT||0|hiddenField|__
LASTFOCUS||1624|hiddenField|__VIEWSTATE|1Atsytn51usXShfT92FZnRfhkyw7616TfovQaG
...
Demo|184|scriptBlock|ScriptPath|/ScriptResource.axd?d=zvkqIRNUspAvS1yKeFhMb_LRgBPQ
LrZDpLmd71civkClsZ5csFf1SkT-
k1NurvxrEjhFFVa7dJqUQpcX913wMJNiJeY5DJdOF5sqxTU0JGDbsEuI_njxenny6ggiBtc
4vOKR16h2V2npds3RA8dURw2&t=57d51992|
```

Note that I cut out a big piece of content including much of the View State of the page from the middle (represented by the three dots) to save some space in this book. If you look at this response, you'll recognize the HTML for the updated `Label` and the `Button`; the two controls that have been defined within the `<ContentTemplate>` of the `UpdatePanel` control. The remaining text is used by the ASP .NET AJAX Framework to maintain page state (using the `__VIEWSTATE` field) and to understand where to place the response in the page. Even though a lot of data still gets sent down the wire, it's far less than the original full page of around 12KB. This results in a faster response and a better user experience.

When you looked at the source of the page in the browser in step 10 you may have noticed that the page still contained the original source, not the updated source modified by the ASP.NET AJAX Framework. This sometimes makes it difficult to build, test, and debug Ajax applications because you cannot really see what data gets sent to the browser. Fortunately, many tools are available that help with this. Besides the aforementioned Fiddler tool, you're advised to take a look at the Microsoft Internet Explorer Developer Toolbar. It ships with Internet Explorer 8 and later and is accessible through the Tools ➪ Developer Tools menu option.

Another great tool for debugging is Firebug, which integrates nicely with the Firefox browser. You can get the tool at `http://getfirebug.com`. Google's Chrome has a similar tool that you can open by clicking the Wrench icon and then choosing Tools ➪ Developer tools.

In this exercise, you used two important AJAX Extensions controls. The ScriptManager—that you placed in UpdatePanel.aspx directly in this exercise—is a requirement for most Ajax functionality in an ASPX page to operate correctly. It serves as the bridge between the client page and the Microsoft ASP.NET AJAX Framework and takes care of things like registering the correct JavaScript files that are used in the browser. The UpdatePanel is then used to define regions you want to update without reloading the entire page. You see both controls in more detail in the following sections.

A Closer Look at the UpdatePanel

The UpdatePanel and its content is the only part of the page that is updated when you click a button (as discussed in the previous exercise). This is the default behavior of an UpdatePanel, where only its inner contents are refreshed by other server controls defined within the <ContentTemplate> element. However, the UpdatePanel can do more than this, as you see in the next section.

Common UpdatePanel Properties

The following table lists some of the important properties of the UpdatePanel that enable you to influence its behavior.

PROPERTY	DESCRIPTION
ChildrenAsTriggers	This property determines whether controls located within the UpdatePanel can cause a refresh of the UpdatePanel. The default value is True, as you saw in the previous exercise. When you set this value to False, you have to set the UpdateMode to Conditional. Note that controls defined within the UpdatePanel still cause a postback to the server with this property set to False; they just don't update the panel automatically anymore.
Triggers	The Triggers collection contains PostBackTrigger and AsyncPostBackTrigger elements. The first is useful if you want to force a complete page refresh, whereas the latter is useful if you want to update an UpdatePanel with a control that is defined outside the panel.
RenderMode	You can set this property to Block (the default) or Inline to indicate whether the UpdatePanel renders itself as a <div> or <span> element.
UpdateMode	This property determines whether the control is always refreshed (the UpdateMode is set to Always) or only under certain conditions, for example, when one of the controls defined in the <Triggers> element is causing a postback (the UpdateMode is set to Conditional). The default for this setting is Always.
ContentTemplate	Although not visible in the Properties Grid for the UpdatePanel, the <ContentTemplate> is an important property of the UpdatePanel. It's the container in which you place controls as children of the UpdatePanel. If you forget this required ContentTemplate, VS gives you a warning.

You see more of the `UpdatePanel` in later exercises in this chapter.

UpdatePanel Caveats

As useful as the `UpdatePanel` seems (and is), its usage comes at a price. Although it appears as if only part of the page is refreshed, the entire page (and all of its form data) is still posted back to the server. At the server, the page still goes through its normal life cycle and then sends back the HTML that is needed to update the page. However, the data that is sent back isn't in a very optimal format because it contains some overhead data (required by ASP.NET AJAX to understand how to interpret it). This means that the `UpdatePanel` carries some overhead in terms of form posts, page processing, and network traffic. Later in this chapter, you see some ways to get data to and from the server from client-side code that minimize this overhead.

As demonstrated in the previous exercise, the `UpdatePanel` control is capable of refreshing parts of a page. Controls that are defined either inside the `UpdatePanel` or outside of it can cause a refresh of the `UpdatePanel`. However, in order to function, the `UpdatePanel` needs a `ScriptManager` control that manages the client-side JavaScript, among other things.

The ScriptManager Control

The `ScriptManager` control serves as the bridge between the client page and the server. It manages script resources (the JavaScript files used at the client), takes care of partial-page updates as shown earlier, and handles interaction with your website for things like WCF services.

You usually place the `ScriptManager` control directly in a content page if you think you need Ajax capabilities on only a handful of pages. You briefly saw how this worked in the previous Try It Out exercise. However, you can also place the `ScriptManager` in a master page so it becomes available throughout the entire site. You do this in a later exercise in this chapter.

The `ScriptManager` class has a number of properties, of which most are used in advanced scenarios. In many situations, like updating sections of a page using the `UpdatePanel` as you just saw, you don't need to change any of the properties of the `ScriptManager` class. In other scenarios, you may need to change or set some of its properties. The following table lists some of the more common properties of the `ScriptManager` control.

PROPERTY	DESCRIPTION
`AllowCustomErrorsRedirect`	This property determines whether errors that occur during an Ajax operation cause the customized error page to be loaded. The default is `True`; with a setting of `False`, the error is shown as a JavaScript alert window in the browser or is hidden from the client when debugging is disabled. Note that if you haven't configured any customized error page, the error is always shown as a JavaScript alert, regardless of the value of this setting. Chapter 18 talks more about setting up customized error pages and debugging your application.

PROPERTY	DESCRIPTION
AsyncPostBackErrorMessage	When you're not using customized error pages, this property enables you to customize the error message that users see when an Ajax error occurs. It enables you to hide the dirty details from the users and instead present them a more friendly error message.
EnablePageMethods	This property determines whether client code is allowed to call methods defined in the page. You see how this works later.
EnablePartialRendering	This property determines whether the ScriptManager supports the partial rendering of the page using UpdatePanel controls. You should leave this setting to True, unless you want to block the partial updates for the entire page.
EnableCdn	With this property set to True, ASP.NET includes links to the client-side framework files on Microsoft's Content Delivery Network, rather than on your own server. This saves you some bandwidth and speeds up the initial load of the page if the user already had a cached copy of the files from visiting another site using these files.
AjaxFrameworkMode	Determines whether the Microsoft AJAX client library is included. This setting enables you to use the ScriptManager for server-related tasks (like registering client scripts) without embedding the client-side framework in the page.
Scripts	The <Scripts> child element of the ScriptManager control enables you to add additional JavaScript files that must be downloaded by the client at run time.
CompositeScript	Just like the <Scripts> element, the <CompositeScript> element enables you to add additional JavaScript files. However, files registered under <CompositeScript> are combined into a single, downloadable file, minimizing network overhead and improving performance.
Services	The <Services> element enables you to define WCF services that are accessible by your client-side pages. You see how to use WCF services in the second half of this chapter.

Although the UpdatePanel and the ScriptManager together are all you need to create flicker-free pages, ASP.NET AJAX offers more to enhance the user's experience in an Ajax-enabled website. One way to improve the user's experience is by using the UpdateProgress control, discussed next. Another option is to use the Timer control, which is discussed later in this chapter.

Providing Feedback to Users

Despite the visual problems that postbacks usually cause, they have one big advantage: the user can see something is happening. The `UpdatePanel` makes this a little more difficult. Users have no visual cue that something is happening until it has happened. To tell your users to hold on for a few seconds while their request is being processed, you can use the `UpdateProgress` control.

The UpdateProgress Control

You connect the `UpdateProgress` control to an `UpdatePanel` using the `AssociatedUpdatePanelID` property. Its contents, defined in the `<ProgressTemplate>` element, are then displayed whenever the associated `UpdatePanel` is busy refreshing. You usually put text such as "Please wait" or an animated image in this template to let the user know something is happening, although any other markup is acceptable as well.

In addition to the `AssociatedUpdatePanelID` and `<ProgressTemplate>` properties, the `UpdateProgress` control features the following properties you typically use.

PROPERTY	DESCRIPTION
`DisplayAfter`	Determines the time in milliseconds that the control waits before it displays its contents. This is useful when the refresh period is so short that a notification message would be overkill. The default is 500 milliseconds, which is half a second.
`DynamicLayout`	Determines whether the control takes up screen real estate when hidden. This maps directly to the CSS `display: none;` (when this setting is `True/true`) or `visibility: hidden;` (when it's `False/false`).

In the following exercise, you see how to combine the `UpdatePanel`, the `ScriptManager`, and the `UpdateProgress` controls to make the contact form user control flicker-free.

TRY IT OUT Flicker-free Pages—Putting It All Together

In this exercise, you modify the user control `ContactForm.ascx` that you created earlier, wrapping the entire control in an `UpdatePanel` so the page doesn't perform a full postback when you enter a message and click the Send button. To help users understand that the page is busy when the message is being sent, you add an `UpdateProgress` panel to the control. Inside this control you place an animated GIF image that is available in the code download for this book. Alternatively, you can go to `www.ajaxload.info` and create your own animated image.

1. Open the `ContactForm.ascx` user control from the `Controls` folder in Markup View and wrap the entire `<table>` element and the `Label` at the bottom of the control in an `UpdatePanel` with a `<ContentTemplate>`. You can do this by typing the code directly in Markup View, by using a code snippet, or by dragging the control from the Toolbox. Make sure the ID of the `UpdatePanel` is set to `UpdatePanel1`. You should end up with the following code:

```
<asp:UpdatePanel ID="UpdatePanel1" runat="server">
  <ContentTemplate>
    <table class="auto-style1" runat="server" id="FormTable">
```

```
    ....
    </table>
    <asp:Label ID="Message" runat="server" Text="Message Sent" Visible="false" />
  </ContentTemplate>
</asp:UpdatePanel>
```

2. Save the changes to the control and then open the Frontend.master file from the MasterPages folder. Between the opening <form> tag and the <div> for the PageWrapper, add a ScriptManager control by dragging it from the Toolbox into the source of the page. You should end up with this code:

```
<body>
  <form id="form1" runat="server">
    <asp:ScriptManager ID="ScriptManager1" runat="server"></asp:ScriptManager>
    <div id="PageWrapper">
```

3. Save the changes to the master page and close it.

4. Open the UpdatePanel.aspx page you created in an earlier Try It Out and remove the ScriptManager control. Because this control is now declared in the master page, you can no longer redefine it in pages that are based on that master. Save and close the page.

5. Open the Contact.aspx page from the About folder in your browser and then fill in the contact form. Note that as soon as you click the Send button, the form disappears and is replaced with the label stating that the message is sent. Just as with the earlier UpdatePanel example, you'll notice no page flicker when the page reloads and displays the text Message Sent.

6. To keep the user updated on the progress while the message is delivered to the mail server, you should add an UpdateProgress control to the page. Inside this control, you add an animated image and some text informing the user the message is being sent. To add the image, locate the folder where you extracted the files that come with this book (at C:\BegASPNET\Resources) with File Explorer (Windows Explorer on Windows 7). Open the Chapter 10 folder and then the Monochrome folder. Drag the PleaseWait.gif file from File Explorer into the Images folder of the Monochrome theme under App_Themes. Repeat this process, but now drag PleaseWait.gif from the DarkGrey folder into its respective theme's Images folder. Figure 10-3 shows how both images should end up.

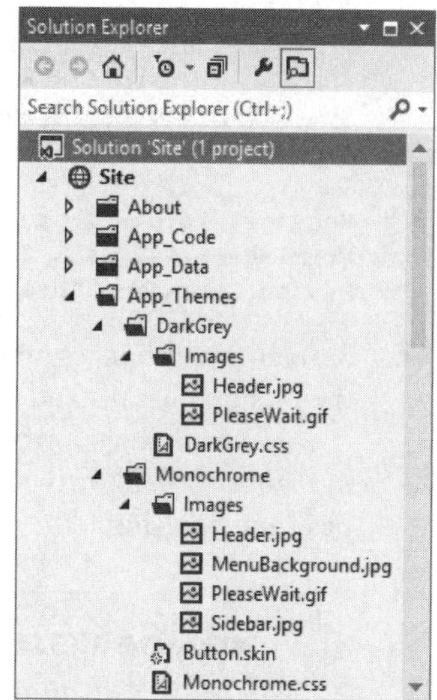

FIGURE 10-3

7. Open the Monochrome.css file, scroll all the way down to the end, and add the following rule:

```
.PleaseWait
{
  height: 32px;
  width: 500px;
  background-image: url(Images/PleaseWait.gif);
  background-repeat: no-repeat;
  padding-left: 40px;
  line-height: 32px;
}
```

8. Copy the exact same rule into the `DarkGrey.css` file for the DarkGrey theme.
9. Switch back to the `ContactForm.ascx` user control and below the closing tag of the `UpdatePanel` at the end of the file, drag an `UpdateProgress` control from the AJAX Extensions category of the Toolbox. Set its `AssociatedUpdatePanelID` to `UpdatePanel1`, the ID of the `UpdatePanel` defined earlier in the page.
10. Between the `<UpdateProgress>` tags create a `<ProgressTemplate>` element, and within this template, create a `<div>` element with its `class` attribute set to `PleaseWait`, the CSS class you created in step 7. Inside the `<div>` element, type some text to inform your users that they should hold on for a while. You should end up with this code:

```
</asp:UpdatePanel>
<asp:UpdateProgress ID="UpdateProgress1" runat="server"
              AssociatedUpdatePanelID="UpdatePanel1">
  <ProgressTemplate>
    <div class="PleaseWait">
      Please Wait...
    </div>
  </ProgressTemplate>
</asp:UpdateProgress>
```

11. To emulate a long delay while sending out the message so you can see the `UpdateProgress` control, add the following line of code to the Code Behind of the control, just after the lines that change the visibility of the controls in the method that sends out the e-mail:

VB.NET

```
Message.Visible = True
FormTable.Visible = False
System.Threading.Thread.Sleep(5000)
```

C#

```
Message.Visible = true;
FormTable.Visible = false;
System.Threading.Thread.Sleep(5000);
```

12. Save all your changes and open the `Contact.aspx` page from the `About` folder once again. Fill in the required details and click the Send button. Shortly after you click the button, you should see the `UpdateProgress` control appear that displays text and an animated image below the form, shown in Figure 10-4. Shortly after that, the `UpdateProgress` control and the entire form should disappear and you should be presented with the Message Sent text.

> **COMMON MISTAKES** *If you don't see the described behavior, your browser may be working with an outdated version of the CSS files. Press Ctrl+F5 or Ctrl+R to get the latest version from the server and try again. Alternatively, you can clear the browser's cache.*

Get in touch with us

Use the form below to get in touch with us. Enter your name, e-mail address, and your home or business phone number to get in touch with us.

Name: Imar Spaanjaars
E-mail address: imar@spaanjaars.com
Repeat e-mail address: imar@spaanjaars.com
Home phone number: 0800-123456
Business phone number: 0900-654321
Comments: Just checking in to tell you I really like this website. Would you consider reviewing the new album from the Chemical Brothers? Thanks,

Send

Please Wait...

FIGURE 10-4

How It Works

With the `UpdatePanel` in the user control, everything that falls within the `ContentTemplate` of the `UpdatePanel` will be updated upon postback, without affecting other parts of the page. This way, you can hide the form with the server controls and replace it with the Message Sent label without causing any page flicker.

To inform the user that his or her message is being sent, you also added an `UpdateProgress` control to the site. By default, this control will be shown when refreshing the `UpdatePanel` it is attached to takes longer than 500 milliseconds (half a second). The `<ProgressTemplate>` element for the control contained a simple `<div>` element with its `class` set to `PleaseWait`. You added the following CSS rule to the two CSS files for the themes:

```
.PleaseWait
{
  height: 32px;
  width: 500px;
  background-image: url(Images/PleaseWait.gif);
  background-repeat: no-repeat;
  padding-left: 40px;
  line-height: 32px;
}
```

This code first sets the dimensions of the Update message to be 500 pixels wide and 32 pixels high. This is enough to span the width of the content block, giving you enough room for a longer message.

The code then adds the animated image as a background image. To prevent the image from being repeated in the background, the `repeat` property is set to `no-repeat`. Then the left padding is set to 40 pixels. This moves the text in the `<div>` to the right, so it appears next to the animated image. Finally, the `line-height` of the text is set to 32 pixels, the same height as the entire `<div>`. This centers the entire text block vertically within the `<div>` element and aligns it nicely with the animated image.

Finally, you added the following line of code to the handler that sends the message:

```
System.Threading.Thread.Sleep(5000);
```

This code halts the execution of the page for 5 seconds (the number you pass to the `Sleep` method is expressed in milliseconds) so you can get a good look at the message in the `UpdateProgress` control. In production code, you should remove this line, because it slows down the page considerably without adding any value to the page.

In addition to user-triggered page updates as you saw with the Send button, you can also trigger page refreshes programmatically at a specified interval, as discussed in the following section.

> ***NOTE*** *When you wrap server-side functionality in an* `UpdatePanel`*, it may sometimes be hard to see if an error has occurred and what the exact error message is. For example, when sending the e-mail fails, you won't see the real error message because it's hidden in the JavaScript. To make it easier to see the error message in case something goes wrong, you can temporarily remove the* `UpdatePanel` *from the page, or comment out its closing and opening tags using the server-side comments tags* `<%--` *and* `--%>` *like this:*
>
> ```
> <%--<asp:UpdatePanel ID="up1" runat="server"><ContentTemplate>--%>
> ... Existing content goes here
> <%--</ContentTemplate></asp:UpdatePanel>--%>
> ```

The Timer Control

The `Timer` control that you find in the AJAX Extensions category of the Toolbox is great for executing server-side code on a repetitive basis. For example, you can use it to update the contents of an `UpdatePanel` every 5 seconds. The contents of this `UpdatePanel` could come from a variety of sources, such as a database with the latest forum posts on a forum or news items on a news site, an XML file with information to rotate advertisements in the browser, stock quotes from a stock web service, and more.

The `Timer` control is pretty simple to use. At a specified interval, the control fires its `Tick` event. Inside an event handler for this event you can execute any code you see fit. The following code snippet shows the markup for a simple `UpdatePanel` and a `Timer` control that you can place inside a content page based on your master page (because the master page already contains the required `ScriptManager`):

```
<asp:UpdatePanel ID="UpdatePanel1" runat="server">
  <ContentTemplate>
    <asp:Label ID="Label1" runat="server"></asp:Label>
    <asp:Timer ID="Timer1" runat="server" Interval="5000" OnTick="Timer1_Tick" />
  </ContentTemplate>
</asp:UpdatePanel>
```

> ***NOTE*** *When you're using VB.NET, you don't need the* `OnTick` *handler on the* `Timer` *control because that is taken care of with the* `Handles` *keyword in the Code Behind file in that language.*

When the timer "ticks" it raises its `Tick` event, which you can handle with the following code:

VB.NET

```
Protected Sub Timer1_Tick(sender As Object, e As EventArgs) Handles Timer1.Tick
  Label1.Text = System.DateTime.Now.ToString()
End Sub
```

C#

```
protected void Timer1_Tick(object sender, EventArgs e)
{
  Label1.Text = System.DateTime.Now.ToString();
}
```

When this code is run in the browser, the label will be updated with the current date and time every 5 seconds. If you want to make it tick slower or faster, you need to adjust its `Interval` property, which specifies the time in milliseconds.

This scenario with an auto-updating panel and the ability to refresh the content with a button click is quite common. The auto-refreshing panel is a non-intrusive way to feed the user the most up-to-date information from the server. In addition, you could offer your users a button to force a refresh of the data at any moment they choose. From a coding perspective, you wouldn't have to change much; you would call the same code (preferably wrapped in a separate method) from the `Timer`'s `Tick` event handler and from the `Button`'s `Click` event handler.

For more information about the `Timer` control, check out the MSDN documentation at `http://tinyurl.com/TimerClass4-5`.

You have now seen the most important server-side controls that the ASP.NET AJAX Framework has to offer. In the remainder of this chapter, you find a discussion of WCF services and page methods in your Ajax-enabled web pages. During the discussion of web services, you see how to use the `ScriptManagerProxy`, the final control in the AJAX Extensions category of the Toolbox.

USING WEB SERVICES AND PAGE METHODS IN AJAX WEBSITES

The ability to call web services and page methods from an Ajax-enabled ASP.NET website is a great addition to your web development toolkit. Being able to call a web service or page method means it's now much easier to access data at the server from client-side code, giving you a great alternative to full postbacks. The next section discusses web services, and a later section digs into ASP.NET page methods.

What Are Web Services?

Web services are essentially methods that you can call over the Internet and that can optionally return data to the calling code. This makes them ideal for exchanging data between different systems. Because web services are based on solid and well-understood standards, they make it easy to exchange data between different types of platforms and systems. For example, with a web service it's possible to exchange data between an ASP.NET website running on Microsoft Windows and a PHP-based site running on Linux. But at the same time, it's also possible to exchange data between an ASP.NET or PHP website and a client browser using JavaScript.

Introducing WCF

To build web services in an ASP.NET website, you use *Windows Communication Foundation* (WCF), Microsoft's platform for service-oriented applications using the .NET Framework. In previous versions of ASP.NET you could also make use of so-called ASMX web services, but these have now been deprecated in favor of WCF. However, this isn't really a problem because WCF can do anything that ASMX web services could do and much more.

WCF supports a number of different underlying network communication technologies such as HTTP, .NET Remoting, Microsoft Message Queuing, and Enterprise Services. This makes it an ideal platform for the exchange of data in a variety of scenarios such as locally on a single machine, on a corporate network, or over the Internet. For public-facing websites such as the Planet Wrox site, HTTP or HTTPS (the secured version of HTTP) is the natural choice because it will work cross-browser and across firewalls.

For information about the other supported technologies, check out this article on the MSDN website at `http://msdn.microsoft.com/library/dd943056.aspx` or get a copy of *Professional WCF 4: Windows Communication Foundation with .NET 4* (Wrox, ISBN: 978-0-470-56314-4).

To build a WCF web service, you add a WCF service (with an `.svc` extension) to your project. As you see later, you have a few different templates available, each serving a different purpose. Inside this service file you define a *Service Contract* and an *Operation Contract*. The Service Contract defines the overall service and the Operation Contract defines the various methods that are available on the service. The following snippet shows a simple WCF service with a single method:

VB.NET

```
<ServiceContract(Namespace:="")>
<AspNetCompatibilityRequirements(
      RequirementsMode:=AspNetCompatibilityRequirementsMode.Allowed)>
Public Class NameService
  <OperationContract()>
  Public Function HelloWorld(name As String) As String
    Return String.Format("Hello {0}", name)
  End Function
End Class
```

C#

```
[ServiceContract(Namespace = "")]
[AspNetCompatibilityRequirements(
```

```
      RequirementsMode = AspNetCompatibilityRequirementsMode.Allowed)]
public class NameService
{
  [OperationContract]
  public string HelloWorld(string name)
  {
    return string.Format("Hello {0}", name);
  }
}
```

You define the Service Contract by applying a `ServiceContract` *attribute* to your class. An attribute is like a little tag or label that you can stick on code elements, like classes, methods, properties, and so on, to mark that piece of code as something special. Other code interacting with the attributed code can then see what attributes that code contains and make decisions based on that information. Don't worry about that too much because you don't have to read those attributes yourself when working with web services. All you need to do is stick the attribute on a class or method to enable it for WCF.

In C# you use square brackets to wrap the attribute, whereas VB.NET uses angle brackets. You may also come across examples where the VB.NET attribute is followed by a space and an underscore, because previous versions of VB.NET required this. You don't need the underscore anymore, although it's perfectly valid to use it anyway.

With this attribute in place, you signal to the run time that you really want to expose this class as a WCF service.

The `AspNetCompatibilityRequirements` attribute that is applied to the service class determines how the WCF service behaves at run time. The `Allowed` value enables your service to run in what's called the ASP.NET Compatibility Mode, which runs the WCF service in a similar way ASMX services were run. When you set the value to `NotAllowed`, your services won't run correctly in your ASP.NET websites.

Besides the attribute on the class, each method you want to expose to the service is marked with the `OperationContract` attribute. This opt-in model enables you to create other methods (for example, helper methods that you call from your service methods) without exposing them to your service.

Calling Services from Client-Side Code

Calling a WCF service from a client HTML page is really simple. ASP.NET takes care of most of the hard work for you by generating the necessary JavaScript to interact with the service. All you have to do is register the service with the `ScriptManager` control and then call it from client-side code. Given the `NameService` you saw earlier, you set up the `ScriptManager` as follows:

```
<asp:ScriptManager ID="ScriptManager1" runat="server">
  <Services>
    <asp:ServiceReference Path="~/WebServices/NameService.svc" />
  </Services>
</asp:ScriptManager>
```

In this example, the service file is called `NameService.svc` and is located in a folder called `WebServices` in the root of your website.

Once you set up the service, you can call the service from client-side JavaScript in an ASPX page like this:

```
NameService.HelloWorld('Imar', helloWorldCallback);

function helloWorldCallback(result)
{
  alert(result);
}
```

Note that this code uses a mix of camel case and Pascal case. To align with the .NET programming guidelines, the service method uses Pascal casing and is written as `HelloWorld`. In JavaScript it's common to write methods using camel case, and thus the callback method is written as `helloWorldCallback` with a lowercase "h." I'll stick to these naming conventions throughout the chapter, which will help you determine if something is a pure client method, or a server-side method. To call a service method, you use *`ServiceName.MethodName`*. So, in the preceding example, `NameService` is the name of the service, and `HelloWorld` is the method you want to call. When you type this code in Visual Studio (and have registered the service in the `ScriptManager` for the master page that the content page is using), you get help from IntelliSense as shown in Figure 10-5.

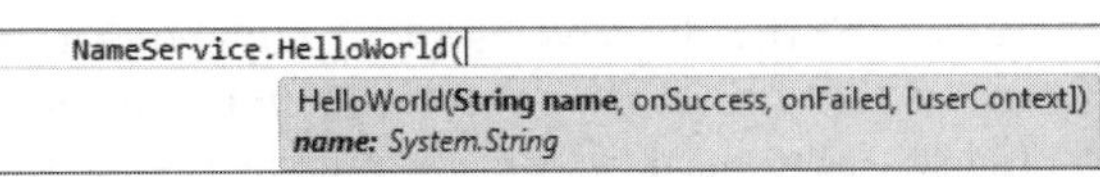

FIGURE 10-5

Although the actual service definition has only a single parameter (the `name` parameter), the client side method in this example has four parameters. The first one is the `name` parameter that I set up in the `HelloWorld` service method. If your service expected more parameters, they would be listed here as well. The second parameter enables you to pass a success *callback method*—a method you define in your code that gets called when the service call completes successfully. In the code example, this method is called `helloWorldCallback`. You can name this method any way you want (as long as it's a valid name in JavaScript), but I prefer to call it *`serviceMethodName`*`Callback` to clearly express for which code it serves as a callback. As a parameter, the callback method receives the value returned from the service. In this example, this result is a simple string, but you see later how you can also pass complex objects. The third parameter is also a callback method and is called when the service call somehow fails (for example, because the service encounters an error or is not available). The final parameter is called `userContext` and enables you to pass additional data to your callback methods. This is useful if you need additional context data to correctly process the success callback. In this example, the first parameter is required and the other three are optional. However, in most real-world scenarios you implement at least the `onSuccess` callback in order to work with the data returned from the service.

In this example, the code in the success callback `helloWorldCallback` is really simple; all it does is alert the value returned from the service. However, it doesn't have to be like this. The values you can return from the service are not limited to simple strings, as you see in the following section.

Exchanging Complex Objects with WCF

Although a simple string can sometimes be enough as the response from a service, you typically need more information. For example, you may want to load the last two reviews from a service call when a user clicks a refresh button. Rather than posting back the entire page, you could call a service, retrieve the reviews from the database, and then display them in the page somehow. Here's an example of how a service that retrieves reviews could look:

VB.NET

```
<ServiceContract(Namespace:="")>
<AspNetCompatibilityRequirements(
      RequirementsMode:=AspNetCompatibilityRequirementsMode.Allowed)>
Public Class ReviewsService

  <OperationContract()>
  Public Function GetLatestReviews() As List(Of Review)
    Dim temp As New List(Of Review) From
    {
      New Review() With {.Id = 1,
       .Title = "21st Century Breakdown by Green Day"},
      New Review() With {.Id = 2,
       .Title = "Sonic Youth: Daydream Nation live in Roundhouse, London"}
    }
    Return temp
  End Function
End Class

Public Class Review
  Public Property Id As Integer
  Public Property Title As String
End Class
```

C#

```
[ServiceContract(Namespace = "")]
[AspNetCompatibilityRequirements(
         RequirementsMode = AspNetCompatibilityRequirementsMode.Allowed)]
public class ReviewsService
{
  [OperationContract]
  public List<Review> GetLatestReviews()
  {
    List<Review> temp = new List<Review>()
    {
      new Review() {Id = 1,
         Title = "21st Century Breakdown by Green Day"},
      new Review() {Id = 2,
         Title = "Sonic Youth: Daydream Nation live in Roundhouse, London"}
    };
    return temp;
  }
}

public class Review
{
  public int Id { get; set; }
  public string Title { get; set; }
}
```

To show you how to work with complex data at the client, this code example returns two hard-coded `Review` instances. In later chapters you see how to work with reviews in a database so you could make this example truly dynamic. For now, it just serves the purpose of showing the reviews at the client.

The code sets up a generic collection of `Review` instances. For now, a `Review` is a simple class with two properties: an `Id` and a `Title`. The collection is then filled using a collection initializer that adds two `Review` instances, each of them created with an object initializer. Refer back to Chapter 5 for more information on collection and object initializers.

When you call the `GetLatestReviews` method from client code, you get back a collection of `Review` instances that you can loop over. The following code shows the `getLatestReviewsCallback` method that accomplishes this:

```
function getLatestReviewsCallback(result)
{
  var listItems = '';
  for (i = 0; i < result.length; i++)
  {
    listItems += '<li>' + result[i].Title + '</li>';
  }
  document.getElementById('Reviews').innerHTML = listItems;
}
```

This code first declares a string that will hold the titles of the reviews. It then loops over the reviews in the `result` variable. JavaScript doesn't support `foreach`, but using a standard `for` loop you can easily access all items in the collection. Within the `for` loop, the review's title is retrieved using `result[i].Title`, which is then wrapped in a pair of `<li>` tags and appended to a string variable. In the end, the string is added as the `innerHTML` of an element called `Reviews` (which could look like this in the code: `<ul id="Reviews"></ul>`) so the review titles end up in a bulleted list.

When you type this code, you'll notice you don't get IntelliSense for the `result` object. VS doesn't know the actual type of the `result` variable, and as such can't help you find properties such as `Id` and `Title`.

Note that this code is a bit clumsy. Using `document.getElementById` and `innerHTML` isn't the best way to write code like this. Therefore, the next chapter introduces you to better alternatives when it discusses jQuery. For now, though, this should suffice, showing the core concept of working with complex objects returned from a WCF service.

It's important to realize that the `Reviews` object you work with in JavaScript is not the exact same object as the one you use in the service. Your VB.NET or C# code targets the .NET Framework at the server, whereas your JavaScript runs at the client. To get the object to the client, WCF *serializes* the collection of reviews into *JavaScript Object Notation* (JSON)—a string representation of your objects that can be used directly in your JavaScript code. You see an example of JSON in a later exercise.

The web services in the Planet Wrox project will only be used to have a client page in the browser talk to the server and exchange data. So, in this site, both the server and the client are in the same web project—one executes at the client (the JavaScript that calls the web server), and the other lives at the server (the web service itself). From a security point of view, this is the easiest solution because both parts trust each other.

If you want your client-side pages to talk to a web service on a different domain, you could host a service on your own site that calls the remote web service. The client browser then calls your service, which in turns calls the remote service. This scenario falls outside the scope of this chapter, though.

You see this WCF theory in practice in the following exercise.

Creating Web Services

Creating WCF services with VS is pretty easy. Just as with all the other document types, VS comes with a template for a WCF service. You add the service to the site using the Add New Item dialog box. You then modify the service code to suit your requirements. Next, you register the service in a `ScriptManager` or `ScriptManagerProxy` and then you're ready to call it from a client web page.

VS comes with a few different templates to create a WCF service. To create one that's callable from a website, you use the AJAX-enabled WCF Service template. When you add a service based on this template, VS adds the necessary configuration code to allow calling this service from a web page to the `Web.config` file for you. In addition, the coding model of this service is a bit easier than the standard WCF Service template because it stores all the code in a single class and file.

TRY IT OUT Creating a Web Service

In this exercise you create a simple "Hello World" web service. This service accepts your name as an input parameter and returns a friendly, personalized greeting. There's not much real-world usage for this exact web service, but because of the simplicity in the service itself, it's easy for you to focus on the underlying concepts.

1. Create a new folder called `WebServices` in the root of your site to group all web services in a single folder. This is not required, but helps in organizing your site.
2. Next, right-click this new folder and choose Add ➪ Add New Item. Click the AJAX-enabled WCF Service item. Because the list of templates can be quite long, you can quickly find the right item by searching for WCF in the search box in the top-right corner of the Add New Item dialog box.

   Make sure that you click the item for your programming language, and call the service **`NameService`**, as shown in Figure 10-6.

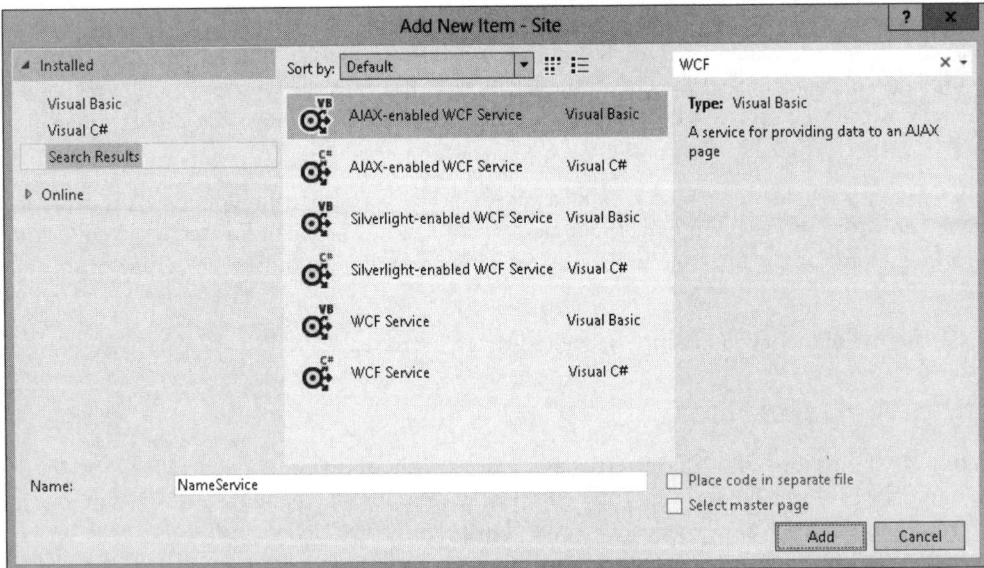

FIGURE 10-6

3. Click Add to add the service to the site. Notice how the `.svc` file is added to the `WebServices` folder and the Code Behind file (`.vb` or `.cs`) is placed in the site's `App_Code` folder shown in Figure 10-7.

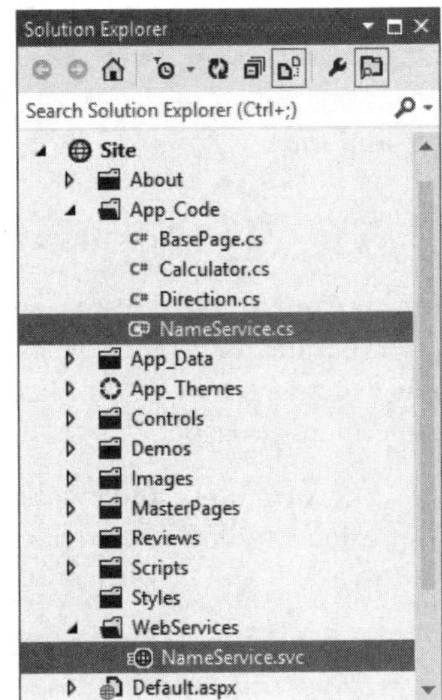

FIGURE 10-7

4. Open the `NameService` Code Behind file from the `App_Code` folder, rename the `DoWork` method to **`HelloWorld`**, and change the code so it accepts a string and returns a personalized greeting. Notice that in VB you need to change the code from a `Sub` to a `Function` and have it return a `String`, and in C# from `void` to a `string` method, because the service method returns a string. You should end up with code like this:

VB.NET

```
Public Class NameService
...
  <OperationContract()>
  Public Function HelloWorld(name As String) As String
    Return String.Format("Hello {0}", name)
  End Function
End Class
```

C#

```
public class NameService
{
  ...
  [OperationContract]
  public string HelloWorld(string name)
```

```
    {
      return string.Format("Hello {0}", name);
    }
}
```

5. That's it. You just created a WCF service that can be called from client-side code. Note that if you try to request the `.svc` file in the browser directly, you get a screen similar to Figure 10-8.

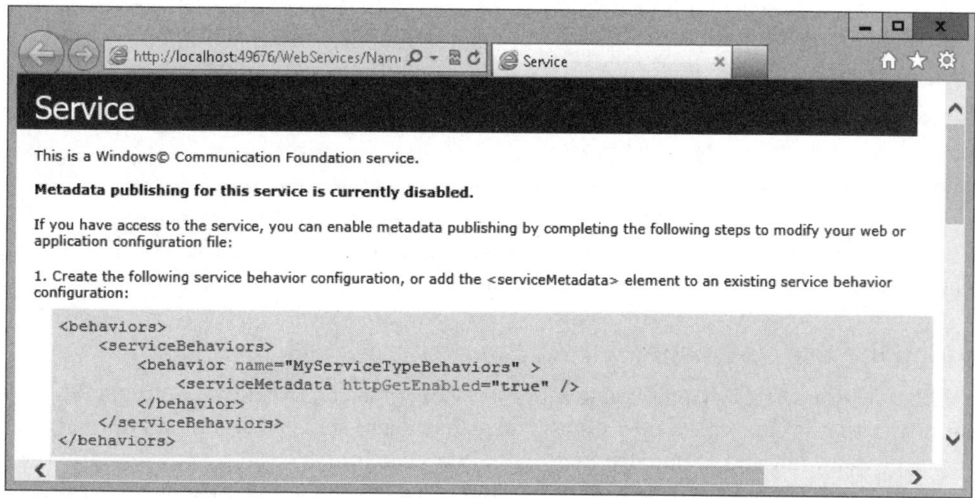

FIGURE 10-8

You get this screen because by default, for security reasons, WCF services don't expose their meta data. This means they don't tell the outside world how they work and how to call them. If you want to test your WCF service you could enable it to publish its meta data by following the instructions on the service page shown in Figure 10-8. Once you've enabled the meta data, you get more information about testing the service using a WCF test client program. I usually don't do this for simple WCF services, though; it's often just as easy to call the service from a client-side page, as you see in a later Try It Out exercise.

How It Works

WCF services are essentially methods that can be called over a network, like the Internet or your local network. They are designed to enable applications to communicate and exchange data with each other. The default underlying message format for an Ajax-enabled WCF service is JSON. This is a very succinct way to exchange data. For example, the two reviews you saw in an earlier example are transferred from the server to the client using the following JSON code:

```
{"d":[{"__type":"Review:#","Id":1,"Title":"21st Century Breakdown
    by Green Day"},{"__type":"Review:#","Id":2,"Title":
    "Sonic Youth: Daydream Nation live in Roundhouse, London"}]}
```

I split the code over multiple lines to make it more legible. In reality, this code was all placed on a single line. If you look at the comments above your service code file you see that you can also have it return XML. However, for most purposes, JSON is an excellent choice.

When you add a web service to your project, not all methods in this file become web-callable automatically. To expose a method as a service, you need to apply the `OperationMethod` attribute:

VB.NET

```
<OperationMethod()>
Public Function HelloWorld(name As String) As String
```

C#

```
[OperationMethod]
public string HelloWorld(string name)
```

With this attribute, the method is visible to the outside world, and can thus be accessed by external systems.

With the service created, the next steps are registering it with the `ScriptManager` and calling it from client code. These two topics are discussed next.

Configuring the ScriptManager

In an earlier section in this chapter you saw that the `ScriptManager` control is a required component in almost all Ajax-related operations. It registers client-side JavaScript files (those used by the Ajax framework and optionally your own), takes care of partial-page updates with the `UpdatePanel`, and handles interaction with the web services you have defined in your website. You can add a `ScriptManager` to an individual page or to the master page so it becomes available throughout your site.

When using web services, you also need to tell the `ScriptManager` that you want to expose your web service to client script. You have two ways to do this:

- In the `ScriptManager` in the master page
- In a content page that uses the web service, using the `ScriptManagerProxy` class

When you are going to use the web service in all or in most pages, you're best off declaring the web service in the master page's `ScriptManager`. You do this by giving the `ScriptManager` control a `<Services>` element that in turn contains one or more `ServiceReference` elements that point to your public services. For example, to make the `NameService.svc` service you created available in all pages in your site, you'd add the following highlighted code to the master page:

```
<asp:ScriptManager ID="ScriptManager1" runat="server">
  <Services>
    <asp:ServiceReference Path="~/WebServices/NameService.svc" />
  </Services>
</asp:ScriptManager>
```

By referencing the service in the master page, it becomes available to all pages based on that master. This also means that each page will download the JavaScript files needed to run this service. This is a waste of bandwidth and resources if your page is not using the web service at all. So, for services that you use on only a few pages, you're better off referencing the service in the page itself.

On a normal page that doesn't use a master page with a ScriptManager, you can simply add a ScriptManager to the Web Form directly. However, if you are using a master page that already has its own ScriptManager (as is the case with the pages in the Planet Wrox website), you need to use a ScriptManagerProxy control. Because you can have only one ScriptManager in a page, you can't add another one in a content page that uses your master page with the ScriptManager. Therefore, the ScriptManagerProxy serves as a bridge between the content page and the ScriptManager in the master page, giving you great flexibility as to where you register your services.

When you have the ScriptManagerProxy in place, you add the exact same <Services> element to it as you saw with the ScriptManager itself:

```
<asp:ScriptManagerProxy ID="ScriptManagerProxy1" runat="server">
  <Services>
    <asp:ServiceReference Path="~/WebServices/NameService.svc" />
  </Services>
</asp:ScriptManagerProxy>
```

The following exercise demonstrates how to register and access your web service from client-side code using the ScriptManagerProxy.

TRY IT OUT Calling Web Services from Client-Side Code

In this exercise you register your web service in a ScriptManagerProxy control so it becomes available in one page only. You then write some client-side JavaScript code that accesses the service and then displays its return value.

1. First, create a page that uses your service and then registers it using a ScriptManagerProxy control. To do this, add a new Web Form in the Demos folder and call it WebServices.aspx. Make sure you base this page on your custom template, so it has the correct master page set and inherits from the BasePage class, and then give it a Title such as **Web Services Demo**. Once you've added the page, drag a ScriptManagerProxy control from the AJAX Extensions category of the Toolbox into the markup of the cpMainContent placeholder.

2. Within the ScriptManagerProxy element, add a <Services> element that in turn contains a ServiceReference with its Path set to the NameService you created earlier. Note that IntelliSense helps you pick the right file as soon as you type **Path="** by showing you a list with files. Click Pick URL at the bottom of the list and browse to the service file in the WebServices folder. You should end up with this code in the WebServices.aspx page:

```
<asp:Content ID="Content2" ContentPlaceHolderID="cpMainContent" runat="Server">
  <asp:ScriptManagerProxy ID="ScriptManagerProxy1" runat="server">
    <Services>
      <asp:ServiceReference Path="~/WebServices/NameService.svc" />
    </Services>
  </asp:ScriptManagerProxy>
</asp:Content>
```

3. Right below the closing tag of the <ScriptManagerProxy>, add an Input (Text) and an Input (Button) by dragging them from the HTML category of the Toolbox. By using plain HTML elements and not ASP.NET Server Controls, you can see that the code you are going to write really

executes at the client. Set the `id` of the text box to `YourName` and the `id` of the button to `SayHello`. Set the `value` of the button to `Say Hello`. You should end up with this markup:

```
</asp:ScriptManagerProxy>
<input id="YourName" type="text" />
<input id="SayHello" type="button" value="Say Hello" />
```

4. Below these two lines, add a client-side JavaScript block with the following code:

```
<input id="SayHello" type="button" value="Say Hello" />
<script type="text/javascript">
  function helloWorld()
  {
    var yourName = document.getElementById('YourName').value;
    NameService.HelloWorld(yourName, helloWorldCallback);
  }

  function helloWorldCallback(result)
  {
    alert(result);
  }
</script>
```

5. Add an `onclick` attribute to the button so that it calls the `helloWorld` method when you click it. Your code should look like this:

```
<input id="SayHello" type="button" value="Say Hello" onclick="helloWorld();" />
```

6. Save all your changes by pressing Ctrl+Shift+S, and then request the `WebServices.aspx` page in your browser. Enter your name and click the Say Hello button. If everything turned out well, you should be greeted with a message from the web service, repeating your name. Figure 10-9 shows the alert window in Apple's Safari.

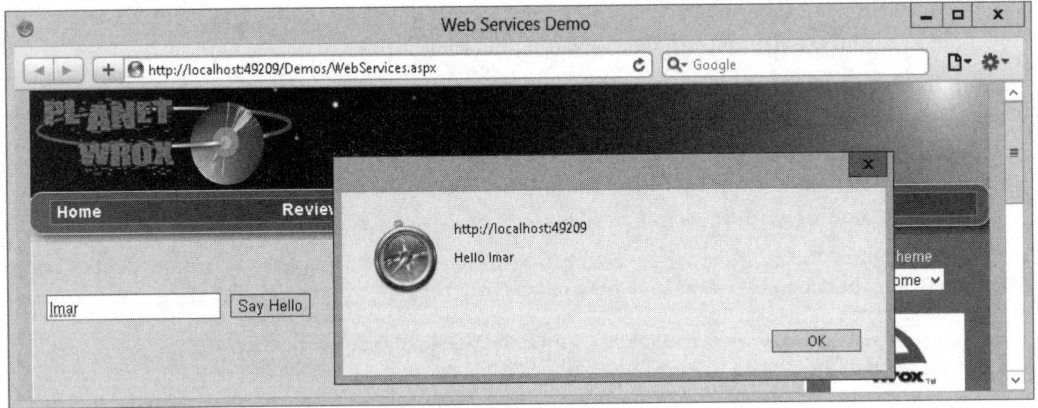

FIGURE 10-9

> ***COMMON MISTAKES*** *If you get an error instead of this message box, or you see a small yellow triangle in the bottom-left corner of the screen, make sure you typed the JavaScript exactly as in the code snippet. JavaScript is case-sensitive, so make sure you get all the capitalization right. Also make sure that the JavaScript block you added in step 4 comes after the input box and button that you defined earlier. Finally, make sure that the path to your web service matches the actual path of your* `.svc` *service file.*

How It Works

To expose a WCF service to the client-side script in your application, you need to register it in the `Web.config` file. In addition, you need to apply the correct attributes to the service class. Both actions are carried out for you when you add an AJAX-enabled WCF service to your project. If you look at the `Web.config` file you see something like this:

```
<system.serviceModel>
  <behaviors>
    <endpointBehaviors>
      <behavior name="NameServiceAspNetAjaxBehavior">
        <enableWebScript />
      </behavior>
    </endpointBehaviors>
  </behaviors>
  <serviceHostingEnvironment aspNetCompatibilityEnabled="true"
         multipleSiteBindingsEnabled="true" />
  <services>
    <service name="NameService">
      <endpoint address=""
              behaviorConfiguration="NameServiceAspNetAjaxBehavior"
        binding="webHttpBinding" contract="NameService" />
    </service>
  </services>
</system.serviceModel>
```

The service element defines a single service; the `NameService` in this case. If your site has more services available, you would add them to the same `<services>` element as the `NameService`. The `binding` and `contract` attributes tell the run time that this service is callable over HTTP and is implemented by the `NameService` class. The `address` attribute is left empty, which means the run time takes care of assigning an address. For more advanced scenarios you can enter a relative or absolute address here. The `behaviorConfiguration` points to a behavior called `NameServiceAspNetAjaxBehavior` defined under the `behaviors` node. WCF separates behaviors from the actual service definition so you can reuse the same behavior across multiple services. In this case, the behavior is created to enable the service to be called by a web page through the `enableWebScript` element.

Once the service is created and registered in the `Web.config` file, you also need to register it with the `ScriptManager`. You could do this in the `<Services>` element of the `ScriptManager` in the master page. The downside of registering the web service in the master page is that its client JavaScript is referenced in each and every page in your site. For a service you only use once or twice, it's much better to add a ScriptManagerProxy to the specific page(s) and register the service there. Within your page, the ScriptManagerProxy control looks and acts like a normal ScriptManager control. However, in reality it's just a proxy control that relays all its settings to the true ScriptManager in the master page, combining the settings for both controls. You used the ScriptManagerProxy control as follows to set up the <Services> element:

```
<asp:ScriptManagerProxy ID="ScriptManagerProxy1" runat="server">
  <Services>
    <asp:ServiceReference Path="~/WebServices/NameService.svc" />
  </Services>
</asp:ScriptManagerProxy>
```

All you need to do is refer to the service by setting the Path property. Just as with other server-side URLs you have seen in this book so far, you can use the tilde (~) syntax to refer to the application's root.

Once you have registered the service, it becomes available in your client-side code. Note that IntelliSense in VS is smart enough to discover the WCF services you have defined and registered. As soon as you typed NameService followed by a dot in a client-side script block, IntelliSense kicked in again and showed the public methods it found. This makes it extremely easy to find the correct services you have defined in your site. This is a huge improvement over old versions of Visual Studio that had only a fixed number of JavaScript-related items in the IntelliSense list. Starting with Visual Studio 2008, IntelliSense is now actually able to look at your code and fill the IntelliSense list with the right variable names, methods, services, and so on that it finds in your code. In VS 2010 and VS 2012, Microsoft improved IntelliSense even further by improving the performance and the accuracy of the items shown in IntelliSense.

To see how the actual page works, and how it accesses the web service, take a look at the code in the <script> block.

The first code you need to look at is the helloWorld method:

```
function helloWorld()
{
  var yourName = document.getElementById('YourName').value;
  NameService.HelloWorld(yourName, helloWorldCallback);
}
```

First, this code gets a reference to the text box you created earlier. You then access its value property to get the name the user entered.

This name is then sent to the web service method HelloWorld with the following code:

```
NameService.HelloWorld(yourName, helloWorldCallback);
```

The first argument of the call to HelloWorld is the argument that the web service method expects: a string holding your name. The second argument, helloWorldCallback, is a reference to another JavaScript method that is triggered when the service returns the result. By design, the call to the web service is made *asynchronously*. This means the call to the service is made in a separate thread and the helloWorld method exits shortly afterward. Because it can potentially take a long time for the web service to respond, you need to designate a method that is responsible for handling the response when it comes back from the service. In this case, the responsible method is called helloWorldCallback.

In addition to this success callback, you could add another one that is triggered when the web service somehow fails; for example, because the network connection is down or because the service threw an exception. In that case, the call to HelloWorld would look like this:

```
NameService.HelloWorld(yourName, helloWorldCallback, helloWorldErrorCallback);
```

The helloWorldErrorCallback function could then look like this:

```
function helloWorldErrorCallback(error)
{
  alert(error.get_message());
}
```

The error argument that is passed to this method has convenient methods and properties to display information about the exception. As in the example, you use get_message() to get at the original exception that occurred at the server. You should use this only during development to figure out the actual error. In Chapter 18 you learn more about dealing with errors at the server so the error details are never sent to the client's browser.

If everything goes according to plan, the call to helloWorld triggers the web service method HelloWorld. This method receives the name and returns a friendly welcome message.

The String.Format method takes a string that contains numeric placeholders wrapped in a pair of curly braces ({}). Then for each numeric value, you supply a string value as subsequent parameters. In the preceding example there is only one placeholder, but you can easily extend the call to the Format method with more parameters. For example, if you wanted to format a string with a first and last name, you'd use this code:

VB.NET

```
Return String.Format("Hello {0} {1}", firstName, lastName)
```

C#

```
return string.Format("Hello {0} {1}", firstName, lastName);
```

The String.Format method is great to make your strings much more readable. Instead of messy string concatenation using & or +, you simply define placeholders in the string, and then supply the values at run time.

Finally, the web service method returns the welcome message as a string. The web service run time then takes care of sending this return value to the calling code and then the helloWorldCallback method is invoked. This method has a result parameter that holds the return value of the web service:

```
function helloWorldCallback(result)
{
  alert(result);
}
```

In the preceding exercise the `result` is a simple string. This means you can use `alert(result)` to directly display the result in a JavaScript alert window.

In other situations, the `result` parameter could hold more complex objects that provide access to its properties or collections with objects, as you saw earlier.

The final thing you need to look at is how everything started in the first place. When you clicked the button, the client-side `helloWorld` function was triggered. This was done by adding an `onclick` attribute to the button that tells the browser which JavaScript method to call when you click the button. Again, better alternatives exist for the `onclick` attribute and the call to `document.getElementById`. Chapter 11, which discusses jQuery, shows you cleaner alternatives.

Obviously, the `NameService` you saw in this chapter has little real-world usage. However, the principles of web services you learned in this chapter are easily applied to more complex services as well, enabling you to access data on the server from client-side JavaScript with just a few lines of code.

You see the `NameService` again in Chapter 18 when debugging is discussed. In that chapter you step through the code line by line so you can see which code executes and in what order.

Although web services are extremely useful and pretty easy to create, they may be a bit of overkill at times. Sometimes you just need to send and receive a tiny bit of information to and from the page you're currently working with. You can do this using *page methods*, which are discussed next.

Introducing Page Methods

Page methods and WCF web services have a few things in common. In both cases, you can call them from the client using very little code. You can send data to them, and receive data back. Additionally, when calling them you can define success and failure callback methods. What's different is that page methods are defined directly in an existing ASPX page instead of a separate WCF service file. You can call them only from script running within that page. That makes them ideal for small, simple functionality that is limited in scope to the current page.

To enable page methods you need to set the property `EnablePageMethods` of the `ScriptManager` control to `True`. You cannot set this property on the `ScriptManagerProxy` class so you need to set it on the `ScriptManager` control directly, which is—in the case of the Planet Wrox website—placed in the master page. Once you have enabled page methods, setting them up and using them is a two-step process:

1. Create a public and *static method* (called a *shared method* in VB.NET) in the Code Behind of the page you're working with. You need to apply the `WebMethod` attribute to this method. The method can optionally receive data through its parameters and optionally return some data.
2. Write the necessary JavaScript to call the page method and work with its result.

   You see how this works in the next exercise.

> ***NOTE*** *A* static method *is a method that you call on a class, rather than on an instance of that class. In Chapter 5 you created the* `Calculator` *class that had four* instance methods. *This means that to use these methods, you need to create an instance of the class first using the* `new` *keyword (*`New` *in VB.NET). If you change the methods to be static methods instead by adding the keyword* `static` *(*`Shared` *in VB.NET) after the* `public/Public` *access modifiers, you could directly call them on the* `Calculator` *class like this:*
>
> ***VB.NET***
>
> ```
> Dim result As Integer = Calculator.Add(4, 5)      ' result is now 9
> ```
>
> ***C#***
>
> ```
> int result = Calculator.Add(4, 5);               // result is now 9
> ```

Static methods are often used for utility methods that don't require an object instance to hold its own state, but as you see next, you also need static methods if you want to implement page methods. Static methods and instance methods each serve a distinct purpose and are often not easily interchangeable. In the case of the `Calculator` class, which doesn't maintain state between method calls, static methods would have been a good option as well. Note that because the page methods are declared as static, you don't have access to other, instance-based members of the class. This means, for instance, that you don't have access to controls like buttons and text boxes.

TRY IT OUT Calling Page Methods from Client-Side Code

In this exercise, you modify the `WebServices.aspx` page and add a second button that calls a page method. To make it easy to compare the two techniques of calling code on the server, the page method you create is similar to the web service you created earlier.

1. Open up the `Frontend.master` master page in Markup View and set the `EnablePageMethods` attribute of the `ScriptManager` control to `True`:

```
<asp:ScriptManager ID="ScriptManager1" runat="server"
        EnablePageMethods="true"></asp:ScriptManager>
```

2. Open the Code Behind of `WebServices.aspx` in the `Demos` folder and add the following server-side method within the `Demos_WebServices` class but outside the existing `Page_Load` method (in C#):

VB.NET

```
<WebMethod()>
Public Shared Function HelloWorld(name As String) As String
  Return String.Format("Hello {0}", name)
End Function
```

C#

```
[WebMethod]
public static string HelloWorld(string name)
{
  return string.Format("Hello {0}", name);
}
```

Notice how this code is somewhat similar to what you defined in the WCF service. What's different is the inclusion of the `static` keyword (`Shared` in VB.NET) and the `WebMethod` attribute you apply to the method.

The `WebMethod` attribute won't be recognized directly. To fix this, type the following `using` or `Imports` statement at the top of the page, below the other statements:

VB.NET

```
Imports System.Web.Services
```

C#

```
using System.Web.Services;
```

Alternatively, click the attribute once in the code and then press Ctrl+. (Ctrl+Dot) to bring up a list with suggested options and choose the first item to have the code inserted for you.

3. Switch to Markup View and create a copy of the HTML button you created earlier, set its `id` to `SayHelloPageMethod`, set its `onclick` handler to `helloWorldPageMethod();`, and change its `value` to better describe what the button does. You should end up with code like this:

```
<input id="SayHelloPageMethod" type="button"
      value="Say Hello with a Page Method" onclick="helloWorldPageMethod();" />
```

4. Implement the `helloWorldPageMethod` method as follows:

```
function helloWorldPageMethod()
{
  var yourName = document.getElementById('YourName').value;
  PageMethods.HelloWorld(yourName, helloWorldCallback);
}
```

You can add the method directly below the `helloWorld` function, in the same script block. Notice there's no need to write a new callback method to handle the return value of the call to `helloWorld`. You can easily reuse the one you created in the web service example because all it does is simply alert the return value.

5. Save all your changes and press Ctrl+F5 to run the page in the browser. Enter your name and click the Say Hello with a Page Method button. You should see the same message as you saw with the web service example.

> ***COMMON MISTAKES*** *If you get an error about* `PageMethods` *not being defined, make sure you added the* `static` *or* `Shared` *keyword to the method's signature and make sure you set* `EnablePageMethods` *to* `True` *on the* `ScriptManager` *control in the master page.*

How It Works

From a client code perspective, almost all code is identical to the web service example except for the actual call to the method. Rather than calling `ServiceName.MethodName` you now need to call `PageMethods.MethodName`, where `PageMethods` is a fixed name to refer to the ASP.NET AJAX JavaScript implementation to call a page method. When you click the button, the ASP.NET AJAX Framework sets up the necessary code to call the method that you defined in the Code Behind. Because the method is marked as static, the ASP.NET run time doesn't need to create an instance of the `Page` class (and consequently doesn't need to go through its entire life cycle) but can simply call the method. This results in a fast and efficient response from the method. However, there is one caveat you need to be aware of: because the method is static and applies to a class, rather than an instance of that class, you can't access instance members, such as the controls defined in the page, from the page method.

Page methods are ideal for sending and retrieving little bits of information that don't require a full postback or don't need the overhead of a web service. You can use them for all kinds of scenarios, including sending user data (such as a username, preferences, pages they have visited, and so on), getting up-to-date data from a database or a web service, and so on.

PRACTICAL AJAX TIPS

Consider these tips to get the most out of ASP.NET AJAX:

- Because the content for an `UpdateProgress` panel is visible only during an Ajax page update, you'll find that it's hard to design its contents. You see the content only for a few seconds or less, and only after you cause a postback to the server. To make it easier to design an `UpdateProgress` panel, you should first design the message outside of the `UpdateProgress` panel. For example, in the exercise from this chapter, you should move the `<div id="PleaseWait">` outside any other controls so it's always visible. You can then change the HTML and the CSS for the `<div>` until it looks exactly right. Then you can move the `<div>` back into the `UpdateProgress` panel so it's shown only during a partial page update.
- Whenever you are using an `UpdatePanel`, consider adding an associated `UpdateProgress` control as well. Even if you don't see the need because the `UpdatePanel` refreshes really fast, it may be worth adding the `UpdateProgress` for people on slow computers or slow networks. Or better yet: add an `UpdateProgress` to the master page in a convenient and visible area of the page (in the Footer section, for example). Don't set `AssociatedUpdatePanelID` to anything so the progress panel will show on any Ajax callback. This way, you don't need lots of different waiting indicators in different areas of your site.
- Don't overuse `UpdatePanel` controls. In many situations, the *perceived* performance of an application increases when using `UpdatePanel` controls even if the true performance is the same. This is a good thing, because your users think your application is faster than without an `UpdatePanel`. However, using too many `UpdatePanel` controls may confuse your users, especially when the controls are not bound to an `UpdateProgress` control that tells your users something is going on. Consider web services and page methods instead, because they can decrease the overhead and the data that gets transferred over the wire.

- You may be tempted to wrap the entire contents of a master page in an `UpdatePanel` control to avoid page flicker when you browse from page to page. However, this won't work because browsing to a new page is a new `GET` request whereas the `UpdatePanel` control works only during postbacks.

SUMMARY

Ajax is a broad and very interesting technology that can really add a lot of value to your site.

The `UpdatePanel` control enables you to create flicker-free pages in no time, whereas the `ScriptManager` control serves as the bridge between the server and the client and is responsible for tasks like registering the necessary client scripts. Other controls in the AJAX Extensions category of the Toolbox include the `ScriptManagerProxy`, the `UpdateProgress`, and the `Timer` controls.

Besides these very useful server-side controls, the ASP.NET AJAX Framework also comes with functionality that enables you to access web services and page methods in your site with just a few lines of code. Both web services and page methods can be used to exchange data with the server without blocking or fully reloading the user interface.

Although Ajax itself is a very compelling technology, it becomes even more useful in richer, data-driven scenarios. For example, using an `UpdatePanel` control around the records returned from a database to avoid page flicker when sorting, filtering, or paging your data greatly enhances the user's browsing experience. You learn how to work with databases in Chapter 12. With the knowledge about Ajax you gained from this chapter, you will quickly create flicker-free, database-driven web pages.

EXERCISES

1. The AJAX Extensions category of the Toolbox defines a `ScriptManager` and a `ScriptManagerProxy`. Explain the difference between these two controls, and explain when you should use the `ScriptManager` and when the `ScriptManagerProxy`.

2. How can you let your users know a partial page update is in progress?

3. To expose a method in your site as a web method that can be called by client-side script, you need to create a class and apply some attributes. Which class do you need to create, and which attributes do you need to apply?

4. What are the steps you need to take to expose and use a method in your page as a page method?

You can find answers to these exercises in Appendix A.

▶ WHAT YOU LEARNED IN THIS CHAPTER

Ajax	Asynchronous JavaScript And XML, a term for a collection of techniques used to create flicker-free web pages and to interact with the server from client-side code
Attribute	A code element that can be applied to other elements such as classes and methods to change their meaning or behavior
Page method	A server-side `static` (`Shared` in VB.NET) method defined in a page that can be called from client script
`ScriptManager` **control**	A core component of the Microsoft ASP.NET AJAX Framework that takes care of managing client script files and server-side Ajax behavior
`ScriptManagerProxy` **control**	The bridge between a content page and the `ScriptManager` control defined in a master page
`UpdatePanel` **control**	A control that helps create flicker-free pages by only updating content defined within its `<ContentTemplate>` element
`UpdateProgress` **control**	A panel (a `<div>` or a `<span>`) that can be shown during the execution of an asynchronous Ajax operation
Web service method	A method that can be called over the Internet or local network by other applications

11

jQuery

WHAT YOU WILL LEARN IN THIS CHAPTER:

- What jQuery is
- What NuGet is and how to use it
- How to use jQuery to enhance your pages, including adding rich visual effects and animations
- How to leverage jQuery to enhance the ASP.NET validation framework

WROX.COM CODE DOWNLOADS FOR THIS CHAPTER

You can find the wrox.com code downloads for this chapter on the Download Code tab at `www.wrox.com/remtitle.cgi?isbn=1118311809`. The code is in the Chapter 11 download.

In previous chapters you were introduced to JavaScript, the de facto language for client-side scripting and interacting with elements in your web pages at the client. Though the examples shown were relatively straightforward, JavaScript can do much more and is quite a powerful programming language. But powerful as it may be, it has a few shortcomings. One of the problems with JavaScript is that not all browsers interpret it the same way. A lot of the JavaScript code you'll write will work in all major browsers, but subtle differences in code and behavior exist that make it difficult to write code that behaves exactly the same in all major browsers. Also, JavaScript lacks some useful features that would come in handy in your day-to-day JavaScript coding. For example, it has built-in methods to find a specific element on a page (using `getElementById` as you saw in Chapters 9 and 10) and to find all elements of a specific HTML tag (using `getElementsByTagName`), but it lacks features like `getElementsByClassName` to get a list of elements with a specific class applied to them.

Fortunately, the Internet developer community has been very active developing frameworks that use JavaScript under the hood and that extend its power, while offering a very rich feature set that helps you create interactive client-side web pages. Over the years, many JavaScript libraries have been developed—most of which are free—including:

- Prototype (`http://prototypejs.org`)
- Scriptaculous, an add-on to Prototype (`http://script.aculo.us`)
- Ext JS (`http://extjs.com`)
- Dojo (`http://dojotoolkit.org`)

One framework that has received a lot of attention is *jQuery*. Initially developed and released by John Resig in January 2006, jQuery has grown to be a very popular client-side framework. It also caught the attention of Microsoft, which decided to start shipping jQuery with Microsoft products. Initially, jQuery shipped with the Microsoft ASP.NET MVC Framework, but it's now also included in Visual Studio 2012.

AN INTRODUCTION TO JQUERY

The main focus of the jQuery library has always been to simplify the way you access the elements in your web pages, provide help in working with client-side events, enable visual effects like animations, and make it easier to use Ajax in your applications. In January 2006, John Resig announced the first version of jQuery, which was followed by an official release of jQuery 1.0 in August 2006. Many more versions would follow, with version 1.7.2 as the latest, stable release at the time of writing.

> ***NOTE*** *jQuery is under active development, and, as such, there's a fair chance that by the time you read this book, a new version of jQuery will have been released. Although the code presented in this chapter is expected to be compatible with future versions, backward-compatibility issues may arise with later versions. If you find that some of your code doesn't work with the jQuery version you are using, consider using the files that come with this chapter's download to rule out any problems with the new version.*

You have a few ways to acquire the jQuery library and add it to your website. First of all, you can download the latest version of jQuery from the official website at `http://jquery.com`. Not only will you find the downloadable files there, but you'll also find the documentation, FAQs, tutorials, and much more information you can use to make the most out of jQuery.

The second way is to use the ASP.NET Web Forms Site template to create a new site, because it already contains a `Scripts` folder with the necessary jQuery files. However, back in Chapter 2 you based the Planet Wrox website on the ASP.NET Empty Web Site template, which doesn't include these files.

The third solution to add jQuery to your site is by using a Content Delivery Network (CDN) as you'll see later.

The final way is to use NuGet, the Library Package Manager that ships with Visual Studio (including the Express editions). NuGet is discussed next.

Introducing NuGet

NuGet is an open source Library Package Manager that comes as a Visual Studio extension and that makes it very easy to add, remove, and update external libraries in your Visual Studio projects and websites. It was initially developed by Microsoft but has now been turned into an Open Source project that accepts contributions from the developer community. Although you'll see NuGet used in the context of a website in VS, NuGet is certainly not for ASP.NET only. You can use it for all types of applications you can build with Visual Studio.

To understand what problems NuGet solves, imagine you want to add an open source library such as jQuery to your ASP.NET website. Although the specifics differ from library to library, you usually need to go through the following steps:

1. Find the website of the library.
2. Find a link to the download of the latest stable version of the library and download it.
3. Unblock the downloaded file using Windows Explorer, unzip it, and add it to your project, optionally creating a specific folder for it.
4. Optionally, add a reference to the library in your project.
5. Optionally, configure the library through the `Web.config` file or other code files.

Using NuGet, you can greatly minimize the steps needed to add libraries to your project. For example, you can add the jQuery library with just five mouse clicks. In addition to adding packages, NuGet also enables you to easily update libraries to their latest versions after you've added them to your website, and it enables you to remove packages again without leaving a trace.

Besides the extension for Visual Studio, NuGet also has its own website at `http://nuget.org`. Here you can browse the catalog of packages, find commands for installing packages (more on that in the next section), read detailed documentation, and more.

To manage libraries with NuGet, you have two options: you can use the Manage NuGet Packages dialog box or use the Package Manager Console.

Using the Manage NuGet Packages Dialog Box

The Manage NuGet Packages dialog box enables you to search for packages online, as well as manage packages you already installed. You access this dialog box by right-clicking your website in the Solution Explorer and choosing Manage NuGet Packages. Alternatively, choose Tools ⇨ Library Package Manager ⇨ Manage NuGet Packages for Solution. Figure 11-1 shows the dialog box in action.

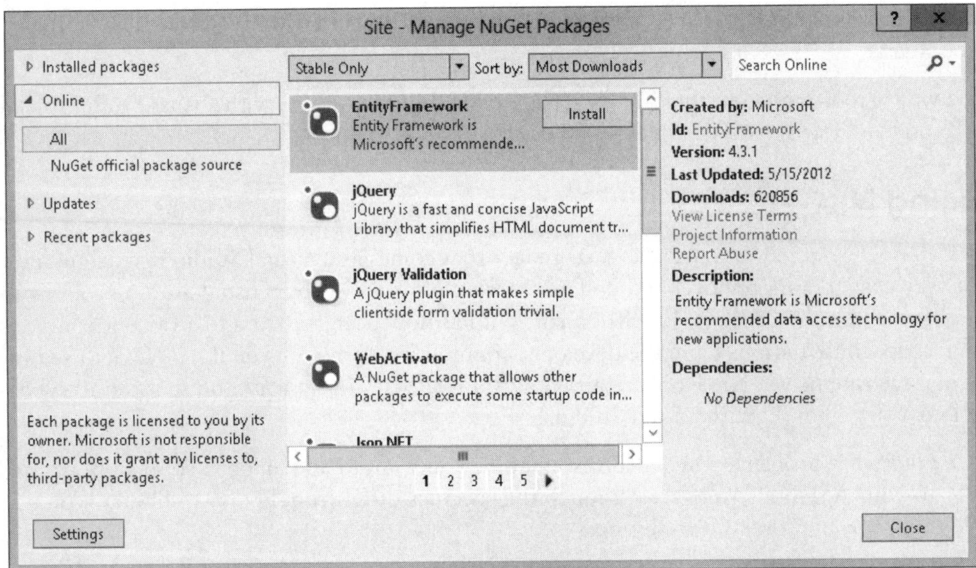

FIGURE 11-1

On the left of the dialog box you can choose from four different types of lists with packages:

- **Installed packages**—This item shows a list of packages that have been installed into your website. You can use this option to find out which version of a package you have installed, uninstall packages, or install the same package into another website or project that is part of the same solution.
- **Online**—This item enables you to search for packages online using the official NuGet package source, or on any additional feeds you may have added (which you can do using Tools ➪ Options ➪ Package Manager ➪ Package Sources). By default, the list shows the most popular packages first (measured by the number of downloads), but you can change the ordering using the drop-down list at the top. To the left of the Sort by drop-down you have the option to display only stable packages, or also include prelease versions of packages. In the upper-right corner you can search for packages by entering (part of) their name. Once you find the package you want to add to your website, select it, click the Install button and the NuGet Package Manager takes care of the installation process. You see more of this in a later exercise.
- **Updates**—This item shows a list of packages for which new versions have been released since you installed the package into your website. Because updates could potentially break an existing website, they are not installed automatically and you need to manually select the packages you want to update.
- **Recent packages**—This item gives you a list of packages you used before. This serves as a shortcut to packages you use often so you don't have to search for them online each time you want to install them in your website.

You can find the full documentation on the Manage NuGet Packages dialog box in the documentation section of the NuGet website at `http://bit.ly/q2PiyM`.

Besides using this dialog box, you can also manage packages using the Package Manager Console.

Using the Package Manager Console

The Package Manager Console enables you to manage your packages from a command-line interface. This is not as user-friendly as using the dialog box, but once you get the hang of using NuGet you'll find that the console can be really useful. Using the console you can access the same features as with the dialog box and more. Figure 11-2 shows the Package Manager Console, which you can access from the main menu by choosing Tools ➪ Library Package Manager ➪ Package Manager Console.

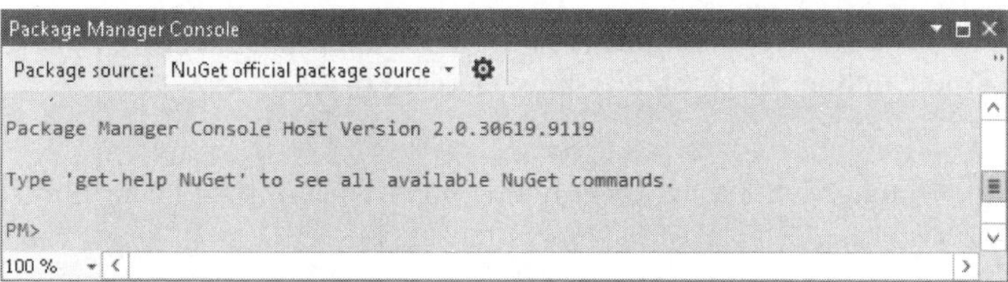

FIGURE 11-2

> ***NOTE*** *NuGet is updated quite often (you'll be notified by Visual Studio when a new release is available) so your version number may be slightly different. That doesn't matter for the functionality described in this book.*

This command-line window supports a number of commands that help you manage packages. To get a list of the available main commands, type **Get-Help NuGet** and press Enter. You'll see a list of commands appear that you can execute at the console. The console has IntelliSense as well to help you complete the commands by pressing the Tab key. In the example of the Help command, simply type Get followed by the Tab key to get a list with all commands that start with `Get`. You can then select the command from the list and complete it by pressing Tab again or by pressing Enter. Because many commands start with `Get`, in this case it's probably quicker to type Get-H and then press Tab, or to type the complete command yourself. However, for longer and more unique command names, using the Tab key can be a great time saver.

Probably the most popular commands are `Get-Package` and `Install-Package`. Using `Get-Package` you can list the packages that are currently installed in your site. To see the list, just type the command and hit Enter. If you try this now, your list will be empty because you haven't installed any packages yet. By using `Get-Package -ListAvailable` you can see a complete list of all available packages. Because thousands of them exist (and the list is growing), you want to filter the list using `-Filter`, like this:

```
Get-Package -ListAvailable -Filter jQuery
```

This lists all the packages that have jQuery in their name. Note that filtering isn't case sensitive. To find prerelease versions of packages that haven't been officially released yet, you use the `-PreRelease` option, like this:

```
Get-Package -ListAvailable -Filter jQuery -PreRelease
```

Once you find the package you want to install, use the `Install-Package` command. As an argument, you need to supply it the name of the package. For example, to install jQuery into your website you execute the following command:

```
Install-Package jQuery
```

After you hit Enter, the Package Manager Console downloads the package and installs it in your website exactly the same as using the Manage NuGet Packages dialog box does.

For a complete overview of all the available commands, look at the official NuGet documentation at `http://docs.nuget.org`. You can find the command-line reference here: `http://bit.ly/q0N57L`.

In the next exercise, you use the Manage NuGet Packages dialog box to install the jQuery library into your website.

TRY IT OUT Using NuGet to Install Packages

In this exercise you see how to find and install the latest jQuery package using the Manage NuGet Packages dialog box. Using the dialog box is the most intuitive and easiest way, so it's a good place to get started with NuGet. In later parts of this book you also use the Console window to install packages.

1. Start by opening the Manage NuGet Packages dialog box. You can do that by right-clicking your site in the Solution Explorer and choosing Manage NuGet Packages. Alternatively, you can choose Tools ➪ Library Package Manager ➪ Manage NuGet Packages for Solution. The dialog box shown in Figure 11-1 appears.
2. If it's not already selected, click the Online item in the list on the left.
3. Because jQuery is so popular, it should appear in the list with packages that are shown by default. If it's not, or if you want to install another package, use the search box at the top-right corner of the dialog box.
4. Click the jQuery library package in the list. Make sure you choose just the jQuery library, and not the jQuery UI (Combined Library) or jQuery Validation package, because these serve a different purpose.
5. Click the Install button. A dialog box pops up that lists the actions that are executed to install the package. Once that dialog box has disappeared, click the Close button to dismiss the Manage NuGet Packages dialog box.

That's it. You just installed jQuery using NuGet.

How It Works

To see how it works, take a look at the `Scripts` folder in your Solution Explorer. You should see an item called `jquery-1.7.2.js`, shown in Figure 11-3. Remember, a new version may have been released since this book was written so your version numbers may be different. During installation, NuGet added three jQuery-related JavaScript files to your `Scripts` folder (which it would have created if it didn't exist.) In addition, it kept track of the installed packages in a file called `packages.config` that has been placed in the root of your website and created a `packages` folder to store a local copy of the downloaded packages. Depending on your settings, this location could differ, but most likely it's located in a folder named after your site in `Documents\Visual Studio 2012\Projects`.

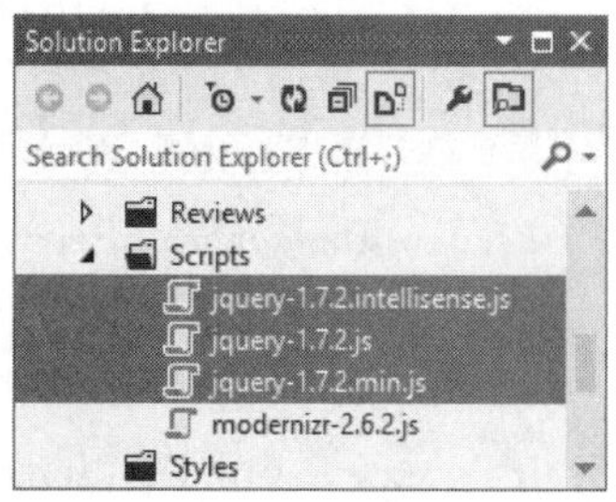

FIGURE 11-3

These three `.js` files all serve a different purpose. The file `jquery-1.7.2.js` contains the core jQuery code in an uncompressed format. This means you can read its code and use it for debugging purposes in cases where you need to see what code the library executes. The file `jquery-1.7.2.intellisense.js` contains the documentation for the code in the jQuery library that is used in the IntelliSense lists and documentation pop-ups. You see how this works later in this chapter. Finally, the file `jquery-1.7.2.min.js` is the core jQuery library in a compressed format. This is the file you'll use in your website because it has the smallest size and is thus the quickest to download.

Now that the jQuery library has been added to the website, the next step is determining where to use it. Because the jQuery library adds to the size of your web pages, it should be a deliberate choice whether or not you include it in your site.

Choosing the Location for Your jQuery Reference

To include jQuery in your website, you have a couple of options:

- Add a reference to the jQuery library in just the web pages or user controls that require it.
- Add a reference to the jQuery library in the master page of your site so it's available in all pages.

Both methods have their own advantages and disadvantages. Adding a reference to the jQuery library in just the pages that need it helps keep the size of your pages down a bit. When your users browse only to pages without jQuery, they'll never have to download the library file, saving them some bandwidth. Note that once they've visited a page that does reference the library, the browser will cache a copy of it, removing the need to download it again on subsequent visits to pages.

Adding the reference to jQuery in the master page of your site is quite convenient, because all pages based on this master page automatically get access to the jQuery functionality. However, this results in a small performance hit on the first page of your site because the library needs to be downloaded from the server. This is the option used in the Planet Wrox website.

In addition to the location where you add your jQuery file, you also have a few options with regard to the way you include the file.

Different Ways to Include the jQuery Library

Because the jQuery library consists of a single file with JavaScript code, you can embed a reference to the library in a page, user control, or master page using the standard `<script>` syntax:

```
<script src="FileName.ext" type="text/javascript"></script>
```

It's important to use a separate closing `</script>` tag because some browsers will choke if you use a self-closing tag.

By default, the NuGet package manager uses (and optionally) creates a `Scripts` folder in the root of the site for JavaScript files such as jQuery, so a reference to the jQuery library (called `jquery-1.7.2.min.js`) will end up like this:

```
<script src="/Scripts/jquery-1.7.2.min.js" type="text/javascript"></script>
```

You can also embed the reference inside the `ScriptManager` control that you added to the master page in the previous chapter. The `ScriptManager` control has a `<Scripts>` child element that lets you register JavaScript files that will be added to the final page in the browser. In its simplest form, a JavaScript file registered in the `ScriptManager` looks like this:

```
<asp:ScriptManager ID="ScriptManager1" runat="server">
  <Scripts>
    <asp:ScriptReference Path="~/Scripts/jquery-1.7.2.min.js" />
  </Scripts>
</asp:ScriptManager>
```

Another alternative is to refer to an online version of the library with Microsoft's Content Delivery Network (CDN) or Google Code. For more information on this, visit Microsoft's CDN site at `www.asp.net/ajax/cdn` or Google's API site at `http://code.google.com/apis/ajaxlibs/`.

The advantages of using online versions of external libraries are improved performance and lowered bandwidth for your servers. Because it is likely that visitors to your site already have downloaded the shared scripts when visiting another site, they don't have to download them again when visiting yours.

In the following exercise, you add the jQuery library to the master page of the Planet Wrox website. With the library set up, the remainder of this chapter teaches you how jQuery works and how to use it in the Planet Wrox website.

> ***NOTE*** *By the time you read this book, a new version of jQuery may have been released. This means that the version number in your jQuery file may be different from what I am showing here. Be sure to update the filenames to match your library files.*

TRY IT OUT Your First jQuery Page

In this exercise, you add the jQuery library to the master page so it's available to all pages in your site.

1. Open the `Frontend.master` file from the `MasterPages` folder and switch it to Markup View if necessary. Locate the `ScriptManager` control and add the following bolded markup to it:

```
<asp:ScriptManager ID="ScriptManager1" runat="server" EnablePageMethods="true">
  <Scripts>
    <asp:ScriptReference Path="~/Scripts/jquery-1.7.2.min.js" />
  </Scripts>
</asp:ScriptManager>
```

   If your `ScriptManager` didn't have a separate closing tag yet, you should add one now (and remove the slash (/) from the opening tag) or the code won't be added correctly.

2. Save and close the master page because you're done with it for now.

3. To try out the jQuery library, create a brand new Web Form in the `Demos` folder based on your custom template. Call the page `jQuery.aspx`, and set its `Title` to **`jQuery Demo`**.

4. With the new page open in Markup View, add the following code to the `Content` block for `cpMainContent`:

```
<asp:Content ID="Content2" ContentPlaceHolderID="cpMainContent" runat="Server">
  <input id="Button1" type="button" value="button" />
  <script type="text/javascript">
    $(document).ready(function() {
      $('#MainContent').css('background-color', 'green')

      $('#Button1').click(function() {
        $('#MainContent').css('background-color', 'red')
                      .animate({ width: '100px', height: '800px' })
      });
    });
  </script>
</asp:Content>
```

   Just like many other programming languages, JavaScript (and thus jQuery) is case sensitive and quite sensitive to missing quotes, brackets, and parentheses, so make sure you type this code exactly as shown here. Alternatively, you can copy and paste the code from the `jQuery.aspx` page that is part of the full source code that comes with this book.

   Note that while typing, IntelliSense pops up, helping you complete the code and giving you information about various methods and parameters in a tooltip. If it doesn't pop up, make sure you added the right `<Scripts>` element to the master page. Also, try saving and closing all open documents and then reopen `jQuery.aspx`.

5. Save the changes to the page and then press Ctrl+F5 to open it up in the browser. Notice how the background color of the `MainContent` element has turned to green. Click the button and notice how the background color changes to red and how the `MainContent` element changes size, ending up with a width of 100 pixels and a height of 800 pixels.

> ***COMMON MISTAKES*** *If you get an error, or you don't see the animation, make sure the link to the jQuery library is added to the master page correctly. Also, check your code for any typos you may have made.*

How It Works

Although the effects shown in this exercise aren't that fancy, a lot is going on under the hood to make this example work. To understand how it works, first look back at the master page where you added a reference to the jQuery library:

```
<asp:ScriptManager ID="ScriptManager1" runat="server" EnablePageMethods="true">
  <Scripts>
    <asp:ScriptReference Path="~/Scripts/jquery-1.7.2.min.js" />
  </Scripts>
</asp:ScriptManager>
```

This tells the script manager to include a `script` element pointing to the jQuery library. If you look in the HTML source for the page in the browser, you should see the following `script` element:

```
<script src="../Scripts/jquery-1.7.2.min.js" type="text/javascript"></script>
```

This in turn tells the browser to download the `jquery-1.7.2.min.js` file from the `Scripts` folder, giving your page access to all functionality included in the jQuery library.

The next thing to look at is the code in the jQuery demo page. First, you added a standard `<script>` block that can contain JavaScript. Inside this block, you added some jQuery code that is fired as soon as the browser is done loading the page. Everything between the opening ({) and closing (}) curly braces is executed when the page is ready:

```
<script type="text/javascript">
  $(document).ready(function() {
    // Remainder of the code skipped
  });
</script>
```

Because the jQuery code interacts with the elements on the page, you often have to wait until the entire page has loaded so the elements you're programming against are available. Adding jQuery code like this is a standard practice to delay execution of the code until the entire page is ready. You see more of this, including a handy shortcut to the "document ready function" `$(document).ready` later in this chapter.

The code that is executed when the page is ready consists of two parts. The first line of code sets the background color of the `MainContent` `<section>` to green:

```
$('#MainContent').css('background-color', 'green')
```

This code gets a reference to the `MainContent` element and then calls the `css` method to change the background color to green. Remember `document.getElementById` from the previous chapter that gets a reference to an element in the page by its `id`? In this example, `$('#MainContent')` is jQuery's equivalent, but as you see later, it's much more powerful.

The second part sets up a click handler for the HTML button you added to the page, similar to how you used `onclick` in Chapter 10. Inside the click handler you see some code that changes the background color of the `MainContent` `<section>` element to red, and changes the height and the width of it using a fluid animation:

```
$('#Button1').click(function() {
        $('#MainContent').css('background-color', 'red')
                  .animate({ width: '100px', height: '800px' })
      });
```

Again, you learn more about how jQuery is able to find the button and the `<section>` element and how the `css` and `animate` methods work later in this chapter, so don't worry too much if none of this is making a lot of sense right now.

When you click the button in the browser, the `MainContent`'s background color is changed to red, and then its width and height are changed to 100 and 800 pixels, respectively.

When you typed the jQuery code you may have noticed you got help from IntelliSense. As soon as you typed `$(` you got a tooltip explaining the information you can pass to this function. Likewise, IntelliSense helps you find and complete the `css` method and the various arguments you need to pass to it, as shown in Figure 11-4.

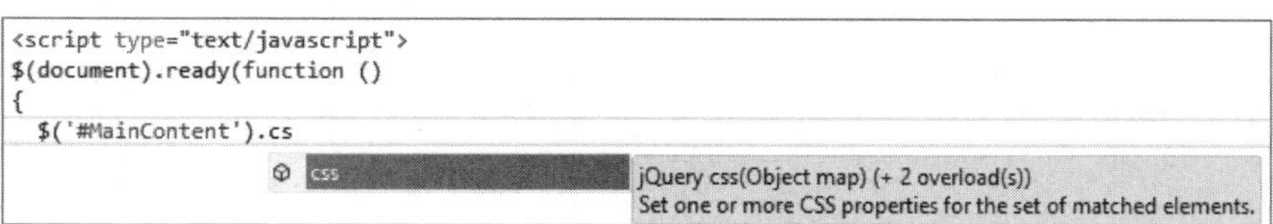

FIGURE 11-4

IntelliSense for jQuery works through the extra file—`jquery-1.7.2.intellisense.js`—you added to the site with NuGet. VS scans the library's folder for files ending in `intellisense.js`, parses them, and then uses the documentation it finds in them to build up the IntelliSense list.

The reason for the separate documentation file is to keep the size of the original jQuery library down. Without the documentation, the library is only 93 KB; with the documentation the file size would be much bigger.

You should never include a link to the IntelliSense version of the library in your pages because it doesn't add any value in the browser.

Now that you've seen some jQuery at work, it's time to get a better understanding of its possibilities and syntax.

JQUERY SYNTAX

To understand and use jQuery, you need to know a few important basics. First, you need to know more about jQuery's core functionality, including the `$` function you've seen before, and its `ready` method that enables you to execute code when the page is done loading in the browser. Next, you need to learn more about jQuery's *selector* and *filter* syntax, which enable you to find elements in a page by criteria that you specify. Once you have a reference to one or more elements in a page, you can apply various methods to them, like the `css` method you saw earlier. You also need to know a little about jQuery *events* that enable you to attach behavior to the events that your HTML elements might fire, like `click`, `mouseover`, and so on. In the next couple of sections, you see all of these main jQuery topics at work.

jQuery Core

Most of the jQuery code you write will be executed when the browser is done loading the page. It's important to wait with executing your code until the page is done loading the *DOM*. The DOM—the document object model—is a hierarchical representation of your web page and contains a tree-like structure of all your HTML elements, script files, CSS, images, and so on. The DOM is always in sync with the page you see in the browser, so if you make a programmatic change to the DOM (for example, with jQuery code), the change is reflected in the page in the browser. If you execute your jQuery code too early (for example, at the very top of the page), the DOM may not have loaded the elements you're referring to in your script, and you may get errors. Fortunately, it's easy to postpone the execution of your code until the DOM is ready using the `ready` function in jQuery. You've already seen the `ready` function at work in the previous Try It Out, but it's shown here again now that you better understand what it's used for:

```
$(document).ready(function() {
  // Code added here is executed when the DOM is ready.
});
```

Any code you add between the opening and closing curly braces is executed when the page is ready for DOM manipulation. jQuery also comes with a shortcut for the `ready` function to make it easier to write code that fires when the DOM is ready. The following snippet is equivalent to the preceding example:

```
$(function() {
  // Code added here is executed when the DOM is ready.
});
```

> ***NOTE*** *It's important that any code referencing the jQuery library is not run before the jQuery library itself is loaded. Because the link to the jQuery library is added after the* `<body>` *tag by the* `ScriptManager`*, you need to find a location later in the page. A good place for this is near the closing* `</body>` *tag defined in the master page.*

Because jQuery code is often specific to a page, it makes sense to add the code to the end of just the pages that require it. To make this a little easier, you can add a `ContentPlaceHolder` in your master page especially for this purpose. The pages that use this master page then have an easy location to write jQuery code. You see how to do this in the next exercise.

In the previous jQuery example you saw some code that selected the `MainContent` `<section>` element and the button in your page. However, jQuery comes with a lot more options to select specific elements in your pages. These options are discussed next.

Selecting Items Using jQuery

In jQuery you use the dollar sign (`$`) as a shortcut to find elements in your page. The elements that are found and returned are referred to as a *matched set*. The basic syntax for the `$` method is this:

```
$('Selector Here')
```

Between the quotes (you can use single or double quotes, as long as you use the same type on each end) you enter one or more selectors, which are discussed later. The `$` method returns zero or more elements that you can then influence using one of the many jQuery methods. For example, to apply some CSS to all `h2` elements, you use the `css` method:

```
$('h2').css('padding-bottom', '10px');
```

This applies a padding of ten pixels at the bottom of all headings at level two in the page. The cool thing about many of the jQuery methods is that, besides applying some design or behavior, they return the matched set again. This enables you to call another method on the same matched set so both are applied. This concept is called *chaining* or *fluent programming* where you use the result of one method as the input of another, enabling you to create a chain of effects. For example, the following code first changes the font size of all level-two headings in the page, and then fades them out until they are invisible in five seconds:

```
$('h2').css('font-size', '40px').fadeOut(5000); // timeout is in milliseconds
```

As you learned in earlier chapters, you should try to avoid using inline CSS properties like this. Instead, you should define CSS classes and assign them to the HTML elements. You see how to do this later in this chapter. You learn more about the different visual effects like `animate` and `fadeOut` after you've seen how selectors and filters work.

Basic Selectors

jQuery *selectors* enable you to find one or more elements in your page's document object model so you can apply all sorts of jQuery methods to these elements. The great thing about jQuery selectors is that you already know how they work. Rather than inventing a new technique to find page elements, the designers of jQuery decided to use an existing selector-based syntax that you are already familiar with: CSS. Remember the CSS selectors from Chapter 3? You can use the exact same ones in jQuery.

The Universal Selector

Just as its CSS counterpart, the Universal selector matches all elements in your page. To set the `font-family` property of the `style` for each element in your page to `Arial`, you use this code:

```
$('*').css('font-family', 'Arial');
```

The Element Selector

This selector returns a reference to zero or more elements that match a specific tag name. For example, this code turns the text color of all headings at level two to blue:

```
$('h2').css('color', 'blue');
```

The ID Selector

This selector finds and retrieves an element by its `id`, the same as you would do in CSS. For example, to set the CSS `class` for a button called `Button1`, you use this code:

```
$('#Button1').addClass('NewClassName');
```

When this code sets the CSS class (using the `addClass` method), the standard CSS rules apply. That means that for this code to work and change the appearance of the button, the `NewClassName` class needs to be available to the page, either through an external CSS file or by an embedded style sheet. Refer to Chapter 3 if you need a refresher on the different cascading style sheet types. However, you'll also see examples where a CSS class is added that doesn't exist in a CSS file. This is convenient to "tag" elements so you can select them again later using a Class selector.

The Class Selector

The Class selector returns a reference to zero or more elements that match a specific class name. Consider this HTML fragment:

```
<h1 class="Highlight">Heading 1</h1>
<h2>Heading 2</h2>
<p class="Highlight">First paragraph</p>
<p>Second paragraph</p>
```

Notice how two of the four elements have a CSS class called `Highlight`. The following jQuery code changes the background color of the first heading and the first paragraph to red, leaving the other elements unmodified:

```
$('.Highlight').css('background-color', 'red');
```

Grouped and Combined Selectors

Just as with CSS, you can group and combine selectors. The following Grouped selector changes the text color of all `h1` and `h2` elements in your page:

```
$('h1, h2').css('color', 'orange');
```

With a Combined selector, you can find specific elements that fall within some others. For example, the following jQuery touches just the paragraphs that fall within the `MainContent` element, leaving all other paragraphs alone:

```
$('#MainContent p').css('border', '1px solid red');
```

To get a feel for the selectors in jQuery and the effects you can apply to the matched set, the next exercise shows you how to use some of the selectors and apply some animations to the matched sets. In later sections of this chapter, you get a more detailed explanation of the different animations; for now, just focus on the selector part of the jQuery code.

TRY IT OUT Using Basic Selectors

In this exercise, you first add an additional `ContentPlaceHolder` control to the main master page so it's easier to add client-side jQuery code to your pages. You then write some jQuery to try out the various selectors.

1. Open up the `Frontend.master` file from the `MasterPages` folder and make sure it's in Markup View.

2. Near the bottom of the page, right before the closing `</form>` tag, drag a `ContentPlaceHolder` from the Toolbox. Set its `ID` to `cpClientScript`. Your code should end up like this:

```
    <footer>Footer Goes Here</footer>
  </div>
  <asp:ContentPlaceHolder ID="cpClientScript" runat="server">
  </asp:ContentPlaceHolder>
</form>
```

3. Save and close the master page because you're done with it for now.

4. Create a new demo page called `BasicSelectors.aspx` in the `Demos` folder. Once again, base it on your own template and give it a meaningful title. Switch the page to Design View, locate the `cpClientScript` placeholder at the bottom, open its Smart Tasks panel, and choose Create Custom Content.

5. Switch to Markup View and add the following HTML to the `cpMainContent` placeholder (don't accidentally add it to the placeholder you just added):

```
<h1>Basic Selectors</h1>
<div class="SampleClass">I am a div.</div>
```

6. Add the following jQuery code demonstrating all six basic selectors to the `cpClientScript` placeholder you created in step 4:

```
<asp:Content ID="Content3" runat="server" ContentPlaceHolderID="cpClientScript">
<script type="text/javascript">
  $(function()
  {
    $('*').css('color', 'Green');                                     // Universal
    $('#Sidebar').css('border-bottom', '2px solid red');              // ID
    $('h1').bind('click', function () { alert('Hello World') });  // Element
    $('.SampleClass').addClass('PleaseWait').hide(5000);             // Class
    $('footer, header').slideUp('slow').slideDown('slow');           // Grouped
    $('#Sidebar img').fadeTo(5000, 0.1);                             // Combined
  });
</script>
</asp:Content>
```

7. Save all your changes and request the page in the browser. All text is now green, the sidebar has an extra bottom border, you see the Please Wait animated icon and text appear and then disappear, the header and footer disappear and then reappear, and finally, during a five-second period, the banner in the sidebar becomes almost transparent. If you click the Basic Selectors heading you get a pop-up saying Hello World.

How It Works

Phew, lots of animation fun. I typically don't recommend adding all these features to your pages at once or you'll be sure to scare away most of your users. However, for this demo it works really well because you can see some of the power of jQuery. You've seen all of the six selectors, but the code that is being executed against their matched sets is probably new to you.

The first selector selects all elements in your page and then applies the `css` method to turn their font color to green. The ID selector then gets a single element and calls the same `css` method to apply a border. The third example uses the Element selector to find the `h1` element and then dynamically binds a `click` handler so that when you click the heading, the code between the curly braces is executed.

Selector four demonstrates the Class selector and shows you how to find elements by their class name. Notice that the CSS class being searched for doesn't have to be an existing CSS class defined in your style sheet. Once the elements are found, the `addClass` method then adds a new class to them, `PleaseWait` in this example, which applies the spinner image as the background to the `<div>` element. The `hide` method then hides the elements again during a five-second timeframe.

Line number five uses the Grouped selector to find both the `footer` and the `header` elements. The `slideUp` method then slowly decreases the height of these elements until they have completely disappeared. In doing so, it remembers the initial size, so when you call `slideDown` again it knows to what size to restore the elements.

The final example uses a Combined selector to find the banner image in the right-hand sidebar. Once it has found the image, it slowly dissolves it (in five seconds) by setting its opacity to 0.1 (10%) so it gets almost invisible.

In a later section in this chapter you see more of the various styling and animation methods that jQuery offers. For now, it's just important that you understand the selector syntax to refer to the elements in your page.

Quite often, simply selecting items in your page is not enough. For instance, when selecting rows in a table you may not want to select all rows at once, but only the odd or even rows, so you can apply a "zebra stripe" effect to the table where odd and even rows have different colors. That's where filters come into play.

Basic Filters

In jQuery you can use filters to further filter the result set from a selector. This opens a lot of possibilities because it enables you to get at elements like the first, last, all even or odd ones, all headings, or items at a specific location. The table after the next exercise lists the most-used basic filters and gives an example of how to use them. To follow along with these examples and many that follow, carry out this exercise, which sets up a test page for most of the jQuery examples.

TRY IT OUT Setting up a jQuery Demo Page

In this exercise, you create a brand new demo page you can use to try out many of the examples in this chapter, simply by replacing a single line of code.

1. Create a new page based on your custom template and call it `jQueryDemos.aspx`. Give the page a title and then in the `cpMainContent` placeholder add the following HTML:

```
<h1 title="First Header">First Header</h1>
<table id="DemoTable">
  <tr><td>Row 1 Cell 1</td><td>Row 1 Cell 2</td></tr>
  <tr><td>Row 2 Cell 1</td><td>Row 2 Cell 2</td></tr>
  <tr><td>Row 3 Cell 1</td><td>Row 3 Cell 2</td></tr>
  <tr><td>Row 4 Cell 1</td><td>Row 4 Cell 2</td></tr>
  <tr><td>Row 5 Cell 1</td><td>Row 5 Cell 2</td></tr>
</table>
<h2>Second <span style="font-style: italic; font-weight: bold;">
              Header</span></h2>
<input id="Button1" type="button" value="button" />
<input id="Text1" type="text" />
<input id="Checkbox1" type="checkbox" />
<input id="Checkbox2" type="checkbox" />
```

   You don't have to type all this code yourself. Instead, you can use VS to write most of it for you. Make good use of the Table menu and the HTML category of the Toolbox.

2. Add a `Content` block for the `cpClientScript` below `cpMainContent` and enter the following code:

```
</asp:Content>
<asp:Content ID="Content3" runat="server" ContentPlaceHolderID="cpClientScript">
<script type="text/javascript">
  $(function()
  {
    // Examples go here
  });
</script>
</asp:Content>
```

3. Replace the line `// Examples go here` with the following code to test out your setup:

```
$('#DemoTable').css('background-color', 'green');
```

4. Save your changes and press Ctrl+F5 to open the page in your browser. If all went well, the background color of the cells in the table turned green.

5. Close your browser and go back to VS. Press Ctrl+Z to undo your last changes until you see the `// Examples go here` line again, and save the page.

How It Works

In this exercise you created a simple `Content` block that can hold your jQuery code. You then defined a code block that fires as soon as the browser is done loading the DOM. Inside this block you wrote a simple selector that selects the table with an `id` of `DemoTable` and then used jQuery's `css` method to change its background color.

In the following table you see a list of jQuery's basic filters. Remember, you can try out each example by replacing the `//Examples go here` line with the code examples given. Then save the page and load it in your browser to see the code at work.

FILTER	PURPOSE

`:first`
`:last`
	Enables you to select the first or last item in a matched set. The following example changes the background color of the first or last row of the table to red:
	`$('#DemoTable tr:first').css('background-color', 'red');`
	`$('#DemoTable tr:last').css('background-color', 'red');`
	First, the table is found using `#DemoTable`. Then all its rows are found using `tr`. Finally, the first or last row is found using the `:first` and `:last` filters.

`:odd` `:even`	Enables you to select the odd or even items in a matched set. The following example changes the background color of the odd rows of the table to red. Because the numbering is zero-based, you actually see the second and fourth rows change color (because they have an index of 1 and 3, respectively). `$('#DemoTable tr:odd').css('background-color', 'red');`

`:eq(index)`
`:lt(index)`
`:gt(index)`
	Matches elements by their index. `:eq` (equals) returns a single element by its index, and `:lt` (less than) and `:gt` (greater than) return items smaller or greater than the given index, respectively. Examples:
	`// Changes the color in the first row (with an index of 0)`
	`$('#DemoTable tr:eq(0)').css('color', 'green');`
	
	`// Changes only the last two rows. The first three`
	`// with an index of 0, 1 and 2 respectively, are skipped.`
	`$('#DemoTable tr:gt(2)').css('color', 'green');`
	
	`// Changes the text color of the first two rows to green.`
	`$('#DemoTable tr:lt(2)').css('color', 'green');`

`:header`	Finds all headers (from `h1` to `h6`) in the page. Example: `$(':header').css('color', 'green');`

For a complete list of all basic filters, check out the jQuery documentation at `http://api.jquery.com/category/selectors/`.

Advanced Filters

Besides the basic filters you just saw, jQuery supports a lot more filters that enable you to get items based on the text they contain, whether or not they are visible, and also on any attributes they may have. Additionally, you can find filters to get at form elements (like buttons, check boxes, radio buttons, and so on) and a number of selectors that enable you to select children, parents, siblings, and descendants. The following table lists the ones you'll use most. The online jQuery documentation gives you access to the complete list, with full working examples showing how they work.

FILTER	PURPOSE
`:contains(text)`	Matches an element by the text it contains. Example: `$('td:contains("Row 3")').css('color', 'green');` If you leave out the `td`, the entire table will be green. This is because the table itself is matched as well (one of its children contains the text Row 3) so the color is applied to the table, which in turn changes the text in each cell to green. Note how I am using double quotes for the text string to avoid closing the single quote from the selector too soon.
`:has(element)`	Matches elements that contain at least one of the given elements. Example: `$(':header:has("span")').css('color', 'green');` This matches only the `h2` because it's a header (`:header`) and contains a <span> element (`has("span")`).

`[attribute]`	Matches an element based on the given attribute. Example:
	`// Matches the button and the text box as both`
	`// have a type attribute but would also`
	`// match other elements with a type attribute`
	`$('[type]').css('color', 'green');`
	To select only input controls with a `type` attribute you can use this:
	`$('input[type]').css('color', 'green');`
	You need to type some text in the text box to see the green font color.

`[attribute=value]`	Matches an element based on an attribute and that attribute's value. Example:
	`// Matches just the text box`
	`$('[type=text]').css('color', 'green');`

`:input`
`:text`
`:password`
`:radio`
`:checkbox`
`:submit`
`:image`
`:reset`
`:button`
`:hidden`
`:file`
	These selectors enable you to match specific client HTML form elements. For example, the code snippet that finds the button and the text box can be rewritten using a Grouped selector as follows:
	`$(':button, :text').css('color', 'green');`
	You can use these filters to do some fancy stuff. For example, to write some functionality that checks all check boxes in a form, you can use:
	`$(':checkbox').attr('checked', true);`
	In order to uncheck all check boxes, you pass `false` as the second argument to the `attr` method.

Powerful as these selectors and filters are, they are pretty useless without a way to act upon their results. Changing the looks and behavior of the items in the matched set is the topic of the next section.

MODIFYING THE DOM WITH JQUERY

Once you have a matched set, you want to do something with it. For example, you may want to apply a CSS `class` or `style` to the items in it. Or you may want to append some behavior to them, like adding a `click` handler that fires some code when the items get clicked. You've already seen some examples of this using the `css` and `bind` methods, but jQuery has a lot more to offer. In the next two sections, you see how to work with the various CSS methods and learn how to set up event handlers.

CSS Methods

CSS is supported in jQuery in a few different ways. First, there's the `css` method that enables you to retrieve a specific CSS value (like the color of an item), and to set one or more CSS properties on a set of elements. Secondly, methods like `addClass`, `removeClass`, `toggleClass`, and `hasClass` enable you to alter or inspect the CSS classes that are applied to elements. Furthermore, a couple of methods enable you to work with the dimensions and position of an element. I discuss only the most common ones, but you can look up the entire list at the jQuery website. The examples once again use the same HTML fragment you saw before, so it's easy to follow along if you want to try them out in your browser.

css(name, value)

This method enables you to set a specific CSS property on a matched element. The `name` argument refers to a CSS property (such as `border`, `color`, and so on) and the `value` defines the style you want to apply. The following example changes the background color of the `h1` element:

```
$('h1').css('background-color', 'green');
```

css(name)

This method retrieves a specific CSS value based on the property you pass to it. The following example alerts '`italic`' because that's the `font-style` of the `<span>` element in the heading level 2:

```
alert($('h2 span').css('font-style'));
```

You can use this value in your jQuery scripts; for example, you can use it to toggle the `font-style` between italic and normal or to set multiple elements to the same style.

css(properties)

This is quite a powerful method because it enables you to set multiple properties on the matched elements in one fell swoop. The following example changes the color of all cells in the table to red, changes the font to Verdana and sets their padding to 10px. You pass the data in what is called an *anonymous object* where you wrap the entire set of properties in a pair of curly braces ({ }), separate each property and value by a colon (:) and each pair by a comma:

```
$('#DemoTable td').css({'color' : 'red', 'font-family' : 'Verdana',
        'padding' : '10px'});
```

addClass, removeClass, and toggleClass

The `addClass` and `removeClass` methods enable you to add and remove classes from elements, respectively. Just as with plain CSS, you're better off using these methods than assigning inline CSS with the `css(properties)` method. This way, it's easier to define CSS classes at a central place, which makes them easier to maintain and reuse. The next example shows how to assign a class to the `h2` element:

```
$('h2').addClass('PleaseWait');
```

If you want to remove the class again, you call `removeClass` like this:

```
$('h2').removeClass('PleaseWait');
```

The `toggleClass` method assigns the class if it's not present yet and removes it otherwise.

All three methods enable you to pass multiple classes by separating them with a space.

attr(attributeName)

The `attr` method enables you to read and set the values of attributes on HTML elements. This version, which accepts a single argument, is used to read an existing value. For the `attributeName` you pass the name of the attribute as a string. The following example alerts First Header, the `title` attribute of the `h1` header:

```
alert($('h1').attr('title'));
```

attr(attributeName, value)

The second version of `attr`, which accepts two arguments, is used to change the value of an attribute. Besides the name of the attribute you want to change, you also need to send the new value for the attribute. The following example checks all check boxes in the demo page:

```
$(':checkbox').attr('checked', true);
```

Together, these CSS methods give you great power to change the look and feel of elements in your page. You can take this one step further by using the rich event system in jQuery that enables you to assign and remove all kinds of handlers to your elements through code.

Handling Events

Events are a very common technique in many programming languages. You've seen .NET events at work in previous chapters where you used them to handle a `Button` control's `Click` event or a `Page`'s `Load` event. JavaScript and the DOM are no exception and events are available in many places. For example, many HTML elements (such as a button defined with `input type="button"`) have a `click` event that fires when you click it. Likewise, they have `mouseover` and `mouseout` events that fire when you move your mouse over or away from them. Normally, when you define the events directly in markup, they look like this:

```
<input type="button" onclick="alert('Hello');" value="Click Me" />
```

Rather than writing the code they trigger inline (the alert function in this example), you can also point them to JavaScript functions you can write yourself. The following example calls a fictitious `SayYourName` function:

```
<input type="button" onclick="SayYourName();" value="Click Me" />
```

jQuery goes one step further, and enables you to hook up events not only to a single element, but to a whole matched set at once. This is extremely powerful because it enables you to bind handlers to a large number of elements with only a few lines of code. Consider, for example, a table with many rows. To make the table a little more visually attractive, you could apply a technique that is called "active item tracking," where the item your mouse is over changes color. Without jQuery you would write `onmouseover` and `onmouseout` handlers on each and every row in the table. This clearly leads to a lot of excessive bloat in the final HTML of the page. With jQuery, all you need is this code, again using the HTML code samples you used before:

```
$(function()
{
  $('#DemoTable tr')
      .bind('mouseover', function() { $(this).css('background-color', 'yellow') });
});
```

This code finds all the table rows within the `#DemoTable` element and then dynamically assigns a function that is called when you hover your mouse over each row. If you hover your mouse over them, the background changes color. But if you move your mouse away, the new color remains. To fix this problem, you can use jQuery's chaining concept, where the result of a jQuery method returns the matched set so you can apply another function to it. To bind the `mouseout` to a new function, simply call `bind` again on the return value of the first call to `bind`:

```
$('#DemoTable tr')
     .bind('mouseover', function() { $(this).css('background-color', 'yellow') })
     .bind('mouseout', function() { $(this).css('background-color', '') });
```

Notice how the semicolon that closed off the line in the previous example has been moved to the final line. Then the second `bind` is simply chained to the previous call to `bind`. It's a bit difficult to see because the code is spread out over multiple lines to accommodate the width of this book, but this code actually comes down to this:

```
$('#DemoTable tr').bind('mouseover', ...). bind('mouseout', ...);
```

This code does three things: first it uses `$('#DemoTable tr')` to find all rows in the table. On the matched set that is returned it calls `bind` to dynamically hook up some behavior that fires when you move your mouse over a row. Then `bind` is called again on the matched set returned by the first call to `bind` to reset the background color when you move your mouse away from the table row. Notice how I am setting the color to an empty string ('') to remove the CSS background property so you can see the original background again.

There's one more important thing to look at in this example and that's the way the background color is set:

```
$(this).css('background-color', 'yellow')
```

The `this` keyword in this example refers to the element to which the item is applied: the table row in this case. Using `$(this)` then gives you a jQuery matched set (containing a single element) to which you can apply regular jQuery methods such as `css`. Instead of using jQuery you can also execute standard JavaScript against the `this` element.

```
this.style.backgroundColor = 'yellow'
```

The table row (and many other HTML elements) has a `style` property that lets you change CSS styles programmatically. Maybe you expected to use `style.background-color` to change the color, but that's not how it works in JavaScript. In that language, the dash (-) is not a valid identifier so in JavaScript all dashes are removed from the property names. Furthermore, each letter following the original dash is written in uppercase. So, `background-color` in CSS becomes `backgroundColor` in JavaScript, `font-family` becomes `fontFamily`, and so forth. Keep these naming rules in mind when you try to set CSS information dynamically through JavaScript and jQuery.

Miscellaneous jQuery Functionality

Before you move on to the next topic of effects with jQuery, you need to understand a few important functions in jQuery. First of all, there's `each`.

The `each` method iterates (or loops) over a collection. This is great if you want to apply some behavior to items in your matched set that you cannot set with a single jQuery function. As an argument to `each` you supply a function that is executed for each item. The following `each` example alerts the contents of each table cell by looping over the items in the matched set and then calling `alert`. Again, you can try this out with your `jQueryDemos.aspx` page.

```
$('#DemoTable td').each(function()
  {
    alert(this.innerHTML);
  });
```

Two other important methods include `parent` and `prev`. These methods are used in DOM traversing, where you can "walk" up and down the document tree finding elements that are either below or above an item, or at the same level.

The `prev` method selects a matched element's direct sibling. To see how this works, take a look at this:

```
alert($('#DemoTable td:contains("Row 1 Cell 2") ').prev()[0].innerHTML);
```

What do you think this alerts? If you guessed "Row 1 Cell 1," you're right. The `$` selector first selects the table cell in the second column of the first row by the text it contains. The `prev` method then returns its first sibling: the cell to the left of it. Because a matched set is a collection even if it contains only a single item, you still need to use an indexer (with `[0]`) to refer to that first item. The table cell then exposes an `.innerHTML` property that returns the content of the cell.

Finally, take a look at `parent`:

```
alert($('#DemoTable td:contains("Row 1 Cell 2") ').parent()[0].innerHTML);
```

If you run this code in the demo page, you get the result shown in Figure 11-5.

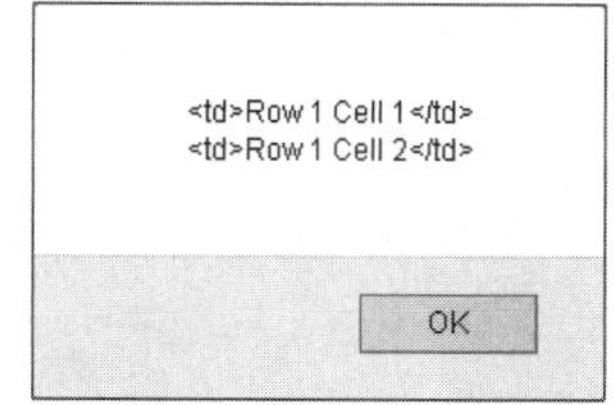
<td>Row 1 Cell 1</td>
<td>Row 1 Cell 2</td>
OK

FIGURE 11-5

If you're not seeing this exact same HTML, make sure that the line that begins with `alert` is the only one inside your document ready function, because the other examples may influence the HTML for the table.

The selector is the same as in the previous example. The `parent` function then points to the `<tr>` around the matched table cell. Alerting the `innerHTML` then returns the HTML for the two cells that this row contains.

Common Mistakes When Working with jQuery

Depending on the complexity of the jQuery functionality you're using, writing the code can be quite challenging. You need to take care of the proper capitalization, parentheses, brackets, commas, and more. When you find your jQuery code doesn't run or has unexpected behavior, check to see if your code is suffering from the following problems.

Your ID Selectors Don't Work

It's likely you forgot to include the # symbol in front of it. `$('DemoTable')` does not select the table with an `id` of `DemoTable`, whereas `$('#DemoTable')` does select it. Another situation where your ID selector might not work is when you've got the casing wrong. ID selectors are case sensitive, so `$('#DemoTable')` is not the same as `$('#demotable')`.

Your ID Selectors Don't Work, Even with a Hash Symbol

In this case, it's likely that the client element doesn't have the `id` you expect. Maybe the ASP.NET run time changed the client `id` by prefixing it with the `id` of its parent? In that case, try setting the `ClientIDMode` on the relevant control to `Static` so the `id` ends up more predictable. Also make sure your code executes inside the document ready function because the elements you're targeting may not be available yet.

None of Your Code Seems to Run

Check your parentheses, curly braces, and quotes. Each pair needs to be balanced, with an equal number of opening and closing items.

So far the code you've seen revolves mostly around finding elements in your page and changing their appearance through CSS or to execute JavaScript. However, jQuery comes with a bag of tricks to animate elements in your page as well. In the next section you see these so-called effects, followed by a Try It Out exercise that shows them in action.

EFFECTS WITH JQUERY

In an earlier example in this chapter you saw how to use `slideUp` and `slideDown` to slowly hide and show elements. But these are only two of the many effect and animation methods that jQuery has available. The following table lists the most common ones you can use. Once again, you're advised to try out all examples using the `jQueryDemos.aspx` page.

METHOD NAME	PURPOSE

`show()`
`hide()`
	Hides or shows the matched elements by decreasing the `height`, `width`, and `opacity` (making them transparent). Both methods enable you to define a fixed speed (slow, normal, and fast) or a number defining the animation time in milliseconds. Examples:
	`$('h1').hide(1000);  //Hide the heading in 1 second`
	`$('h1').show(1000);  //Make it reappear in 1 second`

<table>
<tr><th>METHOD NAME</th><th>PURPOSE</th></tr>
<tr><td><code>toggle()</code></td><td>The <code>toggle</code> method uses <code>show</code> and <code>hide</code> internally and changes the display of the matched elements. That is, visible items are hidden, and vice versa. Example:
<code>$('h1').toggle(2000); // hide or show the h1 in 2 seconds</code></td></tr>
<tr><td><code>slideDown()</code>
<code>slideUp()</code>
<code>slideToggle()</code></td><td>Just like <code>hide</code> and <code>show</code>, these methods make matched elements appear or disappear. However, they do this by adjusting the <code>height</code> from its current size to zero or vice versa, causing the element to "slide up" or "slide down." The <code>slideToggle</code> method slides down hidden elements and slides up visible elements, which makes it easy to show and hide elements repeatedly with a single action. Examples:
<code>$('h1').slideUp(1000);</code>
<code>$('h1').slideDown(1000);</code>
<code>$('h1').slideToggle(1000);</code></td></tr>
<tr><td><code>fadeIn()</code>
<code>fadeOut()</code>
<code>fadeTo()</code></td><td>These methods make the matched elements visible or invisible by changing their opacity. <code>fadeOut</code> sets the opacity to 0, making the item completely transparent, and then sets the CSS <code>display</code> property to <code>none</code>, hiding the item completely. <code>fadeTo</code> lets you specify an opacity (a number between 0 and 1) to determine the transparency level of the elements and <code>fadeIn</code> makes the item visible again and sets the opacity to 1. All three methods enable you to define a fixed speed (slow, normal, and fast) or a number defining the duration of the animation in milliseconds. Examples:
<code>$('h1').fadeOut(1000);   // dissolve the h1 in 1 second</code>
<code>$('h1').fadeIn(1000);   // h1 reappears in 1 second</code>
<code>$('h1').fadeTo(1000, 0.5); // fade to semi-transparent</code></td></tr>
<tr><td><code>animate()</code></td><td>Internally, <code>animate</code> is used for many of the animation methods like <code>show</code> and <code>hide</code>. However, it's also externally available to give you great flexibility in animating your matched elements. With the <code>animate</code> method you can specify a bunch of properties to animate. Consider this example:
<code>$('h1').animate({</code>
<code>   opacity: 0.4,</code>
<code>   marginLeft: '50px',</code>
<code>   fontSize: '50px'</code>
<code> }, 1500);</code>

In one smooth animation with a duration of 1.5 seconds, this code takes the <code>h1</code> element and increases its font size to 50 pixels, sets the opacity to 0.4 to make the element semi-transparent, and changes the left margin to 50 pixels. The first argument of the <code>animate</code> method is an object holding one or more properties you want to animate, each one separated by a comma. Notice how you need to use JavaScript's <code>marginLeft</code> and <code>fontSize</code>, rather than the CSS <code>margin-left</code> and <code>font-size</code> properties. You can only animate properties that take numeric values. That is, you can use properties like <code>margin</code>, <code>fontSize</code>, <code>opacity</code>, and so on, but not properties like <code>color</code> or <code>fontFamily</code>.</td></tr>
</table>

Now that you've seen the most important jQuery concepts, from simple selectors to advanced animation options, you can use this knowledge to make the contact form of the Planet Wrox site a little more attractive.

TRY IT OUT Animating the Contact Form

In this exercise you apply two main animations: one is triggered when the user submits the contact form and slowly slides it up until it disappears. The other animation is used to show and hide the Message Sent label, attracting more attention until it completely disappears.

1. Start by adding an additional text paragraph below the Message Sent label in the `ContactForm.ascx` user control in Markup View. This paragraph will be visible after the form has been submitted, and remains visible, even after the Message Sent text has been hidden. Within the paragraph tags add some text that thanks the user for his response. Add `id` and `runat="server"` attributes to the paragraph (so you can program against it in Code Behind) and set its `Visible` property to `False`. Finally, set the `CssClass` attribute of the `Label` control placed *before* the paragraph to `Attention`. You should end up with this code:

```
<asp:Label ID="Message" runat="server" CssClass="Attention"
           Text="Message Sent" Visible="False" />
<p runat="server" id="MessageSentPara" visible="False">Thank you for your message.
         We'll get in touch with you if necessary.</p>
```

2. Wrap the entire table that holds the form controls in a `<div>` and set its `id` to `TableWrapper`. Tables can't be easily resized using `slideUp` and `slideDown`, but by wrapping the table in a `<div>` you can resize that element instead:

```
<div id="TableWrapper">
<table class="auto-style1" runat="server" id="FormTable">
...
</table>
</div>
```

3. In previous versions of VS, you would not see IntelliSense for jQuery and other script libraries in user controls. That's because VS doesn't know in which pages or master page the control will be used. Because the script references are added to these pages, the user control doesn't know of their existence. You could work around that by adding a reference to the library in the control and hide it in a server-side comment, or remove the reference when you deploy your site. However, VS 2012 introduces a much cleaner solution. By adding a JavaScript file with the special name of `_references.js` to your site, VS gives you IntelliSense for all script file references it finds in that file. To set this up, first add a JavaScript file called `_references.js` to the `Scripts` folder (right-click the folder and choose Add ⇨ JavaScript file.) Then from the `Scripts` folder in the Solution Explorer, drag `jquery-1.7.2.js` into the open JavaScript file. VS adds the following code for you:

```
/// <reference path="jquery-1.7.2.js" />
```

Save and close the file. From now on, you'll see IntelliSense appear for the jQuery library, no matter where you're adding your jQuery code. Visual Studio looks at the file reference you added to this file and looks for matching files with an `intellisense.js` extension, which it uses to build up IntelliSense and the documentation tool tips. You can add other references to _references.js as well to light up IntelliSense for other JavaScript libraries. I really like this feature because it gives you IntelliSense everywhere without messy hacks or double script references. You never have to include a reference to this special file in the pages or controls in your site; it serves purely as a development-time feature.

4. Back in the user control ContactForm.ascx, scroll down to the end of the control's markup, and add a <script> element and the following jQuery code that fires when the form is about to be submitted:

```
<script type="text/javascript">
  $(function() {
    $('form').bind('submit', function()
    {
      if (Page_IsValid)
      {
        $('#TableWrapper').slideUp(3000);
      }
    });
  });
  // Code from step 5 goes here
</script>
```

5. Right before the closing </script> tag and after the closing curly brace, parenthesis, and semicolon of the jQuery document ready function, add the following bold piece of JavaScript:

```
  });
  function pageLoad()
  {
    $('.Attention').animate({ width: '600px' }, 3000).
               animate({ width: '100px' }, 3000).fadeOut('slow');
  }
</script>
```

The pageLoad method (which is part of the client-side JavaScript made available by ASP.NET AJAX) serves the same purpose as jQuery's document ready, with one exception: it also fires after a partial page update, which is what takes place after you submit the form because of the UpdatePanel in the user control.

6. Switch to Code Behind and add the following line of code to the SendButton_Click method. This code makes the text paragraph visible when the form is submitted and the e-mail message is sent:

VB.NET

```
Message.Visible = True
MessageSentPara.Visible = True
FormTable.Visible = False
```

C#

```
Message.Visible = true;
MessageSentPara.Visible = true;
FormTable.Visible = false;
```

7. Save all your changes and close the user control because you're done with it.

8. Open the `Monochrome.css` file from its theme folder and add the following CSS declaration to the bottom of the file:

```
.Attention
{
  border: 4px solid red;
  padding: 10px 0;
  width: 100px;
  margin: auto;
  display: block;
  text-align: center;
}
```

9. Copy the same declaration to the DarkGrey theme's CSS file.

10. Save your changes and then request the Planet Wrox site in your browser. Choose the Contact Us item (under About) from the `Menu` or `TreeView` control, fill in the form, and click Send. Notice how shortly after clicking the button the form slides up slowly until it completely disappears. Figure 11-6 shows the form halfway during the `slideUp` operation.

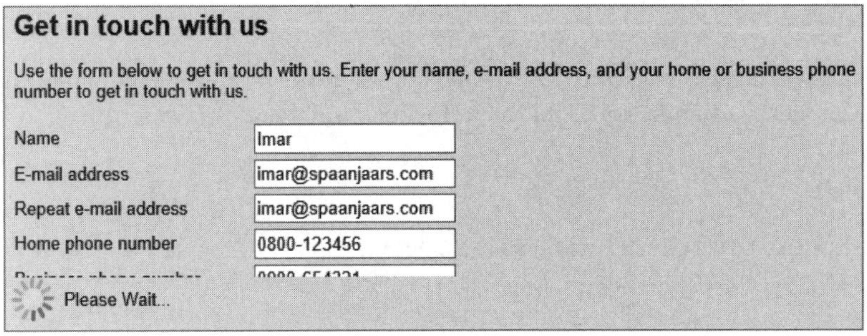

FIGURE 11-6

11. Once the page is done loading, the Message Sent label and the thank you text appear. Notice how the label first grows in size to span the full content width, then shrinks again and finally disappears completely. Figure 11-7 shows the message while it's being resized. If you don't see this animation appear, press Ctrl+F5 or Ctrl+R to get a fresh copy of the CSS file from the server and then fill in the contact form again.

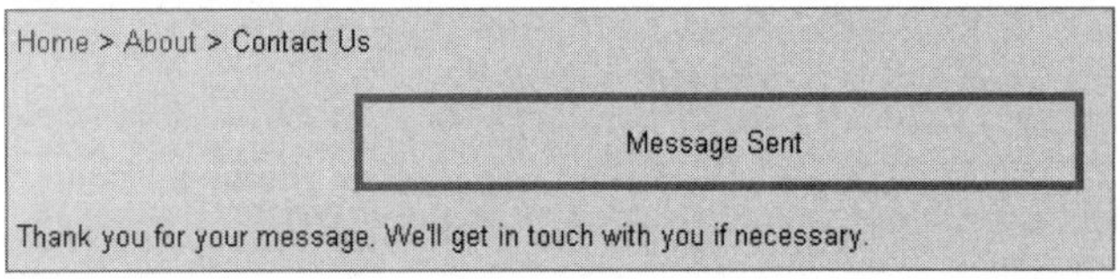

FIGURE 11-7

How It Works

A lot of the steps involved in this exercise deal with things you've already seen: adding `<div>` elements, classes, and CSS declarations. However, there's some jQuery and some Ajax code in this example that's worth examining. First, take a look at the code you added in the jQuery document ready function:

```
$('form').bind('submit', function()
{
  if (Page_IsValid)
  {
    $('#TableWrapper').slideUp(3000);
  }
});
```

The first line dynamically binds some code to the form's `submit` event. This way, the remainder of the code fires when the user clicks the Send button. The check for `Page_IsValid` is necessary to prevent the form from sliding up if the user made a mistake somewhere. Imagine that a user leaves both phone numbers empty and clicks the Send button. This button then tries to submit the form, causing the form's `submit` event to fire. The ASP.NET client framework intercepts this event and validates the form, causing an alert box with an error message to appear. But even though the form is invalid, it continues to handle other submit event handlers, including the one your code set up. If you didn't take precautions, the form would slide up, regardless of whether it was valid. This makes it impossible for the user to complete the form. Fortunately, you can check `Page_IsValid`, which is set to `false` when the form contains invalid data. Only when `Page_IsValid` returns `true` will the `slideUp` method hide the form. During a three-second period (3,000 milliseconds) the form smoothly slides up until it's no longer visible.

Then the server code runs and sends out the message as you've seen in previous chapters. Once the e-mail is sent, the server code sends back the Message Sent label and the paragraph. The message is then animated through this code, which uses a combination of ASP.NET AJAX and jQuery:

```
function pageLoad()
{
  $('.Attention').animate({ width: '600px' }, 3000).
          animate({ width: '100px' }, 3000).fadeOut('slow');
}
```

Rather than using jQuery's `$(function()` to fire code when the page loads, this example uses ASP .NET AJAX's `pageLoad`, and for a very specific reason: this event is fired by the Ajax framework when the page loads the first time, and after every postback, partial or not! This is important, because the Message Sent text is only available after the partial postback caused by the button. Notice that `pageLoad` also fires on the initial request of `Contact.aspx`. However, in that case, the `Label` with the `Attention` class is not present in the page (because its `Visible` property has been set to `False` which results in the control's code not being not sent to the browser) so `$('.Attention')` results in an empty matched set and no animation takes place.

The code that executes here is relatively straightforward. First, using `animate({ width: '600px' }, 3000)` the message is animated to have a width of 600 pixels. The animation takes three seconds to complete. Once the three seconds are over, another chained method animates the message back to 100 pixels. Finally, the `fadeOut` method is used to dissolve the message, after which it completely disappears.

Although some of the code looks quite complex, I hope you agree that with jQuery it's relatively easy to apply some fancy design makeover to your pages. Not every page or form should be abused for these techniques, but when used sparingly, jQuery animations can really add some flavor to your website.

As you saw in the previous sections, jQuery is really powerful. You can use it to find elements in your page, manipulate them through code, change the appearance of elements and create animations. However, jQuery can be used for more than that. The remaining section of this chapter deals with the topic of using jQuery for validation.

JQUERY AND VALIDATION

Remember the validation controls you used in Chapter 9 to validate the contact form? The validation controls work by generating JavaScript that is added to the page. The downside of that approach is that your page becomes unnecessarily large because a lot of repetitive code is added to each page that uses these controls. The developers of ASP.NET have thought of this too and decided to leverage the power of jQuery to improve client-side validation. They have done this through a concept known as *unobtrusive JavaScript*, where the functionality (the code that gets executed) has been separated from the structure and content of the page. Rather than embedding large chunks of JavaScript code in the page, they have written a small JavaScript library that uses jQuery under the hood to perform the validation. This leads to cleaner code and reduces the size of the page. For the Contact Us page, enabling unobtrusive JavaScript validation decreased the size of the final HTML from 20.7 KB to 14.9 KB, a reduction of more than 25 percent.

Configuring the validation framework to use unobtrusive validation with jQuery instead of the built-in code that is generated is a two-step activity:

1. Enable unobtrusive validation in the `Web.config` file.
2. Register the jQuery library with the `ScriptManager` in the `Global.asax` file.

The `Global.asax` file is a special ASP.NET file that you add to the root of the site. Inside this file you can write code that responds to global events that happen within your application. These events work the same as other events you've seen so far, such as the `Button`'s `Click` event. The biggest difference is that these events fire for the entire application (your website) and not for a single control or page. For example, when your ASP.NET application starts up, the `Application_Start` event is fired, enabling you to execute your own code. Other events that fire include `BeginRequest`, which fires for each request to the site and `Application_Error`, which fires when an unhandled exception in your site occurs. You make use of this last event in Chapter 18, which deals with debugging and exception handling.

In the next exercise you see how to add the `Global.asax` file to your site and then enable unobtrusive JavaScript validation.

TRY IT OUT Enabling Unobtrusive JavaScript Validation

In this exercise you revisit the current Contact Us page to look at the code that the controls generate. You'll then add a `Global.asax` file and enable unobtrusive JavaScript validation so you can see the effect this has on the code that is generated.

1. Start by opening the `Contact.aspx` file from the `About` folder and then press Ctrl+F5 to view that page in your browser.

2. View the HTML for the page in the browser by right-clicking the page and choosing View Source or View Page Source.

3. Locate the input field for the user's name and then look at the code for the validator that is placed directly below it. You should see something like this:

```
<span id="cpMainContent_ContactForm_RequiredFieldValidator1"
          class="ErrorMessage" style="visibility:hidden;">*</span>
```

4. Scroll down to the end of the code until you see the large chunk of JavaScript code that is responsible for the validation. For the Name field, you'll see something like this:

```
var cpMainContent_ContactForm_RequiredFieldValidator1 = document.all ?
   document.all["cpMainContent_ContactForm_RequiredFieldValidator1"] :
   document.getElementById(
    "cpMainContent_ContactForm_RequiredFieldValidator1");
cpMainContent_ContactForm_RequiredFieldValidator1.controltovalidate
    = "cpMainContent_ContactForm_Name";
cpMainContent_ContactForm_RequiredFieldValidator1.errormessage
    = "Enter your name";
cpMainContent_ContactForm_RequiredFieldValidator1.evaluationfunction
    = "RequiredFieldValidatorEvaluateIsValid";
cpMainContent_ContactForm_RequiredFieldValidator1.initialvalue = "";
```

For each of the validation controls you see similar code, all adding to the size of the page.

5. Go back to VS, right-click the website in the Solution Explorer, and choose Add ➪ Add New Item. Locate the Global Application Class item. You don't have to enter a name because the default of `Global.asax` is the only allowed name for this file.

6. Add the following code to the `Application_Start` method that is already part of the code template of the `Global.asax` file:

VB

```
Sub Application_Start(ByVal sender As Object, ByVal e As EventArgs)
  ScriptManager.ScriptResourceMapping.AddDefinition("jquery",
      New ScriptResourceDefinition With
        { .Path = "~/Scripts/jquery-1.7.2.min.js" })
End Sub
```

C#

```
void Application_Start(object sender, EventArgs e)
{
  ScriptManager.ScriptResourceMapping.AddDefinition("jquery",
      new ScriptResourceDefinition
      {
        Path = "~/Scripts/jquery-1.7.2.min.js"
      }
  );
}
```

The spelling of the word `jquery` (all lowercase) is case sensitive, so make sure you type it exactly as shown here. If you have a newer version of the jQuery library, don't forget to update the version number.

7. Save your changes and close the file.

8. Next, open up the `Web.config` file and modify the following line of code in the `<appSettings>` element. You added that line in Chapter 9. If you don't have this line of code, add it between the `<appSettings>` tags. Either way, you should end up with this code:

```
<appSettings>
  ...
  <add key="ValidationSettings:UnobtrusiveValidationMode" value="WebForms" />
</appSettings>
```

9. Open up the master page and change the reference to the jQuery library so it points to the `ScriptResourceDefinition` you created in the `Global.asax` file like this:

```
<asp:ScriptManager ID="ScriptManager1" runat="server" EnablePageMethods="true">
  <Scripts>
    <asp:ScriptReference Name="jquery" />
  </Scripts>
</asp:ScriptManager>
```

If you didn't make this change, jQuery would be included twice on pages that use the validation controls; once from the code in `Global.asax`, and once from the reference in the `ScriptManager` control. By having the `ScriptReference` point to the `ScriptResourceDefinition` defined in `Global.asax`, ASP.NET sees that it's pointing to the same JavaScript library and includes the reference only once.

10. Save your changes and then request `Contact.aspx` in your browser. Click the Send button and notice that validation still works. Open up the HTML for the page and locate the input field for the name again. Below that field you should see the following code for the validator:

```
<span data-val-controltovalidate="cpMainContent_ContactForm_Name"
    data-val-errormessage="Enter your name"
    id="cpMainContent_ContactForm_RequiredFieldValidator1"
    class="ErrorMessage" data-val="true"
    data-val-evaluationfunction="RequiredFieldValidatorEvaluateIsValid"
    data-val-initialvalue="" style="visibility:hidden;">*</span>
```

11. Scroll down to the end of the code. Notice all the JavaScript you saw previously has now gone. Instead, at the top of the file you now find a `<script>` element that points to a JavaScript file (one of the links that start with `/ScriptResource.axd`) that contains validation code that uses the jQuery library.

How It Works

By enabling unobtrusive JavaScript validation, the validation controls generate different code. Rather than emitting JavaScript code that carries out the validation, the controls now emit HTML5 data attributes on the validation `<span>`. The HTML5 specification enables you to make up your own attributes on elements as long as you prefix them with `data-`. The unobtrusive validation framework makes use of this feature by adding attributes for things like the error message (in `data-val-error-message`), and the JavaScript function that needs to be executed to validate the input control (in `data-val-evaluationfunction`). When you click the submit button, the validation framework kicks in, finds all controls that need to be validated, and then uses the `data-` attributes to determine what needs to be validated and how. Note that other than the validation controls and the JavaScript they generated previously, not much has changed. Your page still contains the same input controls and submit button. But the way validation takes place has changed radically, and now uses the jQuery library and the `data-`attributes added to the HTML elements.

To enable unobtrusive validation you have to enable a key in `Web.config` that you previously disabled. This key signals the validation framework to switch modes and emit unobtrusive JavaScript code instead. Because the validation relies on jQuery, you also need to register the jQuery library with the `ScriptManager`. Unfortunately, you cannot register the library with the `ScriptManager` control; you have to do this in the `Global.asax` with this code:

VB

```
Sub Application_Start(ByVal sender As Object, ByVal e As EventArgs)
  ScriptManager.ScriptResourceMapping.AddDefinition("jquery",
      New ScriptResourceDefinition With
      { .Path = "~/scripts/jquery-1.7.2.min.js" })
End Sub
```

C#

```
void Application_Start(object sender, EventArgs e)
{
  ScriptManager.ScriptResourceMapping.AddDefinition("jquery",
    new ScriptResourceDefinition
    {
      Path = "~/scripts/jquery-1.7.2.min.js"
    }
  );
}
```

This code uses an object initializer to create a new instance of the `ScriptResourceDefinition` class. It sets its `Path` property to the path of the jQuery library. This instance is then added to the `ScriptManager`'s `ScriptResourceMapping` using the `AddDefinition` method. Finally, by pointing the `ScriptManager` control in the master page to this `ScriptResourceDefinition`, jQuery is included on all pages in your site. Although this looks a bit funky, the outcome is pretty straightforward: a link to the referenced jQuery library is added to the output of the page so the validation framework can use it.

Once you've set this up, you never have to worry about it; you can add validation controls to your page as you did before and jQuery and the validation framework of ASP.NET will handle all validation for you. Note that this change does not impact server-side validation at all; that will continue to function as before.

If by now you think that jQuery really rocks, I completely agree. Although it may be a bit difficult to get used to jQuery in the beginning, once you get the hang of it you'll wonder how you ever did without it. And what's even cooler is that you're not limited to what the jQuery library supports out of the box. jQuery has a pluggable architecture, which means you can write plug-ins for it that extend or enhance jQuery's functionality. At the time of writing, the official jQuery plug-in site was taken offline while they were working on a new site. However, searching the web for "jQuery plug-ins" should bring up many useful plug-ins for all kinds of purposes, ranging from image galleries, validation frameworks, visual tooltips, dialog boxes, and more. You're also encouraged to look at *jQuery UI*, a collection of widgets such as tabs, dialog boxes, calendars, draggable content, and more. You can find the jQuery UI project at `http://jQueryUI.com`. If you like jQuery UI, you should also check out *Juice UI* (at `http://juiceui.com`). Juice UI is an open source collection of ASP.NET controls that render jQuery UI elements in the browser. This way, you get the best of both worlds: a rich and programmable framework at the server and lean and clean client-side HTML that leverages jQuery and jQuery UI.

Up until now, you've been working on fairly static web pages. Although jQuery enables you to create dynamically changing pages at the client, the content that's available on the website is still static. To fix that, you can use a database, the topic of the next four chapters. In the next chapter you get a thorough introduction to databases, and the chapters that follow give you in-depth information on working with data in an ASP.NET environment.

PRACTICAL TIPS ON JQUERY

To get the most out of jQuery, follow these short tips:

- Experiment and experiment. At first, jQuery is a bit of an odd technique to master, mostly because of all its curly braces and parentheses. However, by practicing a lot you can become a jQuery master in no time.
- Visit the `jQuery.com` website. Besides very good documentation with many examples showing off jQuery's capabilities, you also find a wealth of articles and links on using jQuery, including links to sites that feature video content.
- Invest some time in browsing the jQuery UI and Juice UI websites. You may not need what they offer right now, or you may feel you're not ready to take that next step yet, but it's good to know what these products have to offer when you're building your next website with a rich client interface.

SUMMARY

In this chapter you were introduced to jQuery, a very popular, open source, client-side JavaScript framework for interacting with the document object model.

The chapter started off by showing you where to get jQuery and how to add it to your site. You then got a quick example of jQuery, which was followed by an introduction to jQuery selectors and filters that enable you to find relevant elements in your page.

The second part of this chapter was devoted to the numerous methods that jQuery supports to apply effects and animations to your matched sets. You saw how to use methods like `css` to manipulate CSS settings, `parent` and `prev` to navigate through the items in your set, and how to work with events to fire code in response to some action like the click of a button or when a form is submitted.

Near the end of the chapter you learned how to use the many animation methods in jQuery to give your page a more compelling and interactive appearance, and you saw how to leverage the power of jQuery in the ASP.NET validation framework.

EXERCISES

1. Imagine that you want to offer your users the possibility of hiding a certain region of a page. For example, you could offer them a link to hide or show the large banner in the Sidebar element with the click of a button. What jQuery does this require? Bonus points if you can find a way to change the text that triggers the code from Hide to Show and vice versa.

2. What's the difference between `slideUp` and `slideDown`? What important argument do both methods accept?

3. What's the difference between jQuery's document ready function, defined with `$(function() ...)`, and the ASP.NET AJAX `pageLoad` method? How can you make good use of this difference?

4. What's the purpose of the `_references.js` file in the `Scripts` folder?

You can find answers to these exercises in Appendix A.

▶ WHAT YOU LEARNED IN THIS CHAPTER

`_references.js`	The special JavaScript file in the `Scripts` folder that triggers IntelliSense for all JavaScript files it references
Chaining	The concept where the result of one method is used as the input of another to create a chain of effects
Filters	Enable you to further refine your jQuery matched set of elements
`Global.asax`	A central file that is used to handle various application-scoped events such as `Application_Start`, `Application_Error`, and more
jQuery	A popular client-side JavaScript framework that simplifies working with the DOM, visual effects, event handling, and Ajax functionality
Matched set	The set of elements that are returned by a jQuery selector
NuGet	The Library Package Manager for Visual Studio to help you manage third-party libraries in your .NET websites and projects
Selectors	A CSS-like syntax to find elements in your page using jQuery

12

Introduction to Databases

WHAT YOU WILL LEARN IN THIS CHAPTER:

- What a database is and which databases are typically used with ASP .NET pages
- What SQL is, how it looks, and how you use it to manipulate data
- What database relationships are and why they are important
- Which tools you have available to manage database objects (such as tables) and how to use them

WROX.COM CODE DOWNLOADS FOR THIS CHAPTER

You can find the wrox.com code downloads for this chapter on the Download Code tab at `www.wrox.com/remtitle.cgi?isbn=1118311809`. The code is in the Chapter 12 download.

Being able to use a database in your ASP.NET websites is just as critical as understanding HTML and CSS: it's almost impossible to build a modern, full-featured website without it. Databases are useful because they enable you to store and retrieve data in a structured way. The biggest benefit of databases is that you can access them at run time in your site, which means you are no longer limited to just the relatively static files you create at design time in Visual Studio. You can use a database to store reviews, musical genres, pictures, information about users (usernames, e-mail addresses, passwords, and so on), log information about who reads your reviews, news articles, and much more, and then access that data from your ASPX pages.

This gives you great flexibility in the data you present, and the way you present it, enabling you to create highly dynamic websites that can adapt to your visitors' preferences, to the content your site has to offer, or even to the roles or access rights that your users have.

To successfully work with a database in an ASPX page, this chapter teaches you how to access databases using a query language called *SQL*—or *Structured Query Language*. This language enables you to retrieve and manipulate data stored in a database. You also see how to use the database tools to create tables and queries.

Although ASP.NET and the .NET Framework offer you many tools and technologies that enable you to work with databases without requiring a firm knowledge of the underlying concepts like SQL, it's still important to understand them. Once you know how to access a database, you'll find it easier to understand and appreciate other technologies, like the ADO.NET Entity Framework (discussed in Chapter 14), which provides easier access to database operations directly from code.

In the chapters that follow, you apply the things you learn in this chapter. In Chapter 13, you see how to use built-in controls to work with data in your database. In Chapter 14, you learn how to use the ADO.NET Entity Framework as an additional layer on top of your database to access data in an object-oriented way with minimal code. Chapter 15, the last of the data-focused chapters, shows you advanced techniques for working with data.

In the following sections, you see what a database is, and what different kinds of databases are available to you.

WHAT IS A DATABASE?

By its simplest definition, a *database* is a collection of data that is arranged so it can be accessed, managed, and updated easily. For the purposes of this book, and the websites you will build, it's also safe to assume that the data in the database is stored in an electronic format.

The most popular type of database is the *relational database*. It's the type of database that is frequently used in websites and is also the type of database that is used in the remainder of this book. However, the relational database is not the only one. Other types exist, including flat-file, NoSQL, object-relational, and object-oriented databases, but these are less common in Internet applications.

A relational database has the notion of *tables*, where data is stored in rows and columns, much like a spreadsheet. Each row in a table contains the complete information about an item that is stored in the table. Each column, on the other hand, contains information about a specific property of the rows in the table.

The term "relational" refers to the way the different tables in the database can be related to each other. Instead of duplicating the same data over and over again, you store repeating data in its own table and then create a relationship to that data from other tables. Consider the table called `Review` in Figure 12-1. This table could store the album reviews that are presented on the Planet Wrox website.

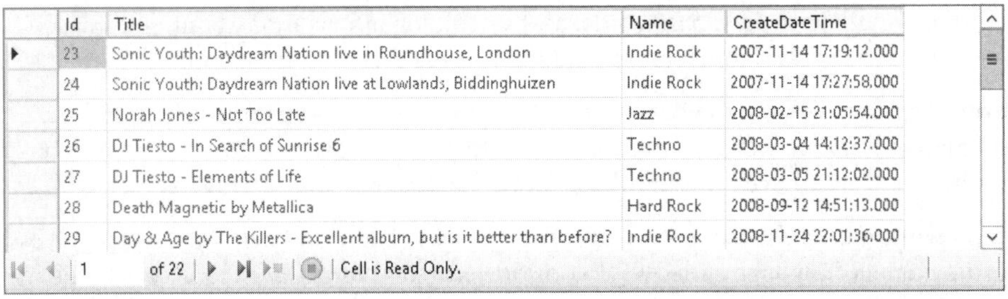

Id	Title	Name	CreateDateTime
23	Sonic Youth: Daydream Nation live in Roundhouse, London	Indie Rock	2007-11-14 17:19:12.000
24	Sonic Youth: Daydream Nation live at Lowlands, Biddinghuizen	Indie Rock	2007-11-14 17:27:58.000
25	Norah Jones - Not Too Late	Jazz	2008-02-15 21:05:54.000
26	DJ Tiesto - In Search of Sunrise 6	Techno	2008-03-04 14:12:37.000
27	DJ Tiesto - Elements of Life	Techno	2008-03-05 21:12:02.000
28	Death Magnetic by Metallica	Hard Rock	2008-09-12 14:51:13.000
29	Day & Age by The Killers - Excellent album, but is it better than before?	Indie Rock	2008-11-24 22:01:36.000

1 of 22 | Cell is Read Only.

FIGURE 12-1

As you can see in Figure 12-1, each review is assigned to a musical genre such as Pop, Indie Rock, or Techno. But what if you wanted to rename the genre Techno to something like Hardcore Techno? You would need to update all the rows that have this genre assigned. If you had other tables that stored a genre, you would need to visit those tables as well and make the changes manually.

A much better solution would be to use a separate table and call it `Genre`, for example. This table could store the name of a genre and an ID (a sequential number, for example) that uniquely identifies each genre. The `Review` table then has a relationship to the `Genre` table and stores only its ID instead of the entire name. The `Genre` table also has a `SortOrder` column, which is used in later examples. Figure 12-2 shows the model for this change.

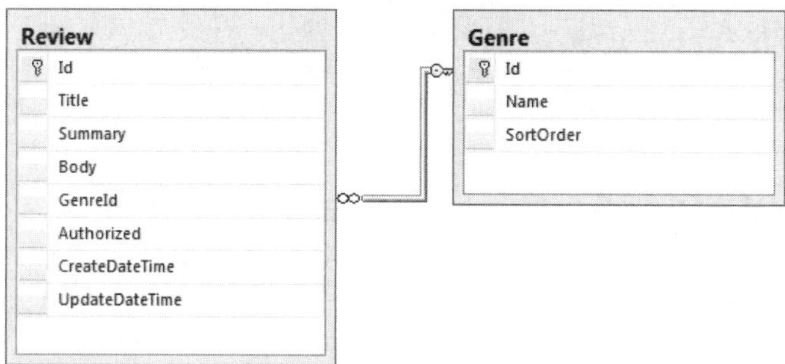

FIGURE 12-2

With just the ID of the genre now stored in the `Review` table, it's easy to rename a genre. All you need to do is change the name of the genre in the `Genre` table, and all tables with a relationship to that genre pick up the change automatically. In database terminology, both `Id` columns in this example are *primary keys* (identified by the lock icon) and are used to uniquely identify each row in the table. `GenreId`, on the other hand, is a *foreign key* which is used to link back to a primary or otherwise unique key in a table. Later in this chapter, you see how to create and make use of relationships in your relational database.

DIFFERENT KINDS OF RELATIONAL DATABASES

You can use many different kinds of databases in your ASP.NET projects, including Microsoft Access, SQL Server, Oracle, SQLite, and MySQL. However, the most commonly used database in ASP.NET websites is probably Microsoft SQL Server. This book focuses on using the Microsoft SQL Server 2012 Express LocalDB edition, because it's free, comes bundled with VS 2012 and has a lot to offer out of the box. Also, because the database format is identical to that of the commercial versions of SQL Server 2012, it's easy to upgrade to those versions at a later stage in the development cycle. This upgrade path is described in more detail in Appendix B.

The only problem with LocalDB is that you can't use all of the database management tools inside Visual Studio. You can create tables and other database objects, but you can't create new queries and diagrams, two features that you'll use regularly when working with databases in your ASP.NET projects.

To overcome this limitation, you should download and install SQL Server Management Studio (SSMS) Express, the free tools to manage all your SQL Server databases, including LocalDB, Express, and the commercial versions of SQL Server (although in the latter case you probably want to use the more feature rich version of the tools that ship with the main product.)

In the next sections you see how to acquire and install SQL Server Management Studio Express. The sections that follow then show you how to use it to manage your databases and the data they contain.

> ***NOTE*** *Installing SQL Server and SSMS can be tricky. If you get stuck, be sure you visit this book's forum at* `http://p2p.wrox.com` *to find a helping hand.*

Installing SQL Server 2012 Express

You can download SQL Server Management Studio Express from the following page at the Microsoft site: `http://tinyurl.com/SqlExpress2012`. If this link no longer works, you can go to `www.microsoft.com/express/database/` instead and click the Download button. Alternatively, you can go to the main downloads page at `www.microsoft.com/downloads` and search for "SQL Server 2012 Management Studio Express."

In all cases, make sure you download and install the 2012 version of Management Studio, and not an older version. Also, if you don't have SQL Server Express installed, download the package that contains both the Express database engine and the Management Studio tools (it should have a name such as Express with Tools or something similar.) You don't need it in the exercises in this and the next three chapters, but it's used in Appendix B that shows you how to configure other versions of Visual Studio. It's quite a large download (around 700 MB if you choose Express with Tools) but well worth the time downloading.

After you have downloaded the Management Studio setup file (optionally with the Express database engine included), run the installer and follow the on-screen instructions. When asked for the Installation Type, choose for a New SQL Server stand-alone installation. This option enables you to choose Management Tools as a component to install later in the Setup Wizard. If you're also installing the database engine, accept `SqlExpress` as the name for the instance. If that name is already taken, it means you already have SQL Server Express installed locally. If this version is SQL Server 2012 (use the Programs and Features option of the control panel in Windows to find out), you can skip installing the Database Engine Services components. If you have a different version installed, you can still install SQL Server 2012 side by side. In that case, choose a name such as `Sql2012Express` for the named instance. From then on, use this name whenever this book refers to `SqlExpress` as the named instance.

Now that SQL Server Management Studio is installed, it's time to look at ways to manage data in SQL Server database. SQL Server supports a query language called SQL that lets you do just that.

USING SQL TO WORK WITH DATABASE DATA

To get data in and out of a database, you need to use *Structured Query Language (SQL)*. This is the de facto language for querying relational databases that almost all relational database systems understand. A number of clear standards exist, with the most popular one being the ANSI 92 SQL standard. Besides the grammar that this standard supports, many database vendors have added their own extensions to the language, giving it a lot more flexibility and power on their own system, at the cost of decreased interoperability with other systems.

Microsoft SQL Server 2012 is no exception, and supports most of the grammar that has been defined in the ANSI 92 SQL standard. On top of this standard, Microsoft has added some proprietary extensions. Collectively, the two are referred to as *T-SQL*, or *Transact SQL*. I'll stick to the term SQL for the remainder of this book.

In the following sections, you see how to use SQL targeting a SQL Server 2012 database to retrieve and manipulate data in your database. However, before you can write your first SQL statement, you need to know how to connect to your database first. The following exercise shows you how to create a sample database from a SQL script file that comes with the downloadable code for this book.

TRY IT OUT Creating the SQL Server Sample Database

In this exercise you learn how to create and work with a database using Visual Studio. To give you something to work with, the code download for this chapter contains a SQL script that creates two tables and a few sample rows in your database. You can use these rows to test out the SQL queries that are shown throughout this chapter. This database is used only for this chapter, and, as such, you don't have to create it to follow along with the Planet Wrox website. However, by creating it with the following instructions you have a nice test database to test out SQL queries.

1. Start by creating a folder called **`Databases`** in the root of your C drive. This serves as a nice central location for your databases, which makes them easier to manage. If you decide to use a different location, make sure the folder is not located in your `Documents` folder or you'll run into permissions problems later. It's recommended to use `C:\Databases` for the walk-throughs in this book.
2. Start SQL Server Management Studio from the Windows Start menu or Start screen.
3. Log in to the SQL Server LocalDB instance by entering **`(localdb)\v11.0`** in the Server Name field as shown in Figure 12-3, and click Connect.

FIGURE 12-3

4. After you log in to the database, you should see the Object Explorer (shown in Figure 12-4) on the left. If you don't see it, choose View ➪ Object Explorer from the main menu or press F8.

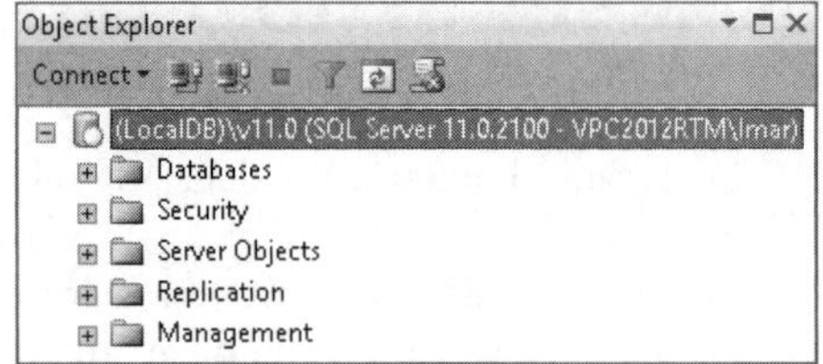

FIGURE 12-4

5. Right-click the Databases node (visible in Figure 12-4) and choose New Database. Type **PlanetWroxTemp** as the name. Don't use PlanetWrox as the name, because you'll be using that for later exercises in the book. In the Database Files section of the screen, type **`C:\Databases`** in the Path column for both rows. You may need to scroll to the right to see the Path column. Your dialog box should end up as shown in Figure 12-5.

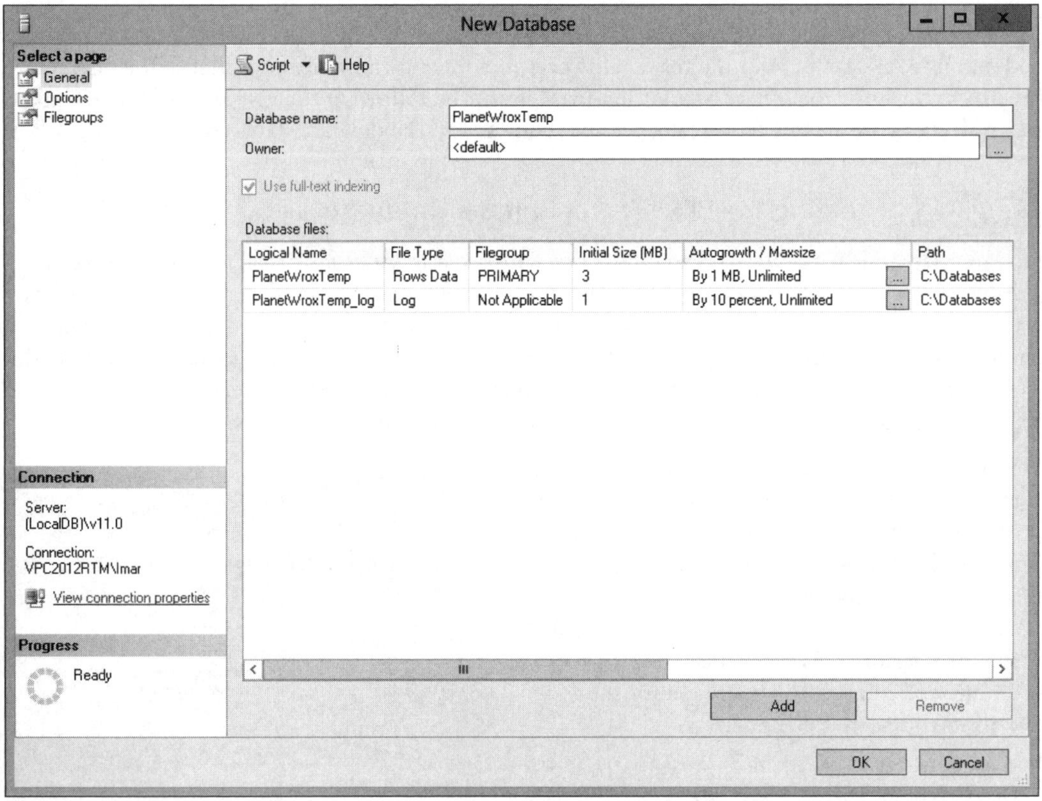

FIGURE 12-5

Click OK to create the database.

6. Press Ctrl+O to bring up a dialog box that lets you select a file. Browse to the folder `C:\BegASPNET\Resources\Chapter 12`. If you don't have this folder, refer to the Introduction of this book to learn how to acquire the code that comes with this book. Select the `Create Planet Wrox Database.sql` file.

7. On the SQL Editor toolbar (shown in Figure 12-6) select the PlanetWroxTemp database from the drop-drown list.

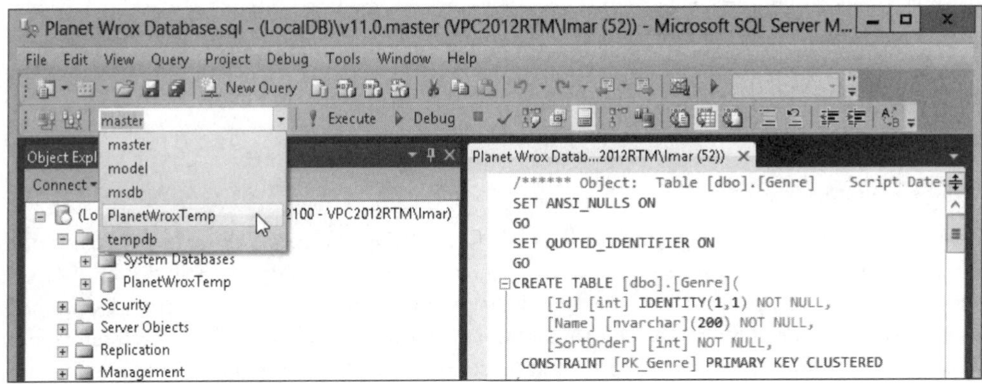

FIGURE 12-6

This makes the PlanetWroxTemp database the active database, so any queries you execute in the query editor window will target that database.

8. Click the Execute button on the SQL Editor toolbar or press F5. This executes the query and creates two tables along with some sample rows. You can take a look at the SQL statements if you want; the concept of inserting the sample rows is explained later in this chapter.

9. On the Object Explorer, click the Refresh icon on the toolbar and then expand Databases, then your new database, and then the Tables node. You should see the `Genre` and `Review` tables appear as shown in Figure 12-7.

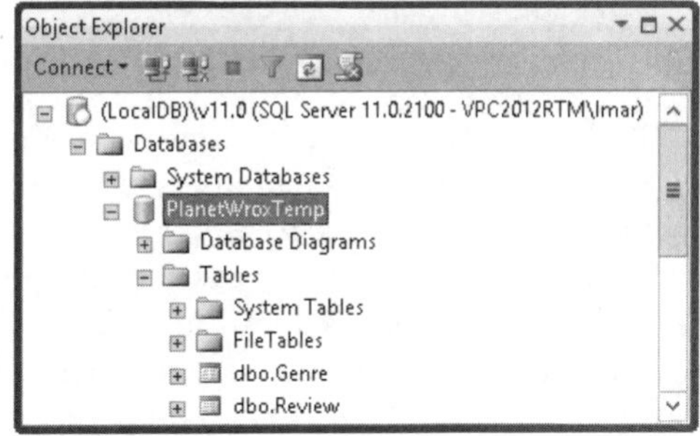

FIGURE 12-7

How It Works

In this exercise you created a new database called PlanetWroxTemp and stored it in the folder `C:\Databases`. The SQL file you executed against this database contains SQL code to create two tables called `Genre` and `Review`. The exact SQL code to create these tables is not so important now; later in this chapter you learn how to create your own tables using SSMS. The file contains SQL `INSERT` statements to add data to these tables. You learn more about the `INSERT` statement in the "Creating Data" section later in this chapter.

When you have a connection to your database in SSMS, you can work with the objects it contains. In the next section you see how you can access and change the data in the tables in your database.

RETRIEVING AND MANIPULATING DATA WITH SQL

When interacting with databases, you'll spend a good deal of time retrieving and manipulating data. Most of it comes down to four distinct types of operations, grouped under the *CRUD* acronym: *Create*, *Read*, *Update*, and *Delete*.

Because these data operations are so crucial, the next couple of sections show you how to use them in detail.

Reading Data

To read data from a database, you typically use a few different concepts. First, you need to indicate the columns that you want to retrieve from the table you are querying. You do that with the `SELECT` statement. You need to indicate the table(s) you want to select the data from using the `FROM` keyword. Then you need a way to filter the data, making sure only the rows you're interested in are returned. You can filter the data using the `WHERE` clause in the SQL statement. Finally, you can order your results using the `ORDER BY` clause.

Selecting Data

To read data from one or more database tables, you use the `SELECT` statement. In its most basic form, the `SELECT` statement looks like this:

```
SELECT ColumnName [, OtherColumnNames] FROM TableName
```

Here, the parts between the square brackets are considered optional. For example, to retrieve all rows from the `Genre` table and select only their `Id` and `Name` columns, you use this SQL statement:

```
SELECT Id, Name FROM Genre
```

Right after the `SELECT` statement comes a comma-separated list of column names. You can have only one or as many columns as you like here. Instead of specifying the column names explicitly, you can also use the asterisk (`*`) character to indicate you want all columns to be returned. However, using `SELECT *` is usually considered a poor programming practice as you're usually selecting more columns than you need, causing unnecessary overhead. It's better to define each column you want to retrieve explicitly. If you want to rename the column in the result set, you use the `AS` keyword, like this:

```
SELECT Id AS GenreId, Name FROM Genre
```

To limit the number of rows retrieved from a table, you use the `TOP` keyword followed by the maximum number of rows. To get predictable results, you typically use an `ORDER BY` clause. Without that, the order of rows is not guaranteed and `TOP` may return different results each time you call it. Here's a quick example that retrieves the first three genres:

```
SELECT TOP 3 Id, Name FROM Genre ORDER BY Name
```

SSMS by default uses `TOP 200` to limit the number of rows retrieved when you open a table.

Right after the `FROM` keyword, you specify the name of the table from which you want to retrieve data. The previous example showed only one table (the `Genre` table), but you see later that you can also specify multiple tables using joins.

> ***NOTE*** *Although the SQL language is not case sensitive, it's common practice to write all keywords such as* `SELECT` *and* `FROM` *in all caps. Additionally, this book uses Pascal casing—where each new word is capitalized—for names of tables, columns, and so on. For example, the date and time a certain review is created are stored in a column called* `CreateDateTime` *in the* `Review` *table.*

Filtering Data

To filter data, you use the `WHERE` clause, with which you indicate the criteria that you want your data to match. For example, to retrieve the ID of the Grunge genre you use the following SQL statement:

```
SELECT Id FROM Genre WHERE Name = 'Grunge'
```

Note that the word Grunge is wrapped in single quotes. This is required for text data types and dates when you filter data or want to send values to an `INSERT` or `UPDATE` statement that enables you to create new or change existing rows, as explained later. You can't use them for numeric or boolean types, though, so to get the name of the genre with an ID of 8 you would use the following statement:

```
SELECT Name FROM Genre WHERE Id = 8
```

The preceding two examples show a `WHERE` clause that uses the equals operator for an exact match. However, you can also use other operators for different criteria. The following table lists a few popular comparison operators you can use in your `WHERE` clauses.

OPERATOR	DESCRIPTION
=	The *equals* operator matches only when the left side and the right side of the comparison are identical.
>	The *greater than* operator matches when the left side of the comparison represents a larger value than the right side.
>=	The *greater than or equal* operator matches when the left side of the comparison is equal to or larger than the right side.
<	The *less than* operator matches when the left side of the comparison represents a smaller value than the right side.
<=	The *less than or equal* operator matches when the left side of the comparison is equal to or smaller than the right side.
<>	The *not equals* operator does the reverse of the equals operator and matches when the left side and the right side of the comparison are different.

To combine multiple `WHERE` criteria, SQL supports a number of logical operators such as `AND` and `OR`. In addition, it supports other operators to search for text and to specify ranges. The following table lists a few of the operators and describes what they are used for.

OPERATOR	DESCRIPTION
`AND`	Enables you to join two expressions. For example, the `WHERE` clause `WHERE Id > 20 AND Id < 30` gives you all rows with IDs that fall between 20 and 30 (with 20 and 30 themselves not included).
`OR`	Enables you to define multiple criteria of which only one has to match (although more matches are allowed). For example, this `WHERE` clause `WHERE GenreId = 5 OR GenreId = 8` gives you all the rows with a `GenreId` of 5 or 8.
`BETWEEN`	Enables you to specify a range of values that you want to match with a lower and upper bound. For example, `WHERE Id BETWEEN 10 AND 35` gives you all rows whose IDs are between 10 and 35 (including 10 and 35 themselves if they exist in the database).
`LIKE`	Used to determine if a value matches a specific pattern. You can use wildcards like `%` to match any string of zero or more characters, and the underscore (_) to match a single character. For example, the `WHERE` clause `WHERE Name LIKE '%rock%'` returns all genres that have `rock` in their name, including Indie Rock, Hard Rock, and so on.

If no rows match the `WHERE` clause, you don't get an error, but you simply get zero results back.

After you have defined your filtering requirements with the `WHERE` clause, you may want to change the order in which the results are returned from the database. You do this with the `ORDER BY` clause.

Ordering Data

The `ORDER BY` clause comes at the end of the SQL statement and can contain one or more column names or expressions, which can optionally include `ASC` or `DESC` to determine if items are sorted in ascending order (with `ASC`, which is the default if you leave out the keyword) or in descending order (using `DESC`).

For example, to retrieve all genres from the `Genre` table and sort them alphabetically by their name in ascending order, you can use this SQL statement:

```
SELECT Id, Name FROM Genre ORDER BY Name
```

Because ascending is the default order, you don't need to specify the `ASC` keyword explicitly, although you could if you wanted to. The next example is functionally equivalent to the preceding example:

```
SELECT Id, Name FROM Genre ORDER BY Name ASC
```

If you wanted to return the same rows but sort them in reverse order on their `Name` column, you use this syntax:

```
SELECT Id, Name FROM Genre ORDER BY Name DESC
```

You can order by columns in the `ORDER BY` statement that are not part of the `SELECT` statement as shown in this snippet:

```
SELECT Id, Name FROM Genre ORDER BY SortOrder DESC
```

In the next exercise, you see how to perform a number of queries against the sample database, giving you a good idea of how different queries affect the results returned from the database.

TRY IT OUT Selecting Data from the Sample Database

In this exercise you use the database that you created in an earlier exercise. This database is used only for the samples in this chapter, so don't worry if you mess things up. Note that all the exercises in this chapter use SQL Server Management Studio to work with your database. In later chapters you see how to use VS to connect to your SQL Server database as well.

1. Open up SQL Server Management Studio if you don't have it open anymore and log in to `(localdb)\v11.0` as shown earlier. Expand the Databases node, then your PlanetWroxTemp database, and then the Tables node. You should see the two tables, `Genre` and `Review`, as shown earlier in Figure 12-7.

2. Right-click the `Genre` table and choose Edit Top 200 Rows. In the Document Window you should now see a list with all the available genres in the `Genre` table, shown in Figure 12-8.

   VPC2012RTM\LOCA...Temp - dbo.Genre

Id	Name	SortOrder
1	Rap and Hip-Hop	14
2	Pop	12
3	Jazz	8
4	Hard Rock	3
5	Indie Rock	7
6	Punk	1
7	Rock	2
8	Grunge	4
9	Alternative Rock	9
10	Reggae	11
11	Industrial	10
12	Techno	5

   1 of 12

   FIGURE 12-8

   Note that this is not just a list with all the rows in the `Genre` table. It's actually the result of a SQL `SELECT` query that is executed when you open the window. To see the query behind this list, ensure that the Query Designer toolbar, shown in Figure 12-9, is displayed on-screen. If the toolbar isn't visible, right-click an existing toolbar and choose Query Designer.

   On this toolbar, click the Show Diagram pane, the Show Criteria pane, and the Show SQL pane buttons to open their respective windows. The first four buttons on the toolbar should now be in a pressed state and the Document Window is split in four regions, with each region corresponding to one of the buttons on the toolbar. Figure 12-10 shows the entire Document Window with the four panes.

   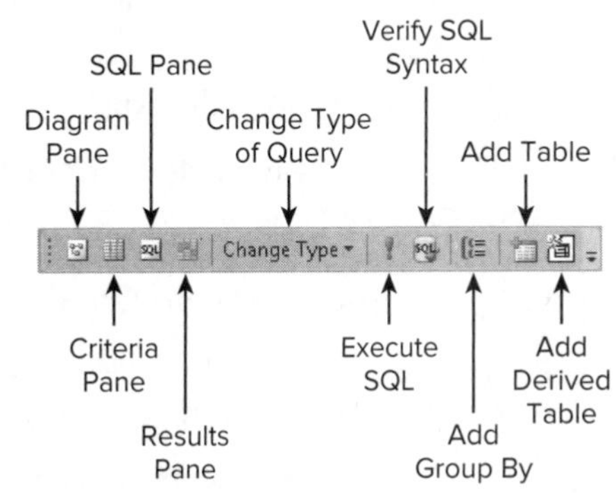

   FIGURE 12-9

   The SQL pane displays the SQL statement that is used to retrieve the genres that are displayed in the Results pane. In this case, the SQL statement reads `SELECT TOP (200) Id, Name, SortOrder FROM Genre` to retrieve all columns and the first 200 rows from the table, but you can easily change that.

3. In the SQL pane, modify the query as follows:

```
SELECT Id, Name, SortOrder FROM Genre WHERE Id
> 4
```

4. To make sure the SQL statement is valid, click the Verify SQL Syntax button on the toolbar and fix any errors your SQL statement may contain. Next, click the Execute SQL button (the one with the

red exclamation mark on it) or press Ctrl+R. In both cases, the SQL statement is executed and the Results pane is updated to show all genres with an ID larger than 4. In your SQL pane, the query is now split over multiple lines to improve legibility. The SQL language enables you to spread your statements over multiple lines without the need for a line continuation character.

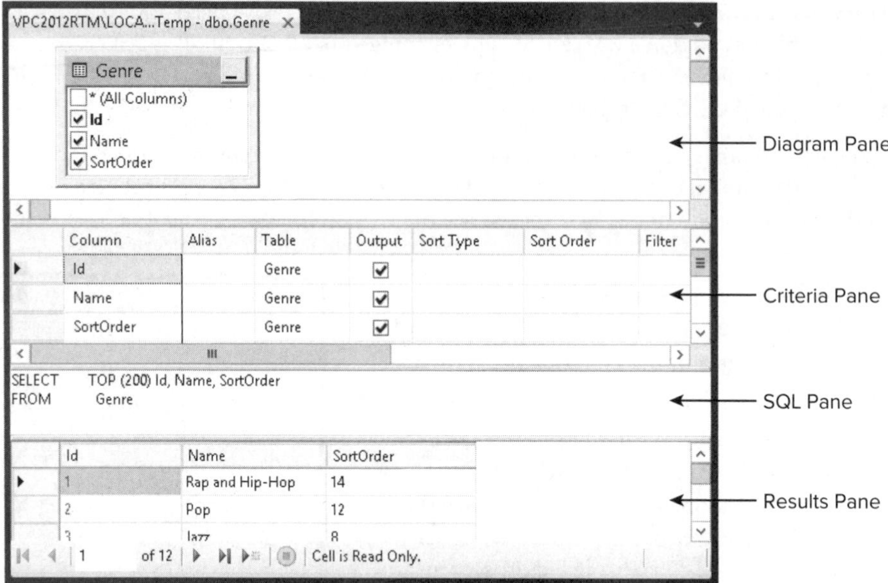

FIGURE 12-10

5. Now take a look at the Diagram pane—the top part of the dialog box in Figure 12-10 that shows your table diagram. In the Diagram pane you can check and uncheck column names to determine whether they end up in the query. Deselect the `SortOrder` column (don't accidentally change the check mark of the Output column in the Criteria pane instead). Note that it also gets removed from the Criteria pane and the SQL statement in the SQL pane (visible in Figure 12-11).

6. Take a look at the Criteria pane in Figure 12-11. It shows the two columns you are selecting. In the Filter column it shows the expression that filters all genres with an ID larger than 4.

   In this pane you can modify the query without manually writing a lot of code. To see how you can apply an additional filter, type **`LIKE '%rock%'`** in the Filter cell for the `Name` row. This limits the results to all genres that contain the word `rock` and that have an ID that is larger than 4. If you press Ctrl+R again, the Results pane is updated to reflect the change in the query.

   Notice how Visual Studio added an N before your search term (see Figure 12-12). You see why this is in the How it Works section following this exercise.

7. To determine the sort order, you can use the Sort Type column. You can do this for visible columns (those that have their Output check box checked end up in the final result set) but also for other columns. To order by the `SortOrder` column, click the cell under `Name` once. It changes and now shows a drop-down list instead. Choose `SortOrder` from the drop-down list. When you click or tab away from the field, SSMS places a check mark in the Output column. You can click that check mark to remove the column again from the output so it remains available for ordering and

filtering, but won't show up in the query results. However, for this exercise you should leave that column selected.

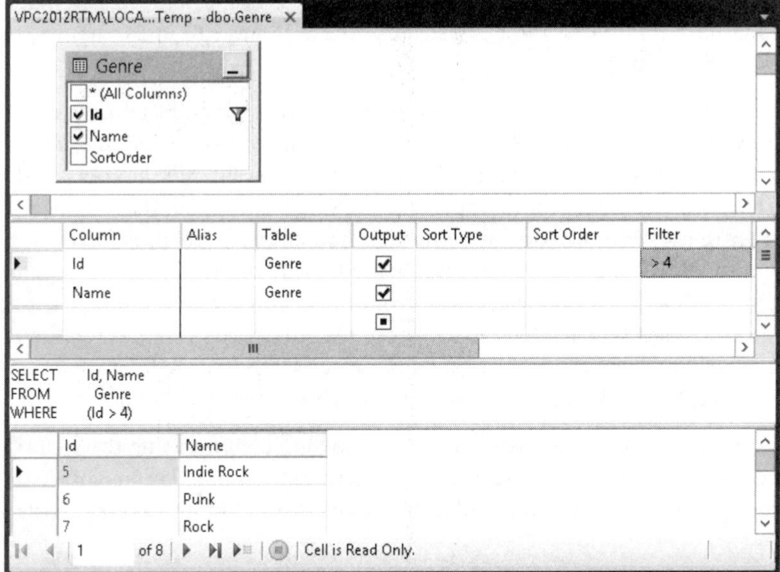

FIGURE 12-11

8. In the Sort Type column, choose Descending from the drop-down list for the `SortOrder`. Your final Criteria pane now looks like Figure 12-12.

Column	Alias	Table	Output	Sort Type	Sort Order	Filter
Id		Genre	☑			> 4
Name		Genre	☑			LIKE N'%rock%'
SortOrder		Genre	☑	Descending	1	

FIGURE 12-12

While you make your changes using the Diagram and Criteria panes, SSMS continuously updates the SQL pane. Your final SQL statement should now include the extra `WHERE` clause and the `ORDER BY` statement:

```
SELECT Id, Name, SortOrder
FROM Genre
WHERE (Id > 4) AND (Name LIKE N'%rock%')
ORDER BY SortOrder DESC
```

9. Press Ctrl+R again (or click the Execute SQL button on the toolbar) and the Results pane shows the rows from the `Genre` table that match your criteria, visible in Figure 12-13.

Note that the rows are now sorted in descending order based on the `SortOrder` column.

FIGURE 12-13

How It Works

The Query Designer in SSMS is a very helpful tool for creating new queries against your database. Instead of hand-coding the entire SQL statement in the SQL pane, you use the Diagram and Criteria panes to create your queries visually. Of course, you can still use the SQL pane to make manual tweaks to the SQL code that SSMS generates for you.

The final query you executed returned all the rows that contain the word *rock* and that had an ID larger than 4. The query shown in step 8 has a `WHERE` clause that consists of two parts: the first part limits the rows returned to those with an ID larger than 4. The second part filtered the rows to those that contain the text *rock*. The two criteria are both applied at the same time using the `AND` keyword, so only rows with an ID larger than 4 *and* the word *rock* in their name are returned. Effectively, this returns the Alternative Rock, Indie Rock, and Rock genres, while leaving out the Hard Rock genre because it has an ID of 4. SSMS adds the capital letter N in front of the filter text to indicate this is a Unicode data type. The Unicode data type enables you to store text for many different foreign languages. In your own queries you can usually leave out the N because SQL Server will figure it out for you. For more information on the N, check out this article: `http://tinyurl.com/39s8wn7`.

At the end, the result set is sorted in descending order on the `SortOrder` column using the syntax `ORDER BY SortOrder DESC`. Notice that `SortOrder` is an arbitrarily chosen name. You can easily give this column a different name, or order on a different column like the `Name` column to retrieve the genres in alphabetical order.

In this example, you saw how to retrieve data from a single table. However, in most real-world applications you get your data from multiple tables that are somehow related to each other. You define this relationship in your SQL syntax using the `JOIN` keyword.

Joining Data

A `JOIN` in your query enables you to express a relationship between one or more tables. For example, you can use a `JOIN` to find all the reviews from the `Review` table that have been published in a specific genre and then select some columns from the `Review` table together with the `Name` of the genre.

The basic syntax for a `JOIN` looks like the following bolded code:

```
SELECT
  SomeColumn
FROM
  LeftTable
INNER JOIN RightTable ON LeftTable.SomeColumn = RightTable.SomeColumn
```

The first part is the standard `SELECT` part of the query that you saw earlier, and the second part introduces the keywords `INNER JOIN` to express the relationship between the two tables. This query only returns the rows in the table `LeftTable` with a corresponding row in `RightTable`. For example, to return the ID and the title of a review together with the name of the genre it belongs to, you use this SQL statement:

```
SELECT
  Review.Id, Review.Title, Genre.Name
FROM
  Review
INNER JOIN Genre ON Review.GenreId = Genre.Id
```

Note that in the `SELECT` statement each column is prefixed with the table name. This makes it clear what table you are referring to and avoids conflicts when multiple tables have similar column names (like the `Id` column that exists in both tables).

In addition to an `INNER JOIN` that returns only matching rows, you can also use an `OUTER JOIN`. The `OUTER JOIN` enables you to retrieve rows from one table regardless of whether they have a matching row in another table. The following example returns a list with all the genres in the system together with the reviews in each genre:

```
SELECT
  Genre.Id, Genre.Name, Review.Title
FROM
  Genre
LEFT OUTER JOIN Review ON Genre.Id = Review.GenreId
```

For each review assigned to a genre, a unique row is returned that contains the review's title. However, even if a genre has no reviews assigned, the row is still returned as shown in Figure 12-14.

Id	Name	Title
5	Indie Rock	Sonic Youth: The Eternal - Takes time to get used but th...
5	Indie Rock	Farm by Dinosaur Jr
6	Punk	21st Century Breakdown by Green Day
7	Rock	*NULL*
8	Grunge	*NULL*
9	Alternative Rock	Love Hate & Then There's you by The Von Bondies

1 of 26 | Cell is Read Only.

FIGURE 12-14

The genre Indie Rock is repeated multiple times, once for each review in the `Review` table that has been assigned to that genre. The Punk genre has only one review attached to it, so it's listed only once. Finally, the Rock and Grunge genres have no reviews associated with them. However, because the SQL statement uses a `LEFT OUTER JOIN`, those two genres (listed on the left side of the `JOIN`) are still returned. Instead of the `Title` of a review, that column now contains a `NULL` value to indicate there is no associated review.

Besides the `LEFT OUTER JOIN`, there is also a `RIGHT OUTER JOIN` that returns all the rows from the table listed at the right side of the `JOIN`.

In addition, you can use other joins including cross joins and self joins. For a detailed description of these types of joins, pick up a copy of the book *Beginning Microsoft SQL Server 2012 Programming* by Paul Atkinson and Robert Vieira, Wrox, 2012 (ISBN: 978-1-1181-0228-2).

You see how to use a very common type of join, the `INNER JOIN`, in the next Try It Out.

TRY IT OUT Joining Data

To join data from two tables, you need to write a `JOIN` statement in your code. To help you write the code, SSMS adds a `JOIN` for you whenever you add related tables to the Diagram pane. However, sometimes this `JOIN` is not correct, so you'll need to check the code to see if it's okay.

1. Still in your test database in SSMS, right-click the `Review` table and choose Edit Top 200 Rows. You'll see all the reviews in the table appear. Next, enable the Diagram, Criteria, and SQL panes by clicking their respective buttons on the Query Designer toolbar.
2. Right-click an open spot of the Diagram pane next to the `Review` table and choose Add Table. Alternatively, choose Query Designer ➪ Add Table from the main menu.
3. In the dialog box that opens, click the `Genre` table and then click the Add button. Finally, click Close.
4. The SQL statement that SSMS generated looks like this:

   ```
   SELECT TOP (200) Review.Id, Review.Title, Review.Summary, Review.Body,
      Review.GenreId, Review.Authorized, Review.CreateDateTime, Review.UpdateDateTime
   FROM Review
   INNER JOIN Genre ON Review.GenreId = Genre.Id
   ```

   SSMS correctly detected the relationship defined in the database between the `GenreId` column of the `Review` table and the `Id` column of the `Genre` table, and applied the correct `JOIN` for you.
5. To see how you can create `JOIN`s yourself without writing code directly, you'll manually re-create the `JOIN`. First, right-click the line that is drawn between the two tables in the Diagram pane and choose Remove. The SQL statement now contains a `CROSS JOIN`.
6. Next, click the `GenreId` column of the `Review` table in the Diagram pane once and drag it onto the `Id` column of the `Genre` table. As soon as you release the mouse, SSMS creates a new `INNER JOIN` in the SQL pane for you with the exact same code as you saw earlier. SQL Server understands the primary and foreign keys that have been set up in the database tables and correctly joins the primary key of the `Genre` table (`Id`) to the foreign key of the `Reviews` table (`GenreId`).
7. Modify the SQL statement so it selects only the `Id` and the `Title` columns from the `Review` table and the `Name` column from the `Genre` table. You can do this by altering the SQL statement manually or by unchecking the columns in the Diagram pane. Your SQL statement should now look like this:

   ```
   SELECT TOP (200) Review.Id, Review.Title, Genre.Name
   FROM Review INNER JOIN Genre ON Review.GenreId = Genre.Id
   ```

8. Finally, press Ctrl+R to execute the query. Your Results pane should now look like Figure 12-15.

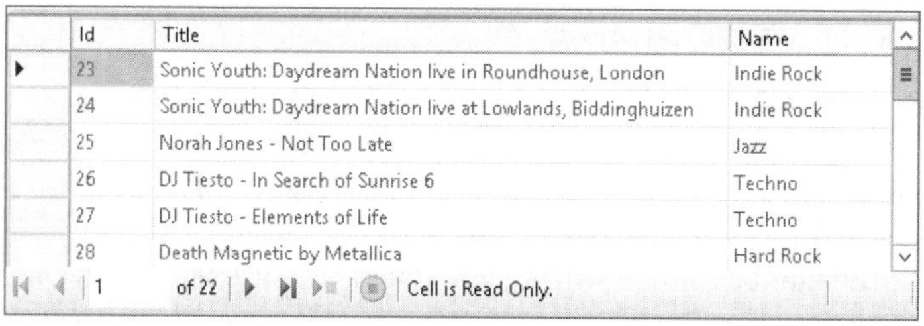

Id	Title	Name
23	Sonic Youth: Daydream Nation live in Roundhouse, London	Indie Rock
24	Sonic Youth: Daydream Nation live at Lowlands, Biddinghuizen	Indie Rock
25	Norah Jones - Not Too Late	Jazz
26	DJ Tiesto - In Search of Sunrise 6	Techno
27	DJ Tiesto - Elements of Life	Techno
28	Death Magnetic by Metallica	Hard Rock

1 of 22 | Cell is Read Only.

FIGURE 12-15

How It Works

By using a `JOIN` in your SQL statement, you tell the database how to relate rows to each other. In this example, you joined the `GenreId` column of the `Review` table to the actual `Id` of the `Genre` table:

```
SELECT
  Review.Id, Review.Title, Genre.Name
FROM
  Review
INNER JOIN Genre ON Review.GenreId = Genre.Id
```

With this `JOIN`, you can retrieve data from multiple tables and present them in a single result set. SQL Server returns the correct genre name for each review, as is shown in Figure 12-15.

In addition to selecting data, you also need to be able to insert data into the database. You do this with the `INSERT` statement.

Creating Data

To insert new rows in a SQL Server table, you use the `INSERT` statement. It comes in a few different flavors, but in its simplest form it looks like this:

```
INSERT INTO TableName (Column1 [, Column2]) VALUES (Value1 [, Value2])
```

Just as with the `WHERE` clause, you need to enclose string and date values in single quotes, but you can enter numbers and boolean values directly in your SQL statement. The following snippet shows how to insert a new row in the `Genre` table:

```
INSERT INTO Genre (Name, SortOrder) VALUES ('Tribal House', 20)
```

The `Id` column of the `Genre` table is set up to generate a value automatically when you insert a new row (you see more of this concept, called *identity columns*, later in this chapter). Because it's generated by SQL Server, it's not part of this query. After you have created some data, you may want to edit it again. You do this with the `UPDATE` statement.

Updating Data

To update data in a table, you use the `UPDATE` statement:

```
UPDATE TableName SET Column1 = NewValue1 [, Column2 = NewValue2] WHERE
      Column3 = Value3
```

With the `UPDATE` statement, you use `Column = Value` constructs to indicate the new value of the specified column. You can have as many of these constructs as you want, with a maximum of one per column in the table. To limit the number of items that get updated, you use the `WHERE` clause, just as with selecting data as you saw earlier. Without a `WHERE` clause, all rows will be affected which is usually not what you want.

The following example updates the row that was inserted with the `INSERT` statement you saw earlier. It sets the `Name` to `Trance` and updates the `SortOrder` to `5` to move the item up a little in sorted lists. It also uses the unique ID of the new row (`13` in this example) in the `WHERE` clause to limit the number of rows that get affected with the `UPDATE` statement.

```
UPDATE Genre SET Name = 'Trance', SortOrder = 5 WHERE Id = 13
```

Obviously, you may also need to delete existing rows. It should come as no surprise that the SQL language uses the `DELETE` statement for this.

Deleting Data

Just as with the `SELECT` and `UPDATE` statements, you can use the `WHERE` clause in a `DELETE` statement to limit the number of rows that get deleted. This `WHERE` clause is often very important, because you will otherwise wipe out the entire table instead of just deleting a few rows. Beware!

When you write a `DELETE` statement, you don't need to specify any column names. All you need to do is indicate the table that you want to delete rows from and an (optional) `WHERE` clause to limit the number of rows that get deleted. The following example deletes the row that was inserted and updated in the previous two examples:

```
DELETE FROM Genre WHERE Id = 13
```

If you leave out the `WHERE` clause, all rows will be deleted from the table.

You see these SQL statements at work in the next exercise.

TRY IT OUT Working with Data in the Sample Database

In this exercise, you put everything you learned so far into practice. In a series of steps, you see how to create a new row in the `Genre` table, select it again to find out its new ID, update it using the `UPDATE` statement, and finally, delete the genre from the database. Although the examples themselves may seem pretty trivial, they are at the core of how SQL works. If you understand the examples from this section, you'll be able to work with the remaining SQL statements in this and coming chapters.

1. Still in SSMS, right-click the `Genre` table and choose Edit Top 200 Rows. If the table was already open with an old query, you need to close it first by pressing Ctrl+F4. This gets rid of the existing SQL statement.

2. Click the first three buttons on the Query Designer toolbar (Diagram, Criteria, and SQL pane) to open up their respective panes.

3. In the SQL pane, remove `TOP (200)` from the SQL statement and then in the Diagram pane, uncheck the `Id` column and leave `Name` and `SortOrder` checked, as shown in Figure 12-16.

   Because the `Id` column gets an auto-generated value from the database, you cannot supply an explicit value for it in an `INSERT` statement.

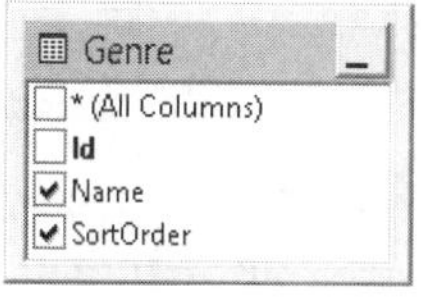

FIGURE 12-16

4. On the Query Designer toolbar click the Change Type button and choose the third option: Insert Values. The query in the SQL pane is updated and now contains a template for the `INSERT` statement:

```
INSERT INTO Genre (Name, SortOrder) VALUES (,)
```

5. Between the parentheses for the `VALUES`, enter a name (between single quotes) and a sort order for your genre separated by a comma:

```
INSERT INTO Genre (Name, SortOrder) VALUES ('Folk', 15)
```

6. Press Ctrl+R to execute the query. You should get a dialog box that tells you that your action caused one row to be affected, as shown in Figure 12-17.

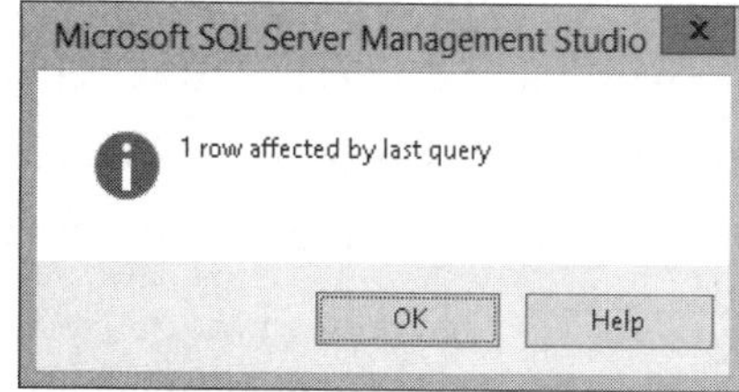

FIGURE 12-17

7. Click OK to dismiss the dialog box.

8. Clear out the entire SQL statement from the SQL pane (you can use Ctrl+A to select the entire SQL statement and then press the Delete key to delete it) and replace it with this code, which selects all the genres and sorts them in descending order:

```
SELECT Id, Name FROM Genre ORDER BY Id DESC
```

9. Press Ctrl+R to execute this `SELECT` statement. The Results pane shows a list of genres with the one you just inserted at the top of the list. Note the ID of the newly inserted row. It should be 13 if you haven't inserted any row before, although it's okay if you have a different ID.

10. Click the Change Type button on the toolbar again, this time choosing Update. Complete the SQL statement that SSMS created for you so it looks like this:

```
UPDATE
  Genre
SET
  Name = 'British Folk',
  SortOrder = 5
WHERE
  Id = 13
```

   Don't forget to replace the number 13 in the SQL statement with the ID you determined in step 9.

11. Press Ctrl+R again to execute the query and you'll get a dialog box informing you that one row has been modified.

12. Once again, clear the SQL pane and then enter and execute the following query by pressing Ctrl+R:

```
SELECT Id, Name FROM Genre WHERE Id = 13
```

Replace the `Id` in the `WHERE` clause with the ID of the row you determined in step 9. You should see the updated row appear.

13. On the Query Designer toolbar, click the Change Type button and choose Delete. SSMS changes the SQL statement so it is now set up to delete the row with an ID of 13:

```
DELETE FROM Genre WHERE (Id = 13)
```

14. Press Ctrl+R to execute the query and delete the row from the database. Click OK to dismiss the confirmation dialog box.

15. To confirm that the row is really deleted, click the Change Type button once more and choose Select. Then choose one or more columns of the `Genre` table in the Diagram pane and press Ctrl+R again. You'll see that this time no rows are returned, confirming that the newly inserted genre has indeed been deleted from the database.

How It Works

In this short exercise, you carried out all four parts of the CRUD acronym, which gave you a look at the life cycle of data in a SQL Server database from creation to deletion.

You started off with an `INSERT` statement:

```
INSERT INTO Genre (Name, SortOrder) VALUES ('Folk', 15)
```

This creates a new row in the `Genre` table. As you see in the next section, the `Id` column of the `Genre` table is an *identity column*, which means that each new row gets a new, sequential ID assigned automatically.

To retrieve that ID, you used a `SELECT` statement with an `ORDER BY` clause that orders the rows on their IDs in descending order, so the most recent ID was put on top of the list. Retrieving the new ID like this in a busy application is not reliable because you may end up with the ID of a row inserted by someone else. You see later in the book how to retrieve the ID in a reliable way, but for the purposes of this exercise, the `ORDER BY` method works well enough.

Armed with the new ID, you executed an `UPDATE` statement to change the `Name` and `SortOrder` of the newly inserted genre. If you want to update only a single column with the `UPDATE` statement—say you want to change only the `Name`—you can simply leave out the other columns. For example, the following `UPDATE` statement changes only the `Name`, leaving all other columns at their original values:

```
UPDATE
  Genre
SET
  Name = 'British Folk'
WHERE
  Id = 13
```

Finally, at the end of the exercise, you executed a `DELETE` statement to get rid of the new row. It's always important to specify a `WHERE` clause when executing a `DELETE` or an `UPDATE` statement to stop you from clearing the entire table or from assigning the same value to all rows.

```
DELETE FROM Genre WHERE (Id = 13)
```

This SQL statement simply deletes the row with an ID of 13. If the row exists, it gets deleted. If the row does not exist, no error is raised, but the dialog box in SSMS shows you that zero rows have been affected. The parentheses are not required in this example, but they help in determining precedence when you have multiple conditions in your `WHERE` clause.

Up to this point, you have seen how to work with existing tables in a database. However, it's also important to understand how to create new tables with relationships yourself. This is discussed in the next section.

CREATING YOUR OWN TABLES

Creating tables in a SQL Server database is easy using the database tools that are part of SSMS. You see how you can create your own tables in the database after the next section, which briefly introduces you to the data types at your disposal in SQL Server.

Data Types in SQL Server

Just as with programming languages like Visual Basic .NET and C#, a SQL Server database uses different data types to store its data. SQL Server 2012 supports more than 30 different data types, most of which look similar to the types used in .NET. The following table lists the most common SQL Server data types together with a description and their .NET counterparts.

SQL 2012 DATA TYPE	DESCRIPTION	.NET DATA TYPE
`bit`	Stores boolean values in a 0 / 1 format (1 = True, 0 = False).	`System.Boolean`
`char / nchar`	Contains fixed-length text. When you store text shorter than the defined length, the text is padded with spaces. The `nchar` stores the data in Unicode format, which enables you to store data for many foreign languages (at the cost of needing twice as much space in the database).	`System.String`
`datetime`	Stores a date and a time in the range 1753/1/1 through 9999/12/31.	`System.DateTime`
`datetime2`	Similar to the `datetime` type, but with a greater precision and range (from 0001/1/1 through 9999/12/31)	`System.DateTime`
`date`	Stores a date without the time element.	`System.DateTime`
`time`	Stores a time without the date element.	`System.TimeSpan`
`decimal`	Enables you to store large, fractional numbers.	`System.Decimal`
`float`	Enables you to store large, fractional numbers.	`System.Double`

continues

(continued)

SQL 2012 DATA TYPE	DESCRIPTION	.NET DATA TYPE
`binary` / `varbinary`	Enables you to store large binary objects such as files. `binary` has a fixed length whereas `varbinary` stores binary objects with a variable length.	`System.Byte[]`
`tinyint`	Used to store integer numbers ranging from 0 to 255.	`System.Byte`
`smallint`	Used to store integer numbers ranging from –32,768 to 32,767.	`System.Int16`
`int`	Used to store integer numbers ranging from –2,147,483,648 to 2,147,483,647.	`System.Int32`
`bigint`	Used to store large integer numbers ranging from –9,223,372,036,854,775,808 to 9,223,372,036,854,775,807.	`System.Int64`
`text` / `ntext`	Used to store large amounts of text. The `ntext` stores the data in Unicode format, which enables you to store data for many foreign languages.	`System.String`
`varchar` / `nvarchar`	Used to store text with a variable length. `nvarchar` stores the data in Unicode format.	`System.String`
`uniqueidentifier`	Stores globally unique identifiers.	`System.Guid`

For a complete list of all the supported data types in SQL Server 2012, check out the MSDN documentation at `http://tinyurl.com/SqlDataTypes`.

Some of these data types enable you to specify the maximum length. When you define a column of type `char`, `nchar`, `varchar`, or `nvarchar` you need to specify the length in characters. For example, an `nvarchar(10)` enables you to store a maximum of 10 characters. For `char` and `nchar`, the value you put in a column is padded with spaces if the value you supply is shorter than the maximum length. The types `varchar` and `nvarchar` also enable you to specify `MAX` as the maximum size. With the `MAX` specifier, you can store data up to 2 GB in a single column. For large pieces of text, like the body of a review, you should consider the `nvarchar(max)` data type. If you have a clear idea about the maximum length for a column (like a ZIP code or a phone number) or you want to explicitly limit the length of it, you should specify that length instead. For example, the title of a review could be stored in an `nvarchar(200)` column to allow up to 200 characters.

Understanding Primary Keys and Identities

To uniquely identify a row in a table, you can set up a *primary key*. A primary key consists of one or more columns in a table that contains a value that is unique across all rows. When you identify a column as a primary key, the database engine ensures that no two rows can end up with the same value. A primary key can consist of just a single column (for example, a numeric column that contains unique numbers for each row in the table such as the `Id` column of the `Genre` table you saw earlier) or it can span multiple columns, where the columns together form a unique ID for the entire row.

SQL Server also supports *identity columns*. An identity column is a numeric column whose sequential values are generated automatically whenever a new row is inserted. They are often used as the primary key for a table. You see how this works in the next section when you create your own tables.

It's not a requirement to give each table a primary key, but it makes your life as a database programmer a lot easier, so it's recommended to always add one to your tables.

Creating tables, primary keys, and identity columns is really easy with SSMS's database tools, as you see in the next Try It Out.

TRY IT OUT Creating Tables in the Table Designer

In this exercise you add two tables to a new database that you use in the Planet Wrox website later. You can delete the test database you created at the beginning of this chapter because you don't need it anymore.

1. Still in SSMS and logged in to the LocalDB SQL Server, right-click the Databases node and choose New Database. In the dialog box that follows, type **`PlanetWrox`** as the name, and then enter **`C:\BegASPNET\Site\App_Data`** as the Path for both rows in the Database Files section of the dialog box (you may need to scroll to the right to see the Path column). This creates the new database in the `App_Data` folder of your website so you can easily connect to it later. Click OK to create the database.

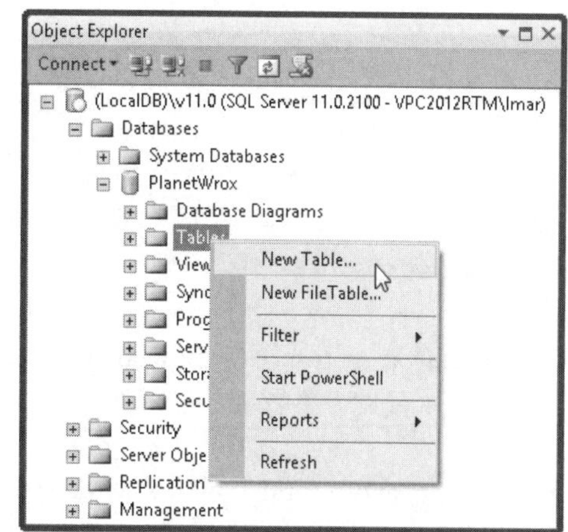

FIGURE 12-18

2. In the Object Explorer, expand Databases and then expand the database you just created. Right-click the Tables node and choose New Table, as shown in Figure 12-18.

3. In the dialog box that follows, you can enter column names and data types that together make up the table definition. Create three columns for the `Id`, `Name`, and `SortOrder` of the `Genre` table so the dialog box ends up as shown in Figure 12-19.

VPC2012RTM\LOCAL...rox - dbo.Table_1*

Column Name	Data Type	Allow Nulls
Id	int	☐
Name	nvarchar(100)	☐
SortOrder	int	☐
		☐

FIGURE 12-19

Make sure you clear the check box for all three items in the Allow Nulls column. This column determines if fields are optional or required. In the case of the `Genre` table, all three columns will be required, so you need to clear the Allow Nulls check box.

4. Next, select the entire row for the `Id` by clicking in the margin on the left (identified by the black arrow in Figure 12-19) and then on the Table Designer toolbar, visible in Figure 12-20, click the second button from the left (with the yellow key on it) to turn the `Id` column into a primary key.

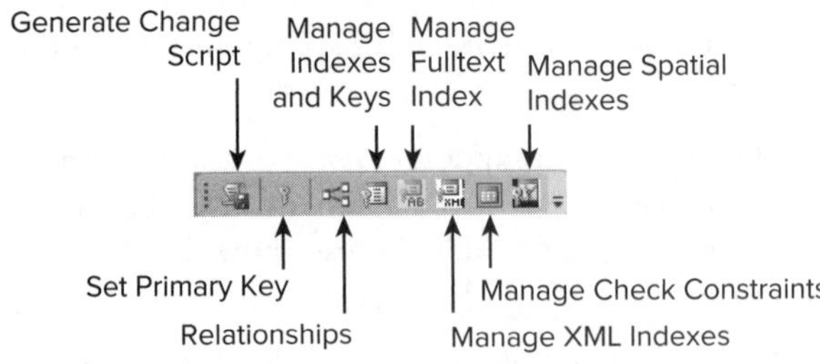

FIGURE 12-20

5. Below the table definition you see the Column Properties, a panel that looks similar to the Properties Grid in VS. With the `Id` column still selected, scroll down a bit on the Column Properties grid until you see Identity Specification. Expand the item and then set (Is Identity) to Yes, as shown in Figure 12-21.

Column Properties

DTS-published	No
Full-text Specification	No
Has Non-SQL Server Subscriber	No
Identity Specification	Yes
(Is Identity)	Yes
Identity Increment	1
Identity Seed	1
Indexable	Yes

(Is Identity)

FIGURE 12-21

6. Press Ctrl+S to save your changes. A dialog box pops up that enables you to provide a name for the table. Type **`Genre`** as the name and click OK to apply your changes. Then press Ctrl+F4 to close the table designer.

7. Create another table by following steps 2 and 3, but this time create a table with the following specifications to hold the CD and concert reviews for the Planet Wrox website.

COLUMN NAME	DATA TYPE	ALLOW NULLS	DESCRIPTION
`Id`	`int`	No	The primary key and identity of the table.
`Title`	`nvarchar(200)`	No	Contains the title of the review.
`Summary`	`nvarchar(max)`	No	Contains a short summary or teaser text for the review.
`Body`	`nvarchar(max)`	Yes	Contains the full body text of the review.

COLUMN NAME	DATA TYPE	ALLOW NULLS	DESCRIPTION
`GenreId`	`int`	No	Contains the ID of a genre that the review belongs to.
`Authorized`	`bit`	No	Determines whether the review is authorized for publication by an administrator. Unauthorized reviews will not be visible on the website.
`CreateDateTime`	`datetime`	No	The date and time the review is created.
`UpdateDateTime`	`datetime`	No	The date and time the review is last updated.

8. Make the `Id` column the primary key again, and set its (Is Identity) property to Yes just as you did in steps 4 and 5.
9. Click the `CreateDateTime` column once and then on the Column Properties grid, type **`getdate()`** in the field for the Default Value or Binding property, as shown in Figure 12-22. This inserts the current date and time for new rows if you don't supply an explicit value.

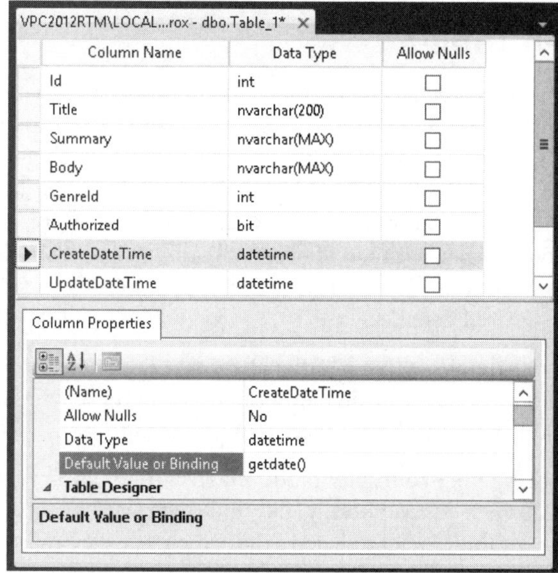

FIGURE 12-22

10. Repeat the preceding step for the `UpdateDateTime` column.
11. When you're done, press Ctrl+S to save the table and call it `Review`. Close the table designer by pressing Ctrl+F4.

How It Works

The Table Designer in SSMS is pretty straightforward. You simply type new column names and define a data type for the column, and you're pretty much done. Some columns, such as the `Id` column in the `Genre` and `Review` tables, require a bit more work. For those columns, you set (Is Identity) to Yes. This means that SQL Server automatically assigns a new sequential number to each new row that you insert. By default, the first row in the table gets an ID of 1, and the ID of subsequent rows is increased by one. You can change the default behavior by setting the Identity Increment and Identity Seed in the Identity Specification element for the column.

You also assigned a *default value* to the `CreateDateTime` and `UpdateDateTime` columns of the `Review` table. Default values are inserted by the database when you don't supply one explicitly in your SQL statements. This means that if your `INSERT` statement does not contain a value for the `CreateDateTime` or `UpdateDateTime` column, the database will insert a default value for you automatically. In the preceding Try It Out, this default value was `getdate()`, which inserts today's date and time automatically. This way, you can easily track when a review was created. In later chapters you see how to update the `UpdateDateTime` column when reviews are updated.

In addition to relationships that are only defined in your own SQL queries as you saw before with the `SELECT` and `JOIN` statements, you can also create relationships in the database. The benefits of relationships and how you can create them in your database are discussed in the next section.

Creating Relationships between Tables

Consider the tables you have created so far. You created a `Genre` table with an `Id` column to uniquely identify a genre row. You also created a `Review` table with a `GenreId` column. Clearly, this column should contain an ID that points to a row in the `Genre` table so you know to which genre a review belongs. Now imagine that you delete a row from the `Genre` table that has reviews attached to it. Without a relationship, the database will let you do that. However, this is causing a great deal of trouble. If you now try to display the genre together with a review, it will fail because there is no longer a matching genre. Similarly, if you want to list all the reviews in your system grouped by genre, you'll miss the ones that belong to the deleted genre.

To avoid these kinds of problems and keep your database in a healthy and consistent state, you can create a relationship between two tables. With a proper relationship set up, the database will stop you from accidentally deleting rows in one table that still have other rows attached to it.

Besides the protection of data, relationships also make your data model clearer. If you look at the database through a diagram (which you use in the next exercise), you'll find that relationships between tables help you better understand how tables are connected, and what data they represent.

You can define a relationship by creating one between the primary key of one table and a column in another table. The column in this second table is referred to as a *foreign key*. In the case of the `Review` and `Genre` tables, the `GenreId` column of the `Review` table points to the primary key column `Id` of the `Genre` table, thus making `GenreId` a foreign key. In the next exercise, you see how to create a relationship between two tables and then execute a SQL statement that shows how the relationship is helping you to protect your data.

TRY IT OUT Creating a Relationship between Two Tables

Before you can visually add a relationship between two tables, you need to add a diagram to your database. A diagram is a visual tool that helps you understand and define your database. On the diagram, you can drag a column from one table to another to create the relationship. In this exercise, you create a relationship between the `Review` and `Genre` tables.

1. On the Object Explorer, expand your Planet Wrox database, right-click the Database Diagrams element (visible in Figure 12-18), and click New Database Diagram. If this is the first time you are adding a diagram to the database, you may get a dialog box asking if you want SSMS to make you the owner of the database. Click Yes to proceed. Don't worry if you don't get this prompt; things will work fine without it. The prompt may be followed by another that indicates that, in order to work with diagrams, SSMS needs to create a few required objects. Again, click Yes to proceed.
2. In the Add Table dialog box that follows, select both tables you created in the previous Try It Out (hold down the Ctrl key while you click each item), click Add to add the tables to the diagram, and then click Close to dismiss the Add Table dialog box.
3. If necessary, arrange the tables in the diagram using drag and drop so they are positioned next to each other.
4. On the `Genre` table, click the left margin of the `Id` column (it should contain the yellow key to indicate this is the primary key of the table) and then drag it onto the `GenreId` column of the `Review` table and release your mouse.
5. Two dialog boxes pop up that enable you to customize the defaults for the relation. In the topmost window, confirm that `Id` is selected from `Genre` as the Primary Key Table and that `GenreId` is selected from `Review` as the Foreign Key Table. Click OK to dismiss the top window. In the dialog box that remains, visible in Figure 12-23, notice how Enforce Foreign Key Constraint is set to Yes. This property ensures that you cannot delete a row from the `Genre` table if it still has reviews attached to it. Click OK to dismiss this dialog box as well.

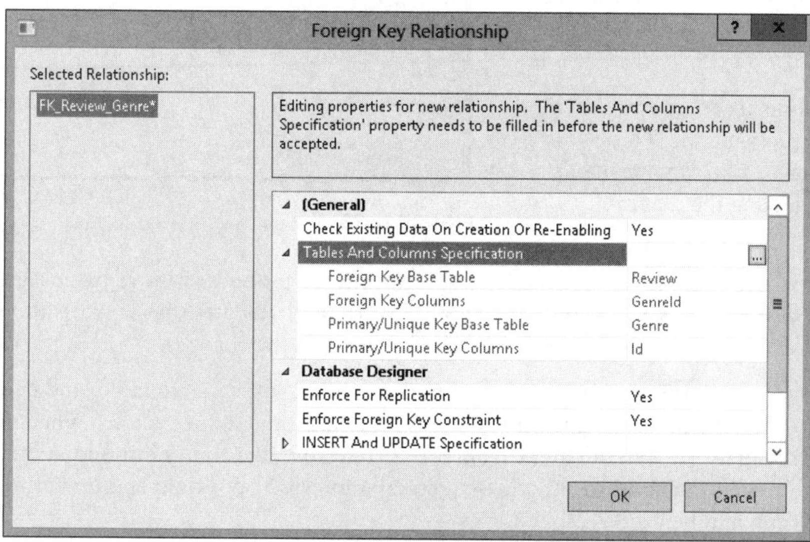

FIGURE 12-23

6. The diagram window should now show a line between the two tables. At the side of the `Genre` table, you should see a yellow key to indicate this table contains the primary key for the relationship. At the other end, you should see the infinity symbol (the number 8 turned 90 degrees) to indicate that the `Review` table can have many rows that use the same `GenreId`. You see the diagram in Figure 12-24.

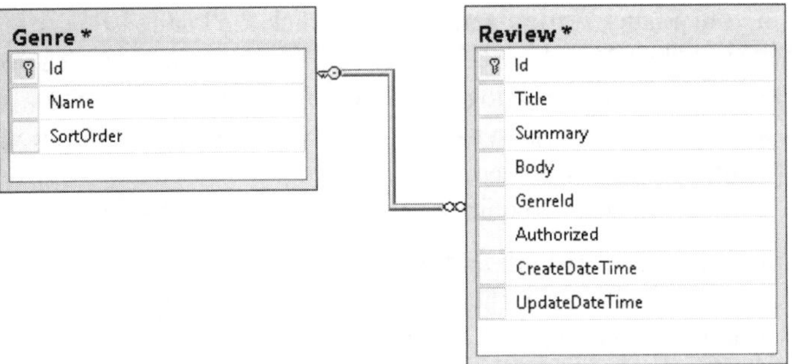

FIGURE 12-24

Note that in your diagram the line heads between the two tables don't necessarily point to the correct columns; they just point to the entire table. This can be confusing sometimes because you may think that other columns are actually related. To confirm the columns participating in the relationship, right-click the line between the two tables and choose Properties. The Table and Columns Specification item shows which columns and tables participate in the relationship, shown in Figure 12-25.

You can drag the line heads up and down to point to the correct column. This doesn't affect the tables, but it makes your intent clearer to others viewing the diagram.

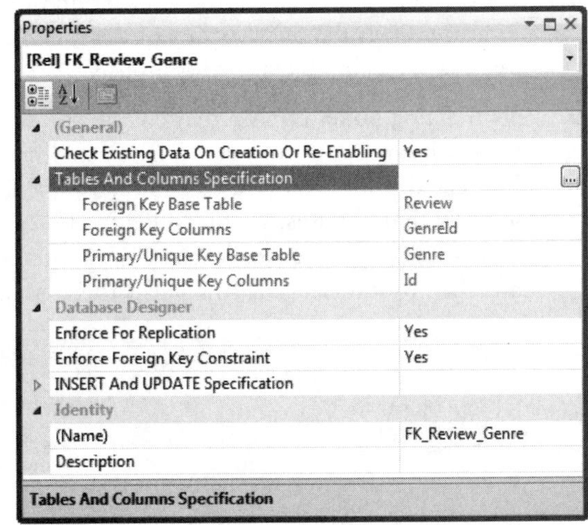

FIGURE 12-25

7. Press Ctrl+S to save the changes to the diagram. You can leave the name set to its default or you can enter a more descriptive name such as **`Reviews and Genres`** and click OK. You'll get another warning that states that you are about to make changes to the `Review` and `Genre` tables. Click Yes to apply the changes.

8. Go back to the Object Explorer, expand the Tables node, right-click the `Genre` table, and choose Edit Top 200 Rows. Enter a few different genres by typing a `Name` and a `SortOrder`. When you press Tab in the `SortOrder` field to tab away from the current row, the row is inserted in the database, and the `Id` column is filled with a unique, sequential number. You should end up with a list similar to the one shown in Figure 12-26.

9. Open the `Review` table from the Database Explorer using the Edit Top 200 Rows command and enter a few review rows. For the `GenreId`, supply some of the new IDs you got when you inserted rows in the `Genre` table. You can just make up the Title, Summary, and Body fields for now and set Authorized to True. Remember, you don't have to enter a value for the date columns. If you leave them out, the database will insert the default value for you. Notice that you can't insert a value in the `Id` column yourself. Because this column is an Identity field, the database supplies values for you automatically. If you get an error about missing values for the date columns, ensure that you entered a proper default value in the previous exercise. When you're done entering a row, click outside the row (on the new, empty row below it, for example) to insert the row in the table. Your list of rows should look similar to Figure 12-27, although your content for the columns, of course, may be different.

VPC2012RTM\LOCAL...Wrox - dbo.Genre

	Id	Name	SortOrder
▸	1	Rap and Hip-Hop	14
	2	Pop	12
	3	Jazz	8
	4	Hard Rock	3
	5	Indie Rock	7
	6	Punk	1
	7	Rock	2
	8	Grunge	4
	9	Alternative Rock	9
	10	Reggae	11
	11	Industrial	10
	12	Techno	5
*	NULL	NULL	NULL

1 of 12

FIGURE 12-26

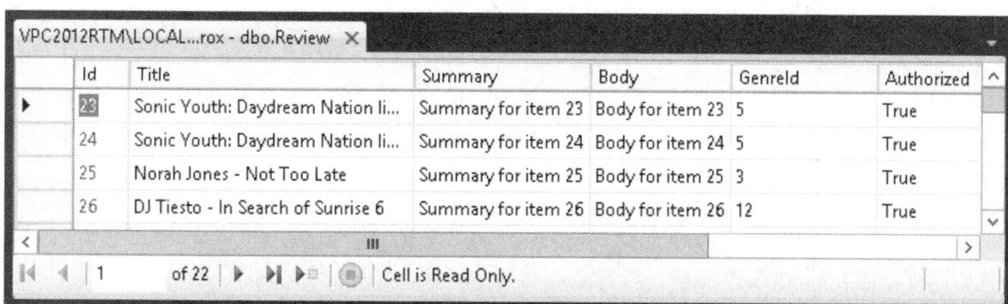

VPC2012RTM\LOCAL...rox - dbo.Review

	Id	Title	Summary	Body	GenreId	Authorized
▸	23	Sonic Youth: Daydream Nation li...	Summary for item 23	Body for item 23	5	True
	24	Sonic Youth: Daydream Nation li...	Summary for item 24	Body for item 24	5	True
	25	Norah Jones - Not Too Late	Summary for item 25	Body for item 25	3	True
	26	DJ Tiesto - In Search of Sunrise 6	Summary for item 26	Body for item 26	12	True

1 of 22 | Cell is Read Only.

FIGURE 12-27

10. Right-click the `Genre` table again and choose Edit Top 200 Rows. Click the SQL pane button on the Query Designer toolbar and then use the Change Type button on the same toolbar to create a `DELETE` query. Modify the query so it deletes one of the genre IDs you used in step 9 to link the reviews to, like this:

```
DELETE FROM Genre WHERE Id = 5
```

This code will attempt to delete the Indie Rock genre. However, because reviews are connected to it, the delete action should fail. Press Ctrl+R to execute the query. Instead of deleting the row from the `Genre` table, SSMS now shows you the dialog box you see in Figure 12-28.

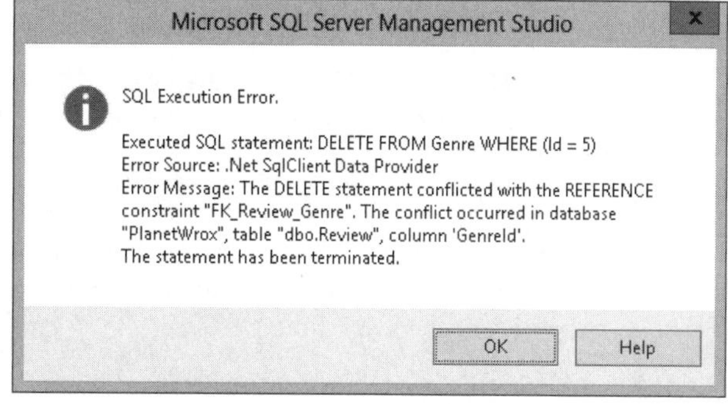

FIGURE 12-28

How It Works

When you create a relationship between two tables, the database will enforce this relationship when you try to insert, update, or delete data. In this example, rows in the `Review` table have a genre that exists in the `Genre` table. When you try to delete a row from the `Genre` table, the database sees that the genre is used by a row in the `Review` table and cancels the delete operation. In Chapter 15 you learn how to handle this situation in your website and present your user with a friendly error message.

Now that you've seen the underlying concepts in dealing with databases, you're ready for the next chapter, which shows you how to work with your database using the many available ASP.NET data controls.

PRACTICAL DATABASE TIPS

The following list provides some practical tips on working with databases:

- Because the database is often at the heart of a website, you need to carefully consider its design. It's especially important to think of a good design up front, before you start building your site on top of it. When you have a number of pages that access your database, it will become harder to make changes—such as removing tables or renaming columns—to the data model.
- Always consider the primary key for your table. I prefer to give each table a column called `Id`. The underlying data type is then an `int` and an identity, which gives each row a unique ID automatically. Instead of an `int`, you can also consider the `uniqueidentifier` data type, which ensures uniqueness even across database or application boundaries. However, a `uniqueidentifier` is much slower than the `int` data type (especially during inserts) so use this only when you need the benefits of the `uniqueidentifier` data type.
- Give your database objects such as tables and columns logical names. Avoid characters such as spaces, underscores, and dashes. A name like `GenreId` is much easier to read than `colGen_ID_3`.
- Don't use `SELECT *` to get all columns from a database. By using `SELECT *` you may be selecting more columns than you actually need. By defining the columns you want to retrieve explicitly, you make your intentions to others clearer and increase the performance of your queries at the same time.
- Always create relationships between tables when appropriate. Although querying for the reviews and genres you saw in this chapter without a relationship between the two tables works just fine, relationships help you enforce the quality of your data. With proper relationships, you minimize the chance of ending up with orphaned or incorrect data.

SUMMARY

The ability to work with databases is a good addition to your set of web development skills. Most of today's dynamic websites use databases, so it's important to understand how to work with them.

To access and manipulate data in a relational database, you use a language called Structured Query Language, or SQL for short. Among other elements, this language defines four important keywords that enable you to perform CRUD—Create, Read, Update, Delete—operations against a database.

The `SELECT` statement enables you to retrieve data from one or more tables. To access more than one table, you can use one of the available `JOIN` types to define a relationship between the tables. To limit the number of rows returned by a query, you can use a `WHERE` clause. To order the items in the result set returned by your query, you use the `ORDER BY` clause. To create new rows in your database you use the `INSERT` statement, and you need an `UPDATE` statement to change existing rows. Finally, to delete rows that you no longer need, you use the `DELETE` statement. Just like the `SELECT` and `UPDATE` statements, `DELETE` takes an optional `WHERE` clause that enables you to limit the number of rows that get deleted.

The second part of this chapter showed you how to use the built-in database tools to create tables with relationships between them. In addition, you saw how a relationship between two tables enables you to protect your data from becoming corrupt or orphaned.

Although this chapter had a strong focus on the SQL that you need to write to access a database, you see in the next chapter that in many cases Visual Studio makes accessing databases pretty easy as well by generating most of the code for you. However, a solid knowledge of SQL helps you in understanding and tweaking the code that is being written for you.

EXERCISES

1. If you try to delete a row from the `Genre` table that has matching rows in the `Review` table, the `DELETE` statement fails. How is this possible?

2. If you try to delete a row from the `Review` table that has its `GenreId` set to the `Id` of an existing genre in the `Genre` table, the `DELETE` statement succeeds. Why?

3. Imagine you want to clean up your database and decide to delete all rows from the `Review` table that have an `Id` of 100 or less. Write a SQL statement that deletes these rows.

4. Imagine you want to delete the genre with an ID of 4. But before you delete the genre, you want to reassign reviews assigned to this genre to another genre with an ID of 11. What SQL statements do you need to accomplish this?

5. Write a SQL statement that updates the Rock genre to read Punk Rock instead. You have at least two ways to write the `WHERE` clause for this statement.

You can find answers to these exercises in Appendix A.

▶ WHAT YOU LEARNED IN THIS CHAPTER

CRUD	The four basic SQL operations to work with data in a database: Create, Read, Update, and Delete
Foreign key	Identifies a column in a table that refers to the primary key of another table to enforce referential integrity
Identity	An automatic, sequential number assigned to new rows
`JOIN`	Enables you to express the relationship between two or more tables in a query to find related data
Primary key	Consists of one or more columns in a table that uniquely identify a row in that table
Relational database	A type of database where data is stored in separate, spreadsheet-like tables that can refer to each other
Relationship	Defines the relation between one or more tables and helps you enforce referential integrity
Table	An object in a database that enables you to store data

13

Displaying and Updating Data

WHAT YOU WILL LEARN IN THIS CHAPTER:

- How to display, insert, edit, and delete data using controls such as `GridView`, `DetailsView`, and `SqlDataSource`
- How to create a rich interface that enables a user to insert and edit data while maintaining data integrity with the ASP.NET validation controls
- The best way to store your connection strings in your application so they are easily updatable

WROX.COM CODE DOWNLOADS FOR THIS CHAPTER

You can find the wrox.com code downloads for this chapter on the Download Code tab at `www.wrox.com/remtitle.cgi?isbn=1118311809`. The code is in the Chapter 13 download.

In this chapter you learn how to display, insert, update, and delete data using the popular data controls that ship with ASP.NET. Besides working with the visual controls that are used to display and edit data in a web page, you also learn how to work with the `SqlDataSource` control that acts as the bridge between the database and your ASPX pages.

The first things you need to look at are the available data controls, discussed in the next section.

DATA CONTROLS

To enable you to work efficiently with the data in your system, ASP.NET offers two sets of data-aware controls: the *data-bound controls* and the *data source controls*.

The first group contains controls that you use to display and edit data, such as the GridView, Repeater, and ListView controls in the user interface. The data source controls are used to retrieve data from a data source, like a database or an XML file, and then offer this data to the data-bound controls. Figure 13-1 shows the complete list of available data controls in the Data category of the Toolbox.

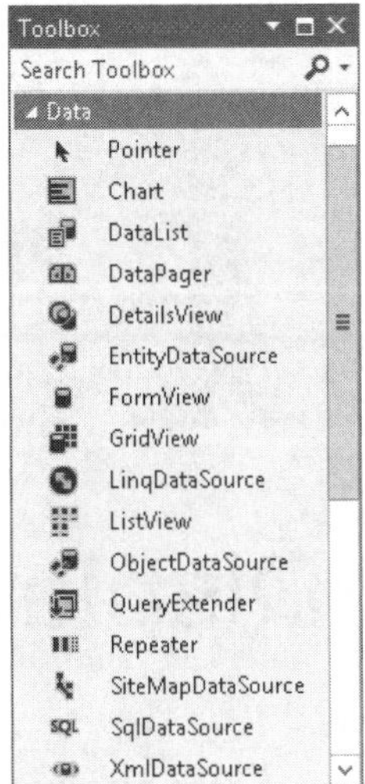

FIGURE 13-1

The following three sections provide a quick overview of all the controls in the Data category. In the remainder of this chapter you get a much more detailed look at some of these controls and how to use them.

Data-Bound Controls

Seven of the controls in the Toolbox depicted in Figure 13-1 are the so-called data-bound controls. You use them to display and edit data on your web pages. The GridView, DataList, ListView, and Repeater are all able to display multiple rows at the same time. As such they are often referred to as *list controls*. The DetailsView and the FormView are designed to show a single row at a time. The DataPager is a helper control used to provide paging capabilities to the ListView controls.

List Controls

Because ASP.NET offers multiple controls to display lists of rows, you may be wondering when to choose what control. The GridView is a very versatile control that supports automatic paging (where rows are spread out over multiple "pages"), sorting, editing, deleting, and selecting. It renders its data like a spreadsheet with rows and columns. Although many possibilities exist to style the looks of these rows and controls (you learn more about this in Chapter 15), you cannot radically change the way the data is presented. Additionally, the GridView does not allow you to insert rows in the underlying data source directly.

Figure 13-2 shows a typical GridView.

	Id	Title	CreateDateTime
Edit Delete Select	44	Wait For Me by Moby	6/30/2009 11:19:24 PM
Edit Delete Select	43	21st Century Breakdown by Green Day	6/23/2009 10:38:58 PM
Edit Delete Select	42	Farm by Dinosaur Jr	6/23/2009 10:36:01 PM
Edit Delete Select	41	First Album by Miss Kittin & The Hacker	6/16/2009 8:50:38 PM
123456			

FIGURE 13-2

The DataList control enables you to present data not only in rows as with the GridView, but in columns as well, enabling you to create a matrix-like presentation of data. The control can be considered deprecated and is replaced with the ListView, which is a lot more powerful. As such, this book doesn't discuss the DataList any further.

The Repeater gives you the greatest flexibility in terms of the HTML that you output to the browser because the control by itself does not add any HTML to the page output. As such, it's often used for HTML ordered or unordered lists (<ol> and <ul>) and other lists where you can't afford to have unwanted HTML mixed with your own. You define the entire client markup through the numerous templates the control exposes. However, this flexibility comes at a price: the control has no built-in capabilities to page, sort, or modify data. You see more of the `Repeater` control in the next chapter.

The `ListView` was introduced in ASP.NET 3.5 and is a best-of-all-worlds combination of the `GridView`, the `DataList`, and the `Repeater`. It has undergone some changes in ASP.NET 4 and 4.5 that make it even easier to work with. The control supports editing, deleting, and paging of data, similar to the `GridView`. It supports multi-column and multi-row layouts like the `DataList` offers, and it enables you to completely control the markup generated by the control, just as the `Repeater` does. It also supports inserting and updating data like the `DetailsView` or `FormView` controls. In the next chapter, you see a lot more of the `ListView` control.

In ASP.NET 4, list controls were extended with a `ClientIDRowSuffix` property that enables you to indicate the column whose value is used to create unique client-side IDs based on data in the database. For this to work, you need to set the `ClientIDMode` property that you saw in earlier chapters to `Predictable`.

In ASP.NET 4.5, the controls have been extended again with a new property: `ItemType`. You see this property at work in the next chapter.

Single Item Controls

The `DetailsView` and `FormView` controls are somewhat similar in that both of them can display a single record at a time. The `DetailsView` uses a built-in tabular format to display the data, whereas the `FormView` uses templates to let you define the look and feel of your data. A simple, template-based `DetailsView` could look like the one shown in Figure 13-3.

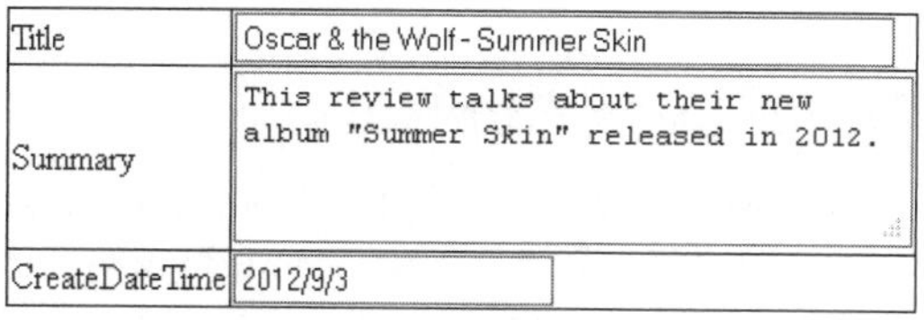

Title	Oscar & the Wolf - Summer Skin
Summary	This review talks about their new album "Summer Skin" released in 2012.
CreateDateTime	2012/9/3

FIGURE 13-3

The `FormView` control and a few of the Login controls you'll see in Chapter 16 have a `RenderOuterTable` property. When you set this property to `False` (it defaults to `True` so you need to set it explicitly) the control doesn't generate a wrapping HTML <table> element. This in turn results in less code and cleaner HTML. Both controls enable you to define the templates for different situations, such as a read-only display of data, and inserting and updating of data. You see how to customize these templates in the second half of this chapter.

Paging Controls

Another useful control is the `DataPager`, which enables paging on other controls. For the time being, you can only use it to extend the `ListView` control, but that might change with future versions of the .NET Framework. The `ListView` and `DataPager` controls are discussed in Chapter 14.

For the data-bound controls to display something useful, you need to assign them a *data source*. To bind this data source to the controls, two main methods are available: You can assign data to the control's `DataSource` property, or you can use one of the separate data source controls. In later chapters, you see how to use the `DataSource` property; the different data source controls are the topic of the following section.

Data Source Controls

The Data category of the Toolbox contains six different data source controls that you can use to bind data to your data-bound controls. The `XmlDataSource` and `SiteMapDataSource` controls are used to bind hierarchical, XML-based data to these controls. You saw `SiteMapDataSource` at work when you created the site map in Chapter 7.

The `ObjectDataSource` control enables you to connect your data-bound controls to separate objects in your application. Instead of tying your data-aware controls directly to a database, you bind data from a separate layer with custom objects to them. Get yourself a copy of Wrox's *Professional ASP.NET 4.5* (ISBN 978-1-118-31182-0) if you want to find out more about the `ObjectDataSource` control.

The final three data source controls are the `SqlDataSource`, the `EntityDataSource`, and the `LinqDataSource` controls. The first two are discussed in this chapter and Chapter 14, respectively. The `LinqDataSource` serves as a data source for LINQ to SQL, a technology similar to the ADO. NET Entity Framework you learn more about in Chapter 14. Because Microsoft is now promoting the Entity Framework instead of LINQ to SQL, I won't discuss the `LinqDataSource` control in this book.

The `QueryExtender` control acts like an add-on to the `LinqDataSource` and `EntityDataSource` controls in that it enables you to create a rich filtering interface to search for specific data without manually writing a lot of code. You can learn more about the `QueryExtender` in this article: `http://bit.ly/92kMPQ`.

Other Data Controls

The final control in the Toolbox is the `Chart` control. It was initially released as an add-on to Visual Studio 2008 but has now been fully integrated into VS 2012. It's designed to render chart graphics ranging from simple bar charts to 3-D pie charts and fancy line diagrams. I won't discuss this control any further, but you can find a series of articles that discuss it in detail here: `http://tinyurl.com/nsnbvv`.

In the next section you see how to use the `SqlDataSource` and the `GridView` to retrieve and display data from a database. Later sections and chapters dig deeper into the other data controls.

DATA SOURCE AND DATA-BOUND CONTROLS WORKING TOGETHER

The `SqlDataSource` control enables you to quickly create functional, database-driven web pages. Without writing a whole lot of code, you can create web pages that enable you to perform all four operations of the CRUD acronym: Create, Read, Update, and Delete data. Although its name may seem to imply that the control can access only Microsoft's SQL Server, that's not the case. The control can access other databases, such as Oracle or MySQL, as well.

Displaying and Editing Data with GridView

To give you an idea of how the `SqlDataSource` control works in conjunction with the data-bound controls, the next Try It Out shows you how to create a very simple data-driven web page that enables you to update and delete the musical genres that are stored in the Genre table in the database. This chapter assumes you have the PlanetWrox.mdf database with the Genre and Review tables in your App_Data folder. It's also assumed that these tables each contain at least a few rows. If you didn't follow the steps in the preceding chapter, use the script file Create Planet Wrox Database.sql supplied in the Resources folder of that chapter to create the necessary tables and records. You still need to create the database at C:\BegASPNET\Site\App_Data as explained in the preceding chapter. It's also a good idea to use this script if your own copy doesn't contain a lot of review and genre rows. This gives you a good set of sample rows to work with.

TRY IT OUT Using the GridView and SqlDataSource Controls

In this exercise you start building the Management section of the website that will be your main entry point to manage things such as reviews and genres in your site. For now, the pages you create in this section are accessible to all users of your site, but Chapter 16 shows you how to block access to this folder to any user that is not an administrator.

You see how to drag a table from the Database Explorer (the Server Explorer in the commercial versions of Visual Studio) onto the page and have VS create a web user interface to manage items in the database for you by automatically generating the necessary code for a GridView and a SqlDataSource. In later exercises in this book you see how to reproduce this behavior manually, giving you more control over the code.

1. Open the Planet Wrox website from its location at C:\BegASPNET\Site in VS.
2. Right-click the MasterPages folder, choose Add ➪ Add New Item, and add a new Master Page called Management.master to the site. Make sure it uses your programming language and that it's not based on an existing master page. Also, make sure it's using Code Behind by checking the Place Code in Separate File option.
3. Change the HTML inside the <form> element to the following code that creates two elements (a <nav> and a <section>) floating next to each other. The first contains a simple list-based menu for the Management section, whereas the second contains the ContentPlaceHolder control that enables content pages to provide custom content:

```
<form id="form1" runat="server">
<div>
  <nav style="width: 200px; float: left;">
    <ul>
      <li><a href="~/Management/Default.aspx" runat="server">
                    Management Home</a></li>
      <li><a href="~/Management/Genres.aspx" runat="server">Manage Genres</a></li>
    </ul>
  </nav>
  <section style="width: 750px; float: left;">
    <asp:ContentPlaceHolder ID="cpMainContent"
             runat="server"></asp:ContentPlaceHolder>
  </section>
</div>
</form>
```

In the next steps, you add the two files linked to from the <nav> element. Save and close the master page.

4. Add a new folder to the root of the site and call it **`Management`**. Right-click this new folder, choose Add ➪ Add New Item, and create a new standard Web Form called **`Default.aspx`**. Don't use your custom template, and make sure the page is based on the new `Management.master` file you just created by checking Select Master Page and then selecting that master page from the `MasterPages` folder. Add some text to the `cpMainContent` content block that welcomes the user to the Management section of the website:

```
<asp:Content ID="Content2" ContentPlaceHolderID="cpMainContent" runat="Server">
  <h1>Planet Wrox Management Section</h1>
  <p>Welcome to the Management section of this web site. Please choose an item
        from the menu on the left to continue.</p>
</asp:Content>
```

   Give the page a title of **`Planet Wrox - Management - Home`**.

5. Create another page in the `Management` folder and call it **`Genres.aspx`**. Base it on the same master page and then change its title to **`Planet Wrox - Management - Genres`** and switch it into Design View.

6. Double-click the `PlanetWrox.mdf` file in the `App_Data` folder. This opens the Database Explorer (or the Server Explorer). If you don't see the Planet Wrox database listed here or you get an error, refer to the preceding chapter, which explains how to set up the database. Remember, there's a script file in the `Resources` folder for the preceding chapter that creates the tables you'll work with in case you don't have your own.

7. Expand the `PlanetWrox.mdf` database, then the Tables node, and then drag the `Genre` table from the Database Explorer and drop it in the `cpMainContent` area of the Genres page in Design View. VS creates a `GridView` and a `SqlDataSource` for you automatically.

8. On the Smart Tasks panel for the `GridView` control that should open automatically (if it doesn't, click the gray arrow on the upper-right corner of the control or right-click the control and choose Show Smart Tag), check all the available check boxes, shown in Figure 13-4.

9. Right-click the `Management` folder in the Solution Explorer and choose Add ➪ Add New Item. Choose Web Configuration File and then click Add to add a `Web.config` file that applies to the `Management` folder only. In the file that opens, add a `<pages>` element under `<system.web>` and set the `theme` attribute to an empty string, effectively disabling the theme for the entire Management section of the site:

```
<configuration>
  <system.web>
    <pages theme="" />
  </system.web>
</configuration>
```

10. Save all your changes and then request `Genres.aspx` from the `Management` folder in your browser. You should see a grid with the genres from the `Genre` table (see Figure 13-5). The links in the left column enable you to edit, delete, and select the relevant genres. Note that you can't delete genres that have one or more reviews attached to them. If you try, you'll get an error instead. Chapter 15 digs much deeper into changing the user interface (UI) to disable the Delete links so users can no longer accidentally click them.

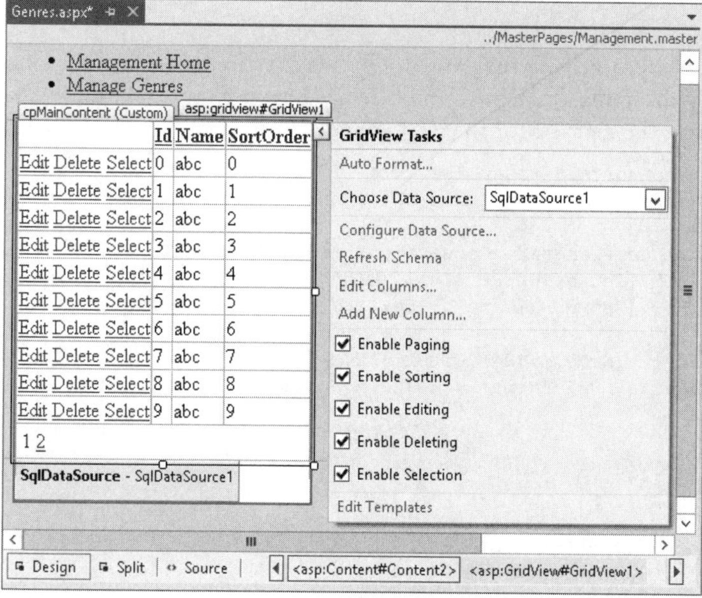

FIGURE 13-4

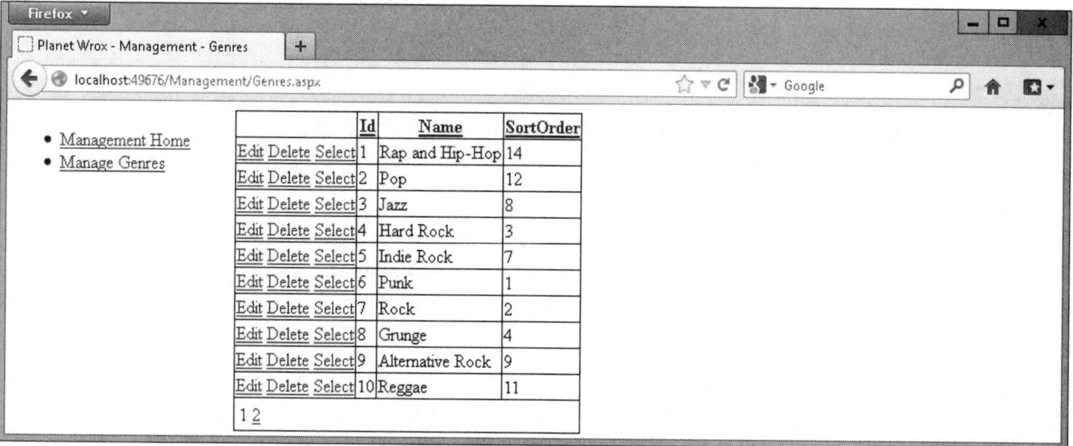

FIGURE 13-5

If the list with genres ends up below the menu on the left, you may need to make your browser window a little wider.

11. You can click the column headers, such as `Name` and `SortOrder` (visible in Figure 13-5), to sort the data in the grid on that column. If you click the same header again, the data is sorted in reverse order. You can move to another page in the grid by clicking the numbers at the bottom.

12. Click the Edit link for one of the genres, change the name in the text box that has appeared, and click the Update link. The `GridView` should now display the new name.

How It Works

You didn't manually write any code to interact with the database in this exercise, but you got a lot of functionality simply by dragging and dropping a database table. To see how it works, take a look at the source that VS generated. First, look at the markup for the `SqlDataSource` control:

```
<asp:SqlDataSource ID="SqlDataSource1" runat="server"
    ConnectionString="<%$ ConnectionStrings:PlanetWroxConnectionString1 %>"
    ProviderName="
           <%$ ConnectionStrings:PlanetWroxConnectionString1.ProviderName %>"
    DeleteCommand="DELETE FROM [Genre] WHERE [Id] = @Id"
    InsertCommand="INSERT INTO [Genre] ([Name], [SortOrder]) VALUES (@Name,
           @SortOrder)"
    SelectCommand="SELECT [Id], [Name], [SortOrder] FROM [Genre]"
    UpdateCommand="UPDATE [Genre] SET [Name] = @Name, [SortOrder] = @SortOrder
           WHERE [Id] = @Id">
  <DeleteParameters>
    <asp:Parameter Name="Id" Type="Int32" />
  </DeleteParameters>
  <InsertParameters>
    <asp:Parameter Name="Name" Type="String" />
    <asp:Parameter Name="SortOrder" Type="Int32" />
  </InsertParameters>
  <UpdateParameters>
    <asp:Parameter Name="Name" Type="String" />
    <asp:Parameter Name="SortOrder" Type="Int32" />
    <asp:Parameter Name="Id" Type="Int32" />
  </UpdateParameters>
</asp:SqlDataSource>
```

I changed the order of the attributes so all the commands are placed together. In your case, you may have the `ProviderName` attribute in a different location. As with all ASP.NET controls, the order of attributes in the control declaration doesn't matter.

A couple of interesting things are worth examining. First, note that the `ConnectionString` and `ProviderName` attributes point to a connection string that has been defined in the `Web.config` file. You see more of this in the next section, including an explanation of the `<%$ %>` syntax used for the attributes.

You then see four commands, each one of them containing a SQL statement that is used for one of the four operations of the CRUD acronym. The `INSERT`, `UPDATE`, and `DELETE` commands contain *parameters*, identified by the at symbol (`@`) prefix. At run time, when the control is asked to perform the relevant data operation, these parameters are substituted by runtime values. The `SqlDataSource` control keeps track of the relevant parameters in the `*Parameters` collections. For example, the `<DeleteParameters>` element contains a single parameter for the `Id` (the primary key) of the genre:

```
<DeleteParameters>
  <asp:Parameter Name="Id" Type="Int32" />
</DeleteParameters>
```

Note that the `Name` of the parameter minus the at symbol (`@`) lines up with the parameter in the SQL statement:

```
DeleteCommand="DELETE FROM [Genre] WHERE [Id] = @Id"
```

Notice how VS has wrapped column and table names in square brackets ([]). You normally only need these if your column or table name contains a special character such as a space or the name matches a reserved word. VS is just cautious and adds them to all columns and tables. You can leave them in, but if you write your own SQL statements you don't have to include them (although you could if you wanted to).

All by itself, the SqlDataSource control can't do much at this stage. It needs a data-bound control that tells it what data operations to execute. In this Try It Out exercise the data-bound control is the GridView that is defined with this code:

```
<asp:GridView ID="GridView1" runat="server" AllowPaging="True" AllowSorting="True"
    AutoGenerateColumns="False" DataKeyNames="Id" DataSourceID="SqlDataSource1"
    EmptyDataText="There are no data records to display.">
  <Columns>
    <asp:CommandField ShowDeleteButton="True" ShowEditButton="True"
        ShowSelectButton="True" />
    <asp:BoundField DataField="Id" HeaderText="Id" ReadOnly="True"
        SortExpression="Id" />
    <asp:BoundField DataField="Name" HeaderText="Name" SortExpression="Name" />
    <asp:BoundField DataField="SortOrder" HeaderText="SortOrder"
        SortExpression="SortOrder" />
  </Columns>
</asp:GridView>
```

The GridView contains a few important attributes. First, the DataKeyNames attribute tells the GridView what the primary key is of the row in the database. It needs this to uniquely identify rows in the grid.

The DataSourceID attribute points to the SqlDataSource control that you saw earlier, whereas AllowPaging and AllowSorting enable their associated features on the GridView.

Under the <Columns> element you see a number of fields set up. First, you see a CommandField. A CommandField is a column in the GridView that enables a user to execute one or more actions for the row to which the CommandField applies. It ends up in the browser as one or more text links or buttons. In this example, ShowDeleteButton, ShowEditButton, and ShowSelectButton have all been set to True. This gives the grid the functionality you see in Figure 13-5. When you click one of the links that have been created by the CommandField, they'll trigger a command at the server. For example, clicking the Edit link puts the GridView in edit mode so you can edit the selected row. Notice how clicking the Select link doesn't seem to change the GridView at all. In Chapter 15 you see how to create styles for the GridView so you can radically change the appearance of the control, including visually distinguishing a selected row from the others.

If you want the GridView to render buttons instead of links, you need to set ButtonType to Button:

```
<asp:CommandField ShowDeleteButton="True" ShowEditButton="True"
      ShowSelectButton="True" ButtonType="Button"></asp:CommandField>
```

The other three fields are so-called *bound fields* and map directly to the columns of the Genre table in the database with their DataField attribute so the GridView knows what data to display where.

The GridView and SqlDataSource controls work together closely to retrieve and modify the data in the underlying data source. To give you an idea of how this works, here's a rundown of the events that took place when you requested the Genres page in the browser and then edited a single genre:

1. You request the page in your browser and the page begins its page life cycle.
2. The GridView knows it is set up to retrieve and display data because it has a DataSourceID attribute that points to a SqlDataSource control. It contacts this data source control and asks it for its data. The SqlDataSource in turn connects to the database and then fires its SelectCommand, the SQL statement that selects the Id, Name, and SortOrder from the Genre table in the database:

```
SelectCommand="SELECT [Id], [Name], [SortOrder] FROM [Genre]"
```

3. When the SqlDataSource receives the requested rows from the database it hands them over to the GridView, which creates an HTML table out of them using the bound fields that have been set up in the <Columns> element. The GridView keeps track of the unique ID for each row that is displayed in the page by storing it in View State.
4. As soon as you click the Edit link, the page posts back. The GridView is able to see what row you clicked by looking at the associated DataKeyNames and retrieving the row's ID from View State. It then gets the latest results from the database by asking the SqlDataSource again to fire its SelectCommand, and, finally, puts the selected row in edit mode so you can change the relevant details. When you click the Update link, the GridView collects the new values from the TextBox controls and then contacts the SqlDataSource again.
5. For each of the parameters in the <UpdateParameters> element of the SqlDataSource, the GridView supplies a value. It retrieves the Id of the genre from the selected row, and then retrieves the new Name and SortOrder values from the TextBox controls in the page.
6. Armed with the relevant data for the Id, Name, and SortOrder, the SqlDataSource then executes its UpdateCommand against the database:

```
UpdateCommand="UPDATE [Genre] SET [Name] = @Name,
              [SortOrder] = @SortOrder WHERE [Id] = @Id"
```

   Each of the parameters prefixed with the at symbol (@) is filled with the values that the GridView supplied. The SQL statement that gets sent to the database ends up looking similar to this:

```
UPDATE [Genre] SET [Name] = 'New Name', [SortOrder] = 1 WHERE [Id] = 1
```

7. Finally, the GridView refreshes the data on the page by once again asking the SqlDataSource to execute its SelectCommand. This way, the GridView now displays the latest data with the update you made.

The other commands work in a similar way and send their own SQL commands to the database.

At the end of the exercise, you added a new Web.config file to the Management folder to reset the theme that is applied to all pages in the Management section. With the theme removed, it's easier to focus on the functionality of the Management section, rather than be distracted by layout issues. In Chapter 15 you create a third theme specifically for the Management folder and apply that theme in the Web.config file in the Management folder. That way, your management pages will have a look and feel that's different from the pages in the front end.

Now that you've seen how to display, edit, and delete data, it's time to learn how to insert new rows in the database using the DetailsView control.

Inserting Data with DetailsView

Just as displaying, updating, and deleting data with the GridView are pretty easy, so is inserting data with the DetailsView control. The DetailsView supports a number of templates that enable you to customize the look and feel of the control in different modes. For example, the control has a <HeaderTemplate>, a <FooterTemplate>, and a <PagerTemplate> element that enable you to define the look of the top and bottom parts of the control. In addition, the control has a <Fields> element that enables you to define the rows that should appear in the control, much like the <Columns> element of the GridView.

The DetailsView is able to display data in a few different modes. First of all, it can display an existing row in read-only mode. In addition, you can use the control to insert new rows and to update existing ones. You control the mode of the DetailsView with the DefaultMode property, which you can set to ReadOnly, Insert, and Edit, respectively. You see how to configure the DetailsView and set the DefaultMode property next.

TRY IT OUT Inserting Data with the DetailsView Control

In this exercise, you see how to use the DetailsView control to let your users insert new rows into the Genre table. As with the GridView example, the next exercise requires no coding from your side. All you need to do is drag and drop a few controls, set a few properties, and you're done. Obviously, these code-free pages have limitations that make them less useful in more advanced scenarios. Therefore, later in this chapter, you see how to extend and customize these controls.

1. Go back to the Genres.aspx page in VS and make sure it's in Design View.
2. Drag and drop a DetailsView control from the Data category of the Toolbox immediately below the GridView. If you have trouble dropping the control below the GridView but above the SqlDataSource control, you can simply drop it *on* the SqlDataSource; VS then adds the markup of the dropped control before the one you drop it on.
3. Open the control's Smart Tasks panel if it didn't open automatically and hook up the control to the existing SqlDataSource1 by selecting that name from the Choose Data Source drop-down list.
4. On the same Smart Tasks panel, select the Enable Inserting item.
5. Open the control's Properties Grid by pressing F4 and then locate the DefaultMode property in the Behavior category. Set the DefaultMode to Insert. The code for the DetailsView should now look like this:

```
<asp:DetailsView ID="DetailsView1" runat="server" AutoGenerateRows="False"
    DataKeyNames="Id" DataSourceID="SqlDataSource1" DefaultMode="Insert"
    Height="50px" Width="125px">
  <Fields>
    <asp:BoundField DataField="Id" HeaderText="Id" InsertVisible="False"
                    ReadOnly="True" SortExpression="Id" />
    <asp:BoundField DataField="Name" HeaderText="Name" SortExpression="Name" />
    <asp:BoundField DataField="SortOrder" HeaderText="SortOrder"
                    SortExpression="SortOrder" />
    <asp:CommandField ShowInsertButton="True" />
  </Fields>
</asp:DetailsView>
```

6. Save the changes to the page, and press Ctrl+F5 to open it up in your browser. Below the GridView you should now see the controls that enable you to insert a new genre, as shown in Figure 13-6.

7. Insert a new genre such as Disco or Dance. Make sure you enter both a name and a sort order (a number) and then click the Insert link. You may need to page to the last page of the GridView by clicking one of the numbers at the bottom of the screen in the Pager bar to see the new row.

	Id	Name	SortOrder
Edit Delete Select	1	Rap and Hip-Hop	14
Edit Delete Select	2	Pop	12
Edit Delete Select	3	Jazz	8
Edit Delete Select	4	Hard Rock	3
Edit Delete Select	5	Indie Rock	7
Edit Delete Select	6	Punk	1
Edit Delete Select	7	Rock	2
Edit Delete Select	8	Grunge	4
Edit Delete Select	9	Alternative Rock	9
Edit Delete Select	10	Reggae	11
1 2			

Name	
SortOrder	
Insert Cancel	

FIGURE 13-6

How It Works

Identical to the other data-bound controls, you hook up the DetailsView to a data source control by setting the DataSourceID property. Because you already have a working SqlDataSource control on the page, you can simply reuse that. The DetailsView exposes different views, for read-only, insert, and edit modes. By setting the DefaultMode to Insert, you force the control to switch to insert mode, which means you automatically get a UI for entering details for the genre, and Insert and Cancel links. The DetailsView control is actually pretty smart. When you point it to the SqlDataSource control, it is able to figure out the DataKeyNames property, which it set to Id:

```
<asp:DetailsView ID="DetailsView1" runat="server" AutoGenerateRows="False"
      DataKeyNames="Id" DataSourceID="SqlDataSource1" ...
```

It also understands that the Id column is an identity column in the database, and therefore hides it in the Insert screen (shown in Figure 13-6) by setting InsertVisible to False. Because the database generates this ID automatically, there is no point in letting the user enter a value for it.

When you enter some values and click the Insert link, a process similar to updating with the GridView takes place. The DetailsView collects the relevant information from the page's controls (the Name and the SortOrder) and forwards them to the SqlDataSource. This control in turn pushes the new values in the parameters for the INSERT statement and then sends the command off to the database, which inserts the new row in the Genre table. If you click the Insert link without entering a name or sort order, you'll get an error. In this and later chapters you see how to modify the data-bound controls to include validation functionality.

When you dropped the Genre table on the Genres.aspx page earlier in this chapter, VS not only created a bunch of controls for you, but it also stored information about the database in your Web.config file. The next section explains how this works and why it is important.

Storing Your Connection Strings in Web.config

The first time you dropped the Genre table on your page, VS created a SqlDataSource control for you. To tell this control what database to access, VS also created a connection string in the

`Web.config` file under the `<connectionStrings>` element and pointed the `SqlDataSource` to this connection string. The setting in `Web.config` looks like this:

```
<connectionStrings>
  <add name="PlanetWroxConnectionString1" connectionString="Data Source=
        (localdb)\v11.0;AttachDbFilename=|DataDirectory|\PlanetWrox.mdf;
              Integrated Security=True"
     providerName="System.Data.SqlClient" />
</connectionStrings>
```

The `SqlDataSource` then accesses this connection string:

```
<asp:SqlDataSource ID="SqlDataSource1" runat="server"
  ConnectionString="<%$ ConnectionStrings:PlanetWroxConnectionString1 %>"
```

This code uses *expression syntax* to refer to the connection string in the `Web.config`. It asks the `Web.config` file for the connection string that listens to the name `PlanetWroxConnectionString1`. It also reads the `providerName` attribute to figure out how its internal code should talk to the database.

> ***NOTE*** *In addition to the expression syntax that uses `<%$ %>` to bind control values to resources like a connection string, you'll also come across similar syntax that uses `<%# %>`. This is called data-binding expression syntax and it enables you to bind control values to data that comes from data sources like a database. You see more about data-binding expression syntax in this and the next two chapters.*

Storing your connection strings in `Web.config` is considered a very good practice. By centralizing your connection strings you make it much easier to modify them when your database changes (for example, when you switch from a development environment to a production server). Never store your connection strings directly in Code Behind files or in the markup section of the page. You'll seriously regret that the day you have to change your connection string and have to wade through all the pages in your site looking for connection strings.

The Express LocalDB edition of SQL Server that you have used so far enables you to work with databases that are *attached* to SQL Server on the fly when you need them. Take a look at the actual connection string to see how this works:

```
Data Source=(localdb)\v11.0;
AttachDbFilename=|DataDirectory|\PlanetWrox.mdf;
Integrated Security=True;
```

This connection string consists of three parts (which are all on one line in your `config` file). The value of the first part contains the data source to identify the SQL Server that is targeted, which in this case is a LocalDB instance of SQL Server 2012. Other valid data sources you may come across include `.` (just a dot, to denote the local machine), `.\SqlExpress`, to target a *named instance* version of SQL Server Express running on the local machine (where `SqlExpress` is the instance name), or something like *MachineName* or *MachineName\InstanceName* to target a remote machine or a named instance on a remote machine.

AttachDbFileName contains a path to your SQL Server Express database. The |DataDirectory| placeholder is expanded to the full and physical path of the App_Data folder at run time. So, when your pages load and the SqlDataSource needs to connect to the database, it will open the file PlanetWrox.mdf in C:\BegASPNET\Site\App_Data\. As an alternative to AttachDbFileName you'll also come across Initial Catalog in other connection strings. The Initial Catalog points to a database available on the SQL Server you are using. You see more of this in Appendix B.

The last part of the connection string has to do with security. With Integrated Security, the account used by the web server is used to connect to the database. In the case of VS and IIS Express, this account is the one you use to log on to your machine. In case you're using the full version of IIS, this account is an account named after an *Application Pool* in IIS, or a special account called Network Service. Chapter 19, which deals with deployment, and Appendix B, which explains how to connect to SQL Server, dig deeper into security-related issues.

So far you have seen most of the database concepts that were introduced in the previous chapter. You saw creating (with the DetailsView in insert mode), reading (with the SelectCommand and the GridView), updating (inline within the GridView and an UpdateCommand), and deleting (with the delete option in the GridView and a DeleteCommand). Moreover, you saw sorting that can be enabled in the GridView with just a single setting. What you haven't seen is *filtering*, a way to limit the data that is presented in the page. In the next section you see how to create a filter that enables you to display reviews that belong to a certain genre. You create the filter in the Management section in a new page called Reviews.aspx, which will be your main entry point for managing the reviews in your website. Subsequent sections build on top of this, gradually expanding the Reviews page with more useful features.

Filtering Data

As you learned in the previous chapter, you use a WHERE clause to filter your data. VS and ASP.NET come with a bunch of tools that make creating filters very easy. To filter data, the SqlDataSource control (and other data source controls) have a <SelectParameters> element that enables you to supply values at run time that are used for filtering. These values can come from a variety of sources, including the ones described in the following table.

WITH A	THE VALUE IS RETRIEVED FROM
ControlParameter	A control in the page, such as a DropDownList or a TextBox.
CookieParameter	A cookie that is stored on the user's computer and that is sent to the server with each request.
FormParameter	A value posted in the form that has been submitted to the server.
Parameter	A variety of sources. With this parameter, you set the value through code.
ProfileParameter	A property on the user's profile. The ASP.NET Profile is discussed in full detail in Chapter 17.
QueryStringParameter	A query string field.
SessionParameter	A value that is stored in a session, which is a server-side, user-specific store of data that exists during a user's visit to a site.

Because these parameters all behave more or less the same, it's easy to use them in your own code. Once you understand how to use one of them, you'll quickly be able to use the others as well. You see the `ControlParameter` at work in the next exercise, where you use a `DropDownList` with all the genres to filter a list of reviews that belong to the chosen genre.

TRY IT OUT Setting Up the Filter

To make long lists of data easier to manage, it's a good idea to offer them to the user in smaller, bite-size blocks. For example, when you need to present a list with reviews in your database, you could enable your users to filter them by genre. A `DropDownList` with the genres to limit the reviews in the `GridView` to those that belong to the selected genre would be the perfect solution for that. You see how to build this next.

1. Create a new Web Form called **`Reviews.aspx`** in the `Management` folder, and make sure it uses Code Behind and is based on the new Management master page. Change the `Title` of the page to **`Planet Wrox - Management - Reviews`**.
2. Add a link to this page in the master page for the Management section:

```
  <li><a href="~/Management/Genres.aspx" runat="server">Manage Genres</a></li>
  <li><a href="~/Management/Reviews.aspx" runat="server">Manage Reviews</a></li>
</ul>
```

3. Go back to `Reviews.aspx` and switch the page into Design View. From the Standard category of the Toolbox, drag a `DropDownList` control into the page. On its Smart Tasks panel, select Enable AutoPostBack and click the Edit Items link. Insert an item with its `Text` set to **`Make a selection`**, and then clear its `Value` that was inserted for you automatically.
4. Once you return from the ListItem Collection Editor dialog box, the Smart Tasks panel for the drop-down list is still open. Click the Choose Data Source item and choose <New data source> from the drop-down list at the top of the screen. The Data Source Configuration Wizard, shown in Figure 13-7, appears.
5. Click Database, leave the ID set to `SqlDataSource1`, and click OK.
6. In the dialog box that follows, select the connection string called `PlanetWroxConnectionString1` from the drop-down list and click Next.
7. Verify that the radio button for Specify Columns from a Table or View is selected. Also ensure that Genre is selected in the drop-down list with table names and then select the `Id` and `Name` columns in the Columns section. Click the ORDER BY button, choose `SortOrder` from the Sort By drop-down list, and click OK. When you're done, your Configure Data Source wizard should look like Figure 13-8.
8. Click Next and then Finish to have VS create the `SqlDataSource` for you. You return to the Data Source Configuration Wizard for the drop-down list where you can now set up a field that is displayed in the drop-down list for the genres and a field that serves as the underlying value in the list. Choose Name as the field to display and leave the second drop-down list set to Id. You should end up with the screen shown in Figure 13-9.

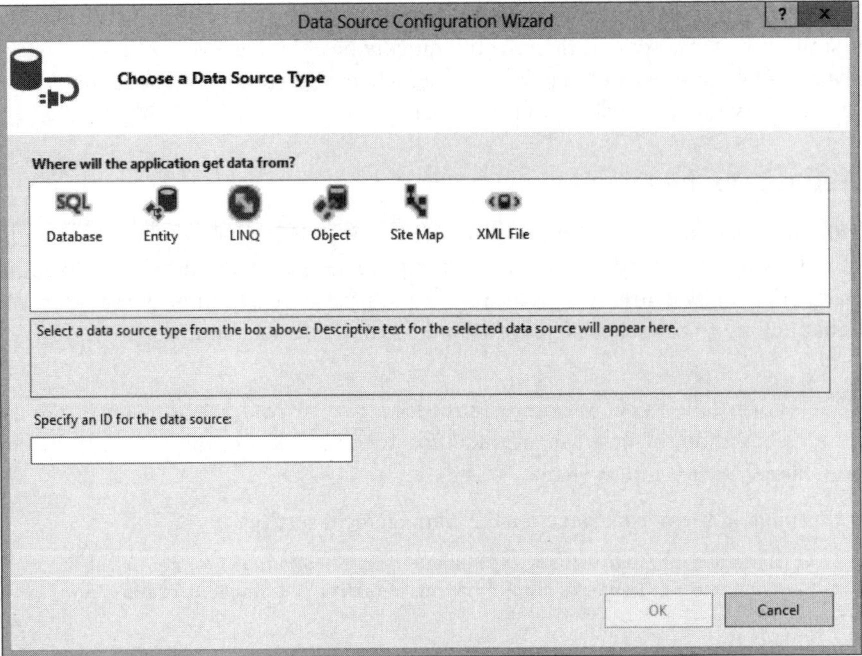

FIGURE 13-7

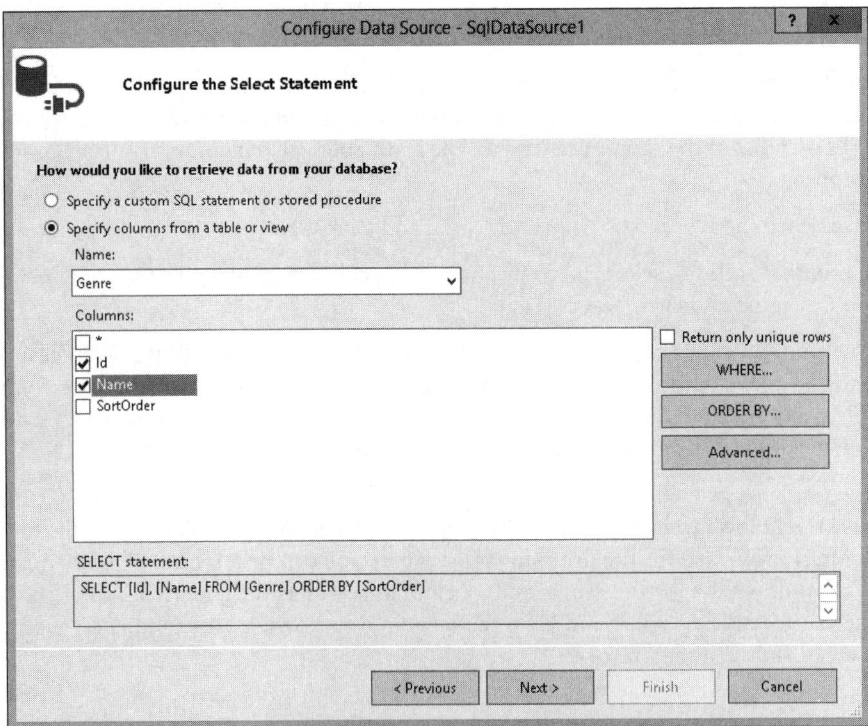

FIGURE 13-8

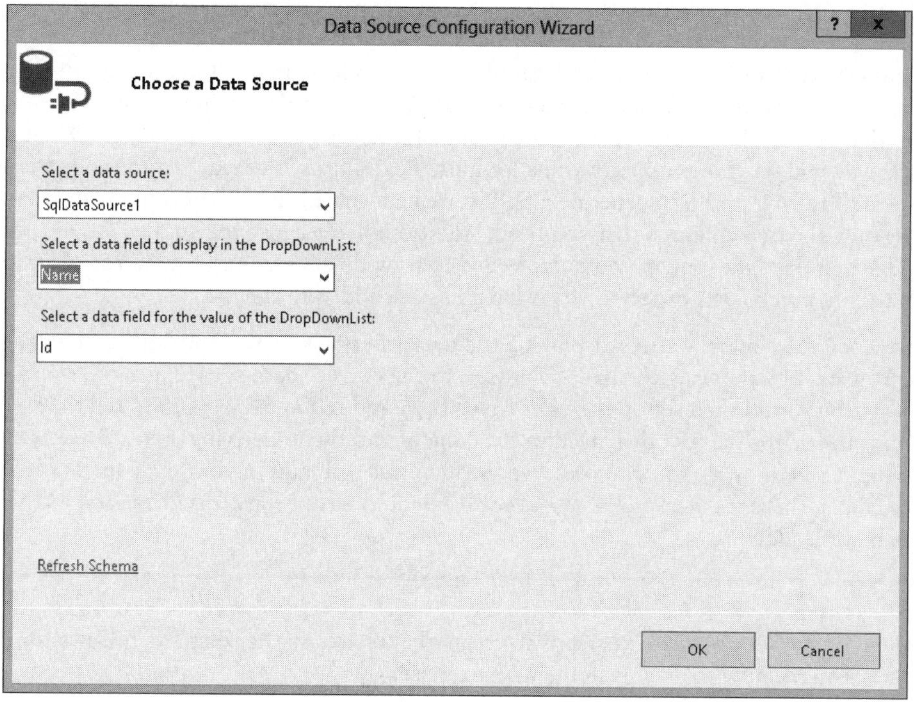

FIGURE 13-9

9. Click OK to close the dialog box and finish setting up the data source for the drop-down list.

10. With the `DropDownList` control still selected in Design View, press F4 to open up its Properties Grid and set the property `AppendDataBoundItems` to `True`. Switch to Markup View, and if the static `ListItem` that instructs your users to select an item does not have a `Value` attribute, add it manually and set it to an empty string. Your final code should look like this:

```
<asp:DropDownList ID="DropDownList1" runat="server" DataSourceID="SqlDataSource1"
      DataTextField="Name" DataValueField="Id" AppendDataBoundItems="true"
      AutoPostBack="True">
  <asp:ListItem Value="">Make a selection</asp:ListItem>
</asp:DropDownList>

<asp:SqlDataSource ID="SqlDataSource1" runat="server"
      ConnectionString="<%$ ConnectionStrings:PlanetWroxConnectionString1 %>"
      SelectCommand="SELECT [Id], [Name] FROM [Genre] ORDER BY [SortOrder]">
</asp:SqlDataSource>
```

11. Save all your changes and press Ctrl+F5 to open the page in the browser. You should now see a drop-down list with all the genres in the database ordered by their `SortOrder` column. Once you choose a new genre from the list, the page posts back to the server. Nothing else happens because you didn't tie any logic to the `DropDownList` control, but you see how to do this in the next exercise.

How It Works

At the end of this exercise you end up with code similar to what VS created automatically when you dropped a `GridView` on the page in an earlier exercise. You have a data-bound control (the `DropDownList`) that gets its data from a data source control (the `SqlDataSource` control). What's different is that the way you set things up gave you a lot more flexibility with regard to the code that is generated. Instead of relying on VS to generate a SQL statement for all the columns in the database, you now choose only the two columns that you need. Additionally, because the `SqlDataSource` doesn't require any updates to the data source, you only needed to provide a `SelectCommand`. You also used the ORDER BY button to control the order in which the items are added to the list.

With the `SqlDataSource` control set up, displaying the data it returns in a `DropDownList` control is pretty easy. You start by pointing the `DropDownList` to the correct data source using the `DataSourceID` attribute, and then set up the `DataTextField` and `DataValueField` to tell the control what columns to use for the text displayed in the control and the underlying value. By setting `AppendDataBoundItems` to `True`, you can preserve the item that you add in your code manually. With this setting turned off, the static item `Make a selection` would have been cleared as soon as the data-bound items were added.

With the filter control set up, the next step is to create the `GridView` that displays reviews for the selected genre. You see how to do this in the next exercise.

TRY IT OUT Applying the Filter

In this Try It Out you add another `SqlDataSource` that gets its data from the `Review` table. By creating a filter (the `WHERE` clause in the SQL statement) you can limit the number of items displayed in the grid to those that belong to a specific genre. The genre chosen in the drop-down list you created in the previous section is sent into the `SqlDataSource` control's `SelectParameters` collection using an `<asp:ControlParameter>`.

1. Switch the `Reviews.aspx` page to Design View and drag a `GridView` from the Data category of the Toolbox on top of the existing `SqlDataSource` control. The `GridView` is added right above it and its Smart Tasks panel opens.
2. In the Choose Data Source drop-down list, choose <New data source>. In the Data Source Configuration Wizard, click Database (just as with the wizard for the genres that is shown in Figure 13-7) and click OK.
3. In the dialog box that follows, select the Planet Wrox connection string from the drop-down list and click Next again.
4. Select the `Review` table in the Name drop-down list and then make sure the asterisk (*) is checked in the Columns list to select all columns. In the preceding chapter I recommended not to use `SELECT *`, but it's OK to do so for this exercise. Later in this chapter you see how to fix this.
5. Click the WHERE button, which enables you to set up a `WHERE` clause using the `SelectParameters`. In the dialog box that follows, enter the details so the screen ends up like Figure 13-10.

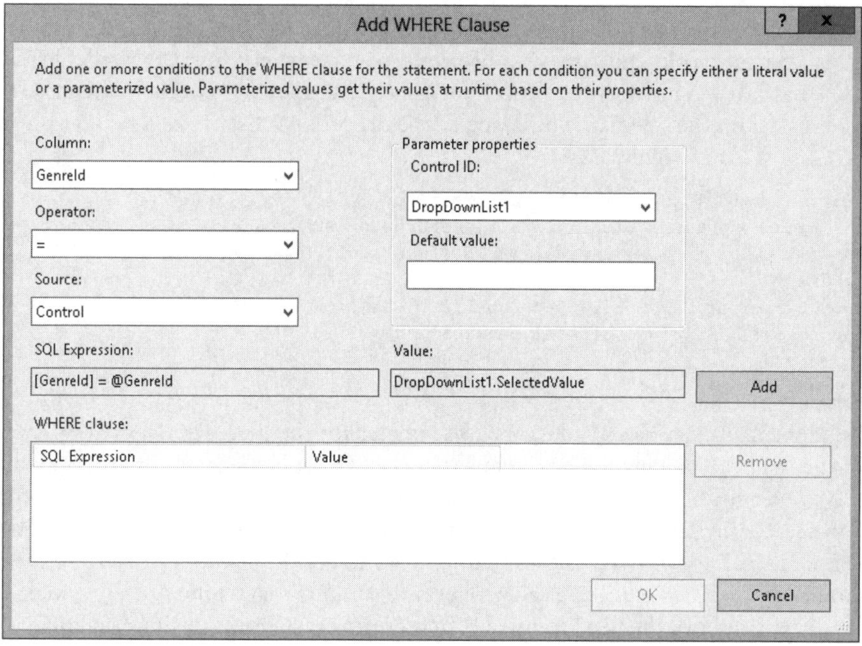

FIGURE 13-10

For some reason, each of your controls may show up twice in the Control ID drop-down list. It doesn't matter which of the `DropDownList1` options you choose.

6. Click the Add button to add the selection to the `WHERE` clause list at the bottom of the screen and click OK.

7. Back in the Configure Data Source wizard, click Next. To test the query, click the Test Query button. If you set up the parameter correctly, a dialog box pops up enabling you to enter a value. Enter a number that you know exists in the `Genre` table (such as 2) and click OK. If rows exist in the `Review` table for the chosen genre, they are displayed in the Test Query window. Finally, click Finish to finalize the wizard. If you get a dialog box about refreshing parameters, click Yes to have the code in Markup View updated for you.

8. Save all your changes and open `Reviews.aspx` in your browser.

> ***COMMON MISTAKES*** *If you get an error stating that the "input string was not in a correct format," ensure that you set the* `Value` *of the static* `ListItem` *in the drop-down list to an empty string (*`""`*) as shown in the preceding exercise.*

9. Select a new item in the drop-down list. The page refreshes, and now shows the reviews that belong to the chosen genre. If the page doesn't refresh, ensure that you set `AutoPostBack` to `True` in the previous exercise. At this stage the page looks rather messy because the `GridView` contains many columns but in the next Try It Out you see how to fix this.

How It Works

For the most part, this exercise works the same as a previous exercise where you displayed a list with the available genres. What's different this time is the way the `SqlDataSource` is able to filter the rows from the `Review` table based on the selection you made in the drop-down list. Take a look at the code for the `SqlDataSource` to see how this works:

```
<asp:SqlDataSource ID="SqlDataSource2" runat="server"
  ConnectionString="<%$ ConnectionStrings:PlanetWroxConnectionString1 %>"
  SelectCommand="SELECT * FROM [Review] WHERE ([GenreId] = @GenreId)">
<SelectParameters>
    <asp:ControlParameter ControlID="DropDownList1" Name="GenreId"
          PropertyName="SelectedValue" Type="Int32" />
  </SelectParameters>
</asp:SqlDataSource>
```

The SQL statement for the `SelectCommand` contains a parameter for the `GenreId` denoted by the `@GenreId` variable in the `SELECT` statement. That means that the SQL statement returns rows from the `Review` table only for a specific genre. At run time, the value for this parameter is retrieved from the control defined in the `ControlParameter` element. In this example, the code is set up to get the value from the `DropDownList1` control. VS knows that in order to get the selected value from the `DropDownList` it should access its `SelectedValue` property, so it adds that as the `PropertyName` for the `ControlParameter`. If you have the need to use a different property, you can simply change it in the `ControlParameter` element's declaration.

With this code set up, the `GridView` asks the `SqlDataSource` for its data. This data source in turn asks the `DropDownList` for the item that the user has selected in the list. This value is inserted in the SQL statement, which is sent to the database. The results that are returned from the database are sent back through the data source to the `GridView`, which uses them to create the HTML table in the browser.

When you choose Make a Selection from the drop-down list, you get an empty page with no rows. In this case, the `DropDownList` returns an empty string as its value (defined in the `Value` property), which is converted to `null`, the database equivalent of nothing. This in turn causes the query to return no rows from the `Review` table.

Until now, you've relied on the code-generation tools of VS to set up the `GridView` and the `DetailsView`. By default, VS creates a column (for the `GridView`) or a field (for the `DetailsView`) for each column that it finds in the data source. It's smart enough to recognize some of the underlying types of the data in the data source so you get a nice `CheckBoxField` for boolean (bit) fields in the database, but that's about it. To further customize the look and feel of these data controls, you need to customize their `Columns` and `Fields` collections.

CUSTOMIZING THE APPEARANCE OF THE DATA CONTROLS

By default, the `GridView` and `DetailsView` render columns or rows automatically based on the data they receive. Alternatively, you can have VS create a number of fields or columns for you when you attach the control to a data source. But, more often than not, you want to change what you see on-screen, be it fewer columns, different column headings, or different controls to display data. Fortunately, this is really easy to do with the Fields editor in VS. In the next section you see how to use this editor to create and modify the different types of built-in columns and fields. In the section that follows, you see how to customize the fields even further with user-defined templates.

Configuring Columns or Fields of Data-Bound Controls

Within the `<Columns>` or `<Fields>` element of the `GridView` and the `DetailsView`, you can add the types of fields shown in the following table.

FIELD TYPE	DESCRIPTION
`BoundField`	The default field for most database types. It renders as simple text in read-only mode, and as a `TextBox` in edit mode.
`ButtonField`	Renders as a link or a button enabling you to execute a command on the server.
`CheckBoxField`	Renders as a read-only check box in read-only mode, and as an editable check box in edit mode.
`CommandField`	Enables you to set up various commands, including editing, inserting, updating, and deleting.
`HyperLinkField`	Renders as a link (an `<a>` element). You can set properties like `DataNavigateUrlFields`, `DataNavigateUrlFormatString`, and `DataTextField` to influence the behavior of the hyperlink. You see more of this in the next exercise.
`ImageField`	Renders as an `<img>` element in the browser.
`TemplateField`	Enables you to define your own look and feel for various templates, like `ItemTemplate`, `InsertItemTemplate`, and `EditItemTemplate`.

Clearly, each field type serves a distinct purpose so you can choose the one that best fits your needs. You see some of these field types in more detail in the next exercise.

TRY IT OUT Customizing GridView Columns

In this exercise, you see how to do the following in the `Reviews.aspx` page:

- Use the Fields editor to customize the fields for the `GridView` with reviews.
- Use a `HyperLink` column to create a link to a details page that enables you to manage the details of a review.
- Format the output of the existing `BoundField` columns.
- Use a custom function in the Code Behind to have full control over the output in a `TemplateField`.

A later exercise shows you how to create the details page to insert new and edit existing reviews.

1. In `Reviews.aspx`, open the Smart Tasks panel for the `SqlDataSource2` control in Design View and click Configure Data Source. Click Next to skip the connection string screen, and then complete the screen as shown in Figure 13-11 by selecting the `Id`, `Title`, `Authorized`, and `CreateDateTime` columns from the `Review` table. Make sure the SQL Statement box also contains the `WHERE` clause filter that you set up earlier. You may have to set this up again using the steps from the previous exercise because VS sometimes seems to lose this information.

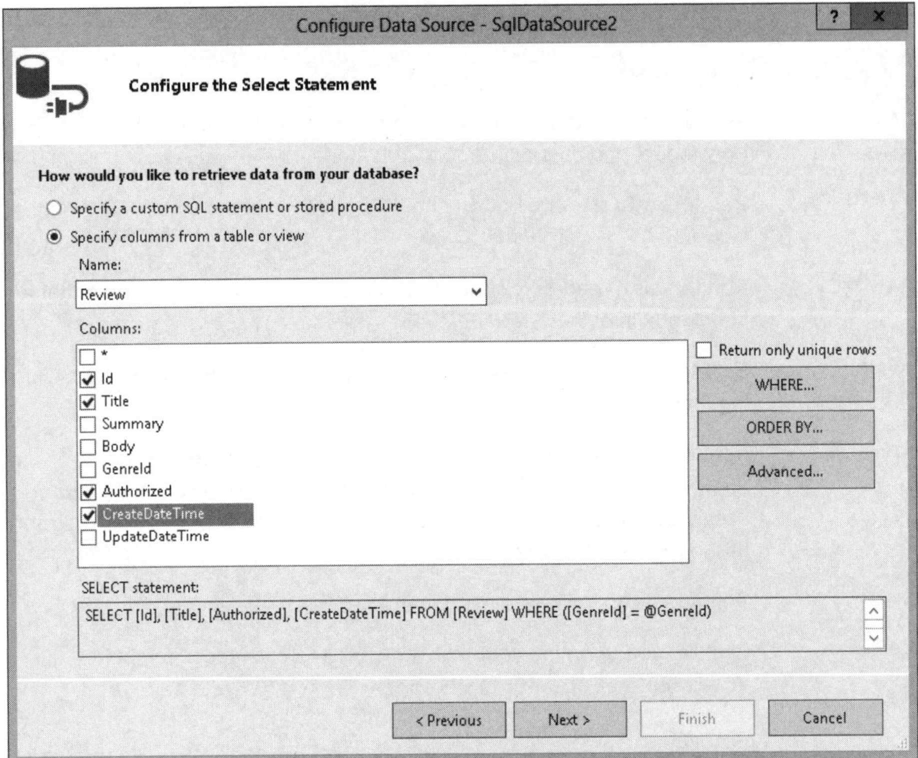

FIGURE 13-11

Click the Advanced button and have VS generate commands for the `INSERT`, `UPDATE`, and `DELETE` statements by checking off the first item. You can leave the Optimistic Concurrency check box—which deals with detecting changes to the row since it was last loaded from the data source—cleared. Click OK to close the Advanced SQL Generation Options dialog box, then click Next and finally Finish to update the SQL statement in the source for the page. When asked whether you want to refresh the fields and keys for the `GridView`, click Yes.

> ***COMMON MISTAKES*** *If both options in the Advanced SQL Generation Options dialog box are grayed out, check your table in the database using SQL Server Management Studio. Make sure that you made the* `Id` *column of the* `Review` *table the primary key and an identity column as explained in the preceding chapter.*

2. At this stage, VS has created columns for the `GridView` in Markup View. To remove those items and define your own, open the Smart Tasks panel for the `GridView` and click Edit Columns. This brings up the Fields dialog box. If the Selected Fields list contains items, use the Delete button (with the big X) to clear the list first.

3. In the Available Fields list, select Authorized under BoundField (not the one under CheckBoxField) and then click the Add button to copy the item to the Selected Fields list. Repeat this step for the `CreateDateTime` field. Your dialog box now looks like Figure 13-12.

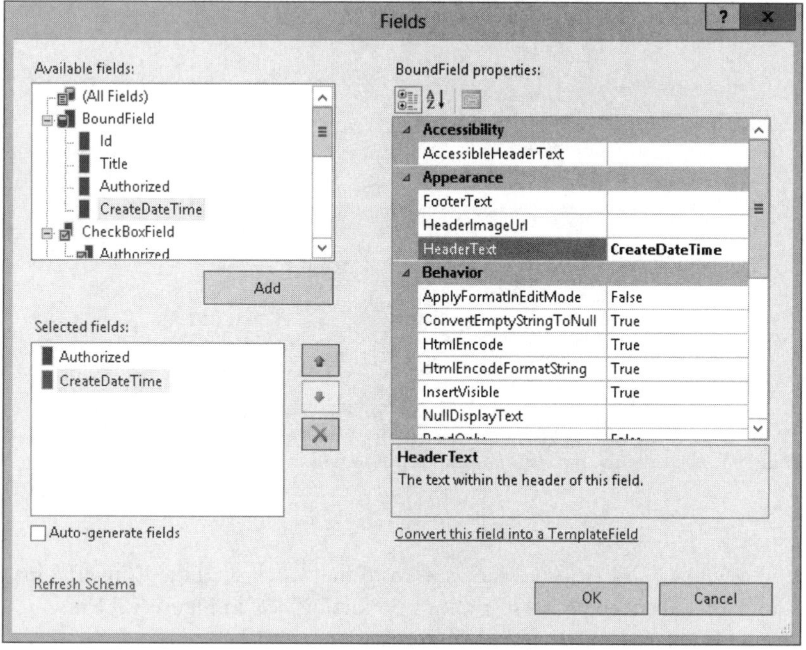

FIGURE 13-12

4. In the Available Fields at the top of the screen, select `HyperLinkField` and then click the Add button to add the item to the Selected Fields list as well. Move the `HyperLinkField` to the top of the list by clicking the button with the up arrow twice. Then, using the Properties Grid on the right, set the following properties on the `HyperLinkField`:

PROPERTY	SET ITS VALUE TO
`HeaderText`	`Title`
`DataNavigateUrlFields`	`Id`
`DataNavigateUrlFormatString`	`AddEditReview.aspx?Id={0}`
`DataTextField`	`Title`

5. In the list with Available Fields, click `CommandField` and click the Add button again. Then set the `HeaderText` of the item you just inserted to `Delete` and `ShowDeleteButton` to `True` using the

Properties Grid. This enables you to delete reviews from the database using the `GridView` later. The Fields dialog box should now look like Figure 13-13.

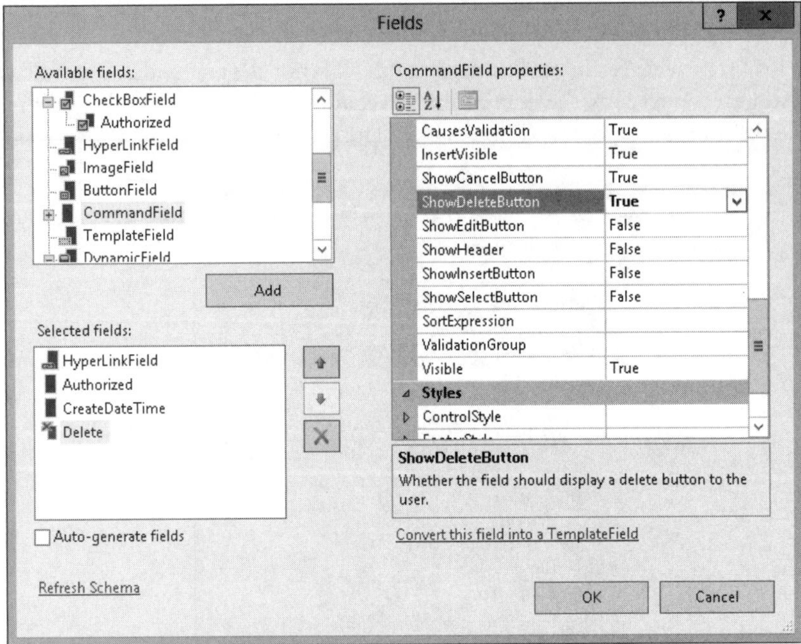

FIGURE 13-13

6. Click the `Authorized` column in the Selected Fields list and then click the blue Convert This Field into a TemplateField link visible at the bottom-right of the dialog box in Figure 13-13.
7. Click the `CreateDateTime` column on the left and set its `DataFormatString` property to `{0:g}`.
8. Click OK to apply the changes to the source code.
9. Switch to Markup View and remove the `<EditItemTemplate>` for the `Authorized` field. The `GridView` displays reviews only in read-only mode, so you don't need this template.
10. Modify the `Label` control in the `ItemTemplate` of the `Authorized` field so it ends up like this:

```
<asp:Label ID="AuthorizedLabel" runat="server"
     Text='<%# GetBooleanText(Eval("Authorized")) %>' />
```

11. Switch to the Code Behind of the page by pressing F7 and add the following function—which returns the text Yes or No depending on the boolean value that you pass—to the top of the class file, right after the `Inherits` line in VB.NET and after the opening curly brace in C#:

VB.NET

```
  Inherits System.Web.UI.Page
Protected Function GetBooleanText(booleanValue As Object) As String
  Dim authorized As Boolean = CType(booleanValue, Boolean)
  If authorized Then
    Return "Yes"
```

```
    Else
      Return "No"
    End If
  End Function
```

C#

```
public partial class Management_Reviews : System.Web.UI.Page
{
  protected string GetBooleanText(object booleanValue)
  {
    bool authorized = (bool)booleanValue;
    if (authorized)
    {
      return "Yes";
    }
    else
    {
      return "No";
    }
  }
```

12. Save all your changes (press Ctrl+Shift+S) and press Ctrl+F5 to open `Reviews.aspx` in the browser. Choose a genre from the drop-down list and you'll see a list of reviews appear. Note that the `Authorized` column now shows the text Yes or No. The `CreateDateTime` column shows the date and time in a short format. Figure 13-14 shows the result for the Indie Rock genre.

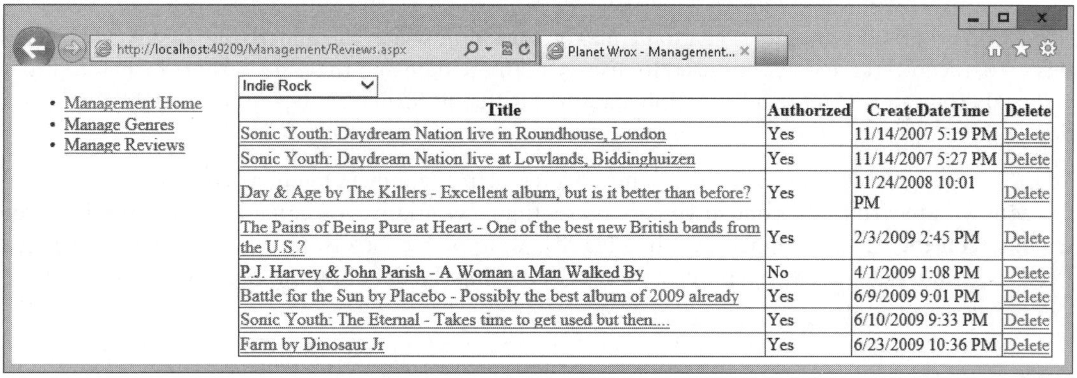

http://localhost:49209/Management/Reviews.aspx — Planet Wrox - Management...

- Management Home
- Manage Genres
- Manage Reviews

Indie Rock

Title	Authorized	CreateDateTime	Delete
Sonic Youth: Daydream Nation live in Roundhouse, London	Yes	11/14/2007 5:19 PM	Delete
Sonic Youth: Daydream Nation live at Lowlands, Biddinghuizen	Yes	11/14/2007 5:27 PM	Delete
Day & Age by The Killers - Excellent album, but is it better than before?	Yes	11/24/2008 10:01 PM	Delete
The Pains of Being Pure at Heart - One of the best new British bands from the U.S.?	Yes	2/3/2009 2:45 PM	Delete
P.J. Harvey & John Parish - A Woman a Man Walked By	No	4/1/2009 1:08 PM	Delete
Battle for the Sun by Placebo - Possibly the best album of 2009 already	Yes	6/9/2009 9:01 PM	Delete
Sonic Youth: The Eternal - Takes time to get used but then....	Yes	6/10/2009 9:33 PM	Delete
Farm by Dinosaur Jr	Yes	6/23/2009 10:36 PM	Delete

FIGURE 13-14

Note that the title in the first column of the `GridView` now links to a page where the ID of the review is passed in the query string field `Id`: `http://localhost:1049/Management/AddEditReview.aspx?Id=1`. You create this Add/Edit page later in this chapter.

How It Works

You started off by modifying the `SelectCommand` for the `SqlDataSource`. Instead of selecting all columns using `SELECT *`, the SQL statement now contains a subset of the columns, making the page load slightly faster:

```
<asp:SqlDataSource ID="SqlDataSource2" runat="server"
      ConnectionString="<%$ ConnectionStrings:PlanetWroxConnectionString1 %>"
```

```
        SelectCommand="SELECT [Id], [Title], [Authorized], [CreateDateTime]
            FROM [Review] WHERE ([GenreId] = @GenreId)">
    ...
</asp:SqlDataSource>
```

You then used the Fields dialog box to modify the different fields that are displayed by the GridView. You created the Title column using a HyperLinkField:

```
<asp:HyperLinkField DataNavigateUrlFields="Id" DataTextField="Title"
     DataNavigateUrlFormatString="AddEditReview.aspx?Id={0}" HeaderText="Title">
</asp:HyperLinkField>
```

The DataNavigateUrlFields property contains a comma-separated list of fields you want to use in the DataNavigateUrlFormatString property. In this case, only one field is used. To display the value of this field you use placeholders such as {0} in the DataNavigateUrlFormatString property. For example, a review with an ID of 10 will end up with a HyperLink column having this NavigateUrl: AddEditReview.aspx?Id=10. With this setup, the {0} is replaced with the value for the first field in the DataNavigateUrlFields property. If you defined more fields separated by a comma, you would access them with {1}, {2}, and so on.

The DataTextField is set to the column Title. This tells the HyperLink to render its Text attribute with the title of the review, as shown in Figure 13-14.

You also set the DataFormatString property of the bound field for the CreateDateTime column:

```
<asp:BoundField DataField="CreateDateTime" DataFormatString="{0:g}"
    HeaderText="CreateDateTime" SortExpression="CreateDateTime" />
```

The DataFormatString enables you to define the format in which the underlying data is displayed. In this case, the lowercase letter g is used to display both the date and the time in short format (without seconds). You can find more information about the different format strings in the MSDN documentation at http://tinyurl.com/DateFormatters45.

You then converted the Authorized column to a template column. A template column gives you full freedom with regard to the content you are presenting. Essentially, you can add almost anything you see fit as content for the column, including HTML and ASPX controls. In this exercise, you changed the Label so that it gets its text from a custom function using the data binding expression syntax <%# %>:

```
<asp:Label ID="AuthorizedLabel" runat="server"
      Text='<%# GetBooleanText(Eval("Authorized")) %>'></asp:Label>
```

Two things are used here to make this work. First, look at the Eval("Authorized") statement. This is called a one-way data *binding expression* and results in the value of the Authorized column being passed as an object to the custom GetBooleanText method. This method in turn converts the incoming value to a Boolean and then returns Yes or No, depending on the value of the Authorized column in the database. This is just a simple example to demonstrate how to call custom methods in your Code Behind during data binding. However, the principle remains the same for more complex methods: you pass one or more arguments to a Code Behind method using Eval("*ColumnName*"). The method in the Code Behind accepts these arguments as objects, casts them to an appropriate type, and then uses them as appropriate. In the end, the method can return a string with any text or HTML you see fit.

The HyperLink for the Title column that you set up points to a page called AddEditReview.aspx. This page enables you to create new and update existing reviews. You see how to create this page in the following section.

UPDATING AND INSERTING DATA

Earlier in this chapter I discussed how to do simple updates with the GridView and the SqlDataSource controls. Although this built-in update behavior is fine in many circumstances, it is not always extensive enough to meet all your demands.

Fortunately, controls like FormView and DetailsView enable you to tweak their look and feel, giving you a lot more flexibility in the way your end users work with their data. In the next section you see how to use the DetailsView to give the user a much easier interface to insert and edit reviews in the database.

Using DetailsView to Insert and Update Data

Earlier in this chapter you learned how to set up a simple DetailsView control and fully rely on VS and the control itself to render the relevant user interface in the browser. Obviously, this default behavior is often not enough. What if you wanted to influence the controls used in the interface? For example, what if you wanted to use a DropDownList instead of a simple TextBox for the genre? And what if you wanted to add one or more validation controls that you learned about in Chapter 9? Or what if you wanted to manage some of the data being sent to the database programmatically? All of this is possible with the DetailsView control, its template-based columns, and the numerous events that the control fires at various stages in its life cycle.

First, however, you need to learn a bit more about the different events that the data-bound and data source controls fire. The following table lists some of the events that the DetailsView, the FormView, and the ListView expose and raise during their lifetime. The GridView has similar events, but they start with Row instead of Item. Because the DataList and Repeater controls do not natively support editing of data, they do not have any of these events.

EVENT	DESCRIPTION
ItemInserting	Fires right before the Insert command is executed against the data source. This is an ideal location to change the data that is about to be sent to the database.
ItemInserted	Fires right after the Insert command has been executed against the data source.
ItemUpdating	Fires right before the Update command is executed against the data source. This is an ideal location to change the data that is about to be sent to the database.
ItemUpdated	Fires right after the Update command has been executed against the data source.
ItemDeleting	Fires right before the Delete command is executed against the data source.
ItemDeleted	Fires right after the Delete command has been executed against the data source.

These six events fire at very convenient moments in the life of the control: right before and right after the data for the operation is sent to the database. You see how to use them in the next Try It Out.

TRY IT OUT Managing Data with the DetailsView Control

In this exercise you create the `AddEditReview.aspx` page that you created a link for earlier in the Reviews page. You add a `DetailsView` to this page, customize most of its fields by implementing template fields, and then handle some of the events of the control to change its behavior. After you're done, you have everything you need to create, list, update, and delete reviews in your website.

1. In the `Management` folder, create a new Web Form and call it **`AddEditReview.aspx`**. Again, select your preferred programming language and base it on the master page for the Management section. Give it a `Title` of **`Planet Wrox - Management - Insert and Update Reviews`**.
2. Switch the page to Design View and drop a `DetailsView` control on the page. In the Smart Tasks panel that opens automatically, choose <New data source> from the Choose Data Source drop-down list. Click the Database icon and then click OK. In the dialog box that follows, choose the connection string from the drop-down list and click Next.
3. Enter the details as displayed in Figure 13-15.

   Note that all fields of the `Review` are selected explicitly, except for the `CreateDateTime` field.

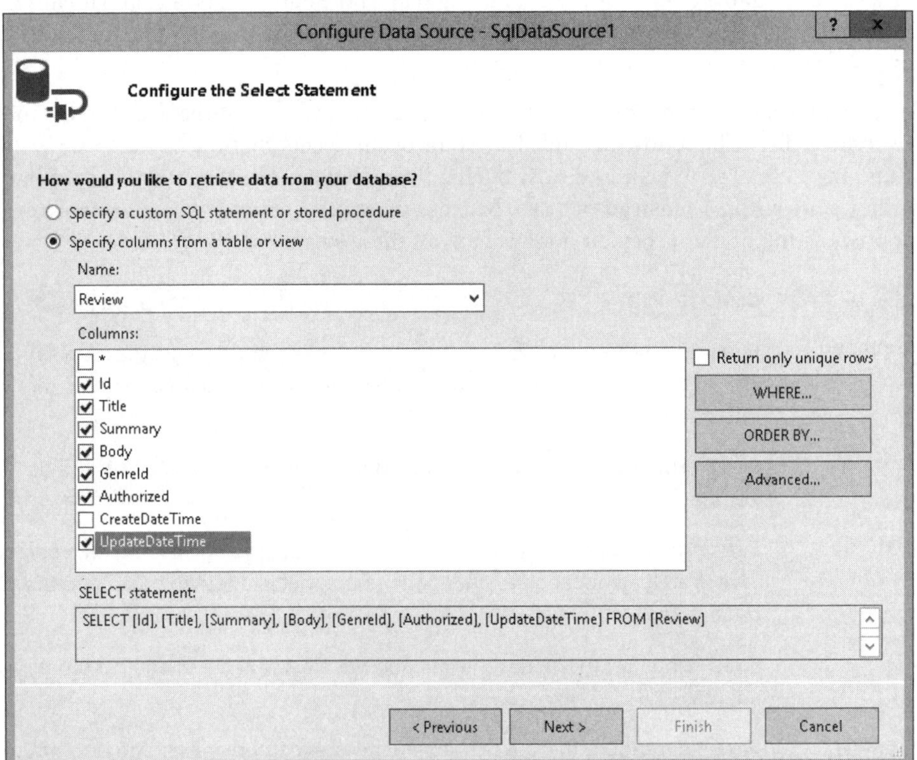

FIGURE 13-15

4. Click the WHERE button to set up a `SelectParameter` that retrieves the review ID from the query string by completing the dialog box as shown in Figure 13-16.

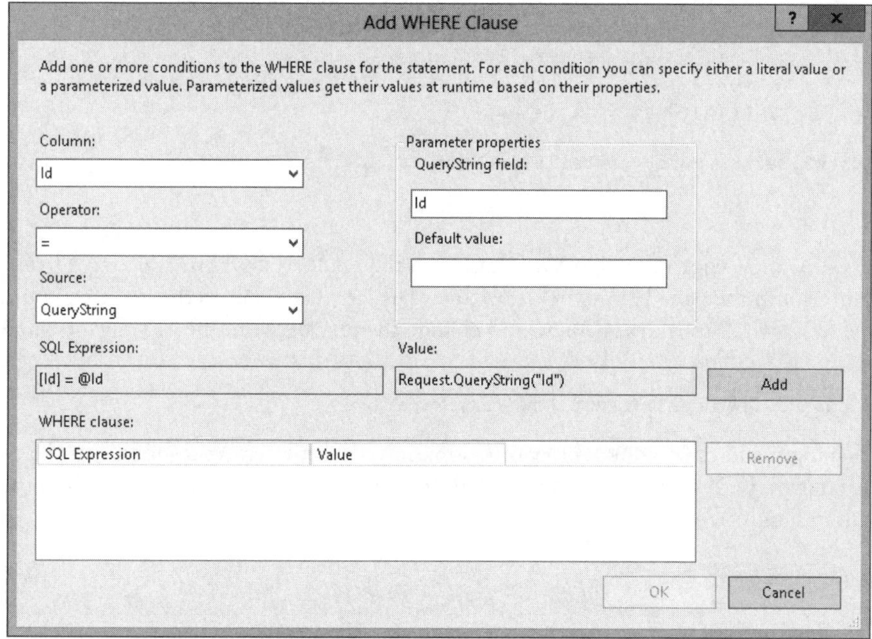

FIGURE 13-16

Don't forget to type **`Id`** in the QueryString field text box.

5. Click the Add button to add the parameter to the WHERE Clause list at the bottom and then click OK to close the dialog box.

6. Back in the Configure Data Source wizard (shown in Figure 13-15), click the Advanced button, select the option to generate `INSERT`, `UPDATE`, and `DELETE` statements, and click OK to close the dialog box. Finally, click Next and then Finish to finalize the data source wizard.

7. On the Smart Tasks panel for the `DetailsView`, select the options for Inserting and Editing as shown in Figure 13-17.

8. On the Properties Grid for the `DetailsView`, set `DefaultMode` to `Insert`.

9. Double-click an empty spot of the page in Design View to set up a `Page_Load` handler and enter the following code:

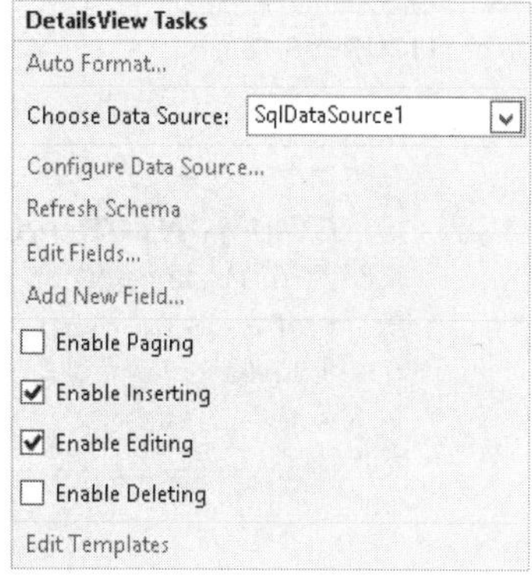

FIGURE 13-17

VB.NET

```
Protected Sub Page_Load(sender As Object, e As EventArgs) Handles Me.Load
  If Request.QueryString.Get("Id") IsNot Nothing Then
```

```
    DetailsView1.DefaultMode = DetailsViewMode.Edit
  End If
End Sub
```

C#

```
protected void Page_Load(object sender, EventArgs e)
{
  if (Request.QueryString.Get("Id") != null)
  {
    DetailsView1.DefaultMode = DetailsViewMode.Edit;
  }
}
```

10. Open the `Reviews.aspx` page in Design View and drag the `AddEditReview.aspx` page from the Solution Explorer onto the page below the `GridView`. This creates a link to this page so you can insert new reviews. Switch to Markup View and change the text between the `<a>` tags to **`Insert New Review`**:

```
<a href="AddEditReview.aspx">Insert New Review</a>
```

11. Save all your changes and open `AddEditReview.aspx` in your browser. You should get the default layout for the control, with simple text boxes for all the columns in the data source. Fill in the fields as shown in Figure 13-18.

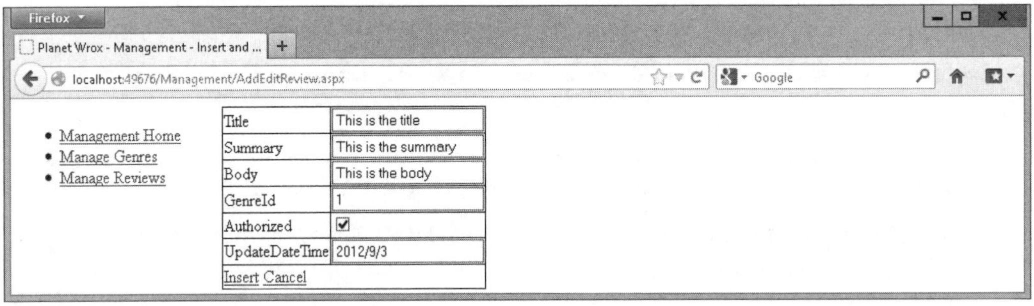

FIGURE 13-18

> ***COMMON MISTAKES*** *If you get an empty screen, make sure you set* `DefaultMode` *to* `Insert`. *Be sure the* `GenreId` *that you enter matches one of the genres in the* `Genre` *table in the database or you'll get an error when you try to insert the item. Also be sure you enter a valid date using the* `yyyy/mm/dd` *format, where* `y` *stands for year,* `m` *for month, and* `d` *for day.*

Click Insert to insert the item in the database. At first, not much seems to happen except that the controls are now all cleared. However, you can now locate the new review through the `Reviews.aspx` page by following these two steps:

- Click the Manage Reviews link in the menu on the left.
- Select the right genre from the drop-down list at the top of the page. If you used the scripts from the preceding chapter to create the data in your database, and you entered `1` for the `GenreId` when inserting the review, the genre is Rap and Hip-Hop.

When you have found your review, you can click its title and you'll be taken to `AddEditReview.aspx`, where you can change the review's details again.

How It Works

Most of this exercise should be familiar by now. The `DetailsView` works the same for inserting as the `DetailsView` for genres you saw earlier. What's different is how updates are handled. The code in the Code Behind looks at the query string and if it finds an `Id` query string parameter, it flips the `DetailsView` into edit mode:

VB.NET

```
If Request.QueryString.Get("Id") IsNot Nothing Then
  DetailsView1.DefaultMode = DetailsViewMode.Edit
End If
```

C#

```
if (Request.QueryString.Get("Id") != null)
{
  DetailsView1.DefaultMode = DetailsViewMode.Edit;
}
```

When the control is in edit mode, it knows what to do. It calls the `SqlDataSource` and requests its data. The `SqlDataSource` in turn retrieves the ID of the review from the query string, accesses the database, and then returns the correct review, which is displayed on the page. When you subsequently click the Update link, the `SqlDataSource` fires its `UpdateCommand` to send the changes to the database.

This exercise provides a nice foundation for the following exercise, where you extend the `DetailsView` by implementing custom templates with validation controls and set up various event handlers to respond to the control's events.

Right now, the page with the `DetailsView` looks quite dull. It would look a lot better and be easier to use if it had the following features:

- A text area instead of a single-line text box for the Summary and Body fields
- A drop-down list for the genre filled with the available genres from the database
- Automatic updating of the `UpdateDateTime` column
- Validation controls to stop you from leaving required fields empty
- Automatic redirection to the `Reviews.aspx` page after an item has been inserted or updated

The next exercise shows you how to implement all of these features.

TRY IT OUT Customizing the DetailsView and Handling Its Events

This walk-through is quite long and has a large number of steps. Remember you can always download the final version of this page from the Wrox website in case you want to compare your result with mine.

1. Make sure `AddEditReview.aspx` is in Design View and bring up the Fields editor for the `DetailsView` control by clicking Edit Fields on its Smart Tasks panel. Locate the `UpdateDateTime` column in the Selected Fields list and set its `Visible` property to `False`.

2. Click the `Title` column in the Selected Fields list and then click the blue link with the text Convert This Field into a TemplateField. Repeat this for the `Summary`, `Body`, and `GenreId` fields and then close the Fields dialog box by clicking OK.

3. Switch to Markup View and add a `TextMode` attribute with its value set to `MultiLine` for the four `TextBox` controls for the `Summary` and `Body` fields. In addition, set their `Width` and `Height` properties to 500 and 100 pixels, respectively. Make sure you do this for both the `EditItemTemplate` and the `InsertItemTemplate`. You should end up with the following code that shows the `Summary` field, but the code for the `Body` field should be similar:

```
<asp:TemplateField HeaderText="Summary" SortExpression="Summary">
  <EditItemTemplate>
    <asp:TextBox ID="TextBox2" TextMode="MultiLine" Width="500" Height="100"
        runat="server" Text='<%# Bind("Summary") %>'></asp:TextBox>
  </EditItemTemplate>
  <InsertItemTemplate>
    <asp:TextBox ID="TextBox2" TextMode="MultiLine" Width="500" Height="100"
        runat="server" Text='<%# Bind("Summary") %>'></asp:TextBox>
  </InsertItemTemplate>
  <ItemTemplate>
    <asp:Label ID="Label2" runat="server"
        Text='<%# Bind("Summary") %>'></asp:Label>
  </ItemTemplate>
</asp:TemplateField>
```

4. Add a `RequiredFieldValidator` in the `EditItemTemplate` and the `InsertItemTemplate` of both the `Title` and the `Summary` rows. You can drag and drop it from the Toolbox directly in Markup View or enter the required code manually. Using a code snippet makes this even easier: position your mouse on an empty, new line below the `TextBox`, type **`requiredfieldvalidator`**, and press Tab. VS inserts a `RequiredFieldValidator` for you and automatically assigns the `ControlToValidate` property with the ID of the previous `TextBox` defined in the code.

   Make sure you hook up all validators to their respective `TextBox` controls in the template by setting the `ControlToValidate` property and providing a useful error message. When you're done, the summary field should look like this:

```
<asp:TemplateField HeaderText="Summary" SortExpression="Summary">
  <EditItemTemplate>
    <asp:TextBox ID="TextBox2" TextMode="MultiLine" Width="500" Height="100"
          runat="server" Text='<%# Bind("Summary") %>'></asp:TextBox>
    <asp:RequiredFieldValidator ControlToValidate="TextBox2"
          runat="server" ErrorMessage="Enter a summary">
    </asp:RequiredFieldValidator>
  </EditItemTemplate>
  <InsertItemTemplate>
```

```
      <asp:TextBox ID="TextBox2" TextMode="MultiLine" Width="500" Height="100"
            runat="server" Text='<%# Bind("Summary") %>'></asp:TextBox>
      <asp:RequiredFieldValidator ControlToValidate="TextBox2"
            runat="server" ErrorMessage="Enter a summary">
      </asp:RequiredFieldValidator>
    </InsertItemTemplate>
    <ItemTemplate>
      <asp:Label ID="Label2" runat="server" Text='<%# Bind("Summary") %>'>
      </asp:Label>
    </ItemTemplate>
  </asp:templatefield>
```

The `Title` and `Body` fields should look similar to `Summary`. The `TextBox` for the `Title` field doesn't have the `TextMode`, `Width`, and `Height` properties applied, whereas the `Body` field is missing the `RequiredFieldValidator`. Other than that, the fields should look pretty similar to the `Summary` field.

5. Switch to Design View and drag a new `SqlDataSource` control next to `SqlDataSource1` that is already on the page. Open the new control's Smart Tasks panel and click Configure Data Source. Select the Planet Wrox connection string from the drop-down list and click Next. Select the `Id` and `Name` columns from the `Genre` table and set up an `ORDER BY` clause on the `SortOrder` column by clicking the ORDER BY button and choosing `SortOrder` from the Sort By drop-down list. When you click OK, the Configure Data Source screen looks like Figure 13-19.

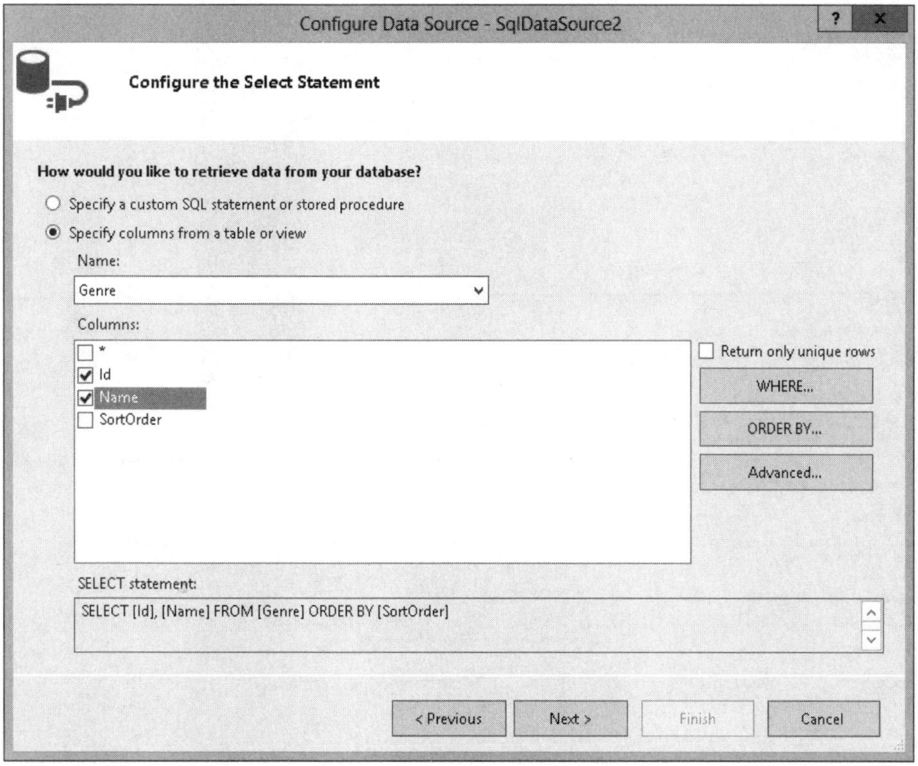

FIGURE 13-19

6. Click Next and then Finish to finalize the Configure Data Source wizard.

7. Select the new `SqlDataSource` (called `SqlDataSource2`) in Design View and change its ID to **`GenresDataSource`** using the Properties Grid so it's easier to recognize in the page.

8. Switch to Markup View, locate the `InsertItemTemplate` for the `GenreId` of the `DetailsView`, and remove its contents (the `TextBox` control). At the place where you removed the `TextBox`, add a `DropDownList` by dragging it from the Toolbox into Markup View. Your code looks like this:

```
<asp:TemplateField HeaderText="GenreId" SortExpression="GenreId">
  <EditItemTemplate>
    <asp:TextBox ID="TextBox4" runat="server"
         Text='<%# Bind("GenreId") %>'></asp:TextBox>
  </EditItemTemplate>
  <InsertItemTemplate>
    <asp:DropDownList ID="DropDownList1" runat="server">
    </asp:DropDownList>
  </InsertItemTemplate>
  ...
</asp:TemplateField>
```

9. Switch to Design View, right-click the `DetailsView`, and choose Edit Template ⇨ Field[4] - GenreId, as shown in Figure 13-20. If you don't see this menu item, you may need to click one of the rows with controls—such as the summary row—first to put the focus on the `DetailsView` correctly.

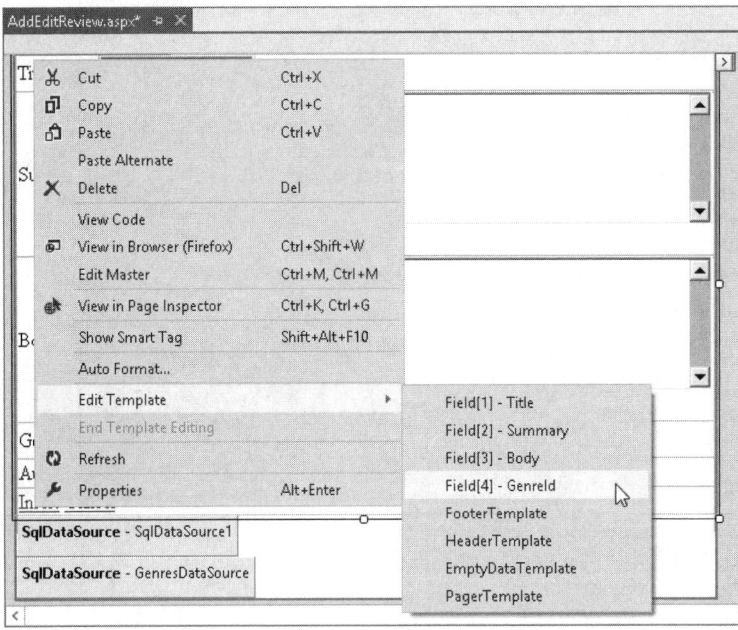

FIGURE 13-20

10. When the control is in template editing mode, you can access the `DropDownList` directly. Open the Smart Tasks panel for the `DropDownList` and select Choose Data Source. In the Data Source Configuration Wizard, choose `GenresDataSource` from the data source drop-down list and `Name` and `Id` from the other two drop-down lists (see Figure 13-21). If `Name` and `Id` don't appear in the drop-down lists, click the blue Refresh Schema link at the bottom of the screen. If you don't see the `GenreDataSource` listed, but you see `SqlDataSource2` instead, make sure you renamed the control correctly as described in step 7.

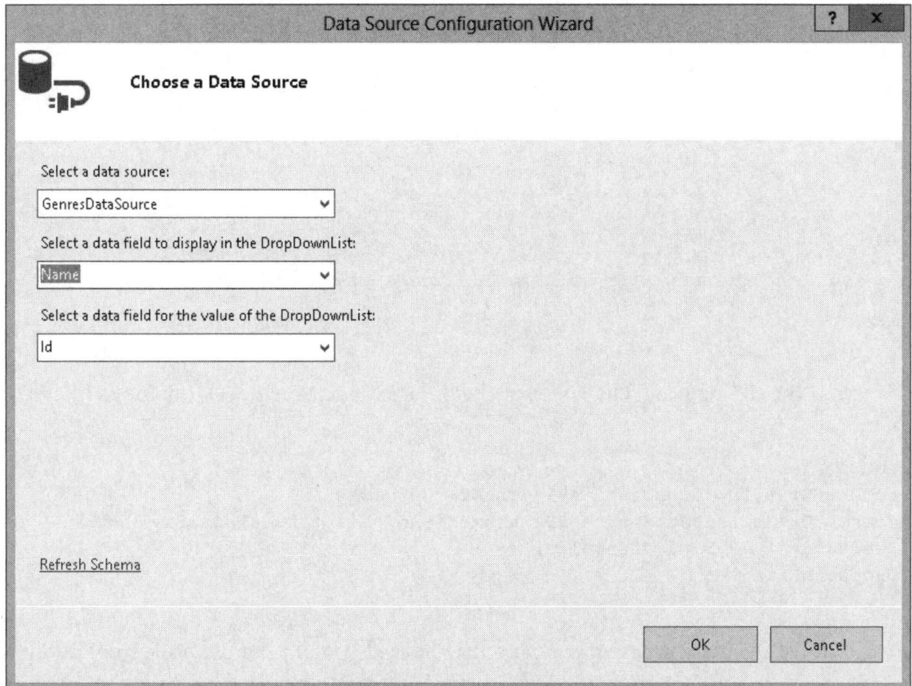

FIGURE 13-21

11. Click OK to close the Data Source Configuration Wizard.
12. Back on the Smart Tasks panel of the `DropDownList` control, click Edit DataBindings. In the dialog box that follows, click `SelectedValue` in the list on the left and then choose `GenreId` from the Bound To drop-down list on the right, as shown in Figure 13-22. If you find that the Field Binding radio button at the top-right of the screen is read-only, click the Refresh Schema link. In the dialog that appears, click OK. When you return to the DataBindings dialog box the item should now be enabled.

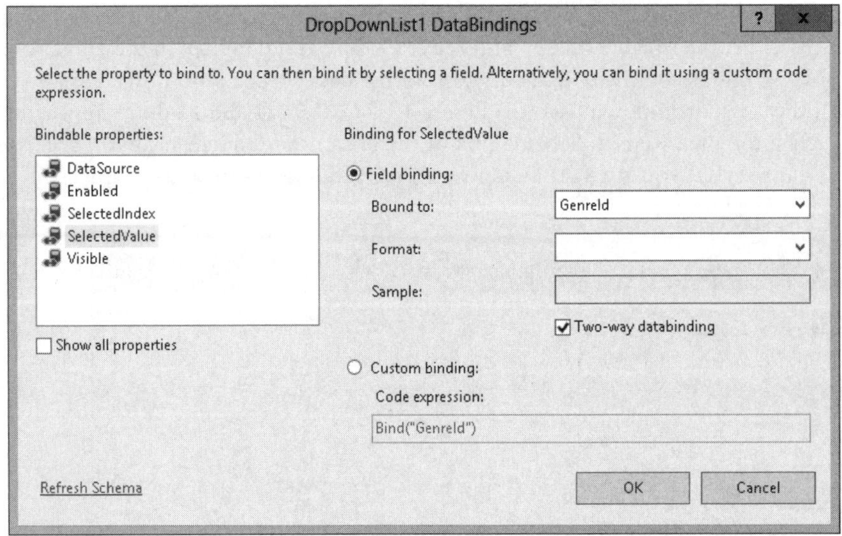

FIGURE 13-22

13. Click OK to close the dialog box. The code for the `InsertItemTemplate` now looks like this in Markup View:

```
<InsertItemTemplate>
  <asp:DropDownList ID="DropDownList1" runat="server"
    DataSourceID="GenresDataSource" DataTextField="Name" DataValueField="Id"
    SelectedValue='<%# Bind("GenreId") %>'>
  </asp:DropDownList>
</InsertItemTemplate>
```

14. Copy the contents of the `InsertItemTemplate` (the bolded code in the previous step) and paste it in the `EditItemTemplate`, overwriting the existing `TextBox` control. This adds the same drop-down list to the `DetailsView` in edit mode.

15. Switch back to Design View, click the `DetailsView`, and press F4 to open up the Properties Grid. Switch to the Events tab of the Properties Grid and double-click the following events. VS switches to the Code Behind file every time you double-click an event, so you need to switch back to the page (using Ctrl+Tab) to add the other events:

- `ItemInserted`
- `ItemInserting`
- `ItemUpdated`
- `ItemUpdating`

When you're done, the event category of the Properties Grid should look like Figure 13-23.

16. Go into the Code Behind and modify the code as follows. Note that the `ItemInserted` and `ItemUpdated` handlers call the `EndEditing` method (that you also need to add to the code), whereas `ItemInserting` and `ItemUpdating` both set the `UpdateDateTime` value:

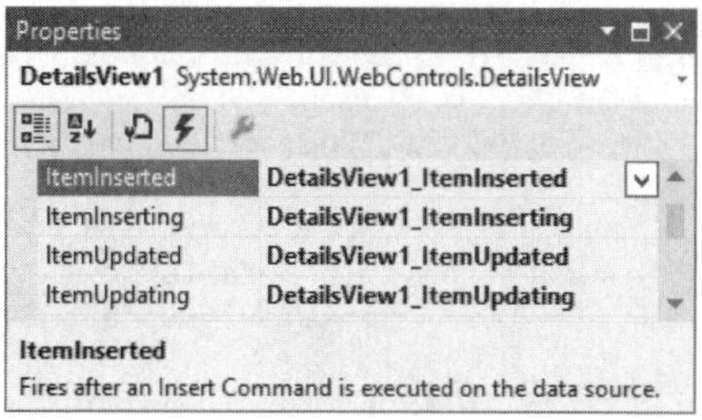

Properties
DetailsView1 System.Web.UI.WebControls.DetailsView

ItemInserted	DetailsView1_ItemInserted
ItemInserting	DetailsView1_ItemInserting
ItemUpdated	DetailsView1_ItemUpdated
ItemUpdating	DetailsView1_ItemUpdating

ItemInserted
Fires after an Insert Command is executed on the data source.

FIGURE 13-23

VB.NET

```
Private Sub EndEditing()
  Response.Redirect("Reviews.aspx")
End Sub

Protected Sub DetailsView1_ItemInserted(sender As Object,
     e As DetailsViewInsertedEventArgs) Handles DetailsView1.ItemInserted
  If e.Exception Is Nothing Then
    EndEditing()
  End If
End Sub

Protected Sub DetailsView1_ItemInserting(sender As Object,
     e As DetailsViewInsertEventArgs) Handles DetailsView1.ItemInserting
  e.Values("UpdateDateTime") = DateTime.Now
End Sub

Protected Sub DetailsView1_ItemUpdated(sender As Object,
     e As DetailsViewUpdatedEventArgs) Handles DetailsView1.ItemUpdated
  If e.Exception Is Nothing Then
    EndEditing()
  End If
End Sub

Protected Sub DetailsView1_ItemUpdating(sender As Object,
     e As DetailsViewUpdateEventArgs) Handles DetailsView1.ItemUpdating
  e.NewValues("UpdateDateTime") = DateTime.Now
End Sub
```

C#

```
private void EndEditing()
{
  Response.Redirect("Reviews.aspx");
}

protected void DetailsView1_ItemInserted(object sender,
          DetailsViewInsertedEventArgs e)
{
  if (e.Exception == null)
  {
    EndEditing();
  }
}
```

```
protected void DetailsView1_ItemInserting(object sender,
          DetailsViewInsertEventArgs e)
{
  e.Values["UpdateDateTime"] = DateTime.Now;
}

protected void DetailsView1_ItemUpdated(object sender,
          DetailsViewUpdatedEventArgs e)
{
  if (e.Exception == null)
  {
    EndEditing();
  }
}

protected void DetailsView1_ItemUpdating(object sender,
          DetailsViewUpdateEventArgs e)
{
  e.NewValues["UpdateDateTime"] = DateTime.Now;
}
```

17. Finally, save all your changes and open `AddEditReview.aspx` in your browser. Leave all fields empty and click the Insert link. Note that the validation controls kick in, preventing you from sending empty values to the server. Next, fill in valid values and click Insert again. You're now taken to `Reviews.aspx`. Locate your review by choosing its genre from the drop-down list and then click its title to edit it. The `DetailsView` should now display all the values you entered previously (see Figure 13-24).

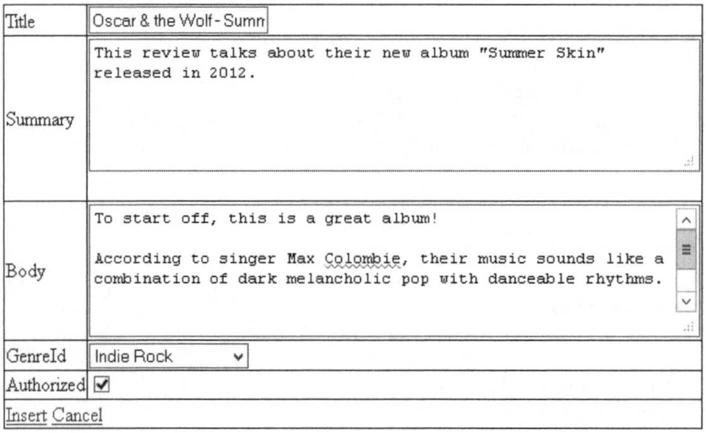

Title	Oscar & the Wolf - Sumn
Summary	This review talks about their new album "Summer Skin" released in 2012.
Body	To start off, this is a great album! According to singer Max Colombie, their music sounds like a combination of dark melancholic pop with danceable rhythms.
GenreId	Indie Rock
Authorized	☑
Insert Cancel	

FIGURE 13-24

How It Works

The `DetailsView` and the `SqlDataSource` controls take care of most of the hard work for you. You set up different templates that enable a user to insert new rows and update existing ones and then the two controls take care of the rest. When you click the Insert link, the controls are validated using JavaScript as you saw in previous chapters. The same validation is carried out at the server by the `DetailsView` control to ensure the submitted data meets the criteria you set. If the data is valid, the `DetailsView` control inserts or updates the data, depending on the mode it's in. To see how this works, take a look at the `InsertItemTemplate` for the `Title` column first:

```
<InsertItemTemplate>
  <asp:TextBox ID="TextBox1" runat="server" Text='<%# Bind("Title") %>'>
  </asp:TextBox>
  <asp:RequiredFieldValidator ControlToValidate="TextBox1"
    runat="server" ErrorMessage="Please enter a title">
  </asp:RequiredFieldValidator>
</InsertItemTemplate>
```

The most important piece of code in this snippet is the way the `Text` property of the `TextBox` is bound. Earlier you saw the one-way binding syntax using `Eval` that basically outputs the value of a bound column. With `Bind`, however, something much more powerful occurs. Basically, `Bind` enables you to express a data binding between a column from the `SqlDataSource` and a control in the page in *two directions*. In this example, the `Title` column of a review is bound to the `TextBox`. This means that when the control must display its data (for example, when updating an existing row), it knows that it must display the `Title` of a review. But more importantly, on postback, after you click the Update link, the control still understands the relationship between the `TextBox` control and the `Title` column. So, when you click Update after making changes to the review in the page, the `DetailsView` collects all the bound data from the form (the `Title`, `Summary`, `Body`, `GenreId`, and whether the item is authorized) and then sends it to the `SqlDataSource` control that has parameters set up for each of the relevant columns of the `Review` table:

```
<asp:SqlDataSource ID="SqlDataSource1" runat="server"
  ...
  <UpdateParameters>
    <asp:Parameter Name="Title" Type="String" />
    <asp:Parameter Name="Summary" Type="String" />
    <asp:Parameter Name="Body" Type="String" />
    <asp:Parameter Name="GenreId" Type="Int32" />
    <asp:Parameter Name="Authorized" Type="Boolean" />
    <asp:Parameter Name="UpdateDateTime" Type="DateTime" />
    <asp:Parameter Name="Id" Type="Int32" />
  </UpdateParameters>
</asp:SqlDataSource>
```

Eventually, the `SqlDataSource` grabs all the parameter values, injects them in the `UpdateCommand`, and then sends them to the database.

This works nicely for all columns of the `Review` table that have a form control attached to them, but what about the other columns? You may have noticed that `CreateDateTime` was not a part of any of the `SqlDataSource` commands. Because the database is set up to insert today's date and time automatically, there's no need to include it in the code. The `UpdateDateTime` column is a different story. Obviously, you don't want your users to enter the value for this column manually. Instead, the system should keep track of it automatically. That's why you hid the control from the user interface by setting its `Visible` property to `False`. However, because the `Insert` and `Update` commands still expect a value for this column, you need to find a different way to insert it. Here's where the `Inserting` and

Updating events come into play. Take a look at the ItemInserting event handler to get a general understanding of how this works:

VB.NET

```
Protected Sub DetailsView1_ItemInserting(sender As Object,
     e As DetailsViewInsertEventArgs) Handles DetailsView1.ItemInserting
  e.Values("UpdateDateTime") = DateTime.Now
End Sub
```

C#

```
protected void DetailsView1_ItemInserting(object sender,
          DetailsViewInsertEventArgs e)
{
  e.Values["UpdateDateTime"] = DateTime.Now;
}
```

As you saw earlier, ItemInserting fires right before the InsertCommand is sent to the database. This is a perfect location to supply (default) values for the columns in your table that have no corresponding control in the user interface, as is the case with UpdateDateTime. This code simply sets the UpdateDateTime value to today's date and time. This value is then sent to the database where it is used to assign a value to the Review table's UpdateDateTime column.

The same principle applies to the ItemUpdating command. Within that event, you need to index the NewValues collection instead of the Values collection, but the principle is the same.

You might argue that in the case of an Insert command, you don't need to set the UpdateDateTime. After all, the database inserts a value for you automatically when you insert a new row. However, to make the distinction between inserting and updating, you need to do a lot more manual work. You have to remove the column from the InsertCommand and then remove the column from the <InsertParameters> collection as well. Although in itself this is not a lot of work, you get into trouble when you later try to modify the SQL commands for the SqlDataSource, because the Insert and Update commands are now out of sync. Simply setting the UpdateDateTime through code, as in this case, solves many of these problems.

When the SqlDataSource control is done with inserting or updating, it fires its ItemInserted or ItemUpdated events, respectively. Inside these events, the code checks if e.Exception is null/Nothing. Without this check, the user would be redirected to the Reviews.aspx page regardless of whether an error occurred. With this check, the user is taken back to Reviews.aspx page by calling EndEditing() only if the database update succeeded:

VB.NET

```
Private Sub EndEditing()
  Response.Redirect("Reviews.aspx")
End Sub
```

C#

```
private void EndEditing()
{
  Response.Redirect("Reviews.aspx");
}
```

A typical reason for an error during the update might be an incorrect genre ID. If you didn't set up the `DropDownList` correctly, the database would be given an invalid genre ID and the `INSERT` or `UPDATE` would fail. By not redirecting when an error occurs, the error message is displayed on-screen so you get a chance to fix it.

With the discussion of the various events that the `DetailsView` control fires, you have come to the end of this chapter. By now, you should have a reasonably good understanding of how to perform CRUD operations using the `GridView`, `DetailsView`, and `SqlDataSource` controls.

Useful as the `SqlDataSource` control may be, many developers don't like or use it. One of the biggest drawbacks of this control is the fact that your SQL statements end up directly in your ASPX pages. This can be really problematic if you start changing your database schema. Even if you think there's no need to do that ever, you can be pretty sure you'll need to change it one day. Once you do that, things are likely to break. For example, if you rename the `Name` column of the `Genre` table to `Description`, your application will break. However, you won't notice that until run time because VS is not able to check the database schema against the command texts defined in the `SqlDataSource` controls. You have a few ways to work around this. One solution is to build strongly typed objects and work with the `ObjectDataSource` control instead. Details of this solution are beyond the scope of this book, but you're invited to check out my website where I've published an article series demonstrating this concept: `http://bit.ly/9woD7D`. The concepts presented in this series are quite advanced, so you may want to postpone digging into it until you've finished this book.

Another alternative is to make use of the ADO.NET Entity Framework, the topic of the next chapter that also shows you how to use the `EntityDataSource` control and the `ListView` and `DataPager` controls to perform similar actions without the need to write embedded SQL statements in your code.

PRACTICAL TIPS FOR DISPLAYING AND UPDATING DATA

The following list provides some practical tips for displaying and updating data:

- Always store your connection strings in the `Web.config` file. Although it may seem easy to store them directly in the `SqlDataSource` control in a page, you'll get in trouble when you need to make changes to your connection string later.
- Always consider adding validation controls to your data entry pages. It makes it a lot easier for your users to find out what data is required, and in what format they should deliver it, while you protect your system from receiving and processing incorrect data.
- If you have long lists of data to present, always consider turning paging on for controls like the `GridView`. Users tend to get lost if you present them with lists containing many items. Generally, a page size of somewhere between 10 and 20 items works best.
- Consider renaming the controls in the page to something other than their default values. For example, in the previous Try It Out exercise you renamed `SqlDataSource2` to `GenresDataSource`. This makes it much easier to see which data source is needed to get information about the genres. With only a few controls in a page this isn't really an issue, but

as soon as your page grows, it is increasingly important to choose distinguishing names for your controls.

- Consider setting the `CssClass` of the validation controls in `AddEditReview.aspx` and hook them up to a CSS class. You can create them in a style sheet in the `Styles` folder in the root for now and link that file to the master page. In a later chapter you create a separate theme for the Management section.

SUMMARY

This chapter built on the general knowledge you gained in Chapter 12 about accessing a database through SQL. It started off with a discussion of the numerous controls in the Data category of the Toolbox in Visual Studio.

These controls can be split into two groups: data-bound controls and data source controls. The first group of controls—including the `GridView`, the `DetailsView`, and the `ListView`—is used to display data in a web page. Most, but not all of them enable you to maintain your data as well, by exposing inserting, updating, and deleting capabilities.

The controls in the other group, the data source controls, have no visual appearance themselves. They serve as a bridge between the user interface and the database. A number of different data source controls exist, each providing access to a specific kind of data store. In this chapter you saw the `SqlDataSource` control, which enables you to retrieve data from many different kinds of relational databases.

EXERCISES

1. If you need to create a user interface that enables a user to display, filter, edit, and delete data coming from a database, what is the best control to use? How do you hook up that control to the database?

2. Which control would you pick if you want to display a simple list of the genres in your database in the following format?

```
<ul>
  <li>Punk</li>
  <li>Hard Rock</li>
  <li>Jazz</li>
  <li>Techno</li>
</ul>
```

3. What's the difference between a `BoundField` and a `TemplateField`? When would you use which of the two?

4. What's the best place to store your connection strings? How do you access the connection strings from that location? And why shouldn't you store them in a page?

You can find answers to these exercises in Appendix A.

▶ WHAT YOU LEARNED IN THIS CHAPTER

Connection string	A string containing information necessary to connect to a database such as SQL Server
Data source controls	A set of ASP.NET controls that serve as a bridge between a data source (a database, an XML file, and so on) and the data-bound controls
Data-binding expression syntax	Syntax used to bind values from data sources to control properties such as labels and text boxes. Example: `Text='<%# Bind("Title") %>'` `Bind` is used for two-way binding, whereas `Eval` is used to display read-only data
Data-bound controls	A set of ASP.NET controls that can display flat and hierarchical data

Expression syntax	A terse syntax to bind a variety of sources, including connection strings from the `Web.config` file, to control properties. Example:
	`ConnectionString=`
	`"<%$ ConnectionStrings:PlanetWroxConnectionString1 %>"`

`InsertParameters`
`UpdateParameters`
`DeleteParameters`
	A set of parameters used to feed data into the data source controls to support insert, update, and delete behavior

Named instance	The name of a specific SQL Server instance. Used to distinguish between multiple installations of SQL Server on the same machine
SelectParameters	A set of parameters that can get their data from other sources (a query string, a cookie, and so on) and that can be used in the data source controls to filter data

14

LINQ and the ADO.NET Entity Framework

WHAT YOU WILL LEARN IN THIS CHAPTER:

- What LINQ is and what its syntax looks like
- The different forms of LINQ that are available and when they are appropriate to use
- How to use the ADO.NET Entity Framework
- How to use the `EntityDataSource` control to access the ADO.NET Entity Framework
- How to use the `ListView` and `DataPager` controls

WROX.COM CODE DOWNLOADS FOR THIS CHAPTER

You can find the wrox.com code downloads for this chapter on the Download Code tab at `www.wrox.com/remtitle.cgi?isbn=1118311809`. The code is in the Chapter 14 download.

Language-Integrated Query (LINQ) is the query language that is tightly integrated with the programming languages used in the .NET Framework. LINQ enables you to query data from within .NET programming languages in the same way that SQL enables you to query data in a database. In fact, the LINQ syntax has been modeled partially after the SQL language, making it easier for programmers familiar with SQL to get started with LINQ.

LINQ comes in a few different implementations, enabling you to access and query a wide variety of sources, including in-memory data, XML files, .NET DataSets, and databases from your VB.NET or C# code. In the next section you get a brief overview of the main LINQ pillars. The remainder of this chapter focuses on the LINQ syntax and on the *ADO.NET Entity Framework (EF)*, a technology that enables you to work with databases without writing a lot of code. The ADO.NET Entity Framework uses LINQ a lot under the hood, so you get a good shot at practicing your new LINQ skills.

INTRODUCING LINQ

LINQ enables you to query data from a wide variety of data sources, directly from your programming code. LINQ is to .NET programming what SQL is to relational databases. With straightforward, declarative syntax you can query collections for objects that match your criteria.

LINQ is not just an add-on that is part of the .NET Framework. On the contrary, LINQ has been designed and implemented as a true part of the programming languages in .NET. This means that LINQ is truly integrated into .NET, giving you a unified way to query data, regardless of where that data comes from. In addition, because it is integrated into the language and not in a certain project type, LINQ is available in all kinds of projects, including web applications, Windows Forms applications, Console applications, and so on. To help developers get familiar with LINQ, its syntax is closely modeled after SQL, the most popular query language for relational databases. This means that LINQ has keywords such as `Select`, `From`, and `Where` to get data from a data source.

To give you an idea of what a LINQ query looks like, here's a quick example that shows a list of Wrox authors whose names contain the capital letter S:

VB.NET

```
Dim authors As String() = New String() {"Hanselman, Scott", "Evjen, Bill",
                          "Haack, Phil", "Vieira, Robert", "Spaanjaars, Imar"}
Dim result = From author In authors
             Where author.Contains("S")
             Order By author
             Select author
For Each author In result
  Label1.Text += author + "<br />"
Next
```

C#

```
using System.Linq;
...
string[] authors = new string[] { "Hanselman, Scott", "Evjen, Bill",
                   "Haack, Phil", "Vieira, Robert", "Spaanjaars, Imar" };
var result = from author in authors
             where author.Contains("S")
             orderby author
             select author;

foreach (var author in result)
{
  Label1.Text += author + "<br />";
}
```

Although the syntax used in this example is probably quite easy to follow, the example itself is really powerful. Given an array of strings containing author names, you can simply select all the authors whose names contain the capital letter S and order them in ascending order. It should come as no surprise that in this example, the `Label` control displays my name and that of Scott Hanselman because only those two names match the `Where` criterion. Notice how in C# the code imports the `System.Linq` namespace. This is necessary to bring the LINQ functionality into scope for your application. If you're finding that some keywords don't show up in IntelliSense or VS gives you compilation errors on your LINQ queries, check that you have this namespace imported at the top of your code file. In a VB website, this namespace is included by default.

Of course, this example is only the beginning. The different types of LINQ discussed in the following three sections enable you to create much more powerful queries against a wide variety of data sources.

Because LINQ is so powerful and has so much potential, it has been integrated into many different areas of the .NET Framework. The following sections introduce the different LINQ implementations.

LINQ to Objects

This is the purest form of language integration. With LINQ to Objects, you can query collections in your .NET applications as you saw in the previous example. You're not limited to arrays because LINQ enables you to query almost any kind of collection that exists in the .NET Framework.

LINQ to XML

LINQ to XML is the new .NET way to read and write XML. Instead of typical XML query languages like XSLT or XPath, you can now write LINQ queries that target XML directly in your application.

LINQ to ADO.NET

ADO.NET is the part of the .NET Framework that enables you to access data and data services like SQL Server and many other different kinds of data sources. ADO.NET is also used under the hood by the `SqlDataSource` control and is commonly used in "raw data access code"—code written in C# or VB.NET that connects to a database without using the declarative data controls. With LINQ to ADO.NET you can query database-related information sets, including LINQ to DataSet, LINQ to SQL, and LINQ to Entities.

LINQ to DataSet enables you to write queries against the `DataSet`, a class that represents an in-memory version of a database.

LINQ to SQL enables you to write object-oriented queries in your .NET projects that target Microsoft SQL Server databases. The LINQ to SQL implementation translates your queries into SQL statements, which are then sent to the database to perform typical CRUD operations. In the 3.5 version of this book, this entire chapter was devoted to LINQ to SQL. However, in the meantime, a lot has happened. Microsoft has indicated that it will no longer actively develop LINQ to SQL. It will remain part of the .NET Framework and Visual Studio for the foreseeable future, but Microsoft probably won't be adding new functionality to it. The reason for this is the great overlap in functionality with the Entity Framework (EF). Almost anything you can do in LINQ to SQL can be done in LINQ to Entities. However, this latter framework is a lot more powerful and offers many more features than LINQ to SQL. Because it's more powerful, the Entity Framework is preferred over LINQ to SQL and as such it's the main topic of this chapter.

For more information about the other types of implementations, check out the official LINQ homepage at `http://bit.ly/18ypUj`.

INTRODUCING THE ADO.NET ENTITY FRAMEWORK

EF is an *Object Relational Mapper (ORM)* that supports the development of data-oriented software applications. With EF, you can take a bunch of database objects like tables and turn them into .NET objects that you can access in your code. You can then use these objects in queries or use them directly in data-binding scenarios. EF also enables you to do the reverse: design an object model first and then let EF create the necessary database structure for you.

Working with EF is pretty easy and quite flexible. Using a diagram designer, you drag and drop objects like tables from your database into your Entity model. The database objects you drop on the diagram become available as .NET objects. For example, if you drop the `Review` table on the diagram, you end up with a strongly typed `Review` class. You can create instances of this class using LINQ queries and other means, as you see later in this chapter.

> ***NOTE*** *The ADO.NET Entity Framework is a large and complex topic by itself. There's a lot more to it than what I can cover in this chapter. For an in-depth look at EF, pick up a copy of the excellent book* Programming Entity Framework, Second Edition *by Julia Lerman.*

When you drop more than one related database table on your diagram, the designer detects the relationships between the tables and then replicates these relationships in your object model. For example, if you had a `Review` instance created in code using some LINQ to Entities query (as you see later), you could access its `Genre` property, which in turn gives you access to properties like `Name`:

VB.NET

```
Label1.Text = myReview.Genre.Name
```

C#

```
Label1.Text = myReview.Genre.Name;
```

Similarly, you can access the associated `Reviews` collection for a specific genre, for example to bind it to a data-bound control:

VB.NET

```
Repeater1.DataSource = myGenre.Reviews
```

C#

```
Repeater1.DataSource = myGenre.Reviews;
```

Don't worry about the actual syntax right now. You see a lot more of it in the remainder of this chapter. What's important to take away from this section is that EF creates a layer between your

.NET application and your SQL Server database. The Entity Designer takes care of most of the work for you, providing access to a clean object model that you can use in your application.

MAPPING YOUR DATA MODEL TO AN OBJECT MODEL

With EF, you map database items such as tables, columns, and relationships in the database to objects and properties in an object model in your application. VS comes with great tools to make this mapping as easy as possible, as you see in the following exercise.

TRY IT OUT A Simple LINQ to Entities Example

In this Try It Out, you see how to add an ADO.NET Entity Data Model file to your project, add database tables to the model, and then write a simple LINQ query to access the data in the underlying tables.

1. Open the Planet Wrox project that you have been working on so far. Right-click the `App_Code` folder, choose Add ➪ Add New Item, and select your programming language on the left. Then click ADO.NET Entity Data Model, type **`PlanetWrox`** as the name, and click Add to add the item to your project. If you don't see the item in the list, check that you right-clicked `App_Code` and not another folder like `App_Data`.
2. On the dialog box that follows, make sure that Generate from Database is selected and click Next.
3. In the Choose Your Data Connection step, make sure `PlanetWroxConnectionString1` is selected in the drop-down and that the check box to store the settings in `Web.config` is checked. Your dialog now looks like Figure 14-1.

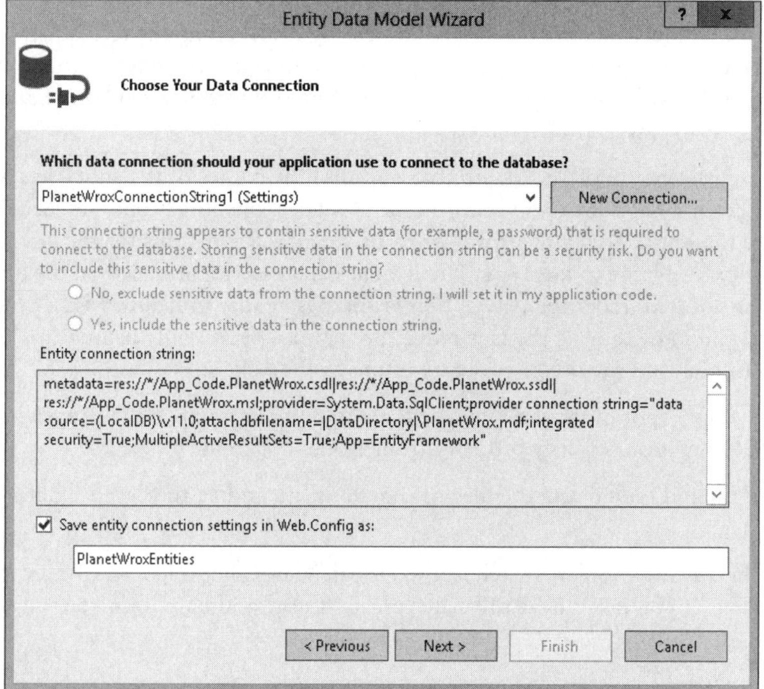

FIGURE 14-1

Click Next to go to the Choose Your Database Objects and Settings dialog box.

4. In this dialog box, expand Tables and then dbo, and then check off the `Genre` and `Review` tables. If you see a `sysdiagrams` table, leave it unchecked. This is a table used by SQL Server internally and you don't need it in your Planet Wrox model. If you're using an English version of VS, you get an option to pluralize or singularize names in the model automatically, which you should leave checked. For other languages you'll need to do this manually, as you see next. Finally, make sure you leave the option to include foreign key columns in the model checked. You see what that option is used for later in this chapter. Click Finish to add the model to your site. If you get a security warning, click Do Not Show This Message Again and then click OK. Visual Studio uses what's called a T4 template to generate the code for you and by default you need to grant permissions to execute this template.

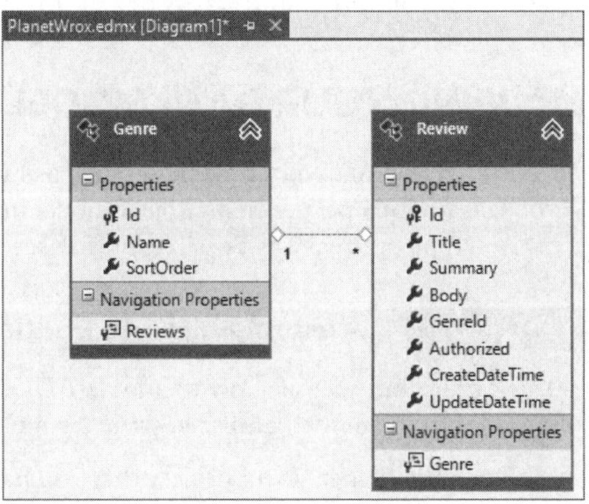

FIGURE 14-2

5. VS adds a file called `PlanetWrox.edmx` and two files with a `.tt` extension and then opens the Entity Designer for you in the main editor window, shown in Figure 14-2. It also created a Bin folder in the root of your site and added an assembly and an XML documentation file needed by the Entity Framework.

   This Entity Designer shows you .NET classes that have been generated based on the tables in your database. VS draws a line connecting the two classes, indicating it picked up the relationship that you created between the underlying tables in Chapter 12. If you don't see the line, or you don't see `Reviews` at the bottom of the `Genre` class or `Genre` at the bottom of the `Reviews` class, make sure you set up your database as explained in Chapter 12.

6. If you're using a non-English version of VS you need to pluralize the names of the entity sets and properties yourself. To do this, click the `Genre` class in the Designer, open its Properties Grid by pressing F4, and change the Entity Set Name from `Genre` to **`Genres`**. Repeat this for the `Review` class and change its Entity Set Name to **`Reviews`**. Finally, click the `Review` property on the diagram for the `Genre` class (located under the Navigation Properties header in Figure 14-2), press F2 to rename the item, and enter **`Reviews`** as the new name. Because a `Review` only belongs to a single `Genre`, you don't need to pluralize the `Genre` property of the `Review` class.

7. Click somewhere on an empty spot of the designer surface and press F4 to open the Properties Grid. Change the Code Generation Strategy property from None to Default.

8. Save and close the diagram and then delete the files `PlanetWrox.tt` and `PlanetWrox.Context.tt` from the `App_Code` folder.

9. Open `All.aspx` from the `Reviews` folder, switch it into Design View, and drag a `GridView` from the Toolbox onto the page. If you don't have this page, create it now and base it on your custom template.

10. Double-click the page in the gray, read-only area to have VS set up a handler for the `Page`'s `Load` event and add the following code. Be sure to read the next paragraph after the code example to learn how to solve an error you may get when typing in this code.

VB.NET

```
Protected Sub Page_Load(sender As Object, e As EventArgs) Handles Me.Load
  Using myEntities As New PlanetWroxEntities()
    Dim authorizedReviews = From review In myEntities.Reviews
                            Where review.Authorized = True
                            Order By review.CreateDateTime Descending
                            Select review
    GridView1.DataSource = authorizedReviews
    GridView1.DataBind()
  End Using
End Sub
```

C#

```
protected void Page_Load(object sender, EventArgs e)
{
  using (PlanetWroxEntities myEntities = new PlanetWroxEntities())
  {
    var authorizedReviews = from review in myEntities.Reviews
                            where review.Authorized == true
                            orderby review.CreateDateTime descending
                            select review;
    GridView1.DataSource = authorizedReviews;
    GridView1.DataBind();
  }
}
```

Notice how you immediately get an error when you type `PlanetWroxEntities` because it's defined in a namespace that is not in scope. You can fix the problem in two ways. You can type `Imports PlanetWroxModel` if you're using VB.NET or `using PlanetWroxModel;` if you're using C# at the top of the code file. Alternatively, you can click the word `PlanetWroxEntities` once and then press Ctrl+. (Ctrl+Dot) to bring up a dialog box that lets you choose the fix for the problem, shown in Figure 14-3 for the C# language. Choose the first item and VS adds the necessary `Imports`/`using` statement for you. In C# you can also right-click the word `PlanetWroxEntities` and then click the Resolve menu to bring up a similar menu.

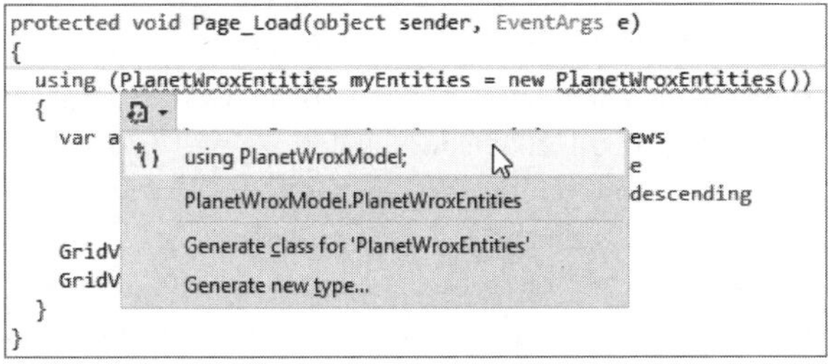

FIGURE 14-3

11. Save all your changes and press Ctrl+F5 to open the page. You'll get a screen full of reviews that have been retrieved from the `Review` table in the database, as shown in Figure 14-4.

The page looks rather messy because of the way the data is presented in the `GridView`, but in later exercises you see how to improve the layout of the grid and the data.

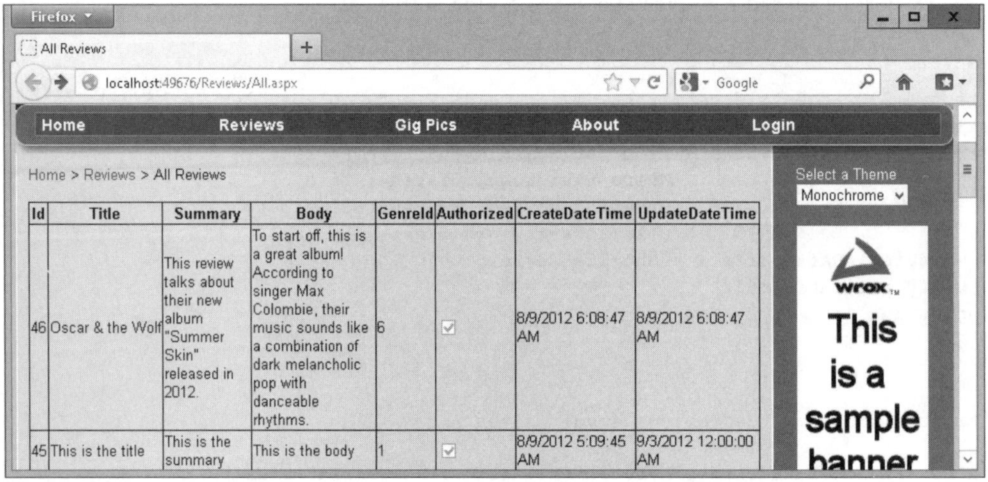

FIGURE 14-4

How It Works

EF comes with an object-relational designer (accessible in VS) that enables you to create an object model that is accessible through code based on the tables in your database. By adding tables to this designer, VS generates code for you that enables you to access the underlying data in the database without writing a lot of code. The classes that are added to the designer are stored in the `.edmx` file and its Code Behind files. The *designer file* (the Code Behind of the `PlanetWrox.edmx` file) contains a class that inherits from `ObjectContext`, the main object in EF that provides access to your database. In the preceding exercise, this class is called `PlanetWroxEntities` (named after the `.edmx` file) and you use it to access the data in the tables you added to the diagram. Although you normally don't need to look at the generated code, you can open the file `PlanetWrox.designer.vb` or `PlanetWrox.designer.cs` file and see what code has been generated for you. The `*.tt` files you deleted enable you to customize the code that is generated based on the underlying data model. However, in most cases you don't have to do this, and you can rely on the default code generation instead. That's why you deleted these files, and configured the EF model to use its default code generation strategy.

The designer is smart enough to detect the relationships in the database and is thus able to create the necessary relationships in code as well, as you saw in Figure 14-2. The model defines two main object types, `Review` and `Genre`, both of which also have collection counterparts called `Reviews` and `Genres`, respectively. These collections are referred to as *entity sets*. Note that on English versions of VS the designer has correctly pluralized the names of the `Review` and `Genre` tables (`Reviews` and `Genres`, respectively), making it easier to see what is a collection (`Reviews`) and what is a single instance of an object (`Review`). For other language versions of VS, you had to apply this logic yourself using the Entity Designer.

After the model has been generated, you can execute *LINQ queries* against it to get data out of the underlying database. To access the data, you need an instance of the `ObjectContext` class, which is created inside the `Using` block in the code. A `Using` block (`using` in C#) is used to wrap code that creates a variable that must be disposed of (cleared from memory) as soon as you're done with it. Because the myEntities variable holds a (scarce) connection to the SQL Server database, it's a good idea to wrap the code that uses it in a Using block, so the object is destroyed at the end of the block and the connection is released. This myEntities object then exposes your data (such as reviews and genres) that you can use in a query:

VB.NET

```
Using myEntities As New PlanetWroxEntities()
  Dim authorizedReviews = From review In myEntities.Reviews
                          Where review.Authorized = True
                          Order By review.CreateDateTime Descending
                          Select review
  ...
End Using
```

C#

```
using (PlanetWroxEntities myEntities = new PlanetWroxEntities())
{
  var authorizedReviews = from review in myEntities.Reviews
                          where review.Authorized == true
                          orderby review.CreateDateTime descending
                          select review;
  ...
}
```

Note that this query looks similar to the SQL that you learned in the previous chapters. Under the hood, the run time converts this LINQ query into its SQL counterpart and executes it against the underlying database. Within this query, the variable review in the From clause is used to refer to the review in the other parts of the query (Where, Order By, and Select), enabling you to specify the select, filter, and ordering criteria.

What's important to realize is that EF uses a mechanism called *lazy loading*, which means sub objects are not loaded until you explicitly tell them to. What this means is that in the previous example the Genre properties of the Review objects you've queried are null in C# and Nothing in VB.NET and don't contain any data. As soon as your code tries to access them, they are loaded by executing another query to the database. This can greatly improve performance if you don't need these sub objects. However, if you're sure you need them in your code beforehand, executing a separate SQL statement for each item results in a lot of overhead. In that case, you can preload the objects with the initial query. To express that you want to include these objects as well, you use the Include method for the types you want to query:

VB.NET

```
Dim authorizedReviews = From review In myEntities.Reviews.Include("Genre")
                        Where review.Authorized = True
...
```

C#

```
var authorizedReviews = from review in myEntities.Reviews.Include("Genre")
                        where review.Authorized == true
...
```

With this addition to the query, the Review objects now have their Genre property correctly filled with data. Though this may seem a little counterintuitive and counterproductive at first, it's actually quite a nice feature. If you don't need the extra Genre property in a specific page, you don't take the performance hit of selecting and returning these objects. If you do need them, all you need to add is a single call to Include.

Besides the Reviews collection the model also contains a Genres collection. When you want to select all the genres in the database, you can use this query:

VB.NET

```
Dim allGenres = From genre In myEntities.Genres
                Order By genre.Name
                Select genre
```

C#

```
var allGenres = from genre in myEntities.Genres
                orderby genre.Name
                select genre;
```

In addition to these two separate objects and their collections, both objects have properties that refer to each other's type. For example, a Review instance has a Genre property that provides additional information about the genre to which the review was assigned. A Genre instance in turn has a Reviews collection property, giving you access to all reviews posted in that genre. You see later how to make use of these properties.

From the keywords used in the first query in this Try It Out, it's probably easy to see what the query does: It gets a list of all the reviews in the system that have been authorized and orders them in descending order on their creation date. The result of the query is then assigned to the authorizedReviews variable. Notice that in both languages you can spread out the query over multiple lines to improve readability. This is not required, but you're encouraged to do it anyway because it makes your queries a lot easier to understand and maintain.

You may notice some strange syntax in the query. The VB.NET example doesn't use an As clause to define the type of the variable. Similarly, the C# snippet uses the var keyword, also without a type name. Although you may not conclude it from these code snippets, in both languages the variable authorizedReviews is still *strongly typed* and not just a variable with an undefined type.

> ***NOTE*** *Strongly typed refers to the fact that the variable's type is explicitly defined when it's declared. Once you've defined the type for a variable (using* Dim *in VB or the type's name in C#) you cannot change it anymore at run time. Strongly typed languages — such as C# and VB.NET — bring many advantages, including the ability to check the types being used at compile time, something that a weakly typed programming language cannot do.*

Because the code didn't state the type for authorizedReviews (the example used Dim or var instead), .NET needs a different solution to determine the type. This is done by a concept called *type inference*, where the compiler is able to infer the type for a variable by looking at the right side of the assignment. In this case, the compiler sees that a list of Review objects will be returned from the query, and correctly types the `authorizedReviews` variable as a *generics* type `IQueryable(Of Review)` in VB.NET syntax or `IQueryable<Review>` in C#. Although this looks a little scary and incomprehensible at first, it becomes much easier to understand if you simply read it as "a bunch of `Review` objects that you can access in queries." In most cases you can also explicitly specify the return type of the variable instead of using `var` or a `Dim` statement without a data type, but exceptions do exist, as you'll see later when anonymous objects are discussed.

These `Review` objects are then assigned to the `DataSource` property of the `GridView`. In previous chapters you saw how to use the `DataSourceID` property to connect a control such as the `GridView` to a data source control like the `SqlDataSource`. By using the `DataSource` property instead, you can assign the actual data yourself, which the control then uses to build up the UI:

VB.NET

```
GridView1.DataSource = authorizedReviews
GridView1.DataBind()
```

C#

```
GridView1.DataSource = authorizedReviews;
GridView1.DataBind();
```

By calling `DataBind()` on the `GridView` you instruct the control to display the individual `Review` objects on the page. Because the `GridView` control's `AutoGenerateColumns` property is `True` by default, the control creates a column for each property it finds on the `Review` object. Later you see how to customize the control and the data that is being assigned to the `DataSource` property.

In the following section you learn more about the LINQ query syntax, the language that drives the querying capabilities of .NET.

INTRODUCING QUERY SYNTAX

The query you saw in the previous example is quite simple; it requests all the authorized reviews from the system and returns them in a sorted order. However, the querying capabilities of LINQ are much more powerful than this. In this section you learn more about the LINQ query syntax that you use to query your object model. Remember, LINQ syntax is not invented just for the Entity Framework. Most of the LINQ concepts that follow can also be used in the other LINQ implementations, such as LINQ to Objects and LINQ to ADO.NET.

Standard Query Operators

LINQ supports a large number of query operators — keywords that enable you to select, order, or filter data that is to be returned from the query. Although all of the examples in this chapter are discussed in the context of EF, you can easily apply them to the other LINQ implementations as well. In the following section you get an overview of the most important standard query operators, each followed by an example. Each of the examples uses the object model and the `ObjectContext` object called `myEntities` you created earlier as the data source to query against.

Select

The Select keyword (select in C#) is used to retrieve objects from the source you are querying. In this example you see how to select an object of an existing type. Later in this chapter you see how to define new object shapes on the fly.

VB.NET

```
Dim allReviews = From r In myEntities.Reviews
                 Select r
```

C#

```
var allReviews = from r in myEntities.Reviews
                 select r;
```

The r variable in this example is referred to as a *range variable* that is only available within the current query. You typically introduce the range variable in the From clause, and then use it again in the Where and Select clauses to filter the data, and to indicate the data you want to select. Although you can choose any name you like, you often see single-letter variables like the r (for Review) or you see the singular form of the collection you are querying (review instead of r in the preceding examples).

From

Although not considered a standard query operator — because it doesn't operate on the data but rather points to the data — the From clause (from in C#) is an important element in a LINQ query, because it defines the collection or data source that the query must act upon. In the previous example, the From clause indicates that the query must be executed against the Reviews collection that is exposed by the myEntities object in EF.

Order By

With Order By (orderby in C#, without the space that VB.NET uses) you can sort the items in the result collection. Order By is followed by an optional Ascending or Descending (ascending and descending in C#) keyword to specify sort order. You can specify multiple criteria by separating them with a comma. The following query returns a list of genres, first sorted by SortOrder in descending order, then sorted on their Name in ascending order (the default):

VB.NET

```
Dim allGenres = From g In myEntities.Genres
                Order By g.SortOrder Descending, g.Name
                Select g
```

C#

```
var allGenres = from g in myEntities.Genres
                orderby g.SortOrder descending, g.Name
                select g;
```

Where

Just like the `WHERE` clause in SQL, the `Where` clause in LINQ (`where` in C#) enables you to filter the objects returned by the query. The following query returns all authorized reviews:

VB.NET

```
Dim authorizedReviews = From r In myEntities.Reviews
                        Where r.Authorized = True
                        Select r
```

C#

```
var authorizedReviews = from r in myEntities.Reviews
                        where r.Authorized == true
                        select r;
```

Note that the `Where` clause uses the language's standard equality operator: a single equals sign (=) in VB.NET and two of them in C#.

Sum, Min, Max, Average, and Count

These aggregation operators enable you to perform mathematical calculations on the objects in the result set. For example, to retrieve the number of reviews, you can execute this query:

VB.NET

```
Dim numberOfReviews = (From r In myEntities.Reviews
                      Select r).Count()
```

C#

```
var numberOfReviews = (from r in myEntities.Reviews
                      select r).Count();
```

Note that the `Count` method is applied to the entire result set. Therefore, you need to wrap the entire statement in parentheses followed by a call to `Count`. Without the parentheses you'll get an error. The `numberOfReviews` variable in this example will be *inferred* as an integer and contains the number of items in the `Review` table.

Take, Skip, TakeWhile, and SkipWhile

`Take` and `Skip` enable you to make sub-selections within the result set. This is ideal for paging scenarios where only the items for the current page are retrieved. `Take` gets the requested number of elements from the result set and then ignores the rest, whereas `Skip` ignores the requested number of elements and then returns the rest.

Within EF, the `Take` and `Skip` operators are translated to SQL statements as well. This means that paging takes place at the database level, and not in the ASP.NET page. This greatly enhances performance of the query, especially with large result sets, because not all elements have to be transferred from the database to the ASP.NET page.

For `Skip` to work in LINQ to Entities, you must add an `Order By` clause (`orderby` in C#) to your query to sort the results before the designated number of rows are skipped. Databases may return results in an unpredictable order if you don't add an explicit `ORDER BY` statement, so adding the `Order By` action in your LINQ to Entities query is needed to get a consistent result from the `Skip` method because rows are sorted first before they are skipped and taken.

The following example shows you how to retrieve the second page of rows, given a page size of 10:

VB.NET

```
Dim someReviews = (From r In myEntities.Reviews
                   Order By r.Title
                   Select r).Skip(10).Take(10)
```

C#

```
var someReviews = (from r in myEntities.Reviews
                   orderby r.Title
                   select r).Skip(10).Take(10);
```

Just as with the `Count` example, the query is wrapped in a pair of parentheses, followed by the calls to `Skip` and `Take` to get the requested rows.

The `TakeWhile` and `SkipWhile` query operators work in a similar fashion, but enable you to take or skip items while a specific condition is true. Unfortunately, they don't work in EF, but you can usually work around that by adding a simple `Where` clause to your query.

Single and SingleOrDefault

The `Single` and `SingleOrDefault` operators enable you to return a single object as a strongly typed instance. This is useful if you know your query returns exactly one row; for example, when you retrieve it by its unique ID. The following example retrieves the review with an ID of 37 from the database:

VB.NET

```
Dim review37 = (From r In myEntities.Reviews
                Where r.Id = 37
                Select r).Single()
```

C#

```
var review37 = (from r in myEntities.Reviews
                where r.Id == 37
                select r).Single();
```

The `Single` operator raises an exception when the requested item is not found or if the query returns more than one instance. If you want the method to return `null` (`Nothing` in VB.NET) — for example, for a `Review` or `Genre` that is not found — or the default value for the relevant data type (such as a 0 for an `Integer`, `False` for a `Boolean`, and so on) instead, use `SingleOrDefault`.

Even though there is only one `Review` with an `Id` of `37` in the database, you will still get a collection of reviews (holding only one element) if you omit the call to `Single`. By using `Single` you force the result set into a single instance of the type you are querying.

First, FirstOrDefault, Last, and LastOrDefault

These operators enable you to return the first or the last element in a specific sequence of objects. Just as with the `Single` method, `First` and `Last` throw an error when the collection is empty, whereas the other two operators return the default value for the relevant data types.

In contrast to `Single`, the `First`, `FirstOrDefault`, `Last`, and `LastOrDefault` operators don't throw an exception when the query returns more than one item. They simply return the first item in the result set.

The `Last` and `LastOrDefault` queries are not supported in EF. However, you can easily accomplish the same behavior with `First` and a `descending` sort order. The following code snippet shows how to retrieve the oldest (the one with the lowest ID) and the most recent review from the database:

VB.NET

```
Dim firstReview = (From r In myEntities.Reviews
                   Order By r.Id
                   Select r).First()

Dim lastReview = (From r In myEntities.Reviews
                  Order By r.Id Descending
                  Select r).First()
```

C#

```
var firstReview = (from r in myEntities.Reviews
                   orderby r.Id
                   select r).First();

var lastReview = (from r in myEntities.Reviews
                  orderby r.Id descending
                  select r).First();
```

Simply by reordering the result set in reverse order before executing `First`, you actually get the last row in the sequence. Note that in both cases, the type returned by the query is a true `Review` object, enabling you to access its properties, such as `Id` and `Title`, directly.

Besides this LINQ Query Syntax, LINQ also supports *method syntax*. For the differences and an example, check out this MSDN article: `http://tinyurl.com/MethodVersusQuery`.

Shaping Data with Anonymous Types

So far, the queries you have seen in the previous sections returned full types. That is, the queries returned a list of `Review` instances (such as the `Select` method), a single instance of `Review` (`Single`, `First`, or `Last`), or a numeric value (such as `Count` and `Average`).

Quite often, however, you don't need all the information from these objects. Figure 14-4 shows a `GridView` with all the properties from the `Review` object. To improve the presentation of this list, you usually want to skip properties like `Body` and `Authorized`, and instead of the genre ID you probably want to display the genre name. Although you could tell the `GridView` to display only the columns you want to see, it would be more efficient if you were able to limit the actual data. This is pretty easy to do with *anonymous types*, another language feature available in C# and VB.NET. An anonymous type is a type whose name and members you don't define up front as you do with other types. Instead, you construct the anonymous type by selecting data and then letting the compiler infer the type for you. The anonymous type can only be accessed within the method that declared it, and as such you cannot return an anonymous type from a method.

If you don't define the actual type and give it a name, how can you access the type and its properties? This is once again done with type inference, where the compiler can see what data is assigned to a variable and then creates a new, anonymous type on the fly.

Creating an anonymous type is easy; instead of selecting the actual object using something like `Select review`, you use the `new` keyword in C# and `New With` in Visual Basic, and then define the properties you want to select between a pair of curly braces:

VB.NET

```
Dim authorizedReviews = From myReview In myEntities.Reviews
                 Where myReview.Authorized = True
                 Select New With {myReview.Id, myReview.Title, myReview.Genre.Name}
```

C#

```
var authorizedReviews = from review in myEntities.Reviews
                        where review.Authorized == true
                        select new { review.Id, review.Title, review.Genre.Name };
```

Although the type is anonymous and cannot be accessed by name directly, the compiler is still able to infer the type, giving you full IntelliSense for the new properties that were selected in the query. Figure 14-5 shows how you access the properties of the anonymous type in the `authorizedReviews` variable, using the `var` keyword in C#.

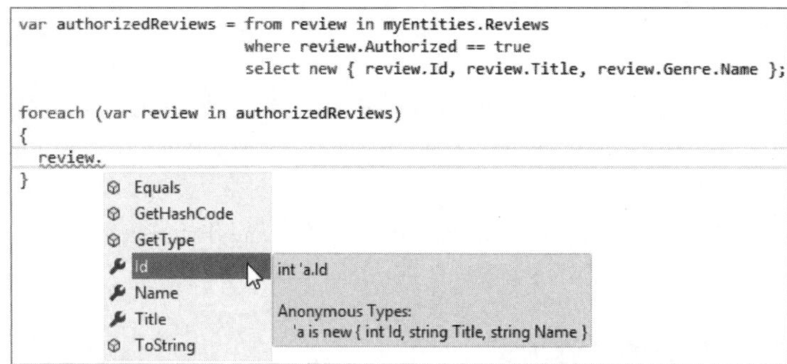

FIGURE 14-5

Note that the preceding query accessed the actual `Genre` property of the `Review`. Besides its `GenreId` (defined as a column in the table `Review` in the database), the `Review` class also has a strongly typed `Genre` property, giving you direct access to the genre's properties, like the `Name`, as the previous query demonstrates.

Besides directly selecting existing properties — as shown in the query that selected the `Id` and `Title` of the `Review` and the `Name` of the `Genre` — you can also make up property values and give them different names as you go. For example, the following query creates a new anonymous type that renames the `Id` as `Number`, limits the `Title` to the first 20 characters, and contains a boolean value that determines whether the item has been updated in the database previously:

VB.NET

```
Dim allReviews = From myReview In myEntities.Reviews
                 Select New With
                 {
                     .Number = myReview.Id,
                     .Title = myReview.Title.Substring(0, 20),
                     myReview.Genre.Name,
                     .HasBeenUpdated = (myReview.UpdateDateTime >
                           myReview.CreateDateTime)
                 }
```

C#

```
var allReviews = from myReview in myEntities.Reviews
                 select new
                 {
                   Number = myReview.Id,
                   Title = myReview.Title.Substring(0, 20),
                   myReview.Genre.Name,
                   HasBeenUpdated = (myReview.UpdateDateTime >
                          myReview.CreateDateTime)
                 };
```

Note the difference between VB.NET and C#; in the VB.NET example, the names of the new properties (`Number`, `Title`, and `HasBeenUpdated`) are prefixed with a period (`.`). C# doesn't have this requirement and lets you write new property names directly. If you don't introduce a new name (as is the case with the genre name in the preceding example), the name of the property you're selecting is used. This means that the genre name is stored in a property called `Name`.

The ability to select extra properties that are not present in the original object gives you great flexibility in the data you display. This example determines whether the current review has been updated by comparing the `CreateDateTime` and `UpdateDateTime` properties. The result of this comparison (a boolean with the value `True` or `False`) is then stored in the property `HasBeenUpdated`. You can select nearly anything you want, including the current date and time, complex calculations, substrings or combinations of properties, and so on.

In the following exercise you see how to create a new anonymous type that has a `Reviews` collection as a property. You use this type to create a list of all the available genres in the database, and the reviews that each genre contains.

TRY IT OUT Working with Queries and Anonymous Types

In this Try It Out you create a page that lists all the available genres, each followed by the list of reviews that have been published in that genre. You use a `Repeater` control to display the list of genres and a nested `BulletedList` to display the inner reviews. When you're done, you should see a list similar to the one displayed in Figure 14-6.

1. Open the `AllByGenre.aspx` page from the `Reviews` folder. Make sure the page is in Markup View and then drag a `Repeater` from the Data category of the Toolbox between the opening and closing tags of the `cpMainContent` content placeholder.

2. Inside the `Repeater` create an `<ItemTemplate>` element that in turn contains an `<h3>` element that contains a `Literal`. You should end up with this code:

```
<asp:Repeater ID="Repeater1" runat="server">
  <ItemTemplate>
    <h3><asp:Literal ID="Literal1" runat="server"></asp:Literal></h3>
  </ItemTemplate>
</asp:Repeater>
```

3. Set the `Text` property of the `Literal` control to **`<%# Eval("Name") %>`**. Instead of double quotes, make sure you use single quotes to delimit the property's value. You need this or otherwise the double quotes surrounding `Name` would prematurely close off the `Text` property.

```
<asp:Literal ID="Literal1" runat="server"
         Text='<%# Eval("Name") %>'></asp:Literal>
```

4. Below the `<h3>` element, drag and drop a `BulletedList` control from the Standard category and set the following properties on the control. You can either enter them directly in Markup View or use the Properties Grid.

PROPERTY NAME	VALUE
`ID`	`ReviewList`
`DataSource`	`<%# Eval("Reviews")%>` (make sure you use single quotes again to wrap this attribute value, as shown in the following code snippet)
`DataTextField`	`Title`
`DisplayMode`	`Text`

You should end up with the following control code:

```
<asp:BulletedList ID="ReviewList" runat="server"
    DataSource='<%# Eval("Reviews")%>' DataTextField="Title"
    DisplayMode="Text"></asp:BulletedList>
```

5. Switch to Design View and double-click the page somewhere in the read-only area defined by the master page to set up a handler for the `Load` event of the page. Within the handler, write the following code. Again, use Ctrl+. (Ctrl + Dot) to let VS insert the right namespace for the `PlanetWroxEntities` class.

VB.NET

```
Imports PlanetWroxModel
... ' Class definition goes here
Protected Sub Page_Load(sender As Object, e As EventArgs) Handles Me.Load
  Using myEntities As New PlanetWroxEntities()
    Dim allGenres = From genre In myEntities.Genres.Include("Reviews")
```

```
                    Order By genre.Name
                    Select New With {genre.Name, genre.Reviews}
    Repeater1.DataSource = allGenres
    Repeater1.DataBind()
  End Using
End Sub
```

C#

```
using PlanetWroxModel;
... // Class definition goes here
protected void Page_Load(object sender, EventArgs e)
{
  using (PlanetWroxEntities myEntities = new PlanetWroxEntities())
  {
    var allGenres = from genre in myEntities.Genres.Include("Reviews")
                    orderby genre.Name
                    select new { genre.Name, genre.Reviews };
    Repeater1.DataSource = allGenres;
    Repeater1.DataBind();
  }
}
```

6. Save the changes to your page and then request it in the browser. You should see a result similar to that shown in Figure 14-6, where each genre appears as a group header above the lists with reviews.

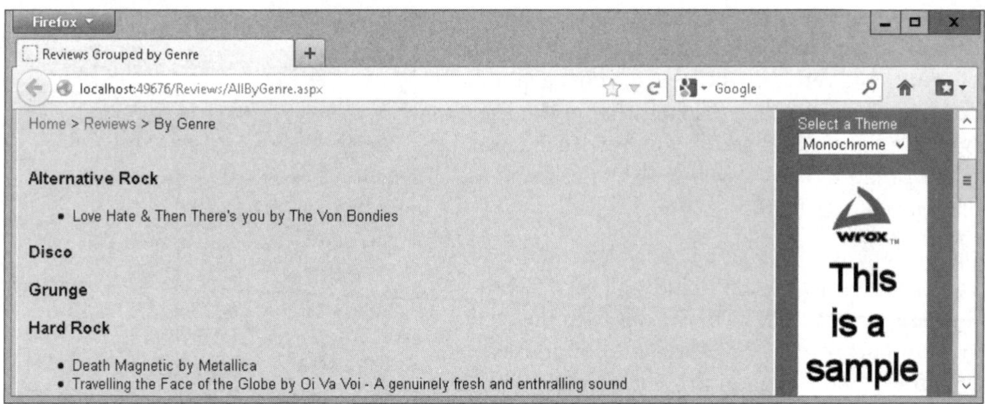

FIGURE 14-6

How It Works

You have two important things to look at in this exercise. First of all, there's the LINQ query that is used to get the genres and reviews from the database. This query (that uses `Include("Reviews")` to prevent lazy loading as you saw earlier) creates a new anonymous type with two properties: the `Name` of the `Genre` as a `String` and a collection of `Review` objects called `Reviews`. The class diagram for the new anonymous type could look like Figure 14-7.

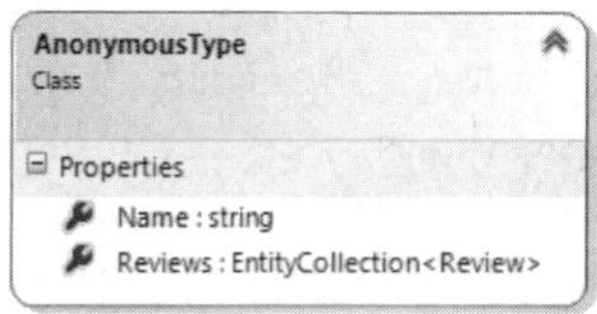

FIGURE 14-7

These Name and Reviews properties are then used in the second important part: the Repeater control with the nested bulleted list. First, take a look at the Repeater:

```
<asp:Repeater ID="Repeater1" runat="server">
  <ItemTemplate>
    <h3><asp:Literal ID="Literal1" runat="server"
              Text='<%# Eval("Name") %>'></asp:Literal></h3>
    <!-- BulletedList here -->
  </ItemTemplate>
</asp:Repeater>
```

Although you haven't worked with the Repeater control before, it may look familiar, because it works in a manner similar to the other data controls. Within the <ItemTemplate> you define the markup that you want repeated for each item in the data source. Using Eval you can get the value of the genre's Name property and assign it to the Literal, which is wrapped in a pair of <h3> tags. A similar construct is used for the BulletedList to feed it a DataSource:

```
<asp:BulletedList ID="BulletedList1" runat="server" DisplayMode="Text"
       DataSource='<%# Eval("Reviews")%>' DataTextField="Title" />
```

In addition to assigning simple properties like the Text of the Literal from the Name of the underlying data item, you can also use Eval to get complex properties. In this example, Eval("Reviews") is used to get the collection of Reviews for the current Genre. The BulletedList control then understands how to handle this data source and retrieves the Title from each individual Review object and then displays that in the list. The diagram in Figure 14-8 shows you how each Genre contains one or more reviews, whose titles are displayed below the name of the genre.

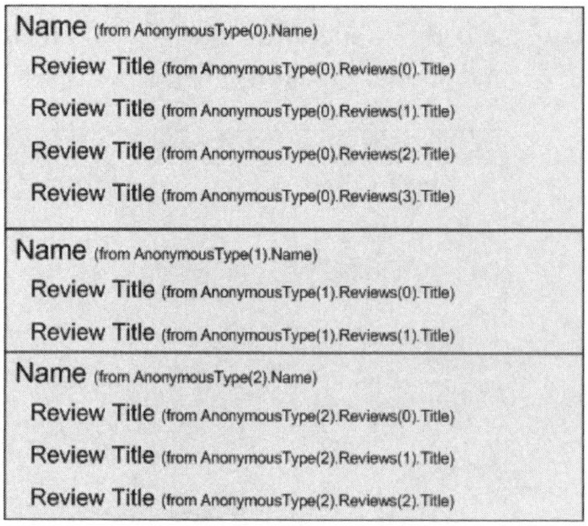

Name (from AnonymousType(0).Name)
Review Title (from AnonymousType(0).Reviews(0).Title)
Review Title (from AnonymousType(0).Reviews(1).Title)
Review Title (from AnonymousType(0).Reviews(2).Title)
Review Title (from AnonymousType(0).Reviews(3).Title)
Name (from AnonymousType(1).Name)
Review Title (from AnonymousType(1).Reviews(0).Title)
Review Title (from AnonymousType(1).Reviews(1).Title)
Name (from AnonymousType(2).Name)
Review Title (from AnonymousType(2).Reviews(0).Title)
Review Title (from AnonymousType(2).Reviews(1).Title)
Review Title (from AnonymousType(2).Reviews(2).Title)

FIGURE 14-8

After you have set up the Repeater and defined the query, you need to start the data-binding process. You do this by assigning the results of the query to the DataSource property of the Repeater, followed by a call to DataBind() as shown in this C# example:

```
Repeater1.DataSource = allGenres;
Repeater1.DataBind();
```

These two lines set things in motion: as soon as you call DataBind(), the query is executed and the relevant genres and reviews are retrieved from the database. In this example, the genres are sorted on their Name, but obviously you can order on other properties, such as SortOrder, as well. The Repeater then loops through each item in the result set (this item is the anonymous type you just saw) and uses that item's Name to fill in the <h3> element with the genre name. The Repeater then assigns the Reviews collection to the inner BulletedList control's DataSource property. This control loops over the available Review instances, using their Title to build up the bulleted list. In this example, you see that genres without reviews are displayed in the list as well. In the "Exercises" section at the end of the chapter, you'll find an exercise that shows you how to hide empty genres.

Although it may take you some time to fully understand the principles behind these LINQ queries and the Entity Framework, I am sure you are beginning to appreciate their power and accessibility. With just a few lines of code and a few controls, you can create powerful data presentation pages.

However, it's possible to create LINQ queries that execute against EF and use them with the ASP .NET Server Controls with even fewer lines of code. You see how this works in the next section, which deals with the `EntityDataSource`, the `ListView`, and the `DataPager` controls.

USING SERVER CONTROLS WITH LINQ QUERIES

So far you have seen one way to bind the results of a LINQ query against EF to a control in your ASPX page: assign the data to the control's `DataSource` property and then call `DataBind`. This way of getting data into the controls has a few shortcomings. First of all, this method does not support the editing, updating, and deleting of data directly. Secondly, because you define the data source in the Code Behind, the `GridView` doesn't know what data you're feeding it until run time, so you get no tool support to set up its columns. These shortcomings are easy to overcome by using the server controls, including the `ListView` and the `EntityDataSource` control.

Using Data Controls with the Entity Framework

In the previous chapter you were introduced to some of the data controls, like the `GridView` and the `SqlDataSource`. But ASP.NET 4.5 ships with more controls that let you create data-driven pages with very few lines of code. Two of these controls provide a visual interface in your ASP.NET pages, and the third one works as a bridge between your data-bound controls and your underlying data sources. The following table briefly introduces you to these controls.

CONTROL	DESCRIPTION
`EntityDataSource`	As with the `SqlDataSource` that you saw in previous chapters, the `EntityDataSource` works as a bridge between your data-bound controls and the underlying data source: EF in this case.
`ListView`	The `ListView` control provides a template-driven visual interface that enables you to display, insert, edit, and delete items in a database, providing full CRUD services.
`DataPager`	The `DataPager` is used together with the `ListView` and enables you to paginate the data in the data source, feeding data to users in bite-sized chunks instead of all rows at once.

The next few sections provide you with more detail about these controls and show you how to use them in a few Try It Out exercises.

Introducing the EntityDataSource Control

As its name implies, the `EntityDataSource` is a close relative of the `SqlDataSource` and other data source controls. The `EntityDataSource` control is to EF what the `SqlDataSource` control is to SQL-based data sources: It provides a declarative way to access your model. Just like the `SqlDataSource` control, `EntityDataSource` gives you easy access to the CRUD operations and additionally makes sorting and filtering of data very easy. The following table describes the main properties and capabilities of this control.

PROPERTY	DESCRIPTION

`EnableDelete`
`EnableInsert`
`EnableUpdate`
	Determine whether the control provides automatic insert, update, and delete capabilities. When enabled, you can use the control together with data-bound controls like the `GridView` or `ListView` to support data management.

`ContextTypeName`	The name of the `ObjectContext` class that the control should use. In the examples in this book, this type name is `PlanetWroxEntities`.
`EntitySetName`	The name of the entity set from the EF model you want to use, such as `Reviews`.

`Select`
`OrderBy`
`Where`
	Enable you to define the query that the `EntityDataSource` control fires against the model. Each of these properties maps to one of the query operators you've seen before.

Together with a data-bound control, the `EntityDataSource` provides you full access to the underlying SQL Server database through LINQ to Entities. The next exercise shows you how to use the control in your ASPX pages.

TRY IT OUT A Simple EntityDataSource Application

In this Try It Out you start building the Gig Pics feature of Planet Wrox, a section of the website where users can upload photos they created during concerts of their favorite bands. You see how to let a user create a new photo album that acts as a container for the pictures that are uploaded. You see how to use the `EntityDataSource` and a `DetailsView` to create a user interface that enables users to enter a name for a new photo album into the system. In later exercises you see how to add pictures to this photo album.

1. Add the following two tables to your database using SQL Server Management Studio. Refer to Chapter 12 for more details about creating tables, primary keys, and identity columns.

PhotoAlbum

COLUMN NAME	DATA TYPE	DESCRIPTION
`Id`	int	The unique ID (identity and primary key) of the photo album
`Name`	nvarchar(100)	The name of the photo album

Picture

COLUMN NAME	DATA TYPE	DESCRIPTION
`Id`	int	The unique ID (identity and primary key) of the picture
`Description`	nvarchar(300)	A description of the picture
`ToolTip`	nvarchar(50)	A tooltip displayed when you hover over a picture
`ImageUrl`	nvarchar(200)	The virtual path to the picture on disk
`PhotoAlbumId`	int	The ID of the photo album this picture belongs to

For both tables, make sure that none of the columns in the two tables are nullable by unchecking their Allow Nulls check boxes. Make the `Id` column the primary key by clicking it once, and then clicking the yellow key icon on the Table Designer toolbar. Additionally, make this column the table's Identity column by setting the (Is Identity) property on the Column Properties Grid to Yes. Refer to Chapter 12 if you're not sure how to do this. Finally, make sure you have the casing of the table and column names right. Later code in this book assumes you wrote the table and column names as shown here.

2. On the Object Explorer, open the database diagram that you created in Chapter 12. Right-click the diagram and choose Add Table. Select the two new tables, click Add, and then click Close. Arrange the two new tables side by side if necessary. Next, drag the `Id` column from the `PhotoAlbum` table onto the `PhotoAlbumId` column of the `Picture` table. Confirm that the Primary Key Table is `PhotoAlbum` with `Id` as the selected column and that `Picture` is the Foreign Key Table with `PhotoAlbumId` as the selected column, as shown in Figure 14-9.

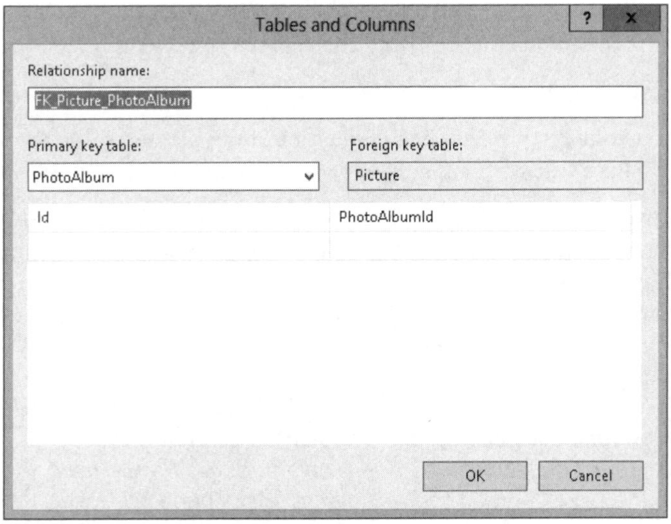

FIGURE 14-9

3. Click OK twice to apply the changes and then save and close the diagram. Click Yes to confirm the changes made to the two tables.

4. Next, switch back to VS, and open the ADO.NET Entity Framework Model file `PlanetWrox.edmx` from the `App_Code` folder by double-clicking it. Right-click an empty spot of the diagram and choose Update Model from Database. In the wizard that appears, expand Tables, then dbo, and then check the two tables you just created: `PhotoAlbum` and `Picture`. Click Finish to have the two tables added to your model. Your diagram should end up like Figure 14-10. Note that I reorganized the diagram by dragging the tables side by side to make it easier to see them.

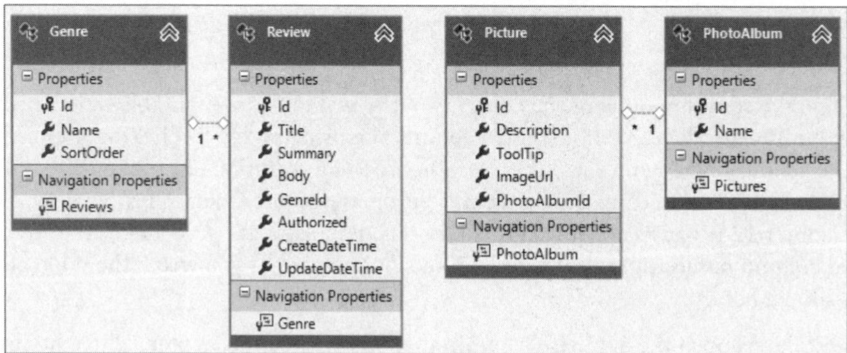

FIGURE 14-10

If you're using a non-English version of VS, you need to pluralize the names of the entity sets and properties again. To do this, click the `Picture` class, open its Properties Grid by pressing F4, and change the Entity Set Name from `Picture` to **`Pictures`**. Repeat this for the `PhotoAlbum` class and change its Entity Set Name to **`PhotoAlbums`**. Finally, click the `Picture` property on the diagram for the `PhotoAlbum` class, press F2 to rename the item, and then enter **`Pictures`** as the new name.

Save all your changes and close the diagram.

5. Create a new Web Form based on your custom template in the root of the site and call it `NewPhotoAlbum.aspx`. Give the page a title of **`Create New Photo Album`**.

6. Switch the page into Design View and from the Data category of the Toolbox, drag a `DetailsView` control and drop it into the `cpMainContent` placeholder. On the `DetailsView` control's Smart Tasks panel, open the Choose Data Source drop-down list and select <New data source>. In the Data Source Configuration Wizard dialog box, click the Entity icon and click OK. In the Named Connection drop-down, choose `PlanetWroxEntities`.

> ***NOTE*** *If you get an error about incorrect metadata, close the dialog box, delete the existing* `EntityDataSource` *control from the page, and manually drag a new one from the Toolbox. On the* `DetailsView` *control's Smart Tasks panel, choose the new data source control. Then open the* `EntityDataSource` *control's Smart Tasks panel and choose Configure Data Source.*

Click Next to go to the Configure Data Selection screen, shown in Figure 14-11. From the EntitySetName drop-down list, choose `PhotoAlbums`.

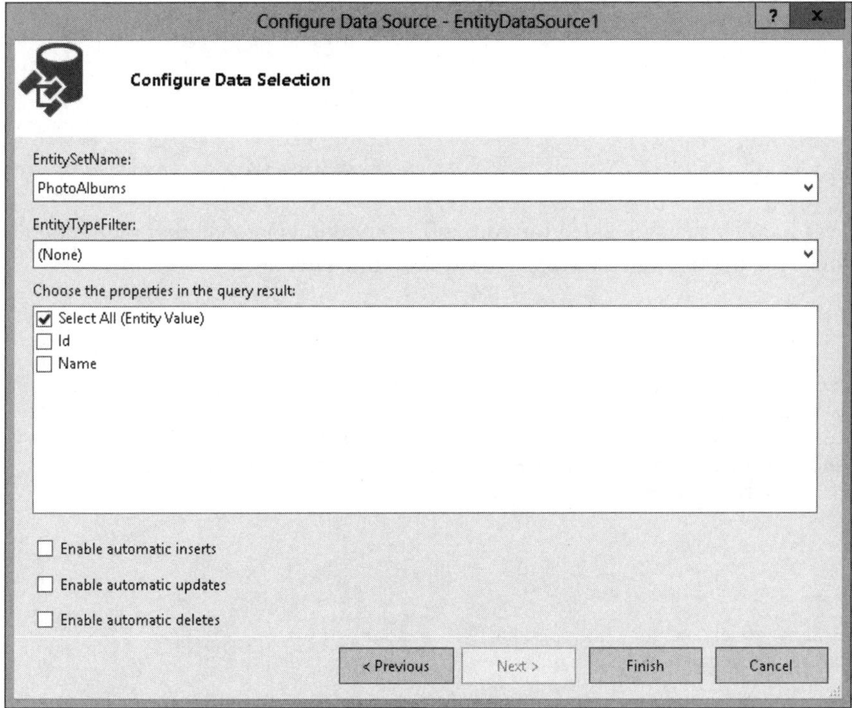

FIGURE 14-11

7. For this exercise, you need insert behavior, so check off the Enable Automatic Inserts check box. Click Finish to close the Configure Data Source wizard.

8. If you don't see the `Id` and `Name` columns in the `DetailsView`, but a general `Databound Col0` instead, click the Refresh Schema link on the control's Smart Tasks panel.

   Enable inserting for the `DetailsView` control by checking the Enable Inserting item on the same Smart Tasks panel.

9. Open the `DetailsView` control's Properties Grid and change the `DefaultMode` from `ReadOnly` to `Insert`.

10. Switch to Markup View, locate the `BoundField` for the `Id` property of the `PhotoAlbum`, and set its `InsertVisible` property to `false` so you don't get a text box for the ID when inserting a new photo album.

```
<asp:BoundField DataField="Id" HeaderText="Id" ReadOnly="True"
          SortExpression="Id" InsertVisible="false" />
```

11. Select the `EntityDataSource` control in Design View, open its Properties Grid, and switch to the Events tab. Double-click the `Inserted` event, visible in Figure 14-12.

12. At the top of the code file, add the following `Imports/using` statement to bring your entities model in scope so you can access classes such as `PhotoAlbum`:

VB.NET

```
Imports PlanetWroxModel
```

C#

```
using PlanetWroxModel;
```

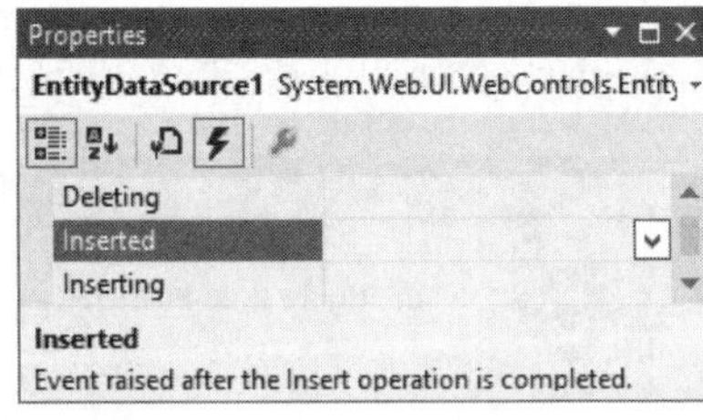

FIGURE 14-12

Then, in the event handler that VS added for you, write the following code that redirects the user to a new page once the photo album has been inserted in the database:

VB.NET

```
Protected Sub EntityDataSource1_Inserted(sender As Object,
     e As EntityDataSourceStatusEventArgs) Handles EntityDataSource1.Inserted
  If (e.Entity IsNot Nothing) Then
    Dim myPhotoAlbum As PhotoAlbum = CType(e.Entity, PhotoAlbum)
    Response.Redirect(String.Format("ManagePhotoAlbum.aspx?PhotoAlbumId={0}",
                    myPhotoAlbum.Id.ToString()))
  End If
End Sub
```

C#

```
protected void EntityDataSource1_Inserted(object sender,
       EntityDataSourceChangedEventArgs e)
{
  if (e.Entity != null)
  {
    PhotoAlbum myPhotoAlbum = (PhotoAlbum)e.Entity;
    Response.Redirect(string.Format("ManagePhotoAlbum.aspx?PhotoAlbumId={0}",
                    myPhotoAlbum.Id.ToString()));
  }
}
```

13. Save all changes and then request `NewPhotoAlbum.aspx` in the browser.

> ***COMMON MISTAKES*** *If the page you get is empty, make sure you set the* `DefaultMode` *property of the* `DetailsView` *to* `Insert`.

Enter a new name for the photo album, such as `Foo Fighters playing live at Lowlands 2012`, and click the Insert link. You'll get a *Resource Not Found* error (because you haven't created `ManagePhotoAlbum.aspx` yet), but you can at least see the ID of the new photo album in the address bar of your browser:

```
http://localhost:9797/ManagePhotoAlbum.aspx?PhotoAlbumId=1
```

How It Works

You started this exercise by adding the `Picture` and `PhotoAlbum` tables to both the database and the EF diagram. These tables are used to store data about photo albums and the pictures they contain. Each individual picture belongs to a `PhotoAlbum` referred to by its `PhotoAlbumId` that points to the `Id` column of the `PhotoAlbum` table in the database. The `Picture` table is designed to only hold data *about* the picture; the actual picture file is stored on disk, as you see later.

To enable users to create a new photo album, you added a `DetailsView` control to the page. To make sure the control can be used to insert new photo albums, you enabled inserting and then set the `DefaultMode` to `Insert`. This forces the control to jump into insert mode, instead of the default read-only mode. You then hooked up an `EntityDataSource` to the `DetailsView`, which takes care of inserting the photo album in the `PhotoAlbum` table. The code for the `EntityDataSource` control looks like this:

```
<asp:EntityDataSource ID="EntityDataSource1" runat="server"
    ConnectionString="name=PlanetWroxEntities" EnableFlattening="False"
    DefaultContainerName="PlanetWroxEntities" EnableInsert="True"
    EntitySetName="PhotoAlbums" OnInserted="EntityDataSource1_Inserted">
</asp:EntityDataSource>
```

The `ConnectionString` attribute points to a named connection string in `Web.config` that is used to access the database. The `EnableFlattening` attribute is used in advanced scenarios when using a version of EF before .NET 4. For .NET 4 and 4.5 you should leave it set to `False`. If you are using Visual Basic.NET, your code won't have the `OnInserted` attribute set.

Note how straightforward the `EntityDataSource` is in this scenario: You point it to a `DefaultContainerName`, the `PlanetWroxEntities` in this example, which is the main entrance for the control to get its data. You also turned on inserting by setting `EnableInsert` to `True`. Additionally, you set the `EntitySetName`, so the control knows what object to use from the EF diagram. For simple inserts, this is all you need to do. When the page loads in the browser, the `DetailsView` renders a user interface that enables you to enter a new name for the photo album. When you click Insert, the data you entered is assembled and forwarded to the `EntityDataSource`. This control in turn creates a new `PhotoAlbum` instance and then saves it in the database by sending the appropriate `INSERT` SQL statement to the database.

In many situations, this standard behavior is not enough. You may need to validate the data that is entered or you may have a need to change the actual data before it gets sent to the database. You see an example of the latter in a subsequent Try It Out when you upload images to the server.

Another common requirement is retrieving the ID of the newly created item, which is then sent to the next page. This exercise used the following code to accomplish that:

VB.NET

```
Dim myPhotoAlbum As PhotoAlbum = CType(e.Entity, PhotoAlbum)
Response.Redirect(String.Format("ManagePhotoAlbum.aspx?PhotoAlbumId={0}",
                  myPhotoAlbum.Id.ToString()))
```

C#

```
PhotoAlbum myPhotoAlbum = (PhotoAlbum)e.Entity;
Response.Redirect(string.Format("ManagePhotoAlbum.aspx?PhotoAlbumId={0}",
                  myPhotoAlbum.Id.ToString()));
```

The cool thing about the `EntityDataSource` control is that it works with strongly typed objects, where the type maps to the tables you added to the model diagram. In this case, you are working with real instances of `PhotoAlbum`, the class that represents the photo albums in the system. This enables you to retrieve the photo album you have inserted in the database in the `Inserted` event of the data source control. The `e` argument exposes a property called `Entity` that contains a reference to the new photo album. Simply by casting it to a real `PhotoAlbum` (by using `CType` in VB.NET or putting the class name in parentheses before it in C#), you can access the properties of the `PhotoAlbum`, including its new ID that has been generated by the database (through the Identity settings on the ID column) and then stored in the `Id` property of the `PhotoAlbum`. The final line in the event handler takes the user to the next page and sends the ID of the new photo album in the query string. This code has been wrapped in an `if` statement that checks if `e.Entity` is not `null` / `Nothing`. If an error occurs while updating the database, the `Entity` property will be null, and the cast to a `PhotoAlbum` will fail. The error you see in the browser will then be about the failed cast, and not about the database error, making it hard to see the root cause of the problem. By using the `if` check, you cast and redirect only when the database update succeeded, whereas you see the database error in case it failed.

Note that you get an error when you leave the name field empty and click Insert. The previous chapter showed you how to modify the `DetailsView` to insert validation controls to its templates.

Now that you can insert new photo albums, the next logical step is to add pictures to the photo album. In the next exercise you see how to create a user interface with the `ListView` control that enables a user to upload new pictures in the photo album.

Introducing the ListView Control

Up until now, you have seen a few data-bound controls at work. You saw the `GridView`, which is quite powerful because it supports updates, deletes, sorting, and paging of data, but lacks inserting and generates a lot of HTML markup. You also saw the `Repeater` control that gives you precise control over the generated HTML, but lacks most advanced features that the other data controls have, such as update and delete behavior and sorting and filtering capabilities. And finally, you saw the `DetailsView` that enables you to insert or update one row at a time.

The `ListView` is a "best of all worlds" control, combining the rich feature set of the `GridView` with the control over the markup that the `Repeater` gives you and adding the insert behavior of the `DetailsView`. The `ListView` enables you to display data in a variety of formats, including a grid (rows and columns like the `GridView`), as a bulleted list (similar to how you set up the `Repeater` earlier in this chapter), and in Flow format, where all the items are placed in the HTML after each other, leaving it up to you to write some CSS to format the data.

The `ListView` displays and manages its data through templates that enable you to control many of the different views that the `ListView` gives you on its underlying data. The following table describes all the available templates that you can add as direct children of the `ListView` control in the markup of the page.

TEMPLATE	DESCRIPTION
`<LayoutTemplate>`	Serves as a container. It enables you to define a location where the individual data items are placed. The data items, presented through the `ItemTemplate` and `AlternatingItemTemplate`, are then added as children of this container.
`<ItemTemplate>` `<AlternatingItemTemplate>`	Define the read-only mode for the control. When used together, they enable you to create a "zebra effect," where odd and even rows have a different appearance (usually a different background color).
`<SelectedItemTemplate>`	Enables you to define the look and feel of the currently active, or selected, item.
`<InsertItemTemplate>` `<EditItemTemplate>`	These two templates enable you to define the user interface for inserting and updating items in the list. You typically place controls like text boxes, drop-down lists, and other server controls in these templates and bind them to the underlying data source.
`<ItemSeparatorTemplate>`	Defines the markup that is placed between the items in the list. Useful if you want to add a line, an image, or any other markup between the items.
`<EmptyDataTemplate>`	Displayed when the control has no data to display. You can add text or other markup and controls to it to tell your users there's no data to display.

`<GroupTemplate>`
`<GroupSeparatorTemplate>`
`<EmptyItemTemplate>`
	Used in advanced presentation scenarios where data can be presented in different groups.

Although this long list of templates seems to suggest you need to write a lot of code to work with the `ListView`, this is not always the case. First of all, VS creates most of the code for you based on the data that is exposed by controls such as the `EntityDataSource`. Secondly, you don't always need all templates, enabling you to minimize the code for the control.

Besides the numerous templates, the control has the following properties that you typically set to influence its behavior.

PROPERTY	DESCRIPTION
`ItemPlaceholderID`	The ID of a server-side control placed within the `LayoutTemplate`. The control referred to by this property is *replaced* by all the repeated data items when the control is displayed on-screen. It can be a true server control like an `<asp:PlaceHolder>` or a simple HTML element with a valid ID and its `runat` attribute set to `server` (for example, `<ul runat="server" id="MainList"></ul>`). If you don't set this property, ASP.NET tries to find a control with an ID of `itemPlaceholder` and uses that control instead.
`DataSourceID`	The ID of a data source control on the page, such as an `EntityDataSource` or a `SqlDataSource` control.
`InsertItemPosition`	The enumeration for this property contains three values — `None`, `FirstItem`, and `LastItem` — to determine the position of the `InsertItemTemplate`: either at the beginning or end of the list, or not visible at all.

Just like the other data-bound controls, the `ListView` has a number of events that fire at specific moments during the control's lifetime. For example, it has `ItemInserting` and `ItemInserted` events that fire right before and after an item has been inserted in the underlying data source. Similarly, it has events that trigger right before and after you update or delete data. You see more about handling these kinds of events in the next chapter.

Besides the templates, properties, and events you just saw, the `ListView` has more to offer. For a detailed explanation of the `ListView` control and all of its members and behavior, check out the MSDN documentation at `http://bit.ly/dCAooK`.

The next exercise shows you how to put all of this information together. You see how to define the various templates and set the relevant properties to control the look and feel of the `ListView` control.

TRY IT OUT Inserting and Deleting Data with the ListView Control

Inserting items with the `ListView` can be just as easy as with the `DetailsView`: You point the control to a data source and let VS create the necessary templates for you. However, in many real-world websites, these default templates won't cut it. You may want to display fewer fields than are available in the data source, validate data before it gets sent to the database, or store data at a different location than the database. For example, you may want to store uploaded images on disk rather than in the database and then store only a reference to the file in the database table. The next exercise shows you how to customize the `ListView` templates and handle the `Inserting` event of the `EntityDataSource` when you build functionality to add pictures to your photo albums.

This exercise has you work with a lot of code that is generated automatically by VS. Most of what you need to do in this exercise is remove code instead of add new code. If you get lost somewhere, or you feel your code does not look like it should, remember this chapter comes with the full source code that you can download from the Wrox website, so you can compare your code with mine.

1. In the root of the website, create a new Web Form based on your custom template. Call it `ManagePhotoAlbum.aspx`, set its `Title` to **`Manage Photo Album`**, and switch it into Design View.

2. From the Data category of the Toolbox, drag a `ListView` control onto the page in the `cpMainContent` placeholder and then hook it up to an `EntityDataSource` control by choosing <New data source> in the Choose Data Source drop-down list on the Smart Tasks panel (just as you did with the `DetailsView` earlier). Click the Entity icon, click OK, choose `PlanetWroxEntities` as the named connection, and click Next.

   In the Configure Data Selection dialog box of the `EntityDataSource` control's wizard, visible in Figure 14-11, choose `Pictures` from the EntitySetName drop-down list.

3. Check the first and the last check box of the three at the bottom of the screen to give the `EntityDataSource` insert and delete support. Finally, click Finish to close the Configure Data Source wizard.

4. Back in Design View, select the `EntityDataSource` control, open its Properties Grid, locate the `Where` property, and open its Expression Editor by clicking the ellipsis for that property. You may recall that the `ManagePhotoAlbum.aspx` page receives the photo album ID through the query string, so you'll need to set up a `QueryStringParameter` in this step to filter the `ListView` to those pictures belonging to the designated photo album. To do this, enter `it.PhotoAlbum.Id = @photoAlbumId` in the Where Expression box at the top of the dialog box. Then click Add Parameter, enter **`PhotoAlbumId`** as the name, choose QueryString from the Parameter Source drop-down, and enter **`PhotoAlbumId`** as the QueryStringField. Next, click the Show Advanced Properties link and change the Type property of the parameter to Int32. Your dialog box should now look like Figure 14-13. When you're done, click OK to dismiss the dialog box.

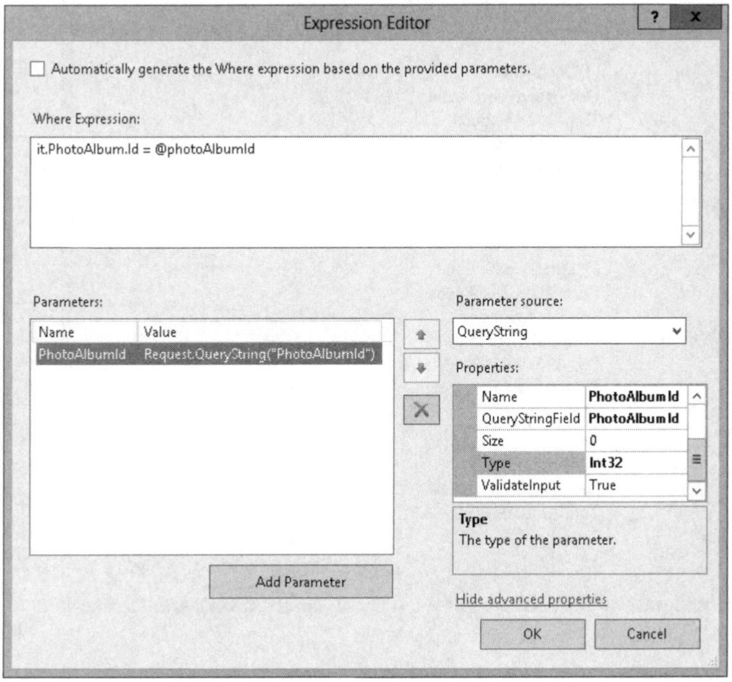

FIGURE 14-13

5. Back in the page, the `ListView` should still appear as a plain rectangle, shown in Figure 14-14, because you haven't provided any template information yet.

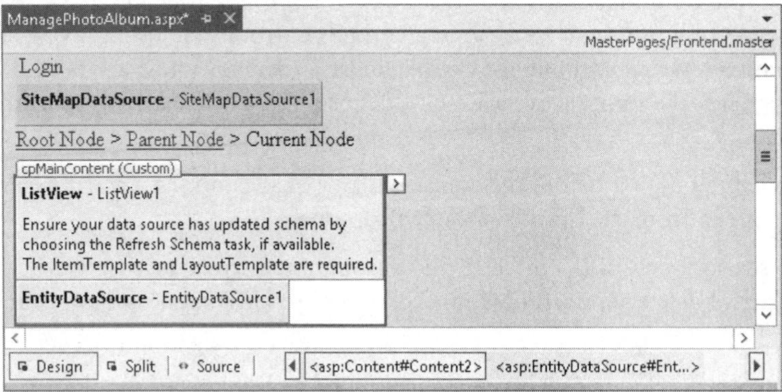

FIGURE 14-14

6. On the Smart Tasks panel of the `ListView`, choose Configure ListView. (If you don't see this link, click Refresh Schema first and reopen the Smart Tasks panel.) A dialog box appears that enables you to choose the layout of the control, a style, and whether or not you want to enable operations such as inserting and updating. Choose Bulleted List as the layout, and check the Enable Inserting and Enable Deleting items so your dialog box ends up as shown in Figure 14-15.

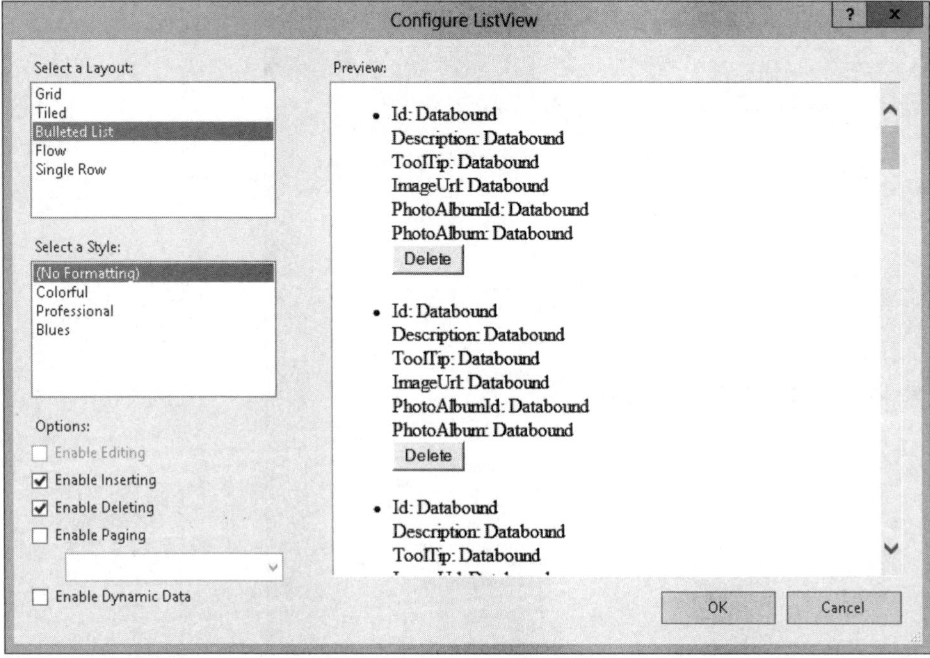

FIGURE 14-15

7. Click OK to close the dialog box. If you get a dialog box that asks if you want to regenerate the `ListView` control, click Yes.

8. Switch to Markup View and remove the code for the following templates. To make this as easy as possible, click the relevant opening tag once, then click the tag in the Tag Selector at the bottom of the Document Window to select the entire element and its content, and then press the Delete key. Alternatively, you can collapse the tag using the plus (+) symbol in the left margin, select the whole line, and delete it at once.

   - `<AlternatingItemTemplate>`
   - `<EditItemTemplate>`
   - `<EmptyDataTemplate>`
   - `<ItemSeparatorTemplate>`
   - `<SelectedItemTemplate>`

   The only three remaining template elements should now be `InsertItemTemplate`, `ItemTemplate`, and `LayoutTemplate`.

9. Locate the `<ul>` element in the `LayoutTemplate` and remove its `ID`, `runat`, and `style` attributes. Then add a `class` attribute and set it to `ItemContainer`. You can also remove the empty `<div>` element that VS added for you below the `<ul>`. Your `<LayoutTemplate>` now contains this code:

```
<LayoutTemplate>
  <ul class="ItemContainer">
    <li runat="server" id="itemPlaceholder" />
  </ul>
</LayoutTemplate>
```

10. Locate the `ItemTemplate` and remove the lines that make up the `Id`, `PhotoAlbumId`, and `PhotoAlbum` columns, bolded in the following code snippet, because you don't need them. Make sure you don't accidentally delete the opening `<li>` tag:

```
<li style="">
  Id:
  <asp:Label ID="IdLabel" runat="server" Text='<%# Eval("Id") %>' />
  <br />
  Description:
  <asp:Label ID="DescriptionLabel" runat="server"
             Text='<%# Eval("Description") %>' />
  <br />
  ToolTip:
  <asp:Label ID="ToolTipLabel" runat="server" Text='<%# Eval("ToolTip") %>' /><br />
  ImageUrl:
  <asp:Label ID="ImageUrlLabel" runat="server"
             Text='<%# Eval("ImageUrl") %>' /><br />
  PhotoAlbumId:
  <asp:Label ID="PhotoAlbumIdLabel" runat="server"
             Text='<%# Eval("PhotoAlbumId") %>' />
  <br />
  PhotoAlbum:
  <asp:Label ID="PhotoAlbumLabel" runat="server" Text='<%# Eval("PhotoAlbum") %>' />
```

```
    <br />
    <asp:Button ID="DeleteButton" runat="server" CommandName="Delete" Text="Delete" />
  </li>
```

11. Repeat the previous step for the `InsertItemTemplate` that is also part of the `ListView` control's markup.

    Compare your code with the following code and make any changes if necessary. Check if your `ListView` has a `DataKeyNames` property set to `Id` and add it if it isn't there. Sometimes VS doesn't add this property, although the code requires it to be there. Also check that the templates contain the correct controls. The order of the templates or the white space can be different in your code.

```
<asp:ListView ID="ListView1" runat="server" DataKeyNames="Id"
               DataSourceID="EntityDataSource1" InsertItemPosition="LastItem">
  <InsertItemTemplate>
    <li style="">
      Description:
      <asp:TextBox ID="DescriptionTextBox" runat="server"
                   Text='<%# Bind("Description") %>' /><br />
      ToolTip:
      <asp:TextBox ID="ToolTipTextBox" runat="server"
                   Text='<%# Bind("ToolTip") %>' /><br />
      ImageUrl:
      <asp:TextBox ID="ImageUrlTextBox" runat="server"
                   Text='<%# Bind("ImageUrl") %>' /><br />
      <asp:Button ID="InsertButton" runat="server"
                  CommandName="Insert" Text="Insert" />
      <asp:Button ID="CancelButton" runat="server"
                  CommandName="Cancel" Text="Clear" />
    </li>
  </InsertItemTemplate>
  <ItemTemplate>
    <li style="">Description:
      <asp:Label ID="DescriptionLabel" runat="server"
                 Text='<%# Eval("Description") %>' /><br />
      ToolTip:
      <asp:Label ID="ToolTipLabel" runat="server"
                 Text='<%# Eval("ToolTip") %>' /><br />
      ImageUrl:
      <asp:Label ID="ImageUrlLabel" runat="server"
                 Text='<%# Eval("ImageUrl") %>' /><br />
      <asp:Button ID="DeleteButton" runat="server"
                  CommandName="Delete" Text="Delete" />
    </li>
   </ItemTemplate>
  <LayoutTemplate>
    <ul class="ItemContainer">
      <li ID="itemPlaceholder" runat="server" />
    </ul>
  </LayoutTemplate>
</asp:ListView>
```

12. Switch back to Design View, select the `EntityDataSource` control, and open its Properties Grid. Switch to the Events tab and double-click the `Inserting` event. At the top of the page add an

Imports or a using statement for the PlanetWroxModel namespace, as you did in the other pages in this chapter. Then in the event handler that VS added for you, write the following code:

VB.NET

```
Protected Sub EntityDataSource1_Inserting(sender As Object,
      e As EntityDataSourceChangingEventArgs) Handles EntityDataSource1.Inserting
  Dim photoAlbumId As Integer =
          Convert.ToInt32(Request.QueryString.Get("PhotoAlbumId"))
  Dim myPicture As Picture = CType(e.Entity, Picture)
  myPicture.PhotoAlbumId = photoAlbumId
End Sub
```

C#

```
protected void EntityDataSource1_Inserting(object sender,
      EntityDataSourceChangingEventArgs e)
{
  int photoAlbumId = Convert.ToInt32(Request.QueryString.Get("PhotoAlbumId"));
  Picture myPicture = (Picture)e.Entity;
  myPicture.PhotoAlbumId = photoAlbumId;
}
```

13. Add the following CSS code to Monochrome.css in the Monochrome theme's folder and save the file:

```
.ItemContainer
{
  width: 600px;
  list-style-type: none;
  clear: both;
}

.ItemContainer li
{
  height: 300px;
  width: 200px;
  float: left;
}

.ItemContainer li img
{
  width: 180px;
  margin: 10px 20px 10px 0;
}
```

14. Add the same code to DarkGrey.css in the DarkGrey theme's folder, but this time set the width of the ItemContainer class to 400px like this:

```
.ItemContainer
{
  width: 400px;
  list-style-type: none;
  clear: both;
}
```

15. Save all your changes, close all open files, and then request `NewPhotoAlbum.aspx` in your browser. Make sure you don't accidentally open `ManagePhotoAlbum.aspx`, because it requires a query string that is sent by `NewPhotoAlbum.aspx`. Enter a new name for the photo album and click Insert. You're taken to `ManagePhotoAlbum.aspx` where you can enter new pictures. For now, all you can do is enter the description of the picture, the tooltip, and a fake URL of the image (just enter some text); you see later how to modify this and let a user upload real pictures to the website. Once you click the Insert button, a new item appears in the list, next to the insert controls. Add a few more items and you'll notice that the insert controls move to a row below the others, as shown in Figure 14-16, which shows the page in Firefox.

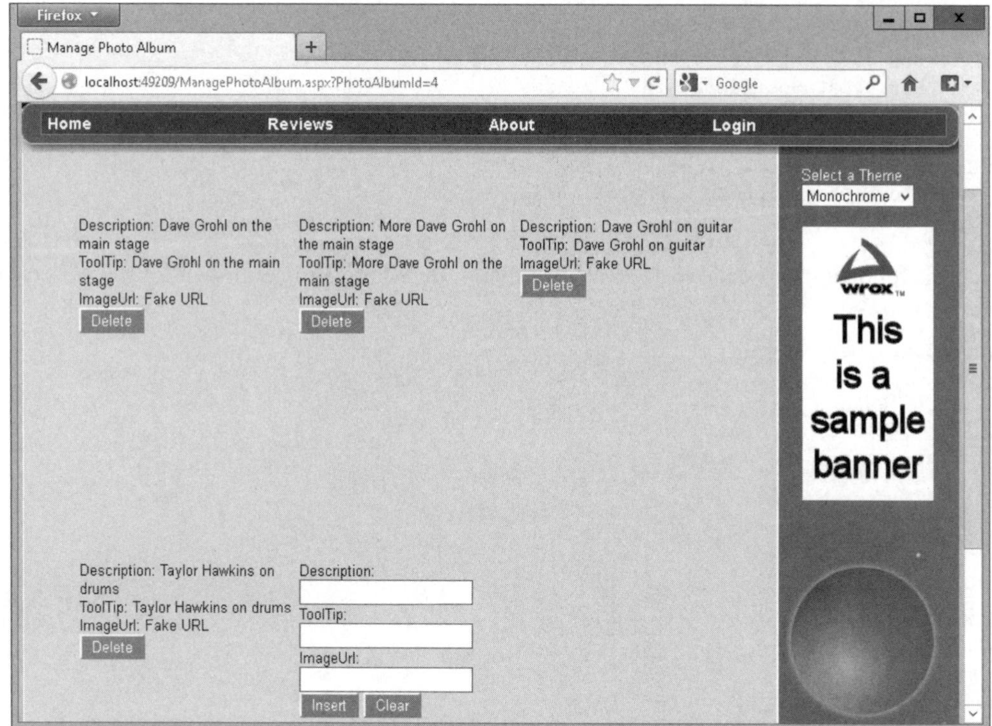

FIGURE 14-16

16. Click the Delete button for an item and see how the item is removed from the list automatically.

17. If you're currently viewing the site in the Monochrome theme, use the drop-down list to switch to DarkGrey. Notice that this theme shows only two images per row instead of the three displayed by the Monochrome theme shown in Figure 14-16.

How It Works

You started this exercise by attaching an `EntityDataSource` control to the `ListView` control. The `EntityDataSource` is configured to work with the `Pictures` entity set. As you saw earlier, each picture is linked to a photo album by its PhotoAlbumId. To have the ManagePhotoAlbum.aspx page display only those pictures that belong to the current photo album (identified by the PhotoAlbumId query string), you set up a WhereParameter:

```
<asp:EntityDataSource ID="EntityDataSource1" runat="server"
    ConnectionString="name=PlanetWroxEntities"
    DefaultContainerName="PlanetWroxEntities" EnableDelete="True"
    EnableFlattening="False" EnableInsert="True" EntitySetName="Pictures"
    Where="it.PhotoAlbum.Id = @photoAlbumId"
    OnInserting="EntityDataSource1_Inserting">
  <WhereParameters>
    <asp:QueryStringParameter Name="PhotoAlbumId"
         QueryStringField="PhotoAlbumId" Type="Int32" />
  </WhereParameters>
</asp:EntityDataSource>
```

You should take note of two important parts in this markup. First, there's the WhereParameters collection that contains a QueryStringParameter that looks at the PhotoAlbumId field in the query string. When the EntityDataSource is about to get its data, it retrieves the value for the parameter from the query string.

The second important part is the Where attribute of the EntityDataSource control. It uses a Where clause to limit the items that are returned from the database:

```
Where="it.PhotoAlbum.Id = @photoAlbumId"
```

This gets all the Pictures from the Picture table that have the requested PhotoAlbumId. The it in the Where clause is an implicit range variable, just like other range variables in queries you've seen before. However, here you need to use it and cannot make up your own name as you can do with your own LINQ queries. At run time, the Where clause is filled in with the actual PhotoAlbumId, retrieved from the query string, which ensures only pictures belonging to the current album are returned.

The first time the page loads after you create a new photo album, there won't be any pictures. However, as soon as you start adding items using the InsertTemplate of the ListView control, you'll see them appear in the list.

To display the pictures on the page, you used the ListView control. Just like other data-bound controls, the ListView is able to display repetitive data in a structured way. In this example, you set the ListView to bulleted list mode, so the control presents its data as a set of <li> elements. You define the container of the items with the <LayoutTemplate>:

```
<LayoutTemplate>
  <ul class="ItemContainer">
    <li ID="itemPlaceholder" runat="server" />
  </ul>
</LayoutTemplate>
```

Note that this <li> has its ID set to itemPlaceholder. This tells the ListView control where to add the individual pictures. At run time, this element will be *replaced* by the actual items from the templates, like <ItemTemplate>.

When the `ListView` control needs to display its data, it creates an item based on the `<ItemTemplate>` for each data item in the data source. In this example, each data item is a strongly typed `Picture` object, which provides access to properties such as `ToolTip` and `Description`:

```
<ItemTemplate>
  <li>
    ...
    ToolTip:
    <asp:Label ID="ToolTipLabel" runat="server" Text='<%# Eval("ToolTip") %>' />
    ...
    <asp:Button ID="DeleteButton" runat="server" CommandName="Delete" />
  </li>
</ItemTemplate>
```

With this code in place, each item in the data source is presented as a series of labels that display relevant properties of the picture. `Eval` *`(PropertyName)`* is used to retrieve the requested value from the object, which is then displayed as the `Label` control's text. Note that at this stage, the `<ItemTemplate>` only displays data *about* the picture. You see how to upload and display real pictures later.

Note the `CommandName` of the `Button` control in the `ItemTemplate`. It's set to `Delete`, which turns this button into a true Delete button. When you click it, the `ListView` figures out what picture you clicked the button for and then instructs the `EntityDataSource` control to delete the associated picture from the database.

The code you added to the theme's CSS files displays the items in an organized way. By setting the `class` attribute of the `<ul>` control to `ItemContainer`, the following CSS is applied to that list:

```
.ItemContainer
{
  width: 600px;
  list-style-type: none;
  clear: both;
}
```

The first property sets the entire width of the list to 600 pixels and the second declaration removes the bullet from the items in the list. Each item in the list is then displayed within a `<li>` element, to which the following CSS is applied:

```
.ItemContainer li
{
  height: 300px;
  width: 200px;
  float: left;
}
```

Each item gets a forced width of 200 pixels. The `float` property tells the `<li>` elements to float next to each other. Within the parent area of 600 pixels you can fit three `<li>` elements of 200 pixels each, causing the fourth and further elements to be placed on their own line. This is a great alternative to presenting data with HTML tables, which generally needs a lot more markup to achieve the same effect.

Finally, each image within the `<li>` element gets a forced width of 180 pixels and 10 pixels of margin at the top and bottom, 20 pixels on the right (to create some room between the images), and none at the left side:

```
.ItemContainer li img
{
```

```
    width: 180px;
    margin: 10px 20px 10px 0;
  }
```

In the DarkGrey theme, the `width` of the `ItemContainer` is set to only 400 pixels. This way, the `<div>` is just wide enough to display two images side by side.

In contrast to many of the other data-bound controls, the `ListView` also supports inserting by defining an `InsertItemTemplate` that contains one or more controls that are bound to properties in the underlying object. For example, the `Description` property of the picture is bound like this:

```
<InsertItemTemplate>
  <li>
    Description:
    <asp:TextBox ID="DescriptionTextBox" runat="server"
                     Text='<%# Bind("Description") %>' /><br />
    ...
</InsertItemTemplate>
```

Instead of `Eval(PropertyName)`, this code uses `Bind(PropertyName)` to set up a *two-way binding* mechanism. This ensures that the ASP.NET run time is able to figure out the relationship between the `Description` property of a `Picture` and the text box called `DescriptionTextBox`, even after a postback. So when you enter some details and click the special Insert button (with its `CommandName` set to `Insert`), a new `Picture` object is constructed, its properties, such as `Description`, `Title`, and `ToolTip`, are filled with the values from the associated server controls in the `InsertItemTemplate`, and then the `Picture` instance is forwarded to the `EntityDataSource` control, which takes care of saving the item in the database and refreshing the list of pictures that are displayed on the page.

Once the `EntityDataSource` control is about to save the picture, it fires its `Inserting` event. In that event handler in this exercise you added some code that linked the new `Picture` instance to the `PhotoAlbumId` like this:

VB.NET

```
Dim photoAlbumId As Integer =
         Convert.ToInt32(Request.QueryString.Get("PhotoAlbumId"))
Dim myPicture As Picture = CType(e.Entity, Picture)
myPicture.PhotoAlbumId = photoAlbumId
```

C#

```
int photoAlbumId = Convert.ToInt32(Request.QueryString.Get("PhotoAlbumId"));
Picture myPicture = (Picture)e.Entity;
myPicture.PhotoAlbumId = photoAlbumId;
```

The Include Foreign Key Columns option you enabled earlier in this chapter has given you a `PhotoAlbumId` property on the `Picture` class that enables you to directly set the ID of the `PhotoAlbum` (which you retrieved from the query string). This in turn relates the picture in the database to a specific photo album in the `PhotoAlbum` table. If you hadn't enabled that option, the property wouldn't have been there, and you would have had to assign a `PhotoAlbum` instance to the `PhotoAlbum` property of the picture by querying the photo album from the database based on its ID. Using the Foreign Key Columns option makes this process a lot easier because you can simply assign the ID of the album you want to add this picture to.

The code in the `ListView` uses `Eval` and `Bind` statements to get data in and out of the `Picture` objects that you're assigning to the controls. ASP.NET 4.5 introduces a new way to set up these bindings, as you see next.

Using Strongly Typed Data-Bound Controls

When VS created the code for the `ListView` for you, it added `Bind` and `Eval` statements like this:

```
<asp:TextBox ID="ToolTipTextBox" runat="server" Text='<%# Bind("ToolTip") %>' />
...
<asp:Label ID="ToolTipLabel" runat="server" Text='<%# Eval("ToolTip") %>' />
```

As you learned in the "How It Works" section of the preceding exercise, `Bind` is for two-way data binding (for insert and edit scenarios) and `Eval` is for read-only scenarios. Notice how the name of the property (`ToolTip` in this example) is a literal string placed between quotes. Using string literals makes your code more prone to errors. First of all, it's easy to misspell the name. Because a string cannot be checked by VS at development time, you won't notice this error until you view the page in the browser. Secondly, if you rename a property, the change is not picked up by the string literal.

Fortunately, ASP.NET 4.5 now has a solution to deal with this problem. The data-bound controls (such as the `ListView`, the `Repeater`, the `GridView`, the `DetailsView`, and the `FormView`) have been turned into *strongly typed data-bound controls*. They have been extended with an `ItemType` property that you can point to the type of object you're assigning to its data source. In the preceding example, this type would have been `PlanetWroxModel.Picture`, the fully qualified name of the `Picture` class. Once you've set this property, the data-bound control gets two new properties, `Item` and `BindItem`, that are of the type you assigned to the `ItemType` property. The first one serves as a replacement for `Eval` and the second one replaces `Bind`. By setting the `ItemType` property and using `Item` and `BindItem`, you get the following benefits:

- IntelliSense now helps you find the correct property of the object you're working with, as shown in Figure 14-17.

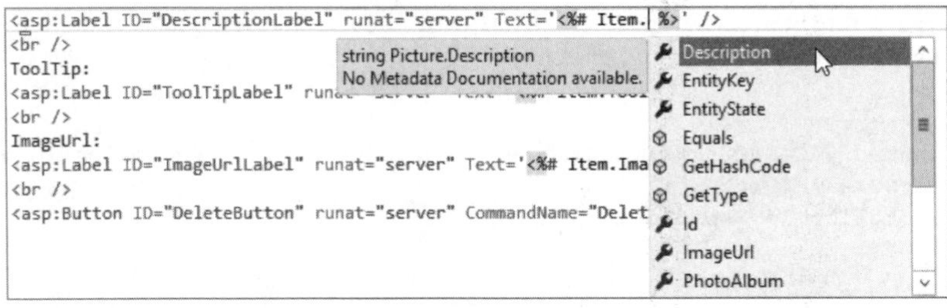

FIGURE 14-17

- When you now misspell the name of a property, or rename it later, you get an error in the Error List, giving you the chance to fix the problem before the page is viewed in the browser.
- External tools (available for the full versions of Visual Studio) will correctly rename the item in the markup when you rename a property on your object.

Although this is an excellent new feature that will help you write better code, you can only use this solution when working with a strongly typed object such as `Picture` from an EF model, or from other classes you or third-party developers create. It won't work in situations such as the following:

- When using the `SqlDataSource` control. This control uses an object under the hood that doesn't expose strongly typed properties that map to columns (such as `ToolTip` or `Description`), and as such you cannot access these columns or properties through the `Item` and `BindItem` properties.
- When using anonymous objects. Because the anonymous object doesn't have a name, you cannot assign its name to the `ItemType` property.

In the following short exercise, you see how to make use of this new strongly typed data-binding capability.

TRY IT OUT Using Strongly Typed Data-Bound Controls

In this exercise you modify the `ListView` control in `ManagePhotoAlbum.aspx` by making it strongly typed. You see how to set the `ItemType` property and how to replace `Bind` and `Eval` with their strongly typed counterparts. When you're done, the page will work exactly as before, but will now be easier to maintain in the future.

1. Start by opening `ManagePhotoAlbum.aspx` in Markup View in VS.
2. Locate the opening tag of the `ListView` and add an `ItemType` property with its value set to `PlanetWroxModel.Picture`. Notice how IntelliSense helps you find the correct item by showing a list with all the types that can be used as the `ItemType`, as shown in Figure 14-18.

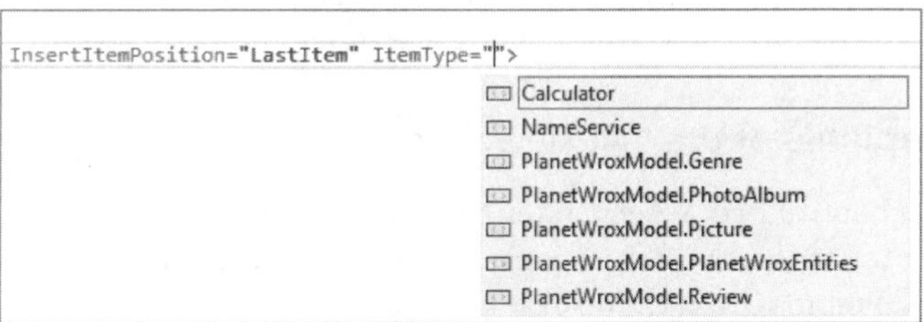

FIGURE 14-18

3. Inside the `InsertItemTemplate` template of the `ListView`, locate the `Bind` statement for the `Description TextBox`, and change it from `Bind("Description")` to `BindItem.Description`. You should end up with this code:

```
<asp:TextBox ID="DescriptionTextBox" runat="server"
       Text='<%# BindItem.Description %>' />
```

4. Repeat the previous step for the `ToolTip TextBox`. The `ImageUrl` gets special treatment later in this chapter, so there's no point in changing it now.

5. Inside the `ItemTemplate` template of the `ListView`, locate the `Eval` statement for the `Description Label` and change it from `Eval("Description")` to `Item.Description`. You should end up with this code:

```
<asp:Label ID="DescriptionLabel" runat="server"
          Text='<%# Item.Description%>' />
```

6. Repeat step 5 for the `ToolTip Label`. Again, the `ImageUrl` gets special treatment later in this chapter, so there's no point in changing it now.

7. Save your changes and request `NewPhotoAlbum.aspx` in the browser. Insert a new album and then add a few pictures by entering a description and tooltip and uploading an image file. Notice how the code still behaves as before.

How It Works

You didn't have to change a lot to make the `ListView` strongly typed and get access to IntelliSense and compile-time checking of your code. All you had to do was add an `ItemType` property to the `ListView` and replace the calls to `Bind` and `Eval` with their `BindItem` and `Item` counterparts. With these changes in place, the control behaves exactly as before. At run time, the control looks at the value of the assigned properties and displays them in the browser. When you submit data back to the server, the reverse takes place: The values you entered in the controls are assigned to the properties of an instance of the `Picture` object, which is then saved in the database by the Entity Framework. It's recommended to use the strongly typed binding capabilities whenever you can, because they'll help you spot errors much sooner and make it easier to type your code.

Right now, users need to type in a URL for an image manually. Obviously, this isn't very user friendly. It would be much easier for them if they could pick an image from their local computer and upload it to the server. You see how to accomplish this in the next exercise.

TRY IT OUT Customizing Templates of the ListView Control

The default templates for the `ListView` control that VS generates based on the information from the `EntityDataSource` are enough only in the most trivial situations. Usually, you need much more control. For example, in the `ItemTemplate` you may want to display an actual `Image` control instead of the plain `ImageUrl` property as text. Likewise, in the `InsertItemTemplate` you may want to display a file upload control instead of a simple text box. In this exercise, you see how to change the standard templates so you can incorporate both features. Additionally, you see how to handle the `Inserting` event of the `EntityDataSource` control to save the uploaded file to disk, and update the database with the URL of the image.

For this example to work, the account used by the web server (the account you use to log on to your machine if you are using IIS Express) needs read and write permissions to the `GigPics` folder that you create in this exercise. The account should already have these permissions on your machine, but if you run into problems with this exercise, refer to the section "Understanding Security in IIS" in Chapter 19.

1. Create a new folder in the root of the website called `GigPics`. This folder will contain concert pictures uploaded by users.

2. Open the ManagePhotoAlbum.aspx page in Markup View and locate the <ItemTemplate> element. Remove the Label that displays the ImageUrl and replace it with an Image control, with its ImageUrl set to the ImageUrl of the picture object.

```
<asp:Image ID="ImageUrl" runat="server" ImageUrl='<%# Item.ImageUrl %>' />
```

Remove the text ImageUrl: that appears right above the image.

3. To enable users to upload images, you need to replace the TextBox for the ImageUrl property with a FileUpload control. You also need to remove the text ImageUrl: again. You do this in the InsertItemTemplate:

```
<asp:TextBox ID="ToolTipTextBox" runat="server"
                Text='<%# BindItem.ToolTip %>' /><br />
<asp:FileUpload ID="FileUpload1" runat="server" />
<br />
<asp:Button ID="InsertButton" runat="server" CommandName="Insert" Text="Insert" />
```

Note that you don't need to bind the property to the control here. Because the uploaded image needs special treatment, you'll write some code in the Code Behind of the page instead of relying on the built-in data-binding capabilities.

4. Set the CausesValidation property of the Cancel button in the <InsertItemTemplate> to false:

```
<asp:Button ID="CancelButton" runat="server" CommandName="Cancel" Text="Clear"
          CausesValidation="false" />
```

5. Similarly, set the CausesValidation property of the Delete button in the <ItemTemplate> to false.

6. Switch to the Code Behind of the page (press F7) and then extend the Inserting event handler with the following code, which saves the file to disk and then updates the ImageUrl property of the Picture instance with its new location:

VB.NET

```
myPicture.PhotoAlbumId = photoAlbumId

Dim FileUpload1 As FileUpload =
              CType(ListView1.InsertItem.FindControl("FileUpload1"), FileUpload)
Dim virtualFolder As String = "~/GigPics/"
Dim physicalFolder As String = Server.MapPath(virtualFolder)
Dim fileName As String = Guid.NewGuid().ToString()
Dim extension As String = System.IO.Path.GetExtension(FileUpload1.FileName)

FileUpload1.SaveAs(System.IO.Path.Combine(physicalFolder, fileName + extension))
myPicture.ImageUrl = virtualFolder + fileName + extension
```

C#

```
myPicture.PhotoAlbumId = photoAlbumId;

FileUpload FileUpload1 =
              (FileUpload)ListView1.InsertItem.FindControl("FileUpload1");
string virtualFolder = "~/GigPics/";
```

```
string physicalFolder = Server.MapPath(virtualFolder);
string fileName = Guid.NewGuid().ToString();
string extension = System.IO.Path.GetExtension(FileUpload1.FileName);

FileUpload1.SaveAs(System.IO.Path.Combine(physicalFolder, fileName + extension));
myPicture.ImageUrl = virtualFolder + fileName + extension;
```

7. Go back to Markup View and add three validation controls to the `InsertItemTemplate`: two `RequiredFieldValidator` controls hooked up to the text boxes for the `Description` and `ToolTip`, and one `CustomValidator` with its `ErrorMessage` set to `Select a valid .jpg file.` Give the `RequiredFieldValidator` controls an ID such as **`reqDesc`** and **`reqToolTip`** and assign the `CustomValidator` an ID of **`cusValImage`**. Finally, set the `TextMode` property of the text box for the `Description` to `MultiLine` and enter a line break (a `<br />`) before the Insert button.

   You should end up with the following code:

```
Description:
<asp:RequiredFieldValidator ID="reqDesc" ControlToValidate="DescriptionTextBox"
      runat="server" ErrorMessage="Enter a description." />
<asp:TextBox ID="DescriptionTextBox" runat="server" TextMode="MultiLine"
       Text='<%# BindItem.Description %>' /><br />
ToolTip:
<asp:RequiredFieldValidator ID="reqToolTip" ControlToValidate="ToolTipTextBox"
      runat="server" ErrorMessage="Enter a tool tip." />
<asp:TextBox ID="ToolTipTextBox" runat="server"
       Text='<%# BindItem.ToolTip %>' /><br />
<asp:FileUpload ID="FileUpload1" runat="server" /><br />
<asp:CustomValidator ID="cusValImage" runat="server"
       ErrorMessage="Select a valid .jpg file." />
<br />
<asp:Button ID="InsertButton" runat="server" CommandName="Insert" Text="Insert" />
```

8. Select the `ListView` control in Design View and set up an event handler for its `ItemInserting` event by double-clicking the event in the Events tab of the Properties Grid. Complete the event handler with the following code:

VB.NET

```
Protected Sub ListView1_ItemInserting(sender As Object,
           e As ListViewInsertEventArgs) Handles ListView1.ItemInserting
  Dim FileUpload1 As FileUpload =
            CType(ListView1.InsertItem.FindControl("FileUpload1"), FileUpload)
  If Not FileUpload1.HasFile OrElse
            Not FileUpload1.FileName.ToLower().EndsWith(".jpg") Then
    Dim cusValImage As CustomValidator =
      CType(ListView1.InsertItem.FindControl("cusValImage"), CustomValidator)
    cusValImage.IsValid = False
    e.Cancel = True
  End If
End Sub
```

C#

```
protected void ListView1_ItemInserting(object sender, ListViewInsertEventArgs e)
{
  FileUpload FileUpload1 =
```

```
        (FileUpload)ListView1.InsertItem.FindControl("FileUpload1");
  if (!FileUpload1.HasFile || !FileUpload1.FileName.ToLower().EndsWith(".jpg"))
  {
    CustomValidator cusValImage =
          (CustomValidator)ListView1.InsertItem.FindControl("cusValImage");
    cusValImage.IsValid = false;
    e.Cancel = true;
  }
}
```

9. Save all your changes, and then request `NewPhotoAlbum.aspx` in your browser (don't accidentally request the `ManagePhotoAlbum.aspx` page that you just worked on). Enter a new name for the photo album and click the Insert link. Insert a few pictures by entering a description and a tooltip, selecting a `.jpg` picture from your hard drive, and clicking the Insert button. Then enter the description and tooltip of another image, but leave the file upload box empty. When you click Insert, you get an error message indicating that you didn't upload a valid `.jpg` file, as shown in Figure 14-19.

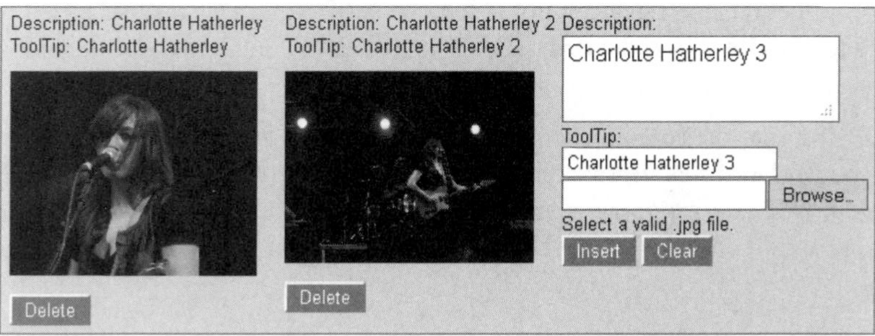

FIGURE 14-19

10. Click the Browse button of the file upload box, browse for a valid `.jpg` file, and click the Insert button once more. The file now gets uploaded successfully.

How It Works

You haven't changed much in the actual process of inserting the `Picture` into the database. The `ListView` control still collects all the relevant data from the page and then sends it to the `EntityDataSource` control, which then inserts the item in the `Picture` table in the database through EF. What is different is the way you set up the templates and the way you handled the events of the `EntityDataSource` and `ListView` controls. Look at the templates first. Inside the `ItemTemplate` you added an `<asp:Image>` to take the place of the plain text label. As you can see in Figure 14-19, this displays the actual image, rather than just its URL.

To enable a user to upload the images, you replaced the `TextBox` control in the `InsertItemTemplate` with a `FileUpload` control. Additionally, you added a few validation controls to force the user to enter the required fields. As soon as you click the Insert button, the page posts back and the `ListView` control fires its `ItemInserting` event. This event is a good place to perform any custom validation. One of the arguments this event handler receives (the `e` argument) is of the type `ListViewInsertEventArgs`, a class that provides context-sensitive information to the `ItemInserting` event. When you detect an error, you can set the `Cancel` property of this `e` argument to `True` (`true` in C#) to tell the `ListView` control you want to cancel the insert operation. Inside this event handler you added some code that "finds" the upload control in the `InsertItem` template. Because you can potentially have multiple controls with the same name (for example, a `FileUpload` control in the `InsertItemTemplate` and one in the `EditItemTemplate`), you cannot access `FileUpload1` directly. Instead, you need to use `FindControl` on the `InsertItem` object to search for the control:

VB.NET

```
Dim FileUpload1 As FileUpload =
          CType(ListView1.InsertItem.FindControl("FileUpload1"), FileUpload)
```

C#

```
FileUpload FileUpload1 =
     (FileUpload)ListView1.InsertItem.FindControl("FileUpload1");
```

When you have a reference to the `FileUpload` control, you can check its `HasFile` property to see if a file has been uploaded. Additionally, you can check `FileUpload1.FileName.ToLower().EndsWith(".jpg")` to see if a file with a `.jpg` extension has been uploaded. To ensure that this test is carried out only when the user has uploaded a file, the code uses `OrElse` in VB and `||` in C# to short-circuit the logic in the `If` statement, as explained in Chapter 5.

If the user doesn't upload a valid file, the code in the `If` block runs. It uses `FindControl` again to find the `CustomValidator` control and sets its `IsValid` property to `False` (`false` in C#). This tells the control to display its `ErrorMessage` property when the page renders. Finally, to stop the `ListView` from continuing the insert operation you need to set the `Cancel` property of the `e` argument to `True` (`true` in C#):

VB.NET

```
e.Cancel = True
```

C#

```
e.Cancel = true;
```

The other validation controls to make sure a title and description are entered work in the same way as you saw in Chapter 9.

If the user uploaded a valid `.jpg` file, the `ListView` continues with its insert operation, which eventually results in an insert action against the `EntityDataSource` control. When that control is about to send the insert operation to EF, it fires its `Inserting` event, giving you a last chance to hook into the process and look at the data. Inside this event handler, you used similar code to find a reference to the `FileUpload` control inside the `InsertItem` template. You then used the following code to determine the physical and virtual folder for the file, its name, and its extension:

VB.NET

```
Dim virtualFolder As String = "~/GigPics/"
Dim physicalFolder As String = Server.MapPath(virtualFolder)
```

```
Dim fileName As String = Guid.NewGuid().ToString()
Dim extension As String = System.IO.Path.GetExtension(FileUpload1.FileName)
```

C#

```
string virtualFolder = "~/GigPics/";
string physicalFolder = Server.MapPath(virtualFolder);
string fileName = Guid.NewGuid().ToString();
string extension = System.IO.Path.GetExtension(FileUpload1.FileName);
```

The variable `virtualFolder` holds the virtual location — starting off the root of the website — of the folder where the uploaded images are stored. Using `Server.MapPath` you can turn this into a physical folder. Assuming you have your project in its default location of `C:\BegASPNET\Site`, the `physicalFolder` variable now contains `C:\BegASPNET\Site\GigPics`.

Next, a new, random filename is generated using `Guid.NewGuid()`. The `Guid` class is able to generate more or less random filenames that are guaranteed to be unique across time and space. This code assigns the variable `fileName` something like `f6d8ed05-2dbe-4aed-868a-de045f9462e3`, which guarantees a unique filename. Finally, the extension of the file is retrieved using the static `GetExtension` method of the `Path` class in the `System.IO` namespace.

At this stage, you have all the required information to store the file on disk, and then update the database. Storing the file on disk is easy using the `SaveAs` method of the `FileUpload` control:

VB.NET

```
FileUpload1.SaveAs(System.IO.Path.Combine(physicalFolder, fileName + extension))
```

C#

```
FileUpload1.SaveAs(System.IO.Path.Combine(physicalFolder, fileName + extension));
```

This code takes the physical folder, the filename, and the extension and passes them to the `Combine` method of the `Path` class that builds up the full path. This path is then sent to the `SaveAs` method, which saves the file at the requested location.

Finally, the `Picture` instance is updated with the new `ImageUrl`:

VB.NET

```
myPicture.ImageUrl = virtualFolder + fileName + extension
```

C#

```
myPicture.ImageUrl = virtualFolder + fileName + extension;
```

This assigns something like `~/GigPics/f6d8ed05-2dbe-4aed-868a-de045f9462e3.jpg` to the `ImageUrl` property, which is the new virtual location of the uploaded image. Right after you insert the new image, the `ListView` is updated and now shows the new image, using the `Image` control with its `ImageUrl` set to the image you just uploaded.

You can imagine that if you upload a large number of images for a single photo album, the page becomes more difficult to manage. This is especially true at the front end, where users may be accessing your site over a slow network connection. Instead of presenting them all the images in the photo album on a single page, you can split up the photo album into multiple pages, enabling users to go from page to page. You see how to do this in the next section, which discusses the `DataPager` control.

Introducing the DataPager Control

The `DataPager` is a separate control that you can use to extend another, data-bound, control. Currently, the .NET Framework lets you use the `DataPager` only to provide paging capabilities to the `ListView` control, but the developer community has been active writing implementations for other controls, like the `GridView`, as well.

You can hook up the `DataPager` to the `ListView` control in two ways: You can either define it within the `<LayoutTemplate>` of the `ListView` control or you can define it entirely outside the `ListView`. In the first case, the `DataPager` knows to what control it should provide paging capabilities automatically. In the latter case, you need to set the `PagedControlID` property of the `DataPager` to the `ID` of a valid `ListView` control. You see how to configure and use the `DataPager` in conjunction with a `ListView` next. Being able to define the `DataPager` outside of the `ListView` control is useful if you want to place it at a different location of the page, such as in the `Footer` or `Sidebar` area, for example.

TRY IT OUT Paging Data with the ListView and DataPager Controls

In this Try It Out you create the front-end page of the Gig Pics feature. Users of your site can choose one of the available photo albums from a drop-down list and then view all the available pictures in a pageable list that is created by a `ListView` and a `DataPager` control. Figure 14-22 shows the final result of this exercise.

1. In the root of your site, create a new folder called `PhotoAlbums`. Inside this folder create a new Web Form based on your custom page template and call it `Default.aspx`. Set the `Title` of the page to **`All Photo Albums`**.
2. Switch to Design View and drop a `DropDownList` control on the page. On the control's Smart Tasks panel, enable `AutoPostBack` and then hook it up to a new `EntityDataSource` control by clicking Choose Data Source, and then choosing <New data source> from the first drop-down list. Click the Entity icon, click OK, and select `PlanetWroxEntities` in the Named Connection drop-down list. Click Next. On the Configure Data Selection dialog box, choose PhotoAlbums from the EntitySetName drop-down list and select the fields `Id` and `Name`, as shown in Figure 14-20.
3. Click Finish to close the Configure Data Source wizard. In the Choose a Data Source dialog box, select `Name` from the Data Field to Display drop-down list and leave `Id` selected in the Data Field for the Value drop-down list. If you don't see the items in the lists, click Refresh Schema first.
4. Click OK to close the Data Source Configuration Wizard.
5. Below the `DropDownList` add a new `ListView` control and connect it to a new `EntityDataSource` by selecting <New data source> from the drop-down list on the control's Smart Tasks panel. Click the Entity icon and click OK. Select `PlanetWroxEntities` in the drop-down and click Next. In the dialog box that follows, choose Pictures from the EntitySetName drop-down list and click Finish.

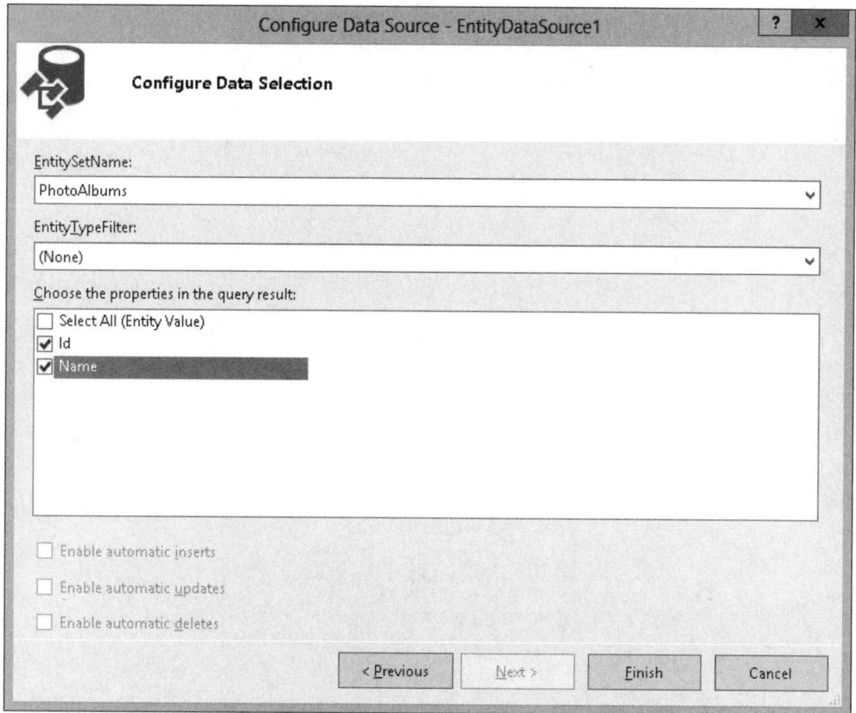

FIGURE 14-20

6. Select the new `EntityDataSource` control (called `EntityDataSource2`) in Design View, open its Properties Grid, and click the button with the ellipsis for the `Where` property to open up the Expression Editor. Check off the check box for an automatically generated Where clause at the top of the dialog box. Click the Add Parameter button and enter **`PhotoAlbumId`** as the name for the parameter. Then choose Control in the Parameter Source drop-down property and choose `DropDownList1` as the ControlID. Finally, click the Show Advanced Properties link and change the `Type` of the parameter to `Int32`. Your Expression Editor should look like Figure 14-21.

   Click OK to close the dialog box.

7. On the `ListView` control's Smart Tasks panel, click Configure ListView (click Refresh Schema and reopen the Smart Tasks panel first if you don't see that option). Select Bulleted List as the layout, and in the Options area choose Enable Paging. The drop-down list below it should default to Next/Previous Pager, which is fine for this exercise.

8. Click OK and VS creates a couple of templates for you.

9. Switch to Markup View and add an `ItemType` attribute to the `ListView` with its value set to `PlanetWroxModel.Picture`. Your `ListView` should end up like this:

```
<asp:ListView ID="ListView1" runat="server" DataKeyNames="Id"
      DataSourceID="EntityDataSource2" ItemType="PlanetWroxModel.Picture">
```

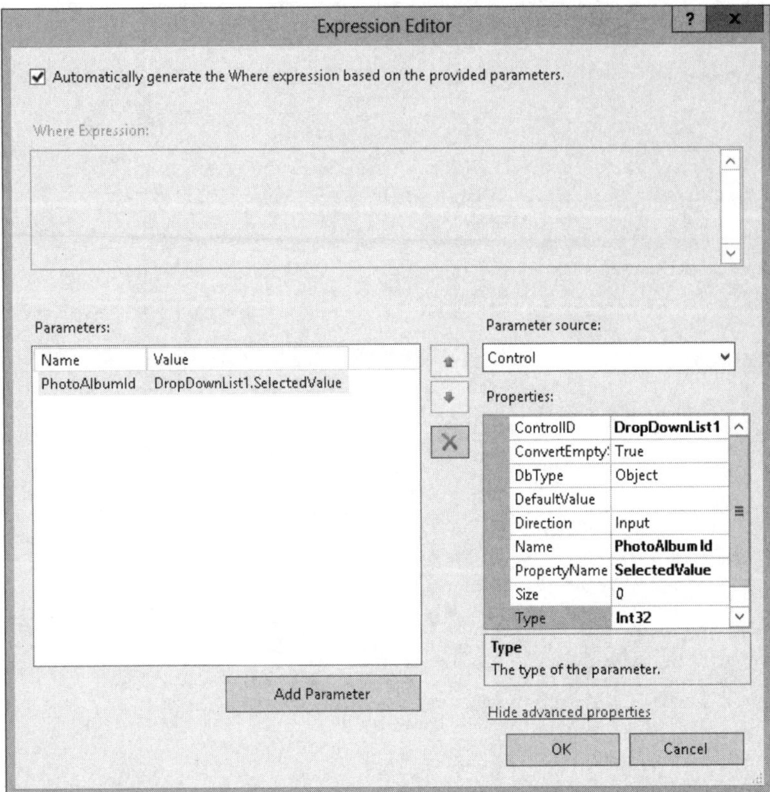

FIGURE 14-21

10. Next, remove the following templates and the code they contain:

- `<AlternatingItemTemplate>`
- `<EditItemTemplate>`
- `<InsertItemTemplate>`
- `<ItemSeparatorTemplate>`
- `<SelectedItemTemplate>`

11. Remove the `ID`, `runat`, and `style` attributes from the `<ul>` in the `LayoutTemplate` and add a `class` attribute and set it to `ItemContainer`. Locate the `DataPager` inside the `LayoutTemplate` and add a `PageSize` attribute set to `3`. Finally, add `clear: both;` to the empty `style` attribute:

```
<LayoutTemplate>
  <ul class="ItemContainer">
    <li id="itemPlaceholder" runat="server" />
  </ul>
  <div style="clear: both;">
    <asp:DataPager ID="DataPager1" runat="server" PageSize="3">
      <Fields>
        <asp:NextPreviousPagerField ButtonType="Button" ShowFirstPageButton="True"
                ShowLastPageButton="True" />
```

```
      </Fields>
    </asp:DataPager>
  </div>
</LayoutTemplate>
```

12. Modify the code in the `ItemTemplate` so it ends up like this:

```
<ItemTemplate>
  <li>
    <asp:Image ID="Image1" runat="server" ImageUrl='<%# Item.ImageUrl %>'
            ToolTip='<%# Item.ToolTip %>' />
    <asp:Label ID="DescriptionLabel" runat="server"
            Text='<%# Item.Description %>' />
  </li>
</ItemTemplate>
```

This creates an `Image` control with its `ImageUrl` and `ToolTip` properties bound to the corresponding properties of the `Picture` object that you're binding to. The `ToolTip` appears when you hover your mouse over the image in the browser. Below the image, a simple `Label` control displays the `Description` of the image. You don't need the other properties that were initially defined in the template for this exercise.

13. Next, wrap the entire code in the `cpMainContent` content block in an `UpdatePanel` with a `ContentTemplate` element to avoid page flicker when paging the list of pictures, or when choosing a new photo album from the list.

```
<asp:Content ID="Content2" ContentPlaceHolderID="cpMainContent" runat="Server">
  <asp:UpdatePanel ID="UpdatePanel1" runat="server">
    <ContentTemplate>
      <asp:DropDownList ID="DropDownList1" runat="server" AutoPostBack="True"
        DataSourceID="EntityDataSource1" DataTextField="Name" DataValueField="Id">
      ...
    </ContentTemplate>
  </asp:UpdatePanel>
</asp:Content>
```

14. Open the `Web.sitemap` file for the site and add a main menu and two submenu items for the Gig Pics section, between the Reviews and About sections:

```
</siteMapNode>
<siteMapNode url="~/PhotoAlbums/" title="Gig Pics" description="All Gig Pics">
  <siteMapNode url="~/PhotoAlbums/Default.aspx" title="Gig Pics"
          description="All Gig Pics" />
  <siteMapNode url="~/NewPhotoAlbum.aspx" title="New Album"
          description="Create a new Photo Album with Gig Pics" />
</siteMapNode>
<siteMapNode url="~/About/Default.aspx" title="About"
            description="About this site">
```

15. Because you added another menu item, you need to change the width of each item in the menu for the Monochrome theme. To do this, open up `Monochrome.css` and change the width for the `.MainMenu ul li` selector from 200 to 160 pixels:

```
.MainMenu ul li
{
  width: 160px;
}
```

16. Save all your changes and then request `Default.aspx` from the `PhotoAlbums` folder in your browser. Choose a photo album from the drop-down list and the page reloads, showing you the relevant pictures in the photo album.

> ***COMMON MISTAKES*** *If nothing happens when you choose a new item from the drop-down list, go back to VS and ensure you set* `AutoPostBack` *on the* `DropDownList` *control to* `True`*.*
>
> *If you don't have any pictures in a photo album, or not enough to fill an entire page, choose New Album from the Gig Pics menu, create a new photo album, and add at least four images to it. Then click the Gig Pics menu item and choose your new photo album from the drop-down list. Note that there is now a paging user interface, enabling you to move forward and backward through the list of pictures in the photo album using the First, Previous, Next, and Last buttons visible at the bottom of the screen in Figure 14-22. Because of the AJAX panel you added, the selection and paging operations now occur completely flicker-free.*

> ***NOTE*** *Your first few albums will end up broken. That's because you didn't supply images when you created them. You can delete the albums (and their associated picture rows) from the database if you want to clean up a bit. In Chapter 16 you develop functionality to delete images from the* `Default.aspx` *page in the* `PhotoAlbums` *folder.*

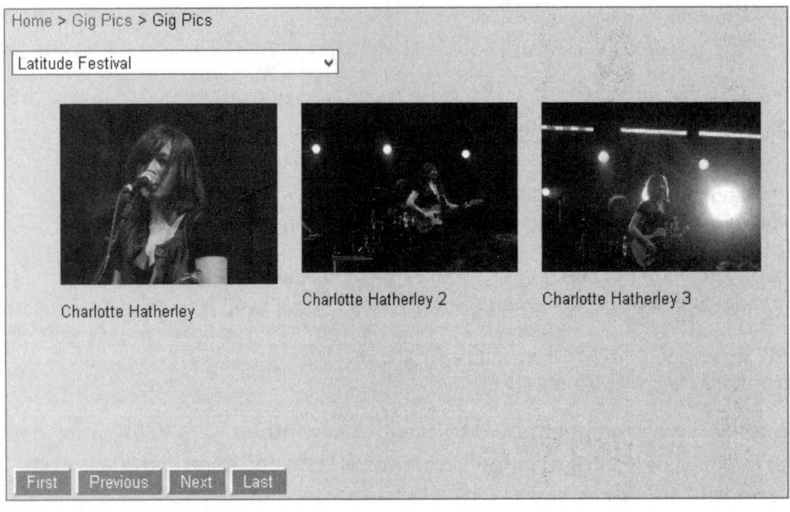

FIGURE 14-22

How It Works

Most of what you have seen in this exercise should be familiar. You connected a DropDownList to an EntityDataSource using a method similar to the one you used to create the Genres drop-down list in the previous chapter. The ListView and its associated EntityDataSource are also similar to what is discussed earlier in this chapter. However, instead of a Where parameter that looks at the query string, the code now uses a Where parameter that looks at the DropDownList:

```
<WhereParameters>
  <asp:ControlParameter ControlID="DropDownList1" Name="PhotoAlbumId"
          PropertyName="SelectedValue" Type="Int32" />
</WhereParameters>
```

Because you set AutoGenerateWhereClause to True on the EntityDataSource control, a Where clause is created on the fly based on these parameters. This is in contrast to an earlier example where you explicitly defined a Where clause. For simple scenarios as in the preceding exercise, relying on the automatically generated Where clause works fine. For more detailed scenarios, it's good to know you can also assign one explicitly.

When the EntityDataSource is about to get its data from the database, it looks at the SelectedValue property of the drop-down list and then retrieves only the pictures that match the requested PhotoAlbumId.

The biggest difference from previous examples is the addition of the DataPager. As demonstrated in this exercise, paging is handled for you automatically. All you need to do is embed a DataPager control somewhere in the LayoutTemplate of the ListView and the rest is taken care of automatically. If you place the DataPager outside the ListView, don't forget to hook it up to the ListView by setting the PagedControlID property. If you prefer links or images over buttons, you can set the ButtonType property of the NextPreviousPagerField element to Link or Image, respectively. If you prefer a numeric pager, replace the NextPreviousPagerField item with a NumericPagerField:

```
<asp:NumericPagerField NextPageText="..." PreviousPageText="..." />
```

In this exercise you set the PageSize to 3 so it's easier to fill more than one page and see the pager at work. In real-world applications the PageSize is usually a bit higher, such as 10 or 20. Because the layout uses a three-column layout for the Monochrome theme and a two-column layout for the DarkGrey theme, you may want to select a value that's dividable by both, such as 18.

A Few Notes about Performance

The preceding exercise has two known performance problems that you should be aware of. First, although the ItemTemplate of the ListView resizes the images to 180 pixels *in the browser* by setting their widths through CSS, the actual image is left unmodified. This means that if you upload a large image, the entire image is still downloaded, only to display as a small thumbnail image. It would be better to create a true thumbnail image at the server, and send that to the browser instead. The chapter entitled "Greeting Cards" in my book *ASP.NET 2.0 Instant Results* (ISBN: 978-0-471-74951-6) has a number of examples on resizing images on the server.

The other potential performance problem lies in the way the data is paged. With the `DataPager` control, the data is paged inside the ASPX page. That means that all data is retrieved from the database and sent to the `EntityDataSource` control. The `DataPager` control then selects the right rows to display on the current page. This works fine for result sets of up to hundreds of rows. However, as soon as the number of items in a photo album or other collection grows above that number, you may find that your pages start to slow down. If that's the case, you may want to look at paging at the database level. The ADO.NET Entity Framework supports this scenario using the `Skip()` and `Take()` methods you've seen before.

PRACTICAL LINQ AND ADO.NET ENTITY FRAMEWORK TIPS

Here are some practical LINQ and ADO.NET Entity Framework tips:

- In this chapter you saw how to create anonymous types to shape the data you want to return from your queries. The compiler and IntelliSense are invaluable tools in determining what data you can return and what properties you have available. Spend some time playing around with the anonymous types, looking at the different options that the IntelliSense lists give you.
- Just as with other data access methods, like the `SqlDataSource` control you saw in the previous chapter, try to filter your data as much as possible. If you know you only need reviews in the Jazz genre, be explicit and incorporate a `Where` clause in your code or `EntityDataSource` control that limits the list of reviews at the database level. This speeds up your queries and data retrieval, improving the overall speed of the application.
- Make use of anonymous types to decrease the memory consumption of your LINQ queries. For example, instead of retrieving the entire `Review` object, use the `New` (`new` in C#) keyword to create a new anonymous type on the fly. Because this new object contains only the properties you really need, you save yourself the overhead of bringing in the full object.

SUMMARY

LINQ is a compelling and exciting technology that ships with .NET. LINQ is an important plumbing technique in many data access scenarios, including database access in ASP.NET web applications using the ADO.NET Entity Framework.

Because LINQ is so important, it has been integrated in many different places in .NET. LINQ is available for objects enabling you to query in-memory collections. Additionally, LINQ is available for XML, ADO.NET, and DataSets, each type providing access to a different data store, but with the same, unified querying language. LINQ is also used as the query language for the ADO.NET Entity Framework.

To work with EF in your ASP.NET web applications you have a couple of different options. First, you can write queries in the Code Behind of a page and then bind the results to a data-bound control using the `DataSource` property and `DataBind` method of the control. Alternatively, you can use the `EntityDataSource` control that serves as the bridge between your data-bound controls and your model. Combined with the new `ListView` and `DataPager` controls, the `EntityDataSource` enables you to create fully functional CRUD pages.

Until now, the database-driven pages you have seen look quite dull. You haven't applied a lot of styling, or provided any conditional formatting, where data is presented differently based on its values. You can do this through control styles and the many events of the data-bound and data source controls. The next chapter shows you how to make use of these styles and events.

EXERCISES

1. Imagine you have a page in the `Reviews` folder called `MostRecent.aspx`. This page should show the 10 most recently added reviews. What would your LINQ query look like if you only wanted to show the review's `Title` property and the name of the genre it belongs to? You should use the `Take` method to limit the result set to 10. If you're having trouble writing the code to get the last reviews, look at the section titled "First, FirstOrDefault, Last, and LastOrDefault," which shows you how to get the last review in the database.

2. What is the major benefit of the `ListView` control over other data controls like `GridView` and `Repeater`?

3. Currently the `Default.aspx` page from the `PhotoAlbums` folder just shows the thumbnails of the pictures. What would you need to do to display the full-size picture on its own page using a LINQ query?

4. When you delete a picture from the `ListView` on the Photo Album page, only the database row is deleted, but the image on disk is left untouched. Make use of the static `System.IO.File.Delete` method to delete the item from disk. Choose an appropriate event of the `EntityDataSource` to handle this and make use of the `Entity` property that is available on the `e` argument of the event.

5. Currently, the `AllByGenre.aspx` page displays the title of the genre, regardless of whether it has any reviews attached to it. How can you hide genres that don't have any reviews? Make use of the `Count` method on the `Reviews` collection to solve this question.

You can find answers to these exercises in Appendix A.

▶ WHAT YOU LEARNED IN THIS CHAPTER

ADO.NET Entity Data Model file	The file that contains the information necessary to map your object model to the tables in your database
Anonymous types	Types that are created on the fly without defining them explicitly
Entity Framework	A technology to create a strongly typed object model with an underlying database that enables you to interact with the data in your database
Entity sets	A collection of objects in your entity model; for example, a `PhotoAlbum` instance has a `Pictures` entity set that contains the pictures in the album.
`EntityDataSource` **control**	An ASP.NET control that serves as a bridge between your ASPX pages and the Entity Framework
Lazy loading	A technique in which data is not loaded from the database until it is accessed at run time
LINQ	Language-Integrated Query; the part of .NET Framework programming languages that provides querying support against all kinds of data collections, including objects, XML, and databases
Range variable	A variable defined in your LINQ query that is subsequently used in the `Select` and `Where` parts
Strong typing	A programming concept in which the type of a variable is explicitly defined when the variable is declared
Type inference	A technique in which the compiler determines the type of a variable based on the data it gets assigned; this enables you to create strongly typed variables without explicitly defining the variable's type first.

15

Working with Data — Advanced Topics

WHAT YOU WILL LEARN IN THIS CHAPTER:

- How to change the formatting of the various data-bound controls using styles, themes, and skins
- How to handle the various events that are fired by the data controls to change their appearance conditionally
- How to hand-code the UI of data access pages to get complete freedom over the pages' structure and markup
- How to use the built-in caching mechanisms to improve the performance of your website

WROX.COM CODE DOWNLOADS FOR THIS CHAPTER

You can find the wrox.com code downloads for this chapter on the Download Code tab at `www.wrox.com/remtitle.cgi?isbn=1118311809`. The code is in the Chapter 15 download.

The previous three chapters introduced you to a lot of new concepts. Chapter 12 discussed databases in general and SQL Server 2012 Express LocalDB edition in particular. That chapter also covered the basic operations to create, read, update, and delete data. Chapter 13 focused mostly on working with the `SqlDataSource` control and the different data-bound controls that you have at your disposal. Finally, Chapter 14 explored the world of the ADO .NET Entity Framework, Microsoft's latest data access technology designed to speed up the way you write data access code.

To help you really understand the core concepts of data access, those three chapters focused mainly on the data source controls and the principles behind them, and much less on the presentation of data with the data-bound controls. Obviously, in a real-world application this is not enough, and you need a way to present data in a clear and attractive way.

The data-bound controls that ship with ASP.NET 4.5 provide many options to change the way data is presented. They enable you to completely change the design (font, colors, spacing, and so on) of the data they are presenting. Additionally, you can tweak these controls to hide specific columns, modify column headers, and even change the look and feel of the controls programmatically.

In the next sections you see how to style your controls using a variety of techniques. Later sections in this chapter show you how to hand-code your data access pages, giving you great flexibility. Near the end of the chapter, caching — a technique to improve the performance of your website — is discussed.

FORMATTING YOUR CONTROLS USING STYLES

Chapters 13 and 14 explained how to work with the numerous data-bound ASP.NET 4.5 controls. You learned how to display and edit lists of data with controls like `GridView`, `Repeater`, and `ListView`, as well as how to work with single record controls such as `DetailsView`.

So far, you've relied on the built-in look and feel of the controls, which often results in dull and plain-looking screens. Figure 15-1 shows the `GridView` that you created in Chapter 13 to manage the genres in the Planet Wrox database in Firefox.

	Id	Name	SortOrder
Edit Delete Select	1	Rap and Hip-Hop	14
Edit Delete Select	2	Pop	12
Edit Delete Select	3	Jazz	8
Edit Delete Select	4	Hard Rock	3
Edit Delete Select	5	Indie Rock	7
Edit Delete Select	6	Punk	1
Edit Delete Select	7	Rock	2
Edit Delete Select	8	Grunge	4
Edit Delete Select	9	Alternative Rock	9
Edit Delete Select	10	Reggae	11
1 2			

FIGURE 15-1

This control relies on the default settings of the browser to display text and links, which usually results in purple and blue links with the default font, such as Times New Roman. Additionally, the columns in the grid are just as wide as necessary to display the text they contain. It would be a lot easier on the eyes if you could present the `GridView` as in Figure 15-2 instead.

	▲ Name	Sort Order
Edit Delete	Alternative Rock	9
Edit Delete	Disco	8
Edit Delete	Grunge	4
Edit Delete	Hard Rock	3
Edit Delete	Indie Rock	7
Edit Delete	Industrial	10
Edit Delete	Jazz	8
Edit Delete	Pop	12
Edit Delete	Punk	1
Edit Delete	Rap and Hip-Hop	14
1 2		

FIGURE 15-2

The column for the Edit and Delete links is now a little wider, separating it clearly from the actual content in the grid. The `Id` column has been hidden and the `Name` column has been made wider as well. The different colors for the header, footer, items, and alternating items make the data in the grid a lot easier to read. Because some genres have reviews attached to them, their Delete links are disabled. And finally, a little glyph has been added to the Name heading to indicate the direction the column is sorted on.

Changing the dull-looking `GridView` from Figure 15-1 into the snazzier one shown in Figure 15-2 is easily accomplished with the use of *ASP.NET styles* and the many events that the data-bound controls fire. In the next section you see how to apply these styles to a single control in a page. In the section that follows you see how to move the styles to a theme, so styles can be reused more easily by all controls in a section of your site. You have already seen some styles at work in Chapter 7, where you used them to style the `Menu` and the `TreeView` controls. However, because styles are used so much for formatting data-bound controls, they really deserve their own section.

An Introduction to Styles

Many of the data-bound and navigation controls have a number of style properties that enable you to modify the look and feel of the control. For example, the `GridView` control has `RowStyle` and `AlternatingRowStyle` properties that enable you to customize the look of an individual row in the grid. Here's an example of a `GridView` with two style elements that renders odd and even rows with different background colors:

```
<asp:GridView ID="GridView1" runat="server">
  <AlternatingRowStyle BackColor="White" />
  <RowStyle BackColor="#EFF3FB" />
</asp:GridView>
```

Likewise, the `DetailsView` has a `CommandRowStyle` property that is used to control the appearance of the command row that holds commands such as `Insert`, `Delete`, `Cancel`, and so on.

Ultimately, each style property inherits from the `Style` class that lives in the `System.Web.UI.WebControls` namespace. Figure 15-3 shows you a filtered view of the diagram for this class with its most common properties visible.

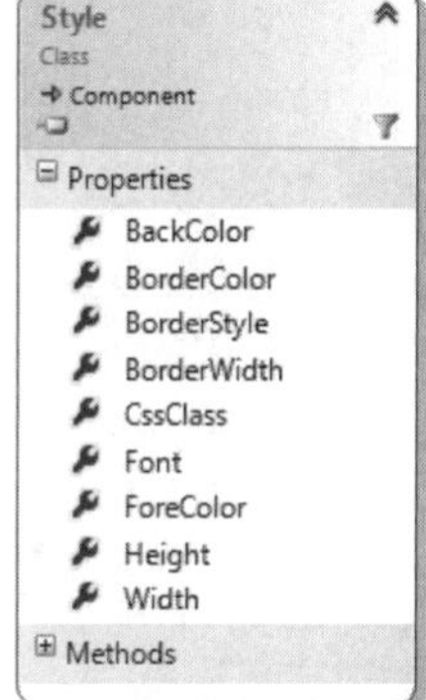

FIGURE 15-3

As you can see from their names, the properties of the `Style` class are used to change style-related information on the objects to which this class is applied. Each of these properties is eventually converted to a CSS property or an HTML attribute, such as `background-color`, `border`, and so on. Other styles, like the styles for the `GridView` control, add various layout-related properties, such as different options to control alignment. The following table lists the most important properties of the various `Style`-derived classes that are available. Note that not every property is available for every style. IntelliSense shows you exactly what properties you can use in a certain style.

PROPERTY	DESCRIPTION
`BackColor` `ForeColor`	These enable you to change the background and text color of the elements. They map to the CSS properties `background-color` and `color`, respectively.

`BorderColor`
`BorderStyle`
`BorderWidth`
	These enable you to change the border of the element to which the style is applied. They map directly to their CSS counterparts `border-color`, `border-style`, and `border-width`.

continues

(continued)

PROPERTY	DESCRIPTION
`CssClass`	This enables you to assign a CSS class instead of inline style information. You should give preference to the `CssClass` property over the individual style properties because they minimize page bloat. You see how to use `CssClass` in a later exercise.
`Font`	This enables you to set the font for the element through the various subproperties like `Font-Names`, `Font-Size`, and `Font-Bold`. These properties end up as various CSS font properties, such as `font-family`, `font-size`, and `font-weight`.
`HorizontalAlign` `VerticalAlign`	These end up as `align` and `valign` attributes on the HTML element to which they are applied and enable you to control the alignment of the contents of the element. For example, you use `HorizontalAlign` to left-, center-, or right-align the text of the column headers of a `GridView`. Note: These properties output HTML attributes that are obsolete in HTML5. Most browsers will still render them as intended, but if HTML5 conformance is important, you shouldn't use these properties, but use your own CSS class assigned with the `CssClass` property.
`Wrap`	This ends up as a `white-space: nowrap;` CSS declaration when set to `False` and determines whether a piece of text is allowed to wrap to a new line.
`Height` `Width`	These enable you to control the height and width of the elements to which they are applied and map directly to their CSS `height` and `width` counterparts.

Check out the MSDN documentation (at `http://bit.ly/Lb3WZd`) for a full description of the `Style` class.

The different data-bound controls each have a different set of styles, although they do share a few. The following table lists the available styles for the `GridView` and describes their purpose. The other data-bound controls have slightly different styles, but from their names you should be able to see what they do and determine what they are used for. Another good way to learn more about the different styles that are available is by using Visual Studio's Auto Format, which inserts a number of styles for you. You see later how to use and improve the styles that are generated by the Auto Format feature.

STYLE	DESCRIPTION
`RowStyle` `AlternatingRowStyle`	These control the look of a single row. By default, the `RowStyle` affects all rows. The `AlternatingRowStyle` is used only on even rows when it's set.
`SelectedRowStyle`	This can be applied to selected rows, and gives you the opportunity to visually present selected rows differently from unselected rows.

STYLE	DESCRIPTION
`EditRowStyle`	This can be applied to rows that are currently in Edit mode. For example, when you click the Edit link for a row in the `GridView` on the Genres page in the Management section, the row switches to Edit mode and this `EditRowStyle` is applied.
`EmptyDataRowStyle`	This enables you to define the look of the row that is displayed when the grid is bound to an empty data source. This style works together with the `EmptyDataText` property of the grid that contains the text displayed when no records exist, or with the `EmptyDataTemplate` that enables you to define your own custom template to be displayed when an empty data source is used.
`HeaderStyle` `FooterStyle`	These control the appearance of the header and footer rows.
`PagerStyle`	This enables you to influence the look of the pager bar displayed in the `GridView` when paging is enabled.

`SortedAscendingCellStyle`
`SortedAscendingHeaderStyle`
`SortedDescendingCellStyle`
`SortedDescendingHeaderStyle`
	Collectively, these styles enable you to change the looks of the header and the entire column when the column is sorted in ascending or descending order.

Some controls, like `Repeater` and `ListView`, have no built-in styles. Because these controls do not contribute any HTML to the page all by themselves and leave it up to you to define the look and feel in the numerous templates these controls have, there is no point in having separate styles; you can simply add the necessary style or class information to the elements you define in their templates.

To show you how to use these styles with your controls, the following exercise guides you through the process of enhancing the `GridView` control in the Genres page of the Management section. In a later exercise, you see how to move the style-related information to a theme and CSS file to improve the reusability of the code and to reduce the amount of HTML sent to the browser on each request.

TRY IT OUT Applying Styles

In this Try It Out, you use the built-in formatting capabilities of VS to change the appearance of the `GridView` control. You see how VS creates the necessary styles for you, each with its relevant styling properties set.

1. Open `Genres.aspx` from the `Management` folder of the main Planet Wrox website that you have been working on so far.
2. Switch to Design View and open the `GridView` control's Smart Tasks panel. Make sure you open that of the `GridView` and not the one for the surrounding `Content` block.

3. At the top of the panel, click the Auto Format link.
4. From the list of format schemes on the left, choose Classic. The Preview on the right is updated and now looks like Figure 15-4.

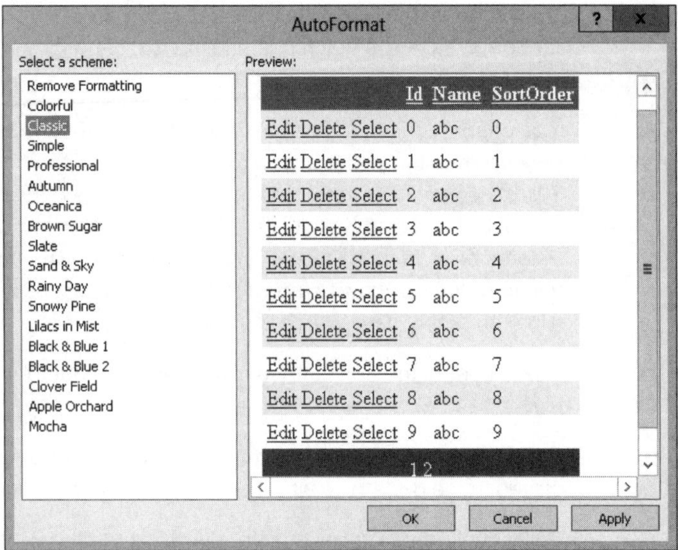

FIGURE 15-4

5. Click OK to have VS generate the necessary templates for you. The `GridView` is updated in Design View immediately, showing the selected format scheme.
6. Switch back to Markup View and inspect the various styles that have been generated. You should see the following styles, some placed before and others placed below the `<Columns>` element:

```
<AlternatingRowStyle BackColor="White" />
...
<EditRowStyle BackColor="#2461BF" />
<FooterStyle BackColor="#507CD1" Font-Bold="True" ForeColor="White" />
... Some styles are not shown here to save some space
<SortedDescendingHeaderStyle BackColor="#4870BE" />
```

7. Save the changes to the page and request it in the browser by pressing Ctrl+F5. You should see the list of genres with the selected formatting scheme applied.
8. Open the HTML source for the page by right-clicking the page in the browser and choosing the View Source or View Page Source command. Scroll down a bit until you see an HTML table with its `id` set to `cpMainContent_GridView1`. You'll see that the table itself has a `style` attribute that sets text color and border properties:

```
<table cellspacing="0" cellpadding="4" id="cpMainContent_GridView1"
      style="color:#333333;border-collapse:collapse;">
```

Additionally, you see that the numerous child elements of the table (table rows and anchor elements) all have different style settings applied. For example, odd and even rows now have the following style applied:

```
<tr style="background-color:#EFF3FB;"> ... </tr>
<tr style="background-color:White;"> ... </tr>
```

Close the source document and click the headers of the `GridView` a few times. The header changes color to indicate the column is now sorted.

How It Works

The different style elements you created in step 5 are converted into their CSS and HTML equivalents. For example, `RowStyle` and `AlternatingRowStyle` have their `BackColor` set to a different background color:

```
<RowStyle BackColor="#EFF3FB" />
<AlternatingRowStyle BackColor="White" />
```

When the control renders its HTML, it applies these backgrounds to the table row of the items and alternating items:

```
<tr style="background-color:#EFF3FB;"> ... </tr>
<tr style="background-color:White;"> ... </tr>
```

The same principle is applied to the other styles in the `GridView`.

If you look at the source of the page in the browser, you see a lot of page bloat, because each individual row has its properties set. This increases the page size, especially with larger results displayed in the `GridView`. To decrease the page size and improve the performance of the page, you could move the style definitions to a page theme and then use CSS and jQuery instead. You see how to do this next.

Combining Styles, Themes, and Skins

Chapter 6 discussed how to create consistent-looking web pages using master pages, themes, and skins. With the basic theme infrastructure set up, it's now easy to add a new theme that applies to the entire Management section. Earlier you saw how to create a skin file to change the appearance of a button; in the following exercise you see how to reuse this concept to create a skin file for the `GridView`, enabling you to style all `GridView` controls in the `Management` folder in one fell swoop.

TRY IT OUT Creating Advanced Style Solutions

In this Try It Out, you move the various `Style` properties from the `Genres.aspx` page into a separate `.skin` file. You also move the inline style information to a separate CSS file. You then use some jQuery to separate data and appearance of the page even further.

1. On the Solution Explorer, right-click the `App_Themes` folder, choose Add ➪ Add ASP.NET Folder ➪ Theme, and type **`Management`** as the new theme name.

2. Right-click this new folder and choose Add ⇨ Add New Item. Add a skin file called **GridView.skin.** You should end up with a Solution Explorer looking like Figure 15-5.

FIGURE 15-5

3. Open the `Genres.aspx` page in Markup View and delete all the style elements you created in the previous exercise except the `HeaderStyle`, the `PagerStyle`, the `SortedAscendingHeaderStyle`, and the `SortedDescendingHeaderStyle`. From the four remaining styles, remove all attributes and replace them with a single `CssClass` attribute named after the style and prefixed with `GridView`. You should end up with the following styles:

```
<HeaderStyle CssClass="GridViewHeaderStyle" />
<PagerStyle CssClass="GridViewPagerStyle" />
<SortedAscendingHeaderStyle CssClass="GridViewSortedAscendingHeaderStyle" />
<SortedDescendingHeaderStyle CssClass="GridViewSortedDescendingHeaderStyle" />
```

Don't worry if VS adds red error lines under the CSS class names. Because the CSS classes aren't defined yet, it can't find them. Later, you add them to the theme's CSS file, where VS still can't find them. They'll work fine at run time, though, so don't worry.

4. Select the styles in the code editor and then cut them to the clipboard using Ctrl+X. Switch to the `GridView.skin` file, delete all existing code (the comment text you saw earlier), and paste the styles into the skin file.

5. Wrap the styles in an `<asp:GridView>` element with its `runat` attribute set to `server` and its `CssClass` attribute set to `GridView`. Don't add an `ID` attribute, because skin files don't need this. You should end up with this code:

```
<asp:GridView runat="server" CssClass="GridView">
  ... styles go here
</asp:GridView>
```

6. Open the resources folder for this chapter (located at `C:\BegASPNET\Resources\Chapter 15` if you followed the instructions in the Introduction section of this book) in File Explorer (Windows Explorer in Windows 7), select the `Images` folder and the `Management.css` file, and press Ctrl+C to copy them. Switch back to VS, click the `Management` folder under `App_Themes`, and press Ctrl+V. Just as the other two themes do, the management theme now has its own style sheet and `Images` folder, shown in Figure 15-6.

The two images are used to change the header for sorted columns in the `GridView`, as you will see later.

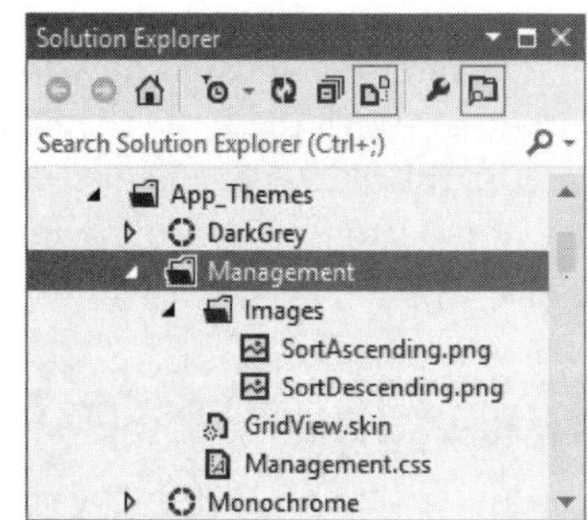

FIGURE 15-6

7. Open the `Web.config` file for the `Management` folder in the root that you added earlier and set the `theme` to `Management`:

```
<system.web>
  <pages theme="Management" />
</system.web>
```

8. Open the `Management.master` file from the `MasterPages` folder, switch to Markup View, and below the `ContentPlaceHolder` in the `<head>` section of the page, drag the `jquery-1.7.2.min.js` file from the `Scripts` folder. VS inserts the following `<script>` element for you:

```
  </asp:ContentPlaceHolder>
  <script src="../Scripts/jquery-1.7.2.min.js"></script>
</head>
```

9. Go back to `Genres.aspx` and in Markup View, under the `Columns` element of the `GridView` control, delete the bound field for the `Id` column. Users typically don't need to see the IDs of items in the user interface because they are often meaningless to them. By removing the `Id` column, you reduce the noise in the page. Set the `ItemStyle-Width` for the `CommandField` to `100px` and for the `Name` column to `200px`. Finally, set `ShowSelectButton` of the `CommandField` to `False`, and set the `HeaderText` of the `SortOrder` field to `Sort Order` with a space between the words. You should end up with this `GridView`:

```
<asp:GridView ID="GridView1" runat="server" AllowPaging="True"
      AllowSorting="True" AutoGenerateColumns="False" DataKeyNames="Id"
      DataSourceID="SqlDataSource1" GridLines="None" CellPadding="4"
      ForeColor="#333333" EmptyDataText="There are no data records to display.">
  <Columns>
    <asp:CommandField ShowDeleteButton="True" ShowEditButton="True"
          ShowSelectButton="False" ItemStyle-Width="100px" />
    <asp:BoundField DataField="Name" HeaderText="Name"
          SortExpression="Name" ItemStyle-Width="200px" />
    <asp:BoundField DataField="SortOrder" HeaderText="Sort Order"
          SortExpression="SortOrder"></asp:BoundField>
  </Columns>
</asp:GridView>
```

10. Scroll down to the end of the page in Markup View and, right before the closing `</asp:Content>` tag, add the following jQuery code wrapped in a `<script>` block:

```
<script type="text/javascript">
  $(function()
  {
    $('.GridView tr:odd:not(.GridViewPagerStyle)').
                         addClass('GridViewAlternatingRowStyle');
  });
</script>
```

11. Save all your changes by pressing Ctrl+Shift+S and then open `Genres.aspx` in the browser. You should now see the list of genres that was presented in Figure 15-2, except for the disabled Delete links, which you add later. Click the header of the Name or Sort Order columns to order the data in the `GridView`. Notice how the `GridView` now shows a little glyph beside the name to indicate the sort direction.

12. Click Manage Reviews in the main Management menu to open the Reviews page. Select a genre from the drop-down list to display a list of reviews. Note that the Reviews list — visible in Figure 15-7 — now also has the same styles applied as the Genres list you saw earlier, except for the alternating row styles applied by jQuery.

Indie Rock

Title	Authorized	CreateDateTime	Delete
Sonic Youth: Daydream Nation live in Roundhouse, London	Yes	11/14/2007 5:19 PM	Delete
Sonic Youth: Daydream Nation live at Lowlands, Biddinghuizen	Yes	11/14/2007 5:27 PM	Delete
Day & Age by The Killers - Excellent album, but is it better than before?	Yes	11/24/2008 10:01 PM	Delete
The Pains of Being Pure at Heart - One of the best new British bands from the U.S.?	Yes	2/3/2009 2:45 PM	Delete
P.J. Harvey & John Parish - A Woman a Man Walked By	No	4/1/2009 1:08 PM	Delete
Battle for the Sun by Placebo - Possibly the best album of 2009 already	Yes	6/9/2009 9:01 PM	Delete
Sonic Youth: The Eternal - Takes time to get used but then....	Yes	6/10/2009 9:33 PM	Delete
Farm by Dinosaur Jr	Yes	6/23/2009 10:36 PM	Delete
Oscar & the Wolf - Summer Skin	Yes	8/9/2012 6:28 AM	Delete

Insert New Review

FIGURE 15-7

How It Works

The concepts from this exercise should be familiar by now. You have seen how to create and apply themes and skins in Chapter 6, and how to use the various control styles in the previous exercise. You also saw the concepts behind jQuery in Chapter 11. What may be new is the way that odd rows in the `GridView` are selected to dynamically change their background color, skipping the footer row using the `not` filter:

```
$('.GridView tr:odd:not(.GridViewPagerStyle)')
```

First, all odd table rows are selected using the selector `.GridView tr:odd`. However, depending on the number of rows in the `GridView`, this may also select the footer row (with the paging controls in it) because the footer is rendered as a `<tr>` as well. To stop the footer from being included you use the `not` filter and pass it an expression on which you want to filter. In this case, the expression is `.GridViewPagerStyle` because that's the class name applied to the footer row. The jQuery code is only applied to the `Genres.aspx` page, but you could move it to the Management master page or copy it to individual pages. Either way, it helps in removing page bloat because you don't have to add a `style` or `class` attribute to each row in the `GridView`. Instead, you can let jQuery figure out what rows are odd and even. If you want, you can create a `ContentPlaceHolder` in the master page for the Management section as you've done with the `Frontend.master` file, in which to put page-specific JavaScript code.

Assigning the image to the sorted column header requires changes to a few selectors. First, each sorted header (ascending or descending) is given some padding:

```
.GridViewSortedAscendingHeaderStyle, .GridViewSortedDescendingHeaderStyle
{
  padding-left: 20px;
}
```

This moves the text in the header cell a bit to the right, making room for the image. Then for both the ascending and descending sort order, there is a separate selector that assigns the image. The selector is applied by ASP.NET by adding a `class` attribute to the relevant HTML elements. The following shows the selector for a column that is sorted in ascending order:

```
.GridViewSortedAscendingHeaderStyle
{
```

```
    background-image: url(Images/SortAscending.png);
  }
```

The `.GridViewHeaderStyle th` selector then stops the background image from repeating, positions the image near the top, and determines the background color and text alignment:

```
  .GridViewHeaderStyle th, .GridViewPagerStyle
  {
    background-color: #BCD1FE;
    background-repeat: no-repeat;
    background-position: 0 5px;
    text-align: left;
  }
```

By moving your control style declarations to a separate skin file that in turn is part of a theme, you have created a very flexible, maintainable solution. If you want to see how the new styles are applied, open the source of the page in the browser using its View Source command. Instead of inline styles, the relevant `class` attributes are applied. If you want to change the layout of all the `GridView` controls in the Management section, all you need to do now is modify the relevant CSS in the `Management.css` file. If you need to make changes to other styles, don't forget to add them to the `GridView.skin` file first.

Obviously, you can still tweak the controls at the page level. Though the skin defines the global look and feel of the `GridView`, you can still set individual properties on columns as you did with the `ItemStyle-Width` in the Genres page.

Although styles, skins, and themes are powerful tools to style your web pages, you'll find that they are often an all-or-nothing solution. For example, if you create `ItemStyle` and `AlternatingItemStyle` elements (rather than using jQuery as you just did), they are applied to each and every row in the grid. What if you wanted to change the look and feel of just a few rows? Or what if you wanted to change some rows based on the actual data that the row is holding? You see how to accomplish conditional formatting and more, using event handling, in the following section.

HANDLING EVENTS

Previous chapters have covered how the ASP.NET controls can raise events. You learned how to handle these events with event-handler code that you typically add to the page's Code Behind file. For example, you wrote code to handle a `Button` control's `Click` event. Additionally, in the preceding chapter, you learned how to react to various events — such as `Inserting` and `Inserted` — that happen just prior to and after interaction with the database. However, most controls expose a lot more events.

A solid understanding of the various events that fire during a control's life cycle and the order in which they fire is important knowledge for an ASP.NET developer. Being able to hook into the control's life cycle, tweaking parts of the output as you go, enables you to create flexible, dynamic web pages that do exactly what you want.

To gain an understanding of the various events and the order in which they fire, the next section explains the basic steps in the ASP.NET control life cycle. You won't see every event that is fired in the process, but instead you see the ones you are most likely to use. Later sections then show you how to make use of these events to change the behavior of your web pages.

The ASP.NET Page and Control Life Cycles Revisited

In Chapter 6 you learned about the stages in a page's life. You learned about different events such as `PreInit`, `Load`, `PreRender`, and `Unload`. Besides these events that are raised by the ASPX page, all the other controls in your ASPX pages can raise their own events. These events can be as simple as a `Button` control's `Click` event (triggered by a user action) or be more complex events, such as `Inserting`, which is raised by controls like the `EntityDataSource` and the `SqlDataSource`, or the `DataBound` event that is raised by various data-bound controls. You see many of these events in the next exercise.

TRY IT OUT Seeing the Page and Control Life Cycles at Work

To give you an idea of the different events that you can hook into during a page or control's life cycle and the order in which they fire, this Try It Out shows you how to set up a page that displays some data from the `Genres` table using an `EntityDataSource`. You also add a button to the page that you can use to trigger a postback to see how that influences things. You then hook up a number of event handlers to a few interesting events of the controls on the page so you can see in what order things are called. You can apply the concepts you learn in this exercise to any other page or control that raises events to get a better understanding of how they operate.

1. Inside the `Demos` folder, create a new file called `Events.aspx`. Make sure it's based on your custom page template so it inherits from `BasePage`. Set the page's `Title` to **`Events Demo`**.
2. Switch the page to Design View, drop a `GridView` into the `cpMainContent` placeholder, and then hook it up to a new `EntityDataSource` control using the `GridView`'s Smart Tasks panel. Use PlanetWroxEntities as the Named Connection and bind the `EntityDataSource` control to the `Genres` entity set. There's no need to set up insert, update, or delete behavior, nor do you need to select specific columns or add a `Where` clause.
3. Back on the `GridView` control's Smart Tasks panel, click Refresh Schema if the `GridView` doesn't show the columns for the `Id`, `Name`, and `SortOrder`. Then enable sorting by selecting the second check box. When you're done, your code should look like this:

```
<asp:GridView ID="GridView1" runat="server" AutoGenerateColumns="False"
        DataKeyNames="Id" DataSourceID="EntityDataSource1" AllowSorting="True">
  <Columns>
    <asp:BoundField DataField="Id" HeaderText="Id"
              ReadOnly="True" SortExpression="Id" />
    <asp:BoundField DataField="Name" HeaderText="Name"
              SortExpression="Name" />
    <asp:BoundField DataField="SortOrder" HeaderText="SortOrder"
              SortExpression="SortOrder" />
  </Columns>
</asp:GridView>
<asp:EntityDataSource ID="EntityDataSource1" runat="server" EntitySetName="Genres"
    ConnectionString="name=PlanetWroxEntities" EnableFlattening="False"
    DefaultContainerName="PlanetWroxEntities">
</asp:EntityDataSource>
```

4. Make sure you're in Markup View, and directly under the opening `Content` tag and before the `GridView` add the following markup that creates a table with one row and two cells, each with a large heading (`h1`) and a `Label` control called `NoPostBack` and `PostBack`, respectively.

```
<table>
  <tr>
    <td><h1>No PostBack</h1><asp:Label ID="NoPostBack" runat="server" /></td>
    <td><h1>PostBack</h1><asp:Label ID="PostBack" runat="server" /></td>
  </tr>
</table>
```

5. Switch to Design View, and below the `GridView` drop a `Button` control and double-click it in Design View to set up an event handler for its `Click` event in the Code Behind.

6. Switch back to Design View and double-click the gray and read-only area of the page to set up a handler for the `Page` control's `Load` event.

7. Switch to Design View again, click the `GridView`, and open its Properties Grid by pressing F4. Switch to the Events tab and double-click the following events to set up handlers for them in the Code Behind. After each handler, switch back to Design View by pressing Ctrl+Tab so you can add the next event.

    - `Sorted`
    - `Sorting`
    - `RowCreated`
    - `DataBinding`
    - `DataBound`
    - `RowDataBound`

8. Repeat the preceding step, but now set up the following events for the `EntityDataSource` control:

    - `ContextCreating`
    - `Selecting`

9. Make sure you are in Code Behind and at the top of the file add the following `Imports/using` statement:

    VB.NET

    ```
    Imports System.Runtime.CompilerServices
    ```

    C#

    ```
    using System.Runtime.CompilerServices;
    ```

    Then below the last event handler (but still within the class definition), add the following method that writes some text to one of the two labels, depending on whether the current page request is the result of a postback:

VB.NET

```
Private Sub WriteMessage(<CallerMemberName> Optional handlerName As String = "")
  If Page.IsPostBack Then
    PostBack.Text &= handlerName & "<br />"
  Else
    NoPostBack.Text &= handlerName & "<br />"
  End If
End Sub
```

C#

```
private void WriteMessage([CallerMemberName] string handlerName = "")
{
  if (Page.IsPostBack)
  {
    PostBack.Text += handlerName + "<br />";
  }
  else
  {
    NoPostBack.Text += handlerName + "<br />";
  }
}
```

10. To each of the event handlers that you have set up, add the following code that calls your custom method. Because you're not passing a value for the optional `handlerName` parameter, .NET automatically inserts the name of the calling method because of the `CallerMemberName` attribute applied to that parameter in the `WriteMessage` method. You see how this works later.

VB.NET

```
Protected Sub Page_Load(sender As Object, e As EventArgs) Handles Me.Load
  WriteMessage()
End Sub
```

C#

```
protected void Page_Load(object sender, EventArgs e)
{
  WriteMessage();
}
```

11. Finally, add the following event handler to the Code Behind manually:

VB.NET

```
Protected Sub Page_PreRenderComplete(sender As Object,
          e As EventArgs) Handles Me.PreRenderComplete
  WriteMessage("Page_PreRenderComplete<br />---------")
End Sub
```

C#

```
protected void Page_PreRenderComplete(object sender, EventArgs e)
{
  WriteMessage("Page_PreRenderComplete<br />---------");
}
```

The `PreRenderComplete` event fires very late in the `Page` control's life cycle, making it an ideal place to put a line at the bottom of the event list. That way you can clearly see what set of events belong to each other, which in turn helps you to figure out what events are triggered during page load or a postback.

12. Save all your changes and open the page in the browser. In addition to the `GridView` with the available genres, you should also see a list with event names under the No PostBack heading:

```
Page_Load
EntityDataSource1_ContextCreating
EntityDataSource1_Selecting
GridView1_DataBinding
GridView1_RowCreated
GridView1_RowDataBound
GridView1_RowCreated
GridView1_RowDataBound
...
GridView1_DataBound
Page_PreRenderComplete
---------
```

Note that the `RowCreated` and `RowDataBound` events are repeated multiple times — once for each genre from the database plus two more. You see later why that is. Click the button below the `GridView` to cause a postback. The No PostBack label won't change, but the PostBack label now shows the following list of event names:

```
GridView1_RowCreated
GridView1_RowCreated
...
GridView1_RowCreated
GridView1_RowCreated
Page_Load
Button1_Click
Page_PreRenderComplete
---------
```

Click one of the column headers of the `GridView` to order the data it is displaying. Notice that the second label's text is extended with a second set of event names. Each set is separated by a line of dashes, created by the `Page_PreRenderComplete` event handler.

How It Works

Technically, this exercise isn't complicated. You set up a bunch of event handlers for the various controls in your page. Inside the event handler you call a method that checks whether the page is currently loading for the first time or is loading due to a postback. To make it easy to add the name of the calling method to the `Label` control, the `handlerName` parameter of the method has a special `CallerMemberName` attribute applied, like this:

VB.NET

```
Private Sub WriteMessage(<CallerMemberName> Optional handlerName As String = "")
```

C#

```
private void WriteMessage([CallerMemberName] string handlerName = "")
```

This attribute is new in .NET 4.5 and can be applied to *optional parameters* (identified in VB.NET with the `Optional` keyword and a default value, and in C# simply by assigning it a default value). When no value is passed to the `WriteMessage` method for this parameter (as is the case for most of the handlers except for the last one you added), .NET fills it for you with the name of the calling method. This is very convenient for debugging purposes because it enables you to easily figure out which method called `WriteMessage`. In previous versions of .NET you had to pass the name of the calling method manually in each call to `WriteMessage`, making this code a bit more tedious to write. Also, because this attribute only has an effect when no value is passed in, you can still supply a value yourself, as is the case with the `Page_PreRenderComplete` handler. Besides the method name, this code also passes the line break and the dashed line and, as such, you have to supply the value yourself.

The `WriteMessage` method then updates one of the two `Label` controls with the name of the event that triggered the event handler.

What's also interesting about this exercise is the order in which the events occur. Take a look at the first list, displayed when the page first loads:

```
Page_Load
EntityDataSource1_ContextCreating
EntityDataSource1_Selecting
GridView1_DataBinding
GridView1_RowCreated
GridView1_RowDataBound
GridView1_RowCreated
GridView1_RowDataBound
...
GridView1_DataBound
Page_PreRenderComplete
---------
```

First `Page_Load` is triggered. Then the `GridView` sees that it's hooked up to an `EntityDataSource` and asks that control for its data. This causes the `ContextCreating` and `Selecting` events to be triggered. When the `GridView` receives the data from the `EntityDataSource`, it fires its `DataBinding` event to signal it's about to bind the data to the control. The `GridView` then starts to create rows. For each item in the data source, it creates a row, fires `RowCreated`, binds the item's data to the row, and finally calls `RowDataBound`. If you carefully count the number of times that `RowCreated` and `RowDataBound` are called, you'll notice that the total number of calls is the actual number of items that are in the data source plus two. This is because the same event is also raised when the control creates its header and footer rows. You see how to distinguish between these rows inside an event handler in a later exercise.

Finally, when the `GridView` is done creating and binding all the rows in the data source, it fires its `DataBound` event.

On postback, the story looks quite different. When you click the button to cause a postback, the following events are raised:

```
...
GridView1_RowCreated
GridView1_RowCreated
GridView1_RowCreated
GridView1_RowCreated
Page_Load
```

```
Button1_Click
Page_PreRenderComplete
----------
```

Note that this list contains no `RowDataBound` or `DataBound` events, and the `EntityDataSource` is also nowhere to be seen. The `GridView` is able to reconstruct the entire control from View State, eliminating the need to access the database again. While getting the data from View State, the `GridView` still needs to re-create each row in the grid, so you still see the `RowCreated` events. Toward the end of the list you see the `Page_Load` event followed by the `Button` control's `Click` event. It's important to understand and remember that user-triggered control events like a `Button` control's `Click` or a `SelectedIndexChanged` of a `DropDownList` occur *after* the `Load` event of the `Page`. Note that this `Load` event isn't the start of the `Page`'s life cycle. Before the `Load` event, the `Page` is already instantiated and has fired its `Init` event. You could add a handler for this event to the code to confirm this.

At the end of the exercise, you clicked a column header to sort the data in the grid. This time, the `GridView` knows it must sort the data that is being displayed. It cannot do that itself, so instead it asks the `EntityDataSource` for a fresh copy of the data in the order the user requested. Just as you did the first time the page loaded, you see the various `RowCreated` and `DataBound` events appear. What's interesting to see is that the `Sorting` and `Sorted` events fire after each other, and before the `EntityDataSource` gets its data. The reason for this is that the `GridView` doesn't handle the sorting here; it merely exposes the sorting parameters (the sort expression and the direction) to other controls. With an `EntityDataSource`, sorting takes place at the database level, but it retrieves the sorting parameters from the `GridView`.

If you want to see other events at work, simply repeat steps 7 and 10 of the preceding exercise, setting up handlers for the various events. To see the effect of View State, try disabling it either at the control level (for example, for the `GridView`) or at the page level. In Chapter 18 you learn a technique called tracing that enables you to find out this information for all controls in your page, including the time it takes to execute the various events.

Although the preceding exercise is quite useless in a real-world application, it should help you gain an understanding of the various control events and the order in which they fire. You can use the exact same principles to hook into the page and make modifications to the page itself, or to any of the controls in the page. In the next exercise you see how to change the appearance of rows in the data source, depending on the data that you are displaying.

The ASP.NET Page Life Cycle and Events in Data Controls

As previously discussed, the `GridView` raises its `RowCreated` and `RowDataBound` events for each row it adds to its output. These events are ideal to peek into the data and then, based on that data, take appropriate action. For example, you can use these events to verify whether a review that is being displayed is authorized. If it's not (meaning it won't be visible in the front-end website), you can change the review's appearance to draw attention to it. Another example of using events would be to hide or disable elements in the interface when it doesn't make sense for them to be visible or active. You see how to disable the Delete link in the Genres `GridView` in the next exercise.

TRY IT OUT Hooking into RowDataBound

In this Try It Out you write an event handler for the `RowDataBound` event of the `GridView` control in the Genres page of the Management section. Within this event, you can diagnose the data item that is being bound to the `GridView` row, enabling you to see if the genre has reviews attached to it or not. If reviews are associated with the genre, you use some code to disable the Delete link so users cannot accidentally try to delete that genre.

1. Open the `Genres.aspx` page from the `Management` folder in Markup View and locate the `SqlDataSource` control. Find the `SelectCommand` and modify the SQL statement so it reads like this:

```
SelectCommand="SELECT Genre.Id, Genre.Name, Genre.SortOrder,
    COUNT(Review.Id) AS NumberOfReviews FROM Genre LEFT OUTER JOIN Review
    ON Genre.Id = Review.GenreId GROUP BY Genre.Id, Genre.Name, Genre.SortOrder"
```

   You can type the entire SQL statement on a single line or break it up over multiple lines as I've done here.

2. Switch to Design View and open the `GridView` control's Smart Tasks panel. Click the Refresh Schema link on the Smart Tasks panel and answer No to the questions about regenerating fields and keys to maintain the current layout of the controls.

   Click Edit Columns on the Smart Tasks panel to bring up the Fields dialog box. Click the `CommandField` item in the Selected Fields list and then click the blue link at the bottom right of the dialog box to convert the field to a `TemplateField`. This way the column is expanded into a template, which makes it easier to access the controls, such as the Delete link, it contains. Click OK to close the Fields dialog box.

3. In Markup View, locate the Delete link (the one with its `CommandName` set to `Delete`) and change its ID to `DeleteLink`:

```
<asp:LinkButton ID="DeleteLink" runat="server" CausesValidation="False"
      CommandName="Delete" Text="Delete"></asp:LinkButton>
```

4. Switch to Design View, open the Properties Grid for the `GridView`, and switch to the Events tab. Set up an event handler for the `RowDataBound` event.

5. At the top of the Code Behind of the Web Form, add the following line of code:

   VB.NET

```
Imports System.Data
```

   C#

```
using System.Data;
```

6. Inside the event handler that VS created for you, add the following code:

   VB.NET

```
Protected Sub GridView1_RowDataBound(sender As Object,
          e As GridViewRowEventArgs) Handles GridView1.RowDataBound
```

```
    Select Case e.Row.RowType
      Case DataControlRowType.DataRow
        Dim myRowView As DataRowView = CType(e.Row.DataItem, DataRowView)
        If Convert.ToInt32(myRowView("NumberOfReviews")) > 0 Then
          Dim deleteLink As LinkButton =
                  TryCast(e.Row.FindControl("DeleteLink"), LinkButton)
          If deleteLink IsNot Nothing Then
            deleteLink.Enabled = False
          End If
        End If
    End Select
  End Sub
```

C#

```
protected void GridView1_RowDataBound(object sender, GridViewRowEventArgs e)
{
  switch (e.Row.RowType)
  {
    case DataControlRowType.DataRow:
      DataRowView myDataRowView = (DataRowView)e.Row.DataItem;
      if (Convert.ToInt32(myDataRowView["NumberOfReviews"]) > 0)
      {
        LinkButton deleteLink = e.Row.FindControl("DeleteLink") as LinkButton;
        if (deleteLink != null)
        {
          deleteLink.Enabled = false;
        }
      }
      break;
  }
}
```

7. Save changes to all open files and then request `Genres.aspx` in the browser. Notice how for genres that have reviews attached to them, the Delete link is now disabled, as shown in Figure 15-8.

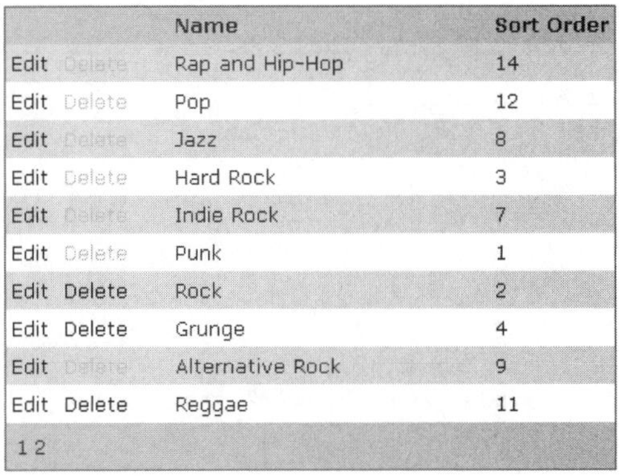

		Name	Sort Order
Edit	Delete	Rap and Hip-Hop	14
Edit	Delete	Pop	12
Edit	Delete	Jazz	8
Edit	Delete	Hard Rock	3
Edit	Delete	Indie Rock	7
Edit	Delete	Punk	1
Edit	Delete	Rock	2
Edit	Delete	Grunge	4
Edit	Delete	Alternative Rock	9
Edit	Delete	Reggae	11
1 2			

FIGURE 15-8

How It Works

Although short, this exercise demonstrates a powerful way to hook into the different events of a control and change the presentation of the underlying control. To see how it works, take a look at the modified SQL code first:

```
SELECT
  Genre.Id, Genre.Name, Genre.SortOrder, COUNT(Review.Id) AS NumberOfReviews
FROM
  Genre LEFT OUTER JOIN
  Review ON Genre.Id = Review.GenreId
GROUP BY
  Genre.Id, Genre.Name, Genre.SortOrder
```

This modified SQL statement gets all the columns from the `Genre` table but introduces a new column, called `NumberOfReviews`, which contains the number of reviews associated with each genre. It does this by executing the SQL `COUNT` function against the `Id` column of the `Review` table. The statement uses `GROUP BY` to group the selected rows into a set of summary rows by collapsing non-unique rows. Because the SQL statement is grouped on all unique columns in the `Genre` table, you get a unique row including the number of reviews for each genre row, whether or not reviews are associated, as shown in Figure 15-9, which displays the result of this query in SSMS.

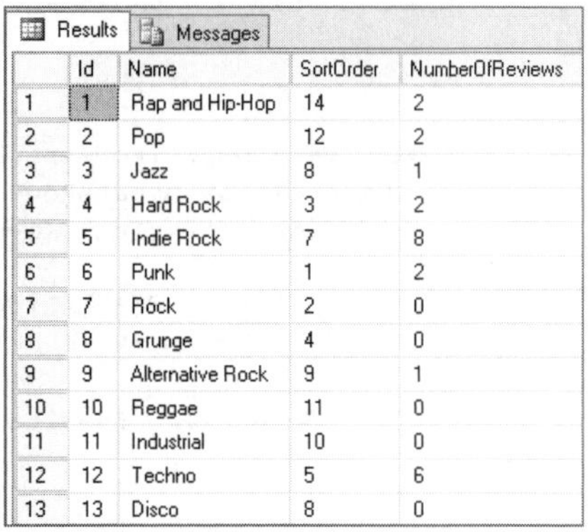

Results | Messages

	Id	Name	SortOrder	NumberOfReviews
1	1	Rap and Hip-Hop	14	2
2	2	Pop	12	2
3	3	Jazz	8	1
4	4	Hard Rock	3	2
5	5	Indie Rock	7	8
6	6	Punk	1	2
7	7	Rock	2	0
8	8	Grunge	4	0
9	9	Alternative Rock	9	1
10	10	Reggae	11	0
11	11	Industrial	10	0
12	12	Techno	5	6
13	13	Disco	8	0

FIGURE 15-9

When this query is executed, the `GridView` in the markup of the page makes use of the first three columns, just as it did in the previous version of this page. But you can access the fourth column as well. You do this in the Code Behind, in the `RowDataBound` event to be exact, which fires for each row after the `GridView` is done binding the data for a specific row:

VB.NET

```
Protected Sub GridView1_RowDataBound(sender As Object,
          e As GridViewRowEventArgs) Handles GridView1.RowDataBound
  Select Case e.Row.RowType
    Case DataControlRowType.DataRow
      ...
  End Select
End Sub
```

C#

```
protected void GridView1_RowDataBound (object sender, GridViewRowEventArgs e)
{
  switch (e.Row.RowType)
  {
    case DataControlRowType.DataRow:
      ...
  }
}
```

The `RowDataBound` event gets passed an instance of `GridViewRowEventArgs`, a class that provides information about the row and data that are being bound at this stage. One of the properties of this class is the `Row` that represents the actual row that is being added to the `GridView`. This row in turn contains a `RowType` enumeration property that you can test to see what kind of row is being added. This enumeration contains six different members that map directly to the different types of rows the `GridView` can contain: `DataRow` for normal and alternating rows, `EmptyDataRow` for empty data rows, `Header` and `Footer` for the header and footer rows that are placed at the top and bottom, `Pager` for the pager bar, and `Separator` for rows separating the data items in the grid. Because you need to change the appearance of an actual data row, the code in the `Case` block only fires for normal and alternating rows.

Inside the `Case` block, the following code is executed:

VB.NET

```
Dim myRowView As DataRowView = CType(e.Row.DataItem, DataRowView)
If Convert.ToInt32(myRowView("NumberOfReviews")) > 0 Then
  Dim deleteLink As LinkButton =
            TryCast(e.Row.FindControl("DeleteLink"), LinkButton)
  If deleteLink IsNot Nothing Then
    deleteLink.Enabled = False
  End If
End If
```

C#

```
DataRowView myDataRowView = (DataRowView)e.Row.DataItem;
if (Convert.ToInt32(myDataRowView["NumberOfReviews"]) > 0)
{
  LinkButton deleteLink = e.Row.FindControl("DeleteLink") as LinkButton;
  if (deleteLink != null)
  {
    deleteLink.Enabled = false;
  }
}
```

The `DataItem` property contains a reference to the data item object that is being bound. When you are using a `SqlDataSource` control, the `DataItem` is presented as a `DataRowView`, a .NET object that encapsulates a row returned from the database. The `DataItem` is therefore cast to a `DataRowView` object and then it's indexed — using `myRowView("NumberOfReviews")` in VB.NET and `myRowView["NumberOfReviews"]` in C# — to get the count of reviews from the `NumberOfReviews` column. If the count is larger than zero, it means reviews are associated with this genre and the Delete link must be disabled. Earlier you converted the `CommandField` to a template field, which added an explicit declaration for the Delete link in your code:

```
<asp:LinkButton ID="DeleteLink" runat="server" CausesValidation="False"
        CommandName="Delete" Text="Delete"></asp:LinkButton>
```

Using `FindControl` on the row that is being data bound, you can then get a reference to the Delete link, convert it to a proper `LinkButton`, and set its `Enabled` property to `False`. Because this code is also called when a row in the `GridView` is in Edit mode (by clicking the Edit link), you need to check if `deleteLink` is `null` (`Nothing` in VB.NET) or not. In case you're editing, the `GridView` row does not contain the `DeleteLink` (because the `EditItemTemplate` is active, and not the `ItemTemplate`) and therefore `FindControl` returns `null`.

When you disable a `LinkButton` by setting `Enabled` to `False` as in this example, ASP.NET applies a CSS class of `aspNetDisabled`:

```
<a id="cpMainContent_GridView1_DeleteLink_0" class="aspNetDisabled">Delete</a>
```

You can then style this disabled link with the CSS class (which you find in `Management.css` that you added earlier) and give it a gray color:

```
a.aspNetDisabled
{
  color : #CCC;
}
```

With this code, you can easily prevent errors that may occur when you try to delete a genre that has associated reviews. However, you may not always be able to prevent an error from occurring during a CRUD operation against a data source control. For example, you may try to delete a genre that initially didn't have any reviews attached. But imagine that right before you try to delete the genre, somebody else inserts a new review for it. When you then try to delete the genre you'll get an error because the genre is now linked to a review. In such cases, the data source controls enable you to diagnose the error that occurred and then take the necessary measures, like providing feedback to the users informing them that their CRUD operation didn't succeed.

Handling Errors That Occur in the Data Source Controls

In Chapter 18 you see a lot more about recognizing and handling errors that occur in your ASP .NET pages. That chapter demonstrates how to catch errors that may occur in your code, and then handle them by logging them or by informing the user. But because the data source controls expose error information as well, it's interesting to look at data access errors in this chapter.

Both the `EntityDataSource` and the `SqlDataSource` controls give you information about errors (*exceptions* in .NET parlance) that may occur during one of the four CRUD operations. With the `EntityDataSource`, the three events that occur after the database has been updated (`Inserted`, `Updated`, and `Deleted`) all provide access to an instance of a class called `EntityDataSourceChangedEventArgs`, whereas the `Selected` event gets passed an `EntityDataSourceSelectedEventArgs`. With the `SqlDataSource` control, all four events accept an instance of `SqlDataSourceStatusEventArgs`. Figure 15-10 shows these three `EventArgs` classes and their properties.

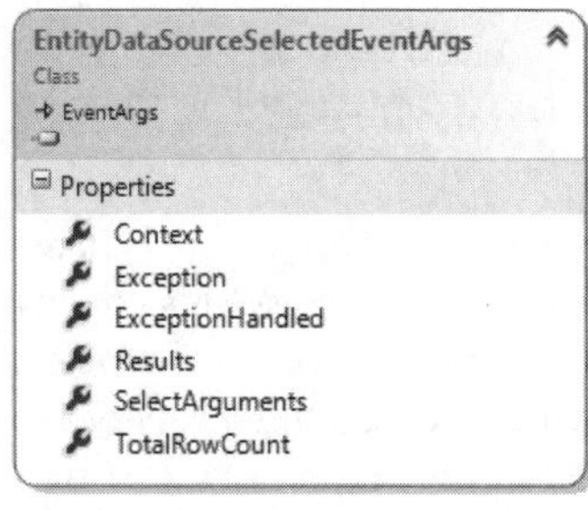

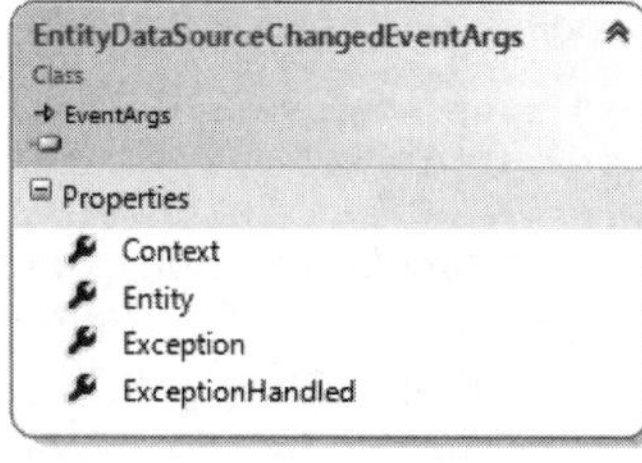

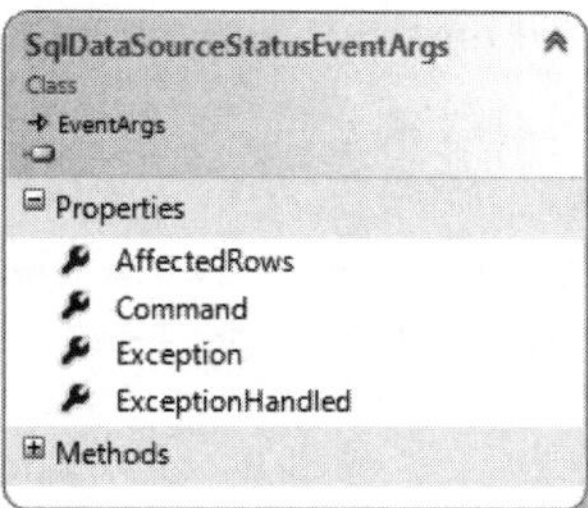

FIGURE 15-10

These classes share two important properties: `Exception` and `ExceptionHandled`. The first contains the actual exception that occurred or `Nothing` (in VB.NET) or `null` (in C#) when everything goes according to plan and no error occurs. You can examine this error and take appropriate action. For example, you can inform the user that something went terribly wrong, or you can send an e-mail to the site's webmaster informing her about the error so appropriate follow-up action can be taken.

If you decide to handle the error in the event handler of the data source control, you should set the `ExceptionHandled` property of the object to `True`. This signals to the ASP.NET run time that you are aware of the exception and have dealt with it adequately. If you omit setting this property, the run time forwards the exception, which is eventually displayed to the user.

In the following exercise, you see how to make use of the `SqlDataSourceStatusEventArgs` class in the `Genres.aspx` page. Rest assured, you can apply the exact same principles from this section to events that are raised by the `EntityDataSource` control as well.

TRY IT OUT Handling Errors when Deleting Rows

In this Try It Out you see how to deal with exceptions that occur in a `GridView` when deleting rows. You'll temporarily comment out the code that disables the Delete link so you can try to delete genres with associated reviews. The code then displays an error message when a user tries to delete a genre that still has reviews attached to it. This exercise mainly serves to demonstrate how to handle exceptions that may be thrown by the data source controls. From an end user's perspective, disabling the Delete link when it's not appropriate, as you did in an earlier exercise, should take care of the problem in most circumstances, but someone else could still insert a new review before you try to delete a genre. The best way to handle this is to combine both solutions: You disable links that are not available, and handle an error gracefully in case someone else has created a review for a genre you just tried to delete.

1. Open `Genres.aspx` from the `Management` folder.
2. Switch to Design View and from the Toolbox drag a `Label` control onto the `GridView`. This places the `Label` that will hold an error message above the `GridView`. Change the ID of the `Label` to `ErrorMessage` and clear its `Text` property. (Right-click the `Text` property label in the Properties Grid and choose Reset. This removes the entire `Text` property and its value from the control's markup.) Set its `CssClass` to `ErrorMessage`. Finally, set its `EnableViewState` property to `false` to ensure the label doesn't maintain its text after postbacks. You should end up with this code:

```
<asp:Label ID="ErrorMessage" runat="server" CssClass="ErrorMessage"
                EnableViewState="false"></asp:Label>
<asp:GridView ID="GridView1" runat="server" AllowPaging="True"
```

3. Open the `Management.css` file from the `Management` theme folder and add the following rule set:

```
.ErrorMessage
{
  color: Red;
  font-weight: bold;
}
```

4. Switch back to `Genres.aspx`, make sure the page is in Design View, and click the `SqlDataSource` control once to select it. Then open its Properties Grid, switch to the Events tab, and set up an event handler for the `Deleted` event by double-clicking the event name in the list of events.

5. At the top of the Code Behind, add the following namespace to bring the `SqlException` class into scope:

   VB.NET

   ```
   Imports System.Data.SqlClient
   ```

   C#

   ```
   using System.Data.SqlClient;
   ```

6. Inside the event handler that VS added for you in step 4, write the following code:

   VB.NET

   ```
   Protected Sub SqlDataSource1_Deleted(sender As Object,
             e As SqlDataSourceStatusEventArgs) Handles SqlDataSource1.Deleted
     If e.Exception IsNot Nothing AndAlso TypeOf (e.Exception) Is SqlException Then
       Dim myException As SqlException = CType(e.Exception, SqlException)
       If myException.Number = 547 Then
         ErrorMessage.Text = "Sorry, you can't delete this genre because " &
                 "it has associated reviews that you need to delete first."
         e.ExceptionHandled = True
       End If
     End If
   End Sub
   ```

   C#

   ```
   protected void SqlDataSource1_Deleted(object sender,
                             SqlDataSourceStatusEventArgs e)
   {
     if (e.Exception != null && e.Exception is SqlException)
     {
       SqlException myException = (SqlException)e.Exception;
       if (myException.Number == 547)
       {
         ErrorMessage.Text = @"Sorry, you can't delete this genre because
                   it has associated reviews that you need to delete first.";
         e.ExceptionHandled = true;
       }
     }
   }
   ```

7. Comment out the code that you added in the previous Try It Out to stop the Delete link from being disabled. For this exercise it's enough to just comment out the line that disables the link:

   VB.NET

   ```
   ' deleteLink.Enabled = False
   ```

   C#

   ```
   // deleteLink.Enabled = false;
   ```

   If you wanted to remove this functionality completely, you could remove the entire event handler. In that case, don't forget to remove the handler from the `GridView`'s markup in C# as well.

8. Save all your changes and then press Ctrl+F5 to open `Genres.aspx` in your browser. Try deleting a genre that you know has associated reviews, such as Rap and Hip-Hop. Instead of deleting the genre, the ASPX page now presents you with the error that is displayed above the `GridView` in Figure 15-11.

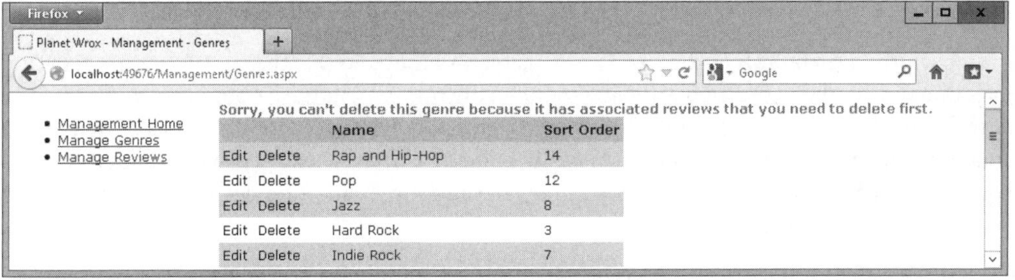

FIGURE 15-11

If the error message doesn't appear in red, press Ctrl+F5 to force a fresh copy of the Management theme's style sheet.

9. Click the Manage Reviews menu item in the Management menu and then select the Rap and Hip-Hop genre from the drop-down list. Delete the reviews in the genre, or edit them and reassign them to a different genre.

10. Go back to `Genres.aspx` and try deleting the Rap and Hip-Hop genre again. This time the genre is successfully deleted from the database.

11. To see the error you would get without this error handling, comment out the line in the Code Behind that sets `ExceptionHandled` to `True`. Save your changes, open the page again in your browser, and try to delete a genre with reviews. You'll get a detailed ASP.NET error instead, shown in Figure 15-12.

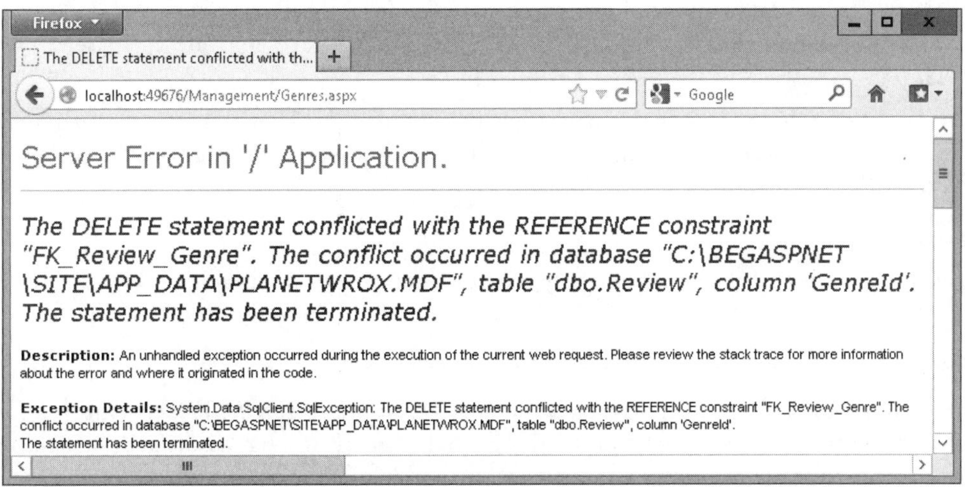

FIGURE 15-12

Notice how this error is almost identical to the one you got near the end of Chapter 12 when you tried to delete a genre manually. Don't forget to enable both lines you commented out in this exercise when you're done, so links are disabled when appropriate and you still get a friendly error message when the genre can't be deleted.

How It Works

When you click the Delete link in the `GridView` visible in Figure 15-11, the `GridView` triggers the `Delete` command on the associated `SqlDataSource` control. As you have seen in previous chapters, this control tries to send a `DELETE` statement to the database. The database then tries to delete the requested genre from the database, but finds out that it can't because the genre has related reviews. This results in a *foreign key constraint error*, which means the genre cannot be deleted because its ID is used as a foreign key in another table.

This foreign key constraint error is then returned from the database and eventually ends up in the `Exception` property of the `e` argument of the `SqlDataSource1_Deleted` handler. The code then checks if there was an error (`e.Exception` is not `Nothing`/`null`) and checks the type of the exception to find out whether it's a `SqlException`:

VB.NET

```
If e.Exception IsNot Nothing AndAlso _
              TypeOf (e.Exception) Is SqlException Then
  ...
End If
```

C#

```
if (e.Exception != null && e.Exception is SqlException)
{
  ...
}
```

When you are working with a SQL Server database, as is the case in the Planet Wrox example, the errors thrown by the database are of type `SqlException` from the `System.Data.SqlClient` namespace that you imported in this exercise. This enables you to clearly separate database errors from other errors.

When SQL Server throws an error, it also passes an error number, which is stored in the `Number` property of the exception. To access that number, you need to cast the exception to a true `SqlException`, which you do with this code:

VB.NET

```
Dim myException As SqlException = CType(e.Exception, SqlException)
```

C#

```
SqlException myException = (SqlException)e.Exception;
```

Finally, the code checks the `Number` property. When it is `547`, it means that SQL Server threw a foreign key constraint error to indicate you cannot delete a genre because it still has associated reviews. When this is the case, the `Label` control's `Text` property is set, and finally the code sets `e.ExceptionHandled` to `True`. This tells the ASP.NET run time that the error has been dealt with, so the user won't get a nasty error page, but a nice and friendly error message at the top of the `GridView` instead. Note that for all other types of exceptions, the user still gets the default ASP.NET error message screen, also called the *Yellow Screen of Death*. Chapter 18 teaches you some techniques to log the error in a central location and present the user with a friendly, human-readable error page instead.

The number `547` seems to be arbitrarily chosen, but it's the number that SQL Server returns for a foreign key constraint exception. In Chapter 18, which deals with debugging, you learn a few tricks that enable you to look into the exceptions that are thrown so you can diagnose the `Number` property for different kinds of exceptions.

In the past few chapters you have seen many examples of accessing a database using one of the built-in data controls like `SqlDataSource` and `EntityDataSource`. Useful and quick to use as they are, they are not suitable for every situation. In cases where they don't fit, you can always hand-code your pages, as you see how to do next.

HAND-CODING DATA ACCESS CODE

The biggest issue I often have with the data controls is the amount of markup that they require. Although, for example, the `ListView` generates most of the code for you, you still end up with a lot of code in the page. This makes it cumbersome and time-consuming to make a lot of modifications to this control. Another issue with these controls is that often you find yourself defining almost identical markup twice: once for an Insert template and once for an Edit template. The final issue I often encounter when working with the data controls is that I do not have complete control over the markup they create. This can make it difficult sometimes to create fancy and complex pages with multiple levels of bound drop-down controls, AJAX `UpdatePanel` controls, image uploads, and more. To overcome these issues, you can hand-code your pages, which gives you full control over the markup in the page and the code in the Code Behind.

Hand-coding isn't as difficult as it seems and you do get a lot of flexibility in return for the extra effort. Though the actual process differs from page to page, here's a general description of the steps you need to carry out to hand-code an Add/Edit page that enables you to enter a new or update an existing item in the database with the same markup:

- Create the user interface by adding a number of controls, such as `TextBox` and `DropDownList`, to a page that enables users to enter new and update existing data.
- Add validation controls to the page so users are forced to enter valid data.
- In the Code Behind, figure out whether you're creating a new or editing an existing item. You can make the distinction by looking at the query string, for example. When you're editing an existing item, you get it from the data source and prepopulate the form controls.
- Handle the Save button to insert or update the item. When you're updating an existing item, you should get the item from the database first and then overwrite the existing values with the new ones from the form. Finally, save the items back to the data store.

In the next Try It Out you build a page that implements this process.

> ***NOTE*** *In the next exercise, you hand-code the user interface and use the ADO.NET Entity Framework to handle all data access for you. It's also common to hand-code the interaction with the database using ADO.NET classes, such as classes that inherit from* `DbConnection`, `DbCommand`, *and* `DbDataReader`. *Although hand-coding the interaction with the database requires a lot more code, it also gives you greater control and more flexibility. Get yourself a copy of Wrox's* Professional ASP.NET 4.5 in C# and VB *(ISBN: 978-1-118-31182-0) for a deeper dive into ADO.NET.*

TRY IT OUT Hand-Coding Data Access Pages

In this exercise you create a new version of the `AddEditReview.aspx` page to replace the existing one that currently uses a `DetailsView` to handle the insert and update process. In the new page you add form controls to enter the review's title, summary, body, and genre and whether or not it's authorized. In the Code Behind of the page you work with the `PlanetWroxEntities` class to handle all data access code. To keep the exercise short you won't be adding any validation controls. However, with the knowledge you gained from Chapter 9, you know what to do to make this page accept valid data only.

1. Start by adding a standard Web Form (don't use your custom template) using Code Behind to the `Management` folder of your site and call it **`AddEditReviewHandCoded.aspx.`** Base the page on the Management master page and give it a meaningful title.

2. Switch to Design View, choose Table ⇨ Insert Table, and insert a table of six rows and two columns. Add controls to the cells of the HTML table and set their properties according to this table:

ROW	COLUMN 1	COLUMN 2
1	Add a `Label` control `Text`: Title	Add a `TextBox` control `ID`: TitleText `Width`: 450px
2	Add a `Label` control `Text`: Summary	Add a `TextBox` control `ID`: SummaryText `Width`: 450px `TextMode`: MultiLine
3	Add a `Label` control `Text`: Body	Add a `TextBox` control `ID`: BodyText `Width`: 450px `TextMode`: MultiLine
4	Add a `Label` control `Text`: Genre	Add a `DropDownList` control `ID`: GenreList

ROW	COLUMN 1	COLUMN 2
5	Add a `Label` control `Text`: Authorized	Add a `CheckBox` control `ID`: Authorized
6	Leave this cell empty	Add a `Button` control `ID`: SaveButton `Text`: Save

When you're done, your page looks similar to Figure 15-13.

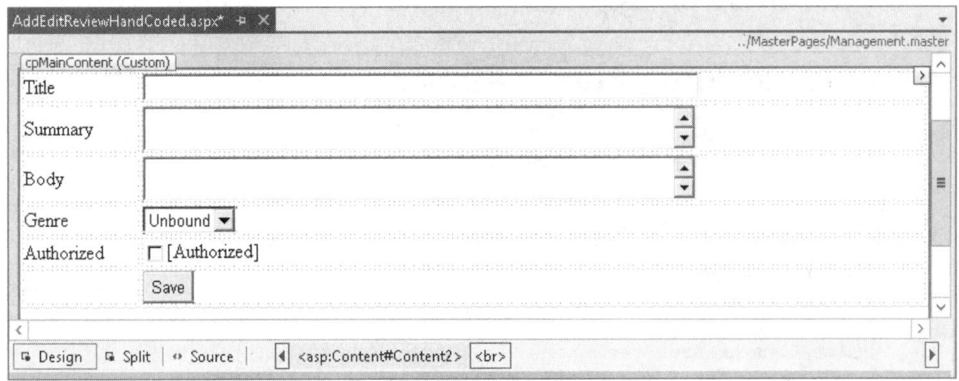

FIGURE 15-13

3. Next, hook up the `DropDownList` to a new `EntityDataSource` control. You should bind it to the `Genres` entity set and use `Id` and `Name` as the `DataValueField` and `DataTextField` properties, respectively. If you don't see the `Name` and `Id` properties listed in the drop-down lists for `DataValueField` and `DataTextField`, remember you can click the Refresh Schema link. Refer to the previous chapter if you're not sure how to hook up the control to an `EntityDataSource`. When you're done, the code for the two controls looks like this:

```
<asp:DropDownList ID="GenreList" runat="server" DataSourceID="EntityDataSource1"
     DataTextField="Name" DataValueField="Id"></asp:DropDownList>
<asp:EntityDataSource ID="EntityDataSource1" runat="server"
     ConnectionString="name=PlanetWroxEntities"
     DefaultContainerName="PlanetWroxEntities" EnableFlattening="False"
     EntitySetName="Genres"></asp:EntityDataSource>
```

4. The next step is to write some code that gets an existing `Review` from the database in case the user is editing an item. The page assumes you are editing an item when the query string contains the item's ID. If it doesn't, it assumes you are creating a new review.

   To set up the code, double-click the gray and read-only area of the page in Design View to set up a handler for the `Page`'s `Load` event, add an `Imports/using` statement at the top of the page for the PlanetWroxModel namespace, and then add the following bold code. Don't forget the _id variable outside Page_Load but inside the class definition.

VB.NET

```
Imports PlanetWroxModel

Partial Class Management_AddEditReviewHandCoded
    Inherits System.Web.UI.Page

  Dim _id As Integer = -1
  Protected Sub Page_Load(sender As Object, e As EventArgs) Handles Me.Load
    If Not String.IsNullOrEmpty(Request.QueryString.Get("Id")) Then
      _id = Convert.ToInt32(Request.QueryString.Get("Id"))
    End If
    If Not Page.IsPostBack And _id > -1 Then
      Using myEntities As New PlanetWroxEntities()
        Dim review = (From r In myEntities.Reviews
                      Where r.Id = _id
                      Select r).SingleOrDefault()

        If review IsNot Nothing Then
          TitleText.Text = review.Title
          SummaryText.Text = review.Summary
          BodyText.Text = review.Body
          GenreList.DataBind()
          Dim myItem As ListItem =
                GenreList.Items.FindByValue(review.GenreId.ToString())
          If myItem IsNot Nothing Then
            myItem.Selected = True
          End If
          Authorized.Checked = review.Authorized
        End If
      End Using
    End If
  End Sub
End Class
```

C#

```
using PlanetWroxModel;

public partial class Management_AddEditReviewHandCoded : System.Web.UI.Page
{
  int _id = -1;
  protected void Page_Load(object sender, EventArgs e)
  {
    if (!string.IsNullOrEmpty(Request.QueryString.Get("Id")))
    {
      _id = Convert.ToInt32(Request.QueryString.Get("Id"));
    }
    if (!Page.IsPostBack && _id > -1)
    {
      using (PlanetWroxEntities myEntities = new PlanetWroxEntities())
```

```
        {
          var review = (from r in myEntities.Reviews
                        where r.Id == _id
                        select r).SingleOrDefault();
          if (review != null)
          {
            TitleText.Text = review.Title;
            SummaryText.Text = review.Summary;
            BodyText.Text = review.Body;
            GenreList.DataBind();
            ListItem myItem =
                     GenreList.Items.FindByValue(review.GenreId.ToString());
            if (myItem != null)
            {
              myItem.Selected = true;
            }
            Authorized.Checked = review.Authorized;
          }
        }
      }
    }
  }
```

If you don't feel like typing all this code, remember you can find a copy of it in the `Chapter 15` folder of the source for this book that you can download from `www.wrox.com`. However, in real-world applications you typically need to type this code, so rather than copying and pasting it now, you're better off finding the most efficient way to enter code like this, letting IntelliSense do most of the work for you.

5. Switch back to Design View and double-click the Save button to set up a handler for the `Button` control's `Click` event. Then back in the Code Behind, add the following code to that handler:

VB.NET

```
Protected Sub SaveButton_Click(sender As Object, e As EventArgs) _
              Handles SaveButton.Click
  Using myEntities As New PlanetWroxEntities()
    Dim myReview As Review
      If _id = -1 Then ' Insert new item
        myReview = New Review()
        myReview.CreateDateTime = DateTime.Now
        myReview.UpdateDateTime = myReview.CreateDateTime
        myEntities.AddToReviews(myReview)
      Else ' update existing item
        myReview = (From r In myEntities.Reviews
                    Where r.Id = _id
                    Select r).Single()
        myReview.UpdateDateTime = DateTime.Now
      End If

      myReview.Title = TitleText.Text
      myReview.Summary = SummaryText.Text
      myReview.Body = BodyText.Text
```

```
      myReview.GenreId = Convert.ToInt32(GenreList.SelectedValue)
      myReview.Authorized = Authorized.Checked

      myEntities.SaveChanges()
      Response.Redirect("Reviews.aspx")
    End Using
End Sub
```

C#

```
protected void SaveButton_Click(object sender, EventArgs e)
{
  using (PlanetWroxEntities myEntities = new PlanetWroxEntities())
  {
    Review myReview;
    if (_id == -1) // Insert new item
    {
      myReview = new Review();
      myReview.CreateDateTime = DateTime.Now;
      myReview.UpdateDateTime = myReview.CreateDateTime;
      myEntities.AddToReviews(myReview);
    }
    else // update existing item
    {
      myReview = (from r in myEntities.Reviews
                  where r.Id == _id
                  select r).Single();
      myReview.UpdateDateTime = DateTime.Now;
    }

    myReview.Title = TitleText.Text;
    myReview.Summary = SummaryText.Text;
    myReview.Body = BodyText.Text;
    myReview.GenreId = Convert.ToInt32(GenreList.SelectedValue);
    myReview.Authorized = Authorized.Checked;

    myEntities.SaveChanges();
    Response.Redirect("Reviews.aspx");
  }
}
```

6. Open the `Reviews.aspx` file from the `Management` folder and change the two occurrences of `AddEditReview.aspx` to **`AddEditReviewHandCoded.aspx`**. You should find one in the `HyperLinkField` for the `Title` and one in the Insert New Review link at the bottom.

7. Save all pending changes by pressing Ctrl+Shift+S. Then right-click the `AddEditReviewHandCoded.aspx` page in the Solution Explorer and choose View in Browser. You should see a screen that enables you to insert a new review, as shown in Figure 15-14, which shows the page in Opera 12.

8. Enter a new review, choose a genre, and click the Save button. You're taken to the Reviews page again. Open your genre, locate your review, and click its title. You're taken to `AddEditReviewHandCoded.aspx`, where all form controls should already be filled in, ready to be edited.

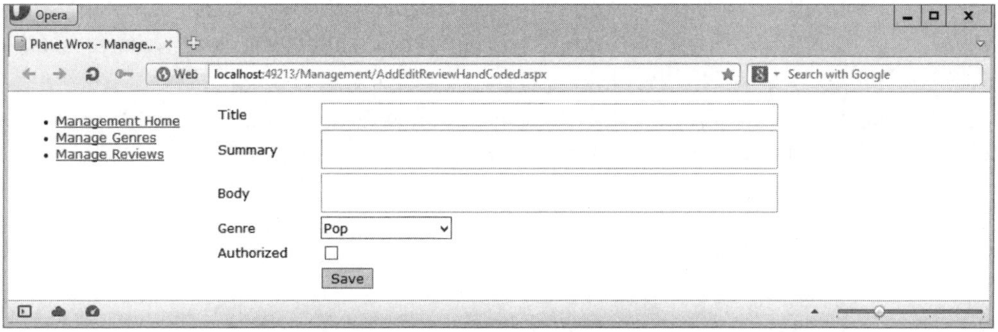

FIGURE 15-14

How It Works

You actually coded quite a lot in this exercise and didn't use many of the ready-made controls, other than those to let the user enter some details and to create the list of genres. Although hand-coding often means more work, you do gain a lot of flexibility, and — when you do it right — you end up with a page that's a lot easier to maintain. In this example, the markup section of the page is much easier to maintain than the previous version that used a `DetailsView`. Gone are the endless attributes on the controls, gone is the duplication that existed between the `InsertItemTemplate` and the `EditItemTemplate`, and gone is the awkward code to handle the `UpdateDateTime` in the Code Behind. What remains is a simple table-based presentation of the necessary form controls. Just like the Contact form you created in Chapter 9, it's easy to modify this page, add validation controls from Chapter 9, and use CSS to change the appearance of the page.

Next up is the code in the Code Behind. I'll discuss saving the form for a new review in the database first. After that I'll show you how to load an existing review from the database and prepopulate the form.

When you fill in the form's controls and click the Save button, the code in the `SaveButton_Click` method fires. This code first creates a new `PlanetWroxEntities` object with a `using` block to enable you to interact with the database through EF. Then when the `_id` variable does not contain an ID of an existing review (you see how the ID is retrieved later), a new `Review` instance is created and added to the `Reviews` collection of the entities object. This would be the case when you are creating a brand new review using the Insert New Review link.

VB.NET

```
myReview = New Review()
myReview.CreateDateTime = DateTime.Now
myReview.UpdateDateTime = myReview.CreateDateTime
myEntities.AddToReviews(myReview)
```

C#

```
myReview = new Review();
myReview.CreateDateTime = DateTime.Now;
myReview.UpdateDateTime = myReview.CreateDateTime;
myEntities.AddToReviews(myReview);
```

Because the review needs a CreateDateTime and an UpdateDateTime, this code sets both. Notice how the UpdateDateTime is filled with the CreateDateTime so both contain the exact same date and time, indicating the item hasn't been modified yet.

If the _id variable did contain a review ID (which means an existing review is being edited and saved), it's queried from the database with a LINQ to Entities query:

VB.NET

```
myReview = (From r In myEntities.Reviews
            Where r.Id = _id
            Select r).Single()
myReview.UpdateDateTime = DateTime.Now
```

C#

```
myReview = (from r in myEntities.Reviews
            where r.Id == _id
            select r).Single();
myReview.UpdateDateTime = DateTime.Now;
```

Whether or not an ID was passed to this page, at this stage the myReview variable contains a Review instance. The remaining code then fills the review's properties by retrieving them from the relevant form controls. For the genre, the code directly assigns the GenreId property instead of querying a complete Genre instance and assigning it to the Genre property of the Review instance. This works because the model has support for foreign key columns, as you learned in the preceding chapter.

Finally, when the object is fully set up, the code calls SaveChanges on the PlanetWroxEntities object. This eventually sends a SQL INSERT or UPDATE instruction to the database to tell it to insert a new or update the existing Review row. Just as with the data source control, calling SaveChanges may throw an error. Chapter 18 digs deeper into handling errors that may occur in your code. After SaveChanges has been called, the user is redirected to the Reviews.aspx page using Response .Redirect:

VB.NET

```
myEntities.SaveChanges()
Response.Redirect("Reviews.aspx")
```

C#

```
myEntities.SaveChanges();
Response.Redirect("Reviews.aspx");
```

Obviously, once you've saved a review in the database, you can edit it again. Once you click one of the existing reviews in the reviews list at Reviews.aspx, you're taken to the Add/Edit page with the ID of the review in the query string. For example, browsing to http://localhost:1049/Management/AddEditReviewHandCoded.aspx?Id=6 enables me to edit the *Death Magnetic* album by Metallica. The page is able to detect the ID in the query string using this code in Page_Load:

VB.NET

```
If Not String.IsNullOrEmpty(Request.QueryString.Get("Id")) Then
  _id = Convert.ToInt32(Request.QueryString.Get("Id"))
End If
```

C#

```
if (!string.IsNullOrEmpty(Request.QueryString.Get("Id")))
{
  _id = Convert.ToInt32(Request.QueryString.Get("Id"));
}
```

Because this `_id` variable is assigned a value in `Page_Load`, it can be used to load an existing item to display in the form, but also to get the item from the database in the `SaveButton`'s `Click` event (which you saw earlier).

If there is an ID (`_id` is assigned a value other than `-1`) and the page is not posted back, the code sets up a new `PlanetWroxEntities` instance inside a `using` block and queries the `Review` instance using the following LINQ to Entities query:

VB.NET

```
Dim review = (From r In myEntities.Reviews
             Where r.Id = _id
             Select r).SingleOrDefault()
```

C#

```
var review = (from r in myEntities.Reviews
             where r.Id == _id
             select r).SingleOrDefault();
```

Once the `Review` instance is found in the database, its properties are used to prepopulate the form controls:

VB.NET

```
If review IsNot Nothing Then
  TitleText.Text = review.Title
  SummaryText.Text = review.Summary
  BodyText.Text = review.Body
  GenreList.DataBind()
  Dim myItem As ListItem = GenreList.Items.FindByValue(review.GenreId.ToString())
  If myItem IsNot Nothing Then
    myItem.Selected = True
  End If
  Authorized.Checked = review.Authorized
End If
```

C#

```
if (review != null)
{
  TitleText.Text = review.Title;
  SummaryText.Text = review.Summary;
  BodyText.Text = review.Body;
  GenreList.DataBind();
  ListItem myItem = GenreList.Items.FindByValue(review.GenreId.ToString());
  if (myItem != null)
  {
    myItem.Selected = true;
  }
  Authorized.Checked = review.Authorized;
}
```

The code checks to make sure `review` is not `Nothing/null` before it tries to access its properties. The chances of the review being `null` in this example are pretty small because you access the Add/Edit page by clicking an existing item in the Reviews page, so you can be pretty sure the item is there. However, this is not always the case, especially not in public-facing pages. Your clients may have a bookmark for a page with a specific ID in the query string. If you then delete that item from the database and your users access the page using the old bookmark, the review can't be found and a so-called Null Reference exception occurs.

The same defensive coding mechanism is used to preselect the genre in the drop-down list. In this case you can be sure the `Genre` still exists in the database because there's a relationship between the `Id` column of the `Genre` table and the `GenreId` of the `Review` table. However, checking to make sure an item exists in a `DropDownList` control before you try to select it is a best practice and helps in avoiding other Null Reference exceptions. Because the `DropDownList` with genres hasn't been populated at this stage, you need to call `DataBind()` first. This forces the `EntityDataSource` control to get the genres and add them to the `DropDownList`. Afterward, the code can successfully find and preselect the appropriate item.

Finally, when you click the Save button for an edited item, the exact same code is fired that was used to insert a new item.

If you were using validation controls (and you really should, as you learned in Chapter 9), you need to check whether or not the page is valid before you proceed with saving the `Review` instance:

VB.NET

```
Protected Sub SaveButton_Click(sender As Object, e As EventArgs) _
        Handles SaveButton.Click
  If (Page.IsValid) Then
    Using myEntities As New PlanetWroxEntities()
```

C#

```
protected void SaveButton_Click(object sender, EventArgs e)
{
  if (Page.IsValid)
  {
    using (PlanetWroxEntities myEntities = new PlanetWroxEntities())
```

This is really all there is to adding and editing new reviews using your own code against the Entities Framework. I realize it may look a little funky at first because you need to reset your head, forget about smart controls and their many properties and events, and think in straight code. However, EF makes this pretty straightforward, and most of it comes down to querying entities, copying values from or to an object's properties, and calling `SaveChanges` to propagate the changes back to the database.

Clearly, this is just the beginning. There's a whole lot more you can do once you start writing your own code, whether or not it targets EF. For more information, get yourself a copy of *Programming Entity Framework Second Edition* by Julia Lerman or *Professional ASP.NET 4.5 in C# and VB* from Wrox (ISBN: 978-1-118-31182-0).

In all the database examples you have seen so far, the code accesses the database for each and every request. Every time some data needs to be displayed, it's retrieved fresh from the database. Clearly, this can be a waste of time and resources like network bandwidth and CPU cycles, especially if the data hasn't changed since the last time you accessed it. In the final section of this chapter, you are introduced to a technique called *caching* that can greatly improve the responsiveness and performance of your application.

CACHING

Caching is one of the best and often easiest ways to improve the performance of an application. It's also an option that is too often overlooked by developers. With caching, a *copy* of your data is stored in a location that can be accessed very quickly. The idea with caching is that fetching data from the cache should be faster than regenerating it or fetching it from the original data source. Therefore, most caching solutions store data in memory, which is usually the fastest way to get the data. The .NET cache is no exception, and enables you to store frequently accessed data in a special location in the computer's memory.

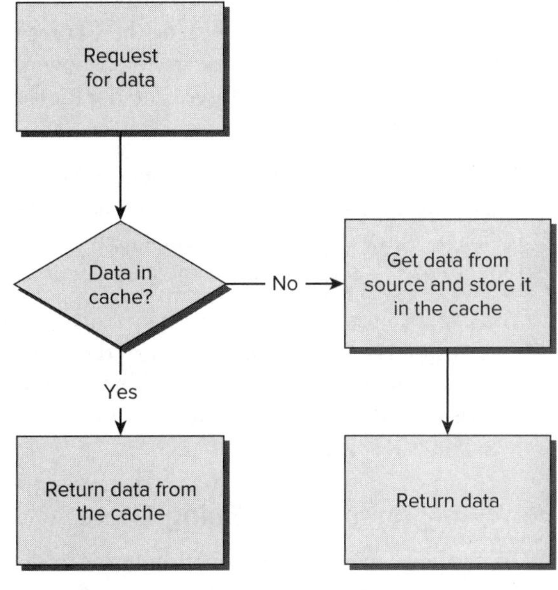

FIGURE 15-15

Typically, the caching principle takes the route displayed in Figure 15-15.

The application queries for some data — for example, a list of genres from the database. Instead of accessing the database directly, the cache is examined to see if it already contains the requested data. If it does, the data is returned from the cache directly. If it's not stored in the cache yet, it is retrieved from the data source (such as a SQL Server database), a copy of the data is stored in the cache for later retrieval, and finally, the data is returned to the calling code.

Though caching is generally a great solution to improve your application, it has a few drawbacks that you need to be aware of. The following section explains a few common pitfalls you can run into when using caching. The section after that shows the different caching mechanisms you have available in your ASP.NET web applications.

Common Pitfalls with Caching Data

When working with cached data you typically encounter two common problem areas:

- You end up with stale — or out-of-date — data.
- You assume an item is present in the cache when it isn't.

In the next sections you see how to avoid these two problems.

Avoiding Stale Data

Stale data is cached data that no longer matches its original source. For example, when you cache the results of a query for all the genres in the database and use that data instead of getting it fresh from the database, a new genre inserted by another user may go unnoticed.

To avoid stale data you need a way to invalidate the cache. With *cache invalidation*, an item is removed from the cache so it can be re-created on the next request. To invalidate cached data, you have a number of options at your disposal. First of all, you can choose to set a short cache duration. For example, you could cache the Genres list for, say, 10 minutes. If another user inserts a new genre during those 10 minutes, it won't show up in your pages. However, after 10 minutes, the list is removed from the cache and re-created with fresh data the next time it is requested. You see how to use time-based caching later.

Another option to invalidate the cache is by using a cache dependency. With a *cache dependency*, you create a relationship between the cached item and the original data source. When the underlying data source changes, the cached item is invalidated so it can be re-created the next time it is requested. You see how to use the `CacheDependency` class later.

You can also use a cache dependency when using a database like Microsoft SQL Server. This means that as soon as the data that is part of the cached query is changed, the cached item is invalidated. Database caching and invalidation is an advanced and broad subject. You find more in the chapter that deals with caching in *Professional ASP.NET 4.5 in C# and VB*, published by Wrox (ISBN: 978-1-118-31182-0).

Don't Rely on the Data Being There

To minimize memory consumption for an application, the caching mechanism in ASP.NET automatically removes old and infrequently used items from the cache from time to time. Also, when the server is consuming too much memory, items may be ejected from the cache as well. Therefore, you shouldn't rely on items being in the cache. They may have been removed by the cache itself when the ASP.NET run time determined that the item was not used often enough and was thus taking up precious space unnecessarily. The entire cache is also cleared when the web application or web server restarts (which happens when you make changes to the `Web.config` file, for example). But items can also be removed because of their dependencies. Therefore, you should never rely on the item being in the cache, even if you set it there yourself earlier in the application's life cycle. Later in this chapter you see how to use the Cache API (application programming interface; the way you can interact with a program) to use the cache programmatically.

Using the Cache API is not the only way to use the cache. The next section shows you the different ways of caching data in ASP.NET.

Different Ways to Cache Data in ASP.NET Web Applications

You can deploy a few different caching strategies in your ASP.NET applications, including output caching, caching with the built-in data source controls, and programmatic caching. All three options are discussed in the remainder of this chapter.

Output Caching

With output caching, the end result of a rendered page is cached. This means that the very first time a page is requested, its final result is added to the cache. Subsequent requests to the same page result in the same HTML being sent. This last sentence is important enough to be repeated: *Subsequent requests to the same page result in the same HTML being sent.* This means the page is not processed at the server again, and no custom code in the Code Behind will fire. The exact same HTML from the first request is simply returned on each subsequent request.

Enabling output caching is extremely simple; just add an `OutputCache` directive below your `Page` directive, as shown in bold under this C# `@ Page` directive (you use the same code if you're using VB.NET, but your `@ Page` directive may look slightly different):

```
<%@ Page Title="About this Site" Language="C#"
        MasterPageFile="~/MasterPages/Frontend.master" AutoEventWireup="true"
        CodeFile="Default.aspx.cs" Inherits="About_Default" %>
<%@ OutputCache Duration="60" VaryByParam="None" %>
```

The `Duration` is the number of seconds you want to cache the page before ASP.NET creates a new copy of it. In the preceding example, the page is cached for a minute.

The `None` value in the `VaryByParam` attribute tells .NET to cache a single version of the page, no matter what query string values you pass to it. Although this is fine for relatively static pages like the About page in the Planet Wrox site, this is typically not an ideal solution for dynamic pages. Imagine a dynamic page that shows the details for a review based on the query string that is being passed to the page. The first time you request the page you may browse to something like:

```
http://localhost:12345/Reviews/ViewDetails.aspx?Id=23
```

ASP.NET generates a page showing review 23 and then caches the entire output of the page. So what happens when you then request this page?

```
http://localhost:12345/Reviews/ViewDetails.aspx?Id=33
```

Instead of seeing the review with an ID of 33, you end up with the review with an ID of 23! To overcome this problem, ASP.NET enables you to cache specific versions of a page. For example, you can instruct the page to cache a copy of the page for each unique query string field that it retrieves. You do this by setting the `VaryByParam` attribute of the directive to a comma-separated list of possible query string or form values. ASP.NET will cache a copy of the page for each unique combination of the fields it finds. As an example, consider a page that accepts the ID of a review in the query string and then displays its details. To cache a copy for each unique review, you add `Id` to the `VaryByParam` attribute like this:

```
<%@ OutputCache Duration="60" VaryByParam="Id" %>
```

For a page showing the details of a specific review, this is perfect. For each unique review, ASP.NET keeps a cached copy. This means that the database will only be hit when the review is not present in the cache. All other requests will be served from the cache.

One of the problems with output caching is that it's often an all-or-nothing scenario. Although it's easy to cache different pages based on, for example, a query string value, you'll need to write custom code to handle other situations like dealing with themes. When a page is requested and cached for the first time, the user's theme is taken into account. If subsequent users have a different theme set they still see the page in the originally requested theme. Another case where output caching can be problematic is when you're using security-related controls such as the LoginView (discussed in the next chapter). These controls can display content based on the currently logged-in user. If that page is cached, other users will see the content that belongs to the first user that requested the page.

One solution to this problem is to not use output caching at the page level and move content that applies to all users to a separate user control, which you then embed in the page as you saw how to do with the Contact Form. For example, a list with news articles or the full list of reviews could be the same for all users. If you move the code for these lists to a user control with output caching enabled, your containing page is still created separately for each user, but the content from the user control is only generated the first time, and then reused for all subsequent requests.

Another solution is to instruct the data source controls to cache data for you, as you see in the next section.

If you're not affected by the drawbacks of output caching (such as when you're not using themes or the security-related controls), output caching is an excellent mechanism to improve the performance of your site.

Caching with Data Source Controls

The biggest benefit of caching with the data source controls is that they only cache dynamic, database-driven data, and not the entire page. That enables you to keep other parts of the page dynamic, such as a banner module or a personalized greeting welcoming the user. Caching is supported by design on most of the data source controls, except for the SiteMapDataSource, LinqDataSource, and EntityDataSource controls.

Caching with the data source controls is very easy: All you need to do is set the EnableCaching property and then specify a CacheDuration. The following code snippet shows a SqlDataSource control that caches its data for 10 minutes:

```
<asp:SqlDataSource ID="SqlDataSource1" runat="server" CacheDuration="600"
      EnableCaching="True"></asp:SqlDataSource>
```

What's cool about caching with the data source controls is that they are smart enough to see if you are making updates to the underlying data. So, when you have set up a SqlDataSource control to cache data for the SelectCommand for 20 minutes, but then make a change to the data by using the InsertCommand, UpdateCommand, or DeleteCommand, the cache is invalidated automatically. This only works when you execute the insert, update, or delete command against the exact same SqlDataSource. If you have one page that displays and caches a list with reviews (such as All.aspx, for example) and then have another page that is used to insert a new review (such as AddEditReview.aspx in the Management folder), this won't work. After you have inserted a new review in the Management section of the site, it won't show up in All.aspx until the cache has expired.

Code-free caching with the data source controls is useful in many situations. However, the data source controls cannot be used in every situation. What if you want to cache the results of data you get from a completely different source? What if you want to cache data you receive in a hand-coded page targeting the Entity Framework, or the contents of a text or an XML file that you frequently need to access? For those cases, ASP.NET gives you programmatic access to the cache.

Programmatic Caching

With programmatic caching, you can store items in the cache through VB.NET or C# code. Obviously, you can also access them again later. To store items, you use the `Add` or the `Insert` method or you index the `Cache` collection directly. The `Add` method is quite powerful (and complex) and enables you to specify a host of options that determine how long the item is cached, what priority it should have compared to other cached items, and what factors trigger the item's removal from the cache.

The `Insert` method, on the other hand, is much easier. It has a few short overloads that enable you to specify the cached item and associate it with a specific key. Another overload also enables you to define dependencies that can be used to invalidate a cached item when the original source is changed. This is great for caching files that don't change very often. You can read a file from disk, and store it in the cache with a dependency on the original file. You then keep reading the file from the cache instead of from disk. When the file on disk is changed, the cached item is invalidated automatically and you can read the original source file again and store it in the cache. The following example shows how to modify the `ContactForm.ascx` user control to store and get the item from the cache until it changes:

VB.NET

```
If Page.IsValid Then
  Dim mailBody As String = TryCast(Cache("ContactFormMailBody"), String)
  If String.IsNullOrEmpty(mailBody) Then
    Dim fileName As String = Server.MapPath("~/App_Data/ContactForm.txt")
    mailBody = System.IO.File.ReadAllText(fileName)
    Cache.Insert("ContactFormMailBody", mailBody, New CacheDependency(fileName))
  End If
  mailBody = mailBody.Replace("##Name##", Name.Text)

  ...
End If
```

C#

```
if (Page.IsValid)
{
  string mailBody = Cache["ContactFormMailBody"] as string;
  if (string.IsNullOrEmpty(mailBody))
  {
    string fileName = Server.MapPath("~/App_Data/ContactForm.txt");
    mailBody = System.IO.File.ReadAllText(fileName);
    Cache.Insert("ContactFormMailBody", mailBody, new CacheDependency(fileName));
  }
  mailBody = mailBody.Replace("##Name##", Name.Text);

  ...
}
```

Notice how a new `CacheDependency` (for which you need to bring the `System.Web.Caching` namespace into scope with an `Imports/using` statement) is created and passed to the `Insert` method. This `CacheDependency` expects the name of the file it is dependent on. As soon as you change the file on disk (using VS or Notepad, for example), ASP.NET removes the item from the cache so it will be read from the original source file again the next time this code is executed.

You remove items from the cache using the `Remove` method that accepts the key of the cached item. You define this key when inserting the item, using either `Add` or `Insert`.

To access the items in the cache, you have a few options available. First of all, you can access the `Cache` collection directly:

VB.NET

```
myReview = TryCast(Cache(myKey), Review)
```

C#

```
Review myReview = Cache[myKey] as Review;
```

Here, the `Cache` collection is indexed using the key stored in the `myKey` variable.

Additionally, you can use the `Get` method that expects the key:

VB.NET

```
myReview = TryCast(Cache.Get(myKey), Review)
```

C#

```
myReview = Cache.Get(myKey) as Review;
```

Because `Get` is a method, the C# example now also uses parentheses around the cache key, making both examples look more like each other.

Finally, you can access items in the cache using the `Item` property that also accepts the key of the cached item.

All three ways to access items in the cache always return an `object` or `Nothing/null` when the item cannot be found. That means that if you know the type you are getting back from the cache, you should cast it to the appropriate type using `TryCast` in VB.NET or the `as` keyword in C# before you can use its properties. The previous two examples show you how the item from the cache is cast to a strongly typed `Review` object first.

To give you an idea of how to use the cache programmatically, the next exercise shows you how to insert a review in the cache, so you don't have to get it from the database every time you need it.

TRY IT OUT Using the Cache API

In this Try It Out exercise you see how to cache a `Review` instance you get from EF using a LINQ to Entities query so it can be retrieved later by its key (which contains the review's ID).

1. Start by adding a new page called `ViewDetails.aspx` in the `Reviews` folder of your web application. Make sure it's based on your custom template. There's no need to set an explicit title, because it will be set programmatically. Instead, remove the `Title=""` attribute from the `Page` directive. There's a funny and old bug in ASP.NET that causes programmatic modifications to the page's `Title` not to stick when this attribute is set to an empty string in Markup View.
2. In Markup View, add three `Label` controls to the `cpMainContent` content placeholder and name the controls as follows:
   - `TitleLabel`

- `SummaryLabel`
- `BodyLabel`

Delete the `Text` attribute and its value from all three labels.

3. Wrap the `TitleLabel` label in an `<h1>` element, and set the `CssClass` property of the `SummaryLabel` control to `Summary`. You should end up with this code:

```
<h1><asp:Label ID="TitleLabel" runat="server"></asp:Label></h1>
<asp:Label CssClass="Summary" ID="SummaryLabel" runat="server"></asp:Label>
<asp:Label ID="BodyLabel" runat="server"></asp:Label>
```

4. Switch to Design View and double-click the read-only area of the page to set up a handler for `Page_Load`.

5. Add an `Imports/using` statement at the top of the page for the `PlanetWroxModel` namespace as you've done before in `AddEditReviewHandCoded.aspx`, and then add the following code to the `Page_Load` event handler that has been created for you:

VB.NET

```
Protected Sub Page_Load(sender As Object, e As EventArgs) Handles Me.Load
  Dim reviewId As Integer = Convert.ToInt32(Request.QueryString.Get("ReviewId"))
  Dim cacheKey As String = "Reviews" + reviewId.ToString()
  Dim myReview As Review = TryCast(Cache(cacheKey), Review)
  If myReview Is Nothing Then
    Using myEntities As New PlanetWroxEntities()
      myReview = (From r In myEntities.Reviews
                  Where r.Id = reviewId
                  Select r).SingleOrDefault()
      If myReview IsNot Nothing Then
        Cache.Insert(cacheKey, myReview, Nothing, DateTime.Now.AddMinutes(20),
                     System.Web.Caching.Cache.NoSlidingExpiration)
      End If
    End Using
  End If

  If myReview IsNot Nothing Then
    TitleLabel.Text = myReview.Title
    SummaryLabel.Text = myReview.Summary
    BodyLabel.Text = myReview.Body
    Title = myReview.Title
    MetaDescription = myReview.Summary
  End If
End Sub
```

C#

```
protected void Page_Load(object sender, EventArgs e)
{
  int reviewId = Convert.ToInt32(Request.QueryString.Get("ReviewId"));
  string cacheKey = "Reviews" + reviewId.ToString();
  Review myReview = Cache[cacheKey] as Review;
  if (myReview == null)
  {
    using (PlanetWroxEntities myEntities = new PlanetWroxEntities())
```

```
    {
      myReview = (from r in myEntities.Reviews
                  where r.Id == reviewId
                  select r).SingleOrDefault();

      if (myReview != null)
      {
        Cache.Insert(cacheKey, myReview, null, DateTime.Now.AddMinutes(20),
                 System.Web.Caching.Cache.NoSlidingExpiration);
      }
    }
  }

  if (myReview != null)
  {
    TitleLabel.Text = myReview.Title;
    SummaryLabel.Text = myReview.Summary;
    BodyLabel.Text = myReview.Body;
    Title = myReview.Title;
    MetaDescription = myReview.Summary;
  }
}
```

6. Open the page `All.aspx` from the `Reviews` folder and delete the `GridView` that you created in the previous chapter. Replace it with a simple `Repeater` control that contains a single `HyperLink` into your new details page:

```
<asp:Content ID="Content2" ContentPlaceHolderID="cpMainContent" runat="Server">
  <asp:Repeater ID="Repeater1" runat="server" ItemType="PlanetWroxModel.Review">
    <ItemTemplate>
      <asp:HyperLink ID="HyperLink1" runat="server"
         NavigateUrl='<%# "ViewDetails.aspx?ReviewId=" + Item.Id.ToString() %>'
         Text='<%# Item.Title %>'></asp:HyperLink>
    </ItemTemplate>
    <SeparatorTemplate><br /></SeparatorTemplate>
  </asp:Repeater>
</asp:Content>
```

7. Switch to the Code Behind of the page and replace the last two calls that used the `GridView` so they end up using the `Repeater` control instead:

VB.NET

```
Repeater1.DataSource = allReviews
Repeater1.DataBind()
```

C#

```
Repeater1.DataSource = allReviews;
Repeater1.DataBind();
```

8. Add the following CSS declaration to the end of the CSS files for the Monochrome and the DarkGrey themes. Since this is a front-end page visited by your users, you don't need to add it to the Management theme:

```
.Summary
{
```

```
  font-style: italic;
  display: block;
}
```

9. Save all changes and then request `All.aspx` from the `Reviews` folder in your browser. Click the title of a review and you're taken to `ViewDetails.aspx` with the ID of the requested review in the query string.

> ***COMMON MISTAKES*** *If you see an error message about an invalid page title, make sure you removed* `Title=""` *from the* `Page` *directive in* `ViewDetails.aspx`*. With the attribute set to an empty string, the title you set in Code Behind won't stick, and then your* `BasePage` *will raise an exception because the title is missing.*

You should now see the details of the review displayed on the page. Press Ctrl+F5 or Ctrl+R to refresh the contents of the page. Although you don't see the difference, the review now comes from the cache. If you want to confirm this is really the case, you can add a `Label` control to the `ViewDetails.aspx` page and then update it with a text saying whether or not the item was in the cache:

VB.NET

```
Label1.Text = "In the cache"
If myReview Is Nothing Then
  Label1.Text = "NOT in the cache"
  Using myEntities As New PlanetWroxEntities()
```

C#

```
Label1.Text = "In the cache";
if (myReview == null)
{
  Label1.Text = "NOT in the cache";
  using (PlanetWroxEntities myEntities = new PlanetWroxEntities())
```

This code initially sets the `Label`'s `Text` to `"In the cache"`. However, if the item isn't found, the `Label` is updated to reflect that observation.

> ***COMMON MISTAKES*** *If you get the error "Page title cannot be 'Untitled Page' or an empty string", make sure you're passing a valid Review ID in the* `ReviewId` *query string parameter to the* `ViewDetails.aspx` *page. You usually get this error when you browse to the details page directly from within VS using Ctrl+F5 rather than through* `All.aspx`*. To work around this situation, you could add code to* `ViewDetails.apsx` *that redirects the user back to* `All.aspx` *when there's not valid value in the* `ReviewId` *query string parameter, which you could check using* `String.IsNullOrEmpty(Request.QueryString.Get("ReviewId")`*. For other unforeseen situations you need to add error-handling code to your page. This is the topic of Chapter 18.*

How It Works

In the `ViewDetails.aspx` page you first added a few labels that hold relevant properties of the `Review`, such as its `Title`, `Summary`, and `Body`. You assigned the `Label` control for the summary a `CssClass` so you can influence its styling from your CSS files. The `.Summary` selector assigns an italic font and sets the `display` property to `block`, forcing the body text that follows onto its own line.

The code in the Code Behind then starts by looking at whether or not it can retrieve the item from the cache:

VB.NET

```
Dim myReview As Review = TryCast(Cache("Reviews" + reviewId.ToString()), Review)
```

C#

```
Review myReview = Cache["Reviews" + reviewId.ToString()] as Review;
```

As the key for the cached item, the code uses a combination of the word `Reviews` and the `Id` of each item. This gives each review a unique key to be used for the cache. If the item cannot be found in the cache (possibly because you're loading the page for the first time or because ASP.NET removed it), the `TryCast` method in VB.NET and the `as` keyword in C# return `Nothing`/`null`. So, by checking the `myReview` variable for that value, you can determine whether the item was in the cache. If it was, you're pretty much done, but if it wasn't you need to get it from the database using a LINQ to Entities query similar to those you've seen before. Note that the query uses the `SingleOrDefault()` operator to limit the query to a single `Review` instance, because there should only be one by the given ID, or to `Nothing`/`null` when the item cannot be found. What you do when the item is not found is up to you; you can display an error message in a `Label` control informing the user that the item is no longer available, or you can redirect to the homepage or another page in your site.

After the item is retrieved from the database, it's inserted into the cache with the following code:

VB.NET

```
Cache.Insert("Reviews" + reviewId.ToString(), myReview, Nothing,
       DateTime.Now.AddMinutes(20), System.Web.Caching.Cache.NoSlidingExpiration)
```

C#

```
Cache.Insert("Reviews" + reviewId.ToString(), myReview, null,
       DateTime.Now.AddMinutes(20), System.Web.Caching.Cache.NoSlidingExpiration);
```

The first parameter of the `Insert` method is the cache key and the second parameter is the object you want to cache: the actual `Review` instance, in this case. The third parameter enables you to hook up your cached item to some dependency, such as a file or a database, so the item is removed from the cache when the dependent object changes. This is not used in this example, so `null` (`Nothing` in VB) is passed. The fourth parameter defines the *absolute expiration date*: the date and time at which the item is considered outdated and has to be removed from the cache. In this example, this date is constructed by adding 20 minutes to the current date and time, meaning the item will be cached for a maximum duration of 20 minutes. The final parameter can be used to set a new expiration time every time the item is accessed. This is a great way to cache frequently used items and ensures that items that are not used often are removed from the cache sooner. However, the previous example is using an absolute expiration date, which means you have to pass the constant value of `System.Web.Caching.Cache.NoSlidingExpiration` as the sliding expiration parameter because the two parameters are mutually exclusive.

At this stage, if the item exists in the database, you have a valid `Review` instance, whether or not it came from the cache. This instance is then used to fill the `Label` controls in the page and the page's `Title` and `MetaDescription` properties:

VB.NET

```
TitleLabel.Text = myReview.Title
SummaryLabel.Text = myReview.Summary
BodyLabel.Text = myReview.Body
Title = myReview.Title
MetaDescription = myReview.Summary
```

C#

```
TitleLabel.Text = myReview.Title;
SummaryLabel.Text = myReview.Summary;
BodyLabel.Text = myReview.Body;
Title = myReview.Title;
MetaDescription = myReview.Summary;
```

Setting the `Title` and `MetaDescription` is good for your users and for the ranking of your page in search engines. The title is used when bookmarking a page, so a clear title helps the user find your page again. Search engines such as Google and Bing use the title in their evaluation of what the page is about. They use the text that you set in the `MetaDescription` (which ends up as a `<meta name="description" />` element in the `<head>` section of the page's HTML) to present the results to the user. This means the text you enter there is often your first point of contact with a user that uses a search engine. As such, it's an important piece of information. Rather than reusing the `Summary` property for this purpose, you could add an additional column (called `SearchEngineDescription`, for example) to the `Reviews` table in the database. You then need to bring this column into the ADO.NET Entity Data Model by right-clicking the EDMX model diagram in the Entity Designer and choosing Update Model from Database. Once you've added this property to the model, don't forget to change the edit pages in the Management section (`AddEditReview.aspx` or `AddEditReviewHandCoded.aspx`) so they support this new property as well. Finally, in the `ViewDetails.aspx` page you can then assign its value to the `MetaDescription` property of the `Page` class.

Besides the `MetaDescription` property, the `Page` class was extended with a `MetaKeywords` property in ASP.NET 4. This property works more or less the same as the `MetaDescription` and enables you to set the keywords for the page. Although the importance of keywords to influence search engine ranking is heavily debated (many say they are not used by search engines at all), it can't hurt to set them. You could add the keywords to the database and model by following the same steps as outlined for the `SearchEngineDescription` property. For a lot more tips on search engine optimization (SEO), consider getting a copy of Wrox's *Professional Search Engine Optimization with ASP.NET: A Developer's Guide to SEO* (ISBN: 978-0-470-13147-3).

The `ViewDetails.aspx` page now performs pretty well; The first time it loads, the item is retrieved from the database and stored in the cache. On subsequent visits to the page, the database is no longer accessed but the item is retrieved from the much faster cache.

PRACTICAL DATA TIPS

Here are some practical tips on working with data in your ASP.NET websites:

- Whenever you use the numerous style properties of the data-bound controls, consider using the `CssClass` property instead of setting the individual style properties directly. This avoids page bloat and makes your site easier to maintain.
- The section about the control's life cycle has an exercise that shows you how to display the various events and the order in which they occur. You could extend the example and write code for even more events. Additionally, you could add more controls to the page and handle their events as well to help you establish a solid understanding of those events. Because a good understanding of those events and their order is often critical in writing web applications, the time you put into this little research project is well spent.
- Whenever you are writing pages that access a database or other slow or scarce resources like files or web services, consider whether they can benefit from caching. Although it's not that hard to add caching at a later stage, it's best to put it in as early as possible.
- Consider hand-coding complex data access pages. Though they are more difficult to write at first, you'll end up with pages that are easier to maintain in the long run.

SUMMARY

This chapter covered some of the more advanced topics on presenting data with the data controls that earlier chapters deliberately skipped to enable you to focus on the core data access concepts.

The chapter started off with a good look at the numerous style elements that most data-bound controls have to influence their appearance. You then learned more about the numerous events that controls can fire. These events can be used to change the appearance of the controls programmatically. Therefore, a solid understanding of the page's life cycle is important knowledge.

The chapter closed with a discussion of the various caching capabilities that ASP.NET supports to help you improve the performance of your websites.

This chapter showed you some advanced ways to handle data in an ASP.NET web application. The following chapter shows you how to protect some of this data — for example, the `Management` folder — from unauthorized users by implementing ASP.NET security.

EXERCISES

1. Imagine you have a simple Web Form with a single `Button` on it. If you click the `Button` in the browser, it causes a postback and at the server its `Click` event is triggered. What happens first — the `Page`'s `Load` event or the `Button` control's `Click` event?

2. Right now, when you insert or edit an item on `AddEditReviewHandCoded.aspx`, you're taken back to `Reviews.aspx` when you're done. It would be nice if the genre for the new or updated review item would already be preselected in the drop-down list. What code do you need to write to implement this feature?

3. What's the proper way to avoid an exception that you handled in a data-bound control's event in the Code Behind from being displayed in the page?

You can find answers to these exercises in Appendix A.

▶ WHAT YOU LEARNED IN THIS CHAPTER

ASP.NET styles	Control properties that inherit from the `Style` class and that let you change the appearance of controls
Caching	A technique used to store copies of data in a location that is quicker to access than the original source in order to improve performance
Cache invalidation	A mechanism where items are removed from the cache when they are no longer valid
Exception	The .NET term for an error (exceptions are discussed in great detail in Chapter 18).
Foreign key constraint error	An error that occurs at the database level when you try to delete a row that other rows depend on
`MetaDescription` **`MetaKeywords`**	These two properties on the `Page` class enable you to set metadata for the page in the browser that can be used by search engines.
Output caching	A form of caching where an entire page or a user control is cached to prevent it from being generated from scratch every time it's accessed
Stale data	A cached copy of some data that no longer accurately represents the original data

16

Security in Your ASP.NET 4.5 Website

WHAT YOU WILL LEARN IN THIS CHAPTER:

- Important terminology you'll encounter when dealing with security
- The ASP.NET application services that drive the security model of ASP.NET
- How you can let users sign up for an account for your site
- How users can reset their passwords or request new ones
- How you can manage the users and roles in your database at development time
- How you can present different content to different users based on their access rights in the system

WROX.COM CODE DOWNLOADS FOR THIS CHAPTER

You can find the wrox.com code downloads for this chapter on the Download Code tab at `www.wrox.com/remtitle.cgi?isbn=1118311809`. The code is in the chapter 16 download.

Until now, you have been creating pages in your website that are accessible to all visitors to your site. There is currently no way to block certain resources like ASPX files or even whole folders for specific users. That means, for example, that currently anyone can access your `Management` folder and start messing with the genres and reviews in the system.

Clearly, this is not something you'd want in a production website. So you need to think of a good security strategy to stop unwanted users from accessing specific content. You also need to look at a mechanism that enables users to sign up for a new account, and at the same time enables you to designate certain users as managers of your website and grant them special access rights.

ASP.NET 4.5 and VS ship with all the tools you need to create a solid and safe security mechanism. In this chapter, you learn how to make use of these tools in your ASP.NET website.

Before you start looking at how security is implemented in the ASP.NET Framework, you need to understand a few important terms that you'll come across in every discussion on security.

INTRODUCING SECURITY

Although security can be quite a complex subject, it often revolves around three straightforward questions:

- Who are you?
- How can you prove that?
- What are you allowed to do in the system?

Identity: Who Are You?

An identity is what makes you, *you*. The answer to what an identity is depends on the context it is used in. As a citizen of a country, your identity revolves around your person, your official name and birth date, and maybe even a Social Security number. However, for a website like `p2p.wrox.com`, Wrox's community website, your identity may be as little as your e-mail address.

No matter what you include in an identity, it is a way to refer to you. But how does anyone else know you? And how can they be sure it's really you when you log on to a website, for example? This is where authentication enters the game.

Authentication: How Can You Prove Who You Are?

Authentication is about providing evidence about who you are. When you need to register for a library card, you may need to show your passport to prove that the name you register the card under really belongs to you. With a website like `p2p.wrox.com,` you need to provide an e-mail address and a password. Together, these two pieces form the evidence that proves your identity. Many other mechanisms are used for authentication, including high-tech fingerprint or iris scans, smart cards and tokens (where the evidence is stored on something tangible), and so on. However, in light of the discussion on security of ASP.NET websites, this chapter sticks to a username and password for authentication. In many cases, e-mail addresses act as usernames because they uniquely identity a user.

Authorization: What Are You Allowed to Do?

Depending on who you are, a system grants you more or fewer privileges to access certain areas. Think about the highly secured headquarters of a national security agency in an action movie, for example. Even if the main character is allowed to enter the building, he is often not allowed to enter specific areas because he lacks the proper authorization (the fact that the hero eventually gains access in those movies using a two-minute hack in the system is beside the point here).

To determine what a user is allowed to do, a system needs to know two things: the *permissions* for the current user and the *authorization rules* for the resource a user is trying to access.

The permissions for the user are based on her username (the identity it represents) and the *roles* (or security groups) the user is optionally assigned to. Similarly, resources can be opened up or blocked for specific users or roles. When there is a match between the current user and the access rules for the resource a user is trying to access, the user is granted access. If the user is blocked specifically, access is denied. Imagine a file that is only accessible to the user Tom and the group Developers. The user Tom can access that file, regardless of whether he is in the Developers role. At the same time, the user Charlotte *must* be in the Developers role in order to access the file.

You see how to work with these concepts in the remainder of this chapter.

A large part of these security concepts in ASP.NET are implemented with the so-called application services, discussed next.

An Introduction to the ASP.NET Application Services

Versions of ASP.NET before ASP.NET 2.0 had some support for security. In ASP.NET 1.*x* applications, you needed to write a lot of code to implement a solid security strategy. The downside of writing this code is that it was often pretty much the same in all your websites. You were more or less forced to write the same code over and over again to implement a security mechanism.

These problems were solved in ASP.NET 2.0, which shipped with the *application services*: a set of services you can use in your website to support management of users, roles, profiles, and more. These services are based on a provider model, something you'll learn more about shortly. The application services are still strongly present in ASP.NET 4.5 and have been updated to simplify configuration and deployment.

ASP.NET 4.5 ships with a number of application services. The most important ones are:

- **Membership** — Enables you to manage and work with user accounts in your system.
- **Roles** — Enables you to manage the roles to which your users can be assigned.
- **Profile** — Enables you to store user-specific data in a back-end database.

Figure 16-1 gives an overview of these services and shows how they are related to your website and the underlying data stores that the services may use.

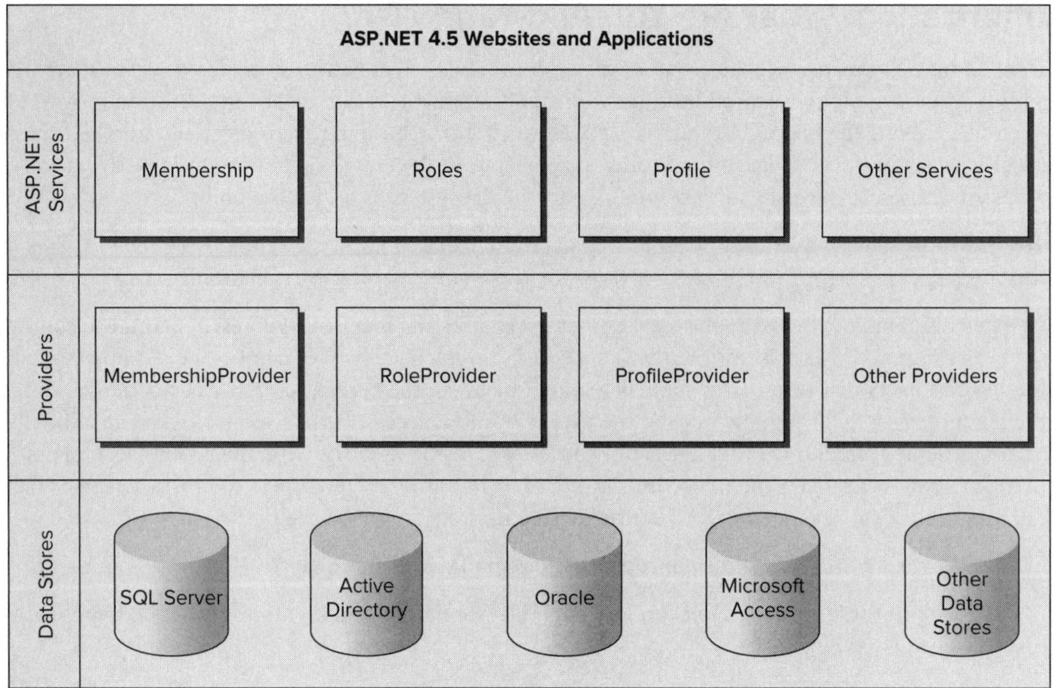

FIGURE 16-1

At the top of the diagram, you see the ASP.NET 4.5 websites and web applications that represent the websites that you build. These websites can contain controls like the login controls (discussed next) that in turn can talk to the ASP.NET application services such as membership and roles. To create a flexible solution, these services don't talk to an underlying data source directly, but instead talk to a configured *provider*. A provider is an interchangeable piece of software that is designed for a specific task. For example, in the case of the membership services, the Membership provider is designed to work with users in the underlying data store. You can configure different providers for the same application service depending on your needs. Previous versions of ASP.NET shipped with a SQL Server provider that enables your membership services to talk to a SQL Server database (both the Express and commercial editions) and an Active Directory provider (that lets you create and manage users in Active Directory on Windows). These providers are still available, but there is now a new alternative. In June 2011, Microsoft released the Universal Providers that work the same as the SQL Server providers, but can be used to target all editions of SQL Server, including SQL Server Compact and SQL Azure. This makes it easy to switch the underlying database, simply by changing the configuration for the application. The Universal Providers are available for .NET 4 and .NET 4.5 and are ideal for Internet-connected websites like `PlanetWrox.com`. If you create a new ASP.NET Web Forms site, the Universal Providers are already set up for you. If you create an empty ASP.NET website instead (as is the case with the Planet Wrox sample project), you need to add the providers yourself using NuGet, as you see in a later exercise.

The beauty of the provider model is that you can swap providers through configuration without any changes to your programming code. If you have your own custom data store, you could write your own provider and plug it into your website to replace one of the default providers with very little effort.

Each provider needs a data store — represented by the bottom part of the diagram in Figure 16-1 — and is written to work with one or more specific data stores. For example, the `DefaultMembershipProvider` (to handle membership services such as creating users, logging in, and resetting passwords) and the `DefaultRoleProvider` (to handle role-related tasks) are designed to work with any version of Microsoft SQL Server, including Express, LocalDB, SQL Server Compact, and SQL Azure. These two providers replace the `SqlMembershipProvider` and the `SqlRoleProvider` that shipped with earlier versions of ASP.NET.

In the remainder of this chapter, you see how to use the `DefaultMembershipProvider` and the `DefaultRoleProvider`. In the next chapter, you work with the `DefaultProfileProvider`. You can configure all three providers to use the same SQL Server database, making it easy to centralize all your user data.

Ideally, you don't deal with these providers directly. Under normal circumstances, the various providers are configured for your website at a central location. You then use these providers by talking to the application services. Although you could access these services directly from code, you often use the ASP.NET built-in login controls to do the hard work for you. These controls are discussed next.

INTRODUCING THE LOGIN CONTROLS

The login controls that ship with ASP.NET 4.5 take away much of the complexity usually associated with writing a security layer in a website. The available login controls effectively encapsulate all the code and logic you need to validate and manage users. These controls work by communicating with the configured provider through the application services, instead of talking to a database directly. To see how this works, the following exercise shows you how to create a simple Login and Sign Up page that enables new users to create an account and then log in. The section that follows then looks at the seven login controls that ship with ASP.NET 4.5.

TRY IT OUT Creating Login and Sign Up Pages

In this Try It Out, you extend the Login page that you created earlier. You also create a new page that enables a user to sign up for an account on the Planet Wrox website.

1. Open your website in VS and then open the Package Console Manager (choose Tools ➪ Library Package Manager ➪ Package Manager Console).

2. Enter the following command at the Package Manager Console prompt and press Enter:

```
Install-Package Microsoft.AspNet.Providers
```

By executing this package, VS downloads the providers, adds an assembly called `System.Web.Providers.dll` to the `Bin` folder of your site and adds configuration information for the providers to `Web.config`. When the command has completed, your Solution Explorer should look like Figure 16-2.

FIGURE 16-2

3. From the root of the site, open the `Login.aspx` page in Markup View. If you don't have that page, create it now, based on your custom template, and set its `Title` to **`Log in to Planet Wrox`**. Then add an `<h1>` element with the same text in the `cpMainContent` placeholder.

4. From the Login category of the Toolbox, drag a `LoginStatus` control and drop it in the page after the `<h1>` element.

5. Switch to Design View and from the Toolbox, drag a `Login` control and drop it on the `LoginStatus`, so it ends up right above it. Both controls are visible in Figure 16-3 (the `LoginStatus` appears as a small Login link below the `Login` control).

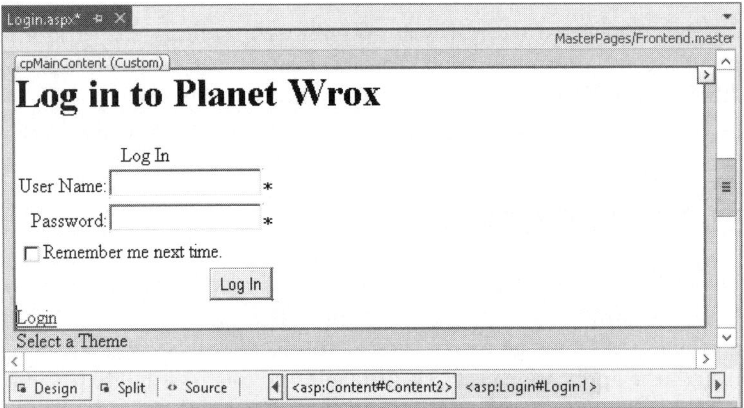

FIGURE 16-3

6. Open the Properties Grid for the `Login` control and set the two properties shown in the following table:

PROPERTY	VALUE
`CreateUserText`	Sign Up for a New Account at Planet Wrox
`CreateUserUrl`	`SignUp.aspx`

7. In the root of the website, create a new Web Form called `SignUp.aspx` based on your custom template and give it a `Title` of **`Sign Up for a New Account at Planet Wrox`**.

8. Switch the page to Design View and from the Toolbox, drag a `CreateUserWizard` control into the main content area for the page. Save and close the page.

9. Open the `Web.config` file from the root of the site and add an `<authentication>` element with its `mode` attribute set to `Forms` as a direct child of the `<system.web>` element.

```
<system.web>
  <authentication mode="Forms" />
  ...
</system.web>
```

10. Still in the Web.config file, take a look at the <connectionStrings> section. Notice how the NuGet package manager added a new connection string for you. You could leave this connection string in there, and everything would work. However, with this connection string, .NET creates a new database and attaches that to SQL Server. From a management perspective, it'll be easier if your user data is stored in the same database as your reviews, genres, pictures, and photo albums. This is quite easy to accomplish, though. First, remove the connection string called DefaultConnection that was added by the package manager. Next, replace the value for the connectionStringName attribute on all four providers (for Profile, Membership, Roles, and Session state) with the name of your Planet Wrox connection string (which should be called PlanetWroxConnectionString1). You should end up with configuration code that looks like the following. Note that I left out a lot of code and only show the code for the Membership provider to save some space. The important part is the connectionStringName attribute on all four providers that points to the Planet Wrox connection string.

```
<connectionStrings>
  <add name="PlanetWroxConnectionString1" connectionString="…
  <add name="PlanetWroxEntities" connectionString="…
</connectionStrings>

<system.web>
  ... Other code here
  <membership defaultProvider="DefaultMembershipProvider">
    <providers>
      <add name="DefaultMembershipProvider"
        ... Other attributes here
        connectionStringName="PlanetWroxConnectionString1"
        enablePasswordRetrieval="false" enablePasswordReset="true"
        .. Other attributes here
      />
    </providers>
  </membership>
  ... Other code here
</system.web>
```

11. Save all your changes, go back to Login.aspx, and press Ctrl+F5 to open that page in your browser. You are greeted with a login box, as shown in Figure 16-4.

    Note that the login status below the Login control is currently set to Login (as a call to action) to indicate you are not logged in yet. If the text says Logout instead, verify that you set authentication to Forms in the Web.config file. Otherwise, Windows authentication is used, which logs you in with your Windows account.

12. Try to log in by entering a random username and password. Obviously, this fails because the account doesn't exist. It may take a few seconds before you see the result because ASP.NET is busy setting up the membership database.

13. Follow the Sign Up link below the Login control to go to SignUp.aspx and then create an account by entering your personal details (see Figure 16-5). By default, the password needs to

have a minimum length of six characters. Note that the password is case sensitive. Write down the username and password you just entered, because you'll need this account information again later.

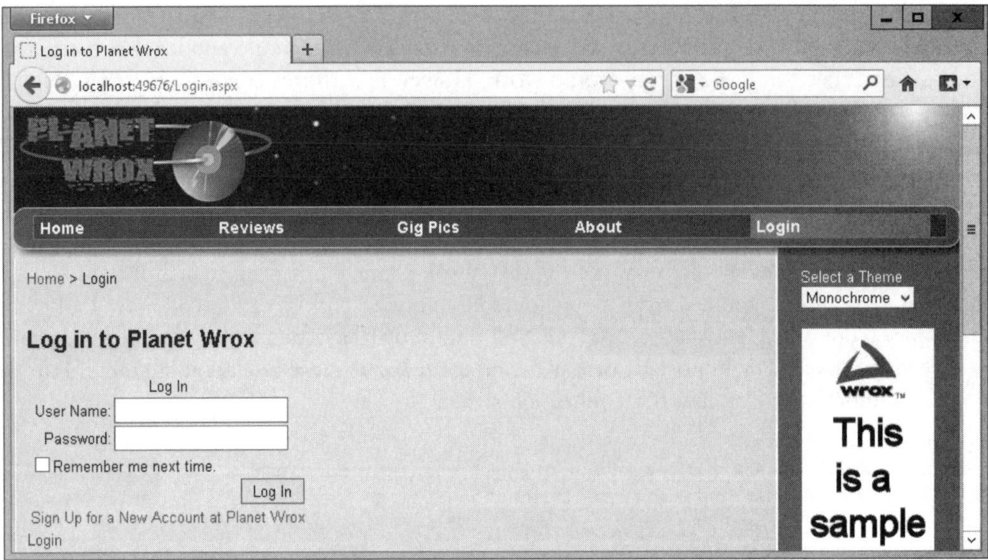

FIGURE 16-4

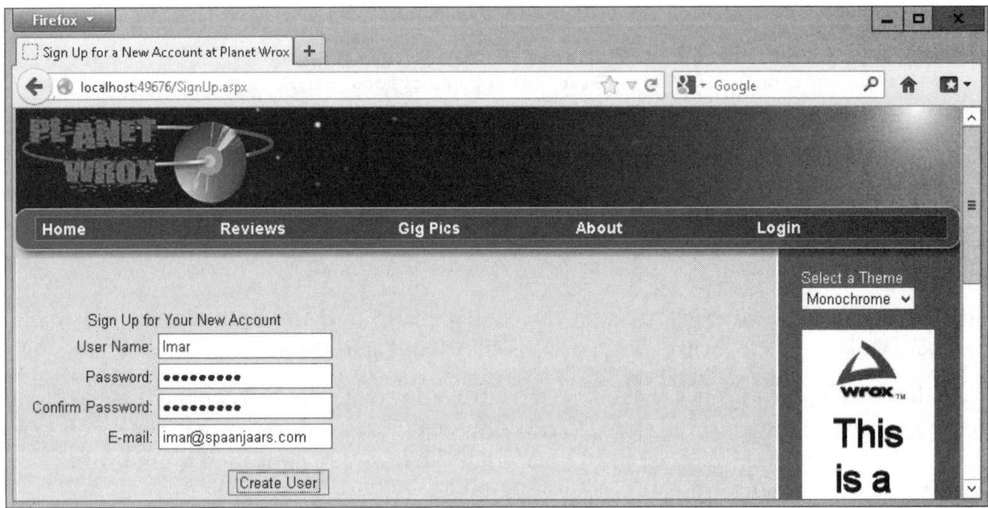

FIGURE 16-5

14. Click the Create User button to have the account created for you. When the page reloads, you get a confirmation that the account was created successfully. Click the Login item from the main `Menu` or `TreeView` (depending on the theme you currently have selected). You are taken to `Login.aspx` again where the LoginStatus control below the Login control now indicates that you are logged in (see Figure 16-6). When you create a new account using the CreateUserWizard, you're logged in automatically, although you can change that behavior by setting the LoginCreatedUser property of the control to false.

FIGURE 16-6

15. Click the Logout link and you are logged out, causing the LoginStatus to display the text Login again. In the Login control, enter the username and password you entered in step 13 and click the Log In button. You're logged in and redirected to the homepage. On the main Menu or TreeView, click Login to return to the Login page again. Note that the LoginStatus has changed and now shows Logout again, illustrating the fact that you successfully logged in.

    At this stage, being logged in doesn't add much value; all you see is the LoginStatus change from Login to Logout. However, later in this chapter you see how to offer different content to logged-in users.

How It Works

Besides adding and configuring a few ASP.NET Server Controls, you didn't do any coding in this exercise. Still, you were able to implement a fully functional login procedure that enables a user to sign up for an account and then log in to the site. So how does all this work? As you learned earlier, the ASP.NET controls talk to the configured application service providers; a software layer that sits between the login controls and the SQL Server database that keeps track of the users.

The very first time you try to log in (or use other login controls that require database access), the provider checks if your application is using a database with the necessary database objects, such as tables. By default, it checks the database by looking at a connection string pointed to by the connectionStringName attribute on the configured Membership provider. If the database from the connection string doesn't exist, or it doesn't contain the necessary tables, .NET executes a SQL script to prepare the database for you. That is why there was a delay when you entered the username and password in step 12. To find out what the database looks like, go back to VS, expand the App_Data folder, and then double-click your PlanetWrox.mdf database. This opens the Database Explorer and shows your database. Expand the Tables node to see which database objects have been added for you, as shown in Figure 16-7.

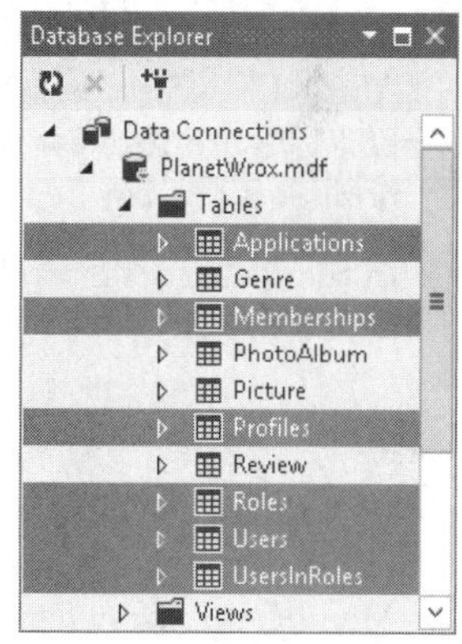

FIGURE 16-7

After this database has been created successfully, the login controls can use it. For example, when you create a new account using the CreateUserWizard control, records are inserted in the Memberships and Users tables. Similarly, when you try to log in, your username and password are checked against these tables.

To force the ASP.NET run time to use forms-based authentication (which the configured Membership provider uses under the hood), you need to set the mode attribute of the authentication element to Forms in the Web.config file:

```
<authentication mode="Forms" />
```

Other options for the `mode` attribute include `Windows` (where security is handled by Windows itself) and `None`, which disables security altogether. In the remainder of this book, the `Forms` option is used exclusively because it's the most common solution for Internet-facing web applications.

The Remember Me Next Time option of the `Login` control is more forgetful than you may think. When you check this option, you are logged in automatically the next time you visit the site, provided your authentication cookie hasn't expired. The first time you log in, the server sets a cookie that is saved for future sessions. However, this cookie expires after 30 minutes, which means a user returning to the site after that period needs to reauthenticate. To extend the period that users remain logged in, you need to set the `timeout` attribute of the `<forms>` element (which itself is a direct child of the `<authentication>` element) in `Web.config`. The `timeout` takes an integer value representing the timeout period in minutes. The following code sets the timeout to 24 hours (1440 minutes):

```
<authentication mode="Forms">
  <forms timeout="1440" />
</authentication>
```

Lower `timeout` values are generally considered safer because they don't provide unlimited or long-lasting access, but longer `timeout` values are more user friendly because users don't need to reauthenticate every time they visit the site.

If you hadn't reconfigured the providers to use the Planet Wrox database, .NET would have created a new one for you.

Now that you have seen how the login controls work in conjunction with the auto-generated SQL Server Express database, it's time to look at the controls in the Login category of the Toolbox in more detail.

The Login Controls

ASP.NET 4.5 ships with seven login controls, each serving a distinct purpose. Figure 16-8 shows the Toolbox with the seven login controls (the pointer is present in all Toolbox categories and is not a login control).

In the sections that follow, each of these controls is explained in more detail.

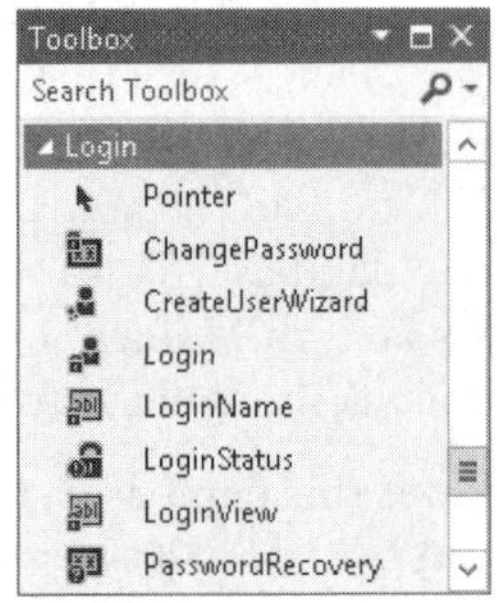

FIGURE 16-8

Login

As you saw in the previous exercise, the `Login` control enables a user to log in to the site. Under the hood, the control talks to the configured Membership provider through the application services to see if the username and password represent a valid user in the system. If the user is validated, a cookie is issued that is sent to the user's browser. On subsequent requests, the browser resubmits the cookie to the server so the system knows it's still dealing with a valid user. The different settings for the Membership provider are all configured in the `<membership />` element of the `Web.config` file. You learn more about this element later in this chapter.

To create a fully functional Login page, you need only the following control declaration:

```
<asp:Login ID="Login1" runat="server" />
```

However, in most situations you want to enhance the appearance and behavior of the control by setting one or more of the properties, shown in the following table.

PROPERTY	DESCRIPTION
DestinationPageUrl	Defines the URL the user is sent to after a successful login attempt. When you leave this property empty, the value is taken from the defaultUrl attribute of the <forms> element in Web.config which defaults to Default.aspx.
CreateUserText	Controls the text that is displayed to invite users to sign up for a new account. If you leave this property empty, the sign up link is not shown.
CreateUserUrl	Controls the URL where users are taken to sign up for a new account.
DisplayRememberMe	Specifies whether the control displays the Remember Me option. When set to False, the check box for this option is not shown.
RememberMeSet	Specifies whether the Remember Me option is initially checked.
PasswordRecoveryText	Controls the text of a link that is displayed to tell users they can reset or recover their password. If you leave this property empty, the link is not shown.
PasswordRecoveryUrl	Specifies the URL where users are taken to get their (new) password.
VisibleWhenLoggedIn	Determines whether the control is visible when the current user is logged in. True by default.

The authentication mechanism of ASP.NET by default assumes you have a page called Login.aspx in the root of your site that is used to let users log in. To be functional, the minimum that this page requires is a Login control. If you want to use a different page, you can specify its path in the <forms /> element under <authentication /> like this:

```
<authentication mode="Forms">
  <forms loginUrl="~/Account/MyLoginPage.aspx" />
</authentication>
```

With this configuration, you tell the ASP.NET run time to load the MyLoginPage.aspx page from the Account folder in the site's root whenever a user needs to present her credentials. Note that on the Login page (configured in the loginUrl), the VisibleWhenLoggedIn property of the Login control has no effect. On the configured Login page, the Login control is always visible. If you want to hide it you can use a LoginView control, as you see in a later exercise.

In addition to these properties, the Login control has a range of Text properties, such as LoginButtonText, RememberMeText, TitleText, and UserNameLabelText, that are used to set the text that appears in the control and in its various child controls like the `Button` and `Label` controls that make up the user interface.

Just as with the data-bound controls, the login controls have numerous style properties that enable you to tweak their appearance. You're encouraged to check out the Styles category of the Properties Grid for the controls to see how you can set the various styling options. Remember, just as with the data-bound controls, you can move much of the styling information to skin and CSS files.

The `Login` control also exposes a few events that you typically don't need to handle, but that can come in handy from time to time. For example, the `LoggedIn` event fires right after the user has logged in and is a good place to send the user to another page dynamically if the `DestinationPageUrl` is not flexible enough.

LoginView

The `LoginView` is a handy control that lets you display different data to different users. It enables you to differentiate between anonymous and logged-in users, and you can even differentiate between users in different roles. The `LoginView` is template-driven and as such lets you define different templates that are shown to different users. The following table describes the two main templates and the special `RoleGroups` element.

TEMPLATE	DESCRIPTION
`AnonymousTemplate`	The content in this template is shown to unauthenticated users only.
`LoggedInTemplate`	The content in this template is shown to logged-in users only. This template is mutually exclusive with the `AnonymousTemplate`. Only one of the two can be visible at any time.
`RoleGroups`	This control can contain one or more `RoleGroup` elements that, in turn, contain a `ContentTemplate` element that defines the content for the specified role. The role or roles that are allowed to see the content are defined in the `Roles` attribute, which takes a comma-separated list of roles. The `RoleGroups` element is mutually exclusive with the `LoggedInTemplate`. That means that if a user is a member of one of the roles for the `RoleGroup`, the content in the `LoggedInTemplate` is not visible. Additionally, only content for the first `RoleGroup` that matches the user's roles is shown.

The `LoginView` control itself doesn't output any markup other than the content you define in the various child elements of the control, which means you can easily embed it between a pair of HTML tags like `<h1>`and `<li>` to create customized headings or list items.

The following code snippet shows a `LoginView` control that defines content for three different users: anonymous visitors to the site, logged-in users, and users that have logged in *and* are members of the Managers role:

```
<asp:LoginView ID="LoginView1" runat="server">
  <AnonymousTemplate>
    Hi there visitor. Would you be interested in signing up for an account?
```

```
      </AnonymousTemplate>
      <LoggedInTemplate>
        Hi there visitor and welcome back to PlanetWrox.com.
      </LoggedInTemplate>
      <RoleGroups>
        <asp:RoleGroup Roles="Managers">
          <ContentTemplate>
            Hi there manager. You can proceed to the Management section.
          </ContentTemplate>
        </asp:RoleGroup>
      </RoleGroups>
    </asp:LoginView>
```

You see how to create and configure roles later in this chapter.

LoginStatus

As demonstrated in the previous Try It Out exercise, the `LoginStatus` control provides information about the current status of the user. It provides a Login link when the user is not authenticated and a Logout link when the user is already logged in. You control the actual text being displayed by setting the `LoginText` and `LogoutText` properties. Alternatively, you can set the `LoginImageUrl` and `LogoutImageUrl` properties to display an image instead of text. When you set both an image and a text, the image is shown and the text is used as the alternative text for the image. Finally, you can set the `LogoutAction` property to determine whether the current page refreshes if the user logs out, or whether the user is taken to another page after logging out. You determine this destination page by setting the `LogoutPageUrl`.

Besides these properties, the control is capable of raising two events, `LoggingOut` and `LoggedOut`, which fire right before and after the user is logged out.

LoginName

`LoginName` is an extremely simple control. All it does is display the name of the logged-in user. To embed the user's name in some text, such as `You are logged in as Imar`, you can use the `FormatString` property. If you include `{0}` in this format string, it will be replaced with the user's name.

You see how this works in the next exercise, which has you modify the login and master pages for the site so they display relevant information about the user.

TRY IT OUT Working with the Login Controls

In this Try It Out, you hide the `Login` control on the `Login.aspx` page when the user is already logged in and display a message instead. Additionally, you add text to the footer of the page that displays the name of the user together with an option to log out again.

1. Open `Login.aspx` and switch to Design View. From the Login category of the Toolbox, drag a new `LoginView` control on top of the `Login` control so it's placed right above it in the page.
2. Open the Smart Tasks panel of the `LoginView` control and make sure that `AnonymousTemplate` is selected in the Views drop-down list, visible in Figure 16-9.

Any content you put in the control is placed in the `AnonymousTemplate` area, because that is now the active template for the control in Design View.

FIGURE 16-9

3. Click the `Login` control once to select it and then press Ctrl+X to cut it to the clipboard. Click inside the small white rectangle that represents the `LoginView` to position your cursor in the control, and then press Ctrl+V to paste the `Login` control into your `LoginView`.
4. Open the Smart Tasks panel of the `LoginView` again and switch to the `LoggedInTemplate` using the Views drop-down list. Click inside the small white rectangle of the control again and type the text **`You are already logged in.`**
5. Switch to Markup View and look at the code. The `Login` control should be placed inside the `AnonymousTemplate`, and the text you typed should be displayed within the `LoggedInTemplate` tags:

```
<asp:LoginView ID="LoginView1" runat="server">
  <AnonymousTemplate>
    <asp:Login ID="Login1" runat="server" CreateUserUrl="SignUp.aspx"
             CreateUserText="Sign Up for a New Account at Planet Wrox">
    </asp:Login>
  </AnonymousTemplate>
  <LoggedInTemplate>
    You are already logged in.
  </LoggedInTemplate>
</asp:LoginView>
```

6. Save and close the page because you're done with it for now.
7. Open the master page `Frontend.master` in Markup View and locate the `<footer>` element at the bottom of the page. Remove the text `Footer Goes Here` and replace it with a new `LoginName` control by dragging it from the Toolbox into the `<footer>` element. Set its `FormatString` property to `Logged in as {0}` by typing in the code directly:

```
<asp:LoginName ID="LoginName1" runat="server" FormatString="Logged in as {0}" />
```

8. From the Toolbox, drag a new `LoginView` control and drop it below the `LoginName` control, but still in the `<footer>` element. Switch to Design View, and on the Smart Tasks panel of the `LoginView`, choose `LoggedInTemplate` from the Views drop-down list. Then in the white rectangle for the active `LoggedInTemplate`, drag and drop a new `LoginStatus` control.
9. Switch to Markup View again and wrap the code for the `LoginStatus` in a pair of parentheses. You should end up with the following code:

```
<footer>
  <asp:LoginName ID="LoginName1" runat="server" FormatString="Logged in as {0}" />
  <asp:LoginView ID="LoginView1" runat="server">
    <LoggedInTemplate>
      (<asp:LoginStatus ID="LoginStatus1" runat="server" />)
```

```
    </LoggedInTemplate>
  </asp:LoginView>
</footer>
```

10. Save all your changes and request `Login.aspx` in your browser. Log in with the account and password you created in a previous exercise (you may need to log out first by clicking the Logout link). If you don't recall the username and password, simply click the Sign Up link to create a new account. Note that as soon as you are logged in, the footer displays the text visible in Figure 16-10.

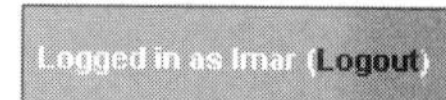

FIGURE 16-10

11. Click the Login item in the `Menu` or `TreeView` to go to the Login page. Instead of the `Login` control you should now see a message indicating that you are already logged in.
12. Click the Logout link in the footer at the bottom of the page. The page refreshes and displays the `Login` control again. Additionally, the text from the footer has now disappeared.

How It Works

You started by adding a `LoginView` to the Login page to wrap the `Login` control and a text message. The `Login` control is shown when the user is not logged in, whereas the text is displayed for logged-in users only.

The code in the footer of the master page contains a `LoginName` control that displays the name of the user that is logged in. It doesn't display anything for anonymous users. To control the text being displayed, you use the `FormatString` property:

```
<asp:LoginName ID="LoginName1" runat="server" FormatString="Logged in as {0}" />
```

At run time, the `{0}` is replaced with the user's name.

By default, the `LoginStatus` you added displays a link to enable users to log in and log out. Because the `Menu` or the `TreeView` already contains a link to the Login page, the footer uses a `LoginView` again to display the Logout text only when the user is currently logged in. If you want to add a Login link as well, you can extend the `LoginView` with an anonymous template and an additional `LoginStatus` or remove the entire `LoginView` so the `LoginStatus` is visible to all users.

In addition to the controls you have seen that enable a user to log in and that use the current user's log-in status to show or hide relevant content, the Login category of the Toolbox contains three more controls that enable users to sign up for a new account on the site, to change an existing password, and to recover a lost password. These controls are discussed next.

CreateUserWizard

You briefly saw `CreateUserWizard` at work in an earlier exercise. But the control has a lot more to offer than the standard behavior you saw in that exercise.

To start with, the control has a long list of `Text` properties, such as `CancelButtonText`, `CompleteSuccessText`, `UserNameLabelText`, and `CreateUserButtonText`, that affect the text used in the control. All properties have good (English) defaults, but you can change them if they don't suit your needs.

The control has a bunch of properties that end in `ImageUrl`, such as `CreateUserButtonImageUrl`. These properties enable you to define images for various user actions instead of the default buttons that the control generates. If you set any of these properties to a valid `ImageUrl`, you also need to set the corresponding `ButtonType`. For example, to change the Create User button to an image, you need to set the `CreateUserButtonImageUrl` to a valid image and set `CreateUserButtonType` to `Image`.

The default value for the `ButtonType` is `Button`, which renders standard buttons by default. You can also set the `ButtonType` to `Link` to have them rendered as standard `LinkButton` controls. The associated text properties introduced at the beginning of this section are displayed on the buttons and the links.

Additionally, the control exposes a number of useful properties that you can set to change its behavior and appearance, shown in the following table.

PROPERTY	DESCRIPTION
`ContinueDestinationPageUrl`	Defines the page where users are taken when they click Continue after signing up.
`DisableCreatedUser`	Determines whether or not the user is marked as disabled when the account is created. When set to `True`, users cannot log in to the site until their account has been enabled. You see how to activate and deactivate user accounts manually later. Defaults to `False`.
`LoginCreatedUser`	Determines whether or not the user is logged in automatically after the account has been created. Defaults to `True`.
`RequireEmail`	Determines whether or not the control asks the user for an e-mail address. Defaults to `True`.
`MailDefinition`	Contains a number of subproperties that enable you to define the (optional) e-mail that gets sent to users after they sign up.

You may notice that the control doesn't have any properties to change the password policy that requires users to type a password of at least six characters. Because multiple controls need access to these settings, you need to configure them on the underlying provider. In the section "Configuring Your Web Application" later in this chapter, you see how this works.

The `CreateUserWizard` control is able to send a confirmation e-mail to users to inform them their new account was created successfully. This e-mail message can also serve as a reminder of their usernames and passwords. In the following exercise, you see how to configure the `MailDefinition` element so the `CreateUserWizard` sends an e-mail message to new users to confirm their account, and sends them their username and password for future reference.

TRY IT OUT Sending Confirmation E-Mail with CreateUserWizard

For this exercise to work, you need to have configured the `<system.net>` element of the `Web.config` file with a valid mail server name or local pickup folder. Refer to Chapter 9 if you don't have these settings and don't know how to configure them.

1. Add a new Text File to the `App_Data` folder and call it `SignUpConfirmation.txt`.
2. Add the following text to the file and then save and close it:

```
Hi <% UserName %>,

Thank you for signing up for a new account at www.PlanetWrox.com.

To log in to the site, use the following details:

User name:       <% UserName %>
Your password:   <% Password %>

We look forward to your contributions.

The Planet Wrox Team
```

   Take care when typing the `UserName` and `Password` placeholders. They are wrapped in a pair of server-side tags (`<%` and `%>`), which are used to give special meaning to these placeholders.

3. Open `SignUp.aspx` and on the Properties Grid of the `CreateUserWizard` control, locate the `MailDefinition` property and expand it. Click the `BodyFileName` property, click the ellipsis to browse for a file, and then select `SignUpConfirmation.txt`, which you created in the `App_Data` folder.
4. Set the `Subject` property to **`Your New Account at PlanetWrox.com`**. When you're done, the Properties Grid should look like Figure 16-11.

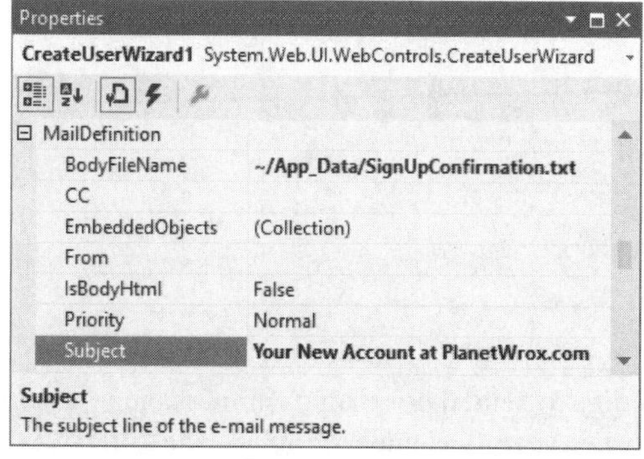

FIGURE 16-11

5. Save all changes and request `SignUp.aspx` in your browser. Enter the required details for a new account and click Create User to sign up for an account. If you get an error about specifying a From address, make sure you assigned a valid e-mail address to the `from` attribute in the `Web.config` file:

```
<smtp deliveryMethod="SpecifiedPickupDirectory" from="planetwrox@example.com">
```

   Refer to Chapter 9 to see how to add this attribute. Make sure you enter a valid e-mail address or the mail server may still reject it.

6. After a while, you should receive an e-mail that contains the welcome text you typed in step 2. Figure 16-12 shows the message with the `UserName` and `Password` placeholders replaced with the details that you entered in step 5.

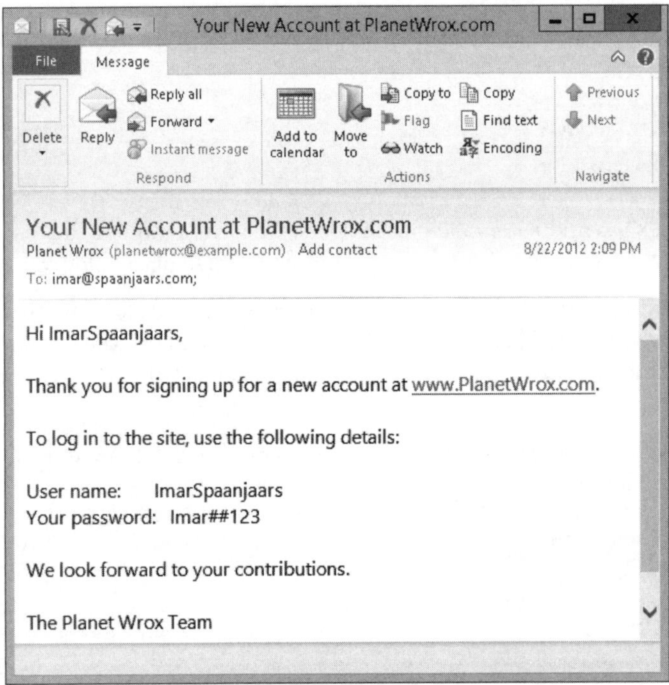

FIGURE 16-12

How It Works

The `CreateUserWizard` comes with built-in functionality to send a confirmation message to the user. It doesn't send the message until you specify the `<MailDefinition>` element. You use the `BodyFileName` property to point to a text file or an HTML file that is used as the e-mail's body.

Within this body, you can use the special placeholders `<% UserName %>` and `<% Password %>`, which are replaced automatically with the actual username and password that the user entered in the signup form.

> **NOTE** *It would be a nice addition if you could check whether a given user name already existed before the user tried to submit the form. You can use the techniques from previous chapters to accomplish this easily. For example, you could use a page method at the server to check whether a given name was already taken. You could then call this page method with some JavaScript as soon as the user moves away from the User Name field. For a step-by-step guide of this solution, take a look at this article on my website:* `http://bit.ly/Ldgr2j`.

The `PasswordRecovery` control, discussed next, also supports a custom mail body and enables you to send the message manually in a handler for the `SendingMail` event.

PasswordRecovery

The `PasswordRecovery` control enables users to retrieve their existing passwords (when the system supports it) or to get a new auto-generated password. In both cases, the password is sent to the e-mail address that the user entered when signing up for an account.

Most of the properties of the `PasswordRecovery` control should be familiar by now. It has a number of `Text` properties, such as `GeneralFailureText` (shown when the password could not be recovered) and `SuccessText`, that enable you to set the text that is displayed by the control. It also has properties that end with `ButtonType`, `ButtonText`, and `ButtonImageUrl`, which enable you to change the look and behavior of the various action buttons of the control. You set the `SuccessPageUrl` to a page in your site if you want to send the user to another page when password recovery succeeds.

As with the `CreateUserWizard`, the `PasswordRecovery` control also has a `MailDefinition` element that can point to a file that you want to send as the mail body. You can use the same placeholders for the username and password to customize the message. If you leave out the `MailDefinition`, the control uses a default mail body, as you see in the next exercise.

ChangePassword

The `ChangePassword` control enables existing and logged-in users to change their passwords. It has a host of properties to change things like text, error messages, and buttons, similar to the `CreateUserWizard` and `PasswordRecovery` controls. It also has a `MailDefinition` element that enables you to send a confirmation of the new password to the user's e-mail address. You see how to use this control in the next exercise.

TRY IT OUT Implementing the Password Functionality

In this Try It Out, you add `PasswordRecovery` and `ChangePassword` controls to the website to enable users to change and recover their passwords. Because changing a password makes sense only for logged-in users, you add the `ChangePassword` control to its own page. In the next chapter, you protect this page so only authenticated users can access it.

1. Open up `Login.aspx` in Markup View and locate the closing `</asp:Login>` tag inside the `<AnonymousTemplate>`. Right after it, type two `<br />` elements (use the `br` code snippet and press Tab to complete the element) to create some room below the `Login` control.

2. Drag a `PasswordRecovery` control from the Toolbox into the code editor, right after the two `<br />` elements you added in step 1.

3. Between the opening and closing tags of the `PasswordRecovery` control, add a `<MailDefinition>` element and then set the `Subject` of the e-mail to **`Your New Password for PlanetWrox.com`**. Your code should now look like this:

```
</asp:Login>
<br />
<br />
<asp:PasswordRecovery ID="PasswordRecovery1" runat="server">
  <MailDefinition Subject="Your New Password for PlanetWrox.com"></MailDefinition>
</asp:PasswordRecovery>
```

4. Save your changes and close the file.

5. In the root of your site, create a new Web Form based on your custom template and call it `MyProfile.aspx`. Set the `Title` of the page to **`My Profile`**.

6. Make sure you're in Markup View and in the `cpMainContent` content placeholder, create an `<h1>` element (type `h1` followed by the Tab key) with its contents set to **`My Profile`**. Right below the heading, type some text that explains that the My Profile page is used for things like changing passwords. Wrap the text in a pair of `<p>` tags to denote a paragraph.

7. Drag a `ChangePassword` control from the Toolbox and drop it after the closing `</p>` tag. You should end up with something like this:

```
<asp:Content ID="Content2" ContentPlaceHolderID="cpMainContent" runat="Server">
  <h1>My Profile</h1>
  <p>The My Profile page allows you to make changes to your personal profile.
      For now, all you can do is change your password below.</p>
  <asp:ChangePassword ID="ChangePassword1" runat="server"></asp:ChangePassword>
```

8. Open the `Web.sitemap` file from the Solution Explorer and add a new element in the About section. Let the `url` point to `~/MyProfile.aspx` and set the `title` and `description` to **`My Profile`**. You should end up with this code:

```
<siteMapNode url="~/About/Default.aspx" title="About"
             description="About this site">
  <siteMapNode url="~/About/Contact.aspx" title="Contact Us"
               description="Contact Us" />
  <siteMapNode url="~/About/AboutUs.aspx" title="About Us"
               description="About Us" />
  <siteMapNode url="~/MyProfile.aspx" title="My Profile"
               description="My Profile" />
</siteMapNode>
```

9. Save all changes and close all open files. Right-click `Login.aspx` in the Solution Explorer and choose View in Browser. Below the `Login` control, you should now see the `PasswordRecovery` control, visible in Figure 16-13.

   Note that if you were already logged in, you need to click the Logout link first.

10. Enter your username in the `PasswordRecovery` control and click the Submit button. You should get an e-mail message with your new, auto-generated password.

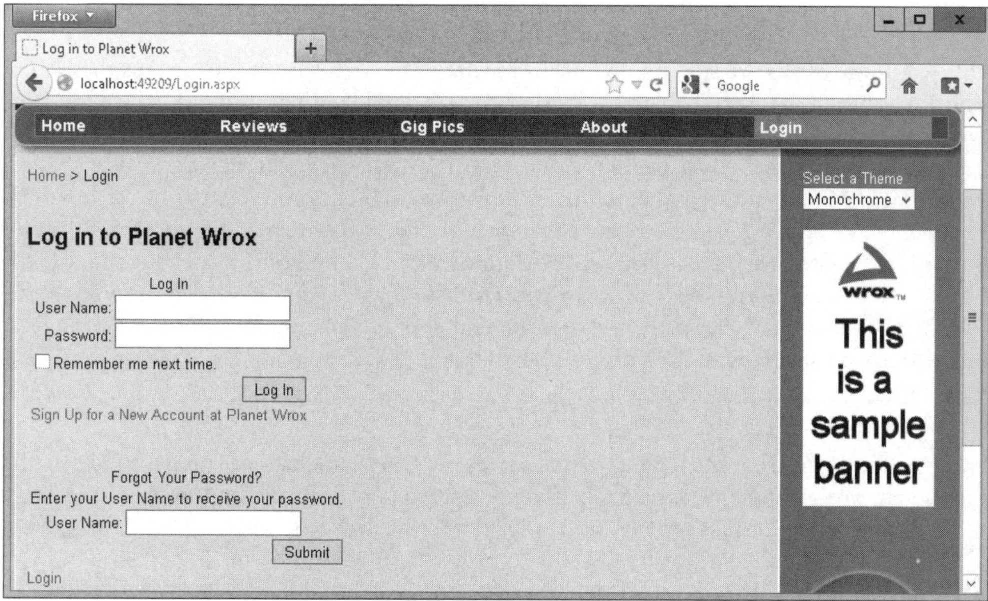

FIGURE 16-13

11. Use this new password to log in to the site. When you're logged in, choose About ➪ My Profile from the `Menu` or the `TreeView`. The `ChangePassword` control visible in Figure 16-14 appears.

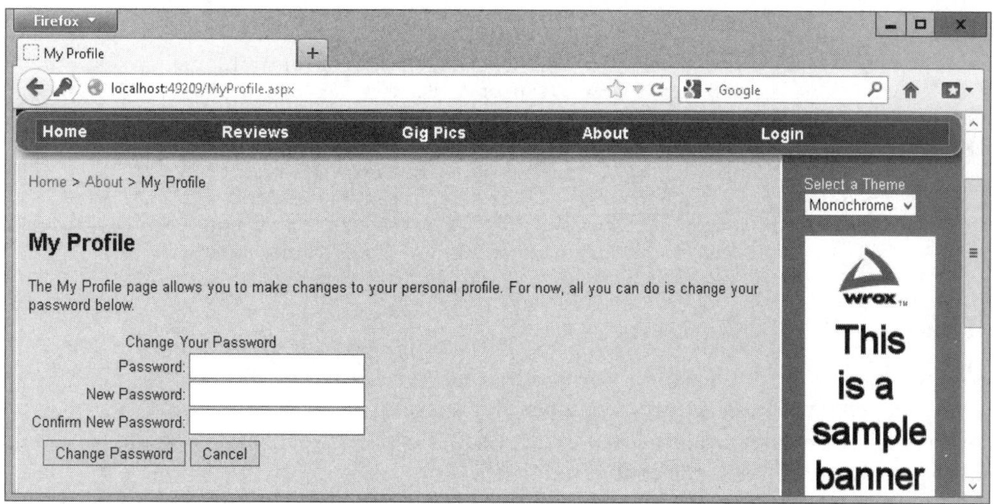

FIGURE 16-14

12. Enter the auto-generated password that was sent to you by e-mail, type a new password that is easier to remember, and then retype the same password. Finally, click Change Password. From now on, you can log in to the site using your new password.

How It Works

By default, your passwords are stored in a *hashed* format in the database, which means they cannot be retrieved. Hashing is an irreversible process that creates a unique fingerprint of your data. Because it's irreversible, there is no way to recreate the password from the hash, which makes it safer to store in a database. When you log in, the password you enter is also hashed and then the two hashes are compared to see if you are allowed to enter. Because the original password cannot be retrieved, the `PasswordRecovery` control generates a new password for you. It then sends this password to the e-mail address that is associated with the username you entered. As the mail body, it uses a standard template that contains the username and the new password. To customize the mail body, you can point the `BodyFileName` of the `MailDefinition` to a text file that contains placeholders for the username and password, just as you saw how to do with the `CreateUserWizard`.

You may have noticed that the login controls use a couple of defaults that you haven't been able to change so far. For example, you need to enter a password with a minimum length of six characters. You can change these settings for the entire application through the `Web.config` file.

Configuring Your Web Application

When you added the Universal Providers, NuGet added a number of configuration settings for the Membership, Roles, Profile, and Session state providers. Here's the code for the Membership provider:

```
<membership defaultProvider="DefaultMembershipProvider">
  <providers>
    <add name="DefaultMembershipProvider"
            type="System.Web.Providers.DefaultMembershipProvider,
            System.Web.Providers, Version=1.0.0.0, Culture=neutral,
            PublicKeyToken=31bf3856ad364e35"
        connectionStringName="PlanetWroxConnectionString1"
        enablePasswordRetrieval="false" enablePasswordReset="true"
        requiresQuestionAndAnswer="false" requiresUniqueEmail="false"
        maxInvalidPasswordAttempts="5" minRequiredPasswordLength="6"
        minRequiredNonalphanumericCharacters="0" passwordAttemptWindow="10"
        applicationName="/"
    />
  </providers>
</membership>
```

This provider configuration features a number of interesting attributes, which are described in the following table. The default values listed in the description column are applied when you don't specify the associated attribute in the configuration file.

ATTRIBUTE	DESCRIPTION
`connectionStringName`	Points to the name of the connection string for the application.
`enablePasswordRetrieval`	Determines whether users are able to retrieve their current password. This option cannot be set when `passwordFormat` is `Hashed` (see `passwordFormat`). Defaults to `false`.

ATTRIBUTE	DESCRIPTION
enablePasswordReset	Determines whether a user is able to request a new password. Defaults to true.
requiresQuestionAndAnswer	Determines whether controls like CreateUserWizard and PasswordRecovery have the user enter a security question and answer. Defaults to true.
applicationName	Provides the unique name of the application. Defaults to a forward slash (/), but you can change it to support multiple websites using the same database with different accounts.
requiresUniqueEmail	Determines whether the system allows duplicate e-mail addresses for user accounts. When set to true, each user must provide a unique username and a unique e-mail address. Defaults to true.
passwordFormat	Determines the way passwords are stored in the database. It supports the following formats: Clear — Passwords are stored as plain text. Encrypted — Passwords are encrypted in a reversible format that enables the system to retrieve the clear text representation of the password again. Hashed — Passwords are encrypted with an irreversible, one-way algorithm. When the passwordFormat is Hashed, users cannot retrieve their original passwords anymore. They can only request a new, auto-generated password. Defaults to Hashed.
maxInvalidPasswordAttempts	Specifies the number of times a user can enter an invalid password or invalid security answer before their account is locked. Defaults to 5.
minRequiredPasswordLength	Determines the minimum length of the password. Defaults to 7.
minRequiredNonalphanumericCharacters	Determines the minimum number of non-alphanumeric characters that must be included in the password. Defaults to 1.
passwordAttemptWindow	Determines the time frame in minutes during which invalid password attempts are counted. Defaults to 10.
passwordStrengthRegularExpression	Enables you to specify a custom regular expression to enforce a strong password.

Check out the complete list of configuration settings for Membership on the MSDN website at http://bit.ly/RFxQZT.

In the following Try It Out, you see what it takes to reconfigure the Membership provider for the Planet Wrox application by changing some of these attributes.

TRY IT OUT Configuring Membership

In this short exercise, you see how to override the default behavior for the Membership provider in the Planet Wrox site to require users to enter a longer and stronger password.

1. Open `Web.config` and locate the `<membership>` element.
2. Change `minRequiredPasswordLength` to `7`.
3. Change `minRequiredNonalphanumericCharacters` to `1`. When you're done, your configuration settings should look like this:

```
<membership defaultProvider="DefaultMembershipProvider">
  <providers>
    <add name="DefaultMembershipProvider"
            type="System.Web.Providers.DefaultMembershipProvider,
            System.Web.Providers, Version=1.0.0.0, Culture=neutral,
            PublicKeyToken=31bf3856ad364e35"
        connectionStringName="PlanetWroxConnectionString1"
        enablePasswordRetrieval="false" enablePasswordReset="true"
        requiresQuestionAndAnswer="false" requiresUniqueEmail="false"
        maxInvalidPasswordAttempts="5" minRequiredPasswordLength="7"
        minRequiredNonalphanumericCharacters="1" passwordAttemptWindow="10"
        applicationName="/"
    />
  </providers>
</membership>
```

4. Save all your changes and request `SignUp.aspx` in the browser.
5. Fill in the form, but for both password fields, type something short like `pass`.
6. Click the Create User button. Note that the control now forces you to enter a password with a minimum length of seven characters that contains at least one non-alphanumeric character. It displays an appropriate error message below the control, shown in Figure 16-15. Note that numbers are not considered non-alphanumeric characters, so you need to make sure your password contains at least one character like `#` or `$` or `*`. For example, `Pa55word` is not a valid password, but `Pass##Word` will be accepted. Also note that the password is case sensitive.

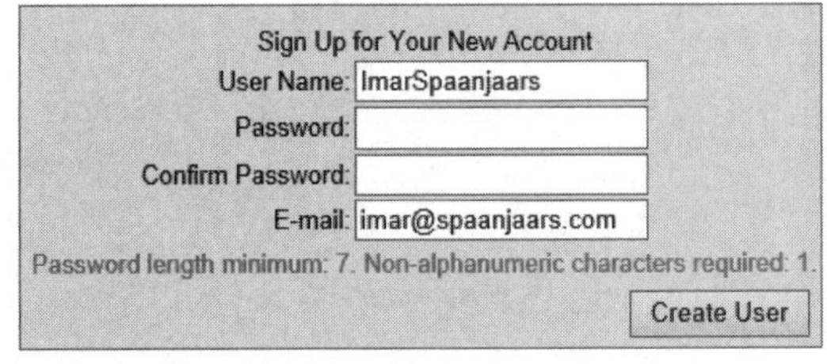

FIGURE 16-15

7. Enter a password of at least seven characters with at least one non-alphanumeric character like `#` or `%` and click the Create User button again. This time your password is accepted and the account is created.

How It Works

The `CreateUserWizard` uses the configured Membership provider under the hood to validate the data and create the user. The provider in turn consults the `Web.config` file for the configuration information such as the minimum password length. When you try to create the user, the provider enforces the rules set in `Web.config` and cancels the user creation process as soon as one of the rules is not fulfilled.

Having the configuration information in `Web.config` is especially useful when you deploy your application to a different server that uses a different database, because all you need to do is change the settings in this file. Chapter 19 and Appendix B show you how to do this.

So far, you have seen how to let users sign up for an account so they can log in. But how can you differentiate between the different users in the system? How can you block access to specific folders such as the `Management` folder for unauthorized users? You do this with the Role Manager, another application service that ships with ASP.NET.

THE ROLE MANAGER

Although it's nice that your users can now sign up and log in to your site, it would be a lot more useful if you could differentiate among your users. That would enable you to grant access rights to one or just a few users to access the `Management` folder so only they can change your reviews and genres. With the Role Manager that ships with ASP.NET, this is pretty easy to do. The Role Manager enables you to assign users to different roles. You can then use these roles to open or block specific functionality in your site. For example, you can block access to the `Management` folder for all users except for those in the Managers role. Additionally, you can display different content based on the roles users have with the `LoginView` as you saw earlier.

The Role Manager Configuration

As with membership, the settings for the Role Manager are placed in `Web.config` files. The default settings added by NuGet when you installed the Universal Providers look like this:

```
<roleManager defaultProvider="DefaultRoleProvider">
  <providers>
    <add name="DefaultRoleProvider"
      type="System.Web.Providers.DefaultRoleProvider, System.Web.Providers,
      Version=1.0.0.0, Culture=neutral, PublicKeyToken=31bf3856ad364e35"
      connectionStringName="PlanetWroxConnectionString1"
      applicationName="/"
    />
  </providers>
</roleManager>
```

The Role Manager is not enabled by default, and to enable it, you need to add an `enabled="true"` attribute to the `<roleManager />` element. In the next exercise, you see a way to enable the Role Manager through the Web Site Administration Tool (WSAT). Just like Membership, the Role Manager uses a provider under the hood.

Besides the settings shown here, the `<roleManager />` element also has a few attributes you can configure. Most of them are related to how the cookies with the role information are created and stored. For most cases, the default configuration should be fine, but check out the complete list of configuration settings for the Role Manager on the MSDN website at `http://bit.ly/LmtmB3` if you have the need to further configure the Role Manager.

With the Membership and Role Manager providers configured and the database created, it's time to manage the users and roles in your system. You have a few ways to accomplish that:

- Using the Web Site Administration Tool, generally referred to as the WSAT
- Using IIS (the Windows web server) on recent Windows editions (you see more about this in Chapter 19)
- Programmatically, using the Role Manager API (application programming interface)

Managing roles using the Role Manager API is beyond the scope of this book. If you want to learn more about it, get a copy of Wrox's *Professional ASP.NET 4.5 in C# and VB* (ISBN: 978-1-118-31182-0).

The Web Site Administration Tool is used for a lot more than managing roles alone, and is discussed in detail in the next section. It is only available from your local machine as a menu shortcut in VS. As such, it's great for setting up the initial users and roles during development, but it isn't suitable for managing users in a production environment.

Managing Users with the WSAT

The WSAT ships with VS and is available from the Website menu. The tool is used for the following tasks:

- Managing users
- Managing roles
- Managing access rules — for example, to determine what user can access which files and folders
- Configuring application, mail, and debug settings
- Taking the site offline so users can't request any pages and get a friendly error message instead

Some of the changes you make with the WSAT are persisted in the `Web.config` file for the application. Other settings, like users and roles, are stored in the database for the configured provider.

In the next exercise you see how to start and use the WSAT. You see how to create a new role and a new user, and how to assign that user to the role.

TRY IT OUT Using the WSAT to Manage User Accounts and Roles

To protect your `Management` folder from users that are not authorized to access it, you need to create a role that is allowed to access this folder. After you have set up this role, you can grant all users in that role access to the folder while keeping all other users out. In this Try It Out, you learn how to create the Managers role and assign a user to it. In a later exercise, you see how to limit access to the `Management` folder to Managers only.

1. From within VS, choose Website ➪ ASP.NET Configuration. Your browser opens and displays the Web Site Administration Tool, shown in Figure 16-16.

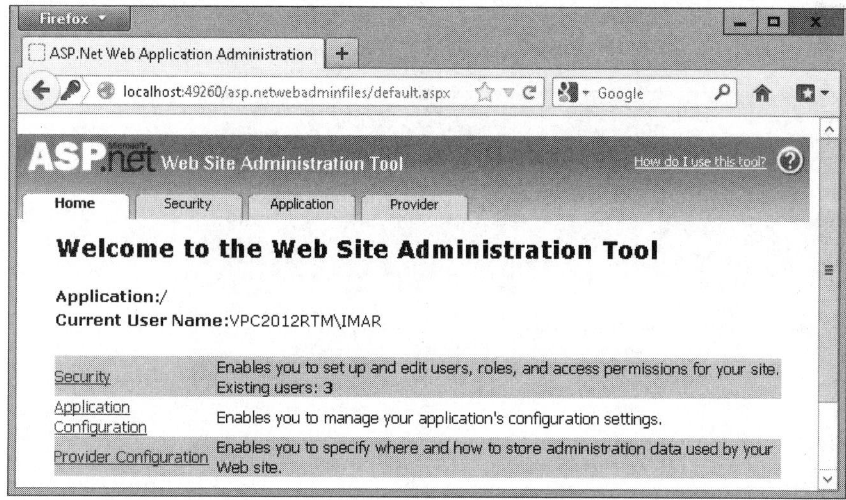

FIGURE 16-16

2. In the top-right corner, you see a Help link that takes you to a help file describing how you can use the tool. Right below the logo of the application, you see four tabs: Home, Security, Application, and Provider. The Home tab takes you back to the start page you see in Figure 16-16. You use the Application tab to configure different application settings, and the Provider tab enables you to reconfigure the chosen provider for the application. In this exercise, all that's important is the Security tab, so go ahead and click it. You should see the screen displayed in Figure 16-17.

   The bottom part of the screen is divided into three parts: Users, Roles, and Access Rules. You see how to use Users and Roles in this exercise. Access Rules is used to block or open up specific parts of your website to users or roles. You won't see how to use it in this chapter, but instead you learn how to change some of these settings in `Web.config` directly in a later exercise.

3. Make sure that under Users, you see the Create User and Manage Users links. If you don't see them, but you see a note about Windows authentication instead, click the Select Authentication Type link, select From the Internet, and click Done. Your screen should now look like Figure 16-17.

4. In the Roles section, click the Enable Roles link. The page reloads and now offers a link with the text Create or Manage Roles. Click that link to open the Create New Role page visible in Figure 16-18.

5. Enter **`Managers`** as the new role name and click the Add Role button. You should see the new role appear. Click the Back button at the bottom-right of the page to return to the main Security page.

6. Click the Create User link in the Users section. You're taken to a page that enables you to enter the details for a new user and assign that user to the Managers role at the same time. Type **`Manager`** as the username. As a password, enter something that meets the password rules you configured earlier. A password like `Manager##123` will do. Enter your e-mail address and then check the check box for the Managers role name in the list of roles on the right.

7. Click Create User to add the user to the system and then click Continue on the confirmation page. At the bottom of the page, click the Back button so you reach the main Security page.
8. On the Security page, click the Manage Users link. You are taken to a page that shows a list of all available users in the system, shown in Figure 16-19.

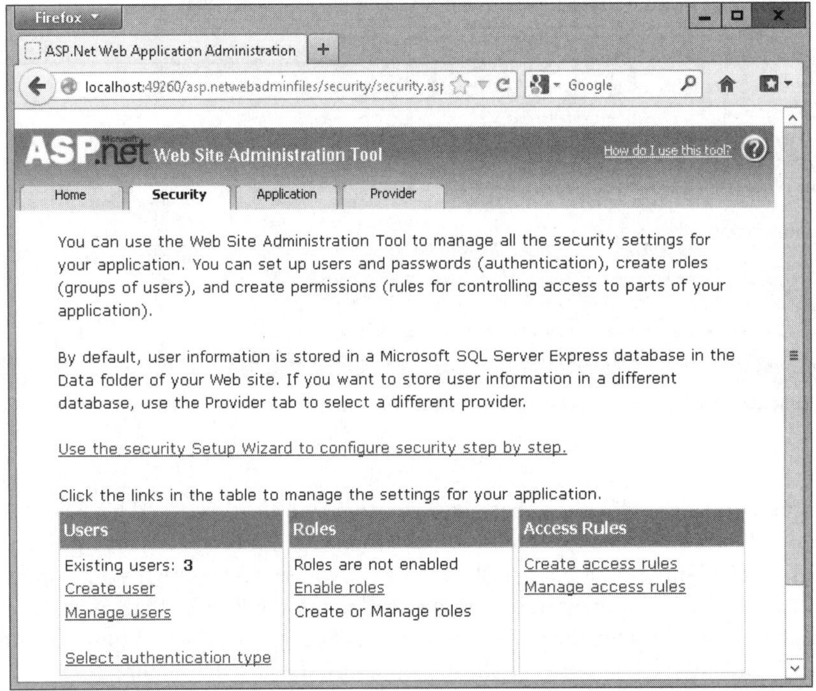

FIGURE 16-17

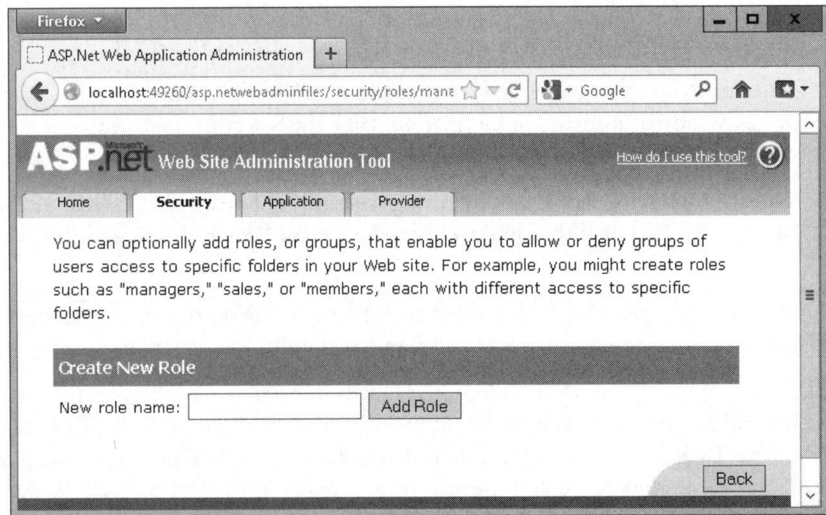

FIGURE 16-18

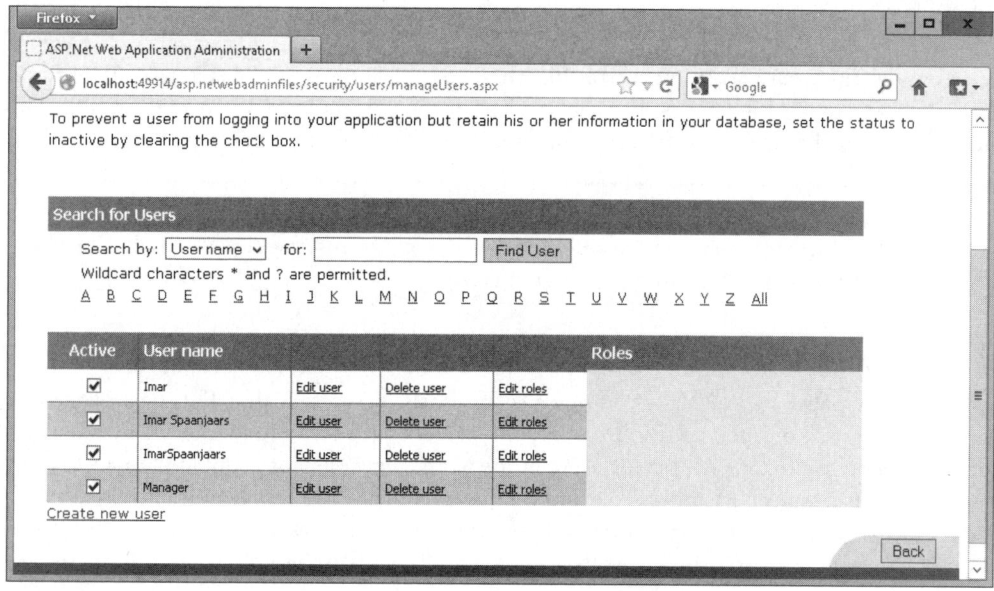

FIGURE 16-19

From here you can edit, enable, disable, or delete existing users. For example, if you previously set `DisableCreatedUser` to `True` in the `CreateUserWizard`, you can enable the user here by checking the check box in front of the username, visible in Figure 16-19. You can change the roles that are assigned to the user by clicking the Edit Roles link. Also, using the filter controls and the alphabet above the user list, you can quickly search for a specific user in case you're dealing with a lot of user accounts.

9. To see where your user and role ended up, close the browser and go back to VS. On the Solution Explorer, double-click the `PlanetWrox.mdf` database in the `App_Data` folder to open it in the Database Explorer window. Then expand the Tables node, right-click the `Roles` table, and choose Show Table Data. The role you created in step 5 should be listed. Open up some of the other tables such as `Memberships` and `UsersInRoles` and inspect the data they contain. In the first table, you should see the user account you created in steps 6 and 7, and the latter table contains a relationship between the new role and user account.

How It Works

Just like the login controls, the WSAT eventually talks to the provider you configured in the `Web.config` file. In the case of the Planet Wrox application, it means it talks to the `DefaultMembershipProvider` and the `DefaultRoleProvider`, which in turn talk to a SQL Server Express LocalDB database identified by your connection string. The users and roles you create are stored in various tables in the database. Users that you create using the WSAT end up in the exact same location as those created with the `CreateUserWizard` control. In fact, the WSAT uses a `CreateUserWizard` to create new user accounts. This means that any user you enter in the WSAT is able to log in using your standard `Login.aspx` page. In a later exercise, you use the Manager account you created in this exercise to log in to the site and access the `Management` folder.

To use the role you created in this exercise, you have a few options at your disposal. First, you can use the role name to block access to specific folders in your web application through settings in the `Web.config` file. Secondly, you can use the role in controls like the `LoginView` to present different content to different users. Finally, you can use the Role API to check whether the current user is in a specific role. This gives you fine control over the content or functionality you can offer to certain privileged users.

You see how to block access to the `Management` folder and modify the `LoginView` in the next section; using the Role API is discussed in a later exercise.

Configuring the Web Application to Work with Roles

On the Security page of the WSAT, you saw a section called Access Rules. This part of the tool enables you to block or open up resources in your site. It enables you to define rules such as "This folder is blocked for anyone except for users in the Managers role," or "Anyone can access this file, except for the users in the Members role and the Joe account." The tool is quite intuitive to use, so it isn't difficult to set up the different rules. However, it has one downside: it stores the security settings in separate `Web.config` files, one for each subfolder you configure.

This makes it somewhat difficult to get an overview of all the different security settings. Fortunately, ASP.NET also enables you to configure the same settings in the main `Web.config` using `<location>` elements. A `<location>` element has a `path` attribute that points to a file or folder you want to configure differently. You can use the `<location>` element for many (but not all) other settings from `Web.config` as well (for example, you could set the `theme` attribute of the `<pages>` element for the `Management` folder in the main `Web.config`). For the following exercise, you only set the child elements of `<location>` to those related to security.

TRY IT OUT Blocking Access to the Management Folder

Obviously, you don't want just anyone to mess with the reviews and genres that you have posted on your website. Therefore, it's important to block access to the `Management` folder to anyone except site managers assigned to the Managers role. In this exercise, you see how to modify `Web.config` to block the folder so only the user account you assigned to the Managers role earlier can access this folder and the files it contains.

1. Open the `Web.config` file at the root of the site. Scroll all the way down to the closing `</configuration>` tag and right *before* it type a `<location>` element. Add a `path` attribute to the element and set its value to **`Management`**. Note that IntelliSense kicks in to help you complete the element and find the attribute. Complete the configuration by entering the following settings:

```
  <location path="Management">
    <system.web>
      <authorization>
        <allow roles="Managers" />
        <deny users="*" />
      </authorization>
    </system.web>
  </location>
</configuration>
```

2. Save and close the `Web.config` file.

3. Open the main master page for the site (`Frontend.master`) in Design View and scroll down to the end of the file. Select the `LoginView` control and open its Smart Tasks panel. At the top of the panel, click the Edit RoleGroups link, shown in Figure 16-20.

FIGURE 16-20

4. In the dialog box that opens, click the Add button to insert a new `RoleGroup` and then set the `Roles` property of this group to `Managers`, as shown in Figure 16-21.

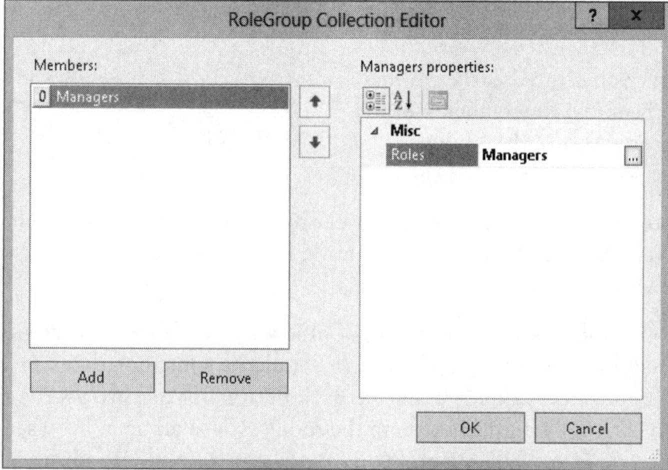

FIGURE 16-21

5. Click OK to insert the `RoleGroup` and return to Design View.

6. Still on the Smart Tasks panel of the `LoginView`, choose `RoleGroup[0] - Managers` from the Views drop-down list. This switches the current template of the control to the `RoleGroup` for Managers, so you can add content that is visible only to Managers.

7. From the Standard category of the Toolbox, drag a `HyperLink` control and drop it into the `LoginView`. Using the Properties Grid, set the `Text` property of this `HyperLink` to **`Manage Site`** and set the `NavigateUrl` to `~/Management/Default.aspx`. (You can use the URL picker for the `HyperLink` by clicking the small button with the ellipsis on it.) Switch to Markup View and after

the closing tag of the `HyperLink` control, type the word **or** followed by a `LoginStatus` control that you can drag from the Toolbox, or copy from the existing code in the `LoggedInTemplate`. Finally, wrap the `HyperLink` and `LoginStatus` in a pair of parentheses just as you did in the `LoggedInTemplate`.

When you are ready, your `LoginView` should contain the following code:

```
<asp:LoginView ID="LoginView1" runat="server">
  ...
  </LoggedInTemplate>
  <RoleGroups>
    <asp:RoleGroup Roles="Managers">
      <ContentTemplate>
        (<asp:HyperLink ID="HyperLink1" runat="server"
            NavigateUrl="~/Management/Default.aspx">Manage Site</asp:HyperLink> or
        <asp:LoginStatus ID="LoginStatus2" runat="server" />)
      </ContentTemplate>
    </asp:RoleGroup>
  </RoleGroups>
  ...
```

8. Save all your changes and then request the homepage (`Default.aspx`) for the site in your browser. Verify that you are currently not logged in (check the footer of the page and, if necessary, click the Logout link).

9. Click the Login link on the `Menu` or `TreeView` and then log in with the Manager account you created earlier in this chapter. Make sure you don't check the Remember Me option. The page refreshes and now shows the Manage Site link in the footer of each page (see Figure 16-22).

FIGURE 16-22

If you don't see the Manage Site and Logout links in the footer region, close all browser windows, go back to the WSAT (using Website ➪ ASP.NET Configuration in VS), and ensure the account you're using is assigned to the Managers role.

10. Click the Manage Site link to open the Management section of the website. Copy the current URL of the page from the browser's address bar to the clipboard (it should be something like `http://localhost:49666/Management/Default.aspx`). Click the Back button of your browser to go back to the homepage and then click the Logout button in the footer. Close all open browser windows and open a new instance of your browser again. (You can do this from the Windows Start menu or Start screen or you can right-click a page in VS and choose View in Browser.)

11. Paste the address you just copied in the address bar of the browser window and press Enter. Instead of going to an address like:

```
http://localhost:49666/Management/Default.aspx
```

you are taken to the Login page:

```
http://localhost:49666/login.aspx?ReturnUrl=%2fManagement%2fDefault.aspx
```

Note that the page you initially requested (`Management/Default.aspx`) is now appended to the query string. The forward slashes (/) in the address have been encoded to their URL-safe counterpart — `%2f` — automatically. Log in with your Manager account and you should see the

Management section appear again. Next, log out again, log in with one of the other accounts, and then try to access the Management folder again. Because that account doesn't have permissions to access that folder, you're redirected to the Login page again.

How It Works

To see how this works, you need to look at a couple of things. First, look at the settings you added to the Web.config file to limit access to the Management folder:

```
<location path="Management">
  <system.web>
    <authorization>
      <allow roles="Managers" />
      <deny users="*" />
    </authorization>
  </system.web>
</location>
```

When the ASP.NET run time processes the request for a page, it checks the various configuration files to see whether the current user is allowed to access that resource. For requests to files in the Management folder, it encounters the rule set in the <location> element. It starts scanning the various allow and deny elements with roles or users attributes to specify the users or roles that are affected by the rule. The roles and users attributes take one or more role or user names, separated by a comma. As soon as a rule is found that matches, the scanning process is stopped and that rule is applied. If no rule is satisfied, access is *granted*! Therefore, it's important to end the rule with a deny rule to block all other users that haven't been granted access previously.

If you'd add an authorization element to the Web.config in the Management folder, the settings you apply there are looked at first because the security model works inside out. That is, it starts by scanning the Web.config file (if present) in the folder that contains the requested page. If it doesn't find the file there or it doesn't contain settings that block or grant access, it goes up in the folder hierarchy searching for configuration files with authorization elements. In the previous exercise, the run-time found the settings in the Web.config file in the root that were then applied to the folder.

When an unauthenticated user logs in, the first rule won't match because the anonymous user is not a member of the Managers role. The user is then denied access because of the deny rule that blocks all users, indicated by the asterisk (*).

After you logged in as a Manager and requested the same resource, the rule set was scanned again. The run time then found the allow element that grants access to the Managers role and immediately let you in. The final rule that blocks access to all other users was not even checked. In addition to specific roles or usernames and the asterisk (*) to refer to all users, you can also use the question mark (?) to refer to unauthenticated — or anonymous — users. So, for example, to let any logged-in user access the Reviews folder regardless of the role they are in, and block access to all other users, you can add the following <location> element to your configuration file:

```
<location path="Reviews">
  <system.web>
    <authorization>
      <deny users="?" />
    </authorization>
  </system.web>
</location>
```

This denies access to all users that are not logged in. Because of the default rule that grants access to the resource if the current user is not matched by an earlier rule, all logged-in users can successfully access files in the `Reviews` folder.

You can specify multiple roles or usernames in the `roles` and `user` attributes by separating them with a comma.

It's important to understand how the `RoleGroups` element of the `LoginView` works. Although you can specify multiple `RoleGroup` elements that may all apply to a certain user, only *the first that matches* is displayed. Consider a user called Alex assigned to the role WebMasters and to the role Managers and a web page with the following `LoginView`:

```
<asp:LoginView ID="LoginView1" runat="server">
  <RoleGroups>
    <asp:RoleGroup Roles="Managers">
      <ContentTemplate>
        <!--Content for Managers here-->
      </ContentTemplate>
    </asp:RoleGroup>
    <asp:RoleGroup Roles="WebMasters">
      <ContentTemplate>
        <!--Content for WebMasters here-->
      </ContentTemplate>
    </asp:RoleGroup>
  </RoleGroups>
</asp:LoginView>
```

With this code, the user Alex only sees the content of the first `RoleGroup`, even though he is also assigned to the WebMasters role.

Programmatically Checking Roles

Although it's easy to use the `LoginView` control to change the content a user is allowed to see at run time, this isn't always enough. At times, you need programmatic control over the data you are presenting based on someone's role membership. You can access information about roles for the current user in a number of ways. First of all, you can access the `IsInRole` method of the `User` property from the current page or user control like this:

VB.NET

```
If User.IsInRole("Managers") Then
  ' This code runs for Managers only
End If
```

C#

```
if (User.IsInRole("Managers"))
{
  // This code runs for Managers only
}
```

Alternatively, you can access the `Roles` class that contains a number of static methods that you can access directly. The following code is functionally equivalent to the previous example:

VB.NET

```
If Roles.IsUserInRole("Managers") Then
  ' This code runs for Managers only
End If
```

C#

```
if (Roles.IsUserInRole("Managers"))
{
  // This code runs for Managers only
}
```

In addition to the `IsUserInRole` method, the `Roles` class contains a lot of other methods that enable you to work with roles programmatically. For example, you can create and delete roles, assign users to and remove users from roles, and you can get a list of users that are assigned to a certain role. For more information about the Roles API, check out the MSDN documentation at `http://tinyurl.com/RolesAPI4-5` or pick up a copy of *Professional ASP.NET 3.5 Security, Membership, and Role Management with C# and VB* by Bilal Haidar (Wrox, ISBN: 978-0-470-37930-1). Although the book targets ASP.NET 3.5, you'll find that most topics discussed in that book still apply to ASP.NET 4.5.

In the following exercise, you learn how to modify the photo albums page so users logged in as Managers are able to delete pictures from a photo album. Other users won't be able to delete a picture because the Delete button will be hidden for them.

TRY IT OUT Checking Roles with IsUserInRole at Run Time

This Try It Out uses a programmatic check for the user's role to hide or show the Delete button. Although you could recreate this example by using a `LoginView` with different templates and `RoleGroups`, this exercise serves as an example of programmatic role checking.

1. Open `Default.aspx` from the `PhotoAlbums` folder in Markup View and right *after* the closing tag of the `ListView` control, enter two HTML breaks (you can use the `br` snippet) followed by a `HyperLink` control (you can use the `hyperlink` snippet). Set its `ID` property to `EditLink` and its `Text` property to **`Edit Photo Album`**. You assign the `NavigateUrl` programmatically in the next step.

```
<br /><br />
<asp:HyperLink ID="EditLink" runat="server" Text="Edit Photo Album" />
```

2. Switch to Design View, select the `ListView` control, open up its Properties Grid, and switch to the Events tab. Double-click `DataBound` to set up a handler for that event. Inside the handler that VS created, add the following code:

VB.NET

```
Protected Sub ListView1_DataBound(sender As Object,
          e As EventArgs) Handles ListView1.DataBound
```

```
    If Not String.IsNullOrEmpty(DropDownList1.SelectedValue) Then
      EditLink.NavigateUrl = String.Format(
           "~/ManagePhotoAlbum.aspx?PhotoAlbumId={0}", DropDownList1.SelectedValue)
      EditLink.Visible = True
    Else
      EditLink.Visible = False
    End If
  End Sub
```

C#

```
protected void ListView1_DataBound(object sender, EventArgs e)
{
  if (!string.IsNullOrEmpty(DropDownList1.SelectedValue))
  {
    EditLink.NavigateUrl = string.Format(
      "~/ManagePhotoAlbum.aspx?PhotoAlbumId={0}", DropDownList1.SelectedValue);
    EditLink.Visible = true;
  }
  else
  {
    EditLink.Visible = false;
  }
}
```

3. Open up `ManagePhotoAlbum.aspx` in the root of the site and switch it to Design View. Select the `ListView` and open its Properties Grid. Switch to the Events tab and double-click the `ItemCreated` event to set up an event handler for that event.

4. If you're using C#, add an `Imports/using` statement for the `System.Web.Security` namespace at the top of the Code Behind file. A VB.NET website imports this namespace by default.

```
using System.Web.Security;
```

5. Add the following code to the event handler that VS created:

VB.NET

```
Protected Sub ListView1_ItemCreated(sender As Object,
         e As ListViewItemEventArgs) Handles ListView1.ItemCreated
  Select Case e.Item.ItemType
    Case ListViewItemType.DataItem
      Dim deleteButton As Button =
                  CType(e.Item.FindControl("DeleteButton"), Button)
      deleteButton.Visible = Roles.IsUserInRole("Managers")
  End Select
End Sub
```

C#

```
protected void ListView1_ItemCreated(object sender, ListViewItemEventArgs e)
{
  switch (e.Item.ItemType)
  {
```

```
      case ListViewItemType.DataItem:
        Button deleteButton = (Button)e.Item.FindControl("DeleteButton");
        deleteButton.Visible = Roles.IsUserInRole("Managers");
        break;
    }
  }
```

6. Save all your changes and then request `Default.aspx` from the `PhotoAlbums` folder in your browser by right-clicking it and then choosing View in Browser. If you're not logged in as a manager, click the Login link in the main `Menu` or `TreeView`, log in with the Manager account you created earlier in this chapter, and return to the Gig Pics page.
7. Choose one of the photo albums from the drop-down list. The page reloads and shows the pictures in the photo album.
8. Click the Edit Photo Album link at the bottom of the page. Figure 16-23 shows how each picture is still associated with a Delete button that deletes the picture when clicked, just as you saw in Chapter 14. Click the Delete button for a picture to confirm that it still works.

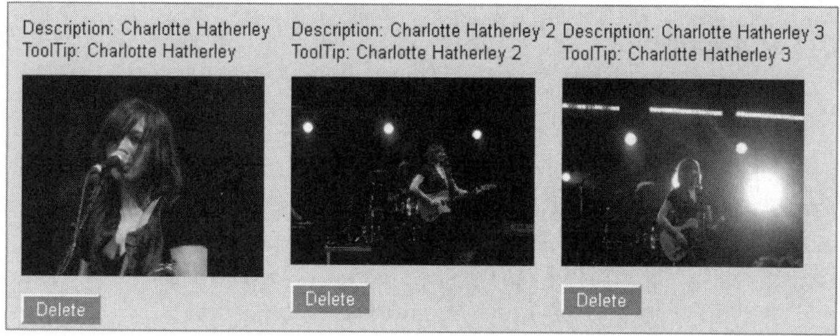

FIGURE 16-23

9. Click the Logout link in the footer again and go to the Login page. Log in with an account you created earlier in this chapter that is not a member of the Managers role. Go to the Gig Pics page again, select an album from the list and click the Edit Photo Album link. This time, you don't see Delete buttons, because the account you're logged in with is not assigned to the Managers role. In the next chapter you see how to modify this page once more to also let owners of an album delete their own pictures. In addition, you'll see how to hide the Edit Photo Album link for users without edit permissions.

How It Works

Most of the code in this exercise shouldn't be new to you. You have seen how you can delete items with the `EntityDataSource` and `ListView` controls. You also learned how to handle events such as `ItemCreated` (that fires for each item that is shown in the `ListView` control) and search for controls in an item using `FindControl`.

What's new in this example is the way you check whether the current user is a member of the Managers role:

VB.NET

```
Dim deleteButton As Button = CType(e.Item.FindControl("DeleteButton"), Button)
deleteButton.Visible = Roles.IsUserInRole("Managers")
```

C#

```
Button deleteButton = (Button)e.Item.FindControl("DeleteButton");
deleteButton.Visible = Roles.IsUserInRole("Managers");
```

The `IsUserInRole` method returns a boolean that indicates whether the current user is a manager. When the method returns `True`, it means that the `Visible` property of the `Button` is set to `True`. When the method returns `False`, the button is hidden and the user is not able to delete pictures from the photo album.

PRACTICAL SECURITY TIPS

The following list provides some practical security tips:

- Although the concept of security is introduced quite late in the book, you shouldn't see it as an afterthought. To ensure that you create a solid and secure application, you should keep security in mind from the very early stages of your website development. Deciding whether you want to have areas that are accessible only to certain users, and whether you are going to force users into getting an account for your site before they get access is best done as early as possible. The later in the process you introduce these concepts, the more difficulties you'll face when integrating this functionality.
- Try to group resources like ASPX pages under folders that represent roles in your system. Take, for example, the `Management` folder in the Planet Wrox website. All pages related to the management of your site are packed together in a single folder, making it very easy to block the entire folder with a single `<location>` element in the `Web.config` file. When the files you want to protect are scattered throughout your website, you'll need more time to configure the application, and you'll end up with a cluttered view of the active security settings.
- When you create roles to differentiate between users on your website, try to limit the number of different roles your system has. You'll find that your system becomes much easier to manage with only a handful of logically grouped roles than with a large number of roles with only one or two users in them.

SUMMARY

You can implement security in your ASP.NET site with several techniques, including Windows authentication (where the web server takes care of authentication) and Forms authentication, which is the de facto standard for many of today's ASP.NET websites.

In general, security encompasses three important concepts: identity, authentication, and authorization. Together, they determine who you are and what you are allowed to do.

The Membership service (that uses a Membership provider under the hood) enables you to create and manage users in a central database using handy controls such as `CreateUserWizard`, `PasswordRecovery`, and `Login`.

The Role Manager (which uses a Role provider under the hood) enables you to group users in various roles to which you can apply permissions. You can check roles programmatically, or use the `LoginView` to present different data depending on the role the user is assigned to.

Users and roles are managed with the WSAT, so you can assign user accounts to different roles, as you saw in this chapter. You can then open up or block specific resources in your website to members in a certain role using simple `<location>` elements in the `Web.config` file.

The various login controls enable you to customize the content that users get to see. In the next chapter you discover how to take this one level further, by creating dynamic pages that adapt based on the user that is accessing them.

EXERCISES

1. What's the difference between authentication and authorization?
2. Right now the `Management` folder is blocked for all users except those in the Managers role. What change do you need to make to the `Web.config` file if you also want to open up the folder for the user John and all people in the Editors role?
3. Imagine you have a website that features a Login page with a single `Login` control. What change to the `Login` control do you need to make to send users to `MyProfile.aspx` in the root after they log in?
4. What's the difference between the `LoginView` and `LoginStatus` controls? When would you use each one?

You can find answers to these exercises in Appendix A.

▶ WHAT YOU LEARNED IN THIS CHAPTER

Application services	A set of ASP.NET services that you can access from your website to handle tasks such as membership, role, and profile management
Authentication	The process of proving your identity to a system
Authorization	The process of determining the permissions a user has in a system
Login controls	The set of security controls that ship with ASP.NET and that enable you to sign up, log in, recover your password, and more
Membership	One of the ASP.NET application services that handles membership-related tasks (including creating users, logging in, and more)
Permissions	Determine the operations a user in the system is allowed to carry out
Provider model	A model where an interchangeable piece of software is used for certain application tasks. Through configuration, you can assign a different piece of software that handles the same tasks (but in a different way).
Role Manager	One of the ASP.NET application services that handles role-related tasks including creating roles, assigning users to roles, and checking their role membership

17

Personalizing Websites

WHAT YOU WILL LEARN IN THIS CHAPTER:

- Details about the Profile feature that ships with ASP.NET
- How to create and consume a user's profile in a website
- How you can recognize your users and how to serve them customized content
- How you can access the profile of other users of your site

WROX.COM CODE DOWNLOADS FOR THIS CHAPTER

You can find the wrox.com code downloads for this chapter on the Download Code tab at `www.wrox.com/remtitle.cgi?isbn=1118311809`. The code is in the Chapter 17 download.

There is only one thing that beats good content on the web—good *personalized* content. In the era of information overload and the huge amount of competitive sites, it's important to know your visitors and understand the possibilities you have to present them personalized content. With a good personalization strategy, you can create a website that lives up to your users' expectations by presenting them with exactly the data they are looking for. Personalization is useful for many different scenarios. For example, on a sports site, you use personalized content to highlight activities from the user's favorite team. On a site that deals with programming, you can personalize content by showing users examples in their preferred programming language(s) only. On a news website, you can let users choose one or more news categories (World, Local, Sports, Business, Financial, and so on) and target the content you show them based on these preferences. You can take this one step further by sending them e-mail updates when a new article is posted in one of those categories.

However, personalization goes further than just storing personal preferences and adapting the content to these preferences. With personalization, you can also keep track of other user details, such as a name, date of birth, visits to the site, items users bought in an online shop, and so on. You can then use these details to further personalize web pages, creating a closer relationship with your visitors.

In the Planet Wrox website, personalization is implemented simply yet effectively. The main Reviews page is designed to show only the reviews for those music genres in which the user is interested. To see all the available reviews, users can still visit the `All.aspx` page, but by visiting the personalized page, they only see reviews in music genres they really like.

Additionally, users can enter personal details about themselves, such as a first and last name, and a short biography. These details are shown on the Photo Albums details page so you know who created a particular photo album.

To enable you to add personalization features to a website, ASP.NET 4.5 ships with an application service called *Profile*. With the Profile service, you can store data for a particular user with very few lines of code.

By the end of this chapter, you'll have enough knowledge about the personalization features brought by Profile to create dynamic and personalized websites.

UNDERSTANDING PROFILE

The ASP.NET Profile is another application service that ships with ASP.NET. It enables you to store and retrieve information about users to your site that goes beyond basic information such as an e-mail address and password that users can enter during sign-up. With Profile, you can store information such as a first and last name, a date of birth, and much more, as you see later in this chapter. By keeping track of the user to which that data belongs, ASP.NET is able to map that data to a user the next time she visits your site, whether that be minutes or weeks later. The cool thing about Profile is that it enables you to store data for registered users as well as anonymous users. So, even if your visitors haven't signed up for an account, you can recognize them and store information about them.

You access the information in a user's profile through a clean API with virtually no code. All you need to do is define the information you want to keep track of in the central `Web.config` file and the Profile service takes care of the rest. All interaction with the database to retrieve or store profile information in the database is handled automatically for you.

Enabling Profile in your web application is a simple, two-step process:

1. Define the information you want to store for a user in the `Web.config` file. Based on this information, the ASP.NET run time generates and compiles a class for you on the fly that gives you access to the properties you defined. It then dynamically expands a property called `Profile` on all web pages in your site , so you can easily access the profile properties from every page in your site.
2. In your application, you program directly to this generated class to get and store the profile information for the *current* user.

The ASP.NET Profile by default is connected to a logged-in user, although you can also save profile data for unauthenticated users, as you will see later in this chapter.

In the following section, you see how to define profile properties in `Web.config` and how to access them in your web pages.

> ***NOTE*** *It's important to realize that the built-in Profile feature works only with Web Site Projects and not with Web Application Projects. For a discussion on the difference between the two, refer to Chapter 2. If you find that none of the examples in this chapter seem to work, check that you haven't accidentally created a Web Application Project. The simplest way to check is to look at the Code Behind file of a Web Form. If you see two Code Behind files (one named after the page with a* `.cs` *or* `.vb` *extension and one with an additional* `Designer` *extension), you have created a Web Application Project. In that case, get yourself a copy of the* `Chapter 16` *folder that is part of the source that comes with this book and use that as the starting point for this chapter.*

Configuring the Profile

You define a profile for your website in the `Web.config` file by creating a `<profile>` element as a direct child of the `<system.web>` element. Between the `<profile>` tags, you need to create a `<properties>` element that is used to define the properties you want to expose from your `Profile` object. Two types of properties exist: simple properties and complex properties, referred to as *profile groups*.

Creating Simple Profile Properties

You define simple properties as direct children of the `<properties>` element using an `<add>` element. The following example demonstrates how to create a property that can be used to hold a user's first name and one to hold a date of birth. The `FirstName` property can be accessed and set for authenticated and anonymous users, whereas the `DateOfBirth` property is accessible only to logged-in users:

```
<system.web>
  ...
  <profile>
    <properties>
      <add name="FirstName" allowAnonymous="True" />
      <add name="DateOfBirth" type="System.DateTime" />
    </properties>
  </profile>
```

Because properties are by default of type `System.String`, there's no need to define an explicit `type` on the property for text-based properties like a first name. However, for other types like a `DateTime`, a `Boolean`, an `Integer`, or your own types, you need to define the type explicitly using the `type` attribute and its *fully qualified name* including its namespace, as shown for the `DateOfBirth` property. The following table lists the most common attributes of the `<add>` element that influence the properties of a profile.

ATTRIBUTE	DESCRIPTION
name	Defines the name of the property, such as FirstName, DateOfBirth, and so forth.
type	Sets the full .NET type name of the property, such as System.String, System.Boolean, System.DateTime, System.Int32 (an Integer in VB.NET and an int in C#), and so on.
allowAnonymous	Specifies whether the property can be written to for anonymous users. The default is false. When you set this attribute to true, you also need to enable anonymousIdentification, discussed later in this chapter.
defaultValue	Defines the default value for the property if it hasn't been set explicitly. When you leave out this attribute, the profile property takes the default value for the underlying type (for example, null for a String, 0 for an Int32, and so on).
readOnly	Specifies whether the profile property can be changed at run time. The default is false, which means you can read from and write to the property.

Besides simple properties, you can also create profile groups that enable you to group other simple properties together.

Creating Profile Groups

Profile groups serve two distinct purposes: first, they enable you to logically group related properties. For example, you can create a group called Address that, in turn, has properties like Street, PostalCode, and City.

Groups also enable you to have properties with the same name, but located in a different group. For example, you can have two groups called VisitAddress and PostalAddress that both feature properties like Street and PostalCode, making it easier for a developer using your Profile object to find the relevant information.

To create a profile group, you add a <group> element to the <properties> element of your profile and then specify a name. The <group> element then contains one or more properties. The following example shows a profile group for a PostalAddress:

```
<properties>
  <add name="FirstName" />
  <group name="PostalAddress">
    <add name="Street" />
    <add name="PostalCode" />
    <add name="City" />
    <add name="Country" />
  </group>
</properties>
```

You can have multiple groups within the `<properties>` tags, but you can have only one level of groups. This means that you can't nest a `<group>` element in another `<group>` or `<add>` element.

Using Non-Standard Data Types

In addition to the data types listed earlier such as `String`, `DateTime`, and `Int32`, you can also use your own types (defined in the `App_Code` folder, for example).

As with the built-in .NET types, you need to refer to your type using its fully qualified name, which includes the namespace and the class name. Imagine that you have a type called `Preference` that contains various properties (implemented as automatic properties in this example) related to the user's preference. To include this type in the profile, you need to wrap it in a namespace first:

VB.NET

```
Namespace PlanetWrox
  Public Class Preference
    Public Property FavoriteColor As String
    ' Other properties go here
  End Class
End Namespace
```

C#

```
namespace PlanetWrox
{
  public class Preference
  {
    public string FavoriteColor { get; set; }
    // Other properties go here
  }
}
```

You then refer to the type in an `<add />` element as follows:

```
<add name="Preferences" type="PlanetWrox.Preference" />
```

A situation where you need a different syntax to refer to a type in the profile setup is when you are using generics. Chapter 5 discusses how to use generics to store role names using a `List` of strings. Here's a quick refresher of the code you saw in that chapter:

VB.NET

```
Dim roles As New List(Of String)
...
roles.Add("Members")
```

C#

```
List<string> roles = new List<string>();
...
roles.Add("Members");
```

To give your profile a property that is of a generic `List` type, you need to use some special syntax. The following setting in `Web.config` creates a profile property called `FavoriteGenres` that stores the user's favorite genres as a `List (Of Integer)` in VB.NET and as a `List<int>` in C#:

```
<add name="FavoriteGenres"
     type="System.Collections.Generic.List`1[System.Int32]" />
```

The first part of the type attribute looks quite normal. The List class lives in the System .Collections.Generic namespace so it makes sense that you need to specify that here as well. However, right after the class name (List) you see `1. This is not a typo, but the .NET way to refer to generic types in plain text. To define a property that is based on a generic type, you need to use the back tick (`) followed by a 1. The back tick is usually found to the left of the 1 key on your keyboard. The `1 is then followed by a pair of square brackets that contains the actual type you want to use for the list. The type specified in the FavoriteGenres profile property maps to these VB.NET and C# counterparts:

VB.NET

```
Dim FavoriteGenres As New List(Of Integer)
```

C#

```
List<int> FavoriteGenres = new List<int>();
```

You see how to make use of this and other profile properties in the following exercises. First, you learn how to configure Profile in Web.config in the next Try It Out. Later exercises show you how to work with these properties, and how to use the various methods of the List class.

TRY IT OUT Creating a Profile

In this Try It Out, you see how to create a profile that is capable of storing a user's first and last name, a date of birth, a short biography, and a list of IDs of the user's favorite genres. This list is later used to show only the reviews that match the user's interest.

1. Open the Web.config file from the root of the site and locate the <profile> element that was added by NuGet in an exercise in the preceding chapter. If you don't have this element yet, refer to the section "Introducing the Login Controls" in Chapter 16 to learn how to configure your site for the application services.
2. Add a new <properties> element as a direct child of <profile>. Make sure you don't accidentally add the new element inside the <providers> element.
3. Complete the <profile> element so it ends up looking like this:

```
<profile defaultProvider="DefaultProfileProvider">
  <properties>
    <add name="FirstName" />
    <add name="LastName" />
    <add name="DateOfBirth" type="System.DateTime" />
    <add name="Bio" />
    <add name="FavoriteGenres"
               type="System.Collections.Generic.List`1[System.Int32]" />
  </properties>
  <providers>
  ...
</profile>
```

4. Save the Web.config. As soon as you save the file, a background process starts to generate a class file that is used for the profile. After the class file has been created and compiled successfully, you can access it programmatically through the Profile property of the Page class.

5. To test the profile, open the `MyProfile.aspx` file that you created in the previous chapter in Design View. Double-click the page to set up an event handler for the `Load` event and add the following code containing your own first and last name:

VB.NET

```
Protected Sub Page_Load(sender As Object, e As EventArgs) Handles Me.Load
  Profile.FirstName = "Your first name here"
  Profile.LastName = "Your last name here"
End Sub
```

C#

```
protected void Page_Load(object sender, EventArgs e)
{
  Profile.FirstName = "Your first name here";
  Profile.LastName = "Your last name here";
}
```

As soon as you type the dot (`.`) after `Profile`, an IntelliSense list appears, showing you the available profile properties (see Figure 17-1).

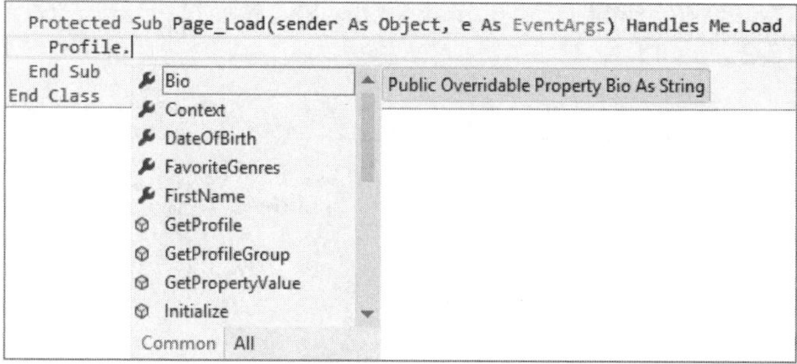

FIGURE 17-1

6. When you are finished typing the code, save and close the file because you're done with it for now.

> ***WARNING*** *If nothing shows up after typing the dot, choose Build ➪ Build Web Site from the main menu or press Ctrl+Shift+B. This forces VS to start a recompilation of the application, including the special class for the* `Profile` *property. You see more about compilation in Chapter 19. After a delay of a few seconds, the properties should now appear in the IntelliSense list for the* `Profile` *property of the* `Page` *class. If they still don't show up, check the Error List (choose View ➪ Error List from the main menu to open up the Error List) to verify that you didn't make any mistakes in the* `Web.config` *file and make sure you are using a Web Site Project and not a Web Application Project.*

7. Switch back to the `Web.config` file and scroll all the way to the end. Create a copy of the `<location>` element that blocks access to the `Management` folder for unauthorized users and paste it

right below the existing element. Then modify the copy so it blocks access to the `MyProfile.aspx` file in the root of the site to all unauthenticated users. You should end up with these settings:

```
  </location>
  <location path="MyProfile.aspx">
    <system.web>
      <authorization>
        <deny users="?"/>
      </authorization>
    </system.web>
  </location>
</configuration>
```

8. In the Solution Explorer, right-click the `MyProfile.aspx` file and choose View in Browser. You can only view this file when you're logged in; if you weren't logged in previously, you are taken to `Login.aspx` first. Log in with the username and password you created in the previous chapter and click Login. You're taken back to `MyProfile.aspx`. Although you don't see anything new in the page, the code in `Page_Load` has run and has created a profile for you in the database.

9. To see this profile, close your browser and go back to Visual Studio. Open the Database Explorer (the Server Explorer in paid versions of VS) and expand the Tables element of the `PlanetWrox.mdf` database. Locate the `Profiles` table, right-click it, and choose Show Table Data. You should see something similar to Figure 17-2.

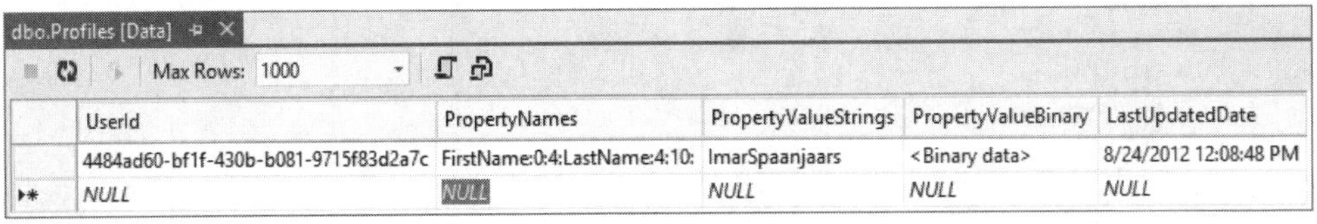

dbo.Profiles [Data]

Max Rows: 1000

	UserId	PropertyNames	PropertyValueStrings	PropertyValueBinary	LastUpdatedDate
	4484ad60-bf1f-430b-b081-9715f83d2a7c	FirstName:0:4:LastName:4:10:	ImarSpaanjaars	<Binary data>	8/24/2012 12:08:48 PM
▶*	NULL	NULL	NULL	NULL	NULL

FIGURE 17-2

This figure shows the profile data for a single user. The first and last name you entered in step 5 are stored in the column `PropertyValueStrings`. Because of the special format this data is stored in, you shouldn't modify this data manually. Instead, you should use Profile to change the underlying data.

How It Works

When you define profile properties in `Web.config`, the ASP.NET run time creates a class for you in the background. This class, called `ProfileCommon`, gives you access to the strongly typed properties such as `FirstName`, `LastName`, and `FavoriteGenres`. The `ProfileCommon` class is then made accessible to the `Page` through its `Profile` property. `ProfileCommon` inherits from `ProfileBase`, the base class defined in the .NET Framework that contains the behavior to access the profile in the database by talking to the configured provider, the *ASP.NET Profile provider.* The provider in turn takes care of all the hard work of persisting the data in the configured database. Just as the Membership and Roles providers you saw in the preceding chapter, the Profile provider uses the connection string defined in the `connectionStringName` attribute of the configured provider.

To define properties, you use <add> elements with a name attribute and an optional type if the property is of a type other than System.String. For example:

```
<add name="FavoriteGenres"
         type="System.Collections.Generic.List`1[System.Int32]" />
```

This property sets up a list that can store Integer values to hold the user's favorite music genres. You see how to use this property in a later exercise.

After you have set up the profile in Web.config and the background class has been compiled, you can access the profile in your pages. For example, you can now set properties such as FirstName through code:

VB.NET

```
Profile.FirstName = "Your first name here"
```

C#

```
Profile.FirstName = "Your first name here";
```

Although not used in this exercise, you access properties in a group in pretty much the same way. All you need to do is prefix the property name with the group name and a dot. Given the example of a PostalAddress, you would store the street for that address like this:

VB.NET

```
Profile.PostalAddress.Street = "Some Street"
```

C#

```
Profile.PostalAddress.Street = "Some Street";
```

Changes made to the profile are saved automatically for you during EndRequest, an event that fires very late during the ASP.NET page life cycle. This way, you can change the profile during many of the stages of the life cycle without having to worry about explicitly saving the profile manually.

In Figure 17-2, you can see how a single row is used to store the entire profile. The first column contains the unique ID of the user to which the profile belongs. The second column contains a list of property names that are saved for the current user, together with a starting index of the value and a length. For example, for the last name you see:

```
LastName:4:10
```

This states that the value for the LastName property, which is stored in the PropertyValueStrings column, starts at position 4 (the fifth character because zero-based positions are used) and has a length of 10 characters. This dense format enables the Profile provider to store many different properties in a single column, which eliminates the need to mess with the database schema any time the profile changes. Earlier versions of the Profile provider used the PropertyValueBinary column to store binary objects such as images. However, the Profile provider converts these to strings and stores them in the PropertyValueStrings column as well.

You learn more about reading from and writing to the profile in the following section.

Using the Profile

As you saw in the previous section, writing to the profile is easy. To change a property like `FirstName`, all you need is a single line of code. The profile keeps track of the changes you have made to it, and, if necessary, automatically saves the changes during `EndRequest`. Reading from the profile is just as easy; all you need to do is access one of its properties. The following snippet shows how to fill a `TextBox` with the first name from the profile:

VB.NET

```
FirstName.Text = Profile.FirstName
```

C#

```
FirstName.Text = Profile.FirstName;
```

Retrieving properties in a group is almost identical. To access the `Street` property discussed in a previous example, you need this code:

VB.NET

```
PostalAddressStreet.Text = Profile.PostalAddress.Street
```

C#

```
PostalAddressStreet.Text = Profile.PostalAddress.Street;
```

Accessing the `FavoriteGenres` property is slightly different. Because this property is a collection, you shouldn't assign a value to it directly. Instead, you use its methods and properties to get data in and out. The following example clears the entire list first, and then adds the IDs of two genres to it:

VB.NET

```
Profile.FavoriteGenres.Clear()
Profile.FavoriteGenres.Add(7)
Profile.FavoriteGenres.Add(11)
```

C#

```
Profile.FavoriteGenres.Clear();
Profile.FavoriteGenres.Add(7);
Profile.FavoriteGenres.Add(11);
```

The following exercise shows you how to store basic data in the user's profile. You see a real-world implementation of using the `FavoriteGenres` list in a later exercise.

TRY IT OUT Storing Basic User Data in the Profile

In this Try It Out, you modify the Profile page so users can save their first and last name, birthday, and a short biography in their profile.

1. Open `MyProfile.aspx` again and switch to Code Behind. Remove the two lines of code in `Page_Load` that set the first and last name.
2. Switch to Design View and position your cursor between the paragraph and the `ChangePassword` control. To position your cursor, click the `ChangePassword` control once to select it, and then

press the left arrow key once. Next, add an HTML table of five rows and three columns by choosing Table ➪ Insert Table.

3. In the second column of each of the first four rows, drag `TextBox` controls and rename them, from the first to the last row, `FirstName`, `LastName`, `DateOfBirth`, and `Bio` by setting their `ID` attribute. Figure 17-3 shows you exactly where the `TextBox` controls should be placed.

4. In the first column of each of the first four rows, drop `Label` controls and set their properties as follows so each label is associated with a `TextBox` in the same row.

TEXT	ASSOCIATEDCONTROLID
`First name`	`FirstName`
`Last name`	`LastName`
`Date of birth`	`DateOfBirth`
`Biography`	`Bio`

5. In the second cell of the fifth row, drag a `Button` and set its `ID` to `SaveButton` and its `Text` to `Save Profile`. Design View should look like Figure 17-3.

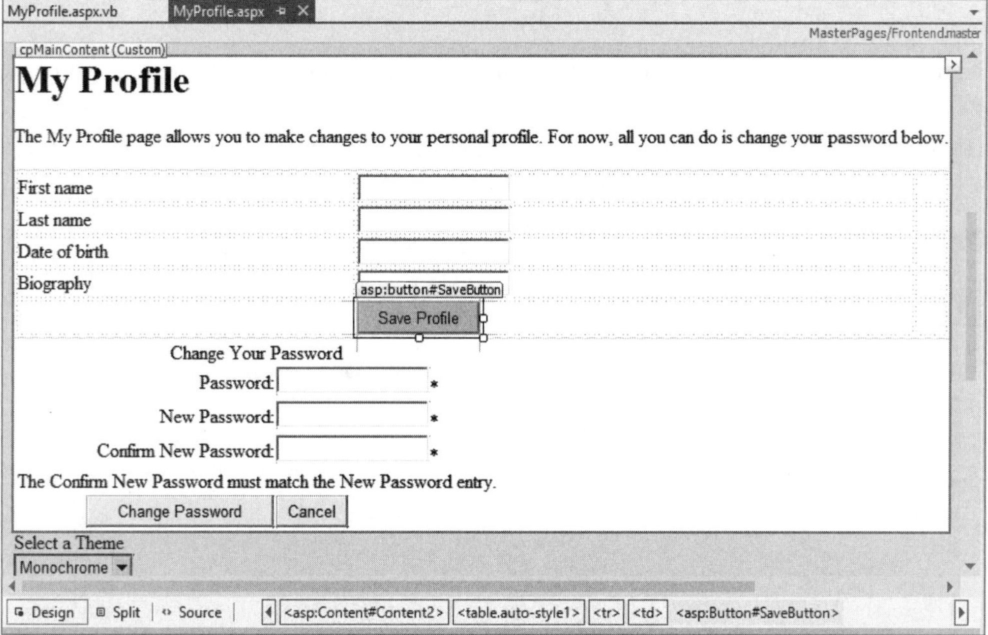

FIGURE 17-3

6. In the last column of each of the first three rows, drag `RequiredFieldValidator` controls. Set their properties as follows, so each validator lines up with a `TextBox` in the same row. Remember:

you can set the `Display` property for all controls at once by selecting the controls while pressing the Ctrl key.

CONTROLTOVALIDATE	DISPLAY	ERRORMESSAGE
FirstName	Dynamic	First name is required.
LastName	Dynamic	Last name is required.
DateOfBirth	Dynamic	Date of birth is required.

7. Next to the validator for the `DateOfBirth` box, drag a `CompareValidator` and set its properties as follows:

PROPERTY	VALUE
Display	Dynamic
ErrorMessage	Please enter a valid date.
ControlToValidate	DateOfBirth
Operator	DataTypeCheck
Type	Date

8. Set the `TextMode` of the `Bio` control to `MultiLine` and set its `Height` and `Width` properties to `75px` and `300px`, respectively.

9. Modify the text above the table to indicate that users can now do more than just change their password alone. Your Design View should look like Figure 17-4.

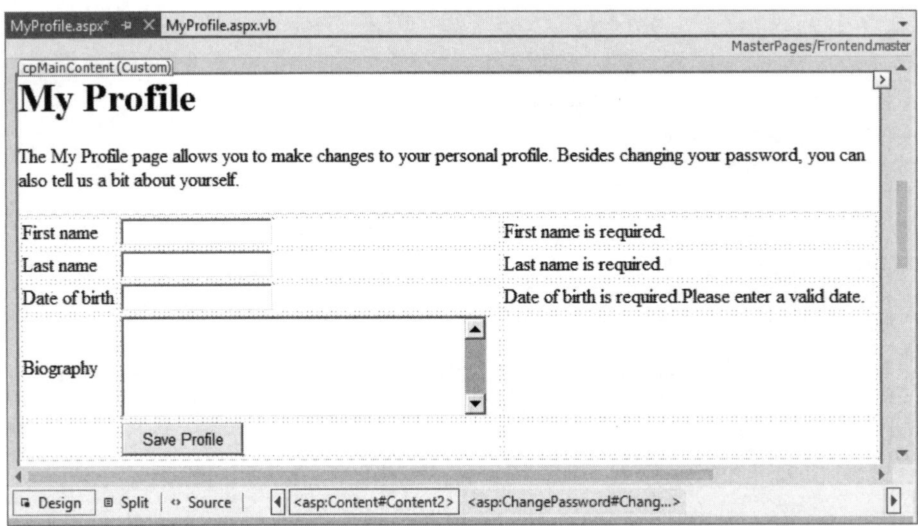

FIGURE 17-4

10. Double-click the Save Profile button and in the `Click` event handler that VS added for you, write the following bolded code:

VB.NET

```
Protected Sub SaveButton_Click(sender As Object,
      e As EventArgs) Handles SaveButton.Click
  If Page.IsValid Then
    Profile.FirstName = FirstName.Text
    Profile.LastName = LastName.Text
    Profile.DateOfBirth = DateTime.Parse(DateOfBirth.Text)
    Profile.Bio = Bio.Text
  End If
End Sub
```

C#

```
protected void SaveButton_Click(object sender, EventArgs e)
{
  if (Page.IsValid)
  {
    Profile.FirstName = FirstName.Text;
    Profile.LastName = LastName.Text;
    Profile.DateOfBirth = DateTime.Parse(DateOfBirth.Text);
    Profile.Bio = Bio.Text;
  }
}
```

11. In the `Page_Load` event handler of the same page, add the following code, which fills in the text box controls with the data from the profile when the page loads:

VB.NET

```
Protected Sub Page_Load(sender As Object, e As EventArgs) Handles Me.Load
  If Not Page.IsPostBack Then
    FirstName.Text = Profile.FirstName
    LastName.Text = Profile.LastName
    DateOfBirth.Text = Profile.DateOfBirth.ToShortDateString()
    Bio.Text = Profile.Bio
  End If
End Sub
```

C#

```
protected void Page_Load(object sender, EventArgs e)
{
  if (!Page.IsPostBack)
  {
    FirstName.Text = Profile.FirstName;
    LastName.Text = Profile.LastName;
    DateOfBirth.Text = Profile.DateOfBirth.ToShortDateString();
    Bio.Text = Profile.Bio;
  }
}
```

12. Save all changes and request the page in the browser. If you're required to log in first, enter your details and click the Login button. You should see the My Profile page reappear with the data you

entered for the first and last names in the previous Try It Out already filled in. In addition, the date of birth field is filled with the default value for a `DateTime`: 1/1/0001. Complete the form with your details and click the Save Profile button.

13. Close your browser and request `MyProfile.aspx` again. Note that your changes have been persisted between the two browser sessions.

How It Works

Much of what you have seen in this exercise should be familiar by now. The page contains a number of `TextBox` controls that are validated using `RequiredFieldValidator` and `CompareValidator` controls. Additionally, the `Label` controls are hooked up to their respective `TextBox` controls using the `AssociatedControlID` property. This makes it easy to put focus on the controls in the browser because clicking a `Label` now puts the cursor in the associated `TextBox`.

When you click the Save Profile button, the values are retrieved from the four `TextBox` controls and stored in the profile. When the page loads the first time, the reverse of this process takes place: the controls are prefilled with the values from the profile. To avoid overwriting the data that the user has entered, the code gets the data from the profile only when the page initially loads, and not during a postback:

VB.NET

```
If Not Page.IsPostBack Then
  FirstName.Text = Profile.FirstName
  ....
End If
```

C#

```
if (!Page.IsPostBack)
{
  FirstName.Text = Profile.FirstName;
  ...
}
```

Although the example itself is pretty trivial, it lays out a nice foundation for a more advanced scenario using the `List` of integers to store the user's preference for certain music genres. You can then use this list of favorite genres to limit the list with reviews to those the user is really interested in. You see how to store the user's preference in Profile in the following exercise; a later exercise shows you how to use the saved data again.

TRY IT OUT Storing Genre Preferences in the Profile

In this Try It Out, you learn how to fill the `FavoriteGenres` property of the user profile. To let the user choose her favorite genres, you display a `CheckBoxList` that is hooked up to an `EntityDataSource` that retrieves the available genres. When the user saves the data, the items that the user checked are then stored in the profile.

1. In `MyProfile.aspx`, add a table row above the one with the Save Profile button. To do this, make sure you're in Design View, right-click an empty spot in the row with the button, and choose Insert ➪ Row Above from the context menu that appears. Alternatively, click the cell to put the cursor in it and press Ctrl+Alt+up arrow.
2. In the second cell of the new row, drag a `CheckBoxList` control from the Standard category of the Toolbox and set its `ID` to `PreferenceList`.
3. In the first cell, drag a `Label` control, set its `Text` to **`Favorite genres`** and its `AssociatedControlID` to `PreferenceList`.
4. Hook up the `CheckBoxList` control to a new `EntityDataSource` as follows. Click Choose Data Source on the `CheckBoxList` control's Smart Tasks panel. Choose <New data source> from the data source drop-down list, then choose the Entity data source type and click OK. In the Configure Data Source wizard for the new data source control, choose `PlanetWroxEntities` as the Named Connection, click Next, and choose Genres as the EntitySetName. In the Select list, check only the items for the `Id` and `Name` properties. Your Configure Data Source dialog box now looks like Figure 17-5.

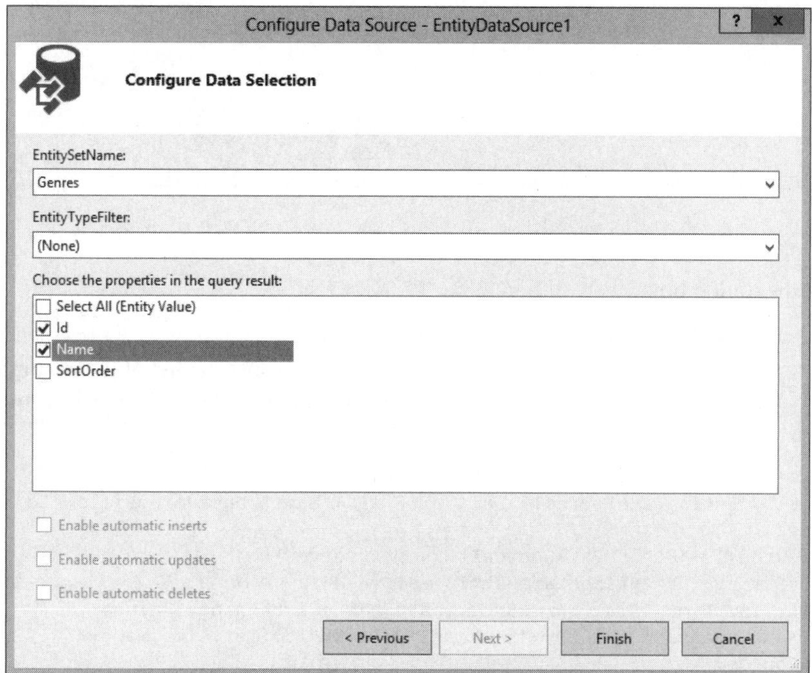

FIGURE 17-5

5. Click Finish to close the dialog box. Back in the Data Source Configuration Wizard for the `CheckBoxList` control, choose `Name` as the data field to display and `Id` as the data field for the

value. If these items don't appear in the drop-down lists, click the blue Refresh Schema link at the bottom of the dialog box first. Your screen now looks like Figure 17-6.

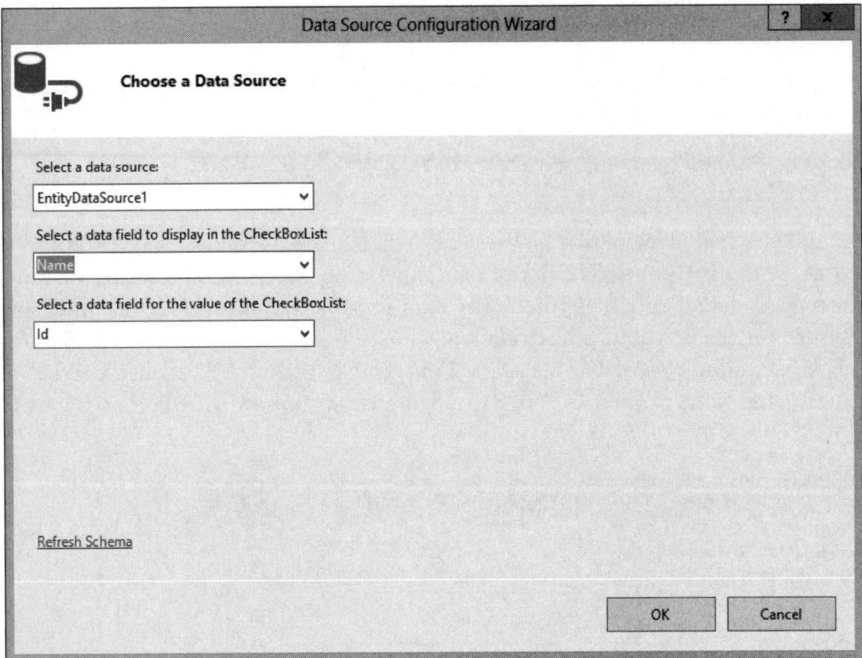

FIGURE 17-6

Click OK to close the dialog box.

6. Back in Design View, click the `EntityDataSource` that was just added and press F4 to open its Properties Grid. Locate the `OrderBy` property and enter **`it.Name`** to sort the list of genres alphabetically. Switch to Markup View and confirm that the code for the `EntityDataSource` control and the `CheckBoxList` looks as follows:

```
<asp:CheckBoxList ID="PreferenceList" runat="server"
      DataSourceID="EntityDataSource1" DataTextField="Name" DataValueField="Id">
</asp:CheckBoxList>
<asp:EntityDataSource ID="EntityDataSource1" runat="server"
      ConnectionString="name=PlanetWroxEntities"
      DefaultContainerName="PlanetWroxEntities" EnableFlattening="False"
      EntitySetName="Genres" OrderBy="it.Name" Select="it.[Id], it.[Name]">
</asp:EntityDataSource>
```

7. In Design View, click the `CheckBoxList` control once, open its Properties Grid, and switch to the Events tab. Double-click the `DataBound` event and add the following code in the Code Behind to preselect the items in the list based on the user's profile settings:

VB.NET

```
Protected Sub PreferenceList_DataBound(sender As Object,
```

```
        e As EventArgs) Handles PreferenceList.DataBound
  For Each myItem As ListItem In PreferenceList.Items
    Dim currentValue As Integer = Convert.ToInt32(myItem.Value)
    If Profile.FavoriteGenres.Contains(currentValue) Then
      myItem.Selected = True
    End If
  Next
End Sub
```

C#

```
protected void PreferenceList_DataBound(object sender, EventArgs e)
{
  foreach (ListItem myItem in PreferenceList.Items)
  {
    int currentValue = Convert.ToInt32(myItem.Value);
    if (Profile.FavoriteGenres.Contains(currentValue))
    {
      myItem.Selected = true;
    }
  }
}
```

8. Extend the `SaveButton_Click` handler with the following code so it also saves the user's preferred genres:

VB.NET

```
Profile.Bio = Bio.Text

' Clear the existing list
Profile.FavoriteGenres.Clear()

' Now add the selected genres
For Each myItem As ListItem In PreferenceList.Items
  If myItem.Selected Then
    Profile.FavoriteGenres.Add(Convert.ToInt32(myItem.Value))
  End If
Next
```

C#

```
Profile.Bio = Bio.Text;

// Clear the existing list
Profile.FavoriteGenres.Clear();

// Now add the selected genres
foreach (ListItem myItem in PreferenceList.Items)
{
  if (myItem.Selected)
  {
    Profile.FavoriteGenres.Add(Convert.ToInt32(myItem.Value));
  }
}
```

9. Save all your changes, request the Profile page in your browser, and log in when required. You should see the list of genres displayed in the browser, each one preceded by a check box. Select a couple of your favorite genres and click the Save Profile button. Browse to another page and choose My Profile again from the main `Menu` or `TreeView`. The genres you selected should still be selected in the page, as shown in Figure 17-7.

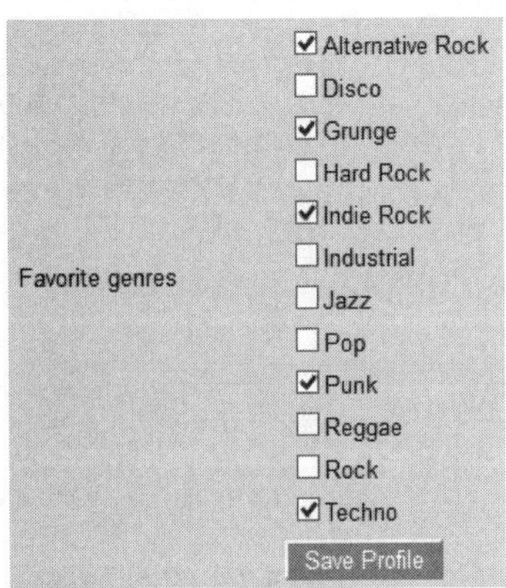

FIGURE 17-7

How It Works

Earlier you defined the `FavoriteGenres` property in the profile as a generic list that can hold integer values. Because this property is a `List`, you do not assign values to it directly; instead, you use its methods like `Add` and `Clear` to add and remove items. Because each genre ID should be stored in the list only once, the list is cleared to remove any selection made earlier and then the selected items are added again:

VB.NET

```
Profile.FavoriteGenres.Clear()
```

C#

```
Profile.FavoriteGenres.Clear();
```

Then when the list is empty, the IDs of the selected genres are added:

VB.NET

```
For Each myItem As ListItem In PreferenceList.Items
  If myItem.Selected Then
    Profile.FavoriteGenres.Add(Convert.ToInt32(myItem.Value))
  End If
Next
```

C#

```
foreach (ListItem myItem in PreferenceList.Items)
{
  if (myItem.Selected)
  {
    Profile.FavoriteGenres.Add(Convert.ToInt32(myItem.Value));
  }
}
```

This code loops through all the items in the `CheckBoxList`. The `Selected` property determines whether the user has selected the item in the Profile page. If it has been selected, the value of the genre is retrieved, converted to an `Integer` (an `int` in C#), and then added to the `FavoriteGenres` list using the `Add` method.

That's really all you need to store complex data like a list of favorite genres in the user's profile. All you need to do is add a bunch of numbers to a list. The .NET run time then takes care of persisting the profile in the database and making it available again in subsequent pages.

Of course, the list with favorite genres isn't really useful until you actually make use of it in the site. In the next exercise, you see how to use the list to limit the list of `Reviews` that users initially see when they visit the default Reviews page.

TRY IT OUT Using Profile in the Reviews Page

Currently your site has two pages in the `Reviews` folder that are capable of displaying reviews: `AllByGenre.aspx` and `All.aspx`. In this Try It Out, you modify the `Default.aspx` page so it displays yet another list of reviews. However, this time the list with reviews is limited to those belonging to the genres that the user has selected in the My Profile page. When anonymous users see the page, they get a message that they haven't set their favorite genres yet.

1. From the `Reviews` folder, open `Default.aspx` in Markup View.
2. Inside the control for the `cpMainContent` placeholder, add the following code that creates a nested `Repeater` with each selected genre as a heading, followed by a list of reviews belonging to that genre:

```
<asp:Repeater ID="GenreRepeater" runat="server">
  <HeaderTemplate>
    <p>Below you find a list with reviews for your favorite music genres.</p>
  </HeaderTemplate>
  <ItemTemplate>
    <h3><asp:Literal ID="Literal1" runat="server"
                Text='<%# Eval("Name") %>'></asp:Literal></h3>
    <asp:Repeater ID="ReviewRepeater" runat="server"
            DataSource='<%# Eval("Reviews")%>' ItemType="PlanetWroxModel.Review">
      <ItemTemplate>
        <asp:HyperLink ID="HyperLink1" runat="server" Text='<%# Item.Title %>'
          NavigateUrl='<%# "ViewDetails.aspx?ReviewId=" + Item.Id.ToString() %>'>
        </asp:HyperLink><br />
      </ItemTemplate>
    </asp:Repeater>
  </ItemTemplate>
</asp:Repeater>
<asp:PlaceHolder ID="NoRecords" runat="server" Visible="False">
  <p>Sorry, no reviews were found. You either didn't set your favorite genres
         or you may need to log in first. </p>
</asp:PlaceHolder>
<p>You can change your genre preferences <a href="~/MyProfile.aspx"
                 runat="server">here</a>.</p>
```

   You can create the `Repeater` controls manually by writing the necessary code, or you can drag and drop them from the Data category of the Toolbox. The inner `Repeater` contains a `HyperLink` control that points to the `ViewDetails.aspx` page that you created in Chapter 15. Note how the inner `Repeater` is strongly typed by setting its `ItemType` to `PlanetWroxModel.Review` (because it's displaying `Review` instances). You can't do this for the outer `Repeater` because its data source is a collection of anonymous objects, set in `Page_Load` in the Code Behind as you see next.

3. Double-click the page in Design View to set up a `Load` handler. Add an `Imports/using` statement at the top of the page for the `PlanetWroxModel` namespace and add the following code to the handler that VS created for you:

VB.NET

```
Imports PlanetWroxModel
...
Protected Sub Page_Load(sender As Object, e As EventArgs) Handles Me.Load
  Using myEntities As PlanetWroxEntities = New PlanetWroxEntities()
    If Profile.FavoriteGenres.Count > 0 Then
      Dim favGenres = From genre In myEntities.Genres.Include("Reviews")
                      Order By genre.Name
                      Where Profile.FavoriteGenres.Contains(genre.Id)
                      Select New With {genre.Name, genre.Reviews}

      GenreRepeater.DataSource = favGenres
      GenreRepeater.DataBind()
    End If

    GenreRepeater.Visible = GenreRepeater.Items.Count > 0
    NoRecords.Visible = Not GenreRepeater.Visible
  End Using
End Sub
```

C#

```
using PlanetWroxModel;
...
protected void Page_Load(object sender, EventArgs e)
{
  using (PlanetWroxEntities myEntities = new PlanetWroxEntities())
  {
    if (Profile.FavoriteGenres.Count > 0)
    {
      var favGenres = from genre in myEntities.Genres.Include("Reviews")
                      orderby genre.Name
                      where Profile.FavoriteGenres.Contains(genre.Id)
                      select new { genre.Name, genre.Reviews };
      GenreRepeater.DataSource = favGenres;
      GenreRepeater.DataBind();
    }
    GenreRepeater.Visible = GenreRepeater.Items.Count > 0;
    NoRecords.Visible = !GenreRepeater.Visible;
  }
}
```

4. Save all your changes and request the page in the browser. If you selected one or more genres in the Profile page previously, and reviews are available for those genres, you should see a list similar to Figure 17-8.

   If you haven't set any preferred genres, or you're not logged in, you get the message shown in Figure 17-9.

By clicking the link in the message, you are taken to the My Profile page so you can set or change your preferred genres. Unauthorized users are asked to log in or sign up for an account before they can access the Profile page.

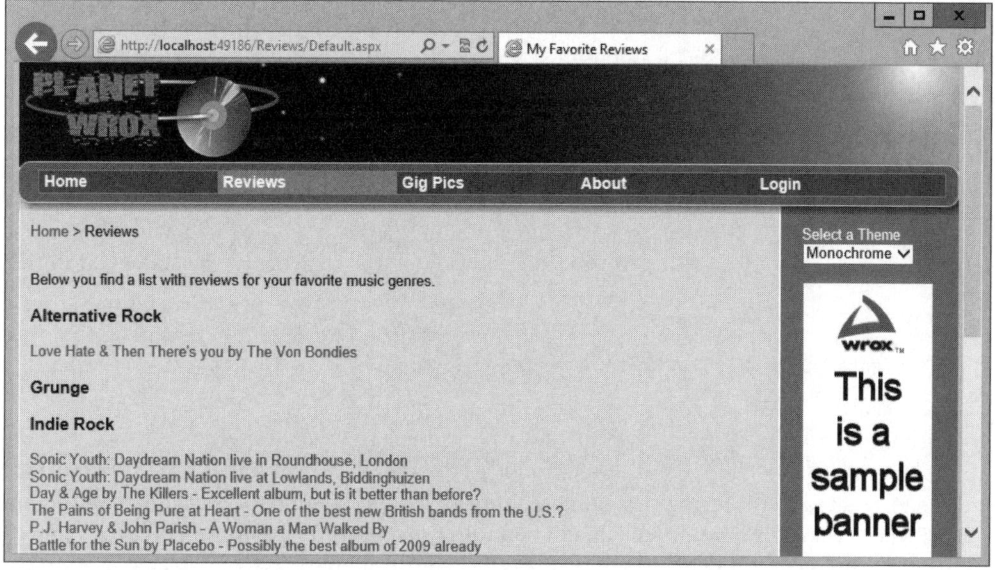

FIGURE 17-8

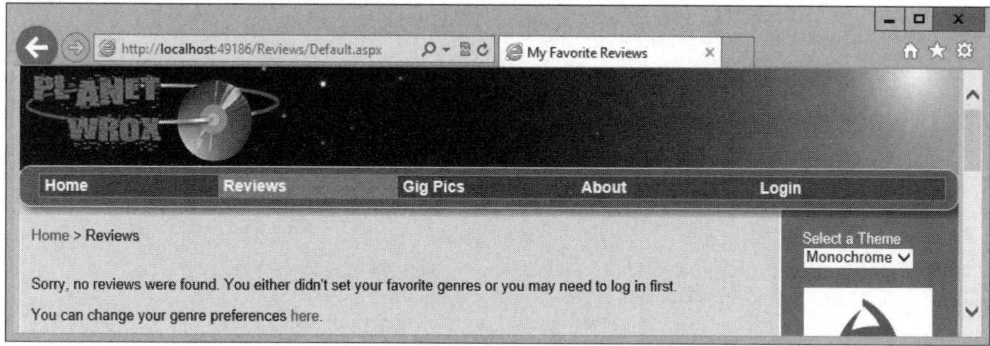

FIGURE 17-9

How It Works

The code in the Code Behind executes a LINQ to Entities query that retrieves all the reviews that belong to the user's favorite genres. For anonymous users, the list of favorite genres will be empty so they always get to see the message about setting their preferences in the Profile page. To avoid an unnecessary call to the database, the query is executed only when the user has selected at least one preferred genre by checking the `Count` property of the `FavoriteGenres` list.

Because the data source of the nested Repeater you added to the Default.aspx page is a collection of Review instances, it has been made strongly typed by setting its ItemType and using its Item property as opposed to using Eval. As you learned previously, this makes it easier to write code and catch errors earlier.

The nested Repeater looks a bit like the code for the AllByGenre.aspx page that has a Repeater that contains a BulletedList control. Just as in that page, the nested Repeater gets its data from the outer Repeater with the DataSource attribute:

```
<asp:Repeater ID="ReviewRepeater" runat="server" ItemType="PlanetWroxModel.Review"
            DataSource='<%# Eval("Reviews")%>'>
  ...
</asp:Repeater>
```

The nested Repeater then uses the list of Reviews to build up the hyperlinks that take you to the details page:

```
<asp:HyperLink ID="HyperLink1" runat="server" Text='<%# Item.Title %>'
    NavigateUrl='<%# "ViewDetails.aspx?ReviewId=" + Item.Id.ToString() %>'>
</asp:HyperLink><br />
```

The HyperLink control gets its Text from the Review instance that it's bound to and uses its Id to build up the NavigateUrl. The ToString method is used on Item.Id to convert the value to a string before it's concatenated to the string that contains the URL. This is done to avoid type conversions in Visual Basic where Item.Id normally results in a number that you can't concatenate to a string directly. As an alternative, if you're following along in VB.NET, you could have used the & character to concatenate the value.

To see how these controls get their data, you need to look at the Code Behind that uses a LINQ query targeting the Entity Framework:

VB.NET

```
Dim favGenres = From genre In myEntities.Genres.Include("Reviews")
                Order By genre.Name
                Where Profile.FavoriteGenres.Contains(genre.Id)
                Select New With {genre.Name, genre.Reviews}
```

C#

```
var favGenres = from genre in myEntities.Genres.Include("Reviews")
                orderby genre.Name
                where Profile.FavoriteGenres.Contains(genre.Id)
                select new { genre.Name, genre.Reviews };
```

Except for the highlighted line of code and the variable name, this LINQ query is identical to the one used in AllByGenre.aspx. What makes this example special is the Where clause that limits the number of reviews to those that the user is really interested in. Note how the Contains method of the generic List class is used here. Although at first it may seem that all genres and reviews are retrieved from the database into the ASPX page and then compared with the values in the profile property called FavoriteGenres, the reverse is actually the case. The Entity Framework is smart enough to collect all the IDs from the FavoriteGenres property first and then include them in the SQL statement that is sent to the database to fetch the requested genres and reviews. This means that filtering of the requested genres takes place at the database level, and not in the ASPX page. This in turn means that fewer rows are transferred from the database to the ASPX page (only those that are really needed), which results in better performance.

The profile property `FavoriteGenres` returns an empty list, rather than throwing an exception for anonymous users. So, even users with no profile can safely view this page. Instead of seeing any reviews, they get a message stating they haven't set their genre preferences yet, or that they need to log in first.

In the end of the `Page_Load` handler, some code determines whether to show or hide the `Repeater` and the `NoRecords` controls:

VB.NET

```
GenreRepeater.Visible = GenreRepeater.Items.Count > 0
NoRecords.Visible = Not GenreRepeater.Visible
```

C#

```
GenreRepeater.Visible = GenreRepeater.Items.Count > 0;
NoRecords.Visible = !GenreRepeater.Visible;
```

If after data binding the outer `Repeater`, its `Items` collection is still empty, it means no genres were found for the current user. If that's the case, the entire `Repeater` is hidden and the `PlaceHolder` is shown. However, if the `Count` property of the `Items` collection is larger than zero, the `Repeater` is made visible and the `PlaceHolder` is hidden.

In Chapter 14, you created a page called `NewPhotoAlbum.aspx` that lets users insert new Gig Pics albums. The current implementation of this page has a few shortcomings. First of all, anyone can insert a new album. There's no way to block anonymous users from creating a new album and uploading pictures.

Secondly, only Managers can remove pictures from an existing photo album. It would be nice if the owner of an album could also remove her own pictures. Now that you know more about security and personalizing web pages, this is pretty easy to implement, as you see in the following exercise.

TRY IT OUT Letting Users Manage Their Own Photo Albums

In this Try It Out you see how to block the `NewPhotoAlbum.aspx` and `ManagePhotoAlbum.aspx` pages from unauthenticated users. Additionally, you see how to record the name of the user who created the photo album and use that name later on to enable users to alter their own photo albums.

1. Open SQL Server Management Studio from the Windows Start menu or Start screen. Open your `PlanetWrox` database, and locate the `PhotoAlbum` table. Right-click it and choose Design. Add a new column called `UserName`, set its data type to `nvarchar(256)`, and leave the Allow Nulls option selected. (This table already contains photo albums without a valid `UserName`, so you can't make the column required at this stage unless you delete these photo albums and their related

pictures from the database first, or manually enter a username for each existing row.) Save your changes to the table and close SSMS.

2. Open the ADO.NET Entity Data Model file `PlanetWrox.edmx` from the `App_Code` folder, right-click an empty space in the designer, and choose Update Model from Database. Wait until VS has analyzed your database and click Finish. The `UserName` column in the database now shows up as a property of the `PhotoAlbum` class (see Figure 17-10).

   Save your changes and close the file.

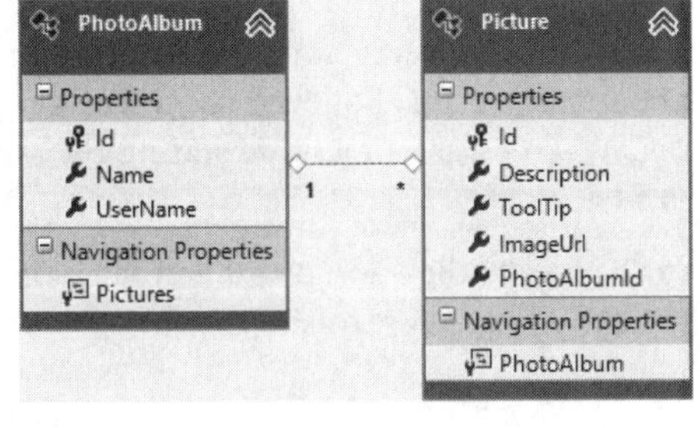

FIGURE 17-10

3. Open the `Web.config` file, and below the existing `<location>` elements, add the following two `<location>` elements to block access to the two referenced files for anonymous users:

```
</location>
<location path="ManagePhotoAlbum.aspx">
  <system.web>
    <authorization>
      <deny users="?" />
    </authorization>
  </system.web>
</location>
<location path="NewPhotoAlbum.aspx">
  <system.web>
    <authorization>
      <deny users="?" />
    </authorization>
  </system.web>
</location>
</configuration>
```

   Save your changes and close the `Web.config` file.

4. Open `NewPhotoAlbum.aspx` in Design View, locate the `EntityDataSource` control, and set up an event handler for its `Inserting` event using the Events tab of the Properties Grid. Add the following code to the handler that VS created for you:

VB.NET

```
Protected Sub EntityDataSource1_Inserting(sender As Object,
       e As EntityDataSourceChangingEventArgs) Handles EntityDataSource1.Inserting
  Dim myPhotoAlbum As PhotoAlbum = CType(e.Entity, PhotoAlbum)
  myPhotoAlbum.UserName = User.Identity.Name
End Sub
```

C#

```
protected void EntityDataSource1_Inserting(object sender,
        EntityDataSourceChangingEventArgs e)
{
  PhotoAlbum myPhotoAlbum = (PhotoAlbum)e.Entity;
  myPhotoAlbum.UserName = User.Identity.Name;
}
```

5. From the PhotoAlbums folder, open Default.aspx and switch to its Code Behind.

6. At the top of the file, add an Imports/using statement for the PlanetWroxModel namespace, and then extend the DataBound event handler with the following code that shows the Edit link when the current user is either a Manager or the owner of the photo album:

VB.NET

```
Protected Sub ListView1_DataBound(sender As Object,
          e As EventArgs) Handles ListView1.DataBound
  If Not String.IsNullOrEmpty(DropDownList1.SelectedValue) Then
    Dim photoAlbumId As Integer = Convert.ToInt32(DropDownList1.SelectedValue)
    Using myEntities As PlanetWroxEntities = New PlanetWroxEntities()
      Dim photoAlbumOwner As String = (From p In myEntities.PhotoAlbums
                                       Where p.Id = photoAlbumId
                                       Select p.UserName).Single()

      If User.Identity.IsAuthenticated And (User.Identity.Name = photoAlbumOwner _
               Or User.IsInRole("Managers")) Then
        EditLink.NavigateUrl = String.Format(
          "~/ManagePhotoAlbum.aspx?PhotoAlbumId={0}", DropDownList1.SelectedValue)
        EditLink.Visible = True
      Else
        EditLink.Visible = False
      End If
    End Using
  Else
    EditLink.Visible = False
  End If
End Sub
```

C#

```
protected void ListView1_DataBound(object sender, EventArgs e)
{
  if (!string.IsNullOrEmpty(DropDownList1.SelectedValue))
  {
    int photoAlbumId = Convert.ToInt32(DropDownList1.SelectedValue);
    using (PlanetWroxEntities myEntities = new PlanetWroxEntities())
    {
      string photoAlbumOwner = (from p in myEntities.PhotoAlbums
                                where p.Id == photoAlbumId
                                select p.UserName).Single();
      if (User.Identity.IsAuthenticated &&
            (User.Identity.Name == photoAlbumOwner || User.IsInRole("Managers")))
      {
        EditLink.NavigateUrl = string.Format(
         "~/ManagePhotoAlbum.aspx?PhotoAlbumId={0}", DropDownList1.SelectedValue);
        EditLink.Visible = true;
      }
      else
      {
        EditLink.Visible = false;
      }
    }
```

```
    }
    else
    {
      EditLink.Visible = false;
    }
  }
```

7. Open the Code Behind of `ManagePhotoAlbum.aspx` in the root. Add the following code to a `Page_Load` handler. If the handler isn't there yet, double-click the page in Design View to have VS set one up for you.

VB.NET

```
Protected Sub Page_Load(sender As Object, e As EventArgs) Handles Me.Load
  Dim photoAlbumId As Integer =
            Convert.ToInt32(Request.QueryString.Get("PhotoAlbumId"))

  Using myEntities As PlanetWroxEntities = New PlanetWroxEntities()
    Dim photoAlbumOwner As String = (From p In myEntities.PhotoAlbums
                                     Where p.Id = photoAlbumId
                                     Select p.UserName).Single()
    If User.Identity.Name <> photoAlbumOwner And
              Not User.IsInRole("Managers") Then
      Response.Redirect("~/")
    End If
  End Using
End Sub
```

C#

```
protected void Page_Load(object sender, EventArgs e)
{
  int photoAlbumId = Convert.ToInt32(Request.QueryString.Get("PhotoAlbumId"));

  using (PlanetWroxEntities myEntities = new PlanetWroxEntities())
  {
    string photoAlbumOwner = (from p in myEntities.PhotoAlbums
                              where p.Id == photoAlbumId
                              select p.UserName).Single();
    if (User.Identity.Name != photoAlbumOwner && !User.IsInRole("Managers"))
    {
      Response.Redirect("~/");
    }
  }
}
```

8. Because the entire page is now blocked for users without the proper permissions, there's no longer the need to hide the individual buttons in the `ListView` control. This means you can remove the code for the `ListView1_ItemCreated` event handler. If you're using C#, don't forget to remove the handler definition from the `ListView`'s control in Markup View as well.

9. Save the changes to all open files (press Ctrl+Shift+S) and request `NewPhotoAlbum.aspx` in your browser. If necessary, log in with an account you created earlier.

10. Enter a new name for the photo album and click Insert. At this stage, the photo album is saved, together with your username. Proceed by adding a few images to your photo album.

11. Click Gig Pics from the main `Menu` or `TreeView` and choose the new photo album you just created from the drop-down list. After the page has reloaded, your new photo album should be displayed, together with the Edit Photo Album link at the bottom of the screen. Clicking the link takes you to `ManagePhotoAlbum.aspx`, which lets you add or remove pictures in your photo album.

12. Click Logout in the footer of the page. Then go to the Gig Pics page again and choose your new photo album from the drop-down list. Note that the Edit Photo Album link is now no longer visible.

How It Works

You started this exercise by adding a column for the user's name to the `PhotoAlbum` table. With this column, you can keep track of the user who created the photo album, giving you the opportunity to display data related to the user together with a photo album. When you run the Update Wizard by choosing Update Model from Database, changes in the database (such as adding a column to a table) are reflected in the model.

In the New Photo Album page, you used this new property by assigning it the name of the current user with this code in the `EntityDataSource1_Inserting` handler:

VB.NET

```
myPhotoAlbum.UserName = User.Identity.Name
```

C#

```
myPhotoAlbum.UserName = User.Identity.Name;
```

The `Page` class has a `User` property that represents the user associated with the current request. This user, in turn, has an `Identity` property that contains the user's `Name`. The `Name` is then assigned to the `UserName` property of the `PhotoAlbum` instance, which is retrieved from `e.Entity`.

At this stage, the name is successfully stored in the database, together with the rest of the photo album. What's left is doing something useful with this name. The first place where you use this name is in the default page of the `PhotoAlbums` folder. There, you used the following LINQ to Entities query to retrieve the `UserName` for a photo album:

VB.NET

```
Dim photoAlbumOwner As String = (From p In myEntities.PhotoAlbums
                                 Where p.Id = photoAlbumId
                                 Select p.UserName).Single()
```

C#

```
string photoAlbumOwner = (from p in myEntities.PhotoAlbums
                          where p.Id == photoAlbumId
                          select p.UserName).Single();
```

This code uses the `Single` method to retrieve the `UserName` for a single photo album; the one specified in `photoAlbumId`. The remainder of the code then determines the visibility of the Edit link if the current user is logged in and is an owner of the photo album or a member of the Managers group. This way, both owners and all Managers can change existing photo albums.

The code in `ManagePhotoAlbum.aspx` performs a similar check to stop unauthorized users from accessing the page directly.

OTHER WAYS OF DEALING WITH PROFILE

In the final section of this chapter, you see two other useful ways of dealing with the Profile feature in ASP.NET. First, you see how to use Profile for anonymous users and then you learn how to access the profile of a user other than the current user.

Anonymous Identification

The Profile feature is extremely easy to configure, yet very powerful. All you need to do to give logged-in users access to their profiles is create a few elements in `Web.config`, and the ASP.NET run time takes care of the rest. But what about anonymous users? What if you wanted to store data for your visitors who haven't signed up for an account or aren't logged in yet? For those users, you need to enable *anonymous identification.* With anonymous identification, ASP.NET creates an anonymous user in the `Users` table for every new visitor to your site. This user then gets a cookie that is linked to the anonymous user account in the database. On every visit, the browser sends the cookie with the request, enabling ASP.NET to associate a user, and thus a profile, with the user for the current request.

To enable an anonymous profile, you need to do two things: turn on anonymous identification and modify some or all profile properties to expose them to anonymous users.

You enable anonymous identification with the following element in `Web.config`, directly under `<system.web>`:

```
<anonymousIdentification enabled="true" cookieName="PlanetWroxAnonymous" />
```

The `enabled` attribute turns on the feature, and the `cookieName` attribute is used to give the application a unique cookie name used to store the user's ID at the client.

After you have turned on anonymous identification, the next step involves modifying properties under the `<profile>` element and setting their `allowAnonymous` attribute to `true`:

```
<add name="FavoriteGenres" type="System.Collections.Generic.List`1[System.Int32]"
          allowAnonymous="true" />
```

This profile property can now be accessed through code for anonymous users as well. If you try to set a profile property without the `allowAnonymous` attribute set to `true` for a user that is not logged on, you'll get an error. It's up to you to only write to these properties from pages that are accessible only to logged-in users. Reading from a property works just fine, although you'll get empty values or the defaults you specified in `Web.config`.

Once you have enabled profile properties for anonymous users, reading from and writing to them is identical to how you deal with normal profile properties. In the "Exercises" section at the end of this chapter, you find code to modify the current theme selector so it uses Profile for anonymous and logged-in users.

Cleaning Up Old Anonymous Profiles

You may wonder what is happening with an anonymous user's profile when the associated user signs up for an account and becomes a registered user. The answer is: nothing. The old profile is discarded and the user gets a new profile that is associated with the registered account. Fortunately, this is easy to fix. Whenever a user changes from an anonymous to an authenticated user (that is, when she logs in), ASP.NET fires the `Profile_OnMigrateAnonymous` event that you can handle. You handle this event in a `Global.asax`, which is used for code that handles application- or session-wide events as you've seen before. Inside an event handler for this event, you can access two profiles for the same user: the old, anonymous profile that is about to get detached from the user and the new profile that is associated with the user who is currently logging in. You can then copy over relevant data and delete the old user account and its related profile data. From then on, you deal with the new profile only. Although not used in the Planet Wrox website, this event handler is a perfect place to copy anonymous profile data from the old profile to the new one, as demonstrated by the following code:

VB.NET

```
Public Sub Profile_OnMigrateAnonymous(sender As Object,
          args As ProfileMigrateEventArgs)
  Dim anonymousProfile As ProfileCommon = Profile.GetProfile(args.AnonymousID)

  ' Copy over anonymous properties only
  Profile.AnonymousProperty = anonymousProfile.AnonymousProperty

  ProfileManager.DeleteProfile(args.AnonymousID)
  AnonymousIdentificationModule.ClearAnonymousIdentifier()
  Membership.DeleteUser(args.AnonymousID, True)
End Sub
```

C#

```
public void Profile_OnMigrateAnonymous(object sender, ProfileMigrateEventArgs args)
{
  ProfileCommon anonymousProfile = Profile.GetProfile(args.AnonymousID);

  // Copy over anonymous properties only
  Profile.AnonymousProperty = anonymousProfile.AnonymousProperty;

  ProfileManager.DeleteProfile(args.AnonymousID);
  AnonymousIdentificationModule.ClearAnonymousIdentifier();
  Membership.DeleteUser(args.AnonymousID, true);
}
```

Note that this code uses `Profile.GetProfile(args.AnonymousID)` to get an instance of the previous, anonymous profile of the user. This gets a reference to the profile of the user before she logged in. `args.AnonymousID` returns a unique identifier for the anonymous user, which has been stored as the user's username in the `Users` table in the database.

The code then continues to copy over the existing, *anonymous* profile properties from the old to the new profile. In this example, only one property—called `AnonymousProperty`—is copied. However, you can modify the code to copy more properties. Note that there is no point in copying over properties that are not accessible by anonymous users. Those types of properties cannot have been set previously, so there's nothing to copy.

The final three lines of code then delete the old profile, clear the anonymous user ID from the cookie and, finally, delete the old, anonymous user account from the database. When this code has finished, the old profile is migrated successfully to the new profile, and all the old profile stuff has been successfully deleted from the database and the user's cookies.

The `ProfileManager` class—which lives in the `System.Web.Profile` namespace that you need to import for the previous example to work—provides you with more useful methods to work with Profile. For example, you can use `DeleteInactiveProfiles` to delete profiles for users who have been inactive for a certain amount of time. For detailed information about the `ProfileManager` class, look at this MSDN web page: `http://tinyurl.com/ManageProfile4-5`.

Looking at Other Users' Profiles

The examples you have seen so far use Profile to access data for the *current* user. However, what if you need to display data for a different user? For example, what if you wanted to display a user's biography below a Gig Pics album? You won't be able to use the `Profile` property of the `Page` class in this case directly because it provides information about the current user, not about the user who created the photo album.

To solve this problem, the `ProfileCommon` class, the base class of the underlying type of the `Profile` property of the `Page` class, comes with a `GetProfile` method. The `GetProfile` method retrieves an existing profile from the database if the name passed to it exists, or it creates a brand new profile if it doesn't exist yet. For example, to get the profile of a user with a username of Carmen, you can use this code:

VB.NET

```
Dim theProfile As ProfileCommon = Profile.GetProfile("Carmen")
```

C#

```
ProfileCommon theProfile = Profile.GetProfile("Carmen");
```

With the `Profile` instance created, you can access its properties as you are used to. The following code assigns the `Bio` property of Carmen's profile to the `Text` property of a `Label` control:

VB.NET

```
BioLabel.Text = theProfile.Bio
```

C#

```
BioLabel.Text = theProfile.Bio;
```

Being able to read someone else's profile is extremely useful. You can use it to show some of the properties of the profile to other users, as you see in the final exercise of this chapter. However, you can also use similar code to update other users' profiles. For example, you could create a page in the

Management section that enables you to manage the profiles of the users that registered at your site. When you do modify other users' profiles, be sure to call the `Save` method when you're done. As you learned earlier, changes to the profile are normally persisted in the database automatically. However, this applies only to the profile of the *current* user. To change and persist the previously retrieved profile, you can use this code:

VB.NET

```
theProfile.Bio = "New Bio for the Carmen account here"
theProfile.Save()
```

C#

```
theProfile.Bio = "New Bio for the Carmen account here";
theProfile.Save();
```

In the following exercise, you put some of this into practice when you show the name of the user who created a specific photo album, together with the biography of the user.

TRY IT OUT Working with Other Users' Profiles

The `Default.aspx` page in the `PhotoAlbums` folder displays the pictures in a specific photo album. You can't see which user created the photo album, so that would be a nice new feature. And to further improve the page, you can also display the user's biography. In this Try It Out, you see how to implement both features.

1. From the `PhotoAlbums` folder, open the `Default.aspx` page in Markup View. Scroll down and locate the two breaks and the `HyperLink` to edit the album you added earlier. Just before the breaks and the `HyperLink` control, drag a `PlaceHolder` control from the Toolbox and set its ID to `PhotoAlbumDetails`. Inside this `PlaceHolder`, drag two `Label` controls and then modify the code manually so it ends up like this:

```
</asp:ListView>
<asp:PlaceHolder ID="PhotoAlbumDetails" runat="server">
  <h2>Photo Album Details</h2>
  Created by:
  <asp:Label ID="UserNameLabel" runat="server" Text=""></asp:Label><br />
  About this user:
  <asp:Label ID="BioLabel" runat="server" Text=""></asp:Label>
</asp:PlaceHolder>
<br /><br />
<asp:HyperLink ID="EditLink" runat="server" Text="Edit Photo Album" />
```

2. Switch to the Code Behind of the page (press F7) and locate the `DataBound` event handler for the `ListView` control. Right after the nested `if` statement that hides the `HyperLink` control when the user doesn't have the necessary permissions, add these lines of code that retrieve the profile for the user who created the photo album and then update the relevant labels:

VB.NET

```
    EditLink.Visible = False
  End If

  If Not String.IsNullOrEmpty(photoAlbumOwner) Then
```

```
      Dim ownerProfile As ProfileCommon = Profile.GetProfile(photoAlbumOwner)
      UserNameLabel.Text = photoAlbumOwner
      BioLabel.Text = ownerProfile.Bio
      PhotoAlbumDetails.Visible = True
    Else
      PhotoAlbumDetails.Visible = False
    End If
  End Using
```

C#

```
      EditLink.Visible = false;
    }

    if (!string.IsNullOrEmpty(photoAlbumOwner))
    {
      ProfileCommon ownerProfile = Profile.GetProfile(photoAlbumOwner);
      UserNameLabel.Text = photoAlbumOwner;
      BioLabel.Text = ownerProfile.Bio;
      PhotoAlbumDetails.Visible = true;
    }
    else
    {
      PhotoAlbumDetails.Visible = false;
    }
  }
```

3. Save all your changes and open the page in your browser.
4. From the drop-down list, choose a photo album you created and you should see the photo album details appear. If you don't see them, make sure you selected a recent photo album from the list. Because you added the `UserName` column to the database at a later stage, some of the photo albums don't have a user associated with them. If the Photo Album Details section remains hidden, create a new photo album and add one or more pictures to it. This ensures that you have at least one photo album with the `UserName` property. If you now select the photo album from the list, you should see the Photo Album Details, as displayed in Figure 17-11.

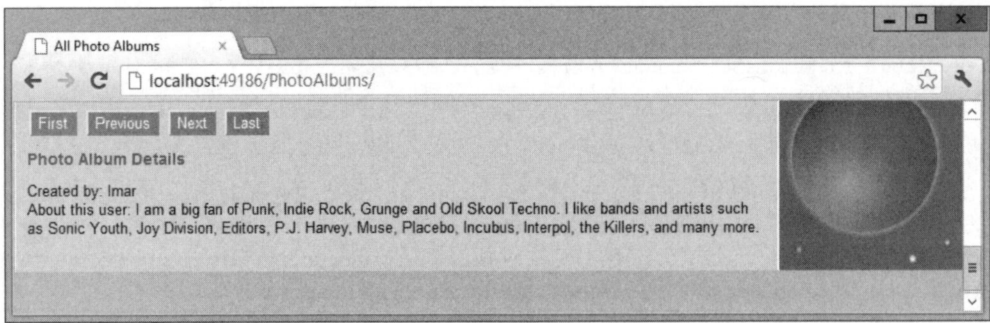

FIGURE 17-11

How It Works

Much of the code in this exercise has been discussed before. After adding a few `Label` controls in the Photo Album page, you retrieved the profile for the owner of the album with this code:

VB.NET

```
Dim ownerProfile As ProfileCommon = Profile.GetProfile(photoAlbumOwner)
```

C#

```
ProfileCommon ownerProfile = Profile.GetProfile(photoAlbumOwner);
```

This code gets a reference to an existing profile using `GetProfile`. The class that is returned is of type `ProfileCommon`; the underlying data type of the `Profile` property with the properties such as `FirstName` and `LastName` you set in the `Web.config` file. When you have the reference, working with it is almost identical to working with normal profiles. The only difference is that you must call `Save` to persist any changes made to the profile in the database as you saw earlier.

PRACTICAL PERSONALIZATION TIPS

The following list provides some personalization tips:

- Don't try to access the profile of the current user in the Login page, because it isn't available yet. The profile is instantiated early in the page's life cycle, so when a `Login` control authenticates a user in a Login page, it's too late to associate that user's profile with the current request. Use the `GetProfile` method of `ProfileCommon` instead or redirect to another page.
- Carefully consider what to store in Profile and what is better stored in your own database tables. Although the single-row structure that ASP.NET uses to store your profile offers you a simple and convenient solution, it's not the most efficient one, especially not with large amounts of data. Don't try to store complete reviews or even photo albums in Profile, but use your own database tables instead.
- The current implementation of Profile makes it difficult to query data from the `Profiles` table in your own queries. For example, it's difficult to answer queries like "Give me all users that prefer the Rock genre" because all the data is stored in a single column. To work around these issues, store data in your own tables (using Entity Framework, for example), or use a different Profile provider that you can download from the Sandbox section of the official ASP.NET website at `www.asp.net/downloads/sandbox/`.

SUMMARY

In this chapter, you learned how to use the Profile feature that ships with ASP.NET 4.5 to store user-related data. You can use Profile to keep track of data for authenticated and for anonymous users.

Setting up a profile is a pretty straightforward operation. You need a `<profile>` element in the `Web.config` file with a `<properties>` child element, and then you add one or more properties using `<add/>` elements. To group related properties, you use the `<group>` element.

When you have set up the profile, you access its properties through the `Profile` property of the `Page` class. This always accesses the profile for the current user. Any changes you make to this profile are persisted for you automatically at the end of the ASP.NET life cycle.

By design, profile properties are accessible only to logged-in users. However, you can easily change this by turning on anonymous identification.

To access the profile of a user other than the one associated with the current request, you can use the `GetProfile` method. Any changes made to this profile are not persisted automatically, so you must call `Save` to send the changes to the database.

Now that your pages contain more and more code, chances are that bugs and problems will creep into your application. In the next chapter you learn how to use exception handling to avoid those problems from ending up in the user interface. You also learn how to debug your code, so you can fix problems before they occur.

EXERCISES

1. The favorite theme feature you created earlier would be a great candidate for a profile property. What code would you need to add to the profile in `Web.config` to make this possible?

2. When you create profile properties in `Web.config`, the compiler extends the `Profile` property only for the Code Behind classes of Web Forms. Therefore, in order to set the favorite theme (or other properties) in the `BasePage`, you need to access the profile in a special way. Instead of accessing the `Profile` property on the `Page` class, you access it through the `HttpContext` like this:

   VB.NET

   ```
   Dim myProfile As ProfileCommon = CType(HttpContext.Current.Profile, ProfileCommon)
   ```

   C#

   ```
   ProfileCommon myProfile = (ProfileCommon) HttpContext.Current.Profile;
   ```

   Given this code, how can you rewrite `Page_PreInit` so it gets the preferred theme from the profile instead of from a cookie?

3. What else do you need to change to finalize storing the theme in the profile instead of a custom cookie?

You can find answers to these exercises in Appendix A.

▶ WHAT YOU LEARNED IN THIS CHAPTER

Anonymous identification	The ASP.NET feature that enables you to track users to your site, even if they haven't signed up for an account or are not logged in
ASP.NET Profile	The ASP.NET application service that enables you to store and retrieve information about users to your site
`EndRequest`	An event fired by the application in which the changes to the profile are persisted in the database
`OnMigrateAnonymous`	An event fired by the ASP.NET Profile feature that you can handle in `Global.asax` to copy anonymous properties into the new profile
Personalization	The process of targeting users with customized content based on their preferences or other information
Profile groups	The mechanism that enables you to group related profile properties
Profile provider	A provider responsible for storing and retrieving profile-related data

18

Exception Handling, Debugging, and Tracing

WHAT YOU WILL LEARN IN THIS CHAPTER:

- How to write code that is able to detect and handle errors that occur at run time, at the same time shielding your users from the error details
- How to detect errors that occur on your production machine so you can take countermeasures
- What debugging is and what debugging tools VS offers
- What tools you can use to gain information about your system and code while it's running in a development or production environment

WROX.COM CODE DOWNLOADS FOR THIS CHAPTER

You can find the wrox.com code downloads for this chapter on the Download Code tab at `www.wrox.com/remtitle.cgi?isbn=1118311809`. The code is in the Chapter 18 download.

You can't make an omelet without breaking eggs and you cannot write code without creating bugs. No matter how hard you try and how good you are, your code will contain problems that affect the behavior of your website.

Of course you should strive to minimize the impact of these bugs, aiming for a "zero bug count." To aid you in this, the ASP.NET run time and Visual Studio provide you with a number of tools.

First of all, the languages supported by .NET implement *exception handling*, a methodology to identify and handle errors that occur at run time. By handling these errors, you can present your users a friendly error message. At the same time, you can log these errors, giving you a chance to fix them before they reoccur. In this chapter, you see how exception handling works, and how to log your errors.

Before your code goes into production, you need to write and debug it first. To help you debug your code, VS comes with a rich toolset that includes ways to step through your code line by line, look at your variables and objects at run time, and even change them as you go. The toolset also provides you with valuable information about the *execution path* your code follows: the path that your application takes through your code, following methods, event handlers, `If` and `Else` statements, and so on. In the next section, you learn more about exception handling, while the debugging tools are discussed later in this chapter.

EXCEPTION HANDLING

Whenever you write code, there is a chance things won't turn out as expected, resulting in code that does not compile, a crash, or otherwise unexpected behavior of your application. Things can go wrong for a large number of reasons: you introduce a typo in your code, the database server you're connecting to at run time suddenly goes down, you got your logic mixed up and accidentally deleted all rows from a database table instead of just one, you try to delete a row from a database table that still has associated rows, you try to write a file to a folder without proper permissions, your users enter incorrect data, and so forth.

To understand these problems and think of ways to anticipate, avoid, and handle them, you first need to understand the different types of errors that may occur in your website. Once you understand the main differences, the remainder of this section is spent discussing ways to prevent and solve them.

Different Types of Errors

You can broadly categorize errors into the following groups:

- **Syntax errors**—Errors that are caused by typos, missing keywords, or otherwise incorrect code.
- **Logic errors**—Errors in applications that seem to run fine but that produce unexpected or unwanted results.
- **Runtime errors**—Errors that cause the application to crash or behave unexpectedly at run time.

Each of these categories is discussed in the following sections, together with information on avoiding and fixing them.

Syntax Errors

Syntax errors, or *compile errors*, are the easiest to find and fix because they happen during development. The IDE tells you when an error occurs and often prevents you from running the application while it still contains errors. Syntax errors are caused by simple typos, missing or duplicate keywords and characters, and so on. The following examples all show errors that are caught at development time by the *compiler*. A compiler is a program that turns the human-readable code you write in VB.NET or C# into machine-readable code that can be executed.

VB.NET

```
mailBody = mailBody.Repalce("##Name##", Name.Text)  ' Replace is misspelled

Response.Write()                                    ' Required parameter
                                                    ' for the Write method
                                                    ' is missing

If i > 10                                           ' Missing keyword Then
  ' Do something here
End If
```

C#

```
mailBody = mailBody.Repalce("##Name##", Name.Text); // Replace is misspelled

Response.Write();                                   // Required parameter for the
                                                    // Write method is missing

if (i > 10)                                         // Missing opening brace or
                                                    // extraneous closing brace
  // Do something here
}
```

Compile errors are always displayed in the Error List (accessible through the View ➪ Error List menu), shown in Figure 18-1 for a C# website.

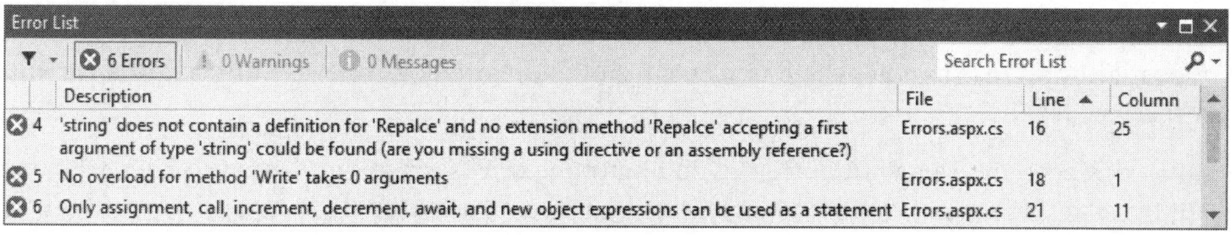

Error List

6 Errors | 0 Warnings | 0 Messages | Search Error List

	Description	File	Line	Column
4	'string' does not contain a definition for 'Repalce' and no extension method 'Repalce' accepting a first argument of type 'string' could be found (are you missing a using directive or an assembly reference?)	Errors.aspx.cs	16	25
5	No overload for method 'Write' takes 0 arguments	Errors.aspx.cs	18	1
6	Only assignment, call, increment, decrement, await, and new object expressions can be used as a statement	Errors.aspx.cs	21	11

FIGURE 18-1

You can force the compiler to give you an up-to-date list of all the compilation errors in your site. To do this, from the main menu choose Build ➪ Build Web Site. When you want to force VS to recompile the entire site (which is slower as it also recompiles files that haven't changed), choose Build ➪ Rebuild Web Site instead.

To go to the location where the error occurred so you can fix it, double-click the error in the Error List. To cycle through the errors and the code where the error occurs, click an error in the Error List and press F8 to go to the next error.

Logic Errors

Logic errors are often harder to find because they compile fine but only happen during the execution of your code. Consider the following buggy example:

VB.NET

```
Dim fromAddress As String = "you@example.com"
Dim toAddress As String = EmailAddress.Text
```

```
myMessage.From = New MailAddress(toAddress)
myMessage.To.Add(New MailAddress(fromAddress))
```

C#

```
string fromAddress = "you@example.com";
string toAddress = EmailAddress.Text;
myMessage.From = new MailAddress(toAddress);
myMessage.To.Add(new MailAddress(fromAddress));
```

Although it's easy to see what the problem is in this example (the `To` and `From` addresses are mixed up), it may be harder to find in a file with 250 lines of code. Additionally, because the compiler happily accepts your mistake, you won't notice the error until you see a message in your Inbox that you thought you sent to your visitors.

The best way to track down and solve logic errors is using the built-in debugging capabilities of VS. You get an in-depth look at these tools later in the chapter.

Runtime Errors

Runtime errors occur at run time, which makes them incredibly difficult to track. Imagine you have a site that contains a bug that's hidden somewhere in a page. You haven't found it yet, but one of your visitors did and she gets a nasty error message (more on those later) instead. What can you do? Probably not much, because there's a fair chance your visitor won't even inform you about the mistake.

So, it's important to have a good error handling strategy in place that enables you to avoid errors when possible, and that handles them gracefully and optionally logs relevant information for you when they occur.

The following section deals with detecting and handling errors, or *exceptions* in .NET parlance; later in this chapter, you learn how to log errors and shield your users from ugly pages with detailed exception messages.

Catching and Handling Exceptions

Normally, when serious exceptions occur, the user is presented with an error message. For example, if you try to send a message to a mail server that isn't up and running, or doesn't allow you to connect to it, you'll get an *exception* that provides details about the error. The exception that you get is an instance of a class that ultimately inherits the `System.Exception` class; the base class for all exceptions. Many exception types exist, each serving a distinct purpose.

By default, this exception bubbles up all the way to the user interface where it's presented as a so-called *Yellow Screen of Death*, a reference to Windows' "Blue Screen of Death" that you get when Windows crashes. You see a real example of this error in the next exercise.

Obviously, it's a lot better if you can anticipate the exception and write some code that prevents it from appearing in the user interface. You could, for example, display a nicely formatted message to users instead, informing them the message could not be sent at this moment.

Fortunately, support for these kinds of scenarios is integrated deeply in the .NET programming languages such as C# and Visual Basic .NET. In these languages, you can make use of `Try Catch Finally` blocks (`try catch finally` in C#) where code that could potentially throw an exception is wrapped in a `Try` block. Note that the VB.NET and C# versions of these keywords only differ in case; I'll refer to the capitalized version in the remainder of the text, except in code blocks.

When an exception occurs, the remainder of the code in the `Try` block is skipped and some code in a `Catch` block can be run to deal with the error. You can have multiple `Catch` blocks that all deal with specific exceptions, but only the first block that matches the exception type will fire. Therefore, it's important to order the various `Catch` blocks from specific to generic in order to handle the exception in the most specific `Catch` block. You see more of this later.

A `Try` or a `Catch` block can be followed by a `Finally` block. Code in a `Finally` block is *always* fired, regardless of whether an exception occurred and, as such, is an ideal location for some clean-up code.

Both `Catch` and `Finally` blocks are optional, although you always need at least one of them.

The code in the following example tries to send an e-mail and then sets the `Text` property of a `Label` to the value of the variable `userMessage`. Note: `myMessage` and `mySmtpClient` are created by code not shown in this example. The `userMessage` variable is assigned a value in either the `Try` block (when the code executed successfully) or in the `Catch` block (when an error occurred). Either way, this `userMessage` is always assigned to the `Label` in the `Finally` block:

VB.NET

```
Dim userMessage As String = String.Empty
Try
  mySmtpClient.Send(myMessage)
  userMessage = "Message sent"
Catch ex As Exception
  userMessage = "An unknown error occurred."
Finally
  Message.Text = userMessage
End Try
```

C#

```
string userMessage = string.Empty;
try
{
  mySmtpClient.Send(myMessage);
  userMessage = "Message sent";
}
catch (Exception ex)
{
  userMessage = "An unknown error occurred.";
}
finally
{
  Message.Text = userMessage;
}
```

In this code example, the `Catch` block is set up to handle an exception of type `System.Exception`, the base class of all exceptions in the .NET Framework. This exception is sent to (or *caught by*) the `Catch` block in the `ex` variable. In C#, you could leave out the `ex` variable if you don't use it in your code:

C#

```
catch (Exception)
{
  userMessage = "An unknown error occurred.";
}
```

The ability to specify an `Exception` type is useful when you think your code can encounter more than one exception. In that case, you can have multiple `Catch` blocks for different `Exception` types. The following code is capable of handling a specific `SmtpException` that may occur during the mail sending operation, and it's also capable of catching all other exceptions using its generic `Catch` block:

VB.NET

```
Try
  mySmtpClient.Send(myMessage)
Catch smtpException As SmtpException
  userMessage = "Sorry, an error occurred while sending your message."
Catch ex As Exception
  ' Something else went wrong.
End Try
```

C#

```
try
{
  mySmtpClient.Send(myMessage);
}
catch (SmtpException smtpException)
{
  userMessage = "Sorry, an error occurred while sending your message.";
}
catch (Exception ex)
{
  // Something else went wrong.
}
```

The order of the exception-handling blocks is important. .NET scans the list of `Catch` blocks from top to bottom and only fires the code in the first block that matches a specific type of exception. In the preceding example, when an `SmtpException` occurs (which is a subclass of `Exception`), it will be caught by the `Catch` block that handles exceptions of type `SmtpException`. Although an `SmtpException` *is* also an `Exception`, the code in the last `Catch` block won't be fired anymore because only the first matching `Catch` block is handled. Therefore, if you reverse the order of the `Catch` blocks in this example, the more generic `Exception` block would be executed, and the code in the `SmtpException` block would never run.

> ***WARNING*** *The preceding example shows how to catch all exceptions using the base* `Exception` *type in the* `Catch` *block. Don't use this in your own websites. Instead, handle only those types of exceptions that you know how to deal with, and let all other, unknown exceptions bubble in the application. Later in this chapter you see how to centrally handle these unhandled exceptions.*

In the following exercise, you see how to use Try Catch Finally in your code.

TRY IT OUT Handling Exceptions

In this Try It Out, you see how to write exception-handling code to catch problems with sending e-mail. These problems may occur when the mail server is down, for example. To simulate a broken mail server, you'll temporarily use a nonexistent mail server name causing your code to crash.

You'll try out the Try Catch Finally code in a separate page in the Demos folder so you can closely watch its behavior. When you understand how it works, you'll modify the ContactForm.ascx user control and incorporate the exception-handling code there. The reason you write this code in the demo page first is that the user control uses an Ajax UpdatePanel that shields users from the dirty details of an exception by default, making it difficult to see what's going on.

1. Create a new file in the Demos folder and call it ExceptionHandling.aspx. Base the page on your custom template and set its Title to **Exception Handling Demo**.
2. Add a Label control to the main content area and set its ID to Message.
3. Switch to Design View and set up an event handler for the Load event of the page by double-clicking the read-only area of the page. Then at the top of the file, add either an Imports or a using statement for the System.Net.Mail namespace:

VB.NET

```
Imports System.Net.Mail
```

C#

```
using System.Net.Mail;
```

4. Add the following code to the event handler that VS created. Notice how this code is almost identical to the code you added in the ContactForm.ascx user control, so you can save yourself some typing by copying parts of the code from that file. Notice how the code passes "DoesNotExist" to the SmtpClient's constructor as an argument for the mail host. This is done deliberately to trigger an exception.

VB.NET

```
Protected Sub Page_Load(sender As Object, e As EventArgs) Handles Me.Load
  Dim myMessage As MailMessage = New MailMessage()
  myMessage.Subject = "Exception Handling Test"
  myMessage.Body = "Test message body"

  myMessage.From = New MailAddress("you@example.com")
  myMessage.To.Add(New MailAddress("you@example.com"))

  Dim mySmtpClient As New SmtpClient("DoesNotExist")
  mySmtpClient.Send(myMessage)
  Message.Text = "Message sent"
End Sub
```

C#

```
protected void Page_Load(object sender, EventArgs e)
```

```
{
  MailMessage myMessage = new MailMessage();
  myMessage.Subject = "Exception Handling Test";
  myMessage.Body = "Test message body";

  myMessage.From = new MailAddress("you@example.com");
  myMessage.To.Add(new MailAddress("you@example.com"));

  SmtpClient mySmtpClient = new SmtpClient("DoesNotExist");
  mySmtpClient.Send(myMessage);
  Message.Text = "Message sent";
}
```

Don't forget to change the two e-mail addresses to your own.

5. Open `Web.config` and comment out the `<system.net>` element (select the entire element and then press Ctrl+K followed by Ctrl+C). You added this element in Chapter 9 to configure your site for sending e-mails. By disabling it temporarily, you can ensure that no settings from the configuration file are used which in turn will force the `SmtpClient` to try to deliver the e-mail at the `DoesNotExist` server which obviously will fail. Save the changes to the file, but keep it open so you can easily undo this change in a later step.

6. Switch back to `ExceptionHandling.aspx` and press Ctrl+F5 to open up the page in your browser. You should see the "Yellow Screen of Death" with an error message. Scroll down in the page to see the Stack Trace, shown in Figure 18-2.

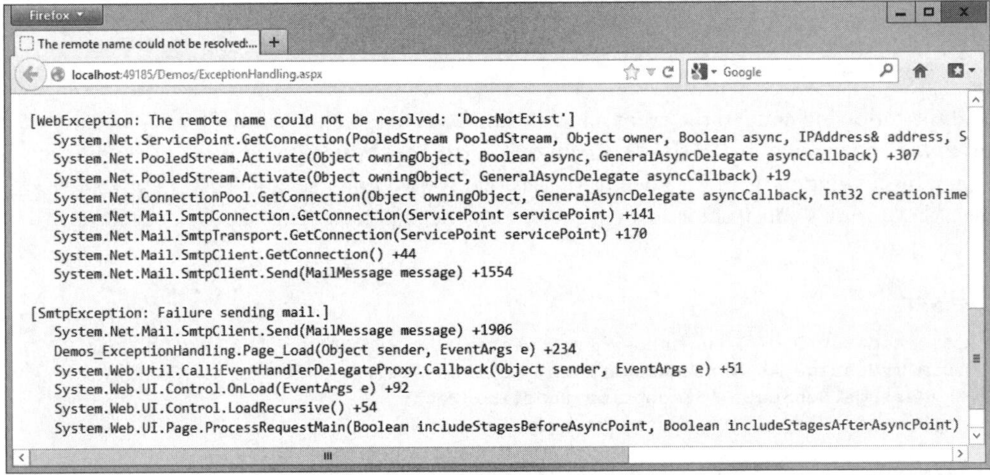

FIGURE 18-2

Note that two exceptions are listed: a `WebException` (to indicate that the name `DoesNotExist` could not be resolved) and a `SmtpException`. The code in the `SmtpClient` encountered and caught the `WebException`, wrapped it in a new `SmtpException` and threw that exception to indicate to your code that a problem occurred.

7. Go back to VS and wrap the code that assigns the addresses and sends the message in a `Try Catch` block:

VB.NET

```
Try
  myMessage.From = New MailAddress("you@example.com")
  myMessage.To.Add(New MailAddress("you@example.com"))
  Dim mySmtpClient As New SmtpClient("DoesNotExist")
  mySmtpClient.Send(myMessage)
  Message.Text = "Message sent"
Catch ex As SmtpException
  Message.Text = "An error occurred while sending your e-mail. Please try again."
End Try
```

C#

```
try
{
  myMessage.From = new MailAddress("you@example.com");
  myMessage.To.Add(new MailAddress("you@example.com"));
  SmtpClient mySmtpClient = new SmtpClient("DoesNotExist");
  mySmtpClient.Send(myMessage);
  Message.Text = "Message sent";
}
catch (SmtpException)
{
  Message.Text = "An error occurred while sending your e-mail. Please try again.";
}
```

Notice how the code still contains an invalid mail server.

8. Save your changes and request the page in your browser again. You should now see a user-friendly error message, visible in Figure 18-3.

FIGURE 18-3

The exception that is thrown is now caught in the `Catch` block. Instead of getting an error page with all the technical details of the exception, the user now gets a friendly message explaining that something went wrong.

9. Go back to `ExceptionHandling.aspx` and fix the code for the `SmtpClient`:

VB.NET

```
Dim mySmtpClient As New SmtpClient()
```

C#

```
SmtpClient mySmtpClient = new SmtpClient();
```

Also, in `Web.config` undo the changes you made earlier by restoring the `<system.net>` element.

10. Save all open changes and request `ExceptionHandling.aspx` in your browser again. You'll now get a message indicating that the e-mail was sent successfully.

11. Open `ContactForm.ascx` from the `Controls` folder, switch to its Code Behind, and wrap the code that creates and sends the message in the following `Try Catch` block. Also, move the line that sets the visibility of the `Message` control to the `Finally` block:

VB.NET

```
Try
  Dim myMessage As New MailMessage()
  ...
  System.Threading.Thread.Sleep(5000)
Catch ex As SmtpException
  Message.Text = "An error occurred while sending your e-mail. Please try again."
Finally
  Message.Visible = True
End Try
```

C#

```
try
{
  MailMessage myMessage = new MailMessage();
  ...
  System.Threading.Thread.Sleep(5000);
}
catch (SmtpException)
{
  Message.Text = "An error occurred while sending your e-mail. Please try again.";
}
finally
{
  Message.Visible = true;
}
```

Notice how the line that sets the `Message` control's `Visible` property to `True` is now in a `Finally` block. This way, the `Label` is made visible, regardless of whether an error occurred.

From now on, whenever an error occurs during the sending of the e-mail, your users will get a normal error message instead of the full error detail page that .NET displays by default.

How It Works

When an exception occurs at run time, .NET checks if the code is wrapped in a `Try Catch` block. If that's the case, it scans the list of `Catch` blocks for an `Exception` type that matches the exception being thrown. Only the first Catch block that matches the Exception is being called; all remaining Catch blocks are ignored. Code in the Try block following the line that caused the exception is not executed anymore.

In this exercise, the code has a Catch block for the SmtpException type, which is executed when an exception of that type—or one of its subtypes—is encountered. As you learned before the exercise, you can have multiple Catch blocks, each one dealing with a specific type of exception. All other exceptions won't be handled by this code. You see how to deal with these other exceptions in a later section.

With these Try Catch Finally blocks, you can write code that helps you deal with errors that you think might happen in your code. It's always a good practice to wrap code that might throw an error in a Try Catch block so you can deal with it gracefully. Some examples of code that may throw an exception include:

- **Sending e-mail**—The mail server may be down, or you may not have the permissions to access it.
- **Accessing a database**—The server may be down, you may not have permission to access it, you may get an error due to foreign key constraint violations as you saw in Chapter 15, and so on.
- **Trying to write an uploaded file to disk**—The disk may be full, you may not have the necessary permissions to write to disk, or you are providing an invalid filename.

Although Try Catch blocks are great to avoid exceptions from bubbling up to the user interface, you should use them with care, because they come at a cost. A Try Catch block is generally slower than code without it, so you shouldn't use a Try Catch block for errors you can avoid otherwise. Consider the following example that divides two numbers:

VB.NET

```
Dim value1 As Integer = Convert.ToInt32(ValueBox1.Text)
Dim value2 As Integer = Convert.ToInt32(ValueBox2.Text)
Try
  result = value1 / value2
  ResultLabel.Text = result.ToString()
Catch ex As DivideByZeroException
  ResultLabel.Text = "Sorry, division by zero is not possible."
End Try
```

C#

```
int value1 = Convert.ToInt32(ValueBox1.Text);
int value2 = Convert.ToInt32(ValueBox2.Text);
try
{
  result = value1 / value2;
  ResultLabel.Text = result.ToString();
}
catch (DivideByZeroException ex)
{
  ResultLabel.Text = "Sorry, division by zero is not possible.";
}
```

In this example, the code is set up to expect a `DivideByZeroException`. This exception is thrown when `value2` contains the value `0`. Although at first it seems like a good idea to implement exception handling here, it's actually much better to write code that checks for this value before the division is carried out, instead of letting an exception occur:

VB.NET

```
If value2 <> 0 Then
  result = value1 / value2
  ResultLabel.Text = result.ToString()
Else
  ResultLabel.Text = "Sorry, division by zero is not possible."
End If
```

C#

```
if (value2 != 0)
{
  result = value1 / value2;
  ResultLabel.Text = result.ToString();
}
else
{
  ResultLabel.Text = "Sorry, division by zero is not possible.";
}
```

Of course it would even be better if you had placed a `CompareValidator` on the page, making sure that `ValueBox2` could never contain the value zero. Chapter 9 explains how to use this control.

Although `Try Catch` blocks are useful to catch exceptions that you anticipate, what about errors you don't? How can you deal with unexpected errors? Because they are unexpected, you won't know when they occur, so it's difficult to write code to handle them.

To solve this problem, the next section shows you how you can globally catch and log unhandled exceptions and send information about them by e-mail. This way, you know they occurred, giving you, the page developer, a chance to fix them before they happen again.

Global Error Handling and Custom Error Pages

To shield your users from the technical details of the exception, you should provide them with a user-friendly error page instead. Fortunately, ASP.NET enables you to define *custom error pages*: ASPX pages that are shown to the user when an exception occurs. You can map different types of errors (server errors, page not found errors, security problems, and so forth) to different pages.

You define the error page or pages you want to show in the `customErrors` element of the `Web.config` file. A typical element looks like this:

```
<customErrors mode="On" defaultRedirect="~/Errors/Error500.aspx"
                        redirectMode="ResponseRewrite">
  <error statusCode="404" redirect="~/Errors/Error404.aspx" />
  <error statusCode="500" redirect="~/Errors/Error500.aspx" />
</customErrors>
```

The `mode` attribute determines whether or not a visitor to your site gets to see a detailed error page. The attribute supports the following three values:

- `On`—Every visitor to your site always sees the custom error page when an error occurs.
- `Off`—The custom error page is never shown and full error details are displayed on the page.
- `RemoteOnly`—The full error details are shown to local users (browsing the site from the same machine as the site runs on), while all other users get to see the custom error page. This setting enables you to see error messages on your site during development, while your users are always presented with the custom error page.

Within the opening and closing tags of the `customErrors` element you define separate `<error />` elements, one for each HTTP status code you want to support. The previous configuration defines two custom pages: one that is shown when the requested page could not be found (a 404 status code) and one that is shown when a server error occurs (a 500 code).

For all other HTTP status codes you haven't defined explicitly, the `defaultRedirect` attribute is used to determine the custom error page.

The `redirectMode` attribute determines the way the new page is shown to the user and is discussed later in this chapter.

Although custom error pages shield your users from the exception details, they don't help in informing *you* that an exception occurred. All these pages do is hide the real error and show a page with a custom error message instead. To be notified about these exceptions, you could write some code that looks at the exception and then sends you an e-mail with the details. Alternatively, you could write code that inserts the error details in a database, or writes them to a text file.

ASP.NET offers you a handy, central location to write code that is triggered when an exception occurs. You write this code in a special event handler called `Application_Error` inside the `Global.asax` file that you saw first in Chapter 11. Inside this event handler, you can collect relevant data about the exception, stick it in an e-mail message, and send it to your own Inbox. This gives you detailed information about exceptions that occur on your site, aiding in fixing the problem as soon as possible. You see how to write this code in the next exercise.

TRY IT OUT Handling Exceptions Site Wide

In this Try It Out you learn how to write code in the `Global.asax` file to send the exception message by e-mail. Additionally, you see how to create global error pages that are shown to your user in case of an error.

1. If you didn't add the `Global.asax` file to your site in Chapter 11, you need to add it first. To do so, right-click the website in the Solution Explorer and choose Add ⇨ Add New Item. In the list with templates, select Global Application Class. Leave its name set to `Global.asax` and click Add.
2. At the top of the `Global.asax` file, right after the `Application` directive, add the following `Import` statement. Note that when adding an `Import` statement in Markup View, both VB.NET and C# use the keyword `Import`, rather than `Imports` and `using` that you normally use in Code Behind:

   VB.NET

   ```
   <%@ Application Language="VB" %>
   <%@ Import Namespace="System.Net.Mail" %>
   ```

C#

```
<%@ Application Language="C#" %>
<%@ Import Namespace="System.Net.Mail" %>
```

3. Inside the `Application_Error` handler that should already be present in the `Global.asax` file, add the following highlighted code that is triggered whenever an unhandled exception occurs in your site. If the handler isn't there, make sure you type all the code from the following snippet, including the parts that are not bolded:

VB.NET

```
Sub Application_Error(ByVal sender As Object, ByVal e As EventArgs)
  If HttpContext.Current.Server.GetLastError() IsNot Nothing Then
    Dim myException As Exception =
                HttpContext.Current.Server.GetLastError().GetBaseException()
    Dim mailSubject As String = "Error in page " & Request.Url.ToString()
    Dim message As String = String.Empty
    message &= "<strong>Message</strong><br />" & myException.Message & "<br />"
    message &= "<strong>Stack Trace</strong><br />" &
            myException.StackTrace & "<br />"
    message &= "<strong>Query String</strong><br />" &
            Request.QueryString.ToString()&"<br />"
    Dim myMessage As MailMessage = New MailMessage("you@example.com",
                  "you@example.com", mailSubject, message)
    myMessage.IsBodyHtml = True
    Dim mySmtpClient As SmtpClient = New SmtpClient()
    mySmtpClient.Send(myMessage)
  End If
End Sub
```

C#

```
void Application_Error(object sender, EventArgs e)
{
  if (HttpContext.Current.Server.GetLastError() != null)
  {
    Exception myException =
            HttpContext.Current.Server.GetLastError().GetBaseException();
    string mailSubject = "Error in page " + Request.Url.ToString();
    string message = string.Empty;
    message += "<strong>Message</strong><br />" + myException.Message + "<br />";
    message += "<strong>Stack Trace</strong><br />" + myException.StackTrace +
              "<br />";
    message += "<strong>Query String</strong><br />" +
              Request.QueryString.ToString() + "<br />";
    MailMessage myMessage = new MailMessage("you@example.com",
              "you@example.com", mailSubject, message);
    myMessage.IsBodyHtml = true;
    SmtpClient mySmtpClient = new SmtpClient();
    mySmtpClient.Send(myMessage);
  }
}
```

Don't forget to change the two e-mail addresses that are passed to the `MailMessage`'s constructor. The first address represents the sender's address, and the second one holds the recipient's address.

4. Save all your changes and close the `Global.asax` file.

5. Next, open up the `Web.config` file, and as a direct child of `<system.web>`, add the following `customErrors` element:

```
<system.web>
  <customErrors mode="On" defaultRedirect="~/Errors/OtherErrors.aspx"
          redirectMode="ResponseRewrite">
    <error statusCode="404" redirect="~/Errors/Error404.aspx" />
  </customErrors>
```

   Save and close the configuration file.

6. Create a new folder in the root of your website and call it `Errors`.

7. Inside this new folder, create two new Web Forms and call them `Error404.aspx` and `OtherErrors.aspx`, respectively. Make sure both of them are based on your custom template so they are using the main master page and inherit from `BasePage`. If you followed the exercises in the previous chapter and now use Profile to store the user's favorite theme, refer to the Common Mistakes section at the end of this exercise to learn about the pitfalls of using the master page and `BasePage` for your custom 404 error page.

8. Set the `Title` of `Error404.aspx` to **`File Not Found`**. Inside the content placeholder for the main content, add the following markup:

```
<asp:Content ID="Content2" ContentPlaceHolderID="cpMainContent" runat="Server">
  <h1>File Not Found</h1>
  <p>The page you requested could not be found. Please check out the
    <a href="~/" runat="server">Homepage</a>
          or choose a different page from the menu.</p>
  <p>The Planet Wrox Team</p>
</asp:Content>
```

9. Switch to Design View, double-click the page to set up a `Page_Load` handler, and add the following code to it:

   VB.NET

```
Protected Sub Page_Load(sender As Object, e As EventArgs) Handles Me.Load
  Response.Status = "404 Not Found"
  Response.StatusCode = 404
  Response.TrySkipIisCustomErrors = True
End Sub
```

   C#

```
protected void Page_Load(object sender, EventArgs e)
{
  Response.Status = "404 Not Found";
  Response.StatusCode = 404;
  Response.TrySkipIisCustomErrors = true;
}
```

10. Open the generic `OtherErrors.aspx` page, set its `Title` to **`An Error Occurred`**, and enter the following content:

```
<asp:Content ID="Content2" ContentPlaceHolderID="cpMainContent" runat="Server">
  <h1>An unknown error occurred</h1>
```

```
  <p>An error occurred in the page you requested. The error has been logged and
               we'll fix it ASAP.</p>
  <p>The Planet Wrox Team</p>
</asp:Content>
```

11. Double-click the page in Design View and add the following code to the `Page_Load` handler:

VB.NET

```
Protected Sub Page_Load(sender As Object, e As EventArgs) Handles Me.Load
  Response.TrySkipIisCustomErrors = True
End Sub
```

C#

```
protected void Page_Load(object sender, EventArgs e)
{
  Response.TrySkipIisCustomErrors = true;
}
```

Because this page will be used for all possible errors except a 404 error, there's no point in setting an explicit `Status` or `StatusCode`.

12. Save the changes to all open files by pressing Ctrl+Shift+S and then close them. Right-click `Default.aspx` in the Solution Explorer and choose View In Browser. Once the page has finished loading, request a nonexistent page like `DefaultTest.aspx` by changing the address bar of the browser to something like `http://localhost:49186/DefaultTest.aspx`. Obviously, the `DefaultTest.aspx` page does not exist, so you get an error. But instead of a detailed error page, you should now get the error page you defined and created in this Try It Out, shown in Figure 18-4.

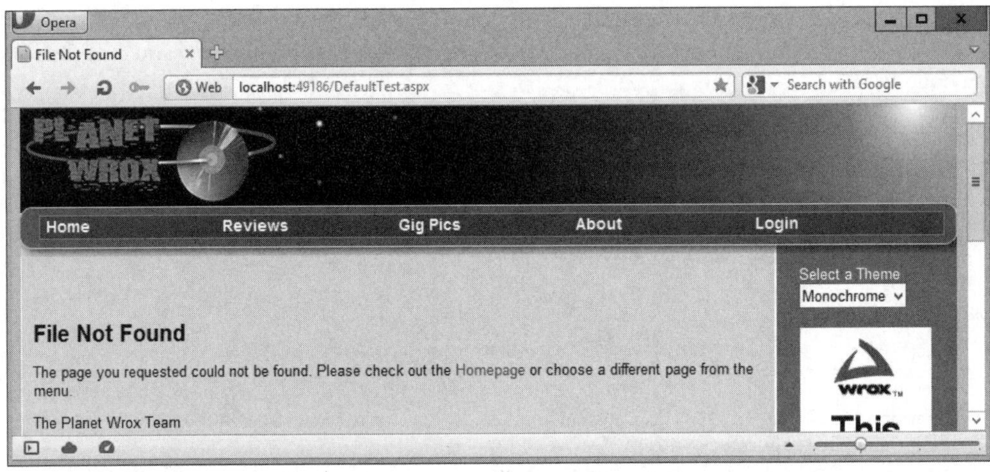

FIGURE 18-4

> **COMMON MISTAKES** *If, instead of this error message, you get a generic "File not found" exception page, check the syntax of the* `customErrors` *section in the* `Web.config` *file. Additionally, check that you can successfully view the actual error pages (*`Error404.aspx` *and* `OtherErrors.aspx`*) by directly requesting them in the browser. If they contain an error (for example, if you forgot to set the page title) they cannot be used as custom error pages.*
>
> *You'll also get the generic error page when you followed the exercises in the preceding chapter and rewrote the preferred theme selector to use Profile. Because of the way a 404 error is handled internally, you cannot use Profile in the error page or the master page it's based on. To work around this problem, re-create the* `Error404.aspx` *page as a standard Web Form not using your master page and* `BasePage` *and things should work fine. You could also set the* `redirectMode` *attribute in the* `Web.config` *to* `ResponseRedirect`*, but from a Search Engine Optimization (SEO) point of view this is not recommended. You'll learn more about the* `redirectMode` *attribute and why* `ResponseRedirect` *is not the optimal solution in the How it Works section.*

Besides the error page in the browser, you should also get a message by e-mail that provides more details about the error. Figure 18-5 shows the message you get when you request a page that does not exist.

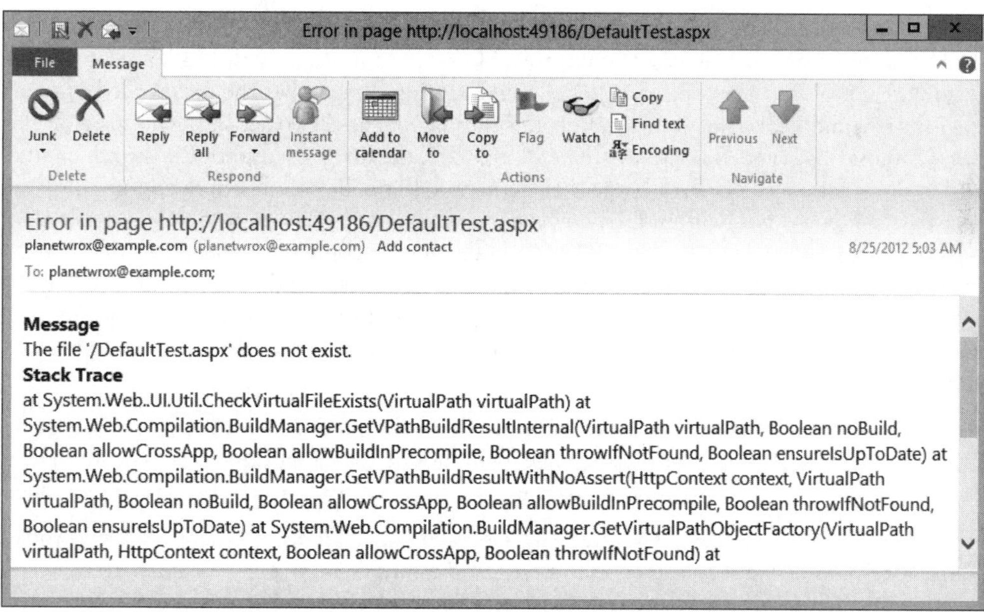

FIGURE 18-5

In the next chapter, you learn how to turn this feature on and off through configuration so you can disable it during development.

How It Works

Two important parts are worth examining in this exercise. The first part is the way the ASP.NET run time hides the "Yellow Screen of Death" with the error details from the user with the use of custom error pages. This serves two purposes. First, it helps you protect potentially private data like passwords or information about database connections that may end up in the error message. Second, it shields your users from cryptic error messages they probably don't understand anyway and gives you the chance to display a good-looking error page instead that integrates with the site's look and feel.

The only thing you need to do to make this work is to enable custom errors in the `Web.config` file and provide one or more pages you want to display for the errors that may occur in your site. The configuration element lets you set up different pages for different exceptions:

```
<customErrors mode="On" defaultRedirect="~/Errors/OtherErrors.aspx"
        redirectMode="ResponseRewrite">
  <error statusCode="404" redirect="~/Errors/Error404.aspx" />
</customErrors>
```

When .NET encounters a 404 exception (when you request a page that cannot be found), the contents of the `Error404.aspx` page are shown. The name and content of this page are completely up to you, giving you the option to provide your own explanation to the user about what went wrong. Note that this works only for file types that are registered with ASP.NET, like `.aspx` files. It won't work out of the box for `.html` files or images when you're not using the Integrated Pipeline mode of IIS, Microsoft's web server. You see more about the Integrated Pipeline mode in the next chapter.

This exercise contains two key elements to improve SEO. First, notice how the `redirectMode` is set to `ResponseRewrite`. The other option is `ResponseRedirect`. Remember the difference between `Server.Transfer` and `Response.Redirect` from Chapter 7? These two settings are based on the same principles. If you set `redirectMode` to `ResponseRedirect`, the browser (and thus a search engine) is *redirected* to the error page. The error page then returns a 404 code so the search engine thinks that the error page itself could not be found. If, however, you set `redirectMode` to `ResponseRewrite`, the originally requested page results in a 404 error code and the contents of the `Error404.aspx` page are streamed to the browser. This enables search engines to correctly update their indexes. The only downside of the `ResponseRewrite` setting is that you can't use Profile in the page or a master page it is based on. As you saw earlier, the best work around is to create a page that is not based on your custom template.

The second part that improves SEO is the code in the Code Behind of `Error404.aspx`. That code sets the HTTP status code to 404 to indicate the page could not be found on the server. Without these two lines of code, search engines won't understand the page doesn't exist and will keep trying to index it.

Notice that only the 404 error code is redirected to its own page. All other exceptions cause the generic `OtherErrors.aspx` to be loaded. You can, however, add multiple `<error />` elements to the `<customErrors>` element, each one for a different status code. For a list of HTTP status codes, check out this knowledge base article: `http://support.microsoft.com/default.aspx/kb/943891`.

Note the call to `Response.TrySkipIisCustomErrors`. This tells IIS that it should not try to render its own custom error pages. Without this setting, you may get IIS's generic error pages instead of the ones you defined here. You won't notice the difference with IIS Express, so this code won't come into play until you deploy your site to a production version of IIS as you'll see in the next chapter.

The other main part of this exercise is the code in `Global.asax` that fires when an unhandled exception occurs. In that case, the `Application_Error` event handler is triggered. Within this handler, you can retrieve the exception that occurred with this code:

VB.NET

```
If HttpContext.Current.Server.GetLastError() IsNot Nothing Then
  Dim myException As Exception =
            HttpContext.Current.Server.GetLastError().GetBaseException()
```

C#

```
if (HttpContext.Current.Server.GetLastError() != null)
{
  Exception myException =
            HttpContext.Current.Server.GetLastError().GetBaseException();
```

To get at the root exception that caused the problem in the first place, you need to call `GetBaseException()` on the `Exception` that is returned by `Server.GetLastError()`. This `Exception` instance, stored in the `myException` variable, then gives you access to useful properties such as `Message` and `StackTrace`. In this exercise, the `StackTrace` displayed in the error e-mail contains information that really isn't of any interest to you. However, with other exceptions, such as one thrown by an incorrect configuration of the mail server or a division by zero exception, the `StackTrace` gives you information about the file that generated the error, the method that caused it, and even the line number in the code, making it easy to find the error and fix it.

The remainder of the code creates an e-mail message with the error details. It also adds information about the query string with this code:

VB.NET

```
message &= "<strong>Query String</strong><br />" &
        Request.QueryString.ToString() & "<br />"
```

C#

```
message += "<strong>Query String</strong><br />" +
        Request.QueryString.ToString() + "<br />";
```

Knowledge of the query string helps in debugging a problem if values from the query string are used. You could extend the code in `Application_Error` and add other useful information such as cookies and form collections. For more information about accessing these kinds of collections, pick up a copy of *Professional ASP.NET 4.5* published by Wrox. Alternatively, look into ELMAH—the Error Logging Modules and Handlers project—at `http://code.google.com/p/elmah/`, which is an open source project run by Atif Aziz that is aimed at catching and logging exceptions. The beauty of the ELMAH project is that it's extremely simple to integrate in your site (no programming required, you just need to add a few lines of configuration code to your `Web.config` file). And even better: there's a NuGet package available that adds the necessary files and configuration for you. Simply run the following command from the Package Manager Console:

```
Install-Package Elmah
```

After you have installed ELMAH, you can get a list of the errors that occurred in the site by requesting a special page called `elmah.axd`:

```
http://localhost:49394/elmah.axd
```

By default, you can access this page only from the local machine. Besides showing the errors in `elmah.axd`, you can also configure ELMAH to store errors in the database, send them by e-mail, provide them as an RSS feed, and much more. Check out the ELMAH project site for more information.

I have been using ELMAH for most of my production websites for the past couple of years, and it has helped me find many bugs that otherwise would have gone unnoticed.

Although the ability to handle and log exceptions at run time is useful, it's of course better to prevent them from happening in the first place. To write solid code with as few bugs as possible, you need good tools to help you understand the execution of your code so you can debug it. VS comes with excellent debugging tools that aid you in this process. You see what these tools are and how to use them in the next section.

THE BASICS OF DEBUGGING

Debugging is the process of finding and fixing bugs in your code. Although that may sound easy, it often isn't. Some bugs are very obvious and easy to spot and thus easy to fix. Others are much harder to find and require knowledge about the execution environment of your program. The debugging tools that ship with Visual Studio help you understand this execution environment by giving you direct access to the inner workings of your program or web page.

Debugging with VS is like snapping your fingers to stop the time. When you do that, everything halts, except for you, so you can walk around in your code, investigate variables, look into objects, try out methods, and even execute new code. To tell VS where to halt, you need to set one or more *breakpoints* in your code. When the code under the breakpoint is about to be executed, VS stops the execution of the application (usually a web page, a user control, or code in the `App_Code` folder) and then puts focus back on VS so you can diagnose the code and its environment.

You set a breakpoint by pressing F9 on the line of code where you want execution to halt. Instead of the F9 shortcut key, you can also click the margin of the code, where the big dot appears in Figure 18-6, or you can choose Debug ➪ Toggle Breakpoint from the main menu. Pressing F9, clicking the same spot in the margin, or choosing the menu item again toggles the presence of the breakpoint. To clear all breakpoints in your entire website, press Ctrl+Shift+F9.

To give you an idea of how debugging works, and what it can do to help you, the following exercise shows you the basic operations of debugging. Later parts of this chapter give you a detailed look at the numerous debugging tools and windows that ship with VS.

TRY IT OUT Debugging Your Application

In this Try It Out, you debug the Calculator page you created in a previous chapter. If you don't have the file, refer to Chapter 5 or download the code for this chapter from `www.wrox.com`. The debugging exercises in this chapter assume you are using Internet Explorer as your browser. If you are using a different default browser, such as Firefox or Opera, the debugging experience will be largely the same, although you may find that VS does not always get the focus automatically while breaking into your code.

1. Open the `CalculatorDemo.aspx` page from the `Demos` folder and switch to Code Behind.
2. Click the first line of code in the `CalculateButton_Click` handler that checks the length of the text in the two `TextBox` controls. Then press F9 to set a breakpoint. The line gets highlighted, as shown in Figure 18-6, and a colored dot appears in the margin of the Document Window.

```
CalculatorDemo.aspx.cs    CalculatorDemo.aspx
Demos_CalculatorDemo    CalculateButton_Click(object sender, EventArgs e)
protected void Page_Load(object sender, EventArgs e)
{
}

protected void CalculateButton_Click(object sender, EventArgs e)
{
  if (ValueBox1.Text.Length > 0 && ValueBox2.Text.Length > 0)
  {
    double result = 0;
    double value1 = Convert.ToDouble(ValueBox1.Text);
    double value2 = Convert.ToDouble(ValueBox2.Text);
100 %
```

FIGURE 18-6

3. Press F5 (instead of Ctrl+F5, which you have been using so far) to open the website in your browser and start the debugging process. Alternatively, choose Debug ➪ Start Debugging from the main menu. If you get the dialog box in Figure 18-7, click OK to have VS modify the `Web.config` file for you.

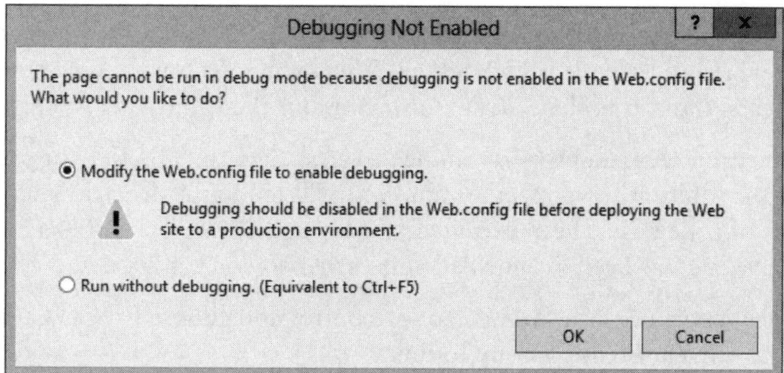

FIGURE 18-7

Depending on your browser's setup, you may be confronted with a dialog box (in Internet Explorer only) about enabling Script Debugging. If you get that dialog box, follow the instructions it displays, return to VS, and click the Yes button.

4. The page should load normally, showing you the two `TextBox` controls, the `DropDownList`, and the `Button`.

> ***COMMON MISTAKES*** *If you get an error stating that the page title is not valid, close your browser, return to VS, give the page a title, save your changes, and press F5 again.*

Enter `5` in the first text box, `7` in the second, and then click the Calculate button. Instead of seeing the answer in your browser, you are now taken back to VS. If you're not taken back to VS directly, you may need to switch to it manually. You'll see the taskbar icon for VS flash to get your attention.

5. In VS, the line with the breakpoint is now highlighted in yellow. Additionally, you see a yellow arrow in the document margin to indicate this line of code is *about to be executed*. However, before it does, you get a chance to look at your controls, variables, and other elements that make up the execution environment. To see the values you entered in the `TextBox` controls, hover your mouse over the `Text` properties in the highlighted lines. You'll see, as shown in Figure 18-8, a small tooltip appear that displays the value you entered.

```
if (ValueBox1.Text.Length > 0 && ValueBox2.Text.Length > 0)
{                     ValueBox1.Text  "5"
  double result = 0;
  double value1 = Convert.ToDouble(ValueBox1.Text);
  double value2 = Convert.ToDouble(ValueBox2.Text);
```

FIGURE 18-8

6. Hover your mouse over some of the variables in the code like `result` and `value1`. Note that you *won't* get a tooltip, because the code hasn't reached the point where these variables are declared. As far as the debugger is concerned, they don't exist.

7. To advance in the code, press F10. This steps over the selected line, executing it. Keep pressing F10 until the line that declares the `value2` variable is highlighted. When you now hover your mouse over `value1`, the tooltip appears, indicating that `value1` now contains the value `5.0`.

8. Hover your mouse over the `SelectedValue` property in the `Select Case` (in VB.NET) or `switch` statement (in C#). Note that the tooltip shows you the value you selected in the drop-down list (the plus symbol). Even if this line of code hasn't been executed, the `DropDownList` control has been instantiated and its `SelectedValue` has been assigned a value earlier so you can look at it here.

9. Right-click the line that assigns the value to the `ResultLabel` control and choose Run to Cursor. This executes all code from the current breakpoint up to this line. Hover your mouse over the `result` variable (you may need to highlight the `result` variable first with your mouse if you are using VB.NET) and note that it displays the value `12.0`, which is the outcome of the calculation, shown in Figure 18-9.

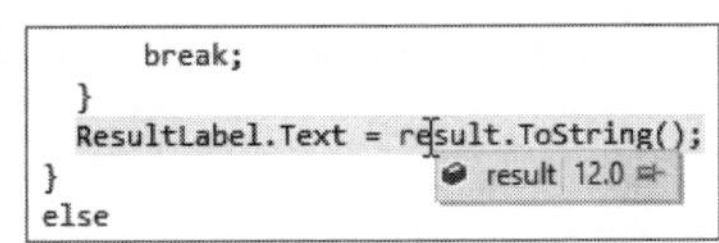
break;
}
ResultLabel.Text = result.ToString();
}
result 12.0
else

FIGURE 18-9

10. Finally, press F5. By pressing this key, the code continues until it finds the next breakpoint. Because you haven't defined another breakpoint in your code, the remainder of the code in the `Click` event handler is executed and the result is displayed in the page.

How It Works

Whenever you press Ctrl+F5 to view a page in a browser as you have done up until this chapter, nothing special happens. VS simply opens the browser, which then requests the page from IIS Express. However, when you press F5 instead, VS gets in debugging mode and respects the breakpoints you have set in your code. Whenever a breakpoint is hit, execution of the code is stopped so you can look at the code and its execution environment, which gives you access to variables, controls, methods, and much more. Note that the code on the line with the breakpoint has not been executed at this point. To continue executing the code, use F10, F11, or F5. You see more of these shortcuts later.

Before you can debug your code, you need to configure the application to support it. You do this by setting the `debug` attribute of the `compilation` element in `Web.config` to `true`:

```
<compilation debug="true">
```

If you're using Visual Basic, you may see two additional attributes on this element: `strict` and `explicit`. By default, `strict` is set to `false`, which means Visual Basic will do silent casts and conversions for you. The `explicit` attribute is set to `true`, which means you need to declare all your variables before you can use them.

Whenever you start debugging and the `debug` attribute of the `<compilation />` is set to `false`, you get the dialog box shown in Figure 18-7 offering to turn it on for you. To avoid the overhead this setting brings, you should always set it to `false` on a production server. You see more of this in the next chapter.

In this exercise you also learned how to use *data tips*, the small tooltip windows that appear when you hover your mouse over selected variables. For simple types, such as an `Integer` or a `String`, all you see is the variable's value. For complex types, such as results returned from a LINQ query, you get a much richer data tip, providing you with a lot more detail.

Useful as the debugging data tips may seem, they are only a small part of the rich debugging features. In the next section, you get an overview of all the debugging tools that ship with VS.

TOOLS SUPPORT FOR DEBUGGING

With a number of shortcut keys and menu items, VS lets you move around the code that you are debugging, giving you the option to execute code line by line or larger blocks of code at once. Additionally, the IDE provides you with a lot of windows that enable you to diagnose and change the execution environment, including the values of variables at run time. You see how to move around code first, which is followed by a discussion on the numerous debugging windows.

Moving Around in Debugged Code

When your code has halted on a breakpoint, you can use a number of keyboard shortcuts to determine what to do next. The following table lists the most common shortcuts.

KEY	DESCRIPTION
F5	Press this key to start debugging, as demonstrated in the previous exercise. When you press this key during debugging, the code continues until the next breakpoint is hit, or until all code is finished executing.
F11	Press this key to execute the current line and step into a member that's being called, if possible. You see how this works later.
F10	Press this key to execute the current line without stepping into the code that is being called, unless that code itself contains a breakpoint.
Shift+F11	Press this key combination to complete the code in the current code block and return to the code that initially called it.
Shift+F5	Press this key combination to stop debugging.
Ctrl+Shift+F5	Press this key combination to restart the debugging process.

In addition to these keyboard shortcuts, you can also use the Debugging toolbar shown in Figure 18-10, which offers similar functionality.

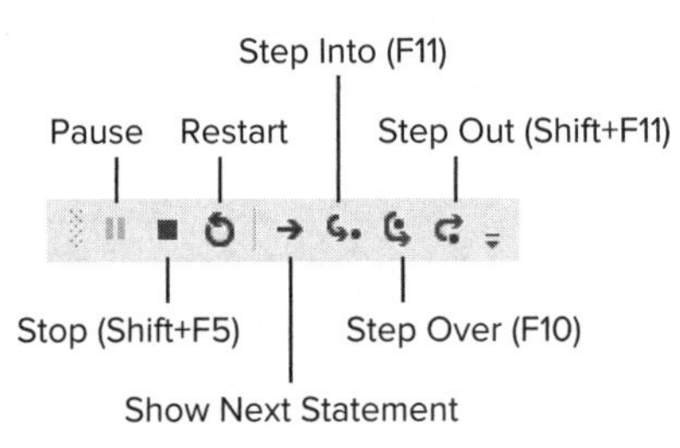

FIGURE 18-10

This toolbar should appear automatically when you start debugging, but if it doesn't, right-click an existing toolbar and choose Debug. To start debugging using the toolbar, press the button with the green arrow on the Standard toolbar.

While you are debugging your code in VS, you have a number of debugging windows at your disposal, which are discussed in the following section.

Debugging Windows

The numerous debugging windows enable you to watch the variables in your application and even change them during run time. Additionally, they provide you with information about where you are in the application and what code was previously executed. All this information helps you understand the execution flow of your application.

You access all the debugging windows through the Debug ➪ Windows menu option. Not all of them are available in the Express edition of Visual Studio. Also, to access most of the windows, your application must be in debug mode first. The next sections show you the different windows that are available. In the exercise that follows, you get a chance to work with them so you understand how to use them and why they are useful.

Watching Variables

Knowing the values of your variables is critical to understanding your application. To help you with this, VS offers three debugging windows that provide you with useful information. All these windows support changing the value of your variables at run time, enable you to use data tips to dig deeper into the objects, and enable you to copy and paste data so you can reuse it somewhere else.

The Watch Window

This is probably the most important window for you to keep an eye on. It enables you to watch variables you're interested in and dig into them. Figure 18-11 shows the Watch window that is currently watching the `value1` variable used in the Calculator page while the `value2` variable is being added to the list.

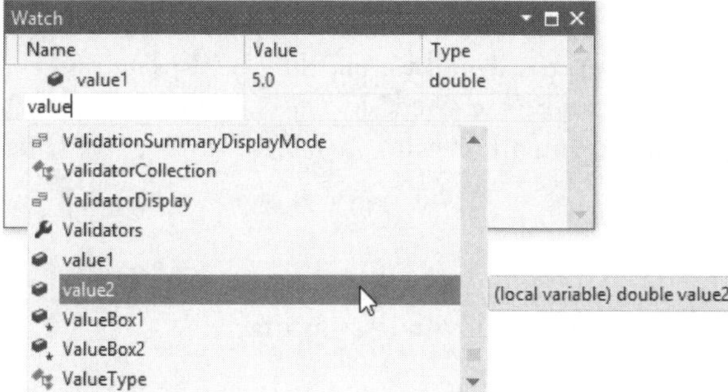

FIGURE 18-11

You can add your variables to the Watch window in a few different ways. First of all, you can click the Watch window once and then start typing a variable name. You can then press Ctrl+Space to bring up the IntelliSense list, making it easy to complete the variable's name. Alternatively, you can right-click a variable in the code editor and choose Add Watch. And finally, you can highlight a variable in the code editor and then drag it into the Watch window.

When your variables are in the Watch window, you can change their values to influence the execution of your code. For example, you could change the value of the `value1` variable to a different number, changing the outcome of the calculation. To change a value, double-click it in the Value column of the Watch window. Alternatively, right-click the watched variable and choose Edit Value.

Besides showing variables' values, you can also use the Watch window to execute code. For example, you could call `ToString()` on the `value1` variable to see what its string representation looks like. To do this, double-click the variable name in the Watch window so it becomes editable, add `.ToString()` as shown in Figure 18-12, and press Enter.

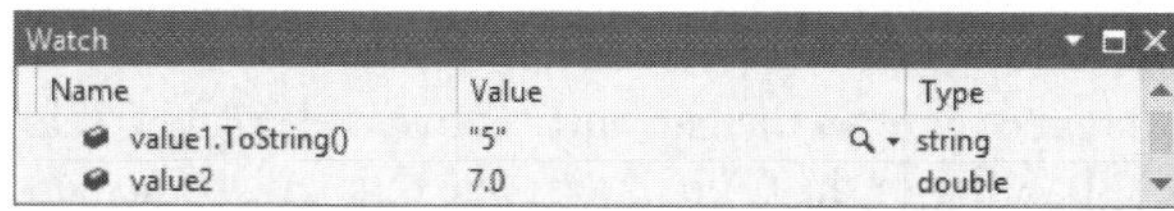

FIGURE 18-12

You are not limited to calling `ToString` in the Watch window. Most expressions that produce a value can be executed here, but there are some exceptions (such as LINQ queries). However, the Immediate window, discussed later, is much more appropriate for executing code on the fly.

In addition to the Watch window, the Autos and Locals windows are available. They work more or less the same as the Watch window.

The Autos Window

The Autos window is available only in the commercial versions of Visual Studio and not in the Express edition. Because it's so similar to the Watch window, this isn't really a problem. The Autos window shows the variables used by the current and previous code statements and is updated automatically as you step through the code.

The Locals Window

The Locals window is also similar to the Watch and Autos windows, but the Locals window shows all variables that are currently in scope (they can be "reached" by the code that is currently executing). This is a useful window, because it shows you all relevant variables without requiring you to add them manually.

Other Windows

Besides windows to watch variables, VS has a few other useful windows available.

The Breakpoints Window

The Breakpoints window gives you an overview of all breakpoints you have set in code throughout your entire website. Unfortunately, this window is not available in the Express edition, so you have to find breakpoints manually by looking at the actual code.

Call Stack Window

The Call Stack window provides you with information about the order in which your code has been executed or called. Each call from one piece of code into another is placed on a *stack of calls* that you can navigate. It looks a bit cryptic at first, but once you understand how it works, it enables you to jump through your code quite easily. Figure 18-13 shows the Call Stack window inside the `Add` method of the `Calculator` class.

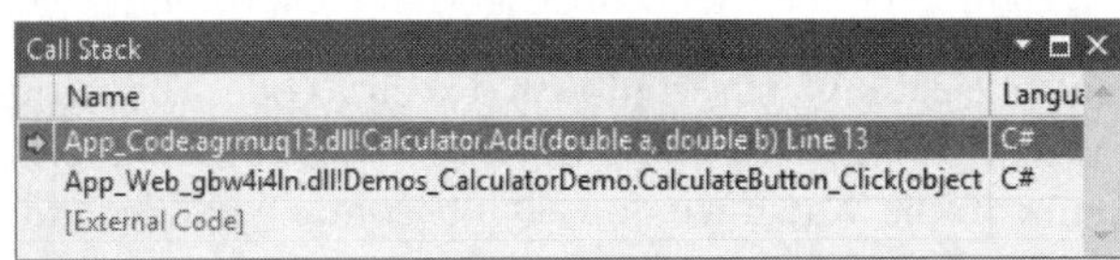

FIGURE 18-13

In the highlighted line, you can see that `Calculator.Add` is the currently active code. Right below it you see `CalculateButton_Click`, the event handler in the Calculator page that called the `Add` method. Double-clicking a line in the Call Stack window takes you to the appropriate code location. At the bottom you see [External Code], which refers to executed code that is not part of your website, such as executing code coming from the .NET Framework. To expand the [External Code] item to see what it contains, right-click the Call Stack window and choose Show External Code.

Immediate Window

The last interesting debugging window is the Immediate window. This window enables you to execute code as if you had written it in a page, for example. You can use this window to test expressions, see what values a function returns, and so on. For example, when you are in debug mode, you can enter the following command in the Immediate window:

VB.NET

```
? New Calculator().Add(3, 4)
```

C#

```
? new Calculator().Add(3, 4);
```

The question mark is used to output to the Immediate window. The code then instantiates a new `Calculator` instance and directly passes the values `3` and `4` to its `Add` method. The code is executed and the `Add` method returns `7`, which is then printed in the Immediate window.

This window is great for quickly testing out code. Instead of writing code you want to test in a page, you can type it directly in the Immediate window and see its output.

In the following Try It Out, you see these debugging windows at work.

TRY IT OUT Extensive Debugging

In this exercise, you look at all the debugging windows that have been discussed earlier. Because a lot of windows and options are available, you won't see a detailed discussion of every step in the process. Instead, you're encouraged to experiment. Try adding more variables to the Watch window, type your own code in the Immediate window, and so on. Experimenting is the best way to discover the large number of debugging capabilities in VS.

1. If you're still in debug mode from the preceding exercise, press Shift+F5 or press the Stop button on the debugging toolbar. Open the Code Behind of `CalculatorDemo.aspx` again and press Ctrl+Shift+F9 to clear all previously set breakpoints in all code files. Click Yes to confirm the deletion.

2. Click the line that declares the variable `value1` and press F9 to set a breakpoint. Your Document Window should look similar to Figure 18-14, which shows the Document Window for the C# project.

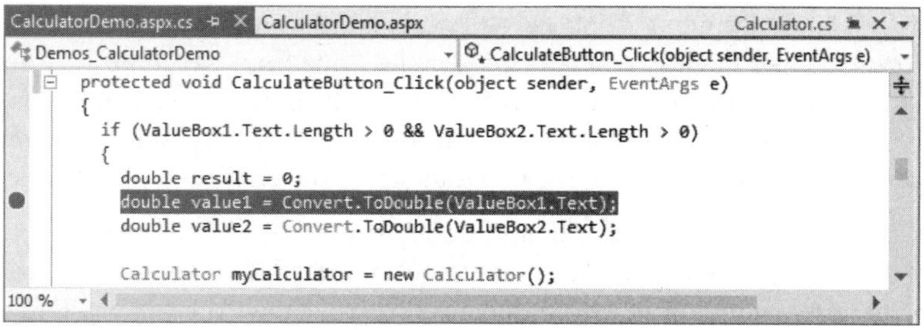

```
CalculatorDemo.aspx.cs   CalculatorDemo.aspx   Calculator.cs
Demos_CalculatorDemo   CalculateButton_Click(object sender, EventArgs e)
protected void CalculateButton_Click(object sender, EventArgs e)
{
  if (ValueBox1.Text.Length > 0 && ValueBox2.Text.Length > 0)
  {
    double result = 0;
    double value1 = Convert.ToDouble(ValueBox1.Text);
    double value2 = Convert.ToDouble(ValueBox2.Text);

    Calculator myCalculator = new Calculator();
100 %
```

FIGURE 18-14

3. Press F5 or choose Debug ➪ Start Debugging from the main menu to start debugging the application. Enter the number **5** in the first text box, ensure that the plus sign is selected in the drop-down list, and enter **7** in the second text box. Then click the Calculate button, and VS breaks at the breakpoint you set in the previous step. If you aren't taken there automatically, switch back to VS manually.

4. Hover your mouse over the `OperatorList` variable that is used a few lines below the current breakpoint and notice how VS displays a data tip with a plus (+) symbol in front of it. This means you can expand the item to get detailed information about the variable. Figure 18-15 displays the expanded data tip for C#.

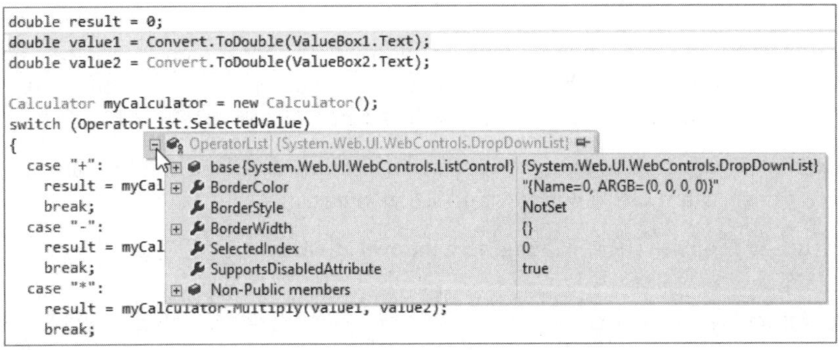

```
double result = 0;
double value1 = Convert.ToDouble(ValueBox1.Text);
double value2 = Convert.ToDouble(ValueBox2.Text);

Calculator myCalculator = new Calculator();
switch (OperatorList.SelectedValue)
{                OperatorList {System.Web.UI.WebControls.DropDownList}
  case "+":        base {System.Web.UI.WebControls.ListControl}  {System.Web.UI.WebControls.DropDownList}
    result = myCal   BorderColor                                "{Name=0, ARGB=(0, 0, 0, 0)}"
    break;           BorderStyle                                NotSet
  case "-":          BorderWidth                                {}
    result = myCal   SelectedIndex                              0
    break;           SupportsDisabledAttribute                  true
  case "*":          Non-Public members
    result = myCalculator.Multiply(value1, value2);
    break;
```

FIGURE 18-15

Note that you can expand other items such as the `BorderWidth` property. If you're using C#, you can also expand `base` to see the `DropDownList` control's base class's properties such as `SelectedValue`. With VB.NET, the properties of the base class have been merged into the main IntelliSense list so you'll see `SelectedValue` at the bottom of the list.

5. Right-click `ValueBox1` in the code at the top that checks the length of the text in the `TextBox` controls and choose Add Watch. The variable is added to the Watch window where you can expand it, similar to how you expanded the data tip. Expand the item, scroll down in the list to the `Text` property, and you'll see its value is set to `"5"`.

6. Double-click the value `"5"` for the `Text` property, change it to `"12"` (including the quotes), and press Enter.

7. Open the Locals window (choose Debug ➪ Windows ➪ Locals if the window isn't visible yet.) Press F10 to execute the line under the breakpoint. This gets the value from `ValueBox1`, converts it to a double, and assigns it to `value1`. Look at the `value1` variable in the Locals window (see Figure 18-16 that shows the window for the C# website). It now contains `12.0`, the value you assigned to the `Text` property of the text box in the previous step, now converted to a double.

   Note that the value of the `value1` variable has changed color as well. This is done to indicate that the item has recently been changed. Also note that because all of this is happening at the server during a postback, the browser is unmodified, and the text box still shows the value `5`. Only when the page has finished rendering to the browser will you see the new value show up.

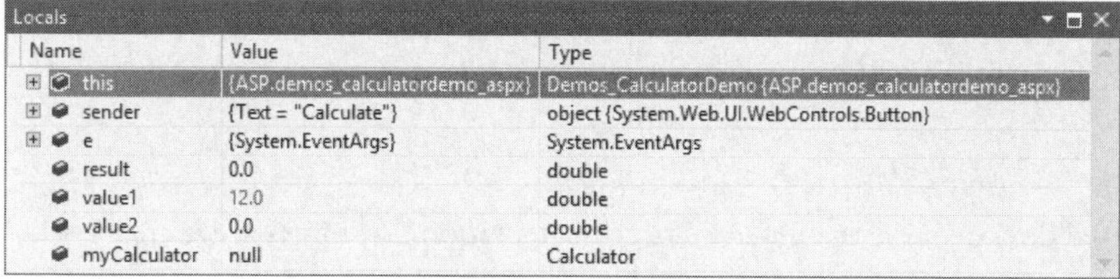

FIGURE 18-16

In Figure 18-16, you also see the other variables that are currently in scope, such as `result`, `myCalculator`, and `this` (`Me` in Visual Basic) that contains a reference to the page that is currently being executed.

8. Press F10 once more so `value2` is updated as well. The color of the value of the `value2` variable has changed to red to indicate it has changed, whereas `value1`'s value is black again. This makes it easy to see what variables are modified by the last statement.

9. Press F10 until you reach the line that calls the `Add` method on the `Calculator` class. Instead of pressing F10 to execute that line, press F11. This steps into the `Add` method so you can see how it performs the calculation. Inside the `Add` method, you can hover over the method's arguments to see their values, as demonstrated in Figure 18-17.

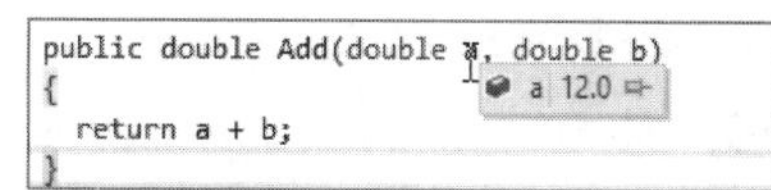

FIGURE 18-17

10. Choose Debug ➪ Windows ➪ Call Stack to bring up the Call Stack window (or press Ctrl+Alt+C) and note that the `Add` method was called by the `CalculateButton`'s `Click` handler, shown in Figure 18-18.

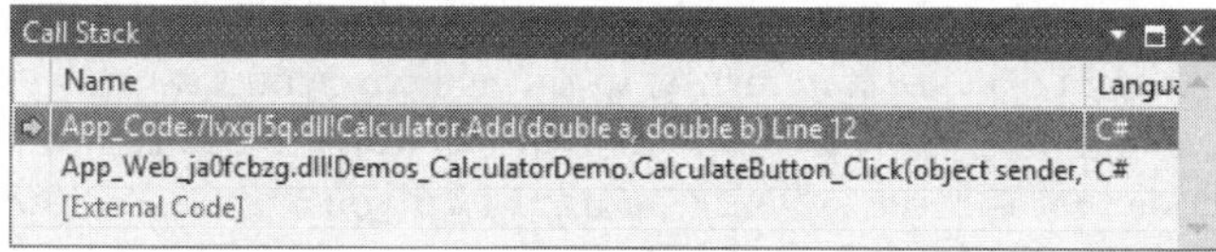

FIGURE 18-18

11. Double-click the second line in the Call Stack window and you are taken back to the Calculator page. The line that called the `Add` method is highlighted in green. Note that this doesn't execute any code; all it does is show you the relevant code. Double-click the first line and you are taken to the `Add` method code again.

12. Press Shift+F11 to step out of the `Add` method and return to the calling code in the Calculator page. If you take another look at the Call Stack window, you'll see the line for the `Add` method has disappeared from the call stack. At this point, the `result` variable does not have a value yet because the line of code hasn't been fully executed.

13. Open the Immediate Window (choose Debug ➪ Windows ➪ Immediate) to test out some code. In the window that appeared, type the following and press Enter:

VB.NET

```
? New Calculator().Multiply(4, 12)
```

C#

```
? new Calculator().Multiply(4, 12);
```

The Immediate window displays the outcome of the calculation, as shown in Figure 18-19.

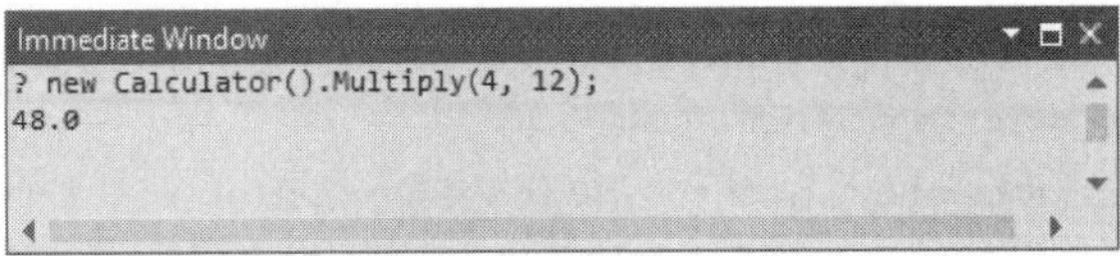

FIGURE 18-19

14. Press F10 to finish executing the line with `Calculate.Add`. The yellow marker in the margin of the code editor jumps to the end of the `Select Case` / `switch` block. Drag the marker back to the line with `Calculate.Add`. This changes the line that is executed next so you can repeat part of the code that has already executed. You can then press F11 again to step into the `Add` method, or press F10 to execute the line directly.
15. Finally, press F5. This executes the remainder of the code in the page. The focus is put on the browser again, which now displays the outcome of the calculation in the `Label` control. If everything turned out as planned, you should see the number `19`: the sum of `12` (the new value you entered for `ValueBox1.Text` in step 6), and `7` (which you entered in step 3).

How It Works

As demonstrated in a previous Try It Out exercise, when you put a breakpoint in your code, execution is halted as soon as the line with the breakpoint is about to be executed. From there, you can jump around in your code, investigate variables, and execute statements. In this exercise you saw how to step in and over code using the F10 and F11 shortcut keys. You usually use F10 to execute a line if you're not interested in seeing the underlying code that is being called. You use F11 if you want to see the code that is being executed, as you saw how to do with the `Add` method.

The data tips and Watch and Locals windows are invaluable tools in examining and changing variables and values. For example, even though you entered `5` in the first text box in the browser, you were able to change that value to `12` during debugging. Any changes you make while debugging are propagated to the rest of the code that still needs to be executed.

The Immediate window lets you try out small snippets of code. This can be useful to try out some ideas, without the need to write it in the code window and debug it. In this exercise, you wrote some code that created a new `Calculator` instance, called the `Multiply` method, and outputted the value using the question mark.

VB.NET

```
? New Calculator().Multiply(4, 12)
```

C#

```
? new Calculator().Multiply(4, 12);
```

Being able to change the line that is executed next by dragging the yellow arrow is very useful. This enables you to skip some code you may not want to run during a debugging session, or to repeat some code you want to see execute again (for example, after changing a variable's value).

Besides debugging code at the server, VS comes with excellent support for debugging client-side JavaScript as well.

DEBUGGING CLIENT-SIDE SCRIPT

So far, you have used the debugging tools to debug ASPX pages and Code Behind. However, that's not all there is to it. VS also has great support for debugging client-side JavaScript. Debugging client-side JavaScript requires that you use Internet Explorer and won't work correctly with other browsers like Firefox or Opera. The cool thing about debugging client-side JavaScript in VS is that you already know how to do it. You can use the same familiar tools that you have seen in this chapter to debug both server-side and client-side code.

The JavaScript that is eventually used by the page in the web browser can come from a lot of different sources. You can have JavaScript in external script files, embedded in the page, in a master page, and even server controls can emit their own JavaScript. This makes it difficult sometimes to break in the right code, because you don't always know where it comes from. Fortunately, VS has a great solution for this; it lets you set breakpoints in the final HTML being displayed in the browser. To show you in what file you're adding breakpoints or what code you are debugging, VS updates the Solution Explorer and displays a list of all files containing client-side script that you can step through as soon as you are in debug mode. Breakpoints you set in these files during debugging are preserved when possible, making debugging a smooth experience.

The easiest way to learn the new client-side JavaScript debugging possibilities is by trying them out, so the next exercise dives right in and shows you how to debug the web service test page that you created in Chapter 10.

TRY IT OUT Debugging JavaScript in Internet Explorer

You need to use Microsoft Internet Explorer to carry out the following exercise because most of the features shown in this Try It Out work only with that browser. If Internet Explorer is currently not your default browser in VS, you can choose your browser from the drop-down list next to the green Start Debugging arrow on the Standard toolbar.

1. If you're still in debug mode from the previous exercise, press Shift+F5 to stop debugging. Then open the `NameService.cs` or `NameService.vb` file from the `App_Code` folder. Locate the `HelloWorld` web method and set a breakpoint on the first and only line of code in the method that returns the personalized greeting. Close the file.
2. Open `WebServices.aspx` from the `Demos` folder in Markup View. Locate the `helloWorld` JavaScript method, click the line that declares the `yourName` variable, and press F9 to set a breakpoint, visible in Figure 18-20.

```
<script type="text/javascript">
  function helloWorld()
  {
    var yourName = document.getElementById('YourName').value;
    NameService.HelloWorld(yourName, helloWorldCallback);
  }
```

FIGURE 18-20

3. Press F5 to start debugging. The page loads in the browser and you get a text box and two buttons. Enter your name in the text box and click the Say Hello button. As soon as you click it, focus is put back on Visual Studio, and the code halts in the JavaScript code block.

> ***COMMON MISTAKES*** *If your client-side JavaScript breakpoint doesn't get hit, close your browser to stop debugging, type the word* **`debugger`** *before the line you set the breakpoint on, and press F5 again. VS does not always correctly debug your client-side JavaScript breakpoints, but it works fine when using the* `debugger` *keyword:*
>
> ```
> debugger
> var yourName = document.getElementById('YourName').value;
> NameService.HelloWorld(yourName, helloWorldCallback);
> ```

4. Press F10 to execute the highlighted line (you need to press it twice if you're using the `debugger` keyword). The value in the text box is now assigned to the `yourName` variable. When you hover your mouse over that variable, a data tip appears.

5. Open the other debugging windows and notice how they all behave identically to what you saw before. You can add JavaScript variables to the Watch window to look at their values, enter JavaScript in the Immediate window for evaluation, and so on. Also note that the Solution Explorer has changed, showing the active client-side files containing script right above the web project (see Figure 18-21).

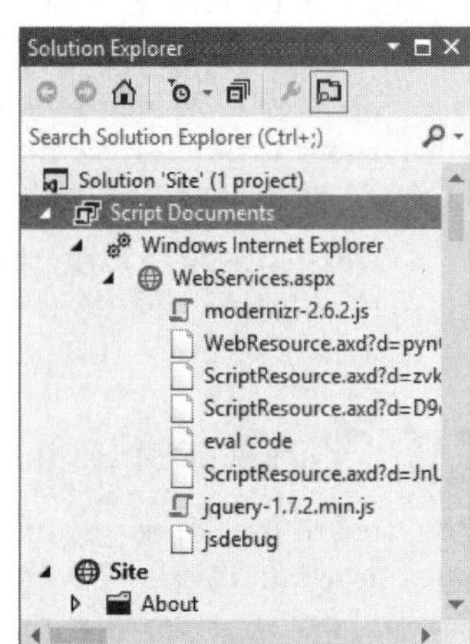

FIGURE 18-21

6. To look inside these documents, you can double-click them under the Windows Internet Explorer node that has appeared in the Solution Explorer. The file `WebServices.aspx` should already be open in the Document Window. At first, the file may look like before. But if you look closely, you can see that this is no longer the original source file with ASP.NET controls mixed up with other markup, but the final HTML rendered in the browser. To warn you that you are looking at the final file, and not the original source, VS has added the text `[dynamic]` and a lock icon to the tab for the file above the Document Window, shown in Figure 18-22.

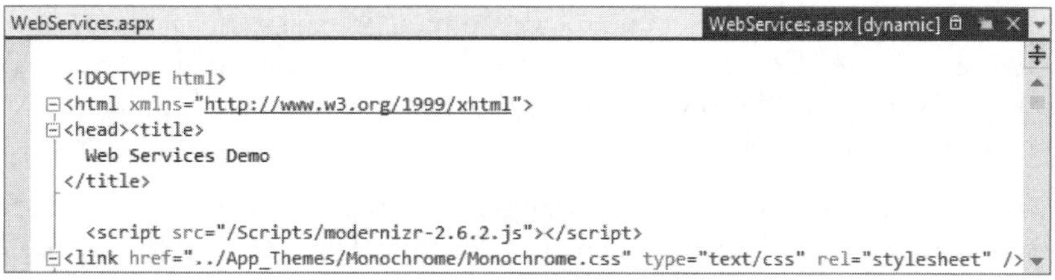

```
WebServices.aspx                                    WebServices.aspx [dynamic]
<!DOCTYPE html>
<html xmlns="http://www.w3.org/1999/xhtml">
<head><title>
  Web Services Demo
</title>

  <script src="/Scripts/modernizr-2.6.2.js"></script>
<link href="../App_Themes/Monochrome/Monochrome.css" type="text/css" rel="stylesheet" />
```

FIGURE 18-22

What's really nice about this is that even though you are looking at a runtime file, VS is still able to relate this runtime file with the original source. This means you can set breakpoints in the runtime file, and they'll be remembered in the original source so they are available for the next debugging session.

7. To see how this works, set a breakpoint on the line with the `alert` statement in the `helloWorldCallback` handler. Once the code returns from the web service that is being called in this exercise, you'll return to this handler again, so you can investigate the value returned by the service.

8. Press F5 to continue executing code. The name you entered in the text box is retrieved and then sent into the `HelloWorld` method of the service. Because you added a breakpoint there in step 1, the code should stop again, enabling you to look at the variable `name` passed to the web method. Although this exercise itself is pretty simple, a lot of magic just happened under the hood. You stepped from some client-side code running in the browser into code running in a web service at the server, all from the same IDE.

9. Press F5 again and you are taken back from the server-side web service into the client-side code where you can see the result of the web service in the `helloWorldCallback` handler.

10. Press F5 once more. The code completes and shows a JavaScript alert window with a greeting containing your name, just as it did in Chapter 10.

11. Close your browser, go back to VS again, and open the `WebServices.aspx` file by double-clicking it in the Solution Explorer. This opens the original source file, and not the dynamic version you saw in step 6 of this exercise. Locate the `helloWorldCallback` handler in the `WebServices.aspx` file. Note that the breakpoint you set in step 7 has been persisted.

How It Works

You have a few interesting points to take away from this exercise. First of all, you should understand the notion of *dynamic files*, or *runtime files*. These files are the final result from your ASPX pages and give you insight in the final HTML, CSS, and JavaScript that ends up in the browser. This is a great help, because it gives you a total view of all relevant content. Remember, the final markup displayed in the browser comes from a variety of resources, including master pages, content pages, external CSS and JavaScript files, and from the various server controls that live in your page. The ability to look at the combined result from a single location makes it easy to see how everything fits together.

Another important point to remember from this exercise is how the IDE offers you fully integrated debugging features, from the client-side code in the user interface, all the way up into the server. To make it easy to set breakpoints, VS doesn't restrict you to adding them in pages at design time only; instead, it also enables you to set them in the dynamic runtime files. When you stop debugging, VS tracks the new breakpoints for you, finds out to what source file they belong, and adds them there again for you, so they are available for the next debugging session.

Although you may not realize it because everything is taking place on the same computer and in the same IDE, you are crossing many boundaries when debugging like this. First, VS enables you to debug client-side script in the browser, so you can hook into that even before any data is sent to the server. When you press F5 in step 8, the code continues and sends the value to the server where it was used in the `HelloWorld` method of the `NameService` class. Once that server-side web method is done, execution returns to the client again, enabling you to break on the `alert` statement that shows the message from the web service.

For some reason, debugging client-side JavaScript in VS 2012 doesn't always work. If you're encountering issues, remember the `debugger` keyword. Just add it before the line you want to break on and VS will halt execution when it encounters this keyword. Don't forget to remove the `debugger` keyword again if you're done with debugging; otherwise, your browser will try to start a script debugger when it encounters this keyword, which is meaningless to most of your users.

So far you've been looking at debugging code. However, VS now has great support to diagnose the HTML of your page as well. You see how this works next.

DEBUGGING WITH THE PAGE INSPECTOR

If you want to build a site that is easy to maintain, you probably make use of many of the features that ASP.NET and the browser offers. For example, you're probably using a master page for the general layout, you store page-specific content in a content page that uses that master page, you may have one or more user controls for content you reuse across your site (such as the Contact Form in the Planet Wrox website), and you may be using themes and skins to separate the design from the rest of your application.

In the browser, all of this code comes together as a single HTML source document that in turn includes references to external resources such as JavaScript and CSS files and images. Because it's a single file, it can be hard to debug that code and understand where a certain piece of HTML came from. In addition, because multiple CSS selectors can influence the layout of your page, it may be hard to track down the file in which a certain piece of CSS is defined. Using the Page Inspector, new to VS 2012, this now becomes much easier.

Introducing the Page Inspector

The Page Inspector is a diagnostics tool that runs inside Visual Studio and that brings a unified experience between your browser, the ASP.NET run time, and your source files. The Page Inspector comes with Visual Studio so you don't need to do anything to make use of it.

Although an upcoming exercise shows you many of the features that the Page Inspector offers, here's a quick description of how you can use it:

- You start the Page Inspector by choosing it as your target browser in the Debug Target drop-down on the Standard toolbar. You then start your site as you normally would using F5 or Ctrl+F5.
- The Page Inspector presents itself as a browser window in the IDE (so you can see what the page looks like), along with a number of tools windows to diagnose your code.
- Once loaded, you can use the Page Inspector's Inspect button to look at the various elements available in your page such as navigation elements, buttons, images, and more.
- While hovering over the elements in the Page Inspector, the code editor window is updated with a preview of the documents that contributed the HTML you're inspecting. As mentioned in the introduction of this section, this could be a master page, a content page, a user control, and so on.
- You can make changes to these documents in VS and then you can refresh the Page Inspector to see them show up in the final page.
- The Page Inspector also helps you find the CSS rules in your CSS files, whether they are defined in a theme's folder or in a custom folder.

If you've ever used Firebug (for Firefox) or the IE or Chrome Developer tools, some of this may sound familiar. These tools also enable you to inspect HTML elements in your page and look at the associated CSS. What makes the Page Inspector different and very special is that it is able to relate the final HTML back to the original ASP.NET source files. This in turn enables editing of the file in the IDE, making changes and previewing the results a breeze.

You get a good look at the Page Inspector and its feature set in the exercise in the next section.

Using the Page Inspector

Getting started with the Page Inspector is pretty simple. Because it ships with VS, it's ready for use. However, it has a few prerequisites. First of all, you need to have Internet Explorer 9 or later installed on your machine. Secondly, your site needs to run against .NET 4 or later. Because the Planet Wrox sample site runs against .NET 4.5, this is not a problem. Thirdly, the Page Inspector needs to be installed and registered correctly on your machine. Because this is done during installation of VS, this is not a problem either. The final prerequisite is that your site needs to be run in debug mode, or you need to add a special key to your `Web.config` to enable the Page Inspector. You enabled debugging for the Planet Wrox site earlier in this chapter, which means you don't have to do anything else for the Page Inspector to work correctly. For cases where you don't have debugging enabled and still want to use the Page Inspector, either enable debugging or add the following key to your `Web.config` in the `appSettings` element:

```
<appSettings>
  <add key="PageInspector:ServerCodeMappingSupport" value="Enabled"/>
</appSettings>
```

If debugging is not enabled or this key is not present, VS gives you a warning when you invoke the Page Inspector and offers to fix the problem automatically for you by turning on debugging.

You see how to use the Page Inspector in the following exercise.

TRY IT OUT Using the Page Inspector to Diagnose your Site

In this exercise, you load a few pages into the Page Inspector and diagnose the underlying HTML. You see how to use the Inspect feature to find the originating source files and how to make changes to the code and refresh the Page Inspector. This should prepare you for cases where you need to hunt for a bug in your site.

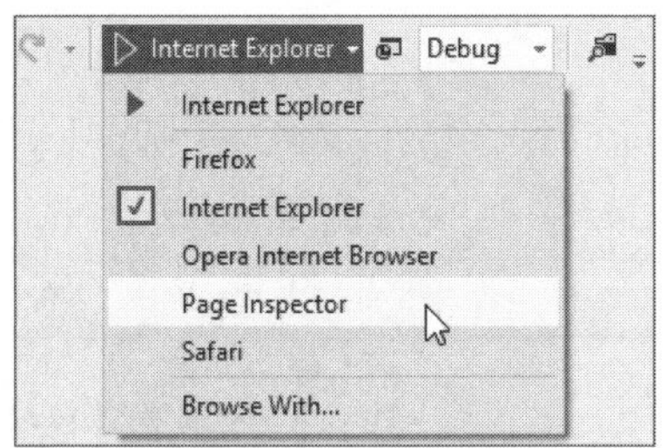

FIGURE 18-23

1. If you're still in debug mode from the previous exercise, press Shift+F5 to stop debugging. Then close all open files and choose Page Inspector from the Target Browser drop-down on the Standard toolbar, shown in Figure 18-23.
2. Press F5 or click the green arrow next to the Target Browser drop-down, shown in Figure 18-23. If you enabled debugging earlier, the Page Inspector should start without further messages. If you haven't enabled debugging earlier, follow the on-screen instructions to properly configure your site. After a few seconds, the Page Inspector is loaded in the Document Window in VS, as shown in Figure 18-24.

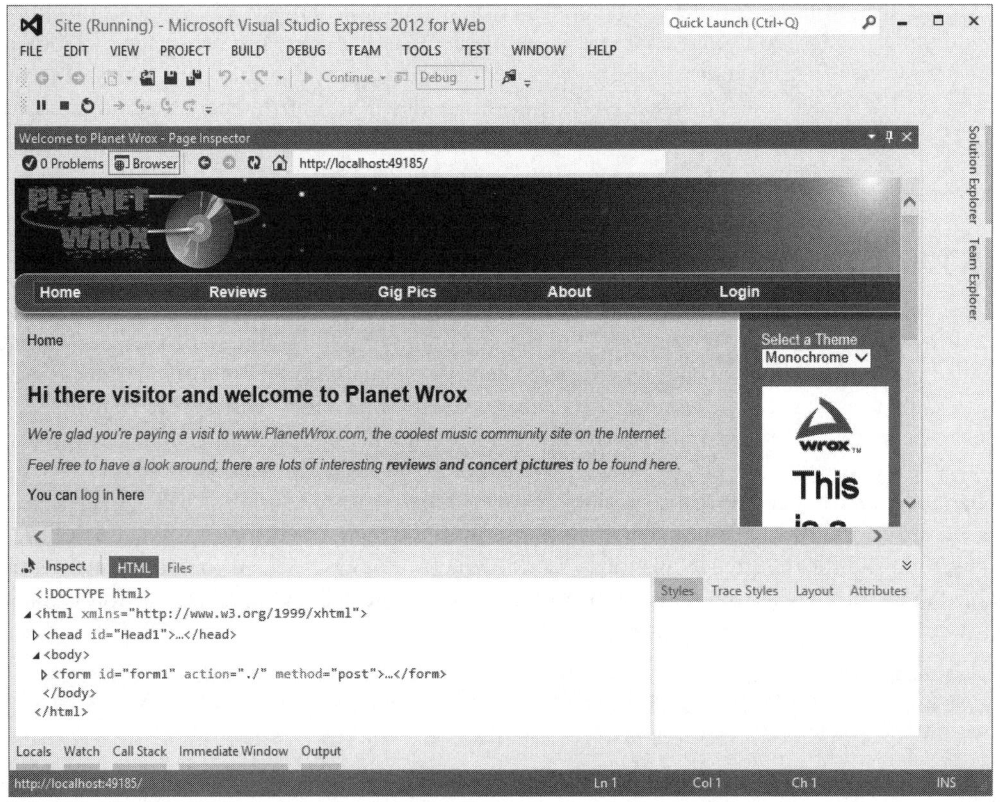

FIGURE 18-24

At the top left of the Page Inspector, you see two buttons labeled 0 Problems and Browser. The Browser view is currently active and shows the site as it would appear in your browser. The Problems button lets you diagnose any problems with the setup of the Page Inspector. If you have covered all prerequisites, the problem count should be zero and you can ignore this button. Otherwise, clicking the button shows you a list of problems and hints on fixing them.

The bottom of the screen is divided in two. The left half shows you the HTML for the page (indicated by the active HTML tab). The Inspect button enables you to point at elements in your page, as you see in a moment. The Files tab shows all server-side files that were used to render this page. For the homepage of the Planet Wrox site, these are `Frontend.master` (the master page), `Default.aspx` (the homepage), and `Banner.ascx` (the Banner user control in the `Sidebar` `<aside>`). Clicking any of these files opens them in the code editor side by side with the Page Inspector.

3. Click the Inspect button and then hover your mouse over elements in the page. When you do that, the code file that generated the element is shown side by side with the Page Inspector. For example, when you hover over the logo, the `Frontend.master` file appears. If you hover over the banner image, the `Banner.ascx` file is loaded, as shown in Figure 18-25.

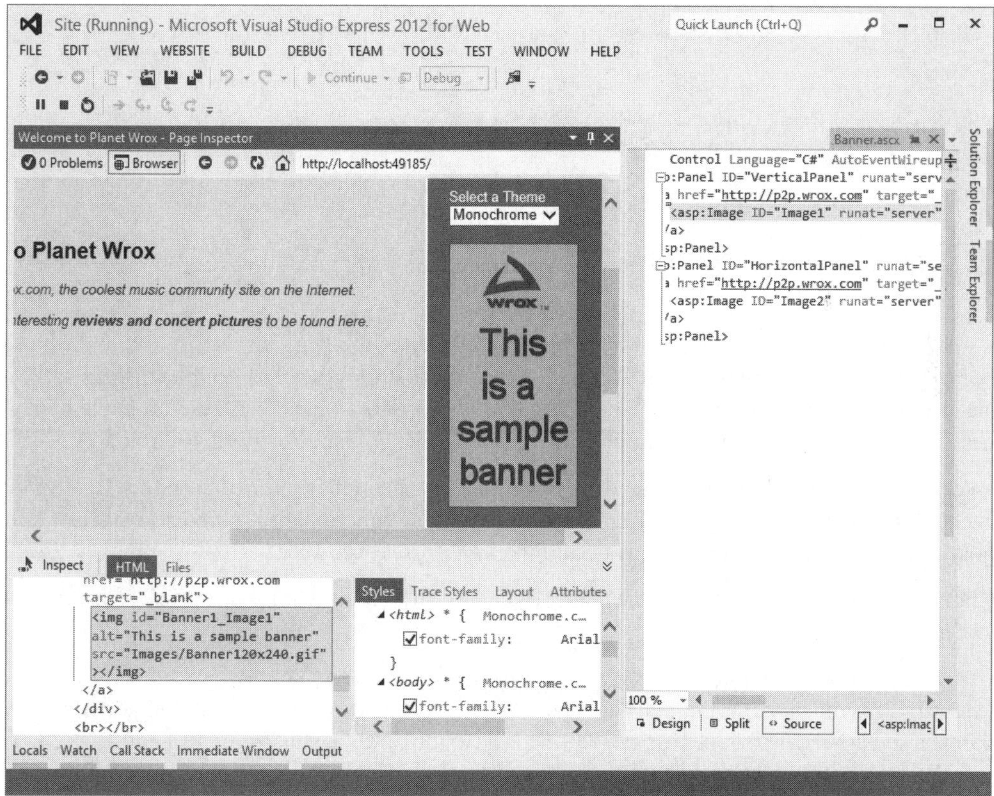

FIGURE 18-25

Not only is the correct file opened, but the active control is selected for you (the highlighted `Image` control in Figure 18-25) as well. In addition, in the client-side HTML at the bottom left, the `img` element is highlighted. This makes it super easy to see how it all fits together: the `<img>` in the browser came from an `Image` control in `Banner.ascx`. If you didn't know the source code of this site that well, finding this out without the Page Inspector would have been much more difficult. You had to diagnose the underlying HTML, find the `<img>` element, look for the control's `id` attribute, and then search the entire site in VS for the text `Image1`.

4. Click once on the `<h1>` element (with the text that welcomes the user). VS opens up `Default.aspx` in Preview mode (indicated by the tab with the page name at the right of the code editor) and correctly highlights the text. Make a change to the header text (for example, change "welcome to Planet Wrox" to "welcome to the Planet Wrox website"). Note that as soon as you start typing, the tab of the page in the code editor moves to the left side, taking the page out of Preview mode and into Edit mode. In addition, the Page Inspector now indicates that the source of the page has changed and that it needs to be reloaded to reflect those changes. This is indicated by a yellow bar above the page, shown in Figure 18-26.

FIGURE 18-26

Click that bar, or press Ctrl+Alt+Enter. The page reloads and now shows the change you made to the page.

5. Look at the HTML for the page in the lower-left corner of the Page Inspector, and make a change. For example, change the page's title in the `<head>` section (you need to double-click the text in order to edit it) or change the text above the theme drop-down list. Changes you make here are not persisted in your source files, and only show up in the Page Inspector until you reload it.

6. Switch to the other theme using the drop-down list in the Sidebar. Notice how this "just works"; because the page runs in Internet Explorer, all client-side functionality, such as JavaScript and form posts, keep working as if the page was running in a normal browser.

7. Choose All Reviews from the `TreeView` or `Menu` and then click the link for one of the reviews to go to the details page.

8. Use the Inspect button and highlight the summary of the review. You may recall from an earlier exercise that you gave the summary label a CSS class called `Summary`, which you added to the theme's style sheet. The Page Inspector noticed that too, and, as illustrated in Figure 18-27, shows you the correct filename in the Styles tab below the Page Inspector. You need to scroll down in order to see the `Summary` class.

```
Styles   Trace Styles   Layout   Attributes
◢* {                                                  DarkGrey.css
   ☑font-family:          Verdana, Arial, Sans-Serif;
 }
◢.Summary {                                           DarkGrey.css
   ☑display:              block;
   ☑font-style:           italic;
 }
```

FIGURE 18-27

Click the `.Summary` selector (not the filename to the right) to open the CSS file that defines the `.Summary` selector. Its code gets highlighted automatically. Make a change to the `.Summary` selector, for example by adding a thin grey border to its bottom:

```
.Summary
{
  font-style: italic;
  display: block;
  border-bottom: 1px solid Grey;
}
```

Just as with the change to the HTML you made, the Page Inspector sees the changes and enables you to refresh the page to see the changes. Click the yellow bar or press Ctrl+Alt+Enter to reload the updated stylesheet.

9. Click the Inspect button and highlight the summary in the text again. Switch to the Trace Styles tab, shown in Figure 18-28. Expand a few items such as `font-size` and `font-style`.

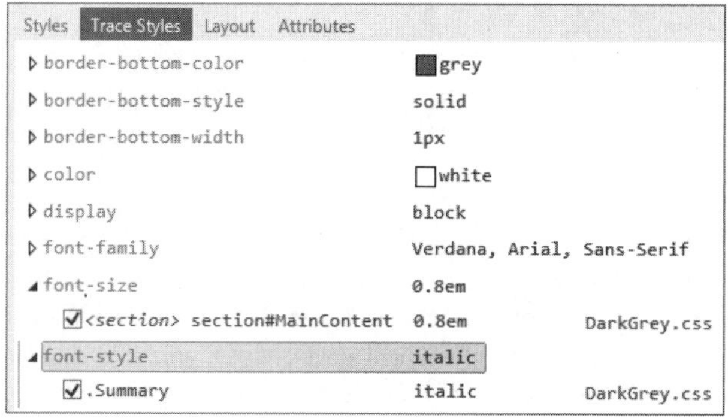

FIGURE 18-28

This screen shows you all the CSS rules that are currently in effect for the selected element. This makes it easy to see the CSS by which the element is styled and where that CSS came from. You can't make changes from this screen to your source files. You can, however, disable some of the rules to see how that affects the page. The changes you make are not persisted and only show up in the Page Inspector until you reload it or browse to another page.

The other two tabs (Layout and Attributes) show you the box model for the selected element and enable you to add additional attributes (a `class` attribute, for example) to the selected element.

10. To stop using the Page Inspector, click the Stop button on the toolbar. You can also press Shift+F5 if the Page Inspector is currently not the active window in the IDE.

How It Works

When you enable the Page Inspector, the .NET run time and the IDE keep track of which file or control contributes which HTML to the final page. It then uses that information to find the responsible file and highlight the relevant code in it when you inspect page elements in the Page Inspector. Changes you make to the source files are detected by the IDE so you can refresh the Page Inspector whenever it's needed.

Useful as debugging your code may be during the development of your site, it lacks the capability to investigate the behavior of your site while it's running in production. Fortunately, ASP.NET has a solution for that as well: tracing.

TRACING YOUR ASP.NET WEB PAGES

Without tracing, finding out the values of variables, objects, the execution path your code follows, and so on at run time is problematic at best. You would probably add a `Label` control to the page, and then write information to it like this:

VB.NET

```
Dim value2 As Double = Convert.ToDouble(ValueBox2.Text)
DebugLabel.Text &= "The value of value2 = " & value2.ToString() & "<br />"
```

C#

```
double value2 = Convert.ToDouble(ValueBox2.Text);
DebugLabel.Text += "The value of value2 = " + value2.ToString() + "<br />";
```

Although this certainly works, it's quite cumbersome. First, you need to write a lot of code to make this work. Secondly, you end up with an ugly `Label` control in your page that you shouldn't forget to remove when you're done with your debugging or tracing. And finally, when you're ready, you should remove all the code that sets the `DebugLabel` label. You could take the easy way out by setting the `Label` control's `Visible` property to `False`, but you would still take the performance hit of assigning the text to the `Label` control.

Tracing in ASP.NET solves all of these problems. It lets your pages, controls, and code write information to a central location, called the *trace*, which can then be shown in the browser. Tracing is built into the ASP.NET Framework, which means you can use it without any manual coding. Additionally, you can add your own information to the trace. In the following section, you see how to use the built-in tracing capabilities, giving you a wealth of information about your page. In a later exercise, you see how to add your own information to the trace.

Using the Standard Tracing Capabilities

Without much work, you can get a lot of good information about the way your pages execute. All you need to do is enable tracing for your pages. You can do this at the page level or at the site level. With tracing enabled at the page level, you can choose one or more specific pages you want to trace. Application-level tracing is useful if you want to look at multiple pages at the same time. This may help you, for example, to find slow pages in your website.

Tracing with Individual Pages

To enable tracing in a page, you need to set its `Trace` attribute in the `Page` directive to `true`:

```
<%@ Page ........ Trace="true" %>
```

When you run a trace-enabled page, you get a long list of details at the bottom of the page. Figure 18-29 shows the ASP.NET trace for the Calculator demo page you have been working with in this chapter.

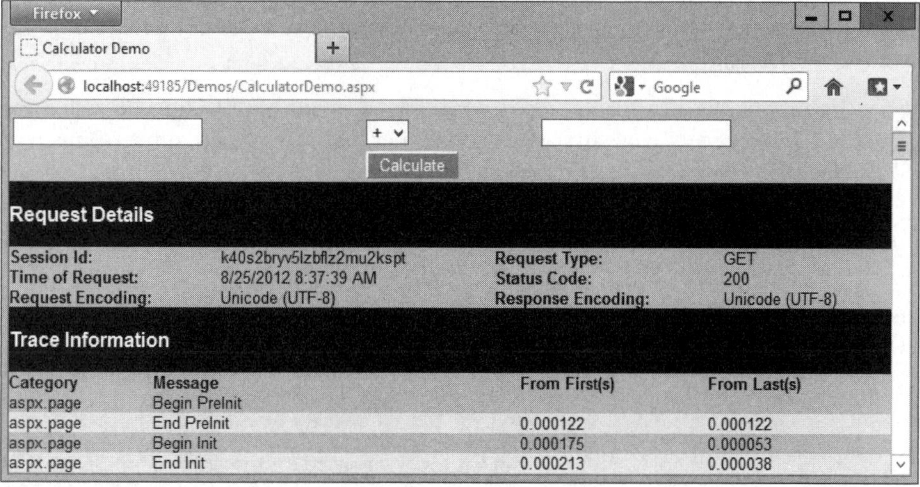

FIGURE 18-29

The trace provides a lot of details about your current page. At the top, you find a summary of the request details, including the current date and time, the method used to retrieve this page (GET or POST), and the status code (status 200 in Figure 18-29, to indicate success).

Below that, you see the Trace Information section. The ASP.NET `Page` class writes to the trace when you enable it. This is similar to the demo page you wrote in Chapter 15 that wrote to a `Label` control from the numerous events triggered during the page's life cycle. For each trace line you see a message, a category it's placed in, and two times. The first time column records the elapsed time in seconds since the first trace message was processed. The first trace message appears at the top of the list. The second time column records the elapsed time in seconds between processing of the current trace message and the preceding trace message.

By default, the data is sorted by time, putting the events in the order in which they occurred. You can also sort them on the category (more on categories in the section that deals with adding your own information to the trace) by changing the `TraceMode` from `SortByTime` to `SortByCategory`:

```
<%@ Page ....... Trace="true" TraceMode="SortByCategory" %>
```

A little further down the page (not visible in Figure 18-29), you see the *control tree*, which presents a hierarchical view of the controls in your page and their size.

Below the control tree, you see the details for a number of important collections, including the Query String, Cookies, Form, Headers, and Server Variables. Additionally, you see information you may have stored in Session or Application state. Being able to see these collections can be a great aid in figuring out a problem. For example, if you have a page that is supposed to read from a cookie, but that crashes and raises an exception as soon as the page loads, you can look at the Cookies collection and see if the page receives the data you expect. These collections are invaluable tools in understanding the execution of your page and can really aid in finding and fixing bugs in your code. In order for tracing to work when dealing with exceptions, you need to turn custom error pages off in the `Web.config` file. Refer to the section "Global Error Handling and Custom Error Pages" to learn more about custom error pages.

Page-level tracing means you need to enable tracing on every page you want to trace. It also means that you need to disable it on every page after you're done. Because this can be cumbersome in a large site, ASP.NET also enables you to trace the entire application.

Tracing the Entire Website

You can enable tracing for the entire website by changing trace settings in the `Web.config` file. You do this by creating a `<trace />` element under `<system.web>`. The following table lists the most important attributes that the `<trace />` element takes.

ATTRIBUTE	DESCRIPTION
`enabled`	Determines whether or not tracing is enabled for the application. By default, tracing is disabled, so you need to set this attribute to `true` explicitly.
`traceMode`	Determines the order in which items are sorted in the trace output. It works identically to the `TraceMode` attribute of the `Page` directive.
`requestLimit`	Determines the number of trace requests that ASP.NET keeps available. When the limit is hit, older trace records will be deleted automatically, leaving only recent trace requests available.
`pageOutput`	Specifies whether the trace information is displayed on the page. When set to `false` (the default), you can only access the tracing information using `Trace.axd`, which is discussed later.

ATTRIBUTE	DESCRIPTION
localOnly	Specifies whether the special Trace.axd handler is accessible from the local host only. From a security point of view, you're best off to leave this set to true, which means the trace is not available to outside users.
mostRecent	Determines whether old trace records are discarded when the number of trace requests hits the requestLimit. When set to false, tracing is disabled automatically when the requestLimit is hit.

When you have enabled tracing, you have two ways to read the trace information. When you have set pageOutput to true, the trace information is appended to each page, similar to what you saw with page-level tracing.

However, to make tracing less obtrusive, you can disable pageOutput and then request tracing information using a special file called Trace.axd. This is a virtual file, which means you won't find it in your website when you go looking for it. However, the ASP.NET run time knows it should provide you with tracing information when you request this special page. Although the file is virtual, you can still protect it using ASP.NET's URL security by adding a <location /> element to the main Web.config file as you've done with other file and folders.

You see how to enable tracing for the site in the following exercise.

TRY IT OUT Enabling Tracing for the Entire Site

In this Try It Out, you see how to enable site-wide tracing. First, you make a few changes to the Web.config file. You then browse your site, filling the trace log with your page requests. Finally, you request the special Trace.axd page to see the available trace log information.

1. Open Web.config and locate the opening <system.web> tag. As a direct child of that element, add the following configuration information to enable tracing:

```
<system.web>
  <trace mostRecent="true" enabled="true" requestLimit="100" pageOutput="false"
        localOnly="true" />
```

   This enables the trace, but doesn't add its output to the page. Instead, you need to request the special Trace.axd page to see the trace information. Additionally, you make your system a little more secure by only allowing requests for the trace information from the local machine. Save and close Web.config.

2. Open the Target Browser drop-down on the Standard toolbar and switch back from the Page Inspector to your preferred browser. Then right-click Default.aspx in the Solution Explorer and choose View in Browser.

3. Click around the site, opening pages, changing the theme, filling in the contact form, and so on.

4. After you have requested at least five pages, change the address bar of your browser as follows so it requests the special `Trace.axd` page:

```
http://localhost:49394/Trace.axd
```

Your port number may be different, but it's important that you request the page `Trace.axd` on localhost. You should get a page similar to Figure 18-30. If the page is empty, press Ctrl+F5 to refresh it.

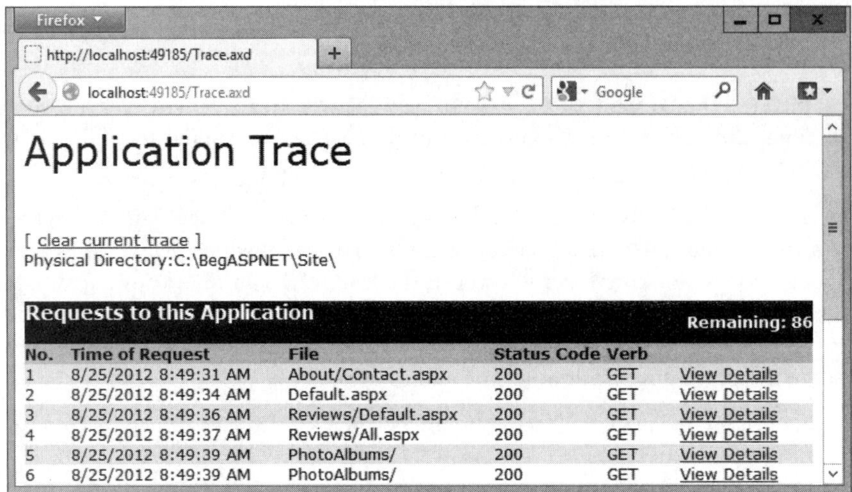

FIGURE 18-30

5. The list of traces is sorted based on time, from oldest to newest. Click the View Details link you see in Figure 18-30 for an ASPX page. You get a page similar to the one shown in Figure 18-29.

6. Disable tracing by setting the `enabled` attribute to `false` in the `Web.config` file, and then try requesting `Trace.axd` again. Notice that ASP.NET doesn't serve the page, but shows your error page instead.

How It Works

The ability to see trace information for pages that have been requested is extremely valuable. The information can help you understand the flow of information from and to a web page. For example, the trace information for the `Contact.aspx` page also shows the information that users have entered in the text box controls on the page. To see what this information looks like, click the View Details link for an item you want to zoom in on.

Although the information that ASP.NET traces for you automatically is extremely useful, you're not limited to just this information. You can also add your own information to the trace log.

Adding Your Own Information to the Trace

Adding your own data to the trace is useful if, for example, you want to see the value of a variable, or want to find out if a specific event fires, and when it fires exactly.

You can add information to the trace by using the `Trace` class. This class exposes two useful methods: `Write` and `Warn`. Both do pretty much the same thing: they add information to the trace that you can optionally put in a category you make up yourself. The only difference between `Write` and `Warn` is that messages written by `Warn` appear in red. You could use the `Warn` method for unexpected situations because the message will draw more attention.

In the following exercise, you see how simple it is to add your own information to the trace using the `Warn` and `Write` methods.

TRY IT OUT Adding Trace Data to Your Pages

In this Try It Out, you add some custom information to the ASP.NET trace. You use the `Write` method to write out trace information in a normal page execution, and use the `Warn` method for unexpected scenarios.

1. Open `CalculatorDemo.aspx`, switch to its Code Behind, and locate the `Click` handler for the Calculate button.
2. Right before the `Select Case` (VB.NET) or `switch` statement (C#), add the following `Trace.Write` call:

   VB.NET

   ```
   Trace.Write(String.Format("Performing the calculation with the {0} operator",
               OperatorList.SelectedValue))
   Select Case OperatorList.SelectedValue
   ```

   C#

   ```
   Trace.Write(string.Format("Performing the calculation with the {0} operator",
               OperatorList.SelectedValue));
   switch (OperatorList.SelectedValue)
   ```

3. Near the bottom of the event handler, modify the `Else` statement for the check that ensures that both `TextBox` controls contain a value:

   VB.NET

   ```
   Else
     Result.Text = String.Empty
     Trace.Warn("Custom Category",
                "TextBox controls are empty; time to add Validation controls?")
   End If
   ```

   C#

   ```
   else
   {
   ```

```
    Result.Text = string.Empty;
    Trace.Warn("Custom Category",
            "TextBox controls are empty; time to add Validation controls?");
  }
```

4. Enable tracing for this page explicitly. You can do this by setting the `Trace` attribute of the `Page` directive in Markup View:

   ```
   <%@ Page Title="Calculator Demo" ... Trace="true" %>
   ```

5. Save all your changes and request the Calculator page in the browser by pressing Ctrl+F5. Enter two numbers and click the Calculate button. Note that your custom information is added to the trace, between the `Begin Raise PostBackEvent` and `End Raise PostBackEvent` trace entries even though tracing is disabled at the site level. Note also that the text is black, and has no category assigned.

6. Clear the text from both `TextBox` controls in the browser and click the Calculate button again. The trace information should now be easier to spot because of its different color and own category name, as shown in Figure 18-31.

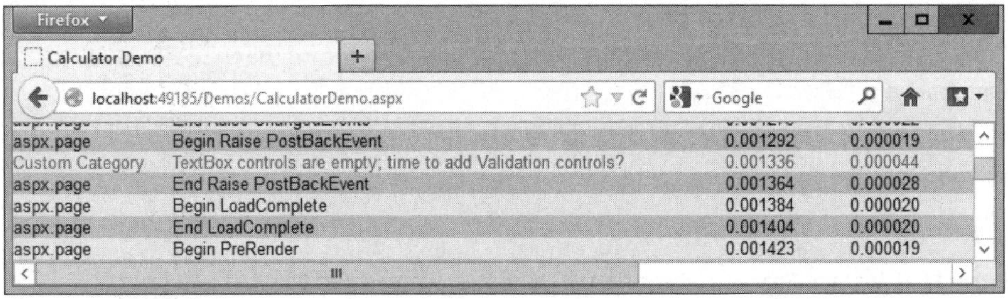

FIGURE 18-31

7. Go back to VS once more and disable tracing for the Calculator page by setting the `Trace` attribute of the `Page` directive to `false`. Save your changes and request the page again. Note that the page still functions correctly, but no longer outputs the trace information.

How It Works

The `Write` and `Warn` methods of the `Trace` class enable you to write additional information to the trace. The ASP.NET run time keeps track of the information and displays it together with the rest of the trace info, either directly at the bottom of the page in the browser with page-level tracing, or through the special `Trace.axd` page you saw earlier.

The `Write` and `Warn` methods each have three overloads. The first one (shown only with `Write` in the previous example) accepts a single string that is displayed in the Message column. The second overload also accepts a category name as demonstrated with the `Warn` method. The final overload, not shown in the Try It Out exercise, also accepts an `Exception` object whose message will be added to the trace output. This is useful to trace the information of an exception in a `Catch` block.

Tracing and Performance

Although it may seem that leaving `Warn` and `Write` statements in your code on your production system may hurt performance, this isn't the case. Because you can disable tracing in the `Web.config` file by setting the `enabled` property of the `trace` element to `false`, you greatly minimize the performance overhead of tracing.

A Security Warning

Tracing can be very useful, but leaving trace information in your production environment can lead to information disclosure. Therefore, you should always either disable tracing by setting its `enabled` attribute in `Web.config` to `false`, or at least by setting the `localOnly` attribute to `true`. In Chapter 19, you learn a trick that enables you to make this change for all sites on your production server, making it easy to block access to the trace functionality.

PRACTICAL DEBUGGING TIPS

The following list provides some practical tips to help you debug your application:

- Never leave `debug="true"` in the `Web.config` file in a production environment. Always set it to `false` to improve performance. In Chapter 19, you see an even better solution to ensure this setting is never set to `true` on a production server.
- Try to avoid *swallowing* exceptions in a `Catch` block. You may be tempted to wrap your code in a `Try/Catch` block and then leave the entire `Catch` block empty. Although this certainly avoids exceptions showing up in the user interface, it makes debugging extremely difficult. Because you are no longer aware a problem occurs, you also cannot write code to prevent the error from happening in the first place. The general rule here is: Catch errors that you can handle successfully, for example by displaying a message to the user. If you can't handle the exception in your code, let it bubble up and log it in the `Application_Error` event handler so you know that the exception occurred.
- If you need to re-throw an exception in a `Catch` block, don't use `Throw ex` (`throw ex` in C#), but use `Throw` (`throw` in C#) only. When you use `Throw ex`, you make it difficult to track the path the code has followed before the exception occurred, but by using `Throw` you maintain this information. Here's the code showing both options:

VB.NET

```
Try
  ...
Catch ex As Exception
  ' Do something with the error here, such as logging it
  Throw ex   ' Bad example; you lose track of the source of the exception
  Throw      ' Good example; forwards the exception
             ' and maintains the call stack
End Try
```

C#

```
try
{
  ...
}
catch (Exception ex)
{
  // Do something with the error here, such as logging it
  throw ex;  // Bad example; you lose track of the source of the exception
  throw;     // Good example; forwards the exception
             // and maintains the call stack
}
```

- Try to avoid exception handling when possible. As you saw in this chapter, it's much better (and faster) to simply avoid an exception in the first place. For example, you can easily avoid the `DivideByZeroException` exception by checking for a value of zero before carrying out the division.
- Be as explicit as possible with the `Exception` types you catch in `Try/Catch` blocks. Try to avoid catching generic `Exception` types and set up multiple, explicit `Catch` blocks for each specific type you anticipate.

SUMMARY

No matter how carefully you program, your site is likely to contain some bugs or throw exceptions at run time. To minimize these exceptions and build a site that runs as smoothly as possible, you can do a number of things.

First of all, you can use exception-handling techniques, where you write code that is able to catch exceptions that you foresee and handle them appropriately.

To help you write code with as few bugs as possible, VS offers you a great set of debugging tools. The ability to break into your code and analyze and change the execution environment from client-side code all the way into the server is a great aid in your bug-slashing adventures.

Even if you have debugged your application thoroughly, there's still a chance your site may have issues in production, whether they are related to performance, logic errors, or other unexpected reasons. In those cases, you can use the ASP.NET tracing facilities that let you track information about running pages. Analyzing this trace information can bring you a long way in fixing the underlying issues.

Now that your website is complete and hopefully bug-free, the next step is to put it online. You see how to deploy your ASP.NET website in the next chapter.

EXERCISES

1. What's the difference between debugging and tracing?

2. Imagine you have some code that could potentially throw an exception. For example, you try to send an e-mail message to a mail server. What kind of exception-handling strategy would you use to avoid the exception from being displayed in the browser? What code would you need?

3. You're taking over a website that has been built by another developer who had never heard of exception handling. Your client is complaining about the quality of the site and the large number of "Yellow Screens of Death" that users see. Besides analyzing the code for the entire application, what would be a quick solution to get information about the errors and the locations where they occur? And how can you shield the site's users from the dirty details of the exception messages?

You can find answers to these exercises in Appendix A.

▶ WHAT YOU LEARNED IN THIS CHAPTER

Breakpoint	A marker you can set in your code to indicate where you want the debugger to halt at run time
Data tips	Tooltips that present simple or rich data about variables during debugging
Debugging	The process of finding and fixing bugs in your code
Exception	The .NET term for an error that may occur in your code
Exception handling	A methodology to identify and handle errors that occur at run time
Stack trace	A visual representation of the current stack of code calls
Trace	Enables ASP.NET controls and your own custom code to write information to a central log location at run time

19

Deploying Your Website

WHAT YOU WILL LEARN IN THIS CHAPTER:

- How to ease the deployment process through simple changes to your code and configuration
- How to prepare your site for deployment by creating a copy using Visual Studio's built-in copy tools
- How to install and configure a web server and your website on your target machine
- How to avoid common errors you may get when deploying a site
- How to copy data stored in your SQL Server database to the target server

WROX.COM CODE DOWNLOADS FOR THIS CHAPTER

You can find the wrox.com code downloads for this chapter on the Download Code tab at `www.wrox.com/remtitle.cgi?isbn=1118311809`. The code is in the Chapter 19 download.

Congratulations! The fact that you're reading this chapter probably means you now have a full-featured, database-driven ASP.NET website that is ready for release into the wild. It's an exciting time for you and your project. Pretty soon your application will be used and judged by your target audience.

To make your website accessible to users worldwide, you need to publish it to a production server that is connected to the Internet. What kind of server this is and where it is located depends on your own requirements and budget. You can host the site on a home server in your attic with a private Internet connection (as I used to do with `http://imar.spaanjaars.com`) or you can host it with an external (and often commercial) party with a direct connection to the Internet backbone.

Either way, you need to do some work to get your site from its development location at `C:\BegASPNET\Site` to a location where it's accessible over the Internet.

This chapter deals with a few topics related to successfully deploying your website. You learn about the process from preparing your site in the development environment to actually running and testing it at your production server.

The chapter then ends with a list of things you need to take care of when deploying your site. You can use this checklist to make sure you configure your production site in the most secure and optimal way.

PREPARING YOUR WEBSITE FOR DEPLOYMENT

When you're working on the first edition of your website in a development environment, managing the site and its source code is pretty straightforward. You have only a single version of the site's source, making it easy to maintain. However, as soon as you put your site in production, you now have two versions of it: one running in the production environment and the one you use for development. This makes it difficult to keep things synchronized. For example, you probably use a different database and connection string in your production environment. You're also likely to use different e-mail addresses for the e-mail that is sent by the site. Finally, you may want to disable sending the error e-mails from the `Global.asax` files in a development environment. If you make all of these changes in the code directly when you put your site on a production server, there's a fair chance that you'll overwrite some settings during the next update, which can lead to unwanted results.

This section shows you how to make managing different versions of the same website a little easier. You see how to move some of the hardcoded settings, such as e-mail addresses, to the `Web.config` file. The code in your application then reads these values at run time. The only difference between your development and production environments is then a single configuration file, making it easy to have different settings in both environments.

Avoiding Hard-Coded Settings

So far, the pages and user controls you have built use some hard-coded settings for things like e-mail addresses. For example, `ContactForm.ascx`, the user control that sends out an e-mail, uses the following code to set the recipient and sender information:

VB.NET

```
myMessage.From = New MailAddress("you@example.com", "Planet Wrox")
myMessage.To.Add(New MailAddress("you@example.com", "Planet Wrox"))
```

C#

```
myMessage.From = New MailAddress("you@example.com", "Planet Wrox");
myMessage.To.Add(New MailAddress("you@example.com", "Planet Wrox"));
```

Hard-coding settings in this manner makes it difficult to give them different values in different environments. Every time you want to roll out your site to production, you need to make sure you're not accidentally overwriting settings you changed for the production environment.

Fortunately, ASP.NET comes with a great solution to avoid these kinds of problems: the `Web.config` file, *expression syntax*, and the `WebConfigurationManager` class you use to read from `Web.config`.

The Web.config File

You've used the `Web.config` file a number of times in this book to store information about connection strings, membership, roles and profile information, and more. You also briefly saw the `<appSettings>` element that enables you to store data in a key/value pair using `<add>` elements. The `<appSettings>` element enables you to store simple information, such as an e-mail address, and retrieve that value by its key. For example, to store an e-mail address, you can add the following to the `Web.config` file:

```
<appSettings>
  <add key="FromAddress" value="webmaster@example.com" />
</appSettings>
```

The `<appSettings>` element is placed outside the `<system.web>` element in the `Web.config` file, yet still within the parent `<configuration>` element.

Obviously, you need a way to access the data in `<appSettings>` at run time. You can do this in a couple of ways, including expression syntax and the `WebConfigurationManager` class, both of which are discussed next.

Expression Syntax

Expression syntax enables you to bind control properties to resources, such as those found in the `<appSettings>` element in `Web.config`, connection strings, localization resource files, and various routing settings used in URL rewrite scenarios. To display data from the `<appSettings>` element, you use the following syntax, where *`AppSettingKeyName`* refers to a key you define in `Web.config`:

```
<%$ AppSettings:AppSettingKeyName %>
```

For example, to display a copyright notice on your pages in a `Literal` control, you can add the following setting to `Web.config`:

```
<add key="Copyright" value="Copyright by Wrox" />
```

You can then display this text in a `Literal` control like this:

```
<asp:Literal ID="Copyright" runat="server" Text="<%$ AppSettings:Copyright %>" />
```

To make it even easier to set properties like `Text` as in the preceding example, Visual Studio comes with the Expression Editor. To access this dialog box, select a control in Design or Markup View, open its Properties Grid, and click the ellipsis for the (Expressions) item, shown in Figure 19-1. You may find that the (Expressions) item does not always show up when in Markup View. If that's the case, switch to Split View or Design View first.

The Expressions dialog for the `Literal` control opens, enabling you to bind control properties to expressions. Visual Studio limits the list of properties of the control to those that can be bound using an expression. To bind the `Text` property of the `Literal` control to an application setting, first click Text on the left side of the dialog box, choose AppSettings from the Expression Type drop-down list on the right, and finally, choose the desired AppSetting from the drop-down list in the Expression Properties section. Figure 19-2 shows the complete Expressions dialog box for a `Literal` control used to display the copyright text.

When you click OK, Visual Studio modifies the `Text` property of the `Literal` control so it contains a reference to the correct application setting.

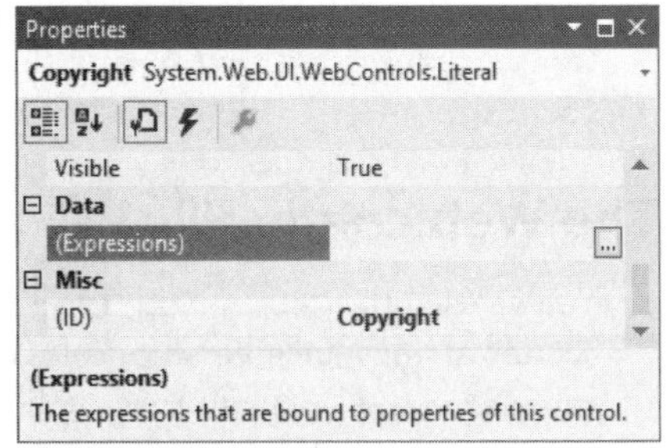

FIGURE 19-1

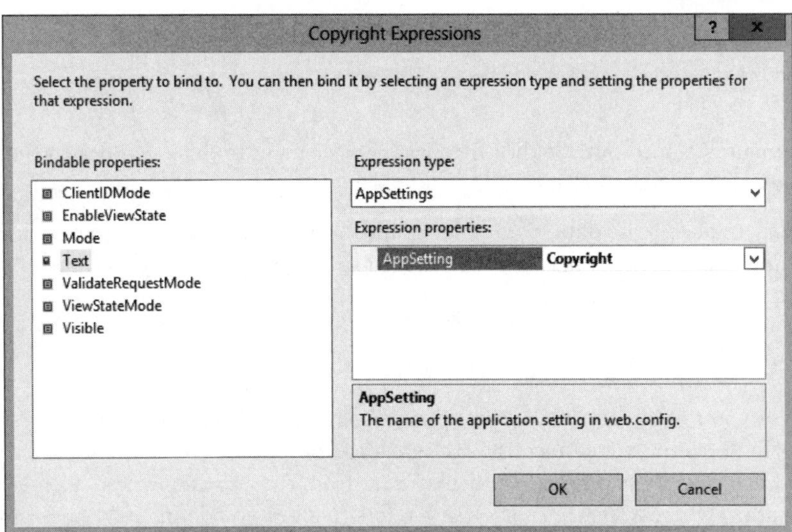

FIGURE 19-2

Getting values from the `Web.config` using expression syntax is useful, but may not cover all your needs. Therefore, it's good to know that you can retrieve the values programmatically as well. To do this, you can use the `WebConfigurationManager` class.

The WebConfigurationManager Class

The `WebConfigurationManager` class from the `System.Web.Configuration` namespace provides access to data that is stored in configuration files. It has special support for the `appSettings` and `connectionStrings` elements of the `Web.config` file, enabling you to retrieve data from those sections with a single line of code. The following snippet shows you how to retrieve the `FromAddress` value you saw earlier from the `<appSettings>` element:

VB.NET

```
Imports System.Web.Configuration
...
Dim fromAddress As String = WebConfigurationManager.AppSettings.Get("FromAddress")
```

C#

```
using System.Web.Configuration;
...
string fromAddress = WebConfigurationManager.AppSettings.Get("FromAddress");
```

The `Get` method always returns data as a string, so you'll need to convert it to a proper type if you're expecting anything other than a string. For example, if you have stored a boolean value in `Web.config` like this:

```
<add key="SendMailOnError" value="true" />
```

you need to use the following code to retrieve and convert the value:

VB.NET

```
Dim sendMail As Boolean =
    Convert.ToBoolean(WebConfigurationManager.AppSettings.Get("SendMailOnError"))
```

C#

```
bool sendMail =
    Convert.ToBoolean(WebConfigurationManager.AppSettings.Get("SendMailOnError"));
```

Although you can access the `WebConfigurationManager` class in the Code Behind of your Web Forms and user controls directly (provided you have imported the `System.Web.Configuration` namespace), I prefer to create static, read-only properties in a custom configuration class that accesses the `Web.config` file to get the values. You see how to do this in the following exercise.

TRY IT OUT Moving Application Settings to Web.config

In this Try It Out, you create a class with a few properties that get their values from the `Web.config` file. You then use the properties of this class in your code to replace the hard-coded values that were used earlier.

1. Inside the `App_Code` folder, create a new class file and call it `AppConfiguration.vb` or `AppConfiguration.cs`. In C#, remove the constructor code, shown in the following code block:

   ```
   public AppConfiguration()
   {
     //
     // TODO: Add constructor logic here
     //
   }
   ```

   Because the class is going to have static properties exclusively, you don't need the constructor.

2. At the top of the class file, add an `Imports/using` statement for the `System.Web.Configuration` namespace:

   VB.NET

   ```
   Imports System.Web.Configuration
   ```

   C#

   ```
   using System.Web.Configuration;
   ```

3. Add a new `Shared` (`static` in C#), read-only property to this class that returns the `FromAddress` from the `Web.config` file. Recall from Chapter 5 that a `Shared/static` member (like a method or a property) operates on the class itself, and not on an instance of that class.

VB.NET

```
Public Class AppConfiguration
  Public Shared ReadOnly Property FromAddress() As String
    Get
      Dim result As String =
            WebConfigurationManager.AppSettings.Get("FromAddress")
      If Not String.IsNullOrEmpty(result) Then
        Return result
      End If
      Throw New Exception("AppSetting FromAddress not found in web.config file.")
    End Get
  End Property
End Class
```

C#

```
public class AppConfiguration
{
  public static string FromAddress
  {
    get
    {
      string result = WebConfigurationManager.AppSettings.Get("FromAddress");
      if (!string.IsNullOrEmpty(result))
      {
        return result;
      }
      throw new Exception("AppSetting FromAddress not found in web.config file.");
    }
  }
}
```

4. Repeat the previous step, but this time create the following three properties by creating a copy of `FromAddress`:

   - `FromName`
   - `ToAddress`
   - `ToName`

   Don't forget to rename all three occurrences of `FromAddress` to the new property name.

5. Still inside the `AppConfiguration` class, create a boolean property called `SendMailOnError`:

VB.NET

```
Public Shared ReadOnly Property SendMailOnError() As Boolean
  Get
    Dim result As String =
            WebConfigurationManager.AppSettings.Get("SendMailOnError")
```

```
    If Not String.IsNullOrEmpty(result) Then
      Return Convert.ToBoolean(result)
    End If
    Throw New Exception(
                "AppSetting SendMailOnError not found in web.config file.")
  End Get
End Property
```

C#

```
public static bool SendMailOnError
{
  get
  {
    string result = WebConfigurationManager.AppSettings.Get("SendMailOnError");
    if (!string.IsNullOrEmpty(result))
    {
      return Convert.ToBoolean(result);
    }
    throw new Exception(
                "AppSetting SendMailOnError not found in web.config file.");
  }
}
```

6. When you're ready with the five properties, save and close the `AppConfiguration` file.
7. Open the Code Behind of `ContactForm.ascx` in the `Controls` folder, locate the code that sets the From and To addresses, and replace the hard-coded values with their `AppConfiguration` counterparts:

   VB.NET

   ```
   myMessage.From = New MailAddress(AppConfiguration.FromAddress,
                    AppConfiguration.FromName)
   myMessage.To.Add(New MailAddress(AppConfiguration.ToAddress,
                    AppConfiguration.ToName))
   ```

   C#

   ```
   myMessage.From = new MailAddress(AppConfiguration.FromAddress,
                    AppConfiguration.FromName);
   myMessage.To.Add(new MailAddress(AppConfiguration.ToAddress,
                    AppConfiguration.ToName));
   ```

   Notice how IntelliSense helps you pick the correct property of your `AppConfiguration` class.
8. This is also a good moment to delete the line of code that calls the `Sleep` method (near the end of the `SendButton_Click` method) that you added there in Chapter 10 to simulate a slow mail server. On your production site, you want this to go as fast as possible.
9. Save your changes and close the file.
10. Open the `Global.asax` file and wrap the entire code in `Application_Error` in an `If` check that ensures that `SendMailOnError` is set to `True`. Additionally, change the hard-coded e-mail addresses to use the `FromAddress` and `ToAddress` from the `AppConfiguration` class instead:

VB.NET

```
Sub Application_Error(ByVal sender As Object, ByVal e As EventArgs)
  If AppConfiguration.SendMailOnError Then
    If HttpContext.Current.Server.GetLastError() IsNot Nothing Then
      ...
      Dim myMessage As MailMessage = New MailMessage(AppConfiguration.FromAddress,
               AppConfiguration.ToAddress, mailSubject, message)
      ...
    End If
  End If
End Sub
```

C#

```
void Application_Error(object sender, EventArgs e)
{
  if (AppConfiguration.SendMailOnError)
  {
    if (HttpContext.Current.Server.GetLastError() != null)
    {
      ...
      MailMessage myMessage = new MailMessage(AppConfiguration.FromAddress,
                    AppConfiguration.ToAddress, mailSubject, message);
      ...

    }
  }
}
```

11. Open `Web.config` and add the following elements to the `<appSettings>` element. Change the e-mail addresses for `FromAddress` and `ToAddress` to your own:

```
<configuration>
  <appSettings>
    ...
    <add key="FromAddress" value="planetwrox@example.com" />
    <add key="FromName" value="Planet Wrox" />
    <add key="ToAddress" value="planetwrox@example.com" />
    <add key="ToName" value="Planet Wrox" />
    <add key="SendMailOnError" value="true" />
  ...
```

12. Save all your changes and press Ctrl+F5 to open the homepage in your browser. Go to the Contact page and fill in the contact form. You should receive an e-mail at the address you specified in the previous step.

13. Request a nonexistent page in your browser. For example, change the page name in the address in the browser's address bar to `DefaultTest.aspx`. You should receive a "File Not Found" message and an e-mail with the exception details, just as in the preceding chapter.

14. Go back to Visual Studio, open `Web.config`, and change the setting for `SendMailOnError` from `true` to `false`:

```
<add key="SendMailOnError" value="false" />
```

15. Save your changes, and again request a page that doesn't exist. Because you changed the `SendMailOnError` setting, you shouldn't get an e-mail with the exception details.

How It Works

The properties of the `AppConfiguration` class look in the `Web.config` file for the requested application settings. When the setting is not defined or does not contain a value, each property throws an exception. This is useful to detect missing application settings at an early stage. Instead of silently returning an empty value, you now get an exception that reminds you to add the required application setting.

At run time, the code accesses these properties like this:

VB.NET

```
myMessage.From = New MailAddress(AppConfiguration.FromAddress,
                                 AppConfiguration.FromName)
```

C#

```
myMessage.From = new MailAddress(AppConfiguration.FromAddress,
                                 AppConfiguration.FromName);
```

Because the properties have been defined as `Shared` (`static` in C#), you can access them directly on the `AppConfiguration` class, without the need to create a new instance of `AppConfiguration` first.

Although you could access the `<appSettings>` element in `Web.config` directly in the code (for example, you could use `WebConfigurationManager.AppSettings.Get("FromAddress")` to get the e-mail address in `ContactForm.ascx` directly), it's better to wrap the `<appSettings>` elements in shared properties in their own class. This solution gives you IntelliSense on the `AppConfiguration` class, making it easy to see what configuration properties are available. It also enables you to write centralized code that throws exceptions when the required application settings cannot be found or that supplies sensible defaults. Notice how the properties throw an exception only when a valid value cannot be returned. If you access `Web.config` directly in your own code, you would need to check for valid values every time you access a setting.

The same principle is used for the `SendMailOnError` setting. When an exception occurs at run time, the code in `Application_Error` now consults the `SendMailOnError` property. This property in turn checks the `<appSettings>` element of `Web.config` to determine if an error message should be e-mailed. Because the `SendMailOnError` property is a boolean, the code uses `Convert.ToBoolean` to convert the string returned from the `Web.config` file into a boolean.

By storing values in `Web.config` instead of hard-coding them, your site becomes easier to maintain and deploy. When you go live, all you need to do is create a copy of `Web.config` for your production environment and change a few settings. This enables you to turn off error logging by e-mail on your development machine easily.

With the hard-coded application settings moved to the central `Web.config` file, the next step in the deployment process is optimizing your external CSS and JavaScript references.

INTRODUCING BUNDLING AND MINIFICATION

Bundling and minification are two new features that have been added to ASP.NET 4.5. Both are designed to improve the performance of your site by minimizing the number and size of your client CSS and JavaScript files. With bundling, the ASP.NET run time combines one or more CSS or JavaScript files into a single request. This minimizes the network overhead as the browser needs to make fewer requests. Minification works by removing irrelevant code from these files. Combining these two techniques greatly enhances the performance of your site.

The cool thing about bundling and minification is that they are really simple to do, and require hardly any code. As an example, imagine you have two CSS files in your `Styles` folder called `1.css` and `2.css`. Without bundling and minification, you may have something like this in your master page:

```
<link href="Styles/1.css" rel="stylesheet" type="text/css" />
<link href="Styles/2.css" rel="stylesheet" type="text/css" />
```

To enable bundling and minification, you change these two lines into the following single line:

```
<link href="Styles/css" rel="stylesheet" type="text/css" />
```

Notice that you no longer specify a filename after the folder name. Instead, you just specify a file extension — `css` in this case. This instructs the ASP.NET run time to take all files with a `.css` extension from the `Styles` folder, bundle them into a single response, and minify them by removing unnecessary content like whitespace and comments. This final result is then streamed to the browser, where it's interpreted in exactly the same way as it was with the two separate files.

You can bundle and minimize JavaScript files the same way by specifying `js` as the file extension rather than `css`.

One problem with the previous code example is that the browser caches the result for the URL `Styles/css`. Even if you change the underlying CSS or JavaScript files, the browser may continue to use the old files. You can overcome this problem by using the `ResolveBundleUrl` method and passing in the path to the CSS or JS files you want to bundle and minify. `ResolveBundleUrl` then generates a unique key for the files that is appended to the query string. As long as the files are unmodified on disk, `ResolveBundleUrl` keeps returning the same key, which tells the browser it's safe to keep using a cached copy of the file. However, as soon as you change one of the files, the key changes as well, which in turn causes the browser to request a fresh copy of the bundle from the server. You see how this works in the next exercise.

Enabling bundling and minification in your ASP.NET website is a three-step process:

1. Install the Microsoft.Web.Optimization package using NuGet.
2. Enable bundling by writing some code in `Global.asax`.
3. Remove existing `<link>` and `<script>` elements pointing to CSS and JavaScript files and replace them with a single `<link>` or `<script>` element per file type pointing at the correct source folder.

The current Planet Wrox website doesn't benefit a lot from bundling and minification because the number of CSS and JavaScript files is quite low. In addition, the CSS for the site is placed in the `Themes` folder, which is not supported by the bundling and minification functionality.

However, to show you how to use bundling and minification in your own sites where it may result in improved performance, in the following exercise you optimize a few style sheets you add to the `Styles` folder so their content is bundled and minified.

TRY IT OUT Using Bundling and Minification

In this exercise, you add two new CSS files to the `Styles` folder. You then enable bundling and minification for this folder so you can see how this affects the CSS code that gets sent to the client.

1. Create a new folder called `Styles` in the root of your site. You may already have this folder from earlier exercises in this book, in which case you can skip this step.
2. Install the Microsoft.Web.Optimization package. To do this, choose Tools ➪ Library Package Manager ➪ Package Manager Console and run the following command:

```
Install-Package Microsoft.Web.Optimization
```

3. Open up your `Global.asax` file and in the `Application_Start` event handler that should already be there, add the following code below the line that creates the `ScriptResourceDefinition`.

VB.NET

```
Microsoft.Web.Optimization.BundleTable.Bundles.EnableDefaultBundles()
```

C#

```
Microsoft.Web.Optimization.BundleTable.Bundles.EnableDefaultBundles();
```

4. Add a new CSS file to your `Styles` folder and call it `Test1.css`. Remove the existing code and add the following code to underline all headings at level one:

```
h1
{
  text-decoration: underline;
}
```

5. Add another CSS file to your `Styles` folder and call it `Test2.css`. Remove the existing code and add the following code to change the color of all headings at level one to green:

```
h1
{
  color: Green;
}
```

6. Open the Frontend master page and directly after the opening `<body>` tag add the following `<link>` element:

```
<body>
<link href="<%=Microsoft.Web.Optimization.BundleTable.Bundles.ResolveBundleUrl(
         "~/Styles/css")%>" rel="stylesheet" type="text/css" />
```

Because of the way `ResolveBundleUrl` works, you can't use it in the `<head>` section of the page and you'll get an error if you try.

7. Save all your changes and request the homepage in your browser. Notice how the heading is now underlined and green.

8. Open the HTML source for the page in the browser and locate the `<link>` element near the opening `<body>` tag. It should look similar to this:

```
<link href="/Styles/css?v=-2048696850486782O5" rel="stylesheet" type="text/css" />
```

   The `v` parameter ensures that the browser always gets a fresh copy of the page if you make a change to the underlying CSS files. The exact value for the `v` parameter will be different on your machine.

9. Request the URL set in the `href` attribute in your browser directly. Your browser's address bar should look similar to this:

```
http://localhost:8631/Styles/css?v=-2048696850486782O5
```

   The CSS code you see should look similar to this:

```
h1{text-decoration:underline}h1{color:green}
```

10. Go back to VS and delete `Test2.css` from the `Styles` folder.
11. Request the homepage in your browser again. The heading should still be underlined, but the green font has now gone.
12. Repeat steps 8 and 9 and notice how both the query string parameter and the CSS have changed to reflect the deleted style sheet.

How It Works

When ASP.NET encounters a request for a folder followed by a file extension (for example, `/Styles/css` or `/Scripts/js`), it takes all files with the extension in the folder, combines them into a single file, and then optimizes the code by removing unneeded code such as comments and irrelevant whitespace. The result of this operation is streamed back to the browser as a single file. To overcome caching issues, you don't point to `/Styles/css` from your server code directly. Instead, you call the `ResolveBundleUrl` method on the `Bundles` collection to create a path that contains a cache key. Whenever the underlying files change, the cache key changes as well, which causes the browser to fetch a fresh copy from the server. To enable the bundling and minification in the first place, you call `EnableDefaultBundles` on the `Bundles` collection during the website's `Start` event in `Global.asax`.

Notice how in the final CSS from step 9 the `underline` property comes first. The standard logic for the bundling mechanism is to put files in alphabetical order. Some exceptions to this rule exist. For example, known frameworks such as jQuery that other code may depend on are included first to avoid dependency issues.

Bundling and minification are fully extensible, meaning you can fully customize the way the files are included and minified. For more information, check out this blog post: `http://tinyurl.com/c63reut`.

Now that you have seen how you optimize your site for the way CSS and script references are handled, you're ready to create a copy of the site for deployment.

COPYING YOUR WEBSITE

During development of your site, you use IIS Express, which ships with Visual Studio. Although this server is great for local development, it's not designed to be used in a production environment. To put your site in production, you need to deploy it to a machine that runs the full version of *Internet Information Services (IIS)*, Microsoft's professional web server. In this section you see how to prepare your site so it can be run under IIS. Later in this chapter, you see how to install and configure IIS.

To deploy your website to a production server, the deployment targets shown in the following table are available, right from within VS.

DEPLOYMENT OPTION	DESCRIPTION
File System	Enables you to create a copy of the site on the local filesystem of your development machine or a networked machine. This option is useful if you want to move the files manually to your production server later.
Local IIS	Enables you to create a copy of your site that will run under your local IIS installation.
FTP Site	Enables you to send the files that make up your web application directly to a remote server using FTP.
Remote Site	Enables you to send the files that make up your web application to a remote IIS server. For this option to work, the remote server needs to have the Front Page Server Extensions installed. Check out the documentation that comes with IIS or consult the administrator of your remote server for more help with this option.

If you are using a commercial version of Visual Studio, you can access these four deployment targets from the two main ways of deployment that Visual Studio offers: Copy Web Site and Publish Web Site. If you're using the free Express edition, you can use only Copy Web Site. The Copy Web Site option simply creates a copy of the site whereas Publish Web Site also compiles all the code into one or more assemblies (`.dll` files), making it impossible to change the code on the server. For a description of the differences between the two, check out this MSDN article: `http://tinyurl.com/9e6gad5`.

> ***NOTE*** *At the very beginning of this book, you learned about the differences between Web Site Projects (WSP) and Web Application Projects (WAP). For this book, I have chosen to use the WSP model because it's easier to work with for beginners and supports a few features not available to WAPs (such as Profile and the dynamic* `App_Code` *folder). Unfortunately, there is one major feature that WAP supports and WSP doesn't: Web Packaging. This is a mechanism to create a setup package of your entire website so it can easily be deployed to a production server, taking the differences in configuration between the development and production machines into account. For more information about Web Packaging in WAPs, check out the list of links on deployment at the Visual Studio Team blog via* `http://tinyurl.com/WebDeploymentOverview`. *Although the articles target Visual Studio 2010, you'll find that the concepts discussed still apply.*

Creating a Simple Copy of Your Website

The Copy Web Site command simply creates a copy of your site using any of the four transportation options. This is a great way to quickly copy your site to another location, including your production server, or even to a portable media device like a USB stick that you can take with you. You can access the Copy Web Site option from the main Website menu or by right-clicking the site in the Solution Explorer.

Before you create a copy, it's a good idea to check the state of your website. You should do a full recompile where Visual Studio compiles all the code and pages in your website. This helps you detect any problems in your website before you deploy it to a production environment.

Deploying a site is also a good moment to do some housekeeping. To avoid slowing down the deployment process and to keep your site as lean and clean as possible, you should delete the files from your website that you don't need in production.

In the next exercise, you see how to use the Copy Web Site command to create a copy of the entire Planet Wrox project. In a later exercise, you use this copy again when you configure IIS for your production website.

TRY IT OUT Using the Copy Web Site Option

In this Try It Out, you use the Copy Web Site option together with the Local File System option to create a copy of the site. The other three transportation options (FTP, Local IIS, and Remote IIS) work similarly. The biggest difference with these options is that they ask you for details about the destination, such as a username and password, or the IIS website you want to use. With the copy you create in this exercise, you can configure an IIS website manually, something you see how to do later in this chapter.

1. Close all open files in Visual Studio and then choose Build ➪ Rebuild Web Site from the main menu. Doing so forces Visual Studio to recompile the entire site even if it already had compiled some parts of it. Visual Studio lists any problems your site may have in the Error List. To verify that your site is error free, open the Error List (choose View ➪ Error List from the main menu) and make sure you don't have any compilation errors. Fix any errors you may have in your site.
2. When the Error List is empty, choose Website ➪ Copy Web Site or right-click the site in the Solution Explorer and choose Copy Web Site.
3. At the top of the dialog box, click the Connect button to bring up a dialog box that enables you to choose the destination location for your site.

   At the left side of the dialog box, make sure that File System is selected. Then on the right side, locate the `C:\BegASPNET` folder, click it once to select it, and then click the Create New Folder button at the top-right corner of the dialog box. Type **`Release`** and press Enter to apply the new name. Figure 19-3 shows the final dialog box.

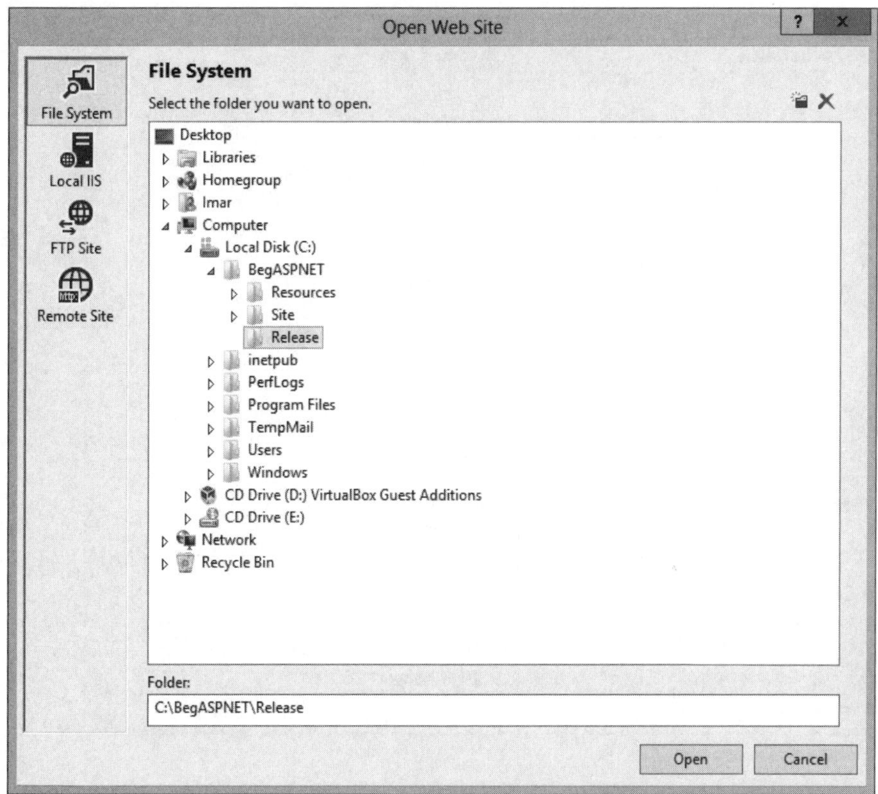

FIGURE 19-3

Click Open to choose `C:\BegASPNET\Release` as the destination location for your copy operation.

4. In the Copy Web Site dialog box, put focus on the list at the left by clicking a file or folder and then press Ctrl+A to select all files in the Source Web Site list.
5. Click the Synchronize Selected Files button (the third button with the two arrows facing in opposite directions) between the two lists, visible in Figure 19-4. This starts the synchronization process. Because the folder displayed on the right side is empty, all files from the left list are copied to the right. When copying is complete, your dialog box should look like Figure 19-4.
6. Next, open File Explorer (on Windows 8) or Windows Explorer (on older versions of Windows) and browse to `C:\BegASPNET\Release`. Verify that all relevant files that make up your site are there.

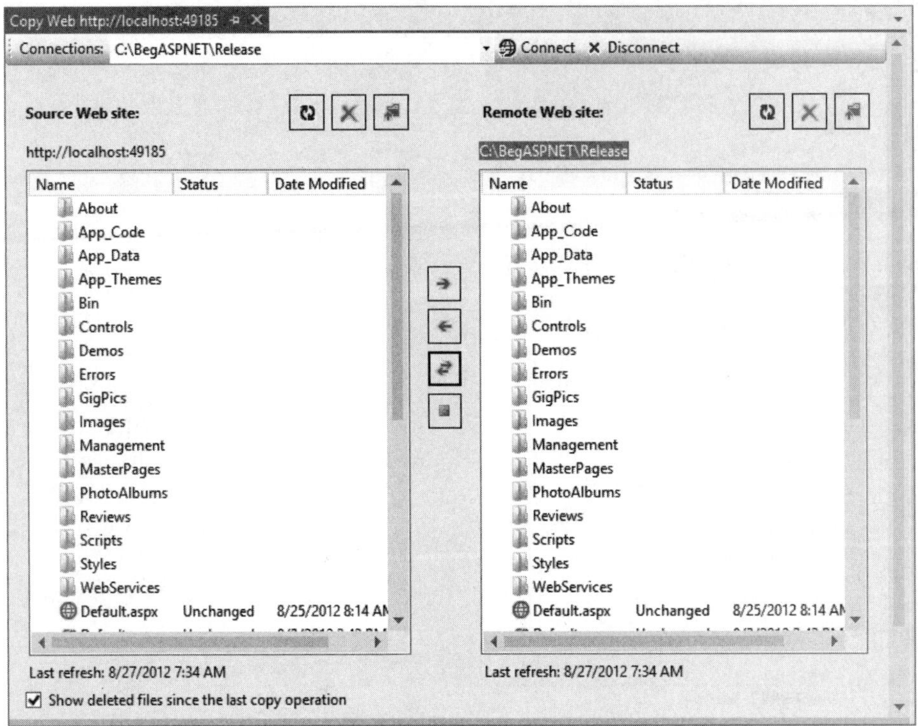

FIGURE 19-4

How It Works

The Copy Web Site option simply creates a copy of all files that make up your site. It can create a copy of the site at different locations, including the local filesystem, an FTP server, and an IIS server. In this exercise, you created a copy at a local hard drive. The first two buttons with arrows between the two file lists in Figure 19-4 enable you to copy files from the source to the remote location or vice versa. The third button, with the two arrows, enables you to *synchronize*, rather than just copy over the files. When you create a copy on your local system this may not seem like a big deal, but when you're creating the copy over a slow FTP connection, you'll be glad this tool uploads only new and changed files, and leaves unmodified files untouched. If the same file has been changed in both the source site and the remote site and you synchronize these files, the tool prompts you to indicate in which direction you want to copy. Likewise, if you synchronize a file that has been deleted in one site, the tool will prompt you to indicate if you want to delete the file from the other site.

In this exercise, you opted to copy the files to the local filesystem. This is a great way to create a copy that is detached from the development environment that can be run on your local machine. You can, of course, copy the same set of files to another machine using an FTP program, a USB stick, and so on. Also, if you host your site externally, your hosting provider may offer a web-based interface to upload these files to its server.

The detached local copy enables you to make modifications to a few files first (like `Web.config`) and then upload everything to your host.

Besides copying a website, the commercial versions of Visual Studio also support *publishing* your website.

Publishing Your Website

The Publish Web Site command, available only in the commercial versions of Visual Studio and not in the Express edition, is similar to the Copy Web Site option in that it creates a copy of the website you can use for deployment. However, it's different in that it enables you to *precompile* the application, which means all the code in the Code Behind of your ASPX pages, controls, code files in `App_Code`, and so on are compiled into *.NET assemblies*; files with a `.dll` extension, stored in the `bin` folder of your site. The main benefits of precompiling are source protection (others with access to the server can't look into your source) and an increased performance the very first time a page is requested. Pages that are not precompiled are compiled on the fly when they are requested the first time, which takes a little bit of time. Remember that regular visitors to your site will never be able to see the source of your application. All they'll be able to see is the final HTML that gets sent to the browser.

The Publish Web Site command is available from the Build menu and brings up the dialog box shown in Figure 19-5.

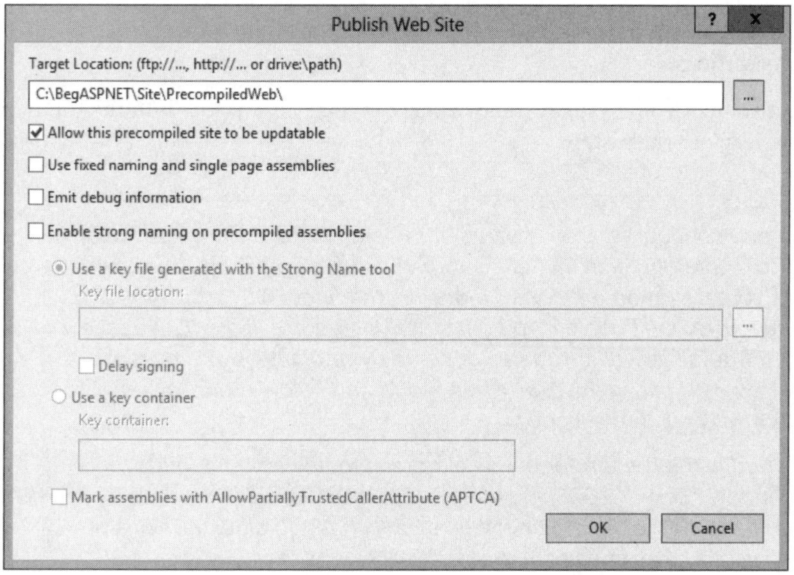

FIGURE 19-5

Clicking the ellipsis at the end of the Target Location brings up the same dialog box shown in Figure 19-3, enabling you to choose a target location. When you select the Allow This Precompiled Site to Be Updateable option, Visual Studio compiles all your VB.NET and C# code into .NET assemblies and places them in a `bin` folder at the root of your site. It leaves the markup in ASPX and ASCX files alone. However, with this option turned off, *all the markup code is compiled into* `.dll` files as well. The actual files still need to be deployed to the server, but their content has been replaced with placeholder text: "*This is a marker file generated by the precompilation tool, and should not be deleted*!" When the page is requested by a browser, the ASP.NET run time finds the appropriate content in the assemblies in the `bin` folder and serves its content as if it were a normal page. This latter option is especially great if you want to prevent other people with access to your server from altering your site after it has been deployed. Because all the source and markup is compiled into `.dll` files, there is no way to change it on the server anymore, other than uploading a new set of published files.

Copying or publishing your website to a new folder on your local system is only one step of the deployment process. The next part is configuring the web server so it knows where to look for your files.

RUNNING YOUR SITE UNDER IIS

Up until now, you've been using IIS Express, which ships with Visual Studio, to debug and test your application. However, because requests to this server are limited to those coming from the localhost to minimize security implications, you'll need to use the full IIS, which comes with most major Windows versions. To have your website run under IIS, you need to perform the following steps:

1. Install and configure IIS.
2. Install and configure the .NET Framework 4.5.
3. Configure security settings.

Depending on the current state of your system, some of these actions are optional. In the following sections, you see how to carry out these steps.

> ***NOTE*** *Installing and configuring a web server can be a complex task. You have many factors to take into account, including your operating system, its configuration, the account you use to log on to your machine, the final SQL Server you're going to use, and more. Don't panic if you get stuck. Instead, visit the IIS website at* `www.iis.net` *for detailed walkthroughs, or come over to this book's own discussion forum at* `http://p2p.wrox.com` *where you'll find fellow programmers (including me) that will help you succeed.*
>
> *The steps described in the remainder of this chapter should work on Windows 7, Windows 8, Windows Server 2008 R2, and Windows Server 2012. For a lot more information about IIS, including help with installing IIS on older versions of Windows not discussed here, check out the official IIS website at* `www.iis.net`.

Installing and Configuring the Web Server

Although IIS ships with most Windows versions, it's not installed by default, so you need to do that first. You also need to make sure that your version of Windows supports IIS. Although the Starter and Home Basic versions of Windows 7 and 8 ship with some parts of IIS, you can't run ASP.NET pages on them, so you need at least the Home Premium edition. On the server-based versions of Windows, IIS is fully supported. If you're hosting your site with an external hosting company, you can skip the following sections on installing IIS.

> ***NOTE*** *Even though IIS is supported on consumer versions of Windows such as Windows 7 and 8, it doesn't mean these operating systems are the best choices for hosting your website. You typically use these versions of Windows for local development and testing, whereas the server versions of Windows (such as Windows Server 2008 R2 and Windows Server 2012) are used for hosting production websites.*

To install and configure IIS on your Windows machine, you need to be logged on as an Administrator. If the account you use to log on to your machine does not have administrative privileges, you need to ask your administrator to install and configure IIS for you.

In addition to installing IIS, you also see how to create and configure the website in IIS. Because of the way security works under Windows, your site probably won't work immediately after you configure IIS unless you change some of the security settings under Windows. You see how to do this in the section "Understanding Security in IIS" and the Try It Out entitled "Configuring the Filesystem."

You'll be able to test out your IIS settings more easily if you already have SQL Server 2012 Express installed. This is the case if you followed along with the exercises in Chapter 12. If you haven't installed SQL Server 2012 Express yet, refer to the section "Installing SQL Server 2012 Express" in Chapter 12 for installation instructions. If you have one of the commercial versions of SQL Server, or have SQL Server on a remote machine, pay special attention to the section "Moving Data to a Remote Server" in this chapter and to Appendix B.

Making Sure IIS Is Installed

The easiest way to install IIS is through the Web Platform Installer (WPI). WPI is installed with Visual Studio so if you're carrying out these steps on your development machine, you already have the WPI. If you're following these steps on another machine (running Windows Server for example), you need to download and install WPI first. You can download WPI from `www.asp.net/download` and install it by clicking the Install Now button. If this link has changed by the time you read this document, go to `www.microsoft.com/web/downloads` instead, or search the web for "Web Platform Installer download" to find one of the other Microsoft locations that lets you download and install WPI.

Once WPI is installed, it starts automatically, or you can run it from the Windows Start menu or Start screen. When it's done loading, switch to the Products tab, at the top of the screen enter **IIS recommended,** and press Enter. WPI should list the IIS Recommended Configuration, as shown in Figure 19-6.

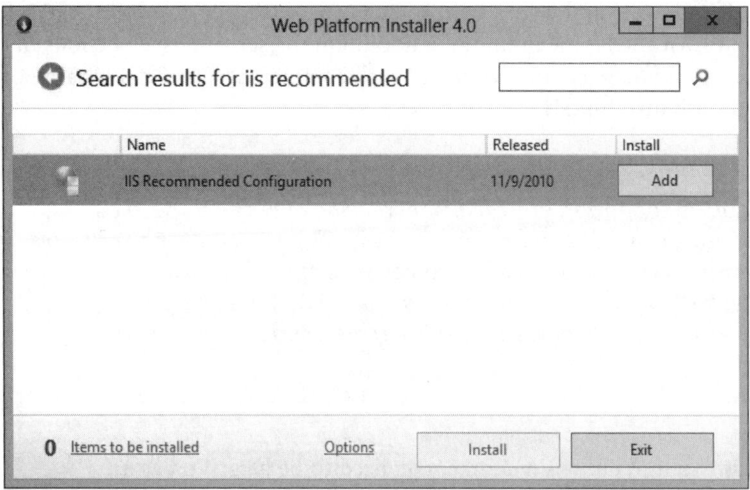

FIGURE 19-6

Click Add to add this item to the list of items to be installed. If the Add button is disabled, parts of IIS are already installed.

Next, use the search box again and search for IIS: ASP.NET. Depending on your version of Windows, this should bring up an item called IIS: ASP.NET or IIS: ASP.NET 4.5 (as well as other, unrelated items). The IIS: ASP.NET or IIS: ASP.NET 4.5 item is needed to run ASP.NET under IIS, and is a critical component to run your site successfully. Select this item and click Add. If you see both items choose IIS: ASP.NET 4.5. Finally, click the Install button at the bottom of the screen and then accept the license terms. After a while, you should get a confirmation that IIS and its components were installed successfully.

For detailed instructions on manually setting up IIS, check out these articles on the official IIS website:

`http://tinyurl.com/IISServer2008`

`http://tinyurl.com/IISServer2012`

When IIS is installed successfully, you need to make sure you have the Microsoft .NET Framework version 4.5 installed.

Installing and Configuring ASP.NET

If you installed Visual Studio 2012 (any edition) on your target machine or you're running Windows 8 or Windows Server 2012, you already have the .NET Framework 4.5 installed. Otherwise, you need to download it. You can use the Web Platform Installer as discussed earlier, or you can download the redistributable package from the Microsoft site at `http://msdn.microsoft.com/en-us/netframework`. Follow the Download or Install link or use the search option and search for "download .NET Framework 4.5." Make sure you download the full version of the .NET 4.5 Framework and not an earlier version or the Client Profile package. After you have downloaded the .NET Framework, run the installer and follow the on-screen instructions.

If you already had the .NET Framework 4.5 on your machine and installed IIS *afterward*, you need to tell IIS about the existence of the framework. Normally, this is done during installation of the .NET Framework, but if you installed IIS later, you need to do this manually. You only need to do this on Windows 7 and Server 2008 R2. For Windows 8 and Server 2012, ASP.NET 4.5 is registered correctly when you install IIS through the WPI. To register ASP.NET in IIS, follow these steps:

1. Open a command prompt in Administrative mode. To do this, click the Start button, type **`cmd`** in the search box, and press Ctrl+Shift+Enter to start the command prompt with elevated permissions. When you confirm the action, the command prompt will open with elevated permissions.
2. Navigate to the .NET Framework version 4 folder by entering the following command and pressing Enter:

   ```
   cd \Windows\Microsoft.NET\Framework\v4.0.30319
   ```

   Because .NET 4.5 is an in-place replacement for .NET 4, this folder uses the 4.0 version number. Note that the actual version number following `v4.0` may be slightly different on your machine if newer versions of the .NET Framework have been released by the time you read this book. Also, if you are using a 64-bit version of Windows, you should use the `Framework64` folder. Use Windows Explorer to find out the correct folder before you enter it at the command prompt.
3. Type **`aspnet_regiis -i`** and press Enter again.

   After a while, you should get a message that ASP.NET 4.5 was registered with IIS successfully.

Now that IIS and the .NET Framework have been installed and configured correctly, the next step is to configure your website under IIS. You see how to do this in the next Try It Out exercise. After the Try It Out, you learn more about configuring security permissions for your system.

TRY IT OUT Configuring Your Site

In this exercise, you see how to configure the standard "Default Web Site" that ships with IIS. Although it's possible to create more than one site under IIS on Windows 7, Windows 8, Windows Server 2008 R2, and Windows Server 2012, this option is not discussed here. Contact your system administrator or read the documentation that comes with IIS to learn more about creating multiple websites under IIS. Most of the steps in Windows 8 are identical to those in Windows 7, Windows Server 2008 R2, and Windows Server 2012. However, the screens you see in the following exercise are taken in Windows 8 and are slightly different on the other operating systems.

If you're doing this exercise on a machine other than the one you used to build the Planet Wrox site, be sure to copy the `BegASPNET` folder to the root of the C drive of the target machine. Also make sure this machine has access to SQL Server 2012, installed either locally or on another remote machine.

1. Open the Internet Information Services (IIS) Manager. You find this item in the Administrative Tools section of the Control Panel, which you can access through its System and Security category. Alternatively, click the Start button or Start screen, type **`inetmgr`**, and press Enter. If you get a question about learning more about WPI, click No (you could click Yes if you wanted to; if you do, you're taken to the main WPI section of the Microsoft website).

2. Expand the tree on the left until you see Application Pools and the Default Web Site, as shown in Figure 19-7.

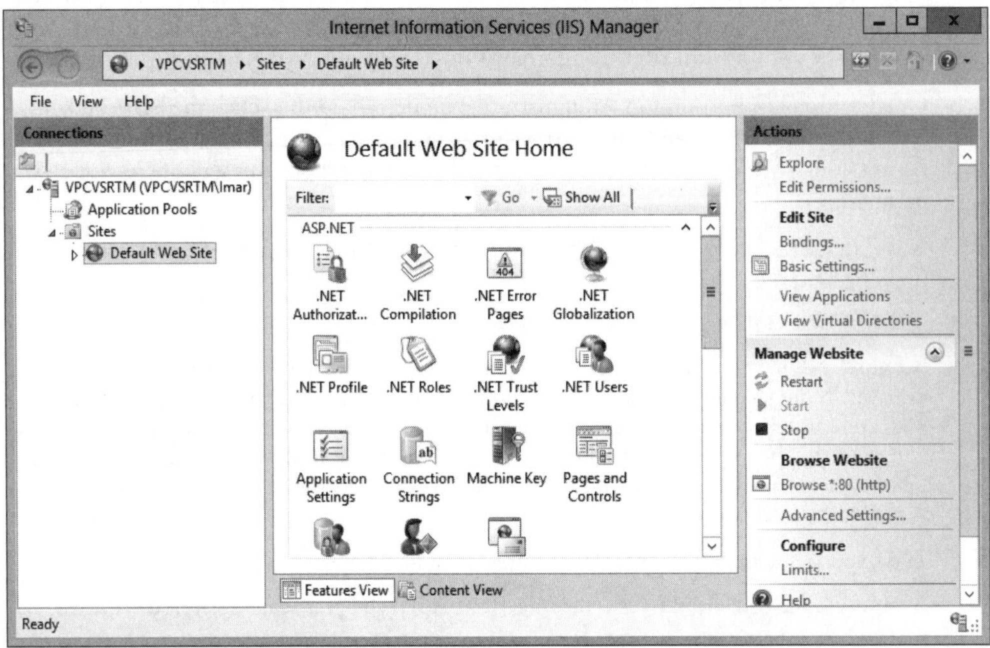

FIGURE 19-7

3. Click the Application Pools item and confirm you have an entry called .NET v4.5 that uses v4.0 as the .NET Framework version and that has its Managed Pipeline Mode set to Integrated. If you don't have this item, click Add Application Pool in the Actions panel on the right and create a new application pool called .NET v4.5 using the .NET Framework v4.0.30319 with Integrated as the Managed Pipeline mode.

> ***NOTE*** *Although the website you built runs on .NET 4.5, you still need to choose .NET v4.0 as the Framework version for the application pool. The reason for this is that ASP.NET 4.5 uses the .NET 4.0 run time which is what you're configuring here.*

4. Select the.NET v4.5 application pool (whether it was already there or not) and click Advanced Settings in the Actions panel on the right. Locate the property called Identity and ensure that it is set to ApplicationPoolIdentity. If it's not, click the button with the ellipsis choose the correct item from the Built-in Account drop-down list and click OK. You use this identity later when configuring security. In the same dialog box, make sure the Load User Profile option is set to True. Your final screen should look like Figure 19-8.

Click OK to close the Advanced Settings dialog box.

5. Click the Default Web Site item to select it and click Advanced Settings in the Actions panel on the right of Figure 19-7.

6. In the Advanced Settings dialog box, click the Physical Path property, click the ellipsis to open up a folder browser, select the folder `C:\BegASPNET\Release`, and click OK to confirm the path.

7. In the same dialog box, click Application Pool, then click the ellipsis, choose the application pool from step 3 labeled .NET v4.5, and click OK. Your Advanced Settings dialog now looks like Figure 19-9.

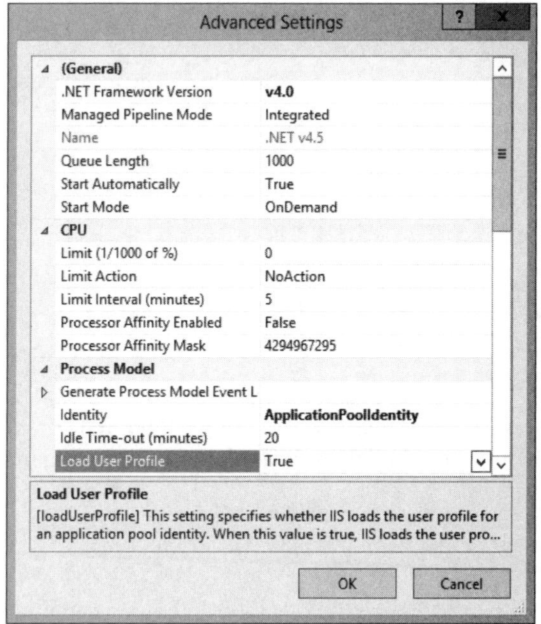

FIGURE 19-8

FIGURE 19-9

Click OK again to close the Advanced Settings dialog box.

8. Next you need to make sure that IIS is configured to use a sensible default document; the document that is served when you request a folder name or the root of the site. The Planet Wrox site uses `Default.aspx`, which is the most common default document name for ASP.NET websites. To check this, make sure Default Web Site is the selected option in the tree on the left. Then double-click the Default Document option in the IIS Features list (below the items you see in Figure 19-7). Make sure that `Default.aspx` is present and at the beginning of the list. If the item is not there,

add it manually. To do this, click the Add link in the Actions panel to add it. Then use the Move Up links to move it to the top of the list. Click Yes when you see the warning about inheriting changes. Your dialog box should look similar to Figure 19-10.

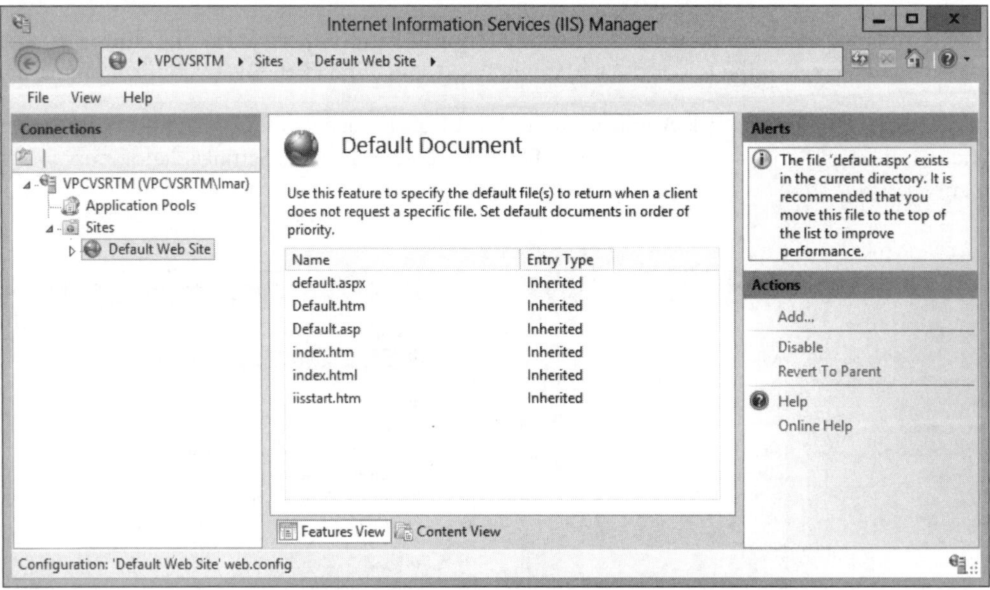

FIGURE 19-10

9. You can now close the Internet Information Services Manager, because the site is configured correctly as far as IIS is concerned. However, it still won't run correctly because you need to configure security permissions on the filesystem, as you see later.

How It Works

Each new IIS installation has a Default Web Site, the site that listens to `http://localhost` by default. In this exercise, you configured this default website to run Planet Wrox, but you can also create a whole new site that can run side by side with other websites. You pointed the root of the site to the `Release` folder that contains your website. With that mapping set up, IIS is able to see what files to serve when you request a URL like `http://localhost`. It means that a URL like `http://localhost/Login.aspx` is mapped to the physical file at `C:\BegASPNET\Release\Login.aspx`. You also assigned the website an application pool — an IIS mechanism to isolate and configure one or more IIS websites in one fell swoop. Two websites running in different application pools do not affect each other in case of a problem such as a crash. In this exercise you selected an application pool that uses the .NET 4.5 Framework and that uses the *Integrated Pipeline* mode. In this mode, IIS and ASP.NET are tightly integrated, which means you can use ASP.NET features (such as Forms Authentication, which you saw in Chapter 16) in standard IIS functionality such as serving static files. For more information about this mode, check out the official IIS website via `http://tinyurl.com/IntegratedPipelineMode`.

At the end of the exercise, you configured a default document, the file that is served when you request a URL without an explicit filename, like `http://localhost/` or `http://localhost/Reviews/`. When you configure `Default.aspx` as the default document, IIS tries to find and serve a file by that name.

The final thing you need to do to make sure your site runs on your local IIS installation is configure the security settings. This is discussed in the following two sections.

Understanding Security in IIS

Because of the seamless integration with IIS Express, you may not realize what happens under the hood, and what security settings are in effect when you browse pages in your site. To use resources in your site, such as ASPX files, Code Behind files, the database in the `App_Data` folder, and the images in your site, your web server needs permissions from Windows to access those resources. This means that you need to configure Windows and grant access to those resources to the account that the web server uses. But what exactly is that account? The specific account that needs permission depends on a number of factors, including the version of Windows, whether you run your site under IIS or IIS Express, and on a number of settings within IIS.

In most cases, however, you have only two scenarios to consider: using IIS Express or the full version of IIS as your web server.

In the former case, the account that IIS Express uses is the account you use to log on to your Windows machine. This account is usually something like `DomainName\UserName` or `MachineName\UserName`. While logged in with this account on Windows, you start up Visual Studio, which in turn starts up IIS Express. This means that the entire web server runs with your credentials. Because it's likely that you're an Administrator or a power user on your local Windows machine and have permissions to access all files that make up your site, things probably worked fine so far without any changes to the security settings.

In the latter case, where IIS is used, things are quite different. By default, an ASP.NET application under IIS runs with a special account created when you installed IIS. This account is called *ApplicationPoolIdentity*.

You won't find the ApplicationPoolIdentity user account on your system directly, because it depends on the name of the configured application pool.

Because the application pool you saw earlier runs in Integrated Pipeline mode, you only need to configure a single user account. If you are running in Classic mode (which isn't necessary for the Planet Wrox website) you also need to configure another account called IUSR. This account is used by IIS to serve non-ASP.NET content such as HTML files and images. Consult the IIS documentation for more information about Classic mode and the IUSR account.

After you have determined the account that you need to configure, the final step is to configure the filesystem.

NTFS Settings for Planet Wrox

Regardless of the account you are using, you need to make changes to the Windows filesystem so the web server is allowed to access your resources.

FOLDER NAME	PERMISSIONS	EXPLANATION
`Release` (located at `C:\BegASPNET\`)	List folder contents Read	The web server account needs to be able to read all the files and folders that make up the website. Child folders, like `Reviews`, need to be set up to inherit these settings.

`App_Data`
`GigPics`
(both located under `C:\BegASPNET\Release`)
	Modify	The web server account needs to be able to read from and write to the Microsoft SQL Server databases in the `App_Data` folder. It also needs to be able to save the uploaded images in the `GigPics` folder.

`C:\TempMail`	Modify	If you're dropping your e-mails locally, you need to configure the `TempMail` folder as well.

If you came here from Chapter 12 to learn how to configure NTFS for the `App_Data` folder, you can ignore the `Release` folder that was created earlier in this chapter. Instead, grant Modify permissions for your own account to the `App_Data` folder of your site at `C:\BegASPNET\Site` as per the instructions in the next exercise. You may need to do the same for the `GigPics` folder, which you could create now at the root of your site, or return to this section after you created the folder in Chapter 14.

In the following exercise, you learn how to configure the security settings for these folders.

TRY IT OUT Configuring the Filesystem

In this Try It Out, you see how to configure the filesystem for the Planet Wrox website. The exercise shows you screenshots from Windows 8, but the other flavors of Windows have similar screens. Search Windows help for "security NTFS" or contact your administrator if you're having problems carrying out the following steps.

1. Start by opening a File Explorer (called Windows Explorer on versions of Windows before Windows 8 and Server 2012) and then locate your C drive.
2. Browse to `C:\BegASPNET`, visible in Figure 19-11.
3. Right-click the `Release` folder, choose Properties, and switch to the Security tab (see Figure 19-12). If you don't see the Security tab, your disk is probably not formatted using NTFS and you can skip this exercise.

4. The next step is to add the web server account. Click the Edit button visible in Figure 19-12, and then click the Add button. Type **IIS AppPool** followed by the name of the application pool. If you followed along with the previous exercises, the application pool is called .NET v4.5 which means the account name is `IIS AppPool\.NET v4.5`. Click OK to add the account.

   With the account selected in the Group or User Names list, ensure that only List Folder Contents and Read are selected. Your dialog box should end up similar to Figure 19-13.

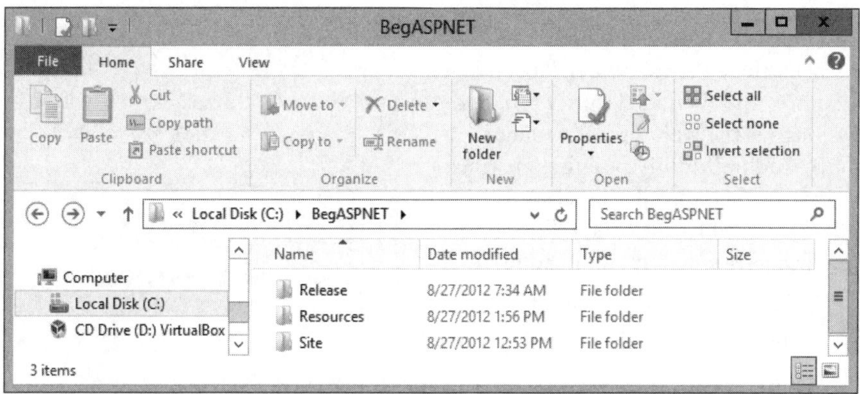

FIGURE 19-11

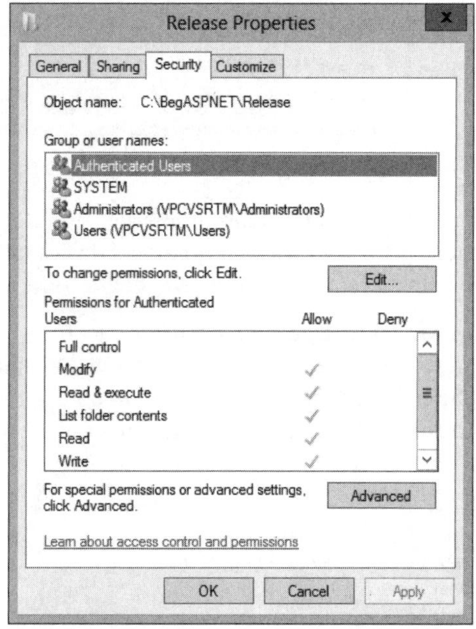

FIGURE 19-12

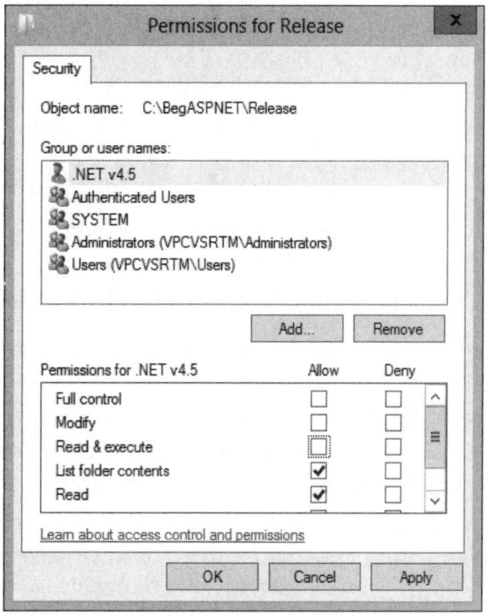

FIGURE 19-13

5. Close the dialog box so you return to the Release Properties dialog box shown in Figure 19-12.
6. Click the Advanced button to open the Advanced Security Settings dialog box again. For Windows 7 and Server 2008 R2, click the Change Permissions button and check the Replace All Child Object Permissions check box. For Windows 8 and Server 2012, you find this check box on the Advanced Security Settings dialog box directly. This forces Windows to apply the same security settings to all sub files and folders, replacing all existing settings. Click OK and then confirm the changes that will be made. Finally, close all remaining open dialog boxes.
7. Back in File Explorer / Windows Explorer, right-click `App_Data` from the `Release` folder, open its Properties dialog box and then its Security tab, and edit the permissions for the web server account you added in step 4 by adding Modify permissions (this in turn causes some of the other permissions to be selected as well). You need to click the Edit button first to bring the Properties dialog box in editable mode. Figure 19-14 shows the completed dialog.

   Click OK to close the dialog box.

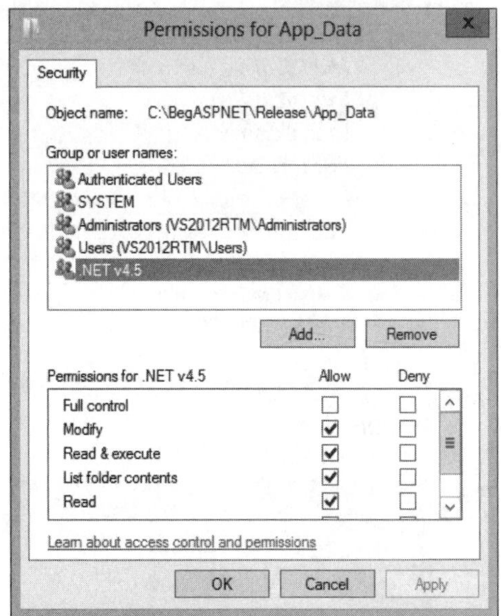

FIGURE 19-14

8. Repeat this step for the `GigPics` folder and optionally for the `TempMail` folder.
9. If you are using IIS on a machine that has SQL Server Express, the final thing you need to do is modify your connection strings. If you don't have SQL Server Express installed, refer to the start of Chapter 12 that shows you how to install SQL Server Express Edition as well as SQL Server Management Studio Express Edition. If you're using a different database server, or if you only have SQL Server Local DB Edition installed and don't want to install SQL Server Express, look at the section "Moving Data to a Remote Server" later in this chapter and look at Appendix B, which explains how to configure a different SQL Server.

   To modify the connection string, open up `Web.config` and replace both occurrences of `(LocalDB)\v11.0` in the connection strings with **`.\SqlExpress`**. This targets a named instance of SQL Server called `SqlExpress` on the local machine (identified by the dot (.)). In addition, add **`User Instance=True`** to both connection strings to run SQL Server under the same user account as the website. Your connection strings should end up like this:

```
<connectionStrings>
  <add name="PlanetWroxConnectionString1" connectionString="Data
    Source=.\SqlExpress;AttachDbFilename=|DataDirectory|\PlanetWrox.mdf;
    Integrated Security=True;User Instance=True"
            providerName="System.Data.SqlClient" />
  <add name="PlanetWroxEntities" connectionString="metadata=
       res://*/App_Code.PlanetWrox.csdl|res://*/App_Code.PlanetWrox.ssdl
      |res://*/App_Code.PlanetWrox.msl;provider=System.Data.SqlClient;
    provider connection string=&quot;data source=.\SqlExpress;
      attachdbfilename=|DataDirectory|\PlanetWrox.mdf;
```

```
        integrated security=True;User Instance=True;
        MultipleActiveResultSets=True;App=EntityFramework&quot;"
    providerName="System.Data.EntityClient" />
</connectionStrings>
```

10. To check if the site works, open a browser and go to `http://localhost`. You should see the Planet Wrox website appear. To verify that everything is in order, browse through the site by requesting pages from the main menu, filling in the contact form, creating a new album, uploading pictures, and so on. If you get an error, refer to the section "Troubleshooting Web Server Errors."

> ***NOTE*** *If you still can't make it work, try configuring the filesystem for the Everyone group. Although, from a security point of view, this is absolutely not the recommended group to use in a production environment, it may help you in finding out whether it's a security issue. If it works for the Everyone account, it's indeed security-related, so you need to make sure you configured the correct accounts. Don't forget to remove the Everyone account later again. If you keep having problems, refer to the next section where you find a number of problems you may run into while deploying as well as a solution.*

How It Works

On a standard Windows system, all files and folders are protected using Windows NTFS. To ensure proper operation of your website, you need to grant the account used by the web server the necessary permissions to the files and folders of your website. For most files and folders, Read permission is enough. However, for a few folders you need to change the permissions. Both `App_Data` and `GigPics` are written to at run time so you need to grant Modify permissions to these folders. In addition, you need to configure `C:\TempMail` if your site drops e-mails there locally.

In order for your site to connect to a database, you changed both connection strings in `Web.config` to target an instance of SQL Server called `SqlExpress`. The Local DB Edition you used before is great for local development, but not for running your production sites. Instead, you can use SQL Server Express Edition or one of the commercial versions of SQL Server. Appendix B digs much deeper into configuring your site to work with versions of SQL Server other than Express.

Troubleshooting Web Server Errors

When you try to access your site in a web browser, you may run into a number of problems. The first thing you need to do to get helpful error messages is to change the `<customErrors>` section in `Web.config` from `On` to `Off` or `RemoteOnly`. This makes it easier to see what's going on. Additionally, you may want to check out the Windows Event Viewer (type `eventvwr` from the Start menu or Start screen) for more details about errors and hints how to solve them.

This section lists the most common problems and provides a fix for them. You should realize a large number of possible reasons exist for the errors you may get, so it's impossible to cover them all here. If you run into a problem you can't solve, turn to this book's forum at the Wrox community site at http://p2p.wrox.com. You'll find many helping hands (including mine) that understand your problem and can help you find a solution for it.

- **It is an error to use a section registered as allowDefinition='MachineToApplication' beyond application level** — You get this error when your website is not at the root of the web server, or you haven't configured the folder as a separate application. Given the current configuration for the Planet Wrox site, you get this error when, for example, you map your site in IIS to `C:\BegASPNET` and then browse to `http://localhost/Release`. To fix this error, make sure that the root of your IIS website points to the folder that contains your main `Web.config` file; `C:\BegASPNET\Release`, in this case. You get the same error when you open an incorrect folder in VS; for example, when you open `C:\BegASPNET` and then browse to `http://localhost:12345/Site`. Instead, open `C:\BegASPNET\Site` as the website in VS. You may also run into this error if a subfolder in your site contains a `Web.config` file that tries to override settings that are meant to be defined at the root of the site only; for example, if you have a `<membership />` element in the `Web.config` file of the `Management` folder.
- **HTTP Error 401.3–Unauthorized** — You get this error when the account used by the web server does not have permission to read the files on disk. To fix this problem, refer to the Try It Out entitled "Configuring the Filesystem" earlier in this chapter and configure the correct permissions.
- **Failed to update database "C:\BEGASPNET\RELEASE\APP_DATA\ASPNETDB.MDF" because the database is read-only** — You get this error when either the database files have been marked as read-only, or if the account used by the web server is not allowed to write to the database files. In the former case, open the file's Properties in File Explorer / Windows Explorer and verify that the Read Only check box is cleared. In the latter case, ensure that the account used by ASP.NET has at least Modify permissions on the `App_Data` folder.
- **HTTP Error 403.14–Forbidden** — Although this error seems to suggest a problem with NTFS permissions at first, it's often caused by an incorrect or missing default document. If you get this error, ensure that the site or folder you are accessing contains a document called `Default.aspx` and that you configured that document name as a default document in IIS.
- **HTTP Error 404.0–Not Found** — You get this error when you try to request a file or folder that doesn't exist, such as `http://localhost/DoesNotExist` or `http://localhost/DoesNotExist.gif`.
- **An error has occurred while establishing a connection to the server. When connecting to SQL Server 2008, this failure may be caused by the fact that under the default settings SQL Server does not allow remote connections. (provider: Named Pipes Provider, error: 40–Could not open a connection to SQL Server)**. Alternatively, you may get the error: **A network-related or instance-specific error occurred while establishing a connection to SQL Server. The server was not found or was not accessible. Verify that the instance name is correct and that SQL Server is configured to allow remote connections. (provider: SQL Network Interfaces, error: 26 - Error Locating Server/Instance Specified)** — You can get these errors for a number of reasons. Although the error message here mentions SQL Server 2008 explicitly, you can also get this error for other versions of SQL Server. Usually, this error is caused by problems reaching the configured database server. You can get it when you misspelled the server's

name in a connection string, the server is down, or the server can only be reached from the local machine and is not accessible over the network. To make sure that SQL Server is running correctly, open the Services section of the Administrative Tools (that you find in the Control Panel). Then look under SQL Server and verify that SQL Server is started. Appendix B explains SQL Server security in more detail and provides solutions to these problems.

- **Failed to generate a user instance of SQL Server due to failure in retrieving the user's local application data path. Please make sure the user has a local user profile on the computer. The connection will be closed** — You can get this error when you forgot to enable the "Load User Profile" option discussed in the Try It Out titled "Configuring your Site."
- **HTTP Error 500.21 - Internal Server Error Handler "PageHandlerFactory-Integrated" has a bad module "ManagedPipelineHandler" in its module list Detailed Error Information** — You get this error when ASP.NET is not registered with IIS. Refer to the section labeled "Installing and Configuring ASP.NET" to learn how to fix this issue.
- **Runtime Error Description: An application error occurred on the server. The current custom error settings for this application prevent the details of the application error from being viewed. Details: To enable the details of this specific error message to be viewable on the local server machine, please create a <customErrors> tag within a "web.config" configuration file located in the root directory of the current web application. This <customErrors> tag should then have its "mode" attribute set to "RemoteOnly". To enable the details to be viewable on remote machines, please set "mode" to "Off"** — You may get this error when a runtime error occurs and the `Web.config` does not contain a `<customErrors>` element. However, you may also get the same error when the `Web.config` file itself contains an error; for example, when you forgot to close an element. To fix this latter category of errors, open the file in Visual Studio and it provides you with more details about the error.

When you are deploying to a machine that also has SQL Server Express edition installed, you are done with the deployment process now. However, if you're dealing with a different SQL Server, the only thing that's left to do is to make sure your new site has the required data. You see how to do this next.

MOVING DATA TO A REMOTE SERVER

Releasing a site to IIS on your local machine is pretty straightforward. You simply copy the data to a new location, configure IIS, change a few security settings, and that's it. Because the site continues to use your local copy of SQL Server, it will run fine.

However, in the real world when you need to move your site to an external server or host, things are not so easy. Although copying the files that make up your site is usually extremely simple using an FTP program, copying data from your SQL Server database to your host is quite often a bit trickier. This is because most web hosts don't support the free Express or LocalDB editions, so you can't just simply copy the `.mdf` files to the `App_Data` folder at your remote host. Instead, these hosts often offer the full versions of SQL Server, which you can access either with a web-based management tool or with tools such as SQL Server Management Studio.

Getting your database data from your local machine to your remote host is typically a two-step process:

1. Create a `.sql` script from your local SQL Server database.
2. Send this script to your host and execute it there.

In the next section, you see how to export your database to a `.sql` file. I won't show you how to run that file at your host to re-create the database because this is different from host to host. Instead, I will give you some general pointers so you know what to look for with your host.

Exporting Your Data to a File

To make it easy to transfer data from your local SQL Server database into a SQL Server database of your web host, SQL Server Management Studio comes with a tool to export your database structure and data to a file. This file then contains all the information required to re-create your database and its data at a remote server.

In the following exercise, you see how to use SSMS to export your database to a file.

TRY IT OUT Exporting the Planet Wrox Database

This exercise assumes you've already downloaded and installed SQL Server Management Studio Express Edition. If you haven't already done this, refer to the start of Chapter 12 for more details.

1. Start SQL Server Management Studio from the Start menu or Start screen. You should see a screen similar to Figure 19-15.
2. Enter **`(localdb)\v11.0`** as the server name and click Login. Your `PlanetWrox` database should already be listed, but if it's not, right-click the Databases node, click Attach, and then browse for the `PlanetWrox.mdf` file in your `C:\BegASPNET\Site\App_Data` folder.
3. Right-click the `PlanetWrox` database and choose Tasks ➪ Generate Scripts. If you get a welcome screen, click Next. Ensure that Script Entire Database and All Database Objects is selected, and then click Next. The dialog box shown in Figure 19-16 appears.

FIGURE 19-15

4. In this screen, you can choose between two Output Type options. The first enables you to create a text file with the necessary SQL statements, and the second option enables you to talk to your shared hosting provider over the Internet directly. If your host supports this, it can give you the necessary information to configure a provider here. For now, choose Save Scripts to a Specific Location. Then click the Advanced button and change the setting for Types of Data to Script to Schema and Data. The default value of Schema Only would only script your database structure, but not the actual records your tables contain. Set Script Use Database to False. With this setting set to True, code will be included to create a database at the `App_Data` folder, which likely won't

work on a machine other than your own. Click OK to close the Advanced Scripting Options dialog box.

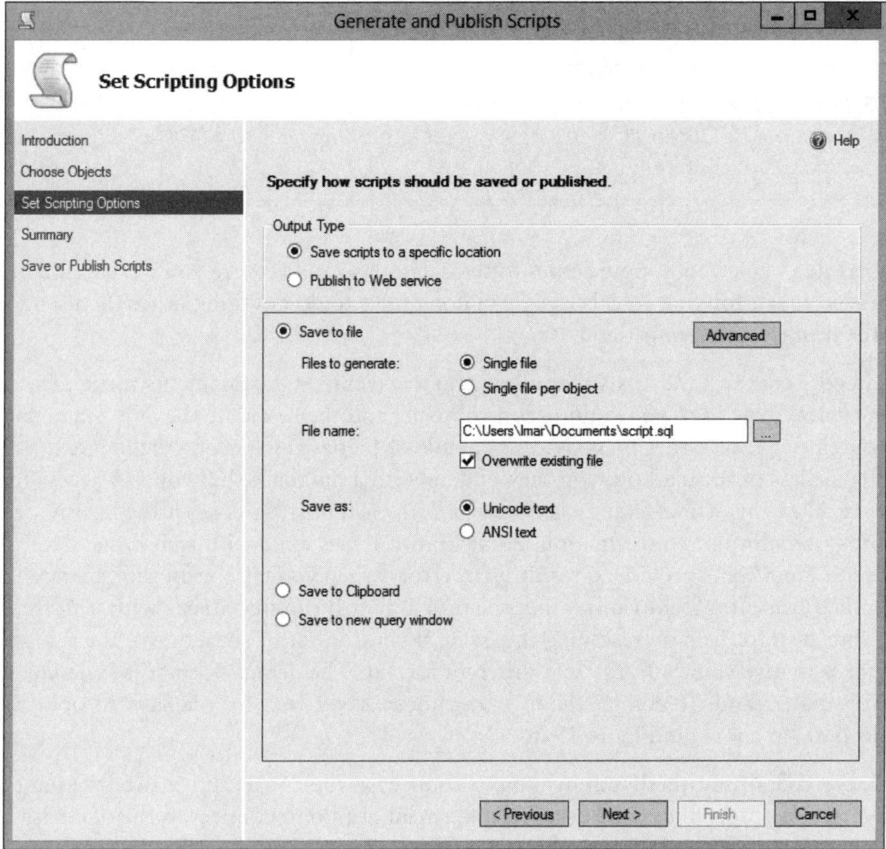

FIGURE 19-16

5. Click Next twice and the wizard generates the SQL script for you in your `Documents` folder (as specified in the File Name box shown in Figure 19-16). Open the file in Notepad and look at the SQL statements it contains. Although most of it probably looks like gibberish to you, it can be used as is to re-create the database structure and data on a compatible SQL Server database.

How It Works

The contents of a database can be separated in two categories: the structure of the database and the actual data. When the scripting tool runs, it investigates the structure of your database first and creates SQL `CREATE` statements for all the items it finds in your database, such as the tables you created in earlier chapters. It then creates `INSERT` statements that re-create all records such as Reviews, Genres, and even users in the target database. By clearing the Script All Objects check box at the beginning of the wizard, you can selectively choose parts of your database, enabling you to script only a few tables, for example.

At the end, the scripting tool assembles all the SQL statements and saves them to a single `.sql` file. This file is now ready to be run at your host to re-create the database.

Re-Creating the Database

Although every host has its own rules and procedures when it comes to providing access to their SQL Server, they can be grouped in three categories.

> **NOTE** *For detailed information about hosting your site with an external hosting party, check out the tutorials in the hosting section of the official ASP.NET site at* `www.asp.net/learn/hosting`.

First, some hosts don't give you remote access to their database and require you to submit a `.sql` file so they can execute it for you. In this case, you don't have to do anything other than send the file and wait for the host to create your database.

The second category contains the hosts that allow you to execute SQL statements through a web interface. You typically log in to your online control panel and then execute the SQL statements created by the scripting tool, either by uploading the file or by pasting its contents in a text area in a web page. Regardless of the method, you then end up with a database that you can access from your application. How this works exactly is different with each host, so consult the hosting service's help or support system for more information. Some known issues exist with web-based database management tools from some providers, resulting in errors when you try to run the generated SQL file. Although the file itself is technically valid, the tool may still run into issues with it. If that's the case, contact your host for help on resolving the issue. If you run into issues, one of the things you may want to try is to save your SQL file in a different format. The default format is Unicode, which not all providers understand. To change the format, choose ANSI Text for the Save As option when exporting your data, as shown in Figure 19-16.

The final category contains hosts that allow you to connect to their SQL Server over the Internet. This enables you to use tools like SQL Server Management Studio to connect to the database at your host right from your desktop and execute the SQL scripts remotely. Refer to the first exercise in the section "Using SQL to Work with Database Data" of Chapter 12 to learn more about executing SQL files against a database using SSMS.

After your database is re-created at your target server, you need to reconfigure your ASP.NET application to use the new database by changing the connection strings in your website. For this to work, you need to modify two connection strings: the `PlanetWroxConnectionString1` and the `PlanetWroxEntities` you created in an earlier chapter. How your connection string must look depends on the database you are using and its configuration. Your hosting company or database administrator typically provides this information. For many examples of proper connection strings, check out `www.connectionstrings.com`. The following snippet provides a simple example that reconfigures your application to use a database server called `DatabaseServer`. This example shows a connection string for a SQL Server that requires you to log in with a username and password (in your configuration file, each connection string should be on a single line):

```
<connectionStrings>
  <add name="PlanetWroxConnectionString1" connectionString="Data
      Source=DatabaseServer;Initial Catalog=PlanetWrox;User Id=YourUserName;
      Password=YourPassword;" providerName="System.Data.SqlClient"/>
```

```
    <add name="PlanetWroxEntities" connectionString="metadata=res://*
        /App_Code.PlanetWrox.csdl|res://*/App_Code.PlanetWrox.ssdl|res://*
        /App_Code.PlanetWrox.msl;provider=System.Data.SqlClient;
        provider connection string=&quot;Data Source=DatabaseServer;
          Initial Catalog=PlanetWrox;User Id=YourUserName;Password=YourPassword;
          MultipleActiveResultSets=True&quot;"
        providerName="System.Data.EntityClient"/>
  </connectionStrings>
```

This points both connection strings for the `PlanetWrox` database to a different SQL Server. Consult Appendix B for more information about configuring your ASP.NET application and SQL Server to operate with each other.

At this stage, you're pretty much done configuring your newly created website. Congratulations! However, before you relax and start enjoying your new website, read the following checklist that helps you secure your site and improve its performance.

THE DEPLOYMENT CHECKLIST

Instead of ending this chapter with general tips about deployment, this section gives you a practical list of things to check when you're ready to put your website in production:

- Make sure you don't have debugging enabled in the `Web.config` file. This causes unnecessary overhead and decreases performance of your website, because code executes slower and important files cannot be cached by the browser. To ensure debugging is disabled, open the `Web.config` file you are using for your production environment, and verify that `debug` is set to `false`:

  ```
  <compilation debug="false">
  ```

- Make sure you have turned on custom errors by setting the `mode` attribute of the `customErrors` element in `Web.config` to either `On` or `RemoteOnly`. In the first case, everyone sees your custom error pages, and in the second case, only users local to the web server can see the error details. Never leave the `mode` set to `Off`, because doing so can lead to information disclosure. The following snippet shows a safe configuration of the `customErrors` element:

  ```
  <customErrors mode="On" defaultRedirect="~/Errors/OtherErrors.aspx">
    Optional <error /> elements go here
  </customErrors>
  ```

- Disable tracing, or at least limit the trace information to users coming from the local machine. The following `<trace />` element from `Web.config` blocks tracing for users coming from machines other than the web server itself. Additionally, it stops the trace information from appearing in the page:

  ```
  <trace mostRecent="true" enabled="true" requestLimit="1000"
          pageOutput="false" localOnly="true"/>
  ```

- Consider setting the `retail` attribute of the deployment element in `machine.config` to `true`:

  ```
  <configuration>
    <system.web>
  ```

```
    <deployment retail="true"/>
  </system.web>
</configuration>
```

This section is used to indicate that the server hosts production-ready versions of your sites, and for all sites on the server, changes all three previous items to a secure setting: debugging and tracing are disabled, and error messages are accessible only to local users.

To make this change, you need to be logged in as an Administrator on your system. Also, be sure to make a backup copy of the file first. Because it serves as the root configuration file for all your ASP.NET websites, you don't want to mess up this file.

- Scan your site for important files that may contain sensitive information (like Word or text documents) and either exclude them from the release version or consider moving them to the `App_Data` folder. Files in that folder cannot be accessed directly. However, your own code can still access the files as you saw in Chapter 9.
- Make sure you turn on error logging. With the error logging code you created in the previous chapter, you are notified whenever an error occurs, enabling you to proactively keep an eye on your server, fixing errors before they get a chance to happen again.
- If you are using themes in your site, make sure you remove the `styleSheetTheme` attribute from the `<pages>` element in `Web.config`. The Planet Wrox website uses themes, but you added the `styleSheetTheme` attribute to enable design-time support in Visual Studio. On your production server, all you need is this:

```
<pages theme="Monochrome">
  ...
</pages>
```

This way, the page won't include the same style sheet twice.

WHAT'S NEXT

Now that you have finished your first ASP.NET website, I am sure you are looking forward to creating your next site. The Planet Wrox site can serve as a basis for new sites you will build. You probably won't use any of its pages in your site directly, but hopefully this book and the Planet Wrox website inspired you enough to build a new website on your own.

Because this book is aimed at beginners, I haven't been able to provide you with a lot of in-depth information on some important topics. Most subjects that have their own chapter in this book easily warrant an entire book on their own. For example, topics like CSS, AJAX, and LINQ are so extensive that Wrox has published many books about them. Now that you've mastered the basics of these technologies, you can dig deeper into them using the following books in the Wrox Professional series:

- *Professional CSS: Cascading Style Sheets for Web Design, 3rd Edition* (ISBN: 978-0-470-89152-0)
- *Professional ASP.NET 2.0 Design: CSS, Themes, and Master Pages* (ISBN: 978-0-470-12448-2)
- *Professional ASP.NET 4.5 in C# and VB* (ISBN: 978-1-118-31182-0)

- *Professional LINQ* (ISBN: 978-0-470-04181-9)
- Professional Microsoft IIS 8 (ISBN: 978-1-118-38804-4)

Of course, the web is also a good place for more information. The following URLs may be helpful in your search for more information about ASP.NET and its related technologies:

- `http://p2p.wrox.com` — The public discussion forum from Wrox where you can go for all your programming-related questions. This book has its own category on that site, enabling you to ask targeted questions. I am a frequent visitor to these forums and I'll do my best to answer each question you may have about this book.
- `http://imar.spaanjaars.com` — My own website where I keep you up to date about various web programming–related topics.
- `http://www.asp.net` — The Microsoft community site for ASP.NET technology. Go here for news on ASP.NET, additional downloads, and tutorials.
- `http://msdn.microsoft.com/asp.net` – The official home for ASP.NET at the Microsoft developers website that gives you a wealth of information on ASP.NET.

SUMMARY

Obviously, deployment is an important action at the end of the development cycle of your new website. However, it's unlikely that you deploy your site only once. As soon as you release the first version of your site, you'll think of other new and cool features you want to add, making the development of your site a continuous process. To accommodate for this, you need to make your site easy to deploy.

One way to do this is by moving hard-coded configuration settings to the `Web.config` file, giving you a single location to change parameters for the site in your development and production environments.

When you're ready to roll out your site, it's a good idea to create a copy of your site and clean that up before you send the files to your target server. Copying and then publishing a site is a breeze with the Copy Web Site and Publish Web Site commands.

Because you will deploy your site against IIS, you need to understand some important settings of this web server. In this chapter, you saw how to configure the Default Web Site and make some configuration changes. Because of the way security works in Windows and IIS, you also need to configure your hard drive so that the accounts used by the web server can read the files in your site, and write to specific folders such as `App_Data` and `GigPics`.

EXERCISES

This chapter has no exercises, because the Planet Wrox site is now completely finished. However, your biggest challenge starts now: building websites with the knowledge you gained from this book. If you ever build a site with the information from this book and want to share it with me, please contact me through my website at `http://imar.spaanjaars.com`. Have fun!

▶ WHAT YOU LEARNED IN THIS CHAPTER

.NET assembly	A file with a `.dll` extension that contains executable and callable .NET code
Application pool	A mechanism to isolate (one or more) websites in IIS to give them their own set of resources
Deployment	The process of releasing a website from your development environment to the production environment
Expression syntax	A technique that enables you to bind control properties to different resources, such as application settings defined in `Web.config`
IIS	Internet Information Services — Microsoft's web server for the Windows platform
Integrated Pipeline mode	With Integrated Pipeline mode turned on for an application pool in IIS, ASP.NET and IIS are tightly integrated together, enabling you to use ASP.NET techniques for non-.NET resources such as static files
Precompilation	The process of compiling a web application into a set of `.dll` files, which can be deployed to a production server; without precompilation, the ASP.NET files are compiled on the fly the first time they are requested
`WebConfigurationManager` class	A .NET Framework class that provides access to data that is stored in configuration files

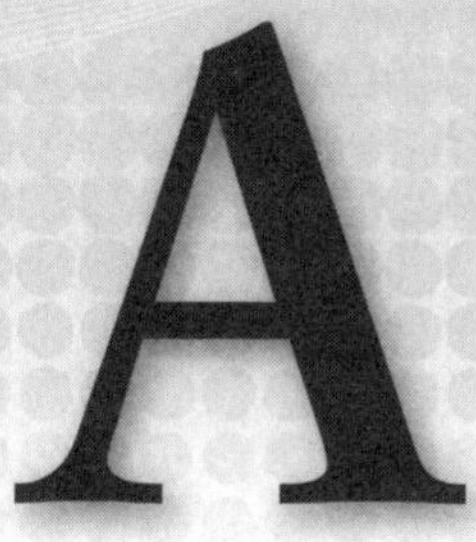

Exercise Answers

CHAPTER 1

Exercise 1 Solution

The markup of a page in Visual Studio contains the raw and unprocessed source for the page, including the HTML, ASP.NET Server Controls, and programming code. The web server then processes the page and sends out the final HTML to the browser. In the browser this HTML is then used to render the user interface.

Exercise 2 Solution

The easiest way to store HTML fragments that you use often is to select them in the Document Window and then drag them to a free space on the Toolbox. When the item is added, you can rename it to a more meaningful name. Now you can simply double-click an item or drag it from the Toolbox into your page whenever you need it.

Exercise 3 Solution

You have a number of ways to reset part of the customization changes you may have made, including:

- Resetting the window layout by choosing Window ➪ Reset Window Layout.
- Resetting the Toolbox by right-clicking it and choosing Reset Toolbox.
- Resetting all settings of Visual Studio using Tools ➪ Settings ➪ Import and Export Settings or Tools ➪ Import and Export Settings, depending on your version of Visual Studio.

Exercise 4 Solution

To change the property of a control on a page, you can click the control in Design or Markup View and then use the Properties Grid (which you can bring up by pressing F4) to change the value of the property. Alternatively, you can change the property directly in Markup View.

CHAPTER 2

Exercise 1 Solution

A number of files fall in the Web Files category, including `.aspx` files (Web Forms that end up as pages in the web browser), `.html` files (that contain static HTML for your site), `.css` files (that contain cascading style sheet information), and `.config` files (that contain configuration information for the website). Refer to the table with the different file types in Chapter 2 for a complete list of files.

Exercise 2 Solution

When you want to make a piece of text both bold and italicized, you need to select the text and then click the Bold button on the Formatting toolbar. Next you need to click the Italic button. The final HTML code in the page should look like this:

```
<strong><em>Welcome to Planet Wrox</em></strong>
```

You may also come across `<b>` and `<i>` elements, which have the same effect. However, these are now considered outdated and you're encouraged to use `<strong>` and `<em>` instead.

Exercise 3 Solution

The first way is using the Solution Explorer. Right-click your site, choose Add ➪ Existing Item, and then browse for the item(s) you want to add.

Secondly, you can drag and drop files from File Explorer or Windows Explorer or from your desktop directly into a VS website. As a third alternative, you could put the files directly in the site's folder using Windows Explorer. For example, files you add to the folder `C:\BegASPNET\Site` become part of your website automatically. If you don't see the new files appear in VS directly, click the Refresh icon on the Solution Explorer toolbar.

Exercise 4 Solution

In VS, you have three different views on your code: Design View, Markup View (also referred to as Source View or Code View), and Split View. The first gives you an impression of how your web page is going to look in the browser, and the second view shows you the raw markup. Split View enables you to see both views at the same time. VS also has different views for other files. For example, programming code for an ASPX page is generally referred to as the Code Behind view or simply the Code Behind.

CHAPTER 3

Exercise 1 Solution

The biggest benefit of an external style sheet is the fact that it can be applied to the entire site. Simply by changing a single rule in that file, you can influence all pages in your site that make use of that rule. With embedded or inline styles, you need to change all the files in your site manually. External style sheets also make it much easier to reuse a certain style with many different elements in your site. Simply create a Class or an ID selector and reuse that wherever you see fit.

Exercise 2 Solution

The rule can look like this:

```
h1
{
  font-family: Arial;
  color: Blue;
  font-size: 18px;
  border-top: 1px solid Blue;
  border-left: 1px solid Blue;
}
```

Note another shorthand version of the `border` property. This one looks similar to the `border` property you saw earlier in this chapter that enabled you to set the size, style, and color of the border at once. In this rule, `border-top` and `border-left` are used to change the left and top borders only; the other two directions, the bottom border and right border, are not affected by this rule.

Exercise 3 Solution

The second declaration is more reusable in your site because it denotes a Class selector as opposed to an ID selector. The latter can only be used once in a single page by an element that has a matching `id` attribute: `MainContent` in this example. The Class selector `BoxWithBorders`, on the other hand, can be used by multiple elements in a single page, because you are allowed to apply an identical class attribute to multiple elements in a page.

Exercise 4 Solution

VS lets you attach a style sheet in the following ways:

- Type in the required `<link>` element in the `<head>` of the page in Markup View directly.
- Drag a CSS file from the Solution Explorer into the `<head>` section of a page in Markup View.
- Drag a CSS file from the Solution Explorer and drop it onto the page in Design View.
- Use the main menu Format ⇨ Attach Style Sheet and then browse to your CSS file.
- Use the Manage Styles or Apply Styles windows and click the Attach Style Sheet link.

CHAPTER 4

Exercise 1 Solution

The mechanism that enables controls to maintain their state is called View State.

Exercise 2 Solution

The ASP.NET run time stores the values for the controls in a hidden field called __VIEWSTATE. This hidden field is sent with each postback to the server, where it's unpacked and then used to repopulate the controls in the page with their previous values.

Exercise 3 Solution

The DropDownList only allows a user to make a single selection whereas the ListBox allows for multiple selections. In addition, the DropDownList only shows one item in the list when it's not expanded, while the ListBox is capable of displaying multiple items simultaneously.

Exercise 4 Solution

In order to have a CheckBox control submit back to the server when you select or clear it in the browser, you need to set the AutoPostBack property to True:

```
<asp:CheckBox ID="CheckBox1" runat="server" AutoPostBack="True" />
```

Exercise 5 Solution

Many of the ASP.NET Server Controls let you change colors using properties like BackColor and ForeColor. Additionally, you can use BorderColor, BorderStyle, and BorderWidth to change the border around a control in the browser. Finally, to affect the size of the control, you need to set its Height and Width properties.

Exercise 6 Solution

Instead of setting individual styles, you're much better off setting the CssClass property that points to a rule set. This way, your pages become easier to maintain, as style-related information is stored in a single place: in the style sheet. At the same time, your page loads faster as not all the style information is sent for each control on each request. Instead, the browser reads in the style sheet once and keeps a locally cached copy.

CHAPTER 5

Exercise 1 Solution

Both the Byte and the SByte data types are designed to hold small, numeric values. Both of them take up exactly the same amount of computer memory, so you're probably best off using the Byte data type. Because it doesn't allow you to store negative numbers, it's clear from the start that it can only contain a number between `0` and `255`. However, it's much better not to store someone's age, but the date of birth instead. That way, you can always extract the age from the date of birth by comparing it with today's date. Because the date of birth is a fixed point in time, it will always reflect someone's age correctly without the need to annually update it.

Exercise 2 Solution

This piece of code toggles the visibility of the `DeleteButton` control. It uses both the assignment operator and the negation operator. First, the negation operator is applied to the current value of `Visible`. When that value is currently `True`, the `Not` (`!` in C#) operator turns it into `False` and vice versa. This result is then assigned back to the `Visible` property. So, where the button was previously hidden, it is now visible. Where it was visible before, it's now made invisible.

Exercise 3 Solution

To create a specialized version of `Person`, you need to create a second class that inherits the `Person` class and extend its behavior by adding the `StudentId` property.

VB.NET

```
Public Class Student
    Inherits Person
  Public Property StudentId As String
End Class
```

C#

```
public class Student : Person
{
  public string StudentId { get; set; }
}
```

CHAPTER 6

Exercise 1 Solution

The `ContentPlaceHolder` element should be placed in the master page. It defines a region that content pages can fill in. The `Content` control should be placed in a content page that is based on the master page. It is used to supply the content for the `ContentPlaceHolder` element that it is connected to.

Exercise 2 Solution

To link a `Content` control to its `ContentPlaceHolder` in the master page, you need to set the `ContentPlaceHolderID`:

```
<asp:Content ID="Content1" ContentPlaceHolderID="IdOfContentPlaceHolder"
              runat="Server">
</asp:Content>
```

Exercise 3 Solution

You have a few ways to do this. First, you can create a named skin with a different CSS class in the same skin file:

```
<asp:Button runat="server" SkinID="RedButton" CssClass="RedButton" />
```

You then hook up the control you want to change to this named skin using the `SkinID` attribute:

```
<asp:Button ID="Button1" runat="server" Text="Button" SkinID="RedButton" />
```

Alternatively, you can disable theming on the `Button` control and give it a different CSS class directly in the ASPX page:

```
<asp:Button ID="Button1" runat="server" EnableTheming="False"
      CssClass="RedButton" Text="Button" />
```

In both solutions, you need a CSS class that sets the background color:

```
.RedButton
{
  background-color: Red;
}
```

Exercise 4 Solution

A `StyleSheetTheme` is applied early in the page's life cycle. This gives controls in the ASPX page the opportunity to override settings they initially got from the `StyleSheetTheme`. This means that the `StyleSheetTheme` just suggests the look and feel of controls, giving the individual controls the ability to override that look.

A `Theme`, on the other hand, overrides any settings applied by the controls. This enables you as a page developer to enforce the look and feel of controls in your site with the settings from the theme. If you still need to change individual controls, you can disable theming by setting `EnableTheming` to `False`.

Exercise 5 Solution

You have three ways to set the `Theme` property in an ASP.NET website. The first option is to set the property directly in the `@ Page` directive so it applies to that page only:

```
<%@ Page Language="C#" ...... Theme="Monochrome" %>
```

To apply a theme to all pages in your site, you set the `theme` attribute of the `<pages>` element in the `Web.config` file:

```
<pages theme="Monochrome" ...
```

The final option you have is to set the theme programmatically. You have to do this in the `PreInit` event of the `Page` class, which you can handle in individual pages in your site or at a central location using the `BasePage` class as you did in Chapter 6.

Exercise 6 Solution

A base page enables you to centralize behavior for all the pages in your site. Instead of recoding the same functionality over and over again in every page, you move this code to the base page so all ASPX pages can use it. When you implement the theme switcher, all you have to do is write some code in the central `BasePage` class. All pages in your site that inherit from this `BasePage` class then automatically set the selected theme, without the need for any additional code.

CHAPTER 7

Exercise 1 Solution

To change the background color of items in the `TreeView` control you can use the `NodeStyle` element as follows:

```
<asp:TreeView ID="TreeView1" runat="server"
             DataSourceID="SiteMapDataSource1" ShowExpandCollapse="False">
  <NodeStyle BackColor="White" />
  ...
</asp:TreeView>
```

Instead of setting the `BackColor` property (which results in an inline style), you're better off setting the `CssClass` property:

```
<NodeStyle CssClass="TreeViewNodeStyle" />
```

You then need to create a separate class in your CSS file:

```
.TreeViewNodeStyle
{
  background-color: White;
}
```

This way, it's easier to manage the styling from a central location.

Exercise 2 Solution

To redirect a user to another page programmatically, you can use `Response.Redirect`, `Response.RedirectPermanent`, and `Server.Transfer`. The first two options send a redirect instruction to the browser and are thus considered client-side redirects. `Server.Transfer`, on the other hand, takes place at the server, enabling you to serve a different page without affecting the user's address bar.

Exercise 3 Solution

To display a `TreeView` that doesn't have the ability to expand or collapse nodes, you need to set its `ShowExpandCollapse` property to `False`.

CHAPTER 8

Exercise 1 Solution

A standard property uses a normal backing variable to store its value, whereas a View State property uses the ViewState collection for this. A normal property is reset on each postback, whereas a View State property is able to maintain its value. This advantage of the View State property comes at a cost, however. Storing the value in View State adds to the size of the page, both during the request and the response. A normal property doesn't have this disadvantage. You should carefully consider what you store in View State to minimize the page size.

Exercise 2 Solution

To make the property maintain its state across postbacks, you need to turn it into a View State property. The required code is almost identical to that of the NavigateUrl, but it uses the Direction data type instead of a String. You need to remove the automatic property and replace it with the following code:

VB.NET

```
Public Property DisplayDirection() As Direction
  Get
    Dim _displayDirection As Object = ViewState("DisplayDirection")
    If _displayDirection IsNot Nothing Then
      Return CType(_displayDirection, Direction)
    Else
      Return Direction.Horizontal ' Not found in View State; return a default value
    End If
  End Get

  Set(Value As Direction)
    ViewState("DisplayDirection") = Value
  End Set
End Property
```

C#

```
public Direction DisplayDirection
{
  get
  {
    object _displayDirection = ViewState["DisplayDirection"];
    if (_displayDirection != null)
    {
      return (Direction)_displayDirection;
    }
    else
    {
      return Direction.Horizontal; // Not found in View State;
                                   // return a default value
    }
  }
  set
```

```
    {
      ViewState["DisplayDirection"] = value;
    }
  }
```

Exercise 3 Solution

Using a custom data type like the `Direction` enumeration has two benefits over using numeric or `String` data types. Because of the way IntelliSense helps you select the right item, you don't have to memorize magic numbers or strings like `0` or `1`. Additionally, the compiler helps you check the spelling, so if you type `Direction.Vrtical` instead of `Direction.Vertical`, you get an error at development time.

CHAPTER 9

Exercise 1 Solution

First, you need to write a property in the Code Behind of the user control, similar to the `DisplayDirection` property you created in the previous chapter for the `Banner` control. This property could look like this:

VB.NET

```
Public Property PageDescription As String
```

C#

```
public string PageDescription { get; set; }
```

You then need to modify the control declaration. For example, in `Contact.aspx`, you can modify the control like this:

```
<uc1:ContactForm ID="ContactForm" runat="server"
               PageDescription="Contact Page"/>
```

Note that the `PageDescription` property contains a short description of the containing page.

Obviously, you can put whatever text you see fit in the property to describe the page. Finally, you need to add the `PageDescription` to the subject or body of the e-mail message. The following code snippet shows you how to extend the subject with the value of this new property:

VB.NET

```
myMessage.Subject = "Response from web site. Page: " & PageDescription
myMessage.From = New MailAddress("you@example.com", "Sender Name")
```

C#

```
myMessage.Subject = "Response from web site. Page: " + PageDescription;
myMessage.From = new MailAddress("you@example.com", "Sender Name");
```

From now on, this custom page description is added to the subject of the mail message. This solution becomes particularly useful if you have multiple Web Forms using this contact form and you want to find out which page was used to send the information.

Exercise 2 Solution

If you don't inspect the `IsValid` property, your system is vulnerable to invalid data. Users can disable JavaScript in their browsers and submit invalid data directly into your page. By checking the `IsValid` property you can tell whether or not it's safe to continue with the submitted data.

Exercise 3 Solution

The `From` property of the `MailMessage` class is of type `MailAddress`, meaning that you can directly assign a single instance of this class to it. Because you can potentially have more than one recipient, the `To` property is a collection of `MailAddress` objects, and so you need to use its `Add` method to add instances of `MailAddress` to it.

Exercise 4 Solution

To call a client-side validation function, you need to set the `ClientValidationFunction` property of the `CustomValidator` like this:

```
<asp:CustomValidator ID="CustomValidator1" runat="server"
      ClientValidationFunction="functionName">*</asp:CustomValidator>
```

The client function that you need to add to the markup of the page must have the following signature:

```
function functionName(source, args)
{ ... }
```

The `source` argument contains a reference to the actual `CustomValidator` control in the client-side HTML code. The `args` argument provides context information about the data and enables you to indicate whether or not the data is valid. The names of the arguments don't have to be `source` and `args`; however, when using these names, the client-side function looks as close to its server-side counterpart as possible. Another common naming scheme, used for almost all other event handlers in ASP.NET, is to use `sender` and `e`, respectively.

Exercise 5 Solution

To tell the validation mechanism whether the data you checked is valid, you set the `IsValid` property of the `args` argument in your custom validation method. This applies to both client- and server-side code. The following snippet shows how this is done in the client-side validation method for the `ContactForm.ascx` control:

```
if (phoneHome.value != '' || phoneBusiness.value != '')
{
  args.IsValid = true;
}
else
{
  args.IsValid = false;
}
```

CHAPTER 10

Exercise 1 Solution

The ScriptManager control is a required component in almost all Ajax-related operations. It takes care of registering client-side JavaScript files, handles interaction with web services defined in your website, and it's responsible for the partial page updates. You usually place the ScriptManager directly in a content page if you think you need Ajax capabilities on only a handful of pages. However, you can also place the ScriptManager in a master page so it becomes available throughout the entire site.

When you have the ScriptManager in the master page you can use the ScriptManagerProxy to register individual web services or script files on content pages. Because you can have only one ScriptManager in a page, you can't add another one in a content page that uses your master page with the ScriptManager. The ScriptManagerProxy serves as a bridge between the content page and the ScriptManager, giving you great flexibility as to where you register your services.

Exercise 2 Solution

You can let your users know a partial page update is in progress by adding an UpdateProgress control to the page. You connect this control to an UpdatePanel using its AssociatedUpdatePanelID. Inside the <ProgressTemplate> you define whatever markup you see fit to inform your user an update is in progress. A typical <ProgressTemplate> contains an animated icon, some text, or both.

Exercise 3 Solution

To create a script-callable service, you first need to add an AJAX-enabled WCF service file to your site using the Add New Item dialog box. The class file that is created for you already has the ServiceContract and AspNetCompatibilityRequirements attributes applied.

VB.NET

```
<ServiceContract(Namespace:="")>
<AspNetCompatibilityRequirements(
          RequirementsMode:=AspNetCompatibilityRequirementsMode.Allowed)>
Public Class NameOfYourService
```

C#

```
[ServiceContract(Namespace = "")]
[AspNetCompatibilityRequirements(
        RequirementsMode = AspNetCompatibilityRequirementsMode.Allowed)]

public class NameOfYourService
```

You then need to decorate each method within this class that you want exposed as a web method with the OperationContract attribute:

VB.NET

```
<OperationContract()>
Public Function NameOfYourMethod(parameters) As DataType
```

C#

```
[OperationContract]
public DataType NameOfYourMethod(parameters)
```

Once you've registered the WCF service in a `ScriptManager` or `ScriptManagerProxy` control, you can call the service as follows from your client-side JavaScript:

```
NameOfYourService.NameOfYourMethod(
        parameters, successCallback, errorCallback);
```

Exercise 4 Solution

To expose and use a page method you need to carry out the following steps:

1. Set `EnablePageMethods` on the `ScriptManager` to `True`.
2. Define a `static` (`Shared` in VB.NET) method in your page and apply the `WebMethod` attribute like this:

   VB.NET

   ```
   <WebMethod()>
   Public Shared Function NameOfYourMethod(parameters) As DataType
     ...
   End Function
   ```

   C#

   ```
   [WebMethod]
   public static DataType NameOfYourMethod(parameters) { ... }
   ```

3. You call the method in JavaScript through the `PageMethods` object and define a callback method to handle the result of the method:

   ```
   PageMethods.NameOfYourMethod(parameters, successCallback, errorCallback);
   ```

CHAPTER 11

Exercise 1 Solution

To accomplish this, you first need to set the `ClientIDMode` of `VerticalPanel` to `Static` in the markup of `Banner.ascx`. This makes it easier to work with the client IDs of the controls inside the panel:

```
<asp:Panel ID="VerticalPanel" runat="server" ClientIDMode="Static">
```

Then you need to add a `<span>` element just below `VerticalPanel` with the text Hide Banner. The `style` attribute changes the mouse cursor into a hand so users understand the text is clickable when they hover over it. You need to add a runat attribute and a server-side ID so you can hide the link in the Code Behind. You also need to give it a class attribute so you can find the element using jQuery. You should end up with this span element:

```
<span id="HideBanner" style="cursor: pointer;" runat="server"
   class="HideBanner">Hide Banner</span>
```

In a script block below the last panel, you need to add the following code:

```
<script type="text/javascript">
  $(function ()
  {
    $('.HideBanner').bind('click', function ()
    {
      $('#VerticalPanel').slideToggle('fast', function ()
      {
        if ($(this).css('display') == 'block')
        {
          $('.HideBanner').text('Hide Banner');
        }
        else
        {
          $('.HideBanner').text('Show Banner');
        }
      });
    });
  });
</script>
```

This code dynamically binds some code to the click event of the <span> element found by using $('.HideBanner'). Then inside the handler for the click, the code finds the whole panel (#VerticalPanel) and calls slideToggle, which hides items in the matched set when they are visible and shows them when they aren't. The if check then uses the css method on the VerticalPanel element (now referred to with the this keyword) and asks for its display property. When it is block it means the banner is visible, and thus the text must be Hide Banner. Otherwise, the text is set to Show Banner. Finally, you need to hide the link when the banner is in horizontal mode in the banner control's Code Behind:

VB.NET

```
Case Direction.Horizontal
  HorizontalPanel.Visible = True
  VerticalPanel.Visible = False
  HorizontalLink.HRef = NavigateUrl
  HideBanner.Visible = False
```

C#

```
case Direction.Horizontal:
  HorizontalPanel.Visible = true;
  VerticalPanel.Visible = false;
  HorizontalLink.HRef = NavigateUrl;
  HideBanner.Visible = false;
  break;
```

Exercise 2 Solution

The slideUp method hides elements by slowly decreasing their height. slideDown shows hidden elements instead by doing the reverse: slowly increasing the height of an element until it's fully visible. Both methods accept, among other arguments, a speed parameter that either accepts a fixed value (slow, normal, or fast) or a number specifying the speed of the animation in milliseconds.

Exercise 3 Solution

jQuery's document ready function fires when the page is finished loading in the browser, only during the initial request. The pageLoad method fires both when the page first loads and after an asynchronous postback, for example, when using an UpdatePanel. This difference enables you to choose the desired behavior. Need to fire some code on initial load and after a postback? Choose pageLoad. Otherwise, choose jQuery's document ready function.

Exercise 4 Solution

You use the special _references.js file in the Scripts folder to enable IntelliSense. VS will read this file and parse all JavaScript files that you added with this syntax:

```
/// <reference path="Path/To/File.js" />
```

This way, you get IntelliSense in files where it would otherwise not be supported (such as user controls) or for JavaScript files that you're not directly linking to in your website.

CHAPTER 12

Exercise 1 Solution

The DELETE statement fails because there is a relationship between the Id of the Genre table and the GenreId of the Review table. As long as this relationship is in effect, you cannot delete genres that still have reviews attached to them. To be able to delete the requested genre, you need to delete the associated reviews first, or assign them to a different genre using an UPDATE statement. Exercise 4 shows you how you can accomplish this.

Exercise 2 Solution

The relationship between the Genre and Review tables is a one-way relationship. The relationship enforces that the GenreId assigned to a review must exist as an Id in the Genre table. At the same time, it blocks you from deleting genres that have reviews attached to them. However, the relationship doesn't stop you from deleting rows from the Review table.

Exercise 3 Solution

To delete reviews with an Id of 100 or less, you need the following SQL statement:

```
DELETE FROM Review WHERE Id <= 100
```

Exercise 4 Solution

Before you can delete the genre, you need to reassign the existing reviews to a new genre first. You can do this with the following UPDATE statement:

```
UPDATE Review SET GenreId = 11 WHERE GenreId = 4
```

This assigns the GenreId of 11 to all reviews that previously had their GenreId set to 4. This in turn means that the genre with an Id of 4 no longer has any reviews attached to it, so you can now remove it with the following SQL statement:

```
DELETE FROM Genre WHERE Id = 4
```

Exercise 5 Solution

To update the name you need to execute an UPDATE statement. To limit the number of affected rows to just the Rock genre, you need to use a WHERE clause. You can use the WHERE clause to filter the rows based on the genre's Id or on its Name. The following SQL statements are functionally equivalent:

```
UPDATE Genre SET Name = 'Punk Rock' WHERE Id = 7
UPDATE Genre SET Name = 'Punk Rock' WHERE Name = 'Rock'
```

This code assumes that the current Rock genre has an Id of 7.

CHAPTER 13

Exercise 1 Solution

The best control for this scenario is the GridView control. It's easy to set up and has built-in support for paging, updating, and deleting of data. Together with a DetailsView control you can offer your users all four CRUD operations. To connect to your database you need to use a SqlDataSource control. Chapter 14 provides you with alternatives for both the GridView and the SqlDataSource.

Exercise 2 Solution

For a simple, unordered list, you're probably best off using a Repeater control hooked up to a SqlDataSource control. The biggest benefit of the Repeater control is that it emits no HTML code of its own, enabling you to control the final markup. A downside of the control is that it doesn't support editing or deletion of data, which isn't a problem if all you need to do is present the data in a list. Chapter 14 shows you how to use the Repeater control.

Exercise 3 Solution

A BoundField is directly tied to a column in your data source and offers only limited ways to customize its appearance. The TemplateField, on the other hand, gives you full control over the way the field is rendered. As such, it's an ideal field for more complex scenarios—for example, when you want to add validation controls to the page, or if you want to let the user work with a different control, like a DropDownList instead of the default TextBox.

Exercise 4 Solution

You should always store your connection strings in the Web.config file. This file has an element called <connectionStrings> that is designed specifically for storing connection strings. By storing them in Web.config, you make it very easy to find your connection strings and modify them. If you store them at the page level, you have to search through your entire project for the relevant connection strings.

You can access the connection strings using expression binding syntax. For example, to set the connection string in a SqlDataSource, you can use code like this:

```
ConnectionString="<%$ ConnectionStrings:PlanetWroxConnectionString1 %>"
```

For this code to work, you need a connection string similar to this in your Web.config file:

```
<connectionStrings>
  <add name="PlanetWroxConnectionString1" connectionString="Data
    Source=(localdb)\v11.0;AttachDbFilename=|DataDirectory|\PlanetWrox.mdf;
        Integrated Security=True"
    providerName="System.Data.SqlClient" />
</connectionStrings>
```

CHAPTER 14

Exercise 1 Solution

To get the 10 most recent reviews from the system, your query needs two important LINQ constructs: first, it needs an Order By (orderby in C#) clause to order the list in descending order. It then needs the Take method to take the first 10 reviews from that result set:

VB.NET

```
Using myEntities As New PlanetWroxEntities()
  Dim recentReviews = (
                        From myReview In myEntities.Reviews
                        Order By myReview.CreateDateTime Descending
                        Select New With {
                           myReview.Title, myReview.Genre.Name
                       }
                     ).Take(10)
  GridView1.DataSource = recentReviews
  GridView1.DataBind()
End Using
```

C#

```
using (PlanetWroxEntities myEntities = new PlanetWroxEntities())
{
  var recentReviews = (from myReview in myEntities.Reviews
                     orderby myReview.CreateDateTime descending
                     select new { myReview.Title, myReview.Genre.Name }).Take(10);
  GridView1.DataSource = recentReviews;
```

```
    GridView1.DataBind();
  }
```

This code also uses the New keyword (new in C#) to create a new, anonymous type that contains only the review's title and the genre's name.

Exercise 2 Solution

The biggest benefit of the ListView control is that it combines the strengths of those other data controls. Just like the GridView control, the ListView control makes it easy to display data in a grid format that users can edit from within the grid. Additionally, the ListView control enables you to insert new rows, behavior that is found in controls like DetailsView and FormView but not in GridView.

Finally, the ListView control gives you full control over the markup that gets sent to the browser, an important feature that only the Repeater control gives you out of the box.

Exercise 3 Solution

First you would need to change the Default.aspx page in the PhotoAlbums folder so it links each thumbnail to a details page and passes the ID of the picture to this new page. In the <ItemTemplate> of the ListView control in Default.aspx, add this HyperLink control around the Image control that was already there:

```
<asp:HyperLink ID="HyperLink1" runat="server"
    NavigateUrl='<%# "PictureDetails.aspx?Id=" + Item.Id.ToString() %>'>
<asp:Image ID="Image1" runat="server" ImageUrl='<%# Item.ImageUrl %>'
    ToolTip='<%# Item.ToolTip %>' />
</asp:HyperLink>
```

Note that the NavigateUrl is built up from the static text PictureDetails.aspx?Id= and the ID of the picture in the database.

Then create a new page called PictureDetails.aspx and add an Image control in the markup:

```
<asp:Content ID="Content2" ContentPlaceHolderID="cpMainContent" runat="server">
  <asp:Image ID="Image1" runat="server" />
</asp:Content>
```

Finally, you need to execute the following LINQ query in the Load event of the page in the Code Behind to set the ImageUrl:

VB.NET

```
Protected Sub Page_Load(sender As Object, e As EventArgs) Handles Me.Load
  Dim pictureId As Integer = Convert.ToInt32(Request.QueryString.Get("Id"))
  Using myEntities As New PlanetWroxEntities()
    Dim imageUrl As String = (From picture In myEntities.Pictures
                              Where picture.Id = pictureId
                              Select picture).Single().ImageUrl
    Image1.ImageUrl = imageUrl
  End Using
End Sub
```

C#

```
protected void Page_Load(object sender, EventArgs e)
{
  int pictureId = Convert.ToInt32(Request.QueryString.Get("Id"));
  using (PlanetWroxEntities myEntities = new PlanetWroxEntities())
  {
    string imageUrl = (from picture in myEntities.Pictures
                       where picture.Id == pictureId
                       select picture).Single().ImageUrl;
    Image1.ImageUrl = imageUrl;
  }
}
```

This code gets the ID of the picture from the query string first and then feeds it to the LINQ query.

The `Single` method is used to retrieve a single picture from the `Picture` table whose `ImageUrl` is then used to display the image in the browser.

Exercise 4 Solution

The best location to delete the image from disk is in the `EntityDataSource` control's `Deleted` event that fires after the item has been deleted from the database. Inside a handler for this event you get a reference to the `Picture` that has been deleted, find its `ImageUrl`, convert the URL to a physical location, and delete the image. To implement this, follow these steps:

1. Open `ManagePhotoAlbum.aspx` from the root of the site in Design View, select the `EntityDataSource` control, open its Properties Grid, and switch to the Events tab.
2. Double-click the `Deleted` event and in Code Behind add the following code to the handler that VS added for you:

   VB.NET

   ```
   Dim myPicture As Picture = CType(e.Entity, Picture)
   Dim fileName As String = Server.MapPath(myPicture.ImageUrl)
   System.IO.File.Delete(fileName)
   ```

   C#

   ```
   Picture myPicture = e.Entity as Picture;
   string fileName = Server.MapPath(myPicture.ImageUrl);
   System.IO.File.Delete(fileName);
   ```

3. Add `ImageUrl` to the list of `DataKeyNames` of the `ListView` control:

   ```
   <asp:ListView ID="ListView1" ... DataKeyNames="Id,ImageUrl" ...>
   ```

This code first finds a reference to the `Picture` using `e.Entity`. It then grabs its virtual `ImageUrl`, converts it to a physical path, and then uses the `Delete` method of the `File` class to get rid of the file on disk. Because the entire image is constructed from View State and not requested from EF, you need to store the ImageUrl in the DataKeyNames property. This adds it to View State so it roundtrips to the browser and is available in the Deleted event.

Exercise 5 Solution

To display only genres that have at least one review, all you need to do is filter out empty genres using Where with a Count method like this:

VB.NET

```
Dim genresWithReviews = From genre In myEntities.Genres
                        Order By genre.Name
                        Where genre.Reviews.Count() > 0
                        Select New With {genre.Name, genre.Reviews}
```

C#

```
var genresWithReviews = from genre in myEntities.Genres
                        orderby genre.Name
                        where genre.Reviews.Count() > 0
                        select new { genre.Name, genre.Reviews };
```

CHAPTER 15

Exercise 1 Solution

The Load event of the Page always fires before user-triggered events such as a Button control's Click.

Exercise 2 Solution

To preselect the correct item in the drop-down list after a user has inserted or edited a review, you need to make two modifications. First, you need to change the Redirect statement in the AddEditReviewHandCoded.aspx page so it includes the ID of the genre:

VB.NET

```
Response.Redirect(String.Format("Reviews.aspx?GenreId={0}",
      GenreList.SelectedValue))
```

C#

```
Response.Redirect(string.Format("Reviews.aspx?GenreId={0}",
      GenreList.SelectedValue));
```

Using String.Format makes this code a bit easier to read as opposed to plain string concatenation using the ampersand (&) in VB.NET and the plus (+) in C#.

If you now insert or edit a new review, you'll see that the ID of the genre is passed back to the Reviews.aspx page. On that page, you can use that ID to preselect the correct item in the

DropDownList control, which you can accomplish with the following code in the Page_Load method:

VB.NET

```
Protected Sub Page_Load(sender As Object, e As EventArgs) Handles Me.Load
  If Not Page.IsPostBack Then
    Dim genreId As String = Request.QueryString.Get("GenreId")
    If Not String.IsNullOrEmpty(genreId) Then
      DropDownList1.DataBind()
      Dim myItem As ListItem = DropDownList1.Items.FindByValue(genreId)
      If myItem IsNot Nothing Then
        myItem.Selected = True
      End If
    End If
  End If
End Sub
```

C#

```
protected void Page_Load(object sender, EventArgs e)
{
  if (!Page.IsPostBack)
  {
    string genreId = Request.QueryString.Get("GenreId");
    if (!string.IsNullOrEmpty(genreId))
    {
      DropDownList1.DataBind();
      ListItem myItem = DropDownList1.Items.FindByValue(genreId);
      if (myItem != null)
      {
        myItem.Selected = true;
      }
    }
  }
}
```

Only when the page loads from a new request (and not from a postback) does this code fire. The code then tries to find a GenreId in the query string. If it can find it, it tries to find an item with that requested value in the DropDownList. Because the DropDownList control hasn't been data bound yet it doesn't contain any items. Therefore, you need to call DataBind() first. This gets the genres from the database using EF and puts them in the DropDownList. Once that's done and the item is found in the Items collection, it's made the active item by setting its Selected property to True/true. The SqlDataSource control watches this DropDownList so when the data source gets its reviews, it does so for the correct genre.

Exercise 3 Solution

The various data-bound controls can raise exceptions that you can handle in their event handlers.

Once you have dealt with the exception appropriately, you need to set the ExceptionHandled property of the e argument to True. The following code snippet shows how a Label control is updated with an error message. ExceptionHandled is then set to stop the Exception from getting passed on into the user interface where it would otherwise result in a "Yellow Screen of Death."

VB.NET

```
Protected Sub SqlDataSource1_Deleted(sender As Object,
            e As SqlDataSourceStatusEventArgs) Handles SqlDataSource1.Deleted
  If e.Exception IsNot Nothing Then
      ErrorMessage.Text = "We're sorry, but something went terribly wrong while " &
           "deleting your genre."
    e.ExceptionHandled = True
  End If
End Sub
```

C#

```
protected void SqlDataSource1_Deleted(object sender,
       SqlDataSourceStatusEventArgs e)
{
  if (e.Exception != null)
  {
    ErrorMessage.Text = @"We're sorry, but something went terribly wrong while
        deleting your genre.";
    e.ExceptionHandled = true;
  }
}
```

CHAPTER 16

Exercise 1 Solution

Authentication is all about proving your identity to a system like a website. After you have been authenticated, *authorization* then determines what you can and cannot do in the system.

Exercise 2 Solution

To expand the access to the Management folder for John and all users in the Editors role, you need to expand the current roles attribute to include Editors, and add an additional allow element with its users attribute set to John:

```
<system.web>
  <authorization>
    <allow roles="Managers, Editors" />
    <allow users="John" />
    <deny users="*" />
  </authorization>
</system.web>
```

The roles attribute enables you to specify multiple roles separated by a comma. To grant the John account access, you need to add an additional allow element and then fill in John's name in the users attribute.

From a maintainability perspective, it would be a lot better to add John to the Managers or Editors role if possible. However, you may end up giving John more rights than you want (he could then access anything that a Manager or an Editor could access). Generally, it's best to manage users through roles as much as possible, but it's good to know that you can grant individual accounts the necessary rights as well (or explicitly take those rights away using a `deny` element).

Exercise 3 Solution

If you want to redirect all users to the same page, all you need to set is the `DestinationPageUrl`:

```
<asp:Login ID="Login1" runat="server" DestinationPageUrl="~/MyProfile.aspx">
```

When a user is logged in successfully, she's taken to `MyProfile.aspx` automatically.

Exercise 4 Solution

The `LoginStatus` simply displays a simple link that indicates whether or not the user is logged in. By default the text that is displayed is Login when the user is currently not logged in, and Logout when the user is already logged in. Clicking the link either sends the user to the default Login page, or logs the user out.

The `LoginView` is somewhat similar in that it displays different content depending on whether the user is currently logged in. However, because the control is completely template driven, you can fully control the content that is displayed. To enable you to differentiate between different user roles, you can use the `RoleGroups` element to set up templates that are shown only to users in specific roles.

CHAPTER 17

Exercise 1 Solution

You would implement the favorite theme as a `String` property and call it `FavoriteTheme`. To ensure that you always have a valid theme, you could also set a default value. Finally, you should make the property accessible to anonymous users. Your final profile property could end up like this:

```
<add name="FavoriteTheme" defaultValue="Monochrome" allowAnonymous="true" />
```

To support anonymous profiles, you need to explicitly enable them by adding an `<anonymousIdentification>` element as a direct child of `<system.web>` in the `Web.config` file:

```
<system.web>
  <anonymousIdentification enabled="true" cookieName="PlanetWroxAnonymous" />
```

Exercise 2 Solution

Given the syntax you saw in the question, you could now access the new property and use it to change the current theme in the `BasePage`:

VB.NET

```
Private Sub Page_PreInit(sender As Object, e As EventArgs) _
```

```
            Handles Me.PreInit
  Dim myProfile As ProfileCommon =
          CType(HttpContext.Current.Profile, ProfileCommon)
  If Not String.IsNullOrEmpty(myProfile.FavoriteTheme) Then
    Page.Theme = myProfile.FavoriteTheme
  End If
End Sub
```

C#

```
private void BasePage_PreInit(object sender, EventArgs e)
{
  ProfileCommon myProfile = (ProfileCommon) HttpContext.Current.Profile;
  if (!string.IsNullOrEmpty(myProfile.FavoriteTheme))
  {
    Page.Theme = myProfile.FavoriteTheme;
  }
}
```

Exercise 3 Solution

To finalize the theme selector using Profile, you also need to change the code in the master page `Frontend.master`. Instead of storing the user-selected theme in a cookie, you should now store it in Profile. Change the code in `Page_Load` as follows:

VB.NET

```
If Not Page.IsPostBack Then
  Dim selectedTheme As String = Page.Theme
  If Not String.IsNullOrEmpty(Profile.FavoriteTheme) Then
    selectedTheme = Profile.FavoriteTheme
  End If
  If Not String.IsNullOrEmpty(selectedTheme) Then
    Dim item As ListItem = ThemeList.Items.FindByValue(selectedTheme)
    If item IsNot Nothing Then
      item.Selected = True
    End If
  End If
End If
Select Case Page.Theme.ToLower()
```

C#

```
if (!Page.IsPostBack)
{
  string selectedTheme = Page.Theme;
  if (!string.IsNullOrEmpty(Profile.FavoriteTheme))
  {
    selectedTheme = Profile.FavoriteTheme;
  }
  if (!string.IsNullOrEmpty(selectedTheme))
  {
      ListItem item = ThemeList.Items.FindByValue(selectedTheme);
      if (item != null)
      {
          item.Selected = true;
```

```
        }
    }
  }
  switch (Page.Theme.ToLower())
```

You can then simplify the code in `ThemeList_SelectedIndexChanged` in the master page to:

VB.NET

```
Protected Sub ThemeList_SelectedIndexChanged(sender As Object,
       e As EventArgs) Handles ThemeList.SelectedIndexChanged
  Profile.FavoriteTheme = ThemeList.SelectedValue
  Response.Redirect(Request.Url.ToString())
End Sub
```

C#

```
protected void ThemeList_SelectedIndexChanged(object sender, EventArgs e)
{
  Profile.FavoriteTheme = ThemeList.SelectedValue;
  Response.Redirect(Request.Url.ToString());
}
```

CHAPTER 18

Exercise 1 Solution

Debugging is the process of watching your code execute in the development environment—investigating variables and looking into objects in order to understand the execution path of your code—looking for bugs with the aim to fix them. Debugging usually takes place at development time in your Visual Studio IDE.

Tracing, on the other hand, provides you with information on the runtime execution of your code. As discussed in this chapter, you can use tracing to get information about events that fire and the order in which they fire. Additionally, you can add your own information to the trace. Because disabling tracing through configuration greatly minimizes the performance overhead associated with it, you can leave your trace calls in the code, making it easy to disable and enable tracing whenever you need it.

Exercise 2 Solution

The best way to stop a possible exception from ending up in the user interface is to wrap your code in a `Try/Catch` block. That way you can display an error message to the user in case something goes wrong. Your code could end up looking like this:

VB.NET

```
Try
  ' Execute code here to send an e-mail.
Catch ex As SmtpException
```

```
  ErrorMessage.Text = "Something went wrong while sending your message."
End Try
```

C#

```
try
{
  // Execute code here to send an e-mail.
}
catch (SmtpException ex)
{
  ErrorMessage.Text = "Something went wrong while sending your message.";
}
```

Exercise 3 Solution

To understand which exceptions occur in the site and find out where they occur (that is, what pages or code files are causing the exceptions) you can log all exceptions using some code in the `Application_Error` event handler. The exception details you can intercept in this method should help you understand the cause of the exception, which in turn should help in finding a fix for it.

To prevent your users from seeing the "Yellow Screen of Death" error messages, you need to use custom error pages. You should create a simple Web Form that tells the user something went wrong.

To tell the ASP.NET run time to show the contents of that file instead of the error message, you need the following element in your `Web.config`:

```
<customErrors mode="On" defaultRedirect="~/Errors/AllOtherErrors.aspx"
          redirectMode="ResponseRewrite">
  <error statusCode="500" redirect="~/Errors/Error500.aspx" />
</customErrors>
```

This element sets up a special page for error code 500 that occurs when your code crashes unexpectedly.

When other exceptions occur, such as a "Page not found" error, users are sent to the more generic `AllOtherErrors.aspx` page.

B

Configuring SQL Server 2012

So far, the exercises in the book assume that you are using Microsoft SQL Express 2012 LocalDB Edition 11.0 as the database for the Planet Wrox project. SQL Express LocalDB Edition 11.0 is great for development because it's free, lightweight, and easy to use. However, it's not designed to be used in a production environment and is limited in terms of processor and memory usage and database size. In cases where the LocalDB edition is not enough, you need to look at its bigger brothers: SQL Server 2012 Express edition or the commercial versions of SQL Server 2012, such as the Standard or Enterprise Editions. In this appendix you learn more about SQL Server 2012, its security model, how to enable your SQL Server 2012 database and ASP.NET 4.5 website to work together, and how to use SQL Server Management Studio Express, a free tool from Microsoft that lets you manage your database.

Although this appendix doesn't discuss earlier versions of SQL Server, you'll find that most of the concepts apply to these older versions as well. In fact, you can also use SQL Server 2012 Management Studio Express to manage older SQL Server 2005 and 2008 databases. This appendix uses SQL Server Express edition because it's a free download, but the same principles apply to the commercial versions of SQL Server.

CONFIGURING SQL SERVER 2012

Before you can configure your database, you need to be aware of the various security concepts that are inevitably associated with databases and web applications. In Chapter 19 you learned how the account used by the web server plays a big role when configuring security settings for the filesystem, and that's no different when connecting to SQL Server. In the following section, you get a quick primer on the different ways to connect to SQL Server. In the section that follows you see how to attach your `.mdf` database files to SQL Server, followed by a discussion of configuring your application and database so they can talk to each other.

Terminology and Concepts

When you connect to a SQL Server database, SQL Server needs to know who you are, so it can enforce the correct access policies on the objects like tables in the database. SQL Server supports two different authentication mechanisms: SQL Server Authentication and Windows Authentication (often called Integrated Security). Both come with a few advantages of their own and require you to write different connection strings to connect to SQL Server. In the following section you see the two most common connection strings, but you're advised to visit `www.connectionstrings.com` for an extensive list of possible connection strings.

SQL Server Authentication

With SQL Server Authentication, SQL Server takes care of user management. You manage the users for your SQL Server database with Microsoft SQL Server Management Studio, either the Express edition (which you see how to use a little later in this appendix) or the full versions that ship with the commercial versions of SQL Server. SQL Server uses a *login* that handles authentication. You define this login at the server level by providing a login name and a password. A login can then be mapped to a *database user* to grant access to a specific database.

To connect your web application to a SQL Server installation that requires you to use SQL Server Authentication, you need to pass a username and password in the connection string of your application. A typical connection string looks like this:

```
Data Source=ServerName;Initial Catalog=DatabaseName;
      User Id=UserName;Password=Password;
```

In this case the `Data Source` points to an *unnamed instance* of SQL Server: the SQL server is addressed by its machine name alone. It's also possible to install SQL Server as a *named instance*. With a named instance, the name of the server is followed by a back slash (\) and the name of a particular SQL Server instance. For example:

```
Data Source=ServerName\InstanceName;Initial Catalog=DatabaseName;
      User Id=UserName;Password=Password;
```

SQL Server Authentication is often used when you need to connect to a remote SQL Server over the Internet because Windows Authentication, discussed next, is not supported in that scenario.

Windows Authentication

With Windows Authentication, the Windows OS takes care of user management. All interaction with the database is done in the context of the calling user so the database knows who's accessing the system. You still need to map a Windows login to a SQL Server database user so SQL Server can determine whether the account has sufficient permissions. I show you how to do this later.

A typical connection string using Windows Authentication looks like this:

```
Data Source=ServerName;Initial Catalog=DatabaseName;Trusted_Connection=True
```

Instead of specifying a username and password, you add `Trusted_Connection=True` to the connection string to indicate you want to connect to the server with the user context of the calling user. You may also come across the setting `Integrated Security=True`, which has the same effect.

Because both authentication methods eventually do the same thing (they enable you to connect to SQL Server), you may wonder which one of the two you should use.

Choosing between Windows and Server Authentication

In general, it's recommended to use Windows Authentication when possible. The fact that you don't need to use a password in the connection string means your application will be a bit safer. You don't need to send the password over the wire, and it's also not stored in a configuration file for your application.

However, SQL Server Authentication is a bit easier to set up. Because you specify the username and password explicitly, you don't need to know the final user account that your application runs under.

Later in this appendix you see how to use both authentication mechanisms to connect to your database. However, you need to look at something else first: the tools used to manage SQL Server.

Using SQL Server Management Studio

You use SQL Server Management Studio to manage your SQL server and databases. It enables you to attach and detach databases to your SQL Server; create new database objects like tables in existing databases; select, create, edit and delete data; and much more.

So far, you've been using the LocalDB version of SQL Server, the developer-friendly version of SQL Server. In addition to LocalDB, Microsoft has another free version of SQL Server called SQL Server Express. The following sections of this appendix show you how to work with this free SQL Server Express edition, because it's very similar in use compared to its commercial and production-ready databases. If you only installed LocalDB, you need to download and install SQL Server Express along with the free SQL Server Management Studio Express. The section, "Installing SQL Server 2012 Express," in Chapter 12 explains how to acquire SQL Server 2012 Express Edition as well as its Management Studio component.

If you are already using a commercial version of SQL Server, you already have access to the full version of SQL Server Management Studio, because it comes bundled with the database engine.

If you are having trouble connecting to a remote SQL Server (for example, an instance of SQL Server that is not on the same physical server as the one on which you're running Management Studio), you may need to enable remote connections for that SQL Server first. This is discussed next.

Enabling Remote Connections in SQL Server

When working with SQL Server, you may receive an error stating that the server was not found, not accessible, or that remote connections may not be configured properly.

Although you may get this error when the database server is down, you also get this error when SQL Server is not configured for remote connections. In a default installation, SQL Server allows only local applications to connect and blocks remote connections automatically. To resolve this, and grant remote systems access to the server as well, follow these steps:

1. Open the SQL Server Configuration Manager from the Start menu or Start screen. Depending on the version of SQL Server you're using, this item may be located under the Microsoft SQL Server 2012/Configuration Tools submenu.

2. In the window that appears, expand SQL Server Network Configuration, locate your instance of SQL Server, and click it to display the list with available protocols. If you're running a 64-Bit version of Windows, you see an additional node with this name, followed by (32-Bit). In that case, find the one that contains the Protocols for SQLEXPRESS node. Figure B-1 shows the list for a SQL Server instance called SQLEXPRESS on a 32-Bit machine.

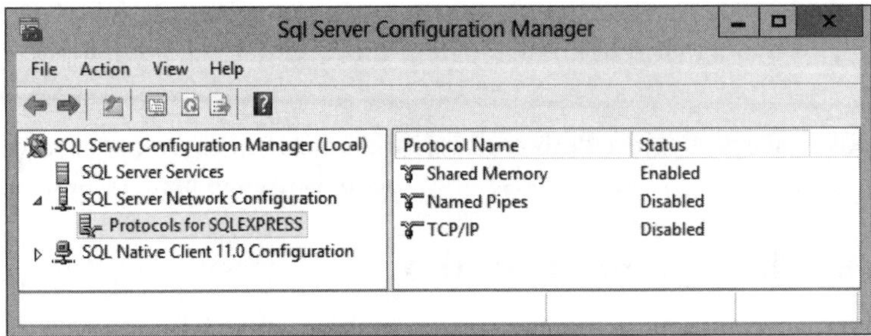

FIGURE B-1

3. In the list with protocols on the right, right-click Named Pipes and choose Enable if its status is currently set to Disabled.
4. Repeat the previous step, but now enable TCP/IP.
5. Restart SQL Server. To do this, click SQL Server Services in the SQL Server Configuration Manager (shown in Figure B-1), then right-click your server and choose Restart. If you get an error about security permissions, you may need to reboot your computer instead.

SQL Server now allows incoming connections from remote machines. However, before you can actually use your databases, you need to attach them to SQL Server first. This is described in the following section.

> ***NOTE*** *If you have trouble connecting to SQL Server, make sure that SQL Server is installed and running. To verify this, open the Control Panel and then open the Administrative Tools section found in the System and Security category. Next, open the Services item and then verify that the SQL Server instance you are connecting to is running. If you installed SQL Server Express on your local machine with the default instance name, the service is called SQL Server (SQLEXPRESS).*

Attaching Databases to SQL Server

SQL Server Express enables you to work with database files in two ways: you can either attach them at run time using a special attribute in the connection string, or you can attach them using tools such as Management Studio before you start using the database.

You've been using the first option in all database-related chapters so far using the LocalDB version of SQL Server. The Planet Wrox connection string you used looks like this:

```
<add name="PlanetWroxConnectionString1"
    connectionString="Data Source=(localdb)\v11.0;
    AttachDbFilename=|DataDirectory|\PlanetWrox.mdf;Trusted_Connection=True;"
          providerName="System.Data.SqlClient" />
```

This connection string points to a database called `PlanetWrox.mdf` located in the website's `App_Data` folder (determined by `|DataDirectory|`). The connection string instructs SQL Server to attach this database file to SQL Server LocalDB on the fly when it's used. When the database is no longer needed, it is detached again. You can use the same connection string to target SQL Server Express by changing the data source to `.\SqlExpress`.

This is a great solution for local development because it enables you to easily create and use SQL Server databases and move them around from project to project. However, with a production database this option isn't good enough and you need to attach the database to SQL Server first. The following steps explain how to attach the `PlanetWrox.mdf` database to an instance of SQL Server in case you have the need. You can follow the exact same steps if you want to use SQL Server Management Studio to perform maintenance tasks on a SQL Server database that you cannot do in Visual Studio (managing users and roles, for example).

1. Create a folder that will hold your new database, such as `C:\Data\SqlServer`.
2. Move the `PlanetWrox.mdf` file and its associated `.ldf` file from the website's `App_Data` folder at `C:\BegASPNET\Release` to this new folder.
3. Enable Modify permissions on the folder where the database resides (`C:\Data\SqlServer`) for the account used by SQL Server (which is the Network Service account by default) and for your own account. Chapter 19 explains how to set these permissions.
4. Open SQL Server Management Studio and log in to your SQL Server instance to which you want to attach the database. Depending on your security settings, you may have to run this process as an administrator. To do this for Windows 7 or Server 2008, right-click the Management Studio Start menu item and choose Run as Administrator. For Windows 8 or Server 2012, right-click the item in the Start screen and then choose Run as Administrator from the Options bar that has appeared.
5. Right-click the Databases node and choose Attach.
6. In the dialog box that follows, click the Add button and then select the `PlanetWrox.mdf` file you moved to `C:\Data\SqlServer` in step 2.
7. Click the value in the Attach As column to make it editable and type **`PlanetWrox`** as the new name that will be given to the database. Once you're done, your dialog box should look like Figure B-2.
8. Click OK to attach the database to SQL Server. If you get an error, make sure your own account (or the Users group you are part of) and the Network Service account both have Modify permissions on the `C:\Data\SqlServer` folder and the `.mdf` files this folder contains. Also, try running SQL Server Management Studio as an administrator as explained in step 4.

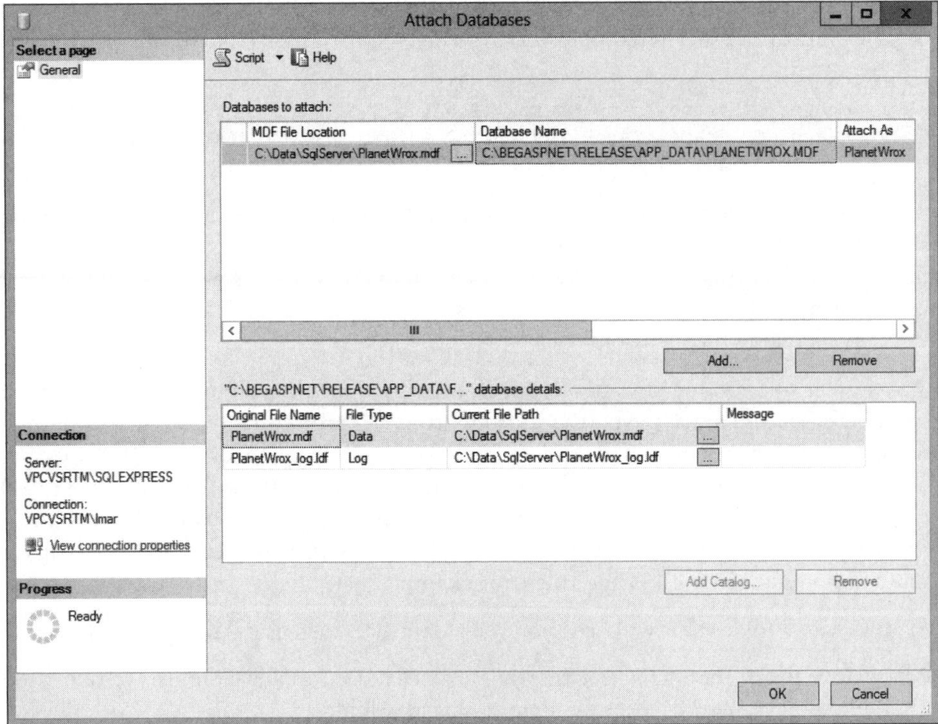

FIGURE B-2

9. Your database is now accessible under the Databases node of Management Studio's Object Explorer. If you expand the Databases element and then look into your database, you should see familiar items like tables that you also saw in the Database Explorer in Visual Studio earlier in the book. Figure B-3 shows the attached database and its tables.

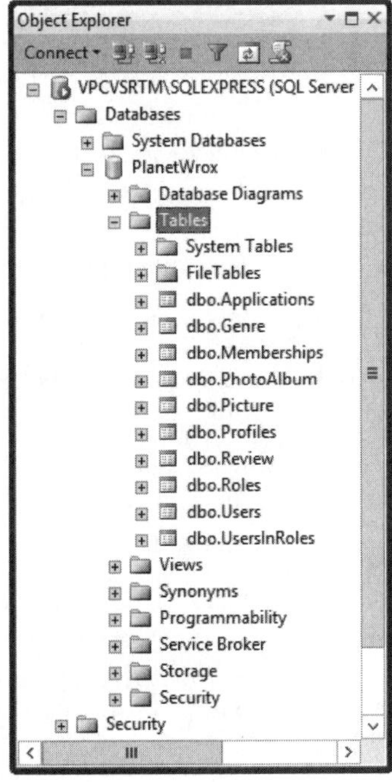

FIGURE B-3

At this stage, only administrative accounts (Windows administrators or the built-in SQL Server administrative account called SA) have access to the database. To have the Planet Wrox website work with these two databases, you need to configure both SQL Server security and your website. You see how to do this next.

Connecting Your Application to SQL Server 2012

In the following section, I show you how to connect to SQL Server from two different but common scenarios: using SQL Server Authentication and using Windows Authentication when IIS and SQL Server are on the same server. For both scenarios, you see how to configure SQL Server, the Planet Wrox website, and if necessary, your Windows accounts.

You're likely to use the first scenario when dealing with an external hosting company that hosts your site. When web hosts offer SQL Server, they often use SQL Server Authentication and, as such, require you to pass a username and password to the database server.

The second scenario is useful if you host the site yourself and have both SQL Server 2012 and IIS on the same machine.

More advanced scenarios, such as using Windows Authentication with IIS and SQL Server on two different machines, are beyond the scope of this appendix. For more information about configuring and securing SQL Server, get yourself a copy of *Professional Microsoft SQL Server 2012 Administration* by Adam Jorgensen, Steven Wort, Ross LoForte, Brian Knight, 2012, (Wrox, ISBN: 978-1-1181-0688-4).

Scenario 1 — Using SQL Server Authentication

From a configuration point of view, this is probably the easiest scenario to configure: all you need to do is make sure that your SQL Server installation supports SQL Server Authentication, create a user in SQL Server, and then use that account in the connection string of the Planet Wrox website. To do this, follow these steps:

1. In SQL Server Management Studio, right-click the server name in the Object Explorer shown in Figure B-3, choose Properties, and switch to the Security category. The dialog box shown in Figure B-4 appears.

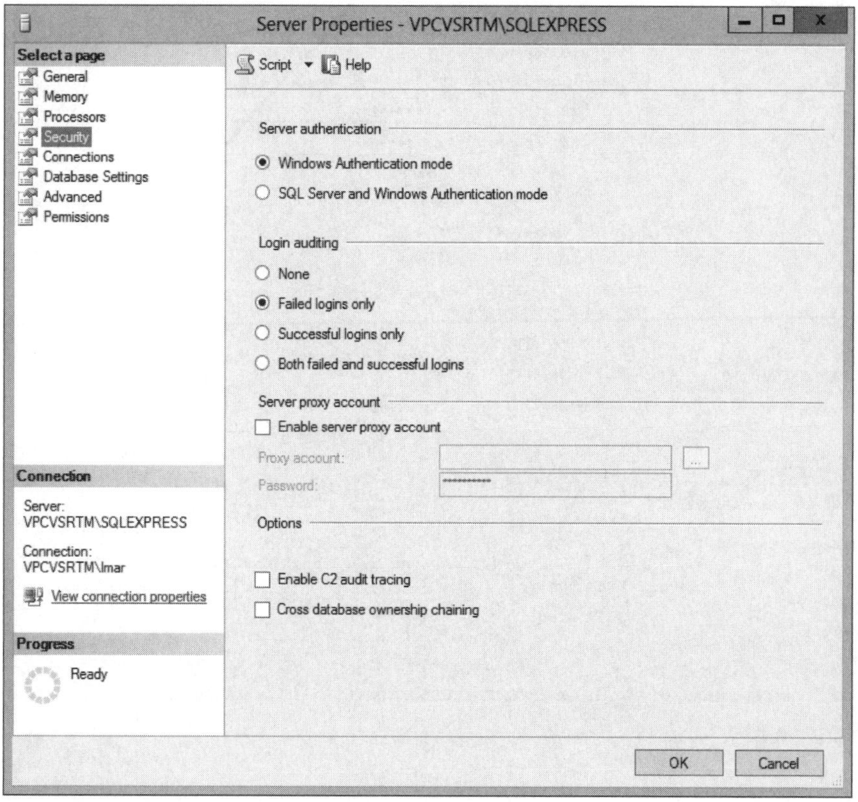

FIGURE B-4

2. If not already selected, choose the SQL Server and Windows Authentication Mode item at the top of the screen. Before you click OK, click the Help item at the top of the screen and read a bit more about SQL and Windows Authentication, and determine if you really need SQL Server Authentication. Windows Authentication is more secure than SQL Server Authentication, so you're advised to use that option whenever possible.

3. If you changed the server authentication, restart SQL Server. You can do this by right-clicking the server in the Object Explorer and choosing Restart. If you get an error about security permissions, you may need to reboot your computer instead.

4. Back in SQL Server Management Studio's Object Explorer, expand the server's Security node visible at the bottom of Figure B-3. Make sure you choose the one under your server name, and not the one belonging to a specific database. Right-click Logins and choose New Login.

5. Type a login name, then select the SQL Server Authentication option, and type a password (twice). In this and the following examples, I'll use `PlanetWroxUser` as the username, and `Pa$$w0rD` (with a zero instead of the letter o) as the password.

6. Clear the Enforce Password Expiration option. This also disables User Must Change Password at Next Login. Your dialog box should end up looking like the one in Figure B-5.

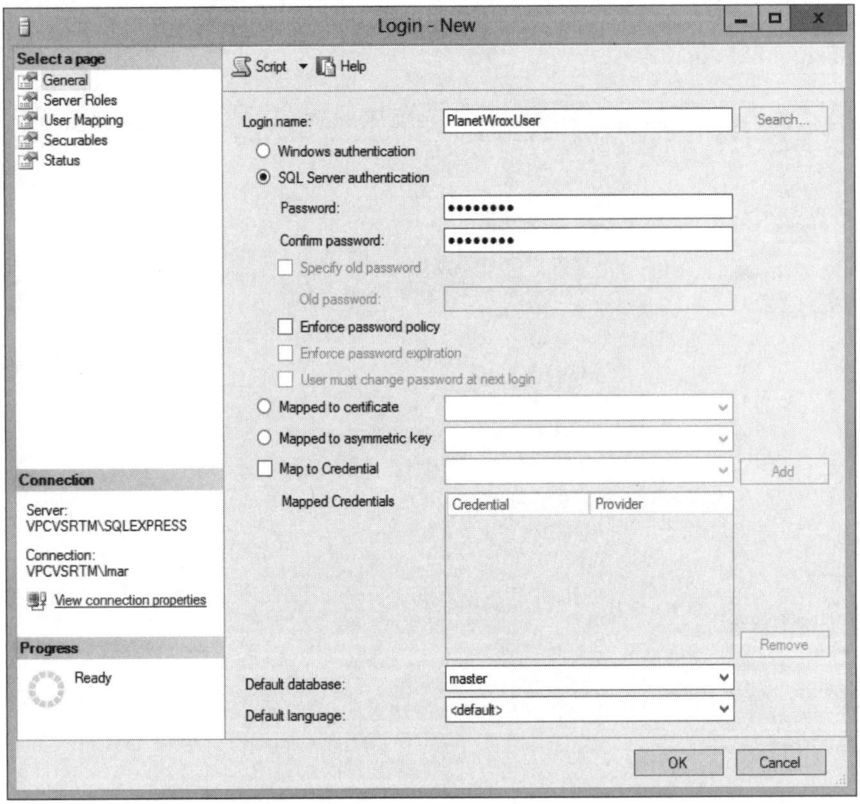

FIGURE B-5

If you want to learn more about the individual settings on this screen, click the Help button at the top of the screen.

7. Click OK to create the new account.

With the account created, the next step is to give this new account the proper permissions to your database:

1. On the Object Explorer, expand Databases, then the PlanetWrox database, followed by the Security node. Finally, right-click the Users node and choose New User.
2. In the User Type drop-down, choose SQL User with Login (this option doesn't exist in earlier versions of Management Studio). In the User Name text box, type **PlanetWroxUser**.
3. In the Login Name text box, type **PlanetWroxUser** again. Alternatively, click the ellipsis button, then click Browse, and select the user from the list that has appeared.
4. Click Membership in the list on the left and you see a box labeled Database Role Membership (in earlier versions of SQL Server Management Studio this box is on the same page where you enter the username.) In this box, you can choose a number of roles that you can grant to your new user. The rule here is: give users as few permissions as possible. A good choice is db_datareader and db_datawriter, which allows the account to both read from and write to tables in the database, so check these two options, visible in Figure B-6.

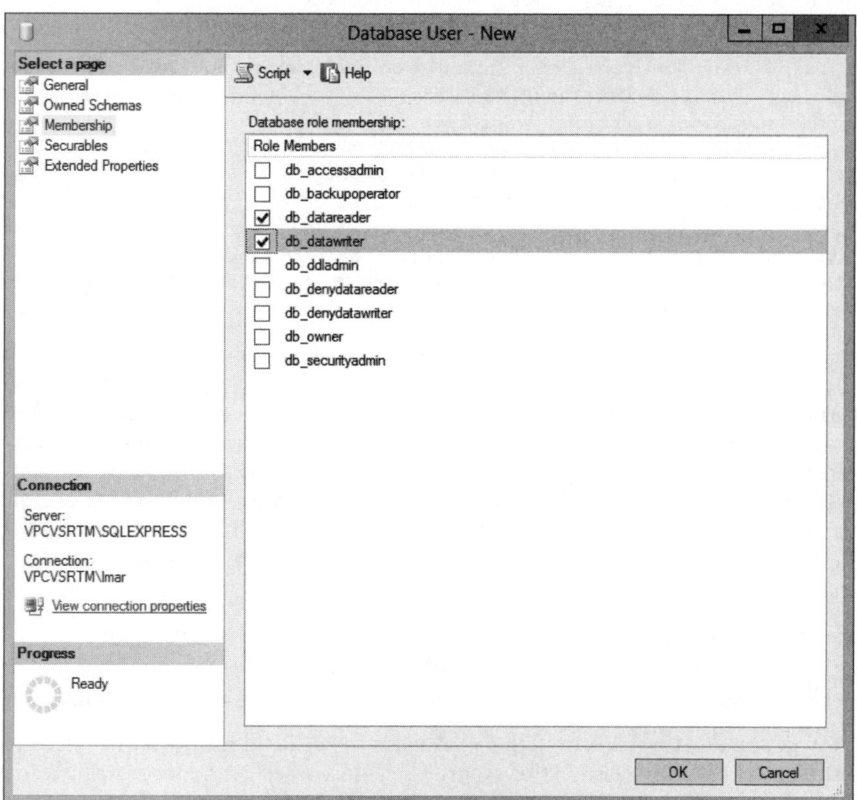

FIGURE B-6

> ***NOTE*** *Check out SQL Server's Books Online for more information about the various roles.*

5. If you want to set fine-grained security options for your database objects, click the Securables option you see in the left-hand part of Figure B-6. This dialog box enables you to determine permissions for the user account on objects in your database like tables, views, and stored procedures. For the Planet Wrox website, you don't need to make any changes in this dialog box.
6. Finally, click OK to create the PlanetWroxUser account and to assign it to the db_datareader and db_datawriter roles.
7. You can close SQL Server Management Studio because you're done with it for now.

Now that SQL Server and your user accounts are configured correctly, the final phase is to configure the website to use this new user account.

1. Open the `Web.config` file of the deployed Planet Wrox application from the `C:\BegASPNET\Release` folder.
2. Modify the `<connectionStrings>` element as follows:

```
<connectionStrings>
  <add name="PlanetWroxConnectionString1" connectionString="Data Source=ServerName;
            Initial Catalog=PlanetWrox;User ID=PlanetWroxUser;password=Pa$$w0rD"
      providerName="System.Data.SqlClient"
  />
  <add name="PlanetWroxEntities" connectionString="
     metadata=res://*/App_Code.PlanetWrox.csdl|res://*/App_Code.PlanetWrox.ssdl|res
     ://*/App_Code.PlanetWrox.msl;provider=System.Data.SqlClient;provider connection
     string=&quot;Data Source=ServerName;Initial Catalog=PlanetWrox;
     User ID=PlanetWroxUser;password=Pa$$w0rD;MultipleActiveResultSets=True&quot;"
    providerName="System.Data.EntityClient"
  />
</connectionStrings>
```

   In your configuration file, each connection string should be on a single line. Don't forget to replace the value *`ServerName`* in the `Data Source` attributes with a valid server name. Depending on your server and configuration, this could be as simple as `(local)` or `.\SqlExpress` to point to a SQL Server on the local machine, `DatabaseServer` to point to a server called `DatabaseServer` on the network, or something like `DatabaseServer\Sql2012` that points to a named instance called `Sql2012` on a machine called `DatabaseServer`.

3. Save the changes and then open the site by starting your browser and going to `http://localhost`. Everything should still work, but the site now no longer uses the databases in the `App_Data` folder; it uses the SQL Server you defined in your connection strings instead.

   If you get an error when browsing to the site on your local host, you may need to turn off custom errors in `Web.config` (for security reasons, set it to `RemoteOnly` instead of to `Off`) to see the actual error message. Possible reasons for an error include an incorrect username, password, or server name in the connection string, and an incorrectly configured database role membership for the PlanetWroxUser account.

Scenario 2 — Using Windows Authentication with IIS and the Database on the Same Machine

This is a common scenario, especially when you're running your site on a local machine that you control yourself. Both the web server (either IIS or the built-in development web server) and SQL Server run on the same physical machine. This scenario makes it easy to use Windows Authentication because both the web server and SQL Server can use the same Windows account. To configure your server for this scenario, follow these steps:

1. Determine the account used by your web server. Refer to Chapter 19 for precise details on how to do this, but you're likely to need the ApplicationPoolIdentity account (called IIS AppPool\.NET v4.5 by default). I am using the account IIS AppPool\.NET v4.5 in the remainder of this section.
2. Next, you need to map this Windows account to a SQL Server login. To do this, open SQL Server Management Studio and log in to your SQL Server instance. Expand the Security node for the server (and not of an individual database), as shown at the bottom of Figure B-3. Then right-click Logins and choose New Login.
3. In the Login Name box, enter `IIS AppPool\.NET v4.5` and click OK to add the new Login.

With the login created, the next step is to map this login to a database user that has the proper permissions to your database:

1. Open the Security node of the PlanetWrox database, right-click the Users node, and choose New User.
2. In the User Type drop-down, choose SQL User with Login (this option doesn't exist in earlier versions of Management Studio). In the User Name text box, type **.NET** v4.5.
3. For the Login Name text box, click the ellipsis button and then click Browse so you can select a username. Choose the account you configured earlier (called IIS AppPool\.NET 4.5) and click OK twice.
4. Click Membership in the list on the left and you see a box labeled Database Role Membership (in earlier versions of SQL Server Management Studio this box is on the same page where you enter the username). In this box, you can choose a number of roles that you can grant to your new user. The rule here is: give users as few permissions as possible. A good choice is db_datareader and db_datawriter, which allows the account to both read from and write to tables in the database, so check these two options, shown earlier in Figure B-6.

> ***NOTE*** *Check out SQL Server's Books Online for more information about the various roles.*

5. If you want to set fine-grained security options for your database objects, click the Securables option visible in Figure B-6. This dialog box enables you to determine permissions for the user account on objects in your database like tables, views, and stored procedures. For the Planet Wrox website, you don't need to make any changes in this dialog box.
6. Finally, click OK to create the database user and assign it to the db_datareader and db_datawriter roles.

Now that SQL Server and your user accounts are configured correctly, the final step is to configure the website to use this new user account.

1. Open the `Web.config` file of the Planet Wrox application from the `C:\BegASPNET\Release` folder.
2. Modify the `<connectionStrings>` element so it ends up like this:

```
<connectionStrings>
  <add name="PlanetWroxConnectionString1" connectionString="Data Source=ServerName;
              Initial Catalog=PlanetWrox;Trusted_Connection=True"
      providerName="System.Data.SqlClient"
  />
  <add name="PlanetWroxEntities" connectionString="
     metadata=res://*/App_Code.PlanetWrox.csdl|res://*/App_Code.PlanetWrox.ssdl|res
     ://*/App_Code.PlanetWrox.msl;provider=System.Data.SqlClient;provider connection
     string=&quot;Data Source=ServerName;Initial Catalog=PlanetWrox;
     Trusted_Connection=True;MultipleActiveResultSets=True&quot;"
    providerName="System.Data.EntityClient"
  />
</connectionStrings>
```

   In your configuration file, each connection string should be on a single line. Don't forget to replace the value *`ServerName`* in the `Data Source` attributes with a valid server name. Depending on your server and configuration, this could be as simple as `(local)` or `.\SqlExpress` to point to a SQL Server on the local machine, `DatabaseServer` to point to a server on the network called DatabaseServer, or something like `DatabaseServer\Sql2012` that points to a named instance called `Sql2012` on a machine called `DatabaseServer`.

3. Save the changes and then open the site by starting your browser and going to `http://localhost`. Everything should still work as expected, but the site now no longer uses the databases in the `App_Data` folder; it uses the SQL Server defined in your connection strings instead through Windows Authentication, as identified by the `Trusted_Connection=True` attribute in the connection string.

   If you get an error when browsing to the site, you may need to turn off custom errors in the `Web.config` file (or set it to `RemoteOnly`) to see the actual error message. Possible reasons for the error are an incorrect server name in the connection string and an incorrectly configured database role membership for the configured account.

Once you find out the correct account and have configured SQL Server correctly, using Windows Authentication isn't that hard. In fact, your connection string now becomes a little easier and more secure, because you don't need to store a username and password in it anymore.

CONFIGURING APPLICATION SERVICES

Earlier in this book you learned that the ASP.NET application services make use of a SQL Server database. You also saw how to make sure your own website and the application services use the same database.

If you chose not to merge your database and the one used by the application services, your site now uses two databases: your own and one called `aspnetdb.mdf`. However, you can still merge them later if you want. In earlier versions of ASP.NET, this involved quite a bit of work including changes to the `Web.config` file and running command-line tools. However, with the updated providers this is now pretty simple. Follow these steps to let the application services use your own database:

1. First, make sure the application services point to a connection string you want to use. To do this, you need to set the `connectionStringName` to a connection string defined in your config file. The following example shows how to do this for the Membership section, but the other services follow a similar pattern:

   ```
   <membership defaultProvider="DefaultMembershipProvider">
     <providers>
       <add name="DefaultMembershipProvider"
        type="System.Web.Providers.DefaultMembershipProvider,
                     System.Web.Providers, Version=1.0.0.0, Culture=neutral,
                     PublicKeyToken=31bf3856ad364e35"
         connectionStringName="PlanetWroxConnectionString1"
         enablePasswordRetrieval="false" enablePasswordReset="true"
         requiresQuestionAndAnswer="false" requiresUniqueEmail="false"
         maxInvalidPasswordAttempts="5" minRequiredPasswordLength="7"
         minRequiredNonalphanumericCharacters="1" passwordAttemptWindow="10"
         applicationName="/"
       />  </providers>
   </membership>
   ```

   Notice how `connectionStringName` points to the connection string called `PlanetWroxConnectionString1`, defined elsewhere in the config file.

2. Make sure the account used by the web server has permissions to alter the database schema. You can accomplish this by adding the account to the **db_ddladmin** group, shown in Figure B-6. This grants the account the permissions to execute *Data Definition Language* statements, which means it can create and alter tables and other objects in the database.

3. Restart IIS. To do this, start the IIS Server Manager (type **inetmgr** in the Start menu or Start screen), click your server name, and then click Restart in the Actions panel on the right. To minimize impact on the server, you could also recycle just the application pool used by the site by right-clicking it and choosing Recycle.

4. Browse to your site and request the Login page. Try to log in with a fake username and password. At this stage, the .NET run time will modify the database and add the necessary tables to it. If you look in the database defined in the connection string used by the membership services, you'll notice it now contains the tables that are used by Membership, Roles, and Profile.

5. For security reasons, you should now remove the account from the **db_ddladmin** group because using Membership at run time does not require these permissions.

INDEX

Symbols

A

B

C

D

F

I

L

M

N

O

P

Q

R

S

T

U

V